W9-CCY-046

THE
Norton Anthology of Poetry

THIRD EDITION · SHORTER

W.W. NORTON & COMPANY, INC.
also publishes

THE NORTON ANTHOLOGY OF AMERICAN LITERATURE
edited by Ronald Gottesman et al.

THE NORTON ANTHOLOGY OF ENGLISH LITERATURE
edited by M. H. Abrams et al.

THE NORTON ANTHOLOGY OF MODERN POETRY
edited by Richard Ellmann and Robert O'Clair

THE NORTON ANTHOLOGY OF SHORT FICTION
edited by R. V. Cassill

THE NORTON ANTHOLOGY OF WORLD MASTERPIECES
edited by Maynard Mack et al.

THE NORTON FACSIMILE OF
THE FIRST FOLIO OF SHAKESPEARE
prepared by Charlton Hinman

THE NORTON INTRODUCTION TO LITERATURE
edited by Carl E. Bain, Jerome Beaty, and J. Paul Hunter

THE NORTON INTRODUCTION TO THE SHORT NOVEL
edited by Jerome Beaty

THE NORTON READER
edited by Arthur M. Eastman et al.

THE NORTON SAMPLER
edited by Thomas Cooley

and the

NORTON CRITICAL EDITIONS

THE Norton Anthology of Poetry

THIRD EDITION · SHORTER

ALEXANDER W. ALLISON
LATE OF THE UNIVERSITY OF MICHIGAN

HERBERT BARROWS
UNIVERSITY OF MICHIGAN

CAESAR R. BLAKE
UNIVERSITY OF TORONTO

ARTHUR J. CARR
WILLIAMS COLLEGE

ARTHUR M. EASTMAN
VIRGINIA POLYTECHNIC INSTITUTE AND STATE UNIVERSITY

HUBERT M. ENGLISH, JR.
UNIVERSITY OF MICHIGAN

With an essay on versification by Jon Stallworthy, Cornell University

W · W · NORTON & COMPANY
New York · London

Since this page cannot legibly accommodate all the copyright notices, the six pages following constitute an extension of the copyright page.

Library of Congress Cataloging in Publication Data
Main entry under title:

The Norton anthology of poetry.

Bibliography: p.
Includes indexes.
1. English poetry. 2. American poetry. I. Allison, Alexander W. (Alexander Ward)
PR1174.N6 1983b 821'.008 83-24952

W. W. Norton & Company, Inc., 500 Fifth Avenue, New York, N.Y. 10110
W. W. Norton & Company Ltd., 37 Great Russell Street, London WC1B 3NU

ISBN 0-393-95224-X

3 4 5 6 7 8 9 0

Andre Deutsch Ltd. Robert Bly: from *Light Around the Body.* Reprinted by permission of Rapp & Whiting Ltd. Roy Fuller: from *Collected Poems* (1962) and *Brutus Orchard* (1957). Galway Kinnell: from *Poems of Night* (1968) and *Body Rags* (1969, first published by Rapp & Carroll). James Dickey: from *Poems 1957–1967* (1967, first published by Rapp & Carroll). Geoffrey Hill: from *For the Unfallen* (1959), *King Log* (1968) and *Mercian Hymns* (1971). Above selections reprinted by permission of Andre Deutsch Ltd.

Devin-Adair Publishers. From *Collected Poems* by Patrick Kavanagh. Permission granted by the Devin-Adair Publishers. Copyright © 1964 by Patrick Kavanagh.

Doubleday & Company, Inc. Theodore Roethke: "Root Cellar" copyright 1943 by Modern Poetry Association, Inc. "My Papa's Waltz" copyright 1942 by Hearst Magazine, Inc. "Elegy for Jane" copyright 1950 by Theodore Roethke. "The Waking" copyright 1953 by Theodore Roethke. "I Knew a Woman" copyright 1954 by Theodore Roethke. "The Far Field" copyright © 1962 by the Administratrix to the Estate. "Wish for a Young Wife" copyright © 1963 by the Administratrix to the Estate. "In a Dark Time" copyright © 1960 by the Administratrix to the Estate. All poems from *The Collected Poems of Theodore Roethke.* The preceding selections reprinted by permission of Doubleday & Company, Inc.

Gerald Duckworth & Co. Ltd. Dorothy Parker: reprinted by permission of Gerald Duckworth & Co. Ltd.

Early English Text Society. Charles d'Orléans: From Early English Text Society Original Series 215, *English Poems of Charles of Orléans,* edited by R. Steele, 1941. Selections reprinted by permission of the Early English Text Society, Oxford.

The Ecco Press. Robert Hass: Robert Hass: "Meditation at Lagunitas" © 1979 by Robert Hass. From *Praise,* The Ecco Press, 1979. Reprinted by permission. Lawrence Raab: "Attack of the Crab Monsters" © 1976 by Lawrence Raab. From *The Collector of Cold Weather,* The Ecco Press, 1976. Reprinted by permission.

Norma Millay Ellis. Edna St. Vincent Millay: From *Collected Poems,* Harper & Row. Copyright 1923, 1934, 1954, 1962 by Edna St. Vincent Millay and Norma Millay Ellis.

Faber and Faber Ltd. W. H. Auden: from *Collected Poems* by W. H. Auden. John Berryman: from (a) *Homage to Mistress Bradstreet,* (b) *Berryman's Sonnets,* (c) *77 Dream Songs,* (d) *His Toy, His Dream, His Rest,* all by John Berryman. T. S. Eliot: from *Collected Poems 1909–1962* by T. S. Eliot. Thom Gunn: from (a) *The Sense of Movement,* (b) *Moly,* (c) *Jack Straw's Castle,* (d) *Touch,* all by Thom Gunn. Seamus Heaney: from (a) *Death of a Naturalist,* (b) *Door into the Dark,* (c) *Wintering Out,* (d) *North,* (e) *Fieldwork,* all by Seamus Heaney. Ted Hughes: from (a) *Lupercal,* (b) *Wodwo,* (c) *Season Songs,* (d) *Moortown,* (e) *Hawk in the Rain,* all by Ted Hughes. Randall Jarrell: from *The Complete Poems* by Randall Jarrell. Philip Larkin: from (a) *The Whitsun Weddings,* (b) *High Windows* by Philip Larkin. Robert Lowell: from (a) *Poems 1938–1949,* (b) *Life Studies,* (c) *For the Union Dead,* (d) *For Lizzie and Harriet,* (e) *Day By Day,* by Robert Lowell. Louis MacNeice: from *The Collected Poems of Louis MacNeice.* Marianne Moore: from *The Complete Poems of Marianne Moore.* Edwin Muir: from *The Collected Poems of Edwin Muir.* Ezra Pound: from (a) *Collected Shorter Poems,* (b) *The Cantos of Ezra Pound.* Theodore Roethke: from *The Collected Poems of Theodore Roethke.* Stephen Spender: from *Collected Poems* by Stephen Spender. Wallace Stevens: from (a) *Opus Posthumous,* (b) *The Collected Poems of Wallace Stevens.* Allan Tate: from *The Collected Poems.* Derek Walcott: from *The Fortunate Traveller* by Derek Walcott, Richard Wilbur: from (a) *Poems 1943–1956,* (b) *Advice to a Prophet,* (c) *Walking to Sleep* by Richard Wilbur.

Farrar, Straus & Giroux, Inc. John Berryman: "The Ball Poem" from *Short Poems*; copyright 1948 by John Berryman, copyright renewed © 1976 by Kate Berryman. "Sonnet 23, They may suppose, because I would not cloy your ear" from *Berryman's Sonnets*; copyright © 1952, 1967 by John Berryman. "Dream Songs #1, #29, #324, #375, and #382" from *The Dream Songs*; copyright © 1959, 1962, 1963, 1964, 1965, 1966, 1967, 1968, 1969 by John Berryman. Elizabeth Bishop: "Jeronimo's House," "At the Fishhouses," "Filling Station," "The Armadillo," "The Fish," and "Sestina" from *Elizabeth Bishop: The Complete Poems 1927–1979*; copyright © 1940, 1941, 1946, 1955, 1956, 1957, 1969, by Elizabeth Bishop, copyright renewed © 1968, 1969, 1974 by Elizabeth Bishop, copyright renewed © 1983 by Alice Methfessel. Louise Bogan: "Medusa" and "Song for the Last Act" from *The Blue Estuaries*; copyright © 1923, 1929, 1930, 1931, 1933, 1934, 1935, 1936, 1937, 1938, 1941, 1949, 1951, 1952, 1954, 1957, 1958, 1962, 1963, 1964, 1965, 1966, 1967, 1968 by Louise Bogan. Thom Gunn: "On the Move" from *Selected Poems*; copyright © 1957, 1958 by Thom Gunn. "Streetsong" from *Moly* and *My Sad Captains*; copyright © 1961, 1971, 1973 by Thom Gunn. Seamus Heaney: "Mid-term Break," "Punishment," and "Sunlight" from *Poems 1965–1975*; copyright © 1966, 1969, 1972, 1975, 1980 by Seamus Heaney. "The Strand at Lough Beg," "Guttural Muse," and Glanmore Sonnets from *Field Work*; copyright © 1976, 1979 by Seamus Heaney. Randall Jarrell: "The Death of the Ball-Turret Gunner" and "A Girl in a Library" from *Randall Jarrell: The Complete Poems*; copyright © 1947, 1951, 1969 by Mrs. Randall Jarrell, copyright renewed © 1974, 1978 by Mrs. Randall Jarrell. Philip Larkin: "Sad Steps" from *High Windows*; © 1974 by Philip Larkin. Robert Lowell: "My Last Afternoon with Uncle Devereux Winslow" and "Skunk Hour" from *Life Studies*; copyright © 1956, 1959 by Robert Lowell, "Water" and "For the Union Dead" from *For the Union Dead*; copyright © 1956; 1960, 1961, 1962, 1963, 1964 by Robert Lowell. "1930's" from *History*; copyright © 1967, 1968, 1969, 1970, 1973 by Robert Lowell. "Harriet" from *For Lizzie and Harriet*; copyright © 1967, 1968, 1969, 1970, 1973 by Robert Lowell. "This Golden Summer," "The Withdrawal," and "Epilogue" from *Day By Day*; copyright © 1975, 1976, 1977 by Robert Lowell. Allen Tate: "Ode to the Confederate Dead" from *Allen Tate: The Collected Poems 1919–1976*; copyright © 1952, 1953, 1970, 1977 by Allen Tate, copyright 1931, 1932, 1937, 1948 by Charles Scribner's Sons, copyright renewed © 1959, 1960, 1965 by Allen Tate. Derek Walcott: "The Gulf" from *The Gulf*; copyright © 1963, 1964, 1965, 1969, 1970 by Derek Walcott. "Europa" and "The Season of Phantasmal Peace" from *The Fortunate Traveller*; copyright © 1980, 1981 by Derek Walcott. James Wright: "Discoveries in Arizona" from *To A Blossoming Pear Tree*; copyright © 1973, 1974, 1975, 1976, 1977 by James Wright. Above selections all reprinted by permission of Farrar, Straus & Giroux, Inc.

Ellis Freedman. Ishmael Reed: Copyright © 1972 Ishmael Reed. Reprinted by permission.

Harcourt Brace Jovanovich, Inc. T. S. Eliot: From *Collected Poems 1909–1962* by T. S. Eliot; copyright, 1936, by Harcourt Brace Jovanovich, Inc.; copyright © 1963, 1964, by T. S. Eliot. Reprinted by permission of the publishers. From *Four Quartets*, copyright 1943 by T. S. Eliot; renewed 1971 by Esme Valerie Eliot. E. E. Cummings: "anyone lived in a pretty how town" and "my father moved through dooms of love" copyright 1940 by E. E. Cummings; renewed 1968 by Marion Morehouse Cummings. Above selections reprinted from *Complete Poems 1913–1962* by E. E. Cummings by permission of Harcourt Brace Jovanovich, Inc. Robert Lowell: "The Quaker Graveyard in Nantucket" and "Mr. Edwards and the Spider" from *Lord Weary's Castle*, copyright 1946, 1974 by Robert Lowell. Carl Sandburg: "Chicago" from *Chicago Poems* by Carl Sandburg, copyright 1916 by Holt, Rinehart and Winston, Inc.; renewed 1944 by Carl Sandburg. "Grass" from *Cornhuskers* by Carl Sandburg, copyright 1918 by Holt, Rinehart and Winston, Inc.; renewed 1946 by Carl Sandburg. Richard Wilbur: "First Snow in Alsace" and "Objects" from *The Beautiful Changes and Other Poems*, copyright 1947, 1975 by Richard Wilbur. "The Death of a Toad" and "Museum Piece" from *Ceremony and Other Poems*, copyright 1950, 1978 by Richard Wilbur. "Boy at the Window" copyright 1952 by *The New Yorker* Magazine, Inc.; renewed 1980 by Richard Wilbur. Reprinted from *Things of This World*. "For K.R. on Her Sixtieth Birthday" copyright © 1968 by Richard Wilbur. Reprinted from his volume *Walking to Sleep* by permission of Harcourt Brace Jovanovich, Inc. "A Storm in April" copyright © 1973 by Richard Wilbur. Reprinted from his volume *The Mind-Reader* by permission of Harcourt Brace Jovanovich, Inc. First published in *The New Yorker*. "Junk" © 1961 by Richard Wilbur. Reprinted from his volume *Advice To A Prophet and Other Poems* by permission of Harcourt Brace Jovanovich, Inc. The above selections all reprinted with the permission of Harcourt Brace Jovanovich, Inc.

Harper & Row, Publishers, Inc. Ted Hughes: From *New Selected Poems* by Ted Hughes: "The Thought-Fox" originally appeared in *The New Yorker*. Copyright © 1957 by Ted Hughes. "The Bull Moses" Copyright © 1959 by Ted Hughes. "Deaf School" Copyright © 1979 by Ted Hughes. William Stafford: *From Stories That Could Be True: New and Collected Poems by William Stafford:* "For the Grave of Daniel Boone" Copyright © 1957 by William Stafford. "Traveling Through the Dark" Copyright © 1960 by William Stafford. "Accountability" Copyright © 1976 by William Stafford. Sylvia Plath: "Daddy" from *Ariel* by Sylvia Plath. Copyright © 1963 by Ted Hughes. From *The Collected Poems of Sylvia Plath*, Edited by Ted Hughes: "Sleep in the Mojave Desert" Copyright © 1962 by Ted Hughes. "Lady Lazarus" Copyright © 1963 by Ted Hughes. "Ariel" Copyright © 1965 by Ted Hughes. "Elm" Copyright © 1963 by Ted Hughes. "Black Rook in Rainy Weather" Copyright © 1960 by Ted Hughes. Gwendolyn Brooks: From *The World of Gwendolyn Brooks* by Gwendolyn Brooks: "kitchenette building" Copyright, 1944, by Gwendolyn Brooks Blakely. "We Real Cool: The Pool Players. Seven at the Golden Shovel." Copyright © 1959 by Gwendolyn Brooks. "Boy Breaking Glass" Copyright © 1967 by Gwendolyn Brooks Blakely. Countee Cullen: "Heritage" from *On These I Stand* by Countee Cullen. Copyright, 1925, by Harper & Row, Publishers, Inc.; renewed, 1953, by Ida M. Cullen. The above selections are reprinted by permission of Harper & Row, Publishers, Inc.

Harvard University Press. Emily Dickinson: reprinted by permission of the publishers and the Trustees of Amherst College from *The Poems of Emily Dickinson*, edited by Thomas H. Johnson, Cambridge, Mass.: The Belknap Press of Harvard University Press, Copyright 1951, © 1955, 1979 by the President and Fellows of Harvard College. Anne Bradstreet: reprinted by permission of the publishers from *The Works of Anne Bradstreet*, edited by Jeannine Hensley, Cambridge, Mass.: The Belknap Press of Harvard University Press, Copyright © 1967 by the President and Fellows of Harvard College.

Estate of Robert Hayden. "Paul Laurence Dunbar" by Robert Hayden. Copyright © 1976 by Robert Hayden. First appeared in *Michigan Quarterly Review* 15 (Winter 1976); also in *American Journal*, Poems by Robert Hayden. Reprinted by permission of Erma Hayden.

David Higham Associates Limited.

Dylan Thomas: from *Collected Poems*, published by J. M. Dent. W. S. Merwin: from *The Drunk in the Furnace, First Four Books of Poems*, and *Moving Target*. Above selections reprinted by permission of David Higham Associates Limited.

Holt, Rinehart and Winston, Publishers. Robert Frost: from *The Poetry of Robert Frost* edited by Edward Connery Lathem. Copyright 1916, 1923, 1928, 1930, 1939, 1947, © 1969 by Holt, Rinehart and Winston. Copyright 1936, 1942, 1944, 1951, © 1956, 1958 by Robert Frost. Copyright © 1964, 1967, 1970, 1975 by Lesley Frost Ballantine. A. E. Housman: From *The Collected Poems of A. E. Housman*. Copyright 1936 by Barclays Bank Ltd. Copyright © 1964 by Robert E. Symons. From "A Shropshire Lad"—Authorised Edition—from *The Collected Poems of A. E. Housman*. Copyright 1939, 1940, © 1965 by Holt, Rinehart and Winston. Copyright © 1967, 1968 by Robert E. Symons. Above selections reprinted by permission of Holt, Rinehart and Winston, Publishers.

Houghton Mifflin Company. Archibald MacLeish: "Ars Poetica," "You, Andrew Marvell," and "Calypso's Island" from *New and Collected Poems 1917–1976* by Archibald MacLeish. Copyright © 1976 by Archibald MacLeish. Galway Kinnell: "First Song" from *Body Rags* by Galway Kinnell. Copyright © 1967 by Galway Kinnell. "The Correspondence School Instructor Says Goodbye to His Poetry Students" from *What A Kingdom It Was* by Galway Kinnell. Copyright © 1960 by Galway Kinnell. Above selections reprinted by permission of Houghton Mifflin Company.

Richard Eberhart: "The Fury of Aerial Bombardment" from *Collected Poems 1930–1976* by Richard Eberhart. Copyright © 1960, 1976 by Richard Eberhart. Jon Stallworthy: "The Almond Tree" from *Root and Branch* by Jon Stallworthy. © Jon Stallworthy 1969. Above selections reprinted by permission of Oxford University Press, Inc.

Oxford University Press, New Zealand. James K. Baxter: "Wild Bees," "Lament for Barney Flanagan," "East Coast Journey," "New Zealand," and "Jerusalem Sonnets" #1 from *Collected Poems of James K. Baxter.* Reprinted by permission of Oxford University Press, Auckland, New Zealand.

P. K. Page. © P. K. Page 1974.

A. D. Peters & Co. Ltd. C. Day Lewis: reprinted by permission of A. D. Peters & Co. Ltd.

Laurence Pollinger Ltd. John Crowe Ransom: from *Selected Poems.* Eyre/Methuen Ltd., publishers; Alfred A. Knopf/Random House Inc., proprietors. Hart Crane: from *The Complete Poems and Selected Letters and Prose.* Oxford University Press, publishers; Liveright Publishing Corporation, proprietors. D. H. Lawrence: from *The Complete Poems of D. H. Lawrence.* Reprinted with permission of Laurence Pollinger Ltd and the Estate of Frieda Lawrence Ravagli. The above selections reprinted with permission of Laurence Pollinger Ltd.

Princeton University Press. Edward Taylor: from *The Poetical Works of Edward Taylor,* ed. with an Introduction and Notes by Thomas H. Johnson. Copyright 1939 by Rockland, 1943 by Princeton University Press. Selections reprinted by permission of Princeton University Press.

Random House, Inc. Alfred A. Knopf, Inc. Sylvia Plath: Copyright © 1961 by Sylvia Plath. Reprinted from *The Colossus and Other Poems,* by Sylvia Plath, by permission of Alfred A. Knopf, Inc. Copyright © 1959 by Sylvia Plath. Reprinted from *The Colossus and Other Poems,* by permission of Alfred A. Knopf, Inc. Wallace Stevens: Copyright 1923 and renewed 1951 by Wallace Stevens. Reprinted from *The Collected Poems of Wallace Stevens,* by permission of Alfred A. Knopf, Inc. Copyright 1936 by Wallace Stevens and renewed 1964 by Holly Stevens. Copyright 1942 by Wallace Stevens and renewed 1970 by Holly Stevens. Copyright 1947 by Wallace Stevens. Reprinted from *The Collected Poems of Wallace Stevens,* by permission of Alfred A. Knopf, Inc. Copyright 1957 by Elsie Stevens and Holly Stevens. Reprinted from *Opus Posthumous,* by permission of Alfred A. Knopf, Inc. Robinson Jeffers: Copyright 1925 and renewed 1953 by Robinson Jeffers. Copyright 1924 and renewed 1952 by Robinson Jeffers. Copyright 1928 and renewed 1956 by Robinson Jeffers. Copyright 1937 and renewed 1965 by Donnan Jeffers and Garth Jeffers. Copyright © 1954 by Robinson Jeffers. Copyright © 1963 by Garth Jeffers and Donnan Jeffers. Copyright © 1963 by Steuben Glass. Reprinted from *The Selected Poetry of Robinson Jeffers,* by permission of Random House, Inc. John Crowe Ransom: Copyright 1924 by Alfred A. Knopf, Inc. and renewed 1952 by John Crowe Ransom. Copyright 1927 by Alfred A. Knopf, Inc. and renewed 1955 by John Crowe Ransom. Copyright 1934 by Alfred A. Knopf, Inc. and renewed 1962 by John Crowe Ransom. Reprinted from *Selected Poems, Third Edition, Revised and Enlarged* by John Crowe Ransom, by permission of Alfred A. Knopf, Inc. Langston Hughes: Copyright 1951 by Langston Hughes. Copyright 1926 by Alfred A. Knopf, Inc. and renewed 1954 by Langston Hughes. Reprinted from *Selected Poems of Langston Hughes,* by Langston Hughes, by permission of Alfred A. Knopf, Inc. From *Shakespeare in Harlem,* by Langston Hughes, Copyright 1942 by Alfred A. Knopf, Inc. and renewed 1970 by Arna Bontemps and George Houston Bass. Reprinted by permission of the publisher. Robert Penn Warren: from *Selected Poems, 1923–1975* by Robert Penn Warren. Copyright © 1976 by Robert Penn Warren. Reprinted by permission of Random House, Inc. From *Being Here: Poems 1977–1980.* Copyright © 1978, 1979, 1980 by Robert Penn Warren. Reprinted by permission of Random House, Inc. Stephen Spender: Copyright 1934 and renewed 1962 by Stephen Spender. Copyright 1946 by Stephen Spender. Reprinted from *Selected Poems,* by permission of Random House, Inc. William Meredith: Copyright 1953 by William Meredith. Reprinted from *The Open Sea,* by permission of Alfred A. Knopf, Inc. Copyright © 1973 by William Meredith. Reprinted from *Hazard, the Painter,* by permission of Alfred A. Knopf, Inc. From *The Cheer.* Copyright © 1980 by William Meredith. Reprinted by permission of Alfred A. Knopf, Inc. W. H. Auden: Copyright 1940 and renewed 1968 by W. H. Auden. Copyright © 1952 by W. H. Auden. Copyright 1941 and renewed 1969 by W. H. Auden. Copyright 1951 by W. H. Auden. Copyright 1945 by W. H. Auden. Reprinted from *W. H. Auden: Collected Poems,* edited by Edward Mendelson, by permission of Random House, Inc. W. D. Snodgrass: Copyright © 1957 by W. D. Snodgrass. Reprinted from *Heart's Needle,* by permission of Alfred A. Knopf, Inc.

Rupert-Hart-Davis. Christopher Smart: lines 697–780 from *Jubilate Agno,* edited by W. H. Bond. Reprinted by permission of Granada Publishing Limited.

Scott, Foresman and Company. Geoffrey Chaucer: From *Chaucer's Poetry: An Anthology for the Modern Reader* edited by E. T. Donaldson. Copyright © 1958, 1975 Scott, Foresman and Company. Reprinted by permission.

Charles Scribner's Sons. Edwin Arlington Robinson: "Miniver Cheevy" in *The Town Down the River.* Copyright 1910 Charles Scribner's Sons; copyright renewed 1938 Ruth Nivison. Reprinted with the permission of Charles Scribner's Sons. "Richard Cory" in *The Children of the Night.* Copyright under the Berne Convention. Reprinted with the permission of Charles Scribner's Sons. Robert Creeley: "A Wicker Basket" and "Heroes" in *For Love: Poems 1950–1965.* Copyright © 1962 Robert Creeley. Reprinted with the permission of Charles Scribner's Sons. Anthony Hecht: "Sestino D'Inverno" and "The Feast of Stephen" in *Millions of Strange Shadows.* Copyright © 1977 by Anthony E. Hecht. Reprinted with the permission of Atheneum Publishers. " 'More Light: More Light!" in *The Hard Hours.* Copyright © 1967 by Anthony E. Hecht. Reprinted with the permission of Atheneum Publishers. James Merrill: "Upon a Second Marriage" in *The Country of a Thousand Years of Peace.* Copyright © 1970 by James Merrill. Reprinted with the permission of Atheneum Publishers. "The Victor Dog" in *Braving the Elements.* Copyright © 1972 by James Merrill. Reprinted with the permission of Atheneum Publishers. "Whitebeard on Videotape" in *Divine Comedies.* Copyright © 1976 by James Merrill. Reprinted with the permission of Atheneum Publishers. John Hollander: "Adam's Task" in *The Night Mirror.* Copyright © 1971 by John Hollander. Reprinted with the permission of Atheneum Publishers. "Swan and Shadow" in *Types of Shape.* Copyright © 1969 by John Hollander. Reprinted with the permission of Atheneum Publishers. W. S. Merwin: "The Drunk in the Furnace" and "Odysseus" in *The Drunk in the Furnace.* Copyright © 1960 by W. S. Merwin. Reprinted with the permission of Atheneum Publishers from *The First Four Books of Poems.* "Separation" in *The Moving Target.* Copyright © 1963 by W. S. Merwin. Reprinted with the permission of Atheneum Publishers.

Seaver Books. Leslie Marmon Silko: Copyright © 1981 by Leslie Marmon Silko. Reprinted from *Storyteller* by Leslie Marmon Silko, published by Seaver Books, New York, 1981.

Simon & Schuster. Margaret Atwood: "Pig Song" from *Selected Poems.* Copyright © 1976 by Margaret Atwood. "You Begin" from *Two-Headed Poems.* Copyright © 1978 by Margaret Atwood. Reprinted by permission of Simon & Schuster, a Division of Gulf & Western Corporation.

Gary Snyder. "Mid-August at Sourdough Mountain Lookout" and "Above Pate Valley" © Gary Snyder 1965.

The Society of Authors. A. E. Housman: The Society of Authors as the literary representative of the Estate of A. E. Housman, and Jonathan Cape Ltd., publishers of A. E. Housman's *Collected Poems.* Walter de la Mare: The Literary Trustees of Walter de la Mare and The Society of Authors as their representative.

The Sterling Lord Agency, Inc. Amiri Baraka (LeRoi Jones): Copyright © 1961, 1969, 1970 by Amiri Baraka (LeRoi Jones). Reprinted by permission of The Sterling Lord Agency, Inc.

James Tate. From *The Lost Pilot.* © James Tate.

Mrs. Myfanwy Thomas. Edward Thomas: From *Collected Poems* by Edward Thomas. Reprinted by permission of Faber & Faber Ltd., W. W. Norton & Company, and Myfanwy Thomas.

University of Illinois Press. Josephine Miles: "Memorial Day" from *Coming to Terms,* by Josephine Miles. Copyright © 1979 by Josephine Miles. Reprinted by permission of the University of Illinois Press.

Viking Penguin Inc. John Ashbery: "Melodic Trains" from *Houseboat Days* by John Ashbery. Copyright © 1975, 1976, 1977 by John Ashbery. "Paradoxes and Oxymorons" from *Shadow Train* by John Ashbery. Copyright © 1980, 1981 by John Ashbery. Dorothy Parker: From *The Portable Dorothy Parker,* revised and enlarged edition, edited by Brendan Gill. Copyright 1926 by Dorothy Parker. Copyright renewed 1954 by Dorothy Parker. D. H. Lawrence: From *The Complete Poems of D. H. Lawrence,* Collected and Edited by Vivian de Sola Pinto and F. Warren Roberts. Copyright © 1964, 1971 by Angelo Ravagli and C. M. Weekly, Executors of The Estate of Frieda Lawrence Ravagli. A. D. Hope: From *Collected Poems 1930–1965* by A. D. Hope. Copyright © 1960, 1962 by A. D. Hope. Copyright 1963, 1966 in all countries of the International Copyright Union by A. D. Hope. Ted Hughes: "A March Calf" from *Season Songs* by Ted Hughes. Copyright © 1973 by Ted Hughes. Above selections reprinted by permission of Viking Penguin Inc.

Watson, Little Limited. D. J. Enright: From *Collected Poems,* published by Oxford University Press. Reprinted with the permission of the publishers, and Watson, Little Limited, agents.

A. P. Watt Ltd. William Butler Yeats: From *The Collected Poems of W. B. Yeats.* Reprinted with the permission of Michael and Anne Yeats, and A. P. Watt Ltd., agents. Rudyard Kipling: Reprinted with the permission of The National Trust, and A. P. Watt Ltd. Robert Graves: From *The Collected Poems of Robert Graves.* Reprinted with the permission of Robert Graves and A. P. Watt Ltd.

Wesleyan University Press. James Dickey: "The Lifeguard" and "In the Tree House at Night" from *Drowning with Others*; copyright © 1961 by James Dickey. All poems first appeared in *The New Yorker.* James Wright: "A Note Left in Jimmy Leonard's Shack" from *Saint Judas*; copyright © 1957 by James Wright. First appeared in *New Orleans Poetry Journal.* "A Blessing" from *The Branch Will Not Break*; copyright © 1961 by James Wright. First appeared in *Poetry.* Above selections reprinted by permission of Wesleyan University Press.

Preface

With the Third Shorter Edition of *The Norton Anthology of Poetry*, we again give readers a wide and deep sampling of the best poetry written in the English language, from early medieval times to the present day. As our friend and adviser M. H. Abrams has said in another context, "a vital literary culture is always on the move," both in the appearance of new works and in the altering response to existing texts. Hence a new edition, which broadens and refines that cultural tradition. Once again, our efforts have been crucially helped by the practical criticism and informed suggestions provided to us by many teachers who have used the anthology in their classes.

In distilling this shorter anthology from the parent Third Edition, we have to some degree altered our principles of selection. We have striven for the same range and comprehensiveness that characterized earlier editions, but we have also concentrated on the needs of instructors and students in introductory poetry courses and have made a number of choices accordingly. The result is a somewhat expanded book which adds over four hundred poems and seventy-five poets to the Shorter Edition for the first time. A little less than half of these have been newly selected from the parent edition; the rest are new to both. The result is, we believe, a more teachable array of poems.

The new Shorter Edition provides, as before, a suitable balance of the older and the newer. Of the new poets and works added, something over half are modern, the rest earlier. There are now twenty-five woman poets, ranging from Elizabeth I to Leslie Marmon Silko: fourteen are new. There is a stronger focus on American poetry. There is a generous selection of Afro-American poems. The representation of Canadian poets has been tripled, while the number of poems written in English in other countries has been signally increased. Finally, we hope that teachers and students will welcome the writers of light verse, new to our ranks.

In addition to reconsidering and adding poets of significance, we have also carefully reviewed the work of poets retained from earlier editions. Almost all writers who have produced important work since our last edition have been updated, and in some cases their selections have been significantly increased to reflect their present status—for example, Richard Wilbur, A. R. Ammons, Adrienne Rich, Sylvia Plath, and Seamus Heaney. But William Shakespeare has been re-examined, too; so also, to name but a few other "classic" poets, have John Milton, Emily Dickinson, William Butler Yeats, and Robert Frost.

Attention to the major poets has not precluded the inclusion of pedagogically useful and stimulating poems by many other poets, nor—at the other end of the scale—significant single poems, from Chidiock Tichborne's "Elegy" all the way to Ishmael Reed's "beware : do not read this poem."

More different *kinds* of poems are thus available for teaching, and nowhere is this better demonstrated than in our offering of longer poems, enabling students to experience poetic forms other than the brief iambic-pentameter lyric. New to the Shorter Edition are Milton's "L'Allegro" and "Il Penseroso," Johnson's "The Vanity of Human Wishes," Whitman's "Crossing Brooklyn Ferry," Stevens's "Thirteen Ways of Looking at a Blackbird," Pound's "Canto I," Eliot's "The Dry Salvages," Hart Crane's "Voyages," and Auden's "In Praise of Limestone." We also make it possible for students to encounter self-contained excerpts that demonstrate some of the great verse achievements in English: the Spenserian stanza, Miltonic blank verse, Byron's *Don Juan* stanza, and the open form of Whitman's *Song of Myself*.

The order is chronological, poets appearing according to their dates of birth and their poems according to the dates of publication in volume form. These dates are printed at the end of the poem, and to the right; when two dates appear together, they indicate published versions which differ in an important way. Dates on the left, when given, are those of composition.

Texts are based on authoritative editions, but have been normalized in spelling and capitalization according to modern American usage—except in the instances in which changes would significantly obscure meter or meaning. The works of Spenser and the Scottish poets, contrivedly archaic or dialectic in spelling, have been left untouched, as have the oldest of the medieval poems, which would remain almost as opaque to modern eyes after normalizing and modernizing as before. The text of Hopkins remains unchanged. For the normalized text of Chaucer selections, as well as for the notes to them, the editors particularly wish to thank Professor E. Talbot Donaldson.

Notes, as Dr. Johnson observed, are necessary, but necessary evils.

They have been provided for information, not criticism; they gloss words and allusions but refrain, as much as possible, from interpretive comment.

It remains to note two added elements which will further facilitate use of the anthology in the classroom. The first is a new essay on versification by Jon Stallworthy of Cornell University. Stallworthy has drawn upon the prosodic glossary and commentary ably provided in the earlier editions by Alexander W. Allison and Arthur J. Carr, but has tailored his essay for students who require a more basic knowledge than that presented in the previous essays. The second is a course guide for instructors, prepared by Debra Fried, also of Cornell. The principal aim of this guide (available on request from the publisher) is to help teachers select poems from the anthology to shape a course or courses along any lines they wish—according to formal elements, subject matter, themes and topics, or the like—and to establish relationships between poets and poems of different genres, periods, and concerns.

So many teachers aided us in so many ways in preparing this edition that we have listed them on a separate page of acknowledgments; to all of them we give our deepest thanks. Once again, we salute M. H. Abrams, whose experience and saving sanity have guided our work throughout. The publisher's editor, John Benedict, wishes to acknowledge his gratitude to his co-workers at Norton: for their special editorial assistance, Kathleen M. Anderson, Mary Cunnane, Carol Flechner, Rachel P. Teplow; and for their signal help in preparing the book speedily and accurately for the press, Sue Crooks, Roberta Flechner, Nelda Freeman, Diane O'Connor.

Note on the Modernizing of Medieval Texts

Changes that have taken place in pronunciation obscure for the modern reader the regular metrical character of some Middle English verse. The most important of these changes is the loss of an unstressed syllable in many word endings. We still pronounce some endings as separate syllables (*roses, wedded*), but for Chaucer the full syllabic value of an ending was available generally, even though its pronunciation was not always mandatory. Moreover, a great many final *–e*'s, vestiges of fuller endings at an earlier stage of the language, were still often pronounced (ə) in the ordinary speech of the day, so that the poet could treat them as syllables or not, according to the requirements of his meter, as *boughte* (pronounced either *bought* or *boughtë*) and *ofte* (pronounced either *oft* or *oftë*).

In modernizing, the editors have tried wherever possible to preserve or devise spellings that do not cut the reader off from the possibility of recovering the original rhythms. A non-modern spelling, especially at the end of a word, means that in the original text there is warrant for supposing that an "extra" syllable might have been pronounced at this point to justify metrical expectation. At the same time the editors have tried to avoid imposing a non-modern reading in those cases where a clear metrical pattern is not manifest.

Acknowledgments

The following critics, advisers, and friends were of especial help in providing critiques of *The Norton Anthology of Poetry* as a whole or in giving expert advice about specific poets and genres: Lianna Babener (Grinnell College); Walter Jackson Bate (Harvard University); Barbara Belyea (University of Calgary); Russell Brown (Scarborough College, University of Toronto); C. Abbott Conway (McGill University); Kevin Crossley-Holland, Hans deGroot (University of Toronto); Elizabeth Dobbs (Grinnell College); Mary Fitz Gerald (University of New Orleans); William D. Ford (Lycoming College); Debra Fried (Cornell University); Albert Gelpi (Stanford University); Barbara Charlesworth Gelpi (Stanford University, and editor of *Signs*); Brian K. Green (University of Stellenbosch); Seraphia Leyda (University of New Orleans); Joanna Lipking (Northwestern University); Nicholas Lorimer (information officer, New Zealand Consulate General); Alasdair D. F. Macrae (University of Stirling); Jacqueline T. Miller (Livingston College, Rutgers University); Perry Nodelman (University of Winnipeg); David Perkins (Harvard University); Dr. James Pipkin (University of Houston); Peter Quartermain (University of British Columbia); Merrill Skaggs (Drew University); Jon Stallworthy (Cornell University); Jennifer Sutherland; A. J. Wainwright (Dalhousie University); Leon Waldorf (University of Illinois at Urbana); Christopher Wallace-Crabbe (University of Melbourne); D. R. M. Wilkinson (University of Groningen).

And the following teacher-scholars aided immeasurably in our plans for the new edition by answering questions about their use of the book in their classrooms: William Blissett (University of Toronto); Patricia Chaffee (Norfolk State University); Richard Edwards (Moorpark College); M. L. Flynn (University of Missouri at Columbia); Milton J. Foley (University of Montevallo); William Galperin (Oregon State University); Elizabeth Greene (Queen's University at Kingston); Donald Gray (Indiana University); Thomas Keeling (University of California, Los Angeles); Frank Lentricchia (University of California, Irvine); Robert Lewis (University of North Dakota); Richard T. Martin (Ohio State University); Thomas F. Merrill (University of Delaware); John Olmstead (Oberlin College); Michael O'Connell (University of California, Santa Barbara); G. E. Powell (University of British Columbia); Duncan Robertson (Queen's University at Kingston); Shirley Steve (Gustavus Adolphus College); Harry C. Stiehl (San Diego State University); Richard Tillinghast (Harvard University); Herbert Tucker (Northwestern University); Michael W. Twomey (Ithaca College).

Acknowledgments

Contents

THE
Norton Anthology of Poetry

THIRD EDITION · SHORTER

ANONYMOUS LYRICS OF THE THIRTEENTH AND FOURTEENTH CENTURIES

Now Go'th Sun Under Wood[1]

Nou goth sonne under wode[2]—
Me reweth, Marie, thi faire rode.
Nou goth sonne under tre—
Me reweth, Marie, thi sone and the.

The Cuckoo Song[3]

Sing, cuccu, nu. Sing, cuccu.
Sing, cuccu. Sing, cuccu, nu.

Sumer is i-cumen in—
Lhude sing, cuccu!
Groweth sed and bloweth med
And springth the wude nu.
Sing, cuccu!

Awe bleteth after lomb,
Lhouth after calve cu,
Bulluc sterteth, bucke verteth—
Murie sing, cuccu!
Cuccu, cuccu.
Wel singes thu, cuccu.
Ne swik thu naver nu!

Ubi Sunt Qui Ante Nos Fuerunt?

Were beth they biforen us weren,[4]
Houndes ladden and hauekes beren
And hadden feld and wode?

1. *Translation:* Now goes the sun under the wood— / I pity, Mary, thy fair face. / Now goes the sun under the tree— / I pity, Mary, thy son and thee.
2. *Wood* and *tree* not only had their modern meanings but also meant *the cross.*
3. *Translation:* Sing, cuckoo, now. Sing, cuckoo. / Sing, cuckoo. Sing, cuckoo, now.
Spring is come in— / Sing loud, cuckoo! / The seed grows, the meadow blooms / And the wood now comes into leaf / Sing, cuckoo!
The ewe bleats after the lamb, / The cow lows after the calf, / The bullock leaps, the buck breaks wind— / Sing merrily, cuckoo! / Cuckoo, cuckoo. / Well singest thou, cuckoo. / Cease thou never now!
4. The poem's first line translates the title. *Translation:* Where be they who before us were, / Who led hounds and bore hawks / And owned fields and woods? / The rich ladies in their bowers, / That wore gold in their coiffures, / and had fair faces,
[That] ate and drank and rejoiced; / Their life was all a game; / Men knelt before them; / They bore themselves exceeding high— / And in the twinkling of an eye / Their souls were lost.
Where is that laughing and that song, / That trailing [of garments] and that proud gait, / Those hawks and those hounds? / All that joy is gone away; / That well has come to wellaway, / To many hard times.
Their paradise they took here, / And now they lie in hell together— / The fire it burns ever. / Long is their "ay" and long their "oh," / Long their "alas" and long their "woe"— / Thence shall they come never.
Suffer here, man, then if thou wilt, / The little pain thou art asked to bear. / Withdraw thine eyes oft [from the things of this world]. / Though thy pain be severe, / If thou think on thy reward, / It shall seem soft to thee.
If that fiend, that foul thing, / Through wicked counsel, through false tempting, / Has cast thee down, / Up and be a good champion! / Stand, and fall no more / For a little blast [for a mere puff of wind].
Take thou the cross for thy staff / And think on him that thereon gave / His life that was so dear. / He gave it for thee; repay him for it / Against his foe. Take thou that staff / And avenge him on that thief.
Of right belief [true faith] take thou the shield / While thou art in the field. / Seek to strengthen thy hand / And keep thy foe at staff's end / And make that traitor say the word [of surrender]. Gain that merry land
Wherein is day without night, / Without end strength and might, / And vengeance on every foe, / With God himself eternal life, / And peace and rest without strife, / Weal without woe.
Maiden mother, heaven's queen, / Thou might and can and ought to be / Our shield against the fiend. / Help us to flee from sins / That we may see thy son / In joy without end. / Amen.

The riche levedies in hoere bour,
That wereden gold in hoere tressour,
With hoere brighte rode,

Eten and drounken and maden hem glad;
Hoere lif was al with gamen i-lad;
Men keneleden hem biforen;
They beren hem wel swithe heye—
And in a twincling of an eye
Hoere soules weren forloren.

Were is that lawing and that song,
That trayling and that proude yong,
Tho hauekes and tho houndes?
Al that joye is went away;
That wele is comen to welaway,
To manie harde stoundes.

Hoere paradis hy nomen here,
And nou they lien in helle i-fere—
The fuir hit brennes hevere.
Long is ay and long is ho,
Long is wy and long is wo—
Thennes ne cometh they nevere.

Dreghy here, man, thenne if thou wilt,
A luitel pine, that me the bit.
Withdrau thine eyses ofte.
They thi pine be ounrede,
And thou thenke on thi mede,
Hit sal the thinken softe.

If that fend, that foule thing,
Thorou wikke roun, thorou fals egging,
Nethere the haveth i-cast,
Oup, and be god chaunpioun!
Stond, ne fal namore adoun
For a luytel blast.

Thou tak the rode to thi staf
And thenk on him that thereonne yaf
His lif that wes so lef.
He hit yaf for the; thou yelde hit him
Ayein his fo. That staf thou nim
And wrek him of that thef.

Of rightte bileve thou nim that sheld
The wiles that thou best in that feld.
Thin hond to strenkthen fonde
And kep thy fo with staves ord
And do that traytre seien that word.
Biget that murie londe

Thereinne is day withouten night,
Withouten ende strenkthe and might,
And wreche of everich fo,
Mid god himselwen eche lif
And pes and rest withoute strif,
Wele withouten wo.

Mayden moder, hevene quene,
Thou might and const and owest to bene
Oure sheld ayein the fende.
Help ous sunne for to flen
That we moten thi sone i-seen
In joye withouten hende.
Amen.

Alison[5]

Bytuene Mersh and Averil,
When spray biginneth to springe,
The lutel foul hath hire wyl
On hyre lud to synge.
Ich libbe in love-longinge
For semlokest of alle thinge—
He may me blisse bringe;
Icham in hire baundoun
An hendy hap ichabbe yhent—
Ichot from hevene it is me sent:
From alle wymmen mi love is lent
And lyht on Alysoun.

On heu hire her is fayr ynoh,
Hire browe broune, hire eye blake—
With lossum chere he on me loh—
With middel smal and wel ymake.
Bote he me wolle to hire take,
Forte buen hire owen make,
Longe to lyven ichulle forsake
And feye fallen adoun
An hendy hap . . .

Nightes when I wende and wake—
Forthi myn wonges waxeth won—
Levedi, al for thine sake
Longinge is ylent me on.
In world nis non so wyter mon
That al hire bounte telle con.
Hire swyre is whittore then the swon,
And feyrest may in toune.
An hendy hap . . .

Icham for wowyng al forwake,
Wery so water in wore,
Lest eny reve me my make

5. *Translation:* Between March and April, / When the twigs begin to leaf, / The little bird is free / To sing her song. / I live in love-longing / For the seemliest of all things— / She may bring me bliss; / I am in her power. / A fair chance I have got— / I know from heaven it is sent me: / From all women my love is turned / And lights on Alison.

In hue her hair is fair enough, / Her brow brown, her eye black— / With a lovely face she laughed upon me— / Her waist small and well-made. / Unless she will take me to her, / To be her own mate, / [The hope] to live long I shall forsake / And, doomed, fall down [to die]. / A fair chance . . .

Nights when I turn and wake— / For which my cheeks wax pale— / Lady, all for thy sake / Longing has lighted on me. / In the world there is no man so wise / That he all her bounty can tell. / Her neck is whiter than the swan, / And [she is] the fairest maid in town. / A fair chance . . .

I am from wooing all worn out [exhausted from staying awake], / Weary as water on the beach, / [For fear] lest any seize from me my mate / [For whom] I have yearned long. / It is better to suffer awhile sorely / Than to mourn evermore. / Kindest of ladies [literally, *under gown*], / Harken to my song. / A fair chance . . .

GEOFFREY CHAUCER
(ca. 1343–1400)

From THE CANTERBURY TALES

The Pardoner's Prologue and Tale

The Introduction

Oure Hoste gan to swere as he were wood;° *insane*
"Harrow,"° quod he, "by nailes[1] and by blood, *help*
This was a fals cherl and a fals justice.[2]
As shameful deeth as herte may devise
Come to thise juges and hir advocats.
Algate° this sely° maide is slain, allas! *at any rate / innocent*
Allas, too dere boughte she beautee!
Wherfore I saye alday° that men may see *always*
The yiftes of Fortune and of Nature
Been cause of deeth to many a creature.
As bothe yiftes that I speke of now,
Men han ful ofte more for harm than prow.° *benefit*
"But trewely, myn owene maister dere,
This is a pitous tale for to heere.
But nathelees, passe over, is no fors:[3]
I praye to God so save thy gentil cors,° *body*
And eek thine urinals and thy jurdones,[4]
Thyn ipocras[5] and eek thy galiones,
And every boiste° ful of thy letuarye°— *box / medicine*
God blesse hem, and oure lady Sainte Marye.
So mote I theen,[6] thou art a propre man,
And lik a prelat, by Saint Ronian![7]
Saide I nat wel? I can nat speke in terme.[8]
But wel I woot, thou doost° myn herte to erme° *make / grieve*
That I almost have caught a cardinacle.[9]
By corpus bones,[1] but if I have triacle.° *medicine*
Or elles a draughte of moiste° and corny° ale, *fresh / malty*
Or but I heere anoon° a merye tale, *at once*
Myn herte is lost for pitee of this maide.
"Thou bel ami,[2] thou Pardoner," he saide,
"Tel us som mirthe or japes° right anoon." *joke*
"It shal be doon," quod he, "by Saint Ronion.
But first," quod he, "here at this ale-stake[3]

1. I.e., God's nails.
2. The Host has been affected by the Physician's sad tale of the Roman maiden Virginia, whose great beauty caused a judge to attempt to obtain her person by means of a trumped-up lawsuit in which he connived with a "churl" who claimed her as his slave; in order to preserve her chastity, her father killed her.
3. I.e., never mind.
4. Jordans (chamber pots): the Host is somewhat confused in his endeavor to use technical medical terms.
5. A medicinal drink named after Hippocrates; "galiones": a medicine, probably invented on the spot by the Host, named after Galen.
6. So might I thrive.
7. St. Ronan or St. Ninian, with a possible play on "runnion" (sexual organ).
8. Speak in technical idiom.
9. Apparently a cardiac condition, confused in the Host's mind with a cardinal.
1. An illiterate oath, mixing "God's bones" with *corpus dei*. "But if": unless.
2. Fair friend.
3. Sign of a tavern.

I wol bothe drinke and eten of a cake."
And right anoon thise gentils gan to crye,
"Nay, lat him telle us of no ribaudye.° *ribaldry*
Tel us som moral thing that we may lere,° *learn*
Som wit,[4] and thanne wol we gladly heere."
"I graunte, ywis," quod he, "but I moot thinke
Upon som honeste° thing whil that I drinke. *decent*

The Prologue

Lordinges—quod he—in chirches whan I preche,
I paine me[5] to han an hautein° speeche, *loud*
And ringe it out as round as gooth a belle,
For I can al by rote[6] that I telle.
My theme is alway oon,[7] and evere was:
Radix malorum est cupiditas.[8]
First I pronounce whennes° that I come, *whence*
And thanne my bulles[9] shewe I alle and some:
Oure lige lordes seel on my patente,[1]
That shewe I first, my body to warente,° *keep safe*
That no man be so bold, ne preest ne clerk,
Me to destourbe of Cristes holy werk.
And after that thanne telle I forth my tales[2]—
Bulles of popes and of cardinales,
Of patriarkes and bisshopes I shewe,
And in Latin I speke a wordes fewe,
To saffron with[3] my predicacioun,° *preaching*
And for to stire hem to devocioun.
Thanne shewe I forth my longe crystal stones,° *jars*
Ycrammed ful of cloutes° and of bones— *rags*
Relikes been they, as weenen° they eechoon. *suppose*
Thanne have I in laton° a shulder-boon *zinc*
Which that was of an holy Jewes sheep.
"Goode men," I saye, "take of my wordes keep:° *notice*
If that this boon be wasshe in any welle,
If cow, or calf, or sheep, or oxe swelle,
That any worm hath ete or worm ystonge,[4]
Take water of that welle and wassh his tonge,
And it is hool° anoon. And ferthermoor, *sound*
Of pokkes° and of scabbe and every soor° *pox / sore*
Shal every sheep be hool that of this welle
Drinketh a draughte. Take keep eek° that I telle: *also*
If that the goode man that the beestes oweth° *owns*
Wol every wike,° er that the cok him croweth, *week*
Fasting drinken of this welle a draughte—
As thilke° holy Jew oure eldres taughte— *that same*
His beestes and his stoor° shal multiplye. *stock*
"And sire, also it heleth jalousye:
For though a man be falle in jalous rage,
Lat maken with this water his potage,° *soup*
And nevere shal he more his wif mistriste,° *mistrust*
Though he the soothe of hir defaute wiste,[5]
Al hadde she[6] taken preestes two or three.

4. I.e., something with significance.
5. Take pains.
6. I know all by heart.
7. I.e., the same.
8. Avarice is the root of evil (I Timothy vi.10).
9. Episcopal mandates; "alle and some": each and every one.
1. I.e., the Pope's seal on my papal license.
2. I go on with my yarn.
3. To add spice to.
4. That has eaten or been bitten by any worm.
5. Knew the truth of her infidelity.
6. Even if she had.

"Here is a mitein° eek that ye may see: *mitten*
He that his hand wol putte in this mitein
He shal have multiplying of his grain,
Whan he hath sowen, be it whete or otes—
So that he offre pens or elles grotes.[7]
"Goode men and wommen, oo thing warne I you:
If any wight be in this chirche now
That hath doon sinne horrible, that he
Dar nat for shame of it yshriven° be, *absolved*
Or any womman, be she yong or old,
That hath ymaked hir housbonde cokewold,° *cuckold*
Swich folk shal have no power ne no grace
To offren to[8] my relikes in this place;
And whoso findeth him out of swich blame,
He wol come up and offre in Goddes name,
And I assoile° him by the auctoritee *absolve*
Which that by bulle ygraunted was to me."
By this gaude° have I wonne, yeer by yeer, *trick*
An hundred mark[9] sith° I was pardoner. *since*
I stonde lik a clerk in my pulpet,
And whan the lewed° peple is down yset, *ignorant*
I preche so as ye han herd bifore,
And telle an hundred false japes° more. *tricks*
Thanne paine I me[1] to strecche forth the nekke,
And eest and west upon the peple I bekke[2]
As dooth a douve,° sitting on a berne;° *dove / barn*
Mine handes and my tonge goon so yerne° *fast*
That it is joye to see my bisinesse.
Of avarice and of swich cursednesse° *sin*
Is al my preching, for to make hem free° *generous*
To yiven hir pens, and namely° unto me, *especially*
For myn entente is nat but for to winne,[3]
And no thing for correccion of sinne:
I rekke° nevere whan that they been beried° *care / buried*
Though that hir soules goon a-blakeberied.[4]
For certes, many a predicacioun° *sermon*
Comth ofte time of yvel entencioun:
Som for plesance of folk and flaterye,
To been avaunced° by ypocrisye, *promoted*
And som for vaine glorye, and som for hate;
For whan I dar noon otherways debate,° *fight*
Thanne wol I stinge him with my tonge smerte
In preching, so that he shal nat asterte° *escape*
To been defamed falsly, if that he
Hath trespassed to[5] my bretheren or to me.
For though I telle nought his propre name,
Men shal wel knowe that it is the same
By signes and by othere circumstaunces.
Thus quite° I folk that doon us displesaunces;[6] *pay back*
Thus spete° I out my venim under hewe° *spit / color*
Of holinesse, to seeme holy and trewe.
But shortly myn entente I wol devise:° *describe*
I preche of no thing but for coveitise;
Therfore my theme is yit and evere was

7. Pennies, groats, coins.
8. To make gifts in reverence of.
9. Marks (pecuniary units).
1. I take pains.
2. I.e., I shake my head.
3. Only to gain.
4. Go blackberrying, i.e., go to hell.
5. Injured.
6. Do us discourtesies.

Radix malorum est cupiditas.
Thus can I preche again that same vice
Which that I use, and that is avarice.
But though myself be gilty in that sinne,
Yit can I make other folk to twinne° *separate*
From avarice, and sore to repente—
But that is nat my principal entente:
I preche no thing but for coveitise.
Of this matere it oughte ynough suffise.
Thanne telle I hem ensamples[7] many oon
Of olde stories longe time agoon,
For lewed° peple loven tales olde— *ignorant*
Swiche thinges can they wel reporte and holde.[8]
What, trowe° ye that whiles I may preche, *believe*
And winne gold and silver for° I teche, *because*
That I wol live in poverte wilfully?
Nay, nay, I thoughte° it nevere, trewely, *intended*
For I wol preche and begge in sondry landes;
I wol nat do no labour with mine handes,
Ne make baskettes and live therby,
By cause I wol nat beggen idelly.[9]
I wol none of the Apostles countrefete:° *imitate*
I wol have moneye, wolle,° cheese, and whete, *wool*
Al were it[1] yiven of the pooreste page,
Or of the pooreste widwe in a village—
Al sholde hir children sterve[2] for famine.
Nay, I wol drinke licour of the vine
And have a joly wenche in every town.
But herkneth, lordinges, in conclusioun,
Youre liking° is that I shal telle a tale: *pleasure*
Now have I dronke a draughte of corny ale,
By God, I hope I shal you telle a thing
That shal by reson been at youre liking;
For though myself be a ful vicious man,
A moral tale yit I you telle can,
Which I am wont to preche for to winne.
Now holde youre pees, my tale I wol biginne.

The Tale

In Flandres whilom° was a compaignye *once*
Of yonge folk that haunteden° folye— *practiced*
As riot, hasard, stewes,[3] and tavernes,
Wher as with harpes, lutes, and gival giternes° *guitars*
They daunce and playen at dees° bothe day and night, *dice*
And ete also and drinke over hir might,[4]
Thurgh which they doon the devel sacrifise
Within that develes temple in cursed wise
By superfluitee° abhominable. *overindulgence*
Hir othes been so grete and so dampnable
That it is grisly for to heere hem swere:
Oure blessed Lordes body they totere[5]—
Hem thoughte that Jewes rente° him nought ynough. *tore*
And eech of hem at otheres sinne lough.° *laughed*

7. *Exempla* (stories illustrating moral principles).
8. Repeat and remember.
9. I.e., without profit.
1. Even though it were.
2. Even though her children should die.
3. Wild parties, gambling, brothels.
4. Beyond their capacity.
5. Tear apart (a reference to oaths sworn by parts of His body, such as "God's bones!" or "God's teeth!").

And right anoon thanne comen tombesteres,° *dancing girls*
Fetis° and smale,° and yonge frutesteres,[6] *shapely / neat*
Singeres with harpes, bawdes,° wafereres[7]— *pimps*
Whiche been the verray develes officeres,
To kindle and blowe the fir of lecherye
That is annexed unto glotonye:[8]
The Holy Writ take I to my witnesse
That luxure° is in win and dronkenesse. *lechery*
Lo, how that dronken Lot[9] unkindely° *unnaturally*
Lay by his doughtres two unwitingly:
So dronke he was he niste° what he wroughte. *didn't know*
Herodes, who so wel the stories soughte,[1]
Whan he of win was repleet at his feeste,
Right at his owene table he yaf his heeste° *command*
To sleen° the Baptist John, ful giltelees. *slay*

Senek[2] saith a good word doutelees:
He saith he can no difference finde
Bitwixe a man that is out of his minde
And a man which that is dronkelewe,° *drunken*
But that woodnesse, yfallen in a shrewe,[3]
Persevereth lenger than dooth dronkenesse.
O glotonye, ful of cursednesse!° *wickedness*
O cause first of oure confusioun!° *downfall*
O original of oure dampnacioun,° *damnation*
Til Crist hadde bought° us with his blood again! *redeemed*
Lo, how dere, shortly for to sayn,
Abought° was thilke° cursed vilainye; *paid for / that same*
Corrupt was al this world for glotonye:
Adam oure fader and his wif also
Fro Paradis to labour and to wo
Were driven for that vice, it is no drede.° *doubt*
For whil that Adam fasted, as I rede,
He was in Paradis; and whan that he
Eet° of the fruit defended° on a tree, *ate / forbidden*
Anoon he was out cast to wo and paine.
O glotonye, on thee wel oughte us plaine!° *complain*

O, wiste a man[4] how manye maladies
Folwen of excesse and of glotonies,
He wolde been the more mesurable° *moderate*
Of his diete, sitting at his table.
Allas, the shorte throte, the tendre mouth,
Maketh that eest and west and north and south,
In erthe, in air, in water, men to swinke,° *work*
To gete a gloton daintee mete and drinke.
Of this matere, O Paul, wel canstou trete:
"Mete unto wombe,° and wombe eek unto mete, *belly*
Shal God destroyen bothe," as Paulus saith.[5]
Allas, a foul thing is it, by my faith,
To saye this word, and fouler is the deede
Whan man so drinketh of the white and rede[6]
That of his throte he maketh his privee° *privy*
Thurgh thilke cursed superfluitee.° *overindulgence*

6. Fruit-selling girls.
7. Girl cake-vendors.
8. I.e., closely related to gluttony.
9. For Lot, see Genesis xix.30–36.
1. For the story of Herod and St. John the Baptist, see Mark vi.17–29. "Who so * * * soughte": i.e., whoever looked it up in the Gospel would find.
2. Seneca, the Roman Stoic philosopher.
3. But that madness, occurring in a wicked man.
4. If a man knew.
5. See I Corinthians vi.13.
6. I.e., white and red wines.

The Apostle[7] weeping saith ful pitously,
"Ther walken manye of which you told have I—
I saye it now weeping with pitous vois—
They been enemies of Cristes crois,° *cross*
Of whiche the ende is deeth—wombe is hir god!"[8]
O wombe, O bely, O stinking cod,° *bag*
Fulfilled° of dong° and of corrupcioun! *filled full / dung*
At either ende of thee foul is the soun.° *sound*
How greet labour and cost is thee to finde!° *provide for*
Thise cookes, how they stampe° and straine and grinde, *pound*
And turnen substance into accident[9]
To fulfillen al thy likerous° talent!° *dainty / appetite*
Out of the harde bones knokke they
The mary,° for they caste nought away *marrow*
That may go thurgh the golet[1] softe and soote.° *sweetly*
Of spicerye° of leef and bark and roote *spices*
Shal been his sauce ymaked by delit,
To make him yit a newer appetit.
But certes, he that haunteth swiche delices° *pleasures*
Is deed° whil that he liveth in tho° vices. *dead / those*
A lecherous thing is win, and dronkenesse
Is ful of striving° and of wrecchednesse. *quarreling*
O dronke man, disfigured is thy face!
Sour is thy breeth, foul artou to embrace!
And thurgh thy dronke nose seemeth the soun
As though thou saidest ay,° "Sampsoun, Sampsoun." *always*
And yit, God woot,° Sampson drank nevere win.[2] *knows*
Thou fallest as it were a stiked swin;[3]
Thy tonge is lost, and al thyn honeste cure,
For dronkenesse is verray sepulture° *burial*
Of mannes wit° and his discrecioun. *intelligence*
In whom that drinke hath dominacioun
He can no conseil° keepe, it is no drede.° *secrets / doubt*
Now keepe you fro the white and fro the rede—
And namely° fro the white win of Lepe[4] *pariticularly*
That is to selle in Fisshstreete or in Chepe:[5]
The win of Spaine creepeth subtilly
In othere wines growing faste° by, *close*
Of which ther riseth swich fumositee° *heady fumes*
That whan a man hath dronken draughtes three
And weeneth° that he be at hoom in Chepe, *supposes*
He is in Spaine, right at the town of Lepe,
Nat at The Rochele ne at Burdeux town,[6]
And thanne wol he sayn, "Sampsoun, Sampsoun."
But herkneth, lordinges, oo° word I you praye, *one*
That alle the soverein actes,[7] dar I saye,
Of victories in the Olde Testament,
Thurgh verray God that is omnipotent,
Were doon in abstinence and in prayere:
Looketh° the Bible and ther ye may it lere.° *behold / learn*

7. I.e., St. Paul.
8. See Philippians iii.18.
9. A philosophic joke, depending on the distinction between inner reality (substance) and outward appearance (accident).
1. Through the gullet.
2. Before Samson's birth an angel told his mother that he would be a Nazarite throughout his life; members of this sect took no strong drink.
3. Stuck pig. "Honeste cure": care for self-respect.
4. A town in Spain.
5. Fishstreet and Cheapside in the London market district.
6. The Pardoner is joking about the illegal custom of adulterating fine wines of Bordeaux and La Rochelle with strong Spanish wine.
7. Distinguished deeds.

Looke Attila, the grete conquerour,[8]
Deide° in his sleep with shame and dishonour, *died*
Bleeding at his nose in dronkenesse:
A capitain sholde live in sobrenesse.
And overal this, aviseth° you right wel *consider*
What was comanded unto Lamuel[9]—
Nat Samuel, but Lamuel, saye I—
Redeth the Bible and finde it expresly,
Of win-yiving° to hem that han[1] justise: *wine-serving*
Namore of this, for it may wel suffise.
And now that I have spoken of glotonye,
Now wol I you defende° hasardrye:° *prohibit / gambling*
Hasard is verray moder° of lesinges,° *mother / lies*
And of deceite and cursed forsweringes,
Blaspheme of Crist, manslaughtre, and wast° also *waste*
Of catel° and of time; and ferthermo, *property*
It is repreve° and contrarye of honour *disgrace*
For to been holden a commune hasardour,° *gambler*
And evere the hyer he is of estat
The more is he holden desolat.[2]
If that a prince useth hasardrye,
In alle governance and policye
He is, as by commune opinioun,
Yholde the lasse° in reputacioun. *less*
Stilbon, that was a wis embassadour,
Was sent to Corinthe in ful greet honour
Fro Lacedomye° to make hir alliaunce, *Sparta*
And whan he cam him happede° parchaunce *it happened*
That alle the gretteste° that were of that lond *greatest*
Playing at the hasard he hem foond,° *found*
For which as soone as it mighte be
He stal him[3] hoom again to his contree,
And saide, "Ther wol I nat lese° my name, *lose*
N'I wol nat take on me so greet defame° *dishonor*
You to allye unto none hasardours:
Sendeth othere wise embassadours,
For by my trouthe, me were levere[4] die
Than I you sholde to hasardours allye.
For ye that been so glorious in honours
Shal nat allye you with hasardours
As by my wil, ne as by my tretee."° *treaty*
This wise philosophre, thus saide he.
Looke eek that to the king Demetrius
The King of Parthes,° as the book[5] saith us, *Parthians*
Sente him a paire of dees° of gold in scorn, *dice*
For he hadde used hasard therbiforn,
For which he heeld his glorye or his renown
At no value or reputacioun.
Lordes may finden other manere play
Honeste° ynough to drive the day away; *honorable*
Now wol I speke of othes false and grete
A word or two, as olde bookes trete:
Greet swering is a thing abhominable,

8. Attila was the leader of the Huns who captured Rome in the 5th century.
9. Lemuel's mother told him that kings should not drink (Proverbs xxxi.4–5).
1. I.e., administer.
2. I.e., dissolute.
3. He stole away.
4. I had rather.
5. The book that relates this and the previous incident is the *Policraticus* of the 12th-century Latin writer, John of Salisbury.

And fals swering is yit more reprevable.° *reprehensible*
The hye God forbad swering at al—
Witnesse on Mathew.[6] But in special
Of swering saith the holy Jeremie,[7]
"Thou shalt swere sooth thine othes and nat lie,
And swere in doom[8] and eek in rightwisnesse,
But idel swering is a cursedness."° *wickedness*
  Biholde and see that in the firste Table[9]
Of hye Goddes heestes° honorable *commandments*
How that the seconde heeste of him is this:
"Take nat my name in idel or amis."
Lo, rather° he forbedeth swich swering *sooner*
Than homicide, or many a cursed thing.
I saye that as by ordre thus it stondeth—
This knoweth that[1] his heestes understondeth
How that the seconde heeste of God is that.
And fertherover,° I wol thee telle al plat° *moreover / flat*
That vengeance shal nat parten° from his hous *depart*
That of his othes is too outrageous.
"By Goddes precious herte!" and "By his nailes!"° *fingernails*
And "By the blood of Crist that is in Hailes,[2]
Sevene is my chaunce, and thyn is cink and traye!"[3]
"By Goddes armes, if thou falsly playe
This daggere shal thurghout thyn herte go!"
This fruit cometh of the bicche bones[4] two—
Forswering, ire, falsnesse, homicide.
Now for the love of Crist that for us dyde,
Lete° youre othes bothe grete and smale. *leave*
But sires, now wol I telle forth my tale.
  Thise riotoures° three of whiche I telle, *revelers*
Longe erst er prime[5] ronge of any belle,
Were set hem in a taverne to drinke,
And as they sat they herde a belle clinke
Biforn a cors° was caried to his grave. *corpse*
That oon of hem gan callen to his knave:° *servant*
"Go bet,"[6] quod he, "and axe° redily° *ask / promptly*
What cors is this that passeth heer forby,
And looke° that thou reporte his name weel."° *be sure / well*
  "Sire," quod this boy, "it needeth neveradeel:[7]
It was me told er ye cam heer two houres.
He was, pardee, an old felawe of youres,
And sodeinly he was yslain tonight,° *last night*
Fordronke° as he sat on his bench upright; *very drunk*
Ther cam a privee° thief men clepeth° Deeth, *stealthy / call*
That in this contree al the peple sleeth,° *slays*
And with his spere he smoot his herte atwo,
And he wente his way withouten wordes mo.
He hath a thousand slain this° pestilence. *during this*
And maister, er ye come in his presence,
Me thinketh that it were necessarye
For to be war of swich an adversarye;
Beeth redy for to meete him everemore:

6. "But I say unto you, Swear not at all" (Matthew v.34).
7. Jeremiah (iv.2).
8. Equity; "rightwisnesse": righteousness.
9. I.e., the first four of the Ten Commandments.
1. I.e., he that.
2. An abbey in Gloucestershire supposed to possess some of Christ's blood.
3. Five and three.
4. I.e., damned dice.
5. Long before 9 A.M.
6. Better, i.e., quick.
7. It isn't a bit necessary.

Thus taughte me my dame.° I saye namore." *mother*
"By Sainte Marye," saide this taverner,
"The child saith sooth, for he hath slain this yeer,
Henne° over a mile, within a greet village, *hence*
Bothe man and womman, child and hine° and page. *farm laborer*
I trowe° his habitacion be there. *believe*
To been avised° greet wisdom it were *wary*
Er that he dide a man a dishonour."
"Ye, Goddes armes," quod this riotour,
"Is it swich peril with him for to meete?
I shal him seeke by way and eek by streete,[8]
I make avow to Goddes digne° bones. *worthy*
Herkneth, felawes, we three been alle ones:° *of one mind*
Lat eech of us holde up his hand to other
And eech of us bicome otheres brother,
And we wol sleen this false traitour Deeth.
He shal be slain, he that so manye sleeth,
By Goddes dignitee, er it be night."
Togidres han thise three hir trouthes plight[9]
To live and dien eech of hem with other,
As though he were his owene ybore° brother. *born*
And up they sterte,° al dronken in this rage, *started*
And forth they goon towardes that village
Of which the taverner hadde spoke biforn.
And many a grisly ooth thanne han they sworn,
And Cristes blessed body they torente:° *tore apart*
Deeth shal be deed° if that they may him hente.° *dead / catch*
Whan they han goon nat fully half a mile,
Right as they wolde han treden° over a stile, *stepped*
An old man and a poore with hem mette;
This olde man ful mekely hem grette,° *greeted*
And saide thus, "Now lordes, God you see."[1]
The pruddeste° of thise riotoures three *proudest*
Answerde again, "What, carl° with sory grace, *churl*
Why artou al forwrapped save thy face?
Why livestou so longe in so greet age?"
This olde man gan looke in his visage,
And saide thus, "For° I ne can nat finde *because*
A man, though that I walked into Inde,
Neither in citee ne in no village,
That wolde chaunge his youthe for myn age;
And therfore moot I han myn age stille,
As longe time as it is Goddes wille.
"Ne Deeth, allas, ne wol nat have my lif.
Thus walke I lik a resteless caitif,° *captive*
And on the ground which is my modres° gate *mother's*
I knokke with my staf both erly and late,
And saye, 'Leve° moder, leet me in: *dear*
Lo, how I vanisshe, flessh and blood and skin.
Allas, whan shal my bones been at reste?
Moder, with you wolde I chaunge° my cheste[2] *exchange*
That in my chambre longe time hath be,
Ye, for an haire-clout[3] to wrappe me.'
But yit to me she wol nat do that grace,
For which ful pale and welked° is my face. *withered*

8. By highway and byway.
9. Pledged their words of honor.
1. May God protect you.
2. Chest for one's belongings, used here as the symbol for life—or perhaps a coffin.
3. Haircloth, for a winding sheet.

But sires, to you it is no curteisye
To speken to an old man vilainye,° *rudeness*
But° he trespasse° in word or elles in deede. *unless / offend*
In Holy Writ ye may yourself wel rede,
'Agains[4] an old man, hoor° upon his heed, *hoar*
Ye shal arise.'[5] Wherfore I yive you reed,° *advice*
Ne dooth unto an old man noon harm now,
Namore than that ye wolde men dide to you
In age, if that ye so longe abide.
And God be with you wher ye go° or ride: *walk*
I moot go thider as I have to go."
"Nay, olde cherl, by God thou shalt nat so,"
Saide this other hasardour anoon.
"Thou partest nat so lightly,° by Saint John! *easily*
Thou speke° right now of thilke traitour Deeth, *spoke*
That in this contree alle oure freendes sleeth:
Have here my trouthe, as thou art his espye,
Tel wher he is, or thou shalt it abye,° *pay for*
By God and by the holy sacrament!
For soothly thou art oon of his assent[6]
To sleen us yonge folk, thou false thief."
"Now sires," quod he, "if that ye be so lief° *anxious*
To finde Deeth, turne up this crooked way,
For in that grove I lafte° him, by my fay,° *left / faith*
Under a tree, and ther he wol abide:
Nat for youre boost° he wol him no thing hide. *boast*
See ye that ook?° Right ther ye shal him finde. *oak*
God save you, that boughte again[7] mankinde,
And you amende." Thus saide this olde man.
And everich of thise riotoures ran
Til he cam to that tree, and ther they founde
Of florins° fine of gold ycoined rounde *coins*
Wel neigh an eighte busshels as hem thoughte—
Ne lenger thanne after Deeth they soughte,
But eech of hem so glad was of the sighte,
For that the florins been so faire and brighte,
That down they sette hem by this precious hoord.
The worste of hem he spak the firste word:
"Bretheren," quod he, "take keep° what that I saye: *heed*
My wit is greet though that I bourde° and playe. *joke*
This tresor hath Fortune unto us yiven
In mirthe and jolitee oure lif to liven,
And lightly° as it cometh so wol we spende. *easily*
Ey, Goddes precious dignitee, who wende[8]
Today that we sholde han so fair a grace?
But mighte this gold be caried fro this place
Hoom to myn hous—or elles unto youres—
For wel ye woot that al this gold is oures—
Thanne were we in heigh felicitee.
But trewely, by daye it mighte nat be:
Men wolde sayn that we were theves stronge,° *flagrant*
And for oure owene tresor doon us honge.[9]
This tresor moste ycaried be by nighte,
As wisely and as slyly as it mighte.
Therfore I rede° that cut° amonges us alle *advise / lots*

4. In the presence of.
5. Cf. Leviticus xix.32.
6. I.e., one of his party.
7. Redeemed.
8. Who would have supposed.
9. Have us hanged.

Be drawe, and lat see wher the cut wol falle;
And he that hath the cut with herte blithe
Shal renne° to the town, and that ful swithe,° *run / quickly*
And bringe us breed and win ful prively;
And two of us shal keepen° subtilly *guard*
This tresor wel, and if he wol nat tarye,
Whan it is night we wol this tresor carye
By oon assent wher as us thinketh best."
That oon of hem the cut broughte in his fest° *fist*
And bad hem drawe and looke wher it wol falle;
And it fil° on the yongeste of hem alle, *fell*
And forth toward the town he wente anoon.
And also° soone as that he was agoon,° *as / gone away*
That oon of hem spak thus unto that other:
"Thou knowest wel thou art my sworen brother;
Thy profit wol I telle thee anoon:
Thou woost wel that oure felawe is agoon,
And here is gold, and that ful greet plentee,
That shal departed° been among us three. *divided*
But nathelees, if I can shape° it so *arrange*
That it departed were among us two,
Hadde I nat doon a freendes turn to thee?"
That other answerde, "I noot[1] how that may be:
He woot that the gold is with us twaye.
What shal we doon? What shal we to him saye?"
"Shal it be conseil?"[2] saide the firste shrewe.° *villain*
"And I shal telle in a wordes fewe
What we shul doon, and bringe it wel aboute."
"I graunte," quod that other, "out of doute,
That by my trouthe I wol thee nat biwraye."° *expose*
"Now," quod the firste, "thou woost wel we be twaye,
And two of us shal strenger° be than oon: *stronger*
Looke whan that he is set that right anoon
Aris as though thou woldest with him playe,
And I shal rive° him thurgh the sides twaye, *pierce*
Whil that thou strugelest with him as in game,
And with thy daggere looke thou do the same;
And thanne shal al this gold departed be,
My dere freend, bitwixe thee and me.
Thanne we may bothe oure lustes° al fulfille, *desires*
And playe at dees° right at oure owene wille." *dice*
And thus accorded been thise shrewes twaye
To sleen the thridde, as ye han herd me saye.
This yongeste, which that wente to the town,
Ful ofte in herte he rolleth up and down
The beautee of thise florins newe and brighte.
"O Lord," quod he, "if so were that I mighte
Have al this tresor to myself allone,
Ther is no man that liveth under the trone° *throne*
Of God that sholde live so merye as I."
And at the laste the feend oure enemy
Putte in his thought that he sholde poison beye,° *buy*
With which he mighte sleen his felawes twaye—
Forwhy° the feend foond him in swich livinge *because*
That he hadde leve° him to sorwe bringe:[3] *permission*

1. Don't know.
2. A secret.
3. Christian doctrine teaches that the devil may not tempt men except with God's permission.

For this was outrely° his fulle entente, *plainly*
To sleen hem bothe, and nevere to repente.
  And forth he gooth—no lenger wolde he tarye—
Into the town unto a pothecarye,° *apothecary*
And prayed him that he him wolde selle
Som poison that he mighte his rattes quelle,° *kill*
And eek ther was a polcat[4] in his hawe° *yard*
That, as he saide, his capons hadde yslawe,° *slain*
And fain he wolde wreke him[5] if he mighte
On vermin that destroyed him[6] by nighte.
  The pothecarye answerde, "And thou shalt have
A thing that, also° God my soule save, *as*
In al this world there is no creature
That ete or dronke hath of this confiture°— *mixture*
Nat but the mountance° of a corn° of whete— *amount / grain*
That he ne shal his lif anoon forlete.° *lose*
Ye, sterve° he shal, and that in lasse° while *die / less*
Than thou wolt goon a paas[7] nat but a mile,
The poison is so strong and violent."
This cursed man hath in his hand yhent° *taken*
This poison in a box and sith° he ran *then*
Into the nexte streete unto a man
And borwed of him large botels three,
And in the two his poison poured he—
The thridde he kepte clene for his drinke,
For al the night he shoop him[8] for to swinke° *work*
In carying of the gold out of that place.
And whan this riotour with sory grace
Hadde filled with win his grete botels three,
To his felawes again repaireth he.
  What needeth it to sermone of it more?
For right as they had cast° his deeth bifore, *plotted*
Right so they han him slain, and that anoon.
And whan that this was doon, thus spak that oon:
"Now lat us sitte and drinke and make us merye,
And afterward we wol his body berye."° *bury*
And with that word it happed him par cas[9]
To take the botel ther the poison was,
And drank, and yaf his felawe drinke also,
For which anoon they storven° bothe two. *died*
  But certes I suppose that Avicen
Wroot nevere in no canon ne in no *fen*[1]
Mo wonder signes[2] of empoisoning
Than hadde thise wrecches two er hir ending:
Thus ended been thise homicides two,
And eek the false empoisonere also.
  O cursed sinne of alle cursednesse!
O traitours homicide, O wikkednesse!
O glotonye, luxure,° and hasardrye! *lechery*
Thou blasphemour of Crist with vilainye
And othes grete of usage° and of pride! *habit*
Allas, mankinde, how may it bitide
That to thy Creatour which that thee wroughte,
And with his precious herte blood thee boughte,° *redeemed*

4. A weasel-like animal.
5. He would gladly avenge himself.
6. I.e., were ruining his farming.
7. Take a walk.
8. He was preparing.
9. By chance.
1. The *Canon of Medicine*, by Avicenna, an 11th-century Arabic philosopher, was divided into sections called "*fens*."
2. More wonderful symptoms.

Thou art so fals and so unkinde,° allas? *unnatural*
 Now goode men, God foryive you youre trespas,
And ware° you fro the sinne of avarice: *guard*
Myn holy pardon may you alle warice°— *save*
So that ye offre nobles or sterlinges,[3]
Or elles silver brooches, spoones, ringes.
Boweth your heed under this holy bulle!
Cometh up, ye wives, offreth of youre wolle!° *wool*
Youre name I entre here in my rolle: anoon
Into the blisse of hevene shul ye goon.
I you assoile° by myn heigh power— *absolve*
Ye that wol offre—as clene and eek as cleer
As ye were born.—And lo, sires, thus I preche.
And Jesu Crist that is oure soules leeche° *physician*
So graunte you his pardon to receive,
For that is best—I wol you nat deceive.

The Epilogue

"But sires, oo word forgat I in my tale:
I have relikes and pardon in my male° *bag*
As faire as any man in Engelond,
Whiche were me yiven by the Popes hond.
If any of you wol of devocioun
Offren and han myn absolucioun,
Come forth anoon, and kneeleth here adown,
And mekely receiveth my pardoun,
Or elles taketh pardon as ye wende,
Al newe and fressh at every miles ende—
So that ye offre alway newe and newe[4]
Nobles or pens whiche that be goode and trewe.
It is an honour to everich that is heer
That ye have a suffisant° pardoner *competent*
T'assoile you in contrees as ye ride,
For aventures whiche that may bitide:
Paraventure ther may falle oon or two
Down of his hors and breke his nekke atwo;
Looke which a suretee° is it to you alle *safeguard*
That I am in youre felaweship yfalle
That may assoile you, bothe more and lasse,[5]
Whan that the soule shal fro the body passe.
I rede° that oure Hoste shal biginne, *advise*
For he is most envoluped° in sinne. *involved*
Com forth, sire Host, and offre first anoon,
And thou shalt kisse the relikes everichoon,° *each one*
Ye, for a grote: unbokele° anoon thy purs." *unbuckle*
 "Nay, nay," quod he, "thanne have I Cristes curs!
Lat be," quod he, "it shal nat be, so theech!° *may I thrive*
Thou woldest make me kisse thyn olde breech° *breeches*
And swere it were a relik of a saint,
Though it were with thy fundament depeint.° *stained*
But, by the crois which that Sainte Elaine foond,[6]
I wolde I hadde thy coilons° in myn hond, *testicles*
In stede of relikes or of saintuarye.° *relic-box*
Lat cutte hem of: I wol thee helpe hem carye.

3. "Nobles" and "sterlinges" were valuable coins.
4. Over and over.
5. Both high and low (i.e., everybody).
6. I.e., by the cross that St. Helena found. Helena, mother of Constantine the Great, was reputed to have found the True Cross.

They shal be shrined in an hogges tord."° *turd*
  This Pardoner answerde nat a word:
So wroth he was no word ne wolde he saye.
  "Now," quod oure Host, "I wol no lenger playe
With thee, ne with noon other angry man."
  But right anoon the worthy Knight bigan,
Whan that he sawgh that al the peple lough,° *laughed*
"Namore of this, for it is right ynough.
Sire Pardoner, be glad and merye of cheere,
And ye, sire Host that been to me so dere,
I praye you that ye kisse the Pardoner,
And Pardoner, I praye thee, draw thee neer,
And as we diden lat us laughe and playe."
Anoon they kiste and riden forth hir waye.

Lyrics and Occasional Verse

To Rosamond

Madame, ye been of alle beautee shrine
As fer as cercled is the mapemounde:[7]
For as the crystal glorious ye shine,
And like ruby been youre cheekes rounde.
Therwith ye been so merye and so jocounde
That at a revel whan that I see you daunce
It is an oinement unto my wounde,
Though ye to me ne do no daliaunce.[8]

For though I weepe of teres ful a tine,° *tub*
Yit may that wo myn herte nat confounde;
Youre semy° vois, that ye so smale outtwine,[9] *small*
Maketh my thought in joye and blis habounde:° *abound*
So curteisly I go with love bounde
That to myself I saye in my penaunce,[1]
"Suffiseth me to love you, Rosemounde,
Though ye to me ne do no daliaunce."

Was nevere pik walwed in galauntine[2]
As I in love am walwed and ywounde,
For which ful ofte I of myself divine
That I am trewe Tristam[3] the secounde;
My love may not refreide nor affounde;[4]
I brenne° ay in amorous plesaunce: *burn*
Do what you list, I wol youre thral° be founde, *slave*
Though ye to me ne do no daliaunce.

Truth

Flee fro the prees° and dwelle with soothfastnesse; *crowd*
Suffise° thyn owene thing, though it be smal; *let suffice*
For hoord hath[5] hate, and climbing tikelnesse;° *insecurity*

7. I.e., to the farthest circumference of the map of the world.
8. I.e., show me no encouragement.
9. That you so delicately spin out.
1. I.e., pangs of unrequited love.
2. Pike rolled in galantine sauce.
3. The famous lover of Isolt (Iseult, Isolde) in medieval legend, renowned for his constancy.
4. Cool nor chill.
5. Hoarding causes.

Prees hath envye, and wele° blent° overal. *prosperity / blinds*
Savoure° no more than thee bihoove shal; *relish*
Rule wel thyself that other folk canst rede:° *advise*
And Trouthe shal delivere,[6] it is no drede.° *doubt*

Tempest thee nought al crooked to redresse[7]
In trust of hire[8] that turneth as a bal;
Muche wele stant in litel bisinesse;[9]
Be war therfore to spurne ayains an al.[1]
Strive nat as dooth the crokke° with the wal. *pot*
Daunte° thyself that dauntest otheres deede: *master*
And Trouthe shal delivere, it is no drede.

That thee is sent, receive in buxomnesse;° *obedience*
The wrastling for the world axeth° a fal; *asks for*
Here is noon hoom, here nis but wildernesse:
Forth, pilgrim, forth! Forth, beest, out of thy stal!
Know thy countree, looke up, thank God of al.
Hold the heigh way and lat thy gost° thee lede: *spirit*
And Trouthe shal delivere, it is no drede.

Therfore, thou Vache,[2] leve thyn olde wrecchednesse
Unto the world; leve[3] now to be thral.
Crye him mercy that of his heigh goodnesse
Made thee of nought, and in especial
Draw unto him, and pray in general,
For thee and eek for othere, hevenelich meede:° *reward*
And Trouthe shal delivere, it is no drede.

Complaint to His Purse

To you, my purs, and to noon other wight,
Complaine I, for ye be my lady dere.
I am so sory, now that ye be light,
For certes, but if[4] ye make me hevy cheere,
Me were as lief[5] be laid upon my beere;° *bier*
For which unto youre mercy thus I crye:
Beeth hevy again, or elles moot° I die. *must*

Now voucheth sauf this day er it be night
That I of you the blisful soun may heere,
Or see youre colour, lik the sonne bright,
That of yelownesse hadde nevere peere.
Ye be my life, ye be myn hertes steere,° *rudder, guide*
Queene of confort and of good compaignye:
Beeth hevy again, or elles moot I die.

Ye purs, that been to me my lives light
And saviour, as in this world down here,
Out of this tonne[6] helpe me thurgh your might,

6. I.e., truth shall make you free.
7. Do not disturb yourself to straighten all that's crooked.
8. Fortune, who turns like a ball in that she is always presenting a different aspect to men.
9. Peace of mind stands in little anxiety.
1. I.e., to kick against the pricks.
2. Probably Sir Philip de la Vache, with a pun on the French for "cow."
3. I.e., cease.
4. Unless.
5. I'd just as soon.
6. Tun, meaning "predicament."

Sith that ye wol nat be my tresorere;° *disburser*
For I am shave as neigh° as any frere.° *close / friar*
But yit I praye unto youre curteisye:
Beeth hevy again, or elles moot I die.

Envoy to Henry IV

O conquerour of Brutus Albioun,[7]
Which that by line and free eleccioun
Been verray king, this song to you I sende:
And ye, that mowen° alle oure harmes amende, *may*
Have minde upon my supplicacioun.

Merciless Beauty

1

Youre yën two wol slee° me sodeinly: *slay*
I may the beautee of hem nat sustene,° *withstand*
So woundeth it thurghout myn herte keene.° *keenly*

And but° youre word wol helen hastily *unless*
Myn hertes wounde, whil that it is greene,[8]
  Youre yën two wol slee me sodeinly:
  I may the beautee of hem nat sustene.

Upon my trouthe, I saye you faithfully
That ye been of my lif and deeth the queene,
For with my deeth the trouthe shal be seene.
  Youre yën two wol slee me sodeinly:
  I may the beautee of hem nat sustene,
  So woundeth it thurghout myn herte keene.

2

So hath youre beautee fro youre herte chaced
Pitee, that me ne availeth nought to plaine:° *complain*
For Daunger halt[9] youre mercy in his chaine.

Giltelees my deeth thus han ye me purchaced;° *procured*
I saye you sooth, me needeth nought to feine:° *dissemble*
  So hath youre beautee fro youre herte chaced
  Pitee, that me ne availeth nought to plaine.

Allas, that nature hath in you compaced° *enclosed*
So greet beautee that no man may attaine
To mercy, though he sterve° for the paine. *die*
  So hath youre beautee fro youre herte chaced
  Pitee, that me ne availeth nought to plaine:
  For Daunger halt youre mercy in his chaine.

3

Sin I fro Love escaped am so fat,
I nevere thenke° to been in his prison lene: *intend*
Sin I am free, I counte him nat a bene.[1]

7. Britain (Albion) was supposed to have been founded by Brutus, the grandson of Aeneas, the founder of Rome.

8. I.e., fresh.

9. Haughtiness holds.

1. I don't consider him worth a bean.

He may answere and saye right this and that;
I do no fors,[2] I speke right as I mene:
Sin I fro Love escaped am so fat,
I nevere thenke to been in his prison lene.

Love hath my name ystrike° out of his sclat,° *struck / slate*
And he is strike out of my bookes clene
For everemo; ther is noon other mene.° *solution*
Sin I fro Love escaped am so fat,
I nevere thenke to been in his prison lene:
Sin I am free, I counte him nat a bene.

CHARLES D'ORLÉANS
(1391–1465)

The Smiling Mouth

The smiling mouth and laughing eyen gray,
The breastes round and long small armes twain,
The handes smooth, the sides straight and plain,
Your feetes lit°—what should I further say? *little*
It is my craft° when ye are far away *practice*
To muse thereon in stinting° of my pain— *soothing*
The smiling mouth and laughing eyen gray,
The breastes round and long small armes twain.
So would I pray you, if I durst or may,
The sight to see as I have seen,
Forwhy° that craft me is most fain,° *because / pleasing*
And will be to the hour in which I day°— *die*
The smiling mouth and laughing eyen gray,
The breastes round and long small armes twain.

Oft in My Thought

Oft in my thought full busily have I sought,
Against the beginning of this fresh new year,
What pretty thing that I best given ought
To her that was mine hearte's lady dear;
But all that thought bitane° is fro° me clear *taken / from*
Since death, alas, hath closed her under clay
And hath this world fornaked° with her here— *stripped bare*
God have her soul, I can no better say.

But for to keep in custom, lo, my thought,
And of my seely° service the manere, *simple*
In showing als° that I forget her not *also*
Unto each wight I shall to my powere
This dead[3] her serve with masses and prayere;
For all too foul a shame were me, mafay,° *by my faith*
Her to forget this time that nigheth near—
God have her soul, I can no better say.

2. I don't care.
3. Dead person, the deceased. *Her* is redundant, as is one of the *its* in line 27.

To her profit now nis° there to be bought — *is not*
None other thing all° will I buy it dear; — *although*
Wherefore, thou Lord that lordest all aloft,
My deedes take, such as goodness steer,
And crown her, Lord, within thine heavenly sphere
As for most truest lady, may I say,
Most good, most fair, and most benign of cheer°— — *countenance*
God have her soul, I can no better say.

When I her praise, or praising of her hear,
Although it whilom° were to me pleasere, — *formerly*
It fill enough it doth mine heart today,
And doth° me wish I clothed had my bier— — *makes*
God have her soul, I can no better say.

ANONYMOUS LYRICS OF THE FIFTEENTH CENTURY

Adam Lay I-bounden

Adam lay i-bounden, bounden in a bond;
Foure thousand winter thought he not too long.
And all was for an apple, an apple that he took,
As clerkes finden written in theire book.

Ne hadde the apple take been,[1] the apple taken been,
Ne hadde never our Lady aye been Heaven's queen.
Blessed be the time that apple taken was,
Therefore we may singen, "*Deo gracias!*"[2]

I Sing of a Maiden

I sing of a maiden
That is makeless:° — *mateless, matchless*
King of alle kinges
To° her son she ches.° — *for / chose*

He came also° stille — *as*
Where his mother was
As dew in Aprille
That falleth on the grass.

He came also stille
To his mother's bower
As dew in Aprille
That falleth on the flower.

He came also stille
Where his mother lay
As dew in Aprille
That falleth on the spray.

1. I.e., if the apple had not been taken.
2. Thanks be to God.

Mother and maiden
Was never none but she—
Well may such a lady
Godes mother be.

This Endris Night

This endris[3] night
I saw a sight,
A star as bright as day,
And ever among[4]
A maiden sung,
"Lullay, by, by, lullay."

That lovely lady sat and sung,
And to her child said,
"My Son, my Brother, my Father dear,
Why liest thou thus in hay?
My sweete brid,° *bird*
Thus it is betid,° *happened*
Though thou be king verray;° *in truth*
But nevertheless
I will not cesse° *cease*
To sing 'By, by, lullay.' "

The child then spake in his talking,
And to his mother said,
"I am kenned° for Heaven's King *known*
In crib though I be laid,
For angels bright
Done° to me light, *gave*
Thou knowest it is no nay;
And of[5] that sight
Thou mayst be light[6]
To sing 'By, by, lullay.' "

"Now, sweet Son, since thou art king,
Why art thou laid in stall?
Why ne thou ordained thy bedding
In some great kinge's hall?
Methinketh it is right
That king or knight
Should lie in good array,
And then among° *in that circumstance*
It were no wrong
To sing 'By, by, lullay.' "

3. "This endris": the other.
4. "Ever among": every now and then.
5. I.e., because of.
6. "Thou mayst be light": feel free.

"Mary mother, I am thy child,
Though I be laid in stall;
Lords and dukes shall worship me,
And so shall kinges all.
Ye shall well see
That kinges three
Shall come the Twelfth Day.
For this behest° *promise*
Give me thy breast
And sing 'By, by, lullay.' "

"Now tell me, sweet Son, I thee pray,
Thou are me lief° and dear, *beloved*
How should I keep thee to thy pay° *liking*
And make thee glad of cheer?° *face*
For all thy will
I would fulfill,
Thou wottest full well in fay,° *faith*
And for all this
I will thee kiss
And sing 'By, by, lullay.' "

"My dear mother, when time it be,
Thou take me up on loft,
And set me upon thy knee,
And handle me full soft,
And in thy arm
Thou hill° me warm, *cover*
And keepe night and day;
If I weep
And may not sleep,
Then sing 'By, by, lullay.' "

"Now, sweet Son, since it is so,
That all thing is at thy will,
I pray thee, grante me a boon,
If it be both right and skill:° *reason*
That child or man
That will or can
Be merry upon my day,
To bliss them bring,
And I shall sing
'Lullay, by, by, lullay.' "

I Have a Young Sister

I have a young sister
Far beyond the sea;
Many be the drowries° *tokens*
That she sente me.

She sente me the cherry
Withouten any stone,
And so she did the dove
Withouten any bone.

She sente me the briar
Withouten any rind;° *bark*
She bade me love my leman° *beloved*
Without longing.

How should any cherry
Be withoute stone?
And how should any dove
Be withoute bone?

How should any briar
Be withoute rind?
How should I love my leman
Without longing?

When the cherry was a flower,
Then hadde it no stone.
When the dove was an egg,
Then hadde it no bone.

When the briar was unbred.[7]
Then hadde it no rind.
When the maiden hath that she loveth,
She is without longing.

I Have a Gentle Cock

I have a gentle° cock, *noble*
Croweth me day;
He doth me risen[8] early
My matins for to say.

I have a gentle cock,
Comen he is of great;° *lofty lineage*
His comb is of red coral,
His tail is of jet.

I have a gentle cock,
Comen he is of kind;° *good stock*
His comb is of red coral,
His tail is of inde.° *indigo*

His legges be of azure,
So gentle and so small;
His spurres are of silver white
Into the wortewale.[9]

His eyen are of crystal,
Locked° all in amber; *set*
And every night he percheth him
In my lady's chamber.

7. I.e., still in the seed.
8. "Doth me risen": makes me rise.
9. Up to the root.

Jolly Jankin

"Kyrie, so kyrie,"
Jankin singeth murie,° *merrily*
With "Aleison."[1]

As I went on Yule Day
In our processïon,
Knew I jolly Jankin
By his merry tone.
Kyrieleison.

Jankin began the office
On the Yule Day,
And yet methinketh it does me good,
So merry gan he say,
"Kyrieleison."

Jankin read the 'Pistle
Full fair and full well,
And yet methinketh it does me good,
As ever have I sel.[2]
Kyrieleison.

Jankin at the Sanctus
Cracketh a merry note,
And yet methinketh it does me good—
I payed for his coat.
Kyrieleison.

Jankin cracketh notes
An hundred on a knot,° *at a time*
And yet he hacketh° them smaller *chops up*
Than wortes° to the pot. *herbs*
Kyrieleison.

Jankin at the Agnus
Beareth the pax-bred;[3]
He twinkled but said nought,
And on my foot he tread.
Kyrieleison.

Benedicamus Domino,[4]
Christ from shame me shield;
Deo gracias thereto—[5]
Alas! I go with child.
Kyrieleison.

1. *Kyrie eleison,* a prayer, "Lord have mercy"; the Epistle (line 13), a reading from Paul or one of the Prophets; the *Sanctus* (line 19), a prayer of rejoicing, "Holy, Holy, Holy"; and the *Agnus* (line 29), an invocation of the Lamb of God, are early, middle, and late parts of the divine office (line 9) or Mass.

2. I.e., as ever I (hope to) have good luck.

3. A tablet ("bred": board) bearing a representation of the Crucifixion, kissed by the priests celebrating the Mass, then by the congregation. "Pax": (the kiss of) peace.

4. Let us bless the Lord.

5. Thanks be to God, as well.

Timor Mortis

In what estate° so ever I be — *condition*
Timor mortis conturbat me.[6]

As I went on a merry morning,
I heard a bird both weep and sing.
This was the tenor of her talking:
"Timor mortis conturbat me."

I asked that bird what she meant.
"I am a musket° both fair and gent;° — *male sparrowhawk / gentle*
For dread of death I am all shent.:° — *ruined*
Timor mortis conturbat me.

"When I shall die, I know no day;
What country or place I cannot say;
Wherefore this song sing I may:
Timor mortis conturbat me.

"Jesu Christ, when he should die,
To his Father he gan say,
'Father,' he said, 'in Trinity,
Timor mortis conturbat me.'

"All Christian people, behold and see:
This world is but a vanity
And replete with necessity.
Timor mortis conturbat me.

"Wake I or sleep, eate or drink,
When I on my last end do think,
For greate fear my soul do shrink:
Timor mortis conturbat me.

"God grant us grace him for to serve,
And be at our end when we sterve,° — *die*
And from the fiend he us preserve.
Timor mortis conturbat me.

The Corpus Christi[7] Carol

Lully, lullay, lully, lullay,
The falcon hath born my make° away. — *mate*

He bore him up, he bore him down,
He bore him into an orchard brown.

In that orchard there was a hall
That was hanged with purple and pall.° — *rich fabric*

6. The title phrase comes from the Office of the Dead: *"Peccantem me quotidie et non poenitentem* timor mortis conturbat me. *Quia in inferno nulla est redemptio misere mei Deus et salva me."* (Since I have been sinning daily and repenting not, *the fear of death distresses me.* Since in hell there is no redemption, have pity on me, God, and save me.)

7. "Corpus Christi": the body of Christ.

And in that hall there was a bed,
It was hanged with gold so red.

And in that bed there lieth a knight,
His woundes bleeding day and night.

By that bed's side there kneeleth a may° *maiden*
And she weepeth both night and day.

And by that bed's side there standeth a stone,
Corpus Christi written thereon.

Western Wind

Western wind, when will thou blow,
  The small rain down can rain?
Christ, if my love were in my arms
  And I in my bed again!

A Lyke-Wake[8] Dirge

This ae° night, this ae night, *one*
  Every night and all,
Fire and sleet[9] and candle-light,
  And Christ receive thy saul.° *soul*

When thou from hence away are past,
To Whinny-muir[1] thou comest at last:

If ever thou gavest hosen and shoon,
Sit thee down and put them on:

If hosen and shoon thou ne'er gavest nane,
The whins shall prick thee to the bare bane:

From Whinny-muir when thou mayst pass,
To Brig° o' Dread thou comest at last: *bridge*

From Brig o' Dread when thou mayst pass,
To purgatory fire thou comest at last:

If ever thou gavest meat or drink,
The fire shall never make thee shrink:

If meat or drink thou ne'er gavest nane,
The fire will burn thee to the bare bane:

This ae night, this ae night,
Fire and sleet and candle-light,

8. The night watch (*wake*) kept over a corpse (*lyke*). The italicized lines are repeated as a refrain throughout the lyrics.
9. Salt, sometimes placed with earth on the breast of the dead as emblematic of soul and body.
1. Prickly-moor. *Whin* is a name given to various prickly shrubs.

Jolly Good Ale and Old

Back and side go bare, go bare,
Both foot and hand go cold;
But, belly, God send thee good ale enough,
Whether it be new or old.

I cannot eat but little meat,
My stomach is not good;
But sure I think that I can drink
With him that wears a hood.[2]
Though I go bare, take ye no care,
I am nothing a-cold;
I stuff my skin so full within
Of jolly good ale and old.

I love no roast but a nut-brown toast,[3]
And a crab° laid in the fire; *crab apple*
A little bread shall do me stead,° *service*
Much bread I not desire.
No frost nor snow, no wind, I trow,° *trust*
Can hurt me if it would,
I am so wrapped and throughly° lapped° *thoroughly / swathed*
Of° jolly good ale and old. *in*

And Tib, my wife, that as her life
Loveth well good ale to seek,
Full oft drinks she till ye may see
The tears run down her cheek.
Then doth she troll° to me the bowl, *pass*
Even as a maltworm° should, *toper*
And saith, "Sweetheart, I took my part
Of this jolly good ale and old."

Now let them drink till they nod and wink,
Even as good fellows should do;
They shall not miss to have the bliss
Good ale doth bring men to.
And all poor souls that have scoured bowls
Or have them lustily trolled—
God save the lives of them and their wives,
Whether they be young or old.

WILLIAM DUNBAR
(ca. 1460–ca. 1525)

Lament for the Makaris° *poets*

I that in heill° was and gladness, *health*
Am troublit now with great seikness,

2. I.e., as much as any friar.

3. Used as a sop with ale or wine.

And feeblit with infirmity:
Timor Mortis conturbat me.[1]

Our plesance here is all vain-glory
This false warld is bot transitory,
The flesh is brukill,° the Fiend is sle;° *frail/sly*
Timor Mortis conturbat me.

The state of man dois change and vary,
Now sound, now seik, now blyth, now sary,
Now dansand merry, now like to die;
Timor Mortis conturbat me.

No state in erd here standis siccar;° *securely*
As with the wind wavis the wicker,° *willow*
Wavis this warldis vanitie;
Timor Mortis conturbat me.

Unto the deid gois all Estatis,
Princes, Prelatis, and Potestatis,° *potentates*
Baith rich and puir of all degree;
Timor Mortis conturbat me.

He takis the knichtis into the field,
Enarmit under helm and shield;
Victor he is at all mêlée;
Timor Mortis conturbat me.

That strang unmerciful tyrand
Takis on the moderis breist soukand° *sucking*
The babe, full of benignite;
Timor Mortis conturbat me.

He takis the champion in the stour,° *battle*
The capitane closit in the tour,
The lady in bour full of beautie;
Timor Mortis conturbat me.

He sparis no lord for his puissance,
Na clerk° for his intelligence; *scholar*
His awful straik may no man flee;
Timor Mortis conturbat me.

Art magicianis, and astrologis,° *astrologers*
Rethoris,° logicianis, and theologis, *rhetoricians*
Them helpis no conclusionis sle;
Timor Mortis conturbat me.

In medicine the most° practicianis, *greatest*
Leechis,° surigianis, and phisicianis, *doctors*
Them-self fra deid° may not supple;° *death/help*
Timor Mortis conturbat me.

I see that makaris amang the lave° *remainder*
Playis here their pageant, syne° gois to grave; *then*

1. "The fear of death confounds me," a line from the Office for the Dead. Cf. the anonymous 15th-century poem with the same refrain, above.

Sparit is nocht their facultie;
Timor Mortis conturbat me.

He has done piteously devour
The noble Chaucer, of makaris flour,
The Monk of Bery, and Gower, all three;
Timor Mortis conturbat me.

The gude Sir Hew of Eglintoun,
And eik° Heriot, and Wintoun, *also*
He has ta'en out of this countrie;
Timor Mortis conturbat me.

That scorpion fell has done infec'
Maister John Clerk and James Affleck,
Fra ballad-making and tragedie;
Timor Mortis conturbat me.

Holland and Barbour he has bereavit;
Alas! that he nought with us leavit
Sir Mungo Lockhart of the Lea;
Timor Mortis conturbat me.

Clerk of Tranent eke he has ta'en,
That made the Aunteris° of Gawain;[2] *adventures*
Sir Gilbert Hay endit has he;
Timor Mortis conturbat me.

He has Blind Harry, and Sandy Traill
Slain with his shour of mortal hail,
Whilk° Patrick Johnstoun micht nocht flee; *which*
Timor Mortis conturbat me.

He has reft° Merser endite,° *taken from/talent*
That did in luve so lively write,
So short, so quick, of sentence hie;
Timor Mortis conturbat me.

He has ta'en Roull of Aberdeen,
And gentle Roull of Corstorphin;
Two better fellowis did no man see;
Timor Mortis conturbat me.

In Dunfermline he has done roune° *whisper*
With Maister Robert Henryson;
Sir John the Ross embraced has he;
Timor Mortis conturbat me.

And he has now ta'en, last of a',
Gude gentle Stobo and Quintin Shaw,
Of wham all wichtis° has pitie: *creatures*
Timor Mortis conturbat me.

Gude Maister Walter Kennedy
In point of deid lies verily,

2. A hero of Arthurian romance.

Great ruth° it were that so suld be; *pity*
Timor Mortis conturbat me.

Sen he has all my brether ta'en,
He will nocht lat me live alane,
On force I maun° his next prey be; *must*
Timor Mortis conturbat me.

Sen for the deid remead° is none, *remedy*
Best is that we for deid dispone,° *prepare*
Eftir our deid that live may we;
Timor Mortis conturbat me.

1508

JOHN SKELTON
(1460–1529)

Mannerly Margery Milk and Ale[1]

Ay, beshrew° you! by my fay,° *curse / faith*
These wanton clerks be nice[2] alway!
Avaunt, avaunt, my popinjay!
What, will ye do nothing but play?
Tilly vally, straw,[3] let be I say!
Gup,[4] Christian Clout, gup, Jack of the Vale!
With Mannerly Margery Milk and Ale.

By God, ye be a pretty pode,° *toad*
And I love you an whole cart-load.
Straw, James Foder, ye play the fode,° *deceiver*
I am no hackney[5] for your rod:° *riding*
Go watch a bull, your back is broad!
Gup, Christian Clout, gup, Jack of the Vale!
With Mannerly Margery Milk and Ale.

Ywis° ye deal uncourteously; *for certain*
What, would ye frumple[6] me? now fy!
What, and ye shall be my pigesnye?° *pet*
By Christ, ye shall not, no hardely:° *indeed*
I will not be japéd° bodily! *fooled with*
Gup, Christian Clout, gup, Jack of the Vale!
With Mannerly Margery Milk and Ale.

Walk forth your way, ye cost me nought;
Now have I found that I have sought:
The best cheap flesh that ever I bought.
Yet, for His love that all hath wrought,
Wed me, or else I die for thought.
Gup, Christian Clout, your breath is stale!

1. On the somewhat uncertain basis of the original musical setting for three voices (and internal evidence), this lyric is sometimes printed as a dialogue between the title character and James Foder (named in line 10), to whom are given lines 4, 8–9, 17, 22–24, and sometimes the refrain lines.
2. "Nice" variously meant foolish, finicky, lascivious.
3. Expressions of contemptuous rejection: fiddlesticks, poppycock, nonsense.
4. Contracted (?) from *go up;* sometimes an exclamation of derision, remonstrance, or surprise, sometimes a command: get along, get out; get up.
5. I.e., an ordinary riding horse (as distinct from a warhorse or a plowhorse).
6. Wrinkle, rumple; muss up.

Go, Mannerly Margery Milk and Ale!
Gup, Christian Clout, gup, Jack of the Vale!
With Mannerly Margery Milk and Ale.

To Mistress Margaret Hussey

Merry Margaret,
As midsummer flower,
Gentle as falcon
Or hawk of the tower:[7]
With solace and gladness,
Much mirth and no madness,
All good and no badness;
So joyously,
So maidenly,
So womanly
Her demeaning
In every thing,
Far, far passing
That I can indite,
Or suffice to write
Of Merry Margaret
As midsummer flower,
Gentle as falcon
Or hawk of the tower.
As patient and still
And as full of good will
As fair Isaphill,[8]
Coriander,[9]
Sweet pomander,[1]
Good Cassander,[2]
Steadfast of thought,
Well made, well wrought,
Far may be sought
Ere that ye can find
So courteous, so kind
As Merry Margaret,
This midsummer flower,
Gentle as falcon
Or hawk of the tower.

POPULAR BALLADS

Lord Randal[1]

1

"O where ha' you been, Lord Randal, my son?
And where ha' you been, my handsome young man?"
"I ha' been at the greenwood; mother, mak my bed soon,
For I'm wearied wi' huntin', and fain wad° lie down." *would*

7. Hawk trained to fly high (*tower*).
8. Hypsipyle, princess of Lemnos, savior of her father's life, comforter of the Argives, mother of twins by Jason.
9. An aromatic herb.
1. A mixture of perfumed or aromatic substances made into a ball.
2. Cassandra, daughter of Priam and Hecuba; according to myth her beauty bedazzled Apollo himself, who conferred on her the gift of prophecy.
1. Child, No. 12.A.

2

"And wha met ye there, Lord Randal, my son?
And wha met you there, my handsome young man?"
"O I met wi' my true-love; mother, mak my bed soon,
For I'm wearied wi' huntin', and fain wad lie down."

3

"And what did she give you, Lord Randal, my son?
And what did she give you, my handsome young man?"
"Eels fried in a pan; mother, mak my bed soon,
For I'm wearied wi' huntin', and fain wad lie down."

4

"And wha gat your leavin's, Lord Randal, my son?
And wha gat your leavin's, my handsome young man?"
"My hawks and my hounds; mother, mak my bed soon,
For I'm wearied wi' huntin', and fain wad lie down."

5

"And what becam of them, Lord Randal, my son?
And what becam of them, my handsome young man?"
"They stretched their legs out and died; mother, mak my bed soon,
For I'm wearied wi' huntin', and fain wad lie down."

6

"O I fear you are poisoned, Lord Randal, my son!
I fear you are poisoned, my handsome young man!"
"O yes, I am poisoned; mother, mak my bed soon,
For I'm sick at the heart, and I fain wad lie down."

7

"What d' ye leave to your mother, Lord Randal, my son?
What d'ye leave to your mother, my handsome young man?"
"Four and twenty milk kye°; mother, mak my bed soon, *kine, cattle*
For I'm sick at the heart, and I fain wad lie down."

8

"What d' ye leave to your sister, Lord Randal, my son?
What d' ye leave to your sister, my handsome young man?"
"My gold and my silver; mother, mak my bed soon,
For I'm sick at the heart, and I fain wad lie down."

9

"What d' ye leave to your brother, Lord Randal, my son?
What d' ye leave to your brother, my handsome young man?"
"My houses and my lands; mother, mak my bed soon,
For I'm sick at the heart, and I fain wad lie down."

10

"What d' ye leave to your true-love, Lord Randal, my son?
What d' ye leave to your true-love, my handsome young man?"
"I leave her hell and fire; mother, mak my bed soon,
For I'm sick at the heart, and I fain wad lie down."

Edward[2]

1

"Why does your brand° sae° drap wi' bluid, *sword / so*
Edward, Edward,
Why does your brand sae drap wi' bluid,
And why sae sad gang° ye, O?" *go*
"O I ha'e killed my hawk sae guid,
Mither, mither,

2. Child, No. 13.B.

O I ha'e killed my hawk sae guid,
And I had nae mair but he, O."

2

"Your hawke's bluid was never sae reid,° *red*
Edward, Edward,
Your hawke's bluid was never sae reid,
My dear son I tell thee, O."
"O I ha'e killed my reid-roan steed,
Mither, mither,
O I ha'e killed my reid-roan steed,
That erst was sae fair and free, O."

3

"Your steed was auld, and ye ha'e gat mair,
Edward, Edward,
Your steed was auld, and ye ha'e gat mair,
Some other dule° ye drie,° O." *grief / suffer*
"O I ha'e killed my fader dear,
Mither, mither,
O I ha'e killed my fader dear,
Alas, and wae° is me, O!" *woe*

4

"And whatten° penance wul ye drie for that, *what sort of*
Edward, Edward?
And whatten penance wul ye dree for that,
My dear son, now tell me O?"
"I'll set my feet in yonder boat,
Mither, mither,
I'll set my feet in yonder boat,
And I'll fare over the sea, O."

5

"And what wul ye do wi' your towers and your ha',
Edward, Edward?
And what wul ye do wi' your towers and your ha',
That were sae fair to see, O?"
"I'll let them stand tul they down fa',
Mither, mither,
I'll let them stand tul they down fa',
For here never mair maun° I be, O." *must*

6

"And what wul ye leave to your bairns° and your wife, *children*
Edward, Edward?
And what wul ye leave to your bairns and your wife,
Whan ye gang over the sea, O?"
"The warlde's room,[3] let them beg thrae° life, *through*
Mither, mither,
The warlde's room, let them beg thrae life,
For them never mair wul I see, O."

7

"And what wul ye leave to your ain mither dear,
Edward, Edward?
And what wul ye leave to your ain mither dear,
My dear son, now tell me, O?"
"The curse of hell frae° me sall° ye bear, *from / shall*
Mither, mither,
The curse of hell frae me sall ye bear,
Sic° counsels ye gave to me, O." *such*

3. I.e., the wide world.

The Three Ravens[4]

1

There were three ravens sat on a tree,
  Down a down, hay down, hay down
There were three ravens sat on a tree,
  With a down
There were three ravens sat on a tree,
They were as black as they might be.
  With a down derry, derry, derry, down, down.

2

The one of them said to his mate,
"Where shall we our breakfast take?"

3

"Down in yonder greene field,
There lies a knight slain under his shield.

4

"His hounds they lie down at his feet,
So well they can their master keep.

5

"His hawks they fly so eagerly,° — *fiercely*
There's no fowl dare him come nigh."

6

Down there comes a fallow[5] doe,
As great with young as she might go.

7

She lift up his bloody head
And kissed his wounds that were so red.

8

She got him up upon her back
And carried him to earthen lake.° — *pit*

9

She buried him before the prime;[6]
She was dead herself ere even-song time.

10

God send every gentleman
Such hawks, such hounds, and such a leman.° — *lover, sweetheart*

The Twa Corbies[7]

1

As I was walking all alane,
I heard twa corbies making a mane;° — *moan*
The tane° unto the t'other say, — *one*
"Where sall° we gang° and dine to-day?" — *shall / go*

2

"In behint you auld fail° dike, — *turf*
I wot there lies a new slain knight;
And naebody kens° that he lies there, — *knows*
But his hawk, his hound, and lady fair.

4. Child, No. 26.
5. A species of deer distinguished by color (fallow: pale brownish or reddish yellow) from the red deer.
6. The first hour of the day, sunrise.
7. Child, No. 26. "Corbies" are ravens.

3
"His hound is to the hunting gane,
His hawk to fetch the wild-fowl hame,
His lady's ta'en another mate,
So we may mak our dinner sweet.

4
"Ye'll sit on his white hause-bane,° *neck-bone*
And I'll pike° out his bonny blue een;° *pick / eyes*
Wi' ae° lock o' his gowden° hair *one / golden*
We'll theek° our nest when it grows bare. *thatch*

5
"Mony a one for him makes mane,
But nane sall ken where he is gane;
O'er his white banes, when they are bare,
The wind sall blaw for evermair."

Sir Patrick Spens[8]

1
The king sits in Dumferling town,
  Drinking the blude-reid° wine: *blood-red*
"O whar will I get guid sailor,
  To sail this ship of mine?"

2
Up and spak an eldern knicht,
  Sat at the king's richt knee:
"Sir Patrick Spens is the best sailor
  That sails upon the sea."

3
The king has written a braid° letter *broad*
  And signed it wi' his hand,
And sent it to Sir Patrick Spens,
  Was walking on the sand.

4
The first line that Sir Patrick read,
  A loud lauch° lauched he; *laugh*
The next line that Sir Patrick read,
  The tear blinded his ee.° *eye*

5
"O wha is this has done this deed,
  This ill deed done to me,
To send me out this time o' the year,
  To sail upon the sea?

6
"Mak haste, mak haste, my mirry men all,
  Our guid ship sails the morn."
"O say na sae,° my master dear, *so*
  For I fear a deadly storm.

7
"Late, late yestre'en I saw the new moon
  Wi' the auld moon in hir arm,
And I fear, I fear, my dear master,
  That we will come to harm."

8. Child, No. 58.A.

8

O our Scots nobles were richt laith° *loath*
To weet° their cork-heeled shoon,° *wet / shoes*
But lang or° a' the play were played *before*
Their hats they swam aboon.[9]

9

O lang, lang may their ladies sit,
Wi' their fans into their hand,
Or ere they see Sir Patrick Spens
Come sailing to the land.

10

O lang, lang may the ladies stand
Wi' their gold kems° in their hair, *combs*
Waiting for their ain dear lords,
For they'll see them na mair.

11

Half o'er, half o'er to Aberdour
It's fifty fadom deep,
And there lies guid Sir Patrick Spens
Wi' the Scots lords at his feet.

The Unquiet Grave[1]

1

"The wind doth blow today, my love,
And a few small drops of rain;
I never had but one true-love,
In cold grave she was lain.

2

"I'll do as much for my true-love
As any young man may;
I'll sit and mourn all at her grave
For a twelvemonth and a day."

3

The twelvemonth and a day being up,
The dead began to speak:
"Oh who sits weeping on my grave,
And will not let me sleep?"

4

" 'T is I, my love, sits on your grave,
And will not let you sleep;
For I crave one kiss of your clay-cold lips,
And that is all I seek."

5

"You crave one kiss of my clay-cold lips,
But my breath smells earthy strong;
If you have one kiss of my clay-cold lips,
Your time will not be long.

6

" 'T is down in yonder garden green,
Love, where we used to walk,
The finest flower that e'er was seen
Is withered to a stalk.

9. I.e., their hats swam above (them).

1. Child, No. 78.A.

7

"The stalk is withered dry, my love,
So will our hearts decay;
So make yourself content, my love,
Till God calls you away."

The Wife of Usher's Well[2]

1

There lived a wife at Usher's Well,
And a wealthy wife was she;
She had three stout and stalwart sons,
And sent them o'er the sea.

2

They hadna been a week from her,
A week but barely ane,
Whan word came to the carlin° wife *peasant*
That her three sons were gane.

3

They hadna been a week from her,
A week but barely three,
Whan word came to the carlin wife
That her sons she'd never see.

4

"I wish the wind may never cease,
Nor fashes° in the flood, *troubles*
Till my three sons come hame to me,
In earthly flesh and blood."

5

It fell about the Martinmass,[3]
When nights are lang and mirk,
The carlin wife's three sons came hame,
And their hats were o' the birk.° *birch*

6

It neither grew in syke° nor ditch, *trench*
Nor yet in any sheugh;° *furrow*
But at the gates o' Paradise,
That birk grew fair eneugh.

7

"Blow up the fire, my maidens,
Bring water from the well;
For a' my house shall feast this night,
Since my three sons are well."

8

And she has made to them a bed,
She's made it large and wide,
And she's ta'en her mantle her about,
Sat down at the bed-side.

9

Up then crew the red, red cock,
And up and crew the gray;
The eldest to the youngest said,
" 'T is time we were away."

10

The cock he hadna crawed but once,
And clapped his wings at a',

2. Child, No. 79.A.
3. The feast of St. Martin (the martyred Pope Martin I, died 655), November 11.

When the youngest to the eldest said,
"Brother, we must awa'.

11

"The cock doth craw, the day doth daw,
The channerin'° worm doth chide; *fretting*
Gin° we be missed out o' our place, *if*
A sair° pain we maun° bide. *sore / must*

12

"Fare ye weel, my mother dear!
Fareweel to barn and byre!° *cowhouse*
And fare ye weel, the bonny lass,
That kindles my mother's fire!"

Bonny Barbara Allan[4]

1

It was in and about the Martinmas[5] time,
When the green leaves were a falling,
That Sir John Græme, in the West Country,
Fell in love with Barbara Allan.

2

He sent his man down through the town,
To the place where she was dwelling:
"O haste and come to my master dear,
Gin° ye be Barbara Allan." *if*

3

O hooly,° hooly rose she up, *slowly, gently*
To the place where he was lying,
And when she drew the curtain by:
"Young man, I think you're dying."

4

"O it's I'm sick, and very, very sick,
And 'tis a' for Barbara Allan."
"O the better for me ye s'° never be, *ye shall*
Though your heart's blood were a-spilling.

5

"O dinna° ye mind, young man," said she, *don't*
"When ye was in the tavern a drinking,
That ye made the healths gae° round and round, *go*
And slighted Barbara Allan?"

6

He turned his face unto the wall,
And death was with him dealing:
"Adieu, adieu, my dear friends all,
And be kind to Barbara Allan."

7

And slowly, slowly raise she up,
And slowly, slowly left him,
And sighing said, she could not stay,
Since death of life had reft him.

8

She had not gane a mile but twa,
When she heard the dead-bell ringing,
And every jow° that the dead-bell geid,° *stroke / gave*
It cried, "Woe to Barbara Allan!"

4. Child, No. 84.A.

5. See footnote 3.

9
"O mother, mother, make my bed!
O make it saft and narrow!
Since my love died for me to-day,
I'll die for him to-morrow."

Mary Hamilton[6]

1
Word's gane to the kitchen,
And word's gane to the ha',
That Marie Hamilton gangs° wi' bairn° *goes / child*
To the hichest° Stewart of a'. *highest*

2
He's courted her in the kitchen,
He's courted her in the ha',
He's courted her in the laigh cellar,[7]
And that was warst of a'.

3
She's tied it in her apron
And she's thrown it in the sea;
Says, "Sink ye, swim ye, bonny wee babe!
You'll ne'er get mair o' me."

4
Down then cam the auld queen,
Goud° tassels tying her hair: *gold*
"O Marie, where's the bonny wee babe
That I heard greet sae sair?"[8]

5
"There was never a babe intill° my room, *in*
As little designs to be;
It was but a touch o' my sair side,
Come o'er my fair body."

6
"O Marie, put on your robes o' black,
Or else your robes o' brown,
For ye maun° gang wi' me the night, *must*
To see fair Edinbro' town."

7
"I winna° put on my robes o' black, *won't*
Nor yet my robes o' brown;
But I'll put on my robes o' white,
To shine through Edinbro' town."

8
When she gaed° up the Cannogate,[9] *went*
She laughed loud laughters three;
But when she cam down the Cannogate
The tear blinded her ee.° *eye*

9
When she gaed up the Parliament stair,
The heel cam aff her shee;

6. Child, No. 173.A.
7. "Laigh cellar": low cellar, basement.
8. "Greet sae sair": cry so sorely.
9. The Canongate is the Edinburgh street leading uphill from Holyrood House (where the queen and the "four Maries" of line 69 lived) to the Tolbooth, which was both jail and judicial chamber and, on occasion, the place where Parliament (line 33) sat.

And lang or° she cam down again *before*
  She was condemned to dee.

10

When she cam down the Cannogate,
  The Cannogate sae free,
Many a lady looked o'er her window,
  Weeping for this lady.

11

"Ye need nae weep for me," she says,
  "Ye need nae weep for me;
For had I not slain mine own sweet babe,
  This death I wadna dee.

12

"Bring me a bottle of wine," she says,
  "The best that e'er ye ha'e,
That I may drink to my weil-wishers,
  And they may drink to me.

13

"Here's a health to the jolly sailors,
  That sail upon the main;
Let them never let on to my father and mother
  But what I'm coming hame.

14

"Here's a health to the jolly sailors,
  That sail upon the sea;
Let them never let on to my father and mother
  That I cam here to dee.

15

"Oh little did my mother think,
  The day she cradled me,
What lands I was to travel through,
  What death I was to dee.

16

"Oh little did my father think,
  The day he held up me,
What lands I was to travel through,
  What death I was to dee.

17

"Last night I washed the queen's feet,
  And gently laid her down;
And a' the thanks I've gotten the night[1]
  To be hanged in Edinbro' town!

18

"Last night there was four Maries,
  The night there'll be but three;
There was Marie Seton, and Marie Beton,
  And Marie Carmichael, and me."

Bonnie George Campbell[2]

1

High upon Highlands,
  And laigh° upon Tay,[3] *low*

1. I.e., tonight
2. Child, No. 210.C.
3. The longest river in Scotland, coming down from the Highlands into the Lowlands and entering the North Sea at Perth.

Bonnie George Campbell
  Rode out on a day.

2

He saddled, he bridled,
  And gallant rode he,
And hame cam his guid horse,
  But never cam he.

3

Out cam his mother dear,
  Greeting° fu' sair,° *weeping / sore[ly]*
And out cam his bonnie bride,
  Riving° her hair. *tearing*

4

"The meadow lies green,
  The corn is unshorn,
But bonnie George Campbell
  Will never return."

5

Saddled and bridled
  And booted rode he,
A plume in his helmet,
  A sword at his knee.

6

But toom° cam his saddle, *empty*
  All bloody to see,
Oh, hame cam his guid horse,
  But never cam he!

Get Up and Bar the Door[4]

1

It fell about the Martinmas[5] time,
  And a gay time it was then,
When our goodwife got puddings to make,
  And she's boiled them in the pan.

2

The wind sae° cauld blew south and north, *so*
  And blew into the floor;
Quoth our goodman to our goodwife,
  "Gae° out and bar the door." *go*

3

"My hand is in my hussyfskap.° *housewifery*
  Goodman, as ye may see;
An° it should nae be barred this hundred year, *if*
  It s'° no be barred for me." *shall*

4

They made a paction 'tween them twa,
  They made it firm and sure,
That the first word whae'er should speak,
  Should rise and bar the door.

5

Then by there came two gentlemen,
  At twelve o'clock at night,
And they could neither see house nor hall,
  Nor coal nor candle-light.

4. Child, No. 275.A.
5. The feast of St. Martin (the martyred Pope Martin I, died 655), November 11.

6

"Now whether is this a rich man's house,
Or whether is it a poor?"
But ne'er a word wad° ane o' them speak, *would*
For barring of the door.

7

And first they ate the white puddings,
And then they ate the black;
Though muckle° thought the goodwife to hersel, *much, a lot*
Yet ne'er a word she spak.

8

Then said the one unto the other,
"Here, man, tak ye my knife;
Do ye tak aff° the auld man's beard, *off*
And I'll kiss the goodwife."

9

"But there's nae water in the house,
And what shall we do then?"
"What ails ye at[6] the pudding-broo,° *-broth*
That boils into the pan?"

10

O up then started our goodman,
An angry man was he:
"Will ye kiss my wife before my een,° *eyes*
And scad° me wi' pudding-bree?"° *scald / -broth*

11

Then up and started our goodwife,
Gied° three skips on the floor: *gave*
"Goodman, you've spoken the foremost word,
Get up and bar the door."

The Bitter Withy

1

As it fell out on a holy day,
The drops of rain did fall, did fall,
Our Saviour asked leave of his mother Mary
If he might go play at ball.

2

"To play at ball, my own dear son,
It's time you was going or gone,
But be sure let me hear no complain of you,
At night when you do come home."

3

It was upling scorn and downling scorn,[7]
Oh, there he met three jolly jerdins;° *boys?*
Oh, there he asked the jolly jerdins
If they would go play at ball.

4

"Oh, we are lords' and ladies' sons,
Born in bower or in hall,
And you are some poor maid's child
Borned in an ox's stall."

5

"If you are lords' and ladies' sons,
Borned in bower or in hall,

6. I.e., what's the matter with.
7. There was scorn everywhere (*upling, downling*).

Then at last I'll make it appear
  That I am above you all."

6

Our Saviour built a bridge with the beams of the sun,
  And over it he gone, he gone he.
And after followed the three jolly jerdins,
  And drownded they were all three.

7

It was upling scorn and downling scorn,
  The mothers of them did whoop and call,
Crying out, "Mary mild, call home your child,
  For ours are drownded all."

8

Mary mild, Mary mild, called home her child,
  And laid our Saviour across her knee,
And with a whole handful of bitter withy° *willow*
  She gave him slashes three.

9

Then he says to his mother, "Oh! the withy, oh! the withy,
  The bitter withy that causes me to smart, to smart,
Oh! the withy, it shall be the very first tree
  That perishes at the heart."

ANONYMOUS ELIZABETHAN AND JACOBEAN POEMS

As You Came from the Holy Land of Walsingham[1]

As you came from the holy land
  Of Walsingham,
Met you not with my true love,
  By the way as you came?

"How should I know your true love
  That have met many a one
As I came from the holy land,
  That have come, that have gone?"

She is neither white nor brown,
  But as the heavens fair;
There is none hath her form so divine,
  On the earth, in the air.

"Such a one did I meet, good sir,
  With angel-like face,
Who like a nymph, like a queen did appear
  In her gait, in her grace."

She hath left me here alone,
  All alone unknown,
Who sometime loved me as her life,
  And called me her own.

1. A shrine in Norfolk, famous as a place of pilgrimage.

"What is the cause she hath left thee alone,
And a new way doth take,
That sometime did thee love as herself,
And her joy did thee make?"

I have loved her all my youth,
But now am old as you see;
Love liketh not the falling fruit,
Nor the withered tree.

For love is a careless child,
And forgets promise past;
He is blind, he is deaf, when he list,° *pleases*
And in faith never fast.

His desire is fickle found,
And a trustless joy;
He is won with a world of despair,
And is lost with a toy.

Such is the love of womenkind,
Or the word, love, abused,
Under which many childish desires
And conceits are excused.

But love, it is a durable fire
In the mind ever burning,
Never sick, never dead, never cold,
From itself never turning.

ca. 1593 1678

Fine Knacks for Ladies

Fine knacks for ladies, cheap, choice, brave and new!
Good pennyworths—but money cannot move:
I keep a fair but for the fair to view;
A beggar may be liberal of love.
Though all my wares be trash, the heart is true,
The heart is true.

Great gifts are guiles and look for gifts again;
My trifles come as treasures from my mind.
It is a precious jewel to be plain;
Sometimes in shell the orient'st° pearls we find. *most lustrous*
Of others take a sheaf, of me a grain!
Of me a grain!

Within this pack pins, points,[2] laces, and gloves,
And divers toys fitting a country fair;
But in my heart, where duty serves and loves,
Turtles° and twins, court's brood, a heavenly pair. *turtledoves*
Happy the heart that thinks of no removes!
Of no removes!

1600

2. A lace (such as a shoelace) with the ends tagged or pointed for convenience in lacing.

Weep You No More, Sad Fountains

Weep you no more, sad fountains;
What need you flow so fast?
Look how the snowy mountains
Heaven's sun doth gently waste.
But my sun's heavenly eyes
View not your weeping,
That now lie sleeping
Softly, now softly lies
Sleeping.

Sleep is a reconciling,
A rest that peace begets.
Doth not the sun rise smiling
When fair at even he sets?
Rest you then, rest, sad eyes,
Melt not in weeping
While she lies sleeping
Softly, now softly lies
Sleeping.

1603

There Is a Lady Sweet and Kind

There is a lady sweet and kind,
Was never face so pleased my mind;
I did but see her passing by,
And yet I love her till I die.

Her gesture, motion and her smiles,
Her wit, her voice, my heart beguiles,
Beguiles my heart, I know not why,
And yet I love her till I die.

Her free behavior, winning looks,
Will make a lawyer burn his books.
I touched her not, alas, not I,
And yet I love her till I die.

Had I her fast betwixt mine arms,
Judge you that think such sports were harms,
Were't any harm? No, no, fie, fie!
For I will love her till I die.

Should I remain confinéd there,
So long as Phoebus[3] in his sphere,
I to request, she to deny,
Yet would I love her till I die.

Cupid is wingéd and doth range;
Her country so my love doth change,
But change she earth, or change she sky,
Yet will I love her till I die.

1607

3. Apollo, god of the sun.

The Silver Swan

The silver swan, who living had no note,
When death approached, unlocked her silent throat;
Leaning her breast against the reedy shore,
Thus sung her first and last, and sung no more:
"Farewell, all joys; Oh death, come close mine eyes;
More geese than swans now live, more fools than wise."

1612

THOMAS WYATT
(1503–1542)

The Long Love That in My Thought Doth Harbor[1]

The long love that in my thought doth harbor,
And in my heart doth keep his residence,
Into my face presseth with bold pretense
And there encampeth, spreading his banner.
She that me learns° to love and suffer *teaches*
And wills that my trust and lust's negligence
Be reined by reason, shame, and reverence
With his hardiness takes displeasure.
Wherewithal unto the heart's forest he fleeth,
Leaving his enterprise with pain and cry,
And there him hideth, and not appeareth.
What may I do, when my master feareth,
But in the field with him to live and die?
For good is the life ending faithfully.

1557

Whoso List to Hunt[2]

Whoso list to hunt, I know where is an hind,
  But as for me, alas, I may no more;
  The vain travail hath wearied me so sore,
  I am of them that furthest come behind.
Yet may I by no means my wearied mind
  Draw from the deer, but as she fleeth afore
  Fainting I follow; I leave off therefore,
  Since in a net I seek to hold the wind.
Who list her hunt, I put him out of doubt,
  As well as I, may spend his time in vain.
  And graven with diamonds in letters plain,
There is written her fair neck round about,
  "*Noli me tangere,*[3] for Caesar's I am,
  And wild for to hold, though I seem tame."

Egerton Ms.

1. Translated from Petrarch. Compare the translation by the Earl of Surrey, *Love That Doth Reign and Live Within My Thought.*
2. This poem, like many of Wyatt's, existed only in manuscript form until comparatively recently.
3. Touch me not.

My Galley Charged with Forgetfulness

My galley charged[4] with forgetfulness
Thorough sharp seas in winter nights doth pass
'Tween rock and rock; and eke° mine enemy, alas, *also*
That is my lord, steereth with cruelness;
And every oar a thought in readiness,
As though that death were light in such a case.
An endless wind doth tear the sail apace
Of forced sighs, and trusty fearfulness.
A rain of tears, a cloud of dark disdain,
Hath done the wearied cords great hinderance;
Wreathed with error and eke with ignorance,
The stars be hid that led me to this pain;
Drowned is reason that should me consort,
And I remain despairing of the port.

1557

Madam, Withouten Many Words

Madam, withouten many words,
Once, I am sure ye will, or no;
And if ye will, then leave your bords,° *jests*
And use your wit, and show it so.

And with a beck ye shall me call,
And if of one that burneth alway,
Ye have any pity at all,
Answer him fair with yea or nay.

If it be yea, I shall be fain;
If it be nay, friends as before;
Ye shall another man obtain,
And I mine own, and yours no more.

1557

They Flee from Me

They flee from me, that sometime did me seek,
With naked foot stalking in my chamber.
I have seen them, gentle, tame, and meek,
That now are wild, and do not remember
That sometime they put themselves in danger
To take bread at my hand; and now they range,
Busily seeking with a continual change.

Thanked be Fortune it hath been otherwise,
Twenty times better; but once in special,
In thin array, after a pleasant guise,
When her loose gown from her shoulders did fall,
And she me caught in her arms long and small,° *slender*

4. Wyatt's meter is so often irregular that it is difficult to say with certainty when he intended an *-ed* ending to be pronounced as a second syllable and when not. Hence no attempt has been made to mark syllabic endings with an accent in any of Wyatt's poems, although in this particular poem such endings appear to be intended in lines 1, 8, 11, and 13.

And therewith all sweetly did me kiss
And softly said, "Dear heart, how like you this?"

It was no dream, I lay broad waking.
But all is turned, thorough my gentleness,
Into a strange fashion of forsaking;
And I have leave to go, of her goodness,
And she also to use newfangleness.
But since that I so kindely[5] am served,
I fain would know what she hath deserved.

1557

My Lute, Awake!

My lute, awake! Perform the last
Labor that thou and I shall waste,
And end that I have now begun;
For when this song is sung and past,
My lute, be still, for I have done.

As to be heard where ear is none,
As lead to grave° in marble stone, *engrave*
My song may pierce her heart as soon.
Should we then sigh or sing or moan?
No, no, my lute, for I have done.

The rocks do not so cruelly
Repulse the waves continually
As she my suit and affection.
So that I am past remedy,
Whereby my lute and I have done.

Proud of the spoil that thou hast got
Of simple hearts, thorough love's shot;
By whom, unkind, thou hast them won,
Think not he hath his bow forgot,
Although my lute and I have done.

Vengeance shall fall on thy disdain
That makest but game on earnest pain.
Think not alone under the sun
Unquit° to cause thy lovers plain, *unrequited*
Although my lute and I have done.

Perchance thee lie withered and old
The winter nights that are so cold,
Plaining in vain unto the moon.
Thy wishes then dare not be told.
Care then who list,° for I have done. *likes*

And then may chance thee to repent
The time that thou hast lost and spent
To cause thy lovers sigh and swoon.
Then shalt thou know beauty but lent,
And wish and want as I have done.

5. I.e., in the normal way of womankind, an older meaning that does not exclude the modern meaning of "kindly."

Now cease, my lute. This is the last
Labor that thou and I shall waste,
And ended is that we begun.
Now is this song both sung and past;
My lute, be still, for I have done.

1557

Mine Own John Poins

Mine own John Poins, since ye delight to know
The cause why that homeward I me draw,
And flee the press of courts, whereso they go,
Rather than to live thrall, under the awe
Of lordly looks, wrapped within my cloak,
To will and lust° learning to set a law; *pleasure*
It is not for because I scorn and mock
The power of them to whom Fortune hath lent
Charge over us, of right to strike the stroke.
But true it is that I have always meant
Less to esteem them than the common sort,
Of outward things that judge in their intent
Without regard what doth inward resort.
I grant sometime that of glory the fire
Doth touch my heart; me list not[6] to report
Blame by honor, and honor to desire.
But how may I this honor now attain
That cannot dye the color black a liar?
My Poins, I cannot frame me tune to feign,
To cloak the truth, for praise without desert,
Of them that list all vice for to retain.
I cannot honor them that sets their part
With Venus and Bacchus[7] all their life long;
Nor hold my peace of them, although I smart.
I cannot crouch nor kneel to do so great a wrong,
To worship them like God on earth alone,
That are as wolves these sely° lambs among. *innocent*
I cannot with my words complain and moan
Nor suffer naught, nor smart without complaint,
Nor turn the word that from my mouth is gone;
I cannot speak and look like a saint,
Use wiles for wit, or make deceit a pleasure;
And call craft counsel, for profit still to paint;
I cannot wrest the law to fill the coffer,
With innocent blood to feed myself fat,
And do most hurt where most help I offer.
I am not he that can allow the state
Of high Caesar, and damn Cato[8] to die,
That with his death did 'scape out of the gate
From Caesar's hands, if Livy do not lie,
And would not live where liberty was lost,
So did his heart the common weal apply.[9]
I am not he, such eloquence to boast

6. "Me list not": I care not.
7. Venus was the goddess of love and Bacchus the god of wine.
8. The Roman historian Livy recounts the death of Cato the Younger, who chose suicide in preference to tyranny.
9. I.e., so did his heart practice the common good.

To make the crow in singing as the swan,
Nor call the lion of coward beasts the most,
That cannot take a mouse as the cat can;
And he that dieth of hunger of the gold,
Call him Alexander,[1] and say that Pan
Passeth Apollo in music manifold;[2]
Praise Sir Thopas for a noble tale,
And scorn the story that the Knight told,[3]
Praise him for counsel that is drunk of ale;
Grin when he laugheth that beareth all the sway,
Frown when he frowneth, and groan when he is pale;
On others' lust to hang both night and day—
None of these points would ever frame in me;
My wit is naught: I cannot learn the way;
And much the less of things that greater be
That asken help of colors of device[4]
To join the mean with each extremity.
With nearest virtue to cloak alway the vice,
And as to purpose, likewise it shall fall
To press the virtue that it may not rise;
As drunkenness good fellowship to call;
The friendly foe, with his double face,
Say he is gentle and courteous therewithal;
And say that favel° hath a goodly grace — *flattery*
In eloquence; and cruelty to name
Zeal of justice, and change in time and place;
And he that suff'reth offense without blame,
Call him pitiful, and him true and plain
That raileth reckless to every man's shame,
Say he is rude that cannot lie and feign,
The lecher a lover, and tyranny
To be the right of a prince's reign.
I cannot, I: no, no, it will not be.
This is the cause that I could never yet
Hang on their sleeves, that weigh, as thou mayst see,
A chip of chance more than a pound of wit.
This maketh me at home to hunt and hawk,
And in foul weather at my book to sit,
In frost and snow then with my bow to stalk.
No man doth mark whereso I ride or go.
In lusty leas° at liberty I walk, — *pleasant meadows*
And of these news I feel nor weal nor woe,
Save that a clog doth hang yet at my heel.
No force° for that, for it is ordered so — *no matter*
That I may leap both hedge and dike full well;
I am not now in France, to judge the wine,
With sav'ry sauce those delicates to feel;
Nor yet in Spain, where one must him incline,
Rather than to be, outwardly to seem.
I meddle not with wits that be so fine;
Nor Flanders' cheer[5] letteth° not my sight to deem — *hinders*

1. Alexander the Great, conqueror of the entire known world, lamented that there was nothing left for him to conquer.
2. The god Pan played simple ditties on his syrinx; Apollo, divine melodies on his lyre.
3. Chaucer's tale of *Sir Thopas* (in *The Canterbury Tales*) is a deliberately dull parody that is cut off after a few stanzas by the Host. The *Knight's Tale* is perhaps the most impressive of all the tales.
4. Artful language that "colors" or falsifies.
5. Flemings were reputed to be heavy drinkers.

Of black and white, nor taketh my wit away
With beastliness, they beasts do so esteem.
Nor am I not where Christ is given in prey
For money, poison, and treason—at Rome
A common practice, used night and day.
But here I am in Kent and Christendom,
Among the Muses, where I read and rhyme;
Where, if thou list, my Poins, for to come,
Thou shalt be judge how I do spend my time.

1536 1557

HENRY HOWARD, EARL OF SURREY
(ca. 1517–1547)

The Soote Season

The soote° season, that bud and bloom forth brings, *sweet*
With green hath clad the hill and eke° the vale; *also*
The nightingale with feathers new she sings;
The turtle° to her make° hath told her tale. *turtledove / mate*
Summer is come, for every spray now springs;
The hart hath hung his old head on the pale;
The buck in brake his winter coat he flings,
The fishes float with new repairéd scale;
The adder all her slough away she slings,
The swift swallow pursueth the flies small;
The busy bee her honey now she mings.° *remembers*
Winter is worn, that was the flowers' bale.° *harm*
And thus I see among these pleasant things,
Each care decays, and yet my sorrow springs.

1557

Love, That Doth Reign and Live Within My Thought[1]

Love, that doth reign and live within my thought,
And built his seat within my captive breast,
Clad in the arms wherein with me he fought,
Oft in my face he doth his banner rest.
But she that taught me love and suffer pain,
My doubtful hope and eke my hot desire
With shamefast° look to shadow and refrain, *shamefaced*
Her smiling grace converteth straight to ire.
And coward Love, then, to the heart apace
Taketh his flight, where he doth lurk and plain,° *complain*
His purpose lost, and dare not show his face.
For my lord's guilt thus faultless bide I pain,
Yet from my lord shall not my foot remove:
Sweet is the death that taketh end by love.

1557

1. Translated from Petrarch. Compare the translation by Sir Thomas Wyatt, *The Long Love That in My Thought Doth Harbor*.

Wyatt Resteth Here

Wyatt resteth here, that quick° could never rest; *living*
Whose heavenly gifts increaséd by disdain,
And virtue sank the deeper in his breast;
Such profit he of envy could obtain.
A head where wisdom mysteries did frame,
Whose hammers beat still in that lively brain
As on a stithy,° where some work of fame *anvil*
Was daily wrought, to turn to Britain's gain.
A visage stern and mild, where both did grow,
Vice to contemn, in virtues to rejoice,
Amid great storms, whom grace assuréd so,
To live upright, and smile at fortune's choice.
A hand that taught what might be said in rhyme;
That reft Chaucer the glory of his wit;
A mark, the which—unperfited,° for time— *uncompleted*
Some may approach, but never none shall hit.
A tongue that served in foreign realms his king;
Whose courteous talk to virtue did enflame
Each noble heart; a worthy guide to bring
Our English youth, by travail, unto fame.
An eye whose judgment no affect° could blind, *passion*
Friends to allure, and foes to reconcile;
Whose piercing look did represent a mind
With virtue fraught, reposéd, void of guile.
A heart where dread yet never so impressed
To hide the thought that might the truth advance;
In neither fortune lost, nor so repressed,
To swell in wealth, nor yield unto mischance.
A valiant corps,° where force and beauty met, *body*
Happy, alas! too happy, but for foes,
Livéd, and ran the race that nature set;
Of manhood's shape, where she the mold did lose.
But to the heavens that simple soul is fled,
Which left with such as covet Christ to know
Witness of faith that never shall be dead,
Sent for our health, but not receivéd so.
Thus, for our guilt, this jewel have we lost;
The earth his bones, the heavens possess his ghost.

1557

QUEEN ELIZABETH I
(1533–1603)

When I Was Fair and Young

When I was fair and young, and favor gracéd me,
Of many was I sought, their mistress for to be;
But I did scorn them all, and answered them therefore,
"Go, go, go seek some otherwhere!
Importune me no more!"

How many weeping eyes I made to pine with woe,
How many sighing hearts, I have no skill to show;
Yet I the prouder grew, and answered them therefore,
"Go, go, go seek some otherwhere!
Importune me no more!"

Then spake fair Venus' son, that proud victorious boy,
And said, "Fine dame, since that you be so coy,
I will so pluck your plumes that you shall say no more,
'Go, go, go seek some otherwhere!
Importune me no more!' "

When he had spake these words, such change grew in my breast
That neither night nor day since that, I could take any rest.
Then lo! I did repent that I had said before,
"Go, go, go seek some otherwhere!
Importune me no more!"

GEORGE GASCOIGNE
(ca. 1535–1577)

And If I Did What Then?

"And if I did what then?
Are you aggrieved therefore?
The sea hath fish for every man,
And what would you have more?"

Thus did my mistress once
Amaze my mind with doubt,
And popped a question for the nonce
To beat my brains about.

Whereto I thus replied:
"Each fisherman can wish
That all the sea at every tide
Were his alone to fish.

And so did I, in vain;
But since it may not be,
Let such fish there as find the gain,
And leave the loss for me.

And with such luck and loss
I will content myself,
Till tides of turning time may toss
Such fishers on the shelf.

And when they stick on sands,
That every man may see,
Then will I laugh and clap my hands,
As they do now at me."

1573

Gascoigne's Lullaby

Sing lullaby, as women do,
Wherewith they bring their babes to rest,
And lullaby can I sing too,
As womanly as can the best.
With lullaby they still the child,
And if I be not much beguiled,
Full many wanton babes have I,
Which must be stilled with lullaby.

First, lullaby, my youthful years,
It is now time to go to bed,
For crooked age and hoary hairs
Have won the haven within my head.
With lullaby then, youth, be still,
With lullaby content they will,
Since courage quails and comes behind,
Go sleep, and so. beguile thy mind.

Next, lullaby, my gazing eyes,
Which wonted were to glance apace.
For every glass may now suffice
To show the furrows in my face.
With lullaby then wink awhile,
With lullaby your looks beguile.
Let no fair face nor beauty bright
Entice you eft° with vain delight. *after*

And lullaby, my wanton will,
Let reason's rule now rein thy thought,
Since all too late I find by skill
How dear I have thy fancies bought.
With lullaby now take thine ease,
With lullaby thy doubts appease.
For trust to this, if thou be still,
My body shall obey thy will.

Eke° lullaby, my loving boy, *also*
My little Robin, take thy rest.
Since age is cold and nothing coy,° *lascivious*
Keep close thy coin, for so is best.
With lullaby be thou content,
With lullaby thy lusts relent.
Let others pay which° hath mo° pence; *who/more*
Thou art too poor for such expense.

Thus, lullaby, my youth, mine eyes,
My will, my ware, and all that was.
I can no mo delays devise,
But welcome pain, let pleasure pass.
With lullaby now take your leave,
With lullaby your dreams deceive,
And when you rise with waking eye,
Remember Gascoigne's lullaby.

1573

CHIDIOCK TICHBORNE
(d. 1586)

Tichborne's Elegy

WRITTEN WITH HIS OWN HAND
IN THE TOWER BEFORE HIS EXECUTION

My prime of youth is but a frost of cares,
My feast of joy is but a dish of pain,
My crop of corn is but a field of tares,° *weeds*
And all my good is but vain hope of gain;
The day is past, and yet I saw no sun,
And now I live, and now my life is done.

My tale was heard and yet it was not told,
My fruit is fallen and yet my leaves are green,
My youth is spent and yet I am not old,
I saw the world and yet I was not seen;
My thread is cut and yet it is not spun,[2]
And now I live, and now my life is done.

I sought my death and found it in my womb,
I looked for life and saw it was a shade,
I trod the earth and knew it was my tomb,
And now I die, and now I was but made;
My glass° is full, and now my glass is run, *hourglass*
And now I live, and now my life is done.

1586

SIR WALTER RALEGH
(ca. 1552–1618)

The Nymph's Reply to the Shepherd[1]

If all the world and love were young,
And truth in every shepherd's tongue,
These pretty pleasures might me move
To live with thee and be thy love.

Time drives the flocks from field to fold
When rivers rage and rocks grow cold,
And Philomel° becometh dumb; *the nightingale*
The rest complains of cares to come.

The flowers do fade, and wanton fields
To wayward winter reckoning yields;
A honey tongue, a heart of gall,
Is fancy's spring, but sorrow's fall.

2. An allusion to the three Fates, who spun the thread that determined the length of man's life and cut it when he was destined to die.

1. Written in reply to Christopher Marlowe's *The Passionate Shepherd to His Love.*

Thy gowns, thy shoes, thy beds of roses,
Thy cap, thy kirtle,[2] and thy posies
Soon break, soon wither, soon forgotten—
In folly ripe, in reason rotten.

Thy belt of straw and ivy buds,
Thy coral clasps and amber studs,
All these in me no means can move
To come to thee and be thy love.

But could youth last and love still breed,
Had joys no date[3] nor age no need,
Then these delights my mind might move
To live with thee and be thy love.

1600

The Passionate Man's Pilgrimage

Give me my scallop-shell[4] of quiet,
My staff of faith to walk upon,
My scrip[5] of joy, immortal diet,
My bottle of salvation,
My gown of glory, hope's true gage,° *pledge*
And thus I'll take my pilgrimage.

Blood must be my body's balmer,
No other balm will there be given,
Whilst my soul like a white palmer[6]
Travels to the land of heaven,
Over the silver mountains,
Where spring the nectar fountains;
And there I'll kiss
The bowl of bliss,
And drink my eternal fill
On every milken hill.
My soul will be a-dry before,
But after it will ne'er thirst more;
And by the happy blissful way
More peaceful pilgrims I shall see
That have shook off their gowns of clay
And go appareled fresh like me.
I'll bring them first
To slake their thirst,
And then to taste those nectar suckets,° *confections*
At the clear wells
Where sweetness dwells,
Drawn up by saints in crystal buckets.

And when our bottles and all we
Are filled with immortality,
Then the holy paths we'll travel,
Strewed with rubies thick as gravel,
Ceilings of diamonds, sapphire floors,
High walls of coral, and pearl bowers,
From thence to heaven's bribeless hall
Where no corrupted voices brawl,

2. A long dress, often worn under an outer garment.
3. I.e., terminal date.
4. A scallop shell or something resembling it was worn as the sign of a pilgrim.
5. Pilgrim's knapsack or bag.
6. A person wearing a palm leaf as a sign that he had made a pilgrimage to the Holy Land.

No conscience molten into gold,
Nor forged accusers bought and sold,
No cause deferred, nor vain-spent journey,
For there Christ is the king's attorney,
Who pleads for all, without degrees,
And he hath angels,[7] but no fees.
When the grand twelve million jury
Of our sins and sinful fury,
'Gainst our souls black verdicts give,
Christ pleads his death, and then we live.
Be thou my speaker, taintless pleader,
Unblotted lawyer, true proceeder;
Thou movest salvation even for alms,
Not with a bribed lawyer's palms.
And this is my eternal plea
To him that made heaven, earth, and sea,
Seeing my flesh must die so soon,
And want a head to dine next noon,
Just at the stroke when my veins start and spread,
Set on my soul an everlasting head.
Then am I ready, like a palmer fit,
To tread those blest paths which before I writ.

1604

The Lie

Go, soul, the body's guest,
Upon a thankless errand;
Fear not to touch the best;
The truth shall be thy warrant.
Go, since I needs must die,
And give the world the lie.

Say to the court, it glows
And shines like rotten wood;
Say to the church, it shows
What's good, and doth no good.
If church and court reply,
Then give them both the lie.

Tell potentates, they live
Acting by others' action;
Not loved unless they give,
Not strong but by a faction.
If potentates reply,
Give potentates the lie.

Tell men of high condition,
That manage the estate,
Their purpose is ambition,
Their practice only hate.
And if they once reply,
Then give them all the lie.

Tell them that brave it most,
They beg for more by spending,
Who, in their greatest cost,
Seek nothing but commending.

7. A punning reference to the gold coin of that name, ten shillings in value.

And if they make reply,
Then give them all the lie.

Tell zeal it wants devotion;
Tell love it is but lust;
Tell time it is but motion;
Tell flesh it is but dust.
And wish them not reply,
For thou must give the lie.

Tell age it daily wasteth;
Tell honor how it alters;
Tell beauty how she blasteth;
Tell favor how it falters.
And as they shall reply,
Give every one the lie.

Tell wit how much it wrangles
In tickle° points of niceness; *delicate*
Tell wisdom she entangles
Herself in overwiseness.
And when they do reply,
Straight give them both the lie.

Tell physic of her boldness;
Tell skill it is pretension;
Tell charity of coldness;
Tell law it is contention.
And as they do reply,
So give them still the lie.

Tell fortune of her blindness;
Tell nature of decay;
Tell friendship of unkindness;
Tell justice of delay.
And if they will reply,
Then give them all the lie.

Tell arts they have no soundness,
But vary by esteeming;
Tell schools they want profoundness,
And stand too much on seeming.
If arts and schools reply,
Give arts and schools the lie.

Tell faith it's fled the city;
Tell how the country erreth;
Tell manhood shakes off pity;
Tell virtue least preferreth.
And if they do reply,
Spare not to give the lie.

So when thou hast, as I
Commanded thee, done blabbing—
Although to give the lie
Deserves no less than stabbing—
Stab at thee he that will,
No stab the soul can kill.

1608

EDMUND SPENSER
(ca. 1552–1599)

From The Faerie Queene

From Book V, Canto II

29

. . . at length nigh to the sea they[1] drew;
By which as they did travell on a day,
They saw before them, far as they could vew,
Full many people gathered in a crew;
Whose great assembly they did much admire.° *wonder at*
For never there the like resort they knew.
So towardes them they coasted,° to enquire *approached*
What thing so many nations met, did there desire.

30

There they beheld a mighty Gyant stand
Upon a rocke, and holding forth on hie
An huge great paire of ballance in his hand,
With which he boasted in his surquedrie,° *arrogance*
That all the world he would weigh equallie,
If ought he had the same to counterpoys.
For want whereof he weighéd vanity,
And fild his ballaunce full of idle toys:
Yet was admired much of fooles, women, and boys.

31

He sayd that he would all the earth uptake,
And all the sea, devided each from either:
So would he of the fire one ballaunce make,
And one of th'ayre, without or wind, or wether:
Then would he ballaunce heaven and hell together,
And all that did within them all containe;
Of all whose weight, he would not misse a fether.
And looke what surplus did of each remaine,
He would to his owne part restore the same againe.

32

For why°, he sayd they all unequall were, *because*
And had encroched uppon others share,
Like as the sea (which plaine he shewéd there)
Had worne the earth, so did the fire the aire,
So all the rest did others parts empaire.
And so were realmes and nations run awry.
All which he undertooke for to repaire,
In sort as they were forméd auncientl y;
And all things would reduce° unto equality. *restore*

33

Therefore the vulgar did about him flocke,
And cluster thicke unto his leasings° vaine, *lies*

1. Artegall, the knight of Justice, and his squire Talus, an "iron man."

Like foolish flies about an hony crocke,
In hope by him great benefite to gaine,
And uncontrolléd freedome to obtaine.
All which when Artegall did see, and heare,
How he mis-led the simple peoples traine,
In sdeignfull° wize he drew unto him neare, *disdainful*
And thus unto him spake, without regard or feare.

34

"Thou that presum'st to weigh the world anew,
And all things to an equall to restore,
In stead of right me seemes great wrong dost shew,
And far above thy forces pitch to sore.
For ere thou limit what is lesse or more
In every thing, thou oughtest first to know,
What was the poyse° of every part of yore: *weight*
And looke then how much it doth overflow,
Or faile thereof, so much is more then just to trow.° *be considered*

35

"For at the first they all created were
In goodly measure, by their Makers might,
And weighéd out in ballaunces so nere,° *exactly*
That not a dram was missing of their right,
The earth was in the middle centre pight,° *set*
In which it doth immoveable abide,
Hemd in with waters like a wall in sight;
And they with aire, that not a drop can slide:
Al which the heavens containe, and in their courses guide.

36

"Such heavenly justice doth among them raine,
That every one doe know their certaine bound,
In which they doe these many yeares remaine,
And mongst them al no change hath yet beene found.
But if thou now shouldst weigh them new° in pound,° *anew / scales*
We are not sure they would so long remaine:
All change is perillous, and all chaunce unsound.
Therefore leave off to weigh them all againe,
Till we may be assur'd they shall their course retaine."

37

"Thou foolishe Elfe°," said then the Gyant wroth, *faerie knight*
"Seest not, how badly all things present bee,
And each estate quite out of order goth?
The sea it selfe doest thou not plainely see
Encroch uppon the land there under thee;
And th'earth it selfe how daily its increast,
By all that dying to it turnéd be?
Were it not good that wrong were then surceast,
And from the most, that some were given to the least?

38

"Therefore I will throw downe these mountaines hie,
And make them levell with the lowly plaine:
These towring rocks, which reach unto the skie,
I will thrust downe into the deepest maine,
And as they were, them equalize againe.
Tyrants that make men subject to their law,
I will suppresse, that they no more may raine;
And Lordings curbe, that commons over-aw;
And all the wealth of rich men to the poore will draw."

39
"Of things unseene how canst thou deeme aright,"
Then answeréd the righteous Artegall,
"Sith° thou misdeem'st so much of things in sight? *since*
What though the sea with waves continuall
Doe eate the earth, it is no more at all:
Ne is the earth the lesse, or loseth ought,
For whatsoever from one place doth fall,
Is with the tide unto an other brought:
For there is nothing lost, that may be found, if sought.

40
"Likewise the earth is not augmented more,
By all that dying into it doe fade.
For of the earth they forméd were of yore,
How ever gay their blossome or their blade
Doe flourish now, they into dust shall vade.° *vanish*
What wrong then is it, if that when they die,
They turne to that, whereof they first were made?
All in the powre of their great Maker lie:
All creatures must obey the voice of the most hie.

41
"They live, they die, like as he doth ordaine,
Ne ever any asketh reason why.
The hils doe not the lowly dales disdaine;
The dales doe not the lofty hils envy.
He maketh Kings to sit in soverainty;
He maketh subjects to their powre obay;
He pulleth downe, he setteth up on hy;
He gives to this, from that he takes away.
For all we have is his: what he list doe, he may.

42
"What ever thing is done, by him is donne,
Ne any may his mighty will withstand;
Ne any may his soveraine power shonne,
Ne loose that he hath bound with stedfast band.
In vaine therefore doest thou now take in hand,
To call to count, or weigh his workes anew,
Whose counsels depth thou canst not understand,
Sith of things subject to thy daily vew
Thou doest not know the causes, nor their courses dew.

43
"For take thy ballaunce, if thou be so wise,
And weigh the winde, that under heaven doth blow;
Or weigh the light, that in the East doth rise;
Or weigh the thought, that from mans mind doth flow.
But if the weight of these thou canst not show,
Weigh but one word which from thy lips doth fall.
For how canst thou those greater secrets know,
That doest not know the least thing of them all?
Ill can he rule the great, that cannot reach the small."

44
Therewith the Gyant much abashéd sayd;
That he of little things made reckoning light,
Yet the least word that ever could be layd
Within his ballaunce, he could way aright.
"Which is," sayd he, "more heavy then in weight,
The right or wrong, the false or else the trew?"

He answered, that he would try it streight,
So he the words into his ballaunce threw,
But streight the winged words out of his ballaunce flew.

45

Wroth wext he then, and sayd, that words were light,
Ne would within his ballaunce well abide.
But he could justly weigh the wrong or right.
"Well then," sayd Artegall, "let it be tride.
First in one ballance set the true aside."
He did so first; and then the false he layd
In th'other scale; but still it downe did slide,
And by no meane could in the weight° be stayd. *scale*
For by no meanes the false will with the truth be wayd.

46

"Now take the right likewise," sayd Artegale,
"And counterpeise the same with so much wrong."
So first the right he put into one scale;
And then the Gyant strove with puissance strong
To fill the other scale with so much wrong.
But all the wrongs that he therein could lay,
Might not it peise; yet did he labour long,
And swat, and chauf'd, and provéd° every way: *tried*
Yet all the wrongs could not a litle right downe way.

47

Which when he saw, he greatly grew in rage,
And almost would his balances have broken:
But Artegall him fairely gan° asswage,° *began / to assuage*
And said, "Be not upon thy balance wroken:° *avenged*
For they doe nought but right or wrong betoken;
But in the mind the doome of right must bee;
And so likewise of words, the which be spoken,
The eare must be the ballance, to decree
And judge, whether with truth or falshood they agree.

48

"But set the truth and set the right aside,
For they with wrong or falshood will not fare;
And put two wrongs together to be tride,
Or else two falses, of each equall share;
And then together doe them both compare.
For truth is one, and right is ever one."
So did he, and then plaine it did appeare,
Whether° of them the greater were attone. *which*
But right sate in the middest of the beame alone.

49

But he the right from thence did thrust away,
For it was not the right, which he did seeke;
But rather strove extremities to way,
Th'one to diminish, th'other for to eeke.° *increase*
For of the meane he greatly did misleeke.° *mislike*
Whom when so lewdly° minded Talus found, *ignorantly*
Approching nigh unto him cheeke by cheeke,
He shouldered him from off the higher ground,
And down the rock him throwing, in the sea him dround.

50

Like as a ship, whom cruell tempest drives
Upon a rocke with horrible dismay,

Her shattered ribs in thousand peeces rives,
And spoyling all her geares and goodly ray,° *array*
Does make her selfe misfortunes piteous pray.
So downe the cliffe the wretched Gyant tumbled;
His battred ballances in peeces lay,
His timbered bones all broken rudely rumbled,
So was the high aspyring with huge ruine humbled.

1596

From Amoretti

Sonnet 10

Unrighteous Lord of love, what law is this,
That me thou makest thus tormented be:
The whiles she lordeth in licentious blisse
Of her freewill, scorning both thee and me.
See how the Tyrannesse doth joy to see
The huge massácres which her eyes do make:
And humbled harts brings captives unto thee,
That thou of them mayst mightie vengeance take.
But her proud hart doe thou a little shake
And that high look, with which she doth comptroll
All this worlds pride, bow to a baser make,° *lowlier manner*
And al her faults in thy black booke enroll.
That I may laugh at her in equall sort,
As she doth laugh at me and makes my pain her sport.

Sonnet 67

Lyke as a huntsman after weary chace,
Seeing the game from him escapt away,
Sits downe to rest him in some shady place,
With panting hounds beguiléd of their pray:
So after long pursuit and vaine assay,
When I all weary had the chace forsooke,
The gentle deare returnd the selfe-same way,
Thinking to quench her thirst at the next brooke.
There she beholding me with mylder looke,
Sought not to fly, but fearelesse still did bide:
Till I in hand her yet halfe trembling tooke,
And with her owne goodwill hir fyrmely tyde.
Strange thing me seemd to see a beast so wyld,
So goodly wonne with her owne will beguyld.

Sonnet 68

Most glorious Lord of lyfe, that on this day,[2]
Didst make thy triumph over death and sin:
And having harrowd hell,[3] didst bring away
Captivity thence captive us to win:[4]
This joyous day, deare Lord, with joy begin,
And grant that we for whom thou diddest dye
Being with thy deare blood clene washt from sin,
May live for ever in felicity.
And that thy love we weighing worthily,

2. Easter.
3. A reference to the apocryphal account of Christ's descent into hell, after his crucifixion, in order to rescue the captive souls of the just.
4. "When he ascended up on high, he led captivity captive" (Ephesians iv.8).

May likewise love thee for the same againe:
And for thy sake that all lyke deare didst buy,
With love may one another entertayne.
So let us love, deare love, lyke as we ought,
Love is the lesson which the Lord us taught.[5]

Sonnet 70

Fresh spring the herald of loves mighty king,
In whose cote armour° richly are displayd   *coat of arms*
All sorts of flowers the which on earth do spring
In goodly colours gloriously arrayd.
Goe to my love, where she is carelesse layd,
Yet in her winters bowre not well awake:
Tell her the joyous time wil not be staid
Unless she doe him by the forelock take.[6]
Bid her therefore her selfe soone ready make,
To wayt on love amongst his lovely crew:
Where every one that misseth then her make,°   *mate*
Shall be by him amearst° with penance dew.   *punished*
Make hast therefore sweet love, whilest it is prime,°   *spring*
For none can call againe the passéd time.

Sonnet 75

One day I wrote her name upon the strand,
But came the waves and washéd it away:
Agayne I wrote it with a second hand,°   *a second time*
But came the tyde, and made my paynes his pray.
"Vayne man," sayd she, "that doest in vaine assay,
A mortall thing so to immortalize,
For I my selve shall lyke to this decay,
And eek° my name bee wypéd out lykewize."   *also*
"Not so," quod° I, "let baser things devize°   *quoth / plan*
To dy in dust, but you shall live by fame:
My verse your vertues rare shall eternize,
And in the hevens wryte your glorious name.
Where whenas death shall all the world subdew,
Our love shall live, and later life renew."

Sonnet 79

Men call you fayre, and you doe credit° it,   *believe*
For that your selfe ye dayly such doe see:
But the trew fayre, that is the gentle wit,
And vertuous mind, is much more praysd of me.
For all the rest, how ever fayre it be,
Shall turne to nought and loose that glorious hew:°   *form*
But onely that is permanent and free
From frayle corruption, that doth flesh ensew.°   *follow*
That is true beautie: that doth argue you
To be divine and borne of heavenly seed:
Derived from that fayre Spirit, from whom al true
And perfect beauty did at first proceed.
He onely fayre, and what he fayre hath made:
All other fayre, lyke flowres, untymely fade.

1595

5. "This is my commandment, That ye love one another, as I have loved you" (John xv.12).

6. "To take time by the forelock" is to act promptly.

Epithalamion[7]

Ye learned sisters[8] which have oftentimes
Beene to me ayding, others to adorne:
Whom ye thought worthy of your gracefull rymes,
That even the greatest did not greatly scorne
To heare theyr names sung in your simple layes,
But joyéd in theyr prayse.
And when ye list your owne mishaps to mourne,
Which death, or love, or fortunes wreck did rayse,
Your string could soone to sadder tenor° turne, *strain*
And teach the woods and waters to lament
Your dolefull dreriment.
Now lay those sorrowfull complaints aside,
And having all your heads with girland crownd,
Helpe me mine owne loves prayses to resound,
Ne let the same of any be envíde:
So Orpheus[9] did for his owne bride,
So I unto my selfe alone will sing,
The woods shall to me answer and my Eccho ring.

Early before the worlds light giving lampe,
His golden beame upon the hils doth spred,
Having disperst the nights unchearefull dampe,
Doe ye awake, and with fresh lustyhed
Go to the bowre° of my belovéd love, *bedchamber*
My truest turtle dove,
Bid her awake; for Hymen[1] is awake,
And long since ready forth his maske to move,
With his bright Tead that flames with many a flake,° *spark*
And many a bachelor to waite on him,
In theyr fresh garments trim.
Bid her awake therefore and soone her dight,° *dress*
For lo the wishéd day is come at last,
That shall for al the paynes and sorrowes past,
Pay to her usury of long delight:
And whylest she doth her dight,
Doe ye to her of joy and solace° sing, *pleasure*
That all the woods may answer and your eccho ring.

Bring with you all the Nymphes that you can heare[2]
Both of the rivers and the forrests greene:
And of the sea that neighbours to her neare,
Al with gay girlands goodly wel beseene.
And let them also with them bring in hand,
Another gay girland
For my fayre love of lillyes and of roses,
Bound truelove wize with a blew silke riband.
And let them make great store of bridale poses,° *posies*
And let them eeke bring store of other flowers
To deck the bridale bowers.
And let the ground whereas her foot shall tread,

7. The title (literally "at the bridal chamber") is the Greek word for "wedding song." Spenser's poem was published with the *Amoretti*.
8. The Muses, sources of inspiration.
9. Whose music was said to move even inanimate objects and to change foul weather to fair.
1. The Greek god of the wedding feast, represented as a young man bearing a torch ("Tead") and leading a "maske" or procession.
2. I.e., that can hear you.

For feare the stones her tender foot should wrong
Be strewed with fragrant flowers all along,
And diapred lyke the discolored mead.[3]
Which done, doe at her chamber dore awayt,
For she will waken strayt,° *straightway*
The whiles doe ye this song unto her sing,
The woods shall to you answer and your Eccho ring.

Ye Nymphes of Mulla[4] which with carefull heed,
The silver scaly trouts doe tend full well,
And greedy pikes which use therein to feed,
(Those trouts and pikes all others doo excell)
And ye likewise which keepe the rushy lake,
Where none doo fishes take,
Bynd up the locks the which hang scatterd light,
And in his waters which your mirror make,
Behold your faces as the christall bright,
That when you come whereas my love doth lie,
No blemish she may spie.
And eke ye lightfoot mayds which keepe the deere,
That on the hoary mountayne use to towre,[5]
And the wylde wolves which seeke them to devoure,
With your steele darts doo chace from comming neer
Be also present heere,
To helpe to decke her and to help to sing,
That all the woods may answer and your eccho ring.

Wake, now my love, awake; for it is time,
The Rosy Morne long since left Tithones bed,[6]
All ready to her silver coche to clyme,
And Phoebus gins to shew his glorious hed.
Hark how the cheerefull birds do chaunt theyr laies
And carroll of loves praise.
The merry Larke hir mattins sings aloft.
The thrush replyes, the Mavis descant[7] playes,
The Ouzell shrills, the Ruddock warbles soft,
So goodly all agree with sweet consent,
To this dayes merriment.
Ah my deere love why doe ye sleepe thus long,
When meeter were that ye should now awake,
T' awayt the comming of your joyous make,° *mate*
And hearken to the birds lovelearnéd song,
The deawy leaves among.
For they of joy and pleasance to you sing,
That all the woods them answer and theyr eccho ring.

My love is now awake out of her dreame,
And her fayre eyes like stars that dimméd were
With darksome cloud, now shew theyr goodly beams
More bright then Hesperus° his head doth rere. *evening star*
Come now ye damzels, daughters of delight,
Helpe quickly her to dight,
But first come ye fayre houres which were begot

3. And variegated like the many-colored meadow.
4. The Awbeg River in Ireland, near Spenser's home.
5. A hawking term meaning "to climb high."
6. The dawn, personified in mythology as the goddess Eos or Aurora, was the wife of Tithonus.
7. Melodic counterpart. The mavis, ouzell (or European blackbird), and ruddock (or robin) are all varieties of thrush.

In Joves sweet paradice, of Day and Night,
Which doe the seasons of the yeare allot,
And al that ever in this world is fayre
Doe make and still° repayre. *continually*
And ye three handmayds of the Cyprian Queene,[8]
The which doe still adorne her beauties pride,
Helpe to addorne my beautifullest bride:
And as ye her array, still throw betweene° *at intervals*
Some graces to be seene,
And as ye use to Venus, to her sing,
The whiles the woods shal answer and your eccho ring.

Now is my love all ready forth to come,
Let all the virgins therefore well awayt,
And ye fresh boyes that tend upon her groome
Prepare your selves; for he is comming strayt.
Set all your things in seemely good aray
Fit for so joyfull day,
The joyfulst day that ever sunne did see.
Faire Sun, shew forth thy favourable ray,
And let thy lifull° heat not fervent be *lifegiving*
For feare of burning her sunshyny face,
Her beauty to disgrace.° *spoil*
O fayrest Phoebus, father of the Muse,
If ever I did honour thee aright,
Or sing the thing, that mote° thy mind delight, *might*
Doe not thy servants simple boone° refuse, *request*
But let this day let this one day be myne,
Let all the rest be thine.
Then I thy soverayne prayses loud wil sing,
That all the woods shal answer and theyr eccho ring.

Harke how the Minstrels gin to shrill aloud
Their merry Musick that resounds from far
The pipe, the tabor,° and the trembling Croud,° *drum / viol*
That well agree withouten breach or jar.° *discord*
But most of all the Damzels doe delite,
When they their tymbrels° smyte, *tambourines*
And thereunto doe daunce and carrol sweet,
That all the sences they doe ravish quite,
The whyles the boyes run up and downe the street,
Crying aloud with strong confuséd noyce,
As if it were one voyce.
Hymen iô[9] *Hymen, Hymen* they do shout,
That even to the heavens theyr shouting shrill
Doth reach, and all the firmament doth fill,
To which the people standing all about,
As in approvance doe thereto applaud
And loud advaunce her laud,
And evermore they *Hymen Hymen* sing,
That al the woods them answer and theyr eccho ring.

Loe where she comes along with portly° pace *stately*
Lyke Phoebe[1] from her chamber of the East,

8. Venus, whose handmaids were the three Graces: Aglaia, Thalia, and Euphrosyne. Their names mean "the brilliant one," "she who brings flowers," and "she who rejoices the heart."
9. A shout of joy or triumph (Greek).
1. Another name for the moon goddess Diana.

Arysing forth to run her mighty race,
Clad all in white, that seemes° a virgin best. *befits*
So well it her beseemes that ye would weene
Some angell she had beene.
Her long loose yellow locks lyke golden wyre,
Sprinckled with perle, and perling° flowres a tweene, *intermingling*
Doe lyke a golden mantle her attyre,
And being crownéd with a girland greene,
Seeme lyke some mayden Queene.
Her modest eyes abashéd to behold
So many gazers, as on her do stare,
Upon the lowly ground affixéd are.
Ne dare lift up her countenance too bold,
But blush to heare her prayses sung so loud,
So farre from being proud.
Nathlesse° doe ye still loud her prayses sing. *nevertheless*
That all the woods may answer and your eccho ring.

Tell me ye merchants daughters did ye see
So fayre a creature in your towne before,
So sweet, so lovely, and so mild as she,
Adornd with beautyes grace and vertues store,° *wealth*
Her goodly eyes lyke Saphyres shining bright,
Her forehead yvory white,
Her cheekes lyke apples which the sun hath rudded,
Her lips lyke cherryes charming men to byte,
Her brest like to a bowle of creame uncrudded,° *uncurdled*
Her paps lyke lyllies budded,
Her snowie necke lyke to a marble towre,
And all her body lyke a pallace fayre,
Ascending uppe with many a stately stayre,
To honors seat and chastities sweet bowre.
Why stand ye still ye virgins in amaze,
Upon her so to gaze,
Whiles ye forget your former lay to sing,
To which the woods did answer and your eccho ring.

But if ye saw that which no eyes can see,
The inward beauty of her lively spright,° *spirit*
Garnisht with heavenly guifts of high degree,
Much more then would ye wonder at that sight,
And stand astonisht lyke to those which red° *saw*
Medusaes mazeful hed.[2]
There dwels sweet love and constant chastity,
Unspotted fayth and comely womanhood,
Regard of honour and mild modesty,
There vertue raynes as Queene in royal throne,
And giveth lawes alone.
The which the base affections° doe obay, *lowly emotions*
And yeeld theyr services unto her will,
Ne thought of thing uncomely ever may
Thereto approch to tempt her mind to ill.
Had ye once seene these her celestial threasures,
And unrevealéd pleasures,
Then would ye wonder and her prayses sing,
That al the woods should answer and your eccho ring.

2. The Gorgon Medusa had serpents for hair; whoever looked upon her was turned to stone.

Open the temple gates unto my love,
Open them wide that she may enter in,
And all the postes adorne as doth behove,[3]
And all the pillours deck with girlands trim,
For to recyve this Saynt with honour dew,
That commeth in to you.
With trembling steps and humble reverence,
She commeth in, before th' almighties vew,
Of her ye virgins learne obedience,
When so ye come into those holy places,
To humble your proud faces:
Bring her up to th' high altar, that she may
The sacred ceremonies there partake,
The which do endlesse matrimony make,
And let the roring Organs loudly play
The praises of the Lord in lively notes,
The whiles with hollow throates
The Choristers the joyous Antheme sing,
That al the woods may answere and their eccho ring.

Behold whiles she before the altar stands
Hearing the holy priest that to her speakes
And blesseth her with his two happy hands,
How the red roses flush up in her cheekes,
And the pure snow with goodly vermill° stayne, *vermilion*
Like crimsin dyde in grayne,[4]
That even th' Angels which continually,
About the sacred Altare doe remaine,
Forget their service and about her fly,
Ofte peeping in her face that seemes more fayre,
The more they on it stare.
But her sad° eyes still fastened on the ground, *sober*
Are governéd with goodly modesty,
That suffers not one looke to glaunce awry,
Which may let in a little thought unsownd.
Why blush ye love to give to me your hand,
The pledge of all our band?° *bond*
Sing ye sweet Angels, Alleluya sing,
That all the woods may answere and your eccho ring.

Now al is done; bring home the bride againe,
Bring home the triumph of our victory,
Bring home with you the glory of her gaine,[5]
With joyance bring her and with jollity.
Never had man more joyfull day then this,
Whom heaven would heape with blis.
Make feast therefore now all this live long day,
This day for ever to me holy is,
Poure out the wine without restraint or stay,
Poure not by cups, but by the belly full,
Poure out to all that wull,° *will*
And sprinkle all the postes and wals with wine,
That they may sweat, and drunken be withall.
Crowne ye God Bacchus with a coronall,° *garland*
And Hymen also crowne with wreathes of vine,
And let the Graces daunce unto the rest;

3. I.e., as is fitting.
4. I.e., dyed with colorfast dye.
5. I.e., of gaining her.

For they can doo it best:
The whiles the maydens doe theyr carroll sing,
To which the woods shal answer and theyr eccho ring.

Ring ye the bels, ye yong men of the towne,
And leave your wonted labors for this day:
This day is holy; doe ye write it downe,
That ye for ever it remember may.
This day the sunne is in his chiefest hight,
With Barnaby the bright,[6]
From whence declining daily by degrees,
He somewhat loseth of his heat and light,
When once the Crab[7] behind his back he sees.
But for this time it ill ordainéd was,
To chose the longest day in all the yeare,
And shortest night, when longest fitter weare:
Yet never day so long, but late° would passe. *finally*
Ring ye the bels, to make it weare away,
And bonefiers make all day,
And daunce about them, and about them sing:
That all the woods may answer, and your eccho ring.

Ah when will this long weary day have end,
And lende me leave to come unto my love?
How slowly do the houres theyr numbers spend?
How slowly does sad Time his feathers move?
Hast thee O fayrest Planet to thy home[8]
Within the Westerne fome:
Thy tyred steedes long since have need of rest.
Long though it be, at last I see it gloome,
And the bright evening star with golden creast
Appeare out of the East.
Fayre childe of beauty, glorious lampe of love
That all the host of heaven in rankes doost lead,
And guydest lovers through the nightés dread,
How chearefully thou lookest from above,
And seemst to laugh atweene thy twinkling light
As joying in the sight
Of these glad many which for joy doe sing,
That all the woods them answer and their eccho ring.

Now ceasse ye damsels your delights forepast;
Enough is it, that all the day was youres:
Now day is doen, and night is nighing fast:
Now bring the Bryde into the brydall boures.
Now night is come, now soone her disaray,
And in her bed her lay;
Lay her in lillies and in violets,
And silken courteins over her display,
And odourd sheetes, and Arras° coverlets. *tapestry*
Behold how goodly my faire love does ly
In proud humility;
Like unto Maia,[9] when as Jove her tooke,

6. St. Barnabas's day (July 11) was also the day of the summer solstice in the calendar in use during Spenser's time.
7. Cancer the Crab, the fourth constellation in the zodiac, through which the sun passes in July.
8. In Ptolemaic astronomy, still often accepted in Spenser's time, the sun was one of the planets, which revolved about the earth.
9. The most beautiful of the Pleiades, who by Jove became the mother of the god Hermes.

In Tempe, lying on the flowry gras,
Twixt sleepe and wake, after she weary was,
With bathing in the Acidalian brooke.
Now it is night, ye damsels may be gon,
And leave my love alone,
And leave likewise your former lay to sing:
The woods no more shal answere, nor your eccho ring.

Now welcome night, thou night so long expected,° *awaited*
That long daies labour doest at last defray,° *requite*
And all my cares, which cruell love collected,
Hast sumd in one, and cancellèd for aye:
Spread thy broad wing over my love and me,
That no man may us see,
And in thy sable mantle us enwrap,
From feare of perrill and foule horror free.
Let no false treason seeke us to entrap,
Nor any dread disquiet once annoy
The safety of our joy:
But let the night be calme and quietsome,
Without tempestuous storms or sad afray:° *dark terror*
Lyke as when Jove with fayre Alcmena[1] lay,
When he begot the great Tirynthian groome:
Or lyke as when he with thy selfe did lie,
And begot Majesty.
And let the mayds and yongmen cease to sing:
Ne let the woods them answer, nor theyr eccho ring.

Let no lamenting cryes, nor dolefull teares,
Be heard all night within nor yet without:
Ne let false whispers, breeding hidden feares,
Breake gentle sleepe with misconceivèd dout.° *fear*
Let no deluding dreames, nor dreadful sights
Make sudden sad affrights;
Ne let housefyres, nor lightnings helpelesse harmes,
Ne let the Pouke,[2] nor other evill sprights,
Ne let mischívous witches with theyr charmes,
Ne let hob Goblins, names whose sence we see not,
Fray us with things that be not.
Let not the shriech Oule, nor the Storke be heard:
Nor the night Raven that still° deadly yels, *continually*
Nor damnèd ghosts cald up with mighty spels,
Nor griesly vultures make us once affeard:
Ne let th' unpleasant Quyre of Frogs still croking
Make us to wish theyr choking.
Let none of these theyr drery accents sing;
Ne let the woods them answer, nor theyr eccho ring.

But let stil Silence trew night watches keepe,
That sacred peace may in assurance rayne,
And tymely sleep, when it is tyme to sleepe,
May poure his limbs forth on your pleasant playne,
The whiles an hundred little wingèd loves,° *cupids*
Like divers fethered doves,
Shall fly and flutter round about your bed,

1. The mother of Hercules, who as groom or servant to the king of Tiryns performed twelve prodigious labors.
2. Puck, also called Hobgoblin. The same Puck appears as the merely mischievous Robin Goodfellow in Shakespeare's *A Midsummer Night's Dream.*

And in the secret darke, that none reproves,
Their prety stealthes shal worke, and snares shal spread
To filch away sweet snatches of delight,
Conceald through covert night.
Ye sonnes of Venus, play your sports at will,
For greedy pleasure, carelesse of your toyes,° *amorous sports*
Thinks more upon her paradise of joyes,
Then what ye do, albe it good or ill.
All night therefore attend your merry play,
For it will soone be day:
Now none doth hinder you, that say or sing,
Ne will the woods now answer, nor your Eccho ring.

Who is the same, which at my window peepes?
Or whose is that faire face, that shines so bright,
Is it not Cinthia,[3] she that never sleepes,
But walkes about high heaven al the night?
O fayrest goddesse, do thou not envy
My love with me to spy:
For thou likewise didst love, though now unthought,[4]
And for a fleece of woll,° which privily, *wool*
The Latmian shephard once unto thee brought,
His pleasures with thee wrought.
Therefore to us be favorable now;
And sith of wemens labours thou hast charge,[5]
And generation goodly dost enlarge,
Encline thy will t' effect our wishfull vow,
And the chast wombe informe with timely seed,
That may our comfort breed:
Till which we cease our hopefull hap to sing,
Ne let the woods us answere, nor our Eccho ring.

And thou great Juno, which with awful° might *awe-inspiring*
The lawes of wedlock still dost patronize,
And the religion° of the faith first plight *sanctity*
With sacred rites hast taught to solemnize:
And eeke for comfort often calléd art
Of women in their smart,° *pains of childbirth*
Eternally bind thou this lovely band,
And all thy blessings unto us impart.
And thou glad Genius,[6] in whose gentle hand,
The bridale bowre and geniall° bed remaine, *marriage*
Without blemish or staine,
And the sweet pleasures of theyr loves delight
With secret ayde doest succour and supply,
Till they bring forth the fruitfull progeny,
Send us the timely fruit of this same night.
And thou fayre Hebe,[7] and thou Hymen free,
Grant that it may so be.
Til which we cease your further prayse to sing,
Ne any woods shal answer, nor your Eccho ring.

3. Yet another name for the moon goddess Diana.
4. The moon was often regarded as a symbol of virginity, in spite of several myths recounting her amours. In the next three lines Spenser, perhaps mistakenly, blends the story about Pan, who loved Diana disguised in the fleece of a white ram, with the story of Endymion ("The Latmian shephard"), whom Diana visited nightly in his sleep.
5. Lucina, the goddess of childbirth, is often identified with both Diana and Juno (see lines 394–95).
6. The universal god of generation. By invoking both Juno and Genius as patrons of the marriage bed, Spenser draws also on the belief that each individual is watched over from birth by a tutelary spirit called "a Genius" (for boys) or "a Juno" (for girls).
7. Daughter of Juno and goddess of youth.

And ye high heavens, the temple of the gods,
In which a thousand torches flaming bright
Doe burne, that to us wretched earthly clods,
In dreadful darknesse lend desiréd light;
And all ye powers which in the same remayne,
More then we men can fayne,° *imagine*
Poure out your blessing on us plentiously,
And happy influence upon us raine,
That we may raise a large posterity,
Which from the earth, which they may long possesse,
With lasting happinesse,
Up to your haughty pallaces may mount,
And for the guerdon° of theyr glorious merit *reward*
May heavenly tabernacles there inherit,
Of blessed Saints for to increase the count.
So let us rest, sweet love, in hope of this,
And cease till then our tymely joyes to sing,
The woods no more us answer, nor our eccho ring.

Song made in lieu of many ornaments,
With which my love should duly have bene dect,
Which cutting off through hasty accidents,
Ye would not stay your dew time to expect,
But promist both to recompens,
Be unto her a goodly ornament,
And for short time an endlesse moniment.

1595

JOHN LYLY
(1554–1606)

Cupid and My Campaspe

Cupid and my Campaspe played
At cards for kisses; Cupid paid.
He stakes his quiver, bow, and arrows,
His mother's[1] doves and team of sparrows,
Loses them too; then down he throws
The coral of his lip, the rose
Growing on 's cheek (but none knows how),
With these the crystal of his brow,
And then the dimple of his chin:
All these did my Campaspe win.
At last he set her both his eyes;
She won, and Cupid blind did rise.
   Oh Love! has she done this to thee?
   What shall, alas, become of me?

1632

Oh, For a Bowl of Fat Canary

Oh, for a bowl of fat Canary,
Rich Palermo, sparkling Sherry,

1. I.e., Venus'.

Some nectar else, from Juno's dairy;[2]
Oh, these draughts would make us merry!

Oh, for a wench (I deal in faces,
And in other daintier things);
Tickled am I with her embraces,
Fine dancing in such fairy rings.

Oh, for a plump fat leg of mutton,
Veal, lamb, capon, pig, and coney;° *rabbit*
None is happy but a glutton,
None an ass but who wants money.

Wines indeed and girls are good,
But brave victuals feast the blood;
For wenches, wine, and lusty cheer,
Jove would leap down to surfeit here.

1640

SIR PHILIP SIDNEY
(1554–1586)

Ye Goatherd Gods[1]

STREPHON.[2] Ye goatherd gods, that love the grassy mountains,
Ye nymphs which haunt the springs in pleasant valleys,
Ye satyrs joyed with free and quiet forests,
Vouchsafe your silent ears to plaining music,
Which to my woes gives still an early morning,
And draws the dolor on till weary evening.

KLAIUS. O Mercury,[3] foregoer to the evening,
O heavenly huntress of the savage mountains,
O lovely star, entitled of the morning,
While that my voice doth fill these woeful valleys,
Vouchsafe your silent ears to plaining music,
Which oft hath Echo tired in secret forests.

STREPHON. I, that was once free burgess° of the forests, *citizen*
Where shade from sun, and sport I sought in evening,
I, that was once esteemed for pleasant music,
Am banished now among the monstrous mountains
Of huge despair, and foul affliction's valleys,
Am grown a screech owl to myself each morning.

KLAIUS. I, that was once delighted every morning,
Hunting the wild inhabiters of forests,

2. Nectar, the drink of the gods, was sometimes thought to resemble mead, a drink made from milk and honey; hence it might be regarded figuratively as coming from the "dairy" of Juno, the queen of the gods.

1. The poem is in the form of a double sestina, two sets of six six-line stanzas, with a triplet concluding the whole. The same six key words end the lines of each stanza; their order is always a permutation of the order in the stanza just preceding: the pattern is 6 1 5 2 4 3, i.e., the last word of line 1 of any stanza is always the same as the last word of line 6 in the preceding stanza. Line 2 always ends like the preceding stanza's line 1; line 3 like line 5; line 4 like line 2; line 5 like line 4; and line 6 like line 3. All six key words appear in the triplet in the same order as that of the first and seventh stanzas.

2. Strephon and Klaius are shepherds in Sidney's heroic romance *Arcadia,* in which this poem appears.

3. The evening star. The "heavenly huntress" is the goddess Diana, the moon.

I, that was once the music of these valleys,
So darkened am that all my day is evening,
Heartbroken so, that molehills seem high mountains
And fill the vales with cries instead of music.

STREPHON. Long since, alas, my deadly swannish[4] music
Hath made itself a crier of the morning,
And hath with wailing strength climbed highest mountains;
Long since my thoughts more desert be than forests,
Long since I see my joys come to their evening,
And state° thrown down to overtrodden valleys. *high position*

KLAIUS. Long since the happy dwellers of these valleys
Have prayed me leave my strange exclaiming music,
Which troubles their day's work and joys of evening;
Long since I hate the night, more hate the morning;
Long since my thoughts chase me like beasts in forests
And make me wish myself laid under mountains.

STREPHON. Meseems° I see the high and stately mountains *it seems to me*
Transform themselves to low dejected valleys;
Meseems I hear in these ill-changéd forests
The nightingales do learn of owls their music;
Meseems I feel the comfort of the morning
Turned to the mortal serene[5] of an evening.

KLAIUS. Meseems I see a filthy cloudy evening
As soon as sun begins to climb the mountains;
Meseems I feel a noisome° scent, the morning *offensive*
When I do smell the flowers of these valleys;
Meseems I hear, when I do hear sweet music,
The dreadful cries of murdered men in forests.

STREPHON. I wish to fire the trees of all these forests;
I give the sun a last farewell each evening;
I curse the fiddling finders-out of music;
With envy I do hate the lofty mountains
And with despite despise the humble valleys;
I do detest night, evening, day, and morning.

KLAIUS. Curse to myself my prayer is, the morning;
My fire is more than can be made with forests,
My state more base than are the basest valleys.
I wish no evenings more to see, each evening;
Shaméd, I hate myself in sight of mountains
And stop mine ears, lest I grow mad with music.

STREPHON. For she whose parts maintained a perfect music,
Whose beauties shined more than the blushing morning,
Who much did pass° in state the stately mountains, *surpass*
In straightness passed the cedars of the forests,
Hath cast me, wretch, into eternal evening
By taking her two suns from these dark valleys.

4. The swan was supposed to sing only just before it died.

5. Damp evening air, thought to produce sickness ("mortal": deadly). The stress is on the first syllable.

KLAIUS. For she, with whom compared, the Alps are valleys,
She, whose least word brings from the spheres their music,
At whose approach the sun rose in the evening,
Who where she went bare° in her forehead morning, *bore*
Is gone, is gone, from these our spoilèd forests,
Turning to deserts our best pastured mountains.

STREPHON. These mountains witness shall, so shall these valleys,
KLAIUS. These forests eke,° made wretched by our music, *also*
Our morning hymn this is, and song at evening.

1577–80 1593

The Nightingale

The nightingale, as soon as April bringeth
Unto her rested sense a perfect waking,
While late bare earth, proud of new clothing, springeth,
Sings out her woes, a thorn her song-book making,
And mournfully bewailing,
Her throat in tunes expresseth
What grief her breast oppresseth
For Tereus' force on her chaste will prevailing.[6]
Oh Philomela fair, Oh take some gladness,
That here is juster cause of plaintful sadness:
Thine earth now springs, mine fadeth;
Thy thorn without, my thorn my heart invadeth.

Alas, she hath no other cause of anguish
But Tereus' love, on her by strong hand wroken,[7]
Wherein she suffering, all her spirits languish;
Full womanlike complains her will was broken.
But I, who daily craving,
Cannot have to content me,
Have more cause to lament me,
Since wanting is more woe than too much having.
O Philomela fair, O take some gladness,
That here is juster cause of plaintful sadness:
Thine earth now springs, mine fadeth;
Thy thorn without, my thorn my heart invadeth.

1581 1598

Ring Out Your Bells

Ring out your bells, let mourning shows be spread,
For Love is dead.
All Love is dead, infected
With plague of deep disdain;
Worth as naught worth rejected,
And Faith fair scorn[8] doth gain.

6. Tereus, the ravisher of Philomela, cut out her tongue to keep her from accusing him. Transformed into a nightingale, she expressed her grief in song.

7. Old past participle of *wreak,* "to urge or force upon."

8. Scorn from the fair.

From so ungrateful fancy,
From such a female franzy,° *frenzy*
From them that use men thus,
Good Lord, deliver us!

Weep, neighbors, weep; do you not hear it said
That Love is dead?
His deathbed peacock's folly,
His winding sheet is shame,
His will false-seeming holy,
His sole exec'tor blame.
From so ungrateful . . .

Let dirge be sung and trentals[9] rightly read,
For Love is dead.
Sir Wrong his tomb ordaineth
My mistress, marble heart,
Which epitaph containeth,
"Her eyes were once his dart."
From so ungrateful . . .

Alas, I lie, rage hath this error bred;
Love is not dead.
Love is not dead, but sleepeth
In her unmatchéd mind,
Where she his counsel keepeth,
Till due desert she find.
Therefore from so vile fancy,
To call such wit a franzy,
Who Love can temper thus,
Good Lord, deliver us!

1581 1598

From Astrophel and Stella

1

Loving in truth, and fain° in verse my love to show, *eager*
That she dear she might take some pleasure of my pain,
Pleasure might cause her read, reading might make her know,
Knowledge might pity win, and pity grace obtain,
I sought fit words to paint the blackest face of woe:
Studying inventions fine, her wits to entertain,
Oft turning others' leaves, to see if thence would flow
Some fresh and fruitful showers upon my sunburned brain.
But words came halting forth, wanting Invention's stay;
Invention, Nature's child, fled stepdame Study's blows;
And others' feet still seemed but strangers in my way.
Thus, great with child to speak, and helpless in my throes,
Biting my truant pen, beating myself for spite:
"Fool," said my Muse to me, "look in thy heart, and write."

31

With how sad steps, Oh Moon, thou climb'st the skies,
How silently, and with how wan a face!
What, may it be that even in heav'nly place

9. A series of thirty masses for the dead.

That busy archer[1] his sharp arrows tries?
Sure, if that long-with-love-acquainted eyes
Can judge of love, thou feel'st a lover's case;
I read it in thy looks: thy languished grace,
To me that feel the like, thy state descries.
Then even of fellowship, Oh Moon, tell me,
Is constant love deemed there but want of wit?
Are beauties there as proud as here they be?
Do they above love to be loved, and yet
Those lovers scorn whom that love doth possess?
Do they call virtue there ungratefulness?

47

What, have I thus betrayed my liberty?
Can those black beams such burning marks engrave
In my free side? or am I born a slave,
Whose neck becomes such yoke of tyranny?
Or want I sense to feel my misery?
Or sprite, disdain of such disdain to have?
Who for long faith, though daily help I crave,
May get no alms but scorn of beggary.
Virtue, awake! Beauty but beauty is;
I may, I must, I can, I will, I do
Leave following that which it is gain to miss.
Let her go. Soft, but here she comes. Go to,
Unkind, I love you not! O me, that eye
Doth make my heart give to my tongue the lie!

48

Soul's joy, bend not those morning stars from me,
Where virtue is made strong by beauty's might,
Where love is chasteness, pain doth learn delight,
And humbleness grows one with majesty.
Whatever may ensue, O let me be
Co-partner of the riches of that sight;
Let not mine eyes be hell-driv'n from that light;
O look, O shine, O let me die and see.
For though I oft my self of them bemoan,
That through my heart their beamy darts be gone,
Whose cureless wounds even now most freshly bleed,
Yet since my death wound is already got,
Dear killer, spare not thy sweet cruel shot;
A kind of grace it is to slay with speed.

49

I on my horse, and Love on me, doth try
Our horsemanships, while by strange work I prove
A horseman to my horse, a horse to Love,
And now man's wrongs in me, poor beast, descry.
The reins wherewith my rider doth me tie
Are humbled thoughts, which bit of reverence move,
Curbed[2] in with fear, but with gilt boss above
Of hope, which makes it seem fair to the eye.
The wand is will; thou, fancy, saddle art,
Girt fast by memory; and while I spur
My horse, he spurs with sharp desire my heart;

1. I.e., Cupid.
2. The curb is a short chain or strap connecting the upper branches of the bit and ornamented, in this case, with a metal *boss* or decorative stud.

And let the day be time enough to mourn
The shipwreck of my ill-adventured youth;
Let waking eyes suffice to wail their scorn
Without the torment of the night's untruth.
Cease, dreams, th' imagery of our day desires,
To model forth the passions of the morrow;
Never let rising sun approve you liars,
To add more grief to aggravate my sorrow.
Still let me sleep, embracing clouds in vain,
And never wake to feel the day's disdain.

46

Let others sing of knights and paladins
In aged accents of untimely° words, *outdated*
Paint shadows in imaginary lines
Which well the reach of their high wits records;
But I must sing of thee and those fair eyes.
Authentic shall my verse in time to come,
When yet th' unborn shall say, "Lo where she lies,
Whose beauty made him speak that else was dumb."
These are the arks, the trophies I erect,
That fortify thy name against old age;
And these thy sacred virtues must protect
Against the dark and time's consuming rage.
Though th' error of my youth they shall discover,
Suffice, they show I lived and was thy lover.

1592

Ulysses and the Siren

SIREN. Come, worthy Greek, Ulysses, come,
Possess these shores with me;
The winds and seas are troublesome,
And here we may be free.
Here may we sit and view their toil
That travail in the deep,
And joy the day in mirth the while,
And spend the night in sleep.

ULYSSES. Fair nymph, if fame or honor were
To be attained with ease,
Then would I come and rest me there,
And leave such toils as these.
But here it dwells, and here must I
With danger seek it forth;
To spend the time luxuriously
Becomes not men of worth.

SIREN. Ulysses, Oh be not deceived
With that unreal name;
This honor is a thing conceived,
And rests on others' fame.
Begotten only to molest
Our peace, and to beguile
The best thing of our life, our rest,
And give us up to toil.

ULYSSES. Delicious nymph, suppose there were
Nor honor nor report,
Yet manliness would scorn to wear
The time in idle sport.
For toil doth give a better touch,
To make us feel our joy;
And ease finds tediousness, as much
As labor yields annoy.

SIREN. Then pleasure likewise seems the shore
Whereto tends all your toil,
Which you forgo to make it more,
And perish oft the while.
Who may disport them diversly,
Find never tedious day,
And ease may have variety
As well as action may.

ULYSSES. But natures of the noblest frame
These toils and dangers please,
And they take comfort in the same
As much as you in ease,
And with the thoughts of actions past
Are recreated still;
When pleasure leaves a touch at last
To show that it was ill.

SIREN. That doth opinion only cause
That's out of custom bred,
Which makes us many other laws
Than ever nature did.
No widows wail for our delights,
Our sports are without blood;
The world, we see, by warlike wights
Receives more hurt than good.

ULYSSES. But yet the state of things require
These motions of unrest,
And these great spirits of high desire
Seem born to turn them best,
To purge the mischiefs that increase
And all good order mar;
For oft we see a wicked peace
To be well changed for war.

SIREN. Well, well, Ulysses, then I see
I shall not have thee here,
And therefore I will come to thee,
And take my fortunes there.
I must be won that cannot win,
Yet lost were I not won;
For beauty hath created been
T' undo, or be undone.

1605

MARK ALEXANDER BOYD (1563–1601)

Fra Bank to Bank

Fra bank to bank, fra wood to wood I rin,
Ourhailit° with my feeble fantasie; *overwhelmed*
Like til a leaf that fallis from a tree,
Or til a reed ourblawin with the win'.

Twa gods [1] guidis me; the ane of them is blin',
Yea and a bairn° brocht up in vanitie; *child*
The next a wife° ingenrit of the sea, *woman*
And lichter° nor° a dauphin with her fin. *more wanton/than*

Unhappy is the man for evermair
That tills the sand and sawis° in the air; *sows*
But twice unhappier is he, I lairn,
That feedis in his hairt a mad desire,
And follows on a woman throw the fire,
Led by a blind and teachit by a bairn.

MICHAEL DRAYTON (1563–1631)

From Idea

To the Reader of these Sonnets

Into these loves who but for passion looks,
At this first sight here let him lay them by
And seek elsewhere, in turning other books,
Which better may his labor satisfy.
No far-fetched sigh shall ever wound my breast,
Love from mine eye a tear shall never wring,
Nor in *Ah me*'s my whining sonnets dressed,
A libertine, fantastically I sing.
My verse is the true image of my mind,
Ever in motion, still desiring change;
And as thus to variety inclined,
So in all humors sportively I range:
My muse is rightly of the English strain,
That cannot long one fashion entertain.

6

How many paltry, foolish, painted things,
That now in coaches trouble every street,
Shall be forgotten, whom no poet sings,
Ere they be well wrapped in their winding-sheet?

1. Venus, goddess of love, supposedly born from the sea, and Cupid, her blind son.

Where I to thee eternity shall give,
When nothing else remaineth of these days,
And queens hereafter shall be glad to live
Upon the alms of thy superfluous praise.
Virgins and matrons reading these my rhymes
Shall be so much delighted with thy story
That they shall grieve they lived not in these times,
To have seen thee, their sex's only glory.
So shalt thou fly above the vulgar throng,
Still to survive in my immortal song.

61

Since there's no help, come let us kiss and part;
Nay, I have done, you get no more of me,
And I am glad, yea glad with all my heart
That thus so cleanly I myself can free;
Shake hands forever, cancel all our vows,
And when we meet at any time again,
Be it not seen in either of our brows
That we one jot of former love retain.
Now at the last gasp of love's latest breath,
When, his pulse failing, passion speechless lies,
When faith is kneeling by his bed of death,
And innocence is closing up his eyes,
Now if thou wouldst, when all have given him over,
From death to life thou mightst him yet recover.

1619

CHRISTOPHER MARLOWE
(1564–1593)

The Passionate Shepherd to His Love[1]

Come live with me and be my love,
And we will all the pleasures prove° *try*
That valleys, groves, hills, and fields,
Woods, or steepy mountain yields.

And we will sit upon the rocks,
Seeing the shepherds feed their flocks,
By shallow rivers to whose falls
Melodious birds sing madrigals.

And I will make thee beds of roses
And a thousand fragrant posies,
A cap of flowers, and a kirtle
Embroidered all with leaves of myrtle;

A gown made of the finest wool
Which from our pretty lambs we pull;
Fair lined slippers for the cold,
With buckles of the purest gold;

1. See the response by Sir Walter Ralegh. *The Nymph's Reply to the Shepherd,* above.

A belt of straw and ivy buds,
With coral clasps and amber studs:
And if these pleasures may thee move,
Come live with me, and be my love.

The shepherds' swains shall dance and sing
For thy delight each May morning:
If these delights thy mind may move,
Then live with me and be my love.

1599, 1600

WILLIAM SHAKESPEARE (1564–1616)

From Sonnets

18

Shall I compare thee to a summer's day?
Thou art more lovely and more temperate:
Rough winds do shake the darling buds of May,
And summer's lease hath all too short a date:
Sometimes too hot the eye of heaven shines,
And often is his gold complexion dimmed;
And every fair from fair sometimes declines,
By chance or nature's changing course untrimmed;[1]
But thy eternal summer shall not fade,
Nor lose possession of that fair thou ow'st;° *ownest*
Nor shall death brag thou wander'st in his shade,
When in eternal lines to time thou grow'st:
So long as men can breathe, or eyes can see,
So long lives this, and this gives life to thee.

29

When, in disgrace with fortune and men's eyes,
I all alone beweep my outcast state,
And trouble deaf heaven with my bootless° cries, *futile*
And look upon myself, and curse my fate,
Wishing me like to one more rich in hope,
Featured like him, like him with friends possessed,
Desiring this man's art and that man's scope,
With what I most enjoy contented least;
Yet in these thoughts myself almost despising,
Haply I think on thee—and then my state,
Like to the lark at break of day arising
From sullen earth, sings hymns at heaven's gate;
For thy sweet love remembered such wealth brings
That then I scorn to change my state with kings.

30

When to the sessions[2] of sweet silent thought
I summon up remembrance of things past,
I sigh the lack of many a thing I sought,
And with old woes new wail my dear time's waste:
Then can I drown an eye, unused to flow,
For precious friends hid in death's dateless° night, *endless*
And weep afresh love's long since canceled woe,

1. Divested of its beauty.

2. Sittings of a court.

And moan the expense° of many a vanished sight: *loss*
Then can I grieve at grievances foregone,
And heavily from woe to woe tell o'er
The sad account of fore-bemoanéd moan,
Which I new pay as if not paid before.
But if the while I think on thee, dear friend,
All losses are restored and sorrows end.

55

Not marble, nor the gilded monuments
Of princes, shall outlive this powerful rhyme;
But you shall shine more bright in these contents
Than unswept stone, besmeared with sluttish time.
When wasteful war shall statues overturn,
And broils root out the work of masonry,
Nor Mars his[3] sword nor war's quick fire shall burn
The living record of your memory.
'Gainst death and all-oblivious enmity
Shall you pace forth; your praise shall still find room
Even in the eyes of all posterity
That wear this world out to the ending doom.° *Judgment Day*
So, till the judgment that yourself arise,
You live in this, and dwell in lovers' eyes.

65

Since brass, nor[4] stone, nor earth, nor boundless sea
But sad mortality o'er-sways their power,
How with this rage shall beauty hold a plea,
Whose action is no stronger than a flower?
O, how shall summer's honey breath hold out
Against the wreckful siege of battering days,
When rocks impregnable are not so stout,
Nor gates of steel so strong, but Time decays?
O fearful meditation! where, alack,
Shall Time's best jewel from Time's chest lie hid?
Or what strong hand can hold his swift foot back?
Or who his spoil of beauty can forbid?
O, none, unless this miracle have might,
That in black ink my love may still shine bright.

71

No longer mourn for me when I am dead
Than you shall hear the surly sullen bell
Give warning to the world that I am fled
From this vile world, with vilest worms to dwell:
Nay, if you read this line, remember not
The hand that writ it; for I love you so,
That I in your sweet thoughts would be forgot,
If thinking on me then should make you woe.
Oh, if, I say, you look upon this verse
When I perhaps compounded am with clay,
Do not so much as my poor name rehearse,
But let your love even with my life decay;
Lest the wise world should look into your moan,
And mock you with me after I am gone.

73

That time of year thou mayst in me behold
When yellow leaves, or none, or few, do hang
Upon those boughs which shake against the cold,

3. I.e., Mars'.

4. I.e., since there is neither brass nor.

Bare ruined choirs, where late the sweet birds sang.
In me thou see'st the twilight of such day
As after sunset fadeth in the west;
Which by and by black night doth take away,
Death's second self, that seals up all in rest.
In me thou see'st the glowing of such fire,
That on the ashes of his youth doth lie,
As the deathbed whereon it must expire,
Consumed with that which it was nourished by.
This thou perceiv'st, which makes thy love more strong,
To love that well which thou must leave ere long.

116

Let me not to the marriage of true minds
Admit impediments. Love is not love
Which alters when it alteration finds,
Or bends with the remover to remove:
Oh, no! it is an ever-fixéd mark,
That looks on tempests and is never shaken;
It is the star to every wandering bark,
Whose worth's unknown, although his height be taken.[5]
Love's not Time's fool, though rosy lips and cheeks
Within his bending sickle's compass come;
Love alters not with his brief hours and weeks,
But bears it out even to the edge of doom.[6]
If this be error and upon me proved,
I never writ, nor no man ever loved.

129

Th' expense of spirit in a waste of shame
Is lust in action; and till action, lust
Is perjured, murderous, bloody, full of blame,
Savage, extreme, rude, cruel, not to trust;
Enjoyed no sooner but despiséd straight:
Past reason hunted; and no sooner had,
Past reason hated, as a swallowed bait,
On purpose laid to make the taker mad:
Mad in pursuit, and in possession so;
Had, having, and in quest to have, extreme;
A bliss in proof,[7] and proved, a very woe;
Before, a joy proposed; behind, a dream.
All this the world well knows; yet none knows well
To shun the heaven that leads men to this hell.

130

My mistress' eyes are nothing like the sun;
Coral is far more red than her lips' red;
If snow be white, why then her breasts are dun;
If hairs be wires, black wires grow on her head.
I have seen roses damasked,° red and white, *variegated*
But no such roses see I in her cheeks;
And in some perfumes is there more delight
Than in the breath that from my mistress reeks.
I love to hear her speak, yet well I know
That music hath a far more pleasing sound;
I grant I never saw a goddess go;° *walk*
My mistress, when she walks, treads on the ground.
And yet, by heaven, I think my love as rare
As any she belied with false compare.

5. I.e., although its elevation may be measured.

6. Judgment Day, the end of the world.

7. I.e., in the experience.

138

When my love swears that she is made of truth,
I do believe her, though I know she lies,
That she might think me some untutored youth,
Unlearnéd in the world's false subtleties.
Thus vainly thinking that she thinks me young,
Although she knows my days are past the best,
Simply I credit her false-speaking tongue:
On both sides thus is simple truth suppressed.
But wherefore says she not she is unjust?
And wherefore say not I that I am old?
Oh, love's best habit is in seeming trust,
And age in love loves not to have years told.
Therefore I lie with her and she with me,
And in our faults by lies we flattered be.

146

Poor soul, the center of my sinful earth,
Lord of[8] these rebel powers that thee array,° *dress, deck out*
Why dost thou pine within and suffer dearth,
Painting thy outward walls so costly gay?
Why so large cost, having so short a lease,
Dost thou upon thy fading mansion spend?
Shall worms, inheritors of this excess,
Eat up thy charge? Is this thy body's end?
Then, soul, live thou upon thy servant's loss,
And let that pine to aggravate° thy store; *increase*
Buy terms divine in selling hours of dross;
Within be fed, without be rich no more.
So shalt thou feed on death, that feeds on men,
And death once dead, there's no more dying then.

1609

When Daisies Pied[9]

Spring

When daisies pied and violets blue
And ladysmocks all silver-white
And cuckoobuds of yellow hue
Do paint the meadows with delight,
The cuckoo then, on every tree,
Mocks married men;[1] for thus sings he,
Cuckoo;
Cuckoo, cuckoo: Oh word of fear,
Unpleasing to a married ear!

When shepherds pipe on oaten straws,
And merry larks are plowmen's clocks,
When turtles tread,[2] and rooks, and daws,
And maidens bleach their summer smocks,
The cuckoo then, on every tree,
Mocks married men; for thus sings he,
Cuckoo;

8. The original text repeats "My sinful earth," apparently a mistake, in place of "Lord of" at the beginning of this line. Other possibilities have been suggested, e.g., "Rebuke," "Thrall to," "Pressed by."

9. From *Love's Labour's Lost*.

1. The cuckoo's song was often taken fancifully as "Cuckold!"

2. I.e., when turtledoves mate.

Cuckoo, cuckoo: Oh word of fear,
Unpleasing to a married ear!

Winter

When icicles hang by the wall
And Dick the shepherd blows his nail[3]
And Tom bears logs into the hall,
  And milk comes frozen home in pail.
When blood is nipped and ways be foul,
Then nightly sings the staring owl,
          Tu-who;
Tu-whit, tu-who: a merry note,
While greasy Joan doth keel[4] the pot.

When all aloud the wind doth blow,
  And coughing drowns the parson's saw,° *wise saying*
And birds sit brooding in the snow,
  And Marian's nose looks red and raw,
When roasted crabs° hiss in the bowl, *crab apples*
Then nightly sings the staring owl,
          Tu-who;
Tu-whit, tu-who: a merry note
While greasy Joan doth keel the pot.

1595? 1598

Blow, Blow, Thou Winter Wind[5]

  Blow, blow, thou winter wind,
  Thou art not so unkind
    As man's ingratitude;
  Thy tooth is not so keen,
  Because thou art not seen,
    Although thy breath be rude.
Heigh-ho! sing, heigh-ho! unto the green holly:
Most friendship is feigning, most loving mere folly:
  Then, heigh-ho, the holly!
    This life is most jolly.

  Freeze, freeze, thou bitter sky,
  That dost not bite so nigh
    As benefits forgot:
  Though thou the waters warp,
  Thy sting is not so sharp
    As friend remembered not.
Heigh-ho! sing, . . .

1599? 1623

It Was a Lover and His Lass[6]

It was a lover and his lass,
  With a hey, and a ho, and a hey nonino,
That o'er the green corn field did pass
  In springtime, the only pretty ring time,
When birds do sing, hey ding a ding, ding:
Sweet lovers love the spring.

3. I.e., breathes on his fingers to warm them.
4. Keep from boiling over by stirring.
5. From *As You Like It.*
6. From *As You Like It.*

Between the acres of the rye,
  With a hey, and a ho, and a hey nonino,
These pretty country folks would lie,
  In springtime, . . .

This carol they began that hour,
  With a hey, and a ho, and a hey nonino,
How that a life was but a flower
  In springtime, . . .

And therefore take the present time,
  With a hey, and a ho, and a hey nonino;
For love is crownéd with the prime
  In springtime, . . .

1599? 1623

Oh Mistress Mine[7]

Oh mistress mine! where are you roaming?
Oh! stay and hear; your true love's coming,
  That can sing both high and low.
Trip no further, pretty sweeting;
Journeys end in lovers meeting,
  Every wise man's son doth know.

What is love? 'tis not hereafter;
Present mirth hath present laughter;
  What's to come is still unsure:
In delay there lies no plenty;
Then come kiss me, sweet and twenty,
  Youth's a stuff will not endure.

1602 1623

When That I Was and a Little Tiny Boy[8]

When that I was and a little tiny boy,
  With hey, ho, the wind and the rain,
A foolish thing was but a toy,° *trifle*
  For the rain it raineth every day.

But when I came to man's estate,
  With hey, ho, . . .
'Gainst knaves and thieves men shut their gate,
  For the rain, . . .

But when I came, alas! to wive,
  With hey, ho, . . .
By swaggering could I never thrive,
  For the rain, . . .

But when I came unto my beds,
  With hey, ho, . . .
With toss-pots still had drunken heads,
  For the rain, . . .

7. From *Twelfth Night.*
8. From *Twelfth Night;* sung by the clown to conclude the play.

A great while ago the world begun,
  With hey, ho, . . .
But that's all one, our play is done,
  And we'll strive to please you every day.

1602 1623

Fear No More the Heat o' the Sun[9]

Fear no more the heat o' the sun,
  Nor the furious winter's rages;
Thou thy worldly task hast done,
  Home art gone, and ta'en thy wages:
Golden lads and girls all must,
As chimney-sweepers, come to dust.

Fear no more the frown o' the great;
  Thou art past the tyrant's stroke;
Care no more to clothe and eat;
  To thee the reed is as the oak:
The scepter, learning, physic, must
All follow this, and come to dust.

Fear no more the lightning flash,
  Nor the all-dreaded thunder stone;[1]
Fear not slander, censure rash;
  Thou hast finished joy and moan:
All lovers young, all lovers must
Consign to thee, and come to dust.

No exorciser harm thee!
Nor no witchcraft charm thee!
Ghost unlaid forbear thee!
Nothing ill come near thee!
Quiet consummation have;
And renownéd be thy grave!

1610? 1623

Full Fathom Five[2]

Full fathom five thy father lies;
  Of his bones are coral made;
Those are pearls that were his eyes:
  Nothing of him that doth fade,
But doth suffer a sea change
Into something rich and strange.
Sea nymphs hourly ring his knell:
  Ding-dong.
Hark! now I hear them—Ding-dong, bell.

1611 1623

9. From *Cymbeline.*
1. Thunder was thought to be caused by meteorites falling from the sky.
2. From *The Tempest.*

THOMAS CAMPION
(1567–1620)

My Sweetest Lesbia[1]

My sweetest Lesbia, let us live and love,
And though the sager sort our deeds reprove,
Let us not weigh them. Heaven's great lamps do dive
Into their west, and straight again revive,
But soon as once set is our little light,
Then must we sleep one ever-during night.

If all would lead their lives in love like me,
Then bloody swords and armor should not be;
No drum nor trumpet peaceful sleeps should move,
Unless alarm came from the camp of love.
But fools do live, and waste their little light,
And seek with pain their ever-during night.

When timely death my life and fortune ends,
Let not my hearse be vexed with mourning friends,
But let all lovers, rich in triumph, come
And with sweet pastimes grace my happy tomb;
And Lesbia, close up thou my little light,
And crown with love my ever-during night.

1601

When to Her Lute Corinna Sings

When to her lute Corinna sings,
Her voice revives the leaden strings,
And doth in highest notes appear
As any challenged echo clear;
But when she doth of mourning speak,
Ev'n with her sighs the strings do break.

And as her lute doth live or die,
Led by her passion, so must I:
For when of pleasure she doth sing,
My thoughts enjoy a sudden spring,
But if she doth of sorrow speak,
Ev'n from my heart the strings do break.

1601

When Thou Must Home

When thou must home to shades of underground,
And there arrived, a new admiréd guest,
The beauteous spirits do engirt thee round,

1. The Roman poet Catullus sang the praises of his Lesbia in a poem here imitated and partly translated by Campion.

White Iope, blithe Helen,[2] and the rest,
To hear the stories of thy finished love
From that smooth tongue whose music hell can move,

Then wilt thou speak of banqueting delights,
Of masques and revels which sweet youth did make,
Of tourneys and great challenges of knights,
And all these triumphs for thy beauty's sake;
When thou hast told these honors done to thee,
Then tell, Oh tell, how thou didst murther me.

1601

Rose-cheeked Laura

Rose-cheeked Laura, come,
Sing thou smoothly with thy beauty's
Silent music, either other
Sweetly gracing.

Lovely forms do flow
From concent° divinely framed; *sounds in harmony*
Heav'n is music, and thy beauty's
Birth is heavenly.

These dull notes we sing
Discords need for helps to grace them;
Only beauty purely loving
Knows no discord,

But still moves delight,
Like clear springs renewed by flowing,
Ever perfect, ever in them-
Selves eternal.

1602

Now Winter Nights Enlarge

Now winter nights enlarge
The number of their hours;
And clouds their storms discharge
Upon the airy towers.
Let now the chimneys blaze
And cups o'erflow with wine,
Let well-tuned words amaze
With harmony divine.
Now yellow waxen lights
Shall wait on honey love
While youthful revels, masques, and courtly sights
Sleep's leaden spells remove.

This time doth well dispense
With[3] lovers' long discourse;
Much speech hath some defense,

2. Iope or Cassiopeia and Helen of Troy, the first renowned for beauty and vanity, the second for beauty and fickleness.
3. Put up with, deal indulgently with.

Though beauty no remorse.
All do not all things well;
Some measures comely tread,
Some knotted riddles tell,
Some poems smoothly read.
The summer hath his joys,
And winter his delights;
Though love and all his pleasures are but toys,
They shorten tedious nights.

1617

There Is a Garden in Her Face

There is a garden in her face,
Where roses and white lilies grow,
A heavenly paradise is that place,
Wherein all pleasant fruits do flow.
There cherries grow, which none may buy
Till "Cherry ripe!"[4] themselves do cry.

Those cherries fairly do enclose
Of orient pearl a double row,
Which when her lovely laughter shows,
They look like rosebuds filled with snow.
Yet them nor peer nor prince can buy,
Till "Cherry ripe!" themselves do cry.

Her eyes like angels watch them still;
Her brows like bended bows do stand,
Threatening with piercing frowns to kill
All that attempt with eye or hand
Those sacred cherries to come nigh,
Till "Cherry ripe!" themselves do cry.

1617

THOMAS NASHE
(1567–1601)

Spring, the Sweet Spring

Spring, the sweet spring, is the year's pleasant king,
Then blooms each thing, then maids dance in a ring,
Cold doth not sting, the pretty birds do sing:
Cuckoo, jug-jug, pu-we, to-witta-woo![1]

The palm and may make country houses gay,
Lambs frisk and play, the shepherds pipe all day,
And we hear aye birds tune this merry lay:
Cuckoo, jug-jug, pu-we, to-witta-woo!

4. A London street vendor's cry.
1. Bird songs of the cuckoo, nightingale, lapwing, owl.

The fields breathe sweet, the daisies kiss our feet,
Young lovers meet, old wives a-sunning sit,
In every street these tunes our ears do greet:
  Cuckoo, jug-jug, pu-we, to-witta-woo!
    Spring, the sweet spring!

1600

A Litany in Time of Plague

Adieu, farewell, earth's bliss;
This world uncertain is;
Fond° are life's lustful joys; *foolish*
Death proves them all but toys;° *trifles*
None from his darts can fly;
I am sick, I must die.
  Lord, have mercy on us!

Rich men, trust not in wealth,
Gold cannot buy you health;
Physic himself must fade.
All things to end are made,
The plague full swift goes by;
I am sick, I must die
  Lord, have mercy on us!

Beauty is but a flower
Which wrinkles will devour;
Brightness falls from the air;
Queens have died young and fair;
Dust hath closed Helen's eye.
I am sick, I must die.
  Lord, have mercy on us!

Strength stoops unto the grave,
Worms feed on Hector brave;
Swords may not fight with fate,
Earth still holds ope her gate.
"Come, come!" the bells do cry.
I am sick, I must die.
  Lord, have mercy on us.

Wit with his wantonness
Tasteth death's bitterness;
Hell's executioner
Hath no ears for to hear
What vain art can reply.
I am sick, I must die.
  Lord, have mercy on us.

Haste, therefore, each degree,
To welcome destiny;
Heaven is our heritage,
Earth but a player's stage;
Mount we unto the sky.
I am sick, I must die.
  Lord, have mercy on us.

1592 1600

ROBERT HAYMAN
(d. 1631?)

Of the Great and Famous Ever-to-be-honored Knight, Sir Francis Drake, and of My Little-Little Self

The Dragon that our seas did raise his crest
And brought back heaps of gold unto his nest,
Unto his foes more terrible than thunder,
Glory of his age, after-ages' wonder,
Excelling all those that excelled before—
It's feared we shall have none such any more—
Effecting all, he sole did undertake,
Valiant, just, wise, mild, honest, godly Drake.
This man when I was little I did meet
As he was walking up Totnes' long street.
He asked me whose I was. I answered him.
He asked me if his good friend were within.
A fair red orange in his hand he had;
He gave it me, whereof I was right glad,
Takes and kissed me, and prays, "God bless my boy,"
Which I record with comfort to this day.
Could he on me have breathéd with his breath
His gifts, Elias-like,[2] after his death,
Then had I been enabled for to do
Many brave things I have a heart unto.
I have as great desire as e'er had he
To joy, annoy, friends, foes; but 'twill not be.

1628

SIR HENRY WOTTON
(1568–1639)

On His Mistress, the Queen of Bohemia[1]

You meaner beauties of the night,
  That poorly satisfy our eyes
More by your number than your light,
  You common people of the skies—
  What are you when the sun shall rise?

You curious chanters of the wood
  That warble forth dame Nature's lays,
Thinking your voices understood
  By your weak accents, what's your praise
  When Philomel° her voice shall raise? *the nightingale*

2. The prophet Elijah, who departed from earth in a chariot of fire, leaving his sacred mantle and a share of his spirit to his disciple Elisha (II Kings ii.9–14).

1. Elizabeth, daughter of King James of England, who in 1613 married Frederic V, Elector Palatine. Frederic became king of Bohemia in 1619.

You violets that first appear,
  By your pure purple mantles known
Like the proud virgins of the year,
  As if the spring were all your own—
  What are you when the rose is blown?° *blossomed*

So, when my mistress shall be seen
  In form and beauty of her mind,
By virtue first, then choice, a queen,
  Tell me if she were not designed
  Th' eclipse and glory of her kind?

1651

JOHN DONNE
(1572–1631)

The Good-Morrow

I wonder, by my troth, what thou and I
Did, till we loved? were we not weaned till then?
But sucked on country pleasures, childishly?
Or snorted we in the Seven Sleepers' den?[1]
'Twas so; but° this, all pleasures fancies be. *except for*
If ever any beauty I did see,
Which I desired, and got, 'twas but a dream of thee.

And now good-morrow to our waking souls,
Which watch not one another out of fear;
For love, all love of other sights controls,
And makes one little room an everywhere.
Let sea-discoverers to new worlds have gone,
Let maps° to others, worlds on worlds have shown, *sky charts*
Let us possess one world, each hath one, and is one.

My face in thine eye, thine in mine appears,
And true plain hearts do in the faces rest;
Where can we find two better hemispheres,
Without sharp north, without declining west?
Whatever dies was not mixed equally;[2]
If our two loves be one, or, thou and I
Love so alike that none do slacken, none can die.

1633

Song

Go and catch a falling star,
  Get with child a mandrake root,[3]
Tell me where all past years are,
  Or who cleft the Devil's foot,

1. Seven early Christians, immured in the persecution of A.D. 249, were believed to have slept for nearly two centuries.
2. In earlier medicine, death was often considered the result of an imbalance in the body's elements.
3. The large, forked root of the mandrake, roughly resembling a human body, was often credited with human attributes. As a medicine, it was supposed to promote conception.

Teach me to hear mermaids singing,
Or to keep off envy's stinging,
And find
What wind
Serves to advance an honest mind.

If thou beest born to strange sights,
Things invisible to see,
Ride ten thousand days and nights,
Till age snow white hairs on thee.
Thou, when thou return'st, wilt tell me
All strange wonders that befell thee,
And swear
Nowhere
Lives a woman true, and fair.

If thou find'st one, let me know,
Such a pilgrimage were sweet;
Yet do not, I would not go,
Though at next door we might meet;
Though she were true when you met her,
And last till you write your letter,
Yet she
Will be
False, ere I come, to two, or three.

1633

Woman's Constancy

Now thou hast loved me one whole day,
Tomorrow when thou leav'st, what wilt thou say?
Wilt thou then antedate some new-made vow?
Or say that now
We are not just those persons which we were?
Or, that oaths made in reverential fear
Of love, and his wrath, any may forswear?
Or, as true deaths true marriages untie,
So lovers' contracts, images of those,
Bind but till sleep, death's image, them unloose?
Or, your own end to justify,
For having purposed change, and falsehood, you
Can have no way but falsehood to be true?
Vain lunatic,[4] against these 'scapes I could
Dispute, and conquer, if I would,
Which I abstain to do,
For by tomorrow, I may think so too.

1633

The Sun Rising

Busy old fool, unruly sun,
Why dost thou thus,
Through windows and through curtains call on us?
Must to thy motions lovers' seasons run?

4. The word has for Donne the additional meaning of *inconstant* or *fickle*, since lunacy (from *luna*, moon) was supposed to be affected by the changing phases of the moon.

Saucy pedantic wretch, go chide
Late school boys and sour prentices,
Go tell court huntsmen that the king will ride,
Call country ants to harvest offices;
Love, all alike, no season knows nor clime,
Nor hours, days, months, which are the rags of time.

Thy beams, so reverend and strong
Why shouldst thou think?
I could eclipse and cloud them with a wink,
But that I would not lose her sight so long;
If her eyes have not blinded thine,
Look, and tomorrow late tell me,
Whether both th' Indias[5] of spice and mine
Be where thou leftst them, or lie here with me.
Ask for those kings whom thou saw'st yesterday,
And thou shalt hear, All here in one bed lay.

She's all states, and all princes, I,
Nothing else is.
Princes do but play us; compared to this,
All honor's mimic, all wealth alchemy.[6]
Thou, sun, art half as happy as we,
In that the world's contracted thus;
Thine age asks ease, and since thy duties be
To warm the world, that's done in warming us.
Shine here to us, and thou art everywhere;
This bed thy center is, these walls, thy sphere.

1633

The Canonization

For God's sake hold your tongue, and let me love,
Or chide my palsy, or my gout,
My five gray hairs, or ruined fortune, flout,
With wealth your state, your mind with arts improve,
Take you a course, get you a place,
Observe His Honor, or His Grace,
Or the King's real, or his stampéd face[7]
Contémplate; what you will, approve,° *try*
So you will let me love.

Alas, alas, who's injured by my love?
What merchant's ships have my sighs drowned?
Who says my tears have overflowed his ground?
When did my colds a forward spring remove?
When did the heats which my veins fill
Add one more to the plaguy bill?[8]
Soldiers find wars, and lawyers find out still
Litigious men, which quarrels move,
Though she and I do love.

Call us what you will, we're made such by love;
Call her one, me another fly,

5. India and the West Indies, whence came spices and gold, respectively.
6. I.e., a fraud.
7. I.e., on coins.
8. Weekly list of plague victims.

We're tapers too, and at our own cost die,[9]
And we in us find th' eagle and the dove.[1]
The phoenix[2] riddle hath more wit° *sense*
By us: we two being one, are it.
So, to one neutral thing both sexes fit.
We die and rise the same, and prove
Mysterious by this love.

We can die by it, if not live by love,
And if unfit for tombs and hearse
Our legend be, it will be fit for verse;
And if no piece of chronicle we prove,
We'll build in sonnets pretty rooms;
As well a well-wrought urn becomes
The greatest ashes, as half-acre tombs;
And by these hymns, all shall approve
Us canonized for love:

And thus invoke us: You whom reverend love
Made one another's hermitage;
You, to whom love was peace, that now is rage;
Who did the whole world's soul contract, and drove
Into the glasses of your eyes
(So made such mirrors, and such spies,
That they did all to you epitomize)
Countries, towns, courts: Beg from above
A pattern of your love!

1633

Song

Sweetest love, I do not go
For weariness of thee,
Nor in hope the world can show
A fitter love for me;
But since that I
Must die at last, 'tis best
To use myself in jest,
Thus by feigned deaths to die.

Yesternight the sun went hence,
And yet is here today;
He hath no desire nor sense,
Nor half so short a way:
Then fear not me,
But believe that I shall make
Speedier journeys, since I take
More wings and spurs than he.

O how feeble is man's power,
That if good fortune fall,
Cannot add another hour,

9. Death was a popular metaphor for sexual intercourse in the 17th century. "At our own cost" reflects the common superstition that each act of lovemaking shortened one's life by a day.

1. Common symbols of strength and peace.

2. A legendary bird, the only one of its kind, represented as living five hundred years in the Arabian desert, being consumed in fire, then rising anew from its own ashes.

Nor a lost hour recall!
But come bad chance,
And we join to'it[3] our strength,
And we teach it art and length,
Itself o'er us to'advance.

When thou sigh'st, thou sigh'st not wind,
But sigh'st my soul away;
When thou weep'st, unkindly kind,
My life's blood doth decay.
It cannot be
That thou lov'st me, as thou say'st,
If in thine my life thou waste;
Thou art the best of me.

Let not thy divining heart
Forethink me any ill;
Destiny may take thy part
And may thy fears fulfill;
But think that we
Are but turned aside to sleep;
They who one another keep
Alive, ne'er parted be.

1633

The Anniversary

All kings, and all their favorites,
All glory'of honors, beauties, wits,
The sun itself, which makes times, as they pass,
Is elder by a year, now, than it was
When thou and I first one another saw:
All other things to their destruction draw,
Only our love hath no decay;
This, no tomorrow hath, nor yesterday;
Running it never runs from us away,
But truly keeps his first, last, everlasting day.

Two graves must hide thine and my corse;
If one might, death were no divorce:
Alas, as well as other princes, we
(Who prince enough in one another be)
Must leave at last in death, these eyes, and ears,
Oft fed with true oaths, and with sweet salt tears;
But souls where nothing dwells but love
(All other thoughts being inmates°) then shall prove° *lodgers / experience*
This, or a love increasèd there above,
When bodies to their graves, souls from their graves remove.

And then we shall be throughly° blest, *thoroughly*
But we no more than all the rest;

3. Donne frequently uses an apostrophe between words to indicate that the neighboring syllables are fused in pronunciation and counted as one metrically. Such contractions occur only under certain phonetic conditions (e.g., when one word ends, and the next begins, with a vowel). They continue to be common in modern speech, although in writing we now limit use of the apostrophe to those contractions which omit letters from the usual spelling of the words (*you're, don't*).

Here upon earth, we're kings, and none but we
Can be such kings, nor of such subjects be;
Who is so safe as we, where none can do
Treason to us, except one of us two?
True and false fears let us refrain,
Let us love nobly,'and live, and add again
Years and years unto years, till we attain
To write threescore, this is the second of our reign.

1633

A Valediction: Of Weeping

Let me pour forth
My tears before thy face whilst I stay here,
For thy face coins them, and thy stamp they bear,
And by this mintage they are something worth,
For thus they be
Pregnant of thee;
Fruits of much grief they are, emblems of more;
When a tear falls, that Thou falls which it bore,
So thou and I are nothing then, when on a diverse shore.

On a round ball
A workman that hath copies by, can lay
An Europe, Afric, and an Asïa,
And quickly make that, which was nothing, all,
So doth each tear
Which thee doth wear,[4]
A globe, yea world, by that impression grow,
Till thy tears mixed with mine do overflow
This world; by waters sent from thee, my heaven dissolvéd so.

O more than moon,
Draw not up seas to drown me in thy sphere;
Weep me not dead, in thine arms, but forbear
To teach the sea what it may do too soon.
Let not the wind
Example find
To do me more harm than it purposeth;
Since thou and I sigh one another's breath,
Whoe'er sighs most is cruelest, and hastes the other's death.

1633

A Valediction: Forbidding Mourning

As virtuous men pass mildly' away,
And whisper to their souls to go,
Whilst some of their sad friends do say
The breath goes now, and some say, No;

So let us melt, and make no noise,
No tear-floods, nor sigh-tempests move,
'Twere profanation of our joys
To tell the laity our love.

4. I.e., doth wear thee.

Moving of th' earth brings harms and fears,
  Men reckon what it did and meant;
But trepidation of the spheres,[5]
  Though greater far, is innocent.

Dull sublunary[6] lovers' love
  (Whose soul is sense) cannot admit
Absence, because it doth remove
  Those things which elemented it.

But we by'a love so much refined
  That our selves know not what it is,
Inter-assuréd of the mind,
  Care less, eyes, lips, and hands to miss.

Our two souls therefore, which are one,
  Though I must go, endure not yet
A breach, but an expansion,
  Like gold to airy thinness beat.

If they be two, they are two so
  As stiff twin compasses are two;
Thy soul, the fixed foot, makes no show
  To move, but doth, if th' other do.

And though it in the center sit,
  Yet when the other far doth roam,
It leans and hearkens after it,
  And grows erect, as that comes home.

Such wilt thou be to me, who must
  Like th' other foot, obliquely run;
Thy firmness makes my circle[7] just,
  And makes me end where I begun.

1633

The Ecstasy[8]

Where, like a pillow on a bed,
  A pregnant bank swelled up to rest
The violet's reclining head,
  Sat we two, one another's best.
Our hands were firmly cémented
  With a fast balm, which thence did spring.
Our eye-beams twisted, and did thread
  Our eyes upon one double string;
So to'intergraft our hands, as yet
  Was all the means to make us one;
And pictures in our eyes to get° *beget*
  Was all our propagation.
As 'twixt two equal armies, Fate

5. A trembling of the celestial spheres, hypothesized by Ptolemaic astronomers to account for unpredicted variations in the paths of the heavenly bodies.
6. Beneath the moon; earthly—hence, changeable.
7. The circle was a symbol of perfection; with a dot in the middle, it was also the alchemist's symbol for gold.
8. Literally, "a standing out." The term was used by religious mystics to describe the experience in which the soul seemed to leave the body and rise superior to it in a state of heightened awareness.

Suspends uncertain victory,
Our souls (which to advance their state,
Were gone out) hung 'twixt her and me.
And whilst our souls negotiate there,
We like sepulchral statues lay;
All day the same our postures were,
And we said nothing all the day.
If any, so by love refined
That he soul's language understood,
And by good love were grown all mind,
Within convenient distance stood,
He (though he knew not which soul spake,
Because both meant, both spake the same)
Might thence a new concoction[9] take,
And part far purer than he came.
This ecstasy doth unperplex,
We said, and tell us what we love;
We see by this it was not sex;
We see we saw not what did move;
But as all several° souls contain *separate*
Mixture of things, they know not what,
Love these mixed souls doth mix again,
And makes both one, each this and that.
A single violet transplant,
The strength, the colour, and the size
(All which before was poor, and scant)
Redoubles still, and multiplies.
When love, with one another so
Interinanimates two souls,
That abler soul, which thence doth flow,
Defects of loneliness controls.
We then, who are this new soul, know,
Of what we are composed, and made,
For, th' atomies° of which we grow, *atoms*
Are souls, whom no change can invade.
But O alas, so long, so far
Our bodies why do we forbear?
They're ours, though they're not we; we are
Th' intelligences, they the spheres.[1]
We owe them thanks because they thus,
Did us to us at first convey,
Yielded their forces, sense, to us,
Nor are dross to us, but allay.° *alloy*
On man heaven's influence works not so
But that it first imprints the air,[2]
So soul into the soul may flow,
Though it to body first repair.
As our blood labors to beget
Spirits as like souls as it can,[3]
Because such fingers need to knit
That subtle knot which makes us man:
So must pure lovers' souls descend

9. Mixture of diverse elements refined by heat (alchemical term).
1. The nine orders of angels ("intelligences") were believed to govern the nine spheres of Ptolemaic astronomy.
2. Influences from the heavenly bodies were conceived of as being transmitted through the medium of the air; also, angels were thought to assume bodies of air in their dealings with men.
3. "Spirits" were vapors believed to permeate the blood and to mediate between the body and the soul.

To' affections, and to faculties
Which sense may reach and apprehend;
Else a great Prince in prison lies.
To'our bodies turn we then, that so
Weak men on love revealed may look;
Love's mysteries in souls do grow,
But yet the body is his book.
And if some lover, such as we,
Have heard this dialogue of one,
Let him still mark us; he shall see
Small change when we're to bodies gone.

1633

The Funeral

Whoever comes to shroud me, do not harm
Nor question much
That subtle wreath of hair which crowns my arm;
The mystery, the sign you must not touch,
For 'tis my outward soul,
Viceroy to that, which then to heaven being gone,
Will leave this to control,
And keep these limbs, her provinces, from dissolution.

For if the sinewy thread my brain lets fall
Through every part
Can tie those parts and make me one of all;
These hairs, which upward grew, and strength and art
Have from a better brain,
Can better do'it; except she meant that I
By this should know my pain,
As prisoners then are manacled, when they're condemned to die.

Whate'er she meant by 'it, bury it with me,
For since I am
Love's martyr, it might breed idolatry,
If into other's hands these relics came;
As 'twas humility
To'afford to it all that a soul can do,
So 'tis some bravery,
That since you would save none of me, I bury some of you.

1633

The Relic

When my grave is broke up again
Some second guest to entertain[4]
(For graves have learned that woman-head° *womanhood*
To be to more than one a bed),
And he that digs it, spies
A bracelet of bright hair about the bone,
Will he not let'us alone,
And think that there a loving couple lies,
Who thought that this device might be some way

4. Re-use of a grave, after an interval of years, was a common 17th-century practice.

To make their souls, at the last busy day,[5]
Meet at this grave, and make a little stay?

If this fall in a time, or land,
Where mis-devotion doth command,
Then he that digs us up, will bring
Us to the Bishop and the King,
To make us relics; then
Thou shalt be'a Mary Magdalen,[6] and I
A something else thereby;
All women shall adore us, and some men;
And since at such time, miracles are sought,
I would have that age by this paper taught
What miracles we harmless lovers wrought.

First, we loved well and faithfully,
Yet knew not what we loved, nor why,
Difference of sex no more we knew,
Than our guardian angels do;
Coming and going, we
Perchance might kiss, but not between those meals;
Our hands ne'er touched the seals,
Which nature, injured by late law, sets free:
These miracles we did; but now, alas,
All measure and all language I should pass,
Should I tell what a miracle she was.

1633

Elegy VII

Nature's lay idiot, I taught thee to love,
And in that sophistry, oh, thou dost prove
Too subtle: Fool, thou didst not understand
The mystic language of the eye nor hand:
Nor couldst thou judge the difference of the air
Of sighs, and say, this lies, this sounds despair:
Nor by the'eye's water call a malady
Desperately hot, or changing feverously.
I had not taught thee then, the alphabet
Of flowers, how they devicefully° being set *ingeniously*
And bound up, might with speechless secrecy
Deliver errands mutely, and mutually.
Remember since° all thy words used to be *when*
To every suitor, "Ay, if my friends agree";
Since, household charms, thy husband's name to teach,
Were all the love-tricks, that thy wit could reach;
And since, an hour's discourse could scarce have made
One answer in thee, and that ill arrayed
In broken proverbs, and torn sentences.
Thou art not by so many duties his,
That from the world's common having severed thee,

5. Judgment Day, when all parts of the body would be reassembled and reunited with the soul in the resurrection.
6. The woman out of whom Christ had cast seven devils (Luke viii.2), traditionally identified with the repentant prostitute of Luke vii.37–50.

Inlaid thee,[7] neither to be seen, nor see,
As mine: who have with amorous delicacies
Refined thee into a blissful paradise.
Thy graces and good words my creatures be;
I planted knowledge and life's tree[8] in thee,
Which oh, shall strangers taste? Must I alas
Frame and enamel plate, and drink in glass?
Chafe° wax for others' seals? break a colt's force *heat*
And leave him then, being made a ready horse?

1633

Elegy XIX. To His Mistress Going to Bed

Come, madam, come, all rest my powers defy,
Until I labor, I in labor lie.
The foe oft-times having the foe in sight,
Is tired with standing though he never fight.
Off with that girdle, like heaven's zone glistering,
But a far fairer world encompassing.
Unpin that spangled breastplate which you wear,
That th' eyes of busy fools may be stopped there.
Unlace yourself, for that harmonious chime
Tells me from you that now it is bed time.
Off with that happy busk,° which I envy, *corset*
That still can be, and still can stand so nigh.
Your gown, going off, such beauteous state reveals,
As when from flowry meads th' hill's shadow steals.
Off with that wiry coronet and show
The hairy diadem which on you doth grow:
Now off with those shoes, and then safely tread
In this love's hallowed temple, this soft bed.
In such white robes, heaven's angels used to be
Received by men; thou, Angel, bring'st with thee
A heaven like Mahomet's Paradise; and though
Ill spirits walk in white, we easily know
By this these angels from an evil sprite:
Those set our hairs, but these our flesh upright.
License my roving hands, and let them go
Before, behind, between, above, below.
O my America! my new-found-land,
My kingdom, safeliest when with one man manned,
My mine of precious stones, my empery,° *empire*
How blest am I in this discovering thee!
To enter in these bonds is to be free;
Then where my hand is set, my seal shall be.
Full nakedness! All joys are due to thee,
As souls unbodied, bodies unclothed must be
To taste whole joys. Gems which you women use
Are like Atlanta's balls,[9] cast in men's views,
That when a fool's eye lighteth on a gem,
His earthly soul may covet theirs, not them.

7. I.e., "laid thee in," set thee aside for his private uses.
8. The first paradise, Eden, included the Tree of Knowledge and the Tree of Life (Genesis ii.9).
9. Atalanta agreed to marry Hippomenes if he could defeat her in a foot race. As she was about to overtake him, he cast in her path three golden apples given to him by Venus. Distracted by their beauty, Atalanta stopped to retrieve them, and Hippomenes won the race.

Like pictures, or like books' gay coverings made
For lay-men, are all women thus arrayed;
Themselves are mystic books, which only we
(Whom their imputed grace will dignify)
Must see revealed. Then, since that I may know,
As liberally as to a midwife, show
Thyself: cast all, yea, this white linen hence,
There is no penance due to innocence.
  To teach thee, I am naked first; why than,° *then*
What needst thou have more covering than a man?

1669

Good Friday, 1613. Riding Westward

Let man's soul be a sphere, and then, in this,
Th' intelligence that moves,[1] devotion is,
And as the other spheres, by being grown
Subject to foreign motions, lose their own,
And being by others hurried every day,
Scarce in a year their natural form obey;
Pleasure or business, so, our souls admit
For their first mover, and are whirled by it.
Hence is 't, that I am carried towards the West
This day, when my soul's form bends towards the East.
There I should see a Sun, by rising, set,
And by that setting endless day beget:
But that Christ on this cross did rise and fall,
Sin had eternally benighted all.
Yet dare I'almost be glad I do not see
That spectacle, of too much weight for me.
Who sees God's face, that is self-life, must die;
What a death were it then to see God die?
It made his own lieutenant, Nature, shrink;
It made his footstool crack, and the sun wink.[2]
Could I behold those hands which span the poles,
And tune all spheres at once, pierced with those holes?
Could I behold that endless height which is
Zenith to us, and to'our antipodes,[3]
Humbled below us? Or that blood which is
The seat of all our souls, if not of His,
Make dirt of dust, or that flesh which was worn
By God, for his apparel, ragg'd and torn?
If on these things I durst not look, durst I
Upon his miserable mother cast mine eye,
Who was God's partner here, and furnished thus
Half of that sacrifice which ransomed us?
Though these things, as I ride, be from mine eye,
They're present yet unto my memory,
For that looks towards them; and Thou look'st towards me,
O Saviour, as Thou hang'st upon the tree.
I turn my back to Thee but to receive

1. An angel was believed to govern the movements of each of the nine celestial spheres in Ptolemaic astronomy. Each sphere, in addition to its own motion, was influenced by the motions of those outside it ("foreign motions," line 4), the outermost being known as the *primum mobile,* "first mover" (line 8).
2. "Thus saith the Lord * * * the earth is my footstool" (Isaiah lxvi.1). An earthquake and an eclipse accompanied the crucifixion of Jesus (Matthew xxvii.45, 51).
3. The zenith is that part of the heavens directly above any point on earth; the antipodes are that part of the earth diametrically opposite such a point.

Corrections, till Thy mercies bid Thee leave.
O think me worth Thine anger; punish me;
Burn off my rusts and my deformity;
Restore Thine image so much, by Thy grace,
That Thou may'st know me, and I'll turn my face.

1633

From Holy Sonnets

1

Thou hast made me, and shall Thy work decay?
Repair me now, for now mine end doth haste;
I run to death, and death meets me as fast,
And all my pleasures are like yesterday.
I dare not move my dim eyes any way,
Despair behind, and death before doth cast
Such terror, and my feeble flesh doth waste
By sin in it, which it towards hell doth weigh.
Only Thou art above, and when towards Thee
By Thy leave I can look, I rise again;
But our old subtle foe so tempteth me
That not one hour myself I can sustain.
Thy grace may wing me to prevent his art,
And Thou like adamant° draw mine iron heart. *loadstone*

1635

5

I am a little world made cunningly
Of elements, and an angelic sprite;
But black sin hath betrayed to endless night
My world's both parts, and O, both parts must die.
You which beyond that heaven which was most high
Have found new spheres, and of new lands can write,[4]
Pour new seas in mine eyes, that so I might
Drown my world with my weeping earnestly,
Or wash it if it must be drowned no more.[5]
But O, it must be burnt! Alas, the fire
Of lust and envy'have burnt it heretofore,
And made it fouler; let their flames retire,
And burn me, O Lord, with a fiery zeal
Of Thee'and Thy house, which doth in eating heal.[6]

1635

7

At the round earth's imagined corners, blow
Your trumpets, angels;[7] and arise, arise
From death, you numberless infinities
Of souls, and to your scattered bodies go;
All whom the flood did, and fire shall,[8] o'erthrow,
All whom war, dearth, age, agues, tyrannies,
Despair, law, chance hath slain, and you whose eyes
Shall behold God, and never taste death's woe.[9]

4. Copernican astronomy (which placed the sun at the center of our system and not the earth, as in Ptolemaic astronomy) had enlarged men's ideas about the extent of the universe, just as recent terrestrial exploration had changed their idea of the world.
5. God promised Noah that he would never again cover the earth with a flood (Genesis ix.11).
6. "* * * the zeal of thine house hath eaten me up" (Psalms lxix.9).
7. "* * * I saw four angels standing on the four corners of the earth, holding the four winds of the earth * * *" (Revelation vii.1).
8. At the end of the world, "* * * the elements shall melt with fervent heat, the earth also and the works that are therein shall be burned up" (II Peter iii.10).
9. "But I tell you of a truth, there be some standing here, which shall not taste of death, till they see the kingdom of God" (Christ's words to his disciples, Luke ix.27).

But let them sleep, Lord, and me mourn a space;
For, if above all these, my sins abound,
'Tis late to ask abundance of Thy grace
When we are there. Here on this lowly ground,
Teach me how to repent; for that's as good
As if Thou'hadst sealed my pardon with Thy blood.

1633

10

Death, be not proud, though some have callèd thee
Mighty and dreadful, for thou are not so;
For those whom thou think'st thou dost overthrow
Die not, poor Death, nor yet canst thou kill me.
From rest and sleep, which but thy pictures be,
Much pleasure; then from thee much more must flow,
And soonest our best men with thee do go,
Rest of their bones, and soul's delivery.
Thou'art slave to fate, chance, kings, and desperate men,
And dost with poison, war, and sickness dwell,
And poppy'or charms can make us sleep as well
And better than thy stroke; why swell'st thou then?
One short sleep past, we wake eternally
And death shall be no more; Death, thou shalt die.

1633

14

Batter my heart, three-personed God; for You
As yet but knock, breathe, shine, and seek to mend;
That I may rise and stand, o'erthrow me,'and bend
Your force to break, blow, burn, and make me new.
I, like an usurped town, to'another due,
Labor to'admit You, but O, to no end;
Reason, Your viceroy'in me, me should defend,
But is captívèd, and proves weak or untrue.
Yet dearly'I love You,'and would be lovéd fain,
But am betrothed unto Your enemy.
Divorce me,'untie or break that knot again;
Take me to You, imprison me, for I,
Except You'enthrall me, never shall be free,
Nor ever chaste, except You ravish me.

1633

Hymn to God My God, in My Sickness

Since I am coming to that holy room
  Where, with Thy choir of saints for evermore,
I shall be made Thy music; as I come
  I tune the instrument here at the door,
  And what I must do then, think here before.

Whilst my physicians by their love are grown
  Cosmographers, and I their map, who lie
Flat on this bed, that by them may be shown
  That this is my southwest discovery[1]
  Per fretum febris, by these straits to die,

1. Magellan had discovered the straits which bear his name in 1520. They lie at the southern tip of South America and are hence southwest from England. *"Per fretum febris"*: through the straits of fever.

I joy, that in these straits, I see my West;[2]
For, though their currents yield return to none,
What shall my West hurt me? As West and East
In all flat maps (and I am one) are one,
So death doth touch the resurrection.

Is the Pacific Sea my home? Or are
The Eastern riches? Is Jerusalem?
Anyan,° and Mágellan, and Gíbraltar, *Bering Straits*
All straits, and none but straits, are ways to them,
Whether where Japhet dwelt, or Cham, or Shem.[3]

We think that Paradise and Calvary,
Christ's cross, and Adam's tree, stood in one place;
Look, Lord, and find both Adams met in me;
As the first Adam's sweat surrounds my face,
May the last Adam's blood my soul embrace.

So, in his purple wrapped, receive me, Lord;
By these his thorns give me his other crown;
And, as to others' souls I preached Thy word,
Be this my text, my sermon to mine own:
Therefore that he may raise the Lord throws down.[4]

1635

BEN JONSON
(1573–1637)

To the Reader

Pray thee, take care, that tak'st my book in hand,
To read it well: that is, to understand.

1616

On My First Daughter

Here lies, to each her parents' ruth,° *sorrow*
Mary, the daughter of their youth;
Yet all heaven's gifts being heaven's due,
It makes the father less to rue.
At six months' end she parted hence
With safety of her innocence;
Whose soul heaven's queen, whose name she bears,
In comfort of her mother's tears,
Hath placed amongst her virgin-train:
Where, while that severed doth remain,
This grave partakes the fleshly birth;
Which cover lightly, gentle earth!

1616

2. "* * * strait is the gate, and narrow is the way, which leadeth unto life * * *" (Matthew vii.14). "West": i.e., death.
3. The three sons of Noah, who settled in Europe, Africa, and Asia respectively after the Flood.
4. Adapted from Psalms cxlvi.8: "* * * the Lord raiseth them that are bowed down."

On My First Son

Farewell, thou child of my right hand,[1] and joy;
My sin was too much hope of thee, loved boy:
Seven years thou'wert lent to me, and I thee pay,
Exacted by thy fate, on the just day.[2]
O could I lose all father now! for why
Will man lament the state he should envý,
To have so soon 'scaped world's and flesh's rage,
And, if no other misery, yet age?
Rest in soft peace, and asked, say, "Here doth lie
Ben Jonson his best piece of poetry."
For whose sake henceforth all his vows be such
As what he loves may never like too much.

1616

On English Monsieur

Would you believe, when you this mónsieur[3] see,
That his whole body should speak French, not he?
That so much scarf of France, and hat, and feather,
And shoe, and tie, and garter should come hether,° *hither*
And land on one whose face durst never be
Toward the sea farther than Half-Way Tree?[4]
That he, untraveled, should be French so much
As Frenchmen in his company should seem Dutch?
Or had his father, when he did him get,
The French disease,[5] with which he labors yet?
Or hung some mónsieur's picture on the wall,
By which his dam conceived him, clothes and all?
Or is it some French statue? No: 'T doth move,
And stoop, and cringe. O then, it needs must prove
The new French tailor's motion,° monthly made, *puppet*
Daily to turn in Paul's,[6] and help the trade.

1616

To John Donne

Who shall doubt, Donne, where° I a poet be, *whether*
When I dare send my epigrams to thee?
That so alone canst judge, so'alone dost make;
And, in thy censures, evenly dost take
As free simplicity to disavow
As thou hast best authority t' allow.
Read all I send, and if I find but one
Marked by thy hand, and with the better stone,[7]

1. A literal translation of the Hebrew *Benjamin,* the boy's name.
2. Jonson's son died on his seventh birthday in 1603.
3. Stress on first syllable; often spelled *monser* in Jonson's time, suggesting an Anglicized pronunciation.
4. Perhaps a landmark between London and Dover, where a traveler would embark for France.
5. I.e., syphilis.
6. St. Paul's Cathedral in London. In the 17th century St. Paul's was a popular gathering place; merchants hired men to walk up and down in the yard advertising their wares.
7. The allusion may be to the Thracian custom of recording the good or evil fortunes of each day by placing a stone counter of corresponding color in an urn. Jonson refers elsewhere to Pliny's description of this custom in his *Natural History,* VII, 40.

My title's sealed. Those that for claps° do write, *applause*
Let pui'nies',[8] porters', players' praise delight,
And, till they burst, their backs like asses load:
A man should seek great glory, and not broad.

1616

Inviting a Friend to Supper

Tonight, grave sir, both my poor house, and I
Do equally desire your company;
Not that we think us worthy such a guest,
But that your worth will dignify our feast
With those that come, whose grace may make that seem
Something, which else could hope for no esteem.
It is the fair acceptance, sir, creates
The entertainment perfect, not the cates.° *food*
Yet shall you have, to rectify your palate,
An olive, capers, or some better salad
Ushering the mutton; with a short-legged hen,
If we can get her, full of eggs, and then
Lemons, and wine for sauce; to these a cony° *rabbit*
Is not to be despaired of, for our money;
And, though fowl now be scarce, yet there are clerks,
The sky not falling, think we may have larks.[9]
I'll tell you of more, and lie, so you will come:
Of partridge, pheasant, woodcock, of which some
May yet be there, and godwit,[1] if we can;
Knot, rail, and ruff too. Howsoe'er, my man
Shall read a piece of Virgil, Tacitus,
Livy, or of some better book to us,
Of which we'll speak our minds, amidst our meat;
And I'll profess no verses to repeat.
To this, if aught appear which I not know of,
That will the pastry, not my paper, show of.
Digestive[2] cheese and fruit there sure will be;
But that which most doth take my Muse and me,
Is a pure cup of rich Canary wine,
Which is the Mermaid's[3] now, but shall be mine;
Of which had Horace, or Anacreon tasted,
Their lives, as do their lines, till now had lasted.
Tobacco,[4] nectar, or the Thespian spring,
Are all but Luther's beer[5] to this I sing.
Of this we will sup free, but moderately,
And we will have no Pooley, or Parrot[6] by,
Nor shall our cups make any guilty men;
But, at our parting we will be as when
We innocently met. No simple word
That shall be uttered at our mirthful board,
Shall make us sad next morning or affright
The liberty that we'll enjoy tonight.

1616

8. Puisnies (pronounced like *punies*), insignificant persons.
9. According to an old proverb, "When the sky falls we shall have larks."
1. The godwit, knot, rail, and ruff are all wading birds related to the curlew or sandpiper. They were formerly regarded as delicacies.
2. Promoting or aiding digestion.
3. A famous tavern—a favorite haunt of Jonson's.
4. Smoking was often called "drinking tobacco."
5. German beer, considered inferior.
6. Notorious government informers.

On Gut

Gut eats all day and lechers all the night;
So all his meat he tasteth over twice;
And, striving so to double his delight,
He makes himself a thoroughfare of vice.
Thus in his belly can he change a sin:
Lust it comes out, that gluttony went in.

1616

Epitaph on Salomon Pavy, a Child of Queen Elizabeth's Chapel[7]

Weep with me, all you that read
  This little story,
And know, for whom a tear you shed,
  Death's self is sorry.
'Twas a child, that so did thrive
  In grace and feature,
As Heaven and Nature seemed to strive
  Which owned the creature.
Years he numbered scarce thirteen
  When Fates turned cruel,
Yet three filled zodiacs[8] had he been
  The stage's jewel,
And did act, what now we moan,
  Old men so duly,
As, sooth, the Parcae[9] thought him one,
  He played so truly.
So, by error, to his fate
  They all consented;
But viewing him since (alas, too late)
  They have repented.
And have sought, to give new birth,
  In baths to steep him;[1]
But, being so much too good for earth,
  Heaven vows to keep him.

1616

Epitaph on Elizabeth, L. H.

Woudst thou hear what man can say
In a little? Reader, stay.
Underneath this stone doth lie
As much beauty as could die;
Which in life did harbor give
To more virtue than doth live.
If at all she had a fault,
Leave it buried in this vault.
One name was Elizabeth;

7. The Children of Queen Elizabeth's Chapel were a company of boy actors. Salomon Pavy had acted in Jonson's plays.
8. I.e., three years.
9. The three Fates, who determined men's destinies.
1. Aeson, the father of Jason, was made young again by a magic bath prepared by Jason's wife Medea.

Th' other, let it sleep with death:
Fitter, where it died, to tell,
Than that it lived at all. Farewell.

1616

To Penshurst[2]

Thou art not, Penshurst, built to envious show,
Of touch° or marble; nor canst boast a row — *touchstone, basanite*
Of polished pillars, or a roof of gold;
Thou hast no lantern,[3] whereof tales are told,
Or stair, or courts; but stand'st an ancient pile,
And, these grudged at, art reverenced the while.
Thou joy'st in better marks, of soil, of air,
Of wood, of water; therein thou art fair.
Thou hast thy walks for health, as well as sport;
Thy mount, to which the dryads° do resort, — *wood nymphs*
Where Pan and Bacchus their high feasts have made,
Beneath the broad beech and the chestnut shade;
That taller tree, which of a nut was set
At his great birth[4] where all the Muses met.
There in the writhéd bark are cut the names
Of many a sylvan,° taken with his flames; — *forest dweller*
And thence the ruddy satyrs oft provoke
The lighter fauns to reach thy Lady's Oak.
Thy copse too, named of Gamage,[5] thou hast there,
That never fails to serve thee seasoned deer
When thou wouldst feast or exercise thy friends.
The lower land, that to the river bends,
Thy sheep, thy bullocks, kine, and calves do feed;
The middle grounds thy mares and horses breed.
Each bank doth yield thee conies;° and the tops, — *rabbits*
Fertile of wood, Ashore and Sidney's copse,
To crown thy open table, doth provide
The purpled pheasant with the speckled side;
The painted partridge lies in every field,
And for thy mess is willing to be killed.
And if the high-swollen Medway[6] fail thy dish,
Thou hast thy ponds, that pay thee tribute fish,
Fat aged carps that run into thy net,
And pikes, now weary their own kind to eat,
As loath the second draught or cast to stay,° — *await*
Officiously° at first themselves betray; — *dutifully*
Bright eels that emulate them, and leap on land
Before the fisher, or into his hand.
Then hath thy orchard fruit, thy garden flowers,
Fresh as the air, and new as are the hours.
The early cherry, with the later plum,
Fig, grape, and quince, each in his time doth come;
The blushing apricot and woolly peach
Hang on thy walls, that every child may reach.
And though thy walls be of the country stone,
They're reared with no man's ruin, no man's groan;

2. The country estate of the Sidney family, in Kent.
3. A glassed or open structure raised above the roof of a house.
4. Sir Philip Sidney's, November 30, 1554.
5. Barbara Gamage, wife of Sir Robert Sidney, Philip's younger brother and the current owner of Penshurst.
6. The local river.

There's none that dwell about them wish them down;
But all come in, the farmer and the clown,° *countryman*
And no one empty-handed, to salute
Thy lord and lady, though they have no suit.
Some bring a capon, some a rural cake,
Some nuts, some apples; some that think they make
The better cheeses bring them, or else send
By their ripe daughters, whom they would commend
This way to husbands, and whose baskets bear
An emblem of themselves in plum or pear.
But what can this (more than express their love)
Add to thy free provisions, far above
The need of such? whose liberal board doth flow
With all that hospitality doth know;
Where comes no guest but is allowed to eat,
Without his fear, and of thy lord's own meat;
Where the same beer and bread, and selfsame wine,
That is his lordship's shall be also mine,
And I not fain° to sit (as some this day *obliged*
At great men's tables), and yet dine away.
Here no man tells° my cups; nor, standing by, *counts*
A waiter doth my gluttony envý,
But gives me what I call, and lets me eat;
He knows below he shall find plenty of meat.
Thy tables hoard not up for the next day;
Nor, when I take my lodging, need I pray
For fire, or lights, or livery;° all is there, *provisions*
As if thou then wert mine, or I reigned here:
There's nothing I can wish, for which I stay.
That found King James when, hunting late this way
With his brave son, the prince, they saw thy fires
Shine bright on every hearth, as the desires
Of thy Penates[7] had been set on flame
To entertain them; or the country came
With all their zeal to warm their welcome here.
What (great I will not say, but) sudden cheer
Didst thou then make 'em! and what praise was heaped
On thy good lady then, who therein reaped
The just reward of her high housewifery;
To have her linen, plate, and all things nigh,
When she was far; and not a room but dressed
As if it had expected such a guest!
These, Penshurst, are thy praise, and yet not all.
Thy lady's noble, friutful, chaste withal.
His children thy great lord may call his own,
A fortune in this age but rarely known.
They are, and have been, taught religion; thence
Their gentler spirits have sucked innocence.
Each morn and even they are taught to pray,
With the whole household, and may, every day,
Read in their virtuous parents' noble parts
The mysteries of manners, arms, and arts.
Now, Penshurst, they that will proportion° thee *compare*
With other edifices, when they see
Those proud, ambitious heaps, and nothing else,
May say their lords have built, but thy lord dwells.

1616

7. Roman household gods.

Song: To Celia

Drink to me only with thine eyes,
And I will pledge with mine;
Or leave a kiss but in the cup,
And I'll not look for wine.
The thirst that from the soul doth rise,
Doth ask a drink divine:
But might I of Jove's nectar sup,
I would not change for thine.

I sent thee late a rosy wreath,
Not so much honoring thee,
As giving it a hope, that there
It could not withered be.
But thou thereon did'st only breathe,
And sent'st it back to me;
Since when it grows and smells, I swear,
Not of itself, but thee.

1616

A Hymn to God the Father

Hear me, O God!
A broken heart,
Is my best part;
Use still thy rod,
That I may prove° *experience*
Therein thy love.

If thou hadst not
Been stern to me,
But left me free,
I had forgot
Myself and thee.

For sin's so sweet,
As minds ill bent
Rarely repent,
Until they meet
Their punishment.

Who more can crave
Than thou hast done,
That gav'st a Son,
To free a slave?
First made of naught,
With all since bought.

Sin, Death, and Hell,
His glorious Name
Quite overcame,
Yet I rebel,
And slight the same.

But I'll come in
Before my loss
Me farther toss,
As sure to win
Under his Cross.

1640

Slow, Slow, Fresh Fount[8]

Slow, slow, fresh fount, keep time with my salt tears;
Yet slower, yet, O faintly, gentle springs!
List to the heavy part the music bears,
Woe weeps out her division,[9] when she sings.
Droop herbs and flowers;
Fall grief in showers;
Our beauties are not ours. O, I could still,
Like melting snow upon some craggy hill,
Drop, drop, drop, drop,
Since nature's pride is now a withered daffodil.

1600

Queen and Huntress[1]

Queen and huntress, chaste and fair,
Now the sun is laid to sleep,
Seated in thy silver chair,
State in wonted manner keep;
Hesperus entreats thy light,
Goddess excellently bright.

Earth, let not thy envious shade
Dare itself to interpose;
Cynthia's shining orb was made
Heaven to clear, when day did close.
Bless us then with wishéd sight,
Goddess excellently bright.

Lay thy bow of pearl apart,
And thy crystal-shining quiver;
Give unto the flying hart
Space to breathe, how short soever.
Thou that mak'st a day of night,
Goddess excellently bright.

1600

Come, My Celia[2]

Come, my Celia, let us prove,° *experience*
While we can, the sports of love;
Time will not be ours forever;

8. From *Cynthia's Revels,* sung by Echo for Narcissus, who fell in love with his own reflection and was changed into the flower that bears his name. The daffodil (line 11) is a species of narcissus.
9. Part in a song.
1. From *Cynthia's Revels,* sung by Hesperus to Cynthia (Diana, goddess of the moon and of the hunt).
2. From *Volpone.* The lecherous Volpone is attempting to seduce Celia, the virtuous wife of Corvino, whom Volpone has gotten out of the way by a stratagem (line 14).

He at length our good will sever.
Spend not then his gifts in vain.
Suns that set may rise again;
But if once we lose this light,
'Tis with us perpetual night.
Why should we defer our joys?
Fame and rumor are but toys.
Cannot we delude the eyes
Of a few poor household spies,
Or his easier ears beguile,
So removéd by our wile?
'Tis no sin love's fruit to steal;
But the sweet thefts to reveal,
To be taken, to be seen,
These have crimes accounted been.

1606

Still to Be Neat[3]

Still to be neat, still to be dressed,
As you were going to a feast;
Still to be powdered, still perfumed;
Lady, it is to be presumed,
Though art's hid causes are not found,
All is not sweet, all is not sound.

Give me a look, give me a face
That makes simplicity a grace;
Robes loosely flowing, hair as free;
Such sweet neglect more taketh me
Then all th' adulteries of art.
They strike mine eyes, but not my heart.

1609

Though I Am Young and Cannot Tell[4]

Though I am young, and cannot tell
  Either what Death or Love is well,
Yet I have heard they both bear darts,
  And both do aim at human hearts.
And then again, I have been told
  Love wounds with heat, as Death with cold;
So that I fear they do but bring
  Extremes to touch, and mean one thing.

As in a ruin we it call
  One thing to be blown up, or fall;
Or to our end like way may have
  By a flash of lightning, or a wave;
So Love's inflaméd shaft or brand
  May kill as soon as Death's cold hand;
Except Love's fires the virtue have
  To fright the frost out of the grave.

1641

3. From *The Silent Woman.*

4. From *The Sad Shepherd.*

To the Memory of My Beloved, the Author Mr. William Shakespeare

AND WHAT HE HATH LEFT US[5]

To draw no envy, Shakespeare, on thy name,
Am I thus ample to thy book and fame,
While I confess thy writings to be such
As neither man nor Muse can praise too much.
'Tis true, and all men's suffrage.° But these ways *consent*
Were not the paths I meant unto thy praise:
For silliest ignorance on these may light,
Which, when it sounds at best, but echoes right;
Or blind affection,° which doth ne'er advance *feeling*
The truth, but gropes, and urgeth all by chance;
Or crafty malice might pretend this praise,
And think to ruin where it seemed to raise.
These are as some infamous bawd or whore
Should praise a matron. What could hurt her more?
But thou art proof against them, and, indeed,
Above th' ill fortune of them, or the need.
I therefore will begin. Soul of the age!
The applause! delight! the wonder of our stage!
My Shakespeare, rise; I will not lodge thee by
Chaucer or Spenser, or bid Beaumont lie
A little further to make thee a room:[6]
Thou art a monument without a tomb,
And art alive still while thy book doth live,
And we have wits to read and praise to give.
That I not mix thee so, my brain excuses,
I mean with great, but disproportioned° Muses; *not comparable*
For, if I thought my judgment were of years,
I should commit thee surely with thy peers,
And tell how far thou didst our Lyly outshine,
Or sporting Kyd, or Marlowe's mighty line.[7]
And though thou hadst small Latin and less Greek,
From thence to honor thee I would not seek
For names, but call forth thund'ring Aeschylus,
Euripides, and Sophocles to us,
Pacuvius, Accius, him of Cordova dead,[8]
To life again, to hear thy buskin[9] tread
And shake a stage; or, when thy socks were on,
Leave thee alone for the comparison
Of all that insolent Greece or haughty Rome
Sent forth, or since did from their ashes come.
Triumph, my Britain; thou hast one to show
To whom all scenes° of Europe homage owe. *stages*
He was not of an age, but for all time!
And all the Muses still were in their prime

5. Prefixed to the first collected edition—the first folio edition of Shakespeare's works, 1623.
6. Chaucer, Spenser, and Beaumont are all buried in Westminster Abbey.
7. John Lyly, Thomas Kyd, and Christopher Marlowe, all Elizabethan dramatists.
8. Marcus Pacuvius and Lucius Accius were Roman tragedians of the second century B.C.; "him of Cordova" is the Roman tragedian Seneca of the first century A.D.
9. The high-heeled boot worn by Greek tragic actors; the "sock" or light shoe was worn in comedies.

When like Apollo he came forth to warm
Our ears, or like a Mercury to charm.
Nature herself was proud of his designs,
And joyed to wear the dressing of his lines,
Which were so richly spun, and woven so fit,
As, since, she will vouchsafe no other wit:
The merry Greek, tart Aristophanes,
Neat Terence, witty Plautus[1] now not please,
But antiquated and deserted lie,
As they were not of Nature's family.
Yet must I not give Nature all; thy Art,
My gentle Shakespeare, must enjoy a part.
For though the poet's matter Nature be,
His Art doth give the fashion; and that he
Who casts to write a living line must sweat
(Such as thine are) and strike the second heat
Upon the muses' anvil; turn the same,
And himself with it, that he thinks to frame,
Or for the laurel he may gain a scorn;
For a good poet's made as well as born.
And such wert thou! Look how the father's face
Lives in his issue, even so the race
Of Shakespeare's mind and manners brightly shines
In his well-turnéd and true-filéd lines,
In each of which he seems to shake a lance,
As brandished at the eyes of ignorance.
Sweet swan of Avon, what a sight it were
To see thee in our waters yet appear,
And make those flights upon the banks of Thames
That so did take Eliza and our James![2]
But stay; I see thee in the hemisphere
Advanced and made a constellation there!
Shine forth, thou star of poets, and with rage
Or influence[3] chide or cheer the drooping stage,
Which, since thy flight from hence, hath mourned like night,
And despairs day, but for thy volume's light.

1623

JOHN WEBSTER
(1580–1625)

Call for the Robin Redbreast and the Wren

Call for the robin redbreast and the wren,
Since o'er shady groves they hover,
And with leaves and flowers do cover
The friendless bodies of unburied men.
Call unto his funeral dole° *sorrow*
The ant, the field mouse, and the mole,
To rear him hillocks that shall keep him warm,
And, when gay tombs are robbed, sustain no harm;
But keep the wolf far thence, that's foe to men,
For with his nails he'll dig them up again.

1612

1. Aristophanes (Greek) and Terence and Plautus (Roman) were comic writers of the fourth to second centuries B.C.

2. Queen Elizabeth and King James.

3. A supposed emanation of power from stars.

Hark, Now Everything Is Still

Hark, now everything is still;
The screech owl and the whistler shrill
Call upon our dame aloud,
And bid her quickly don her shroud.
Much you had of land and rent;
Your length in clay's now competent.
A long war disturbed your mind;
Here your perfect peace is signed.
Of what is 't fools make such vain keeping?
Sin their conception, their birth weeping,
Their life a general mist of error,
Their death a hideous storm of terror.
Strew your hair with powders sweet,
Don clean linen, bathe your feet,
And, the foul fiend more to check,
A crucifix let bless your neck.
'Tis now full tide, 'tween night and day,
End your groan and come away.

1623

WILLIAM BROWNE
(1591?–1643?)

On the Countess Dowager of Pembroke[1]

Underneath this sable hearse
Lies the subject of all verse:
Sidney's sister, Pembroke's mother.
Death, ere thou hast slain another
Fair and learn'd and good as she,
Time shall throw a dart at thee.

Marble piles let no man raise
To her name, for after-days
Some kind woman, born as she,
Reading this, like Niobe[2]
Shall turn marble, and become
Both her mourner and her tomb.

1623

ROBERT HERRICK
(1591–1674)

The Argument[1] of His Book

I sing of brooks, of blossoms, birds, and bowers,
Of April, May, of June, and July flowers.

1. Mary Herbert, sister of Sir Philip Sidney and mother of William Herbert, third earl of Pembroke. She died in 1621.
2. Niobe, queen of Thebes, grieving the deaths of her seven sons and seven daughters at the hands of Apollo and Diana, continued to weep even after she had been turned to stone.

1. I.e., subject matter.

I sing of Maypoles, hock carts, wassails, wakes,[2]
Of bridegrooms, brides, and of their bridal cakes.
I write of youth, of love, and have access
By these to sing of cleanly wantonness.
I sing of dews, of rains, and, piece by piece,
Of balm, of oil, of spice, and ambergris.
I sing of times trans-shifting, and I write
How roses first came red and lilies white.
I write of groves, of twilights, and I sing
The court of Mab[3] and of the fairy king.
I write of hell; I sing (and ever shall)
Of heaven, and hope to have it after all.

1648

The Vine

I dreamed this mortal part of mine
Was metamorphosed to a vine,
Which crawling one and every way
Enthralled° my dainty Lucia. *imprisoned*
Methought her long small° legs and thighs *slender*
I with my tendrils did surprise;
Her belly, buttocks, and her waist
By my soft nervelets° were embraced. *tendrils*
About her head I writhing hung,
And with rich clusters (hid among
The leaves) her temples I behung,
So that my Lucia seemed to me
Young Bacchus ravished by his tree.[4]
My curls about her neck did crawl,
And arms and hands they did enthrall,
So that she could not freely stir
(All parts there made one prisoner).
But when I crept with leaves to hide
Those parts which maids keep unespied,
Such fleeting pleasures there I took
That with the fancy I awoke;
And found (ah me!) this flesh of mine
More like a stock than like a vine.

1648

Delight in Disorder

A sweet disorder in the dress
Kindles in clothes a wantonness.
A lawn about the shoulders thrown
Into a fine distractiön;
An erring lace, which here and there
Enthralls the crimson stomacher;[5]
A cuff neglectful, and thereby
Ribbons to flow confusedly;

2. The hock cart brought in the last load of the harvest. "Wakes": parish festivals as well as watches over the dead.
3. Queen of the fairies.
4. Bacchus was god of wine; his "tree," of course, is the grape vine.
5. An ornamental piece worn under the open (and often laced) front of a bodice.

A winning wave, deserving note,
In the tempestuous petticoat;
A careless shoestring, in whose tie
I see a wild civility;
Do more bewitch me than when art
Is too precise in every part.

1648

Corinna's Going A-Maying

Get up! get up for shame! the blooming morn
Upon her wings presents the god unshorn.[6]
See how Aurora[7] throws her fair
Fresh-quilted colors through the air:
Get up, sweet slug-a-bed, and see
The dew bespangling herb and tree.
Each flower has wept and bowéd toward the east
Above an hour since, yet you not dressed;
Nay, not so much as out of bed?
When all the birds have matins said,
And sung their thankful hymns, 'tis sin,
Nay, profanation to keep in,
Whenas a thousand virgins on this day
Spring, sooner than the lark, to fetch in May.[8]

Rise, and put on your foliage, and be seen
To come forth, like the springtime, fresh and green,
And sweet as Flora.[9] Take no care
For jewels for your gown or hair;
Fear not; the leaves will strew
Gems in abundance upon you;
Besides, the childhood of the day has kept,
Against[1] you come, some orient pearls unwept;
Come and receive them while the light
Hangs on the dew-locks of the night,
And Titan[2] on the eastern hill
Retires himself, or else stands still
Till you come forth. Wash, dress, be brief in praying:
Few beads[3] are best when once we go a-Maying.

Come, my Corinna, come; and, coming mark
How each field turns a street, each street a park
Made green and trimmed with trees; see how
Devotion gives each house a bough
Or branch: each porch, each door ere this,
An ark, a tabernacle is,
Made up of whitethorn neatly interwove,
As if here were those cooler shades of love.
Can such delights be in the street
And open fields, and we not see 't?

6. I.e., Apollo, god of the sun.
7. Goddess of the dawn.
8. Boughs of white hawthorn, traditionally gathered to decorate streets and houses on May Day.
9. Goddess of flowers.
1. I.e., in readiness for the time when. "Orient": lustrous, glowing.
2. The sun.
3. I.e., prayers.

Come, we'll abroad; and let's obey
The proclamation made for May,
And sin no more, as we have done, by staying;
But, my Corinna, come, let's go a-Maying.

There's not a budding boy or girl this day
But is got up and gone to bring in May;
A deal of youth, ere this, is come
Back, and with whitethorn laden home.
Some have dispatched their cakes and cream
Before that we have left to dream;
And some have wept, and wooed, and plighted troth,
And chose their priest, ere we can cast off sloth.
Many a green-gown has been given,
Many a kiss, both odd and even,
Many a glance, too, has been sent
From out the eye, love's firmament;
Many a jest told of the keys betraying
This night, and locks picked; yet we're not a-Maying.

Come, let us go while we are in our prime,
And take the harmless folly of the time.
We shall grow old apace, and die
Before we know our liberty.
Our life is short, and our days run
As fast away as does the sun;
And, as a vapor or a drop of rain
Once lost, can ne'er be found again;
So when or you or I are made
A fable, song, or fleeting shade,
All love, all liking, all delight
Lies drowned with us in endless night.
Then while time serves, and we are but decaying,
Come, my Corinna, come, let's go a-Maying.

1648

The Lily in a Crystal

You have beheld a smiling rose
When virgins' hands have drawn
O'er it a cobweb-lawn;[4]
And here, you see, this lily shows,
Tombed in a crystal stone,
More fair in this transparent case
Than when it grew alone
And had but single grace.

You see how cream but naked is,
Nor dances in the eye
Without a strawberry;
Or some fine tincture, like to this,
Which draws the sight thereto,
More by that wantoning with it
Than when the paler hue
No mixture did admit.

4. A very fine transparent linen.

You see how amber through the streams
More gently strokes the sight,
With some concealed delight,
Than when he darts his radiant beams
Into the boundless air;
Where either too much light his worth
Doth all at once impair
Or set it little forth.

Put purple grapes or cherries in-
To glass, and they will send
More beauty to commend
Them, from that clean and subtle skin,
Than if they naked stood
And had no other pride at all
But their own flesh and blood
And tinctures natural.

Thus lily, rose, grape, cherry, cream,
And strawberry do stir
More love when they transfer
A weak, a soft, a broken beam,
Than if they should discover
At full their proper excellence,
Without some scene° cast over *veil*
To juggle with the sense.

Thus let this crystalled lily be
A rule, how far to teach
Your nakedness must reach;
And that, no further than we see
Those glaring colors laid
By Art's wise hand, but to this end:
They should obey a shade
Lest they too far extend.

So though y'are white as swan or snow
And have the power to move
A world of men to love,
Yet, when your lawns and silks shall flow,
And that white cloud divide
Into a doubtful twilight, then,
Then will your hidden pride
Raise greater fires in men.

1648

To the Virgins, to Make Much of Time

Gather ye rosebuds while ye may,
Old time is still a-flying;
And this same flower that smiles today
Tomorrow will be dying.

The glorious lamp of heaven, the sun,
The higher he's a-getting,
The sooner will his race be run,
And nearer he's to setting.

That age is best which is the first,
When youth and blood are warmer;
But being spent, the worse, and worst
Times still succeed the former.

Then be not coy, but use your time,
And, while ye may, go marry;
For, having lost but once your prime,
You may forever tarry.

1648

Upon Julia's Breasts

Display thy breasts, my Julia, there let me
Behold that circummortal[5] purity;
Between whose glories, there my lips I'll lay,
Ravished in that fair *Via Lactea*.[6]

1648

Upon a Child That Died

Here she lies, a pretty bud,
Lately made of flesh and blood,
Who as soon fell fast asleep
As her little eyes did peep.
Give her strewings, but not stir
The earth that lightly covers her.

1648

To Daffodils

Fair daffodils, we weep to see
You haste away so soon:
As yet the early-rising sun
Has not attained his noon.
Stay, stay,
Until the hasting day
Has run
But to the evensong;
And, having prayed together, we
Will go with you along.

We have short time to stay as you;
We have as short a spring;
As quick a growth to meet decay,
As you or anything.
We die,
As your hours do, and dry
Away
Like to the summer's rain;
Or as the pearls of morning's dew,
Ne'er to be found again.

1648

5. A coinage by Herrick, literally "around or encompassing what is mortal"; therefore, perhaps, beyond or more than mortal.
6. Milky Way.

Upon Julia's Clothes

Whenas in silks my Julia goes,
Then, then, methinks, how sweetly flows
That liquefaction of her clothes.

Next, when I cast mine eyes, and see
That brave vibration, each way free,
O, how that glittering taketh me!

1648

Upon Prue, His Maid

In this little urn is laid
Prudence Baldwin, once my maid,
From whose happy spark here let
Spring the purple violet.

1648

Upon Ben Jonson

Here lies Jonson with the rest
Of the poets; but the best.
Reader, would'st thou more have known?
Ask his story, not this stone.
That will speak what this can't tell
Of his glory. So farewell.

1648

An Ode for Him

Ah, Ben!
Say how or when
Shall we, thy guests,
Meet at those lyric feasts
Made at the Sun,
The Dog, the Triple Tun,[7]
Where we such clusters had
As made us nobly wild, not mad;
And yet each verse of thine
Outdid the meat, outdid the frolic wine.

My Ben!
Or come again,
Or send to us
Thy wit's great overplus;
But teach us yet
Wisely to husband it,
Lest we that talent spend,
And having once brought to an end
That precious stock, the store
Of such a wit the world should have no more.

1648

7. The names of taverns.

To His Conscience

Can I not sin, but thou wilt be
My private protonotary?[8]
Can I not woo thee to pass by
A short and sweet iniquity?
I'll cast a mist and cloud upon
My delicate transgression,
So utter dark, as that no eye
Shall see the hugged impiety.
Gifts blind the wise,[9] and bribes do please,
And wind° all other witnesses; *pervert*
And wilt not thou, with gold, be tied
To lay thy pen and ink aside?
That in the murk° and tongueless night, *murky*
Wanton I may, and thou not write?
It will not be; and therefore now,
For times to come, I'll make this vow:
From aberrations to live free;
So I'll not fear the judge or thee.

1648

The White Island, or Place of the Blest

In this world, the isle of dreams,
While we sit by sorrow's streams,
Tears and terrors are our themes
Reciting:

But when once from hence we fly,
More and more approaching nigh
Unto young eternity,
Uniting:

In that whiter island, where
Things are evermore sincere;
Candor° here and luster there *whiteness*
Delighting:

There no monstrous fancies shall
Out of hell an horror call,
To create, or cause at all,
Affrighting.

There, in calm and cooling sleep
We our eyes shall never steep,
But eternal watch shall keep,
Attending

Pleasures, such as shall pursue
Me immortalized, and you;
And fresh joys, as never too
Have ending.

1648

8. Chief recorder in a law court.
9. Deuteronomy xvi.19: ". . . a gift doth blind the eyes of the wise, and pervert the words of the righteous."

GEORGE HERBERT
(1593–1633)

Redemption

Having been tenant long to a rich lord,
Not thriving, I resolvéd to be bold,
And make a suit unto him, to afford° *grant*
A new small-rented lease, and cancel the old.

In heaven at his manor I him sought;
They told me there that he was lately gone
About some land, which he had dearly bought
Long since on earth, to take possessiön.

I straight returned, and knowing his great birth,
Sought him accordingly in great resorts;
In cities, theaters, gardens, parks, and courts;
At length I heard a ragged noise and mirth
Of thieves and murderers; there I him espied,
Who straight, *Your suit is granted,* said, and died.

1633

Easter Wings

Lord, who createdst man in wealth and store,° *abundance*
Though foolishly he lost the same,
Decaying more and more
Till he became
Most poor:
With thee
O let me rise
As larks, harmoniously,
And sing this day thy victories:
Then shall the fall further the flight in me.

My tender age in sorrow did begin;
And still with sicknesses and shame
Thou didst so punish sin,
That I became
Most thin.
With thee
Let me combine,
And feel this day[1] thy victory;
For, if I imp[2] my wing on thine,
Affliction shall advance the flight in me.

1633

1. The words "this day," which are superfluous in the metrical scheme of the poem, were perhaps included in the early editions to emphasize the occasion, Easter. They are omitted, however, in the only surviving manuscript book of Herbert's poems.

2. A term from falconry: additional feathers were "imped" or grafted onto the wing of a hawk to improve its powers of flight.

Sin (I)

Lord, with what care hast thou begirt us round!
Parents first season us: then schoolmasters
Deliver us to laws; they send us bound
To rules of reason, holy messengers,
Pulpits and Sundays, sorrow dogging sin,
Afflictions sorted, anguish of all sizes,
Fine nets and stratagems to catch us in,
Bibles laid open, millions of surprises,
Blessings beforehand, ties of gratefulness,
The sound of glory ringing in our ears:
Without, our shame; within, our consciences;
Angels and grace, eternal hopes and fears.
Yet all these fences and their whole array
One cunning bosom-sin blows quite away.

1633

Affliction (I)

When first thou didst entice to thee my heart,
I thought the service brave°: *splendid*
So many joys I writ down for my part,
Besides what I might have
Out of my stock of natural delights,
Augmented with thy gracious benefits.

I lookéd on thy furniture so fine,
And made it fine to me;
Thy glorious household stuff did me entwine,
And 'tice me unto thee.
Such stars I counted mine: both heaven and earth
Paid me my wages in a world of mirth.

What pleasures could I want, whose king I served,
Where joys my fellows were?
Thus argued into hopes, my thoughts reserved
No place for grief or fear;
Therefore my sudden soul caught at the place,
And made her youth and fierceness seek thy face:

At first thou gav'st me milk and sweetnesses;
I had my wish and way:
My days were strawed° with flowers and happiness; *strewed*
There was no month but May.
But with my years sorrow did twist and grow.
And made a party unawares for woe.

My flesh began unto my soul in pain,
"Sicknesses cleave my bones;
Consuming agues dwell in every vein,
And tune my breath to groans."
Sorrow was all my soul; I scarce believed,
Till grief did tell me roundly,° that I lived. *bluntly*

When I got health, thou took'st away my life,
 And more; for my friends die:
My mirth and edge was lost: a blunted knife
 Was of more use than I.
Thus thin and lean without a fence or friend,
I was blown through with every storm and wind.

Whereas my birth and spirit rather took
 The way that takes the town,
Thou didst betray me to a lingering book,
 And wrap me in a gown.
I was entangled in the world of strife,
Before I had the power to change my life.

Yet, for I threatened oft the siege to raise,
 Not simpering all mine age,
Thou often didst with academic praise
 Melt and dissolve my rage.
I took thy sweetened pill, till I came where
I could not go away, nor persevere.

Yet lest perchance I should too happy be
 In my unhappiness,
Turning my purge to food, thou throwest me
 Into more sicknesses.
Thus doth thy power cross-bias[3] me, not making
Thine own gift good, yet me from my ways taking.

Now I am here, what thou wilt do with me
 None of my books will show:
I read, and sigh, and wish I were a tree,
 For sure then I should grow
To fruit or shade; at least, some bird would trust
Her household to me, and I should be just.

Yet, though thou troublest me, I must be meek;
 In weakness must be stout:
Well, I will change the service, and go seek
 Some other master out.
Ah, my dear God! though I am clean forgot,
Let me not love thee, if I love thee not.

1633

Prayer (I)

Prayer, the church's banquet, angels' age,
 God's breath in man returning to his birth,
 The soul in paraphrase, heart in pilgrimage,
The Christian plummet sounding heaven and earth;

Engine against th' Almighty, sinner's tower,
 Reversèd thunder, Christ-side-piercing spear,
 The six-days' world[4] transposing in an hour,
A kind of tune, which all things hear and fear;

3. A term from the game of bowls: to cause the natural path of the ball to be altered.
4. God created the world in six days (Genesis i). Also, of course, the six weekdays might be thought of as a "world" distinct from that of the Sabbath.

Softness, and peace, and joy, and love, and bliss,
Exalted manna, gladness of the best,
Heaven in ordinary,[5] man well dressed,
The Milky Way, the bird of Paradise,

Church bells beyond the stars heard, the soul's blood,
The land of spices; something understood.

1633

Jordan (I)[6]

Who says that fictions only and false hair
Become a verse? Is there in truth no beauty?
Is all good structure in a winding stair?
May no lines pass, except they do their duty
Not to a true, but painted chair?[7]

Is it no verse, except enchanted groves
And sudden arbors[8] shadow coarse-spun lines?
Must purling streams refresh a lover's loves?
Must all be veiled while he that reads, divines,
Catching the sense at two removes?

Shepherds are honest people; let them sing:
Riddle who list, for me, and pull for prime:[9]
I envy no man's nightingale or spring;
Nor let them punish me with loss of rhyme,
Who plainly say, *My God, My King*.

1633

Church Monuments

While that my soul repairs to her devotion,
Here I intomb my flesh, that it betimes
May take acquaintance of this heap of dust;
To which the blast of death's incessant motion,
Fed with the exhalation of our crimes,
Drives all at last. Therefore I gladly trust

My body to this school, that it may learn
To spell his elements, and find his birth
Written in dusty heraldry and lines;
Which dissolution sure doth best discern,
Comparing dust with dust, and earth with earth.
These laugh at jet, and marble put for signs,

To sever the good fellowship of dust,
And spoil the meeting. What shall point out them,
When they shall bow, and kneel, and fall down flat
To kiss those heaps, which now they have in trust?

5. In the everyday course of things. More specifically, *ordinary* also meant a daily allowance of food or an established order or form, as of the divine service.
6. A river in the Holy Land, the cleansing waters of which cured leprosy (II Kings v.10).
7. It was customary to bow or "do one's duty" to the king's chair of state even when unoccupied.
8. One aim of garden design was to incorporate attractive features in such a way that they would be revealed unexpectedly in the course of a walk.
9. Draw for a winning card.

Dear flesh, while I do pray, learn here thy stem
And true descent, that when thou shalt grow fat

And wanton in thy cravings, thou mayst know
That flesh is but the glass which holds the dust
That measures all our time; which also shall
Be crumbled into dust. Mark, here below
How tame these ashes are, how free from lust,
That thou mayst fit thyself against thy fall.

1633

The Windows

Lord, how can man preach thy eternal word?
He is a brittle crazy° glass; *flawed*
Yet in thy temple thou dost him afford
This glorious and transcendent place,
To be a window, through thy grace.

But when thou dost anneal in glass thy story,
Making thy life to shine within
The holy preachers, then the light and glory
More reverend grows, and more doth win;
Which else shows waterish, bleak, and thin.

Doctrine and life, colors and light, in one
When they combine and mingle, bring
A strong regard and awe; but speech alone
Doth vanish like a flaring thing,
And in the ear, not conscience, ring.

1633

Virtue

Sweet day, so cool, so calm, so bright,
The bridal of the earth and sky:
The dew shall weep thy fall tonight;
For thou must die.

Sweet rose, whose hue, angry and brave,
Bids the rash gazer wipe his eye:
Thy root is ever in its grave,
And thou must die.

Sweet spring, full of sweet days and roses,
A box where sweets° compacted lie; *perfumes*
My music shows ye have your closes,[1]
And all must die.

Only a sweet and virtuous soul,
Like seasoned timber, never gives;
But though the whole world turn to coal,[2]
Then chiefly lives.

1633

1. A close is a cadence, the conclusion of a musical strain.

2. An allusion to Judgment Day, when the world will end in a general conflagration.

Artillery

As I one evening sat before my cell,
Methought[3] a star did shoot into my lap.
I rose and shook my clothes, as knowing well
That from small fires comes oft no small mishap;
When suddenly I heard one say,
"Do as thou usest, disobey,
Expel good motions from thy breast,
Which have the face of fire, but end in rest."

I, who had heard of music in the spheres,
But not of speech in stars, began to muse;
But turning to my God, whose ministers
The stars and all things are: "If I refuse,
Dread Lord," said I, "so oft my good,
Then I refuse not ev'n with blood
To wash away my stubborn thought;
For I will do or suffer what I ought.

"But I have also stars and shooters too,
Born where thy servants both artilleries use.
My tears and prayers night and day do woo
And work up to thee; yet thou dost refuse.
Not but I am (I must say still)
Much more obliged to do thy will
Than thou to grant mine; but because
Thy promise now hath ev'n set thee thy laws.

"Then we are shooters both, and thou dost deign
To enter combat with us, and contest
With thine own clay. But I would parley fain:
Shun not my arrows, and behold my breast.
Yet if thou shunnest, I am thine:
I must be so, if I am mine.
There is no articling° with thee: *negotiating*
I am but finite, yet thine infinitely."

1633

The Collar

I struck the board° and cried, "No more; *table*
I will abroad!
What? shall I ever sigh and pine?
My lines and life are free, free as the road,
Loose as the wind, as large as store.° *abundance*
Shall I be still in suit?
Have I no harvest but a thorn
To let me blood, and not restore
What I have lost with cordial° fruit? *life-giving*
Sure there was wine
Before my sighs did dry it; there was corn
Before my tears did drown it.

3. It seemed to me.

Is the year only lost to me?
Have I no bays[4] to crown it,
No flowers, no garlands gay? All blasted?
All wasted?
Not so, my heart; but there is fruit,
And thou hast hands.
Recover all thy sigh-blown age
On double pleasures: leave thy cold dispute
Of what is fit and not. Forsake thy cage,
Thy rope of sands,
Which petty thoughts have made, and made to thee
Good cable, to enforce and draw,
And be thy law,
While thou didst wink and wouldst not see.
Away! take heed;
I will abroad.
Call in thy death's-head[5] there; tie up thy fears.
He that forbears
To suit and serve his need,
Deserves his load."
But as I raved and grew more fierce and wild
At every word,
Methought I heard one calling, *Child!*
And I replied, *My Lord.*

1633

The Pulley

When God at first made man,
Having a glass of blessings standing by,
"Let us," said he, "pour on him all we can.
Let the world's riches, which disperséd lie,
Contract into a span."

So strength first made a way;
Then beauty flowed, then wisdom, honor, pleasure.
When almost all was out, God made a stay,
Perceiving that, alone of all his treasure,
Rest in the bottom lay.

"For if I should," said he,
"Bestow this jewel also on my creature,
He would adore my gifts instead of me,
And rest in Nature, not the God of Nature;
So both should losers be.

"Yet let him keep the rest,
But keep them with repining restlessness.
Let him be rich and weary, that at least,
If goodness lead him not, yet weariness
May toss him to my breast."

1633

4. A laurel garland symbolizing honor or renown.
5. A representation of a human skull intended to serve as a *memento mori,* a reminder that all men must die.

The Flower

How fresh, oh Lord, how sweet and clean
Are thy returns! even as the flowers in spring;
To which, besides their own demean,[6]
The late-past frosts tributes of pleasure bring.
Grief melts away
Like snow in May,
As if there were no such cold thing.

Who would have thought my shriveled heart
Could have have recovered greenness? It was gone
Quite underground; as flowers depart
To see their mother-root, when they have blown,° *bloomed*
Where they together
All the hard weather,
Dead to the world, keep house unknown.

These are thy wonders, Lord of power,
Killing and quickening, bringing down to hell
And up to heaven in an hour;
Making a chiming of a passing-bell[7]
We say amiss
This or that is:
Thy word is all, if we could spell.

Oh that I once past changing were,
Fast in thy Paradise, where no flower can wither!
Many a spring I shoot up fair,
Offering° at heaven, growing and groaning thither; *aiming*
Nor doth my flower
Want a spring shower,
My sins and I joining together.

But while I grow in a straight line,
Still upwards bent, as if heaven were mine own,
Thy anger comes, and I decline:
What frost to that? what pole is not the zone
Where all things burn,
When thou dost turn,
And the least frown of thine is shown?

And now in age I bud again,
After so many deaths I live and write;
I once more smell the dew and rain,
And relish versing. Oh, my only light,
It cannot be
That I am he
On whom thy tempests fell all night.

These are thy wonders, Lord of love,
To make us see we are but flowers that glide;
Which when we once can find and prove,
Thou hast a garden for us where to bide;

6. Demeanor; possibly also *demesne*, "estate."
7. A single bell tolled to announce a death.

Who would be more,
Swelling through store,° *possessions*
Forfeit their Paradise by their pride.

1633

The Forerunners

The harbingers[8] are come. See, see their mark:
White is their color, and behold my head.
But must they have my brain? Must they dispark[9]
Those sparkling notions, which therein were bred?
Must dullness turn me to a clod?
Yet have they left me, *Thou art still my God.*

Good men ye be, to leave me my best room,
Ev'n all my heart, and what is lodgéd there:
I pass not,° I, what of the rest become, *I care not*
So *Thou art still my God* be out of fear.
He will be pleaséd with that ditty;
And if I please him, I write fine and witty.

Farewell sweet phrases, lovely metaphors.
But will ye leave me thus? When ye before
Of stews and brothels only knew the doors,
Then did I wash you with my tears, and more,
Brought you to church well dressed and clad:
My God must have my best, ev'n all I had.

Lovely enchanting language, sugar-cane,
Honey of roses, wither wilt thou fly?
Hath some fond lover 'ticed thee to thy bane?
And wilt thou leave the church and love a sty?
Fie, thou wilt soil thy broidered coat,
And hurt thyself, and him that sings the note.

Let foolish lovers, if they will love dung,
With canvas, not with arras, clothe their shame:
Let folly speak in her own native tongue.
True beauty dwells on high: ours is a flame
But borrowed thence to light us thither.
Beauty and beauteous words should go together.

Yet if you go, I pass not; take your way:
For *Thou art still my God* is all that ye
Perhaps with more embellishment can say.
Go, birds of spring: let winter have his fee;
Let a bleak paleness chalk the door,
So all within be livelier than before.

1633

Love (III)

Love bade me welcome: yet my soul drew back,
Guilty of dust and sin.

8. The advance agents of the king and his party on a royal progress or tour. They marked with chalk the doors of those dwellings where the court would be accommodated.

9. I.e., *dis-park,* to turn out, as of a park; there may also be a play on *dis-spark* (from "sparkling notions" in the next line).

But quick-eyed Love, observing me grow slack
From my first entrance in,
Drew nearer to me, sweetly questioning
If I lacked anything.

"A guest," I answered, "worthy to be here":
Love said, "You shall be he."
"I, the unkind, ungrateful? Ah, my dear,
I cannot look on thee."
Love took my hand, and smiling did reply,
"Who made the eyes but I?"

"Truth, Lord; but I have marred them; let my shame
Go where it doth deserve."
"And know you not," says Love, "who bore the blame?"
"My dear, then I will serve."
"You must sit down," says Love, "and taste my meat."
So I did sit and eat.

1633

JAMES SHIRLEY
(1596–1666)

The Glories of Our Blood and State

The glories of our blood and state
Are shadows, not substantial things;
There is no armor against fate;
Death lays his icy hand on kings.
Scepter and crown
Must tumble down
And in the dust be equal made
With the poor crooked scythe and spade.

Some men with swords may reap the field
And plant fresh laurels where they kill,
But their strong nerves at last must yield;
They tame but one another still.
Early or late
They stoop to fate
And must give up their murmuring breath,
When they, pale captives, creep to death.

The garlands wither on your brow,
Then boast no more your mighty deeds;
Upon death's purple altar now
See where the victor-victim bleeds.
Your heads must come
To the cold tomb;
Only the actions of the just
Smell sweet and blossom in their dust.

1659

THOMAS CAREW
(1598?–1639?)

A Song

Ask me no more where Jove bestows,
When June is past, the fading rose;
For in your beauty's orient deep,
These flowers, as in their causes,[1] sleep.

Ask me no more whither do stray
The golden atoms of the day;
For in pure love heaven did prepare
Those powders to enrich your hair.

Ask me no more whither doth haste
The nightingale when May is past;
For in your sweet dividing[2] throat
She winters, and keeps warm her note.

Ask me no more where those stars light,
That downwards fall in dead of night;
For in your eyes they sit, and there
Fixéd become, as in their sphere.

Ask me no more if east or west
The phoenix[3] builds her spicy nest;
For unto you at last she flies,
And in your fragrant bosom dies.

1640

The Spring

Now that the winter's gone, the earth hath lost
Her snow-white robes, and now no more the frost
Candies the grass, or casts an icy cream
Upon the silver lake or crystal stream;
But the warm sun thaws the benumbéd earth
And makes it tender, gives a sacred birth
To the dead swallow, wakes in hollow tree
The drowsy cuckoo and the humble bee.
Now do a choir of chirping minstrels bring
In triumph to the world the youthful spring.
The valleys, hills, and woods in rich array
Welcome the coming of the long'd-for May.
Now all things smile: only my love doth lour,
Nor hath the scalding noonday sun the power
To melt that marble ice which still doth hold
Her heart congeal'd, and makes her pity cold.

1. Aristotelian philosophy regarded that from which a thing is made or comes into being as the "material cause" of the thing.
2. Executing a "division," an embellished musical phrase.
3. A legendary bird, the only one of its kind, represented as living five hundred years in the Arabian desert, being consumed in fire, then rising anew from its own ashes.

The ox, which lately did for shelter fly
Into the stall, doth now securely lie
In open fields; and love no more is made
By the fireside, but in the cooler shade:
Amyntas now doth with his Chloris[4] sleep
Under a sycamore, and all things keep
Time with the season. Only she doth carry
June in her eyes, in her heart January.

1640

Song. To My Inconstant Mistress

When thou, poor excommunicate
From all the joys of love, shalt see
The full reward and glorious fate
Which my strong faith shall purchase me,
Then curse thine own inconstancy.

A fairer hand than thine shall cure
That heart which thy false oaths did wound,
And to my soul a soul more pure
Than thine shall by Love's hand be bound,
And both with equal glory crown'd.

Then shalt thou weep, entreat, complain
To Love, as I did once to thee;
When all thy tears shall be as vain
As mine were then, for thou shalt be
Damned for thy false apostasy.

1640

An Elegy upon the Death of the Dean of Paul's, Dr. John Donne

Can we not force from widowed poetry,
Now thou art dead, great Donne, one elegy
To crown thy hearse? Why yet did we not trust,
Though with unkneaded dough-baked prose, thy dust,
Such as the unscissored[5] lect'rer from the flower
Of fading rhetoric, short-lived as his hour,
Dry as the sand that measures it,[6] should lay
Upon the ashes on the funeral day?
Have we nor tune, nor voice? Didst thou dispense
Through all our language both the words and sense?
'Tis a sad truth. The pulpit may her plain
And sober Christian precepts still retain;
Doctrines it may, and wholesome uses, frame,
Grave homilies and lectures; but the flame
Of thy brave soul, that shot such heat and light
As burnt our earth and made our darkness bright,
Committed holy rapes upon our will,
Did through the eye the melting heart distil,

4. Conventional names for a shepherd and shepherdess.

5. I.e., with uncut hair.

6. I.e., the sand in an hourglass.

And the deep knowledge of dark truths so teach
As sense might judge what fancy could not reach,
Must be desired forever. So the fire
That fills with spirit and heat the Delphic choir,[7]
Which, kindled first by thy Promethean[8] breath,
Glowed here a while, lies quenched now in thy death.
The Muses' garden, with pedantic weeds
O'erspread, was purged by thee; the lazy seeds
Of servile imitation thrown away,
And fresh invention planted; thou didst pay
The debts of our penurious bankrupt age;
Licentious thefts, that make poetic rage
A mimic fury, when our souls must be
Possessed, or with Anacreon's ecstasy,
Or Pindar's,[9] not their own; the subtle cheat
Of sly exchanges, and the juggling feat
Of two-edged words, or whatsoever wrong
By ours was done the Greek or Latin tongue,
Thou hast redeemed, and opened us a mine
Of rich and pregnant fancy, drawn a line
Of masculine expression, which had good
Old Orpheus[1] seen, or all the ancient brood
Our superstitious fools admire, and hold
Their lead more precious than thy burnished gold,
Thou hadst been their exchequer, and no more
They in each other's dung had searched for ore.
Thou shalt yield no precédence, but of time
And the blind fate of language, whose tuned chime
More charms the outward sense; yet thou mayest claim
From so great disadvantage greater fame,
Since to the awe of thy imperious wit
Our troublesome language bends, made only fit
With her tough thick-ribbed hoops, to gird about
Thy giant fancy, which had proved too stout
For their soft melting phrases. As in time
They had the start, so did they cull the prime
Buds of invention many a hundred year,
And left the rifled fields, besides the fear
To touch their harvest; yet from those bare lands
Of what is only thine, thy only hands
(And that their smallest work) have gleanéd more
Than all those times and tongues could reap before.
    But thou art gone, and thy strict laws will be
Too hard for libertines in poetry.
They will recall the goodly exiled train
Of gods and goddesses, which in thy just reign
Were banished nobler poems; now with these
The silenced tales i' th' *Metamorphoses*[2]
Shall stuff their lines and swell the windy page,
Till verse, refined by thee in this last age,
Turn ballad-rhyme, or those old idols be
Adored again with new apostasy.

7. Ie., the choir of poets. Delphi was the site of an oracle of Apollo, the god of poetry.
8. The fire which Prometheus stole from the gods for the benefit of mankind was sometimes interpreted as man's vital spirit.
9. Anacreon and Pindar were famous Greek poets.
1. In Greek mythology, the son of one of the Muses and the greatest of poets and musicians.
2. Earlier poets had drawn heavily on the stories in Ovid's *Metamorphoses* for the materials of their poetry.

O pardon me, that break with untuned verse
The reverend silence that attends thy hearse,
Whose solemn awful murmurs were to thee,
More than these faint lines, a loud elegy,
That did proclaim in a dumb eloquence
The death of all the arts, whose influence,
Grown feeble, in these panting numbers lies
Gasping short-winded accents, and so dies:
So doth the swiftly turning wheel not stand
In th' instant we withdraw the moving hand,
But some small time retain a faint weak course
By virtue of the first impulsive force;
And so whilst I cast on thy funeral pile
Thy crown of bays,[3] oh, let it crack awhile
And spit disdain, till the devouring flashes
Suck all the moisture up; then turn to ashes.
I will not draw thee envy to engross
All thy perfections, or weep all the loss;
Those are too numerous for one elegy,
And this too great to be expressed by me.
Let others carve the rest; it shall suffice
I on thy grave this epitaph incise:

Here lies a king, that ruled as he thought fit
The universal monarchy of wit;
Here lie two flamens,° and both those the best: *priests*
Apollo's first, at last the true God's priest.

1633, 1640

EDMUND WALLER
(1607–1687)

Song

Go, lovely rose!
Tell her that wastes her time and me
That now she knows,
When I resemble° her to thee, *liken*
How sweet and fair she seems to be.

Tell her that's young,
And shuns to have her graces spied,
That hadst thou sprung
In deserts, where no men abide,
Thou must have uncommended died.

Small is the worth
Of beauty from the light retired;
Bid her come forth,
Suffer herself to be desired,
And not blush so to be admired.

3. In classical times a crown of bays or laurel was the reward of the victor in a poetic competition.

Then die! that she
The common fate of all things rare
May read in thee;
How small a part of time they share
That are so wondrous sweet and fair!

1645

JOHN MILTON (1608–1674)

Lycidas

IN THIS MONODY[1] THE AUTHOR BEWAILS A LEARNED FRIEND, UNFORTUNATELY DROWNED IN HIS PASSAGE FROM CHESTER ON THE IRISH SEAS, 1637. AND BY OCCASION FORETELLS THE RUIN OF OUR CORRUPTED CLERGY, THEN IN THEIR HEIGHT.

Yet once more, O ye laurels[2] and once more
Ye myrtles brown,° with ivy never sere,° *dark / withered*
I come to pluck your berries harsh and crude,° *unripe*
And with forced fingers rude,
Shatter your leaves before the mellowing year.
Bitter constraint, and sad occasion dear,° *severe*
Compels me to disturb your season due;
For Lycidas is dead, dead ere his prime,
Young Lycidas, and hath not left his peer.
Who would not sing for Lycidas? He knew
Himself to sing, and build the lofty rhyme.
He must not float upon his watery bier
Unwept, and welter° to the parching wind, *roll about*
Without the meed° of some melodious tear. *tribute*
Begin then, sisters of the sacred well[3]
That from beneath the seat of Jove doth spring,
Begin, and somewhat loudly sweep the string.
Hence with denial vain, and coy excuse;
So may some gentle Muse° *poet*
With lucky words favor my destined urn,
And as he passes turn,
And bid fair peace be to my sable shroud.
For we were nursed upon the selfsame hill,
Fed the same flock, by fountain, shade, and rill.
Together both, ere the high lawns° appeared *pastures*
Under the opening eyelids of the morn,
We drove afield, and both together heard
What time the grayfly winds her sultry horn,
Battening° our flocks with the fresh dews of night, *fattening*
Oft till the star that rose at evening bright
Toward Heaven's descent had sloped his westering wheel.
Meanwhile the rural ditties were not mute,
Tempered to th' oaten flute,

1. An elegy or dirge sung by a single voice. The "learned friend" was Edward King, Milton's fellow student at Cambridge.
2. The laurel, myrtle, and ivy were all traditional materials for poetic garlands.
3. The Muses. The well sacred to them was Aganippe, at the foot of Mt. Helicon, where they danced about the altar of Jove.

Rough satyrs danced, and fauns with cloven heel
From the glad sound would not be absent long,
And old Damoetas[4] loved to hear our song.
But O the heavy change, now thou art gone,
Now thou art gone, and never must return!
Thee, shepherd, thee the woods and desert caves,
With wild thyme and the gadding° vine o'ergrown, *wandering*
And all their echoes mourn.
The willows and the hazel copses green
Shall now no more be seen,
Fanning their joyous leaves to thy soft lays.
As killing as the canker to the rose,
Or taint-worm to the weanling herds that graze,
Or frost to flowers that their gay wardrobe wear,
When first the white thorn blows;° *blooms*
Such, Lycidas, thy loss to shepherd's ear.
Where were ye, nymphs, when the remorseless deep
Closed o'er the head of your loved Lycidas?
For neither were ye playing on the steep,
Where your old Bards, the famous Druids lie,
Nor on the shaggy top of Mona high,
Nor yet where Deva spreads her wizard stream:[5]
Ay me! I fondly° dream— *foolishly*
Had ye been there—for what could that have done?
What could the Muse[6] herself that Orpheus bore,
The Muse herself, for her inchanting son
Whom universal Nature did lament,
When by the rout that made the hideous roar,
His gory visage down the stream was sent,
Down the swift Hebrus to the Lesbian shore?
Alas! What boots° it with uncessant care *profits*
To tend the homely slighted shepherd's trade,
And strictly meditate the thankless Muse?
Were it not better done as others use,
To sport with Amaryllis[7] in the shade,
Or with the tangles of Neaera's hair?
Fame is the spur that the clear spirit doth raise
(That last infirmity of noble mind)
To scorn delights, and live laborious days;
But the fair guerdon° when we hope to find, *reward*
And think to burst out into sudden blaze,
Comes the blind Fury[8] with th' abhorréd shears,
And slits the thin spun life. "But not the praise,"
Phoebus[9] replied, and touched my trembling ears;
"Fame is no plant that grows on mortal soil,
Nor in the glistering foil[1]
Set off to th' world, nor in broad rumor lies,
But lives and spreads aloft by those pure eyes,

4. A conventional pastoral name, here perhaps referring to one of the tutors at Cambridge.
5. The "steep" is probably the mountain Kerig-y-Druidion in northern Wales, a Druid burial ground. Mona is the Isle of Anglesey, Deva the River Dee, called "wizard" because its changes of course were supposed to foretell the country's fortune. All three places are just south of that part of the Irish Sea where King was drowned.
6. Calliope, the Muse of epic poetry. Her son Orpheus, the greatest of all poets and musicians, was torn limb from limb by a band of Thracian Maenads, who flung his head into the River Hebrus, whence it drifted across the Aegean to the island of Lesbos.
7. A conventional pastoral name, like Neaera in the next line.
8. Atropos, the third of the three Fates, who cut the thread of a man's life after it had been spun and measured by her sisters.
9. Apollo, god of poetic inspiration.
1. The setting for a gem, especially one that enhances the appearance of an inferior or false stone.

And perfect witness of all-judging Jove;
As he pronounces lastly on each deed,
Of so much fame in Heaven expect thy meed."
O fountain Arethuse,[2] and thou honored flood,
Smooth-sliding Mincius, crowned with vocal reeds,
That strain I heard was of a higher mood.
But now my oat[3] proceeds,
And listens to the herald of the sea[4]
That came in Neptune's plea.
He asked the waves, and asked the felon winds,
"What hard mishap hath doomed this gentle swain?"
And questioned every gust of rugged wings
That blows from off each beakèd promontory;
They knew not of his story,
And sage Hippotades[5] their answer brings,
That not a blast was from his dungeon strayed,
The air was calm, and on the level brine,
Sleek Panope[6] with all her sisters played.
It was that fatal and perfidious bark
Built in th' eclipse, and rigged with curses dark,
That sunk so low that sacred head of thine.
Next Camus,[7] reverend sire, went footing slow,
His mantle hairy, and his bonnet sedge,
Inwrought with figures dim, and on the edge
Like to that sanguine flower inscribed with woe.[8]
"Ah! who hath reft," quoth he, "my dearest pledge?"
Last came and last did go
The pilot of the Galilean lake,[9]
Two massy keys he bore of metals twain
(The golden opes, the iron shuts amain).
He shook his mitered locks, and stern bespake:
"How well could I have spared for thee, young swain,
Enow° of such as for their bellies' sake, *enough*
Creep and intrude, and climb into the fold!
Of other care they little reckoning make,
Than how to scramble at the shearers' feast,
And shove away the worthy bidden guest.
Blind mouths! That scarce themselves know how to hold
A sheep-hook, or have learned aught else the least
That to the faithful herdsman's art belongs!
What recks it them?[1] What need they? They are sped;
And when they list, their lean and flashy° songs *insipid*
Grate on their scrannel° pipes of wretched straw. *meager*
The hungry sheep look up, and are not fed,
But swoln with wind, and the rank mist they draw,
Rot inwardly, and foul contagion spread,
Besides what the grim wolf with privy paw[2]
Daily devours apace, and nothing said.

2. A fountain in Sicily, associated with the pastoral poems of Theocritus. The Mincius is a river in Italy described in one of Virgil's pastorals.
3. Oaten pipe, song.
4. The merman Triton, who came to plead his master Neptune's innocence of Lycidas' death.
5. Aeolus, son of Hippotas and god of the winds.
6. One of the Nereids, daughters of Nereus, the Old Man of the Sea.
7. The god of the river Cam, representing Cambridge University.
8. The hyacinth, created by Apollo from the blood of the youth Hyacinthus, whom he had killed by accident with a discus. Certain markings on the flower are supposed to be the letters AIAI ("Alas, alas!"), inscribed there by Apollo.
9. St. Peter, the Galilean fisherman, to whom Christ promised the keys of the kingdom of heaven (Matthew xvi.19). He wears the bishop's miter (line 112) as the first head of Christ's church.
1. What does it matter to them?
2. I.e., anti-Protestant forces, either Roman Catholic or Anglican.

But that two-handed engine at the door
Stands ready to smite once, and smite no more."[3]
Return, Alpheus,[4] the dread voice is past,
That shrunk thy streams; return, Sicilian muse,
And call the vales, and bid them hither cast
Their bells and flowerets of a thousand hues.
Ye valleys low where the mild whispers use,° *frequent*
Of shades and wanton winds, and gushing brooks,
On whose fresh lap the swart star[5] sparely looks,
Throw hither all your quaint enameled eyes,
That on the green turf suck the honeyed showers,
And purple all the ground with vernal flowers.
Bring the rathe° primrose that forsaken dies, *early*
The tufted crow-toe, and pale jessamine,
The white pink, and the pansy freaked° with jet, *mottled*
The glowing violet,
The musk-rose, and the well attired woodbine.
With cowslips wan that hang the pensive head,
And every flower that sad embroidery wears:
Bid amaranthus[6] all his beauty shed,
And daffadillies fill their cups with tears,
To strew the laureate hearse° where Lycid lies. *bier*
For so to interpose a little ease,
Let our frail thoughts dally with false surmise.
Ay me! Whilst thee the shores and sounding seas
Wash far away, where'er thy bones are hurled,
Whether beyond the stormy Hebrides,
Where thou perhaps under the whelming tide
Visit'st the bottom of the monstrous world;
Or whether thou, to our moist vows denied,
Sleep'st by the fable of Bellerus old,[7]
Where the great vision of the guarded mount
Looks toward Namancos and Bayona's hold;
Look homeward angel now, and melt with ruth:° *pity*
And, O ye dolphins, waft the hapless youth.
Weep no more, woeful shepherds, weep no more,
For Lycidas your sorrow is not dead,
Sunk though he be beneath the watery floor,
So sinks the day-star° in the ocean bed, *sun*
And yet anon repairs his drooping head,
And tricks° his beams, and with new-spangled ore,° *dresses / gold*
Flames in the forehead of the morning sky:
So Lycidas sunk low, but mounted high,
Through the dear might of him that walked the waves,
Where other groves, and other streams along,
With nectar pure his oozy locks he laves,
And hears the unexpressive° nuptial song,[8] *inexpressible*
In the blest kingdoms meek of joy and love.

3. A satisfactory explanation of these two lines has yet to be made, although many have been attempted. Most have taken the "two-handed engine" as an instrument of retribution against those clergy who neglect their responsibilities (such as the ax of reformation; the two-handed sword of the archangel Michael; the two houses of Parliament; death and damnation).
4. A river god who fell in love with the nymph Arethusa. When she fled to Sicily he pursued her by diving under the sea and coming up in the island. There she was turned into a fountain (see line 85) and their waters mingled.
5. Sirius, the Dog Star, thought to have a swart or malignant influence.
6. A legendary flower, supposed never to fade.
7. A legendary figure supposedly buried at Land's End in Cornwall. The "mount" of the next line is St. Michael's Mount at the tip of Land's End, "guarded" by the archangel Michael, who gazes southward toward Nemancos and the stronghold of Bayona in northwestern Spain.
8. Milton may have been thinking of the "marriage supper of the Lamb" mentioned in Revelation xix.9.

There entertain him all the saints above,
In solemn troops and sweet societies
That sing, and singing in their glory move,
And wipe the tears forever from his eyes.
Now, Lycidas, the shepherds weep no more;
Henceforth thou art the genius° of the shore, *local divinity*
In thy large recompense, and shalt be good
To all that wander in that perilous flood.
Thus sang the uncouth° swain to th' oaks and rills, *unlettered*
While the still morn went out with sandals gray;
He touched the tender stops of various quills,[9]
With eager thought warbling his Doric[1] lay:
And now the sun had stretched out all the hills,
And now was dropped into the western bay;
At last he rose, and twitched his mantle blue:
Tomorrow to fresh woods, and pastures new.

1637

On the Morning of Christ's Nativity

1

This is the month, and this the happy morn,
Wherein the Son of Heaven's Eternal King,
Of wedded maid and virgin mother born,
Our great redemption from above did bring;
For so the holy sages[2] once did sing,
That he our deadly forfeit[3] should release,
And with his Father work us a perpetual peace.

2

That glorious form, that light unsufferable,
And that far-beaming blaze of majesty,
Wherewith he wont at Heaven's high council-table
To sit the midst of Trinal Unity,
He laid aside, and, here with us to be,
Forsook the courts of everlasting day,
And chose with us a darksome house of mortal clay.

3

Say, Heavenly Muse,[4] shall not thy sacred vein
Afford a present to the Infant God?
Hast thou no verse, no hymn, or solemn strain,
To welcome him to this his new abode,
Now while the heaven, by the Sun's team untrod,
Hath took no print of the approaching light,
And all the spangled host keep watch in squadrons bright?

4

See how from far upon the eastern road
The star-led wizards[5] haste with odors sweet!
Oh run, prevent° them with thy humble ode, *go before*
And lay it lowly at his blessed feet;
Have thou the honor first thy Lord to greet,
And join thy voice unto the angel choir
From out his secret altar touched with hallowed fire.

9. The individual reeds in a set of Panpipes.
1. Pastoral, because Doric was the dialect of the Greek pastoral writers Theocritus, Bion, and Moschus.
2. I.e., the Hebrew prophets.
3. The penalty of death, occasioned by the sin of Adam.
4. Urania, the Muse of Astronomy, later identified with divine wisdom and treated by Milton as the source of creative inspiration.
5. The "wise men from the east" (Matthew ii.1).

The Hymn

1

It was the winter wild,
While the heaven-born child
All meanly wrapt in the rude manger lies;
Nature, in awe to him,
Had doffed her gaudy trim,
With her great Master so to sympathize:
It was no season then for her
To wanton with the Sun, her lusty paramour.

2

Only with speeches fair
She woos the gentle air
To hide her guilty front with innocent snow,
And on her naked shame,
Pollute with sinful blame,
The saintly veil of maiden white to throw;
Confounded, that her Maker's eyes
Should look so near upon her foul deformities.

3

But he, her fears to cease,
Sent down the meek-eyed Peace:
She, crowned with olive green, came softly sliding
Down through the turning sphere,[6]
His ready harbinger,
With turtle° wing the amorous clouds dividing; *dove*
And, waving wide her myrtle wand,
She strikes a universal peace through sea and land.

4

No war, or battle's sound,
Was heard the world around;
The idle spear and shield were high uphung;
The hookéd chariot[7] stood,
Unstained with hostile blood;
The trumpet spake not to the arméd throng;
And kings sat still with awful eye,
As if they surely knew their sovran Lord was by.

5

But peaceful was the night
Wherein the Prince of Light
His reign of peace upon the earth began.
The winds, with wonder whist,° *hushed*
Smoothly the waters kissed,
Whispering new joys to the mild Ocean,
Who now hath quite forgot to rave,
While birds of calm[8] sit brooding on the charméd wave.

6

The stars, with deep amaze,
Stand fixed in steadfast gaze,
Bending one way their precious influence,[9]
And will not take their flight,

6. The heavens as a whole, which "turn" once daily about the earth because of the earth's rotation.

7. War chariots were sometimes armed with sickle-like hooks projecting from the hubs of the wheels.

8. Halcyons or kingfishers, which in ancient times were believed to build floating nests at sea about the time of the winter solstice, and to calm the waves during the incubation of their young.

9. Medieval astrologers believed that stars emitted an ethereal liquid ("influence") that had the power to nourish or otherwise affect all things on earth.

For all the morning light,
Or Lucifer[1] that often warned them thence;
But in their glimmering orbs[2] did glow,
Until their Lord himself bespake, and bid them go.

7

And, though the shady gloom
Had given day her room,
The Sun himself withheld his wonted speed,
And hid his head for shame,
As his inferior flame
The new-enlightened world no more should need:
He saw a greater Sun appear
Than his bright throne or burning axletree could bear.

8

The shepherds on the lawn,° *meadow*
Or ere the point of dawn,
Sat simply chatting in a rustic row;
Full little thought they than° *then*
That the mighty Pan[3]
Was kindly come to live with them below:
Perhaps their loves, or else their sheep,
Was all that did their silly° thoughts so busy keep. *simple*

9

When such music sweet
Their hearts and ears did greet
As never was by mortal finger strook,° *struck*
Divinely-warbled voice
Answering the stringéd noise,
As all their souls in blissful rapture took:
The air, such pleasure loth to lose,
With thousand echoes still prolongs each heavenly close.° *cadence*

10

Nature, that heard such sound
Beneath the hollow round
Of Cynthia's seat[4] the airy region thrilling,
Now was almost won
To think her part was done,
And that her reign had here its last fulfilling:
She knew such harmony alone
Could hold all Heaven and Earth in happier uniön.

11

At last surrounds their sight
A globe of circular light,
That with long beams the shamefaced Night arrayed;
The helméd cherubim
And sworded seraphim[5]
Are seen in glittering ranks with wings displayed,
Harping loud and solemn quire,
With unexpressive° notes, to Heaven's new-born Heir. *inexpressible*

12

Such music (as 'tis said)
Before was never made,

1. Probably the morning star, although Milton sometimes uses the word for the sun.
2. The concentric crystalline spheres of Ptolemaic astronomy. Each sphere was supposed to contain one or more of the heavenly bodies in its surface and to revolve about the earth.
3. The Greek shepherd god Pan (whose name means "all") was often associated with Christ.
4. I.e., beneath the sphere of the moon.
5. Seraphim and cherubim (both are plural forms) are the two highest of the nine orders of angels in the medieval classification.

But when of old the sons of morning sung,[6]
While the Creator great
His constellations set,
And the well-balanced world on hinges hung,
And cast the dark foundations deep,
And bid the weltering waves their oozy channel keep.

13

Ring out, ye crystal spheres,
Once bless our human ears,
If ye have power to touch our senses so;
And let your silver chime
Move in melodious time;
And let the bass of heaven's deep organ blow;
And with your ninefold harmony
Make up full consort to th' angelic symphony.

14

For, if such holy song
Enwrap our fancy long,
Time will run back and fetch the age of gold;[7]
And speckled vanity
Will sicken soon and die;
And leprous sin will melt from earthly mold;
And Hell itself will pass away,
And leave her dolorous mansions to the peering day.

15

Yea, Truth and Justice then
Will down return to men,
Orbed in a rainbow; and, like glories wearing,
Mercy will sit between,
Throned in celestial sheen,
With radiant feet the tissued clouds down steering;
And Heaven, as at some festival,
Will open wide the gates of her high palace-hall.

16

But wisest Fate says no,
This must not yet be so;
The Babe lies yet in smiling infancy
That on the bitter cross
Must redeem our loss,
So both himself and us to glorify:
Yet first, to those ychained[8] in sleep,
The wakeful° trump of doom must thunder through the deep, *awakening*

17

With such a horrid clang
As on Mount Sinai rang,[9]
While the red fire and smoldering clouds outbrake:
The aged Earth, aghast,
With terror of that blast,
Shall from the surface to the center shake,
When, at the world's last sessiön,
The dreadful Judge in middle air shall spread his throne.

6. Job speaks of the creation of the universe as the time "when the morning stars sang together, and all the sons of God shouted for joy" (Job xxxviii.7).

7. The Romans believed that Saturn, after his dethronement by Jupiter, fled to Italy and there brought in the Golden Age, a time of perfect peace and happiness.

8. Milton uses the archaic form of the past participle, common in Chaucer and imitated by Spenser, in which *y-* represents a reduced form of the Old English prefix *ge-*.

9. Moses received the Ten Commandments on Mount Sinai: "* * * there were thunders and lightnings * * * and the voice of the trumpet exceeding loud" (Exodus xix.16).

18

And then at last our bliss
Full and perfect is,
But now begins; for from this happy day
Th' old Dragon° under ground, *Satan*
In straiter limits bound,
Not half so far casts his usurpéd sway,
And, wroth to see his kingdom fail,
Swinges° the scaly horror of his folded tail. *lashes*

19

The Oracles are dumb;
No voice or hideous hum
Runs through the archéd roof in words deceiving.
Apollo from his shrine
Can no more divine,
With hollow shriek the steep of Delphos leaving.
No nightly trance, or breathéd spell,
Inspires the pale-eyed priest from the prophetic cell.

20

The lonely mountains o'er,
And the resounding shore,
A voice of weeping heard and loud lament;
From haunted spring, and dale
Edged with poplar pale,
The parting genius° is with sighing sent; *local spirit*
With flower-inwoven tresses torn
The Nymphs in twilight shade of tangled thickets mourn.

21

In consecrated earth,
And on the holy hearth,
The Lars[1] and Lemures moan with midnight plaint;
In urns and altars round,
A drear and dying sound
Affrights the flamens° at their service quaint;° *priests / elaborate*
And the chill marble seems to sweat,
While each peculiar power forgoes his wonted seat.

22

Peor[2] and Baälim
Forsake their temples dim,
With that twice-battered God of Palestine;[3]
And moonéd Ashtaroth,[4]
Heaven's queen and mother both,
Now sits not girt with tapers' holy shine:
The Libyc Hammon[5] shrinks his horn;
In vain the Tyrian maids their wounded Thammuz mourn.[6]

23

And sullen Moloch,[7] fled,
Hath left in shadows dread
His burning idol all of blackest hue;

1. Tutelary gods or spirits of the ancient Romans associated with particular places. Lemures were hostile spirits of the unburied dead.
2. Baal or Baal-Peor, the highest Canaanite god, whose shrine was at Mount Peor. Baalim (the plural form) were lesser gods related to him.
3. Dagon, god of the Philistines, whose statue twice fell to the ground before the ark of the Lord (I Samuel v.1–4).
4. Astarte, a Phoenician goddess identified with the moon.
5. The Egyptian god Ammon, represented as a horned ram. He had a famous temple and oracle at an oasis in the Libyan desert.
6. The death of the god Thammuz, Ashtaroth's lover, symbolized the coming of winter. The Tyrian (Phoenician) women mourned for him in an annual ceremony.
7. A pagan god to whom children were sacrificed. Their cries were drowned out by the clang of cymbals.

In vain with cymbals' ring
They call the grisly king,
In dismal dance about the furnace blue;
The brutish gods of Nile as fast,
Isis, and Orus, and the dog Anubis,[8] haste.

24

Nor is Osiris seen
In Memphian grove or green,
Trampling the unshowered grass with lowings loud;
Nor can he be at rest
Within his sacred chest;
Nought but profoundest Hell can be his shroud;
In vain, with timbreled anthems dark,
The sable-stoléd sorcerers bear his worshiped ark.

25

He feels from Juda's land
The dreaded Infant's hand;
The rays of Bethlehem blind his dusky eyn;° *eyes*
Nor all the gods beside
Longer dare abide,
Not Typhon[9] huge ending in snaky twine:
Our Babe, to show his Godhead true,
Can in his swaddling bands control the damnéd crew.

26

So, when the sun in bed,
Curtained with cloudy red,
Pillows his chin upon an orient° wave, *eastern*
The flocking shadows pale
Troop to th' infernal jail;
Each fettered ghost slips to his several grave,
And the yellow-skirted fays
Fly after the night-steeds, leaving their moon-loved maze.

27

But see! the Virgin blest
Hath laid her Babe to rest.
Time is our tedious song should here have ending:
Heaven's youngest-teeméd star[1]
Hath fixed her polished car,
Her sleeping Lord with handmaid lamp attending;
And all about the courtly stable
Bright-harnessed angels sit in order serviceable.

1629 1645

L'Allegro[2]

Hence loathéd Melancholy
Of Cerberus[3] and blackest midnight born,
In Stygian[4] cave forlorn
'Mongst horrid shapes, and shrieks, and sights unholy,
Find out some uncouth° cell, *unknown*
Where brooding Darkness spreads his jealous wings,
And the night-raven sings;

8. The Egyptian goddess Isis was represented as a cow, the gods Orus and Anubis as a hawk and a dog (hence "brutish"). Osiris (line 213) the creator, who had a shrine at Memphis, was represented as a bull.
9. A hundred-headed monster destroyed by Zeus.
1. I.e., newest-born star, the star that guided the wise men, now imagined as having halted its "car" or chariot over the manger.
2. The cheerful man.
3. The three-headed dog that guarded the gates of hell.
4. Pertaining to the Styx, one of the rivers of the classical underworld.

There under ebon shades, and low-browed rocks,
As ragged as thy locks,
In dark Cimmerian[5] desert ever dwell.
But come thou goddess fair and free,
In Heaven yclept° Euphrosyne,[6] *called*
And by men, heart-easing Mirth,
Whom lovely Venus at a birth
With two sister Graces more
To ivy-crownéd Bacchus[7] bore;
Or whether (as some sager sing)[8]
The frolic wind that breathes the spring,
Zephyr with Aurora playing,
As he met her once a-Maying,
There on beds of violets blue,
And fresh-blown° roses washed in dew, *newly bloomed*
Filled her with thee a daughter fair,
So buxom,° blithe, and debonair.° *merry / pleasant*
Haste thee nymph, and bring with thee
Jest and youthful Jollity,
Quips and Cranks,° and wanton Wiles, *jests*
Nods, and Becks,° and wreathéd Smiles, *curtseys*
Such as hang on Hebe's[9] cheek,
And love to live in dimple sleek;
Sport that wrinkled Care derides,
And Laughter, holding both his sides.
Come, and trip it as ye go
On the light fantastic toe,
And in thy right hand lead with thee,
The mountain nymph, sweet Liberty;
And if I give thee honor due,
Mirth, admit me of thy crew
To live with her and live with thee,
In unreprovéd pleasures free;
To hear the lark begin his flight,
And, singing, startle the dull night,
From his watch-tower in the skies,
Till the dappled dawn doth rise;
Then to come in spite° of sorrow, *contempt*
And at my window bid good morrow,
Through the sweetbriar, or the vine,
Or the twisted eglantine.
While the cock with lively din,
Scatters the rear of darkness thin,
And to the stack, or the barn door,
Stoutly struts his dames before;
Oft listening how the hounds and horn
Cheerly rouse the slumbering morn,
From the side of some hoar hill,
Through the high wood echoing shrill.
Sometime walking not unseen
By hedgerow elms, on hillocks green,
Right against the eastern gate,

5. In classical mythology the Cimmerians lived in a mysterious land somewhere across the ocean, where the sun never shone.
6. One of the three Graces, who were believed to bring joy into men's lives. Her name means "mirth."
7. The god of wine.
8. It is generally believed that the following mythical account of the birth of Euphrosyne is Milton's own invention. Zephyr is the west wind; Aurora, the dawn.
9. The cupbearer of Zeus, a goddess who personified youth.

Where the great sun begins his state,° *progress*
Robed in flames, and amber light,
The clouds in thousand liveries dight;° *dressed*
While the plowman near at hand,
Whistles o'er the furrowed land,
And the milkmaid singeth blithe,
And the mower whets his scythe,
And every shepherd tells his tale,
Under the hawthorn in the dale.
Straight mine eye hath caught new pleasures
Whilst the landscape round it measures,
Russet lawns and fallows gray,
Where the nibbling flocks do stray,
Mountains on whose barren breast
The laboring clouds do often rest;
Meadows trim with daisies pied,° *variegated*
Shallow brooks, and rivers wide.
Towers and battlements it sees
Bosomed high in tufted trees,
Where perhaps some beauty lies,
The cynosure° of neighboring eyes. *North Star*
Hard by, a cottage chimney smokes,
From betwixt two aged oaks,
Where Corydon and Thyrsis[1] met,
Are at their savory dinner set
Of herbs, and other country messes,
Which the neat-handed Phyllis dresses;
And then in haste her bower she leaves,
With Thestylis to bind the sheaves;
Or if the earlier season lead
To the tanned haycock in the mead.
Sometimes with secure° delight *carefree*
The upland hamlets will invite,
When the merry bells ring round
And the jocund rebecks[2] sound
To many a youth and many a maid,
Dancing in the checkered shade;
And young and old come forth to play
On a sunshine holiday,
Till the livelong daylight fail;
Then to the spicy nut-brown ale,
With stories told of many a feat,
How fairy Mab[3] the junkets eat;° *ate*
She was pinched and pulled, she said,
And he, by Friar's lantern° led, *will-o'-the-wisp*
Tells how the drudging goblin[4] sweat
To earn his cream-bowl, duly set,
When in one night, ere glimpse of morn,
His shadowy flail hath threshed the corn
That ten day-laborers could not end;
Then lies him down the lubber° fiend, *loutish*
And, stretched out all the chimney's° length, *fireplace's*
Basks at the fire his hairy strength;
And crop-full out of doors he flings

1. Conventional names in pastoral poetry, like Phyllis (line 86) and Thestylis (line 88).
2. A rebeck is a kind of three-stringed fiddle.
3. Queen of the fairies. The behavior attributed to fairies in this and the following lines reflects traditional rustic lore.
4. Hobgoblin or Robin Goodfellow.

Ere the first cock his matin rings.
Thus done the tales, to bed they creep,
By whispering winds soon lulled asleep.
Towered cities please us then,
And the busy hum of men,
Where throngs of knights and barons bold,
In weeds° of peace high triumphs hold, *garments*
With store of ladies, whose bright eyes
Rain influence,[5] and judge the prize
Of wit, or arms, while both contend
To win her grace, whom all commend.
There let Hymen[6] oft appear
In saffron robe, with taper clear,
And pomp, and feast, and revelry,
With masque, and antique pageantry;
Such sights as youthful poets dream
On summer eves by haunted stream.
Then to the well-trod stage anon,
If Jonson's learned sock[7] be on,
Or sweetest Shakespeare, fancy's child,
Warble his native wood-notes wild.
And ever against eating cares
Lap me in soft Lydian airs[8]
Married to immortal verse
Such as the meeting soul may pierce
In notes, with many a winding bout° *turn*
Of linkéd sweetness long drawn out,
With wanton heed, and giddy cunning,
The melting voice through mazes running;
Untwisting all the chains that tie
The hidden soul of harmony;
That Orpheus' self[9] may heave his head
From golden slumber on a bed
Of heaped Elysian flowers, and hear
Such strains as would have won the ear
Of Pluto, to have quite set free
His half-regained Eurydice.
These delights if thou canst give,
Mirth, with thee I mean to live.

ca. 1631 1645

Il Penseroso[1]

Hence vain deluding Joys,
  The brood of Folly without father bred.
How little you bestead,° *profit*
  Or fill the fixéd mind with all your toys;° *trifles*
Dwell in some idle brain,
  And fancies fond° with gaudy shapes possess, *foolish*
As thick and numberless
  As the gay motes that people the sunbeams,

5. Medieval astrologers believed that the stars emitted an ethereal liquid ("influence") that could powerfully affect the lives of men.
6. God of marriage.
7. The light shoe worn by Greek comic actors, here standing for the comedies of Ben Jonson.
8. Lydian music was noted for its voluptuous sweetness.
9. The great musician of classical mythology, whose wife Eurydice died on their wedding day. He won permission from Pluto, god of the underworld, to lead her back to the land of the living, but only on the condition that he not look to see if she was following him. Unable to resist a backward glance, he lost her forever.
1. The pensive man.

Or likest hovering dreams,
The fickle pensioners° of Morpheus'[2] train. *retainers*
But hail thou Goddess, sage and holy,
Hail, divinest Melancholy,
Whose saintly visage is too bright
To hit° the sense of human sight; *affect*
And therefore to our weaker view,
O'erlaid with black, staid Wisdom's hue.
Black, but such as in esteem,
Prince Memnon's sister[3] might beseem,
Or that starred Ethiope queen[4] that strove
To set her beauty's praise above
The sea nymphs, and their powers offended.
Yet thou art higher far descended;
Thee bright-haired Vesta long of yore
To solitary Saturn bore;[5]
His daughter she (in Saturn's reign
Such mixture was not held a stain).
Oft in glimmering bowers and glades
He met her, and in secret shades
Of woody Ida's inmost grove,
While yet there was no fear of Jove.
Come pensive nun, devout and pure,
Sober, steadfast, and demure,
All in a robe of darkest grain,° *color*
Flowing with majestic train,
And sable stole of cypress lawn[6]
Over thy decent shoulders drawn.
Come, but keep thy wonted state,
With even step and musing gait,
And looks commercing with the skies,
Thy rapt soul sitting in thine eyes:
There held in holy passion still,
Forget thyself to marble, till
With a sad° leaden downward cast, *serious*
Thou fix them on the earth as fast.
And join with thee calm Peace and Quiet,
Spare Fast, that oft with gods doth diet,
And hears the Muses in a ring
Aye round about Jove's altar sing.
And add to these retired Leisure,
That in trim gardens takes his pleasure;
But first, and chiefest, with thee bring,
Him that yon soars on golden wing,
Guiding the fiery-wheeléd throne,
The cherub Contemplation;[7]
And the mute Silence hist° along *beckon*
'Less Philomel[8] will deign a song,
In her sweetest, saddest plight,

2. God of sleep.
3. Memnon, an Ethiopian prince, was called the handsomest of men. His sister was Hemera, whose name means "day."
4. Cassiopeia, who boasted that her beauty (or her daughter's, in some accounts) surpassed that of the daughters of the sea-god Nereus. "Starred" refers to the fact that a constellation bears her name.
5. The parentage here attributed to Melancholy is Milton's invention. Saturn, who ruled on Mt. Ida before being overthrown by his son Jove, was associated with melancholy because of the supposedly "saturnine" influence of the planet which bears his name. His daughter Vesta was the goddess of purity.
6. A gauzy, crepe-like material, usually dyed black and used for mourning garments. Cypress: Cyprus, where the material was originally made.
7. Milton is thinking of the vision of the four cherubim (a high order of angels) stationed beside four wheels of fire under the throne of the Lord (Ezekiel i and x).
8. The nightingale, often associated with a sad or contemplative mood.

Smoothing the rugged brow of night,
While Cynthia[9] checks her dragon yoke
Gently o'er th' accustomed oak;
Sweet bird that shunn'st the noise of folly,
Most musical, most melancholy!
Thee chantress oft the woods among,
I woo to hear thy evensong;
And missing thee, I walk unseen
On the dry smooth-shaven green,
To behold the wandering moon,
Riding near her highest noon,
Like one that had been led astray
Through the Heaven's wide pathless way;
And oft as if her head she bowed,
Stooping through a fleecy cloud.
Oft on a plat° of rising ground, *plot*
I hear the far-off curfew sound,
Over some wide-watered shore,
Swinging slow with sullen roar;
Or if the air will not permit,
Some still removéd place will fit,
Where glowing embers through the room
Teach light to counterfeit a gloom
Far from all resort of mirth,
Save the cricket on the hearth,
Or the bellman's° drowsy charm, *night-watchman's*
To bless the doors from nightly harm;
Or let my lamp at midnight hour
Be seen in some high lonely tower,
Where I may oft outwatch the Bear,[1]
With thrice great Hermes,[2] or unsphere
The spirit of Plato to unfold
What worlds, or what vast regions hold
The immortal mind that hath forsook
Her mansion in this fleshly nook;
And of those demons[3] that are found
In fire, air, flood, or underground,
Whose power hath a true consent° *correspondence*
With planet, or with element.
Some time let gorgeous Tragedy
In sceptered pall° come sweeping by, *robe*
Presenting Thebes, or Pelops' line,
Or the tale of Troy divine.[4]
Or what (though rare) of later age
Ennobled hath the buskined[5] stage.
But, O sad virgin, that thy power
Might raise Musaeus[6] from his bower,
Or bid the soul of Orpheus sing
Such notes as, warbled to the string,
Drew iron tears down Pluto's cheek,

9. Goddess of the moon, sometimes represented as driving a team of dragons.
1. The Great Bear or Big Dipper, which in northern latitudes never sets.
2. Hermes Trismegistus ("thrice-great"), a name given by Neo-Platonists to the Egyptian god Thoth, who was sometimes identified with the Greek Hermes. He was thought to be the actual author of some forty books embodying mystical, theosophical, astrological, and alchemical doctrines. "Unsphere": call back from his present sphere.
3. Supernatural beings inhabiting each of the four "elements": fire, air, water, and earth.
4. The city of Thebes, the descendants of Pelops, and the Trojan War afforded the subjects of most Greek tragedies.
5. The buskin was the high boot worn by Greek tragic actors.
6. A legendary Greek poet, contemporary of Orpheus (line 105), for whose story see the note to *L'Allegro,* line 145.

And made Hell grant what Love did seek.
Or call up him[7] that left half told
The story of Cambuscan bold,
Of Camball, and of Algarsife,
And who had Canacee to wife,
That owned the virtuous° ring and glass, *potent*
And of the wondrous horse of brass,
On which the Tartar king did ride;
And if aught else great bards beside
In sage and solemn tunes have sung,
Of tourneys and of trophies hung,
Of forests and enchantments drear,
Where more is meant than meets the ear.
Thus, Night, oft see me in thy pale career,
Till civil-suited morn[8] appear,
Not tricked and frounced° as she was wont, *curled*
With the Attic boy to hunt,
But kerchiefed in a comely cloud,
While rocking winds are piping loud,
Or ushered with a shower still,
When the gust hath blown his fill,
Ending on the rustling leaves,
With minute-drops from off the eaves.
And when the sun begins to fling
His flaring beams, me, Goddess, bring
To archéd walks of twilight groves,
And shadows brown that Sylvan[9] loves
Of pine or monumental oak,
Where the rude ax with heavéd stroke,
Was never heard the nymphs to daunt,
Or fright them from their hallowed haunt.
There in close covert by some brook,
Where no profaner eye may look,
Hide me from day's garish eye,
While the bee with honeyed thigh,
That at her flowery work doth sing,
And the waters murmuring
With such consort° as they keep, *harmony*
Entice the dewy-feathered sleep;
And let some strange mysterious dream,
Wave at his wings in airy stream,
Of lively portraiture displayed,
Softly on my eyelids laid.
And as I wake, sweet music breathe
Above, about, or underneath,
Sent by some spirit to mortals good,
Or th' unseen genius° of the wood. *indwelling spirit*
But let my due feet never fail
To walk the studious cloister's pale,° *enclosure*
And love the high embowéd roof,
With antic[1] pillars massy proof,
And storied windows richly dight,° *dressed*
Casting a dim religious light.
There let the pealing organ blow,

7. Chaucer, whose *Squire's Tale* leaves unfinished the story of Cambuscan and his three children, Cambala, Algarsyf, and Canacee.
8. Aurora, goddess of the dawn, who loved Cephalus ("the Attic boy," line 124).
9. Sylvanus, god of forests.
1. Fancifully decorated. "Massy proof": massive solidity. "Storied windows" (line 159): windows with representations of Biblical stories in stained glass.

To the full-voicéd choir below,
In service high, and anthems clear,
As may with sweetness, through mine ear,
Dissolve me into ectasies,
And bring all heaven before mine eyes.
And may at last my weary age
Find out the peaceful hermitage,
The hairy gown and mossy cell,
Where I may sit and rightly spell° *speculate*
Of every star that Heaven doth show,
And every herb that sips the dew
Till old experience do attain
To something like prophetic strain.
These pleasures, Melancholy, give,
And I with thee will choose to live.

ca. 1631 1645

On Shakespeare

What needs my Shakespeare for his honored bones
The labor of an age in piléd stones?
Or that his hallowed reliques should be hid
Under a star-ypointing[2] pyramid?
Dear son of Memory,[3] great heir of Fame,
What need'st thou such weak witness of thy name?
Thou in our wonder and astonishment
Hast built thyself a livelong monument.
For whilst, to th' shame of slow-endeavoring art,
Thy easy numbers° flow, and that each heart *verses*
Hath from the leaves of thy unvalued° book *invaluable*
Those Delphic[4] lines with deep impression took,
Then thou, our fancy of itself bereaving,
Dost make us marble with too much conceiving,
And so sepúlchred in such pomp dost lie
That kings for such a tomb would wish to die.

1630 1645

How Soon Hath Time

How soon hath Time, the subtle thief of youth,
   Stoln on his wing my three and twentieth year!
   My hasting days fly on with full career,
   But my late spring no bud or blossom shew'th.° *showeth*
Perhaps my semblance might deceive the truth,
   That I to manhood am arrived so near,
   And inward ripeness doth much less appear,
   That some more timely-happy spirits endu'th.° *endoweth*
Yet be it less or more, or soon or slow,
   It shall be still in strictest measure even° *equal*
   To that same lot, however mean or high,
Toward which Time leads me, and the will of Heaven;
   All is, if I have grace to use it so,
   As ever in my great Taskmaster's eye.

1631 1645

2. Milton uses the archaic form of the past participle, common in Chaucer and imitated by Spenser, in which *y-* represents a reduced form of the Old English prefix *ge-*.

3. Memory (Mneymosyne) was the mother of the Muses.

4. Pertaining to Apollo, god of poetry, who had an oracle at Delphi.

When I Consider How My Light Is Spent[5]

When I consider how my light is spent
Ere half my days, in this dark world and wide,
And that one talent which is death to hide[6]
Lodged with me useless, though my soul more bent
To serve therewith my Maker, and present
My true account, lest he returning chide;
"Doth God exact day-labor, light denied?"
I fondly° ask; but Patience to prevent *foolishly*
That murmur, soon replies, "God doth not need
Either man's work or his own gifts; who best
Bear his mild yoke, they serve him best. His state
Is kingly. Thousands at his bidding speed
And post o'er land and ocean without rest:
They also serve who only stand and wait."

ca. 1652 1673

On the Late Massacre in Piedmont[7]

Avenge, O Lord, thy slaughtered saints, whose bones
Lie scattered on the Alpine mountains cold,
Even them who kept thy truth so pure of old
When all our fathers worshiped stocks° and stones,[8] *idols*
Forget not: in thy book record their groans
Who were thy sheep and in their ancient fold
Slain by the bloody Piedmontese that rolled
Mother with infant down the rocks. Their moans
The vales redoubled to the hills, and they
To Heaven. Their martyred blood and ashes sow
O'er all th' Italian fields where still doth sway
The triple tyrant:[9] that from these may grow
A hundredfold, who having learnt thy way
Early may fly the Babylonian woe.[1]

1655 1673

Cyriack,[2] Whose Grandsire

Cyriack, whose grandsire on the royal bench
Of British Themis,[3] with no mean applause,
Pronounced, and in his volumes taught, our laws,
Which others at their bar so often wrench,
Today deep thoughts resolve with me to drench
In mirth that after no repenting draws;
Let Euclid rest, and Archimedes pause,
And what the Swede intend, and what the French.

5. Milton had become totally blind in 1651.
6. An allusion to the parable of the talents, in which the servant who buried the single talent his lord had given him, instead of investing it, was deprived of all he had and cast "into outer darkness" at the lord's return (Matthew xxv.14–30).
7. Some 1700 members of the Protestant Waldensian sect in the Piedmont in northwestern Italy died as a result of a treacherous attack by the Duke of Savoy's forces on Easter Day, 1655.
8. The Waldenses had existed as a sect, first within the Catholic Church and then as heretics, since the 12th century. They were particularly critical of materialistic tendencies in the Church.
9. The Pope, whose tiara has three crowns.
1. Babylon, as a city of luxury and vice, was often linked with the Papal Court by Protestants, who took the destruction of the city described in Revelation xviii as an allegory of the fate in store for the Roman Church.
2. Cyriack Skinner, a pupil of Milton's and grandson of Sir Edward Coke, the great jurist who had been Chief Justice of the King's Bench under James I.
3. The Greek goddess of justice.

To measure life learn thou betimes,° and know *early*
Toward solid good what leads the nearest way;
For other things mild Heaven a time ordains,
And disapproves that care, though wise in show,
That with superfluous burden loads the day,
And, when God sends a cheerful hour, refrains.

ca. 1655 1673

Methought I Saw

Methought I saw my late espouséd saint[4]
Brought to me like Alcestis[5] from the grave,
Whom Jove's great son to her glad husband gave,
Rescued from Death by force, though pale and faint.
Mine, as whom washed from spot of child-bed taint
Purification in the Old Law did save,[6]
And such, as yet once more I trust to have
Full sight of her in heaven without restraint,
Came vested all in white, pure as her mind.
Her face was veiled; yet to my fancied sight
Love, sweetness, goodness, in her person shined
So clear as in no face with more delight.
But O, as to embrace me she inclined,
I waked, she fled, and day brought back my night.

ca. 1658 1673

From Paradise Lost

Book I

[The Invocation][7]

Of man's first disobedience, and the fruit
Of that forbidden tree whose mortal taste
Brought death into the world, and all our woe,
With loss of Eden, till one greater Man[8]
Restore us, and regain the blissful seat,
Sing, Heavenly Muse,[9] that, on the secret top
Of Oreb, or Sinai, didst inspire
That shepherd who first taught the chosen seed
In the beginning how the Heavens and Earth
Rose out of Chaos: or, if Sion hill
Delight thee more, and Siloa's brook that flowed
Fast by the oracle of God, I thence

4. The "saint," or soul in heaven, is Milton's second wife, Katherine Woodcock, to whom he had been married less than two years (hence "late espouséd") when she died in 1658. Since Milton had become blind in 1651, it is almost certain that he had never seen his wife.
5. The wife who is brought back from the dead to her husband Admetus by Hercules ("Jove's great son") in Euripides' *Alcestis.*
6. Hebrew law (Leviticus xii) prescribed certain sacrificial rituals for the purification of women after childbirth.
7. In these opening lines of *Paradise Lost* Milton follows long-established epic tradition by stating his subject and invoking divine aid in the treatment of it.
8. Christ, the "second Adam."
9. The phrase is rich with complex associations but may be taken in general as representing the Spirit of God, the same Spirit that spoke to Moses ("that shepherd") out of the burning bush on Mount Horeb (also called Sinai) and called upon him to lead Israel ("the chosen seed") out of Egypt. God's Spirit might also be found at Jerusalem in the Temple of Mount Sion ("the oracle of God") overlooking the stream Siloam, here contrasted with such haunts of the pagan Muses as "th' Aonian mount" (Helicon, in Greece). Milton asks this Spirit not only for inspiration but for instruction, since God alone was present "from the first" and knows the whole truth of the events Milton is about to relate.

Invoke thy aid to my adventurous song,
That with no middle flight intends to soar
Above th' Aonian mount, while it pursues
Things unattempted yet in prose or rhyme.
And chiefly thou, O Spirit, that dost prefer
Before all temples th' upright heart and pure,
Instruct me, for thou know'st; thou from the first
Wast present, and, with mighty wings outspread,
Dovelike sat'st brooding on the vast abyss,
And mad'st it pregnant: what in me is dark
Illumine; what is low, raise and support;
That, to the height of this great argument,° *theme*
I may assert Eternal Providence,
And justify the ways of God to men.

1667

SIR JOHN SUCKLING (1609–1642)

Song

Why so pale and wan, fond lover?
  Prithee, why so pale?
Will, when looking well can't move her,
  Looking ill prevail?
  Prithee, why so pale?

Why so dull and mute, young sinner?
  Prithee, why so mute?
Will, when speaking well can't win her,
  Saying nothing do 't?
  Prithee, why so mute?

Quit, quit, for shame; this will not move,
  This cannot take her.
If of herself she will not love,
  Nothing can make her:
  The devil take her!

1638

Upon My Lady Carlisle's Walking in Hampton Court Garden.

Dialogue.[1]

T.C. J.S.

Thom.

Didst thou not find the place inspired,
And flowers, as if they had desired

1. Lucy, countess of Carlisle, was a patron of many poets and evidently a beautiful woman. The "T.C." or "Thom." of this dialogue is the poet Thomas Carew; "J.S." is, of course, John Suckling himself.

No other sun, start from their beds,
And for a sight steal out their heads?
Heardst thou not music when she talked?
And didst not find that as she walked
She threw rare perfumes all about,
Such as bean-blossoms newly out,
Or chafed spices give?—

J.S.

I must confess those perfumes, Tom,
I did not smell; nor found that from
Her passing by ought sprung up new.
The flowers had all their birth from you;
For I passed o'er the self-same walk
And did not find one single stalk
Of anything that was to bring
This unknown after-after-spring.

Thom.

Dull and insensible, couldst see
A thing so near a deity
Move up and down, and feel no change?

J.S.

None, and so great, were alike strange;
I had my thoughts, but not your way.
All are not born, sir, to the bay.[2]
Alas! Tom, I am flesh and blood,
And was consulting how I could
In spite of masks and hoods descry
The parts denied unto the eye.
I was undoing all she wore,
And had she walked but one turn more,
Eve in her first state had not been
More naked or more plainly seen.

Thom.

'Twas well for thee she left the place;
There is great danger in that face.
But hadst thou viewed her leg and thigh,
And upon that discovery
Searched after parts that are more dear
(As fancy seldom stops so near),
No time or age had ever seen
So lost a thing as thou hadst been.

1646

Out upon It!

Out upon it! I have loved
  Three whole days together;
And am like to love three more,
  If it prove fair weather.

2. A crown of bay (or laurel) leaves was the traditional recognition of poetic achievement.

Time shall molt away his wings,
  Ere he shall discover
In the whole wide world again
  Such a constant lover.

But the spite on 't is, no praise
  Is due at all to me:
Love with me had made no stays
  Had it any been but she.

Had it any been but she,
  And that very face,
There had been at least ere this
  A dozen dozen in her place.

1659

ANNE BRADSTREET
(ca. 1612–1672)

The Vanity of All Wordly Things

As he[1] said vanity, so vain say I,
Oh! vanity, O vain all under sky;
Where is the man can say, "Lo, I have found
On brittle earth a consolation sound"?
What isn't in honor to be set on high?
No, they like beasts and sons of men shall die,
And whilst they live, how oft doth turn their fate;
He's now a captive that was king of late.
What isn't in wealth great treasures to obtain?
No, that's but labor, anxious care, and pain.
He heaps up riches, and he heaps up sorrow,
It's his today, but who's his heir tomorrow?
What then? Content in pleasures canst thou find?
More vain than all, that's but to grasp the wind.
The sensual senses for a time they please,
Meanwhile the conscience rage, who shall appease?
What isn't in beauty? No that's but a snare,
They're foul enough today, that once were fair.
What is't in flow'ring youth, or manly age?
The first is prone to vice, the last to rage.
Where is it then, in wisdom, learning, arts?
Sure if on earth, it must be in those parts;
Yet these the wisest man of men did find
But vanity, vexation of mind.
And he that knows the most doth still bemoan
He knows not all that here is to be known.
What is it then? to do as stoics tell,
Nor laugh, nor weep, let things go ill or well?
Such stoics are but stocks, such teaching vain,

1. The preacher of Ecclesiastes i.2: "Vanity of vanity, saith the Preacher, vanity of vanities; all is vanity."

While man is man, he shall have ease or pain.
If not in honor, beauty, age, nor treasure,
Nor yet in learning, wisdom, youth, nor pleasure,
Where shall I climb, sound, seek, search, or find
That *summum bonum*[2] which may stay my mind?
There is a path no vulture's eye hath seen,
Where lion fierce, nor lion's whelps have been,
Which leads unto that living crystal fount,
Who drinks thereof, the world doth naught account.
The depth and sea have said " 'tis not in me,"
With pearl and gold it shall not valued be.
For sapphire, onyx, topaz who would change;
It's hid from eyes of men, they count it strange.
Death and destruction the fame hath heard,
But where and what it is, from heaven's declared;
It brings to honor which shall ne'er decay,
It stores with wealth which time can't wear away.
It yieldeth pleasures far beyond conceit,
And truly beautifies without deceit.
Nor strength, nor wisdom, nor fresh youth shall fade,
Nor death shall see, but are immortal made.
This pearl of price, this tree of life, this spring,
Who is possessed of shall reign a king.
Nor change of state nor cares shall ever see,
But wear his crown unto eternity.
This satiates the soul, this stays the mind,
And all the rest, but vanity we find.

FINIS

1650

The Author to Her Book[3]

Thou ill-formed offspring of my feeble brain,
Who after birth didst by my side remain,
Till snatched from thence by friends, less wise than true,
Who thee abroad, exposed to public view,
Made thee in rags, halting to th' press to trudge,
Where errors were not lessened (all may judge).
At thy return my blushing was not small,
My rambling brat (in print) should mother call,
I cast thee by as one unfit for light,
Thy visage was so irksome in my sight;
Yet being mine own, at length affection would
Thy blemishes amend, if so I could:
I washed thy face, but more defects I saw,
And rubbing off a spot still made a flaw.
I stretched thy joints to make thee even feet,[4]
Yet still thou run'st more hobbling than is meet;
In better dress to trim thee was my mind,
But nought save homespun cloth i' th' house I find.
In this array 'mongst vulgars[5] may'st thou roam.

2. The highest good (Latin).
3. *The Tenth Muse* was published in 1650 without Anne Bradstreet's knowledge. She is thought to have written this poem in 1666, when a second edition was contemplated.
4. I.e., metrical feet; to smooth out the lines.
5. The common people.

In critic's hands beware thou dost not come,
And take thy way where yet thou art not known;
If for thy father asked, say thou hadst none;
And for thy mother, she alas is poor,
Which caused her thus to send thee out of door.

1678

A Letter to Her Husband, Absent upon Public Employment

My head, my heart, mine eyes, my life, nay, more,
My joy, my magazine° of earthly store, *storehouse*
If two be one, as surely thou and I,
How stayest thou there, whilst I at Ipswich[6] lie?
So many steps, head from the heart to sever,
If but a neck, soon should we be together.
I, like the Earth this season, mourn in black,
My Sun is gone so far in's zodiac,
Whom whilst I 'joyed, nor storms, nor frost I felt,
His warmth such frigid colds did cause to melt.
My chilled limbs now numbed lie forlorn;
Return; return, sweet Sol, from Capricorn;[7]
In this dead time, alas, what can I more
Than view those fruits which through thy heat I bore?
Which sweet contentment yield me for a space,
True living pictures of their father's face.
O strange effect! now thou art southward gone,
I weary grow the tedious day so long;
But when thou northward to me shalt return,
I wish my Sun may never set, but burn
Within the Cancer[8] of my glowing breast,
The welcome house of him my dearest guest.
Where ever, ever stay, and go not thence,
Till nature's sad decree shall call thee hence;
Flesh of thy flesh, bone of thy bone,
I here, thou there, yet both but one.

1678

Here Follows Some Verses upon the Burning of Our House July 10th, 1666

Copied Out of a Loose Paper

In silent night when rest I took
For sorrow near I did not look
I wakened was with thund'ring noise
And piteous shrieks of dreadful voice.
That fearful sound of "Fire!" and "Fire!"
Let no man know is my desire.

6. Ipswich, Massachusetts, is north of Boston.
7. Capricorn, the tenth sign of the zodiac, represents winter; "Sol": sun.
8. Cancer, the fourth sign of the zodiac, represents summer.

I, starting up, the light did spy,
And to my God my heart did cry
To strengthen me in my distress
And not to leave me succorless.
Then, coming out, beheld a space
The flame consume my dwelling place.
And when I could no longer look,
I blest His name that gave and took,[9]
That laid my goods now in the dust.
Yea, so it was, and so 'twas just.
It was His own, it was not mine,
Far be it that I should repine;
He might of all justly bereft
But yet sufficient for us left.
When by the ruins oft I past
My sorrowing eyes aside did cast,
And here and there the places spy
Where oft I sat and long did lie:
Here stood that trunk, and there that chest,
There lay that store I counted best.
My pleasant things in ashes lie,
And them behold no more shall I.
Under thy roof no guest shall sit,
Nor at thy table eat a bit.
No pleasant tale shall e'er be told,
Nor things recounted done of old.
No candle e'er shall shine in thee,
Nor bridegroom's voice e'er heard shall be.
In silence ever shall thou lie,
Adieu, Adieu, all's vanity.
Then straight I 'gin my heart to chide,
And did thy wealth on earth abide?
Didst fix thy hope on mold'ring dust?
The arm of flesh didst make thy trust?
Raise up thy thoughts above the sky
That dunghill mists away may fly.
Thou hast an house on high erect,
Framed by that mighty Architect,
With glory richly furnished,
Stands permanent though this be fled.
It's purchaséd and paid for too
By Him who hath enough to do.
A price so vast as is unknown
Yet by His gift is made thine own;
There's wealth enough, I need no more,
Farewell, my pelf,[1] farewell my store.
The world no longer let me love,
My hope and treasure lies above.

1867

9. "The Lord gave, and the Lord hath taken away; blessed be the name of the Lord" (Job i.21).

1. Possessions, usually in the sense of being falsely gained.

RICHARD CRASHAW
(1613–1649)

A Hymn to the Name and Honor of the Admirable Saint Teresa[1]

FOUNDRESS OF THE REFORMATION OF THE DISCALCED[2] CARMELITES, BOTH MEN AND WOMEN. A WOMAN FOR ANGELICAL HEIGHT OF SPECULATION, FOR MASCULINE COURAGE OF PERFORMANCE, MORE THAN A WOMAN; WHO YET A CHILD OUTRAN MATURITY, AND DURST PLOT A MARTYRDOM.

Love, thou art absolute sole lord
Of life and death. To prove the word,
We'll now appeal to none of all
Those thy old soldiers, great and tall,
Ripe men of martyrdom, that could reach down
With strong arms their triumphant crown;
Such as could with lusty breath
Speak loud into the face of death
Their great Lord's glorious name; to none
Of those whose spacious bosoms spread a throne
For Love at large to fill. Spare blood and sweat,
And see Him take a private seat;
Making His mansion in the mild
And milky soul of a soft child.
   Scarce has she learnt to lisp the name
Of Martyr, yet she thinks it shame
Life should so long play with that breath
Which spent can buy so brave a death.
She never undertook to know
What death with love should have to do;
Nor has she e'er yet understood
Why to show love she should shed blood;
Yet though she cannot tell you why,
She can love and she can die.
   Scarce has she blood enough to make
A guilty sword blush for her sake;
Yet has she a heart dares hope to prove
How much less strong is death than love.
   Be love but there, let poor six years
Be posed with the maturest fears
Man trembles at, you straight shall find
Love knows no nonage, nor the mind.
'Tis love, not years or limbs, that can
Make the martyr or the man.
   Love touched her heart, and lo it beats
High, and burns with such brave heats,

1. The remarkable Spanish mystic (1515–82), canonized in 1622. Her autobiography records how, at the age of six, she ran away from home to convert the Moors. In later visions she saw a seraph with a fire-tipped golden dart who pierced her heart repeatedly, causing simultaneously intense pain and joy. It is these "wounds of love" that constitute the "death more mystical and high" referred to in line 76.
2. Barefoot.

Such thirsts to die, as dares drink up
A thousand cold deaths in one cup.
Good reason, for she breathes all fire;
Her weak breast heaves with strong desire
Of what she may with fruitless wishes
Seek for amongst her mother's kisses.
Since 'tis not to be had at home,
She'll travel to a martyrdom.
No home for hers confesses she
But where she may a martyr be.
She'll to the Moors and trade with them
For this unvalued° diadem. *invaluable*
She'll offer them her dearest breath,
With Christ's name in 't, in change for death.
She'll bargain with them, and will give
Them God, teach them how to live
In Him; or, if they this deny,
For Him she'll teach them how to die.
So shall she leave amongst them sown
Her Lord's blood, or at least her own.
Farewell then, all the world, adieu!
Teresa is no more for you.
Farewell, all pleasures, sports, and joys,
Never till now esteemèd toys;
Farewell, whatever dear may be,
Mother's arms, or father's knee;
Farewell house and farewell home,
She's for the Moors and martyrdom!
Sweet, not so fast! lo, thy fair Spouse
Whom thou seek'st with so swift vows
Calls thee back, and bids thee come
T' embrace a milder martyrdom.
Blest powers forbid thy tender life
Should bleed upon a barbarous knife;
Or some base hand have power to rase° *cut*
Thy breast's chaste cabinet, and uncase
A soul kept there so sweet; oh no,
Wise Heav'n will never have it so.
Thou art Love's victim, and must die
A death more mystical and high;
Into Love's arms thou shalt let fall
A still surviving funeral.
His is the dart must make the death
Whose stroke shall taste thy hallowed breath;
A dart thrice dipped in that rich flame
Which writes thy Spouse's radiant name
Upon the roof of heaven, where aye
It shines, and with a sovereign ray
Beats bright upon the burning faces
Of souls which in that name's sweet graces
Find everlasting smiles. So rare,
So spiritual, pure, and fair
Must be th' immortal instrument
Upon whose choice point shall be sent
A life so loved; and that there be
Fit executioners for thee,

The fair'st and first-born sons of fire,
Blest seraphim, shall leave their choir
And turn Love's soldiers, upon thee
To exercise their archery.
   Oh, how oft shalt thou complain
Of a sweet and subtle pain,
Of intolerable joys,
Of a death, in which who dies
Loves his death and dies again,
And would for ever so be slain,
And lives and dies, and knows not why
To live, but that he thus may never leave to die!
   How kindly will thy gentle heart
Kiss the sweetly killing dart!
And close in his embraces keep
Those delicious wounds, that weep
Balsam to heal themselves with. Thus
When these thy deaths, so numerous,
Shall all at last die into one,
And melt thy soul's sweet mansion;
Like a soft lump of incense, hasted
By too hot a fire, and wasted
Into perfuming clouds, so fast
Shalt thou exhale to heaven at last
In a resolving sigh; and then,
Oh, what? Ask not the tongues of men;
Angels cannot tell; suffice,
Thyself shall feel thine own full joys
And hold them fast for ever. There,
So soon as thou shalt first appear,
The moon of maiden stars, thy white
Mistress, attended by such bright
Souls as thy shining self, shall come
And in her first ranks make thee room;
Where 'mongst her snowy family
Immortal welcomes wait for thee.
Oh, what delight when revealed life shall stand
And teach thy lips heaven with his hand,
On which thou now mayst to thy wishes
Heap up thy consecrated kisses.
What joys shall seize thy soul when she,
Bending her blessed eyes on thee,
Those second smiles of heaven, shall dart
Her mild rays through thy melting heart!
   Angels, thy old friends, there shall greet thee,
Glad at their own home now to meet thee.
   All thy good works which went before
And waited for thee at the door
Shall own thee there, and all in one
Weave a constellatiön
Of crowns, with which the King, thy Spouse,
Shall build up thy triumphant brows.
   All thy old woes shall now smile on thee,
And thy pains sit bright upon thee;
All thy sorrows here shall shine,
All thy sufferings be divine;
Tears shall take comfort and turn gems,

And wrongs repent to diadems.
Even thy deaths shall live, and new
Dress the soul that erst they slew;
Thy wounds shall blush to such bright scars
As keep account of the Lamb's wars.
Those rare works where thou shalt leave writ
Love's noble history, with wit
Taught thee by none but Him, while here
They feed our souls, shall clothe thine there.
Each heavenly word by whose hid flame
Our hard hearts shall strike fire, the same
Shall flourish on thy brows, and be
Both fire to us and flame to thee,
Whose light shall live bright in thy face
By glory, in our hearts by grace.
Thou shalt look round about and see
Thousands of crowned souls throng to be
Themselves thy crown; sons of thy vows,
The virgin-births with which thy sovereign Spouse
Made fruitful thy fair soul, go now
And with them all about thee, bow
To Him. "Put on," He'll say, "put on,
My rosy love, that, thy rich zone
Sparkling with the sacred flames
Of thousand souls whose happy names
Heav'n keeps upon thy score. Thy bright
Life brought them first to kiss the light
That kindled them to stars." And so
Thou with the Lamb, thy Lord, shalt go,
And whereso'er He sets His white
Steps, walk with Him those ways of light
Which who in death would live to see
Must learn in life to die like thee.

1652

RICHARD LOVELACE
(1618–1658)

To Althea, from Prison

When Love with unconfinéd wings
Hovers within my gates,
And my divine Althea brings
To whisper at the grates;
When I lie tangled in her hair
And fettered to her eye,
The gods[1] that wanton in the air
Know no such liberty.

When flowing cups run swiftly round,
With no allaying Thames,[2]
Our careless heads with roses bound,

1. Most 17th-century versions read "birds" for "gods."

2. I.e., without dilution (the Thames River flows through London).

Our hearts with loyal flames;
When thirsty grief in wine we steep,
When healths and draughts go free,
Fishes, that tipple in the deep,
Know no such liberty.

When, like committed° linnets, I *caged*
With shriller throat shall sing
The sweetness, mercy, majesty,
And glories of my King;
When I shall voice aloud how good
He is, how great should be,
Enlargéd winds, that curl the flood,
Know no such liberty.

Stone walls do not a prison make,
Nor iron bars a cage;
Minds innocent and quiet take
That for an hermitage.
If I have freedom in my love,
And in my soul am free,
Angels alone, that soar above,
Enjoy such liberty.

1649

To Lucasta, Going to the Wars

Tell me not, sweet, I am unkind
That from the nunnery
Of thy chaste breast and quiet mind,
To war and arms I fly.

True, a new mistress now I chase,
The first foe in the field;
And with a stronger faith embrace
A sword, a horse, a shield.

Yet this inconstancy is such
As you too shall adore;
I could not love thee, dear, so much,
Loved I not honor more.

1649

The Grasshopper

TO MY NOBLE FRIEND, MR. CHARLES COTTON

O thou that swing'st upon the waving hair
  Of some well-filléd oaten beard,
Drunk every night with a delicious tear
  Dropped thee from heaven, where now th' art reared;

The joys of earth and air are thine entire,
  That with thy feet and wings dost hop and fly;
And, when thy poppy° works, thou dost retire *sleeping potion*
  To thy carved acorn-bed to lie.

Up with the day, the sun thou welcom'st then,
  Sport'st in the gilt plats° of his beams, *hair braids*
And all these merry days mak'st merry men,
  Thyself, and melancholy streams.

But ah, the sickle! Golden ears are cropped;
  Ceres and Bacchus[3] bid good night;
Sharp, frosty fingers all your flowers have topped,
  And what scythes spared, winds shave off quite.

Poor verdant fool, and now green ice! thy joys,
  Large and as lasting as thy perch of grass,
Bid us lay in 'gainst winter rain, and poise° *balance*
  Their floods with an o'erflowing glass.

Thou best of men and friends! we will create
  A genuine summer in each other's breast,
And spite of this cold time and frozen fate,
  Thaw us a warm seat to our rest.

Our sacred hearths shall burn eternally,
  As vestal flames;[4] the North Wind, he
Shall strike his frost-stretched wings, dissolve, and fly
  This Etna[5] in epitome.

Dropping December shall come weeping in,
  Bewail th' usurping of his reign:
But when in showers of old Greek[6] we begin,
  Shall cry he hath his crown again!

Night, as clear Hesper,[7] shall our tapers whip
  From the light casements where we play,
And the dark hag from her black mantle strip,
  And stick there everlasting day.

Thus richer than untempted kings are we,
  That, asking nothing, nothing need:
Though lord of all what seas embrace, yet he
  That wants himself is poor indeed.

1649

ANDREW MARVELL
(1621–1678)

Bermudas

Where the remote Bermudas ride,
In th' ocean's bosom unespied,
From a small boat that rowed along,
The listening winds received this song:

3. The grain and the grape, from Ceres, goddess of the harvest, and Bacchus, god of wine.
4. The vestal virgins, consecrated to the Roman goddess Vesta, kept a sacred fire burning perpetually on her altar.
5. A Sicilian volcano.
6. Old Greek wine.
7. The morning star.

"What should we do but sing His praise,
That led us through the watery maze
Unto an isle so long unknown,
And yet far kinder than our own?
Where He the huge sea monsters wracks,° *casts ashore*
That lift the deep upon their backs;
He lands us on a grassy stage,
Safe from the storms, and prelate's rage.[1]
He gave us this eternal spring
Which here enamels everything,
And sends the fowls to us in care,
On daily visits through the air;
He hangs in shades the orange bright,
Like golden lamps in a green night,
And does in the pomegranates close
Jewels more rich than Ormus[2] shows;
He makes the figs our mouths to meet,
And throws the melons at our feet;
But apples° plants of such a price, *pineapples*
No tree could ever bear them twice;
With cedars, chosen by His hand,
From Lebanon, He stores the land;
And makes the hollow seas, that roar,
Proclaim the ambergris[3] on shore;
He cast (of which we rather boast)
The Gospel's pearl upon our coast,
And in these rocks for us did frame
A temple, where to sound His name.
O! let our voice His praise exalt,
Till it arrive at heaven's vault,
Which, thence (perhaps) rebounding, may
Echo beyond the Mexique Bay."[4]
Thus sung they in the English boat,
An holy and a cheerful note;
And all the way, to guide their chime,
With falling oars they kept the time.

1681

To His Coy Mistress

Had we but world enough, and time,
This coyness, lady, were no crime.
We would sit down, and think which way
To walk, and pass our long love's day.
Thou by the Indian Ganges' side
Shoudst rubies[5] find; I by the tide
Of Humber[6] would complain. I would
Love you ten years before the flood,
And you should, if you please, refuse
Till the conversion of the Jews.[7]

1. Marvell indicates Puritan sympathies by associating the wrath of prelates with storms at sea.
2. An island off Persia whence gems were exported.
3. A soapy secretion of the sperm whale, gathered on beaches and used in perfumes.
4. I.e., the Gulf of Mexico.
5. Rubies are talismans, preserving virginity.
6. The Humber flows through Marvell's native town of Hull.
7. To occur, as tradition had it, at the end of recorded history.

My vegetable[8] love should grow
Vaster than empires and more slow;
An hundred years should go to praise
Thine eyes, and on thy forehead gaze;
Two hundred to adore each breast,
But thirty thousand to the rest;
An age at least to every part,
And the last age should show your heart.
For, lady, you deserve this state,° *dignity*
Nor would I love at lower rate.
  But at my back I always hear
Time's wingéd chariot hurrying near;
And yonder all before us lie
Deserts of vast eternity.
Thy beauty shall no more be found;
Nor, in thy marble vault, shall sound
My echoing song; then worms shall try
That long-preserved virginity,
And your quaint° honor turn to dust, *over-subtle*
And into ashes all my lust:
The grave's a fine and private place,
But none, I think, do there embrace.
  Now therefore, while the youthful hue
Sits on thy skin like morning glow,[9]
And while thy willing soul transpires° *breathes out*
At every pore with instant fires,
Now let us sport us while we may,
And now, like amorous birds of prey,
Rather at once our time devour
Than languish in his slow-chapped° power. *slow-jawed*
Let us roll all our strength and all
Our sweetness up into one ball,
And tear our pleasures with rough strife
Thorough the iron gates[1] of life:
Thus, though we cannot make our sun
Stand still,[2] yet we will make him run.

1681

The Gallery

Clora, come view my soul, and tell
Whether I have contrived it well.
Now all its several lodgings lie
Composed into one gallery;
And the great arras-hangings, made
Of various faces, by are laid;
That, for all furniture, you'll find
Only your picture in my mind.

8. A technical term: "possessing, like plants, the power of growth but not of consciousness"; in context, "being magnified without conscious nurture."

9. In these rhyme-words (originally spelled *hew* and *glew*) the vowel sounds are probably similar and possibly identical: an *eh* gliding into an *oo*.

1. The obscurity "iron gates" suggests that the "ball" of line 42 has become a missile from a siege gun, battering its way into a citadel.

2. We lack, that is, the power of Zeus, who, to prolong his enjoyment of the mortal Alcmena, arrested the diurnal course and created a week-long night.

Here thou art painted in the dress
Of an inhuman murderess;
Examining° upon our hearts *testing*
Thy fertile shop of cruel arts:
Engines° more keen than ever yet *instruments*
Adornèd tyrant's cabinet;
Of which the most tormenting are
Black eyes, red lips, and curlèd hair.

But, on the other side, thou'rt drawn
Like to Aurora[3] in the dawn;
When in the east she slumb'ring lies,
And stretches out her milky thighs;
While all the morning choir does sing,
And manna falls, and roses spring;
And, at thy feet, the wooing doves
Sit perfecting their harmless loves.

Like an enchantress here thou show'st,
Vexing thy restless lover's ghost;
And, by a light obscure, dost rave
Over his entrails,[4] in the cave;
Divining thence, with horrid care,
How long thou shalt continue fair;
And (when informed) them throw'st away,
To be the greedy vulture's prey.

But, against° that, thou sit'st afloat *opposite*
Like Venus in her pearly boat.
The halcyons,[5] calming all that's nigh,
Betwixt the air and water fly:
Or, if some rolling wave appears,
A mass of ambergris it bears:
Nor blows more wind than what may well
Convoy the perfume to the smell.

These pictures and a thousand more,
Of thee, my gallery do store;
In all the forms thou canst invent
Either to please me, or torment:
For thou alone to people me,
Art grown a num'rous colony;
And a collection choicer far
Than or° Whitehall's, or Mantua's were.[6] *either*

But, of these pictures and the rest,
That at the entrance likes me best;
Where the same posture, and the look
Remains, with which I first was took:
A tender shepherdess, whose hair
Hangs loosely playing in the air,
Transplanting flowers from the green hill,
To crown her head, and bosom fill.

1681

3. Goddess of the dawn in Greek mythology.
4. An allusion to the Roman practice of divining the future through examination of the entrails of sacrificial victims.
5. Bird's believed to nest on the surface of the sea; hence representative of calm weather.
6. References to well-known collections of paintings, the first assembled by Charles I of England (owner of Whitehall Palace) and the second by Vincenzo Gonzago, duke of Mantua.

The Fair Singer

To make a final conquest of all me,
Love did compose so sweet an enemy,
In whom both beauties to my death agree,
Joining themselves in fatal harmony;
That while she with her eyes my heart does bind,
She with her voice might captivate my mind.

I could have fled from one but singly fair:
My disentangled soul itself might save,
Breaking the curléd trammels of her hair.
But how should I avoid to be her slave,
Whose subtle art invisibly can wreathe
My fetters of the very air I breathe?

It had been easy fighting in some plain,
Where victory might hang in equal choice,
But all resistance against her is vain,
Who has th' advantage both of eyes and voice,
And all my forces needs must be undone,
She having gainéd both the wind and sun.[7]

1681

The Definition of Love[8]

My Love is of a birth as rare
As 'tis, for object, strange and high;
It was begotten by Despair
Upon Impossibility.

Magnanimous Despair alone
Could show me so divine a thing,
Where feeble Hope could ne'er have flown
But vainly flapped its tinsel wing.

And yet I quickly might arrive
Where my extended soul is fixed;
But Fate does iron wedges drive,
And always crowds itself betwixt.

For Fate with jealous eye does see
Two perfect loves, nor lets them close;° *unite*
Their union would her ruin be,
And her tyrannic power depose.[9]

And therefore her decrees of steel
Us as the distant poles have placed
(Though Love's whole world on us doth wheel),[1]
Not by themselves to be embraced,

7. In earlier warfare (especially at sea) the force with the wind and sun behind it had distinct advantages.
8. The poem plays upon a Platonic definition of love as a longing which is unfulfilled.
9. In the old chemistry, it was assumed that an even mixture of pure elements formed an altogether stable compound, proof against all vicissitudes and hence, in context, defying fate.
1. I.e., the relationship (literally, the line) between us forms the axis on which Love's world turns.

Unless the giddy heaven fall,
And earth some new convulsion tear,
And, us to join, the world should all
Be cramped into a planisphere.[2]

As lines, so loves oblique may well
Themselves in every angle greet;[3]
But ours, so truly parallel,
Though infinite, can never meet.

Therefore the love which us doth bind,
But Fate so enviously debars,
Is the conjunction of the mind,
And opposition of the stars.[4]

1681

The Garden

How vainly men themselves amaze° *perplex*
To win the palm, the oak, or bays,[5]
And their incessant° labors see *unceasing*
Crowned from some single herb, or tree,
Whose short and narrow-vergéd[6] shade
Does prudently their toils upbraid;
While all flowers and all trees do close° *join*
To weave the garlands of repose!

Fair Quiet, have I found thee here,
And Innocence, thy sister dear?
Mistaken long, I sought you then
In busy companies of men.
Your sacred plants,° if here below, *cuttings*
Only among the plants will grow;
Society is all but rude[7]
To this delicious solitude.

No white nor red was ever seen
So amorous as this lovely green.
Fond lovers, cruel as their flame,
Cut in these trees their mistress' name:
Little, alas, they know or heed
How far these beauties hers exceed!
Fair trees, wheresoe'er your barks I wound,
No name shall but your own be found.

When we have run our passion's heat,° *course*
Love hither makes his best retreat.
The gods, that mortal beauty chase,
Still in a tree did end their race:

2. A sphere projected on a plane surface, perhaps here conceivable as plane projections of the northern and southern hemispheres on opposite sides of a disc.
3. I.e., may converge to form any angle up to 180 degrees.
4. In this astronomical image, the minds of the lovers are in accord (literally in *conjunction,* or occupying the same celestial longitude), but the stars determining their destinies are entirely hostile (literally in *opposition,* or 180 degrees apart).
5. The wreaths awarded, respectively, for athletic, civic, and poetic accomplishments.
6. Confined, not spreading luxuriantly like the living branch.
7. I.e., all merely barbarous.

Apollo hunted Daphne so,
Only that she might laurel grow;
And Pan did after Syrinx speed,
Not as a nymph, but for a reed.[8]

What wondrous life is this I lead!
Ripe apples drop about my head;
The luscious clusters of the vine
Upon my mouth do crush their wine;
The nectarine and curious° peach *exquisite*
Into by hands themselves do reach;
Stumbling on melons, as I pass,
Insnared with flowers, I fall on grass.

Meanwhile the mind, from pleasure less,
Withdraws into its happiness;[9]
The mind, that ocean where each kind
Does straight its own resemblance find;[1]
Yet it creates, transcending these,
Far other worlds and other seas,
Annihilating all that's made
To a green thought in a green shade.

Here at the fountain's sliding foot,
Or at some fruit tree's mossy root,
Casting the body's vest° aside, *garment*
My soul into the boughs does glide:
There, like a bird, it sits and sings,
Then whets[2] and combs its silver wings,
And, till prepared for longer flight,
Waves in its plumes the various° light. *iridescent*

Such was that happy garden-state,
While man there walked without a mate:
After a place so pure and sweet,
What other help could yet be meet![3]
But 'twas beyond a mortal's share
To wander solitary there:
Two paradises 'twere in one
To live in paradise alone.

How well the skillful gardener drew
Of flowers and herbs this dial[4] new,
Where, from above, the milder sun
Does through a fragrant zodiac run;
And as it works, th' industrious bee
Computes its time as well as we!
How could such sweet and wholesome hours
Be reckoned but with herbs and flowers?

1681

8. In the original myths, as told by Ovid, the nymphs frustrated the pursuing gods by turning into the plants named. In Marvell's version, the gods intended the transformations.
9. I.e., its own intellectual happiness is a greater pleasure than the taste of fruits.
1. Every land creature was thought to have its counterpart sea creature.
2. Sharpens its beak. But birds apparently whetting their beaks are actually cleaning them.
3. God created Eve because "for Adam there was not found an help meet for him" (Genesis ii.20).
4. A plantation of flowers forming a dial face, perhaps surrounding an actual sundial.

HENRY VAUGHAN
(1622–1695)

Regeneration

A ward, and still in bonds, one day
        I stole abroad;
It was high spring, and all the way
    Primrosed and hung with shade;
    Yet was it frost within,
        And surly winds
Blasted my infant buds, and sin
    Like clouds eclipsed my mind.

Stormed thus, I straight perceived my spring
        Mere stage and show,
My walk a monstrous, mountained thing,
    Roughcast with rocks and snow;
    And as a pilgrim's eye,
        Far from relief,
Measures the melancholy sky,
    Then drops and rains for grief,

So sighed I upwards still; at last
        'Twixt steps and falls
I reached the pinnacle, where placed
    I found a pair of scales;
    I took them up and laid
        In th' one, late pains;
The other smoke and pleasures weighed,
    But proved the heavier grains.[1]

With that some cried, "Away!" Straight I
        Obeyed, and led
Full east, a fair, fresh field could spy;
    Some called it Jacob's bed,[2]
    A virgin soil which no
        Rude feet ere trod,
Where, since he stepped there, only go
    Prophets and friends of God.

Here I reposed; but scarce well set,
        A grove descried
Of stately height, whose branches met
    And mixed on every side;
    I entered, and once in,
        Amazed to see 't,
Found all was changed, and a new spring
    Did all my senses greet.

The unthrift sun shot vital gold,
        A thousand pieces,
And heaven its azure did unfold,

1. Units of weight.
2. Sleeping in a field, Jacob saw a ladder reaching from earth to heaven, with angels ascending and descending on it (Genesis xxviii.10–12).

Checkered with snowy fleeces;
The air was all in spice,
And every bush
A garland wore; thus fed my eyes,
But all the ear lay hush.

Only a little fountain lent
Some use for ears,
And on the dumb shades language spent,
The music of her tears;
I drew her near, and found
The cistern full
Of divers stones, some bright and round,
Others ill-shaped and dull.

The first, pray mark, as quick as light
Danced through the flood,
But the last, more heavy than the night,
Naïled to the center stood;
I wondered much, but tired
At last with thought,
My restless eye that still desired
As strange an object brought.

It was a bank of flowers, where I descried
Though 'twas midday,
Some fast asleep, others broad-eyed
And taking in the ray;
Here, musing long, I heard
A rushing wind
Which still increased, but whence it stirred
No where I could not find.

I turned me round, and to each shade
Dispatched an eye
To see if any leaf had made
Least motion or reply,
But while I listening sought
My mind to ease
By knowing where 'twas, or where not,
It whispered, "Where I please."[3]

"Lord," then said I, "on me one breath,
And let me die before my death!"

1650

The Retreat

Happy those early days! when I
Shined in my angel infancy.
Before I understood this place
Appointed for my second race,
Or taught my soul to fancy aught
But a white, celestial thought;
When yet I had not walked above

3. "The wind bloweth where it listeth, and thou hearest the sound thereof, but canst not tell whence it cometh, and whither it goeth: so is every one that is born of the Spirit" (John iii.8).

A mile or two from my first love,
And looking back, at that short space,
Could see a glimpse of His bright face;
When on some gilded cloud or flower
My gazing soul would dwell an hour,
And in those weaker glories spy
Some shadows of eternity;
Before I taught my tongue to wound
My conscience with a sinful sound,
Or had the black art to dispense
A several° sin to every sense, *separate*
But felt through all this fleshly dress
Bright shoots of everlastingness.
  O, how I long to travel back,
And tread again that ancient track!
That I might once more reach that plain
Where first I left my glorious train,
From whence th' enlightened spirit sees
That shady city of palm trees.
But, ah! my soul with too much stay
Is drunk, and staggers in the way.
Some men a forward motion love;
But I by backward steps would move,
And when this dust falls to the urn,
In that state I came, return.

1650

They Are All Gone into the World of Light!

They are all gone into the world of light!
  And I alone sit lingering here;
Their very memory is fair and bright,
  And my sad thoughts doth clear.

It glows and glitters in my cloudy breast
  Like stars upon some gloomy grove,
Or those faint beams in which this hill is dressed
  After the sun's remove.

I see them walking in an air of glory,
  Whose light doth trample on my days;
My days, which are at best but dull and hoary,
  Mere glimmering and decays.

O holy hope, and high humility,
  High as the heavens above!
These are your walks, and you have showed them me
  To kindle my cold love.

Dear, beauteous death! the jewel of the just,
  Shining nowhere but in the dark;
What mysteries do lie beyond thy dust,
  Could man outlook that mark!° *boundary*

He that hath found some fledged bird's nest may know
  At first sight if the bird be flown;
But what fair well or grove he sings in now,
  That is to him unknown.

And yet, as angels in some brighter dreams
Call to the soul when man doth sleep,
So some strange thoughts transcend our wonted themes,
And into glory peep.

If a star were confined into a tomb,
Her captive flames must needs burn there;
But when the hand that locked her up gives room,
She'll shine through all the sphere.

O Father of eternal life, and all
Created glories under Thee!
Resume° Thy spirit from this world of thrall *take back*
Into true liberty!

Either disperse these mists, which blot and fill
My perspective° still as they pass; *telescope*
Or else remove me hence unto that hill
Where I shall need no glass.

1655

JOHN DRYDEN
(1631–1700)

Song from *Troilus and Cressida*

1

Can life be a blessing,
Or worth the possessing,
Can life be a blessing, if love were away?
Ah, no! though our love all night keep us waking,
And though he torment us with cares all the day,
Yet he sweetens, he sweetens our pains in the taking;
There's an hour at the last, there's an hour to repay.

2

In every possessing
The ravishing blessing,
In every possessing the fruit of our pain,
Poor lovers forget long ages of anguish,
Whate'er they have suffered and done to obtain;
'Tis a pleasure, a pleasure to sigh and to languish,
When we hope, when we hope to be happy again.

1679

Mac Flecknoe

OR A SATIRE UPON THE
TRUE-BLUE-PROTESTANT POET, T. S.[1]

All human things are subject to decay,
And when fate summons, monarchs must obey.

1. Thomas Shadwell (1640–92), a comic playwright of respectable talents, who considered himself the dramatic heir of Ben Jonson. He was vain, corpulent, and probably overbearing in manner. Dryden names him *Mac* (son of) *Flecknoe,* making him heir not of Jonson but of the recently dead Irish priest Richard Flecknoe, a poet at once tiresome and prolific. The subtitle (presumably added when the poem, itself non-political, was published in 1682) acknowledges a political controversy fed by Dryden's poems *Absalom and Achitophel* and *The Medal* (a satire on Shaftesbury's acquittal) and Shadwell's rejoinder *The Medal of John Bayes* (John Dryden). Shadwell belonged to the Whig party, the political haven of dissenting Protestants.

This Flecknoe found, who, like Augustus,[2] young
Was called to empire, and had governed long;
In prose and verse, was owned, without dispute,
Through all the realms of Nonsense, absolute.
This aged prince, now flourishing in peace,
And blest with issue of a large increase,
Worn out with business, did at length debate
To settle the succession of the state;
And, pondering which of all his sons was fit
To reign, and wage immortal war with wit,[3]
Cried: " 'Tis resolved; for nature pleads that he
Should only rule, who most resembles me.
Sh——[4] alone my perfect image bears,
Mature in dullness from his tender years:
Sh—— alone, of all my sons, is he
Who stands confirmed in full stupidity.
The rest to some faint meaning make pretense,
But Sh—— never deviates into sense.
Some beams of wit on other souls may fall,
Strike through, and make a lucid interval;
But Sh——'s genuine night admits no ray,
His rising fogs prevail upon the day.
Besides, his goodly fabric fills the eye,
And seems designed for thoughtless majesty:
Thoughtless as monarch oaks that shade the plain,
And, spread in solemn state, supinely reign.
Heywood and Shirley[5] were but types of thee,
Thou last great prophet of tautology.
Even I, a dunce of more renown than they,
Was sent before but to prepare thy way;
And, coarsely clad in Norwich drugget,[6] came
To teach the nations in thy greater name.
My warbling lute, the lute I whilom° strung, *formerly*
When to King John of Portugal I sung,[7]
Was but the prelude to that glorious day,
When thou on silver Thames didst cut thy way,
With well-timed oars before the royal barge,
Swelled with the pride of thy celestial charge;
And big with hymn, commander of a host,
The like was ne'er in Epsom blankets tossed.[8]
Methinks I see the new Arion[9] sail,
The lute still trembling underneath thy nail.
At thy well-sharpened thumb from shore to shore
The treble squeaks for fear, the basses roar;
Echoes from Pissing Alley Sh—— call,
And Sh—— they resound from Aston Hall.
About thy boat the little fishes throng,
As at the morning toast[1] that floats along.
Sometimes, as prince of thy harmonious band,

2. Augustus became Roman emperor at thirty-two and reigned for forty years.
3. *Wit,* here as in other poems of the time, variously denotes the intellect, the poetic imagination, and a general sprightliness of mind.
4. A transparent pretense to anonymity, admitting here and there a scatological suggestion.
5. Playwrights of the time of Charles I, now out of fashion. Dryden suggests that they prefigure Shadwell as the Old-Testament prophets and (in lines 31–34) John the Baptist prefigured the ultimate revelation in Jesus Christ.
6. A coarse cloth.
7. Flecknoe claimed the king of Portugal as his patron.
8. A simultaneous reference to two of Shadwell's plays: *The Virtuoso,* in which a character is tossed in a blanket, and *Epsom Wells.*
9. When the Greek poet Arion was cast into the sea, a dolphin, charmed by his singing, bore him ashore. Shadwell was proud of his musical accomplishments.
1. A euphemism for sewage.

Thou wield'st thy papers in thy threshing hand.
St. André's[2] feet ne'er kept more equal time,
Not ev'n the feet of thy own *Psyche's* rhyme;
Though they in number as in sense excel:
So just, so like tautology, they fell,
That, pale with envy, Singleton[3] forswore
The lute and sword, which he in triumph bore,
And vowed he ne'er would act Villerius[4] more."
Here stopped the good old sire, and wept for joy
In silent raptures of the hopeful boy.
All arguments, but most his plays, persuade,
That for anointed dullness he was made.
Close to the walls which fair Augusta[5] bind
(The fair Augusta much to fears inclined),
An ancient fabric° raised to inform the sight, *building*
There stood of yore, and Barbican it hight:
A watchtower once; but now, so fate ordains,
Of all the pile an empty name remains.
From its old ruins brothel houses rise,
Scenes of lewd loves, and of polluted joys,
Where their vast courts the mother-strumpets keep,
And, undisturbed by watch, in silence sleep.
Near these a Nursery[6] erects its head,
Where queens are formed, and future heroes bred;
Where unfledged actors learn to laugh and cry,
Where infant punks° their tender voices try, *prostitutes*
And little Maximins[7] the gods defy.
Great Fletcher[8] never treads in buskins here,
Nor greater Jonson dares in socks appear;
But gentle Simkin[9] just reception finds
Amidst this monument of vanished minds:
Pure clinches° the suburbian Muse affords, *puns*
And Panton[1] waging harmless war with words.
Here Flecknoe, as a place to fame well known,
Ambitiously designed his Sh———'s throne;
For ancient Dekker[2] prophesied long since,
That in this pile would reign a mighty prince,
Born for a scourge of wit, and flail of sense;
To whom true dullness should some *Psyches* owe,
But worlds of *Misers* from his pen should flow;[3]
Humorists and *Hypocrites* it should produce,
Whole Raymond families, and tribes of Bruce.
Now Empress Fame had published the renown
Of Sh———'s coronation through the town.
Roused by report of Fame, the nations meet,
From near Bunhill, and distant Watling Street.[4]
No Persian carpets spread the imperial way,
But scattered limbs of mangled poets lay;
From dusty shops neglected authors[5] come,

2. St. André, a French dancing-master, was choreographer of Shadwell's opera *Psyche.*
3. John Singleton, a musician of the Theatre Royal.
4. A role in Sir William Davenant's opera, *The Siege of Rhodes.*
5. London. (She "fears" Catholic plots.)
6. A training school for actors.
7. The bombastic emperor in Dryden's own *Tyrannic Love.*
8. Early 17th-century playwright; *buskins,* the high-soled boots worn in Athenian tragedy, are opposed to *socks,* the low shoes worn in comedy.
9. A clown.
1. A punster.
2. Elizabethan playwright satirized by Jonson.
3. In these lines Dryden names plays of (and characters in plays by) Shadwell.
4. These locations, both within a half-mile of the scene of the supposed coronation ("the Nursery"), circumscribe Shadwell's fame within an unfashionable bourgeois part of London.
5. I.e., unsold books, the paper of which, in that time of relative scarcity, found various uses.

Martyrs of pies, and relics of the bum.
Much Heywood, Shirley, Ogilby[6] there lay,
But loads of Sh——— almost choked the way.
Bilked stationers[7] for yeomen stood prepared,
And Herringman was captain of the guard.
The hoary prince in majesty appeared,
High on a throne of his own labors reared.
At his right hand our young Ascanius[8] sate,
Rome's other hope, and pillar of the state.
His brows thick fogs, instead of glories, grace,
And lambent dullness played around his face.
As Hannibal did to the altars come,
Sworn by his sire a mortal foe to Rome,[9]
So Sh——— swore, nor should his vow be vain,
That he till death true dullness would maintain;
And, in his father's right, and realm's defense,
Ne'er to have peace with wit, nor truce with sense.
The king himself the sacred unction° made, *ointment*
As king by office, and as priest by trade.
In his sinister[1] hand, instead of ball,
He placed a mighty mug of potent ale;
Love's Kingdom[2] to his right he did convey,
At once his scepter, and his rule of sway;
Whose righteous lore the prince had practiced young,
And from whose loins recorded *Psyche* sprung.
His temples, last, with poppies[3] were o'erspread,
That nodding seemed to consecrate his head.
Just at that point of time, if fame not lie,
On his left hand twelve reverend owls did fly.
So Romulus, 'tis sung, by Tiber's brook,
Presage of sway from twice six vultures took.[4]
The admiring throng loud acclamations make,
And omens of his future empire take.
The sire then shook the honors° of his head, *locks*
And from his brows damps° of oblivion shed *vapors*
Full on the filial dullness: long he stood,
Repelling from his breast the raging god;
At length burst out in this prophetic mood:
"Heavens bless my son, from Ireland let him reign
To far Barbadoes on the western main;[5]
Of his dominion may no end be known,
And greater than his father's be his throne;
Beyond *Love's Kingdom* let his stretch his pen!"
He paused, and all the people cried, "Amen."
Then thus continued he: "My son, advance
Still in new imprudence, new ignorance.
Success let others teach, learn thou from me
Pangs without birth, and fruitless industry.

6. John Ogilby, a translator of Virgil and Homer; the derided competitor of Dryden and (later) of Pope.
7. Booksellers, impoverished because they had stocked the works of Shadwell and others, were the guard of honor ("yoemen of the guard"). Their "captain," Henry Herringman, however, had been Dryden's publisher as well as Shadwell's.
8. Aeneas' son; hence, like Shadwell, the destined heir.
9. Hannibal, the Carthaginian general who invaded Italy, was dedicated to his hatred of Rome (it was said) at the age of nine.
1. In British coronations the monarch holds in his left ("sinister") hand a globe surmounted by a cross.
2. A "pastoral tragicomedy" by Flecknoe, apparently visualized by Dryden as a rolled-up manuscript held like a scepter.
3. Connoting both intellectual heaviness and Shadwell's addiction to opiates.
4. When the site which Romulus had chosen for Rome was visited by twelve vultures, or twice as many as had visited the site picked by his brother Remus, the kingship ("sway") of Romulus was presaged.
5. I.e., a realm of empty ocean.

Let *Virtuosos* in five years be writ;
Yet not one thought accuse thy toil of wit.
Let gentle George[6] in triumph tread the stage,
Make Dorimant betray, and Loveit rage;
Let Cully, Cockwood, Fopling, charm the pit,
And in their folly show the writer's wit.
Yet still thy fools shall stand in thy defense,
And justify their author's want of sense.
Let 'em be all by thy own model made
Of dullness, and desire no foreign aid;
That they to future ages may be known,
Not copies drawn, but issue of thy own.
Nay, let thy men of wit too be the same,
All full of thee, and differing but in name.
But let no alien S—dl—y[7] interpose,
To lard with wit thy hungry *Epsom* prose.
And when false flowers of rhetoric thou wouldst cull,
Trust nature, do not labor to be dull;
But write thy best, and top; and, in each line,
Sir Formal's[8] oratory will be thine:
Sir Formal, though unsought, attends thy quill,
And does thy northern dedications[9] fill.
Nor let false friends seduce thy mind to fame,
By arrogating Jonson's hostile name.
Let father Flecknoe fire thy mind with praise,
And uncle Ogilby thy envy raise.
Thou art my blood, where Jonson has no part:
What share have we in nature, or in art?
Where did his wit on learning fix a brand,
And rail at arts he did not understand?
Where made he love in Prince Nicander's vein,
Or swept the dust in *Psyche's* humble strain?[1]
Where sold he bargains,[2] 'whip-stitch, kiss my arse,'
Promised a play and dwindled to a farce?
When did his Muse from Fletcher scenes purloin,
As thou whole Eth'rege dost transfuse to thine?
But so transfused, as oil on water's flow,
His always floats above, thine sinks below.
This is thy province, this thy wondrous way,
New humors to invent for each new play:
This is that boasted bias of thy mind,
By which one way, to dullness, 'tis inclined;
Which makes thy writings lean on one side still,
And, in all changes, that way bends thy will.
Nor let thy mountain-belly make pretense
Of likeness; thine's a tympany[3] of sense.
A tun of man in thy large bulk is writ,
But sure thou'rt but a kilderkin of wit.[4]
Like mine, thy gentle numbers feebly creep;
Thy tragic Muse gives smiles, thy comic sleep.

6. George Etherege (ca. 1635–91), playwright who set the tone for stylish Restoration comedy; Dryden proceeds to name five of his characters.

7. Sir Charles Sedley (ca. 1639–1701), Restoration wit who had contributed a prologue and (Dryden suggests) a part of the text to Shadwell's *Epsom Wells*.

8. Sir Formal Trifle was an inflated orator in *The Virtuoso*.

9. I.e., to Shadwell's patron the Duke of Newcastle, whose seat was in northern England.

1. Nicander pays court to the title character Psyche in Shadwell's opera.

2. A "bargain" is a gross rejoinder to an innocent question. The rest of the line, itself a kind of bargain, echoes a farcical character in *The Virtuoso*.

3. A swelling caused by air.

4. Tuns are big casks; kilderkins, little ones.

With whate'er gall thou sett'st thyself to write,
Thy inoffensive satires never bite.
In thy felonious heart though venom lies,
It does but touch thy Irish pen, and dies.
Thy genius calls thee not to purchase fame
In keen iambics,[5] but mild anagram.
Leave writing plays, and choose for thy command
Some peaceful province in acrostic land.
There thou may'st wings display and altars raise,
And torture one poor word ten thousand ways.[6]
Or, if thou wouldst thy different talent suit,
Set thy own songs, and sing them to thy lute."
He said: but his last words were scarcely heard
For Bruce and Longville had a trap prepared,
And down they sent the yet declaiming bard.[7]
Sinking he left his drugget robe behind,
Borne upwards by a subterranean wind.
The mantle fell to the young prophet's part,[8]
With double portion of his father's art.

ca. 1679 1682

To the Memory of Mr. Oldham[9]

Farewell, too little, and too lately known,
Whom I began to think and call my own:
For sure our souls were near allied, and thine
Cast in the same poetic mold with mine.
One common note on either lyre did strike,
And knaves and fools we both abhorred alike.
To the same goal did both our studies° drive; *endeavors*
The last set out the soonest did arrive.
Thus Nisus[1] fell upon the slippery place,
While his young friend performed° and won the race. *completed*
O early ripe! to thy abundant store
What could advancing age have added more?
It might (what nature never gives the young)
Have taught the numbers° of thy native tongue. *metrics*
But satire needs not those, and wit will shine
Through the harsh cadence of a rugged line:
A noble error, and but seldom made,
When poets are by too much force betrayed.
Thy generous fruits, though gathered ere their prime,
Still showed a quickness,° and maturing time *pungency*
But mellows what we write to the dull sweets of rhyme.
Once more, hail and farewell; farewell, thou young,
But ah too short, Marcellus[2] of our tongue;
Thy brows with ivy, and with laurels bound;
But fate and gloomy night encompass thee around.[3]

1684

5. The meter of (Greek) satire; hence satire itself.
6. Ingenuities like those mentioned, frequent in the early century, had been put away as trivial.
7. These characters in *The Virtuoso* so trap Sir Formal Trifle.
8. Like the prophet Elijah's mantle falling on Elisha. See II Kings ii, or Cowley's elegy on Crashaw, line 66*n*.
9. John Oldham (1653–83), author of *Satires Upon the Jesuits,* was a promising young poet, harsh (partly by calculation) in metrics and manner, but earnest and vigorous.
1. A foot racer in Virgil's *Aeneid;* his young friend Euryalus came from behind to reach the goal before him (V.315 ff.).
2. Augustus Caesar's nephew, who died at twenty after a meteoric military career.
3. The Roman elegiac phrase "Hail and farewell!" in line 22; the mention of Marcellus (line 23) and of the classical poet's wreath (line 24); and the echo of Virgil's lament for Marcellus (see *Aeneid* VI.566) conspire to Romanize Oldham.

A Song for St. Cecilia's Day[4]

1

From harmony, from heavenly harmony
This universal frame began:
When Nature[5] underneath a heap
Of jarring atoms lay,
And could not heave her head,
The tuneful voice was heard from high:
"Arise, ye more than dead."
Then cold, and hot, and moist, and dry,
In order to their stations leap,
And Music's power obey.
From harmony, from heavenly harmony
This universal frame began:
From harmony to harmony
Through all the compass of the notes it ran,
The diapason[6] closing full in man.

2

What passion cannot Music raise and quell!
When Jubal[7] struck the corded shell,
His listening brethren stood around,
And, wondering, on their faces fell
To worship that celestial sound.
Less than a god they thought there could not dwell
Within the hollow of that shell
That spoke so sweetly and so well.
What passion cannot Music raise and quell!

3

The trumpet's loud clangor
Excites us to arms,
With shrill notes of anger,
And mortal alarms.
The double double double beat
Of the thundering drum
Cries: "Hark! the foes come;
Charge, charge, 'tis too late to retreat."

4

The soft complaining flute
In dying notes discovers
The woes of hopeless lovers,
Whose dirge is whispered by the warbling lute.

5

Sharp violins proclaim
Their jealous pangs, and desperation,
Fury, frantic indignation,
Depth of pains, and height of passion,
For the fair, disdainful dame.

4. St. Cecilia was a Roman martyr of the 2nd or 3rd century, patron saint of music, customarily represented at the organ (cf. line 52). Her day was November 22.
5. Created nature as distinguished from chaos.
6. The entire range or scale of tones, "all the compass of the notes."
7. "Father of all such as handle the harp and organ" (Genesis iv.21). The "corded" or stringed tortoise "shell" is a harp or lyre.

6

But O! what art can teach,
What human voice can reach,
The sacred organ's praise?
Notes inspiring holy love,
Notes that wing their heavenly ways
To mend the choirs above.

7

Orpheus[8] could lead the savage race;
And trees unrooted left their place,
Sequacious of the lyre;
But bright Cecilia raised the wonder higher:
When to her organ vocal breath was given,
An angel heard, and straight appeared,
Mistaking earth for heaven.

Grand Chorus

As from the power of sacred lays
The spheres began to move,[9]
And sung the great Creator's praise
To all the blest above;
So, when the last and dreadful hour
This crumbling pageant shall devour,
The trumpet shall be heard on high,
The dead shall live, the living die,
And Music shall untune the sky.

1687

THOMAS TRAHERNE
(1637–1674)

Wonder

How like an angel came I down!
How bright are all things here!
When first among His works I did appear
Oh, how their glory me did crown!
The world resembled His eternity,
In which my soul did walk;
And everything that I did see
Did with me talk.

The skies in their magnificence,
The lively, lovely air,
Oh, how divine, how soft, how sweet, how fair!
The stars did entertain my sense,
And all the works of God, so bright and pure,
So rich and great did seem,

8. Son of the Muse Calliope, who played so wonderfully on the lyre that wild beasts ("the savage race") grew tame and followed him, as did even rocks and trees. "Sequacious of": following.
9. As it was harmony that ordered the universe, so it was angelic song ("sacred lays") that put the celestial bodies ("spheres") in motion. The harmonious chord that results from the traditional "music of the spheres" is a hymn of "praise" sung by created nature to its "Creator."

As if they ever must endure
In my esteem.

A native health and innocence
Within my bones did grow;
And while my God did all His glories show,
I felt a vigor in my sense
That was all spirit. I within did flow
With seas of life, like wine;
I nothing in the world did know
But 'twas divine.

Harsh ragged objects were concealed;
Oppressions, tears, and cries,
Sins, griefs, complaints, dissensions, weeping eyes
Were hid, and only things revealed
Which heavenly spirits and the angels prize.
The state of innocence
And bliss, not trades and poverties,
Did fill my sense.

The streets were paved with golden stones,
The boys and girls were mine,
Oh, how did all their lovely faces shine!
The sons of men were holy ones,
In joy and beauty they appeared to me,
And everything I found,
While like an angel I did see,
Adorned the ground.

Rich diamond and pearl and gold
In every place was seen;
Rare splendors, yellow, blue, red, white, and green,
Mine eyes did everywhere behold.
Great wonders clothed with glory did appear,
Amazement was my bliss,
That and my wealth met everywhere;
No joy to° this! *compared to*

Cursed and devised proprieties,[1]
With envy, avarice,
And fraud, those fiends that spoil even paradise,
Flew from the splendor of mine eyes;
And so did hedges, ditches, limits, bounds:
I dreamed not aught of those,
But wandered over all men's grounds,
And found repose.

Proprieties themselves were mine,
And hedges ornaments;
Walls, boxes, coffers, and their rich contents
To make me rich combine.
Clothes, ribbons, jewels, laces, I esteemed
My joys by others worn:
For me they all to wear them seemed
When I was born.

1903

1. Proprietorships, devised or bequeathed in a will.

Shadows in the Water

In unexperienced infancy
Many a sweet mistake doth lie:
Mistake though false, intending° true; *directing to*
A seeming somewhat more than view;
   That doth instruct the mind
   In things that lie behind,
And many secrets to us show
Which afterwards we come to know.

Thus did I by the water's brink
Another world beneath me think;
And while the lofty spacious skies
Reversèd there, abused mine eyes,
   I fancied other feet
   Came mine to touch or meet;
As by some puddle I did play
Another world within it lay.

Beneath the water people drowned,
Yet with another heaven crowned,
In spacious regions seemed to go
As freely moving to and fro:
   In bright and open space
   I saw their very face;
Eyes, hands, and feet they had like mine;
Another sun did with them shine.

'Twas strange that people there should walk,
And yet I could not hear them talk:
That through a little watery chink,
Which one dry ox or horse might drink,
   We other worlds should see,
   Yet not admitted be;
And other confines there behold
Of light and darkness, heat and cold.

I called them oft, but called in vain;
No speeches we could entertain:
Yet did I there expect to find
Some other world, to please my mind.
   I plainly saw by these
   A new antipodes,[2]
Whom, though they were so plainly seen,
A film kept off that stood between.

By walking men's reversèd feet
I chanced another world to meet;
Though it did not to view exceed
A phantom, 'tis a world indeed,
   Where skies beneath us shine,
   And earth by art divine

2. People living at a diametrically opposite point on the globe (literally, "with the feet opposite").

Another face presents below,
Where people's feet against ours go.

Within the regions of the air,
Compassed about with heavens fair,
Great tracts of land there may be found
Enriched with fields and fertile ground;
  Where many numerous hosts
  In those far distant coasts,
For other great and glorious ends
Inhabit, my yet unknown friends.

O ye that stand upon the brink,
Whom I so near me through the chink
With wonder see: what faces there,
Whose feet, whose bodies, do ye wear?
  I my companions see
  In you, another me.
They seemèd others, but are we;
Our second selves these shadows be.

Look how far off those lower skies
Extend themselves! scarce with mine eyes
I can them reach. O ye my friends,
What secret borders on those ends?
  Are lofty heavens hurled
  'Bout your inferior world?
Are yet the representatives
Of other peoples' distant lives?

Of all the playmates which I knew
That here I do the image view
In other selves, what can it mean?
But that below the purling stream
  Some unknown joys there be
  Laid up in store for me;
To which I shall, when that thin skin
Is broken, be admitted in.

ca. 1665 1910

EDWARD TAYLOR
(ca. 1642–1729)

Meditation 8[1]

I kenning° through astronomy divine *discerning, knowing*
  The world's bright battlement, wherein I spy
A golden path my pencil cannot line,
  From that bright throne unto my threshold lie.
  And while my puzzled thoughts about it pore
  I find the bread of life in it at my door.

1. Based on John vi.51: "I am the living bread which came down from heaven: if any man eat of this bread, he shall live for ever: and the bread that I will give is my flesh, which I will give for the life of the world."

When that this bird of paradise put in
This wicker cage (my corpse)[2] to tweedle° praise *sing*
Had pecked the fruit forbad, and so did fling
Away its food, and lost its golden days,
It fell into celestial famine sore,
And never could attain a morsel more.

Alas! alas! Poor bird, what wilt thou do?
The creatures' field no food for souls e'er gave.
And if thou knock at angels' doors they show
An empty barrel; they no soul bread have.
Alas! Poor bird, the world's white loaf is done,
And cannot yield thee here the smallest crumb.

In this sad state, God's tender bowels[3] run
Out streams of grace; and he to end all strife
The purest wheat in heaven, his dear, dear son
Grinds, and kneads up into this bread of life.
Which bread of life from heaven down came and stands
Dished on my table up by angels' hands.

Did God mould up this bread in heaven, and bake,
Which from his table came, and to thine goeth?
Doth he bespeak thee thus: This soul bread take;
Come eat thy fill of this thy God's white loaf?
It's food too fine for angels, yet come, take
And eat thy fill: it's heaven's sugar cake.

What grace is this knead in this loaf? This thing
Souls are but petty things it to admire.
Ye angels, help. This fill would to the brim
Heaven's whelmed-down[4] crystal meal bowl, yea and higher,
This bread of life dropped in thy mouth, doth cry:
Eat, eat me, soul, and thou shalt never die.

1684 1937

Upon Wedlock, and Death of Children

A curious knot God made in paradise,
And drew it out enameled° neatly fresh. *variously colored*
It was the truelove knot, more sweet than spice
And set with all the flowers of grace's dress.
Its wedding knot, that ne'er can be untied;
No Alexander's sword[5] can it divide.

The slips here planted, gay and glorious grow,
Unless an hellish breath do singe their plumes.
Here primrose, cowslips, roses, lilies blow
With violets and pinks that void° perfumes: *give off, exude*
Whose beauteous leaves o'er laid with honey-dew,
And chanting birds chirp out sweet music true.

2. In this context, the living body.
3. I.e., God's powers of mercy and compassion.
4. Turned over upon something so as to cover it.
5. Gordius, king of Phrygia, devised a complicated knot to be undone only by him who was to rule Asia. Alexander the Great cut the knot with a blow of his sword.

When in this knot I planted was, my stock° *stem*
Soon knotted, and a manly flower out brake.
And after it my branch again did knot;
Brought out another flower its sweet breathed mate.
One knot gave one t'other the t'other's place;
Whence chuckling smiles fought in each other's face.

But oh! a glorious hand from glory came
Guarded with angels, soon did crop this flower
Which almost tore the root up of the same
At that unlooked for, dolesome, darksome hour.
In prayer to Christ perfumed it did ascend,
And angels bright did it to heaven tend.

But pausing on't, this sweet perfumed my thought,
Christ would in glory have a flower, choice, prime,
And having choice, chose this my branch forth brought.
Lord take't. I thank thee, thou takest aught of mine,
It is my pledge in glory; part of me
Is now in it, Lord, glorified with thee.

But praying o'er my branch, my branch did sprout
And bore another manly flower, and gay;
And after that another, sweet, brake out,
The which the former hand soon got away.
But oh! the tortures, vomit, screechings, groans,
And six weeks fever would pierce hearts like stones.

Grief o'er doth flow, and nature fault would find
Were not thy will, my spell charm, joy, and gem;
That as I said, I say, take, Lord, they're thine.
I piecemeal pass to glory bright in them.
I joy, may I sweet flowers for glory breed,
Whether thou getst them green, or let them seed.

1937

Upon a Spider Catching a Fly

Thou sorrow, venom elf:
Is this thy play,
To spin a web out of thyself
To catch a fly?
For why?

I saw a pettish° wasp *peevish, petulant*
Fall foul therein,
Whom yet thy whorl-pins[6] did not clasp
Lest he should fling
His sting.

But as afraid, remote
Didst stand hereat
And with thy little fingers stroke
And gently tap
His back.

6. Technically, the flywheel holding the thread on the spindle of a spinning wheel; here, the spider's legs.

Thus gently him didst treat
Lest he should pet,
And in a froppish,° waspish heat *fretful*
Should greatly fret
Thy net.

Whereas the silly fly,
Caught by its leg
Thou by the throat tookst hastily
And hind the head
Bite dead.

This goes to pot,[7] that not
Nature doth call.
Strive not above what strength hath got
Lest in the brawl
Thou fall.

This fray seems thus to us.
Hell's spider gets
His entrails spun to whip-cords[8] thus,
And wove to nets
And sets.

To tangle Adam's race
In's strategems
To their destructions, spoiled, made base
By venom things,
Damned sins.

But mighty, gracious Lord
Communicate
Thy grace to break the cord, afford
Us glory's gate
And state.

We'll nightingale sing like
When perched on high
In glory's cage, thy glory, bright,
And thankfully,
For joy.

1939

JOHN WILMOT, EARL OF ROCHESTER (1647–1680)

A Satire Against Mankind

Were I, who to my cost already am,
One of those strange, prodigious creatures, *Man,*
A spirit free, to choose for my own share,
What case of flesh and blood I pleased to wear,
I'd be a dog, a monkey, or a bear,

7. As in the modern sense, deteriorates.
8. Strong cord or binding, like that made of hemp or catgut.

Or anything but that vain animal,
Who is so proud of being rational.
The senses are too gross,° and he'll contrive *inexact*
A sixth, to contradict the other five:
And before certain instinct will prefer
Reason, which fifty times for one does err.
Reason, an *ignis fatuus*[1] of the mind,
Which leaves the light of Nature, sense, behind.
Pathless and dangerous, wandering ways it takes,
Through Error's fenny bogs, and thorny brakes:
Whilst the misguided follower climbs with pain,
Mountains of whimsies heaped in his own brain:
Stumbling from thought to thought, falls headlong down
Into Doubt's boundless sea, where like to drown
Books bear him up awhile, and make him try
To swim with bladders[2] of philosophy:
In hopes still to o'ertake the skipping light,
The vapor dances in his dazzled sight,
Till spent, it leaves him to eternal night.
Then old age, and experience, hand in hand,
Lead him to death, and make him understand,
After a search so painful, and so long,
That all his life he has been in the wrong;
Huddled in dirt, the reasoning engine lies,
Who was so proud, so witty, and so wise.
Pride drew him in, as cheats their bubbles° catch, *dupes*
And made him venture to be made a wretch:
His wisdom did his happiness destroy,
Aiming to know the world he should enjoy.
And wit was his vain frivolous pretense,
Of pleasing others at his own expense.
For wits are treated just like common whores;
First they're enjoyed, and then kicked out of doors.
The pleasure past, a threatening doubt remains,
That frights the enjoyer with succeeding pains.
Women, and men of wit, are dangerous tools,
And ever fatal to admiring° fools. *wondering*
Pleasure allures, and when the fops escape,
'Tis not that they're beloved, but fortunate;
And therefore what they fear, at heart they hate.
  But now, methinks, some formal Band[3] and Beard
Takes me to task. Come on, sir, I'm prepared:
  "Then, by your favor, anything that's writ
Against this gibing, jingling knack, called wit,
Likes° me abundantly; but you'll take care *pleases*
Upon this point, not to be too severe.
Perhaps my Muse were fitter for this part,
For, I profess, I can be very smart
On wit, which I abhor with all my heart.
I long to lash it, in some sharp essáy,
But your grand indiscretion bids me stay,
And turns my tide of ink another way.
What rage ferments in your degenerate mind,
To make you rail at reason and Mankind?
Blest glorious Man! to whom alone kind heaven

1. Will-o'-the-wisp.
2. Inflated bladders, buoying him up.
3. A Geneva band, worn by the clergy. A Band and Beard is hence a venerable parson.

An everlasting soul has freely given;
Whom his great Maker took such care to make,
That from himself he did the image take,
And this fair frame in shining reason dressed,
To dignify his nature above beast.
Reason, by whose aspiring influence,
We take a flight beyond material sense,
Dive into mysteries, then soaring pierce
The flaming limits of the universe,
Search heaven and hell, find out what's acted there,
And give the world true grounds of hope and fear."
  Hold, mighty man, I cry; all this we know,
From the pathetic pen of Ingelo,
From Patrick's *Pilgrim*, Sibbe's *Soliloquies*,[4]
And 'tis this very reason I despise,
This supernatural gift, that makes a mite
Think he's the image of the Infinite;
Comparing his short life, void of all rest,
To the Eternal and the ever Blest;
This busy, puzzling stirrer up of doubt,
That frames deep mysteries, then finds 'em out,
Filling with frantic crowds of thinking fools,
Those reverend Bedlams,° colleges and schools, *madhouses*
Borne on whose wings, each heavy sot can pierce
The limits of the boundless universe:
So charming ointments[5] make an old witch fly,
And bear a crippled carcass through the sky.
'Tis this exalted power, whose business lies
In nonsense and impossibilities:
This made a whimsical philosopher,
Before the spacious world his tub prefer,[6]
And we have modern cloistered coxcombs, who
Retire to think, 'cause they have nought to do.
But thoughts were given for action's government;
Where action ceases, thought's impertinent.° *irrelevant*
Our sphere of action is life's happiness,
And he who thinks beyond, thinks like an ass.
Thus whilst against false reasoning I inveigh,
I own right reason, which I would obey:
That reason, that distinguishes by sense,
And gives us rules of good and ill from thence;
That bounds desires with a reforming will,
To keep them more in vigor, not to kill.
Your reason hinders, mine helps to enjoy;
Renewing appetites, yours would destroy.
My reason is my friend, yours is a cheat:
Hunger calls out, my reason bids me eat;
Perversely yours, your appetite does mock;
This asks for food, that answers, "What's o'clock?"
This plain distinction, sir, your doubt° secures;° *suspicion / confirms*
'Tis not true reason I despise, but yours.
Thus, I think reason righted: but for Man,

4. Nathaniel Ingello, whose pen is derisively called "pathetic" (heart-rending), wrote an allegorical romance *Bentivolio and Urania*. Simon Patrick's *The Parable of the Pilgrim* (another allegory), and Richard Sibbe's discourses (none actually called *Soliloquies*) were other current instructional works.

5. The magical preparations of witches, usually (as in *Macbeth*) mixtures of outlandish things.

6. Diogenes the Cynic, who (in legend) inhabited a tub.

I'll ne'er recant, defend him if you can.
For all his pride, and his philosophy,
'Tis evident beasts are, in their degree,
As wise at least, and better far than he.
Those creatures are the wisest, who attain,
By surest means, the ends at which they aim.
If therefore Jowler finds, and kills his hares,
Better than Meres supplies committee chairs;[7]
Though one's a statesman, the other but a hound,
Jowler in justice will be wiser found.
You see how far Man's wisdom here extends:
Look next if human nature makes amends;
Whose principles most generous are and just,
And to those whose morals you would sooner trust.
Be judge yourself, I'll bring it to the test,
Which is the basest creature, Man or beast?
Birds feed on birds, beasts on each other prey,
But savage Man alone does Man betray.
Pressed by necessity, *they* kill for food,
Man undoes Man to do himself no good.
With teeth and claws by Nature armed, *they* hunt
Nature's allowance, to supply their want:
But Man, with smiles, embraces, friendships, praise,
Unhumanly, his fellow's life betrays:
With voluntary pains works his distress;
Not through necessity, but wantonness.
For hunger, or for love, *they* bite or tear,
Whilst wretched Man is still in arms for fear:
For fear he arms, and is of arms afraid;
From fear to fear successively betrayed.
Base fear, the source whence his best passions came,
His boasted honor, and his dear-bought fame,
That lust of power, to which he's such a slave,
And for the which alone he dares be brave:
To which his various projects are designed,
Which makes him generous, affable, and kind,
For which he takes such pains to be thought wise,
And screws° his actions, in a forced disguise: *distorts*
Leading a tedious life, in misery,
Under laborious, mean Hypocrisy.
Look to the bottom of his vast design,
Wherein Man's wisdom, power, and glory join;
The good he acts, the ill he does endure,
'Tis all from fear, to make himself secure.
Merely for safety, after fame we thirst,
For all men would be cowards if they durst:
And honesty's against all common sense:
Men must be knaves; 'tis in their own defense.
Mankind's dishonest; if you think it fair,
Amongst known cheats, to play upon the square,
You'll be undone——
Nor can weak truth your reputation save;
The knaves will all agree to call you knave.
Wronged shall he live, insulted o'er, oppressed,
Who dares be less a villain than the rest.

7. Sir Thomas Meres, a Whig member of Parliament.

Thus, sir, you see what human nature craves,
Most men are cowards, all men should be knaves.
The difference lies, as far as I can see,
Not in the thing itself, but the degree;
And all the subject matter of debate,
Is only who's a knave of the first rate.

1675

ANNE FINCH, COUNTESS OF WINCHILSEA
(1661–1720)

A Nocturnal Reverie

In such a night, when every louder wind
Is to its distant cavern safe confined;
And only gentle Zephyr fans his wings,
And lonely Philomel,[1] still waking, sings;
Or from some tree, famed for the owl's delight,
She, hollowing clear, directs the wanderer right:
In such a night, when passing clouds give place,
Or thinly veil the heavens' mysterious face;
When in some river, overhung with green,
The waving moon and trembling leaves are seen;
When freshened grass now bears itself upright,
And makes cool banks to pleasing rest invite,
Whence springs the woodbind, and the bramble-rose,
And where the sleepy cowslip sheltered grows;
Whilst now a paler hue the foxglove takes,
Yet checkers still with red the dusky brakes.[2]
When scattered glow-worms, but in twilight fine,
Show trivial beauties watch their hour to shine;[3]
Whilst Salisbury stands the test of every light,
In perfect charms, and perfect virtue bright:
When odors, which declined repelling day,[4]
Through temperate air uninterrupted stray;
When darkened groves their softest shadows wear,
And falling waters we distinctly hear;
When through the gloom more venerable shows
Some ancient fabric,° awful in repose, *building*
While sunburnt hills their swarthy looks conceal,
And swelling haycocks thicken up the vale:
When the loosed horse now, as his pasture leads,
Comes slowly grazing through the adjoining meads,
Whose stealing pace, and lengthened shade we fear,
Till torn-up forage in his teeth we hear:
When nibbling sheep at large pursue their food,
And unmolested kine rechew the cud;
When curlews[5] cry beneath the village walls,
And to her straggling brood the partridge calls;
Their shortlived jubilee the creatures keep,

1. The nightingale.
2. Thickets; tall ferns or bracken.
3. I.e., show lesser beauties that, unlike Lady Salisbury of the following line, they must make the most of their limited opportunities to shine.
4. When the aromas ("odors") of field and wood, which refused to come forth ("declined") under the hot, "repelling" rays of the sun ("day").
5. A kind of shore bird not unlike a sandpiper.

Which but endures, whilst tyrant man does sleep;
When a sedate content the spirit feels,
And no fierce light disturbs, whilst it reveals;
But silent musings urge the mind to seek
Something, too high for syllables to speak;
Till the free soul to a composedness charmed,
Finding the elements of rage disarmed,
O'er all below a solemn quiet grown,
Joys in the inferior° world, and thinks it like her own: *lower*
In such a night let me abroad remain,
Till morning breaks, and all's confused again;
Our cares, our toils, our clamors are renewed,
Or pleasures, seldom reached, again pursued.

1713

MATTHEW PRIOR
(1664–1721)

To a Lady: She Refusing to Continue a Dispute with Me, and Leaving Me in the Argument

1
Spare, gen'rous victor, spare the slave,
Who did unequal war pursue;
That more than triumph he might have,
In being overcome by you.

2
In the dispute whate'er I said,
My heart was by my tongue belied;
And in my looks you might have read,
How much I argued on your side.

3
You, far from danger as from fear,
Might have sustained an open fight:
For seldom your opinions err;
Your eyes are always in the right.

4
Why, fair one, would you not rely
On reason's force with beauty's joined?
Could I their prevalence deny;
I must at once be deaf and blind.

5
Alas! not hoping to subdue,
I only to the fight aspired:
To keep the beauteous foe in view
Was all the glory I desired.

6
But she, howe'er of vict'ry sure,
Contemns the wreath too long delayed;
And, armed with more immediate Pow'r,
Calls cruel silence to her aid.

7
Deeper to wound, she shuns the fight:
She drops her arms, to gain the field:

Secures her conquest by her flight;
  And triumphs, when she seems to yield.

8

So when the Parthian[6] turned his steed,
  And from the hostile camp withdrew;
With cruel skill the backward reed° *arrow*
  He sent; and as he fled, he slew.

1718

JONATHAN SWIFT (1667–1745)

A Description of the Morning

Now hardly here and there a hackney-coach[1]
Appearing, showed the ruddy morn's approach.
Now Betty from her master's bed had flown,
And softly stole to discompose her own;
The slip-shod 'prentice from his master's door
Had pared the dirt and sprinkled round the floor.
Now Moll had whirled her mop with dext'rous airs,
Prepared to scrub the entry and the stairs.
The youth with broomy stumps began to trace
The kennel-edge,[2] where wheels had worn the place.
The small-coal man[3] was heard with cadence deep,
Till drowned in shriller notes of chimney-sweep:
Duns° at his lordship's gate began to meet; *bill collectors*
And brickdust Moll[4] had screamed through half the street.
The turnkey° now his flock returning sees, *jailer*
Duly let out a-nights to steal for fees:
The watchful bailiffs[5] take their silent stands,
And schoolboys lag with satchels in their hands.

1709

A Description of a City Shower

  Careful observers may foretell the hour
(By sure prognostics) when to dread a shower:
While rain depends,° the pensive cat gives o'er *impends*
Her frolics, and pursues her tail no more.
Returning home at night, you'll find the sink° *sewer*
Strike your offended sense with double stink.
If you be wise, then go not far to dine;
You'll spend in coach hire more than save in wine.
A coming shower your shooting corns presage,
Old achés throb, your hollow tooth will rage.
Sauntering in coffeehouse is Dulman° seen; *dull-man*
He damns the climate and complains of spleen.° *melancholy*
  Meanwhile the South,° rising with dabbled wings, *south wind*
A sable cloud athwart the welkin° flings, *sky*

6. A people of western Asia, whose cavalry fought in the manner Prior describes.
1. A horse-drawn carriage, for hire.
2. Curb of the road.
3. Seller of charcoal.
4. A woman selling powdered brick (used for cleaning knives).
5. I.e., sheriff's deputies.

That swilled more liquor than it could contain,
And, like a drunkard, gives it up again.
Brisk Susan whips her linen from the rope,
While the first drizzling shower is borne aslope:
Such is that sprinkling which some careless quean° *wench*
Flirts on you from her mop, but not so clean:
You fly, invoke the gods; then turning, stop
To rail; she singing, still whirls on her mop.
Not yet the dust had shunned the unequal strife,
But, aided by the wind, fought still for life,
And wafted with its foe by violent gust,
'Twas doubtful which was rain and which was dust.
Ah! where must needy poet seek for aid,
When dust and rain at once his coat invade?
Sole coat, where dust cemented by the rain
Erects the nap, and leaves a mingled stain.
  Now in contiguous drops the flood comes down,
Threatening with deluge this devoted° town. *doomed*
To shops in crowds the daggled° females fly, *spattered*
Pretend to cheapen° goods, but nothing buy. *price*
The Templar° spruce, while every spout's abroach,° *law student / running*
Stays till 'tis fair, yet seems to call a coach.
The tucked-up sempstress walks with hasty strides,
While streams run down her oiled umbrella's sides.
Here various kinds, by various fortunes led,
Commence acquaintance underneath a shed.
Triumphant Tories and desponding Whigs[6]
Forget their feuds, and join to save their wigs.
Boxed in a chair° the beau impatient sits, *sedan chair*
While spouts run clattering o'er the roof by fits,
And ever and anon with frightful din
The leather[7] sounds; he trembles from within.
So when Troy chairmen bore the wooden steed,
Pregnant with Greeks impatient to be freed
(Those bully Greeks, who, as the moderns do,
Instead of paying chairmen, run them through),
Laocoön struck the outside with his spear,
And each imprisoned hero quaked for fear.[8]
  Now from all parts the swelling kennels° flow, *gutters*
And bear their trophies with them as they go:
Filth of all hues and odors seem to tell
What street they sailed from, by their sight and smell.
They, as each torrent drives with rapid force,
From Smithfield or St. Pulchre's shape their course,
And in huge confluence joined at Snow Hill ridge,
Fall from the conduit prone to Holborn Bridge.[9]
Sweepings from butchers' stalls, dung, guts, and blood,
Drowned puppies, stinking sprats,° all drenched in mud, *herring*
Dead cats, and turnip tops, come tumbling down the flood.

1710

6. The Tories (Swift's party) had recently assumed power.
7. Leather roof of the sedan chair.
8. In *Aeneid* II, Laocoön so struck the side of the Trojan horse, frightening the Greeks within.
9. The sewage system referred to is fed first by the refuse of the Smithfield cattle market and drains at last into the open Fleet Ditch at Holborn Bridge.

Stella's Birthday[1]

MARCH 13, 1727

This day, whate'er the fates decree,
Shall still° be kept with joy by me: *always*
This day then, let us not be told
That you are sick, and I grown old,
Nor think on our approaching ills,
And talk of spectacles and pills;
Tomorrow will be time enough
To hear such mortifying stuff.
Yet since from reason may be brought
A better and more pleasing thought,
Which can in spite of all decays
Support a few remaining days:
From not the gravest of divines,
Accept for once some serious lines.
Although we now can form no more
Long schemes of life, as heretofore;
Yet you, while time is running fast,
Can look with joy on what is past.
Were future happiness and pain
A mere contrivance of the brain,
As atheists argue, to entice
And fit their proselytes for vice
(The only comfort they propose,
To have companions in their woes),
Grant this the case, yet sure 'tis hard
That virtue, styled its own reward,
And by all sages understood
To be the chief of human good,
Should acting, die, nor leave behind
Some lasting pleasure in the mind,
Which, by remembrance, will assuage
Grief, sickness, poverty, and age;
And strongly shoot a radiant dart,
To shine through life's declining part.
Say, Stella, feel you no content,
Reflecting on a life well spent?
Your skillful hand employed to save
Despairing wretches from the grave;
And then supporting from your store
Those whom you dragged from death before
(So Providence on mortals waits,
Preserving what it first creates);
Your generous boldness to defend
An innocent and absent friend;
That courage which can make you just,
To merit humbled in the dust:
The detestation you express
For vice in all its glittering dress:

1. The forty-sixth birthday of Swift's devoted companion and protégée Esther Johnson.

That patience under torturing pain,
Where stubborn stoics would complain.
Must these like empty shadows pass,
Or forms reflected from a glass?
Or mere chimeras in the mind,
That fly and leave no marks behind?
Does not the body thrive and grow
By food of twenty years ago?
And, had it not been still supplied,
It must a thousand times have died.
Then who with reason can maintain
That no effects of food remain?
And is not virtue in mankind
The nutriment that feeds the mind?
Upheld by each good action past,
And still continued by the last:
Then who with reason can pretend
That all effects of virtue end?
Believe me, Stella, when you show
That true contempt for things below,
Nor prize your life for other ends
Than merely to oblige your friends,
Your former actions claim their part,
And join to fortify your heart.
For virtue in her daily race,
Like Janus,[2] bears a double face,
Looks back with joy where she has gone,
And therefore goes with courage on.
She at your sickly couch will wait,
And guide you to some better state.
O then, whatever Heaven intends,
Take pity on your pitying friends;
Nor let your ills affect your mind,
To fancy they can be unkind.
Me, surely me, you ought to spare,
Who gladly would your sufferings share;
Or give my scrap of life to you,
And think it far beneath your due;
You, to whose care so oft I owe
That I'm alive to tell you so.

1727

ISAAC WATTS (1674–1748)

Our God, Our Help[1]

Our God, our help in ages past,
Our hope for years to come,
Our shelter from the stormy blast,
And our eternal home:

2. The Roman god of doors, with opposed faces, one looking forward, the other back.

1. Originally entitled "Man Frail and God Eternal," the hymn derives from Psalm 90.

Under the shadow of thy throne
  Thy saints have dwelt secure;
Sufficient is thine arm alone,
  And our defense is sure.

Before the hills in order stood
  Or earth received her frame,[2]
From everlasting thou art God,
  To endless years the same.

Thy word commands our flesh to dust,
  "Return, ye sons of men";
All nations rose from earth at first,
  And turn to earth again.

A thousand ages in thy sight
  Are like an evening gone;
Short as the watch that ends the night
  Before the rising sun.

The busy tribes of flesh and blood,
  With all their lives and cares,
Are carried downwards by thy flood,
  And lost in following years.

Time, like an ever-rolling stream,
  Bears all its sons away;
They fly forgotten, as a dream
  Dies at the opening day.

Like flowery fields the nations stand,
  Pleased with the morning light;
The flowers beneath the mower's hand
  Lie withering e'er 'tis night.

Our God, our help in ages past,
  Our hope for years to come,
Be thou our guard while troubles last,
  And our eternal home.

1719

2. Structure, constitution.

ALEXANDER POPE (1688–1744)

The Rape of the Lock

AN HEROI-COMICAL POEM[1]

Nolueram, Belinda, tuos violare capillos;
sed juvat hoc precibus me tribuisse tuis.[2]
—MARTIAL

Canto I

What dire offense from amorous causes springs,
What mighty contests rise from trivial things,
I sing—This verse to Caryll, Muse! is due:
This, even Belinda may vouchsafe to view:
Slight is the subject, but not so the praise,
If she inspire, and he approve my lays.
Say what strange motive, Goddess! could compel
A well-bred lord to assault a gentle belle?
Oh, say what stranger cause, yet unexplored,
Could make a gentle belle reject a lord?
In tasks so bold can little men engage,
And in soft bosoms dwells such mighty rage?
Sol through white curtains shot a timorous ray,
And oped those eyes that must eclipse the day.[3]
Now lapdogs give themselves the rousing shake,
And sleepless lovers just at twelve awake:
Thrice rung the bell, the slipper knocked the ground,[4]
And the pressed watch returned a silver sound.[5]
Belinda still her downy pillow pressed,
Her guardian Sylph[6] prolonged the balmy rest:
'Twas he had summoned to her silent bed
The morning dream that hovered o'er her head.
A youth more glittering than a birthnight beau[7]
(That even in slumber caused her cheek to glow)
Seemed to her ear his winning lips to lay,
And thus in whispers said, or seemed to say:
"Fairest of mortals, thou distinguished care
Of thousand bright inhabitants of air!
If e'er one vision touched thy infant thought,
Of all the nurse and all the priest have taught,

1. Based on an actual incident. A young man, Lord Petre, had sportively cut off a lock of a Miss Arabella Fermor's hair. She and her family were angered by the prank, and Pope's friend John Caryll (line 3), a relative of Lord Petre's, asked the poet to turn the incident into jest, so that good relations (and possibly negotiations toward a marriage between the principals) might be resumed. Pope responded by treating the incident in a mock epic or "heroi-comical poem." The epic conventions first encountered are the immediate statement of the topic, which the poet says he will "sing" as if in oral recitation, and the request to the Muse (line 7) to grant him the necessary insight.

2. "I did not want, Belinda, to violate your locks, but it pleases me to have paid this tribute to your prayers." Miss Fermor did not in fact request the poem.

3. The eyes of lovely young women—though Belinda herself is still asleep.

4. These are two ways of summoning servants.

5. In the darkened beds, one discovered the approximate time by a watch which chimed the hour and quarter-hour when the stem was pressed.

6. Air-spirit. He accounts for himself in the lines below.

7. Courtier dressed for a royal birthday celebration.

Of airy elves by moonlight shadows seen,
The silver token, and the circled green,[8]
Or virgins visited by angel powers,
With golden crowns and wreaths of heavenly flowers,
Hear and believe! thy own importance know,
Nor bound thy narrow views to things below.
Some secret truths, from learned pride concealed,
To maids alone and children are revealed:
What though no credit doubting wits may give?
The fair and innocent shall still believe.
Know, then, unnumbered spirits round thee fly,
The light militia of the lower sky:
These, though unseen, are ever on the wing,
Hang o'er the box, and hover round the Ring.[9]
Think what an equipage thou hast in air,
And view with scorn two pages and a chair.° *sedan chair*
As now your own, our beings were of old,
And once enclosed in woman's beauteous mold;
Thence, by a soft transition, we repair
From earthly vehicles[1] to these of air.
Think not, when woman's transient breath is fled,
That all her vanities at once are dead:
Succeeding vanities she still regards,
And though she plays no more, o'erlooks the cards.
Her joy in gilded chariots,° when alive, *carriages*
And love of ombre,[2] after death survive.
For when the Fair in all their pride expire,
To their first elements their souls retire:[3]
The sprites of fiery termagants in flame
Mount up, and take a Salamander's name.
Soft yielding minds to water glide away,
And sip, with Nymphs, their elemental tea.[4]
The graver prude sinks downward to a Gnome,
In search of mischief still on earth to roam.
The light coquettes in Sylphs aloft repair,
And sport and flutter in the fields of air.
"Know further yet; whoever fair and chaste
Rejects mankind, is by some Sylph embraced:
For spirits, freed from mortal laws, with ease
Assume what sexes and what shapes they please.[5]
What guards the purity of melting maids,
In courtly balls, and midnight masquerades,
Safe from the treacherous friend, the daring spark,
The glance by day, the whisper in the dark,
When kind occasion prompts their warm desires,

8. The silver token is the coin left by a fairy or elf, and the circled green is a ring of bright green grass, supposed dancing circle of fairies.
9. The box is a theater box; the Ring, the circular carriage course in Hyde Park.
1. Mediums of existence, with a side glance at the fondness of young women for riding in carriages.
2. A popular card game, pronounced *omber*.
3. Namely, to fire, water, earth, and air, the four elements of the old cosmology and the several habitats (in the Rosicrucian myths upon which Pope embroiders) of four different kinds of "spirit." Envisaging these spirits as the transmigrated souls of different kinds of women, Pope causes termagants (scolds) to become fire-spirits or Salamanders (line 60); irresolute women to become water-spirits or Nymphs (line 62); prudes, or women who delight in rejection and negation, to become earth-spirits or Gnomes (line 64); and coquettes to become air-spirits or Sylphs. Since "nymph" could designate either a water-spirit or (in literary usage) a young lady, Pope permits his water-spirits to claim tea as their native element (line 62) and to keep their former company at tea-parties.
4. Pronounced *tay*.
5. Like Milton's angels (*Paradise Lost* I.423 ff.).

When music softens, and when dancing fires?
'Tis but their Sylph, the wise Celestials know,
Though Honor is the word with men below.
"Some nymphs there are, too conscious of their face,
For life predestined to the Gnomes' embrace.
These swell their prospects and exalt their pride,
When offers are disdained, and love denied:
Then gay ideas° crowd the vacant brain, *imaginings*
While peers, and dukes, and all their sweeping train,
And garters, stars, and coronets[6] appear,
And in soft sounds, 'your Grace' salutes their ear.
'Tis these that early taint the female soul,
Instruct the eyes of young coquettes to roll,
Teach infant cheeks a bidden blush to know,
And little hearts to flutter at a beau.
"Oft, when the world imagine women stray,
The Sylphs through mystic mazes guide their way,
Through all the giddy circle they pursue,
And old impertinence expel by new.
What tender maid but must a victim fall
To one man's treat, but for another's ball?
When Florio speaks what virgin could withstand,
If gentle Damon did not squeeze her hand?
With varying vanities, from every part,
They shift the moving toyshop of their heart;
Where wigs with wigs, with sword-knots sword-knots strive,[7]
Beaux banish beaux, and coaches coaches drive.
This erring mortals levity may call;
Oh, blind to truth! the Sylphs contrive it all.
"Of these am I, who thy protection claim,
A watchful sprite, and Ariel is my name.
Late, as I ranged the crystal wilds of air,
In the clear mirror of thy ruling star
I saw, alas! some dread event impend,
Ere to the main this morning sun descend,
But Heaven reveals not what, or how, or where:
Warned by the Sylph, O pious maid, beware!
This to disclose is all thy guardian can:
Beware of all, but most beware of Man!"
He said; when Shock,[8] who thought she slept too long,
Leaped up, and waked his mistress with his tongue.
'Twas then, Belinda, if report say true,
Thy eyes first opened on a billet-doux;[9]
Wounds, charms, and ardors were no sooner read,
But all the vision vanished from thy head.
And now, unveiled, the toilet stands displayed,
Each silver vase in mystic order laid.
First, robed in white, the nymph intent adores,
With head uncovered, the cosmetic powers.
A heavenly image in the glass[1] appears;

6. Insignia of rank and court status.
7. Sword-Knots are ribbons tied to hilts. The verbal repetition and the tangled syntax recall descriptions of the throng and press of battle appearing in English translations of classical epic.
8. A name for lapdogs (like "Poll" for parrots); they looked like little "shocks" of hair.
9. A love letter. The affected language of the fashionable love letter is exhibited in the next line.
1. The mirror. Her image is the object of veneration, the "goddess" named later. Belinda presides over the appropriate rites. Betty, her maid, is the "inferior priestess."

To that she bends, to that her eyes she rears.
The inferior priestess, at her altar's side,
Trembling begins the sacred rites of pride.
Unnumbered treasures ope at once, and here
The various offerings of the world appear;
From each she nicely culls with curious toil,
And decks the goddess with the glittering spoil.
This casket India's glowing gems unlocks,
And all Arabia[2] breathes from yonder box.
The tortoise here and elephant unite,
Transformed to combs, the speckled and the white.
Here files of pins extend their shining rows,
Puffs, powders, patches, Bibles, billet-doux.
Now awful Beauty put on all its arms;
The fair each moment rises in her charms,
Repairs her smiles, awakens every grace,
And calls forth all the wonders of her face;
Sees by degrees a purer blush arise,
And keener lightnings quicken in her eyes.
The busy Sylphs surround their darling care,
These set the head, and those divide the hair,
Some fold the sleeve, whilst others plait the gown;
And Betty's praised for labors not her own.

Canto II

Not with more glories, in the ethereal plain,
The sun first rises o'er the purpled main,
Than, issuing forth, the rival of his beams[3]
Launched on the bosom of the silver Thames.
Fair nymphs and well-dressed youths around her shone,
But every eye was fixed on her alone.
On her white breast a sparkling cross she wore,
Which Jews might kiss, and infidels adore.
Her lively looks a sprightly mind disclose,
Quick as her eyes, and as unfixed as those:
Favors to none, to all she smiles extends;
Oft she rejects, but never once offends.
Bright as the sun, her eyes the gazers strike,
And, like the sun, they shine on all alike.
Yet graceful ease, and sweetness void of pride,
Might hide her faults, if belles had faults to hide:
If to her share some female errors fall,
Look on her face, and you'll forget 'em all.
This nymph, to the destruction of mankind,
Nourished two locks which graceful hung behind
In equal curls, and well conspired to deck
With shining ringlets the smooth ivory neck.
Love in these labyrinths his slaves detains,
And mighty hearts are held in slender chains.
With hairy springes° we the birds betray, *snares*
Slight lines of hair surprise the finny prey,
Fair tresses man's imperial race ensnare,
And beauty draws us with a single hair.
The adventurous Baron the bright locks admired,

2. Source of perfumes.
3. I.e., Belinda. She is en route to Hampton Court, a royal palace some twelve miles up the river Thames from London.

He saw, he wished, and to the prize aspired.
Resolved to win, he meditates the way,
By force to ravish, or by fraud betray;
For when success a lover's toil attends,
Few ask if fraud or force attained his ends.
  For this, ere Phoebus rose, he had implored
Propitious Heaven, and every power adored,
But chiefly Love—to Love an altar built,
Of twelve vast French romances, neatly gilt.
There lay three garters, half a pair of gloves,
And all the trophies of his former loves.
With tender billet-doux he lights the pyre,
And breathes three amorous sighs to raise the fire.
Then prostrate falls, and begs with ardent eyes
Soon to obtain, and long possess the prize:
The powers gave ear, and granted half his prayer,
The rest the winds dispersed in empty air.
  But now secure the painted vessel glides,
The sunbeams trembling on the floating tides,
While melting music steals upon the sky,
And softened sounds along the waters die.
Smooth flow the waves, the zephyrs gently play,
Belinda smiled, and all the world was gay.
All but the Sylph—with careful thoughts oppressed,
The impending woe sat heavy on his breast.
He summons straight his denizens° of air; *inhabitants*
The lucid squadrons round the sails repair:° *assemble*
Soft o'er the shrouds aërial whispers breathe
That seemed but zephyrs to the train beneath.
Some to the sun their insect-wings unfold,
Waft on the breeze, or sink in clouds of gold.
Transparent forms too fine for mortal sight,
Their fluid bodies half dissolved in light,
Loose to the wind their airy garments flew,
Thin glittering textures of the filmy dew,[4]
Dipped in the richest tincture of the skies,
Where light disports in ever-mingling dyes,
While every beam new transient colors flings,
Colors that change whene'er they wave their wings.
Amid the circle, on the gilded mast,
Superior by the head was Ariel placed;
His purple° pinions opening to the sun, *brilliant*
He raised his azure wand, and thus begun:
  "Ye Sylphs and Sylphids, to your chief give ear!
Fays, Fairies, Genii, Elves, and Daemons, hear!
Ye know the spheres and various tasks assigned
By laws eternal to the aërial kind.
Some in the fields of purest ether play,
And bask and whiten in the blaze of day.
Some guide the course of wandering orbs on high,
Or roll the planets through the boundless sky.
Some less refined, beneath the moon's pale light
Pursue the stars that shoot athwart the night,
Or suck the mists in grosser air below,

4. The supposed material of spider webs.

Or dip their pinions in the painted bow,° *rainbow*
Or brew fierce tempests on the wintry main,
Or o'er the glebe° distill the kindly rain. *farmland*
Others on earth o'er human race preside,
Watch all their ways, and all their actions guide:
Of these the chief the care of nations own,
And guard with arms divine the British Throne.
  "Our humbler province is to tend the Fair,
Not a less pleasing, though less glorious care:
To save the powder from too rude a gale,
Nor let the imprisoned essences exhale;
To draw fresh colors from the vernal flowers;
To steal from rainbows e'er they drop in showers
A brighter wash;° to curl their waving hairs, *(cosmetic) wash*
Assist their blushes, and inspire their airs;
Nay oft, in dreams invention we bestow,
To change a flounce, or add a furbelow.
  "This day black omens threat the brightest fair,
That e'er deserved a watchful spirit's care;
Some dire disaster, or by force or slight,
But what, or where, the Fates have wrapped in night:
Whether the nymph shall break Diana's law,[5]
Or some frail china jar receive a flaw,
Or stain her honor or her new brocade,
Forget her prayers, or miss a masquerade,
Or lose her heart, or necklace, at a ball;
Or whether Heaven has doomed that Shock must fall.
Haste, then, ye spirits! to your charge repair:
The fluttering fan be Zephyretta's care;
The drops° to thee, Brillante, we consign; *earrings*
And, Momentilla, let the watch be thine;
Do thou, Crispissa,[6] tend her favorite Lock;
Ariel himself shall be the guard of Shock.
  "To fifty chosen Sylphs, of special note,
We trust the important charge, the petticoat;
Oft have we known that sevenfold fence to fail,
Though stiff with hoops, and armed with ribs of whale.
Form a strong line about the silver bound,
And guard the wide circumference around.
  "Whatever spirit, careless of his charge,
His post neglects, or leaves the fair at large,
Shall feel sharp vengeance soon o'ertake his sins,
Be stopped in vials, or transfixed with pins,
Or plunged in lakes of bitter washes lie,
Or wedged whole ages in a bodkin's° eye; *large needle's*
Gums and pomatums shall his flight restrain,
While clogged he beats his silken wings in vain,
Or alum styptics with contracting power
Shrink his thin essence like a riveled° flower: *shriveled*
Or, as Ixion[7] fixed, the wretch shall feel
The giddy motion of the whirling mill,° *cocoa-mill*
In fumes of burning chocolate shall glow,
And tremble at the sea that froths below!"
  He spoke; the spirits from the sails descend;
Some, orb in orb, around the nymph extend;
Some thread the mazy ringlets of her hair;

5. Of chastity.
6. To "crisp" is to curl (hair).
7. For an affront to Juno, Ixion was bound eternally to a turning wheel.

Some hang upon the pendants of her ear:
With beating hearts the dire event they wait,
Anxious, and trembling for the birth of Fate.

Canto III

Close by those meads, forever crowned with flowers,
Where Thames with pride surveys his rising towers,
There stands a structure of majestic frame,[8]
Which from the neighboring Hampton takes its name.
Here Britain's statesmen oft the fall foredoom
Of foreign tyrants and of nymphs at home;
Here thou, great Anna! whom three realms obey,
Dost sometimes counsel take—and sometimes tea.
Hither the heroes and the nymphs resort,
To taste awhile the pleasures of a court;
In various talk the instructive hours they passed,
Who gave the ball, or paid the visit last;
One speaks the glory of the British Queen,
And one describes a charming Indian screen;
A third interprets motions, looks, and eyes;
At every word a reputation dies.
Snuff, or the fan, supply each pause of chat,
With singing, laughing, ogling, and all that.
Meanwhile, declining from the noon of day,
The sun obliquely shoots his burning ray;
The hungry judges soon the sentence sign,
And wretches hang that jurymen may dine;
The merchant from the Exchange° returns in peace, *stock market*
And the long labors of the toilet cease.
Belinda now, whom thirst of fame invites,
Burns to encounter two adventurous knights,
At ombre[9] singly to decide their doom,
And swells her breast with conquests yet to come.
Straight the three bands prepare in arms° to join, *combat*
Each band the number of the sacred nine.
Soon as she spreads her hand, the aërial guard
Descend, and sit on each important card:
First Ariel perched upon a Matadore,
Then each according to the rank they bore;
For Sylphs, yet mindful of their ancient race,
Are, as when women, wondrous fond of place.
Behold, four Kings in majesty revered,
With hoary whiskers and a forky beard;
And four fair Queens whose hands sustain a flower,
The expressive emblem of their softer power;
Four Knaves in garbs succinct,[1] a trusty band,
Caps on their heads, and halberts in their hand;

8. Hampton Court.
9. This game is like three-handed bridge with some features of poker added. From a deck lacking 8's, 9's and 10's, nine cards are dealt to each player (line 30) and the rest put in a central pool. A declarer called the *Ombre* (Spanish *hombre,* man) commits himself to taking more tricks than either of his opponents individually; hence Belinda would "encounter two knights *singly.*" Declarer, followed by the other players, then selects discards and replenishes his hand with cards drawn sight unseen from the pool (line 45). He proceeds to name his trumps (line 46). The three principal trumps, called *Matadors* (line 47), always include the black aces. When spades are declared, the Matadors are, in order of value, the ace of spades (called *Spadille,* line 49), the deuce of spades (called *Manille,* line 51), and the ace of clubs (called *Basto,* line 53). The remaining spades fill out the trump suit. In the game here described, Belinda leads out her high trumps (lines 49–56), but the suit breaks badly (line 54); the Baron retains the queen (line 67), with which he presently trumps her king of clubs (line 69). He then leads high diamonds until she is on the verge of a set (called *Codille,* line 92). But she makes her bid at the last trick (line 94), taking his ace of hearts with her king (line 95), this being, in ombre, the highest card in the heart suit. The game is played on a green velvet cloth (line 44).
1. Hemmed up short, not flowing.

And parti-colored troops, a shining train,
Draw forth to combat on the velvet plain.
The skillful nymph reviews her force with care;
"Let Spades be trumps!" she said, and trumps they were.
Now move to war her sable Matadores,
In show like leaders of the swarthy Moors.
Spadillio first, unconquerable lord!
Led off two captive trumps, and swept the board.
As many more Manillio forced to yield,
And marched a victor from the verdant field.
Him Basto followed, but his fate more hard
Gained but one trump and one plebeian card.
With his broad saber next, a chief in years,
The hoary Majesty of Spades appears,
Puts forth one manly leg, to sight revealed,
The rest his many-colored robe concealed.
The rebel Knave, who dares his prince engage,
Proves the just victim of his royal rage.
Even mighty Pam,[2] that kings and queens o'erthrew
And mowed down armies in the fights of loo,
Sad chance of war! now distitute of aid,
Falls undistinguished by the victor Spade.
Thus far both armies to Belinda yield;
Now to the Baron fate inclines the field.
His warlike amazon her host invades,
The imperial consort of the crown of Spades.
The Club's black tyrant first her victim died,
Spite of his haughty mien and barbarous pride.
What boots the regal circle on his head,
His giant limbs, in state unwieldy spread?
That long behind he trails his pompous robe,
And of all monarchs only grasps the globe?
The Baron now his Diamonds pours apace;
The embroidered King who shows but half his face,
And his refulgent Queen, with powers combined
Of broken troops an easy conquest find.
Clubs, Diamonds, Hearts, in wild disorder seen,
With throngs promiscuous strew the level green.
Thus when dispersed a routed army runs,
Of Asia's troops, and Afric's sable sons,
With like confusion different nations fly,
Of various habit,° and of various dye,° *dress / color*
The pierced battalions disunited fall
In heaps on heaps; one fate o'erwhelms them all.
The Knave of Diamonds tries his wily arts,
And wins (oh, shameful chance!) the Queen of Hearts.
At this, the blood the virgin's cheek forsook,
A livid paleness spreads o'er all her look;
She sees, and trembles at the approaching ill,
Just in the jaws of ruin, and Codille,
And now (as oft in some distempered state)
On one nice trick depends the general fate.
An Ace of Hearts steps forth: the King unseen
Lurked in her hand, and mourned his captive Queen.
He springs to vengeance with an eager pace,
And falls like thunder on the prostrate Ace.
The nymph exulting fills with shouts the sky,

2. The jack of clubs, paramount trump in the game of loo.

The walls, the woods, and long canals[3] reply.
O thoughtless mortals! ever blind to fate,
Too soon dejected, and too soon elate:
Sudden these honors shall be snatched away,
And cursed forever this victorious day.
For lo! the board with cups and spoons is crowned,
The berries crackle, and the mill turns round;[4]
On shining altars of Japan[5] they raise
The silver lamp; the fiery spirits blaze:
From silver spouts the grateful liquors glide,
While China's earth[6] receives the smoking tide.
At once they gratify their scent and taste,
And frequent cups prolong the rich repast.
Straight hover round the fair her airy band;
Some, as she sipped, the fuming liquor fanned,
Some o'er her lap their careful plumes displayed,
Trembling, and conscious of the rich brocade.
Coffee (which makes the politician wise,
And see through all things with his half-shut eyes)
Sent up in vapors to the Baron's brain
New stratagems, the radiant Lock to gain.
Ah, cease, rash youth! desist ere 'tis too late,
Fear the just Gods, and think of Scylla's fate![7]
Changed to a bird, and sent to flit in air,
She dearly pays for Nisus' injured hair!
But when to mischief mortals bend their will,
How soon they find fit instruments of ill!
Just then, Clarissa drew with tempting grace
A two-edged weapon from her shining case:
So ladies in romance assist their knight,
Present the spear, and arm him for the fight.
He takes the gift with reverence, and extends
The little engine on his fingers' ends;
This just behind Belinda's neck he spread,
As o'er the fragrant steams she bends her head.
Swift to the Lock a thousand sprites repair,
A thousand wings, by turns, blow back the hair,
And thrice they twitched the diamond in her ear,
Thrice she looked back, and thrice the foe drew near.
Just in that instant, anxious Ariel sought
The close recesses of the virgin's thought;
As on the nosegay in her breast reclined,
He watched the ideas rising in her mind,
Sudden he viewed, in spite of all her art,
An earthly lover lurking at her heart.
Amazed, confused, he found his power expired,[8]
Resigned to fate, and with a sigh retired.
The Peer now spreads the glittering forfex° wide, *scissors*
To enclose the Lock; now joins it, to divide.
Even then, before the fatal engine closed,
A wretched Sylph too fondly interposed;
Fate urged the shears, and cut the Sylph in twain

3. Passages between avenues of trees.
4. As coffee beans are roasted and ground.
5. Lacquered tables.
6. Ceramic cups.
7. Scylla cut from the head of her father Nisus the lock of hair on which his life depended and gave it to her lover Minos of Crete, who was Scylla's enemy. For this she was turned into a sea-bird relentlessly pursued by an eagle.
8. Belinda, being strongly attracted to the Baron (line 144), can no longer merely coquette. She hence passes beyond Ariel's control.

(But airy substance soon unites again):[9]
The meeting points the sacred hair dissever
From the fair head, forever, and forever!
Then flashed the living lightning from her eyes,
And screams of horror rend the affrighted skies.
Not louder shrieks to pitying heaven are cast,
When husbands, or when lapdogs breathe their last;
Or when rich china vessels fallen from high,
In glittering dust and painted fragments lie!
"Let wreaths of triumph now my temples twine,"
The victor cried, "the glorious prize is mine!
While fish in streams, or birds delight in air,
Or in a coach and six the British Fair,
As long as *Atalantis*[1] shall be read,
Or the small pillow grace a lady's bed,
While visits shall be paid on solemn days,
When numerous wax-lights in bright order blaze,[2]
While nymphs take treats, or assignations give,
So long my honor, name, and praise shall live!
What Time would spare, from Steel receives its date,° *termination*
And monuments, like men, submit to fate!
Steel could the labor of the Gods destroy,[3]
And strike to dust the imperial towers of Troy;
Steel could the works of mortal pride confound,
And hew triumphal arches to the ground.
What wonder then, fair nymph! thy hairs should feel,
The conquering force of unresisted Steel?"

Canto IV

But anxious cares the pensive nymph oppressed,
And secret passions labored in her breast.
Not youthful kings in battle seized alive,
Not scornful virgins who their charms survive,
Not ardent lovers robbed of all their bliss,
Not ancient ladies when refused a kiss,
Not tyrants fierce that unrepenting die,
Not Cynthia when her manteau's[4] pinned awry,
E'er felt such rage, resentment, and despair,
As thou, sad virgin! for thy ravished hair.
For, that sad moment, when the Sylphs withdrew
And Ariel weeping from Belinda flew,
Umbriel,[5] a dusky, melancholy sprite
As ever sullied the fair face of light,
Down to the central earth, his proper scene,
Repaired to search the gloomy Cave of Spleen.[6]
Swift on his sooty pinions flits the Gnome,
And in a vapor reached the dismal dome.
No cheerful breeze this sullen region knows,
The dreaded east is all the wind that blows.
Here in a grotto, sheltered close from air,

9. Again as with Milton's angels (*Paradise Lost* VI.329–31).
1. A set of memoirs which, under thin disguise, recounted actual scandals.
2. Attending the formal evening visits of the previous line.
3. Troy (named in the next line) was built by Apollo and Poseidon.
4. I.e., robe is.
5. Suggesting *umbra*, shadow; and *umber*, brown. The final *el* of this name is a further reminiscence of Milton's angels: Gabriel, Abdiel, Zophiel.
6. This journey is formally equivalent to Odysseus' and Aeneas' visits to the underworld. "Spleen" refers to the human organ, the supposed seat of melancholy; hence to melancholy itself. Believed to be induced by misty weather such as the east wind brings (lines 18–20), the condition was also called the "vapors." In its severer manifestations it tends toward madness; in its milder forms, it issues in peevishness and suspicion.

And screened in shades from day's detested glare,
She sighs forever on her pensive bed,
Pain at her side, and Megrim° at her head. *migraine*
Two handmaids wait the throne: alike in place,
But differing far in figure and in face.
Here stood Ill-Nature like an ancient maid,
Her wrinkled form in black and white arrayed;
With store of prayers for mornings, nights, and noons,
Her hand is filled; her bosom with lampoons.° *slanders*
There Affectation, with a sickly mien,
Shows in her cheek the roses of eighteen,
Practiced to lisp, and hang the head aside,
Faints into airs, and languishes with pride,
On the rich quilt sinks with becoming woe,
Wrapped in a gown, for sickness and for show.
The fair ones feel such maladies as these,
When each new nightdress gives a new disease.
A constant vapor o'er the palace flies,
Strange phantoms rising as the mists arise;
Dreadful as hermit's dreams in haunted shades,
Or bright as visions of expiring maids.
Now glaring fiends, and snakes on rolling spires,° *coils*
Pale specters, gaping tombs, and purple fires;
Now lakes of liquid gold, Elysian scenes,
And crystal domes, and angels in machines.[7]
Unnumbered throngs on every side are seen
Of bodies changed to various forms by Spleen.
Here living teapots stand, one arm held out,
One bent; the handle this, and that the spout:
A pipkin[8] there, like Homer's tripod, walks;
Here sighs a jar, and there a goose pie talks;
Men prove with child, as powerful fancy works,
And maids, turned bottles, call aloud for corks.
Safe passed the Gnome through this fantastic band,
A branch of healing spleenwort[9] in his hand.
Then thus addressed the Power: "Hail, wayward Queen!
Who rule the sex to fifty from fifteen:
Parent of vapors and of female wit,
Who give the hysteric or poetic fit,
On various tempers act by various ways,
Make some take physic, others scribble plays;
Who cause the proud their visits to delay,
And send the godly in a pet to pray.
A nymph there is that all thy power disdains,
And thousands more in equal mirth maintains.
But oh! if e'er thy Gnome could spoil a grace,
Or raise a pimple on a beauteous face,
Like citron-waters° matrons' cheeks inflame, *orange brandy*
Or change complexions at a losing game;
If e'er with airy horns I planted heads,[1]
Or rumpled petticoats, or tumbled beds,
Or caused suspicion when no soul was rude,
Or discomposed the headdress of a prude,

7. These images are both 1) the hallucinations of insane melancholy and 2) parodies of stage properties and effects.
8. An earthen pot; it walks like the three-legged stools which Vulcan made for the gods in *Iliad* XVIII.
9. A kind of fern, purgative of spleen; suggesting the golden bough which Aeneas bore as a passport to Hades in *Aeneid* VI.
1. I.e., made men imagine they were being cuckolded.

Or e'er to costive lapdog gave disease,
Which not the tears of brightest eyes could ease,
Hear me, and touch Belinda with chagrin:° *annoyance*
That single act gives half the world the spleen."
The Goddess with a discontented air
Seems to reject him though she grants his prayer.
A wondrous bag with both her hands she binds,
Like that where once Ulysses held the winds;[2]
There she collects the force of female lungs,
Sighs, sobs, and passions, and the war of tongues.
A vial next she fills with fainting fears,
Soft sorrows, melting griefs, and flowing tears.
The Gnome rejoicing bears her gifts away,
Spreads his black wings, and slowly mounts to day.
Sunk in Thalestris'[3] arms the nymph he found,
Her eyes dejected and her hair unbound.
Full o'er their heads the swelling bag he rent,
And all the Furies issued at the vent.
Belinda burns with more than mortal ire,
And fierce Thalestris fans the rising fire.
"O wretched maid!" she spreads her hands, and cried
(While Hampton's echoes, "Wretched maid!" replied),
"Was it for this you took such constant care
The bodkin,° comb, and essence to prepare? *hairpin*
For this your locks in paper durance bound,
For this with torturing irons wreathed around?
For this with fillets° strained your tender head, *bands*
And bravely bore the double loads of lead?[4]
Gods! shall the ravisher display your hair,
While the fops envy, and the ladies stare!
Honor forbid! at whose unrivaled shrine
Ease, pleasure, virtue, all, our sex resign.
Methinks already I your tears survey,
Already hear the horrid things they say,
Already see you a degraded toast,
And all your honor in a whisper lost!
How shall I, then, your helpless fame defend?
'Twill then be infamy to seem your friend!
And shall this prize, the inestimable prize,
Exposed through crystal to the gazing eyes,
And heightened by the diamond's circling rays,
On that rapacious hand forever blaze?
Sooner shall grass in Hyde Park Circus[5] grow,
And wits take lodgings in the sound of Bow;[6]
Sooner let earth, air, sea, to chaos fall,
Men, monkeys, lapdogs, parrots, perish all!"
She said; then raging to Sir Plume repairs,
And bids her beau demand the precious hairs
(Sir Plume of amber snuffbox justly vain,
And the nice° conduct° of a clouded cane). *precise / handling*
With earnest eyes, and round unthinking face,
He first the snuffbox opened, then the case,
And thus broke out—"My Lord, why, what the devil!

2. Aeolus, the wind god, enabled Odysseus so to contain all adverse winds in *Odyssey* X.
3. The name of an Amazon.
4. The means by which Belinda's locks were fashioned into a ringlet: lead strips held her curl papers in place.
5. The fashionable carriage course (the "Ring" of I.44).
6. I.e., the sound of the bells of Bowchurch in the unfashionable commercial section of London.

Zounds! damn the lock! 'fore Gad, you must be civil!
Plague on't! 'tis past a jest—nay prithee, pox!
Give her the hair"—he spoke, and rapped his box.
"It grieves me much," replied the Peer again,
"Who speaks so well should ever speak in vain.
But by this Lock, this sacred Lock I swear
(Which never more shall join its parted hair;
Which never more its honors shall renew,
Clipped from the lovely head where late it grew),
That while my nostrils draw the vital air,
This hand, which won it, shall forever wear."
He spoke, and speaking, in proud triumph spread
The long-contended honors° of her head. *ornaments*
But Umbriel, hateful Gnome, forbears not so;
He breaks the vial whence the sorrows flow.
Then see! the nymph in beauteous grief appears,
Her eyes half languishing, half drowned in tears;
On her heaved bosom hung her drooping head,
Which with a sigh she raised, and thus she said:
"Forever cursed be this detested day,
Which snatched my best, my favorite curl away!
Happy! ah, ten times happy had I been,
If Hampton Court these eyes had never seen!
Yet am not I the first mistaken maid,
By love of courts to numerous ills betrayed.
Oh, had I rather unadmired remained
In some lone isle, or distant northern land;
Where the gilt chariot never marks the way,
Where none learn ombre, none e'er taste bohea!° *fine tea*
There kept my charms concealed from mortal eye,
Like roses that in deserts bloom and die.
What moved my mind with youthful lords to roam?
Oh, had I stayed, and said my prayers at home!
'Twas this the morning omens seemed to tell,
Thrice from my trembling hand the patch box[7] fell;
The tottering china shook without a wind,
Nay, Poll sat mute, and Shock was most unkind!
A Sylph too warned me of the threats of fate,
In mystic visions, now believed too late!
See the poor remnants of these slighted hairs!
My hands shall rend what e'en thy rapine spares.
These in two sable ringlets taught to break,
Once gave new beauties to the snowy neck;
The sister lock now sits uncouth, alone,
And in its fellow's fate foresees its own;
Uncurled it hangs, the fatal shears demands,
And tempts once more thy sacrilegious hands.
Oh, hadst thou, cruel! been content to seize
Hairs less in sight, or any hairs but these!"

Canto V

She said: the pitying audience melt in tears.
But Fate and Jove had stopped the Baron's ears.
In vain Thalestris with reproach assails,
For who can move when fair Belinda fails?
Not half so fixed the Trojan could remain,

7. A box for ornamental patches to accent the face.

While Anna begged and Dido raged in vain.[8]
Then grave Clarissa graceful waved her fan;
Silence ensued, and thus the nymph began:
"Say why are beauties praised and honored most,
The wise man's passion, and the vain man's toast?
Why decked with all that land and sea afford,
Why angels called, and angel-like adored?
Why round our coaches crowd the white-gloved beaux,
Why bows the side box from its inmost rows?
How vain are all these glories, all our pains,
Unless good sense preserve what beauty gains;
That men may say when we the front box grace,
'Behold the first in virtue as in face!'
Oh! if to dance all night, and dress all day,
Charmed the smallpox, or chased old age away,
Who would not scorn what housewife's cares produce,
Or who would learn one earthly thing of use?
To patch, nay ogle, might become a saint,
Nor could it sure be such a sin to paint.
But since, alas! frail beauty must decay,
Curled or uncurled, since locks will turn to gray;
Since painted, or not painted, all shall fade,
And she who scorns a man must die a maid;
What then remains but well our power to use,
And keep good humor still whate'er we lose?
And trust me, dear, good humor can prevail
When airs, and flights, and screams, and scolding fail.
Beauties in vain their pretty eyes may roll;
Charms strike the sight, but merit wins the soul."[9]
So spoke the dame, but no applause ensued;
Belinda frowned, Thalestris called her prude.
"To arms, to arms!" the fierce virago cries,
And swift as lightning to the combat flies.
All side in parties, and begin the attack;
Fans clap, silks rustle, and tough whalebones crack;
Heroes' and heroines' shouts confusedly rise,
And bass and treble voices strike the skies.
No common weapons in their hands are found,
Like Gods they fight, nor dread a mortal wound.
So when bold Homer makes the Gods engage,
And heavenly breasts with human passions rage;
'Gainst Pallas, Mars; Latona, Hermes arms;[1]
And all Olympus rings with loud alarms:
Jove's thunder roars, heaven trembles all around,
Blue Neptune storms, the bellowing deeps resound:
Earth shakes her nodding towers, the ground gives way,
And the pale ghosts start at the flash of day!
Triumphant Umbriel on a sconce's height
Clapped his glad wings, and sat to view the fight:
Propped on the bodkin spears, the sprites survey
The growing combat, or assist the fray.
While through the press enraged Thalestris flies,
And scatters death around from both her eyes,

8. Aeneas was determined to leave Carthage for Italy, though the enamored queen Dido raved and her sister Anna pleaded with him to stay.

9. Clarissa's address parallels a speech in *Iliad* XII, wherein Sarpedon tells Glaucus that, as leaders of the army, they must justify their privilege by extraordinary prowess.

1. Mars arms against Pallas, and Hermes against Latona in *Iliad* XX. The tangled syntax is supposed to mirror the press of battle.

A beau and witling perished in the throng,
One died in metaphor, and one in song.
"O cruel nymph! a living death I bear,"
Cried Dapperwit, and sunk beside his chair.
A mournful glance Sir Fopling upwards cast,
"Those eyes are made so killing"—was his last.
Thus on Maeander's flowery margin lies
The expiring swan, and as he sings he dies.
When bold Sir Plume had drawn Clarissa down,
Chloe stepped in, and killed him with a frown;
She smiled to see the doughty hero slain,
But, at her smile, the beau revived again.
Now Jove suspends his golden scales in air,[2]
Weighs the men's wits against the lady's hair;
The doubtful beam long nods from side to side;
At length the wits mount up, the hairs subside.
See, fierce Belinda on the Baron flies,
With more than usual lightning in her eyes;
Nor feared the chief the unequal fight to try,
Who sought no more than on his foe to die.
But this bold lord with manly strength endued,
She with one finger and a thumb subdued:
Just where the breath of life his nostrils drew,
A charge of snuff the wily virgin threw;
The Gnomes direct, to every atom just,
The pungent grains of titillating dust.
Sudden, with starting tears each eye o'erflows,
And the high dome re-echoes to his nose.
"Now meet thy fate," incensed Belinda cried,
And drew a deadly bodkin[3] from her side.
(The same, his ancient personage to deck,
Her great-great-grandsire wore about his neck,
In three seal rings; which after, melted down,
Formed a vast buckle for his widow's gown:
Her infant grandame's whistle next it grew,
The bells she jingled, and the whistle blew;
Then in a bodkin graced her mother's hairs,
Which long she wore, and now Belinda wears.)
"Boast not my fall," he cried, "insulting foe!
Thou by some other shalt be laid as low.
Nor think to die dejects my lofty mind:
All that I dread is leaving you behind!
Rather than so, ah, let me still survive,
And burn in Cupid's flames—but burn alive."
"Restore the Lock!" she cries; and all around
"Restore the Lock!" the vaulted roofs rebound.
Not fierce Othello in so loud a strain
Roared for the handkerchief that caused his pain.[4]
But see how oft ambitious aims are crossed,
And chiefs contend till all the prize is lost!
The lock, obtained with guilt, and kept with pain,
In every place is sought, but sought in vain:
With such a prize no mortal must be blessed,
So Heaven decrees! with Heaven who can contest?

2. He so weighs the fortunes of war in classical epic.
3. Here an ornamental hairpin. Its history suggests that of Agamemnon's scepter in *Iliad* II. "Seal rings" (line 91) are for impressing seals on letters and legal documents.
4. In *Othello* III.iv.

Some thought it mounted to the lunar sphere,
Since all things lost on earth are treasured there.
There heroes' wits are kept in ponderous vases,
And beaux' in snuffboxes and tweezer cases.
There broken vows and deathbed alms are found,
And lovers' hearts with ends of riband bound,
The courtier's promises, and sick man's prayers,
The smiles of harlots, and the tears of heirs,
Cages for gnats, and chains to yoke a flea,
Dried butterflies, and tomes of casuistry.
But trust the Muse—she saw it upward rise,
Though marked by none but quick, poetic eyes
(So Rome's great founder to the heavens withdrew,[5]
To Proculus alone confessed in view);
A sudden star, it shot through liquid° air, *clear*
And drew behind a radiant trail of hair.
Not Berenice's locks first rose so bright,[6]
The heavens bespangling with disheveled light.
The Sylphs behold it kindling as it flies,
And pleased pursue its progress through the skies.
This the beau monde shall from the Mall[7] survey,
And hail with music its propitious ray.
This the blest lover shall for Venus take,
And send up vows from Rosamonda's Lake.
This Partridge[8] soon shall view in cloudless skies,
When next he looks through Galileo's eyes;
And hence the egregious wizard shall foredoom
The fate of Louis, and the fall of Rome.
Then cease, bright nymph! to mourn thy ravished hair,
Which adds new glory to the shining sphere!
Not all the tresses that fair head can boast,
Shall draw such envy as the Lock you lost.
For, after all the murders of your eye,
When, after millions slain, yourself shall die:
When those fair suns shall set, as set they must,
And all those tresses shall be laid in dust,
This Lock the Muse shall consecrate to fame,
And 'midst the stars inscribe Belinda's name.

1712 1714

Epistle to Miss Blount[9]

ON HER LEAVING THE TOWN, AFTER THE CORONATION

As some fond virgin, whom her mother's care
Drags from the town to wholesome country air,
Just when she learns to roll a melting eye,
And hear a spark,[1] yet think no danger nigh;
From the dear man unwilling she must sever,
Yet takes one kiss before she parts forever:
Thus from the world fair Zephalinda[2] flew,

5. Romulus was borne heavenward in a storm-cloud and later deified.
6. The locks which the Egyptian queen Berenice dedicated to her husband's safe return were turned into a constellation.
7. A fashionable walk which (like Rosamonda's Lake [line 136]) was in St. James's Park.
8. A London astrologer who predicted calamities on the enemies of England and Protestantism. "Galileo's eyes": the telescope.
9. Teresa Blount, sister of Pope's life-long friend Martha Blount. The "coronation" was that of George I (1714).
1. Beau, gallant.
2. A fanciful name for Miss Blount.

Saw others happy, and with sighs withdrew;
Not that their pleasures caused her discontent;
She sighed not that they stayed, but that she went.
She went to plain-work,° and to purling[3] brooks, *needlework*
Old-fashioned halls, dull aunts, and croaking rooks:[4]
She went from opera, park, assembly, play,
To morning walks, and prayers three hours a day;
To part her time 'twixt reading and bohea,[5]
To muse, and spill her solitary tea,
Or o'er cold coffee trifle with the spoon,
Count the slow clock, and dine exact at noon;
Divert her eyes with pictures in the fire,
Hum half a tune, tell stories to the squire;
Up to her godly garret after seven,
There starve and pray, for that's the way to heaven.
Some squire, perhaps, you take delight to rack,
Whose game is whist, whose treat a toast in sack;
Who visits with a gun, presents you birds,
Then gives a smacking buss, and cries—"No words!"
Or with his hounds comes hollowing from the stable,
Makes love with nods and knees beneath a table;
Whose laughs are hearty, though his jests are coarse,
And loves you best of all things—but his horse.
In some fair evening, on your elbow laid,
You dream of triumphs in the rural shade;
In pensive thought recall the fancied scene,
See coronations rise on every green:
Before you pass the imaginary sights
Of lords and earls and dukes and gartered knights,
While the spread fan o'ershades your closing eyes;
Then gives one flirt, and all the vision flies.
Thus vanish scepters, coronets, and balls,
And leave you in lone woods, or empty walls!
So when your slave,[6] at some dear idle time
(Not plagued with headaches or the want of rhyme)
Stands in the streets, abstracted from the crew,
And while he seems to study, thinks of you;
Just when his fancy points[7] your sprightly eyes,
Or sees the blush of soft Parthenia[8] rise,
Gay[9] pats my shoulder, and you vanish quite;
Streets, chairs,° and coxcombs[1] rush upon my sight; *sedan chairs*
Vexed to be still in town, I knit my brow,
Look sour, and hum a tune—as you may now.

1717

The Universal Prayer

Father of all! in every age,
In every clime adored,
By saint, by savage, and by sage,
Jehovah, Jove, or Lord!

3. Gently rippling.
4. Crowlike birds.
5. A high-grade Chinese tea.
6. I.e., the speaker, Pope.
7. Focuses or zeroes in on.
8. Like Zephalinda (line 7), a fanciful name for Miss Blount.
9. John Gay, the poet, Pope's friend.
1. Dandies, fops.

Thou Great First Cause,[2] least understood:
  Who all my sense confined
To know but this—that thou art good,
  And that myself am blind:

Yet gave me, in this dark estate,
  To see the good from ill;
And binding Nature fast in fate,
  Left free the human will.

What conscience dictates to be done,
  Or warns me not to do,
This, teach me more than Hell to shun,
  That, more than Heaven pursue.

What blessings thy free bounty gives,
  Let me not cast away;
For God is paid when man receives,
  To enjoy is to obey.

Yet not to earth's contracted span,
  Thy goodness let me bound,
Or think thee Lord alone of man,
  When thousand worlds are round:

Let not this weak, unknowing hand
  Presume thy bolts to throw,[3]
And deal damnation round the land,
  On each I judge thy foe.

If I am right, thy grace impart,
  Still in the right to stay;
If I am wrong, oh teach my heart
  To find that better way.

Save me alike from foolish pride,
  Or impious discontent,
At aught thy wisdom has denied,
  Or aught thy goodness lent.

Teach me to feel another's woe,
  To hide the fault I see;
That mercy I to others show,
  That mercy show to me.

Mean though I am, not wholly so
  Since quickened by thy breath;
Oh lead me wheresoe'er I go,
  Through this day's life or death.

This day, be bread and peace[4] my lot:
  All else beneath the sun,
Thou know'st if best bestowed or not,
  And let thy will be done.

2. God considered as the first principle, creator of all creatures, cause of all truth and goodness.

3. Zeus's weapons, thunderbolts.

4. Perhaps an allusion to the Lord's Prayer.

To thee, whose temple is all space,
Whose altar, earth, sea, skies!
One chorus let all being raise!
All Nature's incense rise!

ca. 1715 1738

Epistle to Dr. Arbuthnot[5]

P. Shut, shut the door, good John![6] (fatigued, I said),
Tie up the knocker, say I'm sick, I'm dead.
The Dog Star[7] rages! nay 'tis past a doubt
All Bedlam, or Parnassus,[8] is let out:
Fire in each eye, and papers in each hand,
They rave, recite, and madden round the land.
What walls can guard me, or what shades can hide?
They pierce my thickets, through my grot[9] they glide,
By land, by water, they renew the charge,
They stop the chariot, and they board the barge.[1]
No place is sacred, not the church is free;
Even Sunday shines no Sabbath day to me:
Then from the Mint[2] walks forth the man of rhyme,
Happy to catch me just at dinner time.
Is there a parson, much bemused in beer,
A maudlin poetess, a rhyming peer,
A clerk foredoomed his father's soul to cross,
Who pens a stanza when he should engross?[3]
Is there who,[4] locked from ink and paper, scrawls
With desperate charcoal round his darkened walls?
All fly to Twit'nam,° and in humble strain *Twickenham*
Apply to me to keep them mad or vain.
Arthur,[5] whose giddy son neglects the laws,
Imputes to me and my damned works the cause:
Poor Cornus[6] sees his frantic wife elope,
And curses wit, and poetry, and Pope.
Friend to my life (which did not you prolong,
The world had wanted many an idle song)
What drop or nostrum° can this plague remove? *drug*
Or which must end me, a fool's wrath or love?
A dire dilemma! either way I'm sped,° *ruined*
If foes, they write, if friends, they read me dead.
Seized and tied down to judge, how wretched I!
Who can't be silent, and who will not lie.
To laugh were want of goodness and of grace,
And to be grave exceeds all power of face.
I sit with sad° civility, I read *sober*
With honest anguish and an aching head,
And drop at last, but in unwilling ears,

5. John Arbuthnot, former physician to Queen Anne, was Pope's physician, and friend and literary collaborator of Pope, Swift, and Gay. He had asked Pope to moderate his attacks on his personal and literary enemies and was hence a logical person to whom to address an apology for writing satire.
6. Pope's servant, John Serle.
7. The summer star Sirius, attendant upon crazing heat. In ancient Rome, late summer was a season for public recitations of poetry.
8. Bedlam is a hospital for the insane; Mt. Parnassus, the haunt of the Muses.
9. Pope's "grotto," one entrance to the grounds of his villa at Twickenham.
1. Pope often traveled from Twickenham to London by water.
2. A sanctuary for debtors. They emerged on Sunday, being everywhere immune from arrest on that day.
3. Prepare legal documents.
4. I.e., one who.
5. Arthur Moore, father of James Moore Smythe, a playwright who had plagiarized some lines from Pope.
6. From Latin *cornu,* horn; hence a cuckold.

This saving counsel, "Keep your piece nine years."[7]
"Nine years!" cries he, who high in Drury Lane,[8]
Lulled by soft zephyrs through the broken pane,
Rhymes ere he wakes, and prints before term° ends, — *the publishing season*
Obliged by hunger and request of friends:
"The piece, you think, is incorrect? why, take it,
I'm all submission, what you'd have it, make it."
Three things another's modest wishes bound,
My friendship, and a prologue, and ten pound.
Pitholeon[9] sends to me: "You know his Grace,
I want a patron; ask him for a place."
Pitholeon libeled me—"but here's a letter
Informs you, sir, 'twas when he knew no better.
Dare you refuse him? Curll[1] invites to dine,
He'll write a *Journal*, or he'll turn divine."
Bless me! a packet.—" 'Tis a stranger sues,
A virgin tragedy, an orphan Muse."
If I dislike it, "Furies, death, and rage!"
If I approve, "Commend it to the stage."
There (thank my stars) my whole commission ends,
The players and I are, luckily, no friends.
Fired that the house° reject him, " 'Sdeath, I'll print it, — *playhouse*
And shame the fools—Your interest, sir, with Lintot!"[3]
Lintot, dull rogue, will think your price too much.
"Not, sir, if you revise it, and retouch."
All my demurs but double his attacks;
At last he whispers, "Do; and we go snacks."° — *shares*
Glad of a quarrel, straight I clap the door,
"Sir, let me see your works and you no more."
'Tis sung, when Midas' ears began to spring
(Midas, a sacred person and a king),
His very minister who spied them first
(Some say his queen) was forced to speak, or burst.[4]
And is not mine, my friend, a sorer case,
When every coxcomb perks them in my face?
A. Good friend, forbear! you deal in dangerous things.
I'd never name queens, ministers, or kings;
Keep close to ears, and those let asses prick;
'Tis nothing—— P. Nothing? if they bite and kick?
Out with it, *Dunciad!* let the secret pass,
That secret to each fool, that he's an ass:
The truth once told (and wherefore should we lie?)
The queen of Midas slept, and so may I.
You think this cruel? take it for a rule,
No creature smarts so little as a fool.
Let peals of laughter, Codrus![5] round thee break,
Thou unconcerned canst hear the mighty crack.
Pit, box, and gallery in convulsions hurled,
Thou stand'st unshook amidst a bursting world.

7. Horace's advice (*Ars Poetica*, 386–89).
8. The theater district, where the speaker occupies a garret.
9. "A foolish poet of Rhodes, who pretended much to Greek" [Pope's note]. He stands for Leonard Welsted, translator of Longinus and an enemy of Pope's.
1. Edmund Curll, an unscrupulous publisher; the bookseller principally derided in the *Dunciad* (above).
2. Referring to attacks on Pope in *The London Journal* and (perhaps) to Welsted's theological writing.
3. Bernard Lintot, an early publisher of Pope's.
4. King Midas, preferring Pan's music to Apollo's, was given ass's ears by the affronted god. His barber (in Chaucer's version of the tale, his wife) discovered the ears and, fairly bursting with the secret, whispered it into a hole in the ground. It is suggested that the prime minister (Walpole) and Queen Caroline know that George II is an ass.
5. A poet ridiculed by Virgil and Juvenal.

Who shames a scribbler? break one cobweb through,
He spins the slight, self-pleasing thread anew:
Destroy his fib or sophistry, in vain;
The creature's at his dirty work again,
Throned in the center of his thin designs,
Proud of a vast extent of flimsy lines.
Whom have I hurt? has poet yet or peer
Lost the arched eyebrow or Parnassian sneer?
And has not Colley[6] still his lord and whore?
His butchers Henley? his freemasons Moore?[7]
Does not one table Bavius still admit?
Still to one bishop Philips seem a wit?
Still Sappho—— A. Hold! for God's sake—you'll offend.
No names—be calm—learn prudence of a friend.
I too could write, and I am twice as tall;
But foes like these!—— P. One flatterer's worse than all.
Of all mad creatures, if the learn'd are right,
It is the slaver kills, and not the bite.
A fool quite angry is quite innocent:
Alas! 'tis ten times worse when they repent.
   One dedicates in high heroic prose,
And ridicules beyond a hundred foes;
One from all Grub Street[8] will my fame defend,
And, more abusive, calls himself my friend.
This prints my letters,[9] that expects a bribe,
And others roar aloud, "Subscribe, subscribe!"[1]
   There are, who to my person pay their court:
I cough like Horace, and, though lean, am short;
Ammon's great son° one shoulder had too high, *Alexander the Great*
Such Ovid's nose, and "Sir! you have an eye—"
Go on, obliging creatures, make me see
All that disgraced my betters met in me.
Say for my comfort, languishing in bed,
"Just so immortal Maro° held his head": *Virgil*
And when I die, be sure you let me know
Great Homer died three thousand years ago.
   Why did I write? what sin to me unknown
Dipped me in ink, my parents', or my own?
As yet a child, nor yet a fool to fame,
I lisped in numbers, for the numbers came.
I left no calling for this idle trade,
No duty broke, no father disobeyed.
The Muse but served to ease some friend, not wife,
To help me through this long disease, my life,
To second, Arbuthnot! thy art and care,
And teach the being° you preserved, to bear. *life*
   A. But why then publish? P. Granville the polite,[2]
And knowing Walsh, would tell me I could write;
Well-natured Garth inflamed with early praise,
And Congreve loved, and Swift endured my lays;
The courtly Talbot, Somers, Sheffield, read;

6. Colley Cibber, poet laureate.
7. John Henley ("Orator Henley") was an independent preacher with a mass following. James Moore Smythe was a member of the Masonic order. Bavius (line 99) is a bad poet referred to by Virgil. The Bishop of Armagh employed Ambrose Philips (line 100 [called "Namby-Pamby" by the wits]) as his secretary. "Sappho" (line 101) is Lady Mary Wortley Montagu.
8. The traditional haunt of hack writers.
9. As Curll had done without permission.
1. Pay for copies in advance of publication.
2. There follow the names of poets and men of letters, Pope's early friends. They were literary elder statesmen, chiefly, who had befriended Dryden in the preceding century.

Even mitered Rochester[3] would nod the head,
And St. John's[4] self (great Dryden's friends before)
With open arms received one poet more.
Happy my studies, when by these approved!
Happier their author, when by these beloved!
From these the world will judge of men and books,
Not from the Búrnets, Óldmixons, and Cookes.[5]
Soft were my numbers; who could take offense
While pure description held the place of sense?
Like gentle Fanny's[6] was my flowery theme,
A painted mistress, or a purling stream.
Yet then did Gildon[7] draw his venal quill;
I wished the man a dinner, and sat still.
Yet then did Dennis[8] rave in furious fret;
I never answered, I was not in debt.
If want provoked, or madness made them print,
I waged no war with Bedlam or the Mint.
Did some more sober critic come abroad?
If wrong, I smiled; if right, I kissed the rod.
Pains, reading, study are their just pretense,
And all they want is spirit, taste, and sense.
Commas and points they set exactly right,
And 'twere a sin to rob them of their mite.
Yet ne'er one sprig of laurel graced these ribalds,
From slashing Bentley down to piddling Tibbalds.[9]
Each wight who reads not, and but scans and spells,
Each word-catcher that lives on syllables,
Even such small critics some regard may claim,
Preserved in Milton's or in Shakespeare's name.
Pretty! in amber to observe the forms
Of hairs, or straws, or dirt, or grubs, or worms!
The things, we know, are neither rich nor rare,
But wonder how the devil they got there.
Were others angry? I excused them too;
Well might they rage; I gave them but their due.
A man's true merit 'tis not hard to find;
But each man's secret standard in his mind,
That casting weight[1] pride adds to emptiness,
This, who can gratify? for who can guess?
The bard whom pilfered pastorals renown,
Who turns a Persian tale for half a crown,[2]
Just writes to make his barrenness appear,
And strains from hard-bound brains eight lines a year:
He, who still wanting, though he lives on theft,
Steals much, spends little, yet has nothing left;
And he who now to sense, now nonsense leaning,
Means not, but blunders round about a meaning:
And he whose fustian's so sublimely bad,
It is not poetry, but prose run mad:

3. The Bishop of Rochester.
4. Pronounced *sinjin.*
5. Thomas Burnet, John Oldmixon and Arthur Cooke had all attacked Pope or his works.
6. Lord Hervey, satirized as Sporus in lines 305 ff.
7. Charles Gildon, a critic who had, as Pope believed, written against him "venally," to curry favor with Addison. (See line 209*n.* below.)
8. John Dennis, who wrote a furious condemnation of Pope's *Essay on Criticism.*
9. Richard Bentley, a classical scholar, had edited *Paradise Lost* with undue license on the ground that Milton was blind and never saw his text. Lewis Theobald, no wit but a closer scholar than Pope, had exposed the faults of Pope's edition of Shakespeare in a subsequent edition of his own.
1. Weight tipping the scales.
2. Ambrose Philips (named in line 100), who had competed with the youthful Pope as a pastoral poet; author of *Persian Tales.*

All these, my modest satire bade translate,
And owned that nine such poets made a Tate.[3]
How did they fume, and stamp, and roar, and chafe!
And swear, not Addison himself was safe.
  Peace to all such! but were there one whose fires
True Genius kindles, and fair Fame inspires;
Blessed with each talent and each art to please,
And born to write, converse, and live with ease:
Should such a man, too fond to rule alone,
Bear, like the Turk, no brother near the throne;[4]
View him with scornful, yet with jealous eyes,
And hate for arts that caused himself to rise;
Damn with faint praise, assent with civil leer,
And without sneering, teach the rest to sneer;
Willing to wound, and yet afraid to strike,
Just hint a fault, and hesitate dislike;
Alike reserved to blame or to commend,
A timorous foe, and a suspicious friend;
Dreading even fools; by flatterers besieged,
And so obliging that he ne'er obliged;
Like Cato, give his little senate laws,[5]
And sit attentive to his own applause;
While wits and Templars° every sentence raise, *law students*
And wonder with a foolish face of praise—
Who but must laugh, if such a man there be?
Who would not weep, if Atticus[6] were he?
  What though my name stood rubric° on the walls? *in red letters*
Or plastered posts, with claps,° in capitals? *posters*
Or smoking forth, a hundred hawkers' load,
On wings of winds came flying all abroad?
I sought no homage from the race that write;
I kept, like Asian monarchs, from their sight:
Poems I heeded (now berhymed so long)
No more than thou, great George! a birthday song.
I ne'er with wits or witlings passed my days
To spread about the itch of verse and praise;
Nor like a puppy daggled through the town
To fetch and carry sing-song up and down;
Nor at rehearsals sweat, and mouthed, and cried,
With handkerchief and orange at my side;
But sick of fops, and poetry, and prate,
To Bufo left the whole Castalian state.[7]
  Proud as Apollo on his forkéd hill,[8]
Sat full-blown Bufo, puffed by every quill;
Fed with soft dedication all day long,
Horace and he went hand in hand in song.
His library (where busts of poets dead
And a true Pindar stood without a head)
Received of wits an undistinguished race,
Who first his judgment asked, and then a place:

3. Nahum Tate, successor to Dryden as poet laureate.
4. The Ottoman Emperors, Europeans believed, regularly killed their principal kinsmen upon ascending the throne.
5. Addison (author of the immensely popular tragedy *Cato*) presided over an admiring company of political and literary partisans at Button's Coffee House.
6. A friend of Cicero's; here a pseudonym for Addison.
7. Pope leaves Bufo the whole republic of letters, named from the spring Castalia, which was sacred to Apollo and the Muses. Bufo is perhaps a composite of Lord Halifax and "Bubo," Bubb Dodington.
8. The twin peaks of Parnassus.

Much they extolled his pictures, much his seat,° *estate*
And flattered every day, and some days eat:° *ate*
Till grown more frugal in his riper days,
He paid some bards with port, and some with praise;
To some a dry° rehearsal was assigned, *without performance*
And others (harder still) he paid in kind.[9]
Dryden alone (what wonder?) came not nigh;
Dryden alone escaped this judging eye:
But still the great have kindness in reserve;
He helped to bury whom he helped to starve.
   May some choice patron bless each gray goose quill!° *quill pen*
May every Bavius have his Bufo still!
So when a statesman wants a day's defense,
Or Envy holds a whole week's war with Sense,
Or simple Pride for flattery makes demands,
May dunce by dunce be whistled off my hands!
Blessed be the great! for those they take away,
And those they left me—for they left me Gay;[1]
Left me to see neglected genius bloom,
Neglected die, and tell it on his tomb;
Of all thy blameless life the sole return
My verse, and Queensberry weeping o'er thy urn!
Oh, let me live my own, and die so too!
("To live and die is all I have to do")
Maintain a poet's dignity and ease,
And see what friends, and read what books I please;
Above a patron, though I condescend
Some times to call a minister my friend.
I was not born for courts or great affairs;
I pay my debts, believe, and say my prayers,
Can sleep without a poem in my head,
Nor know if Dennis be alive or dead.
   Why am I asked what next shall see the light?
Heavens! was I born for nothing but to write?
Has life no joys for me? or (to be grave)
Have I no friend to serve, no soul to save?
"I found him close with Swift"—"Indeed? no doubt,"
Cries prating Balbus, "something will come out."
'Tis all in vain, deny it as I will.
"No, such a genius never can lie still,"
And then for mine obligingly mistakes
The first lampoon Sir Will or Bubo[2] makes.
Poor guiltless I! and can I choose but smile,
When every coxcomb knows me by my style?
   Cursed be the verse, how well soe'er it flow,
That tends to make one worthy man my foe,
Give Virtue scandal, Innocence a fear,
Or from the soft-eyed virgin steal a tear!
But he who hurts a harmless neighbor's peace,
Insults fallen worth, or Beauty in distress,
Who loves a lie, lame Slander helps about,
Who writes a libel, or who copies out:
That fop whose pride affects a patron's name,
Yet absent, wounds an author's honest fame;

9. I.e., he read them his poetry in turn.
1. John Gay, author of *The Beggar's Opera,* associate of Pope and Swift; befriended (line 260) by the Duke and Duchess of Queensberry.
2. Sir William Yonge or Bubb Dodington. Both were Pope's political adversaries as well as, in some degree, silly men.

Who can your merit selfishly approve,
And show the sense of it without the love;
Who has the vanity to call you friend,
Yet wants the honor, injured, to defend;
Who tells whate'er you think, whate'er you say,
And, if he lie not, must at least betray:
Who to the dean and silver bell can swear,
And sees at Cannons what was never there:[3]
Who reads but with a lust to misapply,
Make satire a lampoon, and fiction, lie:
A lash like mine no honest man shall dread,
But all such babbling blockheads in his stead.
Let Sporus[4] tremble—— A. What? that thing of silk,
Sporus, that mere white curd of ass's milk?
Satire or sense, alas! can Sporus feel?
Who breaks a butterfly upon a wheel?
P. Yet let me flap this bug with gilded wings,
This painted child of dirt, that stinks and stings;
Whose buzz the witty and the fair annoys,
Yet wit ne'er tastes, and beauty ne'er enjoys;
So well-bred spaniels civilly delight
In mumbling of the game they dare not bite.
Eternal smiles his emptiness betray,
As shallow streams run dimpling all the way.
Whether in florid impotence he speaks,
And, as the prompter breathes, the puppet squeaks;
Or at the ear of Eve,[5] familiar toad,
Half froth, half venom, spits himself abroad,
In puns, or politics, or tales, or lies,
Or spite, or smut, or rhymes, or blasphemies.
His wit all seesaw between *that* and *this*,
Now high, now low, now master up, now miss,
And he himself one vile antithesis.
Amphibious thing! that acting either part,
The trifling head or the corrupted heart,
Fop at the toilet, flatterer at the board,
Now trips a lady, and now struts a lord.
Eve's tempter thus the rabbins° have expressed, *Hebrew scholars*
A cherub's face, a reptile all the rest;
Beauty that shocks you, parts° that none will trust, *talents*
Wit that can creep, and pride that licks the dust.
Not Fortune's worshiper, nor Fashion's fool,
Not Lucre's° madman, nor Ambition's tool, *Money's*
Not proud, nor servile, be one poet's praise,
That if he pleased, he pleased by manly ways:
That flattery, even to kings, he held a shame,
And thought a lie in verse or prose the same:
That not in fancy's maze he wandered long,
But stooped[6] to truth, and moralized his song:
That not for fame, but Virtue's better end,

3. In his *Epistle to Burlington*, Pope satirized "Timon's Villa," an estate where a silver bell and an obsequious dean invite worshipers to an overstuffed chapel. Mischief-makers had identified this estate with Cannons, the ostentatious home of Pope's well-wisher the Duke of Chandos.
4. Roman eunuch, victim of the Emperor Nero's perversions; in the poem, Lord Hervey, a foppish and effeminate courtier who was Pope's personal, political, and literary enemy. He attested his frailty by drinking ass's milk as a tonic.
5. Like Satan in Eden (*Paradise Lost* IV. 790 ff.). Hervey was Queen Caroline's confidant; the word *familiar* suggests a demonic ministrant.
6. Swooped down perceiving prey (a term from falconry).

He stood the furious foe, the timid friend,
The damning critic, half approving wit,
The coxcomb hit, or fearing to be hit;
Laughed at the loss of friends he never had,
The dull, the proud, the wicked, and the mad;
The distant threats of vengeance on his head,
The blow unfelt, the tear he never shed;
The tale revived, the lie so oft o'erthrown,
The imputed trash, and dullness not his own;
The morals blackened when the writings 'scape,
The libeled person, and the pictured shape;[7]
Abuse on all he loved, or loved him, spread,
A friend in exile, or a father dead;
The whisper,[8] that to greatness still too near,
Perhaps yet vibrates on his sovereign's ear—
Welcome for thee, fair Virtue! all the past!
For thee, fair Virtue! welcome even the last!
A. But why insult the poor, affront the great?
P. A knave's a knave to me in every state:
Alike my scorn, if he succeed or fail,
Sporus at court, or Japhet[9] in a jail,
A hireling scribbler, or a hireling peer,
Knight of the post[1] corrupt, or of the shire,
If on a pillory, or near a throne,
He gain his prince's ear, or lose his own.
Yet soft by nature, more a dupe than wit,
Sappho can tell you how this man was bit:° *deceived*
This dreaded satirist Dennis will confess
Foe to his pride, but friend to his distress:[2]
So humble, he has knocked at Tibbald's door,
Has drunk with Cibber, nay, has rhymed for Moore.
Full ten years slandered, did he once reply?
Three thousand suns went down on Welsted's lie.[3]
To please a mistress one aspersed his life;
He lashed him not, but let her be his wife.
Let Budgell charge low Grub Street on his quill,
And write whate'er he pleased, except his will;[4]
Let the two Curlls, of town and court,[5] abuse
His father, mother, body, soul, and muse.
Yet why? that father held it for a rule,
It was a sin to call our neighbor fool;
That harmless mother thought no wife a whore:
Hear this, and spare his family, James Moore!
Unspotted names, and memorable long,
If there be force in virtue, or in song.
Of gentle blood (part shed in honor's cause,
While yet in Britain honor had applause)
Each parent sprung—— A. What fortune, pray?—— P. Their own,
And better got than Bestia's[6] from the throne.
Born to no pride, inheriting no strife,

7. Cartoons were drawn of Pope's hunched posture.
8. Hervey's whisper to Queen Caroline.
9. Japhet Crook, a forger; his ears were cropped for his crime (line 367).
1. "Knight of the post": professional witness.
2. Pope contributed to a benefit performance for the aging Dennis.
3. A hint that Pope had contributed to the death of the "Unfortunate Lady" celebrated in the *Elegy* above. (The lady seems actually to have been a fiction.)
4. Budgell (perhaps falsely) attributed to Pope a squib in the *Grub-Street Journal* charging that Budgell had forged a will.
5. Edmund Curll, the publisher; and Lord Hervey.
6. A Roman consul who was bribed to arrange a dishonorable peace; in the poem, probably the Duke of Marlborough.

Nor marrying discord in a noble wife,
Stranger to civil and religious rage,
The good man walked innoxious through his age.
No courts he saw, no suits would ever try,
Nor dared an oath, nor hazarded a lie.[7]
Unlearn'd, he knew no schoolman's subtle art,
No language but the language of the heart.
By nature honest, by experience wise,
Healthy by temperance, and by exercise;
His life, though long, to sickness passed unknown,
His death was instant, and without a groan.
Oh, grant me thus to live, and thus to die!
Who sprung from kings shall know less joy than I.
O friend! may each domestic bliss be thine!
Be no unpleasing melancholy mine:
Me, let the tender office long engage,
To rock the cradle of reposing Age,
With lenient arts extend a mother's breath,
Make Languor smile, and smooth the bed of Death,
Explore the thought, explain the asking eye,
And keep a while one parent from the sky!
On cares like these if length of days attend,
May Heaven, to bless those days, preserve my friend,
Preserve him social, cheerful, and serene,
And just as rich as when he served a Queen![8]
A. Whether that blessing be denied or given,
Thus far was right—the rest belongs to Heaven.

1735

LADY MARY WORTLEY MONTAGU (1689–1762)

The Lover: A Ballad

At length, by so much importunity pressed,
Take, C——,[1] at once, the inside of my breast;
This stupid indifference so often you blame
Is not owing to nature, to fear, or to shame;
I am not as cold as a Virgin in lead,[2]
Nor is Sunday's sermon so strong in my head;
I know but too well how time flies along,
That we live but few years and yet fewer are young.

But I hate to be cheated, and never will buy
Long years of repentance for moments of joy.
Oh was there a man (but where shall I find
Good sense and good nature so equally joined?)
Would value his pleasure, contribute to mine,
Not meanly would boast, nor would lewdly design,° *plot*

7. He did not take the special oath required of Catholics wanting to enter public life or the professions, nor did he evade by falsehood the restrictions on Catholics.
8. Arbuthnot, who had sought no professional profit as physician to Queen Anne, continued to earn the same income after her death.

1. Probably Richard Chandler, a friend of Lady Mary. The ideal "lover" of the title, however, is not to be identified with any particular person.
2. I.e., an image of the Virgin Mary, either as a leaden statue or as a stained-glass window framed in lead.

Not over severe, yet not stupidly vain,
For I would have the power though not give the pain;

No pedant yet learnéd, not rakehelly gay
Or laughing because he has nothing to say,
To all my whole sex obliging and free,
Yet never be fond of any but me;
In public preserve the decorum that's just,
And show in his eyes he is true to his trust,
Then rarely approach, and respectfully bow,
Yet not fulsomely pert, nor yet foppishly low.

But when the long hours of public are past
And we meet with champagne and a chicken at last,
May every fond pleasure that hour endear,
Be banished afar both discretion and fear,
Forgetting or scorning the airs of the crowd
He may cease to be formal, and I to be proud,
Till lost in the joy we confess that we live,
And he may be rude, and yet I may forgive.

And that my delight may be solidly fixed,
Let the friend and the lover be handsomely mixed,
In whose tender bosom my soul might confide,
Whose kindness can sooth me, whose counsel could guide.
From such a dear lover as here I describe
No danger should fright me, no millions should bribe;
But till this astonishing creature I know,
As I long have lived chaste, I will keep myself so.

I never will share with the wanton coquette,
Or be caught by a vain affectation of wit.
The toasters and songsters may try all their art
But never shall enter the pass of my heart.
I loathe the lewd rake, the dressed fopling despise;
Before such pursuers the nice° virgin flies; *fastidious*
And as Ovid has sweetly in parables told
We harden like trees, and like rivers are cold.[3]

1747

SAMUEL JOHNSON
(1709–1784)

The Vanity of Human Wishes

IN IMITATION OF THE TENTH SATIRE OF JUVENAL

Let Observation, with extensive view,
Survey mankind, from China to Peru;
Remark each anxious toil, each eager strife,
And watch the busy scenes of crowded life;
Then say how hope and fear, desire and hate

3. In Ovid's *Metamorphoses* Daphne, to escape Apollo, was turned into a laurel; and Arethusa, escaping Alpheus, became a fountain.

O'erspread with snares the clouded maze of fate,
Where wavering man, betrayed by venturous pride
To tread the dreary paths without a guide,
As treacherous phantoms in the mist delude,
Shuns fancied ills, or chases airy good;
How rarely Reason guides the stubborn choice,
Rules the bold hand, or prompts the suppliant voice;
How nations sink, by darling schemes oppressed,
When Vengeance listens to the fool's request.[1]
Fate wings with every wish the afflictive dart,
Each gift of nature, and each grace of art;[2]
With fatal heat impetuous courage glows,
With fatal sweetness elocution flows,
Impeachment stops the speaker's powerful breath,
And restless fire precipitates on death.[3]
  But scarce observed, the knowing and the bold
Fall in the general massacre of gold;
Wide-wasting pest! that rages unconfined,
And crowds with crimes the records of mankind;
For gold his sword the hireling ruffian draws,
For gold the hireling judge distorts the laws;
Wealth heaped on wealth, nor truth nor safety buys,
The dangers gather as the treasures rise.
  Let History tell where rival kings command,
And dubious title shakes the madded land,
When statutes glean the refuse of the sword,
How much more safe the vassal than the lord,
Low skulks the hind beneath the rage of power,
And leaves the wealthy traitor in the Tower,
Untouched his cottage, and his slumbers sound,
Though Confiscation's vultures hover round.
  The needy traveler, serene and gay,
Walks the wild heath, and sings his toil away.
Does envy seize thee? crush the upbraiding joy,
Increase his riches and his peace destroy;
New fears in dire vicissitude invade,
The rustling brake° alarms, and quivering shade, *thicket*
Nor light nor darkness bring his pain relief,
One shows the plunder, and one hides the thief.
  Yet still one general cry the skies assails,
And gain and grandeur load the tainted gales;
Few know the toiling statesman's fear or care,
The insidious rival and the gaping heir.
  Once more, Democritus,[4] arise on earth,
With cheerful wisdom and instructive mirth,
See motley life in modern trappings dressed,
And feed with varied fools the eternal jest:
Thou who couldst laugh where Want enchained Caprice,
Toil crushed Conceit, and man was of a piece;
Where Wealth unloved without a mourner died;
And scarce a sycophant was fed by Pride;
Where ne'er was known the form of mock debate,

1. I.e., when vengeance hangs over a nation, ready to descend on it if the proposals of political fools prevail.
2. The sense of this couplet is that men can be hurried toward misery by their desires and even by their talents and accomplishments.
3. Perhaps, that is, impetuous energy hastens men to their death.
4. Greek philosopher, a fatalist who exalted cheerfulness and derided all immoderate pretensions.

Or seen a new-made mayor's unwieldy state;° *pomp*
Where change of favorites made no change of laws,
And senates heard before they judged a cause;
How wouldst thou shake at Britain's modish tribe,
Dart the quick taunt, and edge the piercing gibe?
Attentive truth and nature to descry,
And pierce each scene with philosophic eye,
To thee were solemn toys or empty show
The robes of pleasures and the veils of woe:
All aid the farce, and all thy mirth maintain,
Whose joys are causeless, or whose griefs are vain.
Such was the scorn that filled the sage's mind,
Renewed at every glance on human kind;
How just that scorn ere yet thy voice declare,
Search every state, and canvass every prayer.
Unnumbered suppliants crowd Preferment's gate,
Athirst for wealth, and burning to be great;
Delusive Fortune hears the incessant call,
They mount, they shine, evaporate, and fall.
On every stage the foes of peace attend,
Hate dogs their flight, and Insult mocks their end.
Love ends with hope, the sinking statesman's door
Pours in the morning worshiper no more;[5]
For growing names the weekly scribbler lies,
To growing wealth the dedicator flies;
From every room descends the painted face,
That hung the bright palladium[6] of the place;
And smoked in kitchens, or in auctions sold,
To better features yields the frame of gold;
For now no more we trace in every line
Heroic worth, benevolence divine:
The form distorted justifies the fall,
And Detestation rids the indignant wall.
But will not Britain hear the last appeal,
Sign her foes' doom, or guard her favorites' zeal?
Through Freedom's sons no more remonstrance rings,
Degrading nobles and controlling kings;
Our supple tribes repress their patriot throats,
And ask no questions but the price of votes,
With weekly libels and septennial ale.[7]
Their wish is full° to riot and to rail. *satisfied*
In full-blown dignity, see Wolsey[8] stand,
Law in his voice, and fortune in his hand:
To him the church, the realm, their powers consign,
Through him the rays of regal bounty shine;
Turned by his nod the stream of honor flows,
His smile alone security bestows:
Still to new heights his restless wishes tower,
Claim leads to claim, and power advances power;
Till conquest unresisted ceased to please,
And rights submitted, left him none to seize.
At length his sovereign frowns—the train of state
Mark the keen glance, and watch the sign to hate.

5. Important personages received petitions and official calls in the morning.
6. An image of Pallas which supposedly preserved Troy from capture as long as it remained in the city; hence, a safeguard.
7. I.e., public attacks in the weekly press and ale distributed at the parliamentary elections held every seventh year.
8. Thomas, Cardinal Wolsey, Lord Chancellor under Henry VIII.

Where'er he turns, he meets a stranger's eye,
His suppliants scorn him, and his followers fly;
At once is lost the pride of awful state,
The golden canopy, the glittering plate,
The regal palace, the luxurious board,
The liveried army, and the menial lord.
With age, with cares, with maladies oppressed,
He seeks the refuge of monastic rest.
Grief aids disease, remembered folly stings,
And his last sighs reproach the faith of kings.
   Speak thou, whose thoughts at humble peace repine,
Shall Wolsey's wealth, with Wolsey's end be thine?
Or liv'st thou now, with safer pride content,
The wisest justice on the banks of Trent?
For why did Wolsey, near the steeps of fate,
On weak foundations raise the enormous weight?
Why but to sink beneath misfortune's blow,
With louder ruin to the gulfs below?
   What gave great Villiers[9] to the assassin's knife,
And fixed disease on Harley's closing life?
What murdered Wentworth, and what exiled Hyde,
By kings protected and to kings allied?
What but their wish indulged in courts to shine,
And power too great to keep or to resign?
   When first the college rolls receive his name,
The young enthusiast quits his ease for fame;
Resistless burns the fever of renown
Caught from the strong contagion of the gown:[1]
O'er Bodley's dome his future labors spread,
And Bacon's mansion trembles o'er his head.[2]
Are these thy views? proceed, illustrious youth,
And Virtue guard thee to the throne of Truth!
Yet should thy soul indulge the generous heat,
Till captive Science yields her last retreat;
Should Reason guide thee with her brightest ray,
And pour on misty Doubt resistless day;
Should no false kindness lure to loose delight,
Nor praise relax, nor difficulty fright;
Should tempting Novelty thy cell refrain,
And Sloth effuse her opiate fumes in vain;
Should Beauty blunt on fops her fatal dart,
Nor claim the triumph of a lettered heart;
Should no disease thy torpid veins invade,
Nor Melancholy's phantoms haunt thy shade;
Yet hope not life from grief or danger free,
Nor think the doom of man reversed for thee:
Deign on the passing world to turn thine eyes,
And pause a while from letters, to be wise;
There mark what ills the scholar's life assail,

9. Duke of Buckingham, court favorite of James I and Charles I; assassinated in 1628. Robert Harley (line 130), Earl of Oxford, a member of the Tory ministry under Queen Anne, was subsequently imprisoned and suffered a decline. Thomas Wentworth, Earl of Strafford, advisor to Charles I, was executed under the Long Parliament. Edward Hyde, Earl of Clarendon, who was Charles II's Lord Chancellor and whose daughter married into the royal family, was impeached and exiled in 1667.

1. Academic gown, put on upon entering the university, with allusion to the shirt of Nessus, the flaming robe which clung to Hercules and drove him to his death.

2. "There is a tradition, that the study of friar Bacon, built on an arch over the bridge, will fall, when a man greater than Bacon shall pass under it" [Johnson's note]. "Bodley's dome" is the Bodleian Library at Oxford; "dome" means *domus,* house.

Toil, envy, want, the patron, and the jail.
See nations slowly wise, and meanly just,
To buried merit raise the tardy bust.
If dreams yet flatter, once again attend,
Hear Lydiat's life, and Galileo's end.[3]
Nor deem, when Learning her last prize bestows,
The glittering eminence exempt from foes;
See when the vulgar 'scapes, despised or awed,
Rebellion's vengeful talons seize on Laud.[4]
From meaner minds though smaller fines content,
The plundered palace, or sequestered° rent; *confiscated*
Marked out by dangerous parts he meets the shock,
And fatal Learning leads him to the block:
Around his tomb let Art and Genius weep,
But hear his death, ye blockheads, hear and sleep.[5]
The festal blazes, the triumphal show,
The ravished standard, and the captive foe,
The senate's thanks, the gázette's pompous tale,
With force resistless o'er the brave prevail.
Such bribes the rapid Greek[6] o'er Asia whirled,
For such the steady Romans shook the world;
For such in distant lands the Britons shine,
And stain with blood the Danube or the Rhine;
This power has praise that virtue scarce can warm,[7]
Till fame supplies the universal charm.
Yet Reason frowns on War's unequal game,
Where wasted nations raise a single name,
And mortgaged states their grandsires' wreaths regret
From age to age in everlasting debt;
Wreaths which at last the dear-bought right convey
To rust on medals, or on stones decay.
On what foundation stands the warrior's pride,
How just his hopes, let Swedish Charles[8] decide;
A frame of adamant, a soul of fire,
No dangers fright him, and no labors tire;
O'er love, o'er fear, extends his wide domain,
Unconquered lord of pleasure and of pain;
No joys to him pacific scepters yield,
War sounds the trump, he rushes to the field;
Behold surrounding kings their powers combine,
And one capitulate, and one resign;[9]
Peace courts his hand, but spreads her charms in vain;
"Think nothing gained," he cries, "till naught remain,
On Moscow's walls till Gothic° standards fly, *Teutonic*
And all be mine beneath the polar sky."
The march begins in military state,
And nations on his eye suspended wait;
Stern Famine guards the solitary coast,

3. Thomas Lydiat (1572–1646), the Oxford mathematician and don, endured lifelong poverty. Galileo, the Italian astronomer, was imprisoned for heresy by the Inquisition; he died blind in 1642.
4. Archbishop of Canterbury under Charles I; executed in 1645 for his devotion to episcopacy.
5. Rest secure, that is, since you lack Laud's learning and gifts.
6. I.e., Alexander.
7. I.e., praise has a power (to activate the brave) which an abstract love of virtue can scarcely begin to kindle.
8. King Charles XII. Peter the Great defeated him at Pultowa in 1709. Escaping, "a needy supplicant," he sought an alliance with the Turkish Sultan. He was killed in an attack on "a petty fortress," Fredrikshald in Norway.
9. Frederick IV of Denmark capitulated, and Augustus II of Poland resigned his throne.

And Winter barricades the realms of Frost;
He comes, nor want nor cold his course delay—
Hide, blushing Glory, hide Pultowa's day:
The vanquished hero leaves his broken bands,
And shows his miseries in distant lands;
Condemned a needy supplicant to wait,
While ladies interpose, and slaves debate.
But did not Chance at length her error mend?
Did no subverted empire mark his end?
Did rival monarchs give the fatal wound?
Or hostile millions press him to the ground?
His fall was destined to a barren strand,
A petty fortress, and a dubious hand;
He left the name at which the world grew pale,
To point a moral, or adorn a tale.
All times their scenes of pompous woes afford,
From Persia's tyrant to Bavaria's lord.[1]
In gay hostility, and barbarous pride,
With half mankind embattled at his side,
Great Xerxes comes to seize the certain prey,
And starves exhausted regions in his way;
Attendant Flattery counts his myriads o'er,
Till counted myriads soothe his pride no more;
Fresh praise is tried till madness fires his mind,
The waves he lashes, and enchains the wind;
New powers are claimed, new powers are still bestowed,
Till rude resistance lops the spreading god;
The daring Greeks deride the martial show,
And heap their valleys with the gaudy foe;
The insulted sea with humbler thought he gains,
A single skiff to speed his flight remains;
The encumbered oar scarce leaves the dreaded coast
Through purple° billows and a floating host. *blood-stained*
The bold Bavarian, in a luckless hour,
Tries the dread summits of Caesarean° power, *imperial*
With unexpected legions bursts away,
And sees defenseless realms receive his sway;
Short sway! fair Austria spreads her mournful charms,
The queen, the beauty, sets the world in arms;
From hill to hill the beacon's rousing blaze
Spreads wide the hope of plunder and of praise;
The fierce Croatian, and the wild Hussar,[2]
With all the sons of ravage crowd the war;
The baffled prince, in honor's flattering bloom,
Of hasty greatness finds the fatal doom;
His foes' derision, and his subjects' blame,
And steals to death from anguish and from shame.
Enlarge my life with multitude of days!
In health, in sickness, thus the suppliant prays;
Hides from himself his state, and shuns to know
That life protracted is protracted woe.
Time hovers o'er, impatient to destroy,

1. "Persia's tyrant" is the emperor Xerxes, whose forces the Greeks defeated by sea at Salamis in 480 B.C. and later, on land, at Plataea. "Bavaria's Lord" is Charles Albert, Elector of Bavaria, who successfully aspired to the crown of the Holy Roman Empire but was deposed in a few years through the political skill of Maria Theresa ("fair Austria," line 245).

2. Hungarian cavalryman.

And shuts up all the passages of joy;
In vain their gifts the bounteous seasons pour,
The fruit autumnal, and the vernal flower;
With listless eyes the dotard views the store,
He views, and wonders that they please no more;
Now pall the tasteless meats, and joyless wines,
And Luxury with sighs her slave resigns.
Approach, ye minstrels, try the soothing strain,
Diffuse the tuneful lenitives° of pain: *softeners*
No sounds, alas! would touch the impervious ear,
Though dancing mountains witnessed Orpheus near;[3]
Nor lute nor lyre his feeble powers attend,
Nor sweeter music of a virtuous friend,
But everlasting dictates crowd his tongue,
Perversely grave, or positively wrong.
The still returning tale, and lingering jest,
Perplex the fawning niece and pampered guest,
While growing hopes scarce awe the gathering sneer,
And scarce a legacy can bribe to hear;
The watchful guests still hint the last offense;
The daughter's petulance, the son's expense,
Improve° his heady rage with treacherous skill, *play upon*
And mold his passions till they make his will.
  Unnumbered maladies his joints invade,
Lay siege to life and press the dire blockade;
But unextinguished avarice still remains,
And dreaded losses aggravate his pains;
He turns, with anxious heart and crippled hands,
His bonds of debt, and mortgages of lands;
Or views his coffers with suspicious eyes,
Unlocks his gold, and counts it till he dies.
  But grant, the virtues of a temperate prime
Bless with an age exempt from scorn or crime;
An age that melts with unperceived decay,
And glides in modest innocence away;
Whose peaceful day Benevolence endears,
Whose night congratulating Conscience cheers;
The general favorite as the general friend:
Such age there is, and who shall wish its end?
  Yet even on this her load Misfortune flings,
To press the weary minutes' flagging wings;
New sorrow rises as the day returns,
A sister sickens, or a daughter mourns.
Now kindred Merit fills the sable bier,
Now lacerated Friendship claims a tear;
Year chases year, decay pursues decay,
Still drops some joy from withering life away;
New forms arise, and different views engage,
Superfluous lags the veteran[4] on the stage,
Till pitying Nature signs the last release,
And bids afflicted Worth retire to peace.
  But few there are whom hours like these await,
Who set unclouded in the gulfs of Fate.
From Lydia's monarch[5] should the search descend,

3. The legendary Thracian bard whose playing could move even trees and hills.
4. I.e., an aged person.
5. Croesus, whom Solon advised to regard no living man as securely happy, was later deposed by the Persian Cyrus.

By Solon cautioned to regard his end,
In life's last scene what prodigies surprise,
Fears of the brave, and follies of the wise!
From Marlborough's eyes the streams of dotage flow,
And Swift expires a driveler and a show.[6]
The teeming mother, anxious for her race,
Begs for each birth the fortune of a face:
Yet Vane could tell what ills from beauty spring;[7]
And Sedley cursed the form that pleased a king.
Ye nymphs of rosy lips and radiant eyes,
Whom Pleasure keeps too busy to be wise,
Whom Joys with soft varieties invite,
By day the frolic, and the dance by night;
Who frown with vanity, who smile with art,
And ask the latest fashion of the heart;
What care, what rules your heedless charms shall save,
Each nymph your rival, and each youth your slave?
Against your fame with Fondness Hate combines,
The rival batters, and the lover mines.° *undermines*
With distant voice neglected Virtue calls,
Less heard and less, the faint remonstrance falls;
Tired with contempt, she quits the slippery reign,
And Pride and Prudence take her seat in vain.
In crowd at once, where none the pass defend,
The harmless freedom, and the private friend.
The guardians yield, by force superior plied:
To Interest, Prudence; and to Flattery, Pride.
Now Beauty falls betrayed, despised, distressed,
And hissing Infamy proclaims the rest.
Where then shall Hope and Fear their objects find?
Must dull Suspense corrupt the stagnant mind?
Must helpless man, in ignorance sedate,
Roll darkling down the torrent of his fate?
Must no dislike alarm, no wishes rise,
No cries invoke the mercies of the skies?
Inquirer, cease; petitions yet remain,
Which Heaven may hear, nor deem religion vain.
Still raise for good the supplicating voice,
But leave to Heaven the measure and the choice.
Safe in His power, whose eyes discern afar
The secret ambush of a specious prayer.
Implore His aid, in His decisions rest,
Secure, whate'er He gives, He gives the best.
Yet when the sense of sacred presence fires,
And strong devotion to the skies aspires,
Pour forth thy fervors for a healthful mind,
Obedient passions, and a will resigned;
For love, which scarce collective man can fill;
For patience sovereign o'er transmuted ill;[8]
For faith, that panting for a happier seat,
Counts death kind Nature's signal of retreat:

6. Both the Duke of Marlborough (the military hero) and Jonathan Swift declined into senility.

7. Anne Vane, the mistress of Frederick Prince of Wales, died in 1736 at the age of thirty-one. Catherine Sedley was mistress to James II.

8. I.e., a capacity for love such that all mankind together can hardly engage it fully; and for patience which, by asserting sovereignty over ills, changes their nature.

These goods for man the laws of Heaven ordain,
These goods He grants, who grants the power to gain;
With these celestial Wisdom calms the mind,
And makes the happiness she does not find.

1749

On the Death of Dr. Robert Levet[9]

Condemned to Hope's delusive mine,
  As on we toil from day to day,
By sudden blasts, or slow decline,
  Our social comforts drop away.

Well tried through many a varying year,
  See Levet to the grave descend;
Officious,° innocent, sincere, *dutiful*
  Of every friendless name the friend.

Yet still he fills Affection's eye,
  Obscurely wise, and coarsely kind;
Nor, lettered Arrogance, deny
  Thy praise to merit unrefined.

When fainting Nature called for aid,
  And hovering Death prepared the blow,
His vigorous remedy displayed
  The power of art without the show.

In Misery's darkest cavern known,
  His useful care was ever nigh,
Where hopeless Anguish poured his groan,
  And lonely Want retired to die.

No summons mocked by chill delay,
  No petty gain disdained by pride,
The modest wants of every day
  The toil of every day supplied.

His virtues walked their narrow round,
  Nor made a pause, nor left a void;
And sure the Eternal Master found
  The single talent[1] well employed.

The busy day, the peaceful night,
  Unfelt, uncounted, glided by;
His frame was firm, his powers were bright,
  Though now his eightieth year was nigh.

Then with no throbbing fiery pain,
  No cold gradations of decay,
Death broke at once the vital chain,
  And freed his soul the nearest way.

1783

9. An unlicensed physician practicing among the poor, who had long lived in Dr. Johnson's house. He was uncouth in appearance and stiff in manner.

1. An allusion to the portion of wealth given in trust in the parable of the talents, Matthew xxv.14–30.

THOMAS GRAY
(1716–1771)

Ode

ON THE DEATH OF A FAVORITE CAT,
DROWNED IN A TUB OF GOLDFISHES

'Twas on a lofty vase's side,
Where China's gayest art had dyed
  The azure flowers that blow;° *bloom*
Demurest of the tabby kind,
The pensive Selima, reclined,
  Gazed on the lake below.

Her conscious tail her joy declared;
The fair round face, the snowy beard,
  The velvet of her paws,
Her coat, that with the tortoise vies,
Her ears of jet, and emerald eyes,
  She saw; and purred applause.

Still had she gazed; but 'midst the tide
Two angel forms were seen to glide,
  The genii° of the stream: *guardian spirits*
Their scaly armor's Tyrian hue
Through richest purple to the view
  Betrayed a golden gleam.[1]

The hapless nymph with wonder saw:
A whisker first and then a claw,
  With many an ardent wish,
She stretched in vain to reach the prize.
What female heart can gold despise?
  What cat's averse to fish?

Presumptuous maid! with looks intent
Again she stretched, again she bent,
  Nor knew the gulf between.
(Malignant Fate sat by and smiled)
The slippery verge her feet beguiled,
  She tumbled headlong in.

Eight times emerging from the flood
She mewed to every watery god,
  Some speedy aid to send.
No dolphin came, no Nereid stirred;[2]
Nor cruel Tom, nor Susan heard;
  A favorite has no friend!

1. "Tyrian" and (in classical reference) "purple" cover a considerable spectrum, including crimson. The fish are seen, through red highlights, as golden.

2. A dolphin appeared to save the singer Arion when he was cast overboard. Nereids are sea-nymphs.

From hence, ye beauties, undeceived,
Know, one false step is ne'er retrieved,
And be with caution bold.
Not all that tempts your wandering eyes
And heedless hearts, is lawful prize;
Nor all that glisters, gold.

1748

Elegy Written in a Country Churchyard

The curfew tolls the knell of parting day,
The lowing herd wind slowly o'er the lea,
The plowman homeward plods his weary way,
And leaves the world to darkness and to me.

Now fades the glimmering landscape on the sight,
And all the air a solemn stillness holds,
Save where the beetle wheels his droning flight,
And drowsy tinklings lull the distant folds;

Save that from yonder ivy-mantled tower
The moping owl does to the moon complain
Of such, as wandering near her secret bower,
Molest her ancient solitary reign.

Beneath those rugged elms, that yew tree's shade,
Where heaves the turf in many a moldering heap,
Each in his narrow cell forever laid,
The rude° forefathers of the hamlet sleep. *rustic*

The breezy call of incense-breathing morn,
The swallow twittering from the straw-built shed,
The cock's shrill clarion, or the echoing horn,° *hunting horn*
No more shall rouse them from their lowly bed.

For them no more the blazing hearth shall burn,
Or busy housewife ply her evening care;
No children run to lisp their sire's return,
Or climb his knees the envied kiss to share.

Oft did the harvest to their sickle yield,
Their furrow oft the stubborn glebe° has broke; *soil*
How jocund did they drive their team afield!
How bowed the woods beneath their sturdy stroke!

Let not Ambition mock their useful toil,
Their homely joys, and destiny obscure;
Nor Grandeur hear with a disdainful smile
The short and simple annals of the poor.

The boast of heraldry,[3] the pomp of power,
And all that beauty, all that wealth e'er gave,
Awaits alike the inevitable hour.
The paths of glory lead but to the grave.

3. I.e., noble family.

Nor you, ye proud, impute to these the fault,
  If Memory o'er their tomb no trophies[4] raise,
Where through the long-drawn aisle and fretted° vault *ornamented*
  The pealing anthem swells the note of praise.

Can storied urn[5] or animated° bust *lifelike*
  Back to its mansion call the fleeting breath?
Can Honor's voice provoke° the silent dust, *call forth*
  Or Flattery soothe the dull cold ear of Death?

Perhaps in this neglected spot is laid
  Some heart once pregnant with celestial fire;
Hands that the rod of empire might have swayed,
  Or waked to ecstasy the living lyre.

But Knowledge to their eyes her ample page
  Rich with the spoils of time did ne'er unroll;
Chill Penury repressed their noble rage,
  And froze the genial current of the soul.

Full many a gem of purest ray serene,
  The dark unfathomed caves of ocean bear:
Full many a flower is born to blush unseen,
  And waste its sweetness on the desert air.

Some village Hampden,[6] that with dauntless breast
  The little tyrant of his fields withstood;
Some mute inglorious Milton here may rest,
  Some Cromwell guiltless of his country's blood.

The applause of listening senates to command,
  The threats of pain and ruin to despise,
To scatter plenty o'er a smiling land,
  And read their history in a nation's eyes,

Their lot forbade: nor circumscribed alone
  Their growing virtues, but their crimes confined;
Forbade to wade through slaughter to a throne,
  And shut the gates of mercy on mankind,

The struggling pangs of conscious truth to hide,
  To quench the blushes of ingenuous shame,
Or heap the shrine of Luxury and Pride
  With incense kindled at the Muse's flame.

Far from the madding° crowd's ignoble strife, *milling*
  Their sober wishes never learned to stray;
Along the cool sequestered vale of life
  They kept the noiseless tenor of their way.

Yet even these bones from insult to protect
  Some frail memorial still erected nigh,
With uncouth rhymes and shapeless sculpture decked,
  Implores the passing tribute of a sigh.

4. Memorials to military heroes; typically, statuary representations of arms captured in battle.
5. Funeral urn with descriptive epitaph.
6. Leader of the opposition to Charles I in the controversy over ship money; killed in battle in the Civil Wars.

Their name, their years, spelt by the unlettered Muse,
The place of fame and elegy supply:
And many a holy text around she strews,
That teach the rustic moralist to die.

For who to dumb Forgetfulness a prey,
This pleasing anxious being e'er resigned,
Left the warm precincts of the cheerful day,
Nor cast one longing lingering look behind?

On some fond breast the parting soul relies,
Some pious drops the closing eye requires;
Even from the tomb the voice of Nature cries,
Even in our ashes live their wonted fires.

For thee, who mindful of the unhonored dead
Dost in these lines their artless tale relate;
If chance, by lonely contemplation led,
Some kindred spirit shall inquire thy fate,

Haply some hoary-headed swain may say,
"Oft have we seen him at the peep of dawn
Brushing with hasty steps the dews away
To meet the sun upon the upland lawn.

"There at the foot of yonder nodding beech
That wreathes its old fantastic roots so high,
His listless length at noontide would he stretch,
And pore upon the brook that babbles by.

"Hard by yon wood, now smiling as in scorn,
Muttering his wayward fancies he would rove,
Now drooping, woeful wan, like one forlorn,
Or crazed with care, or crossed in hopeless love.

"One morn I missed him on the customed hill,
Along the heath and near his favorite tree;
Another came; nor yet beside the rill,
Nor up the lawn, nor at the wood was he;

"The next with dirges due in sad array
Slow through the churchway path we saw him borne.
Approach and read (for thou canst read) the lay,
Graved on the stone beneath yon aged thorn."

The Epitaph

Here rests his head upon the lap of Earth
A youth to Fortune and to Fame unknown.
Fair Science° frowned not on his humble birth, Learning
And Melancholy marked him for her own.

Large was his bounty, and his soul sincere,
Heaven did a recompense as largely send:
He gave to Misery all he had, a tear,
He gained from Heaven ('twas all he wished) a friend.

No farther seek his merits to disclose,
Or draw his frailties from their dread abode
(There they alike in trembling hope repose),
The bosom of his Father and his God.

ca. 1742–50 1751

WILLIAM COLLINS
(1721–1759)

Ode Written in the Beginning of the Year 1746[1]

How sleep the brave who sink to rest
By all their country's wishes blest!
When Spring, with dewy fingers cold,
Returns to deck their hallowed mold,
She there shall dress a sweeter sod
Than Fancy's feet have ever trod.

By fairy hands their knell is rung,
By forms unseen their dirge is sung;
There Honor comes, a pilgrim gray,
To bless the turf that wraps their clay,
And Freedom shall awhile repair,
To dwell a weeping hermit there!

1746

Ode on the Poetical Character

Strophe

As once, if not with light regard,
I read aright that gifted bard
(Him whose school above the rest
His loveliest Elfin Queen has blest).[2]
One, only one, unrivaled fair,
Might hope the magic girdle[3] wear,
At solemn tourney hung on high,
The wish of each love-darting eye;
Lo! to each other nymph in turn applied,
As if, in air unseen, some hovering hand,
Some chaste and angel-friend to virgin-fame.
With whispered spell had burst the starting band,
It left unblest her loathed dishonored side;
Happier, hopeless fair, if never
Her baffled hand with vain endeavor
Had touched that fatal zone to her denied!
Young Fancy thus, to me divinest name,
To whom, prepared and bathed in Heaven

1. The poem celebrates Englishmen who fell resisting the pretender to the throne ("Bonnie Prince Charlie," the grandson of James II) in the previous year.
2. Edmund Spenser.
3. A belt, "band" (line 12), "zone" (line 16), or cest (line 19) described in *Faerie Queene* IV.v: it "gave the virtue of chaste love and wifehood to all that did it bear." "Peerless was she thought" that wore it.

The cest of amplest power is given:
To few the godlike gift assigns,
To gird their blest, prophetic loins,
And gaze her visions wild, and feel unmixed her flame!

Epode

The band, as fairy legends say,
Was wove on that creating day,
When He, who called with thought to birth
Yon tented sky, this laughing earth.
And dressed with springs, and forests tall,
And poured the main engirting all,
Long by the loved Enthusiast[4] wooed,
Himself in some diviner mood,
Retiring, sate with her alone,
And placed her on his sapphire throne;
The whiles, the vaulted shrine around,
Seraphic wires were heard to sound,
Now sublimest triumph swelling,
Now on love and mercy dwelling;
And she, from out the veiling cloud,
Breathed her magic notes aloud:
And thou, thou rich-haired Youth of Morn,[5]
And all thy subject life was born!
The dangerous Passions kept aloof,
Far from the sainted growing woof:[6]
But near it sate ecstatic Wonder,
Listening the deep applauding thunder:
And Truth, in sunny vest arrayed,
By whose the tarsel's° eyes were made; *hawk's*
All the shadowy tribes of Mind,
In braided dance their murmurs joined,
And all the bright uncounted Powers
Who feed on Heaven's ambrosial flowers.
Where is the bard, whose soul can now
Its high presuming hopes avow?
Where he who thinks, with rapture blind,
This hallow'd work for him designed?

Antistrophe

High on some cliff, to Heaven up-piled,
Of rude access, of prospect wild,
Where, tangled round the jealous steep,
Strange shades o'erbrow the valleys deep,
And holy Genii guard the rock,
Its glooms embrown, its springs unlock,
While on its rich ambitious head,
An Eden, like his[7] own, lies spread:
I view that oak, the fancied glades among,
By which as Milton lay, his evening ear,
From many a cloud that dropped ethereal dew,
Nigh sphered in Heaven its native strains could hear:
On which that ancient trump[8] he reached was hung;

4. Literally, one inspired by God; i.e., Fancy.
5. Apollo, the sun, god of poetry.
6. The fabric of the girdle (line 6).
7. Milton's.
8. Milton's epic or sublime trumpet. The line echoes *Il Penseroso*, lines 59–60 ("While Cynthia checks her Dragon yoke, / Gently o'er th'accustomed Oke"), and *Nativity Ode*, line 156 ("The wakefull trump").

Thither oft, his glory greeting,
From Waller's[9] myrtle shades retreating,
With many a vow from Hope's aspiring tongue,
My trembling feet his guiding steps pursue;
In vain—such bliss to one alone,
Of all the sons of soul was known,
And Heaven, and Fancy, kindred powers,
Have now o'erturned the inspiring bowers,
Or curtained close such scene from every future view.

1746

CHRISTOPHER SMART
(1722–1771)

From Jubilate Agno[1]

For I will consider my Cat Jeoffry.
For he is the servant of the Living God, duly and daily serving him.
For at the first glance of the glory of God in the East he worships in his way.
For is this done by wreathing his body seven times round with elegant quickness.
For then he leaps up to catch the musk,[2] which is the blessing of God upon his prayer.
For he rolls upon prank to work it in.
For having done duty and received blessing he begins to consider himself.
For this he performs in ten degrees.
For first he looks upon his forepaws to see if they are clean.
For secondly he kicks up behind to clear away there.
For thirdly he works it upon stretch with the forepaws extended.
For fourthly he sharpens his paws by wood.
For fifthly he washes himself.
For sixthly he rolls upon wash.
For seventhly he fleas himself, that he may not be interrupted upon the beat.[3]
For eighthly he rubs himself against a post.
For ninthly he looks up for his instructions.
For tenthly he goes in quest of food.
For having considered God and himself he will consider his neighbor.
For if he meets another cat he will kiss her in kindness.
For when he takes his prey he plays with it to give it a chance.
For one mouse in seven escapes by his dallying.
For when his day's work is done his business more properly begins.
For he keeps the Lord's watch in the night against the adversary.
For he counteracts the powers of darkness by his electrical skin and glaring eyes.
For he counteracts the Devil, who is death, by brisking about the life.
For in his morning orisons he loves the sun and the sun loves him.
For he is of the tribe of Tiger.
For the Cherub Cat is a term of the Angel Tiger.[4]
For he has the subtlety and hissing of a serpent, which in goodness he suppresses.

9. Edmund Waller. The "myrtle," sacred to Venus, is an emblem of love.
1. "Rejoice in the Lamb"; i.e., in Jesus, the Lamb of God; written while Smart was confined for insanity.
2. Perhaps a scented plant, played with like catnip.
3. Upon his daily round, possibly of hunting.
4. Smart apparently thinks of Jeoffry as an immature or diminutive phase of a larger creature—cherubs being by artistic convention small and childlike.

For he will not do destruction if he is well-fed, neither will he spit without provocation.
For he purrs in thankfulness when God tells him he's a good Cat.
For he is an instrument for the children to learn benevolence upon.
For every house is incomplete without him, and a blessing is lacking in the spirit.
For the Lord commanded Moses concerning the cats at the departure of the Children of Israel from Egypt.
For every family had one cat at least in the bag.[5]
For the English Cats are the best in Europe.
For he is the cleanest in the use of his forepaws of any quadruped.
For the dexterity of his defense is an instance of the love of God to him exceedingly.
For he is the quickest to his mark of any creature.
For he is tenacious of his point.
For he is a mixture of gravity and waggery.
For he knows that God is his Saviour.
For there is nothing sweeter than his peace when at rest.
For there is nothing brisker than his life when in motion.
For he is of the Lord's poor, and so indeed is he called by benevolence perpetually—Poor Jeoffry! poor Jeoffry! the rat has bit thy throat.
For I bless the name of the Lord Jesus that Jeoffry is better.
For the divine spirit comes about his body to sustain it in complete cat.
For his tongue is exceeding pure so that it has in purity what it wants in music.
For he is docile and can learn certain things.
For he can sit up with gravity, which is patience upon approbation.
For he can fetch and carry, which is patience in employment.
For he can jump over a stick, which is patience upon proof positive.
For he can spraggle upon waggle at the word of command.
For he can jump from an eminence into his master's bosom.
For he can catch the cork and toss it again.
For he is hated by the hypocrite and miser.
For the former is afraid of detection.
For the latter refuses the charge.
For he camels his back to bear the first notion of business.
For he is good to think on, if a man would express himself neatly.
For he made a great figure in Egypt for his signal services.
For he killed the Icneumon rat, very pernicious by land.[6]
For his ears are so acute that they sting again.
For from this proceeds the passing quickness of his attention.
For by stroking of him I have found out electricity.
For I perceived God's light about him both wax and fire.
For the electrical fire is the spiritual substance which God sends from heaven to sustain the bodies both of man and beast.
For God has blessed him in the variety of his movements.
For, though he cannot fly, he is an excellent clamberer.
For his motions upon the face of the earth are more than any other quadruped.
For he can tread to all the measures upon the music.
For he can swim for life.
For he can creep.

ca. 1760 1939

5. The Israelites took with them silver and gold ornaments and raiment, as well as flocks and herds (Exodus xi.2 and xii.32,35). Smart adds the cats.
6. The rats encountered by Jeoffry may have impressed Smart as resembling mongooses (one sense of *ichneumon*); or there may be some reference to the ichneumon fly, a wasplike insect parasitic upon caterpillars.

OLIVER GOLDSMITH
(1730–1774)

When Lovely Woman Stoops to Folly

When lovely woman stoops to folly,
And finds too late that men betray,
What charm can soothe her melancholy,
What art can wash her guilt away?

The only art her guilt to cover,
To hide her shame from every eye,
To give repentance to her lover,
And wring his bosom—is to die.

1766

WILLIAM COWPER
(1731–1800)

From Olney Hymns

Light Shining out of Darkness

God moves in a mysterious way,
His wonders to perform;
He plants his footsteps in the sea,
And rides upon the storm.

Deep in unfathomable mines
Of never failing skill,
He treasures up his bright designs,
And works his sovereign will.

Ye fearful saints, fresh courage take,
The clouds ye so much dread
Are big with mercy, and shall break
In blessings on your head.

Judge not the Lord by feeble sense,
But trust him for his grace;
Behind a frowning providence,
He hides a smiling face.

His purposes will ripen fast,
Unfolding every hour;
The bud may have a bitter taste,
But sweet will be the flower.

Blind unbelief is sure to err,
And scan his work in vain;
God is his own interpreter,
And he will make it plain.

1779

Epitaph on a Hare

Here lies, whom hound did ne'er pursue,
  Nor swifter greyhound follow,
Whose foot ne'er tainted° morning dew, *left a scent on*
  Nor ear heard huntsman's hallo',

Old Tiney, surliest of his kind,
  Who, nursed with tender care,
And to domestic bounds confined,
  Was still a wild jack-hare.

Though duly from my hand he took
  His pittance every night,
He did it with a jealous look,
  And, when he could, would bite.

His diet was of wheaten bread,
  And milk, and oats, and straw,
Thistles, or lettuces instead,
  With sand to scour his maw.

On twigs of hawthorn he regaled,° *feasted*
  On pippins' russet peel;
And, when his juicy salads failed,
  Sliced carrot pleased him well.

A Turkey carpet was his lawn,[1]
  Whereon he loved to bound,
To skip and gambol like a fawn,
  And swing his rump around.

His frisking was at evening hours,
  For then he lost his fear;
But most before approaching showers,
  Or when a storm drew near.

Eight years and five round-rolling moons
  He thus saw steal away,
Dozing out all his idle noons,
  And every night at play.

I kept him for his humor's sake,
  For he would oft beguile
My heart of thoughts that made it ache,
  And force me to a smile.

But now, beneath this walnut-shade
  He finds his long, last home,
And waits in snug concealment laid,
  Till gentler Puss shall come.

1. Cowper exercised his hares on his parlor carpet of Turkey red.

He,[2] still more agéd, feels the shocks
  From which no care can save,
And, partner once of Tiney's box,
  Must soon partake his grave.

1783 1784

The Castaway

Obscurest night involved the sky,
  The Atlantic billows roared,
When such a destined wretch as I,
  Washed headlong from on board,
Of friends, of hope, of all bereft,
His floating home forever left.

No braver chief could Albion boast
  Than he with whom he went,[3]
Nor ever ship left Albion's coast,
  With warmer wishes sent.
He loved them both, but both in vain,
Nor him beheld, nor her again.

Not long beneath the whelming brine,
  Expert to swim, he lay;
Nor soon he felt his strength decline,
  Or courage die away;
But waged with death a lasting strife,
Supported by despair of life.

He shouted; nor his friends had failed
  To check the vessel's course,
But so the furious blast prevailed,
  That, pitiless perforce,
They left their outcast mate behind,
And scudded still before the wind.

Some succor yet they could afford;
  And, such as storms allow,
The cask, the coop, the floated cord,
  Delayed not to bestow.
But he (they knew) nor ship, nor shore,
Whate'er they gave, should visit more.

Nor, cruel as it seemed, could he
  Their haste himself condemn,
Aware that flight, in such a sea,
  Alone could rescue them;
Yet bitter felt it still to die
Deserted, and his friends so nigh.

He long survives, who lives an hour
  In ocean, self-upheld;

2. Puss, the longest-lived of Cowper's three hares.

3. Namely, George, Lord Anson, who told the castaway's story in his *Voyage Round the World* (1748).

And so long he, with unspent power,
His destiny repelled;
And ever, as the minutes flew,
Entreated help, or cried, "Adieu!"

At length, his transient respite past,
His comrades, who before
Had heard his voice in every blast,
Could catch the sound no more.
For then, by toil subdued, he drank
The stifling wave, and then he sank.

No poet wept him; but the page
Of narrative sincere,
That tells his name, his worth, his age,
Is wet with Anson's tear.
And tears by bards or heroes shed
Alike immortalize the dead.

I therefore purpose not, or dream,
Descanting on his fate,
To give the melancholy theme
A more enduring date:
But misery still delights to trace
Its semblance in another's case.

No voice divine the storm allayed,
No light propitious shone,
When, snatched from all effectual aid,
We perished, each alone;
But I beneath a rougher sea,
And whelmed in deeper gulfs than he.

1799 1803

WILLIAM BLAKE
(1757–1827)

From Poetical Sketches

Song

How sweet I roam'd from field to field,
And tasted all the summer's pride,
'Till I the prince of love beheld,
Who in the sunny beams did glide!

He shew'd me lilies for my hair,
And blushing roses for my brow;
He led me through his gardens fair,
Where all his golden pleasures grow.

With sweet May dews my wings were wet,
And Phoebus fir'd my vocal rage;[1]

1. Impassioned song. Phoebus is Apollo, god of poetic inspiration.

He caught me in his silken net,
And shut me in his golden cage.

He loves to sit and hear me sing,
Then, laughing, sports and plays with me;
Then stretches out my golden wing,
And mocks my loss of liberty.

1783

To the Evening Star

Thou fair-hair'd angel of the evening,
Now, while the sun rests on the mountains, light
Thy bright torch of love; thy radiant crown
Put on, and smile upon our evening bed!
Smile on our loves; and, while thou drawest the
Blue curtains of the sky, scatter thy silver dew
On every flower that shuts its sweet eyes
In timely sleep. Let thy west wind sleep on
The lake; speak silence with thy glimmering eyes,
And wash the dusk with silver. Soon, full soon,
Dost thou withdraw; then the wolf rages wide,
And the lion glares thro' the dun forest:
The fleeces of our flocks are cover'd with
Thy sacred dew: protect them with thine influence.[2]

1783

From SONGS OF INNOCENCE

Introduction

Piping down the valleys wild
Piping songs of pleasant glee
On a cloud I saw a child,
And he laughing said to me,

"Pipe a song about a Lamb";
So I piped with merry chear.
"Piper pipe that song again"—
So I piped, he wept to hear.

"Drop thy pipe thy happy pipe
Sing thy songs of happy chear";
So I sung the same again
While he wept with joy to hear.

"Piper sit thee down and write
In a book that all may read"—
So he vanish'd from my sight.
And I pluck'd a hollow reed,

And I made a rural pen,
And I stain'd the water clear,
And I wrote my happy songs
Every child may joy to hear.

1789

2. In astrology, the effect that heavenly bodies exert on earthly things and creatures.

The Lamb

Little Lamb, who made thee?
Dost thou know who made thee?
Gave thee life & bid thee feed,
By the stream & o'er the mead;
Gave thee clothing of delight,
Softest clothing wooly bright;
Gave thee such a tender voice,
Making all the vales rejoice!
Little Lamb who made thee?
Dost thou know who made thee?

Little Lamb I'll tell thee,
Little Lamb I'll tell thee!
He° is callèd by thy name, *Christ*
For he calls himself a Lamb:
He is meek & he is mild,
He became a little child:
I a child & thou a lamb,
We are callèd by his name.
Little Lamb God bless thee.
Little Lamb God bless thee.

1789

Holy Thursday [I.]

'Twas on a Holy Thursday,[3] their innocent faces clean,
The children[4] walking two & two, in red & blue & green,
Grey headed beadles[5] walkd before with wands as white as snow,
Till into the high dome of Paul's they like Thames' waters flow.

O what a multitude they seemd, these flowers of London town!
Seated in companies they sit with radiance all their own.
The hum of multitudes was there, but multitudes of lambs,
Thousands of little boys & girls raising their innocent hands.

Now like a mighty wind they raise to heaven the voice of song,
Or like harmonious thunderings the seats of heaven among.
Beneath them sit the aged men, wise guardians of the poor;
Then cherish pity, lest you drive an angel from your door.

1789

The Divine Image

To Mercy, Pity, Peace, and Love,
All pray in their distress:
And to these virtues of delight
Return their thankfulness.

For Mercy, Pity, Peace, and Love,
Is God, our father dear:

3. Probably Ascension Day (40 days after Easter).
4. Here the children of charity schools are depicted in St. Paul's Cathedral, London.
5. Ushers charged with keeping order.

And Mercy, Pity, Peace, and Love,
Is Man, his child and care.

For Mercy has a human heart,
Pity, a human face:
And Love, the human form divine,
And Peace, the human dress.

Then every man of every clime,
That prays in his distress,
Prays to the human form divine,
Love, Mercy, Pity, Peace.

And all must love the human form,
In heathen, Turk, or Jew.
Where Mercy, Love, & Pity dwell,
There God is dwelling too.

1789

The Little Black Boy

My mother bore me in the southern wild,
And I am black, but O! my soul is white;
White as an angel is the English child:
But I am black as if bereav'd of light.

My mother taught me underneath a tree,
And sitting down before the heat of day,
She took me on her lap and kissėd me,
And pointing to the east, began to say:

"Look on the rising sun: there God does live,
And gives his light, and gives his heat away;
And flowers and trees and beasts and men receive
Comfort in morning, joy in the noon day.

"And we are put on earth a little space,
That we may learn to bear the beams of love,
And these black bodies and this sun-burnt face
Is but a cloud, and like a shady grove.

"For when our souls have learn'd the heat to bear,
The cloud will vanish; we shall hear his voice,
Saying: 'Come out from the grove, my love & care,
And round my golden tent like lambs rejoice.' "

Thus did my mother say, and kissėd me;
And thus I say to little English boy:
When I from black and he from white cloud free,
And round the tent of God like lambs we joy,

I'll shade him from the heat till he can bear
To lean in joy upon our father's knee;
And then I'll stand and stroke his silver hair,
And be like him, and he will then love me.

1789

From Songs of Experience

Introduction

Hear the voice of the Bard!
Who Present, Past, & Future sees,
Whose ears have heard
The Holy Word
That walk'd among the ancient trees;[6]

Calling the lapséd Soul
And weeping in the evening dew;
That might controll
The starry pole,
And fallen fallen light renew!

"O Earth O Earth return!
Arise from out the dewy grass;
Night is worn,
And the morn
Rises from the slumberous mass.

"Turn away no more:
Why wilt thou turn away?
The starry floor
The watry shore
Is giv'n thee till the break of day."

1794

A Divine Image

Cruelty has a Human heart
And Jealousy a Human Face,
Terror, the Human Form Divine,
And Secrecy, the Human Dress.

The Human Dress is forgéd Iron,
The Human Form, a fiery Forge,
The Human Face, a Furnace seal'd,
The Human Heart, its hungry Gorge.° *throat*

1790–91 1921

Holy Thursday [II.]

Is this a holy thing to see,
In a rich and fruitful land,
Babes reducd to misery,
Fed with cold and usurous hand?

Is that trembling cry a song?
Can it be a song of joy?
And so many children poor?
It is a land of poverty!

6. "And Adam and Eve heard the voice of the Lord God walking in the garden in the cool of the day" (Genesis iii.8).

And their sun does never shine,
And their fields and bleak & bare,
And their ways are fill'd with thorns;
It is eternal winter there.

For where-e'er the sun does shine,
And where-e'er the rain does fall,
Babe can never hunger there,
Nor poverty the mind appall.

1794

The Clod & the Pebble

"Love seeketh not Itself to please,
Nor for itself hath any care;
But for another gives its ease,
And builds a Heaven in Hells despair."

So sang a little Clod of Clay,
Trodden with the cattle's feet;
But a Pebble of the brook,
Warbled out these metres meet:° *appropriate*

"Love seeketh only Self to please,
To bind another to its delight,
Joys in another's loss of ease,
And builds a Hell in Heaven's despite."

1794

The Sick Rose

O Rose, thou art sick.
The invisible worm
That flies in the night
In the howling storm

Has found out thy bed
Of crimson joy,
And his dark secret love
Does thy life destroy.

1794

A Poison Tree

I was angry with my friend:
I told my wrath, my wrath did end.
I was angry with my foe:
I told it not, my wrath did grow.

And I waterd it in fears,
Night & morning with my tears;
And I sunnéd it with smiles,
And with soft deceitful wiles.

And it grew both day and night,
Till it bore an apple bright.

And my foe beheld it shine,
And he knew that it was mine,

And into my garden stole,
When the night had veild the pole;
In the morning glad I see
My foe outstretchd beneath the tree.

1794

The Tyger

Tyger! Tyger! burning bright
In the forests of the night,
What immortal hand or eye
Could frame thy fearful symmetry?

In what distant deeps or skies
Burnt the fire of thine eyes?
On what wings dare he aspire?
What the hand, dare seize the fire?

And what shoulder, & what art,
Could twist the sinews of thy heart?
And when thy heart began to beat,
What dread hand? & what dread feet?

What the hammer? what the chain?
In what furnace was thy brain?
What the anvil? what dread grasp
Dare its deadly terrors clasp?

When the stars threw down their spears,
And water'd heaven with their tears,
Did he smile his work to see?
Did he who made the Lamb make thee?

Tyger! Tyger! burning bright
In the forests of the night,
What immortal hand or eye
Dare frame thy fearful symmetry?

1794

Ah Sun-flower

Ah Sun-flower! weary of time,
Who countest the steps of the Sun,
Seeking after that sweet golden clime
Where the traveller's journey is done;

Where the Youth pined away with desire,
And the pale Virgin shrouded in snow,
Arise from their graves and aspire,
Where my Sun-flower wishes to go.

1794

The Garden of Love

I went to the Garden of Love,
And saw what I never had seen:
A Chapel was built in the midst,
Where I used to play on the green.

And the gates of this Chapel were shut,
And "Thou shalt not" writ over the door;
So I turn'd to the Garden of Love,
That so many sweet flowers bore,

And I saw it was filled with graves,
And tomb-stones where flowers should be:
And Priests in black gowns were walking their rounds,
And binding with briars my joys & desires.

1794

London

I wander thro' each charter'd[7] street,
Near where the charter'd Thames does flow,
And mark in every face I meet
Marks of weakness, marks of woe.

In every cry of every man,
In every Infant's cry of fear,
In every voice, in every ban,[8]
The mind-forg'd manacles I hear.

How the Chimney-sweeper's cry
Every blackning Church appalls;
And the hapless Soldier's sigh
Runs in blood down Palace walls.

But most thro' midnight streets I hear
How the youthful Harlot's curse
Blasts the new-born Infant's tear,
And blights with plagues the Marriage hearse.

1794

From SONGS AND BALLADS

I Askéd a Thief

I askéd a thief to steal me a peach,
He turned up his eyes;
I ask'd a lithe lady to lie her down,
Holy & meek she cries.

7. Mapped out, legally defined, constricted.
8. A law or notice commanding or forbidding; a published penalty.

As soon as I went
An angel came.
He wink'd at the thief
And smild at the dame—

And without one word said
Had a peach from the tree
And still as a maid
Enjoy'd the lady.

1796 1863

Mock on, Mock on, Voltaire, Rousseau

Mock on, Mock on, Voltaire, Rousseau;[9]
Mock on, Mock on, 'tis all in vain.
You throw the sand against the wind,
And the wind blows it back again.

And every sand becomes a Gem
Reflected in the beams divine;
Blown back, they blind the mocking Eye,
But still in Israel's paths they shine.

The Atoms of Democritus
And Newton's Particles of light[1]
Are sands upon the Red sea shore,[2]
Where Israel's tents do shine so bright.

1800–08 1863

A Question Answered

What is it men in women do require?
The lineaments of Gratified Desire.
What is it women do in men require?
The lineaments of Gratified Desire.

1800–1808 1863

From Milton

And Did Those Feet

And did those feet in ancient time
Walk upon England's mountains green?
And was the holy Lamb of God
On England's pleasant pastures seen?

And did the Countenance Divine
Shine forth upon our clouded hills?
And was Jerusalem builded here,
Among these dark Satanic Mills?[3]

9. Leaders of the pre-Revolutionary French "Enlightenment"; critics of the established order, here representing thinkers who destroy without creating.
1. Democritus (Greek philosopher, fifth century B.C.) and Sir Isaac Newton (1642–1727), both represented as nonsensically reducing nature to inanimate matter.
2. Where God delivered the Israelites from the Egyptians (Exodus xiv).
3. The primary meaning is "millstone"—two heavy cylindrical stones that grind grain into meal between them; "factory" is an extended meaning.

Bring me my Bow of burning gold:
Bring me my Arrows of desire:
Bring me my Spear: O clouds unfold!
Bring me my Chariot of fire!

I will not cease from Mental Fight,
Nor shall my Sword sleep in my hand,
Till we have built Jerusalem
In England's green & pleasant Land.

1804–10

From JERUSALEM

England! Awake! Awake! Awake!

England! awake! awake! awake!
  Jerusalem thy Sister calls!
Why wilt thou sleep the sleep of death?
  And close her from thy ancient walls.

Thy hills & valleys felt her feet,
  Gently upon their bosoms move:
Thy gates beheld sweet Zions ways;
  Then was a time of joy and love.

And now the time returns again:
  Our souls exult & Londons towers,
Receive the Lamb of God to dwell
  In Englands green & pleasant bowers.

1804–09 1818

From FOR THE SEXES: *The Gates of Paradise*

To The Accuser who is The God of This World[4]

Truly My Satan thou art but a Dunce,
And dost not know the Garment from the Man;
Every Harlot was a Virgin once,
Nor canst thou ever change Kate into Nan.

Tho thou are Worshipd by the Names Divine
Of Jesus & Jehovah: thou art still
The Son of Morn in weary Night's decline,
The lost Traveller's Dream under the Hill.

1793–1818

4. God conceived of as a harsh taskmaster and merciless judge; Blake rejected this concept as "Satanic."

ROBERT BURNS
(1759–1796)

To a Mouse

ON TURNING HER UP IN HER NEST WITH THE PLOUGH, NOVEMBER, 1785

Wee, sleekit,° cow'rin, tim'rous beastie, — *sleek*
O, what a panic's in thy breastie!
Thou need na start awa sae hasty,
Wi' bickering° brattle!° — *hurried / scamper*
I wad be laith to rin an' chase thee,
Wi' murd'ring pattle!° — *plowstaff ("paddle")*

I'm truly sorry man's dominion
Has broken Nature's social union,
An' justifies that ill opinion
Which makes thee startle
At me, thy poor earth-born companion,
An' fellow-mortal!

I doubt na, whiles,° but thou may thieve; — *sometimes*
What then? poor beastie, thou maun° live! — *must*
A daimen° icker° in a thrave° — *random / corn-ear / shock*
'S a sma' request:
I'll get a blessin wi' the lave,° — *rest*
And never miss't!

Thy wee bit housie, too, in ruin!
Its silly° wa's the win's are strewin! — *frail*
An' naething, now, to big° a new ane, — *build*
O' foggage° green! — *mosses*
An' bleak December's winds ensuin,
Baith snell° an' keen! — *bitter*

Thou saw the fields laid bare and waste,
An' weary winter comin fast,
An' cozie here, beneath the blast,
Thou thought to dwell,
Till crash! the cruel coulter° past — *plowshare*
Out thro' thy cell.

That wee bit heap o' leaves an' stibble° — *stubble*
Has cost thee mony a weary nibble!
Now thou's turned out, for a' thy trouble,
But° house or hald,° — *without / home ("hold")*
To thole° the winter's sleety dribble, — *endure*
An' cranreuch° cauld! — *hoarfrost*

But, Mousie, thou art no thy lane,[1]
In proving foresight may be vain:

1. "No thy lane": not alone.

The best laid schemes o' mice an' men
Gang° aft a-gley.° *go / astray*
An' lea'e us nought but grief an' pain
For promised joy.

Still thou art blest, compared wi' me!
The present only toucheth thee:
But och! I backward cast my e'e
On prospects drear!
An' forward, tho' I canna see,
I guess an' fear!

1785, 1786

Holy Willie's[2] Prayer

O Thou, wha in the heavens dost dwell,
Wha, as it pleases best thysel',
Sends ane to heaven and ten to hell,
A' for thy glory,
And no for ony guid or ill
They've done afore thee!

I bless and praise thy matchless might,
Whan thousands thou hast left in night,
That I am here afore thy sight,
For gifts an' grace
A burnin' an' a shinin' light,
To a' this place.

What was I, or my generation,
That I should get sic exaltation?
I, wha deserve most just damnation,
For broken laws,
Sax thousand years 'fore my creation,
Thro' Adam's cause.

When frae my mither's womb I fell,
Thou might hae plungéd me in hell,
To gnash my gums, to weep and wail,
In burnin lakes,
Where damnéd devils roar and yell,
Chained to their stakes;

Yet I am here a chosen sample,
To show thy grace is great and ample;
I'm here a pillar in thy temple,
Strong as a rock,
A guide, a buckler, an example
To a' thy flock.

O Lord, thou kens what zeal I bear,
When drinkers drink, and swearers swear.
And singin' there and dancin' here,
Wi' great an' sma':

2. One William Fisher, an elder in the church at Mauchline, the seat of Burns's farm. He habitually censured other men's behavior and doctrine, but was himself rebuked for drunkenness and was suspected of stealing church funds.

For I am keepit by thy fear
Free frae them a'.

But yet, O Lord! confess I must
At times I'm fashed° wi' fleshy lust; *troubled*
An' sometimes too, wi' warldly trust,
Vile self gets in;
But thou remembers we are dust,
Defiled in sin.

O Lord! yestreen,° thou kens, wi' Meg— *last night*
Thy pardon I sincerely beg;
O! may't ne'er be a livin' plague
To my dishonour,
An' I'll ne'er lift a lawless leg
Again upon her.

Besides I farther maun allow,
Wi' Lizzie's lass, three times I trow—
But, Lord, that Friday I was fou,° *full (of liquor)*
When I cam near her,
Or else thou kens thy servant true
Wad never steer° her. *touch ("stir")*

May be thou lets this fleshly thorn
Beset thy servant e'en and morn
Lest he owre high and proud should turn,
That he's sae gifted;
If sae, thy hand maun e'en be borne,
Until thou lift it.

Lord, bless thy chosen in this place,
For here thou hast a chosen race;
But God confound their stubborn face,
And blast their name,
Wha bring thy elders to disgrace
An' public shame.

Lord, mind Gawn Hamilton's[3] deserts,
He drinks, an' swears, an' plays at cartes,
Yet has sae mony takin arts
Wi' great an' sma',
Frae God's ain priest the people's hearts
He steals awa'.

An' when we chastened him therefor,
Thou kens how he bred sic a splore° *row*
As set the warld in a roar
O' laughin' at us;
Curse thou his basket and his store,
Kail° and potatoes. *cabbage*

Lord, hear my earnest cry an' pray'r,
Against that presbytery o' Ayr;

3. Gavin Hamilton, a convivial lawyer friend of Burns's. Accused of Sabbath-breaking and other offenses by the elders of Mauchline church, he was cleared by the Presbytery of Ayr (line 80) with the help of his counsel Robert Aiken (line 85).

Thy strong right hand, Lord, make it bare
Upo' their heads;
Lord, weigh it down, and dinna spare,
For their misdeeds.

O Lord my God, that glib-tongued Aiken,
My very heart and soul are quakin',
To think how we stood sweatin, shakin,
An' pissed wi' dread,
While he, wi' hingin° lips and snakin,° — *hanging / sneering*
Held up his head.

Lord in the day of vengeance try him;
Lord, visit them wha did employ him,
And pass not in thy mercy by them,
Nor hear their pray'r:
But, for thy people's sake, destroy them,
And dinna spare.

But, Lord, remember me and mine
Wi' mercies temp'ral and divine,
That I for gear° and grace may shine — *wealth*
Excelled by nane,
And a' the glory shall be thine,
Amen, Amen!

1785 1808

Green Grow the Rashes

Chorus

Green grow the rashes,° O; — *tall grasses or rushes*
Green grow the rashes, O;
The sweetest hours that e'er I spend,
Are spent amang the lasses, O!

There's nought but care on ev'ry han',
In ev'ry hour that passes, O:
What signifies the life o' man,
An'° 'twere na for the lasses, O. — *if*
(*Chorus*)

The warly° race may riches chase, — *worldly*
An' riches still may fly them, O;
An' though at last they catch them fast,
Their hearts can ne'er enjoy them, O.
(*Chorus*)

But gie me a canny° hour at e'en, — *pleasant*
My arms about my dearie, O;
An' warly cares, an' warly men,
May a' gae tapsalteerie,° O! — *topsy turvy*
(*Chorus*)

For you sae douce,° ye sneer at this, — *prudent*
Ye're nought but senseless asses, O:

The wisest man[4] the warl' saw,
He dearly loved the lasses, O.
(*Chorus*)

Auld nature swears, the lovely dears
Her noblest work she classes, O:
Her prentice han' she tried on man,
An' then she made the lasses, O.
(*Chorus*)

1784 1787

John Anderson, My Jo

John Anderson my jo,° John, *joy*
When we were first acquent,
Your locks were like the raven,
Your bonie brow was brent;[5]
But now your brow is beld, John,
Your locks are like the snow;
But blessings on your frosty pow,° *head*
John Anderson, my jo.

John Anderson my jo, John,
We clamb° the hill thegither; *climbed*
And mony a canty° day, John, *merry*
We've had wi' ane anither:
Now we maun totter down, John,
And hand in hand we'll go,
And sleep thegither at the foot,
John Anderson, my jo.

1789 1790

Bonie Doon

Ye flowery banks o' bonie Doon,
How can ye blume sae fair?
How can ye chant, ye little birds,
And I sae fu' o' care?

Thou'll break my heart, thou bonie bird,
That sings upon the bough;
Thou minds me o' the happy days,
When my fause° luve was true. *false*

Thou'll break my heart, thou bonie bird,
That sings beside thy mate;
For sae I sat, and sae I sang,
And wist° na o' my fate. *knew*

Aft hae I roved by bonie Doon
To see the wood-bine twine,
And ilka° bird sang o' its luve, *every*
And sae did I o' mine.

4. King Solomon, who had many wives.
5. Straight, steep; not rounding off into a bald pate.

Wi' lightsome heart I pu'd a rose
  Frae aff its thorny tree;
And my fause luver staw° my rose *stole*
  But left the thorn wi' me.

1791 1792

A Red, Red Rose

O my luve's like a red, red rose,
  That's newly sprung in June;
O my luve's like the melodie
  That's sweetly played in tune.

As fair art thou, my bonnie lass,
  So deep in luve am I;
And I will luve thee still, my dear,
  Till a' the seas gang dry.

Till a' the seas gang dry, my dear,
  And the rocks melt wi' the sun:
O I will love thee still, my dear,
  While the sands o' life shall run.

And fare thee weel, my only luve,
  And fare thee weel awhile!
And I will come again, my luve,
  Though it were ten thousand mile.

1796

WILLIAM WORDSWORTH
(1770–1850)

Lines

COMPOSED A FEW MILES ABOVE TINTERN ABBEY ON REVISITING THE BANKS OF THE WYE DURING A TOUR. JULY 13, 1798[1]

  Five years have passed; five summers, with the length
Of five long winters! and again I hear
These waters, rolling from their mountain-springs
With a soft inland murmur. Once again
Do I behold these steep and lofty cliffs,
That on a wild secluded scene impress
Thoughts of more deep seclusion; and connect
The landscape with the quiet of the sky.
The day is come when I again repose
Here, under this dark sycamore, and view
These plots of cottage ground, these orchard tufts,
Which at this season, with their unripe fruits,
Are clad in one green hue, and lose themselves
'Mid groves and copses. Once again I see

1. Ruins of a medieval abbey situated in the valley of the river Wye, in Monmouthshire, noted for its scenery.

These hedgerows, hardly hedgerows, little lines
Of sportive wood run wild; these pastoral farms,
Green to the very door; and wreaths of smoke
Sent up, in silence, from among the trees!
With some uncertain notice, as might seem
Of vagrant dwellers in the houseless woods,
Or of some Hermit's cave, where by his fire
The Hermit sits alone.

These beauteous forms,
Through a long absence, have not been to me
As is a landscape to a blind man's eye;
But oft, in lonely rooms, and 'mid the din
Of towns and cities, I have owed to them,
In hours of weariness, sensations sweet,
Felt in the blood, and felt along the heart;
And passing even into my purer mind,
With tranquil restoration—feelings too
Of unremembered pleasure; such, perhaps,
As have no slight or trivial influence
On that best portion of a good man's life,
His little, nameless, unremembered, acts
Of kindness and of love. Nor less, I trust,
To them I may have owed another gift,
Of aspect more sublime; that blessed mood,
In which the burthen of the mystery,
In which the heavy and the weary weight
Of all this unintelligible world,
Is lightened—that serene and blessed mood,
In which the affections gently lead us on—
Until, the breath of this corporeal frame
And even the motion of our human blood
Almost suspended, we are laid asleep
In body, and become a living soul;
While with an eye made quiet by the power
Of harmony, and the deep power of joy,
We see into the life of things.

If this
Be but a vain belief, yet, oh! how oft—
In darkness and amid the many shapes
Of joyless daylight; when the fretful stir
Unprofitable, and the fever of the world,
Have hung upon the beatings of my heart—
How oft, in spirit, have I turned to thee,
O sylvan Wye! thou wanderer through the woods,
How often has my spirit turned to thee!

And now, with gleams of half-extinguished thought,
With many recognitions dim and faint,
And somewhat of a sad perplexity,
The picture of the mind revives again;
While here I stand, not only with the sense
Of present pleasure, but with pleasing thoughts
That in this moment there is life and food
For future years. And so I dare to hope,
Though changed, no doubt, from what I was when first

I came among these hills; when like a roe
I bounded o'er the mountains, by the sides
Of the deep rivers, and the lonely streams,
Wherever nature led—more like a man
Flying from something that he dreads than one
Who sought the thing he loved. For nature then
(The coarser[2] pleasures of my boyish days,
And their glad animal movements all gone by)
To me was all in all.—I cannot paint
What then I was. The sounding cataract
Haunted me like a passion; the tall rock,
The mountain, and the deep and gloomy wood,
Their colors and their forms, were then to me
An appetite; a feeling and a love,
That had no need of a remoter charm,
By thought supplied, nor any interest
Unborrowed from the eye.—That time is past,
And all its aching joys are now no more,
And all its dizzy raptures. Not for this
Faint° I, nor mourn nor murmur; other gifts *become discouraged*
Have followed; for such loss, I would believe,
Abundant recompense. For I have learned
To look on nature, not as in the hour
Of thoughtless youth; but hearing oftentimes
The still, sad music of humanity,
Nor harsh nor grating, though of ample power
To chasten and subdue. And I have felt
A presence that disturbs me with the joy
Of elevated thoughts; a sense sublime
Of something far more deeply interfused,
Whose dwelling is the light of setting suns,
And the round ocean and the living air,
And the blue sky, and in the mind of man:
A motion and a spirit, that impels
All thinking things, all objects of all thought,
And rolls through all things. Therefore am I still
A lover of the meadows and the woods,
And mountains; and of all that we behold
From this green earth; of all the mighty world
Of eye, and ear—both what they half create,
And what perceive; well pleased to recognize
In nature and the language of the sense
The anchor of my purest thoughts, the nurse,
The guide, the guardian of my heart, and soul
Of all my moral being.

Nor perchance,
If I were not thus taught, should I the more
Suffer my genial spirits° to decay: *vital energies*
For thou art with me here upon the banks
Of this fair river; thou my dearest Friend,[3]
My dear, dear Friend; and in thy voice I catch
The language of my former heart, and read
My former pleasures in the shooting lights

2. I.e., primarily physical.
3. Wordsworth's sister Dorothy, who accompanied him on the walking trip here commemorated.

Of thy wild eyes. Oh! yet a little while
May I behold in thee what I was once,
My dear, dear Sister! and this prayer I make,
Knowing that Nature never did betray
The heart that loved her; 'tis her privilege,
Through all the years of this our life, to lead
From joy to joy: for she can so inform
The mind that is within us, so impress
With quietness and beauty, and so feed
With lofty thoughts, that neither evil tongues,
Rash judgments, nor the sneers of selfish men,
Nor greetings where no kindness is, nor all
The dreary intercourse of daily life,
Shall e'er prevail against us, or disturb
Our cheerful faith, that all which we behold
Is full of blessings. Therefore let the moon
Shine on thee in thy solitary walk;
And let the misty mountain winds be free
To blow against thee: and, in after years,
When these wild ecstasies shall be matured
Into a sober pleasure; when thy mind
Shall be a mansion for all lovely forms,
Thy memory be as a dwelling place
For all sweet sounds and harmonies; oh! then,
If solitude, or fear, or pain, or grief
Should be thy portion, with what healing thoughts
Of tender joy wilt thou remember me,
And these my exhortations! Nor, perchance—
If I should be where I no more can hear
Thy voice, nor catch from thy wild eyes these gleams
Of past existence—wilt thou then forget
That on the banks of this delightful stream
We stood together; and that I, so long
A worshiper of Nature, hither came
Unwearied in that service; rather say
With warmer love—oh! with far deeper zeal
Of holier love. Nor wilt thou then forget,
That after many wanderings, many years
Of absence, these steep woods and lofty cliffs,
And this green pastoral landscape, were to me
More dear, both for themselves and for thy sake!

1798

From The Prelude

From *Book I*

Fair seedtime had my soul, and I grew up
Fostered alike by beauty and by fear:
Much favored in my birthplace,[4] and no less
In that belovéd Vale[5] to which erelong
We were transplanted—there were we let loose

4. Cockermouth, in the northern part of the English Lake District.

5. Esthwaite, also in the Lakes.

For sports of wider range. Ere I had told
Ten birthdays, when among the mountain slopes
Frost, and the breath of frosty wind, had snapped
The last autumnal crocus, 'twas my joy
With store of springes° o'er my shoulder hung *snares*
To range the open heights where woodcocks run
Along the smooth green turf. Through half the night,
Scudding away from snare to snare, I plied
That anxious visitation—moon and stars
Were shining o'er my head. I was alone,
And seemed to be a trouble to the peace
That dwelt among them. Sometimes it befell
In these night wanderings, that a strong desire
O'erpowered my better reason, and the bird
Which was the captive of another's toil
Became my prey; and when the deed was done
I heard among the solitary hills
Low breathings coming after me, and sounds
Of undistinguishable motion, steps
Almost as silent as the turf they trod.

Nor less, when spring had warmed the cultured° Vale, *cultivated*
Moved we as plunderers where the mother bird
Had in high places built her lodge; though mean
Our object and inglorious, yet the end
Was not ignoble. Oh! when I have hung
Above the raven's nest, by knots of grass
And half-inch fissures in the slippery rock
But ill sustained, and almost (so it seemed)
Suspended by the blast that blew amain,
Shouldering the naked crag, oh, at that time
While on the perilous ridge I hung alone,
With what strange utterance did the loud dry wind
Blow through my ear! the sky seemed not a sky
Of earth—and with what motion moved the clouds!

Dust as we are, the immortal spirit grows
Like harmony in music; there is a dark
Inscrutable workmanship that reconciles
Discordant elements, makes them cling together
In one society. How strange that all
The terrors, pains, and early miseries,
Regrets, vexations, lassitudes interfused
Within my mind, should e'er have borne a part,
And that a needful part, in making up
The calm existence that is mine when I
Am worthy of myself! Praise to the end!
Thanks to the means which Nature deigned to employ;
Whether her fearless visitings, or those
That came with soft alarm, like hurtless light
Opening the peaceful clouds; or she may use
Severer interventions, ministry
More palpable, as best might suit her aim.

One summer evening (led by her) I found
A little boat tied to a willow tree
Within a rocky cave, its usual home.

Straight I unloosed her chain, and stepping in
Pushed from the shore. It was an act of stealth
And troubled pleasure, nor without the voice
Of mountain echoes did my boat move on;
Leaving behind her still, on either side,
Small circles glittering idly in the moon,
Until they melted all into one track
Of sparkling light. But now, like one who rows,
Proud of his skill, to reach a chosen point
With an unswerving line, I fixed my view
Upon the summit of a craggy ridge,
The horizon's utmost boundary; for above
Was nothing but the stars and the gray sky.
She was an elfin pinnace; lustily
I dipped my oars into the silent lake,
And, as I rose upon the stroke, my boat
Went heaving through the water like a swan;
When, from behind that craggy steep till then
The horizon's bound, a huge peak, black and huge,
As if with voluntary power instinct,
Upreared its head. I struck and struck again,
And growing still in stature the grim shape
Towered up between me and the stars, and still,
For so it seemed, with purpose of its own
And measured motion like a living thing,
Strode after me. With trembling oars I turned,
And through the silent water stole my way
Back to the covert of the willow tree;
There in her mooring place I left my bark,
And through the meadows homeward went, in grave
And serious mood; but after I had seen
That spectacle, for many days, my brain
Worked with a dim and undetermined sense
Of unknown modes of being; o'er my thoughts
There hung a darkness, call it solitude
Or blank desertion. No familiar shapes
Remained, no pleasant images of trees,
Of sea or sky, no colors of green fields;
But huge and mighty forms, that do not live
Like living men, moved slowly through the mind
By day, and were a trouble to my dreams.

Wisdom and Spirit of the universe!
Thou Soul that art the eternity of thought,
That givest to forms and images a breath
And everlasting motion, not in vain
By day or starlight thus from my first dawn
Of childhood didst thou intertwine for me
The passions that build up our human soul;
Not with the mean and vulgar works of man,
But with high objects, with enduring things—
With life and nature—purifying thus
The elements of feeling and of thought,
And sanctifying, by such discipline,
Both pain and fear, until we recognize
A grandeur in the beating of the heart.
Nor was this fellowship vouchsafed to me
With stinted kindness. In November days,

When vapors rolling down the valley made
A lonely scene more lonesome, among woods,
At noon and 'mid the calm of summer nights,
When, by the margin of the trembling lake,
Beneath the gloomy hills homeward I went
In solitude, such intercourse was mine;
Mine was it in the fields both day and night,
And by the waters, all the summer long.

And in the frosty season, when the sun
Was set, and visible for many a mile
The cottage windows blazed through twilight gloom,
I heeded not their summons: happy time
It was indeed for all of us—for me
It was a time of rapture! Clear and loud
The village clock tolled six—I wheeled about,
Proud and exulting like an untired horse
That cares not for his home. All shod with steel,
We hissed along the polished ice in games
Confederate, imitative of the chase
And woodland pleasures—the resounding horn,
The pack loud chiming, and the hunted hare.
So through the darkness and the cold we flew,
And not a voice was idle; with the din
Smitten, the precipices rang aloud;
The leafless trees and every icy crag
Tinkled like iron; while far distant hills
Into the tumult sent an alien sound
Of melancholy not unnoticed, while the stars
Eastward were sparkling clear, and in the west
The orange sky of evening died away.
Not seldom from the uproar I retired
Into a silent bay, or sportively
Glanced sideway, leaving the tumultuous throng,
To cut across the reflex° of a star *reflection*
That fled, and, flying still before me, gleamed
Upon the glassy plain; and oftentimes,
When we had given our bodies to the wind,
And all the shadowy banks on either side
Came sweeping through the darkness, spinning still
The rapid line of motion, then at once
Have I, reclining back upon my heels,
Stopped short; yet still the solitary cliffs
Wheeled by me—even as if the earth had rolled
With visible motion her diurnal round!
Behind me did they stretch in solemn train,
Feebler and feebler, and I stood and watched
Till all was tranquil as a dreamless sleep.

Ye Presences of Nature in the sky
And on the earth! Ye Visions of the hills!
And Souls of lonely places! can I think
A vulgar° hope was yours when ye employed *lowly*
Such ministry, when ye, through many a year
Haunting me thus among my boyish sports,
On caves and trees, upon the woods and hills,
Impressed upon all forms the characters
Of danger or desire; and thus did make

The surface of the universal earth
With triumph and delight, with hope and fear,
Work like a sea?

1798–1800 1850

She Dwelt Among the Untrodden Ways

She dwelt among the untrodden ways
Beside the springs of Dove.[6]
A Maid whom there were none to praise
And very few to love;

A violet by a mossy stone
Half hidden from the eye!
—Fair as a star, when only one
Is shining in the sky.

She lived unknown, and few could know
When Lucy ceased to be;
But she is in her grave, and, oh,
The difference to me!

1800

Three Years She Grew

Three years she grew in sun and shower,
Then Nature said, "A lovelier flower
On earth was never sown;
This Child I to myself will take;
She shall be mine, and I will make
A Lady of my own.

"Myself will to my darling be
Both law and impulse: and with me
The Girl, in rock and plain,
In earth and heaven, in glade and bower,
Shall feel an overseeing power
To kindle or restrain.

"She shall be sportive as the fawn
That wild with glee across the lawn
Or up the mountain springs;
And hers shall be the breathing balm,
And hers the silence and the calm
Of mute insensate things.

"The floating clouds their state shall lend
To her; for her the willow bend;
Nor shall she fail to see
Even in the motions of the Storm
Grace that shall mold the Maiden's form
By silent sympathy.

"The stars of midnight shall be dear
To her; and she shall lean her ear

6. Several rivers in England are named Dove.

In many a secret place
Where rivulets dance their wayward round,
And beauty born of murmuring sound
Shall pass into her face.

"And vital feelings of delight
Shall rear her form to stately height,
Her virgin bosom swell;
Such thoughts to Lucy I will give
While she and I together live
Here in this happy dell."

Thus Nature spake—the work was done—
How soon my Lucy's race was run!
She died, and left to me
This health, this calm, and quiet scene;
The memory of what has been,
And never more will be.

1800

A Slumber Did My Spirit Seal

A slumber did my spirit seal;
I had no human fears:
She seemed a thing that could not feel
The touch of earthly years.

No motion has she now, no force;
She neither hears nor sees;
Rolled round in earth's diurnal course,
With rocks, and stones, and trees.

1800

Resolution and Independence

1

There was a roaring in the wind all night;
The rain came heavily and fell in floods;
But now the sun is rising calm and bright;
The birds are singing in the distant woods;
Over his own sweet voice the Stock-dove broods;
The Jay makes answer as the Magpie chatters;
And all the air is filled with pleasant noise of waters.

2

All things that love the sun are out of doors;
The sky rejoices in the morning's birth;
The grass is bright with rain-drops;—on the moors
The hare is running races in her mirth;
And with her feet she from the plashy earth
Raises a mist; that, glittering in the sun,
Runs with her all the way, wherever she doth run.

3

I was a Traveler then upon the moor;
I saw the hare that raced about with joy;

I heard the woods and distant waters roar;
Or heard them not, as happy as a boy:
The pleasant season did my heart employ:
My old remembrances went from me wholly;
And all the ways of men, so vain and melancholy.

4

But, as it sometimes chanceth, from the might
Of joy in minds that can no further go,
As high as we have mounted in delight
In our dejection do we sink as low;
To me that morning did it happen so;
And fears and fancies thick upon me came;
Dim sadness—and blind thoughts, I knew not, nor could name.

5

I heard the sky-lark warbling in the sky;
And I bethought me of the playful hare:
Even such a happy Child of earth am I;
Even as these blissful creatures do I fare;
Far from the world I walk, and from all care;
But there may come another day to me—
Solitude, pain of heart, distress, and poverty.

6

My whole life I have lived in pleasant thought,
As if life's business were a summer mood;
As if all needful things would come unsought
To genial faith, still rich in genial good;
But how can He expect that others should
Build for him, sow for him, and at his call
Love him, who for himself will take no heed at all?

7

I thought of Chatterton,[7] the marvelous Boy,
The sleepless Soul that perished in his pride;
Of Him[8] who walked in glory and in joy
Following his plow, along the mountain-side:
By our own spirits are we deified:
We Poets in our youth begin in gladness;
But thereof come in the end despondency and madness.

8

Now, whether it were by peculiar grace,
A leading from above, a something given,
Yet it befell, that, in this lonely place,
When I with these untoward thoughts had striven,
Beside a pool bare to the eye of heaven
I saw a Man before me unawares:
The oldest man he seemed that ever wore gray hairs.

9

As a huge stone is sometimes seen to lie
Couched on the bald top of an eminence;
Wonder to all who do the same espy,
By what means it could thither come, and whence;
So that it seems a thing endued with sense:
Like a sea-beast crawled forth, that on a shelf
Of rock or sand reposeth, there to sun itself;

7. Thomas Chatterton (1752–70), a gifted young English poet who committed suicide.

8. Robert Burns (1759–96), who died before achieving his later great renown.

10

Such seemed this Man, not all alive nor dead,
Nor all asleep—in his extreme old age:
His body was bent double, feet and head
Coming together in life's pilgrimage;
As if some dire constraint of pain, or rage
Of sickness felt by him in times long past,
A more than human weight upon his frame had cast.

11

Himself he propped, limbs, body, and pale face,
Upon a long gray staff of shaven wood:
And, still as I drew near with gentle pace,
Upon the margin of that moorish flood
Motionless as a cloud the old Man stood,
That heareth not the loud winds when they call;
And moveth all together, if it move at all.

12

At length, himself unsettling, he the pond
Stirred with his staff, and fixedly did look
Upon the muddy water, which he conned,
As if he had been reading in a book:
And now a stranger's privilege I took;
And, drawing to his side, to him did say,
"This morning gives us promise of a glorious day."

13

A gentle answer did the old Man make,
In courteous speech which forth he slowly drew:
And him with further words I thus bespake,
"What occupation do you there pursue?
This is a lonesome place for one like you."
Ere he replied, a flash of mild surprise
Broke from the sable orbs of his yet-vivid eyes.

14

His words came feebly, from a feeble chest,
But each in solemn order followed each,
With something of a lofty utterance drest—
Choice word and measured phrase, above the reach
Of ordinary men; a stately speech;
Such as grave Livers[9] do in Scotland use,
Religious men, who give to God and man their dues.

15

He told, that to these waters he had come
To gather leeches,[1] being old and poor:
Employment hazardous and wearisome!
And he had many hardships to endure:
From pond to pond he roamed, from moor to moor;
Housing, with God's good help, by choice or chance;
And in this way he gained an honest maintenance.

16

The old Man still stood talking by my side;
But now his voice to me was like a stream

9. Those who live austerely and gravely. See Wordsworth's "The Excursion," Book I, lines 113–117; the reference is to a Scottish family:
Pure livers were they all, austere and grave,
And fearing God; the very children taught
Stern self-respect, a reverence for God's word,
And an habitual piety, maintained
With strictness scarcely known on English ground.

1. Aquatic bloodsuckers, once widely used for medicinal bloodletting.

Scarce heard; nor word from word could I divide;
And the whole body of the Man did seem
Like one whom I had met with in a dream;
Or like a man from some far region sent,
To give me human strength, by apt admonishment.

17

My former thoughts returned: the fear that kills;
And hope that is unwilling to be fed;
Cold, pain, and labor, and all fleshly ills;
And mighty Poets in their misery dead.
—Perplexed, and longing to be comforted,
My question eagerly did I renew,
"How is it that you live, and what is it you do?"

18

He with a smile did then his words repeat;
And said, that, gathering leeches, far and wide
He traveled; stirring thus about his feet
The waters of the pools where they abide.
"Once I could meet with them on every side;
But they have dwindled long by slow decay;
Yet still I persevere, and find them where I may."

19

While he was talking thus, the lonely place,
The old Man's shape, and speech—all troubled me:
In my mind's eye I seemed to see him pace
About the weary moors continually,
Wandering about alone and silently.
While I these thoughts within myself pursued,
He, having made a pause, the same discourse renewed.

20

And soon with this he other matter blended,
Cheerfully uttered, with demeanor kind,
But stately in the main; and when he ended,
I could have laughed myself to scorn to find
In that decrepit Man so firm a mind.
"God," said I, "be my help and stay secure;
I'll think of the Leech-gatherer on the lonely moor!"

1802 1807

It Is a Beauteous Evening

It is a beauteous evening, calm and free,
The holy time is quiet as a Nun
Breathless with adoration; the broad sun
Is sinking down in its tranquility;
The gentleness of heaven broods o'er the Sea:
Listen! the mighty Being is awake,
And doth with his eternal motion make
A sound like thunder—everlastingly.
Dear Child! dear Girl! that walkest with me here,
If thou appear untouched by solemn thought,
Thy nature is not therefore less divine:

Thou liest in Abraham's bosom[2] all the year,
And worship'st at the Temple's inner shrine,[3]
God being with thee when we know it not.

1807

London, 1802

Milton! thou shouldst be living at this hour:
England hath need of thee: she is a fen
Of stagnant waters: altar, sword, and pen,
Fireside, the heroic wealth of hall and bower,
Have forfeited their ancient English dower
Of inward happiness. We are selfish men;
Oh! raise us up, return to us again;
And give us manners, virtue, freedom, power.
Thy soul was like a Star, and dwelt apart;
Thou hadst a voice whose sound was like the sea:
Pure as the naked heavens, majestic, free,
So didst thou travel on life's common way,
In cheerful godliness; and yet thy heart
The lowliest duties on herself did lay.

1807

Composed upon Westminster Bridge, September 3, 1802

Earth has not anything to show more fair:
Dull would he be of soul who could pass by
A sight so touching in its majesty;
This City now doth, like a garment, wear
The beauty of the morning; silent, bare,
Ships, towers, domes, theaters, and temples lie
Open unto the fields, and to the sky;
All bright and glittering in the smokeless air.
Never did sun more beautifully steep
In his first splendor, valley, rock, or hill;
Ne'er saw I, never felt, a calm so deep!
The river glideth at his own sweet will:
Dear God! the very houses seem asleep;
And all that mighty heart is lying still!

1807

My Heart Leaps Up

My heart leaps up when I behold
  A rainbow in the sky:
So was it when my life began;
So is it now I am a man;
So be it when I shall grow old,
  Or let me die!
The Child is father of the Man;
And I could wish my days to be
Bound each to each by natural piety.

1807

2. Where souls in heaven rest (as in Luke, xvi.22).

3. The holy of holies (as in the ancient temple in Jerusalem); where God is present.

Ode

INTIMATIONS OF IMMORTALITY FROM RECOLLECTIONS OF EARLY CHILDHOOD

The Child is father of the Man;
And I could wish my days to be
Bound each to each by natural piety.[4]

1

There was a time when meadow, grove, and stream,
The earth, and every common sight,
To me did seem
Appareled in celestial light,
The glory and the freshness of a dream.
It is not now as it hath been of yore—
Turn whereso'er I may,
By night or day,
The things which I have seen I now can see no more.

2

The Rainbow comes and goes,
And lovely is the Rose,
The Moon doth with delight
Look round her when the heavens are bare,
Waters on a starry night
Are beautiful and fair;
The sunshine is a glorious birth;
But yet I know, where'er I go,
That there hath passed away a glory from the earth.

3

Now, while the birds thus sing a joyous song,
And while the young lambs bound
As to the tabor's sound,[5]
To me alone there came a thought of grief:
A timely utterance gave that thought relief,
And I again am strong:
The cataracts blow their trumpets from the steep;
No more shall grief of mine the season wrong;
I hear the Echoes through the mountains throng,
The Winds come to me from the fields of sleep,
And all the earth is gay;
Land and sea
Give themselves up to jollity,
And with the heart of May
Doth every Beast keep holiday—
Thou Child of Joy,
Shout round me, let me hear thy shouts, thou happy Shepherd-boy!

4

Ye blessèd Creatures, I have heard the call
Ye to each other make; I see
The heavens laugh with you in your jubilee;
My heart is at your festival,
My head hath its coronal,
The fullness of your bliss, I feel—I feel it all.

4. Final lines of Wordsworth's *My Heart Leaps Up.*

5. "Tabor": a small drum.

Oh, evil day! if I were sullen
While Earth herself is adorning,
This sweet May morning,
And the Children are culling
On every side,
In a thousand valleys far and wide,
Fresh flowers; while the sun shines warm,
And the Babe leaps up on his Mother's arm—
I hear, I hear, with joy I hear!
—But there's a Tree, of many, one,
A single Field which I have looked upon,
Both of them speak of something that is gone:
The Pansy at my feet
Doth the same tale repeat:
Whither is fled the visionary gleam?
Where is it now, the glory and the dream?

5

Our birth is but a sleep and a forgetting:
The Soul that rises with us, our life's Star,
Hath had elsewhere its setting,
And cometh from afar:
Not in entire forgetfulness,
And not in utter nakedness,
But trailing clouds of glory do we come
From God, who is our home:
Heaven lies about us in our infancy!
Shades of the prison-house begin to close
Upon the growing Boy
But he
Beholds the light, and whence it flows,
He sees it in his joy;
The Youth, who daily farther from the east
Must travel, still is Nature's Priest,
And by the vision splendid
Is on his way attended;
At length the Man perceives it die away,
And fade into the light of common day.

6

Earth fills her lap with pleasures of her own;
Yearnings she hath in her own natural kind,
And, even with something of a Mother's mind,
And no unworthy aim,
The homely° Nurse doth all she can *simple, kindly*
To make her foster child, her Inmate Man,
Forget the glories he hath known,
And that imperial palace whence he came.

7

Behold the Child among his newborn blisses,
A six-years' Darling of a pygmy size!
See, where 'mid work of his own hand he lies,
Fretted° by sallies of his mother's kisses, *vexed*
With light upon him from his father's eyes!
See, at his feet, some little plan or chart,
Some fragment from his dream of human life,
Shaped by himself with newly-learnéd art;
A wedding or a festival,
A mourning or a funeral;

And this hath now his heart,
And unto this he frames his song;
Then will he fit his tongue
To dialogues of business, love, or strife;
But it will not be long
Ere this be thrown aside,
And with new joy and pride
The little Actor cons another part;
Filling from time to time his "humorous stage"[6]
With all the Persons, down to palsied Age,
That Life brings with her in her equipage;
As if his whole vocation
Were endless imitation.

8

Thou, whose exterior semblance doth belie
Thy Soul's immensity;
Thou best Philosopher, who yet dost keep
Thy heritage, thou Eye among the blind,
That, deaf and silent, read'st the eternal deep,
Haunted forever by the eternal mind—
Mighty Prophet! Seer blest!
On whom those truths do rest,
Which we are toiling all our lives to find,
In darkness lost, the darkness of the grave;
Thou, over whom thy Immortality
Broods like the Day, a Master o'er a Slave,
A Presence which is not to be put by;
Thou little Child, yet glorious in the might
Of heaven-born freedom on thy being's height,
Why with such earnest pains dost thou provoke
The years to bring the inevitable yoke,
Thus blindly with thy blessedness at strife?
Full soon thy Soul shall have her earthly freight,
And custom lie upon thee with a weight,
Heavy as frost, and deep almost as life!

9

O joy! that in our embers
Is something that doth live,
That nature yet remembers
What was so fugitive!
The thought of our past years in me doth breed
Perpetual benediction: not indeed
For that which is most worthy to be blest;
Delight and liberty, the simple creed
Of Childhood, whether busy or at rest,
With new-fledged hope still fluttering in his breast—
Not for these I raise
The song of thanks and praise;
But for those obstinate questionings
Of sense and outward things,
Fallings from us, vanishings;
Blank misgivings of a Creature
Moving about in worlds not realized,
High instincts before which our mortal Nature
Did tremble like a guilty Thing surprised;
But for those first affections,

6. I.e., playing the parts of characters with various temperaments, called "humors" by Elizabethan poets and playwrights.

Those shadowy recollections,
Which, be they what they may,
Are yet the fountain light of all our day,
Are yet a master light of all our seeing;
Uphold us, cherish, and have power to make
Our noisy years seem moments in the being
Of the eternal Silence: truths that wake,
To perish never;
Which neither listlessness, nor mad endeavor,
Nor Man nor Boy,
Nor all that is at enmity with joy,
Can utterly abolish or destroy!
Hence in a season of calm weather
Though inland far we be,
Our Souls have sight of that immortal sea
Which brought us hither,
Can in a moment travel thither,
And see the Children sport upon the shore,
And hear the mighty waters rolling evermore.

10

Then sing, ye Birds, sing, sing a joyous song!
And let the young Lambs bound
As to the tabor's sound!
We in thought will join your throng,
Ye that pipe and ye that play,
Ye that through your hearts today
Feel the gladness of the May!
What though the radiance which was once so bright
Be now forever taken from my sight,
Though nothing can bring back the hour
Of splendor in the grass, of glory in the flower;
We will grieve not, rather find
Strength in what remains behind;
In the primal sympathy
Which having been must ever be;
In the soothing thoughts that spring
Out of human suffering;
In the faith that looks through death,
In years that bring the philosophic mind.

11

And O, ye Fountains, Meadows, Hills, and Groves,
Forebode not any severing of our loves!
Yet in my heart of hearts I feel your might;
I only have relinquished one delight
To live beneath your more habitual sway.
I love the Brooks which down their channels fret,
Even more than when I tripped lightly as they;
The innocent brightness of a newborn Day
Is lovely yet;
The clouds that gather round the setting sun
Do take a sober coloring from an eye
That hath kept watch o'er man's mortality;
Another race hath been, and other palms° are won. *symbols of victory*
Thanks to the human heart by which we live,
Thanks to its tenderness, its joys, and fears,
To me the meanest° flower that blows° can give *most ordinary / blooms*
Thoughts that do often lie too deep for tears.

1802–4 1807

I Wandered Lonely As a Cloud

I wandered lonely as a cloud
That floats on high o'er vales and hills,
When all at once I saw a crowd,
A host, of golden daffodils;
Beside the lake, beneath the trees,
Fluttering and dancing in the breeze.

Continuous as the stars that shine
And twinkle on the milky way,
They stretched in never-ending line
Along the margin of a bay:
Ten thousand saw I at a glance,
Tossing their heads in sprightly dance.

The waves beside them danced; but they
Outdid the sparkling waves in glee;
A poet could not but be gay,
In such a jocund° company; *cheerful*
I gazed—and gazed—but little thought
What wealth the show to me had brought:

For oft, when on my couch I lie
In vacant or in pensive mood,
They flash upon that inward eye
Which is the bliss of solitude;
And then my heart with pleasure fills,
And dances with the daffodils.

1807

Elegiac Stanzas[7]

SUGGESTED BY A PICTURE OF PEELE CASTLE, IN A STORM, PAINTED BY SIR GEORGE BEAUMONT

I was thy neighbor once, thou rugged Pile!
Four summer weeks I dwelt in sight of thee:
I saw thee every day; and all the while
Thy Form was sleeping on a glassy sea.

So pure the sky, so quiet was the air!
So like, so very like, was day to day!
Whene'er I looked, thy Image still was there;
It trembled, but it never passed away.

How perfect was the calm! it seemed no sleep;
No mood, which season takes away, or brings:
I could have fancied that the mighty Deep
Was even the gentlest of all gentle Things.

7. In memory of the poet's brother, John, who had recently died in a shipwreck (see lines 36–39).

Ah! THEN, if mine had been the Painter's hand,
To express what then I saw; and add the gleam,
The light that never was, on sea or land,
The consecration, and the Poet's dream;

I would have planted thee, thou hoary Pile
Amid a world how different from this!
Beside a sea that could not cease to smile;
On tranquil land, beneath a sky of bliss.

Thou shouldst have seemed a treasure house divine
O peaceful years; a chronicle of heaven—
Of all the sunbeams that did ever shine
The very sweetest had to thee been given.

A Picture had it been of lasting ease,
Elysian[8] quiet, without toil or strife;
No motion but the moving tide, a breeze,
Or merely silent Nature's breathing life.

Such, in the fond illusion of my heart,
Such Picture would I at that time have made,
And seen the soul of truth in every part,
A steadfast peace that might not be betrayed.

So once it would have been—'tis so no more;
I have submitted to a new control:
A power is gone, which nothing can restore;
A deep distress hath humanized my Soul.

Not for a moment could I now behold
A smiling sea, and be what I have been:
The feeling of my loss will ne'er be old;
This, which I know, I speak with mind serene.

Then, Beaumont, Friend! who would have been the Friend,
If he had lived, of him whom I deplore,° *lament*
This work of thine I blame not, but commend;
This sea in anger, and that dismal shore.

O 'tis a passionate Work!—yet wise and well,
Well chosen is the spirit that is here;
That Hulk which labors in the deadly swell,
This rueful sky, this pageantry of fear!

And this huge Castle, standing here sublime,
I love to see the look with which it braves,
Cased in the unfeeling armor of old time,
The lightning, the fierce wind, and trampling waves.

Farewell, farewell the heart that lives alone,
Housed in a dream, at distance from the Kind!° *mankind*
Such happiness, wherever it be known,
Is to be pitied; for 'tis surely blind.

8. In Greek myth the souls of the blest dwelt in the Elysian Fields.

But welcome fortitude, and patient cheer,
And frequent sights of what is to be borne!
Such sights, or worse, as are before me here.
Not without hope we suffer and we mourn.

1807

The World Is Too Much with Us

The world is too much with us; late and soon,
Getting and spending, we lay waste our powers;
Little we see in Nature that is ours;
We have given our hearts away, a sordid boon!° *gift*
This Sea that bares her bosom to the moon,
The winds that will be howling at all hours,
And are up-gathered now like sleeping flowers,
For this, for everything, we are out of tune;
It moves us not.—Great God! I'd rather be
A Pagan suckled in a creed outworn;
So might I, standing on this pleasant lea,
Have glimpses that would make me less forlorn;
Have sight of Proteus rising from the sea;
Or hear old Triton blow his wreathèd horn.[9]

1807

The Solitary Reaper

Behold her, single in the field,
Yon solitary Highland Lass!
Reaping and singing by herself;
Stop here, or gently pass!
Alone she cuts and binds the grain,
And sings a melancholy strain;
O listen! for the Vale profound
Is overflowing with the sound.

No Nightingale did ever chaunt
More welcome notes to weary bands
Of travelers in some shady haunt,
Among Arabian sands;
A voice so thrilling ne'er was heard
In springtime from the Cuckoo bird,
Breaking the silence of the seas
Among the farthest Hebrides.

Will no one tell me what she sings?—
Perhaps the plaintive numbers flow
For old, unhappy, far-off things,
And battles long ago;
Or is it some more humble lay,
Familiar matter of today?

9. In Greek myth Proteus, the "Old Man of the Sea," rises from the sea at midday and can be forced to read the future by anyone who holds him while he takes many frightening shapes. Triton is the son of the sea-god Neptune; the sound of his conch-shell horn calms the waves.

Some natural sorrow, loss, or pain,
That has been, and may be again?

Whate'er the theme, the Maiden sang
As if her song could have no ending;
I saw her singing at her work,
And o'er the sickle bending—
I listened, motionless and still;
And, as I mounted up the hill,
The music in my heart I bore,
Long after it was heard no more.

1807

Surprised by Joy

Surprised by joy—impatient as the Wind
I turned to share the transport—Oh! with whom
But thee,[1] deep buried in the silent tomb,
That spot which no vicissitude can find?
Love, faithful love, recalled thee to my mind—
But how could I forget thee? Through what power,
Even for the least division of an hour,
Have I been so beguiled as to be blind
To my most grievous loss!—That thought's return
Was the worst pang that sorrow ever bore,
Save one, one only, when I stood forlorn,
Knowing my heart's best treasure was no more;
That neither present time, nor years unborn
Could to my sight that heavenly face restore.

1815

Mutability

From low to high doth dissolution climb,
And sink from high to low, along a scale
Of awful notes, whose concord shall not fail;
A musical but melancholy chime,
Which they can hear who meddle not with crime,
Nor avarice, nor over-anxious care.
Truth fails not; but her outward forms that bear
The longest date do melt like frosty rime,° *thin coating*
That in the morning whitened hill and plain
And is no more; drop like the tower sublime
Of yesterday, which royally did wear
His crown of weeds, but could not even sustain
Some casual shout that broke the silent air,
Or the unimaginable touch of Time.

1822

Scorn Not the Sonnet

Scorn not the sonnet; critic, you have frowned,
Mindless of its just honors; with this key

1. The poet's daughter Catharine, who died at the age of four, in 1812.

Shakespeare unlocked his heart; the melody
Of this small lute gave ease to Petrarch's[2] wound;
A thousand times this pipe did Tasso[3] sound;
With it Camöens soothed an exile's grief;[4]
The sonnet glittered a gay myrtle leaf
Amid the cypress with which Dante crowned
His visionary brow; a glow-worm lamp,
It cheered mild Spenser, called from Faeryland
To struggle through dark ways; and, when a damp° *dark mist*
Fell round the path of Milton, in his hand
The thing became a trumpet; whence he blew
Soul-animating strains—alas, too few!

1827

Extempore Effusion upon the Death of James Hogg[5]

When first, descending from the moorlands,
I saw the Stream of Yarrow glide
Along a bare and open valley,
The Ettrick Shepherd was my guide.

When last along its banks I wandered,
Through groves that had begun to shed
Their golden leaves upon the pathways,
My steps the Border-minstrel[6] led.

The mighty Minstrel breathes no longer,
'Mid moldering ruins low he lies;
And death upon the braes° of Yarrow, *banks*
Has closed the Shepherd-poet's eyes:

Nor has the rolling year twice measured,
From sign to sign, its steadfast course,
Since every mortal power of Coleridge[7]
Was frozen at its marvelous source;

The rapt One,[8] of the godlike forehead,
The heaven-eyed creature sleeps in earth:
And Lamb,[9] the frolic and the gentle,
Has vanished from his lonely hearth.

Like clouds that rake the mountain summits,
Or waves that own no curbing hand,
How fast has brother followed brother,
From sunshine to the sunless land!

Yet I, whose lids from infant slumber
Were earlier raised, remain to hear

2. Italian poet (1304–74) whose "wound" was his unconsummated love for "Laura."
3. Italian poet (1544–95).
4. Camoëns, a Portuguese poet (1524?–80), was banished from the royal court.
5. Scottish poet (1770–1835) born in Ettrick; for a time he was a shepherd. An *extempore effusion* is a poem composed rapidly, without premeditation.
6. Sir Walter Scott, famous Scottish poet and novelist (1771–1832).
7. Wordsworth's friend and collaborator, who died in 1834.
8. Coleridge (alluding to his "mystical" philosophy).
9. Charles Lamb (1775–1834), essayist and critic, friend of Wordsworth and Coleridge.

A timid voice, that asks in whispers,
"Who next will drop and disappear?"

Our haughty life is crowned with darkness,
Like London with its own black wreath,
On which with thee, O Crabbe![1] forth-looking,
I gazed from Hampstead's breezy heath.

As if but yesterday departed,
Thou too art gone before; but why,
O'er ripe fruit, seasonably gathered,
Should frail survivors heave a sigh?

Mourn rather for that holy Spirit,
Sweet as the spring, as ocean deep;
For her[2] who, ere her summer faded,
Has sunk into a breathless sleep.

No more of old romantic sorrows,
For slaughtered Youth or lovelorn Maid!
With sharper grief is Yarrow smitten,
And Ettrick mourns with her their Poet dead.

1835

SAMUEL TAYLOR COLERIDGE (1772–1834)

Kubla Khan[1]

OR A VISION IN A DREAM. A FRAGMENT

In Xanadu did Kubla Khan
A stately pleasure dome decree:
Where Alph, the sacred river, ran
Through caverns measureless to man
   Down to a sunless sea.

1. George Crabbe (1754–1832), poet, acquaintance of Wordsworth.
2. Felicia Hemans (1793–1835), popular poetess, noted for her beauty and conversation.

1. The first *khan,* or ruler, of the Mongol dynasty in 13th-century China. The topography and place-names are fictitious. In a prefatory note to the poem, Coleridge gave the following background: "In the summer of the year 1797, the author, then in ill health, had retired to a lonely farmhouse between Porlock and Linton, on the Exmoor confines of Somerset and Devonshire. In consequence of a slight indisposition, an anodyne had been prescribed, from the effects of which he fell asleep in his chair at the moment that he was reading the following sentence, or words of the same substance, in *Purchas's Pilgrimage:* "Here the Khan Kubla commanded a palace to be built, and a stately garden thereunto. And thus ten miles of fertile ground were inclosed with a wall." The author continued for about three hours in a profound sleep, at least of the external sense, during which time he has the most vivid confidence that he could not have composed less than from two to three hundred lines; if that indeed can be called composition in which all the images rose up before him as *things,* with a parallel production of the correspondent expressions, without any sensation or consciousness of effort. On awaking he appeared to himself to have a distinct recollection of the whole, and taking his pen, ink, and paper, instantly and eagerly wrote down the lines that are here preserved. At this moment he was unfortunately called out by a person on business from Porlock, and detained by him above an hour, and on his return to his room, found, to his no small surprise and mortification, that though he still retained some vague and dim recollection of the general purport of the vision, yet, with the exception of some eight or ten scattered lines and images, all the rest had passed away like the images on the surface of a stream into which a stone has been cast, but, alas! without the after restoration of the latter!"

So twice five miles of fertile ground
With walls and towers were girdled round:
And there were gardens bright with sinuous rills,
Where blossomed many an incense-bearing tree;
And here were forests ancient as the hills,
Enfolding sunny spots of greenery.

But oh! that deep romantic chasm which slanted
Down the green hill athwart a cedarn cover!
A savage place! as holy and enchanted
As e'er beneath a waning moon was haunted
By woman wailing for her demon lover!
And from this chasm, with ceaseless turmoil seething,
As if this earth in fast thick pants were breathing,
A mighty fountain momently was forced:
Amid whose swift half-intermitted burst
Huge fragments vaulted like rebounding hail,
Or chaffy grain beneath the thresher's flail:
And 'mid these dancing rocks at once and ever
It flung up momently the sacred river.
Five miles meandering with a mazy motion
Through wood and dale the sacred river ran,
Then reached the caverns measureless to man,
And sank in tumult to a lifeless ocean:
And 'mid this tumult Kubla heard from far
Ancestral voices prophesying war!

The shadow of the dome of pleasure
Floated midway on the waves;
Where was heard the mingled measure
From the fountain and the caves.
It was a miracle of rare device,
A sunny pleasure dome with caves of ice!

A damsel with a dulcimer[2]
In a vision once I saw:
It was an Abyssinian maid,
And on her dulcimer she played,
Singing of Mount Abora.
Could I revive within me
Her symphony and song,
To such a deep delight 'twould win me,
That with music loud and long,
I would build that dome in air,
That sunny dome! those caves of ice!
And all who heard should see them there,
And all should cry, Beware! Beware!
His flashing eyes, his floating hair!
Weave a circle round him thrice,
And close your eyes with holy dread,
For he on honey-dew hath fed,
And drunk the milk of Paradise.

1797–98 1816

2. A harp-like instrument.

Frost at Midnight

The Frost performs its secret ministry,
Unhelped by any wind. The owlet's cry
Came loud—and hark, again! loud as before.
The inmates of my cottage, all at rest,
Have left me to that solitude, which suits
Abstruser musings: save that at my side
My cradled infant[3] slumbers peacefully.
'Tis calm indeed! so calm, that it disturbs
And vexes meditation with its strange
And extreme silentness. Sea, hill, and wood,
This populous village! Sea, and hill, and wood,
With all the numberless goings-on of life,
Inaudible as dreams! the thin blue flame
Lies on my low-burnt fire, and quivers not;
Only that film,[4] which fluttered on the grate,
Still flutters there, the sole unquiet thing.
Methinks its motion in this hush of nature
Gives it dim sympathies with me who live,
Making it a companionable form,
Whose puny flaps and freaks the idling Spirit
By its own moods interprets, everywhere
Echo or mirror seeking of itself,
And makes a toy of Thought.

But O! how oft,
How oft, at school, with most believing mind,
Presageful,° have I gazed upon the bars, *foretelling*
To watch that fluttering *stranger!* and as oft
With unclosed lids, already had I dreamt
Of my sweet birthplace, and the old church tower,
Whose bells, the poor man's only music, rang
From morn to evening, all the hot Fair-day,[5]
So sweetly, that they stirred and haunted me
With a wild pleasure, falling on mine ear
Most like articulate sounds of things to come!
So gazed I, till the soothing things, I dreamt,
Lulled me to sleep, and sleep prolonged my dreams!
And so I brooded all the following morn,
Awed by the stern preceptor's° face, mine eye *schoolmaster's*
Fixed with mock study on my swimming book:[6]
Save if the door half opened, and I snatched
A hasty glance, and still my heart leaped up,
For still I hoped to see the *stranger's* face,
Townsman, or aunt, or sister more beloved,
My playmate when we both were clothed alike![7]

Dear Babe, that sleepest cradled by my side,
Whose gentle breathings, heard in this deep calm,
Fill up the intersperséd vacancies
And momentary pauses of the thought!
My babe so beautiful! it thrills my heart

3. Coleridge's son Hartley.
4. Bits of soot fluttering in a fireplace; in folklore, said to foretell the arrival of an unexpected guest, and hence called *strangers* (lines 26, 41).
5. Market-day, often a time of festivities.
6. I.e., seen unclearly because of emotion.
7. In early childhood, when boys and girls wore the same kind of infants' clothing.

With tender gladness, thus to look at thee,
And think that thou shalt learn far other lore,
And in far other scenes! For I was reared
In the great city, pent 'mid cloisters dim,
And saw nought lovely but the sky and stars.
But *thou,* my babe! shalt wander like a breeze
By lakes and sandy shores, beneath the crags
Of ancient mountain, and beneath the clouds,
Which image in their bulk both lakes and shores
And mountain crags: so shalt thou see and hear
The lovely shapes and sounds intelligible
Of that eternal language, which thy God
Utters, who from eternity doth teach
Himself in all, and all things in himself.
Great universal Teacher! he shall mold
Thy spirit, and by giving make it ask.

Therefore all seasons shall be sweet to thee,
Whether the summer clothe the general° earth *generative, vernal*
With greenness, or the redbreast sit and sing
Betwixt the tufts of snow on the bare branch
Of mossy apple tree, while the nigh thatch
Smokes in the sun-thaw; whether the eave-drops fall
Heard only in the trances of the blast,
Or if the secret ministry of frost
Shall hang them up in silent icicles,
Quietly shining to the quiet Moon.

1798

The Rime of the Ancient Mariner

IN SEVEN PARTS

Facile credo, plures esse Naturas invisibles quam visibiles in rerum universitate. Sed horum [sic] *omnium familiam quis nobis enarrabit? et gradus et cognationes et discrimina et singulorum munera? Quid agunt? quae loca habitant? Harum rerum notitiam semper ambivit ingenium humanum, nunquam attigit. Juvat, interea, non diffiteor, quandoque in animo, in tabulâ, majoris et melioris mundi imaginem contemplari: ne mens assuefacta hodiernae vitae minutiis se contrahat nimis, et tota subsidat in pusillas cogitationes. Sed veritati interea invigilandum est, modusque servandus, ut certa ab incertis, diem a nocte, distinguamus.*

—T. BURNET[8]

Part I

An ancient Mariner meeteth three Gallants bidden to a wedding feast, and detaineth one.

It is an ancient Mariner
And he stoppeth one of three.
—"By thy long gray beard and glittering eye,
Now wherefore stopp'st thou me?

The Bridegroom's doors are opened wide,
And I am next of kin;
The guests are met, the feast is set:
May'st hear the merry din."

8. From *Archaeologiae Philosophiae,* p. 68. "I can easily believe that there are more invisible than visible beings in the universe. But of their families, degrees, connections, distinctions, and functions, who shall tell us? How do they act? Where are they found? About such matters the human mind has always circled without attaining knowledge. Yet I do not doubt that sometimes it is well for the soul to contemplate as in a picture the image of a larger and better world, lest the mind, habituated to the small concerns of daily life, limit itself too much and sink entirely into trivial thinking. But meanwhile we must be on watch for the truth, avoiding extremes, so that we may distinguish certain from uncertain, day from night." Burnet was a 17th-century English theologian.

He holds him with his skinny hand,
"There was a ship," quoth he.
"Hold off! unhand me, graybeard loon!"
Eftsoons° his hand dropped he. *straightway*

The Wedding Guest is spell-bound by the eye of the old seafaring man, and constrained to hear his tale.

He holds him with his glittering eye—
The Wedding Guest stood still,
And listens like a three years' child:
The Mariner hath his will.

The Wedding Guest sat on a stone:
He cannot choose but hear;
And thus spake on that ancient man,
The bright-eyed Mariner.

"The ship was cheered, the harbor cleared,
Merrily did we drop
Below the kirk,° below the hill, *church*
Below the lighthouse top.

The Mariner tells how the ship sailed southward with a good wind and fair weather, till it reached the line.

The Sun came up upon the left,
Out of the sea came he!
And he shone bright, and on the right
Went down into the sea.

Higher and higher every day,
Till over the mast at noon—"
The Wedding Guest here beat his breast,
For he heard the loud bassoon.

The Wedding Guest heareth the bridal music; but the Mariner continueth his tale.

The bride hath paced into the hall,
Red as a rose is she;
Nodding their heads before her goes
The merry minstrelsy.

The Wedding Guest he beat his breast,
Yet he cannot choose but hear;
And thus spake on that ancient man,
The bright-eyed Mariner.

The ship driven by a storm toward the South Pole.

"And now the STORM-BLAST came, and he
Was tyrannous and strong;
He struck with his o'ertaking wings,
And chased us south along.

With sloping masts and dipping prow,
As who pursued with yell and blow
Still treads the shadow of his foe,
And forward bends his head,
The ship drove fast, loud roared the blast,
And southward aye we fled.

And now there came both mist and snow,
And it grew wondrous cold:
And ice, mast-high, came floating by,
As green as emerald.

The land of ice, and of fearful sounds where no living thing was to be seen.

And through the drifts the snowy clifts° *cliffs*
Did send a dismal sheen:
Nor shapes of men nor beasts we ken—
The ice was all between.

The ice was here, the ice was there,
The ice was all around:
It cracked and growled, and roared and howled,
Like noises in a swound!° *swoon*

Till a great sea bird, called the Albatross, came through the snow-fog, and was received with great joy and hospitality.

At length did cross an Albatross,
Thorough the fog it came;
As if it had been a Christian soul,
We hailed it in God's name.

It ate the food it ne'er had eat,
And round and round it flew.
The ice did split with a thunder-fit;
The helmsman steered us through!

And lo! the Albatross proveth a bird of good omen, and followeth the ship as it returned northward through fog and floating ice.

And a good south wind sprung up behind;
The Albatross did follow,
And every day, for food or play,
Came to the mariners' hollo!

In mist or cloud, on mast or shroud,
It perched for vespers nine;
Whiles all the night, through fog-smoke white,
Glimmered the white Moon-shine."

The ancient Mariner inhospitably killeth the pious bird of good omen.

"God save thee, ancient Mariner!
From the fiends, that plague thee thus!—
Why look'st thou so?"—With my crossbow
I shot the ALBATROSS.

Part II

The Sun now rose upon the right:
Out of the sea came he,
Still hid in mist, and on the left
Went down into the sea.

And the good south wind still blew behind,
But no sweet bird did follow,
Nor any day for food or play
Came to the mariners' hollo!

His shipmates cry out against the ancient Mariner, for killing the bird of good luck.

And I had done a hellish thing,
And it would work 'em woe:
For all averred, I had killed the bird
That made the breeze to blow.
Ah wretch! said they, the bird to slay,
That made the breeze to blow!

But when the fog cleared off, they justify the same, and thus make themselves accomplices in the crime.

Nor dim nor red, like God's own head,
The glorious Sun uprist:° *arose*
Then all averred, I had killed the bird
That brought the fog and mist.
'Twas right, said they, such birds to slay,
That bring the fog and mist.

The fair breeze continues; the ship enters the Pacific Ocean, and sails northward, even till it reaches the Line.

The fair breeze blew, the white foam flew,
The furrow followed free;
We were the first that ever burst
Into that silent sea.

The ship hath been suddenly becalmed.

Down dropped the breeze, the sails dropped down,
'Twas sad as sad could be;
And we did speak only to break
The silence of the sea!

All in a hot and copper sky,
The bloody Sun, at noon,
Right up above the mast did stand,
No bigger than the Moon.

Day after day, day after day,
We stuck, nor breath nor motion;
As idle as a painted ship
Upon a painted ocean.

And the Albatross begins to be avenged.

Water, water, everywhere,
And all the boards did shrink;
Water, water, everywhere,
Nor any drop to drink.

The very deep did rot: O Christ!
That ever this should be!
Yea, slimy things did crawl with legs
Upon the slimy sea.

About, about, in reel and rout
The death-fires danced at night;
The water, like a witch's oils,
Burnt green, and blue and white.

And some in dreams assuréd were
Of the Spirit that plagued us so;
Nine fathom deep he had followed us
From the land of mist and snow.

A Spirit had followed them; one of the invisible inhabitants of this planet, neither departed souls nor angels; concerning whom the learned Jew, Josephus, and the Platonic Constantinopolitan, Michael Psellus, may be consulted. They are very numerous, ana there is no climate or element without one or more.

And every tongue, through utter drought,
Was withered at the root;
We could not speak, no more than if
We had been choked with soot.

The shipmates, in their sore distress, would fain throw the whole guilt on the ancient Mariner: in sign whereof they hang the dead sea bird round his neck.

Ah! well-a-day! what evil looks
Had I from old and young!
Instead of the cross, the Albatross
About my neck was hung.

Part III

There passed a weary time. Each throat
Was parched, and glazed each eye.
A weary time! a weary time!
How glazed each weary eye,
When looking westward, I beheld
A something in the sky.

The ancient Mariner beholdeth a sign in the element afar off.

At first it seemed a little speck,
And then it seemed a mist;
It moved and moved, and took at last
A certain shape, I wist.° *knew*

A speck, a mist, a shape, I wist!
And still it neared and neared:
As if it dodged a water sprite,
It plunged and tacked and veered.

At its nearer approach, it seemeth him to be a ship; and at a dear ransom he freeth his speech from the bonds of thirst.

With throats unslaked, with black lips baked,
We could nor laugh nor wail;
Through utter drought all dumb we stood!
I bit my arm, I sucked the blood,
And cried, A sail! a sail!

With throats unslaked, with black lips baked,
Agape they heard me call:

A flash of joy;

Gramercy!° they for joy did grin, *thank heavens!*
And all at once their breath drew in,
As they were drinking all.

And horror follows. For can it be a ship that comes onward without wind or tide?

See! see! (I cried) she tacks no more!
Hither to work us weal;° *benefit*
Without a breeze, without a tide,
She steadies with upright keel!

The western wave was all aflame.
The day was well nigh done!
Almost upon the western wave
Rested the broad bright Sun;
When that strange shape drove suddenly
Betwixt us and the Sun.

It seemeth him but the skeleton of a ship.

And straight the Sun was flecked with bars,
(Heaven's Mother send us grace!)
As if through a dungeon grate he peered
With broad and burning face.

And its ribs are seen as bars on the face of the setting Sun.

Alas! (thought I, and my heart beat loud)
How fast she nears and nears!
Are those *her* sails that glance in the Sun,
Like restless gossameres?

The Specter-Woman and her Deathmate, and no other on board the skeleton ship.

Are those *her* ribs through which the Sun
Did peer, as through a grate?
And is that Woman all her crew?
Is that a DEATH? and are there two?
Is DEATH that woman's mate?

Like vessel, like crew!

Her lips were red, *her* looks were free,
Her locks were yellow as gold:
Her skin was as white as leprosy,
The Nightmare LIFE-IN-DEATH was she,
Who thicks man's blood with cold.

Death and Life-in-Death have diced for the ship's crew, and she (the latter) winneth the ancient Mariner.

The naked hulk alongside came,
And the twain were casting dice;
"The game is done! I've won! I've won!"
Quoth she, and whistles thrice.

No twilight within the courts of the Sun.

The Sun's rim dips; the stars rush out:
At one stride comes the dark;
With far-heard whisper, o'er the sea,
Off shot the specter-bark.

At the rising of the Moon,

We listened and looked sideways up!
Fear at my heart, as at a cup,
My lifeblood seemed to sip!
The stars were dim, and thick the night,
The steersman's face by his lamp gleamed white;
From the sails the dew did drip—
Till clomb above the eastern bar
The hornéd Moon, with one bright star
Within the nether tip.

One after another,

One after one, by the star-dogged Moon,
Too quick for groan or sigh,
Each turned his face with ghastly pang,
And cursed me with his eye.

His shipmates drop down dead.

Four times fifty living men,
(And I heard nor sigh nor groan)
With heavy thump, a lifeless lump,
They dropped down one by one.

But Life-in-Death begins her work on the ancient Mariner.

The souls did from their bodies fly—
They fled to bliss or woe!
And every soul, it passed me by,
Like the whizz of my cross-bow!

Part IV

The Wedding Guest feareth that a Spirit is talking to him;

"I fear thee, ancient Mariner!
I fear thy skinny hand!
And thou art long, and lank, and brown,
As is the ribbed sea-sand.

I fear thee and thy glittering eye,
And thy skinny hand, so brown."—
Fear not, fear not, thou Wedding Guest!
This body dropped not down.

But the ancient Mariner assureth him of his bodily life, and proceedeth to relate his horrible penance.

Alone, alone, all, all alone,
Alone on a wide wide sea!
And never a saint took pity on
My soul in agony.

He despiseth the creatures of the calm,

The many men, so beautiful!
And they all dead did lie:
And a thousand thousand slimy things
Lived on; and so did I.

And envieth that they *should live, and so many lie dead.*

I looked upon the rotting sea,
And drew my eyes away;
I looked upon the rotting deck,
And there the dead men lay.

I looked to heaven, and tried to pray;
But or ever a prayer had gushed,
A wicked whisper came, and made
My heart as dry as dust.

I closed my lids, and kept them close,
And the balls like pulses beat,
For the sky and the sea, and the sea and the sky
Lay like a load on my weary eye,
And the dead were at my feet.

But the curse liveth for him in the eye of the dead men.

The cold sweat melted from their limbs,
Nor rot nor reek did they:
The look with which they looked on me
Had never passed away.

An orphan's curse would drag to hell
A spirit from on high;
But oh! more horrible than that
Is the curse in a dead man's eye!
Seven days, seven nights, I saw that curse,
And yet I could not die.

In his loneliness and fixedness he yearneth towards the journeying Moon, and the stars that still sojourn, yet still move onward; and everywhere the blue sky belongs to them, and is their appointed rest, and their native country and their own natural homes, which they enter unannounced, as lords that are certainly expected and yet there is a silent joy at their arrival.

The moving Moon went up the sky,
And nowhere did abide:
Softly she was going up,
And a star or two beside—

Her beams bemocked the sultry main,
Like April hoar-frost spread;
But where the ship's huge shadow lay,
The charméd water burnt alway
A still and awful red.

By the light of the Moon he beholdeth God's creatures of the great calm.

Beyond the shadow of the ship,
I watched the water snakes:
They moved in tracks of shining white,
And when they reared, the elfish light
Fell off in hoary° flakes. *gray or white*

Within the shadow of the ship
I watched their rich attire:
Blue, glossy green, and velvet black,
They coiled and swam; and every track
Was a flash of golden fire.

Their beauty and their happiness.

He blesseth them in his heart.

O happy living things! no tongue
Their beauty might declare:
A spring of love gushed from my heart,
And I blessed them unaware:
Sure my kind saint took pity on me,
And I blessed them unaware.

The spell begins to break.

The self-same moment I could pray;
And from my neck so free
The Albatross fell off, and sank
Like lead into the sea.

Part V

Oh sleep! it is a gentle thing,
Beloved from pole to pole!
To Mary Queen the praise be given!
She sent the gentle sleep from Heaven,
That slid into my soul.

By grace of the holy Mother, the ancient Mariner is refreshed with rain.

The silly° buckets on the deck, *lowly, harmless*
That had so long remained,
I dreamt that they were filled with dew;
And when I awoke, it rained.

My lips were wet, my throat was cold,
My garments all were dank;
Sure I had drunken in my dreams,
And still my body drank.

I moved, and could not feel my limbs:
I was so light—almost
I thought that I had died in sleep,
And was a blesséd ghost.

He heareth sounds and seeth strange sights and commotions in the sky and the element.

And soon I heard a roaring wind:
It did not come anear;
But with its sound it shook the sails,
That were so thin and sere.

The upper air burst into life!
And a hundred fire-flags sheen,° *shone*
To and fro they were hurried about!
And to and fro, and in and out,
The wan stars danced between.

And the coming wind did roar more loud,
And the sails did sigh like sedge;[9]
And the rain poured down from one black cloud;
The Moon was at its edge.

The thick black cloud was cleft, and still
The Moon was at its side:
Like waters shot from some high crag,
The lightning fell with never a jag,
A river steep and wide.

The bodies of the ship's crew are inspirited, and the ship moves on;

The loud wind never reached the ship,
Yet now the ship moved on!
Beneath the lightning and the Moon
The dead men gave a groan.

They groaned, they stirred, they all uprose,
Nor spake, nor moved their eyes;
It had been strange, even in a dream,
To have seen those dead men rise.

The helmsman steered, the ship moved on;
Yet never a breeze up-blew;
The mariners all 'gan work the ropes,
Where they were wont to do;
They raised their limbs like lifeless tools—
We were a ghastly crew.

The body of my brother's son
Stood by me, knee to knee:
The body and I pulled at one rope,
But he said nought to me.

But not by the souls of the men, nor by demons of earth or middle air, but by a blessèd troop of angelic spirits, sent down by the invocation of the guardian saint.

"I fear thee, ancient Mariner!"
Be calm, thou Wedding Guest!
'Twas not those souls that fled in pain,
Which to their corses° came again, *corpses*
But a troop of spirits blest:

For when it dawned—they dropped their arms,
And clustered round the mast;
Sweet sounds rose slowly through their mouths,
And from their bodies passed.

Around, around, flew each sweet sound,
Then darted to the Sun;
Slowly the sounds came back again,
Now mixed, now one by one.

Sometimes a-dropping from the sky
I heard the sky-lark sing;
Sometimes all little birds that are,
How they seemed to fill the sea and air
With their sweet jargoning!° *warbling*

9. Rushlike plants bordering streams and lakes.

And now 'twas like all instruments,
Now like a lonely flute;
And now it is an angel's song,
That makes the heavens be mute.

It ceased; yet still the sails made on
A pleasant noise till noon,
A noise like of a hidden brook
In the leafy month of June,
That to the sleeping woods all night
Singeth a quiet tune.

Till noon we quietly sailed on,
Yet never a breeze did breathe:
Slowly and smoothly went the ship,
Moved onward from beneath.

The lonesome Spirit from the South Pole carries on the ship as far as the Line, in obedience to the angelic troop, but still requireth vengeance.

Under the keel nine fathom deep,
From the land of mist and snow,
The spirit slid: and it was he
That made the ship to go.
The sails at noon left off their tune,
And the ship stood still also.

The Sun, right up above the mast,
Had fixed her to the ocean:
But in a minute she 'gan stir,
With a short uneasy motion—
Backwards and forwards half her length
With a short uneasy motion.

Then like a pawing horse let go,
She made a sudden bound:
It flung the blood into my head,
And I fell down in a swound.

The Polar Spirit's fellow demons, the invisible inhabitants of the element, take part in his wrong; and two of them relate, one to the other, that penance long and heavy for the ancient Mariner hath been accorded to the Polar Spirit, who returneth southward.

How long in that same fit I lay,
I have not° to declare; *cannot*
But ere my living life returned,
I heard and in my soul discerned
Two voices in the air.

"Is it he?" quoth one, "Is this the man?
By him who died on cross,
With his cruel bow he laid full low
The harmless Albatross.

The spirit who bideth by himself
In the land of mist and snow,
He loved the bird that loved the man
Who shot him with his bow."

The other was a softer voice,
As soft as honey-dew:

Quoth he, "The man hath penance done,
And penance more will do."

Part VI

FIRST VOICE

"But tell me, tell me! speak again,
Thy soft response renewing—
What makes that ship drive on so fast?
What is the ocean doing?"

SECOND VOICE

"Still as a slave before his lord,
The ocean hath no blast;
His great bright eye most silently
Up to the Moon is cast—

If he may know which way to go;
For she guides him smooth or grim.
See, brother, see! how graciously
She looketh down on him."

The Mariner hath been cast into a trance; for the angelic power causeth the vessel to drive northward faster than human life could endure.

FIRST VOICE

"But why drives on that ship so fast,
Without or wave or wind?"

SECOND VOICE

"The air is cut away before,
And closes from behind.

Fly, brother, fly! more high, more high!
Or we shall be belated:
For slow and slow that ship will go,
When the Mariner's trance is abated."

The supernatural motion is retarded; the Mariner awakes, and his penance begins anew.

I woke, and we were sailing on
As in a gentle weather:
'Twas night, calm night, the moon was high;
The dead men stood together.

All stood together on the deck,
For a charnel-dungeon fitter:
All fixed on me their stony eyes,
That in the Moon did glitter.

The pang, the curse, with which they died,
Had never passed away:
I could not draw my eyes from theirs,
Nor turn them up to pray.

The curse is finally expiated.

And now this spell was snapped: once more
I viewed the ocean green,
And looked far forth, yet little saw
Of what had else been seen—

Like one, that on a lonesome road
Doth walk in fear and dread,
And having once turned round walks on,

And turns no more his head;
Because he knows, a frightful fiend
Doth close behind him tread.

But soon there breathed a wind on me,
Nor sound nor motion made:
Its path was not upon the sea,
In ripple or in shade.

It raised my hair, it fanned my cheek
Like a meadow-gale of spring—
It mingled strangely with my fears,
Yet it felt like a welcoming.

Swiftly, swiftly flew the ship,
Yet she sailed softly too:
Sweetly, sweetly blew the breeze—
On me alone it blew.

And the ancient Mariner beholdeth his native country.

Oh! dream of joy! is this indeed
The lighthouse top I see?
Is this the hill? is this the kirk?
Is this mine own countree?

We drifted o'er the harbor-bar,
And I with sobs did pray—
O let me be awake, my God!
Or let me sleep alway.

The harbor-bay was clear as glass,
So smoothly it was strewn!
And on the bay the moonlight lay,
And the shadow of the Moon.

The rock shone bright, the kirk no less,
That stands above the rock:
The moonlight steeped in silentness
The steady weathercock.

The angelic spirits leave the dead bodies,

And the bay was white with silent light,
Till rising from the same,
Full many shapes, that shadows were,
In crimson colors came.

And appear in their own forms of light.

A little distance from the prow
Those crimson shadows were:
I turned my eyes upon the deck—
Oh, Christ! what saw I there!

Each corse lay flat, lifeless and flat,
And, by the holy rood!° *cross of Christ*
A man all light, a seraph°-man, *angel-like*
On every corse there stood.

This seraph-band, each waved his hand:
It was a heavenly sight!
They stood as signals to the land,
Each one a lovely light;

This seraph-band, each waved his hand,
No voice did they impart—
No voice; but oh! the silence sank
Like music on my heart.

But soon I heard the dash of oars,
I heard the Pilot's cheer;
My head was turned perforce away
And I saw a boat appear.

The Pilot and the Pilot's boy,
I heard them coming fast:
Dear Lord in Heaven! it was a joy
The dead men could not blast.

I saw a third—I heard his voice:
It is the Hermit good!
He singeth loud his godly hymns
That he makes in the wood.
He'll shrieve[1] my soul, he'll wash away
The Albatross's blood.

Part VII

The Hermit of the Wood

This Hermit good lives in that wood
Which slopes down to the sea.
How loudly his sweet voice he rears!
He loves to talk with marineres
That come from a far countree.

He kneels at morn, and noon, and eve—
He hath a cushion plump:
It is the moss that wholly hides
The rotted old oak stump.

The skiff-boat neared: I heard them talk,
"Why, this is strange, I trow!
Where are those lights so many and fair,
That signal made but now?"

Approacheth the ship with wonder.

"Strange, by my faith!" the Hermit said—
"And they answered not our cheer!
The planks looked warped! and see those sails,
How thin they are and sere!
I never saw aught like to them,
Unless perchance it were

Brown skeletons of leaves that lag
My forest-brook along;
When the ivy tod° is heavy with snow, *bushy clump*
And the owlet whoops to the wolf below,
That eats the she-wolf's young."

"Dear Lord! it hath a fiendish look,"
The Pilot made reply,
"I am a-feared"—"Push on, push on!"
Said the Hermit cheerily.

1. Set free from sin.

The boat came closer to the ship,
But I nor spake nor stirred;
The boat came close beneath the ship,
And straight a sound was heard.

The ship suddenly sinketh.

Under the water it rumbled on,
Still louder and more dread:
It reached the ship, it split the bay;
The ship went down like lead.

The ancient Mariner is saved in the Pilot's boat.

Stunned by that loud and dreadful sound,
Which sky and ocean smote,
Like one that hath been seven days drowned
My body lay afloat;
But swift as dreams, myself I found
Within the Pilot's boat.

Upon the whirl, where sank the ship,
The boat spun round and round;
And all was still, save that the hill
Was telling of the sound.

I moved my lips—the Pilot shrieked
And fell down in a fit;
The holy Hermit raised his eyes,
And prayed where he did sit.

I took the oars: the Pilot's boy,
Who now doth crazy go,
Laughed loud and long, and all the while
His eyes went to and fro.
"Ha! ha!" quoth he, "full plain I see,
The Devil knows how to row."

And now, all in my own countree,
I stood on the firm land!
The Hermit stepped forth from the boat,
And scarcely he could stand.

The ancient Mariner earnestly entreateth the Hermit to shrieve him; and the penance of life falls on him.

"O shrieve me, shrieve me, holy man!"
The Hermit crossed[2] his brow.
"Say quick," quoth he, "I bid thee say—
What manner of man art thou?"

Forthwith this frame of mine was wrenched
With a woeful agony,
Which forced me to begin my tale;
And then it left me free.

And ever and anon throughout his future life an agony constraineth him to travel from land to land;

Since then, at an uncertain hour,
That agony returns:
And till my ghastly tale is told,
This heart within me burns.

I pass, like night, from land to land;
I have strange power of speech;
That moment that his face I see,

2. Made the sign of the cross upon.

I know the man that must hear me:
To him my tale I teach.

What loud uproar bursts from that door!
The wedding guests are there:
But in the garden-bower the bride
And bridemaids singing are:
And hark the little vesper bell,
Which biddeth me to prayer!

O Wedding Guest! this soul hath been
Alone on a wide wide sea:
So lonely 'twas, that God himself
Scarce seemèd there to be.

O sweeter than the marriage feast,
'Tis sweeter far to me,
To walk together to the kirk
With a goodly company!

To walk together to the kirk,
And all together pray,
While each to his great Father bends,
Old men, and babes, and loving friends
And youths and maidens gay!

And to teach, by his own example, love and reverence to all things that God made and loveth.

Farewell, farewell! but this I tell
To thee, thou Wedding Guest!
He prayeth well, who loveth well
Both man and bird and beast.

He prayeth best, who loveth best
All things both great and small;
For the dear God who loveth us,
He made and loveth all.

The Mariner, whose eye is bright,
Whose beard with age is hoar,
Is gone: and now the Wedding Guest
Turned from the bridegroom's door.

He went like one that hath been stunned,
And is of sense forlorn:° *deprived*
A sadder and a wiser man,
He rose the morrow morn.

1798 1817

Dejection: An Ode

Late, late yestreen I saw the new Moon,
With the old Moon in her arms;
And I fear, I fear, my master dear!
We shall have a deadly storm.
Ballad of Sir Patrick Spence

1

Well! If the bard was weather-wise, who made
The grand old ballad of Sir Patrick Spence,
This night, so tranquil now, will not go hence

Unroused by winds, that ply a busier trade
Than those which mold yon cloud in lazy flakes,
Or the dull sobbing draft, that moans and rakes
Upon the strings of this Aeolian lute,[3]
Which better far were mute.
For lo! the New-moon winter-bright!
And overspread with phantom light,
(With swimming phantom light o'erspread
But rimmed and circled by a silver thread)
I see the old Moon in her lap, foretelling
The coming-on of rain and squally blast.
And oh! that even now the gust were swelling,
And the slant night shower driving loud and fast!
Those sounds which oft have raised me, whilst they awed,
And sent my soul abroad,
Might now perhaps their wonted° impulse give, *usual*
Might startle this dull pain, and make it move and live!

2

A grief without a pang, void, dark, and drear,
A stifled, drowsy, unimpassioned grief,
Which finds no natural outlet, no relief,
In word, or sigh, or tear—
O Lady! in this wan and heartless mood,
To other thoughts by yonder throstle wooed,
All this long eve, so balmy and serene,
Have I been gazing on the western sky,
And its peculiar tint of yellow green:
And still I gaze—and with how blank an eye!
And those thin clouds above, in flakes and bars,
That give away their motion to the stars;
Those stars, that glide behind them or between,
Now sparkling, now bedimmed, but always seen:
Yon crescent Moon, as fixed as if it grew
In its own cloudless, starless lake of blue;
I see them all so excellently fair,
I see, not feel, how beautiful they are!

3

My genial spirits° fail; *vital energies*
And what can these avail
To lift the smothering weight from off my breast?
It were a vain endeavor,
Though I should gaze forever
On that green light that lingers in the west:
I may not hope from outward forms to win
The passion and the life, whose fountains are within.

4

O Lady! we receive but what we give,
And in our life alone does Nature live:
Ours is her wedding garment, ours her shroud!
And would we aught behold, of higher worth,
Than that inanimate cold world allowed
To the poor loveless ever-anxious crowd,
Ah! from the soul itself must issue forth
A light, a glory, a fair luminous cloud
Enveloping the Earth—

3. The wind-harp (named after Aeolus, classical god of winds) has a sounding board equipped with a set of strings that vibrate in response to air currents.

And from the soul itself must there be sent
A sweet and potent voice, of its own birth,
Of all sweet sounds the life and element!

5

O pure of heart! thou need'st not ask of me
What this strong music in the soul may be!
What, and wherein it doth exist,
This light, this glory, this fair luminous mist,
This beautiful and beauty-making power.
Joy, virtuous Lady! Joy that ne'er was given,
Save to the pure, and in their purest hour,
Life, and Life's effluence, cloud at once and shower,
Joy, Lady! is the spirit and the power,
Which wedding Nature to us gives in dower
A new Earth and new Heaven,
Undreamt of by the sensual and the proud—
Joy is the sweet voice, Joy the luminous cloud—
We in ourselves rejoice!
And thence flows all that charms or ear or sight,
All melodies the echoes of that voice,
All colors a suffusion from that light.

6

There was a time when, though my path was rough,
This joy within me dallied with distress,
And all misfortunes were but as the stuff
Whence Fancy made me dreams of happiness:
For hope grew round me, like the twining vine,
And fruits, and foliage, not my own, seemed mine.
But now afflictions bow me down to earth:
Nor care I that they rob me of my mirth;
But oh! each visitation
Suspends what nature gave me at my birth,
My shaping spirit of Imagination.

For not to think of what I needs must feel,
But to be still and patient, all I can;
And happly by abstruse research to steal
From my own nature all the natural man—
This was my sole resource, my only plan:
Till that which suits a part infects the whole,
And now is almost grown the habit of my soul.

7

Hence, viper thoughts, that coil around my mind,
Reality's dark dream!
I turn from you, and listen to the wind,
Which long has raved unnoticed. What a scream
Of agony by torture lengthened out
That lute sent forth! Thou Wind, that rav'st without,
Bare crag, or mountain tairn,° or blasted tree, *pool*
Or pine grove whither woodman never clomb,
Or lonely house, long held—the witches' home,
Methinks were fitter instruments for thee,
Mad lutanist! who in this month of showers,
Of dark-brown gardens, and of peeping flowers,
Mak'st devils' yule,[4] with worse than wintry song,
The blossoms, buds, and timorous leaves among.

4. A winter storm in spring; hence, an unnatural or "devils' " Christmas.

Thou actor, perfect in all tragic sounds!
Thou mighty poet, e'en to frenzy bold!
What tell'st thou now about?
'Tis of the rushing of an host in rout,
With groans, of trampled men, with smarting wounds—
At once they groan with pain, and shudder with the cold!
But hush! there is a pause of deepest silence!
And all that noise, as of a rushing crowd,
With groans, and tremulous shudderings—all is over—
It tells another tale, with sounds less deep and loud!
A tale of less affright,
And tempered with delight,
As Otway's self had framed the tender lay—
'Tis of a little child
Upon a lonesome wild,
Not far from home, but she hath lost her way:
And now moans low in bitter grief and fear,
And now screams loud, and hopes to make her mother hear.

8

'Tis midnight, but small thoughts have I of sleep:
Full seldom may my friend such vigils keep!
Visit her, gentle Sleep! with wings of healing,
And may this storm be but a mountain birth,
May all the stars hang bright above her dwelling,
Silent as though they watched the sleeping Earth!
With light heart may she rise,
Gay fancy, cheerful eyes,
Joy lift her spirit, joy attune her voice;
To her may all things live, from pole to pole,
Their life the eddying of her living soul!
O simple spirit, guided from above,
Dear Lady! friend devoutest of my choice,
Thus mayest thou ever, evermore rejoice.

1802 1817

On Donne's Poetry

With Donne, whose muse on dromedary trots,
Wreathe iron pokers into truelove knots;
Rhyme's sturdy cripple, fancy's maze and clue,
Wit's forge and fire-blast, meaning's press and screw.[5]

1836

Epitaph

Stop, Christian passer-by!—Stop, child of God,
And read with gentle breast. Beneath this sod
A poet lies, or that which once seemed he.
O lift one thought in prayer for S. T. C.;
That he who many a year with toil of breath
Found death in life, may here find life in death!
Mercy for° praise—to be forgiven for fame *instead of*
He asked, and hoped, through Christ. Do thou the same!

1834

5. As in *jackscrew*, an instrument for applying great pressure gradually.

WALTER SAVAGE LANDOR
(1775–1864)

Rose Aylmer[1]

Ah what avails the sceptered race,
  Ah what the form divine!
What every virtue, every grace!
  Rose Aylmer, all were thine.
Rose Aylmer, whom these wakeful eyes
  May weep, but never see,
A night of memories and of sighs
  I consecrate to thee.

1806, 1831, 1846

Past Ruined Ilion Helen[2] Lives

Past ruined Ilion Helen lives,
  Alcestis[3] rises from the shades;
Verse calls them forth; 'tis verse that gives
  Immortal youth to mortal maids.

Soon shall Oblivion's deepening veil
  Hide all the peopled hills you see,
The gay, the proud, while lovers hail
  In distant ages you and me.

The tear for fading beauty check,
  For passing glory cease to sigh;
One form shall rise above the wreck,
  One name, Ianthe, shall not die.

1831

Dirce

Stand close around, ye Stygian set,[4]
  With Dirce in one boat conveyed!
Or Charon, seeing may forget
  That he is old and she a shade.

1831, 1846

To My Child Carlino[5]

They are verses written by a gentleman who resided long in this country, and who much regretted the necessity of leaving it.

—BOCCACCIO

Carlino! what art thou about, my boy?
Often I ask that question, though in vain;
For we are far apart: ah! therefore 'tis
I often ask it; not in such a tone

1. The Honorable Rose Whitworth Aylmer (1779–1800), whom Landor had known in Wales, died suddenly in Calcutta on March 2, 1800.
2. Helen of Troy ("Ilion").
3. Alcestis sacrificed her life for her husband, who was stricken with a mortal illness. She acted in accordance with Apollo's promise that he might thus be saved; she was then brought back from the underworld by Hercules.
4. The shades of the dead who were ferried by Charon over the river Styx to Hades.
5. The poem is addressed to Charles Savage Landor (1825–1917), youngest of Landor's three sons, at a time when Landor was in England and the three boys were in Italy.

As wiser fathers do, who know too well.
Were we not children, you and I together?
Stole we not glances from each other's eyes?
Swore we not secrecy in such misdeeds?
Well could we trust each other. Tell me, then,
What thou art doing. Carving out thy name,
Or haply mine, upon my favorite seat,
With the new knife I sent thee oversea?
Or hast thou broken it, and hid the hilt
Among the myrtles, starred with flowers, behind?
Or under that high throne whence fifty lilies
(With sworded tuberoses dense around)
Lift up their heads at once . . . not without fear
That they were looking at thee all the while?
Does Cincirillo follow thee about?
Inverting one swart foot suspensively,
And wagging his dread jaw, at every chirp
Of bird above him on the olive-branch?
Frighten him then away! 'twas he who slew
Our pigeons, our white pigeons, peacock-tailed,
That feared not you and me . . . alas, nor him!
I flattened his striped sides along my knee,
And reasoned with him on his bloody mind,
Till he looked blandly, and half-closed his eyes
To ponder on my lecture in the shade.
I doubt his memory much, his heart a little,
And in some minor matters (may I say it?)
Could wish him rather sager. But from thee
God hold back wisdom yet for many years!
Whether in early season or in late
It always comes high priced. For thy pure breast
I have no lesson; it for me has many.
Come, throw it open then! What sports, what cares
(Since there are none too young for these) engage
Thy busy thoughts? Are you again at work,
Walter[6] and you, with those sly laborers,
Geppo, Giovanni, Cecco, and Poeta,
To build more solidly your broken dam
Among the poplars, whence the nightingale
Inquisitively watched you all day long?
I was not of your council in the scheme,
Or might have saved you silver without end,
And sighs too without number. Art thou gone
Below the mulberry, where that cold pool
Urged to devise a warmer, and more fit
For mighty swimmers, swimming three abreast?
Or art thou panting in this summer noon
Upon the lowest step before the hall,
Drawing a slice of watermelon, long
As Cupid's bow, athwart thy wetted lips
(Like one who plays Pan's pipe) and letting drop
The sable seeds from all their separate cells,
And leaving bays profound and rocks abrupt,
Redder than coral round Calypso's[7] cave?

1837 1846

6. Walter Savage Landor (1822–99), the poet's second son.
7. The nymph or goddess who welcomed Odysseus in her island, Ogygia, after the wreck of his ship, and held him there for seven years.

Dying Speech of an Old Philosopher

I strove with none, for none was worth my strife:
  Nature I loved, and, next to Nature, Art:
I warmed both hands before the fire of Life;
  It sinks; and I am ready to depart.

1849

GEORGE GORDON, LORD BYRON
(1788–1824)

Written After Swimming from Sestos to Abydos[1]

1

If, in the month of dark December,
  Leander, who was nightly wont
(What maid will not the tale remember?)
  To cross thy stream, broad Hellespont!

2

If, when the wintry tempest roared,
  He sped to Hero, nothing loath,
And thus of old thy current poured,
  Fair Venus! how I pity both!

3

For *me,* degenerate modern wretch,
  Though in the genial month of May,
My dripping limbs I faintly stretch,
  And think I've done a feat today.

4

But since he crossed the rapid tide,
  According to the doubtful story,
To woo—and—Lord knows what beside,
  And swam for Love, as I for Glory;

5

'Twere hard to say who fared the best:
  Sad mortals! thus the gods still plague you!
He lost his labor, I my jest;
  For he was drowned, and I've the ague.° *chills and fever*

1812

She Walks in Beauty

1

She walks in beauty, like the night
  Of cloudless climes and starry skies;
And all that's best of dark and bright
  Meet in her aspect and her eyes:
Thus mellowed to that tender light
  Which heaven to gaudy day denies.

1. The Hellespont, or Dardanelles, is the strait separating Europe from Asia Minor, between Abydos on the Greek shore and Sestos on the Asian. In Greek legend, Leander used to swim from Abydos to visit his sweetheart Hero at Sestos.

2

One shade the more, one ray the less,
  Had half impaired the nameless grace
Which waves in every raven tress,
  Or softly lightens o'er her face;
Where thoughts serenely sweet express
  How pure, how dear their dwelling place.

3

And on that cheek, and o'er that brow,
  So soft, so calm, yet eloquent,
The smiles that win, the tints that glow,
  But tell of days in goodness spent,
A mind at peace with all below,
  A heart whose love is innocent!

1815

When We Two Parted

When we two parted
  In silence and tears,
Half broken-hearted
  To sever for years,
Pale grew thy cheek and cold,
  Colder thy kiss;
Truly that hour foretold
  Sorrow to this.

The dew of the morning
  Sunk chill on my brow—
It felt like the warning
  Of what I feel now.
Thy vows are all broken,
  And light is thy fame;
I hear thy name spoken,
  And share in its shame.

They name thee before me,
  A knell to mine ear;
A shudder comes o'er me—
  Why wert thou so dear?
They know not I knew thee,
  Who knew thee too well—
Long, long shall I rue thee,
  Too deeply to tell.

In secret we met—
  In silence I grieve,
That thy heart could forget,
  Thy spirit deceive.
If I should meet thee
  After long years,
How should I greet thee?—
  With silence and tears.

1813 1816

Prometheus

Titan![2] to whose immortal eyes
The sufferings of mortality,
Seen in their sad reality,
Were not as things that gods despise;
What was thy pity's recompense?
A silent suffering, and intense;
The rock, the vulture, and the chain,
All that the proud can feel of pain,
The agony they do not show,
The suffocating sense of woe,
Which speaks but in its loneliness,
And then is jealous lest the sky
Should have a listener, nor will sigh
Until its voice is echoless.

Titan! to thee the strife was given
Between the suffering and the will,
Which torture where they cannot kill;
And the inexorable heaven,
And the deaf tyranny of fate,
The ruling principle of hate,
Which for its pleasure doth create
The things it may annihilate,
Refused thee even the boon to die:
The wretched gift eternity
Was thine—and thou hast borne it well.
All that the Thunderer wrung from thee
Was but the menace which flung back
On him the torments of thy rack;
The fate thou didst so well foresee,
But would not to appease him tell;
And in thy silence[3] was his sentence,
And in his soul a vain repentance,
And evil dread so ill dissembled,
That in his hand the lightnings trembled.

Thy godlike crime was to be kind,
To render with thy precepts less
The sum of human wretchedness,
And strengthen man with his own mind;
But baffled as thou wert from high,
Still in thy patient energy,
In the endurance, and repulse
Of thine impenetrable spirit,
Which earth and heaven could not convulse,
A mighty lesson we inherit:
Thou art a symbol and a sign
To mortals of their fate and force;
Like thee, man is in part divine,
A troubled stream from a pure source;

2. An ancient Greek deity who stole fire from the heavens and gave it to mankind. His punishment, imposed by Jove ("the Thunderer," line 26) was to be chained to a cliff and torn by vultures so long as he defied Jove.

3. Prometheus knew but would not reveal the secret of Jove's eventual downfall.

And Man in portions can foresee
His own funereal destiny;
His wretchedness, and his resistance,
And his sad unallied existence;
To which his spirit may oppose
Itself—and equal to all woes,
And a firm will, and a deep sense,
Which even in torture can descry
Its own concentered recompense,
Triumphant where it dares defy,
And making death a victory.

1816

So We'll Go No More A-Roving

1

So we'll go no more a-roving
So late into the night,
Though the heart be still as loving,
And the moon be still as bright.

2

For the sword outwears its sheath,
And the soul wears out the breast,
And the heart must pause to breathe,
And Love itself have rest.

3

Though the night was made for loving,
And the day returns too soon,
Yet we'll go no more a-roving
By the light of the moon.

1817 1836

From Don Juan[4]

From *Canto the First*

1

I want° a hero: an uncommon want, *lack*
When every year and month sends forth a new one,
Till, after cloying the gazettes[5] with cant,
The age discovers he is not the true one;
Of such as these I should not care to vaunt,
I'll therefore take our ancient friend Don Juan—
We all have seen him, in the pantomime,[6]
Sent to the Devil somewhat ere his time.

* * *

5

Brave men were living before Agamemnon[7]
And since, exceeding valorous and sage,
A good deal like him too, though quite the same none;
But then they shone not on the poet's page,

4. The hero is a legendary Spanish nobleman, a notorious seducer of women; in most versions, but not Byron's, finally carried off to hell. Canto I comprises 222 stanzas; Stanzas 1–117, excerpted here, conclude with the end of the romance between Don Juan and Donna Julia.
5. Official notices or newspapers.
6. I.e., on the stage, in one or another of many adaptations.
7. Commander of the Greeks at the siege of Troy.

And so have been forgotten:—I condemn none,
But can't find any in the present age
Fit for my poem (that is, for my new one);
So, as I said, I'll take my friend Don Juan.

6

Most epic poets plunge "*in medias res*"[8]
(Horace makes this the heroic turnpike road),
And then your hero tells, when'er you please,
What went before—by way of episode,
While seated after dinner at his ease,
Beside his mistress in some soft abode,
Palace, or garden, paradise, or cavern,
Which serves the happy couple for a tavern.

7

That is the usual method, but not mine—
My way is to begin with the beginning;
The regularity of my design
Forbids all wandering as the worst of sinning,
And therefore I shall open with a line
(Although it cost me half an hour in spinning),
Narrating somewhat of Don Juan's father,
And also of his mother, if you'd rather.

8

In Seville was he born, a pleasant city,
Famous for oranges and women—he
Who has not seen it will be much to pity,
So says the proverb—and I quite agree;
Of all the Spanish towns is none more pretty,
Cadiz perhaps—but that you soon may see;
Don Juan's parents lived beside the river,
A noble stream, and called the Guadalquivir.

9

His father's name was José—*Don,* of course,—
A true Hidalgo,[9] free from every stain
Of Moor or Hebrew blood, he traced his source
Through the most Gothic gentlemen of Spain;[1]
A better cavalier ne'er mounted horse,
Or, being mounted, e'er got down again,
Than José, who begot our hero, who
Begot—but that's to come—Well, to renew:

10

His mother was a learnéd lady, famed
For every branch of every science known—
In every Christain language ever named,
With virtues equaled by her wit alone:
She made the cleverest people quite ashamed,
And even the good with inward envy groan,
Finding themselves so very much exceeded,
In their own way, by all the things that she did.

11

Her memory was a mine: she knew by heart
All Calderon and greater part of Lopé,[2]
So, that if any actor missed his part,

8. Into the middle of the subject.
9. Spanish noble of minor degree.
1. Descended from the Visigoths, who conquered Spain in the fifth century A.D.
2. Calderón (1600–81) and Lopé de Vega (1562–1635) pre-eminent Spanish dramatists.

She could have served him for the prompter's copy;
For her Feinagle's[3] were an useless art,
And he himself obliged to shut up shop—he
Could never make a memory so fine as
That which adorned the brain of Donna Inez.

12

Her favorite science was the mathematical,
Her noblest virtue was her magnanimity,
Her wit (she sometimes tried at wit) was Attic[4] all,
Her serious sayings darkened to sublimity;
In short, in all things she was fairly what I call
A prodigy—her morning dress was dimity,
Her evening silk, or, in the summer, muslin,
And other stuffs, with which I won't stay puzzling.

13

She knew the Latin—that is, "the Lord's prayer,"
And Greek—the alphabet—I'm nearly sure;
She read some French romances here and there,
Although her mode of speaking was not pure;
For native Spanish she had no great care,
At least her conversation was obscure;
Her thoughts were theorems, her words a problem,
As if she deemed that mystery would ennoble 'em.

* * *

22

'Tis pity learnéd virgins ever wed
With persons of no sort of education,
Or gentlemen, who, though well born and bred,
Grow tired of scientific conversation:
I don't choose to say much upon this head,
I'm a plain man, and in a single station,
But—Oh! ye lords of ladies intellectual,
Inform us truly, have they not hen-pecked you all?

23

Don José and his lady quarrelled—*why,*
Not any of the many could divine,
Though several thousand people chose to try,
'Twas surely no concern of theirs nor mine;
I loath that low vice—curiosity;
But if there's anything in which I shine,
'Tis in arranging all my friends' affairs,
Not having, of my own, domestic cares.

24

And so I interfered, and with the best
Intentions, but their treatment was not kind;
I think the foolish people were possessed,
For neither of them could I ever find,
Although their porter afterwards confessed—
But that's no matter, and the worst's behind,
For little Juan o'er me threw, down stairs,
A pail of housemaid's water unawares.

25

A little curly-headed, good-for-nothing,
And mischief-making monkey from his birth;

3. Inventor of a method of memorization, who lectured in England in 1811.

4. Athenian: i.e., refined, learned.

His parents ne'er agreed except in doting
  Upon the most unquiet imp on earth;
Instead of quarrelling, had they been but both in
  Their senses, they'd have sent young master forth
To school, or had him soundly whipped at home,
To teach him manners for the time to come.

26

Don José and the Donna Inez led
  For some time an unhappy sort of life,
Wishing each other, not divorced, but dead;
  They lived respectably as man and wife,
Their conduct was exceedingly well-bred,
  And gave no outward signs of inward strife,
Until at length the smothered fire broke out,
And put the business past all kind of doubt.

27

For Inez called some druggists and physicians,
  And tried to prove her loving lord was *mad,*
But as he had some lucid intermissions,
  She next decided he was only *bad;*
Yet when they asked her for her depositions,
  No sort of explanation could be had,
Save that her duty both to man and God
Required this conduct—which seemed very odd.

28

She kept a journal, where his faults were noted,
  And opened certain trunks of books and letters,
All which might, if occasion served, be quoted;
  And then she had all Seville for abettors,
Besides her good old grandmother (who doted);
  The hearers of her case became repeaters,
Then advocates, inquisitors, and judges,
Some for amusement, others for old grudges.

29

And then this best and meekest woman bore
  With such serenity her husband's woes,
Just as the Spartan ladies did of yore,
  Who saw their spouses killed, and nobly chose
Never to say a word about them more—
  Calmly she heard each calumny that rose,
And saw *his* agonies with such sublimity,
That all the world exclaimed, "What magnanimity!"

* * *

32

Their friends had tried at reconciliation,
  Then their relations, who made matters worse.
('Twere hard to tell upon a like occasion
  To whom it may be best to have recourse—
I can't say much for friend or yet relation):
  The lawyers did their utmost for divorce,
But scarce a fee was paid on either side
Before, unluckily, Don José died.

33

He died: and most unluckily, because,
  According to all hints I could collect
From Counsel learnéd in those kinds of laws,
  (Although their talk's obscure and circumspect)

His death contrived to spoil a charming cause;° *legal case*
  A thousand pities also with respect
To public feeling, which on this occasion
Was manifested in a great sensation.

* * *

37

Dying intestate,° Juan was sole heir *leaving no will*
  To a chancery suit,[5] and messuages,° and lands, *household lands*
Which, with a long minority[6] and care,
  Promised to turn out well in proper hands:
Inez became sole guardian, which was fair,
  And answered but to Nature's just demands;
An only son left with an only mother
Is brought up much more wisely than another.

38

Sagest of women, even of widows, she
  Resolved that Juan should be quite a paragon,
And worthy of the noblest pedigree,
  (His Sire was of Castile, his Dam from Aragon):
Then, for accomplishments of chivalry,
  In case our Lord the King should go to war again,
He learned the arts of riding, fencing, gunnery,
And how to scale a fotress—or a nunnery.

39

But that which Donna Inez most desired,
  And saw into herself each day before all
The learnéd tutors whom for him she hired,
  Was, that his breeding should be strictly moral:
Much into all his studies she inquired,
  And so they were submitted first to her, all,
Arts, sciences—no branch was made a mystery
To Juan's eyes, excepting natural history.

40

The languages, especially the dead,
  The sciences, and most of all the abstruse,
The arts, at least all such as could be said
  To be the most remote from common use,
In all these he was much and deeply read:
  But not a page of anything that's loose,
Or hints continuation of the species,
Was ever suffered, lest he should grow vicious.

41

His classic studies made a little puzzle,
  Because of filthy loves of gods and goddesses,
Who in the earlier ages raised a bustle,
  But never put on pantaloons or bodices;
His reverend tutors had at times a tussle,
  And for their Aeneids, Iliads, and Odysseys,
Were forced to make an odd sort of apology,
For Donna Inez dreaded the Mythology.

42

Ovid's a rake, as half his verses show him,
  Anacreon's morals are a still worse sample,
Catullus scarcely has a decent poem,

5. Drawn-out legal proceedings over inheritance of property.

6. Before he should come of age.

I don't think Sappho's Ode a good example,[7]
Although Longinus[8] tells us there is no hymn
Where the Sublime soars forth on wings more ample;
But Virgil's songs are pure, except that horrid one
Beginning with "*Formosum Pastor Corydon.*"[9]

43

Lucretius' irreligion is too strong
For early stomachs, to prove wholesome food;
I can't help thinking Juvenal was wrong,
Although no doubt his real intent was good,
For speaking out so plainly in his song,
So much indeed as to be downright rude;
And then what proper person can be partial
To all those nauseous epigrams of Martial?[1]

44

Juan was taught from out the best edition,
Expurgated by learnéd men, who place,
Judiciously, from out the schoolboy's vision,
The grosser parts; but, fearful to deface
Too much their modest bard by this omission,
And pitying sore his mutilated case,
They only add them all in an appendix,[2]
Which saves, in fact, the trouble of an index;

* * *

52

For my part I say nothing—nothing—but
This I will say—my reasons are my own—
That if I had an only son to put
To school (as God be praised that I have none),
'Tis not with Donna Inez I would shut
Him up to learn his catechism[3] alone,
No—no—I'd send him out betimes to college,
For there it was I picked up my own knowledge.

53

For there one learns—'tis not for me to boast,
Though I acquired—but I pass over *that,*
As well as all the Greek I since have lost:
I say that there's the place—but "*Verbum sat,*"[4]
I think I picked up too, as well as most,
Knowledge of matters—but no matter *what*—
I never married—but, I think, I know
That sons should not be educated so.

54

Young Juan now was sixteen years of age,
Tall, handsome, slender, but well knit: he seemed
Active, though not so sprightly, as a page;
And everybody but his mother deemed
Him almost man; but she flew in a rage
And bit her lips (for else she might have screamed)

7. These lines name Greek and Roman classic and erotic poets.
8. The presumed author (first century A.D.) of a treatise on "the sublime" in literature.
9. "Handsome Shepherd Corydon": opening words of Virgil's Second Eclogue (a pastoral poem), concerned with love between young men.
1. Like Lucretius (line 337) and Juvenal (line 339), a Roman poet. Lucretius was a philosophic atheist; Juvenal and Martial were severe and sometimes obscene satirists.
2. "Fact! There is, or was, such an edition, with all the obnoxious epigrams of Martial placed by themselves at the end" [Byron's note].
3. A brief summary of Christian teaching.
4. A word to the wise suffices.

If any said so—for to be precocious
Was in her eyes a thing the most atrocious.

55

Amongst her numerous acquaintance, all
Selected for discretion and devotion,
There was the Donna Julia, whom to call
Pretty were but to give a feeble notion
Of many charms in her as natural
As sweetness to the flower, or salt to Ocean,
Her zone° to Venus, or his bow to Cupid, *girdle, waist*
(But this last simile is trite and stupid.)

56

The darkness of her Oriental eye
Accorded with her Moorish origin;
(Her blood was not all Spanish; by the by,
In Spain, you know, this is a sort of sin;)
When proud Granada fell, and, forced to fly,
Boabdil[5] wept: of Donna Julia's kin
Some went to Africa, some stayed in Spain—
Her great great grandmamma chose to remain.

57

She married (I forget the pedigree)
With an Hidalgo, who transmitted down
His blood less noble than such blood should be;
At such alliances his sires would frown,
In that point so precise in each degree
That they bred *in and in,* as might be shown,
Marrying their cousins—nay, their aunts, and nieces,
Which always spoils the breed, if it increases.

58

This heathenish cross restored the breed again,
Ruined its blood,[6] but much improved its flesh;
For from a root the ugliest in Old Spain
Sprung up a branch as beautiful as fresh;
The sons no more were short, the daughters plain:
But there 's a rumour which I fain would hush,
'Tis said that Donna Julia's grandmamma
Produced her Don more heirs at love than law.

59

However this might be, the race went on
Improving still through every generation,
Until it centered in an only son,
Who left an only daughter; my narration
May have suggested that this single one
Could be but Julia (whom on this occasion
I shall have much to speak about), and she
Was married, charming, chaste, and twenty-three.

60

Her eye (I'm very fond of handsome eyes)
Was large and dark, suppressing half its fire
Until she spoke, then through its soft disguise
Flashed an expression more of pride than ire,
And love than either; and there would arise
A something in them which was not desire,

5. The last Mohammedan ruler of Granada, a province of Spain.

6. Blood-line, i.e., pure lineage.

But would have been, perhaps, but for the soul
Which struggled through and chastened down the whole.

61

Her glossy hair was clustered o'er a brow
Bright with intelligence, and fair, and smooth;
Her eyebrow's shape was like the aërial bow,° *rainbow*
Her cheek all purple° with the beam of youth, *rosy*
Mounting, at times, to a transparent glow,
As if her veins ran lightning; she, in sooth,
Possessed an air and grace by no means common:
Her stature tall—I hate a dumpy woman.

62

Wedded she was some years, and to a man
Of fifty, and such husbands are in plenty;
And yet, I think, instead of such a ONE
'Twere better to have TWO of five-and-twenty,
Especially in countries near the sun:
And now I think on't, "*mi vien in mente,*"[7]
Ladies even of the most uneasy virtue
Prefer a spouse whose age is short of thirty.

63

'Tis a sad thing, I cannot choose but say,
And all the fault of that indecent sun,
Who cannot leave alone our helpless clay,
But will keep baking, broiling, burning on,
That howsoever people fast and pray,
The flesh is frail, and so the soul undone:
What men call gallantry, and gods adultery,
Is much more common where the climate's sultry.

64

Happy the nations of the moral North!
Where all is virtue, and the winter season
Sends sin, without a rag on, shivering forth
('Twas snow that brought St. Anthony to reason);[8]
Where juries cast up what a wife is worth,
By laying whate'er sum, in mulct,° they please on *as a fine*
The lover, who must pay a handsome price,
Because it is a marketable vice.

65

Alfonso was the name of Julia's lord,
A man well looking for his years, and who
Was neither much beloved nor yet abhorred:
They lived together as most people do,
Suffering each other's foibles by accord,
And not exactly either *one* or *two;*
Yet he was jealous, though he did not show it,
For Jealousy dislikes the world to know it.

* * *

69

Juan she saw, and, as a pretty child,
Caressed him often—such a thing might be
Quite innocently done, and harmless styled,
When she had twenty years, and thirteen he;
But I am not so sure I should have smiled

7. It comes to my mind.
8. St. Anthony recommended the application of snow as a remedy for lust.

When he was sixteen, Julia twenty-three;
These few short years make wondrous alterations,
Particularly amongst sun-burnt nations.

70

Whate'er the cause might be, they had become
Changed; for the dame grew distant, the youth shy,
Their looks cast down, their greetings almost dumb,
And much embarrassment in either eye;
There surely will be little doubt with some
That Donna Julia knew the reason why,
But as for Juan, he had no more notion
Than he who never saw the sea of Ocean.

71

Yet Julia's very coldness still was kind,
And tremulously gentle her small hand
Withdrew itself from his, but left behind
A little pressure, thrilling, and so bland
And slight, so very slight, that to the mind
'Twas but a doubt; but ne'er magician's wand
Wrought change with all Armida's[9] fairy art
Like what this light touch left on Juan's heart.

72

And if she met him, though she smiled no more,
She looked a sadness sweeter than her smile,
As if her heart had deeper thoughts in store
She must not own, but cherished more the while
For that compression in its burning core;
Even Innocence itself has many a wile,
And will not dare to trust itself with truth,
And Love is taught hypocrisy from youth.

* * *

76

She vowed she never would see Juan more,
And next day paid a visit to his mother,
And looked extremely at the opening door,
Which, by the Virgin's grace, let in another;
Grateful she was, and yet a little sore—
Again it opens, it can be no other,
'Tis surely Juan now—No! I'm afraid
That night the Virgin was no further prayed.

77

She now determined that a virtuous woman
Should rather face and overcome temptation,
That flight was base and dastardly, and no man
Should ever give her heart the least sensation,
That is to say, a thought beyond the common
Preference, that we must feel, upon occasion,
For people who are pleasanter than others,
But then they only seem so many brothers.

78

And even if by chance—and who can tell?
The Devil's so very sly—she should discover
That all within was not so very well,
And, if still free,[1] that such or such a lover

9. An enchantress who seduces Christian knights in Tasso's *Jerusalem Delivered.*
1. I.e., if she were not already married.

Might please perhaps, a virtuous wife can quell
  Such thoughts, and be the better when they're over;
And if the man should ask, 'tis but denial:
I recommend young ladies to make trial.

79

And, then, there are such things as Love divine,
  Bright and immaculate, unmixed and pure,
Such as the angels think so very fine,
  And matrons, who would be no less secure,
Platonic, perfect, "just such love as mine;"
  Thus Julia said—and thought so, to be sure;
And so I'd have her think, were *I* the man
On whom her reveries celestial ran.

* * *

86

So much for Julia! Now we'll turn to Juan.
  Poor little fellow! he had no idea
Of his own case, and never hit the true one;
  In feelings quick as Ovid's Miss Medea,[2]
He puzzled over what he found a new one,
  But not as yet imagined it could be a
Thing quite in course, and not at all alarming,
Which, with a little patience, might grow charming.

* * *

90

Young Juan wandered by the glassy brooks,
  Thinking unutterable things; he threw
Himself at length within the leafy nooks
  Where the wild branch of the cork forest grew;
There poets find materials for their books,
  And every now and then we read them through,
So that their plan and prosody are eligible,
Unless, like Wordsworth, they prove unintelligible.

91

He, Juan (and not Wordsworth), so pursued
  His self-communion with his own high soul,
Until his mighty heart, in its great mood,
  Had mitigated part, though not the whole
Of its disease; he did the best he could
  With things not very subject to control,
And turned, without perceiving his condition,
Like Coleridge, into a metaphysician.

92

He thought about himself, and the whole earth,
  Of man the wonderful, and of the stars,
And how the deuce they ever could have birth;
  And then he thought of earthquakes, and of wars,
How many miles the moon might have in girth,
  Of air-balloons, and of the many bars
To perfect knowledge of the boundless skies;—
And then he thought of Donna Julia's eyes.

93

In thoughts like these true Wisdom may discern
  Longings sublime, and aspirations high,

2. In Ovid's *Metamorphoses,* the young Medea finds herself irresistibly infatuated with the hero Jason.

Which some are born with, but the most part learn
  To plague themselves withal, they know not why:
'Twas strange that one so young should thus concern
  His brain about the action of the sky;
If *you* think 'twas Philosophy that this did,
I can't help thinking puberty assisted.

94

He pored upon the leaves, and on the flowers,
  And heard a voice in all the winds; and then
He thought of wood-nymphs and immortal bowers,
  And how the goddesses came down to men:
He missed the pathway, he forgot the hours,
  And when he looked upon his watch again,
He found how much old Time had been a winner—
He also found that he had lost his dinner.

* * *

103

'Twas on a summer's day—the sixth of June:
  I like to be particular in dates,
Not only of the age, and year, but moon;
  They are a sort of post-house, where the Fates
Change horses, making History change its tune,
  Then spur away o'er empires and o'er states,
Leaving at last not much besides chronology,
Excepting the post-obits[3] of theology.

104

'Twas on the sixth of June, about the hour
  Of half-past six—perhaps still nearer seven—
When Julia sate within as pretty a bower
  As e'er held houri[4] in that heathenish heaven
Described by Mahomet, and Anacreon Moore,[5]
  To whom the lyre and laurels have been given,
With all the trophies of triumphant song—
He won them well, and may he wear them long!

105

She sate, but not alone; I know not well
  How this same interview had taken place,
And even if I knew, I should not tell—
  People should hold their tongues in any case;
No matter how or why the thing befell,
  But there were she and Juan, face to face—
When two such faces are so, 'twould be wise,
But very difficult, to shut their eyes.

106

How beautiful she looked! her conscious heart[6]
  Glowed in her cheek, and yet she felt no wrong:
Oh Love! how perfect is thy mystic art,
  Strengthening the weak, and trampling on the strong!
How self-deceitful is the sagest part
  Of mortals whom thy lure hath led along!
The precipice she stood on was immense,
So was her creed° in her own innocence. *trust*

3. Loans repaid from the estate of a person after his death; probably referring to rewards or punishments in the afterlife.
4. A beautiful maiden said to entertain faithful Muslims in Paradise.
5. Byron's friend, Thomas Moore, author of oriental tales in his long poem *Lalla Rookh,* and translator of love poems by the ancient Greek poet Anacreon.
6. Deep emotion.

107

She thought of her own strength, and Juan's youth,
  And of the folly of all prudish fears,
Victorious Virtue, and domestic Truth,
  And then of Don Alfonso's fifty years:
I wish these last had not occurred, in sooth,
  Because that number rarely much endears,
And through all climes, the snowy and the sunny,
Sounds ill in love, whate'er it may in money.

* * *

113

The sun set, and up rose the yellow moon:
  The Devil's in the moon for mischief; they
Who called her CHASTE, methinks, began too soon
  Their nomenclature; there is not a day,
The longest, not the twenty-first of June,
  Sees half the business in a wicked way,
On which three single hours of moonshine smile—
And then she looks so modest all the while!

114

There is a dangerous silence in that hour,
  A stillness, which leaves room for the full soul
To open all itself, without the power
  Of calling wholly back its self-control;
The silver light which, hallowing tree and tower,
  Sheds beauty and deep softness o'er the whole,
Breathes also to the heart, and o'er it throws
A loving languor, which is not repose.

115

And Julia sate with Juan, half embraced
  And half retiring from the glowing arm,
Which trembled like the bosom where 'twas placed;
  Yet still she must have thought there was no harm,
Or else 'twere easy to withdraw her waist;
  But then the situation had its charm,
And then——God knows what next—I can't go on;
I'm almost sorry that I e'er begun.

116

Oh Plato! Plato! you have paved the way,
  With your confounded fantasies, to more
Immoral conduct by the fancied sway
  Your system feigns o'er the controlless core
Of human hearts, than all the long array
  Of poets and romancers:—You're a bore,
A charlatan, a coxcomb—and have been,
At best, no better than a go-between.

117

And Julia's voice was lost, except in sighs,
  Until too late for useful conversation;
The tears were gushing from her gentle eyes,
  I wish, indeed, they had not had occasion;
But who, alas! can love, and then be wise?
  Not that Remorse did not oppose Temptation;
A little still she strove, and much repented,
And whispering "I will ne'er consent"—consented.

1819

On This Day I Complete My Thirty-sixth Year

Missolonghi,[7] January 22, 1824

'Tis time this heart should be unmoved,
Since others it hath ceased to move:
Yet, though I cannot be beloved,
Still let me love!

My days are in the yellow leaf;
The flowers and fruits of love are gone;
The worm, the canker,° and the grief — *deep infection*
Are mine alone!

The fire that on my bosom preys
Is lone as some volcanic isle;
No torch is kindled at its blaze—
A funeral pile.

The hope, the fear, the jealous care,
The exalted portion of the pain
And power of love, I cannot share,
But wear the chain.

But 'tis not *thus*—and 'tis not *here*—
Such thoughts should shake my soul, nor *now*,
Where glory decks the hero's bier,
Or binds his brow.

The sword, the banner, and the field,
Glory and Greece, around me see!
The Spartan, borne upon his shield,
Was not more free.

Awake! (not Greece—she *is* awake!)
Awake, my spirit! Think through *whom*
Thy life-blood tracks its parent lake,
And then strike home!

Tread those reviving passions down,
Unworthy manhood!—unto thee
Indifferent should the smile or frown
Of beauty be.

If thou regrett'st thy youth, *why live?*
The land of honorable death
Is here:—up to the field, and give
Away thy breath!

Seek out—less often sought than found—
A soldier's grave, for thee the best;
Then look around, and choose thy ground,
And take thy rest.

1824

7. In Greece, where Byron had gone to support the Greek war for independence from Turkey, and where he died, April 19, 1824.

PERCY BYSSHE SHELLEY
(1792–1822)

Hymn to Intellectual Beauty[1]

1

The awful shadow of some unseen Power
Floats though unseen among us—visiting
This various world with as inconstant wing
As summer winds that creep from flower to flower—
Like moonbeams that behind some piny mountain shower,
It visits with inconstant glance
Each human heart and countenance;
Like hues and harmonies of evening—
Like clouds in starlight widely spread—
Like memory of music fled—
Like aught that for its grace may be
Dear, and yet dearer for its mystery.

2

Spirit of BEAUTY, that dost consecrate
With thine own hues all thou dost shine upon
Of human thought or form—where art thou gone?
Why dost thou pass away and leave our state,
This dim vast vale of tears, vacant and desolate?
Ask why the sunlight not forever
Weaves rainbows o'er yon mountain river,
Why aught should fail and fade that once is shown,
Why fear and dream and death and birth
Cast on the daylight of this earth
Such gloom—why man has such a scope
For love and hate, despondency and hope?

3

No voice from some sublimer world hath ever
To sage or poet these responses given—
Therefore the names of Daemon, Ghost, and Heaven,
Remain the records of their vain endeavor,
Frail spells—whose uttered charm might not avail to sever,
From all we hear and all we see,
Doubt, chance, and mutability.
Thy light alone—like mist o'er mountains driven,
Or music by the night wind sent
Through strings of some still instrument,
Or moonlight on a midnight stream,
Gives grace and truth to life's unquiet dream.

4

Love, Hope, and Self-esteem, like clouds depart
And come, for some uncertain moments lent.
Man were immortal, and omnipotent,
Didst thou, unknown and awful as thou art,
Keep with thy glorious train° firm state within his heart. *company*

1. Beauty perceived not by the senses but by spiritual illumination.

Thou messenger of sympathies,
That wax and wane in lovers' eyes—
Thou—that to human thought art nourishment,
Like darkness to a dying flame!
Depart not as thy shadow came,
Depart not—lest the grave should be,
Like life and fear, a dark reality.

5

While yet a boy I sought for ghosts, and sped
Through many a listening chamber, cave and ruin,
And starlight wood, with fearful steps pursuing
Hopes of high talk with the departed dead.
I called on poisonous names[2] with which our youth is fed;
I was not heard—I saw them not—
When musing deeply on the lot
Of life, at that sweet time when winds are wooing
All vital things that wake to bring
News of birds and blossoming—
Sudden, thy shadow fell on me;
I shrieked, and clasped my hands in ecstasy!

6

I vowed that I would dedicate my powers
To thee and thine—have I not kept the vow?
With beating heart and streaming eyes, even now
I call the phantoms of a thousand hours
Each from his voiceless grave: they have in visioned bowers
Of studious zeal or love's delight
Outwatched with me the envious night—
They know that never joy illumed my brow
Unlinked with hope that thou wouldst free
This world from its dark slavery,
That thou—O awful LOVELINESS,
Wouldst give whate'er these words cannot express.

7

The day becomes more solemn and serene
When noon is past—there is a harmony
In autumn, and a luster in its sky,
Which through the summer is not heard or seen,
As if it could not be, as if it had not been!
Thus let thy power, which like the truth
Of nature on my passive youth
Descended, to my onward life supply
Its calm—to one who worships thee,
And every form containing thee,
Whom, SPIRIT fair, thy spells did bind
To fear himself, and love all human kind.

1817

Ozymandias[3]

I met a traveler from an antique land
Who said: Two vast and trunkless legs of stone
Stand in the desert . . . Near them, on the sand,

2. Possibly alluding to attempts to summon spirits of the dead by means of magic rites.
3. Greek name for the Egyptian monarch Ramses II (13th century B.C.), who is said to have erected a huge statue of himself.

Half sunk, a shattered visage lies, whose frown,
And wrinkled lip, and sneer of cold command,
Tell that its sculptor well those passions read
Which yet survive, stamped on these lifeless things,
The hand that mocked them, and the heart that fed:
And on the pedestal these words appear:
"My name is Ozymandias, king of kings:
Look on my works, ye Mighty, and despair!"
Nothing beside remains. Round the decay
Of that colossal wreck, boundless and bare
The lone and level sands stretch far away.

1818

Stanzas Written in Dejection, Near Naples

1

The sun is warm, the sky is clear,
  The waves are dancing fast and bright,
Blue isles and snowy mountains wear
  The purple noon's transparent might,
  The breath of the moist earth is light,
Around its unexpanded buds;
  Like many a voice of one delight,
The winds, the birds, the ocean floods,
The City's voice itself is soft like Solitude's.

2

I see the Deep's untrampled floor
  With green and purple seaweeds strown;
I see the waves upon the shore,
  Like light dissolved in star-showers, thrown:
  I sit upon the sands alone—
The lightning of the noontide ocean
  Is flashing round me, and a tone
Arises from its measured motion;
How sweet! did any heart now share in my emotion.

3

Alas! I have nor hope nor health,
  Nor peace within nor calm around,
Nor that content surpassing wealth
  The sage in meditation found,
  And walked with inward glory crowned—
Nor fame, nor power, nor love, nor leisure.
  Others I see whom these surround—
Smiling they live, and call life pleasure;
To me that cup has been dealt in another measure.

4

Yet now despair itself is mild,
  Even as the winds and waters are;
I could lie down like a tired child,
  And weep away the life of care
  Which I have borne and yet must bear,
Till death like sleep might steal on me,
  And I might feel in the warm air
My cheek grow cold, and hear the sea
Breathe o'er my dying brain its last monotony.

5

Some might lament that I were cold,
As I, when this sweet day is gone,
Which my lost heart, too soon grown old,
Insults with this untimely moan;
They might lament—for I am one
Whom men love not—and yet regret,
Unlike this day, which, when the sun
Shall on its stainless glory set,
Will linger, though enjoyed, like joy in memory yet.

1818 1824

England in 1819

An old, mad, blind, despised, and dying king[4]—
Princes, the dregs of their dull race,[5] who flow
Through public scorn—mud from a muddy spring;
Rulers who neither see, nor feel, nor know,
But leechlike to their fainting country cling,
Till they drop, blind in blood, without a blow;
A people starved and stabbed in the untilled field—
An army, which liberticide[6] and prey
Makes as a two-edged sword to all who wield;
Golden and sanguine[7] laws which tempt and slay;
Religion Christless, Godless—a book sealed;
A Senate—Time's worst statute[8] unrepealed—
Are graves, from which a glorious Phantom[9] may
Burst, to illumine our tempestuous day.

1819 1839

Ode to the West Wind

1

O wild West Wind, thou breath of Autumn's being,
Thou, from whose unseen presence the leaves dead
Are driven, like ghosts from an enchanter fleeing,

Yellow, and black, and pale, and hectic red,
Pestilence-stricken multitudes: O thou,
Who chariotest to their dark wintry bed

The wingéd seeds, where they lie cold and low,
Each like a corpse within its grave, until
Thine azure sister of the Spring shall blow

Her clarion[1] o'er the dreaming earth, and fill
(Driving sweet buds like flocks to feed in air)
With living hues and odors plain and hill:

Wild Spirit, which art moving everywhere;
Destroyer and preserver; hear, oh, hear!

4. George III (1738–1820), who lived for years in a state of advanced senility. The "Princes" of line 2 are George III's sons, including the Prince-Regent, later George IV, whom Shelley detested.
5. The "Hanoverian" line of English monarchs, beginning in 1714 with George I.
6. Destruction of liberty.
7. Sanguinary; causing bloodshed.
8. I.e., probably the Act of Union (1801) uniting Ireland to England and excluding Roman Catholics from exercising full citizenship.
9. I.e., the spirit of liberty.
1. Melodious trumpet-call.

2

Thou on whose stream, mid the steep sky's commotion,
Loose clouds like earth's decaying leaves are shed,
Shook from the tangled boughs of Heaven and Ocean,

Angels[2] of rain and lightning: there are spread
On the blue surface of thine aëry surge,
Like the bright hair uplifted from the head

Of some fierce Maenad,[3] even from the dim verge
Of the horizon to the zenith's height,
The locks of the approaching storm. Thou dirge

Of the dying year, to which this closing night
Will be the dome of a vast sepulcher,
Vaulted with all thy congregated might

Of vapors, from whose solid atmosphere
Black rain, and fire, and hail will burst: oh, hear!

3

Thou who didst waken from his summer dreams
The blue Mediterranean, where he lay,
Lulled by the coil of his crystálline streams,

Beside a pumice isle in Baiae's bay,[4]
And saw in sleep old palaces and towers
Quivering within the wave's intenser day,

All overgrown with azure moss and flowers
So sweet, the sense faints picturing them! Thou
For whose path the Atlantic's level powers

Cleave themselves into chasms, while far below
The sea-blooms and the oozy woods which wear
The sapless foliage of the ocean, know

Thy voice, and suddenly grow gray with fear,
And tremble and despoil themselves: oh, hear!

4

If I were a dead leaf thou mightest bear;
If I were a swift cloud to fly with thee;
A wave to pant beneath thy power, and share

The impulse of thy strength, only less free
Than thou, O uncontrollable! If even
I were as in my boyhood, and could be

The comrade of thy wanderings over Heaven,
As then, when to outstrip thy skyey speed
Scarce seemed a vision; I would ne'er have striven

As thus with thee in prayer in my sore need.
Oh, lift me as a wave, a leaf, a cloud!
I fall upon the thorns of life! I bleed!

2. In Greek derivation, messengers or divine messengers.
3. Frenzied dancer, worshipper of Dionysus, a god of wine and fertility.
4. Near Naples, Italy.

A heavy weight of hours has chained and bowed
One too like thee: tameless, and swift, and proud.

5

Make me thy lyre,[5] even as the forest is:
What if my leaves are falling like its own!
The tumult of thy mighty harmonies

Will take from both a deep, autumnal tone,
Sweet though in sadness. Be thou, Spirit fierce,
My spirit! Be thou me, impetuous one!

Drive my dead thoughts over the universe
Like withered leaves to quicken a new birth!
And, by the incantation of this verse,

Scatter, as from an unextinguished hearth
Ashes and sparks, my words among mankind!
Be through my lips to unawakened earth

The trumpet of a prophecy! O Wind,
If Winter comes, can Spring be far behind?

1820

The Cloud

I bring fresh showers for the thirsting flowers,
    From the seas and the streams;
I bear light shade for the leaves when laid
    In their noonday dreams.
From my wings are shaken the dews that waken
    The sweet buds every one,
When rocked to rest on their mother's breast,
    As she dances about the sun.
I wield the flail of the lashing hail,
    And whiten the green plains under,
And then again I dissolve it in rain,
    And laugh as I pass in thunder.

I sift the snow on the mountains below,
    And their great pines groan aghast;
And all the night 'tis my pillow white,
    While I sleep in the arms of the blast.
Sublime on the towers of my skyey bowers,
    Lightning my pilot[6] sits;
In a cavern under is fettered the thunder,
    It struggles and howls at fits;° *intermittently*
Over earth and ocean, with gentle motion,
    This pilot is guiding me,
Lured by the love of the genii that move
    In the depths of the purple sea;
Over the rills, and the crags, and the hills,
    Over the lakes and the plains,
Wherever he dream, under mountain or stream,

5. Small harp traditionally used to accompany songs and recited poems.
6. Electrical energy, here represented as directing the cloud in response to the attraction of opposite charges ("genii," line 23) under the sea.

The Spirit he loves remains;
And I all the while bask in Heaven's blue smile,
Whilst he is dissolving in rains.

The sanguine Sunrise, with his meteor eyes,
And his burning plumes outspread,
Leaps on the back of my sailing rack,[7]
When the morning star shines dead;
As on the jag of a mountain crag,
Which an earthquake rocks and swings,
An eagle alit one moment may sit
In the light of its golden wings.
And when Sunset may breathe, from the lit sea beneath,
Its ardors of rest and of love,
And the crimson pall of eve may fall
From the depth of Heaven above,
With wings folded I rest, on mine aëry nest,
As still as a brooding dove.

That orbéd maiden with white fire laden,
Whom mortals call the Moon,
Glides glimmering o'er my fleecelike floor,
By the midnight breezes strewn;
And wherever the beat of her unseen feet,
Which only the angels hear,
May have broken the woof° of my tent's thin roof, *fabric*
The stars peep behind her and peer;
And I laugh to see them whirl and flee,
Like a swarm of golden bees,
When I widen the rent in my wind-built tent,
Till the calm rivers, lakes, and seas,
Like strips of the sky fallen through me on high,
Are each paved with the moon and these.

I bind the Sun's throne with a burning zone,° *belt*
And the Moon's with a girdle of pearl;
The volcanoes are dim, and the stars reel and swim,
When the whirlwinds my banner unfurl.
From cape to cape, with a bridgelike shape,
Over a torrent sea,
Sunbeam-proof, I hang like a roof—
The mountains its columns be.
The triumphal arch through which I march
With hurricane, fire, and snow,
When the Powers of the air are chained to my chair,
Is the million-colored bow;
The sphere-fire above its soft colors wove,
While the moist Earth was laughing below.

I am the daughter of Earth and Water,
And the nursling of the Sky;
I pass through the pores of the ocean and shores;
I change, but I cannot die.
For after the rain when with never a stain
The pavilion of Heaven is bare,

7. Wind-driven clouds.

And the winds and sunbeams with their convex° gleams *upward-arching*
Build up the blue dome of air,
I silently laugh at my own cenotaph,[8]
And out of the caverns of rain,
Like a child from the womb, like a ghost from the tomb,
I arise and unbuild it again.

1820

To a Skylark

Hail to thee, blithe Spirit!
Bird thou never wert,
That from Heaven, or near it,
Pourest thy full heart
In profuse strains of unpremeditated art.

Higher still and higher
From the earth thou springest
Like a cloud of fire;
The blue deep thou wingest,
And singing still dost soar, and soaring ever singest.

In the golden lightning
Of the sunken sun,
O'er which clouds are bright'ning,
Thou dost float and run;
Like an unbodied joy whose race is just begun.

The pale purple even
Melts around thy flight;
Like a star of Heaven,
In the broad daylight
Thou art unseen, but yet I hear thy shrill delight,

Keen as are the arrows
Of that silver sphere,° *star*
Whose intense lamp narrows
In the white dawn clear
Until we hardly see—we feel that it is there.

All the earth and air
With thy voice is loud,
As, when night is bare,
From one lonely cloud
The moon rains out her beams, and Heaven is overflowed.

What thou art we know not;
What is most like thee?
From rainbow clouds there flow not
Drops so bright to see
As from thy presence showers a rain of melody.

Like a Poet hidden
In the light of thought,
Singing hymns unbidden,

8. Monument honoring a person who is buried elsewhere.

Till the world is wrought
To sympathy with hopes and fears it heeded not:

Like a high-born maiden
In a palace tower,
Soothing her love-laden
Soul in secret hour
With music sweet as love, which overflows her bower:

Like a glowworm golden
In a dell of dew,
Scattering unbeholden
Its aërial hue
Among the flowers and grass, which screen it from the view!

Like a rose embowered
In its own green leaves,
By warm winds deflowered,
Till the scent it gives
Makes faint with too much sweet those heavy-wingéd thieves:

Sound of vernal showers
On the twinkling grass,
Rain-awakened flowers,
All that ever was
Joyous, and clear, and fresh, thy music doth surpass:

Teach us, Sprite° or Bird, *spirit*
What sweet thoughts are thine:
I have never heard
Praise of love or wine
That panted forth a flood of rapture so divine.

Chorus Hymeneal,[9]
Or triumphal chant,
Matched with thine would be all
But an empty vaunt,
A thing wherein we feel there is some hidden want.

What objects are the fountains
Of thy happy strain?
What fields, or waves, or mountains?
What shapes of sky or plain?
What love of thine own kind? what ignorance of pain?

With thy clear keen joyance
Languor cannot be:
Shadow of annoyance
Never came near thee:
Thou lovest—but ne'er knew love's sad satiety.

Waking or asleep,
Thou of death must deem
Things more true and deep
Than we mortals dream,
Or how could thy notes flow in such a crystal stream?

9. As for a wedding.

We look before and after,
And pine for what is not:
Our sincerest laughter
With some pain is fraught;
Our sweetest songs are those that tell of saddest thought.

Yet if we could scorn
Hate, and pride, and fear;
If we were things born
Not to shed a tear,
I know not how thy joy we ever should come near.

Better than all measures
Of delightful sound,
Better than all treasures
That in books are found,
Thy skill to poet were, thou scorner of the ground!

Teach me half the gladness
That thy brain must know,
Such harmonious madness
From my lips would flow
The world should listen then—as I am listening now.

1820

Adonais[1]

AN ELEGY ON THE DEATH OF JOHN KEATS, AUTHOR OF ENDYMION, HYPERION, ETC.

'Αστὴρ πρὶν μὲν ἔλαμπες ἐνὶ ζωοῖσιν 'Εῷος·
νῦν δὲ θανὼν λάμπεις ''Εσπερος ἐν φθιμένοις.[2]

—PLATO

1

I weep for Adonais—he is dead!
Oh, weep for Adonais! though our tears
Thaw not the frost which binds so dear a head!
And thou, sad Hour, selected from all years
To mourn our loss, rouse thy obscure compeers,
And teach them thine own sorrow, say: with me
Died Adonais; till the Future dares
Forget the Past, his fate and fame shall be
An echo and a light unto eternity!

2

Where wert thou mighty Mother,[3] when he lay,
When thy Son lay, pierced by the shaft which flies
In darkness? where was lorn Urania
When Adonais died? With veiléd eyes,
'Mid listening Echoes, in her Paradise
She sate, while one, with soft enamored breath,
Rekindled all the fading melodies,
With which, like flowers that mock the corse° beneath, *corpse*
He had adorned and hid the coming bulk of death.

1. A name derived from *Adonis,* in Greek legend a young hunter beloved of Aphrodite (Venus) and killed by a wild boar. The root meaning of his name, *Adon,* is "the lord," and in the form *Adonai* appears in Hebrew scriptures as a synonym for *God.*

2. "Thou wert the morning star among the living,/Ere thy fair light had fled—/Now, having died, thou art as Hesperus, giving/New splendor to the dead" [Shelley's translation]; Venus is both Hesperus, the evening star, and also the morning star.

3. Urania, "heavenly one," Venus invoked as the Muse of noble poetry. Adonais is represented as her son.

3

Oh, weep for Adonais—he is dead!
Wake, melancholy Mother, wake and weep!
Yet wherefore? Quench within their burning bed
Thy fiery tears, and let thy loud heart keep
Like his, a mute and uncomplaining sleep;
For he is gone, where all things wise and fair
Descend:—oh, dream not that the amorous Deep
Will yet restore him to the vital air;
Death feeds on his mute voice, and laughs at our despair.

4

Most musical of mourners, weep again!
Lament anew, Urania!—He[4] died,
Who was the Sire of an immortal strain,
Blind, old, and lonely, when his country's pride,
The priest, the slave, and the liberticide,
Trampled and mocked with many a loathéd rite
Of lust and blood; he went, unterrified,
Into the gulf of death; but his clear Sprite° *spirit*
Yet reigns o'er earth; the third among the sons of light.[5]

5

Most musical of mourners, weep anew!
Not all to that bright station dared to climb;
And happier they their happiness who knew,
Whose tapers yet burn through that night of time
In which suns perished; others more sublime,
Struck by the envious wrath of man or God,
Have sunk, extinct in their refulgent prime;
And some yet live, treading the thorny road,
Which leads, through toil and hate, to Fame's serene abode.

6

But now, thy youngest, dearest one, has perished,
The nursling of thy widowhood, who grew,
Like a pale flower by some sad maiden cherished,
And fed with true-love tears, instead of dew;
Most musical of mourners, weep anew!
Thy extreme° hope, the loveliest and the last, *highest, latest*
The bloom, whose petals nipped before they blew
Died on the promise of the fruit, is waste;
The broken lily lies—the storm is overpast.

7

To that high Capital,[6] where kingly Death
Keeps his pale court in beauty and decay,
He came; and bought, with price of purest breath,
A grave among the eternal.—Come away!
Haste, while the vault of blue Italian day
Is yet his fitting charnel-roof! while still
He lies, as if in dewy sleep he lay;
Awake him not! surely he takes his fill
Of deep and liquid rest, forgetful of all ill.

8

He will awake no more, oh, never more!—
Within the twilight chamber spreads apace
The shadow of white Death, and at the door

4. Milton, who also invoked the aid of Urania (see *Paradise Lost,* I.6–16).
5. Rivaled as a poet by only two predecessors, Homer and Dante.
6. Rome, where Keats died.

Invisible Corruption waits to trace
His extreme way to her dim dwelling-place;
The eternal Hunger sits, but pity and awe
Soothe her pale rage, nor dares she to deface
So fair a prey, till darkness and the law
Of change, shall o'er his sleep the mortal curtain draw.

9

Oh, weep for Adonais!—The quick Dreams,
The passion-wingéd Ministers of thought,
Who were his flocks, whom near the living streams
Of his young spirit he fed, and whom he taught
The love which was its music, wander not—
Wander no more, from kindling brain to brain,
But droop there, whence they sprung; and mourn their lot
Round the cold heart, where, after their sweet pain,
They ne'er will gather strength, or find a home again.

10

And one with trembling hand clasps his cold head,
And fans him with her moonlight wings, and cries,
"Our love, our hope, our sorrow, is not dead;
See, on the silken fringe of his faint eyes,
Like dew upon a sleeping flower, there lies
A tear some Dream has loosened from his brain."
Lost Angel of a ruined Paradise!
She knew not 'twas her own; as with no stain
She faded, like a cloud which had outwept its rain.

11

One from a lucid urn of starry dew
Washed his light limbs as if embalming them;
Another clipped her profuse locks, and threw
The wreath upon him, like an anadem,° *garland*
Which frozen tears instead of pearls begem;
Another in her willful grief would break
Her bow and wingéd reeds, as if to stem
A greater loss with one which was more weak;
And dull the barbéd fire against his frozen cheek.

12

Another Splendor on his mouth alit,
That mouth, whence it was wont to draw the breath
Which gave it strength to pierce the guarded wit,[7]
And pass into the panting heart beneath
With lightning and with music: the damp death
Quenched its caress upon its icy lips;
And, as a dying meteor stains a wreath
Of moonlight vapor, which the cold night clips,° *envelops*
It flushed through his pale limbs, and passed to its eclipse.

13

And others came . . . Desires and Adorations,
Wingéd Persuasions and veiled Destinies,
Splendors, and Glooms, and glimmering Incarnations
Of hopes and fears, and twilight Phantasies;
And Sorrow, with her family of Sighs,
And Pleasure, blind with tears, led by the gleam
Of her own dying smile instead of eyes,
Came in slow pomp;—the moving pomp might seem
Like pageantry of mist on an autumnal stream.

7. The defensive analytical mind.

14

All he had loved, and molded into thought
From shape, and hue, and odor, and sweet sound,
Lamented Adonais. Morning sought
Her eastern watch-tower, and her hair unbound,
Wet with the tears which should adorn the ground,
Dimmed the aërial eyes that kindle day;
Afar the melancholy thunder moaned,
Pale Ocean in unquiet slumber lay,
And the wild Winds flew round, sobbing in their dismay.

15

Lost Echo[8] sits amid the voiceless mountains,
And feeds her grief with his remembered lay,
And will no more reply to winds or fountains,
Or amorous birds perched on the young green spray,
Or herdsman's horn, or bell at closing day;
Since she can mimic not his lips, more dear
Than those for whose disdain she pined away
Into a shadow of all sounds:—a drear
Murmur, between their songs, is all the woodmen hear.

16

Grief made the young Spring wild, and she threw down
Her kindling buds, as if she Autumn were,
Or they dead leaves; since her delight is flown
For whom should she have waked the sullen year?
To Phoebus was not Hyacinth[9] so dear,
Nor to himself Narcissus, as to both
Thou, Adonais; wan they stand and sere
Amid the faint companions of their youth,
With dew all turned to tears; odor, to sighing ruth.° *pity*

17

Thy spirit's sister, the lorn nightingale,
Mourns not her mate with such melodious pain;
Not so the eagle, who like thee could scale
Heaven, and could nourish in the sun's domain
Her mighty youth,[1] with morning, doth complain,
Soaring and screaming round her empty nest,
As Albion° wails for thee: the curse of Cain[2] *England*
Light on his head who[3] pierced thy innocent breast,
And scared the angel soul that was its earthly guest!

18

Ah, woe is me! Winter is come and gone,
But grief returns with the revolving year;
The airs and streams renew their joyous tone;
The ants, the bees, the swallows reappear;
Fresh leaves and flowers deck the dead Seasons' bier;
The amorous birds now pair in every brake,° *thicket*
And build their mossy homes in field and brere;° *briar*
And the green lizard, and the golden snake,
Like unimprisoned flames, out of their trance awake.

19

Through wood and stream and field and hill and Ocean,
A quickening life from the Earth's heart has burst

8. A nymph who loved Narcissus and who pined away into a mere voice when that youth fell in love with his own reflection in a pool.
9. Youth loved by Apollo ("Phoebus"), who killed him by accident.
1. In folklore an eagle could recapture its youth by soaring close to the sun.
2. God's curse upon Cain for having slain his brother Abel was that nothing should grow for him and that he should be homeless. (Genesis, iii.11–12.)
3. The anonymous critic whose venomous review of Keats's *Endymion* had hastened, Shelley believed, Keats's death.

As it has ever done, with change and motion,
From the great morning of the world when first
God dawned on Chaos; in its stream immersed
The lamps of Heaven flash with a softer light;
All baser things pant with life's sacred thirst;
Diffuse themselves; and spend in love's delight,
The beauty and the joy of their renewéd might.

20

The leprous corpse touched by this spirit tender
Exhales itself in flowers of gentle breath;
Like incarnations of the stars, when splendor
Is changed to fragrance, they illumine death
And mock the merry worm that wakes beneath;
Nought we know, dies. Shall that alone which knows
Be as a sword consumed before the sheath
By sightless[4] lightning?—the intense atom[5] glows
A moment, then is quenched in a most cold repose.

21

Alas! that all we loved of him should be,
But for our grief, as if it had not been.
And grief itself be mortal! Woe is me!
Whence are we, and why are we? of what scene
The actors or spectators? Great and mean
Meet massed in death, who lends what life must borrow.
As long as skies are blue, and fields are green,
Evening must usher night, night urge the morrow,
Month follow month with woe, and year wake year to sorrow.

22

He will awake no more, oh, never more!
"Wake thou," cried Misery, "childless Mother, rise
Out of thy sleep, and slake, in thy heart's core,
A wound more fierce than his with tears and sighs."
And all the Dreams that watched Urania's eyes,
And all the Echoes whom their sister's song
Had held in holy silence, cried, "Arise!"
Swift as a Thought by the snake Memory stung,
From her ambrosial rest the fading Splendor sprung.

23

She rose like an autumnal Night, that springs
Out of the East, and follows wild and drear
The golden Day, which, on eternal wings,
Even as a ghost abandoning a bier,
Has left the Earth a corpse. Sorrow and fear
So struck, so roused, so rapt Urania;
So saddened round her like an atmosphere
Of stormy mist; so swept her on her way
Even to the mournful place where Adonais lay.

24

Out of her secret Paradise she sped,
Through camps and cities rough with stone, and steel,
And human hearts, which to her aery tread
Yielding not, wounded the invisible
Palms of her tender feet where'er they fell:
And barbéd tongues, and thoughts more sharp than they,

4. Unseeing and unseen.
5. Indivisible and indestructible unit of anything that exists.

Rent the soft Form they never could repel,
Whose sacred blood, like the young tears of May,
Paved with eternal flowers that undeserving way.

25

In the death-chamber for a moment Death,
Shamed by the presence of that living Might,
Blushed to annihilation, and the breath
Revisited those lips, and life's pale light
Flashed through those limbs, so late her dear delight.
"Leave me not wild and drear and comfortless,
As silent lightning leaves the starless night!
Leave me not!" cried Urania: her distress
Roused Death: Death rose and smiled, and met her vain caress.

26

"Stay yet awhile! speak to me once again;
Kiss me, so long but as a kiss may live;
And in my heartless breast and burning brain
That word, that kiss, shall all thoughts else survive,
With food of saddest memory kept alive,
Now thou art dead, as if it were a part
Of thee, my Adonais! I would give
All that I am to be as thou now art,
But I am chained to Time, and cannot thence depart!

27

"O gentle child, beautiful as thou wert,
Why didst thou leave the trodden paths of men
Too soon, and with weak hands though mighty heart
Dare the unpastured dragon in his den?
Defenseless as thou wert, oh! where was then
Wisdom the mirrored shield, or scorn the spear?[6]
Or hadst thou waited the full cycle, when
Thy spirit should have filled its crescent sphere,
The monsters of life's waste had fled from thee like deer.

28

"The herded wolves, bold only to pursue;
The obscene ravens, clamorous o'er the dead;
The vultures, to the conqueror's banner true,
Who feed where Desolation first has fed,
And whose wings rain contagion;—how they[7] fled,
When like Apollo, from his golden bow,
The Pythian of the age[8] one arrow sped
And smiled!—The spoilers tempt no second blow,
They fawn on the proud feet that spurn them lying low.

29

"The sun comes forth, and many reptiles spawn;
He sets, and each ephemeral insect then
Is gathered into death without a dawn,
And the immortal stars awake again;
So is it in the world of living men:
A godlike mind soars forth, in its delight
Making earth bare and veiling heaven, and when
It sinks, the swarms that dimmed or shared its light
Leave to its kindred lamps the spirit's awful night."

6. An allusion to Perseus, who killed the monster Medusa, evading her gaze, which could turn him into stone, by using his shield as a mirror.

7. Critics, here characterized as beasts and birds of prey.

8. Byron, Shelley's friend, who attacked the critics in *English Bards and Scotch Reviewers;* here compared to Apollo the Pythian, who slew the monster Python near Delphi.

30

Thus ceased she: and the mountain shepherds came
Their garlands sere, their magic mantles rent;
The Pilgrim of Eternity,[9] whose fame
Over his living head like Heaven is bent,
An early but enduring monument,
Came, veiling all the lightnings of his song
In sorrow; from her wilds Ierne° sent *Ireland*
The sweetest lyrist of her saddest wrong,[1]
And love taught grief to fall like music from his tongue.

31

Midst others of less note, came one frail Form,[2]
A phantom among men; companionless
As the last cloud of an expiring storm,
Whose thunder is its knell; he, as I guess,
Had gazed on Nature's naked loveliness,
Actaeon-like,[3] and now he fled astray
With feeble steps o'er the world's wilderness,
And his own thoughts, along that rugged way,
Pursued, like raging hounds, their father and their prey.

32

A pardlike[4] Spirit beautiful and swift—
A Love in desolation masked;—a Power
Girt round with weakness;—it can scarce uplift
The weight of the superincumbent hour;
It is a dying lamp, a falling shower,
A breaking billow;—even whilst we speak
Is it not broken? On the withering flower
The killing sun smiles brightly: on a cheek
The life can burn in blood, even while the heart may break.

33

His head was bound with pansies overblown,
And faded violets, white, and pied,° and blue; *multicolored*
And a light spear topped with a cypress cone,
Round whose rude shaft dark ivy-tresses grew
Yet dripping with the forest's noonday dew,
Vibrated, as the ever-beating heart
Shook the weak hand that grasped it; of that crew
He came the last, neglected and apart;
A herd-abandoned deer, struck by the hunter's dart.

34

All stood aloof, and at his partial moan[5]
Smiled through their tears; well knew that gentle band
Who in another's fate now wept his own;
As in the accents of an unknown land,
He sung new sorrow; sad Urania scanned
The Stranger's mien, and murmured: "Who art thou?"
He answered not, but with a sudden hand
Made bare his branded and ensanguined brow,
Which was like Cain's or Christ's—oh! that it should be so!

35

What softer voice is hushed over the dead?
Athwart what brow is that dark mantle thrown?

9. Byron, as author of *Childe Harold's Pilgrimage.*
1. Thomas Moore (1779–1852), poet, author of *Irish Melodies.*
2. Shelley, as poet-mourner, here wearing emblems of the god Dionysus.
3. Actaeon, a young hunter, offended the goddess Diana by discovering her while she was bathing. She transformed him into a stag, and he was torn to pieces by his hounds.
4. Leopard-like; the leopard was sacred to Dionysus.
5. Expressing a bond of sympathy (partiality) toward Adonais.

What form leans sadly o'er the white death-bed,
In mockery° of monumental stone, *imitation*
The heavy heart heaving without a moan?
If it be He,[6] who, gentlest of the wise,
Taught, soothed, loved, honored the departed one;
Let me not vex, with inharmonious sighs,
The silence of that heart's accepted sacrifice.

36

Our Adonais has drunk poison—oh!
What deaf and viperous murderer could crown
Life's early cup with such a draught of woe?
The nameless worm[7] would now itself disown:
It felt, yet could escape the magic tone
Whose prelude held° all envy, hate and wrong, *held off*
But what was howling in one breast alone,
Silent with expectation of the song,
Whose master's hand is cold, whose silver lyre unstrung.

37

Live thou, whose infamy is not thy fame!
Live! fear no heavier chastisement from me,
Thou noteless blot on a remembered name!
But be thyself, and know thyself to be!
And ever at thy season be thou free
To spill the venom when thy fangs o'erflow:
Remorse and Self-contempt shall cling to thee;
Hot Shame shall burn upon thy secret brow,
And like a beaten hound tremble thou shalt—as now.

38

Nor let us weep that our delight is fled
Far from these carrion kites° that scream below; *scavenger hawks*
He wakes or sleeps with the enduring dead;
Thou canst not soar where he is sitting now.
Dust to the dust! but the pure spirit shall flow
Back to the burning fountain whence it came,
A portion of the Eternal, which must glow
Through time and change, unquenchably the same,
Whilst thy[8] cold embers choke the sordid hearth of shame.

39

Peace, peace! he is not dead, he doth not sleep—
He hath awakened from the dream of life—
'Tis we, who lost in stormy visions, keep
With phantoms an unprofitable strife,
And in mad trance strike with our spirit's knife
Invulnerable nothings.—*We* decay
Like corpses in a charnel; fear and grief
Convulse us and consume us day by day,
And cold hopes swarm like worms within our living clay.

40

He has outsoared the shadow of our night;
Envy and calumny and hate and pain,
And that unrest which men miscall delight,
Can touch him not and torture not again;
From the contagion of the world's slow stain
He is secure, and now can never mourn

6. Leigh Hunt (1784–1859), poet and critic, friend of Keats and Shelley.
7. Serpent; the anonymous reviewer (see line 152).
8. The reviewer's.

A heart grown cold, a head grown gray in vain;
Nor, when the spirit's self has ceased to burn,
With sparkless ashes load an unlamented urn.

41

He lives, he wakes—'tis Death is dead, not he;
Mourn not for Adonais.—Thou young Dawn,
Turn all thy dew to splendor, for from thee
The spirit thou lamentest is not gone;
Ye caverns and ye forests, cease to moan!
Cease ye faint flowers and fountains, and thou Air,
Which like a morning veil thy scarf hadst thrown
O'er the abandoned Earth, now leave it bare
Even to the joyous stars which smile on its despair!

42

He is made one with Nature: there is heard
His voice in all her music, from the moan
Of thunder, to the song of night's sweet bird;
He is a presence to be felt and known
In darkness and in light, from herb and stone,
Spreading itself where'er that Power may move
Which has withdrawn his being to its own;
Which wields the world with never wearied love,
Sustains it from beneath, and kindles it above.

43

He is a portion of the loveliness
Which once he made more lovely: he doth bear
His part, while the one Spirit's plastic° stress *formative*
Sweeps through the dull dense world, compelling there
All new successions to the forms they wear;
Torturing the unwilling dross° that checks its flight *coarse matter*
To its own likeness, as each mass may bear;
And bursting in its beauty and its might
From trees and beasts and men into the Heaven's light.

44

The splendors of the firmament of time
May be eclipsed, but are extinguished not;
Like stars to their appointed height they climb,
And death is a low mist which cannot blot
The brightness it may veil. When lofty thought
Lifts a young heart above its mortal lair,
And love and life contend in it, for what
Shall be its earthly doom, the dead live there
And move like winds of light on dark and stormy air.

45

The inheritors of unfulfilled renown
Rose from their thrones, built beyond mortal thought,
Far in the Unapparent. Chatterton[9]
Rose pale, his solemn agony had not
Yet faded from him; Sidney,[1] as he fought
And as he fell and as he lived and loved
Sublimely mild, a Spirit without spot,
Arose; and Lucan,[2] by his death approved:° *vindicated*
Oblivion as they rose shrank like a thing reproved.

9. Thomas Chatterton (1752–70), a gifted young poet who committed suicide.
1. Sir Philip Sidney (1554–1586), a poet, critic, courtier, and soldier, fatally wounded in battle.
2. Lucan, a young Roman poet, took his own life rather than die under sentence of the notorious emperor Nero, against whom he had conspired.

46

And many more, whose names on Earth are dark
But whose transmitted effluence cannot die
So long as fire outlives the parent spark,
Rose, robed in dazzling immortality.
"Thou art become as one of us," they cry,
"It was for thee yon kingless sphere has long
Swung blind in unascended majesty,
Silent alone amid an Heaven of Song.
Assume thy wingéd throne, thou Vesper of our throng!"

47

Who mourns for Adonais? Oh, come forth,
Fond wretch! and know thyself and him aright.
Clasp with thy panting soul the pendulous[3] Earth;
As from a center, dart thy spirit's light
Beyond all worlds, until its spacious might
Satiate the void circumference: then shrink
Even to a point within our day and night;
And keep thy heart light lest it make thee sink
When hope has kindled hope, and lured thee to the brink.

48

Or go to Rome, which is the sepulcher,
Oh, not of him, but of our joy: 'tis nought
That ages, empires, and religions there
Lie buried in the ravage they have wrought;
For such as he can lend—they borrow not
Glory from those who made the world their prey;
And he is gathered to the kings of thought
Who waged contention with their time's decay,
And of the past are all that cannot pass away.

49

Go thou to Rome,—at once the Paradise,
The grave, the city, and the wilderness;
And where its wrecks like shattered mountains rise,
And flowering weeds, and fragrant copses dress
The bones of Desolation's nakedness
Pass, till the Spirit of the spot shall lead
Thy footsteps to a slope of green access
Where, like an infant's smile, over the dead
A light of laughing flowers along the grass is spread,

50

And gray walls moulder round, on which dull Time
Feeds, like slow fire upon a hoary brand;
And one keen pyramid[4] with wedge sublime,
Pavilioning the dust of him who planned
This refuge for his memory, doth stand
Like flame transformed to marble; and beneath,
A field is spread, on which a newer band
Have pitched in Heaven's smile their camp of death,
Welcoming him we lose with scarce extinguished breath.

51

Here pause: these graves are all too young as yet
To have outgrown the sorrow which consigned
Its charge to each; and if the seal is set,

3. Floating poised in space.
4. Tomb of Gaius Cestius, an officer of ancient Rome, beside the Protestant cemetery where Keats and Shelley are buried.

Here, on one fountain of a mourning mind,
Break it not thou! too surely shalt thou find
Thine own well full, if thou returnest home,
Of tears and gall. From the world's bitter wind
Seek shelter in the shadow of the tomb.
What Adonais is, why fear we to become?

52

The One remains, the many change and pass;
Heaven's light forever shines, Earth's shadows fly;
Life, like a dome of many-colored glass,
Stains the white radiance of Eternity,
Until Death tramples it to fragments.—Die,
If thou wouldst be with that which thou dost seek!
Follow where all is fled!—Rome's azure sky,
Flowers, ruins, statues, music, words, are weak
The glory they transfuse with fitting truth to speak.

53

Why linger, why turn back, why shrink, my Heart?
Thy hopes are gone before: from all things here
They have departed; thou shouldst now depart!
A light is past from the revolving year,
And man, and woman; and what still is dear
Attracts to crush, repels to make thee wither.
The soft sky smiles,—the low wind whispers near:
'Tis Adonais calls! oh, hasten thither,
No more let life divide what Death can join together.

54

That Light whose smile kindles the Universe,
That Beauty in which all things work and move,
That Benediction which the eclipsing Curse
Of birth can quench not, that sustaining Love
Which through the web of being blindly wove
By man and beast and earth and air and sea,
Burns bright or dim, as each are mirrors of
The fire for which all thirst; now beams on me,
Consuming the last clouds of cold mortality.

55

The breath whose might I have invoked in song
Descends on me; my spirit's bark is driven,
Far from the shore, far from the trembling throng
Whose sails were never to the tempest given;
The massy earth and spherèd skies are riven!
I am borne darkly, fearfully, afar;
Whilst burning through the inmost veil of Heaven,
The soul of Adonais, like a star,
Beacons from the abode where the Eternal are.

1821

To Night

1

Swiftly walk o'er the western wave,
Spirit of Night!
Out of the misty eastern cave,
Where, all the long and lone daylight,
Thou wovest dreams of joy and fear,

Which make thee terrible and dear—
        Swift be thy flight!

2

Wrap thy form in a mantle gray,
        Star-inwrought!
Blind with thine hair the eyes of Day;
Kiss her until she be wearied out,
Then wander o'er city, and sea, and land,
Touching all with thine opiate wand—
        Come, long-sought!

3

When I rose and saw the dawn,
        I sighed for thee;
When light rode high, and the dew was gone,
And noon lay heavy on flower and tree,
And the weary Day turned to his rest,
Lingering like an unloved guest,
        I sighed for thee.

4

Thy brother Death came, and cried,
        "Wouldst thou me?"
Thy sweet child Sleep, the filmy-eyed,
Murmured like a noontide bee,
"Shall I nestle near thy side?
Wouldst thou me?"—And I replied,
        "No, not thee!"

5

Death will come when thou art dead,
        Soon, too soon—
Sleep will come when thou art fled;
Of neither would I ask the boon
I ask of thee, belovéd Night—
Swift be thine approaching flight,
        Come soon, soon!

1824

To Jane:[5] The Keen Stars Were Twinkling

1

  The keen stars were twinkling,
And the fair moon was rising among them,
    Dear Jane!
  The guitar was tinkling,
But the notes were not sweet till you sung them
    Again.

2

  As the moon's soft splendor
O'er the faint cold starlight of Heaven
    Is thrown,
  So your voice most tender
To the strings without soul had then given
    Its own.

3

  The stars will awaken,
Though the moon sleep a full hour later,
    Tonight;

5. Jane Williams and her husband Edward were intimate friends of Shelley's.

No leaf will be shaken
Whilst the dews of your melody scatter
Delight.

4

Though the sound overpowers,
Sing again, with your dear voice revealing
A tone
Of some world far from ours,
Where music and moonlight and feeling
Are one.

1822 1832

From Hellas:[6] *Two Choruses*

Worlds on Worlds

Worlds on worlds are rolling ever
From creation to decay,
Like the bubbles on a river
Sparkling, bursting, borne away.
But they[7] are still immortal
Who, through birth's orient portal
And death's dark chasm hurrying to and fro,
Clothe their unceasing flight
In the brief dust and light
Gathered around their chariots as they go;
New shapes they still may weave,
New gods, new laws receive,
Bright or dim are they as the robes they last
On Death's bare ribs had cast.

A power from the unknown God,[8]
A Promethean conqueror,[9] came;
Like a triumphal path he trod
The thorns of death and shame.
A mortal shape to him
Was like the vapor dim
Which the orient planet animates with light;
Hell, Sin, and Slavery came,
Like bloodhounds mild and tame,
Nor preyed, until their Lord had taken flight;
The moon of Mahomet[1]
Arose, and it shall set:
While blazoned as on Heaven's immortal noon
The cross leads generations on.

Swift as the radiant shapes of sleep
From one whose dreams are Paradise
Fly, when the fond wretch wakes to weep,
And Day peers forth with her blank eyes;
So fleet, so fain, so fair,

6. *Hellas,* an ancient name for Greece, is the title of a drama in which Shelley celebrates the contemporary Greek struggle for independence, which he saw as heralding the return of the legendary "Age of Saturn" or "Age of Gold," the first, best period of human history.
7. "The first stanza contrasts the immortality of the living and thinking beings which inhabit the planets, and to use a common and inadequate phrase, *clothe themselves in matter,* with the transience of the noblest manifestations of the external world" [Shelley's note].
8. At Athens St. Paul proclaimed the "unknown god," i.e., the One God of the Hebraic and Christian faiths (Acts xvii.22–28).
9. Christ; likened to the Greek Titan Prometheus, who befriended and suffered for mankind.
1. Crescent moon, symbol of Mohammedanism.

The Powers of earth and air
Fled from the folding-star[2] of Bethlehem:
Apollo, Pan, and Love,
And even Olympian Jove[3]
Grew weak, for killing Truth had glared on them;
Our hills and seas and streams,
Dispeopled of their dreams,
Their waters turned to blood, their dew to tears,
Wailed for the golden years.

1822

The World's Great Age

The world's great age begins anew,
The golden years return,
The earth doth like a snake[4] renew
Her winter weeds[5] outworn:
Heaven smiles, and faiths and empires gleam,
Like wrecks of a dissolving dream.

A brighter Hellas rears its mountains
From waves serener far;
A new Peneus[6] rolls his fountains
Against the morning star.
Where fairer Tempes[7] bloom, there sleep
Young Cyclads[8] on a sunnier deep.

A loftier Argo[9] cleaves the main,
Fraught with a later prize;
Another Orpheus[1] sings again,
And loves, and weeps, and dies.
A new Ulysses leaves once more
Calypso[2] for his native shore.

Oh, write no more the tale of Troy,
If earth Death's scroll must be!
Nor mix with Laian rage[3] the joy
Which dawns upon the free:
Although a subtler Sphinx renew
Riddles of death Thebes never knew.

Another Athens shall arise,
And to remoter time
Bequeath, like sunset to the skies,
The splendor of its prime;
And leave, if nought so bright may live,
All earth can take or Heaven can give.

2. Star that rises at the hour when sheep are brought to the fold at evening.
3. Gods worshipped in Greece until Christianity displaced them.
4. Shedding its skin after hibernation, a symbol of regeneration.
5. Clothes, especially mourning garments.
6. Greek river of legendary beauty.
7. Valley of the Peneus.
8. Or Cyclades, islands in the Aegean Sea.
9. In Greek legend, the first of seagoing vessels, on which Jason sailed to gain the "prize" (line 14) of the Golden Fleece.
1. Legendary Greek poet and musician of magical genius whose playing on the lyre caused his wife, Eurydice, to be released from the realm of the dead on condition that he would not look at her until they had reached the upper world. Breaking his pledge at the last moment, he lost her forever.
2. Island-nymph with whom Ulysses (Odysseus) lived for seven years during his return to Ithaca from the Trojan War.
3. Ignorant of his own identity, Oedipus in a rage killed King Laius of Thebes (in fact his father). Oedipus then delivered Thebes from the power of a sphinx by answering her riddles and won Jocasta (in fact his mother) as his wife and queen.

Saturn and Love their long repose
Shall burst, more bright and good
Than all who fell, than One who rose,
Than many unsubdued:[4]
Not gold, not blood, their altar dowers,
But votive tears and symbol flowers.

Oh, cease! must hate and death return?
Cease! must men kill and die?
Cease! drain not to its dregs the urn
Of bitter prophecy.
The world is weary of the past,
Oh, might it die or rest at last!

1822

JOHN CLARE
(1793–1864)

Badger

When midnight comes a host of dogs and men
Go out and track the badger to his den,
And put a sack within the hole, and lie
Till the old grunting badger passes by.
He comes and hears—they let the strongest loose.
The old fox hears the noise and drops the goose.
The poacher shoots and hurries from the cry,
And the old hare half wounded buzzes by.
They get a forkéd stick to bear him down
And clap the dogs and take him to the town,
And bait him all the day with many dogs,
And laugh and shout and fright the scampering hogs.
He runs along and bites at all he meets:
They shout and hollo down the noisy streets.

He turns about to face the loud uproar
And drives the rebels to their very door.
The frequent stone is hurled where'er they go;
When badgers fight, then everyone's a foe.
The dogs are clapped and urged to join the fray;
The badger turns and drives them all away.
Though scarcely half as big, demure and small,
He fights with dogs for hours and beats them all.
The heavy mastiff, savage in the fray,
Lies down and licks his feet and turns away.
The bulldog knows his match and waxes cold,
The badger grins and never leaves his hold.
He drives the crowd and follows at their heels
And bites them through—the drunkard swears and reels.

The frighted women take the boys away,
The blackguard laughs and hurries on the fray.

4. Saturn and Love are the restored deities of the "world's great age"; "all who fell" are the deities who "fell" when Christ arose from the dead; the "many unsubdued" are idols still worshipped throughout the world.

He tries to reach the woods, an awkward race,
But sticks and cudgels quickly stop the chase.
He turns again and drives the noisy crowd
And beats the many dogs in noises loud.
He drives away and beats them every one,
And then they loose them all and set them on.
He falls as dead and kicked by boys and men,
Then starts and grins and drives the crowd again;
Till kicked and torn and beaten out he lies
And leaves his hold and crackles, groans, and dies.

1835–37 1920

Farewell

Farewell to the bushy clump close to the river
And the flags where the butter-bump° hides in forever; *bittern*
Farewell to the weedy nook, hemmed in by waters;
Farewell to the miller's brook and his three bonny daughters;
Farewell to them all while in prison I lie—
In the prison a thrall sees naught but the sky.

Shut out are the green fields and birds in the bushes;
In the prison yard nothing builds, blackbirds or thrushes.
Farewell to the old mill and dash of the waters,
To the miller and, dearer still, to his three bonny daughters.

In the nook, the larger burdock grows near the green willow;
In the flood, round the moor-cock dashes under the billow;
To the old mill farewell, to the lock, pens, and waters,
To the miller himsel', and his three bonny daughters.

1842–64 1920

I Am

I am: yet what I am none cares or knows
My friends forsake me like a memory lost,
I am the self-consumer of my woes—
They rise and vanish in oblivious host,
Like shadows in love's frenzied, stifled throes—
And yet I am, and live—like vapors tossed

Into the nothingness of scorn and noise,
Into the living sea of waking dreams,
Where there is neither sense of life or joys,
But the vast shipwreck of my life's esteems;
Even the dearest, that I love the best,
Are strange—nay, rather stranger than the rest.

I long for scenes, where man hath never trod,
A place where woman never smiled or wept—
There to abide with my Creator, God,
And sleep as I in childhood sweetly slept,
Untroubling, and untroubled where I lie,
The grass below— above the vaulted sky.

1842–64 1865

JOHN KEATS
(1795–1821)

On First Looking into Chapman's Homer[1]

Much have I traveled in the realms of gold,
  And many goodly states and kingdoms seen;
  Round many western islands have I been
Which bards in fealty° to Apollo[2] hold. *allegiance*
Oft of one wide expanse had I been told
  That deep-browed Homer ruled as his demesne;° *domain*
  Yet did I never breathe its pure serene° *atmosphere*
Till I heard Chapman speak out loud and bold:
Then felt I like some watcher of the skies
  When a new planet swims into his ken;
Or like stout Cortez[3] when with eagle eyes
  He stared at the Pacific—and all his men
Looked at each other with a wild surmise—
  Silent, upon a peak in Darien.

1816

On Sitting Down to Read *King Lear* Once Again

O golden-tongued Romance with serene lute!
  Fair plumèd Siren!° Queen of far away! *enchantress*
  Leave melodizing on this wintry day,
Shut up thine olden pages, and be mute:
Adieu! for once again the fierce dispute
  Betwixt damnation and impassioned clay
  Must I burn through; once more humbly assay
The bitter-sweet of this Shakespearean fruit.
Chief Poet! and ye clouds of Albion,[4]
  Begetters of our deep eternal theme,
When through the old oak forest I am gone,
  Let me not wander in a barren dream,
But when I am consumèd in the fire,
Give me new Phoenix[5] wings to fly at my desire.

1818 1838

When I Have Fears

When I have fears that I may cease to be
  Before my pen has gleaned my teeming brain,
Before high-pilèd books, in charact'ry,° *written symbols*
  Hold like rich garners the full-ripened grain;
When I behold, upon the night's starred face,
  Huge cloudy symbols of a high romance,

1. Translations from Homer, in particular *Odyssey*, Book V., by George Chapman, a contemporary of Shakespeare's.
2. God of poetic inspiration.
3. Spanish conqueror of Mexico; in fact, Balboa, not Cortez, was the first European to see the Pacific, from Darien, in Panama.
4. Ancient name for England, especially referring to pre-Roman Britain, the era of King Lear.
5. Fabled Arabian bird that, after living for centuries, consumes itself in fire and is reborn.

And think that I may never live to trace
  Their shadows, with the magic hand of chance;
And when I feel, fair creature of an hour,
  That I shall never look upon thee more,
Never have relish in the faery° power — *magical*
  Of unreflecting love!—then on the shore
Of the wide world I stand alone, and think
Till Love and Fame to nothingness do sink.

1818 — 1848

To Homer[6]

Standing aloof in giant ignorance,[7]
  Of thee I hear and of the Cyclades,[8]
As one who sits ashore and longs perchance
  To visit dolphin-coral in deep seas.
So thou wast blind!—but then the veil was rent;
  For Jove[9] uncurtain'd Heaven to let thee live,
And Neptune made for thee a spumy tent,
  And Pan made sing for thee his forest-hive;
Aye, on the shores of darkness there is light,
  And precipices show untrodden green;
There is a budding morrow in midnight;
  There is a triple sight in blindness keen;
Such seeing hadst thou, as it once befel
To Dian,[1] Queen of Earth, and Heaven, and Hell.

1818? — 1848

The Eve of St. Agnes[2]

1

St. Agnes' Eve—Ah, bitter chill it was!
The owl, for all his feathers, was a-cold;
The hare limped trembling through the frozen grass,
And silent was the flock in woolly fold:
Numb were the Beadsman's[3] fingers, while he told
His rosary, and while his frosted breath,
Like pious incense from a censer old,
Seemed taking flight for heaven, without a death,
Past the sweet Virgin's picture, while his prayer he saith.

2

His prayer he saith, this patient, holy man;
Then takes his lamp, and riseth from his knees,
And back returneth, meager, barefoot, wan,
Along the chapel aisle by slow degrees:
The sculptured dead, on each side, seem to freeze,
Imprisoned in black, purgatorial rails:

6. By tradition, blind; here a symbol of poetic illumination.
7. Keats could not read Homer's Greek.
8. Islands near the Greek coast.
9. Jove, Neptune, and Pan: Homer's gods of heaven, sea, and land.
1. The "three-formed" goddess presiding in the moon, in forests, and the underworld.
2. January 20, proverbially the coldest winter night. St. Agnes, martyred in the 4th century A.D., is patroness of virgins. Traditionally, a maiden who observes the ritual of St. Agnes' Eve will see a vision of her husband-to-be.
3. From Middle English *bede,* meaning *prayer.* A needy dependent, paid a small stipend to pray regularly for his benefactor. "Rosary" (line 6): a string of beads on which a series of short prayers are counted ("told," line 5).

Knights, ladies, praying in dumb orat'ries,[4]
He passeth by; and his weak spirit fails
To think how they may ache in icy hoods and mails.

3

Northward he turneth through a little door,
And scarce three steps, ere Music's golden tongue
Flattered to tears this aged man and poor;
But no—already had his deathbell rung:
The joys of all his life were said and sung:
His was harsh penance on St. Agnes' Eve:
Another way he went, and soon among
Rough ashes sat he for his soul's reprieve,
And all night kept awake, for sinner's sake to grieve.

4

That ancient Beadsman heard the prelude soft;
And so it chanced, for many a door was wide,
From hurry to and fro. Soon, up aloft,
The silver, snarling trumpets 'gan to chide:
The level chambers, ready with their pride,
Were glowing to receive a thousand guests:
The carvéd angels, ever eager-eyed,
Stared, where upon their heads the cornice rests,
With hair blown back, and wings put crosswise on their breasts.

5

At length burst in the argent revelry,[5]
With plume, tiara, and all rich array,
Numerous as shadows haunting faerily
The brain, new stuffed, in youth, with triumphs gay
Of old romance. These let us wish away,
And turn, sole-thoughted, to one Lady there,
Whose heart had brooded, all that wintry day,
On love, and winged St. Agnes' saintly care,
As she had heard old dames full many times declare.

6

They told her how, upon St. Agnes' Eve,
Young virgins might have visions of delight,
And soft adorings from their loves receive
Upon the honeyed middle of the night,
If ceremonies due they did aright;
As, supperless to bed they must retire,
And couch supine their beauties, lily white;
Nor look behind, nor sideways, but require
Of Heaven with upward eyes for all that they desire.

7

Full of this whim was thoughtful Madeline:
The music, yearning like a God in pain,
She scarcely heard: her maiden eyes divine,
Fixed on the floor, saw many a sweeping train
Pass by—she heeded not at all: in vain
Came many a tiptoe, amorous cavalier,
And back retired; not cooled by high disdain;
But she saw not: her heart was otherwhere:
She sighed for Agnes' dreams, the sweetest of the year.

8

She danced along with vague, regardless eyes,
Anxious her lips, her breathing quick and short:

4. Small chapels in a larger one.

5. Brightly-dressed revelers.

The hallowed hour was near at hand: she sighs
Amid the timbrels,° and the thronged resort *hand drums*
Of whisperers in anger, or in sport;
'Mid looks of love, defiance, hate, and scorn,
Hoodwinked with faery fancy; all amort,[6]
Save to St. Agnes and her lambs unshorn,[7]
And all the bliss to be before tomorrow morn.

9

So, purposing each moment to retire,
She lingered still. Meantime, across the moors,
Had come young Porphyro, with heart on fire
For Madeline. Beside the portal doors,
Buttressed from moonlight,[8] stands he, and implores
All saints to give him sight of Madeline,
But for one moment in the tedious hours,
That he might gaze and worship all unseen;
Perchance speak, kneel, touch, kiss—in sooth such things have been.

10

He ventures in: let no buzzed whisper tell:
All eyes be muffled, or a hundred swords
Will storm his heart, Love's fev'rous citadel:
For him, those chambers held barbarian hordes,
Hyena foemen, and hot-blooded lords,
Whose very dogs would execrations howl
Against his lineage: not one breast affords
Him any mercy, in that mansion foul,
Save one old beldame,° weak in body and in soul. *old woman*

11

Ah, happy chance! the aged creature came,
Shuffling along with ivory-headed wand,
To where he stood, hid from the torch's flame,
Behind a broad hall-pillar, far beyond
The sound of merriment and chorus bland:° *harmonizing*
He startled her; but soon she knew his face,
And grasped his fingers in her palsied hand,
Saying, "Mercy, Porphyro! hie thee from this place;
They are all here tonight, the whole bloodthirsty race!

12

"Get hence! get hence! there's dwarfish Hildebrand;
He had a fever late, and in the fit
He curséd thee and thine, both house and land:
Then there's that old Lord Maurice, not a whit
More tame for his gray hairs—Alas me! flit!
Flit like a ghost away."—"Ah, Gossip[9] dear,
We're safe enough; here in this armchair sit,
And tell me how"—"Good Saints! not here, not here;
Follow me, child, or else these stones will be thy bier."

13

He followed through a lowly archéd way,
Brushing the cobwebs with his lofty plume,
And as she muttered "Well-a—well-a-day!"
He found him in a little moonlight room,
Pale, latticed, chill, and silent as a tomb.
"Now tell me where is Madeline," said he,

6. Dead; i.e., oblivious.
7. Symbolically associated with St. Agnes; new wool offered at the Mass commemorating the saint was later spun and woven by the nuns (lines 115–117).
8. I.e., concealed in dark shadows.
9. Old kinswoman or household retainer.

"O tell me, Angela, by the holy loom
Which none but secret sisterhood may see,
When they St. Agnes' wool are weaving piously."

14

"St Agnes! Ah! it is St. Agnes' Eve—
Yet men will murder upon holy days:
Thou must hold water in a witch's sieve,
And be liege lord of all the Elves and Fays,[1]
To venture so: it fills me with amaze
To see thee, Porphyro!—St. Agnes' Eve!
God's help! my lady fair the conjuror plays[2]
This very night: good angels her deceive!
But let me laugh awhile, I've mickle° time to grieve." *much*

15

Feebly she laugheth in the languid moon,
While Porphyro upon her face doth look,
Like puzzled urchin on an aged crone
Who keepeth closed a wondrous riddle-book,
As spectacled she sits in chimney nook.
But soon his eyes grew brilliant, when she told
His lady's purpose; and he scarce could brook° *check*
Tears, at the thought of those enchantments cold,
And Madeline asleep in lap of legends old.

16

Sudden a thought came like a full-blown rose,
Flushing his brow, and in his painéd heart
Made purple riot: then doth he propose
A stratagem, that makes the beldame start:
"A cruel man and impious thou art:
Sweet lady, let her pray, and sleep, and dream
Alone with her good angels, far apart
From wicked men like thee. Go, go!—I deem
Thou canst not surely be the same that thou didst seem."

17

"I will not harm her, by all saints I swear,"
Quoth Porphyro: "O may I ne'er find grace
When my weak voice shall whisper its last prayer,
If one of her soft ringlets I displace,
Or look with ruffian passion in her face:
Good Angela, believe me by these tears;
Or I will, even in a moment's space,
Awake, with horrid shout, my foemen's ears,
And beard them, though they be more fanged than wolves and bears."

18

"Ah! why wilt thou affright a feeble soul?
A poor, weak, palsy-stricken, churchyard thing,[3]
Whose passing bell[4] may ere the midnight toll;
Whose prayers for thee, each morn and evening,
Were never missed."—Thus plaining,° doth she bring *complaining*
A gentler speech from burning Porphyro;
So woeful and of such deep sorrowing,
That Angela gives promise she will do
Whatever he shall wish, betide her weal or woe.

1. I.e., to hold water in a sieve and to command elves and fairies ("Fays"), Porphyro would have to be a magician.
2. I.e., is trying magic spells.
3. I.e., soon to die.
4. Tolled when a person died ("passed away").

19

Which was, to lead him, in close secrecy,
Even to Madeline's chamber, and there hide
Him in a closet, of such privacy
That he might see her beauty unespied,
And win perhaps that night a peerless bride,
While legioned faeries paced the coverlet,
And pale enchantment held her sleepy-eyed.
Never on such a night have lovers met,
Since Merlin paid his Demon all the monstrous debt.[5]

20

"It shall be as thou wishest," said the Dame:
"All cates° and dainties shall be storéd there *delicacies*
Quickly on this feast[6] night: by the tambour frame[7]
Her own lute thou wilt see: no time to spare,
For I am slow and feeble, and scarce dare
On such a catering trust my dizzy head.
Wait here, my child, with patience; kneel in prayer
The while: Ah! thou must needs the lady wed,
Or may I never leave my grave among the dead."

21

So saying, she hobbled off with busy fear.
The lover's endless minutes slowly passed:
The dame returned, and whispered in his ear
To follow her; with aged eyes aghast
From fright of dim espial. Safe at last,
Through many a dusky gallery, they gain
The maiden's chamber, silken, hushed, and chaste;
Where Porphyro took covert, pleased amain.° *greatly*
His poor guide hurried back with agues in her brain.

22

Her falt'ring hand upon the balustrade,
Old Angela was feeling for the stair,
When Madeline, St. Agnes' charméd maid,
Rose, like a missioned spirit, unaware:
With silver taper's light, and pious care,
She turned, and down the aged gossip led
To a safe level matting. Now prepare,
Young Porphyro, for gazing on that bed;
She comes, she comes again, like ringdove frayed° and fled. *affrighted*

23

Out went the taper as she hurried in;
Its little smoke, in pallid moonshine, died:
She closed the door, she panted, all akin
To spirits of the air, and visions wide:
No uttered syllable, or, woe betide!
But to her heart, her heart was voluble,
Paining with eloquence her balmy side;
As though a tongueless nightingale should swell
Her throat in vain, and die, heart-stifled, in her dell.

24

A casement high and triple-arched there was,
All garlanded with carven imag'ries
Of fruits, and flowers, and bunches of knot-grass,
And diamonded with panes of quaint device,

5. Possibly alluding to the tale that Merlin, in Arthurian legend a great wizard, lies bound for ages by a spell that he gave to an evil woman to buy her love.
6. The festival, or Mass, honoring St. Agnes.
7. A circular embroidery frame.

Innumerable of stains and splendid dyes,
As are the tiger-moth's deep-damasked wings;
And in the midst, 'mong thousand heraldries,
And twilight saints, and dim emblazonings,
A shielded scutcheon blushed with blood of queens and kings.[8]

25

Full on this casement shone the wintry moon,
And threw warm gules[9] on Madeline's fair breast,
As down she knelt for heaven's grace and boon;° *gift*
Rose-bloom fell on her hands, together pressed,
And on her silver cross soft amethyst,
And on her hair a glory, like a saint:
She seemed a splendid angel, newly dressed,
Save wings, for heaven—Porphyro grew faint:
She knelt, so pure a thing, so free from mortal taint.

26

Anon his heart revives: her vespers done,
Of all its wreathéd pearls her hair she frees;
Unclasps her warméd jewels one by one;
Loosens her fragrant bodice; by degrees
Her rich attire creeps rustling to her knees:
Half-hidden, like a mermaid in sea-weed,
Pensive awhile she dreams awake, and sees,
In fancy, fair St. Agnes in her bed,
But dares not look behind, or all the charm is fled.

27

Soon, trembling in her soft and chilly nest,
In sort of wakeful swoon, perplexed she lay,
Until the poppied warmth of sleep oppressed
Her soothéd limbs, and soul fatigued away;
Flown, like a thought, until the morrow-day;
Blissfully havened both from joy and pain;
Clasped like a missal where swart Paynims[1] pray;
Blinded alike from sunshine and from rain,
As though a rose should shut, and be a bud again.

28

Stol'n to this paradise, and so entranced,
Porphyro gazed upon her empty dress,
And listened to her breathing, if it chanced
To wake into a slumberous tenderness;
Which when he heard, that minute did he bless,
And breathed himself: then from the closet crept,
Noiseless as fear in a wide wilderness,
And over the hushed carpet, silent, stepped,
And 'tween the curtains peeped, where, lo!—how fast she slept.

29

Then by the bedside, where the faded moon
Made a dim, silver twilight, soft he set
A table, and, half anguished, threw thereon
A cloth of woven crimson, gold, and jet—
O for some drowsy Morphean amulet![2]
The boisterous, midnight, festive clarion,
The kettledrum, and far-heard clarinet,
Affray his ears, though but in dying tone—
The hall door shuts again, and all the noise is gone.

8. A shield representing a coat of arms ("scutcheon") showed the red pigments ("blushed") indicating royal ancestry.
9. Heraldic red; here, in stained glass.
1. Dark pagans.
2. An object, such as an engraved stone, exerting the power of Morpheus, god of sleep.

30

And still she slept an azure-lidded sleep,
In blanchéd linen, smooth, and lavendered,
While he from forth the closet brought a heap
Of candied apple, quince, and plum, and gourd;
With jellies soother than the creamy curd,
And lucent syrups, tinct° with cinnamon; *tinctured*
Manna and dates, in argosy transferred
From Fez;[3] and spicéd dainties, every one,
From silken Samarcand to cedared Lebanon.[4]

31

These delicates he heaped with glowing hand
On golden dishes and in baskets bright
Of wreathéd silver: sumptuous they stand
In the retiréd quiet of the night,
Filling the chilly room with perfume light.—
"And now, my love, my seraph° fair, awake! *angel*
Thou art my heaven, and I thine eremite:[5]
Open thine eyes, for meek St. Agnes' sake,
Or I shall drowse beside thee, so my soul doth ache."

32

Thus whispering, his warm, unnervéd arm
Sank in her pillow. Shaded was her dream
By the dusk curtains: 'twas a midnight charm
Impossible to melt as icéd stream:
The lustrous salvers° in the moonlight gleam; *serving dishes*
Broad golden fringe upon the carpet lies:
It seemed he never, never could redeem
From such a steadfast spell his lady's eyes;
So mused awhile, entoiled in wooféd° fantasies. *enwoven*

33

Awakening up, he took her hollow lute—
Tumultuous—and, in chords that tenderest be,
He played an ancient ditty, long since mute,
In Provence called "*La belle dame sans merci*"[6]
Close to her ear touching the melody;
Wherewith disturbed, she uttered a soft moan:
He ceased—she panted quick—and suddenly
Her blue affrayéd eyes wide open shone:
Upon his knees he sank, pale as smooth-sculptured stone.

34

Her eyes were open, but she still beheld,
Now wide awake, the vision of her sleep:
There was a painful change, that nigh expelled
The blisses of her dream so pure and deep,
At which fair Madeline began to weep,
And moan forth witless words with many a sigh;
While still her gaze on Porphyro would keep,
Who knelt, with joinéd hands and piteous eye,
Fearing to move or speak, she looked so dreamingly.

35

"Ah, Porphyro!" said she, "but even now
Thy voice was at sweet tremble in mine ear,
Made tunable with every sweetest vow;
And those sad eyes were spiritual and clear:

3. Morocco.
4. Places associated with ancient luxury and wealth.
5. Hermit, religious devotee.
6. The lady beautiful but without mercy.

How changed thou art! how pallid, chill, and drear!
Give me that voice again, my Porphyro,
Those looks immortal, those complainings dear!
Oh leave me not in this eternal woe,
For if thou diest, my Love, I know not where to go."

36

Beyond a mortal man impassioned far
At these voluptuous accents, he arose,
Ethereal, flushed, and like a throbbing star
Seen mid the sapphire heaven's deep repose;
Into her dream he melted, as the rose
Blendeth its odor with the violet—
Solution sweet: meantime the frost-wind blows
Like Love's alarum° pattering the sharp sleet *signal, call to arms*
Against the windowpanes; St. Agnes' moon hath set.

37

'Tis dark: quick pattereth the flaw-blown° sleet: *gust-blown*
"This is no dream, my bride, my Madeline!"
'Tis dark: the icéd gusts still rave and beat:
"No dream, alas! alas! and woe is mine!
Porphyro will leave me here to fade and pine.—
Cruel! what traitor could thee hither bring?
I curse not, for my heart is lost in thine,
Though thou forsakest a deceivéd thing—
A dove forlorn and lost with sick unprunéd[7] wing."

38

"My Madeline! sweet dreamer! lovely bride!
Say, may I be for aye thy vassal blest?
Thy beauty's shield, heart-shaped and vermeil° dyed? *vermilion*
Ah, silver shrine, here will I take my rest
After so many hours of toil and quest,
A famished pilgrim—saved by miracle.
Though I have found, I will not rob thy nest
Saving of thy sweet self; if thou think'st well
To trust, fair Madeline, to no rude infidel.

39

"Hark! 'tis an elfin-storm from faery land,
Of haggard° seeming, but a boon indeed: *wild, ugly*
Arise—arise! the morning is at hand—
The bloated wassaillers° will never heed— *drunken revelers*
Let us away, my love, with happy speed;
There are no ears to hear, or eyes to see—
Drowned all in Rhenish and the sleepy mead:[8]
Awake! arise! my love, and fearless be,
For o'er the southern moors I have a home for thee."

40

She hurried at his words, beset with fears,
For there were sleeping dragons all around,
At glaring watch, perhaps, with ready spears—
Down the wide stairs a darkling way they found.—
In all the house was heard no human sound.
A chain-dropped lamp was flickering by each door;
The arras, rich with horseman, hawk, and hound,
Fluttered in the besieging wind's uproar;
And the long carpets rose along the gusty floor.

7. Unpreened; i.e., disarranged, rumpled.
8. Rhine wine, and fermented honey and water.

41

They glide, like phantoms, into the wide hall;
Like phantoms, to the iron porch, they glide;
Where lay the Porter, in uneasy sprawl,
With a huge empty flagon by his side:
The wakeful bloodhound rose, and shook his hide,
But his sagacious eye an inmate owns:° *recognizes*
By one, and one, the bolts full easy slide:
The chains lie silent on the footworn stones;
The key turns, and the door upon its hinges groans.

42

And they are gone: aye, ages long ago
These lovers fled away into the storm.
That night the Baron dreamt of many a woe,
And all his warrior-guests, with shade and form
Of witch, and demon, and large coffin-worm,
Were long be-nightmared. Angela the old
Died palsy-twitched, with meager face deform;
The Beadsman, after thousand aves[9] told,
For aye unsought for slept among his ashes cold.

1819 1820

On the Sonnet

If by dull rhymes our English must be chained,
And, like Andromeda,[1] the Sonnet sweet
Fettered, in spite of painéd loveliness;
Let us find out, if we must be constrained,
Sandals more interwoven and complete
To fit the naked foot of poesy;
Let us inspect the lyre, and weigh the stress
Of every chord, and see what may be gained
By ear industrious, and attention meet;
Misers of sound and syllable, no less
Than Midas[2] of his coinage, let us be
Jealous° of dead leaves in the bay-wreath crown;[3] *intolerant*
So, if we may not let the Muse be free,
She will be bound with garlands of her own.

1819 1848

La Belle Dame sans Merci[4]

O what can ail thee, Knight at arms,
Alone and palely loitering?
The sedge has withered from the Lake
And no birds sing!

O what can ail thee, Knight at arms,
So haggard, and so woebegone?

9. As in *Ave Maria* (Hail Mary), a salutation to the Virgin.
1. A beautiful princess chained naked to a rock as a sacrifice to a sea-monster; rescued by the hero Perseus.
2. A fabulously wealthy king who wished to turn all that he touched into gold; granted his wish by the gods, he quickly repented it.
3. Awarded as prize to a true poet.
4. The lady beautiful but without mercy. This is an earlier (and widely preferred) version of a poem first published in 1820.

The squirrel's granary is full
And the harvest's done.

I see a lily on thy brow
With anguish moist and fever dew,
And on thy cheeks a fading rose
Fast withereth too.

"I met a Lady in the Meads,° *meadows*
Full beautiful, a faery's child,
Her hair was long, her foot was light
And her eyes were wild.

"I made a Garland for her head,
And bracelets too, and fragrant Zone;° *girdle*
She looked at me as she did love
And made sweet moan.

"I set her on my pacing steed
And nothing else saw all day long,
For sidelong would she bend and sing
A faery's song.

"She found me roots of relish sweet,
And honey wild, and manna dew,
And sure in language strange she said
'I love thee true.'

"She took me to her elfin grot
And there she wept and sighed full sore,
And there I shut her wild wild eyes
With kisses four.

"And there she lulléd me asleep,
And there I dreamed, Ah Woe betide!
The latest° dream I ever dreamt *last*
On the cold hill side.

"I saw pale Kings, and Princes too,
Pale warriors, death-pale were they all;
They cried, 'La belle dame sans merci
Hath thee in thrall!'

"I saw their starved lips in the gloam
With horrid warning gapéd wide,
And I awoke, and found me here
On the cold hill's side.

"And this is why I sojourn here,
Alone and palely loitering;
Though the sedge is withered from the Lake
And no birds sing."

April 1819 1888

Ode to a Nightingale

1

My heart aches, and a drowsy numbness pains
My sense, as though of hemlock[5] I had drunk,
Or emptied some dull opiate to the drains
One minute past, and Lethe-wards[6] had sunk:
'Tis not through envy of thy happy lot,
But being too happy in thine happiness—
That thou, light-wingéd Dryad of the trees,
In some melodious plot
Of beechen green, and shadows numberless,
Singest of summer in full-throated ease.

2

O, for a draught of vintage! that hath been
Cooled a long age in the deep-delvéd earth,
Tasting of Flora[7] and the country green,
Dance, and Provençal song,[8] and sunburnt mirth!
O for a beaker full of the warm South,
Full of the true, the blushful Hippocrene,[9]
With beaded bubbles winking at the brim,
And purple-stainéd mouth;
That I might drink, and leave the world unseen,
And with thee fade away into the forest dim:

3

Fade far away, dissolve, and quite forget
What thou among the leaves hast never known,
The weariness, the fever, and the fret
Here, where men sit and hear each other groan;
Where palsy shakes a few, sad, last gray hairs,
Where youth grows pale, and specter-thin, and dies,
Where but to think is to be full of sorrow
And leaden-eyed despairs,
Where Beauty cannot keep her lustrous eyes,
Or new Love pine at them beyond tomorrow.

4

Away! away! for I will fly to thee,
Not charioted by Bacchus and his pards,[1]
But on the viewless° wings of Poesy, *invisible*
Though the dull brain perplexes and retards:
Already with thee! tender is the night,
And haply the Queen-Moon is on her throne,
Clustered around by all her starry Fays;° *fairies*
But here there is no light,
Save what from heaven is with the breezes blown
Through verdurous glooms and winding mossy ways.

5

I cannot see what flowers are at my feet,
Nor what soft incense hangs upon the boughs,
But, in embalméd° darkness, guess each sweet *perfumed*
Wherewith the seasonable month endows

5. Opiate made from a poisonous herb.
6. Towards the river Lethe, whose waters in Hades bring the dead forgetfulness.
7. Roman goddess of springtime and flowers.
8. Of the late-medieval troubadours of Provence, in southern France.
9. The fountain of the Muses (goddesses of poetry and the arts) on Mt. Helicon in Greece; its waters induce poetic inspiration.
1. "Bacchus": god of wine, often depicted in a chariot drawn by leopards ("pards").

The grass, the thicket, and the fruit tree wild;
White hawthorn, and the pastoral eglantine;[2]
Fast fading violets covered up in leaves;
And mid-May's eldest child,
The coming musk-rose, full of dewy wine,
The murmurous haunt of flies on summer eves.

6

Darkling° I listen; and for many a time *in darkness*
I have been half in love with easeful Death,
Called him soft names in many a musèd rhyme,
To take into the air my quiet breath;
Now more than ever seems it rich to die,
To cease upon the midnight with no pain,
While thou art pouring forth thy soul abroad
In such an ecstasy!
Still wouldst thou sing, and I have ears in vain—
To thy high requiem become a sod.

7

Thou wast not born for death, immortal Bird!
No hungry generations tread thee down;
The voice I hear this passing night was heard
In ancient days by emperor and clown:
Perhaps the selfsame song that found a path
Through the sad heart of Ruth,[3] when, sick for home,
She stood in tears amid the alien corn;
The same that ofttimes hath
Charmed magic casements, opening on the foam
Of perilous seas, in faery lands forlorn.

8

Forlorn! the very word is like a bell
To toll me back from thee to my sole self!
Adieu! the fancy cannot cheat so well
As she is famed to do, deceiving elf.
Adieu! adieu! thy plaintive anthem fades
Past the near meadows, over the still stream,
Up the hill side; and now 'tis buried deep
In the next valley-glades:
Was it a vision, or a waking dream?
Fled is that music:—Do I wake or sleep?

May 1819 1820

Ode on Melancholy

1

No, no, go not to Lethe,[4] neither twist
Wolfsbane, tight-rooted, for its poisonous wine;
Nor suffer thy pale forehead to be kissed
By nightshade,[5] ruby grape of Proserpine;[6]
Make not your rosary of yew-berries,[7]
Nor let the beetle, nor the death-moth be
Your mournful Psyche, nor the downy owl[8]

2. Sweetbrier; wood roses.
3. In the Old Testament, a woman of great loyalty and modesty who, as a stranger in Judah, won a husband while gleaning in the barley-fields ("the alien corn," line 67).
4. River whose waters in Hades bring forgetfulness to the dead.
5. "Nightshade" and "wolfsbane" are poisonous herbs from which sedatives and opiates were extracted.
6. Queen of Hades.
7. Symbols of mourning; often growing in cemeteries.
8. Beetles, moths, and owls have been traditionally associated with darkness, death and burial; "Psyche" means *Soul,* sometimes symbolized by a moth that escapes the mouth in sleep or at death.

A partner in your sorrow's mysteries;
For shade to shade will come too drowsily,
And drown the wakeful anguish of the soul.

2

But when the melancholy fit shall fall
Sudden from heaven like a weeping cloud,
That fosters the droop-headed flowers all,
And hides the green hill in an April shroud;
Then glut thy sorrow on a morning rose,
Or on the rainbow of the salt sand-wave,
Or on the wealth of globéd peonies;
Or if thy mistress some rich anger shows,
Imprison her soft hand, and let her rave,
And feed deep, deep upon her peerless eyes.

3

She[9] dwells with Beauty—Beauty that must die;
And Joy, whose hand is ever at his lips
Bidding adieu; and aching Pleasure nigh,
Turning to Poison while the bee-mouth sips:
Aye, in the very temple of Delight
Veiled Melancholy has her sov'reign shrine,
Though seen of none save him whose strenuous tongue
Can burst Joy's grape against his palate fine;[1]
His soul shall taste the sadness of her might,
And be among her cloudy trophies[2] hung.

May 1819 1820

Ode on a Grecian Urn

1

Thou still unravished bride of quietness,
Thou foster child of silence and slow time,
Sylvan historian, who canst thus express
A flowery tale more sweetly than our rhyme:
What leaf-fringed legend haunts about thy shape
Of deities or mortals, or of both,
In Tempe or the dales of Arcady?[3]
What men or gods are these? What maidens loath?
What mad pursuit? What struggle to escape?
What pipes and timbrels? What wild ecstasy?

2

Heard melodies are sweet, but those unheard
Are sweeter; therefore, ye soft pipes, play on;
Not to the sensual ear, but, more endeared,
Pipe to the spirit ditties of no tone:
Fair youth, beneath the trees, thou canst not leave
Thy song, nor ever can those trees be bare;
Bold Lover, never, never canst thou kiss,
Though winning near the goal—yet, do not grieve;
She cannot fade, though thou hast not thy bliss,
Forever wilt thou love, and she be fair!

3

Ah, happy, happy boughs! that cannot shed
Your leaves, nor ever bid the Spring adieu;

9. The goddess Melancholy.
1. Keen, subtle.
2. Symbols of victory, such as banners, hung in religious shrines.
3. Tempe and Arcady (or Arcadia), in Greece, are traditional symbols of perfect pastoral landscapes.

And, happy melodist, unwearièd,
Forever piping songs forever new;
More happy love! more happy, happy love!
Forever warm and still to be enjoyed,
Forever panting, and forever young;
All breathing human passion far above,
That leaves a heart high-sorrowful and cloyed,
A burning forehead, and a parching tongue.

4

Who are these coming to the sacrifice?
To what green altar, O mysterious priest,
Lead'st thou that heifer lowing at the skies,
And all her silken flanks with garlands dressed?
What little town by river or sea shore,
Or mountain-built with peaceful citadel,
Is emptied of this folk, this pious morn?
And, little town, thy streets forevermore
Will silent be; and not a soul to tell
Why thou art desolate, can e'er return.

5

O Attic[4] shape! Fair attitude! with brede° — *woven pattern*
Of marble men and maidens overwrought,
With forest branches and the trodden weed;
Thou, silent form, dost tease us out of thought
As doth eternity: Cold Pastoral!
When old age shall this generation waste,
Thou shalt remain, in midst of other woe
Than ours, a friend to man, to whom thou say'st,
"Beauty is truth, truth beauty,"[5]—that is all
Ye know on earth, and all ye need to know.

May 1819 — 1820

To Autumn

1

Season of mists and mellow fruitfulness,
Close bosom-friend of the maturing sun;
Conspiring with him how to load and bless
With fruit the vines that round the thatch-eaves run;
To bend with apples the mossed cottage-trees,
And fill all fruit with ripeness to the core;
To swell the gourd, and plump the hazel shells
With a sweet kernel; to set budding more,
And still more, later flowers for the bees,
Until they think warm days will never cease,
For Summer has o'er-brimmed their clammy cells.

2

Who hath not seen thee oft amid thy store?
Sometimes whoever seeks abroad may find
Thee sitting careless on a granary floor,
Thy hair soft-lifted by the winnowing wind;[6]
Or on a half-reaped furrow sound asleep,

4. Greek, especially Athenian.
5. The quotation marks around this phrase are absent from some other versions also having good authority. This discrepancy has led some readers to ascribe only this phrase to the voice of the Urn; others ascribe to the Urn the whole of the two concluding lines.
6. "Winnowing": blowing the grain clear of the lighter chaff.

Drowsed with the fume of poppies, while thy hook[7]
Spares the next swath and all its twinéd flowers:
And sometimes like a gleaner thou dost keep
Steady thy laden head across a brook;
Or by a cider-press, with patient look,
Thou watchest the last oozings hours by hours.

3

Where are the songs of Spring? Aye, where are they?
Think not of them, thou hast thy music too—
While barréd clouds bloom the soft-dying day,
And touch the stubble-plains with rosy hue;
Then in a wailful choir the small gnats mourn
Among the river sallows,° borne aloft *low-growing willows*
Or sinking as the light wind lives or dies;
And full-grown lambs loud bleat from hilly bourn;° *field*
Hedge crickets sing; and now with treble soft
The redbreast whistles from a garden-croft;[8]
And gathering swallows twitter in the skies.

September 19, 1819 1820

Bright Star

Bright star, would I were steadfast as thou art—
Not in lone splendor hung aloft the night
And watching, with eternal lids apart,
Like nature's patient, sleepless Eremite,° *hermit, devotee*
The moving waters at their priestlike task
Of pure ablution round earth's human shores,
Or gazing on the new soft fallen mask
Of snow upon the mountains and the moors—
No—yet still steadfast, still unchangeable,
Pillowed upon my fair love's ripening breast,
To feel forever its soft fall and swell,
Awake forever in a sweet unrest,
Still, still to hear her tender-taken breath,
And so live ever—or else swoon to death.

1819 1838

This Living Hand[9]

This living hand, now warm and capable
Of earnest grasping, would, if it were cold
And in the icy silence of the tomb,
So haunt thy days and chill thy dreaming nights
That thou wouldst wish thine own heart dry of blood
So in my veins red life might stream again,
And thou be conscience-calmed—see here it is—
I hold it towards you.

1819? 1898

7. Small curved blade for cutting grain; sickle.
8. Small field, as for a vegetable garden, near a house.
9. Written on a manuscript page of Keats's unfinished poem, *The Cap and Bells.*

RALPH WALDO EMERSON
(1803–1882)

Concord Hymn

SUNG AT THE COMPLETION OF THE BATTLE MONUMENT,[1] JULY 4, 1837

By the rude bridge that arched the flood,
Their flag to April's breeze unfurled,
Here once the embattled farmers stood
And fired the shot heard round the world.

The foe long since in silence slept;
Alike the conqueror silent sleeps;
And Time the ruined bridge has swept
Down the dark stream which seaward creeps.

On this green bank, by this soft stream,
We set to-day a votive stone;
That memory may their deed redeem,
When, like our sires, our sons are gone.

Spirit, that made those heroes dare
To die, and leave their children free,
Bid Time and Nature gently spare
The shaft we raise to them and thee.

1837, 1876

The Rhodora

ON BEING ASKED, WHENCE IS THE FLOWER?

In May, when sea-winds pierced our solitudes,
I found the fresh Rhodora in the woods,
Spreading its leafless blooms in a damp nook,
To please the desert and the sluggish brook.
The purple petals, fallen in the pool,
Made the black water with their beauty gay;
Here might the red-bird come his plumes to cool,
And court the flower that cheapens his array.
Rhodora! if the sages ask thee why
This charm is wasted on the earth and sky,
Tell them, dear, that if eyes were made for seeing,
Then Beauty is its own excuse for being:
Why thou wert there, O rival of the rose!
I never thought to ask, I never knew;
But, in my simple ignorance, suppose
The self-same Power that brought me there brought you.

1834 1839, 1847

1. Commemorating the battles of Lexington and Concord, April 19, 1775.

Hamatreya[2]

Bulkeley, Hunt, Willard, Hosmer, Meriam, Flint,[3]
Possessed the land which rendered to their toil
Hay, corn, roots, hemp, flax, apples, wool and wood.
Each of these landlords walked amidst his farm,
Saying, ' 'T is mine, my children's and my name's.
How sweet the west wind sounds in my own trees!
How graceful climb those shadows on my hill!
I fancy these pure waters and the flags° *water plants*
Know me, as does my dog: we sympathize;
And, I affirm, my actions smack of the soil.'

Where are these men? Asleep beneath their grounds:
And strangers, fond as they, their furrows plough.
Earth laughs in flowers, to see her boastful boys
Earth proud, proud of the earth which is not theirs;
Who steer the plough, but cannot steer their feet
Clear of the grave.
They added ridge to valley, brook to pond,
And sighed for all that bounded their domain;
'This suits me for a pasture, that's my park;
We must have clay, lime, gravel, granite-ledge,
And misty lowland, where to go for peat.
The land is well—lies fairly to the south.
'T is good, when you have crossed the sea and back,
To find the sitfast acres where you left them.'
Ah! the hot owner sees not Death, who adds
Him to his land, a lump of mould the more.
Hear what the Earth says:

Earth-song

Mine and yours;
Mine, not yours.
Earth endures;
Stars abide—
Shine down in the old sea;
Old are the shores;
But where are old men?
I who have seen much,
Such have I never seen.

The lawyer's deed
Ran sure,
In tail,[4]
To them, and to their heirs
Who shall succeed,
Without fail,
Forevermore.

Here is the land,
Shaggy with wood,
With its old valley,
Mound and flood.

2. A variant of the Hindu name *Maitreya*.
3. First settlers of Concord, Massachusetts.
4. I.e., entailed; to *entail* is to limit by legal means (usually a will) the inheritance of an estate to a specified line of heirs.

But the heritors?
Fled like the flood's foam.
The lawyer, and the laws,
And the kingdom,
Clean swept herefrom.

They called me theirs.
Who so controlled me;
Yet every one
Wished to stay, and is gone,
How am I theirs,
If they cannot hold me,
But I hold them?

When I heard the Earth-song,
I was no longer brave;
My avarice cooled
Like lust in the chill of the grave.

1847

Ode

INSCRIBED TO W. H. CHANNING[5]

Though loath to grieve
The evil time's sole patriot,
I cannot leave
My honied thought
For the priest's cant,
Or statesman's rant.

If I refuse
My study for their politique,
Which at the best is trick,
The angry Muse
Puts confusion in my brain.

But who is he that prates
Of the culture of mankind,
Of better arts and life?
Go, blindworm, go,
Behold the famous States
Harrying Mexico
With rifle and with knife![6]

Or who, with accent bolder,
Dare praise the freedom-loving mountaineer?
I found by thee, O rushing Contoocook![7]
And in thy valleys, Agiochook![8]
The jackals of the Negro-holder.

The God who made New Hampshire
Taunted the lofty land

5. Unitarian clergyman, transcendentalist, and activist in social causes, particularly the anti-slavery movement.
6. A reference to the war between the United States and Mexico (1846–48) chiefly over the question of the boundaries of Texas. To some Americans, the United States' position was immoral.
7. Part of the Merrimack River in New Hampshire.
8. The White Mountains of New Hampshire.

With little men;
Small bat and wren
House in the oak:
If earth-fire cleave
The upheaved land, and bury the folk,
The southern crocodile would grieve.
Virtue palters;° Right is hence; *hesitates, equivocates*
Freedom praised, but hid;
Funeral eloquence
Rattles the coffin-lid.

What boots thy zeal,
O glowing friend,
That would indignant rend
The northland from the south?
Wherefore? to what good end?
Boston Bay and Bunker Hill
Would serve things still;
Things are of the snake.

The horseman serves the horse,
The neatherd serves the neat,[9]
The merchant serves the purse,
The eater serves his meat;
'T is the day of the chattel,
Web to weave, and corn to grind;
Things are in the saddle,
And ride mankind.

There are two laws discrete,
Not reconciled,
Law for man, and law for things;
The last builds town and fleet,
But it runs wild,
And doth the man unking.

'T is fit the forest fall,
The steep be graded,
The mountain tunnelled,
The sand shaded,
The orchard planted,
The glebe tilled,
The prairie granted,
The steamer built.

Let man serve law for man;
Live for friendship, live for love,
For truth's and harmony's behoof;° *benefit*
The state may follow how it can,
As Olympus follows Jove.

  Yet do not I implore
The wrinkled shopman to my surrounding woods,
Nor bid the unwilling senator
Ask votes of thrushes in the solitudes.
Every one to his chosen work;
Foolish hands may mix and mar;

9. Archaic terms for *cowherd* and *cow*.

Wise and sure the issues are.
Round they roll till dark is light,
Sex to sex, and even to odd;
The over-god
Who marries Right to Might,
Who peoples, unpeoples,
He who exterminates
Races by stronger races,
Black by white faces,
Knows to bring honey
Out of the lion;[1]
Grafts gentlest scion
On pirate and Turk.

The Cossack eats Poland,[2]
Like stolen fruit;
Her last noble is ruined,
Her last poet mute:
Straight, into double band
The victors divide;
Half for freedom strike and stand;—
The astonished Muse finds thousands at her side.

1847

Brahma[3]

If the red slayer think he slays,
  Or if the slain think he is slain,
They know not well the subtle ways
  I keep, and pass, and turn again.

Far or forgot to me is near;
  Shadow and sunlight are the same;
The vanished gods to me appear;
  And one to me are shame and fame.

They reckon ill who leave me out;
  When me they fly, I am the wings;
I am the doubter and the doubt,
  And I the hymn the Brahmin sings.

The strong gods pine for my abode,
  And pine in vain the sacred Seven,[4]
But thou, meek lover of the good!
  Find me, and turn thy back on heaven.

1856 1857, 1867

Days

Daughters of Time, the hypocritic Days,
Muffled and dumb like barefoot dervishes,

1. The allusion in lines 83–87 is to Samson, who killed a lion and returned later to find the carcass filled with honey (Judges xiv.5–10).
2. Russian military despotism, established in Poland after the popular insurrections of 1830–31, was challenged by a new Polish uprising (lines 94–96) in 1846.
3. The supreme God of Hindu mythology and, in later theological developments, the divine reality itself, once thought to comprehend the entire universe which is the manifestation of that reality.
4. Perhaps the seven saints high in the Brahman hierarchy, but lesser than Brahma.

And marching single in an endless file,
Bring diadems and fagots in their hands.
To each they offer gifts after his will,
Bread, kingdom, stars, and sky that holds them all.

I, in my pleached garden,[5] watched the pomp,
Forgot my morning wishes, hastily
Took a few herbs and apples, and the Day
Turned and departed silent. I, too late,
Under her solemn fillet° saw the scorn. *hair band*

1857, 1867

ELIZABETH BARRETT BROWNING (1806–1861)

Sonnets from the Portuguese[1]

1

I thought once how Theocritus had sung[2]
Of the sweet years, the dear and wished-for years,
Who each one in a gracious hand appears
To bear a gift for mortals, old or young:
And, as I mused it in his antique tongue,
I saw, in gradual vision through my tears,
The sweet, sad years, the melancholy years,
Those of my own life, who by turns had flung
A shadow across me. Straightway I was 'ware,
So weeping, how a mystic Shape did move
Behind me, and drew me backward by the hair;[3]
And a voice said in mastery, while I strove,—
"Guess now who holds thee?"—"Death," I said. But, there,
The silver answer rang,—"Not Death, but Love."

43

How do I love thee? Let me count the ways.
I love thee to the depth and breadth and height
My soul can reach, when feeling out of sight
For the ends of Being and ideal Grace.
I love thee to the level of everyday's
Most quiet need, by sun and candle-light.
I love thee freely, as men strive for Right;
I love thee purely, as they turn from Praise.
I love thee with the passion put to use
In my old griefs, and with my childhood's faith.
I love thee with a love I seemed to lose
With my lost saints—I love thee with the breath,
Smiles, tears, of all my life!—and, if God choose,
I shall but love thee better after death.

1845–46 1850

5. To pleach is to entwine, plait, or arrange foliage artificially.

1. The "Sonnets from the Portuguese" were written between 1845, when Miss Barrett met Robert Browning, and 1846, when they were married. An earlier poem, "Catrina to Camoëns," in which Miss Barrett had assumed the persona of the girl who was loved by the sixteenth-century Portuguese poet Camoëns, suggested the lightly disguising title when the sonnets were published in 1850.

2. In Idyll XV of Theocritus, the Greek pastoral poet of the 3rd century B.C., a singer describes (lines 100–5) the Hours, who have brought Adonis back from the underworld, as "the dear soft-footed Hours, slowest of all the Blessed Ones; but their coming is always longed for, and they bring something for all men."

3. In Book I of the *Iliad*, just as Achilles is drawing his sword to raise it against his leader, Agamemnon, Pallas Athene, standing behind him and hence invisible to the others, catches him by his hair to warn him.

A Musical Instrument

What was he doing, the great god Pan,[4]
  Down in the reeds by the river?
Spreading ruin and scattering ban,[5]
Splashing and paddling with hoofs of a goat,
And breaking the golden lilies afloat
  With the dragonfly on the river.

He tore out a reed, the great god Pan,
  From the deep cool bed of the river;
The limpid water turbidly ran,
And the broken lilies a-dying lay,
And the dragonfly had fled away,
  Ere he brought it out of the river.

High on the shore sat the great god Pan
  While turbidly flowed the river;
And hacked and hewed as a great god can,
With his hard bleak steel at the patient reed,
Till there was not a sign of the leaf indeed
  To prove it fresh from the river.

He cut it short, did the great god Pan
  (How tall it stood in the river!),
Then drew the pith, like the heart of a man,
Steadily from the outside ring,
And notched the poor dry empty thing
  In holes, as he sat by the river.

"This is the way," laughed the great god Pan
  (Laughed while he sat by the river),
"The only way, since gods began
To make sweet music, they could succeed."
Then, dropping his mouth to a hole in the reed,
  He blew in power by the river.

Sweet, sweet, sweet, O Pan!
  Piercing sweet by the river!
Blinding sweet, O great god Pan!
The sun on the hill forgot to die,
And the lilies revived, and the dragonfly
  Came back to dream on the river.

Yet half a beast is the great god Pan,
  To laugh as he sits by the river,
Making a poet out of a man;
The true gods sigh for the cost and pain—
For the reed which grows nevermore again
  As a reed with the reeds in the river.

1860 1862

4. In Greek mythology, an Arcadian god, in shape half goat, half human, son of Hermes; his function was to make the flocks fertile; he is also musical, his instrument the reed flute, and later pastoral poets made him the patron of their art. One of his loves was the nymph Syrinx; trying to escape him, she sought help from the river-nymphs, who turned her into a reed-bed: and from a reed Pan made his flute.

5. Baleful influence.

HENRY WADSWORTH LONGFELLOW (1807–1882)

Mezzo Cammin[1]

WRITTEN AT BOPPARD ON THE RHINE AUGUST 25, 1842, JUST BEFORE LEAVING FOR HOME

Half of my life is gone, and I have let
The years slip from me and have not fulfilled
The aspiration of my youth, to build
Some tower of song with lofty parapet.
Not indolence, nor pleasure, nor the fret
Of restless passions that would not be stilled,
But sorrow, and care that almost killed,[2]
Kept me from what I may accomplish yet;
Though, halfway up the hill, I see the Past
Lying beneath me with its sounds and sights,
A city in the twilight dim and vast,
With smoking roofs, soft bells, and gleaming lights,
And hear above me on the autumnal blast
The cataract of Death far thundering from the heights.

1842 1846

The Jewish Cemetery at Newport

How strange it seems! These Hebrews in their graves,
Close by the street of this fair seaport town,
Silent beside the never-silent waves,
At rest in all this moving up and down!

The trees are white with dust, that o'er their sleep
Wave their broad curtains in the southwind's breath,
While underneath these leafy tents they keep
The long, mysterious Exodus[3] of Death.

And these sepulchral stones, so old and brown,
That pave with level flags their burial-place,
Seem like the tablets of the Law, thrown down
And broken by Moses at the mountain's base.[4]

The very names recorded here are strange,
Of foreign accent, and of different climes;
Alvares and Rivera[5] interchange
With Abraham and Jacob of old times.

"Blessed be God! for he created Death!"
The mourners said, "and Death is rest and peace;"
Then added, in the certainty of faith,
"And giveth Life that nevermore shall cease."

1. A phrase from the first line of Dante's *Divina Commedia: "Nel mezzo del cammin di nostra vita"* (midway upon the journey of our life).
2. Probably an allusion to the death of Longfellow's wife in 1835.
3. The Exodus is the flight of Moses and the Israelites from Egypt.
4. Moses, angered by the disobedience of the Israelites, broke the tablets of the Law which had been given them.
5. Many of the early Jewish families in New England were from Spain and Portugal.

Closed are the portals of their Synagogue,
No Psalms of David now the silence break,
No Rabbi reads the ancient Decalogue° *Ten Commandments*
In the grand dialect the Prophets spake.

Gone are the living, but the dead remain,
And not neglected; for a hand unseen,
Scattering its bounty, like a summer rain,
Still keeps their graves and their remembrance green.

How came they here? What burst of Christian hate,
What persecution, merciless and blind,
Drove o'er the sea—that desert desolate—
These Ishmaels and Hagars of mankind?[6]

They lived in narrow streets and lanes obscure,
Ghetto and Judenstrass,[7] in mirk and mire;
Taught in the school of patience to endure
The life of anguish and the death of fire.

All their lives long, with the unleavened bread
And bitter herbs of exile and its fears,
The wasting famine of the heart they fed,
And slaked its thirst with marah[8] of their tears.

Anathema maranatha![9] was the cry
That rang from town to town, from street to street;
At every gate the accursed Mordecai[1]
Was mocked and jeered, and spurned by Christian feet.

Pride and humiliation hand in hand
Walked with them through the world where'er they went;
Trampled and beaten were they as the sand,
And yet unshaken as the continent.

For in the background figures vague and vast
Of patriarchs and of prophets rose sublime,
And all the great traditions of the Past
They saw reflected in the coming time.

And thus forever with reverted look
The mystic volume of the world they read,
Spelling it backward, like a Hebrew book,
Till life became a Legend of the Dead.

But ah! what once has been shall be no more!
The groaning earth in travail and in pain
Brings forth its races, but does not restore,
And the dead nations never rise again.

1852 1854, 1858

6. Hagar, concubine of Abraham, wandered in the desert with Ishmael, her son by Abraham, after she was sent away by Abraham and Sarah (see Genesis xxi.9–21).
7. German for "Street of Jews."
8. The Hebrew word for "bitter" or "bitterness"; salt water (symbolizing tears), unleavened bread, and bitter herbs are all part of the Passover meal.
9. A Greek-Aramaic phrase signifying a terrible curse, applied specifically (as in I Corinthians xvi.22) to the Jews.
1. A Jew whose foster daughter, Esther, became the queen of Ahasuerus (Xerxes), king of Persia. When Haman, Ahasuerus' favored advisor, sought to destroy Mordecai and the Jews, Mordecai stood at the king's gate crying out against the persecution. See Esther iii.

EDWARD FITZGERALD (1809–1883)

The Rubáiyát of Omar Khayyám of Naishápúr[1]

1

Wake! For the Sun, who scattered into flight
The Stars before him from the Field of Night,
Drives Night along with them from Heav'n, and strikes
The Sultán's Turret with a Shaft of Light.

2

Before the phantom of False morning died,
Methought a Voice within the Tavern cried,
"When all the Temple is prepared within,
"Why nods the drowsy Worshipper outside?"

3

And, as the Cock crew, those who stood before
The Tavern shouted—"Open then the Door!
"You know how little while we have to stay,
"And, once departed, may return no more."

4

Now the New Year[2] reviving old Desires,
The thoughtful Soul to Solitude retires,
Where the WHITE HAND OF MOSES on the Bough
Puts out, and Jesus from the Ground suspires.[3]

5

Irám[4] indeed is gone with all his Rose,
And Jamshýd's Sev'n-ringed Cup[5] where no one knows;
But still a Ruby kindles in the Vine,
And many a Garden by the Water blows.

6

And David's lips are lockt; but in divine
High-piping Pehleví,[6] with "Wine! Wine! Wine!
"Red Wine!"—the Nightingale cries to the Rose
That sallow cheek of hers to incarnadine.

7

Come, fill the Cup, and in the fire of Spring
Your Winter-garment of Repentance fling:
The Bird of Time has but a little way
To flutter—and the Bird is on the Wing.

8

Whether at Naishápúr or Babylon,
Whether the Cup with sweet or bitter run,

1. Omar Khayyám, Persian poet, mathematician, and astronomer (ca. 1050–1132?), lived at Nishapur, in the province of Khurasan. FitzGerald translated his epigrammatic quatrains (*Rubáiyát*, plural of *ruba'i*, quatrain) which he first published in 1859; in three subsequent editions (the fourth edition is printed here) FitzGerald made many alterations of detail, arrangement, and number of stanzas.
2. "Beginning with the Vernal Equinox, it must be remembered" [FitzGerald's note].
3. The blossoming of trees is compared to the whiteness of Moses' hand as it is described in Exodus iv.6, and the sweetness of flowers to the sweetness of the breath of Jesus.
4. "A royal Garden now sunk somewhere in the Sands of Arabia" [FitzGerald's note].
5. In Persian mythology, Jamshýd was a king of the peris (celestial beings), who, because he had boasted of his immortality, was compelled to live on earth in human form for 700 years, becoming one of the kings of Persia. His cup, the invention of Kai-Kosru (line 38), another Persian king, great-grandson of Kai-Kobad (line 36), was decorated with signs enabling its possessor to foretell the future.
6. The ancient literary language of Persia.

The Wine of Life keeps oozing drop by drop,
The Leaves of Life keep falling one by one.

9

Each Morn a thousand Roses brings, you say;
Yes, but where leaves the Rose of Yesterday?
And this first Summer month that brings the Rose
Shall take Jamshýd and Kaikobád away.

10

Well, let it take them! What have we to do
With Kaikobád the Great, or Kaikhosrú?
Let Zál and Rustum[7] bluster as they will,
Or Hátim[8] call to Supper—heed not you.

11

With me along the strip of Herbage strown
That just divides the desert from the sown,
Where name of Slave and Sultán is forgot—
And Peace to Mahmúd[9] on his golden Throne!

12

A Book of Verses underneath the Bough,
A Jug of Wine, a Loaf of Bread—and Thou
Beside me singing in the Wilderness—
Oh, Wilderness were Paradise enow!

13

Some for the Glories of This World; and some
Sigh for the Prophet's[1] Paradise to come;
Ah, take the Cash, and let the Credit go,
Nor heed the rumble of a distant Drum!

14

Look to the blowing Rose about us—"Lo,
"Laughing," she says, "into the world I blow,
"At once the silken tassel of my Purse
"Tear, and its Treasure on the Garden throw."

15

And those who husbanded the Golden grain,
And those who flung it to the winds like Rain,
Alike to no such aureate Earth are turned
As, buried once, Men want dug up again.

16

The Worldly Hope men set their Hearts upon
Turns Ashes—or it prospers; and anon,
Like Snow upon the Desert's dusty Face,
Lighting a little hour or two—is gone.

17

Think, in this battered Caravanserai° *inn*
Whose Portals are alternate Night and Day,
How Sultán after Sultán with his Pomp
Abode his destined Hour, and went his way.

18

They say the Lion and the Lizard keep
The Courts where Jamshýd gloried and drank deep:

7. "The 'Hercules' of Persia, and Zál his Father" [FitzGerald's note].
8. Hátim Tai: a Persian chieftain, an archetype of oriental hospitality.
9. Sultan Máhmúd of Ghazni, in Afghanistan (971–1031), renowned both as ruler and as the conqueror of India.
1. I.e., Mohammed's.

And Bahrám,[2] that great Hunter—the Wild Ass
Stamps o'er his Head, but cannot break his Sleep.

19

I sometimes think that never blows so red
The Rose as where some buried Caesar bled;
That every Hyacinth the Garden wears
Dropt in her Lap from some once lovely Head.

20

And this reviving Herb whose tender Green
Fledges the river-lip on which we lean—
Ah, lean upon it lightly! for who knows
From what once lovely Lip it springs unseen!

21

Ah, my Belovéd, fill the Cup that clears
TODAY of past Regrets and future Fears:
Tomorrow!—Why, Tomorrow I may be
Myself with Yesterday's Sev'n thousand Years.

22

For some we loved, the loveliest and the best
That from his Vintage rolling Time hath prest,
Have drunk their Cup a Round or two before,
And one by one crept silently to rest.

23

And we, that make merry in the Room
They left, and Summer dresses in new bloom,
Ourselves must we beneath the Couch of Earth
Descend—ourselves to make a Couch—for whom?

24

Ah, make the most of what we yet may spend,
Before we too into the Dust descend;
Dust into Dust, and under Dust to lie,
Sans Wine, sans Song, sans Singer, and sans End!

25

Alike for those who for TODAY prepare,
And those that after some TOMORROW stare,
A Muezzín[3] from the Tower of Darkness cries,
"Fools! your Reward is neither Here nor There."

26

Why, all the Saints and Sages who discussed
Of the Two Worlds so wisely—they are thrust
Like foolish Prophets forth; their Words to Scorn
Are scattered, and their Mouths are stopt with Dust.

27

Myself when young did eagerly frequent
Doctor and Saint, and heard great argument
About it and about: but evermore
Came out by the same door where in I went.

28

With them the seed of Wisdom did I sow,
And with mine own hand wrought to make it grow;
And this was all the Harvest that I reaped—
"I came like Water, and like Wind I go."

29

Into this Universe, and *Why* not knowing
Nor *Whence*, like Water willy-nilly flowing;

2. A Sassanian king who, according to legend, met his death while hunting the wild ass.

3. The crier who calls the hours of prayer from tower or minaret.

And out of it, as Wind along the Waste,
I know not *Whither,* willy-nilly blowing.

30

What, without asking, hither hurried *Whence?*
And, without asking, *Whither* hurried hence!
Oh, many a Cup of this forbidden Wine[4]
Must drown the memory of that insolence!

31

Up from Earth's Center through the Seventh Gate
I rose, and on the Throne of Saturn[5] sate,
And many a Knot unraveled by the Road;
But not the Master-knot of Human Fate.

32

There was the Door to which I found no Key;
There was the Veil through which I might not see:
Some little talk awhile of Me and Thee
There was—and then no more of Thee and Me.

33

Earth could not answer; nor the Seas that mourn
In flowing Purple, of their Lord forlorn;
Nor rolling Heaven, with all his Signs revealed
And hidden by the sleeve of Night and Morn.

34

Then of the Thee in Me who works behind
The Veil, I lifted up my hands to find
A lamp amid the Darkness; and I heard,
As from Without—"The Me within Thee blind!"

35

Then to the Lip of this poor earthen Urn
I leaned, the Secret of my Life to learn:
And Lip to Lip it murmured—"While you live,
"Drink! for, once dead, you never shall return."

36

I think the Vessel, that with fugitive
Articulation answered, once did live,
And drink; and Ah! the passive Lip I kissed,
How many Kisses might it take—and give!

37

For I remember stopping by the way
To watch a Potter thumping his wet Clay:
And with its all-obliterated Tongue
It murmured—"Gently, Brother, gently, pray!"

38

And has not such a Story from of Old
Down Man's successive generations rolled
Of such a clod of saturated Earth
Cast by the Maker into Human mold?

39

And not a drop that from our Cups we throw
For Earth to drink of, but may steal below
To quench the fire of Anguish in some Eye
There hidden—far beneath, and long ago.

40

As then the Tulip for her morning sup
Of Heav'nly Vintage from the soil looks up,

4. Alcohol is forbidden to Mohammedans.
5. "Lord of the Seventh Heaven" [FitzGerald's note]. In ancient astronomy, Saturn was the most remote of the seven known planets; hence, Omar had reached the bounds of astronomical knowledge.

Do you devoutly do the like, till Heav'n
To Earth invert you—like an empty Cup.

41

Perplext no more with Human or Divine,
Tomorrow's tangle to the winds resign,
And lose your fingers in the tresses of
The Cypress-slender Minister of Wine.[6]

42

And if the Wine you drink, the Lip you press,
End in what All begins and ends in—Yes;
Think then you are TODAY what YESTERDAY
You were—TOMORROW you shall not be less.

43

So when that Angel of the darker Drink
At last shall find you by the river-brink,
And, offering his Cup, invite your Soul
Forth to your Lips to quaff—you shall not shrink.

44

Why, if the Soul can fling the Dust aside,
And naked on the Air of Heaven ride,
Were't not a Shame—were't not a Shame for him
In this clay carcase crippled to abide?

45

'Tis but a Tent where takes his one day's rest
A Sultán to the realm of Death addrest;
The Sultán rises, and the dark Ferrásh[7]
Strikes, and prepares it for another Guest.

46

And fear not lest Existence closing your
Account, and mine, should know the like no more;
The Eternal Sákí° from that Bowl has poured *cup-bearer*
Millions of Bubbles like us, and will pour.

47

When You and I behind the Veil are past,
Oh, but the long, long while the World shall last,
Which of our Coming and Departure heeds
As the Sea's self should heed a pebble-cast.

48

A Moment's Halt—a momentary taste
Of BEING from the Well amid the Waste—
And Lo!—the phantom Caravan has reached
The NOTHING it set out from—Oh, make haste!

49

Would you that spangle of Existence spend
About THE SECRET—quick about it, Friend!
A Hair perhaps divides the False and True—
And upon what, prithee, may life depend?

50

A Hair perhaps divides the False and True;
Yes; and a single Alif[8] were the clue—
Could you but find it—to the Treasure-house,
And peradventure to THE MASTER too;

51

Whose secret Presence, through Creation's veins
Running Quicksilver-like eludes your pains;

6. The maidservant who pours the wine.
7. The servant charged with setting up and striking the tent.
8. First letter of Arabic alphabet, consisting of a single vertical stroke.

Taking all shapes from Máh to Máhi;[9] and
They change and perish all—but He remains;

52

A moment guessed—then back behind the Fold
Immerst of Darkness round the Drama rolled
Which, for the Pastime of Eternity,
He doth Himself contrive, enact, behold.

53

But if in vain, down on the stubborn floor
Of Earth, and up to Heav'n's unopening Door,
You gaze Today, while You are You—how then
Tomorrow, You when shall be You no more?

54

Waste not your Hour, nor in the vain pursuit
Of This and That endeavor and dispute;
Better be jocund with the fruitful Grape
Than sadden after none, or bitter, Fruit.

55

You know, my Friends, with what a brave Carouse
I made a Second Marriage in my house;
Divorced old barren Reason from my Bed,
And took the Daughter of the Vine to Spouse.

56

For "Is" and "Is-not" though with Rule and Line
And "Up-and-down" by Logic I define,
Of all that one should care to fathom, I
Was never deep in anything but—Wine.

57

Ah, but my Computations, People say,
Reduced the Year to better reckoning?[1]—Nay,
'Twas only striking from the Calendar
Unborn Tomorrow, and dead Yesterday.

58

And lately, by the Tavern Door agape,
Came shining through the Dusk an Angel Shape
Bearing a Vessel on his Shoulder; and
He bid me taste of it; and 'twas—the Grape!

59

The Grape that can with Logic absolute
The Two-and-Seventy jarring Sects[2] confute:
The sovereign Alchemist that in a trice
Life's leaden metal into Gold transmute:

60

The mighty Mahmúd, Allah-breathing Lord,[3]
That all the misbelieving and black Horde
Of Fears and Sorrows that infest the Soul
Scatters before him with his whirlwind Sword.

61

Why, be this Juice the growth of God, who dare
Blaspheme the twisted tendril as a Snare?
A Blessing, we should use it, should we not?
And if a Curse—why, then, Who set it there?

62

I must abjure the Balm of Life, I must,
Scared by some After-reckoning ta'en on trust,

9. From lowest to highest.
1. Omar was one of the learned men who had been charged with reforming the calendar.
2. "The 72 sects into which Islamism so soon split" [FitzGerald's note].
3. "This alludes to Máhmúd's Conquest of India and its swarthy Idolators" [FitzGerald's note].

Or lured with Hope of some Diviner Drink,
To fill the Cup—when crumbled into Dust!

63

Oh threats of Hell and Hopes of Paradise!
One thing at least is certain—*This* Life flies;
One thing is certain and the rest is Lies;
The Flower that once has blown for ever dies.

64

Strange, is it not? that of the myriads who
Before us passed the door of Darkness through,
Not one returns to tell us of the Road,
Which to discover we must travel too.

65

The Revelations of Devout and Learned
Who rose before us, and as Prophets burned,
Are all but Stories, which, awoke from Sleep
They told their comrades, and to Sleep returned.

66

I sent my Soul through the Invisible,
Some letter of that Afterlife to spell:
And by and by my Soul returned to me,
And answered "I Myself am Heav'n and Hell:"

67

Heav'n but the Vision of fulfilled Desire,
And Hell the Shadow from a Soul on fire,
Cast on the Darkness into which Ourselves,
So late emerged from, shall so soon expire.

68

We are no other than a moving row
Of Magic Shadow-shapes that come and go
Round with the Sun-illumined Lantern held
In Midnight by the Master of the Show;

69

But helpless Pieces of the Game He plays
Upon his Checkerboard of Nights and Days;
Hither and thither moves, and checks, and slays,
And one by one back in the Closet lays.

70

The Ball no question makes of Ayes and Noes,
But Here or There as strikes the Player goes;
And He that tossed you down into the Field,
He knows about it all—HE knows—HE knows!

71

The Moving Finger writes; and, having writ,
Moves on: nor all your Piety nor Wit
Shall lure it back to cancel half a Line,
Nor all your Tears wash out a Word of it.

72

And that inverted Bowl they call the Sky,
Whereunder crawling cooped we live and die,
Lift not your hands to *It* for help—for It
As impotently moves as you or I.

73

With Earth's first Clay They did the Last Man knead,
And there of the Last Harvest sowed the Seed:
And the first Morning of Creation wrote
What the Last Dawn of Reckoning shall read.

74
YESTERDAY *This* Day's Madness did prepare;
TOMORROW's Silence, Triumph, or Despair:
Drink! for you know not whence you came, nor why:
Drink! for you know not why you go, nor where.

75
I tell you this—When, started from the Goal,
Over the flaming shoulders of the Foal[4]
Of Heav'n, Parwín and Mushtarí[5] they flung,
In my predestined Plot of Dust and Soul.

76
The Vine had struck a fiber: which about
If clings my Being—let the Dervish[6] flout;
Of my Base metal may be filed a Key,
That shall unlock the Door he howls without.

77
And this I know: whether the one True Light
Kindle to Love, or Wrath consume me quite,
One Flash of It within the Tavern caught
Better than in the Temple lost outright.

78
What! out of senseless Nothing to provoke
A conscious Something to resent the yoke
Of unpermitted Pleasure, under pain
Of Everlasting Penalties, if broke!

79
What! from his helpless Creature be repaid
Pure Gold for what he lent him dross-allayed—
Sue for a Debt he never did contract,
And cannot answer—Oh the sorry trade!

80
Oh Thou, who didst with pitfall and with gin° *trap*
Beset the Road I was to wander in,
Thou wilt not with Predestined Evil round
Enmesh, and then impute my Fall to Sin!

81
Oh Thou, who Man of baser Earth didst make,
And ev'n with Paradise devise the Snake:
For all the Sin wherewith the Face of Man
Is blackened—Man's forgiveness give—and take!

82
As under cover of departing Day
Slunk hunger-stricken Ramazán[7] away,
Once more within the Potter's house alone
I stood, surrounded by the Shapes of Clay.

83
Shapes of all Sorts and Sizes, great and small,
That stood along the floor and by the wall;
And some loquacious Vessels were; and some
Listened perhaps, but never talked at all.

4. The constellation known as the Colt (*Equuleus*) or Foal.
5. "The Pleiads and Jupiter" [FitzGerald's note]; Omar ascribes his fate to the position of the stars and planets at the time of his birth.
6. Member of any of several Muslim orders taking vows of austerity and poverty.
7. The Mohammedans' annual thirty-day fast, during which no food may be taken from dawn to sunset.

84
Said one among them—"Surely not in vain
"My substance of the common Earth was ta'en
"And to this Figure molded, to be broke,
"Or trampled back to shapeless Earth again."

85
Then said a Second—"Ne'er a peevish Boy
"Would break the Bowl from which he drank in joy;
"And He that with his hand the Vessel made
"Will surely not in after Wrath destroy."

86
After a momentary silence spake
Some Vessel of a more ungainly Make;
"They sneer at me for leaning all awry:
"What! did the Hand then of the Potter shake?"

87
Whereat some one of the loquacious Lot—
I think a Súfi° pipkin—waxing hot— *mystic*
"All this of Pot and Potter—Tell me then,
"Who is the Potter, pray, and who the Pot?"

88
"Why," said another, "Some there are who tell
"Of one who threatens he will toss to Hell
"The luckless Pots he marred in making—Pish!
"He's a Good Fellow, and 'twill all be well."

89
"Well," murmured one, "Let whoso make or buy,
"My Clay with long Oblivion is gone dry:
"But fill me with the old familiar Juice,
"Methinks I might recover by and by."

90
So while the Vessels one by one were speaking,
The little Moon[8] looked in that all were seeking:
And then they jogged each other, "Brother! Brother!
"Now for the Porter's shoulder-knot[9] a-creaking!"

91
Ah, with the Grape my fading Life provide,
And wash the Body whence the Life has died,
And lay men shrouded in the living Leaf,
By some not unfrequented Garden-side.

92
That ev'n my buried Ashes such a snare
Of Vintage shall fling up into the Air
As not a True-believer passing by
But shall be overtaken unaware.

93
Indeed the Idols I have loved so long
Have done my credit in this World much wrong:
Have drowned my Glory in a shallow Cup,
And sold my Reputation for a Song.

94
Indeed, indeed, Repentance oft before
I swore—but was I sober when I swore?
And then and then came Spring, and Rose-in-hand
My threadbare Penitence apieces tore.

8. The new moon, which signaled the end of Ramazán.

9. The knot on the porter's shoulder-strap from which the wine-jars were hung.

95
And much as Wine has played the Infidel,
And robbed me of my Robe of Honor—Well,
I wonder often what the Vintners buy
One half so precious as the stuff they sell.

96
Yet Ah, that Spring should vanish with the Rose!
That Youth's sweet-scented manuscript should close!
The Nightingale that in the branches sang,
Ah whence, and whither flown again, who knows!

97
Would but the Desert of the Fountain yield
One glimpse—if dimly, yet indeed, revealed,
To which the fainting Traveler might spring,
As springs the trampled herbage of the field!

98
Would but some wingéd Angel ere too late
Arrest the yet unfolded Roll of Fate,
And make the stern Recorder otherwise
Enregister, or quite obliterate!

99
Ah Love! could you and I with Him conspire
To grasp this sorry Scheme of Things entire,
Would not we shatter it to bits—and then
Remold it nearer to the Heart's Desire!

100
Yon rising Moon that looks for us again—
How oft hereafter will she wax and wane;
How oft hereafter rising look for us
Through this same Garden—and for *one* in vain!

101
And when like her, oh Sákí, you shall pass
Among the Guests Star-scattered on the Grass,
And in your joyous errand reach the spot
Where I made One—turn down an empty Glass!

TAMÁM[1]

1859, 1879

EDGAR ALLAN POE
(1809–1849)

Sonnet—To Science

Science! true daughter of Old Time thou art!
Who alterest all things with thy peering eyes.
Why preyest thou thus upon the poet's heart,
Vulture, whose wings are dull realities?
How should he love thee? or how deem thee wise?
Who wouldst not leave him in his wandering
To seek for treasure in the jeweled skies,
Albeit he soared with an undaunted wing?

1. It is ended.

Hast thou not dragged Diana[1] from her car?
And driven the Hamadryad[2] from the wood
To seek a shelter in some happier star?
Hast thou not torn the Naiad° from her flood, *river nymph*
The Elfin from the green grass, and from me
The summer dream beneath the tamarind tree?[3]

1829 1829, 1845

To Helen

Helen, thy beauty is to me
Like those Nicean barks of yore,
That gently, o'er a perfumed sea,
The weary, way-worn wanderer bore
To his own native shore.

On desperate seas long wont to roam,
Thy hyacinth hair,[4] thy classic face,
Thy Naiad airs have brought me home
To the glory that was Greece
And the grandeur that was Rome.

Lo! in yon brilliant window-niche
How statue-like I see thee stand!
The agate lamp within thy hand,
Ah! Psyche,[5] from the regions which
Are Holy Land!

1823 1831, 1845

The City in the Sea

Lo! Death has reared himself a throne
In a strange city lying alone
Far down within the dim West,
Where the good and the bad and the worst and the best
Have gone to their eternal rest.
There shrines and palaces and towers
(Time-eaten towers that tremble not!)
Resemble nothing that is ours.
Around, by lifting winds forgot,
Resignedly beneath the sky
The melancholy waters lie.

No rays from the holy heaven come down
On the long night-time of that town;
But light from out the lurid sea
Streams up the turrets silently—
Gleams up the pinnacles far and free—

1. To the Romans, the virgin goddess of the hunt, revered for her chastity and protectiveness. Her "car" is the moon.
2. Wood nymph said to live and die with the tree she inhabits.
3. An oriental tree the fruit of which is used medicinally and for food.
4. Presumably, hair like that of the slain youth Hyacinthus, beloved of Apollo.
5. Having lost her lover Cupid because she insisted on seeing him when he preferred to come to her unseen at night (she dropped oil accidentally from her lamp while he was sleeping), Psyche appealed for help in finding Cupid to Venus, who required, among other things, that Psyche bring back unopened a box from the underworld.

Up domes—up spires—up kingly halls—
Up fanes—up Babylon-like[6] walls—
Up shadowy long-forgotten bowers
Of sculptured ivy and stone flowers—
Up many and many a marvelous shrine
Whose wreathéd friezes intertwine
The viol, the violet, and the vine.

Resignedly beneath the sky
The melancholy waters lie.
So blend the turrets and shadows there
That all seem pendulous in air,
While from a proud tower in the town
Death looks gigantically down.

There open fanes and gaping graves
Yawn level with the luminous waves;
But not the riches there that lie
In each idol's diamond eye—
Not the gaily-jeweled dead
Tempt the waters from their bed;
For no ripples curl, alas!
Along that wilderness of glass—
No swellings tell that winds may be
Upon some far-off happier sea—
No heavings hint that winds have been
On seas less hideously serene.

But lo, a stir is in the air!
The wave—there is a movement there!
As if the towers had thrust aside,
In slightly sinking, the dull tide—
As if their tops had feebly given
A void within the filmy Heaven.
The waves have now a redder glow—
The hours are breathing faint and low—
And when, amid no earthly moans,
Down, down that town shall settle hence,
Hell, rising from a thousand thrones,
Shall do it reverence.

1831, 1845

Annabel Lee

It was many and many a year ago,
    In a kingdom by the sea,
That a maiden there lived whom you may know
    By the name of Annabel Lee;
And this maiden she lived with no other thought
    Than to love and be loved by me.

She was a child and *I* was a child,
    In this kingdom by the sea,
But we loved with a love that was more than love—
    I and my Annabel Lee—

6. Babylon traditionally symbolizes the wicked city doomed (see, for example, Isaiah xiv.4–23 and Revelation xvi.18–19).

With a love that the wingéd seraphs of Heaven
Coveted her and me.

And this was the reason that, long ago,
In this kingdom by the sea,
A wind blew out of a cloud by night
Chilling my Annabel Lee;
So that her highborn kinsmen came
And bore her away from me,
To shut her up in a sepulchre
In this kingdom by the sea.

The angels, not half so happy in Heaven,
Went envying her and me:
Yes! that was the reason (as all men know,
In this kingdom by the sea)
That the wind came out of the cloud, chilling
And killing my Annabel Lee.

But our love it was stronger by far than the love
Of those who were older than we—
Of many far wiser than we—
And neither the angels in Heaven above
Nor the demons down under the sea,
Can ever dissever my soul from the soul
Of the beautiful Annabel Lee:

For the moon never beams without bringing me dreams
Of the beautiful Annabel Lee;
And the stars never rise but I see the bright eyes
Of the beautiful Annabel Lee;
And so, all the night-tide, I lie down by the side
Of my darling, my darling, my life and my bride,
In her sepulchre there by the sea—
In her tomb by the side of the sea.

1849, 1850

ALFRED, LORD TENNYSON (1809–1892)

Mariana

"Mariana in the moated grange."
—MEASURE FOR MEASURE[1]

With blackest moss the flower-plots
Were thickly crusted, one and all;
The rusted nails fell from the knots
That held the pear to the gable-wall.
The broken sheds look'd sad and strange:
Unlifted was the clinking latch;
Weeded and worn the ancient thatch
Upon the lonely moated grange.

1. Cf. Shakespeare's *Measure for Measure,* 3.1.277.

She only said, "My life is dreary,
He cometh not," she said;
She said, "I am aweary, aweary,
I would that I were dead!"

Her tears fell with the dews at even;
Her tears fell ere the dews were dried;
She could not look on the sweet heaven,
Either at morn or eventide.
After the flitting of the bats,
When thickest dark did trance the sky,
She drew her casement-curtain by,
And glanced athwart the glooming flats.
She only said, "The night is dreary,
He cometh not," she said;
She said, "I am aweary, aweary,
I would that I were dead!"

Upon the middle of the night,
Waking she heard the night-fowl crow;
The cock sung out an hour ere light;
From the dark fen the oxen's low
Came to her; without hope of change,
In sleep she seem'd to walk forlorn,
Till cold winds woke the gray-eyed morn
About the lonely moated grange.
She only said, "The day is dreary,
He cometh not," she said;
She said, "I am aweary, aweary,
I would that I were dead!"

About a stone-cast from the wall
A sluice with blacken'd waters slept,
And o'er it many, round and small,
The cluster'd marish-mosses crept.
Hard by a poplar shook alway,
All silver-green with gnarled bark:
For leagues no other tree did mark
The level waste, the rounding gray.
She only said, "My life is dreary,
He cometh not," she said;
She said, "I am aweary, aweary,
I would that I were dead!"

And ever when the moon was low,
And the shrill winds were up and away,
In the white curtain, to and fro,
She saw the gusty shadow sway.
But when the moon was very low,
And wild winds bound within their cell,
The shadow of the poplar fell
Upon her bed, across her brow.
She only said, "The night is dreary,
He cometh not," she said;
She said, "I am aweary, aweary,
I would that I were dead!"

All day within the dreamy house,
The doors upon their hinges creak'd;
The blue fly sung in the pane; the mouse
Behind the moldering wainscot shriek'd,
Or from the crevice peer'd about.
Old faces glimmer'd thro' the doors,
Old footsteps trod the upper floors,
Old voices called her from without.
She only said, "My life is dreary,
He cometh not," she said;
She said, "I am aweary, aweary,
I would that I were dead!"

The sparrow's chirrup on the roof,
The slow clock ticking, and the sound
Which to the wooing wind aloof
The poplar made, did all confound
Her sense; but most she loathed the hour
When the thick-moted sunbeam lay
Athwart the chambers, and the day
Was sloping toward his western bower.
Then, said she, "I am very dreary,
He will not come," she said;
She wept, "I am aweary, aweary,
Oh God, that I were dead!"

1830

The Lotos-Eaters[2]

"Courage!" he[3] said, and pointed toward the land,
"This mounting wave will roll us shoreward soon."
In the afternoon they came unto a land
In which it seeméd always afternoon.
All round the coast the languid air did swoon,
Breathing like one that hath a weary dream.
Full-faced above the valley stood the moon;
And, like a downward smoke, the slender stream
Along the cliff to fall and pause and fall did seem.

A land of streams! some, like a downward smoke,
Slow-dropping veils of thinnest lawn,[4] did go;
And some through wavering lights and shadows broke,
Rolling a slumbrous sheet of foam below.
They saw the gleaming river seaward flow
From the inner land; far off, three mountain-tops,
Three silent pinnacles of aged snow,
Stood sunset-flushed; and, dewed with showery drops,
Up-clomb the shadowy pine above the woven copse.

The charméd sunset lingered low adown
In the red West; through mountain clefts the dale
Was seen far inland, and the yellow down
Bordered with palm, and many a winding vale

2. In Greek legend, a people who ate the fruit of the lotos, the effect of which was to induce drowsy languor and forgetfulness. The visit of Odysseus and his men to their island is described in the *Odyssey*, IX.82–97.
3. I.e., Odysseus.
4. Sheer cotton fabric.

And meadow, set with slender galingale;[5]
A land where all things always seemed the same!
And round about the keel with faces pale,
Dark faces pale against that rosy flame,
The mild-eyed melancholy Lotos-eaters came.

Branches they bore of that enchanted stem,
Laden with flower and fruit, whereof they gave
To each, but whoso did receive of them
And taste, to him the gushing of the wave
Far far away did seem to mourn and rave
On alien shores; and if his fellow spake,
His voice was thin, as voices from the grave;
And deep-asleep he seemed, yet all awake,
And music in his ears his beating heart did make.

They sat them down upon the yellow sand,
Between the sun and moon upon the shore;
And sweet it was to dream of fatherland,
Of child, and wife, and slave; but evermore
Most weary seemed the sea, weary the oar,
Weary the wandering fields of barren foam.
Then someone said, "We will return no more;"
And all at once they sang, "Our island home
Is far beyond the wave; we will no longer roam."

Choric Song

1

There is sweet music here that softer falls
Than petals from blown roses on the grass,
Or night-dews on still waters between walls
Of shadowy granite, in a gleaming pass;
Music that gentlier on the spirit lies,
Than tired eyelids upon tired eyes;
Music that brings sweet sleep down from the blissful skies.
Here are cool mosses deep,
And through the moss the ivies creep,
And in the stream the long-leaved flowers weep,
And from the craggy ledge the poppy hangs in sleep.

2

Why are we weighed upon with heaviness,
And utterly consumed with sharp distress,
While all things else have rest from weariness?
All things have rest: why should we toil alone,
We only toil, who are the first of things,
And make perpetual moan,
Still from one sorrow to another thrown;
Nor ever fold our wings,
And cease from wanderings,
Nor steep our brows in slumber's holy balm;
Nor harken what the inner spirit sings,
"There is no joy but calm!"—
Why should we only toil, the roof and crown of things?

3

Lo! in the middle of the wood,
The folded leaf is wooed from out the bud

5. A reed-like plant, a species of sedge.

With winds upon the branch, and there
Grows green and broad, and takes no care,
Sun-steeped at noon, and in the moon
Nightly dew-fed; and turning yellow
Falls, and floats adown the air.
Lo! sweetened with the summer light,
The full-juiced apple, waxing over-mellow,
Drops in a silent autumn night.
All its allotted length of days
The flower ripens in its place,
Ripens and fades, and falls, and hath no toil,
Fast-rooted in the fruitful soil.

4

Hateful is the dark-blue sky,
Vaulted o'er the dark-blue sea.
Death is the end of life; ah, why
Should life all labor be?
Let us alone. Time driveth onward fast
And in a little while our lips are dumb.
Let us alone. What is it that will last?
All things are taken from us, and become
Portions and parcels of the dreadful past.
Let us alone. What pleasure can we have
To war with evil? Is there any peace
In ever climbing up the climbing wave?
All things have rest, and ripen toward the grave
In silence—ripen, fall, and cease:
Give us long rest or death, dark death, or dreamful ease.

5

How sweet it were, hearing the downward stream,
With half-shut eyes ever to seem
Falling asleep in a half-dream!
To dream and dream, like yonder amber light,
Which will not leave the myrrh-bush on the height;
To hear each other's whispered speech;
Eating the Lotos day by day,
To watch the crisping ripples on the beach,
And tender curving lines of creamy spray;
To lend our hearts and spirits wholly
To the influence of mild-minded melancholy;
To muse and brood and live again in memory,
With those old faces of our infancy
Heaped over with a mound of grass,
Two handfuls of white dust, shut in an urn of brass!

6

Dear is the memory of our wedded lives,
And dear the last embraces of our wives
And their warm tears; but all hath suffered change;
For surely now our household hearths are cold,
Our sons inherit us, our looks are strange,
And we should come like ghosts to trouble joy.
Or else the island princes[6] over-bold
Have eat our substance, and the minstrel sings
Before them of the ten years' war in Troy,
And our great deeds, as half-forgotten things.

6. The princes who had remained behind in Ithaca while Odysseus was at Troy.

Is there confusion in the little isle?[7]
Let what is broken so remain.
The Gods are hard to reconcile;
'Tis hard to settle order once again.
There *is* confusion worse than death,
Trouble on trouble, pain on pain,
Long labor unto aged breath,
Sore tasks to hearts worn out by many wars
And eyes grown dim with gazing on the pilot-stars.

7

But, propt on beds of amaranth[8] and moly,
How sweet—while warm airs lull us, blowing lowly—
With half-dropt eyelid still,
Beneath a heaven dark and holy,
To watch the long bright river drawing slowly
His waters from the purple hill—
To hear the dewy echoes calling
From cave to cave through the thick-twined vine—
To watch the emerald-colored water falling
Through many a woven acanthus-wreath divine!
Only to hear and see the far-off sparkling brine,
Only to hear were sweet, stretched out beneath the pine.

8

The Lotos blooms below the barren peak,
The Lotos blows by every winding creek;
All day the wind breathes low with mellower tone;
Through every hollow cave and alley lone
Round and round the spicy downs the yellow Lotos-dust is blown.
We have had enough of action, and of motion we,
Rolled to starboard, rolled to larboard, when the surge was seething free,
Where the wallowing monster spouted his foam-fountains in the sea.
Let us swear an oath, and keep it with an equal mind,
In the hollow Lotos-land to live and lie reclined
On the hills like Gods together, careless of mankind.
For they lie beside their nectar, and the bolts are hurled
Far below them in the valleys, and the clouds are lightly curled
Round their golden houses, girdled with the gleaming world;
Where they smile in secret, looking over wasted lands,
Blight and famine, plague and earthquake, roaring deeps and fiery sands,
Clanging fights, and flaming towns, and sinking ships, and praying hands.
But they smile, they find a music centered in a doleful song
Steaming up, a lamentation and an ancient tale of wrong,
Like a tale of little meaning though the words are strong;
Chanted from an ill-used race of men that cleave the soil,
Sow the seed, and reap the harvest with enduring toil,
Storing yearly little dues of wheat, and wine and oil;
Till they perish and they suffer—some, 'tis whispered—down in hell
Suffer endless anguish, others in Elysian valleys dwell,
Resting weary limbs at last on beds of asphodel.[9]
Surely, surely, slumber is more sweet than toil, the shore
Than labor in the deep mid-ocean, wind and wave and oar;
O, rest ye, brother mariners, we will not wander more.

1832, 1842

7. I.e., Ithaca.
8. A legendary flower, reputed not to fade; moly, an herb of magical properties.
9. Any one of a number of plants of the lily family.

Break, Break, Break

Break, break, break,
On thy cold gray stones, O Sea!
And I would that my tongue could utter
The thoughts that arise in me.

O, well for the fisherman's boy,
That he shouts with his sister at play!
O, well for the sailor lad,
That he sings in his boat on the bay!

And the stately ships go on
To their haven under the hill;
But O for the touch of a vanished hand,
And the sound of a voice that is still!

Break, break, break,
At the foot of thy crags, O Sea!
But the tender grace of a day that is dead
Will never come back to me.

1834 1842

Ulysses[1]

It little profits that an idle king,
By this still hearth, among these barren crags,
Matched with an aged wife, I mete and dole
Unequal laws unto a savage race,
That hoard, and sleep, and feed, and know not me.
I cannot rest from travel; I will drink
Life to the lees. All times I have enjoyed
Greatly, have suffered greatly, both with those
That loved me, and alone; on shore, and when
Through scudding drifts the rainy Hyades[2]
Vext the dim sea. I am become a name;
For always roaming with a hungry heart
Much have I seen and known—cities of men
And manners, climates, councils, governments,
Myself not least, but honored of them all,—
And drunk delight of battle with my peers,
Far on the ringing plains of windy Troy.
I am a part of all that I have met;
Yet all experience is an arch wherethrough
Gleams that untraveled world whose margin fades
For ever and for ever when I move.
How dull it is to pause, to make an end,
To rust unburnished, not to shine in use!
As though to breathe were life! Life piled on life
Were all too little, and of one to me

1. Tennyson's Ulysses (Greek *Odysseus*), restless after his return to Ithaca, eager to renew the life of great deeds he had known during the Trojan war and the adventures of his ten-year journey home, resembles the figure of Ulysses presented by Dante, *Inferno* XXVI.

2. A group of stars in the constellation Taurus, believed to foretell the coming of rain when they rose with the sun.

Little remains; but every hour is saved
From that eternal silence, something more,
A bringer of new things; and vile it were
For some three suns to store and hoard myself,
And this gray spirit yearning in desire
To follow knowledge like a sinking star,
Beyond the utmost bound of human thought.
  This is my son, mine own Telemachus,
To whom I leave the scepter and the isle,
Well-loved of me, discerning to fulfill
This labor, by slow prudence to make mild
A rugged people, and through soft degrees
Subdue them to the useful and the good.
Most blameless is he, centered in the sphere
Of common duties, decent not to fail
In offices of tenderness, and pay
Meet adoration to my household gods,
When I am gone. He works his work, I mine.
  There lies the port; the vessel puffs her sail;
There gloom the dark, broad seas. My mariners,
Souls that have toiled, and wrought, and thought with me,
That ever with a frolic welcome took
The thunder and the sunshine, and opposed
Free hearts, free foreheads—you and I are old;
Old age hath yet his honor and his toil.
Death closes all; but something ere the end,
Some work of noble note, may yet be done,
Not unbecoming men that strove with gods.
The lights begin to twinkle from the rocks;
The long day wanes; the slow moon climbs; the deep
Moans round with many voices. Come, my friends,
'Tis not too late to seek a newer world.
Push off, and sitting well in order smite
The sounding furrows; for my purpose holds
To sail beyond the sunset, and the baths
Of all the western stars, until I die.
It may be that the gulfs will wash us down;
It may be we shall touch the Happy Isles,[3]
And see the great Achilles, whom we knew.
Though much is taken, much abides; and though
We are not now that strength which in old days
Moved earth and heaven, that which we are, we are,
One equal temper of heroic hearts,
Made weak by time and fate, but strong in will
To strive, to seek, to find, and not to yield.

1833 1842

Songs from The Princess

The Splendor Falls

The splendor falls on castle walls
  And snowy summits old in story;
The long light shakes across the lakes,

3. The Islands of the Blessed, or Elysium, the abode after death of those favored by the gods, especially heroes and patriots: supposed, in earlier myth, to be located beyond the western limits of the known world.

And the wild cataract leaps in glory.
Blow, bugle, blow, set the wild echoes flying,
Blow, bugle; answer, echoes, dying, dying, dying.

O, hark, O, hear! how thin and clear,
And thinner, clearer, farther going!
O, sweet and far from cliff and scar[4]
The horns of Elfland faintly blowing!
Blow, let us hear the purple glens replying,
Blow, bugle; answer, echoes, dying, dying, dying.

O love, they die in yon rich sky,
They faint on hill or field or river;
Our echoes roll from soul to soul,
And grow for ever and for ever.
Blow, bugle, blow, set the wild echoes flying,
And answer, echoes, answer, dying, dying, dying.

1850

Tears, Idle Tears

Tears, idle tears, I know not what they mean,
Tears from the depth of some divine despair
Rise in the heart, and gather to the eyes,
In looking on the happy autumn-fields,
And thinking of the days that are no more.

Fresh as the first beam glittering on a sail,
That brings our friends up from the underworld,
Sad as the last which reddens over one
That sinks with all we love below the verge;
So sad, so fresh, the days that are no more.

Ah, sad and strange as in dark summer dawns
The earliest pipe of half-awakened birds
To dying ears, when unto dying eyes
The casement slowly grows a glimmering square;
So sad, so strange, the days that are no more.

Dear as remembered kisses after death,
And sweet as those by hopeless fancy feigned
On lips that are for others; deep as love,
Deep as first love, and wild with all regret;
O Death in Life, the days that are no more!

1847

Now Sleeps the Crimson Petal

Now sleeps the crimson petal, now the white;
Nor waves the cypress in the palace walk;
Nor winks the gold fin in the porphyry font.
The firefly wakens; waken thou with me.

Now droops the milk-white peacock like a ghost,
And like a ghost she glimmers on to me.

Now lies the Earth all Danaë[5] to the stars,
And all thy heart lies open unto me.

4. Isolated rock, or rocky height.
5. Daughter of a king of Argos in ancient Greece who, warned by an oracle that she would bear a son who would kill him, shut her up in a bronze chamber, where she was visited by Zeus in a shower of gold.

Now slides the silent meteor on, and leaves
A shining furrow, as thy thoughts in me.

Now folds the lily all her sweetness up,
And slips into the bosom of the lake.
So fold thyself, my dearest, thou, and slip
Into my bosom and be lost in me.

1847

From In Memoriam A. H. H.[6]

OBIIT. MDCCCXXXIII

1

I held it truth, with him who sings
To one clear harp in divers tones,[7]
That men may rise on stepping-stones
Of their dead selves to higher things.

But who shall so forecast the years
And find in loss a gain to match?
Or reach a hand through time to catch
The far-off interest of tears?

Let Love clasp Grief lest both be drowned,
Let darkness keep her raven gloss.
Ah, sweeter to be drunk with loss,
To dance with Death, to beat the ground,

Than that the victor Hours should scorn
The long result of love, and boast,
"Behold the man that loved and lost,
But all he was is overworn."

2

Old yew, which graspest at the stones
That name the underlying dead,
Thy fibers net the dreamless head,
Thy roots are wrapt about the bones.

The seasons bring the flowers again,
And bring the firstling to the flock;
And in the dusk of thee the clock
Beats out the little lives of men.

O, not for thee the glow, the bloom,
Who changest not in any gale,
Nor branding summer suns avail
To touch thy thousand years of gloom;

And gazing on thee, sullen tree,
Sick for thy stubborn hardihood,
I seem to fail from out my blood
And grow incorporate into thee.

6. Arthur Henry Hallam (1811–1833) had been Tennyson's close friend at Cambridge, they had traveled together in France and Germany, and Hallam had been engaged to the poet's sister. To his associates at Cambridge, Hallam had seemed to give the most brilliant promise of greatness. In the summer of 1833, when he had been traveling on the Continent with his father, Hallam died of a stroke at Vienna.

7. I.e., Goethe.

7

Dark house, by which once more I stand
  Here in the long unlovely street,[8]
  Doors, where my heart was used to beat
So quickly, waiting for a hand,

A hand that can be clasped no more—
  Behold me, for I cannot sleep,
  And like a guilty thing I creep
At earliest morning to the door.

He is not here; but far away
  The noise of life begins again,
  And ghastly through the drizzling rain
On the bald street breaks the blank day.

11

Calm is the morn without a sound,
  Calm as to suit a calmer grief,
  And only through the faded leaf
The chestnut pattering to the ground;

Calm and deep peace on this high wold,° *upland plain*
  And on these dews that drench the furze,
  And all the silvery gossamers
That twinkle into green and gold;

Calm and still light on yon great plain
  That sweeps with all its autumn bowers,
  And crowded farms and lessening towers,
To mingle with the bounding main;

Calm and deep peace in this wide air,
  These leaves that redden to the fall,
  And in my heart, if calm at all,
If any calm, a calm despair;

Calm on the seas, and silver sleep,
  And waves that sway themselves in rest,
  And dead calm in the noble breast
Which heaves but with the heaving deep.

19

The Danube to the Severn gave
  The darkened heart that beat no more;[9]
  They laid him by the pleasant shore,
And in the hearing of the wave.

There twice a day the Severn fills;
  The salt sea-water passes by,
  And hushes half the babbling Wye,[1]
And makes a silence in the hills.

The Wye is hushed nor moved along,
  And hushed my deepest grief of all,

8. I.e., Wimpole St., where Hallam had been living after he left Cambridge.
9. Vienna, where Hallam died, is on the Danube; the Severn empties into the Bristol Channel near Clevedon, Somersetshire, Hallam's burial place.
1. The Wye, a tributary of the Severn, also runs into the Bristol Channel; the incoming tide deepens the river and makes it quiet, but as the tide ebbs the Wye once more becomes voluble.

When filled with tears that cannot fall,
I brim with sorrow drowning song.

The tide flows down, the wave again
Is vocal in its wooded walls;
My deeper anguish also falls,
And I can speak a little then.

50

Be near me when my light is low,
When the blood creeps, and the nerves prick
And tingle; and the heart is sick,
And all the wheels of being slow.

Be near me when the sensuous frame
Is racked with pangs that conquer trust;
And Time, a maniac scattering dust,
And Life, a Fury slinging flame.

Be near me when my faith is dry,
And men the flies of latter spring,
That lay their eggs, and sting and sing
And weave their petty cells and die.

Be near me when I fade away,
To point the term of human strife,
And on the low dark verge of life
The twilight of eternal day.

67

When on my bed the moonlight falls,
I know that in thy place of rest
By that broad water of the west
There comes a glory on the walls:[2]

Thy marble bright in dark appears,
As slowly steals a silver flame
Along the letters of thy name,
And o'er the number of thy years.

The mystic glory swims away,
From off my bed the moonlight dies;
And closing eaves of wearied eyes
I sleep till dusk is dipped in gray;

And then I know the mist is drawn
A lucid veil from coast to coast,
And in the dark church like a ghost
Thy tablet glimmers to the dawn.

88

Wild bird, whose warble, liquid sweet,
Rings Eden through the budded quicks,[3]
O, tell me where the senses mix,
O, tell me where the passions meet,

Whence radiate: fierce extremes employ
Thy spirits in the darkening leaf,

2. Hallam's tomb is inside Clevedon Church, just south of Clevedon, Somersetshire, on a hill overlooking the Bristol Channel.
3. Hawthorn hedge-row.

And in the midmost heart of grief
Thy passion clasps a secret joy;

And I—my harp would prelude woe—
I cannot all command the strings;
The glory of the sum of things
Will flash along the chords and go.

95

By night we lingered on the lawn,
For underfoot the herb was dry;
And genial warmth; and o'er the sky
The silvery haze of summer drawn;

And calm that let the tapers burn
Unwavering: not a cricket chirred;
The brook alone far-off was heard,
And on the board the fluttering urn.[4]

And bats went round in fragrant skies,
And wheeled or lit the filmy shapes
That haunt the dusk, with ermine capes
And woolly breasts and beaded eyes;

While now we sang old songs that pealed
From knoll to knoll, where, couched at ease,
The white kine glimmered, and the trees
Laid their dark arms about the field.

But when those others, one by one,
Withdrew themselves from me and night,
And in the house light after light
Went out, and I was all alone,

A hunger seized my heart; I read
Of that glad year which once had been,
In those fallen leaves which kept their green,
The noble letters of the dead.

And strangely on the silence broke
The silent-speaking words, and strange
Was love's dumb cry defying change
To test his worth; and strangely spoke

The faith, the vigor, bold to dwell
On doubts that drive the coward back,
And keen through wordy snares to track
Suggestion to her inmost cell.

So word by word, and line by line,
The dead man touched me from the past,
And all at once it seemed at last
The living soul was flashed on mine,

And mine in this was wound, and whirled
About empyreal heights of thought,

4. I.e., on the table a tea- or coffee-urn heated by a fluttering flame beneath.

And came on that which is, and caught
The deep pulsations of the world,

Eonian music[5] measuring out
The steps of Time—the shocks of Chance—
The blows of Death. At length my trance
Was canceled, stricken through with doubt.

Vague words! but ah, how hard to frame
In matter-molded forms of speech,
Or even for intellect to reach
Through memory that which I became;

Till now the doubtful dusk revealed
The knolls once more where, couched at ease,
The white kine glimmered, and the trees
Laid their dark arms about the field;

And sucked from out the distant gloom
A breeze began to tremble o'er
The large leaves of the sycamore,
And fluctuate all the still perfume,

And gathering freshlier overhead
Rocked the full-foliaged elms, and swung
The heavy-folded rose, and flung
The lilies to and fro, and said,

"The dawn, the dawn," and died away;
And East and West, without a breath,
Mixt their dim lights, like life and death,
To broaden into boundless day.

119

Doors, where my heart was used to beat
So quickly, not as one that weeps
I come once more; the city sleeps;
I smell the meadow in the street;

I hear a chirp of birds; I see
Betwixt the black fronts long-withdrawn
A light-blue lane of early dawn,
And think of early days and thee,

And bless thee, for thy lips are bland,
And bright the friendship of thine eyes;
And in my thoughts with scarce a sigh
I take the pressure of thine hand.

121

Sad Hesper o'er the buried sun
And ready, thou, to die with him,
Thou watchest all things ever dim
And dimmer, and a glory done.

The team is loosened from the wain,° *wagon*
The boat is drawn upon the shore;

5. I.e., the rhythm of the universe which has persisted for eons.

Thou listenest to the closing door,
And life is darkened in the brain.

Bright Phosphor, fresher for the night,
By thee the world's great work is heard
Beginning, and the wakeful bird;
Behind thee comes the greater light.

The market boat is on the stream,
And voices hail it from the brink;
Thou hear'st the village hammer clink,
And see'st the moving of the team.

Sweet Hesper-Phosphor, double name[6]
For what is one, the first, the last,
Thou, like my present and my past,
Thy place is changed; thou art the same.

130

Thy voice is on the rolling air;
I hear thee where the waters run;
Thou standest in the rising sun,
And in the setting thou art fair.

What are thou then? I cannot guess;
But though I seem in star and flower
To feel thee some diffusive power,
I do not therefore love thee less.

My love involves the love before;
My love is vaster passion now;
Though mixed with God and Nature thou,
I seem to love thee more and more.

Far off thou art, but ever nigh;
I have thee still, and I rejoice;
I prosper, circled with thy voice;
I shall not lose thee though I die.

1833–50 1850

The Eagle

FRAGMENT

He clasps the crag with crooked hands;
Close to the sun in lonely lands,
Ringed with the azure world, he stands.

The wrinkled sea beneath him crawls;
He watches from his mountain walls,
And like a thunderbolt he falls.

1851

6. Hesper, the evening star, and Phosphor, the morning star, are both the planet Venus.

Tithonus[7]

The woods decay, the woods decay and fall,
The vapors weep their burthen to the ground,
Man comes and tills the field and lies beneath,
And after many a summer dies the swan.
Me only cruel immortality
Consumes; I wither slowly in thine arms,
Here at the quiet limit of the world,
A white-haired shadow roaming like a dream
The ever-silent spaces of the East,
Far-folded mists, and gleaming halls of morn.
   Alas! for this gray shadow, once a man—
So glorious in his beauty and thy choice,
Who madest him thy chosen, that he seemed
To his great heart none other than a God!
I asked thee, "Give me immortality."
Then didst thou grant mine asking with a smile,
Like wealthy men who care not how they give.
But thy strong Hours indignant worked their wills,
And beat me down and marred and wasted me,
And though they could not end me, left me maimed
To dwell in presence of immortal youth.
Immortal age beside immortal youth,
And all I was in ashes. Can thy love,
Thy beauty, make amends, though even now,
Close over us, the silver star[8] thy guide,
Shines in those tremulous eyes that fill with tears
To hear me? Let me go; take back thy gift.
Why should a man desire in any way
To vary from the kindly race of men,
Or pass beyond the goal of ordinance
Where all should pause, as is most meet for all?
   A soft air fans the cloud apart; there comes
A glimpse of that dark world where I was born.
Once more the old mysterious glimmer steals
From thy pure brows, and from thy shoulders pure,
And bosom beating with a heart renewed.
Thy cheek begins to redden through the gloom,
Thy sweet eyes brighten slowly close to mine,
Ere yet they blind the stars, and the wild team
Which love thee, yearning for thy yoke, arise,
And shake the darkness from their loosened manes,
And beat the twilight into flakes of fire.
   Lo! ever thus thou growest beautiful
In silence, then before thine answer given
Departest, and thy tears are on my cheek.
   Why wilt thou ever scare me with thy tears,
And make me tremble lest a saying learnt,
In days far-off, on that dark earth, be true?
"The Gods themselves cannot recall their gifts."
   Ay me! ay me! with what another heart
In days far-off, and with what other eyes

7. A Trojan prince beloved by Aurora (Greek *Eos*), goddess of the dawn, who took him as her spouse. She begged Zeus to grant him eternal life, but forgot to ask also for the gift of eternal youth.
8. I.e., the morning star.

I used to watch—if I be he that watched—
The lucid outline forming round thee; saw
The dim curls kindle into sunny rings;
Changed with thy mystic change, and felt my blood
Glow with the glow that slowly crimsoned all
Thy presence and thy portals, while I lay,
Mouth, forehead, eyelids, growing dewy-warm
With kisses balmier than half-opening buds
Of April, and could hear the lips that kissed
Whispering I knew not what of wild and sweet,
Like that strange song I heard Apollo sing,
While Ilion like a mist rose into towers.[9]
  Yet hold me not for ever in thine East;
How can my nature longer mix with thine?
Coldly thy rosy shadows bathe me, cold
Are all thy lights, and cold my wrinkled feet
Upon thy glimmering thresholds, when the steam
Floats up from those dim fields about the homes
Of happy men that have the power to die,
And grassy barrows of the happier dead.
Release me, and restore me to the ground.
Thou seest all things, thou wilt see my grave;
Thou wilt renew thy beauty morn by morn,
I earth in earth forget these empty courts,
And thee returning on thy silver wheels.

1833, 1859 1860

Frater Ave Atque Vale[1]

Row us out from Desenzano, to your Sirmione row!
So they rowed, and there we landed—"O venusta Sirmio!"[2]
There to me through all the groves of olive in the summer glow,
There beneath the Roman ruin where the purple flowers grow,
Came that "Ave atque Vale" of the poet's hopeless woe,
Tenderest of Roman poets nineteen-hundred years ago,
"Frater Ave atque Vale"—as we wandered to and fro
Gazing at the Lydian laughter of the Garda Lake below[3]
Sweet Catullus's all-but-island, olive-silvery Sirmio!

1880 1885

Crossing the Bar

Sunset and evening star,
  And one clear call for me!
And may there be no moaning of the bar,
  When I put out to sea,

But such a tide as moving seems asleep,
  Too full for sound and foam,

9. According to legend, the walls and towers of Ilion (Troy) were raised by the sound of Apollo's song, as related by Ovid, *Heroides*, XVI.179.

1. The title (Brother, hail and farewell) repeats the concluding phrase of poem number CI, in which Catullus records the journey to visit his brother's tomb in Asia Minor. Tennyson's poem, written on a visit to the little peninsula of Sirmio, on Lake Garda in Northern Italy, shortly after his own brother had died, echoes phrases from another poem (XXXI) in which Catullus describes his pleasure in returning to Sirmio after a long absence.

2. O lovely Sirmio.

3. Catullus's line, "And rejoice, O Lydian waves of the lake" (XXXI: 13) alludes to the old belief that the Estruscans of the Garda region had originated in Lydia, in Asia Minor.

When that which drew from out the boundless deep
   Turns again home.

Twilight and evening bell,
   And after that the dark!
And may there be no sadness of farewell,
   When I embark;

For though from out our bourne of Time and Place
   The flood may bear me far,
I hope to see my Pilot face to face
   When I have crossed the bar.

1889

ROBERT BROWNING
(1812–1889)

My Last Duchess[1]

FERRARA

That's my last duchess painted on the wall,
Looking as if she were alive. I call
That piece a wonder, now: Frà Pandolf's hands
Worked busily a day, and there she stands.
Will't please you sit and look at her? I said
"Frà Pandolf" by design, for never read
Strangers like you that pictured countenance,
The depth and passion of its earnest glance,
But to myself they turned (since none puts by
The curtain I have drawn for you, but I)
And seemed as they would ask me, if they durst,
How such a glance came there; so, not the first
Are you to turn and ask thus. Sir, 'twas not
Her husband's presence only, called that spot
Of joy into the Duchess' cheek: perhaps
Frà Pandolf chanced to say "Her mantle laps
"Over my lady's wrist too much," or "Paint
"Must never hope to reproduce the faint
"Half-flush that dies along her throat": such stuff
Was courtesy, she thought, and cause enough
For calling up that spot of joy. She had
A heart—how shall I say?—too soon made glad,
Too easily impressed; she like whate'er
She looked on, and her looks went everywhere.
Sir, 'twas all one! My favor at her breast,
The dropping of the daylight in the West,
The bough of cherries some officious fool
Broke in the orchard for her, the white mule

1. The events of Browning's poem parallel historical events, but its emphasis is rather on truth to Renaissance attitudes than on historic specificity. Alfonso II d'Este, Duke of Ferrara (born 1533), in Northern Italy, had married his first wife, daughter of Cosimo I de'Medici, Duke of Florence, in 1558, when she was fourteen; she died on April 21, 1561, under suspicious circumstances, and soon afterwards he opened negotiations for the hand of the nieee of the Count of Tyrol, the seat of whose court was at Innsbruck, in Austria. "Fra Pandolf" and "Claus of Innsbruck" are types rather than specific artists.

She rode with round the terrace—all and each
Would draw from her alike the approving speech,
Or blush, at least. She thanked men—good! but thanked
Somehow—I know not how—as if she ranked
My gift of a nine-hundred-years-old name
With anybody's gift. Who'd stoop to blame
This sort of trifling? Even had you skill
In speech—which I have not—to make your will
Quite clear to such an one, and say, "Just this
"Or that in you disgusts me; here you miss,
"Or there exceed the mark"—and if she let
Herself be lessoned so, nor plainly set
Her wits to yours, forsooth, and made excuse,
—E'en then would be some stooping; and I choose
Never to stoop. Oh sir, she smiled, no doubt,
Whene'er I passed her; but who passed without
Much the same smile? This grew; I gave commands;
Then all smiles stopped together. There she stands
As if alive. Will 't please you rise? We'll meet
The company below, then. I repeat,
The Count your master's known munificence
Is ample warrant that no just pretense
Of mine for dowry will be disallowed;
Though his fair daughter's self, as I avowed
At starting, is my object. Nay, we'll go
Together down, sir. Notice Neptune, though,
Taming a sea-horse, thought a rarity,
Which Claus of Innsbruck cast in bronze for me!

1842

Soliloquy of the Spanish Cloister

1

Gr-r-r—there go, my heart's abhorrence!
  Water your damned flower-pots, do!
If hate killed men, Brother Lawrence,
  God's blood, would not mine kill you!
What? your myrtle-bush wants trimming?
  Oh, that rose has prior claims—
Needs its leaden vase filled brimming?
  Hell dry you up with its flames!

2

At the meal we sit together:
  Salve tibi![2] I must hear
Wise talk of the kind of weather,
  Sort of season, time of year:
Not a plenteous cork-crop: scarcely
  Dare we hope oak-galls,[3] *I doubt:*
What's the Latin name for "parsley"?
  What's the Greek name for Swine's Snout?

3

Whew! We'll have our platter burnished,
  Laid with care on our own shelf!
With a fire-new spoon we're furnished,
  And a goblet for ourself,

2. Hail to thee!
3. Growths produced on oak-leaves by gallflies.

Rinsed like something sacrificial
  Ere 'tis fit to touch our chaps—
Marked with L for our initial!
  (He-he! There his lily snaps!)

4

Saint, forsooth! While brown Dolores
  Squats outside the Convent bank
With Sanchicha, telling stories,
  Steeping tresses in the tank,
Blue-black, lustrous, thick like horsehairs,
  —Can't I see his dead eye glow,
Bright as 'twere a Barbary corsair's?[4]
  (That is, if he'd let it show!)

5

When he finishes refection,° *dinner*
  Knife and fork he never lays
Cross-wise, to my recollection,
  As do I, in Jesu's praise.
I the Trinity illustrate,
  Drinking watered orange-pulp—
In three sips the Arian[5] frustrate;
  While he drains his at one gulp.

6

Oh, those melons? If he's able
  We're to have a feast! so nice!
One goes to the Abbot's table,
  All of us get each a slice.
How go on your flowers? None double?
  Not one fruit-sort can you spy?
Strange! And I, too, at such trouble,
  Keep them close-nipped on the sly!

7

There's a great text in Galatians,[6]
  Once you trip on it, entails
Twenty-nine distinct damnations,
  One sure, if another fails:
If I trip him just a-dying,
  Sure of heaven as sure can be,
Spin him around and send him flying
  Off to hell, a Manichee?[7]

8

Or, my scrofulous French novel
  On grey paper with blunt type!
Simply glance at it, you grovel
  Hand and foot in Belial's[8] gripe:
If I double down its pages
  At the woeful sixteenth print,
When he gathers his greengages,
  Ope a sieve and slip it in't?

9

Or, there's Satan! one might venture
  Pledge one's soul to him, yet leave

4. "Barbary corsair": Pirate from the Berber countries on the north coast of Africa.
5. Arius, a fourth-century Alexandrian heretic, denied the doctrine of the Trinity.
6. The line has sometimes been taken as referring to Galatians iii.10; but see Galatians v.14–15, with its ironic applicability to the spirit of the monologue, and also v.16–24.
7. The Manichean heresy, which the speaker hopes to lure Brother Lawrence into accepting, claimed that the world was divided between forces of good and forces of evil.
8. Hebrew personification of lawlessness, hence one of the names for the Devil.

Such a flaw in the indenture
  As he'd miss till, past retrieve,
Blasted lay that rose-acacia
  We're so proud of![9] *Hy, Zy, Hine*[1] . . .
'St, there's vespers! *Plena gratiâ*
  Ave, Virgo![2] Gr-r-r—you swine!

1842

Home-Thoughts, From Abroad

1

Oh, to be in England
Now that April's there,
And whoever wakes in England
Sees, some morning, unaware,
That the lowest boughs and the brushwood sheaf
Round the elm-tree bole are in tiny leaf,
While the chaffinch sings on the orchard bough
In England—now!

2

And after April, when May follows,
And the whitethroat builds, and all the swallows!
Hark, where my blossomed pear-tree in the hedge
Leans to the field and scatters on the clover
Blossoms and dewdrops—at the bent spray's edge—
That's the wise thrush; he sings each song twice over,
Lest you should think he never could recapture
The first fine careless rapture!
And though the fields look rough with hoary dew
All will be gay when noontide wakes anew
The buttercups, the little children's dower
—Far brighter than this gaudy melon-flower!

1845

The Bishop Orders His Tomb at Saint Praxed's Church[3]

ROME, 15—

Vanity, saith the preacher, vanity![4]
Draw round my bed: is Anselm keeping back?
Nephews—sons mine . . . ah God, I know not! Well—
She, men would have to be your mother once,
Old Gandolf envied me, so fair she was!
What's done is done, and she is dead beside,
Dead long ago, and I am Bishop since,
And as she died so must we die ourselves,
And thence ye may perceive the world's a dream.
Life, how and what is it? As here I lie
In this state-chamber, dying by degrees,
Hours and long hours in the dead night, I ask

9. The speaker seems to say that, if all else fails, he might secure Brother Lawrence's damnation by pledging his own soul to the Devil in return—but being careful to leave a flaw in the contract that would invalidate it.
1. Possibly an incantation used in calling up the Devil.
2. *"Plena gratiâ / Ave, Virgo"*: the speaker reverses the opening words of the *Ave Maria:* "Hail Mary, full of grace."

3. The church of Santa Prassede, in Rome, dedicated to a Roman virgin, dates from the fifth century but was rebuilt early in the ninth and restored at later times. The 16th-century Bishop who speaks here is a fictional figure, as is his predecessor, Gandolf.
4. An echo of Ecclesiastes i.2: "Vanity of vanities, saith the Preacher, vanity of vanities; all is vanity."

"Do I live, am I dead?" Peace, peace seems all.
Saint Praxed's ever was the church for peace;
And so, about this tomb of mine. I fought
With tooth and nail to save my niche, ye know:
—Old Gandolf cozened° me, despite my care; *cheated*
Shrewd was that snatch from out the corner south
He graced his carrion with, God curse the same!
Yet still my niche is not so cramped but thence
One sees the pulpit o' the epistle-side,[5]
And somewhat of the choir, those silent seats,
And up into the aery dome where live
The angels, and a sunbeam's sure to lurk:
And I shall fill my slab of basalt there,
And 'neath my tabernacle[6] take my rest,
With those nine columns round me, two and two,
The odd one at my feet where Anselm stands:
Peach-blossom marble all, the rare, the ripe
As fresh-poured red wine of a mighty pulse.
—Old Gandolf with his paltry onion-stone,
Put me where I may look at him! True peach,
Rosy and flawless: how I earned the prize!
Draw close: that conflagration of my church
—What then? So much was saved if aught were missed!
My sons, ye would not be my death? Go dig
The white-grape vineyard where the oil-press stood,
Drop water gently till the surface sink,
And if ye find . . . Ah God, I know not, I! . . .
Bedded in store of rotten fig-leaves soft,
And corded up in a tight olive-frail,° *olive basket*
Some lump, ah God, of *lapis lazuli*,[7]
Big as a Jew's head cut off at the nape,
Blue as a vein o'er the Madonna's breast . . .
Sons, all have I bequeathed you, villas, all,
That brave Frascati[8] villa with its bath,
So, let the blue lump poise between my knees,
Like God the Father's globe on both his hands
Ye worship in the Jesu Church[9] so gay,
For Gandolf shall not choose but see and burst!
Swift as a weaver's shuttle fleet our years:[1]
Man goeth to the grave, and where is he?
Did I say basalt for my slab, sons? Black—
'Twas ever antique-black I meant! How else
Shall ye contrast my frieze to come beneath?
The bas-relief in bronze ye promised me,
Those Pans and Nymphs ye wot of, and perchance
Some tripod, thyrsus,[2] with a vase or so,
The Saviour at his sermon on the mount,
Saint Praxed in a glory,[3] and one Pan
Ready to twitch the Nymph's last garment off,
And Moses with the tables . . . but I know
Ye mark me not! What do they whisper thee,

5. The right-hand side as one faces the altar, the side from which the Epistles of the New Testament were read.
6. Canopy over his tomb.
7. A vivid blue stone, one of the so-called hard stones, used for ornament.
8. A resort town in the mountains.
9. The splendid baroque church, Il Gesù. The sculptured group of the Trinity includes a terrestrial globe carved from the largest known block of lapis lazuli.
1. See, Job vii.6 ("My days are swifter than a weaver's shuttle, and are spent without hope").
2. A staff ornamented with ivy or vine-leaves, carried by followers of Bacchus, the Roman god of wine and revelry.
3. Rays of gold, signifying sanctity, around the head or body of the saint portrayed.

Child of my bowels, Anselm? Ah, ye hope
To revel down my villas while I gasp
Bricked o'er with beggar's moldy travertine[4]
Which Gandolf from his tomb-top chuckles at!
Nay, boys, ye love me—all of jasper, then!
'T is jasper ye stand pledged to, lest I grieve
My bath must needs be left behind, alas!
One block, pure green as a pistachio-nut,
There's plenty jasper somewhere in the world—
And have I not Saint Praxed's ear to pray
Horses for ye, and brown Greek manuscripts,
And mistresses with great smooth marbly limbs?
—That's if ye carve my epitaph aright,
Choice Latin, picked phrase, Tully's[5] every word,
No gaudy ware like Gandolf's second line—
Tully, my masters? Ulpian[6] serves his need!
And then how I shall lie through centuries,
And hear the blessed mutter of the mass,
And see God made and eaten all day long,[7]
And feel the steady candle-flame, and taste
Good strong thick stupefying incense-smoke!
For as I lie here, hours of the dead night,
Dying in state and by such slow degrees,
I fold my arms as if they clasped a crook,[8]
And stretch my feet forth straight as stone can point,
And let the bedclothes, for a mortcloth,[9] drop
Into great laps and folds of sculptor's-work:
And as yon tapers dwindle, and strange thoughts
Grow, with a certain humming in my ears,
About the life before I lived this life,
And this life too, popes, cardinals and priests,
Saint Praxed at his sermon on the mount,[1]
Your tall pale mother with her talking eyes,
And new-found agate urns as fresh as day,
And marble's language, Latin pure, discreet,
—Aha, ELUCESCEBAT[2] quoth our friend?
No Tully, said I, Ulpian at the best!
Evil and brief hath been my pilgrimage.
All *lapis*, all, son! Else I give the Pope
My villas! Will ye ever eat my heart?
Ever your eyes were as a lizard's quick,
They glitter like your mother's for my soul,
Or ye would heighten my impoverished frieze,
Piece out its starved design, and fill my vase
With grapes, and add a vizor and a Term,[3]
And to the tripod ye would tie a lynx
That in his struggle throws the thyrsus down,
To comfort me on my entablature
Whereon I am to lie till I must ask
"Do I live, am I dead?" There, leave me, there!

4. Ordinary limestone used in building.
5. Familiar name for Cicero (Marcus Tullius Cicero).
6. His Latin would be stylistically inferior to that of Cicero.
7. Refers to the doctrine of transubstantiation.
8. I.e., the Bishop's crozier, with its emblematic resemblance to a shepherd's crook.
9. The pall with which the coffin is draped.
1. As the Bishop's mind wanders, he attributes Christ's Sermon on the Mount to Santa Prassede.
2. A word from Gandolf's epitaph (a form of the Latin verb meaning "to shine forth"); the Bishop claims that this form is inferior to *elucebat*, which Cicero would have used.
3. "Vizor": a mask; "Term": a pillar adorned with a bust. Both are motifs of classical sculpture imitated by the Renaissance.

For ye have stabbed me with ingratitude
To death—ye wish it—God, ye wish it! Stone—
Gritstone, a-crumble! Clammy squares which sweat
As if the corpse they keep were oozing through—
And no more *lapis* to delight the world!
Well, go! I bless ye. Fewer tapers there,
But in a row: and, going, turn your backs
—Ay, like departing altar-ministrants,
And leave me in my church, the church for peace,
That I may watch at leisure if he leers—
Old Gandolf, at me, from his onion-stone,
As still he envied me, so fair she was!

1845, 1849

Fra Lippo Lippi[4]

I am poor brother Lippo, by your leave!
You need not clap your torches to my face.
Zooks, what's to blame? you think you see a monk!
What, 'tis pas midnight, and you go the rounds,
And here you catch me at an alley's end
Where sportive ladies leave their doors ajar?
The Carmine's my cloister:[5] hunt it up,
Do—harry out, if you must show your zeal,
Whatever rat, there, haps on his wrong hole,
And nip each softling of a wee white mouse,
Weke, weke, that's crept to keep him company!
Aha, you know your betters! Then, you'll take
Your hand away that's fiddling on my throat,
And please to know me likewise. Who am I?
Why, one, sir, who is lodging with a friend
Three streets off—he's a certain . . . how d'ye call?
Master—a . . . Cosimo of the Medici,[6]
I' the house that caps the corner. Boh! you were best!
Remember and tell me, the day you're hanged,
How you affected such a gullet's-gripe![7]
But you, sir, it concerns you that your knaves
Pick up a manner nor discredit you:
Zooks, are we pilchards,° that they sweep the streets *fish*
And count fair prize what comes into their net?
He's Judas to a tittle, that man is![8]
Just such a face! Why, sir, you make amends.
Lord, I'm not angry! Bid your hangdogs go
Drink out this quarter-florin to the health
Of the munificent House that harbors me
(And many more beside, lads! more beside!)
And all's come square again. I'd like his face—
His, elbowing on his comrade in the door
With the pike and lantern—for the slave that holds
John Baptist's head a-dangle by the hair
With one hand ("Look you, now," as who should say)

4. Florentine painter (ca. 1406–69), whose life Browning knew from Vasari's *Lives of the Most Eminent Painters, Sculptors, and Architects,* and from other sources, and whose paintings he had learned to know at first hand during his years in Florence.

5. Fra Lippo had entered the Carmelite cloister while still a boy. He gave up monastic vows on June 6, 1421, but was clothed by the monastery until 1431 and was called "Fra Filippo" in documents until his death.

6. Cosimo de'Medici (1389–1464), Fra Lippo's wealthy patron and an important political power in Florence.

7. I.e., grip on my throat.

8. Of one of the watchmen who have arrested him, he says he looks exactly like Judas.

And his weapon in the other, yet unwiped!
It's not your chance to have a bit of chalk,
A wood-coal or the like? or you should see!
Yes, I'm the painter, since you style me so.
What, brother Lippo's doings, up and down,
You know them and they take you? like enough!
I saw the proper twinkle in your eye—
'Tell you, I liked your looks at very first.
Let's sit and set things straight now, hip to haunch.
Here's spring come, and the nights one makes up bands
To roam the town and sing out carnival,
And I've been three weeks shut within my mew,[9]
A-painting for the great man, saints and saints
And saints again. I could not paint all night—
Ouf! I leaned out of window for fresh air.
There came a hurry of feet and little feet,
A sweep of lute-strings, laughs, and whifts of song—
Flower o' the broom,
Take away love, and our earth is a tomb!
Flower o' the quince,
I let Lisa go, and what good in life since?
Flower o' the thyme—and so on. Round they went.
Scarce had they turned the corner when a titter
Like the skipping of rabbits by moonlight—
        three slim shapes,
And a face that looked up . . . zooks, sir, flesh and blood,
That's all I'm made of! Into shreds it went,
Curtain and counterpane and coverlet,
All the bed-furniture—a dozen knots,
There was a ladder! Down I let myself,
Hands and feet, scrambling somehow, and so dropped,
And after them. I came up with the fun
Hard by Saint Laurence,[1] hail fellow, well met—
Flower o' the rose,
If I've been merry, what matter who knows?
And so as I was stealing back again
To get to bed and have a bit of sleep
Ere I rise up to-morrow and go work
On Jerome knocking at his poor old breast[2]
With his great round stone to subdue the flesh,
You snap me of the sudden. Ah, I see!
Though your eye twinkles still, you shake your head—
Mine's shaved—a monk, you say—the sting's in that!
If Master Cosimo announced himself,
Mum's the word naturally; but a monk!
Come, what am I a beast for? tell us, now!
I was a baby when my mother died
And father died and left me in the street.
I starved there, God knows how, a year or two
On fig-skins, melon-parings, rinds and shucks,
Refuse and rubbish. One fine frosty day,
My stomach being empty as your hat,
The wind doubled me up and down I went.
Old Aunt Lapaccia trussed me with one hand,
(Its fellow was a stinger as I knew)

9. I.e., within the confines of my quarters (in the Medici palace).
1. The church of San Lorenzo, not far from the Medici palace.
2. I.e., on a painting of St. Jerome in the Desert.

And so along the wall, over the bridge,
By the straight cut to the convent. Six words there,
While I stood munching my first bread that month:
"So, boy, you're minded," quoth the good fat father
Wiping his own mouth, 't was refection-time—
"To quit this very miserable world?
"Will you renounce" . . . "the mouthful of bread?" thought I;
By no means! Brief, they made a monk of me;
I did renounce the world, its pride and greed,
Palace, farm, villa, shop and banking-house,
Trash, such as these poor devils of Medici
Have given their hearts to—all at eight years old.
Well, sir, I found in time, you may be sure,
'T was not for nothing—the good bellyful,
The warm serge and the rope that goes all round,
And day-long blessed idleness beside!
"Let's see what the urchin's fit for"—that came next.
Not overmuch their way, I must confess.
Such a to-do! They tried me with their books:
Lord, they'd have taught me Latin in pure waste!
Flower o' the clove,
All the Latin I construe is, "amo" I love!
But, mind you, when a boy starves in the streets
Eight years together, as my fortune was,
Watching folk's faces to know who will fling
The bit of half-stripped grape-bunch he desires,
And who will curse or kick him for his pains—
Which gentleman processional and fine,
Holding a candle to the Sacrament,
Will wink and let him lift a plate and catch
The droppings of the wax to sell again,
Or holla for the Eight[3] and have him whipped—
How say I? nay, which dog bites, which lets drop
His bone from the heap of offal in the street—
Why, soul and sense of him grow sharp alike,
He learns the look of things, and none the less
For admonition from the hunger-pinch.
I had a store of such remarks, be sure,
Which, after I found leisure, turned to use.
I drew men's faces on my copy-books,
Scrawled them within the antiphonary's[4] marge,
Joined legs and arms to the long music-notes,
Found eyes and nose and chin for A's and B's,
And made a string of pictures of the world
Betwixt the ins and outs of verb and noun,
On the wall, the bench, the door. The monks looked black.
"Nay," quoth the Prior, "turn him out, d'ye say?
"In no wise. Lose a crow and catch a lark.
"What if at last we get our man of parts,
"We Carmelites, like those Camaldolese[5]
"And Preaching Friars,[6] to do our church up fine
"And put the front on it that ought to be!"
And hereupon he bade me daub away.
Thank you! my head being crammed, the walls a blank,
Never was such prompt disemburdening.

3. The Florentine magistrates.
4. The book containing the antiphons, or responses chanted in the liturgy.
5. Members of a religious order at Camaldoli, in the Apennines.
6. I.e., Dominicans.

First, every sort of monk, the black and white,
I drew them, fat and lean: then, folk at church,
From good old gossips waiting to confess
Their cribs of barrel-droppings, candle-ends—
To the breathless fellow at the altar-foot,
Fresh from his murder, safe and sitting there
With the little children round him in a row
Of admiration, half for his beard and half
For that white anger of his victim's son
Shaking a fist at him with one fierce arm,
Signing[7] himself with the other because of Christ
(Whose sad face on the cross sees only this
After the passion of a thousand years)
Till some poor girl, her apron o'er her head,
(Which the intense eyes looked through) came at eve
On tiptoe, said a word, dropped in a loaf,
Her pair of earrings and a bunch of flowers
(The brute took growling), prayed, and so was gone.
I painted all, then cried " 'Tis ask and have;
"Choose, for more's ready!"—laid the ladder flat,
And showed my covered bit of cloister-wall.
The monks closed in a circle and praised loud
Till checked, taught what to see and not to see,
Being simple bodies—"That's the very man!
"Look at the boy who stoops to pat the dog!
"That woman's like the Prior's niece who comes
"To care about his asthma: it's the life!"
But there my triumph's straw-fire flared and funked;
Their betters took their turn to see and say:
The Prior and the learned pulled a face
And stopped all that in no time. "How? what's here?
"Quite from the mark of painting, bless us all!
"Faces, arms, legs and bodies like the true
"As much as pea and pea! it's devil's-game!
"Your business is not to catch men with show,
"With homage to the perishable clay,
"But lift them over it, ignore it all,
"Make them forget there's such a thing as flesh.
"Your business is to paint the souls of men—
"Man's soul, and it's a fire, smoke . . . no, it's not . . .
"It's vapor done up like a new-born babe—
"(In that shape when you die it leaves your mouth)
"It's . . . well, what matters talking, it's the soul!
"Give us no more of body than shows soul!
"Here's Giotto,[8] with his Saint a-praising God,
"That sets us praising—why not stop with him?
"Why put all thoughts of praise out of our head
"With wonder at lines, colors, and what not?
"Paint the soul, never mind the legs and arms!
"Rub all out, try at it a second time.
"Oh, that white smallish female with the breasts,
"She's just my niece . . . Herodias,[9] I would say—
"Who went and danced and got men's heads cut off!
"Have it all out!" Now, is this sense, I ask?

7. Making the sign of the cross with one hand, because of the image of Christ on the altar.
8. The great Florentine painter (1267–1337).
9. Sister-in-law of the tetrarch Herod. She had demanded that John the Baptist be imprisoned: when her daughter Salome so pleased the king with her dancing that he promised her anything she asked, Herodias instructed her to ask for the head of John the Baptist on a platter (Matthew xiv.1–12).

A fine way to paint soul, by painting body
So ill, the eye can't stop there, must go further
And can't fare worse! Thus, yellow does for white
When what you put for yellow's simply black,
And any sort of meaning looks intense
When all beside itself means and looks nought.
Why can't a painter lift each foot in turn,
Left foot and right foot, go a double step,
Make his flesh liker and his soul more like,
Both in their order? Take the prettiest face,
The Prior's niece . . . patron-saint—is it so pretty
You can't discover if it means hope, fear,
Sorrow or joy? won't beauty go with these?
Suppose I've made her eyes all right and blue,
Can't I take breath and try to add life's flash,
And then add soul and heighten them threefold?
Or say there's beauty with no soul at all—
(I never saw it—put the case the same—)
If you get simple beauty and nought else,
You get about the best thing God invents:
That's somewhat: and you'll find the soul you have missed,
Within yourself, when you return him thanks.
"Rub all out!" Well, well, there's my life, in short,
And so the thing has gone on ever since.
I'm grown a man no doubt, I've broken bounds:
You should not take a fellow eight years old
And make him swear to never kiss the girls.
I'm my own master, paint now as I please—
Having a friend, you see, in the Corner-house![1]
Lord, it's fast holding by the rings in front—
Those great rings serve more purposes than just
To plant a flag in, or tie up a horse!
And yet the old schooling sticks, the old grave eyes
Are peeping o'er my shoulder as I work,
The heads shake still—"It's art's decline, my son!
"You're not of the true painters, great and old;
"Brother Angelico's the man, you'll find;
"Brother Lorenzo[2] stands his single peer:
"Fag on at flesh, you'll never make the third!"
Flower o' the pine,
You keep your mistr . . . manners, and I'll stick to mine!
I'm not the third, then: bless us, they must know!
Don't you think they're the likeliest to know,
They with their Latin? So, I swallow my rage,
Clench my teeth, suck my lips in tight, and paint
To please them—sometimes do and sometimes don't;
For, doing most, there's pretty sure to come
A turn, some warm eve finds me at my saints—
A laugh, a cry, the business of the world—
(*Flower o' the peach,*
Death for us all, and his own life for each!)
And my whole soul revolves, the cup runs over,
The world and life's too big to pass for a dream,
And I do these wild things in sheer despite,
And play the fooleries you catch me at,
In pure rage! The old mill-horse, out at grass

1. I.e., the Medici palace.
2. Fra Angelico (1387–1455), and Fra Lorenzo Monaco (1370–1425).

After hard years, throws up his stiff heels so,
Although the miller does not preach to him
The only good of grass is to make chaff.
What would men have? Do they like grass or no—
May they or mayn't they? all I want's the thing
Settled for ever one way. As it is,
You tell too many lies and hurt yourself:
You don't like what you only like too much,
You do like what, if given you at your word,
You find abundantly detestable.
For me, I think I speak as I was taught;
I always see the garden and God there
A-making man's wife: and, my lesson learned,
The value and significance of flesh,
I can't unlearn ten minutes afterwards.

You understand me: I'm a beast, I know.
But see, now—why, I see as certainly
As that the morning-star's about to shine,
What will hap some day. We've a youngster here
Comes to our convent, studies what do,
Slouches and stares and lets no atom drop:
His name is Guidi—he'll not mind the monks—
They call him Hulking Tom,[3] he lets them talk—
He picks my practice up—he'll paint apace,
I hope so—though I never live so long,
I know what's sure to follow. You be judge!
You speak no Latin more than I, belike;
However, you're my man, you've seen the world
—The beauty and the wonder and the power,
The shapes of things, their colors, lights and shades,
Changes, surprises—and God made it all!
—For what? Do you feel thankful, ay or no,
For this fair town's face, yonder river's line,
The mountain round it and the sky above,
Much more the figures of man, woman, child,
These are the frame to? What's it all about?
To be passed over, despised? or dwelt upon,
Wondered at? oh, this last of course!—you say.
But why not do as well as say, paint these
Just as they are, careless what comes of it?
God's works—paint anyone, and count it crime
To let a truth slip. Don't object, "His works
"Are here already; nature is complete:
"Suppose you reproduce her (which you can't)
"There's no advantage! you must beat her, then."
For, don't you mark? we're made so that we love
First when we see them painted, things we have passed
Perhaps a hundred times nor cared to see;
And so they are better, painted—better to us,
Which is the same thing. Art was given for that;
God uses us to help each other so,
Lending our minds out. Have you noticed, now,
Your cullion's hanging face? A bit of chalk,

3. The painter Tommaso Guidi (1401–28), known as Masaccio (from *Tomasaccio,* meaning "Big Tom" or "Hulking Tom"). The series of frescoes which he painted in Santa Maria del Carmine, of key importance in the history of Florentine painting, was completed by Fra Lippo's son, Filippino Lippi, and it is in fact more likely that Fra Lippo learned from Masaccio than that he saw him as a promising newcomer.

And trust me but you should, though! How much more,
If I drew higher things with the same truth!
That were to take the Prior's pulpit-place,
Interpret God to all of you! Oh, oh,
It makes me mad to see what men shall do
And we in our graves! This world's no blot for us,
Nor blank; it means intensely, and means good:
To find its meaning is my meat and drink.
"Ay, but you don't so instigate to prayer!"
Strikes in the Prior: "when your meaning's plain
"It does not say to folk—remember matins,
"Or, mind you fast next Friday!" Why, for this
What need of art at all? A skull and bones,
Two bits of stick nailed crosswise, or, what's best,
A bell to chime the hour with, does as well.
I painted a Saint Laurence six months since
At Prato,[4] splashed the fresco in fine style:
"How looks my painting, now the scaffold's down?"
I ask a brother: "Hugely," he returns—
"Already not one phiz of your three slaves
"Who turn the Deacon off his toasted side,[5]
"But's scratched and prodded to our heart's content,
"The pious people have so eased their own
"With coming to say prayers there in a rage:
"We get on fast to see the bricks beneath.
"Expect another job this time next year,
"For pity and religion grow i' the crowd—
"Your painting serves its purpose!" Hang the fools!

—That is—you'll not mistake an idle word
Spoke in a huff by a poor monk, God wot,
Tasting the air this spicy night which turns
The unaccustomed head like Chianti wine!
Oh, the church knows! don't misreport me, now!
It's natural a poor monk out of bounds
Should have his apt word to excuse himself:
And hearken how I plot to make amends.
I have bethought me: I shall paint a piece
. . . There's for you! Give me six months, then go, see
Something in Sant' Ambrogio's![6] Bless the nuns!
They want a cast o' my office. I shall paint
God in the midst, Madonna and her babe,
Ringed by a bowery flowery angel-brood,
Lilies and vestments and white faces, sweet
As puff on puff of grated orris-root
When ladies crowd to Church at midsummer.
And then i' the front, of course a saint or two—
Saint John, because he saves the Florentines,[7]
Saint Ambrose, who puts down in black and white
The convent's friends and gives them a long day,
And Job, I must have him there past mistake,
The man of Uz (and Us without the z,
Painters who need his patience). Well, all these

4. Smaller town near Florence, where Fra Lippo painted some of his most important pictures.
5. Saint Lawrence was martyred by being roasted on a gridiron; according to legend, he urged his executioners to turn him over, saying that he was done on one side.
6. Fra Lippo painted the *Coronation of the Virgin,* here described, for the high altar of Sant' Ambrogio in 1447.
7. San Giovanni is the patron saint of Florence.

Secured at their devotion, up shall come
Out of a corner when you least expect,
As one by a dark stair into a great light,
Music and talking, who but Lippo! I!
Mazed, motionless and moonstruck—I'm the man!
Back I shrink—what is this I see and hear?
I, caught up with my monk's-things by mistake,
My old serge gown and rope that goes all round,
I, in this presence, this pure company!
Where's a hole, where's a corner for escape?
Then steps a sweet angelic slip of a thing
Forward, puts out a soft palm—"Not so fast!"
—Addresses the celestial presence, "nay—
"He made you and devised you, after all,
"Though he's none of you! Could Saint John there draw—
"His camel-hair[8] make up a painting-brush?
"We come to brother Lippo for all that,
"Iste perfecit opus!"[9] So, all smile—
I shuffle sideways with my blushing face
Under the cover of a hundred wings
Thrown like a spread of kirtles[1] when you're gay
And play hot cockles,[2] all the doors being shut,
Till, wholly unexpected, in there pops
The hothead husband! Thus I scuttle off
To some safe bench behind, not letting go
The palm of her, the little lily thing
That spoke the good word for me in the nick,
Like the Prior's niece . . . Saint Lucy, I would say.
And so all's saved for me, and for the church
A pretty picture gained. Go, six months hence!
Your hand, sir, and good-bye: no lights, no lights!
The street's hushed, and I know my own way back,
Don't fear me! there's the gray beginning. Zooks!

1855

A Toccata of Galuppi's[3]

1

Oh Galuppi, Baldassare, this is very sad to find!
I can hardly misconceive you; it would prove me deaf and blind;
But although I take your meaning, 'tis with such a heavy mind!

2

Here you come with your old music, and here's all the good it brings.
What, they lived once thus at Venice where the merchants were the kings,
Where Saint Mark's is, where the Doges used to wed the sea with rings?[4]

8. John the Baptist is often portrayed wearing a rough robe of camel's hair, in accord with Mark i.6.

9. It is more likely that the figure which Browning took to be that of the painter is that of the patron, the Very Reverend Francesco Marenghi, who ordered the painting in 1441, and that the words on the scroll before him (*"Is [te] perfecit opus,"* This man accomplished the work) refer to the commissioning of the project.

1. Women's gowns or skirts.

2. A game in which a blindfolded player must guess who has struck him.

3. The poem presents the reflections of a 19th-century Englishman, as he plays a toccata by the 18th-century Venetian composer Baldassare Galuppi. (A toccata is a "touch-piece," the word derived from the Italian verb *toccare,* to touch: "a composition intended to exhibit the touch and execution of the performer," and hence often having the character of "showy improvisation" [*Grove's Dictionary of Music and Musicians*]. In stanzas 7–9, the quoted words represent the thoughts, feelings, or casual remarks of the earlier Venetian audience, now dispersed by death.

4. Each year the Doge, chief magistrate of the Venetian republic, threw a ring into the sea with the ceremonial words, "We wed thee, O sea, in sign of true and everlasting dominion."

3

Ay, because the sea's the street there; and 'tis arched by . . . what you call
. . . Shylock's bridge[5] with houses on it, where they kept the carnival:
I was never out of England—it's as if I saw it all.

4

Did young people take their pleasure when the sea was warm in May?
Balls and masks begun at midnight, burning ever to mid-day,
When they made up fresh adventures for the morrow, do you say?

5

Was a lady such a lady, cheeks so round and lips so red—
On her neck the small face buoyant, like a bellflower on its bed,
O'er the breast's superb abundance where a man might base his head?

6

Well, and it was graceful of them—they'd break talk off and afford
—She, to bite her mask's black velvet—he, to finger on his sword,
While you sat and played Toccatas, stately at the clavichord?[6]

7

What? Those lesser thirds so plaintive, sixths diminished, sigh on sigh,
Told them something? Those suspensions, those solutions—"Must we die?"
Those commiserating sevenths—"Life might last! we can but try!"

8

"Were you happy?" "Yes." "And are you still as happy?" "Yes. And you?"
"Then, more kisses!" "Did *I* stop them, when a million seemed so few?"
Hark, the dominant's persistence till it must be answered to!

9

So, an octave struck the answer. Oh, they praised you, I dare say!
"Brave Galuppi! that was music! good alike at grave and gay!
"I can always leave off talking when I hear a master play!"

10

Then they left you for their pleasure: till in due time, one by one,
Some with lives that came to nothing, some with deeds as well undone,
Death stepped tacitly and took them where they never see the sun.

11

But when I sit down to reason, think to take my stand nor swerve,
While I triumph o'er a secret wrung from nature's close reserve,
In you come with your cold music[7] till I creep through every nerve.

12

Yes, you, like a ghostly cricket, creaking where a house was burned:
"Dust and ashes, dead and done with, Venice spent what Venice earned.
"The soul, doubtless, is immortal—where a soul can be discerned.

13

"Yours for instance: you know physics, something of geology,
"Mathematics are your pastime; souls shall rise in their degree;
"Butterflies may dread extinction—you'll not die, it cannot be!

14

"As for Venice and her people, merely born to bloom and drop,
"Here on earth they bore their fruitage, mirth and folly were the crop:
"What of soul was left, I wonder, when the kissing had to stop?

15

"Dust and ashes!" So you creak it, and I want the heart to scold.
Dear dead women, with such hair, too—what's become of all the gold
Used to hang and brush their bosoms? I feel chilly and grown old.

ca. 1847 1855

5. The Rialto Bridge over the Grand Canal.
6. "A keyboard instrument, precursor of the piano" [Webster].
7. In stanzas 12–15, the quoted words are the words he imagines the composer as speaking to him.

Andrea del Sarto[8]

CALLED "THE FAULTLESS PAINTER"

But do not let us quarrel any more,
No, my Lucrezia; bear with me for once:
Sit down and all shall happen as you wish.
You turn your face, but does it bring your heart?
I'll work then for your friend's friend, never fear,
Treat his own subject after his own way,
Fix his own time, accept too his own price,
And shut the money into this small hand
When next it takes mine. Will it? tenderly?
Oh, I'll content him—but tomorrow, Love!
I often am much wearier than you think,
This evening more than usual, and it seems
As if—forgive now—should you let me sit
Here by the window with your hand in mine
And look a half-hour forth on Fiesole,[9]
Both of one mind, as married people use,
Quietly, quietly the evening through
I might get up tomorrow to my work
Cheerful and fresh as ever. Let us try.
Tomorrow, how you shall be glad for this!
Your soft hand is a woman of itself,
And mine the man's bared breast she curls inside.
Don't count the time lost, neither; you must serve
For each of the five pictures we require:
It saves a model. So! keep looking so—
My serpenting beauty, rounds on rounds!
—How could you ever prick those perfect ears,
Even to put the pearl there! oh, so sweet—
My face, my moon, my everybody's moon,
Which everybody looks on and calls his,
And, I suppose, is looked on by in turn,
While she looks—no one's: very dear, no less.
You smile? why, there's my picture ready made,
There's what we painters call our harmony!
A common grayness silvers everything,
All in a twilight, you and I alike
—You, at the point of your first pride in me
(That's gone you know)—but I, at every point;
My youth, my hope, my art, being all toned down
To yonder sober pleasant Fiesole.
There's the bell clinking from the chapel-top;
That length of convent-wall across the way
Holds the trees safer, huddled more inside;
The last monk leaves the garden; days decrease,
And autumn grows, autumn in everything.
Eh? the whole seems to fall into a shape

8. Andrea del Sarto (1486–1530), the Florentine painter, spent his entire life in Florence except for a year's sojourn at the court of the French king, Francis I, at Fontainebleau, 1518–19. He had been married since 1517 to Lucrezia del Fede, a widow, and in response to her pleading he left Fontainebleau, with the understanding that he would soon return to complete work for which he had been paid. But he did not return, and he spent money which the king had given him to purchase works of art in Italy on a house in Florence for him and Lucrezia. These and other facts Browning derived from Vasari's *Life* of Andrea (in his *Lives of the Most Eminent Painters, Sculptors, and Architects*). But the poem also depends inevitably on Browning's own response to Andrea's art.

9. A small town on the crown of a hill above Florence.

As if I saw alike my work and self
And all that I was born to be and do,
A twilight-piece. Love, we are in God's hand.
How strange now, looks the life he makes us lead;
So free we seem, so fettered fast we are!
I feel he laid the fetter: let it lie!
This chamber for example—turn your head—
All that's behind us! You don't understand
Nor care to understand about my art,
But you can hear at least when people speak:
And that cartoon,[1] the second from the door
—It is the thing, Love! so such things should be—
Behold Madonna! I am bold to say.
I can do with my pencil what I know,
What I see, what at bottom of my heart
I wish for, if I ever wish so deep—
Do easily, too—when I say, perfectly,
I do not boast, perhaps: yourself are judge,
Who listened to the Legate's[2] talk last week,
And just as much they used to say in France.
At any rate 'tis easy, all of it!
No sketches first, no studies, that's long past:
I do what many dream of, all their lives,
—Dream? strive to do, and agonize to do,
And fail in doing. I could count twenty such
On twice your fingers, and not leave this town,
Who strive—you don't know how the others strive
To paint a little thing like that you smeared
Carelessly passing with your robes afloat—
Yet do much less, so much less, Someone says,
(I know his name, no matter)—so much less!
Well, less is more, Lucrezia: I am judged.
There burns a truer light of God in them,
In their vexed beating stuffed and stopped-up brain,
Heart, or whate'er else, than goes on to prompt
This low-pulsed forthright craftsman's hand of mine.
Their works drop groundward, but themselves, I know,
Reach many a time a heaven that's shut to me,
Enter and take their place there sure enough,
Though they come back and cannot tell the world.
My works are nearer heaven, but I sit here.
The sudden blood of these men! at a word—
Praise them, it boils, or blame them, it boils too.
I, painting from myself and to myself,
Know what I do, am unmoved by men's blame
Or their praise either. Somebody remarks
Morello's[3] outline there is wrongly traced,
His hue mistaken; what of that? or else,
Rightly traced and well ordered; what of that?
Speak as they please, what does the mountain care?
Ah, but a man's reach should exceed his grasp,
Or what's a heaven for? All is silver-gray
Placid and perfect with my art: the worse!
I know both what I want and what might gain,
And yet how profitless to know, to sigh

1. A preparatory drawing, on heavy paper, of the same size as the painting to be executed from it in oil or fresco.

2. The Pope's representative.

3. Monte Morello, a mountain lying a little to the northwest of Florence in the Apennines.

"Had I been two, another and myself,
Our head would have o'erlooked the world!" No doubt.
Yonder's a work now, of that famous youth
The Urbinate[4] who died five years ago.
('Tis copied, George Vasari[5] sent it me.)
Well, I can fancy how he did it all,
Pouring his soul, with kings and popes to see,
Reaching, that heaven might so replenish him,
Above and through his art—for it gives way;
That arm is wrongly put—and there again—
A fault to pardon in the drawing's lines,
Its body, so to speak: its soul is right,
He means right—that, a child may understand.
Still, what an arm! and I could alter it:
But all the play, the insight and the stretch—
Out of me, out of me! And wherefore out?
Had you enjoined them on me, given me soul,
We might have risen to Rafael, I and you!
Nay, Love, you did give all I asked, I think—
More than I merit, yes, by many times.
But had you—oh, with the same perfect brow,
And perfect eyes, and more than perfect mouth,
And the low voice my soul hears, as a bird
The fowler's° pipe, and follows to the snare— *bird-catcher's*
Had you, with these the same, but brought a mind!
Some women do so. Had the mouth there urged
"God and the glory! never care for gain.
The present by the future, what is that?
Live for fame, side by side with Agnolo![6]
"Rafael is waiting: up to God, all three!"
I might have done it for you. So it seems:
Perhaps not. All is as God over-rules.
Beside, incentives come from the soul's self;
The rest avail not. Why do I need you?
What wife had Rafael, or has Agnolo?
In this world, who can do a thing, will not;
And who would do it, cannot, I perceive:
Yet the will's somewhat—somewhat, too, the power—
And thus we half-men struggle. At the end,
God, I conclude, compensates, punishes.
'Tis safer for me, if the award be strict,
That I am something underrated here,
Poor this long while, despised, to speak the truth.
I dared not, do you know, leave home all day,
For fear of chancing on the Paris lords.
The best is when they pass and look aside;
But they speak sometimes; I must bear it all.
Well may they speak! That Francis, that first time,
And that long festal year at Fontainebleau!
I surely then could sometimes leave the ground,
Put on the glory, Rafael's daily wear,
In that humane great monarch's golden look—
One finger in his beard or twisted curl
Over his mouth's good mark that made the smile,
One arm about my shoulder, round my neck,
The jingle of his gold chain in my ear,

4. The painter Raphael (1483–1520), so called because he was born at Urbino.
5. Giorgio Vasari, the biographer, himself a painter and an architect, had been Andrea's pupil.
6. I.e., Michelangelo (1475–1564).

I painting proudly with his breath on me,
All his court round him, seeing with his eyes,
Such frank French eyes, and such a fire of souls
Profuse, my hand kept plying by those hearts—
And, best of all, this, this, this face beyond,
This in the background, waiting on my work,
To crown the issue with a last reward!
A good time, was it not, my kingly days?
And had you not grown restless . . . but I know—
'Tis done and past; 'twas right, my instinct said;
Too live the life grew, golden and not gray,
And I'm the weak-eyed bat no sun should tempt
Out of the grange° whose four walls make his world. *country house*
How could it end in any other way?
You called me, and I came home to your heart.
The triumph was—to reach and stay there; since
I reached it ere the triumph, what is lost?
Let my hands frame your face in your hair's gold,
You beautiful Lucrezia that are mine!
"Rafael did this, Andrea painted that;
"The Roman's is the better when you pray,
"But still the other's Virgin was his wife—"
Men will excuse me. I am glad to judge
Both pictures in your presence; clearer grows
My better fortune, I resolve to think.
For, do you know, Lucrezia, as God lives,
Said one day Agnolo, his very self,
To Rafael . . . I have known it all these years . . .
(When the young man was flaming out his thoughts
Upon a palace-wall for Rome to see,
Too lifted up in heart because of it)
"Friend, there's a certain sorry little scrub
Goes up and down our Florence, none cares how,
Who, were he set to plan and execute
As you are, pricked on by your popes and kings,
Would bring the sweat into that brow of yours!"
To Rafael's! And indeed the arm is wrong.
I hardly dare . . . yet, only you to see,
Give the chalk here—quick, thus the line should go!
Ay, but the soul! he's Rafael! rub it out!
Still, all I care for, if he spoke the truth,
(What he? why, who but Michel Agnolo?
Do you forget already words like those?)
If really there was such a chance, so lost,
Is, whether you're—not grateful—but more pleased.
Well, let me think so. And you smile indeed!
This hour has been an hour! Another smile?
If you would sit thus by me every night
I should work better, do you comprehend?
I mean that I should earn more, give you more.
See, it is settled dusk now; there's a star;
Morello's gone, the watch-lights show the wall,
The cue-owls[7] speak the name we call them by.
Come from the window, love—come in, at last,
Inside the melancholy little house
We built to be so gay with. God is just.
King Francis may forgive me: oft at nights

7. A Mediterranean owl whose name derives from its cry, *ki-ou*.

When I look up from painting, eyes tired out,
The walls become illumined, brick from brick
Distinct, instead of mortar, fierce bright gold,
That gold of his I did cement them with!
Let us but love each other. Must you go?
That Cousin here again? he waits outside?
Must see you—you, and not with me? Those loans?
More gaming debts to pay? you smiled for that?
Well, let smiles buy me! have you more to spend?
While hand and eye and something of a heart
Are left me, work's my ware, and what's it worth?
I'll pay my fancy. Only let me sit
The gray remainder of the evening out,
Idle, you call it, and muse perfectly
How I could paint, were I but back in France,
One picture, just one more—the Virgin's face,
Not yours this time! I want you at my side
To hear them—that is, Michel Agnolo—
Judge all I do and tell you of its worth.
Will you? Tomorrow, satisfy your friend.
I take the subjects for his corridor,
Finish the portrait out of hand—there, there,
And throw him in another thing or two
If he demurs; the whole should prove enough
To pay for this same Cousin's freak. Beside,
What's better and what's all I care about,
Get you the thirteen scudi[8] for the ruff!
Love, does that please you? Ah, but what does he,
The Cousin! what does he to please you more?

I am grown peaceful as old age tonight.
I regret little, I would change still less.
Since there my past life lies, why alter it?
The very wrong to Francis! it is true
I took his coin, was tempted and complied,
And built this house and sinned, and all is said.
My father and my mother died of want.
Well, had I riches of my own? you see
How one gets rich! Let each one bear his lot.
They were born poor, lived poor, and poor they died:
And I have labored somewhat in my time
And not been paid profusely. Some good son
Paint my two hundred pictures—let him try!
No doubt, there's something strikes a balance. Yes,
You loved me quite enough, it seems tonight.
This must suffice me here. What would one have?
In heaven, perhaps, new chances, one more chance—
Four great walls in the New Jerusalem,[9]
Meted on each side by the angel's reed,
For Leonard,[1] Rafael, Agnolo and me
To cover—the three first without a wife,
While I have mine! So—still they overcome
Because there's still Lucrezia—as I choose.

Again the Cousin's whistle! Go, my Love.

1855

8. A *scudo* (*shield,* in Italian) was a silver coin bearing a shield.

9. Mentioned in Revelation xxi.10–21.

1. I.e., Leonardo da Vinci (1452–1519).

EDWARD LEAR
(1812–1888)

There Was an Old Man with a Beard

There was an Old Man with a beard,
Who said, "It is just as I feared!—
Two Owls and a Hen, four Larks and a Wren,
Have all built their nests in my beard!"

1846

There Was an Old Man in a Tree

There was an Old Man in a tree,
Who was horribly bored by a Bee;
When they said, "Does it buzz?" he replied, "Yes, it does!"
"It's a regular brute of a Bee!"

1846

There Was an Old Man Who Supposed

There was an Old Man who supposed,
That the street door was partially closed;
But some very large rats, ate his coats and his hats,
While that futile old gentleman dozed.

1846

The Owl and the Pussy-Cat

1

The Owl and the Pussy-cat went to sea
   In a beautiful pea-green boat,
They took some honey, and plenty of money,
   Wrapped up in a five-pound note.
The Owl looked up to the stars above,
   And sang to a small guitar,
"O lovely Pussy! O Pussy, my love,
      What a beautiful Pussy you are,
         You are,
         You are!
   What a beautiful Pussy you are!"

2

Pussy said to the Owl, "You elegant fowl!
   How charmingly sweet you sing!
O let us be married! too long we have tarried:
   But what shall we do for a ring?"
They sailed away, for a year and a day,
   To the land where the Bong-tree grows

And there in a wood a Piggy-wig stood
With a ring at the end of his nose,
His nose,
His nose,
With a ring at the end of his nose.

3
"Dear Pig, are you willing to sell for one shilling
Your ring?" Said the Piggy, "I will."
So they took it away, and were married next day
By the Turkey who lives on the hill.
They dined on mince, and slices of quince,
Which they ate with a runcible spoon;[1]
And hand in hand, on the edge of the sand,
They danced by the light of the moon,
The moon,
The moon,
They danced by the light of the moon.

1871

HENRY DAVID THOREAU (1817–1862)

I Am a Parcel of Vain Strivings Tied

I am a parcel of vain strivings tied
By a chance bond together,
Dangling this way and that, their links
Were made so loose and wide,
Methinks,
For milder weather.

A bunch of violets without their roots,
And sorrel intermixed,
Encircled by a wisp of straw
Once coiled about their shoots,
The law
By which I'm fixed.

A nosegay which Time clutched from out
Those fair Elysian fields,[2]
With weeds and broken stems, in haste,
Doth make the rabble rout
That waste
The day he yields.

And here I bloom for a short hour unseen,
Drinking my juices up,
With no root in the land
To keep my branches green,
But stand
In a bare cup.

1841

1. Fork with three broad, curved prongs and sharpened edge. Lear coined the word "runcible" and used it often in his nonsense verse.

2. In Greek mythology, the home of the blessed in the afterlife.

EMILY BRONTË
(1818–1848)

Remembrance [1]

Cold in the earth—and the deep snow piled above thee,
Far, far removed, cold in the dreary grave!
Have I forgot, my only Love, to love thee,
Severed at last by Time's all-severing wave?

Now, when alone, do my thoughts no longer hover
Over the mountains, on that northern shore,
Resting their wings where heath and fern leaves cover
Thy noble heart forever, ever more?

Cold in the earth—and fifteen wild Decembers,
From those brown hills, have melted into spring;
Faithful, indeed, is the spirit that remembers
After such years of change and suffering!

Sweet Love of youth, forgive, if I forget thee,
While the world's tide is bearing me along;
Other desires and other hopes beset me,
Hopes which obscure, but cannot do thee wrong!

No later light has lightened up my heaven,
No second morn has ever shone for me;
All my life's bliss from thy dear life was given,
All my life's bliss is in the grave with thee.

But, when the days of golden dreams had perished,
And even Despair was powerless to destroy,
Then did I learn how existence could be cherished,
Strengthened, and fed without the aid of joy.

Then did I check the tears of useless passion—
Weaned my young soul from yearning after thine;
Sternly denied its burning wish to hasten
Down to that tomb already more than mine.

And, even yet, I dare not let it languish,
Dare not indulge in memory's rapturous pain;
Once drinking deep of that divinest anguish,
How could I seek the empty world again?

1845 1846

The Prisoner

"Still let my tyrants know, I am not doomed to wear
Year after year in gloom, and desolate despair;

1. One of the Gondal poems. As children, Emily and Anne Brontë had written poems and stories about the inhabitants of Gondal, an imaginary island in the North Pacific, and Emily, at least, continued to write Gondal poems throughout her life.

A messenger of Hope comes every night to me,
And offers for short life, eternal liberty.

"He comes with western winds, with evening's wandering airs,
With that clear dusk of heaven that brings the thickest stars,
Winds take a pensive tone, and stars a tender fire,
And visions rise, and change, that kill me with desire.

"Desire for nothing known in my maturer years,
When Joy grew mad with awe, at counting future tears.
When, if my spirit's sky was full of flashes warm,
I knew not whence they came, from sun or thunderstorm.

"But, first, a hush of peace—a soundless calm descends;
The struggle of distress, and fierce impatience ends;
Mute music soothes my breast—unuttered harmony,
That I could never dream, till Earth was lost to me.

"Then dawns the Invisible; the Unseen its truth reveals;
My outward sense is gone, my inward essence feels:
Its wings are almost free—its home, its harbor found,
Measuring the gulf, it stoops and dares the final bound.

"O! dreadful is the check—intense the agony—
When the ear begins to hear, and the eye begins to see;
When the pulse begins to throb, the brain to think again;
The soul to feel the flesh, and the flesh to feel the chain.

"Yet I would lose no sting, would wish no torture less;
The more that anguish racks, the earlier it will bless;
And robed in fires of hell, or bright with heavenly shine,
If it but herald death, the vision is divine!"

1845 1846

No Coward Soul Is Mine

No coward soul is mine,
No trembler in the world's storm-troubled sphere!
I see Heaven's glories shine,
And Faith shines equal, arming me from Fear.

O God within my breast,
Almighty ever-present Deity!
Life, that in me hast rest
As I, undying Life, have power in thee!

Vain are the thousand creeds
That move men's hearts, unutterably vain;
Worthless as withered weeds,
Or idlest froth, amid the boundless main

To waken doubt in one
Holding so fast by thy infinity,
So surely anchored on
The steadfast rock of Immortality.

With wide-embracing love
Thy spirit animates eternal years,
Pervades and broods above,
Changes, sustains, dissolves, creates and rears.

Though earth and moon were gone,
And suns and universes ceased to be,
And thou were left alone,
Every Existence would exist in thee.

There is not room for Death,
Nor atom that his might could render void
Since thou art Being and Breath,
And what thou art may never be destroyed.

1850

HERMAN MELVILLE (1819–1891)

Shiloh[1]

A REQUIEM (APRIL 1862)

Skimming lightly, wheeling still,
The swallows fly low
Over the field in clouded days,
The forest-field of Shiloh—
Over the field where April rain
Solaced the parched one stretched in pain
Through the pause of night
That followed the Sunday fight
Around the church of Shiloh—
The church so lone, the log-built one,
That echoed to many a parting groan
And natural prayer
Of dying foemen mingled there—
Foemen at morn, but friends at eve—
Fame or country least their care:
(What like a bullet can undeceive!)
But now they lie low,
While over them the swallows skim,
And all is hushed at Shiloh.

1866

The Maldive Shark

About the Shark, phlegmatical one,
Pale sot of the Maldive sea,
The sleek little pilot-fish, azure and slim,
How alert in attendance be.
From his saw-pit of mouth, from his charnel of maw,

1. The battle at Shiloh church in Tennessee on April 6 and 7, 1862, was one of the bloodiest of the Civil War.

They have nothing of harm to dread,
But liquidly glide on his ghastly flank
Or before his Gorgonian[2] head;
Or lurk in the port of serrated teeth
In white triple tiers of glittering gates,
And there find a haven when peril's abroad,
An asylum in jaws of the Fates!
They are friends; and friendly they guide him to prey,
Yet never partake of the treat–
Eyes and brains to the dotard lethargic and dull,
Pale ravener of horrible meat.

1888

WALT WHITMAN
(1819–1892)

From Song of Myself

1

I celebrate myself, and sing myself,
And what I assume you shall assume,
For every atom belonging to me as good belongs to you.

I loaf and invite my soul,
I lean and loaf at my ease observing a spear of summer grass.

My tongue, every atom of my blood, formed from this soil, this air,
Born here of parents born here from parents the same, and their parents the same,
I, now thirty-seven years old in perfect health begin,
Hoping to cease not till death.

Creeds and schools in abeyance,
Retiring back a while sufficed at what they are, but never forgotten,
I harbor for good or bad, I permit to speak at every hazard,
Nature without check with original energy.

6

A child said *What is the grass?* fetching it to me with full hands;
How could I answer the child? I do not know what it is any more than he.

I guess it must be the flag of my disposition, out of hopeful green stuff woven.

Or I guess it is the handkerchief of the Lord,
A scented gift and remembrancer designedly dropped,
Bearing the owner's name someway in the corners, that we may see and remark, and say *Whose?*

Or I guess the grass is itself a child, the produced babe of the vegetation.

Or I guess it is a uniform hieroglyphic,
And it means, Sprouting alike in broad zones and narrow zones,
Growing among black folks as among white,

2. In classical mythology, Gorgon was one of three sisters (Medusa was another) whose face and snake-entwined hair could turn the viewer to stone; hence, a thing so frightening as to freeze its beholder.

Kanuck, Tuckahoe, Congressman, Cuff,[1] I give them the same, I receive them the same.
And now it seems to me the beautiful uncut hair of graves.

Tenderly will I use you curling grass,
It may be you transpire from the breasts of young men,
It may be if I had known them I would have loved them,
It may be you are from old people, or from offspring taken soon out of their mothers' laps,
And here you are the mothers' laps.

This grass is very dark to be from the white heads of old mothers,
Darker than the colorless beards of old men,
Dark to come from under the faint red roofs of mouths.

O I perceive after all so many uttering tongues,
And I perceive they do not come from the roofs of mouths for nothing.

I wish I could translate the hints about the dead young men and women.
And the hints about old men and mothers, and the offspring taken soon out of their laps.

What do you think has become of the young and old men?
And what do you think has become of the women and children?

They are alive and well somewhere,
The smallest sprout shows there is really no death,
And if ever there was it led forward life, and does not wait at the end to arrest it,
And ceased the moment life appeared.

All goes onward and outward, nothing collapses,
And to die is different from what anyone supposed, and luckier.

11

Twenty-eight young men bathe by the shore,
Twenty-eight young men and all so friendly;
Twenty-eight years of womanly life and all so lonesome.

She owns the fine house by the rise of the bank,
She hides handsome and richly dressed aft° the blinds of the window. (*behind*)

Which of the young men does she like the best?
Ah the homeliest of them is beautiful to her.

Where are you off to, lady? for I see you,
You splash in the water there, yet stay stock still in your room.

Dancing and laughing along the beach came the twenty-ninth bather,
The rest did not see her, but she saw them and loved them.

The beards of the young men glistened with wet, it ran from their long hair,
Little streams, passed all over their bodies.

An unseen hand also passed over their bodies,
It descended trembling from their temples and ribs.

1. Denotes a Negro. *Kanuck:* French Canadian; *Tuckahoe:* backwoods Virginian.

The young men float on their backs, their white bellies bulge to the sun, they do not ask who seizes fast to them,
They do not know who puffs and declines with pendant and bending arch,
They do not think whom they souse with spray.

24

Walt Whitman, a kosmos, of Manhattan the son,
Turbulent, fleshly, sensual, eating, drinking and breeding,
No sentimentalist, no stander above men and women or apart from them,
No more modest than immodest.

Unscrew the locks from the doors!
Unscrew the doors themselves from their jambs!

Whoever degrades another degrades me,
And whatever is done or said returns at last to me.

Through me the afflatus° surging and surging, through me the current and index. *inspiration*
I speak the password primeval, I give the sign of democracy,
By God! I will accept nothing which all cannot have their counterpart of on the same terms.

Through me many long dumb voices,
Voices of the interminable generations of prisoners and slaves,
Voices of the diseased and despairing and of thieves and dwarfs,
Voices of cycles of preparation and accretion,
And of the threads that connect the stars, and of wombs and of the father-stuff,
And of the rights of them the others are down upon,
Of the deformed, trivial, flat, foolish, despised,
Fog in the air, beetles rolling balls of dung.

Through me forbidden voices,
Voices of sexes and lusts, voices veiled and I remove the veil,
Voices indecent by me clarified and transfigured.

I do not press my fingers across my mouth,
I keep as delicate around the bowels as around the head and heart,
Copulation is no more rank to me than death is.

I believe in the flesh and the appetites,
Seeing, hearing, feeling, are miracles, and each part and tag of me is a miracle.

Divine am I inside and out, and I make holy whatever I touch or am touched from,
The scent of these armpits aroma finer than prayer,
This head more than churches, bibles, and all the creeds.

If I worship one thing more than another it shall be the spread of my own body, or any part of it,
Translucent mold of me it shall be you!
Shaded ledges and rests it shall be you!
Firm masculine colter [2] it shall be you!
Whatever goes to the tilth [3] of me it shall be you!

2. A cutting edge fastened to a plow ahead of the plowshare.

3. Arable land, topsoil.

You my rich blood! your milky stream pale strippings of my life!
Breast that presses against other breasts it shall be you!
My brain it shall be your occult convolutions!
Root of washed sweet-flag! timorous pond-snipe! nest of guarded duplicate eggs! it shall be you!
Mixed tussled hay of head, beard, brawn, it shall be you!
Trickling sap of maple, fiber of manly wheat, it shall be you!
Suns so generous it shall be you!
Vapors lighting and shading my face it shall be you!
You sweaty brooks and dews it shall be you!
Winds whose soft-tickling genitals rub against me it shall be you!
Broad muscular fields, branches of live oak, loving lounger in my winding paths, it shall be you!
Hands I have taken, face I have kissed, mortal I have ever touched, it shall be you.

I dote on myself, there is that lot of me and all so luscious,
Each moment and whatever happens thrills me with joy,
I cannot tell how my ankles bend, nor whence the cause of my faintest wish,
Nor the cause of the friendship I emit, nor the cause of the friendship I take again.

That I walk up my stoop, I pause to consider if it really be,
A morning-glory at my window satisfies me more than the metaphysics of books.

To behold the daybreak!
The little light fades the immense and diaphanous shadows,
The air tastes good to my palate.

Hefts of the moving world at innocent gambols silently rising, freshly exuding,
Scooting obliquely high and low.

Something I cannot see puts upward libidinous prongs,
Seas of bright juice suffuse heaven.

The earth by the sky staid with, the daily close of their junction,
The heaved challenge from the east that moment over my head,
The mocking taunt, See then whether you shall be master!

1855 1881

When I Heard the Learn'd Astronomer

When I heard the learn'd astronomer,
When the proofs, the figures, were ranged in columns before me,
When I was shown the charts and diagrams, to add, divide, and measure them,
When I sitting heard the astronomer where he lectured with much applause in the lecture-room,
How soon unaccountable I became tired and sick,
Till rising and gliding out I wander'd off by myself,
In the mystical moist night-air, and from time to time,
Look'd up in perfect silence at the stars.

1865, 1865

Crossing Brooklyn Ferry

1

Flood-tide below me! I see you face to face!
Clouds of the west—sun there half an hour high—I see you also face to face.
Crowds of men and women attired in the usual costumes, how curious you are to me!
On the ferry-boats the hundreds and hundreds that cross, returning home, are more curious to me than you suppose,
And you that shall cross from shore to shore years hence are more to me, and more in my meditations, than you might suppose.

2

The impalpable sustenance of me from all things at all hours of the day,
The simple, compact, well-join'd scheme, myself disintegrated, every one disintegrated yet part of the scheme,
The similitudes of the past and those of the future,
The glories strung like beads on my smallest sights and hearings, on the walk in the street and the passage over the river,
The current rushing so swiftly and swimming with me far away,
The others that are to follow me, the ties between me and them,
The certainty of others, the life, love, sight, hearing of others.

Others will enter the gates of the ferry and cross from shore to shore,
Others will watch the run of the flood-tide,
Others will see the shipping of Manhattan north and west, and the heights of Brooklyn to the south and east,
Others will see the islands large and small;
Fifty years hence, others will see them as they cross, the sun half an hour high,
A hundred years hence, or ever so many hundred years hence, others will see them,
Will enjoy the sunset, the pouring-in of the flood-tide, the falling-back to the sea of the ebb-tide.

3

It avails not, time nor place—distance avails not,
I am with you, you men and women of a generation, or ever so many generations hence,
Just as you feel when you look on the river and sky, so I felt,
Just as any of you is one of a living crowd, I was one of a crowd,
Just as you are refresh'd by the gladness of the river and the bright flow, I was refresh'd,
Just as you stand and lean on the rail, yet hurry with the swift current, I stood yet was hurried,
Just as you look on the numberless masts of ships and the thick-stemm'd pipes of steamboats, I look'd.

I too many and many a time cross'd the river of old,
Watched the Twelfth-month° sea-gulls, saw them high in the air floating with motionless wings, oscillating their bodies, *December*
Saw how the glistening yellow lit up parts of their bodies and left the rest in strong shadow,
Saw the slow-wheeling circles and the gradual edging toward the south,
Saw the reflection of the summer sky in the water,
Had my eyes dazzled by the shimmering track of beams,

Look'd at the fine centrifugal spokes of light round the shape of my head in the sunlit water,
Look'd on the haze on the hills southward and south-westward,
Look'd on the vapor as it flew in fleeces tinged with violet,
Look'd toward the lower bay to notice the vessels arriving,
Saw their approach, saw aboard those that were near me,
Saw the white sails of schooners and sloops, saw the ships at anchor,
The sailors at work in the rigging or out astride the spars,
The round masts, the swinging motion of the hulls, the slender serpentine pennants,
The large and small steamers in motion, the pilots in their pilot-houses,
The white wake left by the passage, the quick tremulous whirl of the wheels,
The flags of all nations, the falling of them at sunset,
The scallop-edged waves in the twilight, the ladled cups, the frolicsome crests and glistening,
The stretch afar growing dimmer and dimmer, the gray walls of the granite storehouses by the docks,
On the river the shadowy group, the big steam-tug closely flank'd on each side by the barges, the hay-boat, the belated lighter,[4]
On the neighboring shore the fires from the foundry chimneys burning high and glaringly into the night,
Casting their flicker of black contrasted with wild red and yellow light over the tops of houses, and down into the clefts of streets.

4

These and all else were to me the same as they are to you,
I loved well those cities, loved well the stately and rapid river,
The men and women I saw were all near to me,
Others the same—others who look back on me because I look'd forward to them,
(The time will come, though I stop° here to-day and to-night.) *stay*

5

What is it then between us?
What is the count of the scores or hundreds of years between us?

Whatever it is, it avails not—distance avails not, and place avails not,
I too lived, Brooklyn of ample hills was mine,
I too walk'd the streets of Manhattan island, and bathed in the waters around it,
I too felt the curious abrupt questionings stir within me,
In the day among crowds of people sometimes they came upon me,
In my walks home late at night or as I lay in my bed they came upon me,
I too had been struck from the float forever held in solution,
I too had receiv'd identity by my body,
That I was I knew was of my body, and what I should be I knew I should be of my body.

6

It is not upon you alone the dark patches fall,
The dark threw its patches down upon me also,
The best I had done seem'd to me blank and suspicious,
My great thoughts as I supposed them, were they not in reality meager?
Nor is it you alone who know what it is to be evil,
I am he who knew what it was to be evil,
I too knitted the old knot of contrariety,
Blabb'd, blush'd, resented, lied, stole, grudg'd,

4. Barge used for loading and unloading ships.

Had guile, anger, lust, hot wishes I dared not speak,
Was wayward, vain, greedy, shallow, sly, cowardly, malignant,
The wolf, the snake, the hog, not wanting in me,
The cheating look, the frivolous word, the adulterous wish, not wanting,
Refusals, hates, postponements, meanness, laziness, none of these wanting,
Was one with the rest, the days and haps of the rest,
Was call'd by my nighest name by clear loud voices of young men as they saw me approaching or passing,
Felt their arms on my neck as I stood, or the negligent leaning of their flesh against me as I sat,
Saw many I loved in the street or ferry-boat or public assembly, yet never told them a word,
Lived the same life with the rest, the same old laughing, gnawing, sleeping,
Play'd the part that still looks back on the actor or actress,
The same old role, the role that is what we make it, as great as we like,
Or as small as we like, or both great and small.

7

Closer yet I approach you,
What thought you have of me now, I had as much of you—I laid in my stores in advance,
I consider'd long and seriously of you before you were born.

Who was to know what should come home to me?
Who knows but I am enjoying this?
Who knows, for all the distance, but I am as good as looking at you now, for all you cannot see me?

8

Ah, what can ever be more stately and admirable to me than mast-hemm'd Manhattan?
River and sunset and scallop-edg'd waves of flood-tide?
The sea-gulls oscillating their bodies, the hay-boat in the twilight, and the belated lighter?
What gods can exceed these that clasp me by the hand, and with voices I love call me promptly and loudly by my nighest name as I approach?
What is more subtle than this which ties me to the woman or man that looks in my face?
Which fuses me into you now, and pours my meaning into you?

We understand then do we not?
What I promis'd without mentioning it, have you not accepted?
What the study could not teach—what the preaching could not accomplish is accomplish'd, is it not?

9

Flow on, river! flow with the flood-tide, and ebb with the ebb-tide!
Frolic on, crested and scallop-edg'd waves!
Gorgeous clouds of the sunset! drench with your splendor me, or the men and women generations after me!
Cross from shore to shore, countless crowds of passengers!
Stand up, tall masts of Mannahatta![5] stand up, beautiful hills of Brooklyn!
Throb, baffled and curious brain! throw out questions and answers!
Suspend here and everywhere, eternal float of solution!
Gaze, loving and thirsting eyes, in the house or street or public assembly!
Sound out, voices of young men! loudly and musically call me by my nighest name!
Live, old life! play the part that looks back on the actor or actress!

5. Variant for the Indian word normally spelled Manhattan.

Play the old role, the role that is great or small according as one makes it!
Consider, you who peruse me, whether I may not in unknown ways be looking upon you;
Be firm, rail over the river, to support those who lean idly, yet haste with the hasting current;
Fly on, sea birds! fly sideways, or wheel in large circles high in the air;
Receive the summer sky, you water, and faithfully hold it till all downcast eyes have time to take it from you!
Diverge, fine spokes of light, from the shape of my head, or any one's head, in the sunlit water!
Come on, ships from the lower bay! pass up or down, white-sail'd schooners, sloops, lighters!
Flaunt away, flags of all nations! be duly lower'd at sunset!
Burn high your fires, foundry chimneys! cast black shadows at nightfall! cast red and yellow light over the tops of the houses!
Appearances, now or henceforth, indicate what you are,
You necessary film, continue to envelop the soul,
About my body for me, and your body for you, be hung our divinest aromas,
Thrive, cities—bring your freight, bring your shows, ample and sufficient rivers,
Expand, being than which none else is perhaps more spiritual,
Keep your places, objects than which none else is more lasting.

You have waited, you always wait, you dumb, beautiful ministers,
We receive you with free sense at last, and are insatiate henceforward,
Not you any more shall be able to foil us, or withhold yourselves from us,
We use you, and do not cast you aside—we plant you permanently within us,
We fathom you not—we love you—there is perfection in you also,
You furnish your parts toward eternity,
Great or small, you furnish your parts toward the soul.

1856 1881

Vigil Strange I Kept on the Field One Night

Vigil strange I kept on the field one night;
When you my son and my comrade dropt at my side that day,
One look I but gave which your dear eyes return'd with a look I shall never forget,
One touch of your hand to mine O boy, reach'd up as you lay on the ground,
Then onward I sped in the battle, the even-contested battle,
Till late in the night reliev'd to the place at last again I made my way,
Found you in death so cold dear comrade, found your body son of responding kisses, (never again on earth responding,)
Bared your face in the starlight, curious the scene, cool blew the moderate night-wind,
Long there and then in vigil I stood, dimly around me the battle-field spreading,
Vigil wondrous and vigil sweet there in the fragrant silent night,
But not a tear fell, not even a long-drawn sigh, long I gazed,
Then on the earth partially reclining sat by your side leaning my chin in my hands,
Passing sweet hours, immortal and mystic hours with you dearest comrade—not a tear, not a word,
Vigil of silence, love and death, vigil for you my son and my soldier,
As onward silently stars aloft, eastward new ones upward stole,
Vigil final for you brave boy, (I could not save you, swift was your death,

I faithfully loved you and cared for you living, I think we shall surely meet again,)
Till at latest lingering of the night, indeed just as the dawn appear'd,
My comrade I wrapt in his blanket, envelop'd well his form,
Folded the blanket well, tucking it carefully over head and carefully under feet,
And there and then and bathed by the rising sun, my son in his grave, in his rude-dug grave I deposited,
Ending my vigil strange with that, vigil of night and battle-field dim,
Vigil for boy of responding kisses, (never again on earth responding,)
Vigil for comrade swiftly slain, vigil I never forget, how as day brighten'd,
I rose from the chill ground and folded my soldier well in his blanket,
And buried him where he fell.

1865 1867

Beat! Beat! Drums!

Beat! beat! drums! blow! bugles! blow!
Through the windows—through doors—burst like a ruthless force,
Into the solemn church, and scatter the congregation,
Into the school where the scholar is studying;
Leave not the bridegroom quiet—no happiness must he have now with his bride,
Nor the peaceful farmer any peace, ploughing his field or gathering his grain,
So fierce you whirr and pound you drums—so shrill you bugles blow.

Beat! beat! drums!—blow! bugles! blow!
Over the traffic of cities—over the rumble of wheels in the streets;
Are beds prepared for sleepers at night in the houses? no sleepers must sleep in those beds,
No bargainers' bargains by day—no brokers or speculators—would they continue?
Would the talkers be talking? would the singer attempt to sing?
Would the lawyer rise in the court to state his case before the judge?
Then rattle quicker, heavier drums—you bugles wilder blow.
Beat! beat! drums!—blow! bugles! blow!
Make no parley—stop for no expostulation,
Mind not the timid—mind not the weeper or prayer,
Mind not the old man beseeching the young man,
Let not the child's voice be heard, nor the mother's entreaties,
Make even the trestles to shake the dead where they lie awaiting the hearses,
So strong you thump O terrible drums—so loud you bugles blow.

1861 1867

Out of the Cradle Endlessly Rocking

Out of the cradle endlessly rocking,
Out of the mocking-bird's throat, the musical shuttle,
Out of the Ninth-month[6] midnight,
Over the sterile sands and the fields beyond, where the child leaving his bed wander'd alone, bareheaded, barefoot,
Down from the shower'd halo,
Up from the mystic play of shadows twining and twisting as if they were alive,

6. The Quaker designation for September may here also suggest the human cycle of fertility and birth, in contrast with "sterile sands" in the next line.

Out from the patches of briers and blackberries,
From the memories of the bird that chanted to me,
From your memories sad brother, from the fitful risings and fallings I heard,
From under that yellow half-moon late-risen and swollen as if with tears,
From those beginning notes of yearning and love there in the mist,
From the thousand responses of my heart never to cease,
From the myriad thence-arous'd words,
From the word stronger and more delicious than any,
From such as now they start the scene revisiting,
As a flock, twittering, rising, or overhead passing,
Borne hither, ere all eludes me, hurriedly,
A man, yet by these tears a little boy again,
Throwing myself on the sand, confronting the waves,
I, chanter of pains and joys, uniter of here and hereafter,
Taking all hints to use them, but swiftly leaping beyond them,
A reminiscence sing.

Once Paumanok,[7]
When the lilac-scent was in the air and Fifth-month grass was growing,
Up this seashore in some briers,
Two feather'd guests from Alabama, two together,
And their nest, and four light-green eggs spotted with brown,
And every day the he-bird to and fro near at hand,
And every day the she-bird crouch'd on her nest, silent, with bright eyes,
And every day I, a curious boy, never too close, never disturbing them,
Cautiously peering, absorbing, translating.

Shine! shine! shine!
Pour down your warmth, great sun!
While we bask, we two together.

Two together!
Winds blow south, or winds blow north,
Day come white, or night come black,
Home, or rivers and mountains from home,
Singing all time, minding no time,
While we two keep together.

Till of a sudden,
May-be kill'd, unknown to her mate,
One forenoon the she-bird crouch'd not on the nest,
Nor return'd that afternoon, nor the next,
Nor ever appear'd again.

And thenceforward all summer in the sound of the sea,
And at night under the full of the moon in calmer weather,
Over the hoarse surging of the sea,
Or flitting from brier to brier by day,
I saw, I heard at intervals the remaining one, the he-bird,
The solitary guest from Alabama.

Blow! blow! blow!
Blow up sea-winds along Paumanok's shore;
I wait and I wait till you blow my mate to me.

Yes, when the stars glisten'd,
All night long on the prong of a moss-scallop'd stake,

7. The Indian name for Long Island.

Down almost amid the slapping waves,
Sat the lone singer wonderful causing tears.

He call'd on his mate,
He pour'd forth the meanings which I of all men know.

Yes my brother I know,
The rest might not, but I have treasur'd every note,
For more than once dimly down to the beach gliding,
Silent, avoiding the moonbeams, blending myself with the shadows,
Recalling now the obscure shapes, the echoes, the sounds and sights after their sorts,
The white arms out in the breakers tirelessly tossing,
I, with bare feet, a child, the wind wafting my hair,
Listen'd long and long.

Listen'd to keep, to sing, now translating the notes,
Following you my brother.

Soothe! soothe! soothe!
Close on its wave soothes the wave behind,
And again another behind embracing and lapping, every one close,
But my love soothes not me, not me.

Low hangs the moon, it rose late,
It is lagging—O I think it is heavy with love, with love.

O madly the sea pushes upon the land,
With love, with love.

O night! do I not see my love fluttering out among the breakers?
What is that little black thing I see there in the white?

Loud! loud! loud!
Loud I call to you, my love!

High and clear I shoot my voice over the waves,
Surely you must know who is here, is here,
You must know who I am, my love.

Low-hanging moon!
What is that dusky spot in your brown yellow?
O it is the shape, the shape of my mate!
O moon do not keep her from me any longer.

Land! land! O land!
Whichever way I turn, O I think you could give me my mate back again if you only would,
For I am almost sure I see her dimly whichever way I look.

O rising stars!
Perhaps the one I want so much will rise, will rise with some of you.

O throat! O trembling throat!
Sound clearer through the atmosphere!

Pierce the woods, the earth,
Somewhere listening to catch you must be the one I want.

Shake out carols!
Solitary here, the night's carols!
Carols of lonesome love! death's carols!
Carols under that lagging, yellow, waning moon!
O under that moon where she droops almost down into the sea!
O reckless despairing carols.

But soft! sink low!
Soft! let me just murmur,
And do you wait a moment you husky-nois'd sea,
For somewhere I believe I heard my mate responding to me,
So faint, I must be still, be still to listen,
But not altogether still, for then she might not come immediately to me.

Hither my love!
Here I am! here!
With this just-sustain'd note I announce myself to you,
This gentle call is for you my love, for you.

Do not be decoy'd elsewhere,
That is the whistle of the wind, it is not my voice,
That is the fluttering, the fluttering of the spray,
Those are the shadows of leaves.

O darkness! O in vain!
O I am very sick and sorrowful.

O brown halo in the sky near the moon, drooping upon the sea!
O troubled reflection in the sea!
O throat! O throbbing heart!
And I singing uselessly, uselessly all the night.

O past! O happy life! O songs of joy!
In the air, in the woods, over fields,
Loved! loved! loved! loved! loved!
But my mate no more, no more with me!
We two together no more.

The aria sinking,
All else continuing, the stars shining,
The winds blowing, the notes of the bird continuous echoing,
With angry moans the fierce old mother incessantly moaning,
On the sands of Paumanok's shore gray and rustling,
The yellow half-moon enlarged, sagging down, drooping, the face of the sea almost touching,
The boy ecstatic, with his bare feet the waves, with his hair the atmosphere dallying,
The love in the heart long pent, now loose, now at last tumultuously bursting,
The aria's meaning, the ears, the soul, swiftly depositing,
The strange tears down the cheeks coursing,
The colloquy there, the trio, each uttering,
The undertone, the savage old mother incessantly crying,
To the boy's soul's questions sullenly timing, some drown'd secret hissing,
To the outsetting bard.

Demon or bird! (said the boy's soul,)
Is it indeed toward your mate you sing? or is it really to me?
For I, that was a child, my tongue's use sleeping, now I have heard you,
Now in a moment I know what I am for, I awake,
And already a thousand singers, a thousand songs, clearer, louder and more sorrowful than yours,
A thousand warbling echoes have started to life within me, never to die.

O you singer solitary, singing by yourself, projecting me,
O solitary me listening, never more shall I cease perpetuating you,
Never more shall I escape, never more the reverberations,
Never more the cries of unsatisfied love be absent from me,
Never again leave me to be the peaceful child I was before what there in the night,
By the sea under the yellow and sagging moon,
The messenger there arous'd, the fire, the sweet hell within,
The unknown want, the destiny of me.

O give me the clew! (it lurks in the night here somewhere,)
O if I am to have so much, let me have more!

A word then, (for I will conquer it,)
The word final, superior to all,
Subtle, sent up—what is it?—I listen;
Are you whispering it, and have been all the time, you sea-waves?
Is that it from your liquid rims and wet sands?

Whereto answering, the sea,
Delaying not, hurrying not,
Whisper'd me through the night, and very plainly before daybreak,
Lisp'd to me the low and delicious word death,
And again death, death, death, death,
Hissing melodious, neither like the bird nor like my arous'd child's heart,
But edging near as privately for me rustling at my feet,
Creeping thence steadily up to my ears and laving me softly all over,
Death, death, death, death, death.

Which I do not forget,
But fuse the song of my dusky demon and brother,
That he sang to me in the moonlight on Paumanok's gray beach,
With the thousand responsive songs at random,
My own songs awaked from that hour,
And with them the key, the word up from the waves,
The word of the sweetest song and all songs,
That strong and delicious word which, creeping to my feet,
(Or like some old crone rocking the cradle, swathed in sweet garments, bending aside,)
The sea whisper'd me.

1859 1881

When Lilacs Last in the Dooryard Bloom'd

1

When lilacs last in the dooryard bloom'd,
And the great star early droop'd in the western sky in the night,
I mourn'd, and yet shall mourn with ever-returning spring.

Ever-returning spring, trinity sure to me you bring,
Lilac blooming perennial and drooping star in the west,
And thought of him I love.

2

O powerful western fallen star!
O shades of night—O moody, tearful night!
O great star disappear'd—O the black murk that hides the star!
O cruel hands that hold me powerless—O helpless soul of me!
O harsh surrounding cloud that will not free my soul.

3

In the dooryard fronting an old farm-house near the white-wash'd palings,
Stands the lilac-bush tall-growing with heart-shaped leaves of rich green,
With many a pointed blossom rising delicate, with the perfume strong I love,
With every leaf a miracle—and from this bush in the dooryard,
With delicate-color'd blossoms and heart-shaped leaves of rich green,
A sprig with its flower I break.

4

In the swamp in secluded recesses,
A shy and hidden bird is warbling a song.

Solitary the thrush,
The hermit withdrawn to himself, avoiding the settlements,
Sings by himself a song.

Song of the bleeding throat,
Death's outlet song of life, (for well dear brother I know,
If thou wast not granted to sing thou would'st surely die.)

5

Over the breast of the spring, the land, amid cities,
Amid lanes and through old woods, where lately the violets peep'd from the
ground, spotting the gray debris,
Amid the grass in the fields each side of the lanes, passing the endless grass,
Passing the yellow-spear'd wheat, every grain from its shroud in the dark-
brown fields uprisen,
Passing the apple-tree blows of white and pink in the orchards,
Carrying a corpse to where it shall rest in the grave,
Night and day journeys a coffin.

6

Coffin that passes through lanes and streets,[8]
Through day and night with the great cloud darkening the land,
With the pomp of the inloop'd flags with the cities draped in black,
With the show of the States themselves as of crape-veil'd women standing,
With processions long and winding and the flambeaus of the night,
With the countless torches lit, with the silent sea of faces and the unbared
heads,
With the waiting depot, the arriving coffin, and the sombre faces,
With dirges through the night, with the thousand voices rising strong and
solemn,
With all the mournful voices of the dirges pour'd around the coffin,
The dim-lit churches and the shuddering organs—where amid these you
journey,
With the tolling tolling bells' perpetual clang,
Here, coffin that slowly passes,
I give you my sprig of lilac.

8. The funeral cortège of Lincoln traveled from Washington to Springfield, Illinois, stopping at cities and towns all along the way for the people to honor the murdered President.

7

(Nor for you, for one alone,
Blossoms and branches green to coffins all I bring,
For fresh as the morning, thus would I chant a song for you O sane and sacred death.

All over bouquets of roses,
O death, I cover you over with roses and early lilies,
But mostly and now the lilac that blooms the first,
Copious I break, I break the sprigs from the bushes,
With loaded arms I come, pouring for you,
For you and the coffins all of you O death.)

8

O western orb sailing the heaven,
Now I know what you must have meant as a month since I walk'd,
As I walk'd in silence the transparent shadowy night,
As I saw you had something to tell as you bent to me night after night,
As you droop'd from the sky low down as if to my side, (while the other stars all look'd on,)
As we wander'd together the solemn night, (for something I know not what kept me from sleep,)
As the night advanced, and I saw on the rim of the west how full you were of woe,
As I stood on the rising ground in the breeze in the cool transparent night,
As I watch'd where you pass'd and was lost in the netherward black of the night,
As my soul in its trouble dissatisfied sank, as where you sad orb,
Concluded, dropt in the night, and was gone.

9

Sing on there in the swamp,
O singer bashful and tender, I hear your notes, I hear your call,
I hear, I come presently, I understand you,
But a moment I linger, for the lustrous star has detain'd me,
The star my departing comrade holds and detains me.

10

O how shall I warble myself for the dead one there I loved?
And how shall I deck my song for the large sweet soul that has gone?
And what shall my perfume be for the grave of him I love?

Sea-winds blown from east and west,
Blown from the Eastern sea and blown from the Western sea, till there on the prairies meeting,
These and with these and the breath of my chant,
I'll perfume the grave of him I love.

11

O what shall I hang on the chamber walls?
And what shall the pictures be that I hang on the walls,
To adorn the burial-house of him I love?

Pictures of growing spring and farms and homes,
With the Fourth-month eve at sundown, and the gray smoke lucid and bright,
With floods of the yellow gold of the gorgeous, indolent, sinking sun, burning, expanding the air,
With the fresh sweet herbage under foot, and the pale green leaves of the trees prolific,

In the distance the flowing glaze, the breast of the river, with a wind-dapple here and there,
With ranging hills on the banks, with many a line against the sky, and shadows,
And the city at hand with dwellings so dense, and stacks of chimneys,
And all the scenes of life and the workshops, and the workmen homeward returning.

12

Lo, body and soul—this land,
My own Manhattan with spires, and the sparkling and hurrying tides, and the ships,
The varied and ample land, the South and the North in the light, Ohio's shores and flashing Missouri,
And ever the far-spreading prairies cover'd with grass and corn.

Lo, the most excellent sun so calm and haughty,
The violet and purple morn with just-felt breezes,
The gentle soft-born measureless light,
The miracle spreading bathing all, the fulfill'd noon,
The coming eve delicious, the welcome night and the stars,
Over my cities shining all, enveloping man and land.

13

Sing on, sing on you gray-brown bird,
Sing from the swamps, the recesses, pour your chant from the bushes,
Limitless out of the dusk, out of the cedars and pines.

Sing on dearest brother, warble your reedy song,
Loud human song, with voice of uttermost woe.

O liquid and free and tender!
O wild and loose to my soul—O wondrous singer!
You only I hear—yet the star holds me, (but will soon depart,)
Yet the lilac with mastering odor holds me.

14

Now while I sat in the day and look'd forth,
In the close of the day with its light and the fields of spring, and the farmers preparing their crops,
In the large unconscious scenery of my land with its lakes and forests,
In the heavenly aerial beauty, (after the perturb'd winds and the storms,)
Under the arching heavens of the afternoon swift passing, and the voices of children and women,
The many-moving sea-tides, and I saw the ships how they sail'd,
And the summer approaching with richness, and the fields all busy with labor,
And the infinite separate houses, how they all went on, each with its meals and minutia of daily usages,
And the streets how their throbbings throbb'd, and the cities pent—lo, then and there,
Falling upon them all and among them all, enveloping me with the rest,
Appear'd the cloud, appear'd the long black trail,
And I knew death, its thought, and the sacred knowledge of death.

Then with the knowledge of death as walking one side of me,
And the thought of death close-walking the other side of me,

And I in the middle as with companions, and as holding the hands of companions,
I fled forth to the hiding receiving night that talks not,
Down to the shores of the water, the path by the swamp in the dimness,
To the solemn shadowy cedars and ghostly pines so still.

And the singer so shy to the rest receiv'd me,
The gray-brown bird I know receiv'd us comrades three,
And he sang the carol of death, and a verse for him I love.

From deep secluded recesses,
From the fragrant cedars and the ghostly pines so still,
Came the carol of the bird.

And the charm of the carol rapt me,
As I held as if by their hands my comrades in the night,
And the voice of my spirit tallied the song of the bird.

Come lovely and soothing death,
Undulate round the world, serenely arriving, arriving,
In the day, in the night, to all, to each,
Sooner or later delicate death.

Prais'd be the fathomless universe,
For life and joy, and for objects and knowledge curious,
And for love, sweet love—but praise! praise! praise!
For the sure-enwinding arms of cool-enfolding death.

Dark mother always gliding near with soft feet,
Have none chanted for thee a chant of fullest welcome?
Then I chant it for thee, I glorify thee above all,
I bring thee a song that when thou must indeed come, come unfalteringly.

Approach strong deliveress,
When it is so, when thou hast taken them I joyously sing the dead,
Lost in the loving floating ocean of thee,
Laved in the flood of thy bliss O death.

From me to thee glad serenades,
Dances for thee I propose saluting thee, adornments and feastings for thee,
And the sights of the open landscape and the high-spread sky are fitting,
And life and the fields, and the huge and thoughtful night.

The night in silence under many a star,
The ocean shore and the husky whispering wave whose voice I know,
And the soul turning to thee O vast and well-veil'd death,
And the body gratefully nestling close to thee.

Over the tree-tops I float thee a song,
Over the rising and sinking waves, over the myriad fields and the prairies wide,
Over the dense-pack'd cities all and the teeming wharves and ways,
I float this carol with joy, with joy to thee O death.

15

To the tally of my soul,
Loud and strong kept up the gray-brown bird,
With pure deliberate notes spreading filling the night.

Loud in the pines and cedars dim,
Clear in the freshness moist and the swamp-perfume,
And I with my comrades there in the night.

While my sight that was bound in my eyes unclosed,
As to long panoramas of visions.

And I saw askant the armies,
I saw as in noiseless dreams hundreds of battle-flags,
Borne through the smoke of the battles and pierc'd with missiles I saw them,
And carried hither and yon through the smoke, and torn and bloody,
And at last but a few shreds left on the staffs, (and all in silence,)
And the staffs all splinter'd and broken.

I saw battle-corpses, myriads of them,
And the white skeletons of young men, I saw them,
I saw the debris and debris of all the slain soldiers of the war,
But I saw they were not as was thought,
They themselves were fully at rest, they suffer'd not,
The living remain'd and suffer'd, the mother suffer'd,
And the wife and the child and the musing comrade suffer'd,
And the armies that remain'd suffer'd.

16

Passing the visions, passing the night,
Passing, unloosing the hold of my comrades' hands,
Passing the song of the hermit bird and the tallying song of my soul,
Victorious song, death's outlet song, yet varying ever-altering song,
As low and wailing, yet clear the notes, rising and falling, flooding the night,
Sadly sinking and fainting, as warning and warning, and yet again bursting with joy,
Covering the earth and filling the spread of the heaven,
As that powerful psalm in the night I heard from recesses,
Passing, I leave thee lilac with heart-shaped leaves,
I leave thee there in the door-yard, blooming, returning with spring.

I cease from my song for thee,
From my gaze on thee in the west, fronting the west, communing with thee,
O comrade lustrous with silver face in the night.

Yet each to keep and all, retrievements out of the night,
The song, the wondrous chant of the gray-brown bird,
And the tallying chant, the echo arous'd in my soul,
With the lustrous and drooping star with the countenance full of woe,
With the holders holding my hand nearing the call of the bird,
Comrades mine and I in the midst, and their memory ever to keep, for the dead I loved so well,
For the sweetest, wisest soul of all my days and lands—and this for his dear sake,
Lilac and star and bird twined with the chant of my soul,
There in the fragrant pines and the cedars dusk and dim.

1865–66 1881

A Noiseless Patient Spider

A noiseless patient spider,
I mark'd where on a little promontory it stood isolated,
Mark'd how to explore the vacant vast surrounding,
It launch'd forth filament, filament, filament, out of itself,
Ever unreeling them, ever tirelessly speeding them.

And you O my soul where you stand,
Surrounded, detached, in measureless oceans of space,
Ceaselessly musing, venturing, throwing, seeking the spheres to connect them,
Till the bridge you will need be form'd, till the ductile anchor hold,
Till the gossamer thread you fling catch somewhere, O my soul.

1868 1881

To a Locomotive in Winter

Thee for my recitative,
Thee in the driving storm even as now, the snow, the winter-day declining,
Thee in thy panoply, thy measur'd dual throbbing and thy beat convulsive,
Thy black clyindric body, golden brass and silvery steel,
Thy ponderous side-bars, parallel and connecting rods, gyrating, shuttling at thy sides,
Thy metrical, now swelling pant and roar, now tapering in the distance,
Thy great protruding head-light fix'd in front,
Thy long, pale, floating vapor-pennants, tinged with delicate purple,
The dense and murky clouds out-belching from thy smoke-stack,
Thy knitted frame, thy springs and valves, the tremulous twinkle of thy wheels,
Thy train of cars behind, obedient, merrily following,
Through gale or calm, now swift, now slack, yet steadily careering;
Type of the modern—emblem of motion and power—pulse of the continent,
For once come serve the Muse and merge in verse, even as here I see thee,
With storm and buffeting gusts of wind and falling snow,
By day thy warning ringing bell to sound its notes,
By night thy silent signal lamps to swing.

Fierce-throated beauty!
Roll through my chant with all thy lawless music, thy swinging lamps at night,
Thy madly-whistled laughter, echoing, rumbling like an earthquake, rousing all,
Law of thyself complete, thine own track firmly holding,
(No sweetness debonair of tearful harp or glib piano thine,)
Thy trills of shrieks by rocks and hills return'd,
Launch'd o'er the prairies wide, across the lakes,
To the free skies unpent and glad and strong.

1876 1881

MATTHEW ARNOLD
(1822–1888)

Shakespeare

Others abide our question. Thou art free.
We ask and ask—thou smilest and art still,
Out-topping knowledge. For the loftiest hill,
Who to the stars uncrowns his majesty,

Planting his stedfast footsteps in the sea,
Making the heaven of heavens his dwelling-place,
Spares but the cloudy border of his base
To the foiled searching of mortality;

And thou, who didst the stars and sunbeams know,
Self-schooled, self-scanned, self-honored, self-secure,
Didst tread on earth unguessed at—better so!

All pains the immortal spirit must endure,
All weakneess which impairs, all griefs which bow,
Find their sole speech in that victorious brow.

1849

To Marguerite

Yes! in the sea of life enisled,
With echoing straits between us thrown,
Dotting the shoreless watery wild,
We mortal millions live *alone.*
The islands feel the enclasping flow,
And then their endless bounds they know.

But when the moon their hollows lights,
And they are swept by balms of spring,
And in their glens, on starry nights,
The nightingales divinely sing;
And lovely notes, from shore to shore,
Across the sounds and channels pour—

Oh! then a longing like despair
Is to their farthest caverns sent;
For surely once, they feel, we were
Parts of a single continent!
Now round us spreads the watery plain—
Oh might our marges meet again!

Who ordered, that their longing's fire
Should be, as soon as kindled, cooled?
Who renders vain their deep desire?—
A God, a God their severance ruled!
And bade betwixt their shores to be
The unplumbed, salt, estranging sea.

1852

The Scholar-Gypsy[1]

Go, for they call you, shepherd, from the hill;
Go, shepherd, and untie the wattled cotes![2]
No longer leave thy wistful flock unfed,
Nor let thy bawling fellows rack their throats,
Nor the cropped herbage shoot another head.
But when the fields are still,
And the tired men and dogs all gone to rest,
And only the white sheep are sometimes seen
Cross and recross the strips of moon-blanched green,
Come, shepherd, and again begin the quest!

Here, where the reaper was at work of late—
In this high field's dark corner, where he leaves
His coat, his basket, and his earthen cruse,° *vessel*
And in the sun all morning binds the sheaves,
Then here, at noon, comes back his stores to use—
Here will I sit and wait,
While to my ear from uplands far away
The bleating of the folded flocks is borne,
With distant cries of reapers in the corn°— *grain*
All the live murmur of a summer's day.

Screened is this nook o'er the high, half-reaped field,
And here till sundown, shepherd! will I be.
Through the thick corn the scarlet poppies peep,
And round green roots and yellowing stalks I see
Pale pink convolvulus in tendrils creep;
And air-swept lindens yield
Their scent, and rustle down their perfumed showers
Of bloom on the bent grass where I am laid,
And bower me from the August sun with shade;
And the eye travels down to Oxford's towers.

And near me on the grass lies Glanvil's book—
Come, let me read the oft-read tale again!
The story of the Oxford scholar poor,
Of pregnant parts[3] and quick inventive brain,
Who, tired of knocking at preferment's door,
One summer-morn forsook
His friends, and went to learn the gypsy-lore,
And roamed the world with that wild brotherhood,

1. " 'There was very lately a lad in the University of Oxford, who was by his poverty forced to leave his studies there; and at last to join himself to a company of vagabond gypsies. Among these extravagant people, by the insinuating subtlety of his carriage, he quickly got so much of their love and esteem as that they discovered to him their mystery. After he had been a pretty while well exercised in the trade, there chanced to ride by a couple of scholars, who had formerly been of his acquaintance. They quickly spied out their old friend among the gypsies; and he gave them an account of the necessity which drove him to that kind of life, and told them that the people he went with were not such impostors as they were taken for, but that they had a traditional kind of learning among them, and could do wonders by the power of imagination, their fancy binding that of others: that himself had learned much of their art, and when he had compassed the whole secret, he intended, he said, to leave their company, and give the world an account of what he had learned.'—Glanvil's *Vanity of Dogmatizing*, 1661" [Arnold's note]

2. Sheepfolds made of woven boughs (wattles).

3. I.e., of quick intellectual abilities.

And came, as most men deemed, to little good,
But came to Oxford and his friends no more.

But once, years after, in the country-lanes,
Two scholars, whom at college erst he knew,
Met him, and of his way of life enquired;
Whereat he answered, that the gypsy-crew,
His mates, had arts to rule as they desired
The workings of men's brains,
And they can bind them to what thoughts they will.
"And I," he said, "the secret of their art,
When fully learned, will to the world impart;
But it needs heaven-sent moments for this skill."

This said, he left them, and returned no more.—
But rumors hung about the country-side,
That the lost Scholar long was seen to stray,
Seen by rare glimpses, pensive and tongue-tied,
In hat of antique shape, and cloak of gray.
The same the gypsies wore.
Shepherds had met him on the Hurst[4] in spring;
At some lone alehouse in the Berkshire moors,
On the warm ingle-bench, the smock-frocked boors° *rustics*
Had found him seated at their entering,

But, 'mid their drink and clatter, he would fly.
And I myself seem half to know thy looks,
And put the shepherds, wanderer! on thy trace;
And boys who in lone wheatfields scare the rooks
I ask if thou hast passed their quiet place;
Or in my boat I lie
Moored to the cool bank in the summer-heats,
'Mid wide grass meadows which the sunshine fills,
And watch the warm, green-muffled Cumner hills,
And wonder if thou haunt'st their shy retreats.

For most, I know, thou lov'st retired ground!
Thee at the ferry Oxford riders blithe,
Returning home on summer-nights, have met
Crossing the stripling Thames at Bab-lock-hithe,
Trailing in the cool stream thy fingers wet,
As the punt's rope chops round;[5]
And leaning backward in a pensive dream,
And fostering in thy lap a heap of flowers
Plucked in shy fields and distant Wychwood bowers,
And thine eyes resting on the moonlit stream.

And then they land, and thou art seen no more!
Maidens, who from the distant hamlets come
To dance around the Fyfield elm in May,
Oft through the darkening fields have seen thee roam,
Or cross a stile into the public way.
Oft thou hast given them store

4. A hill near Oxford. (All place-names in the poem, with the obvious exception of the Mediterranean localities of the last two stanzas, refer to the countryside around Oxford.)

5. "As the punt's rope chops round": i.e., as the rope tying the small boat to the bank shifts around.

Of flowers—the frail-leafed, white anemone,
Dark bluebells drenched with dews of summer eves,
And purple orchises with spotted leaves—
But none hath words she can report of thee.

And, above Godstow Bridge, when hay-time's here
In June, and many a scythe in sunshine flames,
Men who through those wide fields of breezy grass
Where black-winged swallows haunt the glittering Thames,
To bathe in the abandoned lasher[6] pass,
Have often passed thee near
Sitting upon the river bank o'ergrown;
Marked thine outlandish garb, thy figure spare,
Thy dark vague eyes, and soft abstracted air—
But, when they came from bathing, thou wast gone!

At some lone homestead in the Cumner hills,
Where at her open door the housewife darns,
Thou hast been seen, or hanging on a gate
To watch the threshers in the mossy barns.
Children, who early range these slopes and late
For cresses from the rills,
Have known thee eying, all an April-day,
The springing pastures and the feeding kine;
And marked thee, when the stars come out and shine,
Through the long dewy grass move slow away.

In autumn, on the skirts of Bagley Wood—
Where most the gypsies by the turf-edged way
Pitch their smoked tents, and every bush you see
With scarlet patches tagged and shreds of gray,
Above the forest-ground called Thessaly—
The blackbird, picking food,
Sees thee, nor stops his meal, nor fears at all;
So often has he known thee past him stray,
Rapt, twirling in thy hand a withered spray,
And waiting for the spark from heaven to fall.

And once, in winter, on the causeway chill
Where home through flooded fields foot-travelers go,
Have I not passed thee on the wooden bridge,
Wrapt in thy cloak and battling with the snow,
Thy face tow'rd Hinksey and its wintry ridge?
And thou hast climbed the hill,
And gained the white brow of the Cumner range;
Turned once to watch, while thick the snowflakes fall,
The line of festal light in Christ-Church hall—
Then sought thy straw in some sequestered grange.

But what—I dream! Two hundred years are flown
Since first thy story ran through Oxford halls,
And the grave Glanvil did the tale inscribe
That thou wert wandered from the studious walls
To learn strange arts, and join a gypsy-tribe;
And thou from earth art gone
Long since, and in some quiet churchyard laid—
Some country-nook, where o'er thy unknown grave

6. Slack water above a weir or dam, or the weir itself.

Tall grasses and white flowering nettles wave,
Under a dark, red-fruited yew-tree's shade.

—No, no, thou hast not felt the lapse of hours!
For what wears out the life of mortal men?
'Tis that from change to change their being rolls;
'Tis that repeated shocks, again, again,
Exhaust the energy of strongest souls
And numb the elastic powers.
Till having used our nerves with bliss and teen,° *vexation*
And tired upon a thousand schemes our wit,
To the just-pausing Genius[7] we remit
Our worn-out life, and are—what we have been.

Thou hast not lived, why should'st thou perish, so?
Thou hadst *one* aim, *one* business, *one* desire;
Else wert thou long since numbered with the dead!
Else hadst thou spent, like other men, thy fire!
The generations of thy peers are fled,
And we ourselves shall go;
But thou possessest an immortal lot,
And we imagine thee exempt from age
And living as thou liv'st on Glanvil's page,
Because thou hadst—what we, alas! have not.

For early didst thou leave the world, with powers
Fresh, undiverted to the world without,
Firm to their mark, not spent on other things;
Free from the sick fatigue, the languid doubt,
Which much to have tried, in much been baffled, brings.
O life unlike to ours!
Who fluctuate idly without term or scope,
Of whom each strives, nor knows for what he strives,
And each half lives a hundred different lives;[8]
Who wait like thee, but not, like thee, in hope.

Thou waitest for the spark from heaven! and we,
Light half-believers of our casual creeds,
Who never deeply felt, nor clearly willed,
Whose insight never has borne fruit in deeds,
Whose vague resolves never have been fulfilled;
For whom each year we see
Breeds new beginnings, disappointments new;
Who hesitate and falter life away,
And lose tomorrow the ground won today—
Ah! do not we, wanderer! await it too?

Yes, we await it! but it still delays,
And then we suffer! and amongst us one,[9]
Who most has suffered, takes dejectedly
His seat upon the intellectual throne;
And all his store of sad experience he
Lays bare of wretched days;

7. In classical mythology, the protecting spirit assigned to each being to see it through the world and finally to usher it out.

8. I.e., half-heartedly lives a hundred different lives.

9. Both Goethe and Tennyson have been suggested as being meant here.

Tells us his misery's birth and growth and signs,
And how the dying spark of hope was fed,
And how the breast was soothed, and how the head,
And all his hourly varied anodynes.

This for our wisest! and we others pine,
And wish the long unhappy dream would end,
And waive all claim to bliss, and try to bear;
With close-lipped patience for our only friend,
Sad patience, too near neighbor to despair—
But none has hope like thine!
Thou through the fields and through the woods dost stray,
Roaming the countryside, a truant boy,
Nursing thy project in unclouded joy,
And every doubt long blown by time away.

O born in days when wits were fresh and clear,
And life ran gaily as the sparkling Thames;
Before this strange disease of modern life,
With its sick hurry, its divided aims,
Its head o'ertaxed, its palsied hearts, was rife—
Fly hence, our contact fear!
Still fly, plunge deeper in the bowering wood!
Averse, as Dido did with gesture stern
From her false friend's approach in Hades turn,[1]
Wave us away, and keep thy solitude!

Still nursing the unconquerable hope,
Still clutching the inviolable shade,
With a free, onward impulse brushing through,
By night, the silvered branches of the glade—
Far on the forest-skirts, where none pursue,
On some mild pastoral slope
Emerge, and resting on the moonlit pales° *fences*
Freshen thy flowers as in former years
With dew, or listen with enchanted ears,
From the dark dingles,° to the nightingales! *valleys*

But fly our paths, our feverish contact fly!
For strong the infection of our mental strife,
Which, though it gives no bliss, yet spoils for rest;
And we should win thee from thy own fair life,
Like us distracted, and like us unblest.
Soon, soon thy cheer would die,
Thy hopes grow timorous, and unfixed thy powers,
And thy clear aims be cross and shifting made;
And then thy glad perennial youth would fade,
Fade, and grow old at last, and die like ours.

Then fly our greetings, fly our speech and smiles!
—As some grave Tyrian[2] trader, from the sea,
Descried at sunrise an emerging prow
Lifting the cool-haired creepers stealthily,

1. Dido, queen of Carthage, had been deserted by Aeneas after giving her love to him. Aeneas later encountered her in the underworld, among the shades of those who have died of unhappy love, but when he greeted her she turned her back on him.

2. A native of the ancient Phoenician city of Tyre, in the eastern Mediterranean.

The fringes of a southward-facing brow
Among the Aegean isles;
And saw the merry Grecian coaster come,
Freighted with amber grapes, and Chian[3] wine,
Green, bursting figs, and tunnies steeped in brine—
And knew the intruders on his ancient home,

The young light-hearted masters of the waves—
And snatched his rudder, he shook out more sail;
And day and night held on indignantly
O'er the blue Midland waters with the gale,
Betwixt the Syrtes[4] and soft Sicily,
To where the Atlantic raves
Outside the western straits;[5] and unbent sails
There, where down cloudy cliffs, through sheets of foam,
Shy traffickers, the dark Iberians[6] come;
And on the beach undid his corded bales.

1853

Dover Beach

The sea is calm tonight.
The tide is full, the moon lies fair
Upon the straits; on the French coast the light
Gleams and is gone; the cliffs of England stand,
Glimmering and vast, out in the tranquil bay.
Come to the window, sweet is the night-air!
Only, from the long line of spray
Where the sea meets the moon-blanched land,
Listen! you hear the grating roar
Of pebbles which the waves draw back, and fling,
At their return, up the high strand,
Begin, and cease, and then again begin,
With tremulous cadence slow, and bring
The eternal note of sadness in.

Sophocles long ago
Heard it on the Aegean, and it brought
Into his mind the turbid ebb and flow
Of human misery;[7] we
Find also in the sound a thought,
Hearing it by this distant northern sea.

The Sea of Faith
Was once, too, at the full, and round earth's shore
Lay like the folds of a bright girdle furled.
But now I only hear
Its melancholy, long, withdrawing roar,
Retreating, to the breath
Of the night-wind, down the vast edges drear
And naked shingles[8] of the world.

3. From the island of Chios, famous for its wine.
4. Two gulfs on the North African coast, one off Cyrenaica, the other off Tunisia.
5. I.e., the Straits of Gibraltar.
6. Ancient name for the inhabitants of Spain.
7. Compare Sophocles' *Antigone*, lines 583–91.
8. Beaches covered with water-worn small stones and pebbles.

Ah, love, let us be true
To one another! for the world, which seems
To lie before us like a land of dreams,
So various, so beautiful, so new,
Hath really neither joy, nor love, nor light,
Nor certitude, nor peace, nor help for pain;
And we are here as on a darkling plain
Swept with confused alarms of struggle and flight,
Where ignorant armies clash by night.

1867

DANTE GABRIEL ROSSETTI (1828–1882)

The Blessed Damozel[1]

The blessed damozel leaned out
From the gold bar of Heaven;
Her eyes were deeper than the depth
Of waters stilled at even;
She had three lilies in her hand,
And the stars in her hair were seven.

Her robe, ungirt from clasp to hem,
No wrought flowers did adorn,
But a white rose of Mary's gift,
For service meetly worn;
Her hair that lay along her back
Was yellow like ripe corn.° *wheat, grain*

Herseemed she scarce had been a day
One of God's choristers;
The wonder was not yet quite gone
From that still look of hers;
Albeit, to them she left, her day
Had counted as ten years.

(To one, it is ten years of years.
. . . Yet now, and in this place,
Surely she leaned o'er me—her hair
Fell all about my face. . . .
Nothing: the autumn fall of leaves.
The whole year sets apace.)

It was the rampart of God's house
That she was standing on;
By God built over the sheer depth
The which is Space begun;
So high, that looking downward thence
She scarce could see the sun.

It lies in Heaven, across the flood
Of ether, as a bridge.

1. Older form of *damsel,* meaning "young unmarried lady," preferred by Romantic and later writers because it avoids the simpler, homelier associations of *damsel.*

Beneath, the tides of day and night
With flame and darkness ridge
The void, as low as where this earth
Spins like a fretful midge.

Around her, lovers, newly met
In joy no sorrow claims,
Spoke evermore among themselves
Their rapturous new names;
And the souls mounting up to God
Went by her like thin flames.

And still she bowed herself and stooped
Out of the circling charm;
Until her bosom must have made
The bar she leaned on warm,
And the lilies lay as if asleep
Along her bended arm.

From the fixed place of Heaven she saw
Time like a pulse shake fierce
Through all the worlds. Her gaze still strove
Within the gulf to pierce
Its path; and now she spoke as when
The stars sang in their spheres.

The sun was gone now; the curled moon
Was like a little feather
Fluttering far down the gulf; and now
She spoke through the still weather.
Her voice was like the voice the stars
Had when they sang together.

(Ah sweet! Even now, in that bird's song,
Strove not her accents there,
Fain to be hearkened? When those bells
Possessed the midday air,
Strove not her steps to reach my side
Down all the echoing stair?)

"I wish that he were come to me,
For he will come," she said.
"Have I not prayed in Heaven?—on earth,
Lord, Lord, has he not prayed?
Are not two prayers a perfect strength?
And shall I feel afraid?

"When round his head the aureole clings,
And he is clothed in white,
I'll take his hand and go with him
To the deep wells of light;
We will step down as to a stream,
And bathe there in God's sight.

"We two will stand beside that shrine,
Occult, withheld, untrod,
Whose lamps are stirred continually
With prayer sent up to God;

And see our old prayers, granted, melt
Each like a little cloud.

"We two will lie i' the shadow of
That living mystic tree
Within whose secret growth the Dove
Is sometimes felt to be,
While every leaf that His plumes touch
Saith His Name audibly.

"And I myself will teach to him,
I myself, lying so,
The songs I sing here; which his voice
Shall pause in, hushed and slow,
And find some knowledge at each pause,
Of some new thing to know."

(Alas! We two, we two, thou say'st!
Yea, one wast thou with me
That once of old. But shall God lift
To endless unity
The soul whose likeness with thy soul
Was but its love for thee?)

"We two," she said, "will seek the groves
Where the lady Mary is,
With her five handmaidens, whose names
Are five sweet symphonies,
Cecily, Gertrude, Magdalen,
Margaret and Rosalys.

"Circlewise sit they, with bound locks
And foreheads garlanded;
Into the fine cloth white like flame
Weaving the golden thread,
To fashion the birth-robes for them
Who are just born, being dead.

"He shall fear, haply, and be dumb:
Then will I lay my cheek
To his, and tell about our love,
Not once abashed or weak:
And the dear Mother will approve
My pride, and let me speak.

"Herself shall bring us, hand in hand,
To Him round whom all souls
Kneel, the clear-ranged unnumbered heads
Bowed with their aureoles:
And angels meeting us shall sing
To their citherns and citoles.[2]

"There will I ask of Christ the Lord
Thus much for him and me:—
Only to live as once on earth
With Love—only to be,

2. Antique musical instruments: the cithern (17th century), a guitar-like instrument with wire strings; the citole, a stringed instrument dating from the 13th–15th century.

As then awhile, forever now
   Together, I and he."

She gazed and listened and then said,
   Less sad of speech than mild,
"All this is when he comes." She ceased.
   The light thrilled towards her, filled
With angels in strong level flight.
   Her eyes prayed, and she smiled.

(I saw her smile.) But soon their path
   Was vague in distant spheres:
And then she cast her arms along
   The golden barriers,
And laid her face between her hands,
   And wept. (I heard her tears.)

1846 1850

The Woodspurge

The wind flapped loose, the wind was still,
Shaken out dead from tree and hill:
I had walked on at the wind's will—
I sat now, for the wind was still.

Between my knees my forehead was—
My lips, drawn in, said not Alas!
My hair was over in the grass,
My naked ears heard the day pass.

My eyes, wide open, had the run
Of some ten weeds to fix upon;
Among those few, out of the sun,
The woodspurge flowered, three cups in one.

From perfect grief there need not be
Wisdom or even memory:
One thing then learnt remains to me—
The woodspurge has a cup of three.

1856 1870

From The House of Life

A Sonnet

A Sonnet is a moment's monument,—
   Memorial from the Soul's eternity
   To one dead deathless hour. Look that it be,
Whether for lustral° rite or dire portent, *purificatory*
Of its own arduous fullness reverent:
   Carve it in ivory or in ebony,
   As Day or Night may rule; and let Time see
Its flowering crest impearled and orient.

A Sonnet is a coin: its face reveals
   The soul—its converse, to what Power 'tis due:

Whether for tribute to the august appeals
Of Life, or dower in Love's high retinue,
It serve; or, 'mid the dark wharf's cavernous breath,
In Charon's[3] palm it pay the toll to Death.

19. *Silent Noon*

Your hands lie open in the long fresh grass—
The finger-points look through like rosy blooms:
Your eyes smile peace. The pasture gleams and glooms
'Neath billowing skies that scatter and amass.
All round our nest, far as the eye can pass,
Are golden kingcup-fields with silver edge
Where the cow-parsley skirts the hawthorn-hedge.
'Tis visible silence, still as the hour-glass.

Deep in the sun-searched growths the dragonfly
Hangs like a blue thread loosened from the sky:
So this winged hour is dropt to us from above.
Oh! clasp we to our hearts, for deathless dower,
This close-companioned inarticulate hour
When twofold silence was the song of love.

70. *The Hill Summit*

This feast-day of the sun, his altar there
In the broad west has blazed for vesper-song;
And I have loitered in the vale too long
And gaze now a belated worshipper.
Yet may I not forget that I was 'ware,
So journeying, of his face at intervals
Transfigured where the fringed horizon falls,
A fiery bush with coruscating hair.

And now that I have climbed and won this height,
I must tread downward through the sloping shade
And travel the bewildered tracks till night.
Yet for this hour I still may here be stayed
And see the gold air and the silver fade
And the last bird fly into the last night.

83. *Barren Spring*

Once more the changed year's turning wheel returns:
And as a girl sails balanced in the wind,
And now before and now again behind
Stoops as it swoops, with cheek that laughs and burns—
So Spring comes merry towards me here, but earns
No answering smile from me, whose life is twined
With the dead boughs that winter still must bind,
And whom to-day the Spring no more concerns.

Behold, this crocus is a withering flame;
This snowdrop, snow; this apple-blossom's part
To breed the fruit that breeds the serpent's art.
Nay, for these Spring-flowers, turn thy face from them,
Nor gaze till on the year's last lily-stem
The white cup shrivels round the golden heart.

1847–80 1870, 1881

3. Charon received a coin, an *obolus*, for ferrying the shades of the newly dead across the river Styx to Hades.

GEORGE MEREDITH
(1828–1909)

Modern Love[1]

1

By this he knew she wept with waking eyes:
That, at his hand's light quiver by her head,
The strange low sobs that shook their common bed
Were called into her with a sharp surprise,
And strangled mute, like little gaping snakes,
Dreadfully venomous to him. She lay
Stone-still, and the long darkness flowed away
With muffled pulses. Then, as midnight makes
Her giant heart of Memory and Tears
Drink the pale drug of silence, and so beat
Sleep's heavy measure, they from head to feet
Were moveless, looking through their dead black years,
By vain regret scrawled over the blank wall.
Like sculptured effigies they might be seen
Upon their marriage-tomb,[2] the sword between;
Each wishing for the sword that severs all.

17

At dinner, she is hostess, I am host.
Went the feast ever cheerfuller? She keeps
The Topic over intellectual deeps
In buoyancy afloat. They see no ghost.
With sparkling surface-eyes we ply the ball:
It is in truth a most contagious game:
HIDING THE SKELETON, shall be its name.
Such play as this the devils might appall!
But here's the greater wonder; in that we,
Enamored of an acting naught can tire,
Each other, like true hypocrites, admire;
Warm-lighted looks, Love's ephemerioe,[3]
Shoot gaily o'er the dishes and the wine.
We waken envy of our happy lot.
Fast, sweet, and golden, shows the marriage-knot.
Dear guests, you now have seen Love's corpse-light shine.

30

What are we first? First, animals; and next
Intelligences at a leap; on whom
Pale lies the distant shadow of the tomb,
And all that draweth on the tomb for text.
Into which state comes Love, the crowning sun:
Beneath whose light the shadow loses form.
We are the lords of life, and life is warm.
Intelligence and instinct now are one.
But nature says: "My children most they seem
When they least know me: therefore I decree

1. *Modern Love* is a sequence of fifty sixteen-line sonnets, a kind of novel in verse about the breakup of a marriage. For most of the sequence the husband is the speaker, but the opening and closing sections are told in the third person.

2. I.e., as motionless as sculptured stone statues on a tomb. In medieval legend, a naked sword between lovers symbolized chastity.

3. Short-lived creatures.

That they shall suffer." Swift doth young Love flee,
And we stand wakened, shivering from our dream.
Then if we study Nature we are wise.
Thus do the few who live but with the day:
The scientific animals are they—
Lady, this is my sonnet to your eyes.[4]

48

Their sense is with their senses all mixed in,
Destroyed by subtleties these women are![5]
More brain, O Lord, more brain! or we shall mar
Utterly this fair garden we might win.
Behold! I looked for peace, and thought it near.
Our inmost hearts had opened, each to each.
We drank the pure daylight of honest speech.
Alas! that was the fatal draught, I fear.
For when of my lost Lady came the word,
This woman, O this agony of flesh!
Jealous devotion bade her break the mesh,
That I might seek that other like a bird.
I do adore the nobleness! despise
The act! She has gone forth, I know not where.
Will the hard world my sentience of her share?
I feel the truth; so let the world surmise.

49

He found her by the ocean's moaning verge,
Nor any wicked change in her discerned;
And she believed his old love had returned,
Which was her exultation, and her scourge.
She took his hand, and walked with him, and seemed
The wife he sought, though shadow-like and dry.
She had one terror, lest her heart should sigh,
And tell her loudly she no longer dreamed.
She dared not say, "This is my breast: look in."
But there's a strength to help the desperate weak.
That night he learned how silence best can speak
The awful things when Pity pleads for Sin.
About the middle of the night her call
Was heard, and he came wondering to the bed.
"Now kiss me, dear! it may be, now!" she said.
Lethe[6] had passed those lips, and he knew all.

50

Thus piteously Love closed what he begat:
The union of this ever-diverse pair!
These two were rapid falcons in a snare,
Condemned to do the flitting of the bat.
Lovers beneath the singing sky of May,
They wandered once; clear as the dew on flowers:
But they fed not on the advancing hours:
Their hearts held cravings for the buried day.
Then each applied to each that fatal knife,

4. A poetic convention of love sonnets was the praise of one of the lady's features, such as her eyes. Meredith uses it as an ironic close to a statement of his theory of evolution.

5. Earlier, the couple had at last talked together about the wife's affair with another man, and had become reconciled. But when the husband tells her of his own recent passing affair with his "lost Lady" (line 9), she resolves to give him up to his mistress. Her resolve is a noble one but, in his view, without "sense" or "brain."

6. River of forgetfulness in Hades, the mythological Greek underworld.

Deep questioning, which probes to endless dole.° *sorrow*
Ah, what a dusty answer gets the soul
When hot for certainties in this our life!—
In tragic hints here see what evermore
Moves dark as yonder midnight ocean's force,
Thundering like ramping° hosts of warrior horse, *rearing*
To throw that faint thin line upon the shore!

1862

Lucifer in Starlight

On a starred night Prince Lucifer uprose.
Tired of his dark dominion, swung the fiend
Above the rolling ball, in cloud part screened,
Where sinners hugged their specter of repose.
Poor prey to his hot fit of pride were those.
And now upon his western wing he leaned,
Now his huge bulk o'er Afric's sands careened,
Now the black planet shadowed Arctic snows.
Soaring through wider zones that pricked his scars
With memory of the old revolt from Awe,[7]
He reached a middle height, and at the stars,
Which are the brain of heaven, he looked, and sank.
Around the ancient track marched, rank on rank,
The army of unalterable law.

1883

Winter Heavens

Sharp is the night, but stars with frost alive
Leap off the rim of earth across the dome.
It is a night to make the heavens our home
More than the nest whereto apace we strive.
Lengths down our road each fir-tree seems a hive,
In swarms outrushing from the golden comb.
They waken waves of thoughts that burst to foam:
The living throb in me, the dead revive.
Yon mantle clothes us: there, past mortal breath,
Life glistens on the river of the death.
It folds us, flesh and dust; and have we knelt,
Or never knelt, or eyed as kine° the springs *cattle*
Of radiance, the radiance enrings:
And this is the soul's haven to have felt.

1888

7. I.e., God. Satan is reminded of the wounds he suffered when his revolt against God was crushed and he was hurled from heaven into hell.

EMILY DICKINSON*
(1830–1886)

49

I never lost as much but twice,
And that was in the sod.
Twice have I stood a beggar
Before the door of God!

Angels—twice descending
Reimbursed my store—
Burglar! Banker—Father!
I am poor once more!

1890

185

"Faith" is a fine invention
When Gentlemen can *see*—
But *Microscopes* are prudent
In an Emergency.

ca. 1860 1891

214

I taste a liquor never brewed—
From Tankards scooped in Pearl—
Not all the Vats upon the Rhine[1]
Yield such an Alcohol!

Inebriate of Air—am I—
And Debauchee of Dew—
Reeling—thro endless summer days—
From inns of Molten Blue—

When "Landlords" turn the drunken Bee
Out of the Foxglove's door—
When Butterflies—renounce their "drams"—
I shall but drink the more!

Till Seraphs[2] swing their snowy Hats—
And Saints—to windows run—
To see the little Tippler
Leaning against the—Sun—

ca. 1860 1861

* The order and numbering of the poems are those established by Thomas H. Johnson in his *Poems of Emily Dickinson* (1955).

1. I.e., wine from Germany.
2. Winged angels believed to guard God's throne.

216

Safe in their Alabaster[3] Chambers—
Untouched by Morning
And untouched by Noon—
Sleep the meek members of the Resurrection—
Rafter of satin,
And Roof of stone.

Light laughs the breeze
In her Castle above them—
Babbles the Bee in a stolid Ear,
Pipe the Sweet Birds in ignorant cadence—
Ah, what sagacity perished here!

version of 1859 1862

216[4]

Safe in their Alabaster Chambers—
Untouched by Morning—
And untouched by Noon—
Lie the meek members of the Resurrection—
Rafter of Satin—and Roof of Stone!

Grand go the Years—in the Crescent—above them—
Worlds scoop their Arcs—
And Firmaments—row—
Diadems—drop—and Doges[5]—surrender—
Soundless as dots—on a Disc of Snow—

version of 1861 1890

249

Wild Nights—Wild Nights!
Were I with thee
Wild Nights should be
Our luxury!

Futile—the Winds—
To a Heart in port—
Done with the Compass—
Done with the Chart!

3. Transluscent white mineral.

4. This poem has been familiar to readers of Emily Dickinson in a three-stanza version which we now know was never her conception of the poem. Thomas H. Johnson's account of the composition of the poem traces Emily's characteristic trying and retrying of various articulations of her poetic idea. The 1859 version was sent to Sue Dickinson, Emily's sister-in-law, for advice, and Sue evidently did not like it much. The notes between the two women (they lived in adjoining houses) show Emily's labors over the poem, and her 1861 version was an attempt to meet her own and Sue's exactions. Johnson believes Emily Dickinson was never fully satisfied with the poem. It was printed once during her lifetime (1862) in the 1859 version, but when she began her famous correspondence with Thomas W. Higginson, the literary critic and editor, she sent a modified version of the 1861 poem. When Higginson edited Emily Dickinson's poetry for posthumous publication (1890), he combined the two versions, and it is this three-stanza poem that readers had known as Dickinson's until Johnson's definitive edition of the poems in 1955.

5. Chief magistrates in the republics of Venice and Genoa from the 11th through the 16th centuries.

Rowing in Eden—
Ah, the Sea!
Might I but moor—Tonight—
In Thee!

ca. 1861 1891

258

There's a certain Slant of light,
Winter Afternoons—
That oppresses, like the Heft
Of Cathedral Tunes—

Heavenly Hurt, it gives us—
We can find no scar,
But internal difference,
Where the Meanings, are—

None may teach it—Any—
'Tis the Seal[6] Despair—
An imperial affliction
Sent us of the Air—

When it comes, the Landscape listens—
Shadows—hold their breath—
When it goes, 'tis like the Distance
On the look of Death—

ca. 1861 1890

280

I felt a Funeral, in my Brain,
And Mourners to and fro
Kept treading—treading—till it seemed
That Sense was breaking through—

And when they all were seated,
A Service, like a Drum—
Kept beating—beating—till I thought
My Mind was going numb—

And then I heard them lift a Box
And creak across my Soul
With those same Boots of Lead, again,
Then Space—began to toll,

As all the Heavens were a Bell,
And Being, but an Ear,
And I, and Silence, some strange Race
Wrecked, solitary, here—

And then a Plank in Reason, broke,
And I dropped down, and down—

6. In the double sense of (1) an official sign of confirmation and (2) a device used to imprint an official mark.

And hit a World, at every plunge,
And Finished knowing—then—

ca. 1861 1896

303

The Soul selects her own Society—
Then—shuts the Door—
To her divine Majority—
Present no more—

Unmoved—she notes the Chariots—pausing—
At her low Gate—
Unmoved—an Emperor be kneeling
Upon her Mat—

I've known her—from an ample nation—
Choose One—
Then—close the Valves of her attention—
Like Stone—

ca. 1862 1890

305

The difference between Despair
And Fear—is like the One
Between the instant of a Wreck—
And when the Wreck has been—

The Mind is smooth—no Motion—
Contented as the Eye
Upon the Forehead of a Bust—
That knows—it cannot see—

ca. 1862 1914

328

A Bird came down the Walk—
He did not know I saw—
He bit an Angleworm in halves
And ate the fellow, raw,

And then he drank a Dew
From a convenient Grass—
And then hopped sidewise to the Wall
To let a Beetle pass—

He glanced with rapid eyes
That hurried all around—
They looked like frightened Beads, I thought—
He stirred his Velvet Head

Like one in danger, Cautious,
I offered him a Crumb
And he unrolled his feathers
And rowed him softer home—

Than Oars divide the Ocean,
Too silver for a seam—
Or Butterflies, off Banks of Noon
Leap, plashless° as they swim. *splashless*

ca. 1862 1891

341

After great pain, a formal feeling comes—
The Nerves sit ceremonious, like Tombs—
The stiff Heart questions was it He, that bore,
And Yesterday, or Centuries before?

The Feet, mechanical, go round—
Of Ground, or Air, or Ought[7]—
A Wooden way
Regardless grown,
A Quartz contentment, like a stone—

This is the Hour of Lead—
Remembered, if outlived,
As Freezing persons, recollect the Snow—
First—Chill—then Stupor—then the letting go—

ca. 1862 1929

465

I heard a Fly buzz—when I died—
The Stillness in the Room
Was like the Stillness in the Air—
Between the Heaves of Storm—

The Eyes around—had wrung them dry—
And Breaths were gathering firm
For that last Onset—when the King
Be witnessed—in the Room—

I willed my Keepsakes—Signed away
What portion of me be
Assignable—and then it was
There interposed a Fly—

With Blue—uncertain stumbling Buzz—
Between the light—and me—
And then the Windows failed—and then
I could not see to see—

ca. 1862 1896

712

Because I could not stop for Death—
He kindly stopped for me—
The Carriage held but just Ourselves—
And Immortality.

7. Nothing, a void.

We slowly drove—He knew no haste
And I had put away
My labor and my leisure too,
For His Civility—

We passed the School, where Children strove
At Recess—in the Ring—
We passed the Fields of Gazing Grain—
We passed the Setting Sun—

Or rather—He passed Us—
The Dews drew quivering and chill—
For only Gossamer, my Gown—
My Tippet°—only Tulle— *shoulder cape*

We paused before a House that seemed
A Swelling of the Ground—
The Roof was scarcely visible—
The Cornice—in the Ground—

Since then—'tis Centuries—and yet
Feels shorter than the Day
I first surmised the Horses' Heads
Were toward Eternity—

ca. 1863 1890

986

A narrow Fellow in the Grass
Occasionally rides—
You may have met Him—did you not
His notice sudden is—

The Grass divides as with a Comb—
A spotted shaft is seen—
And then it closes at your feet
And opens further on—

He likes a Boggy Acre
A Floor too cool for Corn—
Yet when a Boy, and Barefoot—
I more than once at Noon
Have passed, I thought, a Whip lash
Unbraiding in the Sun
When stooping to secure it
It wrinkled, and was gone—

Several of Nature's People
I know, and they know me—
I feel for them a transport
Of cordiality—

But never met this Fellow
Attended, or alone
Without a tighter breathing
And Zero at the Bone—

ca. 1865 1866

1129

Tell all the Truth but tell it slant—
Success in Circuit lies
Too bright for our infirm Delight
The Truth's superb surprise

As Lightning to the Children eased
With explanation kind
The Truth must dazzle gradually
Or every man be blind—

ca. 1868 1945

1463

A Route of Evanescence
With a revolving Wheel—
A Resonance of Emerald—
A Rush of Cochineal[8]—
And every Blossom on the Bush
Adjusts its tumbled Head—
The mail from Tunis,[9] probably,
An easy Morning's Ride—

ca. 1879 1891

1540

As imperceptibly as Grief
The Summer lapsed away—
Too imperceptible at last
To seem like Perfidy—
A Quietness distilled
As Twilight long begun,
Or Nature spending with herself
Sequestered Afternoon—
The Dusk drew earlier in—
The Morning foreign shone—
A courteous, yet harrowing Grace,
As Guest, that would be gone—
And thus, without a Wing
Or service of a Keel
Our Summer made her light escape
Into the Beautiful.

ca. 1865 1891

1545

The Bible is an antique Volume—
Written by faded Men
At the suggestion of Holy Specters—
Subjects—Bethlehem—
Eden—the ancient Homestead—
Satan—the Brigadier—

8. Red dye.

9. City on the north coast of Africa.

Judas—the Great Defaulter—
David—the Troubadour—
Sin—a distinguished Precipice
Others must resist—
Boys that "believe" are very lonesome—
Other Boys are "lost"—
Had but the Tale a warbling Teller—
All the Boys would come—
Orpheus' Sermon[1] captivated—
It did not condemn—

ca. 1882 1924

CHRISTINA ROSSETTI
(1830–1894)

Song

When I am dead, my dearest,
 Sing no sad songs for me;
Plant thou no roses at my head,
 Nor shady cypress tree:
Be the green grass above me
 With showers and dewdrops wet;
And if thou wilt, remember,
 And if thou wilt, forget.

I shall not see the shadows,
 I shall not feel the rain;
I shall not hear the nightingale
 Sing on, as if in pain:
And dreaming through the twilight
 That doth not rise nor set,
Haply I may remember,
 And haply may forget.

1848 1862

In an Artist's Studio

One face looks out from all his canvases,
 One selfsame figure sits or walks or leans:
 We found her hidden just behind those screens,
That mirror gave back all her loveliness.
A queen in opal or in ruby dress,
 A nameless girl in freshest summer-greens,
 A saint, an angel—every canvas means
The same one meaning, neither more nor less.
He feeds upon her face by day and night,
 And she with true kind eyes looks back on him,
Fair as the moon and joyful as the light:
 Not wan with waiting, not with sorrow dim;

1. The music of the legendary Greek musician Orpheus attracted and controlled beasts, rocks, and trees.

Not as she is, but was when hope shone bright;
Not as she is, but as she fills his dream.

1856 1896

Up-Hill

Does the road wind up-hill all the way?
Yes, to the very end.
Will the day's journey take the whole long day?
From morn to night, my friend.

But is there for the night a resting-place?
A roof for when the slow dark hours begin.
May not the darkness hide it from my face?
You cannot miss that inn.

Shall I meet other wayfarers at night?
Those who have gone before.
Then must I knock, or call when just in sight?
They will not keep you standing at that door.

Shall I find comfort, travel-sore and weak?
Of labor you shall find the sum.
Will there be beds for me and all who seek?
Yea, beds for all who come.

1858 1862

Passing Away, Saith the World, Passing Away

Passing away, saith the World, passing away:
Chances, beauty and youth sapped day by day:
Thy life never continueth in one stay.
Is the eye waxen dim, is the dark hair changing to gray
That hath won neither laurel nor bay?[1]
I shall clothe myself in Spring and bud in May:
Thou, root-stricken, shalt not rebuild thy decay
On my bosom for aye.
Then I answered: Yea.

Passing away, saith my Soul, passing away:
With its burden of fear and hope, of labor and play;
Hearken what the past doth witness and say:
Rust in thy gold, a moth is in thine array,
A canker is in thy bud, thy leaf must decay.
At midnight, at cockcrow, at morning, one certain day
Lo the bridegroom shall come and shall not delay:
Watch thou and pray.
Then I answered: Yea.

Passing away, saith my God, passing away:
Winter passeth after the long delay:

1. In ancient Greece, victors in the Pythian games were crowned with a wreath made from the leaves of the laurel, and later such wreaths were bestowed on the winners of academic or poetic honors. "Bay" is synonymous with laurel.

New grapes on the vine, new figs on the tender spray,
Turtle calleth turtle in Heaven's May.
Tho' I tarry, wait for Me, trust Me, watch and pray.
Arise, come away, night is past and lo it is day,
My love, My sister, My spouse, thou shalt hear Me say.
Then I answered: Yea.

1860 1862

LEWIS CARROLL (CHARLES LUTWIDGE DODGSON)

(1832–1898)

Jabberwocky[1]

There was a book lying near Alice on the table, and while she sat watching the White King (for she was still a little anxious about him, and had the ink all ready to throw over him, in case he fainted again), she turned over the leaves, to find some part that she could read, "—for it's all in some language I don't know," she said to herself. It was like this:

JABBERWOCKY.

'Twas brillig, and the slithy toves
Did gyre and gimble in the wabe;
All mimsy were the borogoves,
And the mome raths outgrabe.

She puzzled over this for some time, but at last a bright thought struck her. "Why, it's a Looking-glass book, of course! And, if I hold it up to a glass, the words will all go the right way again."

This was the poem that Alice read:

Jabberwocky

'Twas brillig, and the slithy toves
  Did gyre and gimble in the wabe:
All mimsy were the borogoves,
  And the mome raths outgrabe.

1. From *Through the Looking-Glass,* Chapter I.

"Beware the Jabberwock, my son!
  The jaws that bite, the claws that catch!
Beware the Jubjub bird, and shun
  The frumious Bandersnatch!"

He took his vorpal sword in hand:
  Long time the manxome foe he sought—
So rested he by the Tumtum tree,
  And stood awhile in thought.

And, as in uffish thought he stood,
  The Jabberwock, with eyes of flame,
Came whiffling through the tulgey wood,
  And burbled as it came!

One, two! One, two! And through and through
  The vorpal blade went snicker-snack!
He left it dead, and with its head
  He went galumphing back.

"And hast thou slain the Jabberwock?
  Come to my arms, my beamish boy!
O frabjous day! Callooh! Callay!"
  He chortled in his joy.

'Twas brillig, and the slithy toves
  Did gyre and gimble in the wabe:
All mimsy were the borogoves,
  And the mome raths outgrabe.

[*Humpty Dumpty's Explication of* Jabberwocky][2]

"You seem very clever at explaining words, Sir," said Alice. "Would you kindly tell me the meaning of the poem *Jabberwocky*?"

"Let's hear it," said Humpty Dumpty. "I can explain all the poems that ever were invented—and a good many that haven't been invented just yet."

This sounded very hopeful, so Alice repeated the first verse:

" 'Twas brillig, and the slithy toves
  Did gyre and gimble in the wabe;
All mimsy were the borogoves,
  And the mome raths outgrabe."

"That's enough to begin with," Humpty Dumpty interrupted: "there are plenty of hard words there. 'Brillig' means four o'clock in the afternoon—the time when you begin *broiling* things for dinner."

"That'll do very well," said Alice: "and 'slithy'?"[3]

"Well, 'slithy' means 'lithe and slimy.' 'Lithe' is the same as 'active.' You see it's like a portmanteau—there are two meanings packed up into one word."

"I see it now," Alice remarked thoughtfully: "and what are 'toves'?"

"Well, 'toves' are something like badgers—they're something like lizards—and they're something like corkscrews."

2. From *Through the Looking-Glass,* Chapter VI.

3. Concerning the pronunciation of these words, Carroll later said: "The 'i' in 'slithy' is long, as in 'writhe'; and 'toves' is pronounced so as to rhyme with 'groves.' Again, the first 'o' in 'borogoves' is pronounced like the 'o' in 'borrow.' I have heard people try to give it the sound of the 'o' in 'worry.' Such is Human Perversity."

"They must be very curious creatures."

"They are that," said Humpty Dumpty: "also they make their nests under sundials—also they live on cheese."

"And what's to 'gyre' and to 'gimble'?"

"To 'gyre' is to go round and round like a gyroscope. To 'gimble' is to make holes like a gimlet."

"And the 'wabe' is the grass plot round a sundial, I suppose?" said Alice, surprised at her own ingenuity.

"Of course it is. It's called 'wabe,' you know, because it goes a long way before it, and a long way behind it——"

"And a long way beyond it on each side," Alice added.

"Exactly so. Well then, 'mimsy' is 'flimsy and miserable' (there's another portmanteau for you). And a 'borogove' is a thin shabby-looking bird with its feathers sticking out all round—something like a live mop."

"And then 'mome raths'?" said Alice. "If I'm not giving you too much trouble.'"

"Well, a 'rath' is a sort of green pig: but 'mome' I'm not certain about. I think it's short for 'from home'—meaning that they'd lost their way, you know."

"And what does 'outgrabe' mean?"

"Well, 'outgribing' is something between bellowing and whistling, with a kind of sneeze in the middle: however, you'll hear it done, maybe—down in the wood yonder—and when you've once heard it you'll be *quite* content. Who's been repeating all that hard stuff to you?"

"I read it in a book," said Alice.

1871

The White Knight's Song[4]

Haddock's Eyes or *The Aged Aged Man* or
Ways and Means or *A-Sitting On A Gate*

I'll tell thee everything I can;
  There's little to relate.
I saw an aged, aged man,
  A-sitting on a gate.
"Who are you, aged man?" I said.
  "And how is it you live?"
And his answer trickled through my head
  Like water through a sieve.

He said "I look for butterflies
  That sleep among the wheat;
I make them into mutton-pies,
  And sell them in the street.
I sell them unto men," he said,
  "Who sail on stormy seas;
And that's the way I get my bread—
  A trifle, if you please."

But I was thinking of a plan
  To dye one's whiskers green,
And always use so large a fan
  That it could not be seen.

4. The Knight is a character in *Through the Looking-Glass*; the song is in part a parody of Wordsworth's "Resolution and Independence."

So, having no reply to give
  To what the old man said,
I cried, "Come, tell me how you live!"
  And thumped him on the head.

His accents mild took up the tale;
  He said, "I go my ways,
And when I find a mountain-rill,
  I set it in a blaze;
And thence they make a stuff they call
  Rowland's Macassar Oil—[5]
Yet twopence-halfpenny is all
  They give me for my toil."

But I was thinking of a way
  To feed oneself on batter,
And so go on from day to day
  Getting a little fatter.
I shook him well from side to side,
  Until his face was blue;
"Come, tell me how you live," I cried
  "And what it is you do!"

He said, "I hunt for haddocks' eyes
  Among the heather bright,
And work them into waistcoat-buttons
  In the silent night.
And these I do not sell for gold
  Or coin of silvery shine,
But for a copper halfpenny,
  And that will purchase nine.

"I sometimes dig for buttered rolls,
  Or set limed twigs for crabs;
I sometimes search the grassy knolls
  For wheels of hansom-cabs.
And that's the way" (he gave a wink)
  "By which I get my wealth—
And very gladly will I drink
  Your Honor's noble health."

I heard him then, for I had just
  Completed my design
To keep the Menai bridge[6] from rust
  By boiling it in wine.
I thanked him much for telling me
  The way he got his wealth,
But chiefly for his wish that he
  Might drink my noble health.

And now, if e'er by chance I put
  My fingers into glue,
Or madly squeeze a right-hand foot
  Into a left-hand shoe,

5. A patented hairdressing.

6. A large bridge in Wales.

Or if I drop upon my toe
   A very heavy weight,
I weep, for it reminds me so
Of that old man I used to know—
Whose look was mild, whose speech was slow,
Whose hair was whiter than the snow,
Whose face was very like a crow,
With eyes, like cinders, all aglow,
Who seemed distracted with his woe,
Who rocked his body to and fro,
And muttered mumblingly and low,
As if his mouth were full of dough,
Who snorted like a buffalo—
That summer evening long ago
   A-sitting on a gate.

1871

WILLIAM MORRIS
(1834–1896)

The Earthly Paradise[1]

Of heaven or hell I have no power to sing,
I cannot ease the burden of your fears,
Or make quick-coming death a little thing,
Or bring again the pleasure of past years,
Nor for my words shall ye forget your tears,
Or hope again for aught that I can say,
The idle singer of an empty day.

But rather, when, aweary of your mirth,
From full hearts still unsatisfied ye sigh,
And, feeling kindly unto all the earth,
Grudge every minute as it passes by,
Made the more mindful that the sweet days die—
Remember me a little then I pray,
The idle singer of an empty day.

The heavy trouble, the bewildering care
That weighs us down who live and earn our bread,
These idle verses have no power to bear;
So let me sing of names rememberéd,
Because they, living not, can ne'er be dead,
Or long time take their memory quite away
From us poor singers of an empty day.

Dreamer of dreams, born out of my due time,
Why should I strive to set the crooked straight?
Let it suffice me that my murmuring rhyme
Beats with light wing against the ivory gate,[2]
Telling a tale not too importunate

1. The dedicatory stanzas to Morris's poem *The Earthly Paradise* (1868–70), consisting of a prologue and twenty-four tales on classical and medieval—especially Norse—subjects.

2. In Homer, dreams came through one or the other of two gates: through the gates of ivory, those which were untrue; through the gates of horn, those which were true.

To those who in the sleepy region stay,
Lulled by the singer of an empty day.

Folk say, a wizard to a northern king
At Christmas-tide such wondrous things did show,
That through one window men beheld the spring,
And through another saw the summer glow,
And through a third the fruited vines a-row,
While still, unheard, but in its wonted way,
Piped the drear wind of that December day.

So with this Earthly Paradise it is,
If ye will read aright, and pardon me,
Who strive to build a shadowy isle of bliss
Midmost the beating of the steely sea,
Where tossed about all hearts of men must be;
Whose ravening monsters mighty men shall slay,
Not the poor singer of an empty day.

1868–70

W. S. GILBERT
(1836–1911)

I Am the Very Model of a Modern Major-General[1]

I am the very model of a modern Major-General,
I've information vegetable, animal, and mineral,
I know the kings of England, and I quote the fights historical,
From Marathon to Waterloo, in order categorical;[2]
I'm very well acquainted too with matters mathematical,
I understand equations, both the simple and quadratical,
About binomial theorem I'm teeming with a lot o' news—
With many cheerful facts about the square of the hypotenuse.[3]

ALL With many cheerful facts, etc.

GEN. I'm very good at integral and differential calculus,
I know the scientific names of beings animalculous;[4]
In short, in matters vegetable, animal, and mineral,
I am the very model of a modern Major-General.

ALL In short, in matters vegetable, animal, and mineral,
He is the very model of a modern Major-General.

GEN. I know our mythic history, King Arthur's and Sir Caradoc's,
I answer hard acrostics, I've a pretty taste for paradox,
I quote in elegiacs all the crimes of Heliogabalus,
In conics I can floor peculiarities parabolous.[5]

1. Sung by the Major-General on his entrance in Act I of *The Pirates of Penzance*.
2. The Greeks defeated the Persians in a famous battle at Marathon in 490 B.C.; the duke of Wellington won his decisive victory over Napoleon at Waterloo in 1815.
3. All these are mathematical terms.
4. Microscopic organisms.
5. More examples of the Major-General's abstruse bits of knowledge: Sir Caradoc was a legendary figure in British history, supposedly one of King Arthur's knights; "acrostics" are word puzzles (forerunners of crossword puzzles;) "elegiacs" were a classical verse form of praise, quite unsuitable to describe the life of the most depraved of the Roman emperors; "conics" are the study of three-dimensional figures, of which the parabola is one.

I can tell undoubted Raphaels from Gerard Dows and Zoffanies,
I know the croaking chorus from the *Frogs* of Aristophanes,
Then I can hum a fugue of which I've heard the music's din afore,
And whistle all the airs from that infernal nonsense *Pinafore*.[6]

ALL And whistle all the airs, etc.

GEN. Then I can write a washing bill in Babylonic cuneiform,
And tell you every detail of Caractacus's uniform;[7]
In short, in matters vegetable, animal, and mineral,
I am the very model of a modern Major-General.

ALL In short, in matters vegetable, animal, and mineral,
He is the very model of a modern Major-General.

GEN. In fact, when I know what is meant by "mamelon" and "ravelin,"
When I can tell at sight a chassepôt rifle from a javelin,
When such affairs as sorties and surprises I'm more wary at,
And when I know precisely what is meant by "commissariat,"
When I have learnt what progress has been made in modern gunnery,
When I know more of tactics than a novice in a nunnery:[8]
In short, when I've a smattering of elemental strategy,
You'll say a better Major-Gener*al* has never *sat* a gee—[9]

ALL You'll say a better, etc.

GEN. For my military knowledge, though I'm plucky and adventury,
Has only been brought down to the beginning of the century;
But still in matters vegetable, animal, and mineral,
I am the very model of a modern Major-General.

ALL But still in matters vegetable, animal, and mineral,
He is the very model of a modern Major-General.

1879

When You're Lying Awake with a Dismal Headache[1]

Love, unrequited, robs me of my rest:
  Love, hopeless love, my ardent soul encumbers:
Love, nightmare-like, lies heavy on my chest,
  And weaves itself into my midnight slumbers!

When you're lying awake with a dismal headache, and repose is taboo'd by anxiety,

6. Raphael was one of the great painters of the early Italian Renaissance, as opposed to Gerhard Dou and Johann Zoffany, undistinguished 17th and 18th-century painters; in the *Frogs,* by Aristophanes, the great classical comic playwright, a chorus of frogs chants "Brekke-ko-ax, ko-ax, ko-ax"; a "fugue" is a learned (and, incidentally, multivoiced) musical composition; the last line of the verse is Gilbert's sly dig at the immense popularity of the previous Gilbert and Sullivan operetta, *H.M.S. Pinafore* (1878).

7. Cuneiform was a form of writing (made by pressing a stick into clay) practiced in ancient Babylonia; Caractacus is an alternate form of "Caradoc."

8. The Major-General has just listed his "smattering" of military terms: a "mamelon" is a fortified mound, while a "ravelin" is a detached outwork also used in fortification; the "chassepôt rifle" was a bolt-action rifle, very recently invented in Gilbert's time, while a "javelin" is a light spear that has been used in warfare for centuries; "sorties" and "surprises" both refer to sudden military attacks; a "commissariat" is the system for supplying an army with food.

9. Horse (usually a work horse).

1. Sung by the Lord Chancellor in Act II of *Iolanthe*.

I conceive you may use any language you choose to indulge in, without impropriety;
For your brain is on fire—the bedclothes conspire of usual slumber to plunder you:
First your counterpane° goes, and uncovers your toes, and your sheet slips demurely from under you; *bedspread*
Then the blanketing tickles—you feel like mixed pickles—so terribly sharp is the pricking,
And you're hot, and you're cross, and you tumble and toss till there's nothing 'twixt you and the ticking.
Then the bedclothes all creep to the ground in a heap, and you pick 'em all up in a tangle;
Next your pillow resigns and politely declines to remain at its usual angle!
Well, you get some repose in the form of a doze, with hot eye-balls and head ever aching,
But your slumbering teems with such horrible dreams that you'd very much better be waking;
For you dream you are crossing the Channel,[2] and tossing about in a steamer from Harwich—
Which is something between a large bathing machine[3] and a very small second-class carriage—
And you're giving a treat (penny ice and cold meat) to a party of friends and relations—
They're a ravenous horde—and they all came on board at Sloane Square and South Kensington Stations.[4]
And bound on that journey you find your attorney (who started that morning from Devon);
He's a bit undersized, and you don't feel surprised when he tells you he's only eleven.
Well, you're driving like mad with this singular lad (by the by, the ship's now a four-wheeler[5]),
And you're playing round games, and he calls you bad names when you tell him that "ties pay the dealer";[6]
But this you can't stand, so you throw up your hand, and you find you're as cold as an icicle,
In your shirt and your socks (the black silk with gold clocks[7]), crossing Salisbury Plain on a bicycle:
And he and the crew are on bicycles too—which they've somehow or other invested in—
And he's telling the tars° all the particu*lars* of a company he's interested in— *sailors*
It's a scheme of devices, to get at low prices all goods from cough mixtures to cables
(Which tickled the sailors), by treating retailers as though they were all vege*ta*bles—
You get a good spadesman to plant a small tradesman (first take off his boots with a boot-tree[8]),
And his legs will take root, and his fingers will shoot, and they'll blossom and bud like a fruit-tree—

2. The English Channel, between Britain and France; its waters are often turbulent.
3. A bathhouse which could be wheeled into the water at a beach, enabling people to change for swimming in private; a "second-class carriage" on a train was, obviously, less comfortable than first class.
4. London railway stations.
5. Horse carriage with four wheels.
6. A "round game" is any card game in which each player plays for himself or herself; "ties pay the dealer" would therefore mean that two winners with the same score could not keep their winnings but would have to pay them back to the dealer.
7. Ornamental figures woven into a stocking.
8. Bootjack—a device for helping to pull off one's boots.

From the greengrocer tree you get grapes and green pea, cauliflower, pineapple, and cranberries,
While the pastrycook plant cherry brandy will grant, apple puffs, and three-corners, and Banburys—
The shares are a penny, and ever so many are taken by Rothschild and Baring,[9]
And just as a few are allotted to you, you awake with a shudder despairing—
You're a regular wreck, with a crick in your neck, and no wonder you snore, for your head's on the floor, and you've needles and pins from your soles to your shins, and your flesh is a-creep, for your left leg's asleep, and you've cramp in your toes, and a fly on your nose, and some fluff in your lung, and a feverish tongue, and a thirst that's intense, and a general sense that you haven't been sleeping in clover;
But the darkness has passed, and it's daylight at last, and the night has been long—ditto ditto my song—and thank goodness they're both of them over!

1882

Titwillow[1]

On a tree by a river a little tom-tit
Sang "Willow, titwillow, titwillow!"
And I said to him, "Dicky-bird, why do you sit
Singing 'Willow, titwillow, titwillow'?"
"Is it weakness of intellect, birdie?" I cried,
"Or a rather tough worm in your little inside?"
With a shake of his poor little head, he replied,
"Oh, willow, titwillow, titwillow!"

He slapped at his chest, as he sat on that bough,
Singing "Willow, titwillow, titwillow!"
And a cold perspiration bespangled his brow,
Oh, willow, titwillow, titwillow!
He sobbed and he sighed, and a gurgle he gave,
Then he plunged himself into the billowy wave,
And an echo arose from the suicide's grave—
"Oh, willow, titwillow, titwillow!"

Now I feel just as sure as I'm sure that my name
Isn't Willow, titwillow, titwillow,
That 'twas blighted affection that made him exclaim
"Oh, willow, titwillow, titwillow!"
And if you remain callous and obdurate, I
Shall perish as he did, and you will know why,
Though I probably shall not exclaim as I die,
"Oh, willow, titwillow, titwillow!"

1885

9. Prominent banking house.

1. Sung by Ko-Ko in Act II of *The Mikado*.

ALGERNON CHARLES SWINBURNE
(1837–1909)

Chorus from *Atalanta in Calydon*

Before the Beginning of Years

Before the beginning of years
   There came to the making of man
Time, with a gift of tears;
   Grief, with a glass that ran;
Pleasure, with pain for leaven;
   Summer, with flowers that fell;
Remembrance fallen from heaven,
   And madness risen from hell;
Strength without hands to smite;
   Love that endures for a breath:
Night, the shadow of light,
   And life, the shadow of death.
And the high gods took in hand
   Fire, and the falling of tears,
And a measure of sliding sand
   From under the feet of the years;
And froth and drift of the sea;
   And dust of the laboring earth;
And bodies of things to be
   In the houses of death and of birth;
And wrought with weeping and laughter,
   And fashioned with loathing and love
With life before and after
   And death beneath and above,
For a day and a night and a morrow,
   That his strength might endure for a span
With travail and heavy sorrow,
   The holy spirit of man.
From the winds of the north and the south
   They gathered as unto strife;
They breathed upon his mouth,
   They filled his body with life;
Eyesight and speech they wrought
   For the veils of the soul therein,
A time for labor and thought,
   A time to serve and to sin;
They gave him light in his ways,
   And love, and a space for delight,
And beauty and length of days,
   And night, and sleep in the night.
His speech is a burning fire;
   With his lips he travaileth;
In his heart is a blind desire,
   In his eyes foreknowledge of death;
He weaves, and is clothed with derision;
   Sows, and he shall not reap;
His life is a watch or a vision
   Between a sleep and a sleep.

1865

The Garden of Proserpine[1]

Here, where the world is quiet;
Here, where all trouble seems
Dead winds' and spent waves' riot
In doubtful dreams of dreams;
I watch the green field growing
For reaping folk and sowing,
For harvest-time and mowing,
A sleepy world of streams.

I am tired of tears and laughter,
And men that laugh and weep;
Of what may come hereafter
For men that sow to reap:
I am weary of days and hours,
Blown buds of barren flowers,
Desires and dreams and powers
And everything but sleep.

Here life has death for neighbor,
And far from eye or ear
Wan waves and wet winds labor,
Weak ships and spirits steer;
They drive adrift, and whither
They wot not who make thither;
But no such winds blow hither,
And no such things grow here.

No growth of moor or coppice,
No heather-flower or vine,
But bloomless buds of poppies,
Green grapes of Proserpine,
Pale beds of blowing rushes
Where no leaf blooms or blushes
Save this whereout she crushes
For dead men deadly wine.

Pale, without name or number,
In fruitless fields of corn,° *wheat*
They bow themselves and slumber
All night till light is born;
And like a soul belated,
In hell and heaven unmated,
By cloud and mist abated
Comes out of darkness morn.

Though one were strong as seven,
He too with death shall dwell,
Nor wake with wings in heaven,
Nor weep for pains in hell;
Though one were fair as roses,
His beauty clouds and closes;

1. Persephone, in Roman mythology Proserpine, the daughter of Zeus and Demeter, had been abducted by Hades (the Roman Pluto), god of the underworld, over which she ruled with him thereafter as his queen.

And well though love reposes,
  In the end it is not well.

Pale, beyond porch and portal,
  Crowned with calm leaves, she stands
Who gathers all things mortal
  With cold immortal hands;
Her languid lips are sweeter
Than love's who fears to greet her
To men that mix and meet her
  From many times and lands.

She waits for each and other,
  She waits for all men born;
Forgets the earth her mother,
  The life of fruits and corn;
And spring and seed and swallow
Take wing for her and follow
Where summer song rings hollow
  And flowers are put to scorn.

There go the loves that wither,
  The old loves with wearier wings;
And all dead years draw thither,
  And all disastrous things;
Dead dreams of days forsaken,
Blind buds that snows have shaken,
Wild leaves that winds have taken,
  Red strays of ruined springs.

We are not sure of sorrow,
  And joy was never sure;
Today will die tomorrow;
  Time stoops to no man's lure;[2]
And love, grown faint and fretful,
With lips but half regretful
Sighs, and with eyes forgetful
  Weeps that no love endure.

From too much love of living,
  From hope and fear set free,
We thank with brief thanksgiving
  Whatever gods may be
That no life lives for ever;
That dead men rise up never;
That even the weariest river
  Winds somewhere safe to sea.

Then star nor sun shall waken,
  Nor any change of light:
Nor sound of waters shaken,
  Nor any sound or sight:
Nor wintry leaves nor vernal,
Nor days nor things diurnal;
Only the sleep eternal
  In an eternal night.

1866

2. In falconry, the lure is a device used to recall the hawk to the falconer's wrist.

A Forsaken Garden

In a coign of the cliff between lowland and highland,
  At the sea-down's edge between windward and lee,
Walled round with rocks as an inland island,
  The ghost of a garden fronts the sea.
A girdle of brushwood and thorn encloses
  The steep square slope of the blossomless bed
Where the weeds that grew green from the graves of its roses
      Now lie dead.

The fields fall southward, abrupt and broken,
  To the low last edge of the long lone land.
If a step should sound or a word be spoken,
  Would a ghost not rise at the strange guest's hand?
So long have the grey bare walks lain guestless,
  Through branches and briars if a man make way,
He shall find no life but the sea-wind's, restless
      Night and day.

The dense hard passage is blind and stifled
  That crawls by a track none turn to climb
To the strait waste place that the years have rifled
  Of all but the thorns that are touched not of time.
The thorns he spares when the rose is taken;
  The rocks are left when he wastes the plain.
The wind that wanders, the weeds wind-shaken,
      These remain.

Not a flower to be pressed of the foot that falls not;
  As the heart of a dead man the seed-plots are dry;
From the thicket of thorns whence the nightingale calls not,
  Could she call, there were never a rose to reply.
Over the meadows that blossom and wither
  Rings but the note of a sea-bird's song;
Only the sun and the rain come hither
      All year long.

The sun burns sere° and the rain dishevels *dry*
  One gaunt bleak blossom of scentless breath.
Only the wind here hovers and revels
  In a round where life seems barren as death.
Here there was laughing of old, there was weeping,
  Haply, of lovers none ever will know,
Whose eyes went seaward a hundred sleeping
      Years ago.

Heart handfast in heart as they stood, "Look thither,"
  Did he whisper? "look forth from the flowers to the sea,
For the foam-flowers endure when the rose-blossoms wither,
  And men that love lightly may die—but we?"
And the same wind sang and the same waves whitened,
  And or ever the garden's last petals were shed,
In the lips that had whispered, the eyes that had lightened,
      Love was dead.

Or they loved their life through, and then went whither?
And were one to the end—but what end who knows?
Love deep as the sea as a rose must wither,
As the rose-red seaweed that mocks the rose.
Shall the dead take thought for the dead to love them?
What love was ever as deep as a grave?
They are loveless now as the grass above them
Or the wave.

All are at one now, roses and lovers,
Not known of the cliffs and the fields and the sea.
Not a breath of the time that has been hovers
In the air now soft with a summer to be.
Not a breath shall there sweeten the seasons hereafter
Of the flowers or the lovers that laugh now or weep,
When as they that are free now of weeping and laughter
We shall sleep.

Here death may deal not again for ever;
Here change may come not till all change end.
From the graves they have made they shall rise up never,
Who have left nought living to ravage and rend.
Earth, stones, and thorns of the wild ground growing,
While the sun and the rain live, these shall be;
Till a last wind's breath upon all these blowing
Roll the sea.

Till the slow sea rise and the sheer cliff crumble,
Till terrace and meadow the deep gulfs drink,
Till the strength of the waves of the high tides humble
The fields that lessen, the rocks that shrink,
Here now in his triumph where all things falter,
Stretched out on the spoils that his own hand spread,
As a god self-slain on his own strange altar,
Death lies dead.

1876 1878

THOMAS HARDY
(1840–1928)

Hap

If but some vengeful god would call to me
From up the sky, and laugh: "Thou suffering thing,
Know that thy sorrow is my ecstasy,
That thy love's loss is my hate's profiting!"

Then would I bear it, clench myself, and die,
Steeled by the sense of ire unmerited;
Half-eased in that a Powerfuller than I
Had willed and meted me the tears I shed.

But not so. How arrives it joy lies slain,
And why unblooms the best hope ever sown?
—Crass Casualty obstructs the sun and rain,

And dicing Time for gladness casts a moan. . . .
These purblind Doomsters had as readily strown
Blisses about my pilgrimage as pain.

1866 1898

Thoughts of Phena[1]

AT NEWS OF HER DEATH

Not a line of her writing have I,
Not a thread of her hair,
No mark of her late time as dame in her dwelling, whereby
I may picture her there;
And in vain do I urge my unsight
To conceive my lost prize
At her close, whom I knew when her dreams were upbrimming with light,
And with laughter her eyes.

What scenes spread around her last days,
Sad, shining, or dim?
Did her gifts and compassions enray and enarch her sweet ways
With an aureate nimb?° *nimbus*
Or did life-light decline from her years,
And mischances control
Her full day-star; unease, or regret, or forebodings, or fears
Disennoble her soul?

Thus I do but the phantom retain
Of the maiden of yore
As my relic; yet haply the best of her—fined° in my brain *refined*
It may be the more
That no line of her writing have I,
Nor a thread of her hair,
No mark of her late time as dame in her dwelling, whereby
I may picture her there.

March 1890 1898

I Look into My Glass

I look into my glass,
And view my wasting skin,
And say, "Would God it came to pass
My heart had shrunk as thin!"

For then, I, undistrest
By hearts grown cold to me,
Could lonely wait my endless rest
With equanimity.

But Time, to make me grieve,
Part steals, lets part abide;
And shakes this fragile frame at eve
With throbbings of noontide.

1898

1. The name under which, at various places in his writings, Hardy lightly concealed the identity of Tryphena Sparks, a young woman with whom he had a liaison in the late 1860s and early 1870s; she terminated their engagement in 1873. (See J. O. Bailey, *The Poetry of Thomas Hardy,* 1970, pp. 35–37.)

Drummer Hodge[2]

1

They throw in drummer Hodge, to rest
Uncoffined—just as found:
His landmark is a kopje-crest[3]
That breaks the veldt around;
And foreign constellations west
Each night above his mound.

2

Young Hodge the Drummer never knew—
Fresh from his Wessex home—
The meaning of the broad Karoo,
The Bush, the dusty loam,
And why uprose to nightly view
Strange stars amid the gloam.

3

Yet portion of that unknown plain
Will Hodge forever be;
His homely Northern breast and brain
Grow to some Southern tree,
And strange-eyed constellations reign
His stars eternally.

1902

A Broken Appointment

You did not come,
And marching Time drew on, and wore me numb.
Yet less for loss of your dear presence there
Than that I thus found lacking in your make
That high compassion which can overbear
Reluctance for pure lovingkindness' sake
Grieved I, when, as the hope-hour stroked its sum,
You did not come.

You love not me,
And love alone can lend you loyalty;
—I know and knew it. But, unto the store
Of human deeds divine in all but name,
Was it not worth a little hour or more
To add yet this: Once you, a woman, came
To soothe a time-torn man; even though it be
You love not me?

1902

2. The poem presents an incident from the Boer War (1899–1902) and when first published bore the note: "One of the Drummers killed was a native of a village near Casterbridge," i.e., Dorchester, the principal city of the region of southern England to which, in his novels and poems, Hardy gave its medieval name of Wessex.

3. In Afrikaans, the language of the Dutch settlers in South Africa, the crest of a small hill. The veldt (line 4) is open country, unenclosed pasture land; the Karoo (line 9), barren tracts of plateau-land.

The Darkling Thrush

I leant upon a coppice[4] gate
When Frost was specter-gray,
And Winter's dregs made desolate
The weakening eye of day.
The tangled bine-stems[5] scored the sky
Like strings of broken lyres,
And all mankind that haunted nigh
Had sought their household fires.

The land's sharp features seemed to be
The Century's corpse outleant,
His crypt the cloudy canopy,
The wind his death-lament.
The ancient pulse of germ and birth
Was shrunken hard and dry,
And every spirit upon earth
Seemed fervorless as I.

At once a voice arose among
The bleak twigs overhead
In a full-hearted evensong
Of joy illimited;
An aged thrush, frail, gaunt, and small,
In blast-beruffled plume,
Had chosen thus to fling his soul
Upon the growing gloom.

So little cause for carolings
Of such ecstatic sound
Was written on terrestrial things
Afar or nigh around,
That I could think there trembled through
His happy good-night air
Some blessed Hope, whereof he knew
And I was unaware.

December 31, 1900 1902

The Ruined Maid

"O'Melia, my dear, this does everything crown!
Who could have supposed I should meet you in Town?
And whence such fair garments, such prosperi-ty?"
"O didn't you know I'd been ruined?" said she.

"You left us in tatters, without shoes or socks,
Tired of digging potatoes, and spudding up docks;[6]
And now you've gay bracelets and bright feathers three!"
"Yes: that's how we dress when we're ruined," said she.

4. Thicket or wood consisting of small trees.
5. Shoots or stems of a climbing plant.
6. Digging up weedy herbs.

"At home in the barton° you said 'thee' and 'thou,' *farm*
And 'thik oon,' and 'theäs oon,' and 't'other'; but now
Your talking quite fits 'ee for high compa-ny!"
"Some polish is gained with one's ruin," said she.

"Your hands were like paws then, your face blue and bleak
But now I'm bewitched by your delicate cheek,
And your little gloves fit as on any la-dy!"
"We never do work when we're ruined," said she.

"You used to call home-life a hag-ridden dream,
And you'd sigh, and you'd sock; but at present you seem
To know not of megrims° or melancho-ly!" *low spirits*
"True. One's pretty lively when ruined," said she.

"I wish I had feathers, a fine sweeping gown,
And a delicate face, and could strut about Town!"
"My dear—a raw country girl, such as you be,
Cannot quite expect that. You ain't ruined," said she.

1866 1902

In Tenebris[7]

"Percussus sum sicut foenum, et aruit cor meum"[8]
—PSALM cii

Wintertime nighs;
But my breavement-pain
It cannot bring again:
Twice no one dies.

Flower-petals flee;
But, since it once hath been,
No more that severing scene
Can harrow me.

Birds faint in dread:
I shall not lose old strength
In the lone frost's black length:
Strength long since fled!

Leaves freeze to dun;
But friends can not turn cold
This season as of old
For him with none.

Tempests may scath;
But love can not make smart
Again this year his heart
Who no heart hath.

Black is night's cope;
But death will not appal
One who, past doubtings all,
Waits in unhope.

1902

7. The first poem of a series of three with this title (*In Darkness*).

8. "My heart is smitten, and withered like grass" (King James version).

The Convergence of the Twain

LINES ON THE LOSS OF THE TITANIC[9]

1
In a solitude of the sea
Deep from human vanity,
And the Pride of Life that planned her, stilly couches she.

2
Steel chambers, late the pyres
Of her salamandrine fires,[1]
Cold currents thrid,° and turn to rhythmic tidal lyres. *thread*

3
Over the mirrors meant
To glass the opulent
The sea-worm crawls—grotesque, slimed, dumb, indifferent.

4
Jewels in joy designed
To ravish the sensuous mind
Lie lightless, all their sparkles bleared and black and blind.

5
Dim moon-eyed fishes near
Gaze at the gilded gear
And query: "What does this vaingloriousness down here?"

6
Well: while was fashioning
This creature of cleaving wing,
The Immanent Will that stirs and urges everything

7
Prepared a sinister mate
For her—so gaily great—
A Shape of Ice, for the time far and dissociate.

8
And as the smart ship grew
In stature, grace, and hue,
In shadowy silent distance grew the Iceberg too.

9
Alien they seemed to be:
No mortal eye could see
The intimate welding of their later history,

10
Or sign that they were bent
By paths coincident
On being anon twin halves of one august event,

11
Till the Spinner of the Years
Said "Now!" And each one hears,
And consummation comes, and jars two hemispheres.

1912

9. The White Star liner R.M.S. *Titanic* was sunk, with great loss of life, as the result of collision with an iceberg on its maiden voyage from Southampton to New York on April 15, 1912.

1. The ship's fires, which burn though immersed in water, are compared to the salamander, a lizard-like creature which according to fable could live in the midst of fire.

Channel Firing

That night your great guns, unawares,
Shook all our coffins as we lay,
And broke the chancel window-squares,
We thought it was the Judgment-day

And sat upright. While drearisome
Arose the howl of wakened hounds:
The mouse let fall the altar-crumb,
The worms drew back into the mounds,

The glebe cow[2] drooled. Till God called, "No;
It's gunnery practice out at sea
Just as before you went below;
The world is as it used to be:

"All nations striving strong to make
Red war yet redder. Mad as hatters
They do no more for Christés sake
Than you who are helpless in such matters.

"That this is not the judgment-hour
For some of them's a blessed thing,
For if it were they'd have to scour
Hell's floor for so much threatening. . . .

"Ha, ha. It will be warmer when
I blow the trumpet (if indeed
I ever do; for you are men,
And rest eternal sorely need)."

So down we lay again. "I wonder,
Will the world ever saner be,"
Said one, "than when He sent us under
In our indifferent century!"

And many a skeleton shook his head.
"Instead of preaching forty year,"
My neighbor Parson Thirdly said,
"I wish I had stuck to pipes and beer."

Again the guns disturbed the hour,
Roaring their readiness to avenge,
As far inland as Stourton Tower,
And Camelot, and starlit Stonehenge.[3]

April 1914 1914

2. Cow pastured on the glebe, a piece of land attached to a vicarage or rectory.
3. Stourton Tower, built in 1772, and locally known as "Alfred's Tower," stands on the highest point of the estate of Stourhead, in Wiltshire, close to the Somersetshire border. Camelot, the seat of King Arthur's court, has been variously associated with Winchester and with certain places in Somersetshire. Stonehenge is a circular grouping of megalithic monuments on Salisbury Plain, Wiltshire, dating back to the late Neolithic or early Bronze age.

The Voice

Woman much missed, how you call to me, call to me,
Saying that now you are not as you were
When you had changed from the one who was all to me,
But as at first, when our day was fair.

Can it be you that I hear? Let me view you, then,
Standing as when I drew near to the town
Where you would wait for me: yes, as I knew you then,
Even to the original air-blue gown!

Or is it only the breeze, in its listlessness
Traveling across the wet mead to me here,
You being ever dissolved to wan wistlessness,° *headlessness*
Heard no more again far or near?

Thus I; faltering forward,
Leaves around me falling,
Wind oozing thin through the thorn from norward,
And the woman calling.

December 1912 1914

In Time of "The Breaking of Nations"[4]

1

Only a man harrowing clods
In a slow silent walk
With an old horse that stumbles and nods
Half asleep as they stalk.

2

Only thin smoke without flame
From the heaps of couch-grass;
Yet this will go onward the same
Though Dynasties pass.

3

Yonder a maid and her wight
Come whispering by:
War's annals will cloud into night
Ere their story die.

1915 1916

GERARD MANLEY HOPKINS
(1844–1889)

The Habit of Perfection

Elected Silence, sing to me
And beat upon my whorlèd ear,
Pipe me to pastures still and be
The music that I care to hear.

4. See Jeremiah li.20: "Thou art my battle ax and weapons of war: for with thee will I break in pieces the nations, and with thee will I destroy kingdoms."

Shape nothing, lips; be lovely-dumb:
It is the shut, the curfew sent
From there where all surrenders come
Which only makes you eloquent.

Be shellèd, eyes, with double dark
And find the uncreated light:[1]
This ruck and reel which you remark
Coils, keeps, and teases simple sight.

Palate, the hutch of tasty lust,
Desire not to be rinsed with wine:
The can° must be so sweet, the crust *tankard, cup*
So fresh that come in fasts divine!

Nostrils, your careless breath that spend
Upon the stir and keep of pride,
What relish shall the censers[2] send
Along the sanctuary side!

O feel-of-primrose hands, O feet
That want the yield of plushy sward,
But you shall walk the golden street
And you unhouse and house the Lord.[3]

And, Poverty, be thou the bride
And now the marriage feast begun,
And lily-coloured clothes provide
Your spouse not laboured-at nor spun.[4]

1866 1918

God's Grandeur

The world is charged with the grandeur of God.
  It will flame out, like shining from shook foil;[5]
  It gathers to a greatness, like the ooze of oil
Crushed.[6] Why do men then now not reck his rod?
Generations have trod, have trod, have trod;
  And all is seared with trade; bleared, smeared with toil;
  And wears man's smudge and shares man's smell: the soil
Is bare now, nor can foot feel, being shod.

And for all this, nature is never spent;
  There lives the dearest freshness deep down things;
And though the last lights off the black West went
  Oh, morning, at the brown brink eastward, springs—
Because the Holy Ghost over the bent
  World broods with warm breast and with ah! bright wings.

1877 1895

1. W. H. Gardner, in his notes to the poem, explains "uncreated light" as "the *lux increata* of the Schoolmen, the creative energy of God's mind."
2. Vessels in which incense is burned.
3. I.e., the hands will open and close the pyx, the vessel containing the host, the consecrated bread, used in the sacrament.
4. See Matthew vi.28–29: "* * * Consider the lilies of the field, how they grow; they toil not, neither do they spin."
5. In a letter to Robert Bridges (January 4, 1883), Hopkins says: "* * * I mean foil in its sense of leaf or tinsel, and no other word whatever will give the effect I want. Shaken goldfoil gives off broad glares like sheet lightning and also, and this is true of nothing else, owing to its zigzag dints and crossings and network of small many cornered facets, a sort of fork lightning too."
6. I.e., as when olives are crushed for their oil.

The Windhover[7]

TO CHRIST OUR LORD

I caught this morning morning's minion,° king- *darling, favorite*
dom of daylight's dauphin,[8] dapple-dawn-drawn Falcon, in his riding
Of the rolling level underneath him steady air, and striding
High there, how he rung upon the rein of a wimpling° wing *rippling*
In his ecstasy! then off, off forth on swing,
As a skate's heel sweeps smooth on a bow-bend: the hurl and gliding
Rebuffed the big wind. My heart in hiding
Stirred for a bird,—the achieve of, the mastery of the thing!

Brute beauty and valour and act, oh, air, pride, plume, here
Buckle![9] AND the fire that breaks from thee then, a billion
Times told lovelier, more dangerous, O my chevalier![1]

No wonder of it: shéer plód makes plough down sillion° *furrow*
Shine, and blue-bleak embers, ah my dear,
Fall, gall themselves, and gash gold-vermilion.

1877 1918

Pied Beauty[2]

Glory be to God for dappled things—
For skies of couple-colour as a brinded° cow; *streaked, brindled*
For rose-moles all in stipple upon trout that swim;
Fresh-firecoal chestnut-falls;[3] finches' wings;
Landscape plotted and pieced—fold, fallow, and plough;[4]
And áll trádes, their gear and tackle and trim.
All things counter, original, spare, strange;
Whatever is fickle, freckled (who knows how?)
With swift, slow; sweet, sour; adazzle, dim;
He fathers-forth whose beauty is past change:
Praise him.

1877 1918

Felix Randal

Felix Randal the farrier,° O is he dead then? my duty all ended, *blacksmith*
Who have watched his mould of man, big-boned and hardy-handsome
Pining, pining, till time when reason rambled in it and some
Fatal four disorders, fleshed there, all contended?

Sickness broke him. Impatient, he cursed at first, but mended
Being anointed and all; though a heavenlier heart began some

7. "A name for the kestrel [a species of small hawk], from its habit of hovering or hanging with its head to the wind" [O.E.D.].
8. The eldest son of the king of France was called the *dauphin:* hence, the word here means heir to a splendid, kingly condition.
9. The word "buckle" brings to a single focus the several elements of line 8, in both their literal sense, as descriptive of a single, sudden movement of the airborne bird, and in their symbolic sense as descriptive of Christ and with further reference to the poet himself and the lesson he draws from his observation. It may be read either as indicative or imperative, and in one or another of its possible meanings: "to fasten," "to join closely," "to equip for battle," "to grapple with, engage," but also "to cause to bend, give way, crumple."
1. Knight, nobleman, champion.
2. Having two or more colors, in patches or blotches.
3. W. H. Gardner cites a note from Hopkins's *Journals:* "Chestnuts as bright as coals or spots of vermilion."
4. The land makes a pattern of varicolored patches by reason of its several uses, as for pasture, or being left fallow for a season, or being plowed and sown.

Months earlier, since I had our sweet reprieve and ransom
Tendered to him.[5] Ah well, God rest him all road ever he offended![6]

This seeing the sick endears them to us, us too it endears.
My tongue had taught thee comfort, touch had quenched thy tears,
Thy tears that touched my heart, child, Felix, poor Felix Randal;

How far from then forethought of, all thy more boisterous years,
When thou at the random[7] grim forge, powerful amidst peers,
Didst fettle[8] for the great grey drayhorse his bright and battering sandal!

1880 1918

Spring and Fall

TO A YOUNG CHILD

Márgarét, áre you gríeving
Over Goldengrove unleaving?
Leáves, líke the things of man, you
With your fresh thoughts care for, can you?
Áh! ás the heart grows older
It will come to such sights colder
By and by, nor spare a sigh
Though worlds of wanwood leafmeal lie;[9]
And yet you *will* weep and know why.
Now no matter, child, the name:
Sórrow's spríngs áre the same.
Nor mouth had, no nor mind, expressed
What heart heard of, ghost° guessed: *spirit, soul*
It ís the blight man was born for,
It is Margaret you mourn for.

1880 1893

[As Kingfishers Catch Fire, Dragonflies Draw Flame]

As kingfishers catch fire, dragonflies draw flame;[1]
As tumbled over rim in roundy wells
Stones ring; like each tucked° string tells, each hung bell's *touched, plucked*
Bow swung finds tongue to fling out broad its name;
Each mortal thing does one thing and the same:
Deals out that being indoors each one dwells;[2]
Selves[3]—goes itself; *myself* it speaks and spells,
Crying *What I do is me: for that I came.*

I say more: the just man justices;
Keeps gráce: thát keeps all his goings graces;
Acts in God's eye what in God's eye he is—
Chríst. For Christ plays in ten thousand places,
Lovely in limbs, and lovely in eyes not his
To the Father through the features of men's faces.

1882? 1918

5. I.e., since I had a priest visit him to hear his confession and give absolution.
6. I.e., for any way in which he may have offended.
7. Ramshackle, as applied to the forge itself; but also meaning that the man's life as a blacksmith was merely one casual earthly life as opposed to the sure way of Christian salvation.
8. To line or cover with a refractory material; hence, to shoe.
9. "Wanwood": *pale* or *dim*—the groves are pale because of their light-colored autumn foliage, or dim because of the filtered light. "Leafmeal" (a word coined by Hopkins by analogy with *piecemeal*): *leaf by leaf*, or *leaf mold*—in the first sense, the foliage lies about the grove, having fallen leaf by leaf; in the second, foliage gradually decays to leaf mold.
1. I.e., as their bright colors flash in the light.
2. I.e., gives utterance to the essential nature that dwells within ("indoors") each individual being.
3. I.e., gives being to its own individuality.

[Carrion Comfort]

Not, I'll not, carrion[4] comfort, Despair, not feast on thee;
Not untwist—slack they may be—these last strands of man
In me ór, most weary, cry *I can no more*. I can;
Can something, hope, wish day come, not choose not to be.
But ah, but O thou terrible, why wouldst thou rude° on me *roughly*
Thy wring-world right foot[5] rock? lay a lionlimb against me? scan
With darksome devouring eyes my bruisèd bones? and fan,
O in turns of tempest, me heaped there; me frantic to avoid thee and flee?

Why? That my chaff might fly; my grain lie, sheer and clear.
Nay in all that toil, that coil, since (seems) I kissed the rod,
Hand[6] rather, my heart lo! lapped strength, stole joy, would laugh, chéer.
Cheer whom though? The hero whose heaven-handling flung me, fóot tród
Me? or me that fought him? O which one? is it each one? That night, that year
Of now done darkness I wretch lay wrestling with (my God!) my God.

1885 1918

[No Worst, There Is None. Pitched Past Pitch of Grief]

No worst, there is none. Pitched past pitch of grief,
More pangs will, schooled at forepangs, wilder wring.
Comforter, where, where is your comforting?
Mary, mother of us, where is your relief?

My cries heave, herds-long; huddle in a main, a chief-
woe, world-sorrow; on an age-old anvil wince and sing—
Then lull, then leave off. Fury had shrieked 'No ling-
ering! Let me be fell:° force° I must be brief'. *fierce, deadly/perforce*

O the mind, mind has mountains; cliffs of fall
Frightful, sheer, no-man-fathomed. Hold them cheap
May who ne'er hung there. Nor does long our small
Durance deal with that steep or deep. Here! creep,
Wretch, under a comfort serves in a whirlwind: all
Life death does end and each day dies with sleep.

1885 1918

[My Own Heart Let Me More Have Pity On]

My own heart let me more have pity on; let
Me live to my sad self hereafter kind,
Charitable; not live this tormented mind
With this tormented mind tormenting yet.

I cast for comfort I can no more get
By groping round my comfortless, than blind
Eyes in their dark can day or thirst can find
Thirst's all-in-all in all a world of wet.[7]

4. Dead and putrefying flesh.
5. I.e., the foot capable of causing the world to writhe or twist.
6. I.e., the hand that wields the rod.
7. I.e., as shipwrecked persons adrift without drinking water cannot quench their thirst, even though they are surrounded by "wet." The noun *world* is common to all three instances: the speaker's "comfortless" world, the blind man's "dark" world, the "world of wet" in which the shipwrecked are adrift.

Soul, self; come, poor Jackself,[8] I do advise
You, jaded, let be; call off thoughts awhile
Elsewhere; leave comfort root-room;[9] let joy size

At God knows when to God knows what;[1] whose smile
's not wrung,[2] see you; unforeseen times rather—as skies
Betweenpie mountains[3]—lights a lovely mile.

1885 1918

[Thou Art Indeed Just, Lord . . .]

Justus quidem tu es, Domine, si disputem tecum: verumtamen justa loquar ad te: Quare via impiorum prosperatur? & c.[4]

Thou art indeed just, Lord, if I contend
With thee; but, sir, so what I plead is just.
Why do sinners' ways prosper? and why must
Disappointment all I endeavour end?
Wert thou my enemy, O thou my friend,
How wouldst thou worse, I wonder, than thou dost
Defeat, thwart me? Oh, the sots and thralls of lust
Do in spare hours more thrive than I that spend,
Sir, life upon thy cause. See, banks and brakes
Now, leavèd how thick! lacèd they are again
With fretty chervil,[5] look, and fresh wind shakes
Them; birds build—but not I build; no, but strain,
Time's eunuch, and not breed one work that wakes.
Mine, O thou lord of life, send my roots rain.

1889 1893

A. E. HOUSMAN (1859–1936)

Loveliest of Trees, the Cherry Now

Loveliest of trees, the cherry now
Is hung with bloom along the bough,
And stands about the woodland ride
Wearing white for Eastertide.

Now, of my threescore years and ten,
Twenty will not come again,
And take from seventy springs a score,
It only leaves me fifty more.

8. The humble self—"Jack" used in a pitying, deprecating sense (as in *jack-of-all-trades*).
9. Room for its roots to grow.
1. "Size" (line 11): grow, increase in size; "At God knows when": at unpredictable times; "to God knows what": until it reaches an unpredictable condition.
2. Cannot be forced, but must come as it will.
3. "Betweenpie" (a verb of Hopkins's invention [see *Pied Beauty*]): the brightness of skies seen between mountains, which makes a variegated patterning of light and dark.
4. The Latin epigraph is from the Vulgate version of Jeremiah xii.1; the first three lines of Hopkins's poem translate it. The "&c" indicates that the whole of Jeremiah xii is relevant to the poem, which, while it does not continue to translate it directly, parallels it frequently.
5. An herb of the carrot or parsley family, with curled leaves.

And since to look at things in bloom
Fifty springs are little room,
About the woodlands I will go
To see the cherry hung with snow.

1896

When I Watch the Living Meet

When I watch the living meet,
  And the moving pageant file
Warm and breathing through the street
  Where I lodge a little while,

If the heats of hate and lust
  In the house of flesh are strong,
Let me mind the house of dust
  Where my sojourn shall be long.

In the nation that is not
  Nothing stands that stood before;
There revenges are forgot,
  And the hater hates no more;

Lovers lying two and two
  Ask not whom they sleep beside,
And the bridegroom all night through
  Never turns him to the bride.

1896

To an Athlete Dying Young

The time you won your town the race
We chaired you through the market-place;
Man and boy stood cheering by,
And home we brought you shoulder-high.

Today, the road all runners come,
Shoulder-high we bring you home,
And set you at your threshold down,
Townsman of a stiller town.

Smart lad, to slip betimes away
From fields where glory does not stay
And early though the laurel grows
It withers quicker than the rose.

Eyes the shady night has shut
Cannot see the record cut,
And silence sounds no worse than cheers
After earth has stopped the ears:

Now you will not swell the rout
Of lads that wore their honors out,

Runners whom renown outran
And the name died before the man.

So set, before its echoes fade,
The fleet foot on the sill of shade,
And hold to the low lintel up
The still-defended challenge-cup.

And round that early-laureled head
Will flock to gaze the strengthless dead,
And find unwithered on its curls
The garland briefer than a girl's.

1896

Is My Team Plowing

"Is my team plowing,
  That I was used to drive
And hear the harness jingle
  When I was man alive?"

Ay, the horses trample,
  The harness jingles now;
No change though you lie under
  The land you used to plow.

"Is football playing
  Along the river shore,
With lads to chase the leather,
  Now I stand up no more?"

Ay, the ball is flying,
  The lads play heart and soul;
The goal stands up, the keeper
  Stands up to keep the goal.

"Is my girl happy,
  That I thought hard to leave,
And has she tired of weeping
  As she lies down at eve?"

Ay, she lies down lightly,
  She lies not down to weep:
Your girl is well contented.
  Be still, my lad, and sleep.

"Is my friend hearty,
  Now I am thin and pine,
And has he found to sleep in
  A better bed than mine?"

Yes, lad, I lie easy,
  I lie as lads would choose;
I cheer a dead man's sweetheart,
  Never ask me whose.

1896

On Wenlock Edge the Wood's in Trouble

On Wenlock Edge[1] the wood's in trouble;
His forest fleece the Wrekin[2] heaves;
The gale, it plies the saplings double,
And thick on Severn[3] snow the leaves.

'Twould blow like this through holt and hanger[4]
When Uricon[5] the city stood:
'Tis the old wind in the old anger,
But then it threshed another wood.

Then, 'twas before my time, the Roman
At yonder heaving hill would stare:
The blood that warms an English yeoman,
The thoughts that hurt him, they were there.

There, like the wind through woods in riot,
Through him the gale of life blew high;
The tree of man was never quiet:
Then 'twas the Roman, now 'tis I.

The gale, it plies the saplings double,
It blows so hard, 'twill soon be gone:
To-day the Roman and his trouble
Are ashes under Uricon.

1896

From Far, from Eve and Morning

From far, from eve and morning
And yon twelve-winded sky,[6]
The stuff of life to knit me
Blew hither: here am I.

Now—for a breath I tarry
Nor yet disperse apart—
Take my hand quick and tell me,
What have you in your heart.

Speak now, and I will answer;
How shall I help you, say;
Ere to the wind's twelve quarters
I take my endless way.

1896

With Rue My Heart Is Laden

With rue my heart is laden
For golden friends I had,

1. A range of hills in Shropshire.
2. A prominent, isolated hill in Shropshire.
3. The river Severn.
4. A holt is a wood or wooden hill; a hanger is a steep wooded slope.
5. The Roman town Uriconium, on the site of the modern town of Wroxeter, Shropshire.
6. I.e., winds blowing from the twelve compass points.

For many a rose-lipt maiden
  And many a lightfoot lad.

By brooks too broad for leaping
  The lightfoot boys are laid;
The rose-lipt girls are sleeping
  In fields where roses fade.

1896

"Terence,[7] This Is Stupid Stuff . . ."

"Terence, this is stupid stuff:
You eat your victuals fast enough;
There can't be much amiss, 'tis clear,
To see the rate you drink your beer.
But oh, good Lord, the verse you make,
It gives a chap the belly-ache.
The cow, the old cow, she is dead;
It sleeps well, the hornéd head:
We poor lads, 'tis our turn now
To hear such tunes as killed the cow.
Pretty friendship 'tis to rhyme
Your friends to death before their time
Moping melancholy mad:
Come, pipe a tune to dance to, lad."

Why, if 'tis dancing you would be,
There's brisker pipes than poetry.
Say, for what were hop-yards meant,
Or why was Burton built on Trent?[8]
Oh many a peer of England brews
Livelier liquor than the Muse,
And malt does more than Milton can
To justify God's ways to man.
Ale, man, ale's the stuff to drink
For fellows whom it hurts to think:
Look into the pewter pot
To see the world as the world's not.
And faith, 'tis pleasant till 'tis past:
The mischief is that 'twill not last.
Oh I have been to Ludlow[9] fair
And left my necktie God knows where,
And carried halfway home, or near,
Pints and quarts of Ludlow beer:
Then the world seemed none so bad,
And I myself a sterling lad;
And down in lovely muck I've lain,
Happy till I woke again.
Then I saw the morning sky:
Heigho, the tale was all a lie;
The world, it was the old world yet,
I was I, my things were wet,

7. Housman had at first planned to call the volume in which this poem appeared *The Poems of Terence Hearsay.*

8. Burton-on-Trent, a town in Staffordshire whose principal industry is the brewing of ale.

9. A town in Shropshire.

And nothing now remained to do
But begin the game anew.

Therefore, since the world has still
Much good, but much less good than ill,
And while the sun and moon endure
Luck's a chance, but trouble's sure,
I'd face it as a wise man would,
And train for ill and not for good.
'Tis true, the stuff I bring for sale
Is not so brisk a brew as ale:
Out of a stem that scored the hand
I wrung it in a weary land.
But take it: if the smack is sour,
The better for the embittered hour;
It should do good to heart and head
When your soul is in my soul's stead;
And I will friend you, if I may,
In the dark and cloudy day.

There was a king reigned in the East:
There, when kings will sit to feast,
They get their fill before they think
With poisoned meat and poisoned drink.
He gathered all that springs to birth
From the many-venomed earth;
First a little, thence to more,
He sampled all her killing store;
And easy, smiling, seasoned sound,
Sate the king when healths went round.
They put arsenic in his meat
And stared aghast to watch him eat;
They poured strychnine in his cup
And shook to see him drink it up:
They shook, they stared as white's their shirt:
Them it was their poison hurt.
—I tell the tale that I heard told.
Mithridates, he died old.[1]

1896

Crossing Alone the Nighted Ferry

Crossing alone the nighted ferry
With the one coin for fee,[2]
Whom, on the wharf of Lethe waiting,
Count you to find? Not me.

The brisk fond lackey to fetch and carry,
The true, sick-hearted slave,
Expect him not in the just city
And free land of the grave.

1936

1. Mithridates VI, king of Pontus in Asia Minor in the first century B.C., produced in himself an immunity to certain poisons by administering them to himself in small, gradual doses.
2. The shades of the dead were ferried over the river Styx to Hades by Charon, paying him an obolus (a Greek coin) as fee. Lethe, in Greek mythology, was another of the rivers of the underworld: its water, drunk by souls about to be reincarnated, would cause them to forget their previous existence.

Here Dead Lie We Because We Did Not Choose

Here dead lie we because we did not choose
  To live and shame the land from which we sprung.
Life, to be sure, is nothing much to lose;
  But young men think it is, and we were young.

1936

RUDYARD KIPLING
(1865–1936)

Tommy[1]

I went into a public-'ouse to get a pint o' beer,
The publican° 'e up an' sez, "We serve no red-coats here."   *bar-keeper*
The girls be'ind the bar they laughed an' giggled fit to die,
I outs into the street again an' to myself sez I:
    O it's Tommy this, an' Tommy that, an' "Tommy, go away";
    But it's "Thank you, Mister Atkins," when the band begins to play—
    The band begins to play, my boys, the band begins to play,
    O it's "Thank you, Mister Atkins," when the band begins to play.

I went into a theater as sober as could be,
They gave a drunk civilian room, but 'adn't none for me;
They sent me to the gallery or round the music-'alls,[2]
But when it comes to fightin', Lord! they'll shove me in the stalls!
    For it's Tommy this, an' Tommy that, an' "Tommy, wait outside";
    But its "Special train for Atkins" when the trooper's on the tide—
    The troopship's on the tide, my boys, the troopship's on the tide,
    O it's "Special train for Atkins" when the trooper's on the tide.

Yes, makin' mock o' uniforms that guard you while you sleep
Is cheaper than them uniforms, an' they're starvation cheap;
An' hustlin' drunken soldiers when they're goin' large a bit
Is five times better business than paradin' in full kit.
    Then it's Tommy this, an' Tommy that, an' "Tommy, 'ow's yer soul?"
    But it's "Thin red line of 'eroes"[3] when the drums begin to roll—
    The drums begin to roll, my boys, the drums begin to roll,
    O it's "Thin red line of 'eroes" when the drums begin to roll.

We aren't no thin red 'eroes, nor we aren't no blackguards too,
But single men in barricks, most remarkable like you;
An' if sometimes our conduck isn't all your fancy paints,
Why, single men in barricks don't grow into plaster saints;
    While it's Tommy this, an' Tommy that, an' "Tommy, fall be'ind,"
    But it's "Please to walk in front, sir," when there's trouble in the wind—
    There's trouble in the wind, my boys, there's trouble in the wind,
    O it's "Please to walk in front, sir," when there's trouble in the wind.

1. Derived from "Thomas Atkins," as the typical name for a soldier in the British army.
2. Cheaper seats in a theater, in the balcony; the best seats, in the orchestra, are the stalls.
3. W. H. Russell, a London *Times* correspondent, had used the phrase "thin red line tipped with steel" to describe the 93rd Highlanders infantry regiment as they stood to meet the advancing Russian cavalry at Balaclava (1854), in the Crimean War.

You talk o' better food for us, an' schools, an' fires, an' all:
We'll wait for extry rations if you treat us rational.
Don't mess about the cook-room slops, but prove it to our face
The Widow's Uniform[4] is not the soldier-man's disgrace.
    For it's Tommy this, an' Tommy that, an' "Chuck him out, the brute!"
    But it's "Savior of 'is country" when the guns begin to shoot;
    An' it's Tommy this, an' Tommy that, an' anything you please;
    An' Tommy ain't a bloomin' fool—you bet that Tommy sees!

1890

Recessional[5]

1897[6]

God of our fathers, known of old,
  Lord of our far-flung battle-line,
Beneath whose awful Hand we hold
  Dominion over palm and pine—
Lord God of Hosts, be with us yet,
Lest we forget—lest we forget!

The tumult and the shouting dies;
  The Captains and the Kings depart:
Still stands Thine ancient sacrifice,
  An humble and a contrite heart.[7]
Lord God of Hosts, be with us yet,
Lest we forget—lest we forget!

Far-called, our navies melt away;
  On dune and headland sinks the fire:[8]
Lo, all our pomp of yesterday
  Is one with Nineveh and Tyre![9]
Judge of the Nations, spare us yet,
Lest we forget—lest we forget!

If, drunk with sight of power, we loose
  Wild tongues that have not Thee in awe,
Such boastings as the Gentiles use,
  Or lesser breeds without the Law—[1]
Lord God of Hosts, be with us yet,
Lest we forget—lest we forget!

For heathen heart that puts her trust
  In reeking tube and iron shard,
All valiant dust that builds on dust,
  And guarding, calls not Thee to guard,
For frantic boast and foolish word—
Thy mercy on Thy People, Lord!

1897 1899

4. I.e., the queen's uniform. In his poems and stories Kipling occasionally referred to Queen Victoria as "The Widow at Windsor."
5. A piece of music or a hymn to be played or sung at the close of a religious service.
6. The year of Queen Victoria's Diamond Jubilee, celebrating the sixtieth year of her reign, the occasion serving also to celebrate the current great extent, power, and prosperity of the British Empire.
7. Cf. Psalms li.17.
8. On the night of the anniversary of Victoria's accession to the throne, bonfires were lit on high points throughout Great Britain.
9. Nineveh, ancient capital of Assyria, and Tyre, capital of Phoenicia, were once great cities that later dwindled to insignificance.
1. Cf. Romans ii.14.

WILLIAM BUTLER YEATS*
(1865–1939)

The Stolen Child

Where dips the rocky highland
Of Sleuth Wood[1] in the lake,
There lies a leafy island
Where flapping herons wake
The drowsy water-rats;
There we've hid our faery vats,
Full of berries
And of reddest stolen cherries.
Come away, O human child!
To the waters and the wild
With a faery, hand in hand,
For the world's more full of weeping than you can understand.

Where the wave of moonlight glosses
The dim grey sands with light,
Far off by furthest Rosses
We foot it all the night,
Weaving olden dances,
Mingling hands and mingling glances
Till the moon has taken flight;
To and fro we leap
And chase the frothy bubbles,
While the world is full of troubles
And is anxious in its sleep.
Come away, O human child!
To the waters and the wild
With a faery, hand in hand,
For the world's more full of weeping than you can understand.

Where the wandering water gushes
From the hills above Glen-Car,
In pools among the rushes
That scarce could bathe a star,
We seek for slumbering trout
And whispering in their ears
Give them unquiet dreams;
Leaning softly out
From ferns that drop their tears
Over the young streams.
Come away, O human child!
To the waters and the wild
With a faery, hand in hand,
For the world's more full of weeping than you can understand.

*Yeats's poems are arranged here in the order in which they appear in *The Collected Poems of William Butler Yeats* (1940).

1. Place names throughout the poem refer to the area near Sligo, in the west of Ireland: Rosses Point on Sligo Bay, and Glen-Car, a small lake near Sligo.

Away with us he's going,
The solemn-eyed:
He'll hear no more the lowing
Of the calves on the warm hillside
Or the kettle on the hob
Sing peace into his breast,
Or see the brown mice bob
Round and round the oatmeal-chest.
For he comes, the human child!
To the waters and the wild
With a faery, hand in hand,
From a world more full of weeping than he can understand.

1889

The Lake Isle of Innisfree

I will arise and go now, and go to Innisfree,
And a small cabin build there, of clay and wattles[2] made:
Nine bean-rows will I have there, a hive for the honey-bee,
And live alone in the bee-loud glade.

And I shall have some peace there, for peace comes dropping slow,
Dropping from the veils of the morning to where the cricket sings;
There midnight's all a glimmer, and noon a purple glow,
And evening full of the linnet's wings.

I will arise and go now, for always night and day
I hear lake water lapping with low sounds by the shore;
While I stand on the roadway, or on the pavements gray,
I hear it in the deep heart's core.

1892

When You Are Old[3]

When you are old and gray and full of sleep,
And nodding by the fire, take down this book,
And slowly read, and dream of the soft look
Your eyes had once, and of their shadows deep;

How many loved your moments of glad grace,
And loved your beauty with love false or true,
But one man loved the pilgrim soul in you,
And loved the sorrows of your changing face;

And bending down beside the glowing bars,
Murmur, a little sadly, how Love fled
And paced upon the mountains overhead
And hid his face amid a crowd of stars.

1893

2. Rods interwoven with twigs or branches to form a framework for walls or roof.
3. The poem's point of departure is a sonnet by the French poet Pierre Ronsard (1524–85) that begins *"Quand vous serez bien vieille, au soir à la chandelle"* (When you are very old, in the evening, by candlelight . . .), but is a free adaptation rather than a translation.

Adam's Curse[4]

We sat together at one summer's end,
That beautiful mild woman, your close friend,[5]
And you and I, and talked of poetry.
I said, "A line will take us hours maybe;
Yet if it does not seem a moment's thought,
Our stitching and unstitching has been naught.
Better go down upon your marrow-bones
And scrub a kitchen pavement, or break stones
Like an old pauper, in all kinds of weather;
For to articulate sweet sounds together
Is to work harder than all these, and yet
Be thought an idler by the noisy set
Of bankers, schoolmasters, and clergymen
The martyrs call the world."

And thereupon
That beautiful mild woman for whose sake
There's many a one shall find out all heartache
On finding that her voice is sweet and low
Replied, "To be born woman is to know—
Although they do not talk of it at school—
That we must labor to be beautiful."

I said, "It's certain there is no fine thing
Since Adam's fall but needs much laboring.
There have been lovers who thought love should be
So much compounded of high courtesy
That they would sigh and quote with learned looks
Precedents out of beautiful old books;
Yet now it seems an idle trade enough."

We sat grown quiet at the name of love;
We saw the last embers of daylight die,
And in the trembling blue-green of the sky
A moon, worn as if it had been a shell
Washed by time's waters as they rose and fell
About the stars and broke in days and years.

I had a thought for no one's but your ears:
That you were beautiful, and that I strove
To love you in the old high way of love;
That it had all seemed happy, and yet we'd grown
As weary-hearted as that hollow moon.

1904

The Wild Swans at Coole[6]

The trees are in their autumn beauty,
The woodland paths are dry,

4. Genesis iii.17–19.

5. The two women who figure in the poem are Maud Gonne and, rather than a friend, her sister Kathleen.

6. Coole Park, the estate in western Ireland of Lady Augusta Gregory, Yeats's patroness and friend.

Under the October twilight the water
Mirrors a still sky;
Upon the brimming water among the stones
Are nine-and-fifty swans.

The nineteenth autumn has come upon me
Since I first made my count;[7]
I saw, before I had well finished,
All suddenly mount
And scatter wheeling in great broken rings
Upon their clamorous wings.

I have looked upon those brilliant creatures,
And now my heart is sore.
All's changed since I, hearing at twilight,
The first time on this shore,
The bell-beat of their wings above my head,
Trod with a lighter tread.

Unwearied still, lover by lover,
They paddle in the cold
Companionable streams or climb the air;
Their hearts have not grown old;
Passion or conquest, wander where they will,
Attend upon them still.

But now they drift on the still water,
Mysterious, beautiful;
Among what rushes will they build,
By what lake's edge or pool
Delight men's eyes when I awake some day
To find they have flown away?

1917

An Irish Airman Foresees His Death[8]

I know that I shall meet my fate
Somewhere among the clouds above;
Those that I fight I do not hate,
Those that I guard I do not love;
My country is Kiltartan Cross,[9]
My countrymen Kiltartan's poor,
No likely end could bring them loss
Or leave them happier than before.
Nor law, nor duty bade me fight,
Nor public men, nor cheering crowds,
A lonely impulse of delight
Drove to this tumult in the clouds;
I balanced all, brought all to mind,
The years to come seemed waste of breath,
A waste of breath the years behind
In balance with this life, this death.

1919

7. Yeats had first visited Coole Park in 1897; the poem was written in October 1916.
8. The airman, who was killed in action in Italy in January 1918, is Major Robert Gregory, son of Yeats's friend and patron Lady Augusta Gregory.
9. A village near the Gregory estate, Coole Park, in County Galway, western Ireland.

The Scholars

Bald heads forgetful of their sins,
Old, learned, respectable bald heads
Edit and annotate the lines
That young men, tossing on their beds,
Rhymed out in love's despair
To flatter beauty's ignorant ear.

All shuffle there; all cough in ink;
All wear the carpet with their shoes;
All think what other people think;
All know the man their neighbor knows.
Lord, what would they say
Did their Catullus walk that way?

1917

Easter 1916[1]

I have met them at close of day
Coming with vivid faces
From counter or desk among gray
Eighteenth-century houses.
I have passed with a nod of the head
Or polite meaningless words,
Or have lingered awhile and said
Polite meaningless words,
And thought before I had done
Of a mocking tale or a gibe
To please a companion
Around the fire at the club,
Being certain that they and I
But lived where motley is worn:
All changed, changed utterly:
A terrible beauty is born.

That woman's days were spent
In ignorant good will,
Her nights in argument
Until her voice grew shrill.
What voice more sweet than hers
When, young and beautiful,
She rode to harriers?[2]
This man had kept a school
And rode our wingéd horse;[3]
This other his helper and friend

1. An Irish Nationalist uprising had been planned for Easter Sunday 1916, and although the German ship which was bringing munitions had been intercepted by the British, attempts to postpone the uprising failed; it began in Dublin on Easter Monday. "Fifteen hundred men seized key points and an Irish republic was proclaimed from the General Post Office. After the initial surprise prompt British military action was taken, and when over 300 lives had been lost the insurgents were forced to surrender on 29 April * * * The seven signatories of the republican proclamation, including [Pádraic] Pearse and [James] Connolly, and nine others were shot after court martial between 3 and 12 May; 75 were reprieved and over 2000 held prisoners" [From "Ireland: History," by D. B. Quinn, in *Chambers's Encyclopedia*].

2. Countess Constance Georgina Markiewicz, *née* Gore-Booth, about whom Yeats wrote *On a Political Prisoner* and a later poem, *In Memory of Eva Gore-Booth and Con Markiewicz.*

3. Pádraic Pearse, headmaster of St. Enda's School, and a prolific writer of poems, plays, and stories as well as of essays on Irish politics and Gaelic literature. "This other" was Thomas MacDonough, also a schoolteacher.

Was coming into his force;
He might have won fame in the end,
So sensitive his nature seemed,
So daring and sweet his thought.
This other man I had dreamed
A drunken, vainglorious lout.[4]
He had done most bitter wrong
To some who are near my heart,
Yet I number him in the song;
He, too, has resigned his part
In the casual comedy;
He, too, has been changed in his turn,
Transformed utterly:
A terrible beauty is born.

Hearts with one purpose alone
Through summer and winter seem
Enchanted to a stone
To trouble the living stream.
The horse that comes from the road,
The rider, the birds that range
From cloud to tumbling cloud,
Minute by minute they change;
A shadow of cloud on the stream
Changes minute by minute;
A horse-hoof slides on the brim,
And a horse plashes within it;
The long-legged moor-hens dive,
And hens to moor-cocks call;
Minute by minute they live:
The stone's in the midst of all.

Too long a sacrifice
Can make a stone of the heart.
O when may it suffice?
That is Heaven's part, our part
To murmur name upon name,
As a mother names her child
When sleep at last has come
On limbs that had run wild.
What is it but nightfall?
No, no, not night but death;
Was it needless death after all?
For England may keep faith
For all that is done and said.
We know their dream; enough
To know they dreamed and are dead;
And what if excess of love
Bewildered them till they died?
I write it out in a verse—
MacDonagh and MacBride
And Connolly and Pearse
Now and in time to be,
Wherever green is worn,
Are changed, changed utterly:
A terrible beauty is born.

September 25, 1916 1916

4. Major John MacBride, who had married Maud Gonne (the woman with whom Yeats had for years been hopelessly in love) in 1903 and separated from her in 1905.

The Second Coming

Turning and turning in the widening gyre[5]
The falcon cannot hear the falconer;
Things fall apart; the center cannot hold;
Mere anarchy is loosed upon the world,
The blood-dimmed tide is loosed, and everywhere
The ceremony of innocence is drowned;
The best lack all conviction, while the worst
Are full of passionate intensity.

Surely some revelation is at hand;
Surely the Second Coming is at hand;
The Second Coming! Hardly are those words out
When a vast image out of *Spiritus Mundi*[6]
Troubles my sight: somewhere in sands of the desert
A shape with lion body and the head of a man,[7]
A gaze blank and pitiless as the sun,
Is moving its slow thighs, while all about it
Reel shadows of the indignant desert birds.
The darkness drops again; but now I know
That twenty centuries of stony sleep
Were vexed to nightmare by a rocking cradle,
And what rough beast, its hour come round at last,
Slouches towards Bethlehem to be born?

1921

A Prayer for My Daughter[8]

Once more the storm is howling, and half hid
Under this cradle-hood and coverlid
My child sleeps on. There is no obstacle
But Gregory's wood and one bare hill
Whereby the haystack- and roof-leveling wind,
Bred on the Atlantic, can be stayed;
And for an hour I have walked and prayed
Because of the great gloom that is in my mind.

I have walked and prayed for this young child an hour
And heard the sea-wind scream upon the tower,[9]

5. The gyre—the cone whose shape is traced in the falcon's sweep upward and out in widening circles from the falconer who should control its flight—involves a reference to the geometrical figure of the interpenetrating cones, the "fundamental symbol" Yeats used to diagram his cyclical view of history. (See the opening pages of "The Great Wheel," in *A Vision* [1937]). He saw the cycle of Greco-Roman civilization as having been brought to a close by the advent of Christianity, and in the violence of his own times—"the growing murderousness of the world"—he saw signs that the 2000-year cycle of Christianity was itself about to end, and to be replaced by a system anithetical to it.

6. Or *Anima Mundi,* the Great Memory. "Before the mind's eye, whether in sleep or waking, came images that one was to discover presently in some book one had never read, and after looking in vain for explanation to the current theory of forgotten personal memory, I came to believe in a great memory passing on from generation to generation * * * Our daily thought was certainly but the line of foam at the shallow edge of a vast luminous sea" [*Per Amica Silentia Lunae,* "Anima Mundi," § ii].

7. In the Introduction to his play *The Resurrection* (in *Wheels and Butterflies,* 1935), Yeats describes the way in which the sphinx image had first manifested itself to him: "Our civilisation was about to reverse itself, or some new civilisation about to be born from all that our age had rejected * * *; because we had worshipped a single god it would worship many * * * Had I begun *On Baile's Strand* or not when I began to imagine, as always at my left side just out of the range of the sight, a brazen winged beast (afterwards described in my poem *The Second Coming*) that I associated with laughing, ecstatic destruction?"

8. Yeats's daughter, Anne Butler Yeats, was born on February 26, 1919.

9. Yeats's tower, which he called Thoor Ballylee.

And under the arches of the bridge, and scream
In the elms above the flooded stream;
Imagining in excited reverie
That the future years had come,
Dancing to a frenzied drum,
Out of the murderous innocence of the sea.

May she be granted beauty and yet not
Beauty to make a stranger's eye distraught,
Or hers before a looking glass, for such,
Being made beautiful overmuch,
Consider beauty a sufficient end,
Lose natural kindness and maybe
The heart-revealing intimacy
That chooses right, and never find a friend.

Helen[1] being chosen found life flat and dull
And later had much trouble from a fool,
While that great Queen,[2] that rose out of the spray,
Being fatherless could have her way
Yet chose a bandy-leggèd smith for man.
It's certain that fine women eat
A crazy salad with their meat,
Whereby the Horn of Plenty is undone.

In courtesy I'd have her chiefly learned;
Hearts are not had as a gift but hearts are earned
By those that are not entirely beautiful;
Yet many, that have played the fool
For beauty's very self, has charm made wise,
And many a poor man that has roved,
Loved and thought himself beloved,
From a glad kindness cannot take his eyes.

May she become a flourishing hidden tree
That all her thoughts may like the linnet[3] be,
And have no business but dispensing round
Their magnanimities of sound,
Nor but in merriment begin a chase,
Nor but in merriment a quarrel.
Oh, may she live like some green laurel
Rooted in one dear perpetual place.

My mind, because the minds that I have loved,
The sort of beauty that I have approved,
Prosper but little, has dried up of late,
Yet knows that to be choked with hate
May well be of all evil chances chief.
If there's no hatred in a mind
Assault and battery of the wind
Can never tear the linnet from the leaf.

1. Helen of Troy, whose beauty was legendary. The daughter of Zeus and Leda, she married Menelaus, brother of the Greek leader, Agamemnon. She was abducted by Paris, son of the king of Troy; the Greeks undertook an expedition to Troy to bring her back, besieged the city for ten years, and finally took it. Helen was reunited with Menelaus.

2. Aphrodite, Greek goddess of love. "Fatherless" in the sense that, in Hesiod's version of the myth, "she sprang from the foam (*aphros*) of the sea that gathered about the severed member of Uranus when Cronos . . . mutilated him" (*Oxford Companion to Classical Literature*). She was married to Hephaestus, the smith, lame from birth, who forged thunderbolts for the gods.

3. Small European bird of the finch family.

An intellectual hatred is the worst,
So let her think opinions are accursed.
Have I not seen the loveliest woman born[4]
Out of the mouth of Plenty's horn,
Because of her opinionated mind
Barter that horn and every good
By quiet natures understood
For an old bellows full of angry wind?

Considering that, all hatred driven hence,
The soul recovers radical innocence
And learns at last that it is self-delighting,
Self-appeasing, self-affrighting,
And that its own sweet will is Heaven's will;
She can, though every face should scowl
And every windy quarter howl
Or every bellows burst, be happy still.

And may her bridegroom bring her to a house
Where all's accustomed, ceremonious;
For arrogance and hatred are the wares
Peddled in the thoroughfares.
How but in custom and in ceremony
Are innocence and beauty born?
Ceremony's a name for the rich horn,
And custom for the spreading laurel tree.

1919 1921

Sailing to Byzantium[5]

1

That is no country for old men. The young
In one another's arms, birds in the trees
—Those dying generations—at their song,
The salmon-falls, the mackerel-crowded seas,
Fish, flesh, or fowl, commend all summer long
Whatever is begotten, born, and dies.

4. Doubtless Maud Gonne, whom Yeats had loved hopelessly since meeting her in 1889, and who had married Major John MacBride in 1903; often to Yeats's dismay, she was a very daring activist in the cause of Irish liberation.

5. Of the ancient city of Byzantium—on the site of modern Istanbul, capital of the Eastern Roman Empire, and the center, especially in the fifth and sixth centuries, of highly developed and characteristic forms of art and architecture—Yeats made a many-faceted symbol, which, since it is a symbol, should not be brought within the limits of too narrowly specific interpretation. Byzantine painting and the mosaics which decorated its churches (Yeats had seen later derivatives of these mosaics in Italy, at Ravenna and elsewhere) were stylized and formal, making no attempt at the full naturalistic rendering of human forms, so that the city and its art can appropriately symbolize a way of life in which art is frankly accepted and proclaimed as artifice. As artifice, as a work of the intellect, this art is not subject to the decay and death which overtake the life of "natural things." But while such an opposition of artifice and nature is central to the poem, there are references to Byzantium in Yeats's prose which suggest the wider range of meaning that the city held for him. In *A Vision,* particularly, he makes of it an exemplar of a civilization which had achieved "Unity of Being": "I think if I could be given a month of Antiquity and leave to spend it where I chose, I would spend it in Byzantium a little before Justinian [who ruled at Byzantium from 527 to 565] opened St. Sophia and closed the Academy of Plato. I think I could find in some little wine-shop some philosophical worker in mosaic who could answer all my questions, the supernatural descending nearer to him than to Plotinus even, for the pride of his delicate skill would make what was an instrument of power to princes and clerics, a murderous madness in the mob, show as a lovely flexible presence like that of a perfect human body * * * I think that in early Byzantium, maybe never before or since in recorded history, religious, aesthetic and practical life were one, that architect and artificers * * * spoke to the multitude and the few alike. The painter, the mosaic worker, the worker in gold and silver, the illuminator of sacred books, were almost impersonal, almost perhaps without the consciousness of individual design, absorbed in their subject-matter and that the vision of a whole people."

Caught in that sensual music all neglect
Monuments of unaging intellect.

2

An aged man is but a paltry thing,
A tattered coat upon a stick, unless
Soul clap its hands and sing, and louder sing
For every tatter in its mortal dress,
Nor is there singing school but studying
Monuments of its own magnificence;
And therefore I have sailed the seas and come
To the holy city of Byzantium.

3

O sages standing in God's holy fire
As in the gold mosaic of a wall,
Come from the holy fire, perne in a gyre,[6]
And be the singing-masters of my soul.
Consume my heart away; sick with desire
And fastened to a dying animal
It knows not what it is; and gather me
Into the artifice of eternity.

4

Once out of nature I shall never take
My bodily form from any natural thing,
But such a form as Grecian goldsmiths make
Of hammered gold and gold enameling
To keep a drowsy Emperor awake;
Or set upon a golden bough to sing
To lords and ladies of Byzantium
Of what is past, or passing, or to come.

1927

Leda and the Swan[7]

A sudden blow: the great wings beating still
Above the staggering girl, her thighs caressed
By the dark webs, her nape caught in his bill,
He holds her helpless breast upon his breast.

How can those terrified vague fingers push
The feathered glory from her loosening thighs?
And how can body, laid in that white rush,
But feel the strange heart beating where it lies?

A shudder in the loins engenders there
The broken wall, the burning roof and tower
And Agamemnon dead.
Being so caught up,
So mastered by the brute blood of the air,

6. Out of the noun *pern* (usually *pirn*), a weaver's bobbin, spool, or reel, Yeats makes a verb meaning to move in the spiral pattern taken by thread being unwound from a bobbin or being wound upon it. Here the speaker entreats the sages to descend to him in this manner, to come down into the gyres of history, the cycles of created life, out of their eternity in "the simplicity of fire" where is "all music and all rest." (For "the two realities, the terrestrial and the condition of fire," see *Per Amica Silentia Lunae,* "Anima Mundi," § x.)

7. Leda, possessed by Zeus in the guise of a swan, gave birth to Helen of Troy and the twins Castor and Pollux. (Leda was also the mother of Clytemnestra, Agamemnon's wife, who murdered him on his return from the war at Troy.) Helen's abduction by Paris from her husband, Menelaus, brother of Agamemnon, was the cause of the Trojan war. Yeats saw Leda as the recipient of an annunciation that would found Greek civilization, as the Annunciation to Mary would found Christianity.

Did she put on his knowledge with his power
Before the indifferent beak could let her drop?

1923 1924

Among School Children

1

I walk through the long schoolroom questioning;
A kind old nun in a white hood replies;
The children learn to cipher and to sing,
To study reading-books and histories,
To cut and sew, be neat in everything
In the best modern way—the children's eyes
In momentary wonder stare upon
A sixty-year-old smiling public man.

2

I dream of a Ledaean body,[8] bent
Above a sinking fire, a tale that she
Told of a harsh reproof, or trivial event
That changed some childish day to tragedy—
Told, and it seemed that our two natures blent
Into a sphere from youthful sympathy,
Or else, to alter Plato's parable,
Into the yolk and white of the one shell.[9]

3

And thinking of that fit of grief or rage
I look upon one child or t'other there
And wonder if she stood so at that age—
For even daughters of the swan can share
Something of every paddler's heritage—
And had that color upon cheek or hair,
And thereupon my heart is driven wild:
She stands before me as a living child.

4

Her present image floats into the mind—
Did Quattrocento finger[1] fashion it
Hollow of cheek as though it drank the wind
And took a mess of shadows for its meat?
And I though never of Ledaean kind
Had pretty plumage once—enough of that,
Better to smile on all that smile, and show
There is a comfortable kind of old scarecrow.

5

What youthful mother, a shape upon her lap
Honey of generation had betrayed,[2]
And that must sleep, shriek, struggle to escape
As recollection or the drug decide,
Would think her son, did she but see that shape

8. I.e., the body of a woman the poet has known and loved and who has seemed to him as beautiful as Leda or her daughter, Helen of Troy.

9. In Plato's *Symposium*, one of the speakers, to explain the origin of human love, recounts the legend according to which human beings were originally double their present form until Zeus, fearful of their power, decided to cut them in two, which he did "as men cut sorb-apples in two when they are preparing them for pickling, or as they cut eggs in two with a hair." Since then, "each of us is * * * but the half of a human being, * * * each is forever seeking his missing half."

1. I.e., the hand of an Italian artist of the fifteenth century.

2. In a note to the poem, Yeats says: "I have taken the 'honey of generation' from Porphyry's essay on 'The Cave of the Nymphs' but find no warrant in Porphyry for considering it the 'drug' that destroys the 'recollection' of pre-natal freedom * * * " In the essay explaining the symbolism of a passage from the Thirteenth Book of the *Odyssey*, Porphyry (ca. A.D. 232–305) makes such statements as that "the sweetness of honey signifies * * * the same thing as the pleasure arising from copulation," the pleasure "which draws souls downward to generation."

With sixty or more winters on its head,
A compensation for the pang of his birth,
Or the uncertainty of his setting forth?

6

Plato thought nature but a spume that plays
Upon a ghostly paradigm of things;[3]
Solider Aristotle played the taws
Upon the bottom of a king of kings;[4]
World-famous golden-thighed Pythagoras
Fingered upon a fiddle-stick or strings
What a star sang and careless Muses heard:[5]
Old clothes upon old sticks to scare a bird.

7

Both nuns and mothers worship images,
But those the candles light are not as those
That animate a mother's reveries,
But keep a marble or a bronze repose.
And yet they too break hearts—O Presences
That passion, piety or affection knows,
And that all heavenly glory symbolize—
O self-born mockers of man's enterprise;

8

Labor is blossoming or dancing where
The body is not bruised to pleasure soul,
Nor beauty born out of its own despair,
Nor blear-eyed wisdom out of midnight oil.
O chestnut-tree, great-rooted blossomer,
Are you the leaf, the blossom or the bole?
O body swayed to music, O brightening glance,
How can we know the dancer from the dance?

1927

Byzantium[6]

The unpurged images of day recede;
The Emperor's drunken soldiery are abed;
Night resonance recedes, night-walkers' song
After great cathedral gong;
A starlit or a moonlit dome disdains[7]

3. In Plato's idealistic philosophy the world of nature, of appearances, that we know is but the copy of a world of ideal, permanently enduring prototypes.

4. The philosophy of Aristotle differed most markedly from that of Plato in that it emphasized the systematic investigation of verifiable phenomena. Aristotle was tutor to the son of King Philip of Macedonia, later Alexander the Great. "Played the taws": whipped.

5. A Greek philosopher (sixth century B.C.), about whom clustered many legends even in his own lifetime, as that he was the incarnation of Apollo, that he had a golden hip- or thigh-bone, and so on. Central to the Pythagorean school of philosophy (along with the doctrine of the transmigration of souls) was the premise that the universe is mathematically regular, which premise had as one of its starting points the Pythagoreans' observations of the exact mathematical relationships underlying musical harmony.

6. Under the heading "Subject for a Poem, April 30th," Yeats wrote in his *1930 Diary:* "Describe Byzantium as it is in the system [that is, his system in *A Vision*] towards the end of the first Christian millennium. A walking mummy. Flames at the street corners where the soul is purified, birds of hammered gold singing in the golden trees, in the harbor [dolphins], offering their backs to the wailing dead that they may carry them to Paradise."

7. If the dome is seen as "starlit" at the dark of the moon and as "moonlit" at the full, then these terms may be seen as referring to Phase 1 and Phase 15, respectively, of the twenty-eight phases of the moon in the system of *A Vision.* As Michael Robartes says in *The Phases of the Moon,* "* * * There's no human life at the full or the dark," these being "the superhuman phases," opposite to one another on the Wheel of Being. Phase 1 is the phase of complete objectivity, the soul being "completely absorbed by its supernatural environment," waiting to be formed, in a state of "complete plasticity." Phase 15 is the state of complete subjectivity, when the soul is completely absorbed in an achieved state, "a phase of complete beauty." Thus, the world of "mere complexities," the world in which man is in a state of becoming, is banished from the poem at the beginning, as the "unpurged images of day" have been banished.

All that man is,
All mere complexities,
The fury and the mire of human veins.

Before me floats an image, man or shade,
Shade more than man, more image than a shade;
For Hades' bobbin bound in mummy-cloth
May unwind the winding path;[8]
A mouth that has no moisture and no breath
Breathless mouths may summon;[9]
I hail the superhuman;
I call it death-in-life and life-in-death.

Miracle, bird or golden handiwork,
More miracle than bird or handiwork,
Planted on the starlit golden bough,
Can like the cocks of Hades crow,[1]
Or, by the moon embittered, scorn aloud
In glory of changeless metal
Common bird or petal
And all complexities of mire or blood.

At midnight on the Emperor's pavement flit
Flames that no faggot feeds, nor steel has lit,
Nor storm disturbs, flames begotten of flame,
Where blood-begotten spirits come
And all complexities of fury leave,
Dying into a dance,
An agony of trance,
An agony of flame that cannot singe a sleeve.

Astraddle on the dolphin's mire and blood,
Spirit after spirit! The smithies break the flood.
The golden smithies of the Emperor!
Marbles of the dancing floor
Break bitter furies of complexity,
Those images that yet
Fresh images beget,
That dolphin-torn, that gong-tormented sea.

1930 1932

Crazy Jane Talks with the Bishop

I met the Bishop on the road
And much said he and I.
"Those breasts are flat and fallen now,

8. The soul and/or body of the dead. The comparison to the bobbin or spindle is at first visual, to describe the figure of the dead, wrapped in a winding-sheet or mummy-cloth, but it also emphasizes the idea that the soul may unwind the thread of its fate by retracing its path, returning to the world to serve as guide, instructor, inspiration.

9. The two lines have been read in two different ways, depending on which of the two phrases ("a mouth * * *" or "breathless mouths * * *") is seen as subject and which as object of "may summon." Taking "breathless mouths" as subject: mouths of the living, breathless with the intensity of the act of invocation, may call up the mouths of the dead to instruct them.

1. A symbol of rebirth and resurrection. In a book on Roman sculpture which Yeats is believed to have known, *Apotheosis and After Life* (1915), Mrs. Arthur Strong says: "* * * The great vogue of the cock on later Roman tombstones is due * * * to the fact that as herald of the sun he becomes by an easy transition the herald of rebirth and resurrection." In the next sentence she mentions another visual symbol which figures in the poem's last stanza: "The dolphins and marine monsters, another frequent decoration, form a mystic escort of the dead to the Islands of the Blest * * *"

Those veins must soon be dry;
Live in a heavenly mansion,
Not in some foul sty."

"Fair and foul are near of kin,
And fair needs foul," I cried.
"My friends are gone, but that's a truth
Nor grave nor bed denied,
Learned in bodily lowliness
And in the heart's pride.

"A woman can be proud and stiff
When on love intent;
But Love has pitched his mansion in
The place of excrement;
For nothing can be sole or whole
That has not been rent."

1933

Lapis Lazuli[2]

(FOR HARRY CLIFTON)

I have heard that hysterical women say
They are sick of the palette and fiddle-bow,
Of poets that are always gay,
For everybody knows or else should know
That if nothing drastic is done
Aeroplane and Zeppelin will come out,
Pitch like King Billy[3] bomb-balls in
Until the town lie beaten flat.

All perform their tragic play,
There struts Hamlet, there is Lear,
That's Ophelia, that Cordelia;
Yet they, should the last scene be there,
The great stage curtain about to drop,
If worthy their prominent part in the play,
Do not break up their lines to weep.
They know that Hamlet and Lear are gay;
Gaiety transfiguring all that dread.
All men have aimed at, found and lost;
Black out; Heaven blazing into the head:
Tragedy wrought to its uttermost.
Though Hamlet rambles and Lear rages,
And all the drop-scenes drop at once
Upon a hundred thousand stages,
It cannot grow by an inch or an ounce.

On their own feet they came, or on shipboard,
Camelback, horseback, ass-back, mule-back,

2. A deep-blue semi-precious stone. In a letter dated July 6, 1935, Yeats wrote, "* * * Someone has sent me a present of a great piece [of lapis lazuli] carved by some Chinese sculptor into the semblance of a mountain with temple, trees, paths and an ascetic and pupil about to climb the mountain. Ascetic, pupil, hard stone, eternal theme of the sensual east. The heroic cry in the midst of despair. But no, I am wrong, the east has its solutions always and therefore knows nothing of tragedy. It is we, not the east, that must raise the heroic cry."

3. At the Battle of the Boyne on July 1, 1690, William III, king of England since 1689, had defeated the forces of the deposed king, James II.

Old civilizations put to the sword.
Then they and their wisdom went to rack:
No handiwork of Callimachus,[4]
Who handled marble as if it were bronze,
Made draperies that seemed to rise
When sea-wind swept the corner, stands;
His long lamp-chimney shaped like the stem
Of a slender palm, stood but a day;
All things fall and are built again,
And those that build them again are gay.

Two Chinamen, behind them a third,
Are carved in lapis lazuli,
Over them flies a long-legged bird,
A symbol of longevity;
The third, doubtless a serving-man,
Carries a musical instrument.

Every discoloration of the stone,
Every accidental crack or dent,
Seems a water-course or an avalanche,
Or lofty slope where it still snows
Though doubtless plum or cherry-branch
Sweetens the little half-way house
Those Chinamen climb towards, and I
Delight to imagine them seated there;
There, on the mountain and the sky,
On all the tragic scene they stare.
One asks for mournful melodies;
Accomplished fingers begin to play.
Their eyes mid many wrinkles, their eyes,
Their ancient, glittering eyes, are gay.

1938

Long-Legged Fly

That civilization may not sink,
Its great battle lost,
Quiet the dog, tether the pony
To a distant post;
Our master Caesar is in the tent
Where the maps are spread,
His eyes fixed upon nothing,
A hand under his head.
Like a long-legged fly upon the stream
His mind moves upon silence.

That the topless towers be burnt
And men recall that face,[5]
Move most gently if move you must
In this lonely place.
She thinks, part woman, three parts a child,
That nobody looks; her feet

4. Greek sculptor of the fifth century B.C., of whom Yeats says in *A Vision* that only one example of his work remains, a marble chair, and goes on to mention "that bronze lamp [in the Erechtheum, a temple of the guardian deities of Athens] shaped like a palm, known to us by a description in Pausanias * * *"

5. An echo of Marlowe's lines on Helen of Troy in *Dr. Faustus:* "Was this the face that launched a thousand ships, / And burnt the topless towers of Ilium?"

Practice a tinker shuffle
Picked up on a street.
Like a long-legged fly upon the stream
Her mind moves upon silence.

That girls at puberty may find
The first Adam in their thought,
Shut the door of the Pope's chapel,[6]
Keep those children out.
There on that scaffolding reclines
Michael Angelo.
With no more sound than the mice make
His hand moves to and fro.
Like a long-legged fly upon the stream
His mind moves upon silence.

1939

The Circus Animals' Desertion

1

I sought a theme and sought for it in vain,
I sought it daily for six weeks or so.
Maybe at last, being but a broken man,
I must be satisfied with my heart, although
Winter and summer till old age began
My circus animals were all on show,
Those stilted boys, that burnished chariot,[7]
Lion and woman and the Lord knows what.

2

What can I but enumerate old themes?
First that sea-rider Oisin[8] led by the nose
Through three enchanted islands, allegorical dreams,
Vain gaiety, vain battle, vain repose,
Themes of the embittered heart, or so it seems,
That might adorn old songs or courtly shows:
But what cared I that set him on to ride,
I, starved for the bosom of his faery bride?

And then a counter-truth filled out its play,
The Countess Cathleen[9] was the name I gave it;
She, pity-crazed, had given her soul away,
But masterful Heaven had intervened to save it.
I thought my dear[1] must her own soul destroy,
So did fanaticism and hate enslave it,
And this brought forth a dream and soon enough
This dream itself had all my thought and love.

6. On the ceiling of the Sistine Chapel, so called because it was built under Pope Sixtus IV, Michelangelo painted a series of biblical scenes, including the creation of Adam.
7. The images of lines 7–8 may refer to motifs from specific earlier works by Yeats (in his play *The Unicorn from the Stars,* for instance, a gilded state coach, adorned with lion and unicorn, is being built on stage), but it is at least as likely that they are merely generalized images, in line with the title and argument of the poem, of the people and things to be encountered in the heightened, unreal world of a circus.
8. The hero of Yeats's long allegorical (and symbolic) poem, *The Wanderings of Oisin* (pronounced "Usheen"), 1889, is led by the fairy Niamh (pronounced Nee-ave) in succession to the three Islands of Dancing (changeless joy) Victories (also called "Of Many Fears), and Forgetfulness.
9. Yeats's first play, 1892. In it the people, in a time of famine, are selling their souls to emissaries of the devil. To save their souls, the Countess Cathleen sells hers "for a great price." She dies, but an angel announces that she is "passing to the floor of peace."
1. Maud Gonne, whom Yeats had loved since first meeting her in 1889, and who had married John MacBride in 1903; she was a daring, even violent, activist in the cause of Irish liberation.

And when the Fool and Blind Man stole the bread
Cuchulain fought the ungovernable sea;[2]
Heart-mysteries there, and yet when all is said
It was the dream itself enchanted me:
Character isolated by a deed
To engross the present and dominate memory.
Players and painted stage took all my love,
And not those things that they were emblems of.

3

Those masterful images because complete
Grew in pure mind, but out of what began?
A mound of refuse or the sweeping of a street,
Old kettles, old bottles, and a broken can,
Old iron, old bones, old rags, that raving slut
Who keeps the till. Now that my ladder's gone,
I must lie down where all the ladders start,
In the foul rag-and-bone shop of the heart.

1939

Under Ben Bulben[3]

1

Swear by what the sages spoke
Round the Mareotic Lake[4]
That the Witch of Atlas knew,
Spoke and set the cocks a-crow.[5]

Swear by those horsemen, by those women
Complexion and form prove superhuman,
That pale, long-visaged company
That air in immortality
Completeness of their passions won;
Now they ride the wintry dawn
Where Ben Bulben sets the scene.[6]

Here's the gist of what they mean.

2

Many times man lives and dies
Between his two eternities,
That of race and that of soul,
And ancient Ireland knew it all.
Whether man die in his bed
Or the rifle knocks him dead,

2. In another early play, *On Baile's Strand* (1904), Cuchulain (pronounced Cuhoolin) unwittingly kills his own son; maddened, he rushes out to fight the waves. As the people run to the shore to watch, the fool and the blind man hurry off to steal the bread from their ovens.

3. A mountain in County Sligo, in the west of Ireland, which overlooks Drumcliff Churchyard, where Yeats is buried. The last three lines of the poem are carved on his tombstone.

4. Lake Mareotis, a salt lake in northern Egypt, near which the members of the Thebaid, among them St. Anthony (A.D. 251–356) had withdrawn to contemplation. About the Thebaid, in his *1930 Diary*, Yeats wrote, "* * * men went on pilgrimage to Saint Anthony that they might learn about their spiritual states, what was about to happen and why it happened, and Saint Anthony would reply neither out of traditional casuistry nor common sense but from spiritual powers."

5. In Shelley's poem *The Witch of Atlas*, the protagonist, a spirit of love, beauty, and freedom, visits Egypt and the Mareotic Lake in the course of her magic journeyings. The knowledge and belief that Yeats describes as common to her and to the sages "set the cocks a-crow" in the sense that, like "the cocks of Hades" and the golden bird in *Byzantium*, they summon to a spiritual rebirth.

6. In another late poem, *Alternative Song for the Severed Head in "The King of the Great Clock Tower,"* Yeats re-introduces some of the Irish mythological or legendary heroes and heroines who figure in his early poems—Cuchulain, Niam, and others—with whom the supernatural riders of these lines may be identified.

A brief parting from those dear
Is the worst man has to fear.
Though gravediggers' toil is long,
Sharp their spades, their muscles strong,
They but thrust their buried men
Back in the human mind again.

3

You that Mitchel's prayer have heard,
"Send war in our time, O Lord!"[7]
Know that when all words are said
And a man is fighting mad,
Something drops from eyes long blind,
He completes his partial mind,
For an instant stands at ease,
Laughs aloud, his heart at peace.
Even the wisest man grows tense
With some sort of violence
Before he can accomplish fate,
Know his work or choose his mate.

4

Poet and sculptor, do the work,
Nor let the modish painter shirk
What his great forefathers did,
Bring the soul of man to God,
Make him fill the cradles right.

Measurement began our might:[8]
Forms a stark Egyptian thought,
Forms that gentler Phidias wrought.
Michael Angelo left a proof
On the Sistine Chapel roof,
Where but half-awakened Adam
Can disturb globe-trotting Madam
Till her bowels are in heat,
Proof that there's a purpose set
Before the secret working mind:
Profane perfection of mankind.

Quattrocento[9] put in paint
On backgrounds for a God or Saint
Gardens where a soul's at ease;
Where everything that meets the eye,
Flowers and grass and cloudless sky,
Resemble forms that are or seem
When sleepers wake and yet still dream,
And when it's vanished still declare,
With only bed and bedstead there,
That heavens had opened.
Gyres[1] run on;
When that greater dream had gone

7. John Mitchel (1815–75), the Irish patriot, wrote in his *Jail Journal, or Five Years in British Prisons* (published in New York, 1854): "Czar, I bless thee, I kiss the hem of thy garment. I drink to thy health and longevity. Give us war in our time, O Lord" [Quoted by T. R. Henn, *The Lonely Tower*].

8. The achievements of Western civilization—now, according to the poem, being challenged or destroyed—began with the exact mathematical rules which the Egyptians followed in working out the proportions of their sculptured figures—rules which Phidias (line 44), the great Greek sculptor of the fifth century B.C., used, and which have been implicit in the greatest Western art up to the present, when "confusion [falls] upon our thought."

9. The Italian fifteenth century.

1. I.e., the cycles of history.

Calvert and Wilson, Blake and Claude,
Prepared a rest for the people of God,
Palmer's phrase, but after that[2]
Confusion fell upon our thought.

5

Irish poets, learn your trade,
Sing whatever is well made,
Scorn the sort now growing up
All out of shape from toe to top,
Their unremembering hearts and heads
Base-born products of base beds.
Sing the peasantry, and then
Hard-riding country gentlemen,
The holiness of monks, and after
Porter-drinkers' randy laughter;
Sing the lords and ladies gay
That were beaten into the clay
Through seven heroic centuries;
Cast your mind on other days
That we in coming days may be
Still the indomitable Irishry.

6

Under bare Ben Bulben's head
In Drumcliff churchyard Yeats is laid.
An ancestor was rector there
Long years ago, a church stands near,
By the road an ancient cross.
No marble, no conventional phrase;
On limestone quarried near the spot
By his command these words are cut:

Cast a cold eye
On life, on death.
Horseman, pass by!

September 4, 1938 1939

ERNEST DOWSON
(1867–1900)

Non sum qualis eram bonae sub regno Cynarae[1]

Last night, ah, yesternight, betwixt her lips and mine
There fell thy shadow, Cynara! thy breath was shed
Upon my soul between the kisses and the wine;
And I was desolate and sick of an old passion,
Yea, I was desolate and bowed my head:
I have been faithful to thee, Cynara! in my fashion.

All night upon mine heart I felt her warm heart beat,
Night-long within mine arms in love and sleep she lay;

2. The verse paragraph assembles five artists who had provided Yeats with images and with ideals of what art should be. Claude Lorrain (1600–82), the great French landscape painter, was a central standard for landscape painters up to the early 19th century, including those mentioned here, especially Richard Wilson (1714–82). Edward Calvert (1799–1883) and Samuel Palmer (1805–81), visionaries, landscape painters, and engravers, had found inspiration in many aspects of Blake's life and work.

1. Horace, *Odes,* IV.i, lines 3–4: the poet urges Venus to spare him new efforts in her service: "I am not as I was under the reign of the good Cynara."

Surely the kisses of her bought red mouth were sweet;
But I was desolate and sick of an old passion,
When I awoke and found the dawn was gray:
I have been faithful to thee, Cynara! in my fashion.

I have forgot much, Cynara! gone with the wind,
Flung roses, roses riotously with the throng,
Dancing, to put thy pale, lost lilies out of mind;
But I was desolate and sick of an old passion,
Yea, all the time, because the dance was long:
I have been faithful to thee, Cynara! in my fashion.

I cried for madder music and for stronger wine,
But when the feast is finished and the lamps expire,
Then falls thy shadow, Cynara! the night is thine;
And I am desolate and sick of an old passion,
Yea hungry for the lips of my desire:
I have been faithful to thee, Cynara! in my fashion.

1891 1896

EDWIN ARLINGTON ROBINSON (1869–1935)

Richard Cory

Whenever Richard Cory went down town,
We people on the pavement looked at him:
He was a gentleman from sole to crown,
Clean favored, and imperially slim.

And he was always quietly arrayed,
And he was always human when he talked;
But still he fluttered pulses when he said,
"Good-morning," and he glittered when he walked.

And he was rich—yes, richer than a king—
And admirably schooled in every grace:
In fine, we thought that he was everything
To make us wish that we were in his place.

So on we worked, and waited for the light,
And went without the meat, and cursed the bread;
And Richard Cory, one calm summer night,
Went home and put a bullet through his head.

1896

Miniver Cheevy

Miniver Cheevy, child of scorn,
Grew lean while he assailed the seasons;
He wept that he was ever born,
And he had reasons.

Miniver loved the days of old
When swords were bright and steeds were prancing;
The vision of a warrior bold
Would set him dancing.

Miniver sighed for what was not,
And dreamed, and rested from his labors;
He dreamed of Thebes and Camelot,
And Priam's neighbors.[1]

Miniver mourned the ripe renown
That made so many a name so fragrant;
He mourned Romance, now on the town,
And Art, a vagrant.

Miniver loved the Medici,[2]
Albeit he had never seen one;
He would have sinned incessantly
Could he have been one.

Miniver cursed the commonplace
And eyed a khaki suit with loathing;
He missed the medieval grace
Of iron clothing.

Miniver scorned the gold he sought,
But sore annoyed was he without it;
Miniver thought, and thought, and thought,
And thought about it.

Miniver Cheevy, born too late,
Scratched his head and kept on thinking;
Miniver coughed, and called it fate,
And kept on drinking.

1910

Eros Turannos[3]

She fears him, and will always ask
What fated her to choose him;
She meets in his engaging mask
All reasons to refuse him;
But what she meets and what she fears
Are less than are the downward years,
Drawn slowly to the foamless weirs
Of age, were she to lose him.

Between a blurred sagacity
That once had power to sound him,
And Love, that will not let him be
The Judas[4] that she found him,
Her pride assuages her almost,

1. Thebes was a Greek city, anciently famous in history and legend; Camelot is said to have been the site of King Arthur's court; Priam was king of Troy during the Trojan War.

2. A family of merchant-princes of the Italian Renaissance, rulers of Florence for nearly two centuries; they were known both for cruelty and for their support of learning and art.

3. Tyrannical Love.

4. The disciple who betrayed Christ.

As if it were alone the cost.
He sees that he will not be lost,
And waits and looks around him.

A sense of ocean and old trees
Envelopes and allures him;
Tradition, touching all he sees,
Beguiles and reassures him;
And all her doubts of what he says
Are dimmed with what she knows of days—
Till even prejudice delays
And fades, and she secures him.

The falling leaf inaugurates
The reign of her confusion;
The pounding wave reverberates
The dirge of her illusion;
And home, where passion lived and died,
Becomes a place where she can hide,
While all the town and harbor side
Vibrate with her seclusion.

We tell you, tapping on our brows,
The story as it should be,
As if the story of a house
Were told, or ever could be;
We'll have no kindly veil between
Her visions and those we have seen,
As if we guessed what hers have been,
Or what they are or would be.

Meanwhile we do no harm; for they
That with a god have striven,
Not hearing much of what we say,
Take what the god has given;
Though like waves breaking it may be,
Or like a changed familiar tree,
Or like a stairway to the sea
Where down the blind are driven.

1916

Mr. Flood's Party

Old Eben Flood, climbing alone one night
Over the hill between the town below
And the forsaken upland hermitage
That held as much as he should ever know
On earth again of home, paused warily.
The road was his with not a native near;
And Eben, having leisure, said aloud,
For no man else in Tilbury Town to hear:

"Well, Mr. Flood, we have the harvest moon
Again, and we may not have many more;
The bird is on the wing, the poet says,[5]

5. Alludes to the seventh stanza of *The Rubáiyát of Omar Khayyám* as translated by Edward Fitzgerald: "Come, fill the Cup, and in the fire of Spring/Your Winter-garment of Repentance fling:/The Bird of Time has but a little way/To flutter—and the Bird is on the Wing."

And you and I have said it here before.
Drink to the bird." He raised up to the light
The jug that he had gone so far to fill,
And answered huskily: "Well, Mr. Flood,
Since you propose it, I believe I will."

Alone, as if enduring to the end
A valiant armor of scarred hopes outworn,
He stood there in the middle of the road
Like Roland's ghost winding a silent horn.[6]
Below him, in the town among the trees,
Where friends of other days had honored him,
A phantom salutation of the dead
Rang thinly till old Eben's eyes were dim.

Then, as a mother lays her sleeping child
Down tenderly, fearing it may awake,
He set the jug down slowly at his feet
With trembling care, knowing that most things break;
And only when assured that on firm earth
It stood, as the uncertain lives of men
Assuredly did not, he paced away,
And with his hand extended paused again:

"Well, Mr. Flood, we have not met like this
In a long time; and many a change has come
To both of us, I fear, since last it was
We had a drop together. Welcome home!"
Convivially returning with himself,
Again he raised the jug up to the light;
And with an acquiescent quaver said:
"Well, Mr. Flood, if you insist, I might.

"Only a very little, Mr. Flood—
For auld lang syne. No more, sir; that will do."
So, for the time, apparently it did,
And Eben evidently thought so too;
For soon amid the silver loneliness
Of night he lifted up his voice and sang,
Secure, with only two moons listening,
Until the whole harmonious landscape rang—

"For auld lang syne." The weary throat gave out,
The last word wavered; and the song being done,
He raised again the jug regretfully
And shook his head, and was again alone.
There was not much that was ahead of him,
And there was nothing in the town below—
Where strangers would have shut the many doors
That many friends had opened long ago.

1920

6. Guarding the pass of Roncevaux against a stronger enemy, the knight Roland refused to blow his horn for help from Charlemagne's army until it was too late. His heroic death is recounted in the medieval poem *The Song of Roland.*

PAUL LAURENCE DUNBAR
(1872–1906)

We Wear the Mask

We wear the mask that grins and lies,
It hides our cheeks and shades our eyes—
This debt we pay to human guile;
With torn and bleeding hearts we smile,
And mouth with myriad subtleties.

Why should the world be over-wise,
In counting all our tears and sighs?
Nay, let them only see us, while
We wear the mask.

We smile, but, O great Christ, our cries
To thee from tortured souls arise.
We sing, but oh the clay is vile
Beneath our feet, and long the mile;
But let the world dream otherwise,
We wear the mask!

1896

Little Brown Baby

Little brown baby wif spa'klin' eyes,
Come to yo' pappy an' set on his knee.
What you been doin', suh—makin' san' pies?
Look at dat bib—you's ez du'ty ez me.
Look at dat mouf—dat's merlasses, I bet;
Come hyeah, Maria, an' wipe off his han's.
Bees gwine to ketch you an' eat you up yit,
Bein' so sticky an sweet—goodness lan's!

Little brown baby wif spa'klin' eyes,
Who's pappy's darlin' an' who's pappy's chile?
Who is it all de day nevah once tries
Fu' to be cross, er once loses dat smile?
Whah did you git dem teef? My, you's a scamp!
Whah did dat dimple come f'om in yo' chin?
Pappy do' know you—I b'lieves you's a tramp;
Mammy, dis hyeah's some ol' straggler got in!

Let's th'ow him outen de do' in de san',
We do' want stragglers a-layin' 'roun' hyeah;
Let's gin him 'way to de big buggah-man;
I know he's hidin' erroun' hyeah right neah.
Buggah-man, buggah-man, come in de do',
Hyeah's a bad boy you kin have fu' to eat.
Mammy an' pappy do' want him no mo',
Swaller him down f'om his haid to his feet!

Dah, now, I t'ought dat you'd hug me up close.
Go back, ol' buggah, you sha'n't have dis boy.
He ain't no tramp, ner no straggler, of co'se;
He's pappy's pa'dner an' playmate an' joy.
Come to you' pallet now—go to yo' res';
Wisht you could allus know ease an' cleah skies;
Wisht you could stay jes' a chile on my breas'—
Little brown baby wif spa'klin' eyes!

1899?

WALTER DE LA MARE (1873–1956)

The Listeners

"Is there anybody there?" said the Traveler,
Knocking on the moonlit door;
And his horse in the silence champed the grasses
Of the forest's ferny floor:
And a bird flew up out of the turret,
Above the Traveler's head:
And he smote upon the door again a second time;
"Is there anybody there?" he said.
But no one descended to the Traveler;
No head from the leaf-fringed sill
Leaned over and looked into his gray eyes,
Where he stood perplexed and still.
But only a host of phantom listeners
That dwelt in the lone house then
Stood listening in the quiet of the moonlight
To that voice from the world of men:
Stood thronging the faint moonbeams on the dark stair,
That goes down to the empty hall,
Hearkening in an air stirred and shaken
By the lonely Traveler's call.
And he felt in his heart their strangeness,
Their stillness answering his cry,
While his horse moved, cropping the dark turf,
'Neath the starred and leafy sky;
For he suddenly smote on the door, even
Louder, and lifted his head:—
"Tell them I came, and no one answered,
That I kept my word," he said.
Never the least stir made the listeners,
Though every word he spake
Fell echoing through the shadowiness of the still house
From the one man left awake:
Ay, they heard his foot upon the stirrup,
And the sound of iron on stone,
And how the silence surged softly backward,
When the plunging hoofs were gone.

1912

ROBERT FROST
(1874–1963)

Mending Wall

Something there is that doesn't love a wall,
That sends the frozen-ground-swell under it,
And spills the upper boulders in the sun;
And makes gaps even two can pass abreast.
The work of hunters is another thing:
I have come after them and made repair
Where they have left not one stone on a stone,
But they would have the rabbit out of hiding,
To please the yelping dogs. The gaps I mean,
No one has seen them made or heard them made,
But at spring mending-time we find them there.
I let my neighbor know beyond the hill;
And on a day we meet to walk the line
And set the wall between us once again.
We keep the wall between us as we go.
To each the boulders that have fallen to each.
And some are loaves and some so nearly balls
We have to use a spell to make them balance:
'Stay where you are until our backs are turned!'
We wear our fingers rough with handling them.
Oh, just another kind of outdoor game,
One on a side. It comes to little more:
There where it is we do not need the wall:
He is all pine and I am apple orchard.
My apple trees will never get across
And eat the cones under his pines, I tell him.
He only says, 'Good fences make good neighbors.'
Spring is the mischief in me, and I wonder
If I could put a notion in his head:
'*Why* do they make good neighbors? Isn't it
Where there are cows? But here there are no cows.
Before I built a wall I'd ask to know
What I was walling in or walling out,
And to whom I was like to give offense.
Something there is that doesn't love a wall,
That wants it down.' I could say 'Elves' to him,
But it's not elves exactly, and I'd rather
He said it for himself. I see him there
Bringing a stone grasped firmly by the top
In each hand, like an old-stone savage armed.
He moves in darkness as it seems to me,
Not of woods only and the shade of trees.
He will not go behind his father's saying,
And he likes having thought of it so well
He says again, 'Good fences make good neighbors.'

1914

The Wood-Pile

Out walking in the frozen swamp one gray day,
I paused and said, 'I will turn back from here.
No, I will go on farther—and we shall see.'
The hard snow held me, save where now and then
One foot went through. The view was all in lines
Straight up and down of tall slim trees
Too much alike to mark or name a place by
So as to say for certain I was here
Or somewhere else: I was just far from home.
A small bird flew before me. He was careful
To put a tree between us when he lighted,
And say no word to tell me who he was
Who was so foolish as to think what *he* thought.
He thought that I was after him for a feather—
The white one in his tail; like one who takes
Everything said as personal to himself.
One flight out sideways would have undeceived him.
And then there was a pile of wood for which
I forgot him and let his little fear
Carry him off the way I might have gone,
Without so much as wishing him good-night.
He went behind it to make his last stand.
It was a cord of maple, cut and split
And piled—and measured, four by four by eight.
And not another like it could I see.
No runner tracks in this year's snow looped near it.
And it was older sure than this year's cutting,
Or even last year's or the year's before.
The wood was gray and the bark warping off it
And the pile somewhat sunken. Clematis
Had wound strings round and round it like a bundle.
What held it though on one side was a tree
Still growing, and on one a stake and prop,
These latter about to fall. I thought that only
Someone who lived in turning to fresh tasks
Could so forget his handiwork in which
He spent himself, the labor of his axe,
And leave it there far from a useful fireplace
To warm the frozen swamp as best it could
With the slow smokeless burning of decay.

1914

The Road Not Taken

Two roads diverged in a yellow wood,
And sorry I could not travel both
And be one traveler, long I stood
And looked down one as far as I could
To where it bent in the undergrowth;

Then took the other, as just as fair,
And having perhaps the better claim,
Because it was grassy and wanted wear;

Though as for that, the passing there
Had worn them really about the same,

And both that morning equally lay
In leaves no step had trodden black.
Oh, I kept the first for another day!
Yet knowing how way leads on to way,
I doubted if I should ever come back.

I shall be telling this with a sigh
Somewhere ages and ages hence:
Two roads diverged in a wood, and I—
I took the one less traveled by,
And that has made all the difference.

1916

The Oven Bird

There is a singer everyone has heard,
Loud, a mid-summer and a mid-wood bird,
Who makes the solid tree trunks sound again.
He says that leaves are old and that for flowers
Mid-summer is to spring as one to ten.
He says the early petal-fall is past
When pear and cherry bloom went down in showers
On sunny days a moment overcast;
And comes that other fall we name the fall.
He says the highway dust is over all.
The bird would cease and be as other birds
But that he knows in singing not to sing.
The question that he frames in all but words
Is what to make of a diminished thing.

1916

Birches

When I see birches bend to left and right
Across the lines of straighter darker trees,
I like to think some boy's been swinging them.
But swinging doesn't bend them down to stay.
As ice-storms do. Often you must have seen them
Loaded with ice a sunny winter morning
After a rain. They click upon themselves
As the breeze rises, and turn many-colored
As the stir cracks and crazes their enamel.
Soon the sun's warmth makes them shed crystal shells
Shattering and avalanching on the snow-crust—
Such heaps of broken glass to sweep away
You'd think the inner dome of heaven had fallen.
They are dragged to the withered bracken by the load,
And they seem not to break; though once they are bowed
So low for long, they never right themselves:
You may see their trunks arching in the woods
Years afterwards, trailing their leaves on the ground
Like girls on hands and knees that throw their hair
Before them over their heads to dry in the sun.
But I was going to say when Truth broke in

With all her matter-of-fact about the ice-storm
I should prefer to have some boy bend them
As he went out and in to fetch the cows—
Some boy too far from town to learn baseball,
Whose only play was what he found himself,
Summer or winter, and could play alone.
One by one he subdued his father's trees
By riding them down over and over again
Until he took the stiffness out of them,
And not one but hung limp, not one was left
For him to conquer. He learned all there was
To learn about not launching out too soon
And so not carrying the tree away
Clear to the ground. He always kept his poise
To the top branches, climbing carefully
With the same pains you use to fill a cup
Up to the brim, and even above the brim.
Then he flung outward, feet first, with a swish,
Kicking his way down through the air to the ground.
So was I once myself a swinger of birches.
And so I dream of going back to be.
It's when I'm weary of considerations,
And life is too much like a pathless wood
Where your face burns and tickles with the cobwebs
Broken across it, and one eye is weeping
From a twig's having lashed across it open.
I'd like to get away from earth awhile
And then come back to it and begin over.
May no fate willfully misunderstand me
And half grant what I wish and snatch me away
Not to return. Earth's the right place for love:
I don't know where it's likely to go better.
I'd like to go by climbing a birch tree,
And climb black branches up a snow-white trunk
Toward heaven, till the tree could bear no more,
But dipped its top and set me down again.
That would be good both going and coming back.
One could do worse than be a swinger of birches.

1916

Stopping by Woods on a Snowy Evening

Whose woods these are I think I know
His house is in the village though;
He will not see me stopping here
To watch his woods fill up with snow.

My little horse must think it queer
To stop without a farmhouse near
Between the woods and frozen lake
The darkest evening of the year.

He gives his harness bells a shake
To ask if there is some mistake.
The only other sound's the sweep
Of easy wind and downy flake.

The woods are lovely, dark and deep.
But I have promises to keep,
And miles to go before I sleep,
And miles to go before I sleep.

1923

Spring Pools

These pools that, though in forests, still reflect
The total sky almost without defect,
And like the flowers beside them, chill and shiver,
Will like the flowers beside them soon be gone,
And yet not out by any brook or river,
But up by roots to bring dark foliage on.
The trees that have it in their pent-up buds
To darken nature and be summer woods—
Let them think twice before they use their powers
To blot out and drink up and sweep away
These flowery waters and these watery flowers
From snow that melted only yesterday.

1928

West-running Brook

'Fred, where is north?'
'North? North is there, my love.
The brook runs west.'
'West-running Brook then call it.'
(West-running Brook men call it to this day.)
'What does it think it's doing running west
When all the other country brooks flow east
To reach the ocean? It must be the brook
Can trust itself to go by contraries
The way I can with you—and you with me—
Because we're—we're—I don't know what we are.
What are we?'
'Young or new?'
'We must be something.
We've said we two. Let's change that to we three.
As you and I are married to each other,
We'll both be married to the brook. We'll build
Our bridge across it, and the bridge shall be
Our arm thrown over it asleep beside it.
Look, look, it's waving to us with a wave
To let us know it hears me.'
'Why, my dear,
That wave's been standing off this jut of shore—'
(The black stream, catching on a sunken rock,
Flung backward on itself in one white wave,
And the white water rode the black forever,
Not gaining but not losing, like a bird
White feathers from the struggle of whose breast
Flecked the dark stream and flecked the darker pool
Below the point, and were at last driven wrinkled
In a white scarf against the far shore alders.)
'That wave's been standing off this jut of shore

Ever since rivers, I was going to say,
Were made in heaven. It wasn't waved to us.'

'It wasn't, yet it was. If not to you
It was to me—in an annunciation.'

'Oh, if you take it off to lady-land,
As't were the country of the Amazons[1]
We men must see you to the confines of
And leave you there, ourselves forbid to enter,—
It is your brook! I have no more to say.'

'Yes, you have, too. Go on. You thought of something.'

'Speaking of contraries, see how the brook
In that white wave runs counter to itself.
It is from that in water we were from
Long, long before we were from any creature.
Here we, in our impatience of the steps,
Get back to the beginning of beginnings,
The stream of everything that runs away.
Some say existence like a Pirouot
And Pirouette, forever in one place,
Stands still and dances, but it runs away,
It seriously, sadly, runs away
To fill the abyss' void with emptiness.
It flows beside us in this water brook,
But it flows over us. It flows between us
To separate us for a panic moment.
It flows between us, over us, and *with* us.
And it is time, strength, tone, light, life and love—
And even substance lapsing unsubstantial;
The universal cataract of death
That spends to nothingness—and unresisted,
Save by some strange resistance in itself,
Not just a swerving, but a throwing back,
As if regret were in it and were sacred.
It has this throwing backward on itself
So that the fall of most of it is always
Raising a little, sending up a little.
Our life runs down in sending up the clock.
The brook runs down in sending up our life.
The sun runs down in sending up the brook.
And there is something sending up the sun.
It is this backward motion toward the source,
Against the stream, that most we see ourselves in,
The tribute of the current to the source.
It is from this in nature we are from.
It is most us.'
                    'Today will be the day
You said so.'
                    'No, today will be the day
You said the brook was called West-running Brook.'
'Today will be the day of what we both said.'

1928

1. Legendary female warriors who inhabited a country without men.

Design

I found a dimpled spider, fat and white,
On a white heal-all,[2] holding up a moth
Like a white piece of rigid satin cloth—
Assorted characters of death and blight
Mixed ready to begin the morning right,
Like the ingredients of a witches' broth—
A snow-drop spider, a flower like froth,
And dead wings carried like a paper kite.

What had that flower to do with being white,
The wayside blue and innocent heal-all?
What brought the kindred spider to that height,
Then steered the white moth thither in the night?
What but design of darkness to appall?—
If design govern in a thing so small.

1936

Provide, Provide

The witch that came (the withered hag)
To wash the steps with pail and rag,
Was once the beauty Abishag,[3]

The picture pride of Hollywood.
Too many fall from great and good
For you to doubt the likelihood.

Die early and avoid the fate.
Or if predestined to die late,
Make up your mind to die in state.

Make the whole stock exchange your own!
If need be occupy a throne,
Where nobody can call *you* crone.

Some have relied on what they knew;
Others on being simple true.
What worked for them might work for you.

No memory of having starred
Atones for later disregard,
Or keeps the end from being hard.

Better to go down dignified
With boughten friendship at your side
Than none at all. Provide, provide!

1934 1936

2. One of a variety of plants thought to have curative powers.

3. A beautiful maiden brought to comfort King David in his old age (1 Kings i.2–4).

Come In

As I came to the edge of the woods,
Thrush music—hark!
Now if it was dusk outside,
Inside it was dark.

Too dark in the woods for a bird
By sleight of wing
To better its perch for the night,
Though it still could sing.

The last of the light of the sun
That had died in the west
Still lived for one song more
In a thrush's breast.

Far in the pillared dark
Thrush music went—
Almost like a call to come in
To the dark and lament.

But no, I was out for stars;
I would not come in.
I meant not even if asked,
And I hadn't been.

1942

The Most of It

He thought he kept the universe alone;
For all the voice in answer he could wake
Was but the mocking echo of his own
From some tree-hidden cliff across the lake.
Some morning from the boulder broken beach
He would cry out on life, that what it wants
Is not its own love back in copy speech,
But counter-love, original response.
And nothing ever came of what he cried
Unless it was the embodiment that crashed
In the cliff's talus[4] on the other side,
And then in the far distant water splashed,
But after a time allowed for it to swim,
Instead of proving human when it neared
And someone else additional to him,
As a great buck it powerfully appeared,
Pushing the crumpled water up ahead,
And landed pouring like a waterfall,
And stumbled through the rocks with horny tread,
And forced the underbrush—and that was all.

1942

4. Sloping bank of rock fragments at the foot of a cliff.

The Gift Outright

The land was ours before we were the land's.
She was our land more than a hundred years
Before we were her people. She was ours
In Massachusetts, in Virginia,
But we were England's, still colonials,
Possessing what we still were unpossessed by,
Possessed by what we now no more possessed.
Something we were withholding made us weak
Until we found it was ourselves
We were withholding from our land of living,
And forthwith found salvation in surrender.
Such as we were we gave ourselves outright
(The deed of gift was many deeds of war)
To the land vaguely realizing westward,
But still unstoried, artless, unenhanced,
Such as she was, such as she would become.

1942

Directive

Back out of all this now too much for us,
Back in a time made simple by the loss
Of detail, burned, dissolved, and broken off
Like graveyard marble sculpture in the weather,
There is a house that is no more a house
Upon a farm that is no more a farm
And in a town that is no more a town.
The road there, if you'll let a guide direct you
Who only has at heart your getting lost,
May seem as if it should have been a quarry—
Great monolithic knees the former town
Long since gave up pretense of keeping covered.
And there's a story in a book about it:
Besides the wear of iron wagon wheels
The ledges show lines ruled southeast northwest,
The chisel work of an enormous Glacier
That braced his feet against the Arctic Pole.
You must not mind a certain coolness from him
Still said to haunt this side of Panther Mountain.
Nor need you mind the serial ordeal
Of being watched from forty cellar holes
As if by eye pairs out of forty firkins.
As for the woods' excitement over you
That sends light rustle rushes to their leaves,
Charge that to upstart inexperience.
Where were they all not twenty years ago?
They think too much of having shaded out
A few old pecker-fretted apple trees.
Make yourself up a cheering song of how
Someone's road home from work this once was,
Who may be just ahead of you on foot
Or creaking with a buggy load of grain.
The height of the adventure is the height

Of country where two village cultures faded
Into each other. Both of them are lost.
And if you're lost enough to find yourself
By now, pull in your ladder road behind you
And put a sign up CLOSED to all but me.
Then make yourself at home. The only field
Now left's no bigger than a harness gall.
First there's the children's house of make believe,
Some shattered dishes underneath a pine,
The playthings in the playhouse of the children.
Weep for what little things could make them glad.
Then for the house that is no more a house,
But only a belilaced cellar hole,
Now slowly closing like a dent in dough.
This was no playhouse but a house in earnest.
Your destination and your destiny's
A brook that was the water of the house,
Cold as a spring as yet so near its source,
Too lofty and original to rage.
(We know the valley streams that when aroused
Will leave their tatters hung on barb and thorn.)
I have kept hidden in the instep arch
Of an old cedar at the waterside
A broken drinking goblet like the Grail
Under a spell so the wrong ones can't find it,
So can't get saved, as Saint Mark says they mustn't.[5]
(I stole the goblet from the children's playhouse.)
Here are your waters and your watering place.
Drink and be whole again beyond confusion.

1947

CARL SANDBURG
(1878–1967)

Chicago

Hog Butcher for the World,
Tool Maker, Stacker of Wheat,
Player with Railroads and the Nation's Freight Handler;
Stormy, husky, brawling,
City of the Big Shoulders:

They tell me you are wicked and I believe them, for I have seen your painted women under the gas lamps luring the farm boys.
And they tell me you are crooked and I answer: Yes, it is true I have seen the gunman kill and go free to kill again.
And they tell me you are brutal and my reply is: On the faces of women and children I have seen the marks of wanton hunger.
And having answered so I turn once more to those who sneer at this my city, and I give them back the sneer and say to them:
Come and show me another city with lifted head singing so proud to be alive and coarse and strong and cunning.

5. Cf. Mark iv.11–12, in which Christ says, "To you has been given the secret of the kingdom of God, but for those outside everything is in parables; so that they may indeed see but not perceive, and may indeed hear but not understand; lest they should turn again, and be forgiven." *The Grail:* the holy grail, a cup used by Jesus at the last supper, the object of many quests in Arthurian romance.

Flinging magnetic curses amid the toil of piling job on job, here is a tall bold slugger set vivid against the little soft cities;
Fierce as a dog with tongue lapping for action, cunning as a savage pitted against the wilderness,
Bareheaded,
Shoveling,
Wrecking,
Planning,
Building, breaking, rebuilding,
Under the smoke, dust all over his mouth, laughing with white teeth,
Under the terrible burden of destiny laughing as a young man laughs,
Laughing even as an ignorant fighter laughs who has never lost a battle,
Bragging and laughing that under his wrist is the pulse, and under his ribs the heart of the people,
Laughing!
Laughing the stormy, husky, brawling laughter of Youth, half-naked, sweating, proud to be Hog Butcher, Tool Maker, Stacker of Wheat, Player with Railroads and Freight Handler to the Nation.

1916

Grass

Pile the bodies high at Austerlitz and Waterloo.[1]
Shovel them under and let me work—
I am the grass; I cover all.

And pile them high at Gettysburg[2]
And pile them high at Ypres and Verdun.[3]
Shovel them under and let me work.
Two years, ten years, and passengers ask the conductor:
What place is this?
Where are we now?

I am the grass.
Let me work.

1918

EDWARD THOMAS
(1878–1917)

The Owl

Downhill I came, hungry, and yet not starved;
Cold, yet had heat within me that was proof
Against the North wind; tired, yet so that rest
Had seemed the sweetest thing under a roof.

Then at the inn I had food, fire, and rest,
Knowing how hungry, cold, and tired was I.

1. Napoleon's victory over the Russians and Austrians near Austerlitz, in Moravia, was won on December 2, 1805; his final defeat, at the hands of the Duke of Wellington leading the allied forces, occurred at Waterloo, Belgium, June 18, 1815.
2. The great American Civil War battle begun July 1, 1863, and won three days later by the Union forces.
3. Ypres was the site of a World War I battle (1917), usually regarded as costly and fruitless; Verdun was a French town and fortress strategic to the German offensive in 1916–17, but successfully defended by the Allies.

All of the night was quite barred out except
An owl's cry, a most melancholy cry

Shaken out long and clear upon the hill,
No merry note, nor cause of merriment,
But one telling me plain what I escaped
And others could not, that night, as in I went.

And salted was my food, and my repose,
Salted and sobered, too, by the bird's voice
Speaking for all who lay under the stars,
Soldiers and poor, unable to rejoice.

1917

The Gypsy

A fortnight before Christmas Gypsies were everywhere:
Vans were drawn up on wastes, women trailed to the fair.
"My gentleman," said one, "you've got a lucky face."
"And you've a luckier," I thought, "if such a grace
And impudence in rags are lucky." "Give a penny
For the poor baby's sake." "Indeed I have not any
Unless you can give change for a sovereign,[1] my dear."
"Then just half a pipeful of tobacco can you spare?"
I gave it. With that much victory she laughed content.
I should have given more, but off and away she went
With her baby and her pink sham flowers to rejoin
The rest before I could translate to its proper coin
Gratitude for her grace. And I paid nothing then,
As I pay nothing now with the dipping of my pen
For her brother's music when he drummed the tambourine
And stamped his feet, which made the workmen passing grin,
While his mouth-organ changed to a rascally Bacchanal dance
"Over the hills and far away." This and his glance
Outlasted all the fair, farmer, and auctioneer,
Cheap-jack,° balloon-man, drover with crooked stick, and steer, *peddler*
Pig, turkey, goose, and duck, Christmas corpses to be.
Not even the kneeling ox had eyes like the Romany.° *gypsy*
That night he peopled for me the hollow wooded land,
More dark and wild than stormiest heavens, that I searched and scanned
Like a ghost new-arrived. The gradations of the dark
Were like an underworld of death, but for the spark
In the Gypsy boy's black eyes as he played and stamped his tune,
"Over the hills and far away," and a crescent moon.

1918

WALLACE STEVENS (1879–1955)

The Snow Man

One must have a mind of winter
To regard the frost and the boughs
Of the pine-trees crusted with snow;

1. Formerly, a British gold coin, value one pound, so called because it bore the effigy of the ruler on one face.

And have been cold a long time
To behold the junipers shagged with ice,
The spruces rough in the distant glitter

Of the January sun; and not to think
Of any misery in the sound of the wind,
In the sound of a few leaves,

Which is the sound of the land
Full of the same wind
That is blowing in the same bare place
For the listener, who listens in the snow,
And, nothing himself, beholds
Nothing that is not there and the nothing that is.

1923

The Emperor of Ice-Cream

Call the roller of big cigars,
The muscular one, and bid him whip
In kitchen cups concupiscent curds.
Let the wenches dawdle in such dress
As they are used to wear, and let the boys
Bring flowers in last month's newspapers.
Let be be finale of seem.
The only emperor is the emperor of ice-cream.

Take from the dresser of deal.
Lacking the three glass knobs, that sheet
On which she embroidered fantails [1] once
And spread it so as to cover her face.
If her horny feet protrude, they come
To show how cold she is, and dumb.
Let the lamp affix its beam.
The only emperor is the emperor of ice-cream.

1923

Sunday Morning

1

Complacencies of the peignoir, and late
Coffee and oranges in a sunny chair,
And the green freedom of a cockatoo
Upon a rug mingle to dissipate
The holy hush of ancient sacrifice.
She dreams a little, and she feels the dark
Encroachment of that old catastrophe,
As a calm darkens among water-lights.
The pungent oranges and bright, green wings
Seem things in some procession of the dead,
Winding across wide water, without sound.
The day is like wide water, without sound,
Stilled for the passing of her dreaming feet
Over the seas, to silent Palestine,
Dominion of the blood and sepulchre.

1. That is, fantail pigeons.

2

Why should she give her bounty to the dead?
What is divinity if it can come
Only in silent shadows and in dreams?
Shall she not find in comforts of the sun,
In pungent fruit and bright, green wings, or else
In any balm or beauty of the earth,
Things to be cherished like the thought of heaven?
Divinity must live within herself:
Passions of rain, or moods in falling snow;
Grievings in loneliness, or unsubdued
Elations when the forest blooms; gusty
Emotions on wet roads on autumn nights;
All pleasures and all pains, remembering
The bough of summer and the winter branch.
These are the measures destined for her soul.

3

Jove in the clouds had his inhuman birth.
No mother suckled him, no sweet land gave
Large-mannered motions to his mythy mind
He moved among us, as a muttering king,
Magnificent, would move among his hinds,° *shepherds*
Until our blood, commingling, virginal,
With heaven, brought such requital to desire
The very hinds discerned it, in a star.
Shall our blood fail? Or shall it come to be
The blood of paradise? And shall the earth
Seem all of paradise that we shall know?
The sky will be much friendlier then than now,
A part of labor and a part of pain,
And next in glory to enduring love,
Not this dividing and indifferent blue.

4

She says, "I am content when wakened birds,
Before they fly, test the reality
Of misty fields, by their sweet questionings;
But when the birds are gone, and their warm fields
Return no more, where, then, is paradise?"
There is not any haunt of prophecy,
Nor any old chimera of the grave,
Neither the golden underground, nor isle
Melodious, where spirits gat them home,
Nor visionary south, nor cloudy palm
Remote on heaven's hill, that has endured
As April's green endures; or will endure
Like her remembrance of awakened birds,
Or her desire for June and evening, tipped
By the consummation of the swallow's wings.

5

She says, "But in contentment I still feel
The need of some imperishable bliss."
Death is the mother of beauty; hence from her,
Alone, shall come fulfilment to our dreams
And our desires. Although she strews the leaves
Of sure obliteration on our paths,
The path sick sorrow took, the many paths
Where triumph rang its brassy phrase, or love
Whispered a little out of tenderness,

She makes the willow shiver in the sun
For maidens who were wont to sit and gaze
Upon the grass, relinquished to their feet.
She causes boys to pile new plums and pears
On disregarded plate.[2] The maidens taste
And stray impassioned in the littering leaves.

6

Is there no change of death in paradise?
Does ripe fruit never fall? Or do the boughs
Hang always heavy in that perfect sky,
Unchanging, yet so like our perishing earth,
With rivers like our own that seek for seas
They never find, the same receding shores
That never touch with inarticulate pang?
Why set the pear upon those river-banks
Or spice the shores with odors of the plum?
Alas, that they should wear our colors there,
The silken weavings of our afternoons,
And pick the strings of our insipid lutes!
Death is the mother of beauty, mystical,
Within whose burning bosom we devise
Our earthly mothers waiting, sleeplessly.

7

Supple and turbulent, a ring of men
Shall chant in orgy on a summer morn
Their boisterous devotion to the sun,
Not as a god, but as a god might be,
Naked among them, like a savage source.
Their chant shall be a chant of paradise,
Out of their blood, returning to the sky;
And in their chant shall enter, voice by voice,
The windy lake wherein their lord delights,
The trees, like serafin,° and echoing hills, *celestial beings*
That choir among themselves long afterward.
They shall know well the heavenly fellowship
Of men that perish and of summer morn.
And whence they came and whither they shall go
The dew upon their feet shall manifest.

8

She hears, upon that water without sound,
A voice that cries, "The tomb in Palestine
Is not the porch of spirits lingering.
It is the grave of Jesus, where he lay."
We live in an old chaos of the sun,
Or old dependency of day and night,
Or island solitude, unsponsored, free,
Of that wide water, inescapable.
Deer walk upon our mountains, and the quail
Whistle about us their spontaneous cries;
Sweet berries ripen in the wilderness;
And, in the isolation of the sky,
At evening, casual flocks of pigeons make
Ambiguous undulations as they sink,
Downward to darkness, on extended wings.

1915 1923

2. "Plate is used in the sense of so-called family plate. Disregarded refers to the disuse into which things fall that have been possessed for a long time. I mean, therefore, that death releases and renews" [*Letters of Wallace Stevens*, New York, 1966, pp. 183–184].

Anecdote of the Jar

I placed a jar in Tennessee,
And round it was, upon a hill.
It made the slovenly wilderness
Surround that hill.

The wilderness rose up to it,
And sprawled around, no longer wild.
The jar was round upon the ground
And tall and of a port in air.

It took dominion everywhere.
The jar was gray and bare.
It did not give of bird or bush,
Like nothing else in Tennessee.

1923

To the One of Fictive Music

Sister and mother and diviner love,
And of the sisterhood of the living dead
Most near, most clear, and of the clearest bloom,
And of the fragrant mothers the most dear
And queen, and of diviner love the day
And flame and summer and sweet fire, no thread
Of cloudy silver sprinkles in your gown
Its venom of renown, and on your head
No crown is simpler than the simple hair.

Now, of the music summoned by the birth
That separates us from the wind and sea,
Yet leaves us in them, until earth becomes,
By being so much of the things we are,
Gross effigy and simulacrum, none
Gives motion to perfection more serene
Than yours, out of our imperfections wrought,
Most rare, or ever of more kindred air
In the laborious weaving that you wear.

For so retentive of themselves are men
That music is intensest which proclaims
The near, the clear, and vaunts the clearest bloom,
And of all vigils musing the obscure,
That apprehends the most which sees and names,
As in your name, an image that is sure,
Among the arrant spices of the sun,
O bough and bush and scented vine, in whom
We give ourselves our likest issuance.

Yet not too like, yet not so like to be
Too near, too clear, saving a little to endow
Our feigning with the strange unlike, whence
springs

The difference that heavenly pity brings.
For this, musician, in your girdle fixed
Bear other perfumes. On your pale head wear
A band entwining, set with fatal stones.
Unreal, give back to us what once you gave:
The imagination that we spurned and crave.

1923

Thirteen Ways of Looking at a Blackbird

1

Among twenty snowy mountains,
The only moving thing
Was the eye of the blackbird.

2

I was of three minds,
Like a tree
In which there are three blackbirds.

3

The blackbird whirled in the autumn winds.
It was a small part of the pantomime.

4

A man and a woman
Are one.
A man and a woman and a blackbird
Are one.

5

I do not know which to prefer,
The beauty of inflections
Or the beauty of innuendoes,
The blackbird whistling
Or just after.

6

Icicles filled the long window
With barbaric glass.
The shadow of the blackbird
Crossed it to and fro.
The mood
Traced in the shadow
An indecipherable cause.

7

O thin men of Haddam,[3]
Why do you imagine golden birds?

3. A town in Connecticut. Stevens explains: "the thin men of Haddam are entirely fictitious. * * * I just like the name. It is an old whaling town, I believe. In any case, it has a completely Yankee sound" (*Letters*, p. 340).

Do you not see how the blackbird
Walks around the feet
Of the women about you?

8

I know noble accents
And lucid, inescapable rhythms;
But I know, too,
That the blackbird is involved
In what I know.

9

When the blackbird flew out of sight,
It marked the edge
Of one of many circles.

10

At the sight of blackbirds
Flying in a green light,
Even the bawds of euphony
Would cry out sharply.

11

He rode over Connecticut
In a glass coach.
Once, a fear pierced him,
In that he mistook
The shadow of his equipage
For blackbirds.

12

The river is moving.
The blackbird must be flying.

13

It was evening all afternoon.
It was snowing
And it was going to snow.
The blackbird sat
In the cedar-limbs.

1923

The Idea of Order at Key West

She sang beyond the genius of the sea.
The water never formed to mind or voice,
Like a body wholly body, fluttering
Its empty sleeves; and yet its mimic motion
Made constant cry, caused constantly a cry,
That was not ours although we understood,
Inhuman, of the veritable ocean.

The sea was not a mask. No more was she.
The song and water were not medleyed sound
Even if what she sang was what she heard,
Since what she sang was uttered word by word.
It may be that in all her phrases stirred
The grinding water and the gasping wind;
But it was she and not the sea we heard.
For she was the maker of the song she sang.
The ever-hooded, tragic-gestured sea
Was merely a place by which she walked to sing.
Whose spirit is this? we said, because we knew
It was the spirit that we sought and knew
That we should ask this often as she sang.

If it was only the dark voice of the sea
That rose, or even colored by many waves;
If it was only the outer voice of sky
And cloud, of the sunken coral water-walled,
However clear, it would have been deep air,
The heaving speech of air, a summer sound
Repeated in a summer without end
And sound alone. But it was more than that,
More even than her voice, and ours, among
The meaningless plungings of water and the wind,
Theatrical distances, bronze shadows heaped
On high horizons, mountainous atmospheres
Of sky and sea.
It was her voice that made
The sky acutest at its vanishing.
She measured to the hour its solitude.
She was the single artificer of the world
In which she sang. And when she sang, the sea,
Whatever self it had, became the self
That was her song, for she was the maker. Then we,
As we beheld her striding there alone,
Knew that there never was a world for her
Except the one she sang and, singing, made.

Ramon Fernandez,[4] tell me, if you know,
Why, when the singing ended and we turned
Toward the town, tell why the glassy lights,
The lights in the fishing boats at anchor there,
As the night descended, tilting in the air,
Mastered the night and portioned out the sea,
Fixing emblazoned zones and fiery poles,
Arranging, deepening, enchanting night.

Oh! Blessed rage for order, pale Ramon,
The maker's rage to order words of the sea,
Words of the fragrant portals, dimly-starred,
And of ourselves and of our origins,
In ghostlier demarcations, keener sounds.

1935

4. Stevens pointed out to two of his correspondents that in choosing this name he had simply combined two common Spanish names at random, without conscious reference to Ramon Fernandez the critic: "Ramon Fernandez was not intended to be anyone at all."

The Poems of Our Climate

1

Clear water in a brilliant bowl,
Pink and white carnations. The light
In the room more like a snowy air,
Reflecting snow. A newly-fallen snow
At the end of winter when afternoons return.
Pink and white carnations—one desires
So much more than that. The day itself
Is simplified: a bowl of white,
Cold, a cold porcelain, low and round,
With nothing more than the carnations there.

2

Say even that this complete simplicity
Stripped one of all one's torments, concealed
The evilly compounded, vital I
And made it fresh in a world of white,
A world of clear water, brilliant-edged,
Still one would want more, one would need more,
More than a world of white and snowy scents.

3

There would still remain the never-resting mind,
So that one would want to escape, come back
To what had been so long composed.
The imperfect is our paradise.
Note that, in this bitterness, delight,
Since the imperfect is so hot in us,
Lies in flawed words and stubborn sounds.

1942

The House Was Quiet and the World Was Calm

The house was quiet and the world was calm.
The reader became the book; and summer night

Was like the conscious being of the book.
The house was quiet and the world was calm.

The words were spoken as if there was no book,
Except that the reader leaned above the page,

Wanted to lean, wanted much most to be
The scholar to whom his book is true, to whom

The summer night is like a perfection of thought.
The house was quiet because it had to be.

The quiet was part of the meaning, part of the mind:
The access of perfection to the page.

And the world was calm. The truth in a calm world,
In which there is no other meaning, itself

Is calm, itself is summer and night, itself
Is the reader leaning late and reading there.

1947

Continual Conversation with a Silent Man

The old brown hen and the old blue sky,
Between the two we live and die—
The broken cartwheel on the hill.

As if, in the presence of the sea,
We dried our nets and mended sail
And talked of never-ending things,

Of the never-ending storm of will,
One will and many wills, and the wind,
Of many meanings in the leaves,

Brought down to one below the eaves,
Link, of that tempest, to the farm,
The chain of the turquoise hen and sky

And the wheel that broke as the cart went by.
It is not a voice that is under the eaves.
It is not speech, the sound we hear

In this conversation, but the sound
Of things and their motion: the other man,
A turquoise monster moving round.

1947

E. J. PRATT
(1883–1964)

From Stone to Steel

From stone to bronze, from bronze to steel
Along the road-dust of the sun,
Two revolutions of the wheel
From Java to Geneva run.[1]

The snarl Neanderthal is worn
Close to the smiling Aryan[2] lips,
The civil polish of the horn
Gleams from our praying finger tips.

The evolution of desire
Has but matured a toxic wine,

1. Java, now part of Indonesia, was the site of fossil excavations, where the bones of an early type of prehistoric man ("Neanderthal," line 5) were found. Geneva, in Switzerland, was the headquarters of the League of Nations, an organization intended to foster peace, from 1919 until the outbreak of World War II.
2. According to Nazi racial theory, the Aryan "race" was superior to all others.

Drunk long before its heady fire
Reddened Euphrates or the Rhine.[3]

Between the temple and the cave
The boundary lies tissue-thin:
The yearlings still the altars crave
As satisfaction for a sin.

The road goes up, the road goes down—
Let Java or Geneva be—
But whether to the cross or crown,
The path lies through Gethsemane.[4]

1932

WILLIAM CARLOS WILLIAMS
(1883–1963)

The Young Housewife

At ten A.M. the young housewife
moves about in negligee behind
the wooden walls of her husband's house.
I pass solitary in my car.

Then again she comes to the curb
to call the ice-man, fish-man, and stands
shy, uncorseted, tucking in
stray ends of hair, and I compare her
to a fallen leaf.

The noiseless wheels of my car
rush with a crackling sound over
dried leaves as I bow and pass smiling.

1917

Danse Russe

If when my wife is sleeping
and the baby and Kathleen
are sleeping
and the sun is a flame-white disc
in silken mists
above shining trees,—
if I in my north room
dance naked, grotesquely
before my mirror
waving my shirt round my head
and singing softly to myself:
"I am lonely, lonely.
I was born to be lonely,

3. The Euphrates was one of the two great river valleys of ancient Mesopotamian civilization; the Rhine flows through western Germany and the Netherlands.

4. The garden where Christ prayed while his disciples slept, and where Judas betrayed him (Matthew xxvi.36–56).

I am best so!"
If I admire my arms, my face,
my shoulders, flanks, buttocks
against the yellow drawn shades,—

Who shall say I am not
the happy genius[1] of my household?

1917

To Waken An Old Lady

Old age is
a flight of small
cheeping birds
skimming
bare trees
above a snow glaze.
Gaining and failing
they are buffeted
by a dark wind—
But what?
On harsh weedstalks
the flock has rested,
the snow
is covered with broken
seedhusks
and the wind tempered
by a shrill
piping of plenty.

1921

The Red Wheelbarrow

so much depends
upon

a red wheel
barrow

glazed with rain
water

beside the white
chickens.

1923

Queen-Ann's-Lace

Her body is not so white as
anemone petals nor so smooth—nor
so remote a thing. It is a field
of the wild carrot taking
the field by force; the grass
does not raise above it.
Here is no question of whiteness,
white as can be, with a purple mole

1. The presiding spirit and shaper of destinies.

at the center of each flower.
Each flower is a hand's span
of her whiteness. Wherever
his hand has lain there is
a tiny purple blemish. Each part
is a blossom under his touch
to which the fibres of her being
stem one by one, each to its end,
until the whole field is a
white desire, empty, a single stem,
a cluster, flower by flower,
a pious wish to whiteness gone over—
or nothing.

1925

This Is Just to Say

I have eaten
the plums
that were in
the icebox

and which
you were probably
saving
for breakfast

Forgive me
they were delicious
so sweet
and so cold

1934

Poem

As the cat
climbed over
the top of

the jamcloset
first the right
forefoot

carefully
then the hind
stepped down

into the pit of
the empty
flowerpot

1934

The Yachts

contend in a sea which the land partly encloses
shielding them from the too-heavy blows
of an ungoverned ocean which when it chooses

tortures the biggest hulls, the best man knows
to pit against its beatings, and sinks them pitilessly.
Mothlike in mists, scintillant in the minute

brilliance of cloudless days, with broad bellying sails
they glide to the wind tossing green water
from their sharp prows while over them the crew crawls

ant-like, solicitously grooming them, releasing,
making fast as they turn, lean far over and having
caught the wind again, side by side, head for the mark.

In a well guarded arena of open water surrounded by
lesser and greater craft which, sycophant, lumbering
and flittering follow them, they appear youthful, rare

as the light of a happy eye, live with the grace
of all that in the mind is fleckless, free and
naturally to be desired. Now the sea which holds them

is moody, lapping their glossy sides, as if feeling
for some slightest flaw but fails completely.
Today no race. Then the wind comes again. The yachts

move, jockeying for a start, the signal is set and they
are off. Now the waves strike at them but they are too
well made, they slip through, though they take in canvas.

Arms with hands grasping seek to clutch at the prows.
Bodies thrown recklessly in the way are cut aside.
It is a sea of faces about them in agony, in despair

until the horror of the race dawns staggering the mind,
the whole sea become an entanglement of watery bodies
lost to the world bearing what they cannot hold. Broken,

beaten, desolate, reaching from the dead to be taken up
they cry out, failing, failing! their cries rising
in waves still as the skillful yachts pass over.

1935

The Dance

In Breughel's[2] great picture, The Kermess,
the dancers go round, they go round and
around, the squeal and the blare and the
tweedle of bagpipes, a bugle and fiddles
tipping their bellies (round as the thick-
sided glasses whose wash they impound)
their hips and their bellies off balance
to turn them. Kicking and rolling about
the Fair Grounds, swinging their butts, those
shanks must be sound to bear up under such
rollicking measures, prance as they dance
in Breughel's great picture, The Kermess.

1944

2. Pieter Breughel (died 1569), Flemish painter of peasant life.

The Ivy Crown

The whole process is a lie,
unless,
crowned by excess,
it break forcefully,
one way or another,
from its confinement—
or find a deeper well.
Antony and Cleopatra
were right;
they have shown
the way. I love you
or I do not live
at all.

Daffodil time
is past. This is
summer, summer!
the heart says,
and not even the full of it.
No doubts
are permitted—
though they will come
and may
before our time
overwhelm us.
We are only mortal
but being mortal
can defy our fate.
We may
by an outside chance
even win! We do not
look to see
jonquils and violets
come again
but there are,
still,
the roses!

Romance has no part in it.
The business of love is
cruelty *which,*
by our wills,
we transform
to live together.
It has its seasons,
for and against,
whatever the heart
fumbles in the dark
to assert
toward the end of May.
Just as the nature of briars
is to tear flesh,
I have proceeded
through them.

Keep
the briars out,
they say.
You cannot live
and keep free of
briars.

Children pick flowers.
Let them.
Though having them
in hand
they have no further use for them
but leave them crumpled
at the curb's edge.

At our age the imagination
across the sorry facts
lifts us
to make roses
stand before thorns.
Sure
love is cruel
and selfish
and totally obtuse—
at least, blinded by the light,
young love is.
But we are older,
I to love
and you to be loved,
we have,
no matter how,
by our wills survived
to keep
the jeweled prize
always
at our finger tips.
We will it so
and so it is
past all accident.

1955

D. H. LAWRENCE
(1885–1930)

Piano

Softly, in the dusk, a woman is singing to me;
Taking me back down the vista of years, till I see
A child sitting under the piano, in the boom of the tingling strings
And pressing the small, poised feet of a mother who smiles as she sings.

In spite of myself, the insidious mastery of song
Betrays me back, till the heart of me weeps to belong
To the old Sunday evenings at home, with winter outside
And hymns in the cozy parlor, the tinkling piano our guide.

So now it is vain for the singer to burst into clamor
With the great black piano appassionato. The glamour
Of childish days is upon me, my manhood is cast
Down in the flood of remembrance, I weep like a child for the past.

1918

Snake

A snake came to my water-trough
On a hot, hot day, and I in pajamas for the heat,
To drink there.

In the deep, strange-scented shade of the great dark carob-tree
I came down the steps with my pitcher
And must wait, must stand and wait, for there he was at the trough before me.

He reached down from a fissure in the earth-wall in the gloom
And trailed his yellow-brown slackness soft-bellied down, over the edge of the stone trough
And rested his throat upon the stone bottom,
And where the water had dripped from the tap, in a small clearness,
He sipped with his straight mouth,
Softly drank through his straight gums, into his slack long body,
Silently.

Someone was before me at my water-trough,
And I, like a second comer, waiting.

He lifted his head from his drinking, as cattle do,
And looked at me vaguely, as drinking cattle do,
And flickered his two-forked tongue from his lips, and mused a moment,
And stooped and drank a little more,
Being earth-brown, earth-golden from the burning bowels of the earth
On the day of Sicilian July, with Etna smoking.

The voice of my education said to me
He must be killed,
For in Sicily the black, black snakes are innocent, the gold are venomous.

And voices in me said, If you were a man
You would take a stick and break him now, and finish him off.

But must I confess how I liked him,
How glad I was he had come like a guest in quiet, to drink at my water-trough

And depart peaceful, pacified, and thankless,
Into the burning bowels of this earth?

Was it cowardice, that I dared not kill him?
Was it perversity, that I longed to talk to him?
Was it humility, to feel so honored?
I felt so honored.

And yet those voices:
If you were not afraid, you would kill him!

And truly I was afraid, I was most afraid,
But even so, honored still more
That he should seek my hospitality
From out the dark door of the secret earth.

He drank enough
And lifted his head, dreamily, as one who has drunken,
And flickered his tongue like a forked night on the air, so black,
Seeming to lick his lips,
And looked around like a god, unseeing, into the air,
And slowly turned his head,
And slowly, very slowly, as if thrice adream,
Proceeded to draw his slow length curving round
And climb again the broken bank of my wall-face.

And as he put his head into that dreadful hole,
And as he slowly drew up, snake-easing his shoulders, and entered farther,
A sort of horror, a sort of protest against his withdrawing into that horrid black hole,
Deliberately going into the blackness, and slowly drawing himself after,
Overcame me now his back was turned.

I looked round, I put down my pitcher,
I picked up a clumsy log
And threw it at the water-trough with a clatter.

I think it did not hit him,
But suddenly that part of him that was left behind convulsed in undignified haste.
Writhed like lightning, and was gone
Into the black hole, the earth-lipped fissure in the wall-front,
At which, in the intense still noon, I stared with fascination.

And immediately I regretted it.
I thought how paltry, how vulgar, what a mean act!
I despised myself and the voices of my accursed human education.

And I thought of the albatross[1]
And I wished he would come back, my snake.

For he seemed to me again like a king,
Like a king in exile, uncrowned in the underworld,
Now due to be crowned again.

And so, I missed my chance with one of the lords
Of life.
And I have something to expiate;
A pettiness.

Taormina.
1923

The English Are So Nice!

The English are so nice
So awfully nice
They are the nicest people in the world.

1. In Coleridge's *Rime of the Ancient Mariner.*

And what's more, they're very nice about being nice
About your being nice as well!
If you're not nice they soon make you feel it.

Americans and French and Germans and so on
They're all very well
But they're not *really* nice, you know.
They're not nice in *our* sense of the word, are they now?

That's why one doesn't have to take them seriously.
We must be nice to them, of course,
Of course, naturally.
But it doesn't really matter what you say to them,
They don't really understand
You can just say anything to them:
Be nice, you know, just nice
But you must never take them seriously, they wouldn't understand,
Just be nice, you know! oh, fairly nice,
Not too nice of course, they take advantage
But nice enough, just nice enough
To let them feel they're not quite as nice as they might be.

1932

Andraitx[2]—Pomegranate Flowers

It is June, it is June
The pomegranates are in flower,
The peasants are bending cutting the bearded wheat.

The pomegranates are in flower
Beside the high road, past the deathly dust,
And even the sea is silent in the sun.

Short gasps of flame in the green of night, way off
The pomegranates are in flower,
Small sharp red fires in the night of leaves.

And noon is suddenly dark, is lustrous, is silent and dark
Men are unseen, beneath the shading hats;
Only, from out the foliage of the secret loins
Red flamelets here and there reveal
A man, a woman there.

1932

Bavarian Gentians

Not every man has gentians in his house
in Soft September, at slow, sad Michaelmas.

Bavarian gentians, big and dark, only dark
darkening the daytime, torch-like with the smoking blueness of Pluto's gloom,
ribbed and torch-like, with their blaze of darkness spread blue
down flattening into points, flattened under the sweep of white day

2. A town on the island of Majorca.

torch-flower of the blue-smoking darkness, Pluto's dark-blue daze,
black lamps from the halls of Dis,[3] burning dark blue,
giving off darkness, blue darkness, as Demeter's pale lamps give off light,
lead me then, lead the way.

Reach me a gentian, give me a torch!
let me guide myself with the blue, forked torch of this flower
down the darker and darker stairs, where blue is darkened on blueness
even where Persephone goes, just now, from the frosted September
to the sightless realm where darkness is awake upon the dark
and Persephone herself is but a voice
or a darkness invisible enfolded in the deeper dark
of the arms Plutonic, and pierced with the passion of dense gloom,
among the splendor of torches of darkness, shedding darkness on the lost
  bride and her groom.

1932

The Ship of Death[4]

1

Now it is autumn and the falling fruit
and the long journey towards oblivion.

The apples falling like great drops of dew
to bruise themselves an exit from themselves.

And it is time to go, to bid farewell
to one's own self, and find an exit
from the fallen self.

2

Have you built your ship of death, O have you?
O build your ship of death, for you will need it.

The grim frost is at hand, when the apples will fall
thick, almost thundrous, on the hardened earth.

And death is on the air like a smell of ashes!
Ah! can't you smell it?

And in the bruised body, the frightened soul
finds itself shrinking, wincing from the cold
that blows upon it through the orifices.

3

And can a man his own quietus make
with a bare bodkin?[5]

With daggers, bodkins, bullets, man can make
a bruise or break of exit for his life;
but is that a quietus, O tell me, is it quietus?

3. Another Roman name for Pluto (Greek Hades), ruler of the underworld. He had abducted Persephone (Roman Proserpine) the daughter of Demeter (Roman Ceres), goddess of growing vegetation and living nature; Persephone ruled with him as queen of the underworld, but returned to spend six months of each year with her mother in the world above.

4. In *Etruscan Places,* the book which describes his visit to the Etruscan painted tombs in Central Italy, in the spring of 1927, Lawrence mentions that originally, before the tombs were pillaged, there would be found in the last chamber among "the sacred treasures of the dead, the little bronze ship that should bear [the soul of the dead] over to the other world * * * "

5. From *Hamlet,* III.i.75–6.

Surely not so! for how could murder, even self-murder
ever a quietus make?

4

O let us talk of quiet that we know,
that we can know, the deep and lovely quiet
of a strong heart at peace!

How can we this, our own quietus, make?

5

Build then the ship of death, for you must take
the longest journey, to oblivion.

And die the death, the long and painful death
that lies between the old self and the new.

Already our bodies are fallen, bruised, badly bruised,
already our souls are oozing through the exit
of the cruel bruise.

Already the dark and endless ocean of the end
is washing in through the breaches of our wounds,
already the flood is upon us.

Oh build your ship of death, your little ark
and furnish it with food, with little cakes, and wine
for the dark flight down oblivion.

6

Piecemeal the body dies, and the timid soul
has her footing washed away, as the dark flood rises.

We are dying, we are dying, we are all of us dying
and nothing will stay the death-flood rising within us
and soon it will rise on the world, on the outside world.

We are dying, we are dying, piecemeal our bodies are dying
and our strength leaves us,
and our soul cowers naked in the dark rain over the flood,
cowering in the last branches of the tree of our life.

7

We are dying, we are dying, so all we can do
is now to be willing to die, and to build the ship
of death to carry the soul on the longest journey.

A little ship, with oars and food
and little dishes, and all accoutrements
fitting and ready for the departing soul.

Now launch the small ship, now as the body dies
and life departs, launch out, the fragile soul
in the fragile ship of courage, the ark of faith
with its store of food and little cooking pans
and change of clothes,
upon the flood's black waste
upon the waters of the end
upon the sea of death, where still we sail
darkly, for we cannot steer, and have no port.

There is no port, there is nowhere to go
only the deepening blackness darkening still
blacker upon the soundless, ungurgling flood
darkness at one with darkness, up and down
and sideways utterly dark, so there is no direction any more.
and the little ship is there; yet she is gone.
She is not seen, for there is nothing to see her by.
She is gone! gone! and yet
somewhere she is there.
Nowhere!

8

And everything is gone, the body is gone
completely under, gone, entirely gone.
The upper darkness is heavy as the lower,
between them the little ship
is gone
she is gone.

It is the end, it is oblivion.

9

And yet out of eternity, a thread
separates itself on the blackness,
a horizontal thread
that fumes a little with pallor upon the dark.

Is it illusion? or does the pallor fume
A little higher?
Ah wait, wait, for there's the dawn,
the cruel dawn of coming back to life
out of oblivion.

Wait, wait, the little ship
drifting, beneath the deathly ashy grey
of a flood-dawn.

Wait, wait! even so, a flush of yellow
and strangely, O chilled wan soul, a flush of rose.

A flush of rose, and the whole thing starts again.

10

The flood subsides, and the body, like a worn sea-shell
emerges strange and lovely.
And the little ship wings home, faltering and lapsing
on the pink flood,
and the frail soul steps out, into her house again
filling the heart with peace.

Swings the heart renewed with peace
even of oblivion.

Oh build your ship of death, oh build it!
for you will need it.
For the voyage of oblivion awaits you.

1932

EZRA POUND
(1885–1972)

Portrait d'une Femme[1]

Your mind and you are our Sargasso Sea,[2]
London has swept about you this score years
And bright ships left you this or that in fee:
Ideas, old gossip, oddments of all things,
Strange spars of knowledge and dimmed wares of price.
Great minds have sought you—lacking someone else.
You have been second always. Tragical?
No. You preferred it to the usual thing:
One dull man, dulling and uxorious,
One average mind—with one thought less, each year.
Oh, you are patient, I have seen you sit
Hours, where something might have floated up.
And now you pay one. Yes, you richly pay.
You are a person of some interest, one comes to you
And takes strange gain away:
Trophies fished up; some curious suggestion;
Fact that leads nowhere; and a tale or two,
Pregnant with mandrakes,[3] or with something else
That might prove useful and yet never proves,
That never fits a corner or shows use,
Or finds its hour upon the loom of days:
The tarnished, gaudy, wonderful old work;
Idols and ambergris[4] and rare inlays,
These are your riches, your great store; and yet
For all this sea-hoard of deciduous things,
Strange woods half sodden, and new brighter stuff:
In the slow float of differing light and deep,
No! there is nothing! In the whole and all,
Nothing that's quite your own.
Yet this is you.

1912

The Seafarer[5]

FROM THE ANGLO-SAXON

May I for my own self song's truth reckon,
Journey's jargon, how I in harsh days
Hardship endured oft.

1. Portrait of a Lady.
2. A region of the North Atlantic partially covered with accumulations of floating gulf-weed.
3. A plant, of narcotic properties, and sometimes believed to be aphrodisiac, whose forked root was traditionally thought to resemble the human body.
4. Secretion of the whale, used in perfumery.
5. Pound's poem translates the first 99 lines of an Old English poem, 124 lines long, by an unknown author and of unknown date. For the most part it follows the text closely, usually line for line, but departs from the sense of the original, for a phrase or two, at a few points. Pound's aim is not primarily to give an academically "correct" translation, but to make a version of the original that will give a true sense of its form and spirit, "to get the swing and mood of the subject," as he says in another connection.

Bitter breast-cares have I abided,
Known on my keel many a care's hold,
And dire sea-surge, and there I oft spent
Narrow nightwatch nigh the ship's head
While she tossed close to cliffs. Coldly afflicted,
My feet were by frost benumbed.
Chill its chains are; chafing sighs
Hew my heart round and hunger begot
Mere-weary° mood. Lest man know not — *sea-weary*
That he on dry land loveliest liveth,
List how I, care-wretched, on ice-cold sea,
Weathered the winter, wretched outcast
Deprived of my kinsmen;
Hung with hard ice-flakes, where hail-scur° flew, — *hail-storms*
There I heard naught save the harsh sea
And ice-cold wave, at whiles the swan cries,
Did for my games the gannet's clamor,
Sea-fowls' loudness was for me laughter,
The mews' singing all my mead-drink.
Storms, on the stone-cliffs beaten, fell on the stern
In icy feathers;[6] full oft the eagle screamed
With spray on his pinion.

Not any protector
May make merry man faring needy.
This he little believes, who aye in winsome life
Abides 'mid burghers some heavy business,
Wealthy and wine-flushed, how I weary oft
Must bide above brine.
Neareth nightshade, snoweth from north,
Frost froze the land, hail fell on earth then,
Corn of the coldest. Nathless° there knocketh now — *notwithstanding*
The heart's thought that I on high streams
The salt-wavy tumult traverse alone.
Moaneth alway my mind's lust
That I fare forth, that I afar hence
Seek out a foreign fastness.
For this there's no mood-lofty man over earth's midst,
Not though he be given his good, but will have in his
youth greed;
Nor his deed to the daring, nor his king to the faithful
But shall have his sorrow for sea-fare
Whatever his lord will.
He hath not heart for harping, nor in ring-having
Nor winsomeness to wife, nor world's delight
Nor any whit else save the wave's slash,
Yet longing comes upon him to fare forth on the water.
Bosque° taketh blossom, cometh beauty of berries,[7] — *grove*
Fields to fairness, land fares brisker,
All this admonisheth man eager of mood,
The heart turns to travel so that he then thinks
On flood-ways to be far departing.
Cuckoo calleth with gloomy crying,
He singeth summerward, bodeth sorrow,

6. Strictly: "Storms there beat on the stone cliffs, there the tern answers them, its feathers icy."

7. In the original, the sense of the second half of the line is "towns become fair."

The bitter heart's blood. Burgher knows not—
He the prosperous man—what some perform
Where wandering them widest draweth.
So that but now my heart burst from my breastlock,
My mood 'mid the mere-flood,° *sea-flood*
Over the whale's acre, would wander wide.
On earth's shelter cometh oft to me,
Eager and ready, the crying lone-flyer,
Whets for the whale-path the heart irresistibly,
O'er tracks of ocean; seeing that anyhow
My lord deems to me this dead life
On loan and on land,[8] I believe not
That any earth-weal eternal standeth
Save there be somewhat calamitous
That, ere a man's tide go, turn it to twain.
Disease or oldness or sword-hate
Beats out the breath from doom-gripped body.
And for this, every earl whatever, for those speaking
after—
Laud of the living, boasteth some last word,
That he will work ere he pass onward,
Frame on the fair earth 'gainst foes his malice,
Daring ado,° . . . *brave deeds*
So that all men shall honor him after
And his laud beyond them remain 'mid the English,[9]
Aye, for ever, a lasting life's-blast,
Delight 'mid the doughty.
Days little durable,
And all arrogance of earthen riches,
There come now no kings nor Cæsars
Nor gold-giving lords like those gone.
Howe'er in mirth most magnified,
Whoe'er lived in life most lordliest,
Drear all this excellence, delights undurable!
Waneth the watch, but the world holdeth.
Tomb hideth trouble. The blade is layed low.[1]
Earthly glory ageth and seareth.
No man at all going the earth's gait,
But age fares against him, his face paleth,
Gray-haired he groaneth, knows gone companions,
Lordly men, are to earth o'ergiven,
Nor may he then the flesh-cover, whose life ceaseth,
Nor eat the sweet nor feel the sorry,
Nor stir hand nor think in mid heart,
And though he strew the grave with gold,
His born brothers, their buried bodies
Be an unlikely treasure hoard.

1912

8. Behind Pound's phrase "on loan and on land" is the O. E. "læne on lond," "briefly on earth." ("Because the Lord's joys are warmer to me than this dead life, brief on the earth.") But Pound has chosen to play down the Christian elements in the poem, perhaps believing that they are inconsistent with its essential spirit.

9. In the original, the sense is "with the angels," not "mid the English."

1. In the original, the sense of lines 87–8 is "The weak live on and hold over this world,/ Possess it through trouble. Glory is laid low."

The Garden

En robe de parade.[2]
—SAMAIN

Like a skein of loose silk blown against a wall
She walks by the railing of a path in Kensington Gardens,[3]
And she is dying piecemeal
of a sort of emotional anemia.

And round about there is a rabble
Of the filthy, sturdy, unkillable infants of the very poor.
They shall inherit the earth.

In her is the end of breeding.
Her boredom is exquisite and excessive.
She would like some one to speak to her,
And is almost afraid that I
will commit that indiscretion.

1916

Ts'ai Chi'h[4]

The petals fall in the fountain,
the orange-colored rose-leaves,
Their ochre clings to the stone.

1916

In a Station of the Metro

The apparition of these faces in the crowd;
Petals on a wet, black bough.

1916

The River-Merchant's Wife: a Letter

While my hair was still cut straight across my forehead
I played about the front gate, pulling flowers.
You came by on bamboo stilts, playing horse,
You walked about my seat, playing with blue plums.
And we went on living in the village of Chokan:
Two small people, without dislike or suspicion.

At fourteen I married My Lord you.
I never laughed, being bashful.
Lowering my head, I looked at the wall.
Called to, a thousand times, I never looked back.

At fifteen I stopped scowling,
I desired my dust to be mingled with yours
Forever and forever and forever.
Why should I climb the look out?

2. "Dressed as for a state occasion." The phrase is from a poem by the French poet Albert Samain (1858–1900), *The Infanta.*
3. Extensive public gardens in the residential district west of Hyde Park, London.
4. Ts'ai Chi'h, or more usually Ts'ao Chih, is the name of a Chinese poet who lived from 192–232, and Pound's using it as the title of his poem perhaps indicates that in it he is adopting the mode of Ts'ao Chih's "five-character poems," or even translating one of them.

At sixteen you departed,
You went into far Ku-to-yen, by the river of swirling eddies,
And you have been gone five months.
The monkeys make sorrowful noise overhead.

You dragged your feet when you went out.
By the gate now, the moss is grown, the different mosses,
Too deep to clear them away!
The leaves fall early this autumn, in wind.
The paired butterflies are already yellow with August
Over the grass in the West garden;
They hurt me. I grow older.
If you are coming down through the narrows of the river Kiang,
Please let me know beforehand,
And I will come out to meet you
As far as Cho-fu-Sa.

By *Rihaku*[5]
1915

Hugh Selwyn Mauberley

LIFE AND CONTACTS[6]

I. E. P. Ode Pour L'Election de son Sépulchre[7]

For three years, out of key with his time,
He strove to resuscitate the dead art
Of poetry; to maintain "the sublime"
In the old sense. Wrong from the start—

No, hardly, but seeing he had been born
In a half savage country, out of date;
Bent resolutely on wringing lilies from the acorn;
Capaneus;[8] trout for factitious° bait; *false; artificial*

Ἴδμεν γάρ τοι πάνθ' ὅσ' ἐνὶ Τροίῃ[9]
Caught in the unstopped ear;
Giving the rocks small lee-way
The chopped seas held him, therefore, that year.

His true Penelope[1] was Flaubert,[2]
He fished by obstinate isles;
Observed the elegance of Circe's[3] hair
Rather than the mottoes on sundials.

5. *Rihaku* is the transcription from the Japanese of the name of one of the greatest of the Chinese poets of the T'ang Dynasty, Li Po (ca. 700–762.).

6. *Hugh Selwyn Mauberley (Life and Contacts)* comprises two sets of poems; the first, reprinted here, consists of thirteen poems; the second consists of five poems headed "Mauberley/1920." There are many connections not only among the poems in each set, but also between the two sets. The entire volume bore an epigraph from the fourth Eclogue of the 3rd-century Latin poet Nemesianus: *Vocat aestus in umbram* ("The heat urges us into the shade").

7. Cf. Pierre Ronsard (1524–1585). Odes IV, iv, *"De l'élection de son sépulchre"* ["Concerning the choice of his tomb"], in which the poet describes the kind of burial place, and the kind of frame, he would like to have.

8. In classical mythology, one of the Seven against Thebes, heroes who led an expedition against Thebes in an unsuccessful attempt to set one of their number, Polynices, on the throne. Capaneus, climbing on the walls and defying even Zeus to harm him, was struck by a thunderbolt.

9. Idmen gár toi pánth'hós éni Troíei, from the song sung by the Sirens to lure Odysseus's ship onto the rocks: "For we know everything which [the Greeks and the Trojans have suffered] in Troy [by the will of the Gods]." (Odyssey xii. 184 ff.) Circe had told Odysseus how to avoid the danger: his men must have their ears stopped with wax, after they have bound him hand and foot—he alone hears their song.

1. The faithful wife to whom Odysseus returned after the ten years of adventure that followed the ten-year siege of Troy.

2. French realist novelist (1821–1880), a meticulous craftsman, author of *Madame Bovary, L'Education sentimentale,* etc.

3. An enchantress, living on the island of Aeaea, with whom Odysseus stayed for a year. She turned his men into swine, but he was able to resist her spell with the help of the herb moly, given to him by Hermes.

Unaffected by "the march of events,"
He passed from men's memory in *l'an trentiesme*
De son eage;[4] the case presents
No adjunct to the Muses' diadem.

II

The age demanded an image
Of its accelerated grimace,
Something for the modern stage,
Not, at any rate, an Attic[5] grace;

Not, not certainly, the obscure reveries
Of the inward gaze;
Better mendacities
Than the classics in paraphrase!

The "age demanded" chiefly a mold in plaster,
Made with no loss of time,
A prose kinema,[6] not, not assuredly, alabaster
Or the "sculpture" of rhyme.

III

The tea-rose tea-gown, etc.
Supplants the mousseline of Cos,[7]
The pianola "replaces"
Sappho's barbitos.[8]

Christ follows Dionysus,[9]
Phallic and ambrosial
Made way for macerations;[1]
Caliban casts out Ariel.[2]

All things are a flowing,
Sage Heracleitus says;[3]
But a tawdry cheapness
Shall outlast our days.

Even the Christian beauty
Defects—after Samothrace;[4]
We see τὸ καλὸν[5]
Decreed in the market place.

Faun's flesh is not to us,
Nor the saint's vision.
We have the press for wafer;
Franchise for circumcision.

4. From the part satiric, part elegiac poem *"Le grand testament"* (1461), in which the French poet François Villon (1431–1489?), writing in prison, reviews his life, castigates his enemies, thinks of his friends, etc.: "In the thirtieth year of my age./When I have drunk down all my shame . . ."
5. Athenian—of simple, pure, classical style.
6. Transliteration of the Greek word for "motion," a root word in the early term for motion pictures, "cinematograph."
7. The muslin worn in ancient times by the women of the Greek island of Cos.
8. The Greek poetess, born on the island of Lesbos c. 612 B.C. *Barbitos* (Greek): lyre.
9. The god of an ecstatic, emotional religion among the early Greeks, as well as the god of wine (later Bacchus).

1. Mortifications of the flesh.
2. Two figures from Shakespeare's *The Tempest,* Caliban almost an animal, Ariel totally spiritual.
3. Heraclitus of Ephesus, the early Greek philosopher (fl. c. 500 B.C.), whose central doctrine was that all things are in a state of flux ("everything flows").
4. An Aegean island where was found the masterpiece of Hellenistic sculpture, the Winged Victory (early 2nd century B.C.?), now in the Louvre. That Pound has this feature of Samothrace in mind here is given at least slight support by the fact that the Winged Victory figures in a prose piece by Rémy de Gourmont, *"Stratagèmes,"* which has a role in Poem XI of this sequence.
5. Tò kalón (Greek): "The Beautiful."

All men, in law, are equals.
Free of Pisistratus,[6]
We choose a knave or an eunuch
To rule over us.

O bright Apollo,
τίν ἄνδρα, τίν ἥρωα, τίνα θεὸν,[7]
What god, man, or hero
Shall I place a tin wreath upon!

IV

These fought in any case,
and some believing,
pro domo,[8] in any case . . .

Some quick to arm,
some for adventure,
some from fear of weakness,
some from fear of censure,
some for love of slaughter, in imagination,
learning later . . .
some in fear, learning love of slaughter;

Died some, pro patria,
non "dulce" non "et decor" . . .[9]
walked eye-deep in hell
believing in old men's lies, then unbelieving
came home, home to a lie,
home to many deceits,
home to old lies and new infamy;
usury age-old and age-thick
and liars in public places.

Daring as never before, wastage as never before.
Young blood and high blood,
fair cheeks, and fine bodies;

fortitude as never before

frankness as never before,
disillusions as never told in the old days,
hysterias, trench confessions,
laughter out of dead bellies.

V

There died a myriad,
And of the best, among them,
For an old bitch gone in the teeth,
For a botched civilization,

6. Athenian tyrant (in the sense of absolute ruler, but without later connotations of one who rules cruelly or oppressively), d. 527 B.C. "His long rule weakened the grip of the aristocrats upon their followers, encouraged individualism in many circles, and brought the cultural enlightenment and financial prosperity in which a movement towards democracy became possible" *(Oxford Classical Dictionary)*.

7. Part of a line from the second Olympic ode of the Greek poet Pindar (518–438 B.C.), transliterated : tín ándra, tín héroa, tína theòn [keladésimon]: "What man, what hero, what god [shall we celebrate]?"

8. From the Latin phrase *pro domo sua,* "for one's own home."

9. The famous line from one of Horace's *Odes* (III.ii.13): *Dulce et decorum est pro patria mori* ("Sweet and fitting it is to die for one's country").

Charm, smiling at the good mouth,
Quick eyes gone under earth's lid,

For two gross of broken statues,
For a few thousand battered books.

Yeux Glauques[1]

Gladstone[2] was still respected,
When John Ruskin produced
"King's Treasuries";[3] Swinburne
And Rossetti still abused.

Fetid Buchanan[4] lifted up his voice
When that faun's head of hers
Became a pastime for
Painters and adulterers.

The Burne-Jones cartons[5]
Have preserved her eyes;
Still, at the Tate, they teach
Cophetua to rhapsodize;

Thin like brook water,
With a vacant gaze.
The English Rubaiyat was stillborn[6]
In those days.

The thin, clear gaze, the same
Still darts out faunlike from the half-ruined face,
Questing and passive. . . .
"Ah, poor Jenny's case" . . .[7]

Bewildered that a world
Shows no surprise
At her last maquero's[8]
Adulteries.

1. French, "sea-green eyes." Pound's poem focuses on the eyes of Elizabeth Siddal, wife of D. G. Rossetti and the model used for many of his paintings as well as for those of other Pre-Raphaelite painters, including Burne-Jones, in whose painting "King Cophetua and the Beggar Maid" (1884; now in the Tate Gallery, London; see stanza 3 below) she appears as the beggar maid (painted from studies made earlier; Elizabeth Siddal died in 1862). William Michael Rossetti described her as "Tall, finely formed, with a lofty neck, and regular yet somewhat uncommon features, greenish-blue unsparkling eyes. . . ."
2. William Ewart Gladstone was Prime Minister for four separate terms between 1868 and 1894.
3. John Ruskin's *Sesame and Lilies,* consisting of two parts ("Sesame: Of Kings' Treasuries" and "Lilies: Of Queens' Gardens") was published in 1865, with a drawing by Burne-Jones on the title page. Its subject was "the treasures hidden in books: . . . the way we find them and the way we lose them," the way we lose them being through a Philistine indifference to art, religion, and moral purpose.
4. Robert W. Buchanan's controversial attack on Swinburne, Morris, and Rossetti, but especially Rossetti, appeared pseudonymously in *The Contemporary Review* for October 1871.
5. For "cartoons," in the sense of preliminary studies from which a finished painting is made.
6. FitzGerald's translation of *The Rubáiyát of Omar Khayyám* was first published in 1859. It did not sell and was remaindered at a penny a copy outside the publisher's shop, where Swinburne and Rossetti discovered it and bought several copies to give away; returning to buy more, they found that the price had begun to go up.
7. Buchanan's criticism of Rossetti had discussed one poem in particular, "Jenny," claiming that its scene had appealed to the poet less for human tenderness than for its "inherent quality of animalism." The poem presents the thoughts of a young man who has gone with Jenny, a prostitute, to her room after a dance and spends the night with her sleeping head resting on his knee. It has an epigraph from *The Merry Wives of Windsor:* " 'Vengeance of Jenny's case! Fie on her! Never name her, child!'—Mrs. Quickly." Shakespeare has her continue, ". . . If she be a whore." The Jenny of Rossetti's poem has nothing to do with Elizabeth Siddal, but one phrase describing Jenny—"whose eyes are as blue as the skies"—may be the link, in Pound's poem, between Jenny and the eyes of Rossetti's wife and model.
8. For the French slang term for pimp, *"maquereau."*

"Siena Mi Fe'; Disfecemi Maremma"[9]

Among the pickled fetuses and bottled bones,
Engaged in perfecting the catalogue,
I found the last scion of the
Senatorial families of Strasbourg, Monsieur Verog.[1]

For two hours he talked of Gallifet;[2]
Of Dowson; of the Rhymers' Club;[3]
Told me how Johnson (Lionel) died[4]
By falling from a high stool in a pub . . .

But showed no trace of alcohol
At the autopsy, privately performed—
Tissue preserved—the pure mind
Arose toward Newman[5] as the whiskey warmed.

Dowson found harlots cheaper than hotels;
Headlam[6] for uplift; Image[7] impartially imbued
With raptures for Bacchus, Terpsichore and the Church.
So spoke the author of "The Dorian Mood,"

M. Verog, out of step with the decade,
Detached from his contemporaries,
Neglected by the young,
Because of these reveries.

Brennbaum[8]

The skylike limpid eyes,
The circular infant's face,
The stiffness from spats to collar
Never relaxing into grace;

The heavy memories of Horeb, Sinai[9] and the forty
years,[1]

9. "Siena made me; the Maremma undid me." (*Purgatorio,* V. 133.) Words spoken to Dante by the spirit of Pia de' Tolomei, encountered in Purgatory among those who had repented only at the last moment and without absolution. Although innocent, she had been imprisoned by her husband in a fortress in the Maremma, and died there, either by poison or from malaria. The line carries with it the idea of exile from one's native place; the subject of Pound's poem had been born in Alsace.
1. Pound's model for Verog was Victor Gustav Plarr (1863–1929) friend of such Nineties poets as Yeats, Ernest Dowson, and Lionel Johnson, like them a member of the Rhymers' Club. Besides his own poems (*In the Dorian Mood,* 1896) and biographical work arising out of his post as librarian to the Royal College of Surgeons, he published a brief memoir of Ernest Dowson, covering the years of their friendship (1888–1897).
2. Galliffet (1830–1909), a French general who distinguished himself at the head of the *Chasseurs d'Afrique* at the battle of Sedan, in the Franco-Prussian War, 1870.
3. Founded in 1891, it consisted of from 12 to 14 members who met at the Cheshire Cheese in Fleet St., London, for literary discussion.
4. Lionel Johnson (1867–1902) was received into the Church of Rome in 1891 and published his first collection of poems in 1895. He died from an injury sustained by falling in the street.
5. John Henry Cardinal Newman (1801–1890), who joined the Church of Rome in 1845, author of *Apologia pro Vita Sua* (1864–65).
6. Rev. Stewart Headlam (1847–1924), liberal clergyman who was for many years a vicar in the East End of London, writer on social and religious questions; although he scarcely knew Wilde, he had helped post bail for him at the time of his arrest in 1895.
7. Selwyn Image (1849–1930), artist, poet, and clergyman; his work appeared in such Nineties periodicals as *The Hobby Horse* and *The Savoy.* Bacchus is the Roman god of wine, Terpsichore the Greek muse of the dance.
8. The model for Brennbaum is pretty clearly Max Beerbohm, brilliant satirist in his books (*Zuleika Dobson,* 1911, and *A Christmas Garland,* 1912), but even more widely known for his satiric drawings and caricatures of the literary and political great. He was known as "The Incomparable Max," but Pound, in an essay on Remy de Gourmont, calls him "the impeccable Beerbohm." The Beerbohms were of German descent, however, not Jewish.
9. The young Moses, keeping Jethro's sheep, led them "to the backside of the desert, and came to the mountain of God, even to Horeb," where the angel of the Lord appeared to him out of the burning bush (Exodus iii.1–2). On the top of Mt. Sinai, Moses received the Ten Commandments from God (Exodus xix. 20 ff.).
1. The 40 years spent by the Israelites in the wilderness, after the Exodus from Egypt.

Showed only when the daylight fell
Level across the face
Of Brennbaum "The Impeccable."

Mr. Nixon[2]

In the cream gilded cabin of his steam yacht
Mr. Nixon advised me kindly, to advance with fewer
Dangers of delay. "Consider
Carefully the reviewer.

"I was as poor as you are;
"When I began I got, of course,
"Advance on royalties, fifty at first," said Mr. Nixon,
"Follow me, and take a column,
"Even if you have to work free.

"Butter reviewers. From fifty to three hundred
"I rose in eighteen months;
"The hardest nut I had to crack
"Was Dr. Dundas.

"I never mentioned a man but with the view
"Of selling my own works.
"The tip's a good one, as for literature
"It gives no man a sinecure.

"And no one knows, at sight, a masterpiece.
"And give up verse, my boy,
"There's nothing in it."

. . . .

Likewise a friend of Bloughram's once advised me:
Don't kick against the pricks,
Accept opinion. The "Nineties" tried your game
And died, there's nothing in it.

X

Beneath the sagging roof
The stylist[3] has taken shelter,
Unpaid, uncelebrated,
At last from the world's welter

Nature receives him;
With a placid and uneducated mistress
He exercises his talents
And the soil meets his distress.

The haven from sophistications and contentions
Leaks through its thatch;
He offers succulent cooking;
The door has a creaking latch.

2. This portrait of the calculatingly successful writer is generally thought to refer to Arnold Bennett (1867–1931), the novelist, who did indeed own a yacht. "Dr. Dundas" and the "friend of Bloughram's" are stock figures not susceptible of identification, but in the latter there may be intended a reference to the wily arguments of the bishop, in Browning's "Bishop Blougram's Apology," who lives on the Church whose doctrines he does not entirely believe.

3. In direct contrast with the preceding portrait, this one may be based on Ford Madox Ford (1873–1939), experimental novelist, editor of *The English Review,* and interested in the theory of "The New Novel" as practiced by James and Conrad. The poem depicts his circumstances at one particular period in his life.

XI

"Conservatrix of Milésien"[4]
Habits of mind and feeling,
Possibly. But in Ealing[5]
With the most bank-clerkly of Englishmen?

No, "Milésian" is an exaggeration.
No instinct has survived in her
Older than those her grandmother
Told her would fit her station.

XII

"Daphne with her thighs in bark
Stretches toward me her leafy hands,"[6]–
Subjectively. In the stuffed-satin drawing room
I await The Lady Valentine's commands,

Knowing my coat has never been
Of precisely the fashion
To stimulate, in her,
A durable passion;

Doubtful, somewhat, of the value
Of well-gowned approbation
Of literary effort,
But never of The Lady Valentine's vocation:

Poetry, her border of ideas,
The edge, uncertain, but a means of blending
With other strata
Where the lower and higher have ending;

A hook to catch the Lady Jane's attention,
A modulation toward the theatre,
Also, in the case of revolution,
A possible friend and comforter.

. . . .

Conduct, on the other hand, the soul
"Which the highest cultures have nourished"
To Fleet St.[7] where
Dr. Johnson[8] flourished;

Beside this thoroughfare
The sale of half-hose has

4. Pound was fond of a phrase which occurs in a story by Rémy de Gourmont, *"Stratagèmes,"* in *Histoires magiques*. Riffling through his recollections of women he has possessed, the narrator thinks of the role of knowingly induced pain in lovemaking; women who know how to bite, he says, shouldn't be despised, they are *conservatrices de traditions milésiennes* ("preservers of Milesian traditions")—Milesian from Miletus, ancient Greek city in Asia Minor and the native city of one Aristides (c. 100 B.C.), the writer or collector of a lost group of erotic stories, stories in what has come to be called "the Milesian genre."
5. Staid residential district in West London.
6. The first two lines translate two lines from Gautier's *"Le Château du souvenir"* ("The Castle of Memory"): the speaker is in a salon decorated with the exploits of Apollo. (Daphne, pursued by Apollo, was turned into a laurel to enable her to escape; the tree became sacred to Apollo, its leaves the symbol of literary honor.)
7. The center of London journalism.
8. Dr. Samuel Johnson (1709–1784), the great critic after whom the latter half of the 18th century is know as "The Age of Johnson," and who participated in many journalistic enterprises, both as contributor (for example, to *The Gentlemen's Magazine*) and as founder (of *The Rambler*).

Long since superseded the cultivation
Of Pierian[9] roses.

Envoi (1919)

Go, dumb-born book,
Tell her that sang me once that song of Lawes:[1]
Hadst thou but song
As thou hast subjects known,
Then were there cause in thee that should condone
Even my faults that heavy upon me lie,
And build her glories their longevity.

Tell her that sheds
Such treasure in the air,
Recking naught else but that her graces give
Life to the moment,
I would bid them live
As roses might, in magic amber laid,
Red overwrought with orange and all made
One substance and one color
Braving time.

Tell her that goes
With song upon her lips
But sings not out the song, nor knows
The maker of it, some other mouth,
May be as fair as hers,
Might, in new ages, gain her worshipers,
When our two dusts with Waller's shall be laid,
Siftings on siftings in oblivion,
Till change hath broken down
All things save Beauty alone.

1920

From THE CANTOS

I[2]

And then went down to the ship,
Set keel to breakers, forth on the godly sea, and
We set up mast and sail on that swart ship,
Bore sheep aboard her, and our bodies also
Heavy with weeping, and winds from sternward
Bore us out onward with bellying canvas,
Circe's this craft, the trim-coifed goddess.
Then sat we amidships, wind jamming the tiller,
Thus with stretched sail, we went over sea till day's end.
Sun to his slumber, shadows o'er all the ocean,

9. Pieria was a district on the northern slopes of Mt. Olympus, where the cult of the Muses originated.

1. Henry Lawes (1596–1662), the composer who had set to music "Go, lovely rose," the best known poems of the Cavalier poet Edmund Waller (1606–1687), the phrasing and movement of which are echoed in this poem.

2. The First of Pound's *Cantos,* the complex work of epic proportions which occupied him for something like fifty years, is taken up, through line 67, with Pound's translation of an episode from Book XI of the *Odyssey,* not directly from the Greek but from the 16th-century Latin translation of Andreas Divus. Book XI describes Odysseus' trip to the underworld, on the advice of Circe, to consult the spirit of Tiresias, the blind Theban prophet, who will give him instructions for the final stages of his return to Ithaca.

Came we then to the bounds of deepest water,
To the Kimmerian lands,[3] and peopled cities
Covered with close-webbed mist, unpierced ever
With glitter of sun-rays
Nor with stars stretched, nor looking back from heaven
Swartest night stretched over wretched men there.
The ocean flowing backward, came we then to the place
Aforesaid by Circe.
Here did they rites, Perimedes and Eurylochus,[4]
And drawing sword from my hip
I dug the ell-square pitkin;° *small trench*
Poured we libations unto each the dead,
First mead and then sweet wine, water mixed with white flour.
Then prayed I many a prayer to the sickly death's-heads;
As set in Ithaca, sterile bulls of the best
For sacrifice, heaping the pyre with goods,
A sheep to Tiresias only, black and a bell-sheep.
Dark blood flowed in the fosse,° *trench, ditch*
Souls out of Erebus,[5] cadaverous dead, of brides
Of youths and of the old who had borne much;
Souls stained with recent tears, girls tender,
Men many, mauled with bronze lance heads,
Battle spoil, bearing yet dreory[6] arms,
These many crowded about me; with shouting,
Pallor upon me, cried to my men for more beasts;
Slaughtered the herds, sheep slain of bronze;
Poured ointment, cried to the gods,
To Pluto the strong, and praised Proserpine;[7]
Unsheathed the narrow sword,
I sat to keep off the impetuous impotent dead,
Till I should hear Tiresias.
But first Elpenor[8] came, our friend Elpenor,
Unburied, cast on the wide earth,
Limbs that we left in the house of Circe,
Unwept, unwrapped in sepulchre, since toils urged other.
Pitiful spirit. And I cried in hurried speech:
"Elpenor, how art thou come to this dark coast?
"Cam'st thou afoot, outstripping seamen?"
And he in heavy speech:
"Ill fate and abundant wine. I slept in Circe's ingle.
"Going down the long ladder unguarded,
"I fell against the buttress,
"Shattered the nape-nerve, the soul sought Avernus.[9]
"But thou, O King, I bid remember me, unwept, unburied,
"Heap up mine arms, be tomb by sea-bord, and inscribed:
"*A man of no fortune, and with a name to come.*
"And set my oar up, that I swung mid fellows."

And Anticlea[1] came, whom I beat off, and then Tiresias Theban,
Holding his golden wand, knew me, and spoke first:

3. The Cimmerians were a mythical people living in darkness and mist on the farthest borders of the known world.
4. Two of Odysseus' men, who, like Odysseus in the lines that follow, are performing the propitiatory rites prescribed by Circe.
5. The underworld.
7. "Dripping with blood" (from old English *dreorig*).
7. Pluto, lord of the underworld, and Proserpine, his queen.
8. One of Odysseus' men who, in the manner he goes on to describe, had died on the night before they were to leave Circe's island.
9. A lake near Cumae (now near Naples) believed by the ancients to be the entrance to the infernal regions; also a name, as probably here, for the underworld itself.
1. Odysseus' mother, whose appearance is treated at greater length in *The Odyssey*.

"A second time?[2] why? man of ill star,
"Facing the sunless dead and this joyless region?
"Stand from the fosse,[3] leave me my bloody bever[4]
"For soothsay."
        And I stepped back,
And he strong with the blood, said then: "Odysseus
"Shalt return through spiteful Neptune, over dark seas,
"Lose all companions." And then Anticlea came.
Lie quiet Divus. I mean, that is Andreas Divus,[5]
In officina Wecheli, 1538, out of Homer.
And he sailed, by Sirens and thence outward and away
And unto Circe.[6]
        Venerandam,[7]
In the Cretan's phrase, with the golden crown, Aphrodite,
Cypri munimenta sortita est, mirthful, oricalchi,[8] with golden
Girdles and breast bands, thou with dark eyelids
Bearing the golden bough of Argicida.[9] So that:[1]

1921 1930

H. D. (HILDA DOOLITTLE) (1886–1961)

Sea Violet

The white violet
is scented on its stalk,
the sea-violet
fragile as agate,
lies fronting all the wind
among the torn shells
on the sand-bank.

The greater blue violets
flutter on the hill,
but who would change for these

2. "A second time" correctly translates Divus' adverb *iterum*, but Homer's adverb has here the sense not of "again" but rather of "here, too," i.e., "Why have you come here, too, in addition to all your other wanderings?" Odysseus had not been in the underworld, or met Tiresias, before.
3. The trench, or small pit, that Odysseus and his men have dug and in which the blood from the sacrifice has collected.
4. Drink, potation (cf. beverage).
5. The 16th-century Italian whose translation of the *Odyssey* had been published "in officina Wechel," at the printing shop of Chrétien Wechel, Paris, in 1538.
6. After this visit to the underworld, Odysseus had returned to Circe and then, forewarned by her, had successfully sailed past the Sirens.
7. "Worthy of worship," applied to Aphrodite. This, like the Latin words and phrases in the next lines, derives from a Latin translation of two Hymns to Aphrodite (among the so-called Homeric Hymns, dating from the 8th to 6th century B.C., anciently believed to be by Homer), a translation made by Georgius Dartona Cretensis, contained, Pound tells us, in the volume in which he had found Divus's translation of the *Odyssey*. Of the two Hymns to Aphrodite, the longer, from which Pound takes the reference to Hermes (*Argicida*) in the last line, consists, in Greek, of 293 lines of dactylic hexameter, recounting the union of Aphrodite and Anchises, from which union the Trojan leader Aeneas was to be born. The other is a slight hymn of worship, 21 lines long, which begins with the words that figure, in Latin or in English, in the closing lines of the Canto: "Reverend golden-crowned beautiful Aphrodite/I shall sing, who has received as her lot the citadels of all sea-girt Cyprus. . . ."
8. *Oricalchi:* brass. The Hours, in the shorter poem, have adorned Aphrodite with earrings, flower-formed, of brass and precious gold.
9. An epithet for Hermes, "slayer of Argos" (i.e., of the many-eyed herdsman set to watch Io). Aphrodite, deceiving Anchises at first, says that she is a mortal maiden, that the "slayer of Argos, with wand of gold" has brought her to be Anchises' bride.
1. The Canto ends on the colon, going immediately into Canto II, which begins with the words, "Hang it all, Robert Browning,/ There can be but one 'Sordello.' "

who would change for these
one root of the white sort?

Violet
your grasp is frail
on the edge of the sand-hill,
but you catch the light—
frost, a star edges with its fire.

1916

Wine Bowl

I will rise
from my troth
with the dead,
I will sweeten my cup
and my bread
with a gift;
I will chisel a bowl for the wine,
for the white wine
and red;
I will summon a Satyr[1] to dance,
a Centaur,
a Nymph
and a Faun;
I will picture
a warrior King,
a Giant,
a Naiad,
a Monster;
I will cut round the rim of the crater,
some simple
familiar thing,
vine leaves
or the sea-swallow's wing;
I will work at each separate part
till my mind is worn out
and my heart:
in my skull,
where the vision had birth,
will come wine,
would pour song
of the hot earth,
of the flower and the sweet
of the hill,
thyme,
meadow-plant,
grass-blade and sorrel;
in my skull,
from which vision took flight,
will come wine

1. Here, and in the lines following, figures from classical mythology are evoked. *Nymphs* were minor nature goddesses; those who lived in springs, fountains, rivers and lakes were called *naiads*. In Greek mythology, *satyrs* were woodland spirits in the form of men with the legs of goats and with pointed ears or horns. The Romans identified satyrs with their own woodland spirits, the *fauns*. *Centaurs* had the faces and chests of men, and the bodies of horses. Satyrs are usually associated with lechery; centaurs, with savagery.

will pour song
of the cool night,
of the silver and blade of the moon,
of the star,
of the sun's kiss at midnoon;
I will challenge the reed-pipe
and stringed lyre,
to sing sweeter,
pipe wilder,
praise louder
the fragrance and sweet
of the wine jar,
till each lover
must summon another,
to proffer a rose
where all flowers are,
in the depths of the exquisite crater;
flower will fall upon flower
till the red shower
inflame all
with intimate fervor;
till:
men who travel afar
will look up,
sensing grape
and hill-slope
in the cup;
men who sleep by the wood
will arise,
hearing ripple and fall
of the tide,
being drawn by the spell of the sea;
the bowl will ensnare and enchant
men who crouch by the hearth
till they want
but the riot of stars in the night;
those who dwell far inland
will seek ships;
the deep-sea fisher,
plying his nets,
will forsake them
for wheat-sheaves and loam;
men who wander
will yearn for their home,
men at home
will depart.

I will rise
from my troth with the dead,
I will sweeten my cup
and my bread
with a gift;
I will chisel a bowl for the wine,
for the white wine
and red.

1931

ROBINSON JEFFERS (1887–1962)

Shine, Perishing Republic

While this America settles in the mold of its vulgarity, heavily thickening to empire,
And protest, only a bubble in the molten mass, pops and sighs out, and the mass hardens,

I sadly smiling remember that the flower fades to make fruit, the fruit rots to make earth.
Out of the mother; and through the spring exultances, ripeness and decadence; and home to the mother.

You making haste haste on decay: not blameworthy; life is good, be it stubbornly long or suddenly
A mortal splendor: meteors are not needed less than mountains: shine, perishing republic.

But for my children, I would have them keep their distance from the thickening center; corruption
Never has been compulsory, when the cities lie at the monster's feet there are left the mountains.

And boys, be in nothing so moderate as in love of man, a clever servant, insufferable master.
There is the trap that catches noblest spirits, that caught—they say—God, when he walked on earth.

1924

Hurt Hawks

1

The broken pillar of the wing jags from the clotted shoulder,
The wing trails like a banner in defeat,
No more to use the sky forever but live with famine
And pain a few days: cat nor coyote
Will shorten the week of waiting for death, there is game without talons.
He stands under the oak-bush and waits
The lame feet of salvation; at night he remembers freedom
And flies in a dream, the dawns ruin it.
He is strong and pain is worse to the strong, incapacity is worse.
The curs of the day come and torment him
At distance, no one but death the redeemer will humble that head,
The intrepid readiness, the terrible eyes.
The wild God of the world is sometimes merciful to those
That ask mercy, not often to the arrogant.
You do not know him, you communal people, or you have forgotten him;
Intemperate and savage, the hawk remembers him;
Beautiful and wild, the hawks, and men that are dying, remember him.

2

I'd sooner, except the penalties, kill a man than a hawk; but
the great redtail° *red-tailed hawk*
Had nothing left but unable misery
From the bone too shattered for mending, the wing that trailed under
his talons when he moved.
We had fed him six weeks, I gave him freedom,
He wandered over the foreland hill and returned in the evening,
asking for death,
Not like a beggar, still eyed with the old
Implacable arrogance. I gave him the lead gift in the twilight. What
fell was relaxed,
Owl-downy, soft feminine feathers; but what
Soared: the fierce rush: the night-herons by the flooded river cried
fear at its rising
Before it was quite unsheathed from reality.

1928

Carmel Point[1]

The extraordinary patience of things!
This beautiful place defaced with a crop of suburban houses—
How beautiful when we first beheld it,
Unbroken field of poppy and lupin walled with clean cliffs;
No intrusion but two or three horses pasturing,
Or a few milch cows rubbing their flanks on the outcrop rock-heads—
Now the spoiler has come: does it care?
Not faintly. It has all time. It knows the people are a tide
That swells and in time will ebb, and all
Their works dissolve. Meanwhile the image of the pristine beauty
Lives in the very grain of the granite,
Safe as the endless ocean that climbs our cliff.—As for us:
We must uncenter our minds from ourselves;
We must unhumanize our views a little, and become confident
As the rock and ocean that we were made from.

1954

Birds and Fishes

Every October millions of little fish come along the shore,
Coasting this granite edge of the continent
On their lawful occasions: but what a festival for the sea-fowl.
What a witches' sabbath[2] of wings
Hides the dark water. The heavy pelicans shout "Haw!" like Job's friend's
warhorse[3]
And dive from the high air, the cormorants[4]
Slip their long black bodies under the water and hunt like wolves
Through the green half-light. Screaming, the gulls watch,
Wild with envy and malice, cursing and snatching. What hysterical greed!

1. On the California coast, below San Francisco.
2. Orgiastic midnight assembly of witches and sorcerers, traditionally held, on such nights as Halloween, to renew allegiance to the devil.
3. See Job xxxix:19–25: "He saith among the trumpets Ha, ha; and he smelleth the battle afar off, the thunder of the captains and the shouting." "He" refers to the horse.
4. Aquatic birds with dark plumage

What a filling of pouches! the mob
Hysteria is nearly human—these decent birds!—as if they were finding
Gold in the street. It is better than gold,
It can be eaten: and which one in all this fury of wild-fowl pities the fish?
No one certainly. Justice and mercy
Are human dreams, they do not concern the birds nor the fish nor eternal God.
However—look again before you go.
The wings and wild hungers, the wave-worn skerries, the bright quick minnows
Living in terror to die in torment—
Man's fate and theirs—and the island rocks and immense ocean beyond, and Lobos[5]
Darkening above the bay: they are beautiful?
That is their quality: not mercy, not mind, not goodness, but the beauty of God.

1963

MARIANNE MOORE
(1887–1972)

Poetry

I, too, dislike it: there are things that are important beyond all this fiddle.
Reading it, however, with a perfect contempt for it, one discovers in
it after all, a place for the genuine.
Hands that can grasp, eyes
that can dilate, hair that can rise
if it must, these things are important not because a

high-sounding interpretation can be put upon them but because they are
useful. When they become so derivative as to become unintelligible,
the same thing may be said for all of us, that we
do not admire what
we cannot understand: the bat
holding on upside down or in quest of something to

eat, elephants pushing, a wild horse taking a roll, a tireless wolf under
a tree, the immovable critic twitching his skin like a horse that feels a flea, the base-
ball fan, the statistician—
nor is it valid
to discriminate against "business documents and

school-books";[1] all these phenomena are important. One must make a distinction
however: when dragged into prominence by half poets, the result is not poetry,
nor till the poets among us can be
"literalists of

5. Point Lobos, just below Carmel.

1. "*Diary of Tolstoy* (Dutton), p. 84. 'Where the boundary between prose and poetry lies, I shall never be able to understand. The question is raised in manuals of style, yet the answer to it lies beyond me. Poetry is verse: prose is not verse. Or else poetry is everything with the exception of business documents and school books'" [Moore's note].

the imagination" [2]—above
insolence and triviality and can present

for inspection, "imaginary gardens with real toads in them," shall we have
it. In the meantime, if you demand on the one hand,
the raw material of poetry in
all its rawness and
that which is on the other hand
genuine, you are interested in poetry.

1921

No Swan So Fine

"No water so still as the
dead fountains of Versailles."[3] No swan,
with swart blind look askance
and gondoliering legs,[4] so fine
as the chintz china one with fawn-
brown eyes and toothed gold
collar on to show whose bird it was.

Lodged in the Louis Fifteenth
candelabrum-tree[5] of cockscomb-
tinted buttons, dahlias,
sea-urchins, and everlastings,[6]
it perches on the branching foam
of polished sculptured
flowers—at ease and tall. The king is dead.

1932, 1951

Peter

Strong and slippery,
built for the midnight grass-party
confronted by four cats, he sleeps his time away—
the detached first claw on the foreleg corresponding
to the thumb, retracted to its tip; the small tuft of fronds
or katydid-legs above each eye numbering all units
in each group; the shadbones[7] regularly set about the mouth
to droop or rise in unison like porcupine-quills.
He lets himself be flattened out by gravity,
as seaweed is tamed and weakened by the sun,
compelled when extended, to lie stationary.
Sleep is the result of his delusion that one must
do as well as one can for oneself,
sleep—epitome of what is to him the end of life.
Demonstrate on him how the lady placed a forked stick
on the innocuous neck-sides of the dangerous southern snake.
One need not try to stir him up; his prune-shaped head

2. "Yeats: *Ideas of Good and Evil* (A. H. Bullen), p. 182. 'The limitation of [Blake's] view was from the very intensity of his vision; he was a too literal realist of imagination, as others are of nature; and because he believed that the figures seen by the mind's eye, when exalted by inspiration, were "eternal existences," symbols of divine essences, he hated every grace of style that might obscure their lineaments' " [Moore's note].

3. Famed palace of French kings in the late 17th and early 18th centuries, now a museum.

4. Italian gondoliers paddle from the stern to propel their gondolas.

5. "A pair of Louis XV candelabra with Dresden figures of swans belonging to Lord Balfour" [Moore's note].

6. Plants whose flowers may be dried without losing their form or color; also, the flowers from such plants.

7. Long, very fine bones of the shad fish.

and alligator-eyes are not party to the joke.
Lifted and handled, he may be dangled like an eel
or set up on the forearm like a mouse;
his eyes bisected by pupils of a pin's width,
are flickeringly exhibited, then covered up.
May be? I should have said might have been;
when he has been got the better of in a dream—
as in a fight with nature or with cats, we all know it.
Profound sleep is not with him a fixed illusion.
Springing about with froglike accuracy, with jerky cries
when taken in hand, he is himself again;
to sit caged by the rungs of a domestic chair
would be unprofitable—human. What is the good of hypocrisy?
it is permissible to choose one's employment,
to abandon the nail, or roly-poly,
when it shows signs of being no longer a pleasure,
to score the nearby magazine with a double line of strokes.
He can talk but insolently says nothing. What of it?
When one is frank, one's very presence is a compliment.
It is clear that he can see the virtue of naturalness,
that he does not regard the published fact as a surrender.
As for the disposition invariably to affront,
an animal with claws should have an opportunity to use them.
The eel-like extension of trunk into tail is not an accident.
To leap, to lengthen out, divide the air, to purloin, to pursue.
To tell the hen: fly over the fence, go in the wrong way
in your perturbation—this is life;
to do less would be nothing but dishonesty.

1935

EDWIN MUIR
(1887–1959)

The Animals

They do not live in the world,
Are not in time and space.
From birth to death hurled
No word do they have, not one
To plant a foot upon,
Were never in any place.

For with names the world was called
Out of the empty air,[1]
With names was built and walled,
Line and circle and square,
Dust and emerald;
Snatched from deceiving death
By the articulate breath.

But these have never trod
Twice the familiar track,
Never never turned back
Into the memoried day.

1. Genesis i.5, i.8, and i.10 illustrate the naming of the elements of the world as they were created ("And God called the light Day, and the darkness he called Night. . . . And God called the firmament Heaven. . . . And God called the dry land Earth. . . .")

All is new and near
In the unchanging Here
Of the fifth great day of God,[2]
That shall remain the same,
Never shall pass away.

On the sixth day we came.

1952

The Brothers[3]

Last night I watched my brothers play,
The gentle and the reckless one,
In a field two yards away.
For half a century they were gone
Beyond the other side of care
To be among the peaceful dead.
Even in a dream how could I dare
Interrogate that happiness
So wildly spent yet never less?
For still they raced about the green
And were like two revolving suns;
A brightness poured from head to head,
So strong I could not see their eyes
Or look into their paradise.
What were they doing, the happy ones?
Yet where I was they once had been.

I thought, How could I be so dull,
Twenty thousand days ago,
Not to see they were beautiful?
I asked them, Were you really so
As you are now, that other day?
And the dream was soon away.

For then we played for victory
And not to make each other glad.
A darkness covered every head,
Frowns twisted the original face,
And through that mask we could not see
The beauty and the buried grace.

I have observed in foolish awe
The dateless mid-days of the law
And seen indifferent justice done
By everyone on everyone.
And in a vision I have seen
My brothers playing on the green.

1956 1960

2. Genesis i.20–25 describes the creation of the fish of the sea, the fowls of the air, and the beasts of the earth on the fifth day.
3. Two of Muir's three brothers had died before he himself was 18, and what he says of them here, in a poem completed toward the end of his own life, and which records a dream-vision of his brothers during their life together in Orkney, shares in what he has to say in his *Autobiography* (1954) about the sources of his poetry: "I must have been influenced by something, since we all are, but when I try to find out what it was that influenced me, I can only think of the years of childhood which I spent on my father's farm in the little island of Wyre in Orkney, and the beauty I apprehended then, before I knew there was beauty. These years had come alive, after being forgotten for so long, and when I wrote about horses they were my father's plow-horses as I saw them when I was four or five: and a poem on Achilles pursuing Hector round the walls of Troy was really a resuscitation of the afternoon when I ran away, in real terror, from another boy as I returned from school."

T. S. ELIOT (1888–1965)

The Love Song of J. Alfred Prufrock

S'io credesse che mia risposta fosse
A persona che mai tornasse al mondo,
Questa fiamma staria senza più scosse.
Ma perciocche giammai di questo fondo
Non tornò vivo alcun, s'i'odo il vero,
Senza tema d'infamia ti rispondo.[1]

Let us go then, you and I,
When the evening is spread out against the sky
Like a patient etherized upon a table;
Let us go, through certain half-deserted streets,
The muttering retreats
Of restless nights in one-night cheap hotels
And sawdust restaurants with oyster-shells:
Streets that follow like a tedious argument
Of insidious intent
To lead you to an overwhelming question. . .
Oh, do not ask, "What is it?"
Let us go and make our visit.

In the room the women come and go
Talking of Michelangelo.

The yellow fog that rubs its back upon the window-panes
The yellow smoke that rubs its muzzle on the window-panes
Licked its tongue into the corners of the evening,
Lingered upon the pools that stand in drains,
Let fall upon its back the soot that falls from chimneys,
Slipped by the terrace, made a sudden leap,
And seeing that it was a soft October night,
Curled once about the house, and fell asleep.

And indeed there will be time
For the yellow smoke that slides along the street,
Rubbing its back upon the window-panes;
There will be time, there will be time
To prepare a face to meet the faces that you meet;
There will be time to murder and create,
And time for all the works and days[2] of hands
That lift and drop a question on your plate;
Time for you and time for me,
And time yet for a hundred indecisions,

1. Dante, *Inferno,* XXVII.61–66. These words are spoken by Guido da Montefeltro, whom Dante and Virgil have encountered in the Eighth Chasm, that of the False Counselors, where each spirit is concealed within a flame which moves as the spirit speaks: "If I thought my answer were given/to anyone who would ever return to the world,/this flame would stand still without moving any further./ But since never from this abyss/has anyone ever returned alive, if what I hear is true,/ without fear of infamy I answer thee."

2. Possibly alludes to the title of a didactic work on the seasonal pursuits of country life, *Works and Days,* by the Greek poet Hesiod (eighth century B.C.).

And for a hundred visions and revisions,
Before the taking of a toast and tea.

In the room the women come and go
Talking of Michelangelo.

And indeed there will be time
To wonder, "Do I dare?" and, "Do I dare?"
Time to turn back and descend the stair,
With a bald spot in the middle of my hair—
[They will say: "How his hair is growing thin!"]
My morning coat, my collar mounting firmly to the chin,
My necktie rich and modest, but asserted by a simple pin—
[They will say: "But how his arms and legs are thin!"]
Do I dare
Disturb the universe?
In a minute there is time
For decisions and revisions which a minute will reverse.

For I have known them all already, known them all:
Have known the evenings, mornings, afternoons,
I have measured out my life with coffee spoons;
I know the voices dying with a dying fall
Beneath the music from a farther room.
  So how should I presume?

And I have known the eyes already, known them all—
The eyes that fix you in a formulated phrase,
And when I am formulated, sprawling on a pin,
When I am pinned and wriggling on the wall,
Then how should I begin
To spit out all the butt-ends of my days and ways?
  And how should I presume?

And I have known the arms already, known them all—
Arms that are braceleted and white and bare
[But in the lamplight, downed with light brown hair!]
Is it perfume from a dress
That makes me so digress?
Arms that lie along a table, or wrap about a shawl.
  And should I then presume?
  And how should I begin?

. . . . .

Shall I say, I have gone at dusk through narrow streets
And watched the smoke that rises from the pipes
Of lonely men in shirt-sleeves, leaning out of windows? . . .

I should have been a pair of ragged claws
Scuttling across the floors of silent seas.

. . . . .

And the afternoon, the evening, sleeps so peacefully!
Smoothed by long fingers,
Asleep . . . tired . . . or it malingers,
Stretched on the floor, here beside you and me.
Should I, after tea and cakes and ices,
Have the strength to force the moment to its crisis?

But though I have wept and fasted, wept and prayed,
Though I have seen my head [grown slightly bald] brought in upon a
   platter,[3]
I am no prophet—and here's no great matter;
I have seen the moment of my greatness flicker,
And I have seen the eternal Footman hold my coat, and snicker,
And in short, I was afraid.

And would it have been worth it, after all,
After the cups, the marmalade, the tea,
Among the porcelain, among some talk of you and me,
Would it have been worth while,
To have bitten off the matter with a smile,
To have squeezed the universe into a ball
To roll it toward some overwhelming question,
To say: "I am Lazarus,[4] come from the dead,
Come back to tell you all, I shall tell you all"—
If one, settling a pillow by her head,
   Should say: "That is not what I meant at all.
   That is not it, at all."

And would it have been worth it, after all,
Would it have been worth while,
After the sunsets and the dooryards and the sprinkled streets,
After the novels, after the teacups, after the skirts that trail along the floor—
And this, and so much more?—
It is impossible to say just what I mean!
But as if a magic lantern threw the nerves in patterns on a screen:
Would it have been worth while
If one, settling a pillow or throwing off a shawl,
And turning toward the window, should say:
   "That is not it at all,
   That is not what I meant, at all."

. . . . .

No! I am not Prince Hamlet, nor was meant to be;
Am an attendant lord, one that will do
To swell a progress,[5] start a scene or two,
Advise the prince; no doubt, an easy tool,
Deferential, glad to be of use,
Politic, cautious, and meticulous;
Full of high sentence,° but a bit obtuse; *sententiousness*
At times, indeed, almost ridiculous—
Almost, at times, the Fool.

I grow old . . . I grow old . . .
I shall wear the bottoms of my trousers rolled.

Shall I part my hair behind? Do I dare to eat a peach?
I shall wear white flannel trousers, and walk upon the beach.
I have heard the mermaids singing, each to each.

I do not think that they will sing to me.

3. See the story of the martyrdom of St. John the Baptist (Matthew xiv.1–12), whose head was presented to Salome on a plate at the order of the tetrarch Herod.
4. See John xi, and xii. 1–2.
5. In Elizabethan sense: state journey.

I have seen them riding seaward on the waves
Combing the white hair of the waves blown back
When the wind blows the water white and black.

We have lingered in the chambers of the sea
By sea-girls wreathed with seaweed red and brown
Till human voices wake us, and we drown.

1917

Preludes

1

The winter evening settles down
With smell of steaks in passageways.
Six o'clock.
The burnt-out ends of smoky days.
And now a gusty shower wraps
The grimy scraps
Of withered leaves about your feet
And newspapers from vacant lots;
The showers beat
On broken blinds and chimney-pots,
And at the corner of the street
A lonely cab-horse steams and stamps.
And then the lighting of the lamps.

2

The morning comes to consciousness
Of faint stale smells of beer
From the sawdust-trampled street
With all its muddy feet that press
To early coffee-stands.
With the other masquerades
That time resumes,
One thinks of all the hands
That are raising dingy shades
In a thousand furnished rooms.

3

You tossed a blanket from the bed,
You lay upon your back, and waited;
You dozed, and watched the night revealing
The thousand sordid images
Of which your soul was constituted;
They flickered against the ceiling.
And when all the world came back
And the light crept up between the shutters
And you heard the sparrows in the gutters,
You had such a vision of the street
As the street hardly understands;
Sitting along the bed's edge, where
You curled the papers from your hair,
Or clasped the yellow soles of feet
In the palms of both soiled hands.

4

His soul stretched tight across the skies
That fade behind a city block,
Or trampled by insistent feet
At four and five and six o'clock;

And short square fingers stuffing pipes,
And evening newspapers, and eyes
Assured of certain certainties,
The conscience of a blackened street
Impatient to assume the world.

I am moved by fancies that are curled
Around these images, and cling:
The notion of some infinitely gentle
Infinitely suffering thing.

Wipe your hand across your mouth, and laugh;
The worlds revolve like ancient women
Gathering fuel in vacant lots.

1917

Sweeney Among the Nightingales

ὤμοι, πέπληγμαι καιρίαν πληγὴν ἔσω.[6]

Apeneck Sweeney spreads his knees
Letting his arms hang down to laugh,
The zebra stripes along his jaw
Swelling to maculate° giraffe. *spotted*

The circles of the stormy moon
Slide westward toward the River Plate,[7]
Death and the Raven[8] drift above
And Sweeney guards the hornéd gate.[9]

Gloomy Orion[1] and the Dog
Are veiled; and hushed the shrunken seas;
The person in the Spanish cape
Tries to sit on Sweeney's knees

Slips and pulls the table cloth
Overturns a coffee-cup,
Reorganized upon the floor
She yawns and draws a stocking up;

The silent man in mocha brown
Sprawls at the window-sill and gapes;
The waiter brings in oranges
Bananas figs and hothouse grapes;

The silent vertebrate in brown
Contracts and concentrates, withdraws;
Rachel *née* Rabinovitch
Tears at the grapes with murderous paws;

6. Aeschylus, *Agamemnon,* line 1343. Agamemnon's cry, heard from inside the palace, as Clytemnestra strikes her first blow: "Oh, I have been struck a direct deadly blow, within!"
7. Rio de la Plata, an estuary of the Paraná and Uruguay rivers, between Uruguay and Argentina.
8. The southern constellation Corvus.
9. In Greek legend, dreams came to mortals through two sets of gates: the gates of horn, for dreams which were true, the gates of ivory, for dreams which were untrue.
1. A constellation in which is seen the figure of a hunter, with belt and sword; near it, the dog-star, Sirius, represents the hunter's dog.

She and the lady in the cape
Are suspect, thought to be in league;
Therefore the man with heavy eyes
Declines the gambit, shows fatigue,

Leaves the room and reappears
Outside the window, leaning in,
Branches of wistaria
Circumscribe a golden grin;

The host with someone indistinct
Converses at the door apart,
The nightingales are singing near
The Convent of the Sacred Heart,

And sang within the bloody wood
When Agamemnon cried aloud,
And let their liquid siftings fall
To stain the stiff dishonored shroud.

1919

The Waste Land[2]

"Nam Sibyllam quidem Cumis ego ipse oculis meis vidi in ampulla pendere, et cum illi pueri dicerent: Σίβυλλα τί θέλεις; respondebat illa: ἀποθανεῖν θέλω."[3]

FOR EZRA POUND
il miglior fabbro.[4]

I. The Burial of the Dead[5]

April is the cruelest month, breeding
Lilacs out of the dead land, mixing
Memory and desire, stirring
Dull roots with spring rain.
Winter kept us warm, covering
Earth in forgetful snow, feeding
A little life with dried tubers.
Summer surprised us, coming over the Starnbergersee[6]
With a shower of rain; we stopped in the colonnade,

2. On its first publication in book form, T. S. Eliot provided *The Waste Land* with notes directing the reader to the sources of many of its allusions and explaining certain phases of its plan. Eliot's notes are included below. His general note to the poem is as follows: "Not only the title, but the plan and a good deal of the incidental symbolism of the poem were suggested by Miss Jessie L. Weston's book on the Grail legend: *From Ritual to Romance* (Cambridge). Indeed, so deeply am I indebted, Miss Weston's book will elucidate the difficulties of the poem much better than my notes can do; and I recommend it (apart from the great interest of the book itself) to any who think such elucidation of the poem worth the trouble. To another work of anthropology I am indebted in general, one which has influenced our generation profoundly; I mean *The Golden Bough* [by Sir James Frazer; 12 volumes, 1890–1915]; I have used especially the two volumes *Adonis, Attis, Osiris*. Anyone who is acquainted with these works will immediately recognize in the poem certain references to vegetation ceremonies."

3. "For indeed I myself have seen, with my own eyes, the Sibyl hanging in a bottle at Cumae, and when those boys would say to her: 'Sibyl, what do you want?' she would reply, 'I want to die.' " From the *Satyricon* of Petronius (d. A.D. 66), chapter 48. According to legend the Sibyl, a prophetess who was immortal but subject to the withering of age, was kept in a bottle or cage suspended in the temple of Hercules at Cumae (near Naples).

4. "The better craftsman." The poet Guido Guinizelli, encountered by Dante in Purgatory, answers the latter's praise of him with praise of his predecessor, the Provençal poet Arnaut Daniel, as being "the better craftsman in the maternal tongue" (*Purgatorio,* XXVI.117).

5. From the burial service of the Anglican Church.

6. Lake a few miles south of Munich. The Hofgarten (line 10) is a public garden in Munich, partly surrounded by a colonnaded walk.

And went on in sunlight, into the Hofgarten,
And drank coffee, and talked for an hour.
Bin gar keine Russin, stamm' aus Litauen, echt deutsch.[7]
And when we were children, staying at the archduke's,
My cousin's, he took me out on a sled,
And I was frightened. He said, Marie,
Marie, hold on tight. And down we went.
In the mountains, there you feel free.
I read, much of the night, and go south in the winter.

What are the roots that clutch, what branches grow
Out of this stony rubbish? Son of man,[8]
You cannot say, or guess, for you know only
A heap of broken images, where the sun beats,
And the dead tree gives no shelter, the cricket no relief,[9]
And the dry stone no sound of water. Only
There is shadow under this red rock,
(Come in under the shadow of this red rock),
And I will show you something different from either
Your shadow at morning striding behind you
Or your shadow at evening rising to meet you;
I will show you fear in a handful of dust.
Frisch weht der Wind
Der Heimat zu
Mein Irisch Kind,
Wo weilest du?[1]
"You gave me hyacinths first a year ago;
"They called me the hyacinth girl."
—Yet when we came back, late, from the Hyacinth garden,
Your arms full, and your hair wet, I could not
Speak, and my eyes failed, I was neither
Living nor dead, and I knew nothing,
Looking into the heart of light, the silence.
Oed' und leer das Meer.[2]

Madame Sosostris,[3] famous clairvoyante,
Had a bad cold, nevertheless
Is known to be the wisest woman in Europe,
With a wicked pack of cards.[4] Here, said she,
Is your card, the drowned Phoenician Sailor,

7. "I am by no means a Russian, I come from Lithuania, am really German."
8. "Cf. Ezekiel II, i" [Eliot's note].
9. "Cf. Ecclesiastes XII, v" [Eliot's note].
1. "V. *Tristan und Isolde,* I, verses 5–8" [Eliot's note]. The sailor's song from Wagner's opera: "Fresh blows the wind/Towards home./My Irish child,/Where are you lingering?"
2. "Id. III, verse 24" [Eliot's note]. "Empty and waste the sea": that is, the ship bringing Isolde back to the dying Tristan is nowhere in sight.
3. An invented, generic name for a fortune-teller, perhaps meant to have Egyptian overtones.
4. "I am not familiar with the exact constitution of the Tarot pack of cards, from which I have obviously departed to suit my own convenience. The Hanged Man, a member of the traditional pack, fits my purpose in two ways: because he is associated in my mind with the Hanged God of Frazer, and because I associate him with the hooded figure in the passage of the disciples to Emmaus in Part V. The Phoenician Sailor and the Merchant appear later; also the 'crowds of people,' and Death by Water is executed in Part IV. The Man with Three Staves (an authentic member of the Tarot pack) I associate, quite arbitrarily, with the Fisher King himself" [Eliot's note]. The tarot cards are playing-cards, whose origin goes back to the 14th century in Italy, still in use both for playing and for fortune-telling, as here. The Hanged Man hangs by one foot from the top bar of a trapeze-like construction. The individual figures which the fortune-teller refers to as appearing on her cards have subtle and complex relations to figures who appear in the poem on other levels and to the three principal figures of the Fisher King myth (the impotent King of the waste land, the Deliverer, and the Woman). Besides the relationships which Eliot suggests in his note above, "Belladonna, * * * the lady of situations," looks ahead to the neurotic woman of the opening lines of Part II. The Hanged Man, whom Madame Sosostris cannot find, is the fertility god whose death would bring new life to his people.

(Those are pearls that were his eyes.[5] Look!)
Here is Belladonna, the Lady of the Rocks,
The lady of situations.
Here is the man with three staves, and here the Wheel,
And here is the one-eyed merchant, and this card,
Which is blank, is something he carries on his back,
Which I am forbidden to see. I do not find
The Hanged Man. Fear death by water.
I see crowds of people, walking round in a ring.
Thank you. If you see dear Mrs. Equitone,
Tell her I bring the horoscope myself:
One must be so careful these days.

Unreal City,[6]
Under the brown fog of a winter dawn,
A crowd flowed over London Bridge, so many,
I had not thought death had undone so many.[7]
Sighs, short and infrequent, were exhaled,[8]
And each man fixed his eyes before his feet.
Flowed up the hill and down King William Street,
To where Saint Mary Woolnoth kept the hours
With a dead sound on the final stroke of nine.[9]
There I saw one I knew, and stopped him, crying: "Stetson!
"You who were with me in the ships at Mylae![1]
"That corpse you planted last year in your garden,
"Has it begun to sprout? Will it bloom this year?
"Or has the sudden frost disturbed its bed?
"Oh keep the Dog far hence, that's friend to men,
"Or with his nails he'll dig it up again![2]
"You! hypocrite lecteur!—mon semblable,—mon frère!"[3]

II. A Game of Chess[4]

The Chair she sat in, like a burnished throne,[5]
Glowed on the marble, where the glass

5. From Ariel's song in Shakespeare's *The Tempest,* I.ii, "Full fathom five thy father lies."

6. "Cf. Baudelaire: 'Fourmillante cité, cité pleine de rêves,/Où le spectre en plein jour raccroche le passant' " [Eliot's note]. The lines are from *Les Sept vieillards* (*The Seven Old Men*), one of the poems in *Les Fleurs du mal* (1857): "Swarming city, city filled with dreams,/Where the specter in broad daylight accosts the passerby."

7. "Cf. Inferno III, 55–57: 'si lunga tratta/di gente, ch' io non avrei mai creduto/che morte tanta n'avesse disfatta' " [Eliot's note]. On his arrival in the Inferno, Dante sees the vast crowd of those who "lived without infamy and without praise, * * * such a long procession of people, that I would never have believed that death had undone so many."

8. "Cf. Inferno IV, 25–27: 'Quivi, secondo che per ascoltare,/non avea pianto, ma' che di sospiri,/che l'aura eterna facevan tremare' " [Eliot's note]. Descending into the first circle of Hell, peopled by those whose virtues did not outweigh the fact that they had not been baptized, or that they had lived before the advent of Christ, Dante hears a noise of lamentation: "Here, if one trusted to hearing, there was no weeping but so many sighs as caused the everlasting air to tremble."

9. "A phenomenon which I have often noticed" [Eliot's note]. King William Street leads into London Bridge; St. Mary Woolnoth stood in an angle formed by that street and Lombard Street. These and other London place-names in the poem refer to the East End—the City, the usual name for London's financial and business center.

1. Sicilian seaport, near which the Romans gained a naval victory over the Carthaginians in 260 B.C.

2. "Cf. the Dirge in Webster's *White Devil*" [Eliot's note]. The Dirge begins, "Call for the robin redbreast and the wren," and ends, "But keep the wolf far thence, that's foe to men;/For with his nails he'll dig them up again."

3. "V. Baudelaire, Preface to *Fleurs du Mal*" [Eliot's note]. Baudelaire's prefatory poem is entitled *To the Reader,* and it takes him through a list of the evils which beset him—foolishness, error, sin, miserliness—evoking at the end the most monstrous vice of all, Ennui: "You, reader, know the delicate monster,/—Hypocritical reader,—my counterpart,—my brother!"

4. The title alludes to two plays by Thomas Middleton (1570–1627), *A Game at Chesse* and *Women Beware Women,* both of which involve sexual intrigue. In the second, a game of chess is used to mark a seduction, the moves in the game paralleling the steps in the seduction.

5. "Cf. *Antony and Cleopatra,* II, ii, l. 190" [Eliot's note]. Enobarbus' long description of Cleopatra's first meeting with Antony on the River Cydnus begins: "The barge she sat in, like a burnished throne/Burned on the water * * *"

Held up by standards wrought with fruited vines
From which a golden Cupidon peeped out
(Another hid his eyes behind his wing)
Doubled the flames of sevenbranched candelabra
Reflecting light upon the table as
The glitter of her jewels rose to meet it,
From satin cases poured in rich profusion;
In vials of ivory and colored glass
Unstoppered, lurked her strange synthetic perfumes,
Unguent, powdered, or liquid—troubled, confused
And drowned the sense in odors; stirred by the air
That freshened from the window, these ascended
In fattening the prolonged candle-flames,
Flung their smoke into the laquearia,[6]
Stirring the pattern on the coffered ceiling.
Huge sea-wood fed with copper
Burned green and orange, framed by the colored stone,
In which sad light a carvéd dolphin swam.
Above the antique mantel was displayed
As though a window gave upon the sylvan scene[7]
The change of Philomel, by the barbarous king[8]
So rudely forced; yet there the nightingale[9]
Filled all the desert with inviolable voice
And still she cried, and still the world pursues,
"Jug Jug" to dirty ears.
And other withered stumps of time
Were told upon the walls; staring forms
Leaned out, leaning, hushing the room enclosed.
Footsteps shuffled on the stair.
Under the firelight, under the brush, her hair
Spread out in fiery points
Glowed into words, then would be savagely still.

"My nerves are bad to-night. Yes, bad. Stay with me.
"Speak to me. Why do you never speak. Speak.
  "What are you thinking of? What thinking? What?
"I never know what you are thinking. Think."

I think we are in rats' alley[1]
Where the dead men lost their bones.

"What is that noise?"
                    The wind under the door.[2]
"What is that noise now? What is the wind doing?"
                    Nothing again nothing.

6. "Laquearia. V. *Aeneid,* I, 726: dependent lychni laquearibus aureis/Incensi, et noctem flammis funalia vincunt" [Eliot's note]. "Laquearia" are the panels of a coffered ceiling, and the two lines read: "Glowing lamps hang from the gold-paneled ceiling, and the torches conquer the darkness with their flames." They come from the description of the banquet hall in Dido's palace at Carthage, just after Dido has been inspired by Venus with the passion for Aeneas, her guest, which will end (as Cleopatra's passion for Antony was to end) in her suicide.

7. "Sylvan scene. V. Milton, *Paradise Lost,* IV, 140" [Eliot's note]. The phrase occurs in the description of Eden as it looks to Satan when he sees it for the first time.

8. "V. Ovid, *Metamorphoses,* VI, Philomela" [Eliot's note]. In Ovid's version of the myth, Tereus, king of Thrace, is married to Procne but falls in love with her sister, Philomela, whom he ravishes; he cuts out her tongue to silence her, but she weaves her story into an embroidered cloth. Procne avenges herself and her sister by murdering her child, Itys, and serving his flesh to his father at a banquet. The sisters are saved, as the maddened king pursues them, by being changed to birds: Procne into a swallow, Philomela into a nightingale.

9. "Cf. Part III, l. 204" [Eliot's note].

1. "Cf. Part III, l. 195" [Eliot's note].

2. "Cf. Webster: 'Is the wind in that door still?' " [Eliot's note], referring to John Webster's play, *The Devil's Law Case,* III.ii. 162.

"Do
"You know nothing? Do you see nothing? Do you remember
"Nothing?"

I remember
Those are pearls that were his eyes.[3]
"Are you alive, or not? Is there nothing in your head?"

But
O O O O that Shakespeherian Rag—
It's so elegant
So intelligent
"What shall I do now? What shall I do?"
"I shall rush out as I am, and walk the street
"With my hair down, so. What shall we do tomorrow?
"What shall we ever do?"
The hot water at ten.
And if it rains, a closed car at four.
And we shall play a game of chess,
Pressing lidless eyes and waiting for a knock upon the door.[4]

When Lil's husband got demobbed,° I said— *demobilized*
I didn't mince my words, I said to her myself,
HURRY UP PLEASE ITS TIME[5]
Now Albert's coming back, make yourself a bit smart.
He'll want to know what you done with that money he gave you
To get yourself some teeth. He did, I was there.
You have them all out, Lil, and get a nice set,
He said, I swear, I can't bear to look at you.
And no more can't I, I said, and think of poor Albert,
He's been in the army four years, he wants a good time,
And if you don't give it him, there's others will, I said.
Oh is there, she said. Something o' that, I said.
Then I'll know who to thank, she said, and give me a straight look.
HURRY UP PLEASE ITS TIME
If you don't like it you can get on with it, I said.
Others can pick and choose if you can't.
But if Albert makes off, it won't be for lack of telling.
You ought to be ashamed, I said, to look so antique.
(And her only thirty-one.)
I can't help it, she said, pulling a long face,
It's them pills I took, to bring it off, she said.
(She's had five already, and nearly died of young George.)
The chemist° said it would be all right, but I've never been the same. *druggist*
You *are* a proper fool, I said.
Well, if Albert won't leave you alone, there it is, I said,
What you get married for if you don't want children?
HURRY UP PLEASE ITS TIME
Well, that Sunday Albert was home, they had a hot gammon,° *smoked ham*
And they asked me in to dinner, to get the beauty of it hot—
HURRY UP PLEASE ITS TIME
HURRY UP PLEASE ITS TIME
Goonight Bill. Goonight Lou. Goonight May. Goonight.
Ta ta. Goonight. Goonight.
Good night, ladies, good night, sweet ladies, good night, good night.[6]

3. See Part I, line 48 and note.
4. "Cf. the game of chess in Middleton's *Women Beware Women*" [Eliot's note].
5. A typical injunction of a London bartender, telling his customers that it is closing-time.
6. Compare Ophelia's speech, *Hamlet*, IV.v. 71–72: "Good night, ladies, good night. Sweet ladies, good night, good night."

III. The Fire Sermon[7]

The river's tent is broken: the last fingers of leaf
Clutch and sink into the wet bank. The wind
Crosses the brown land, unheard. The nymphs are departed.
Sweet Thames, run softly, till I end my song.[8]
The river bears no empty bottles, sandwich papers,
Silk handkerchiefs, cardboard boxes, cigarette ends
Or other testimony of summer nights. The nymphs are departed.
And their friends, the loitering heirs of city directors;
Departed, have left no addresses.
By the waters of Leman I sat down and wept[9] . . .
Sweet Thames, run softly till I end my song,
Sweet Thames, run softly, for I speak not loud or long.
But at my back in a cold blast I hear[1]
The rattle of the bones, and chuckle spread from ear to ear.
A rat crept softly through the vegetation
Dragging its slimy belly on the bank
While I was fishing in the dull canal
On a winter evening round behind the gashouse
Musing upon the king my brother's wreck[2]
And on the king my father's death before him.
White bodies naked on the low damp ground
And bones cast in a little low dry garret,
Rattled by the rat's foot only, year to year.
But at my back from time to time I hear[3]
The sound of horns and motors, which shall bring[4]
Sweeney to Mrs. Porter in the spring.
O the moon shone bright on Mrs. Porter[5]
And on her daughter
They wash their feet in soda water
Et O ces voix d'enfants, chantant dans la coupole![6]

Twit twit twit
Jug jug jug jug jug jug

7. The title is that of the Buddha's Fire Sermon (see Eliot's note to line 308, below), in which he preached that "all things are on fire, * * * with the fire of passion, * * * with the fire of hatred, with the fire of infatuation; with birth, old age, death, sorrow, lamentation, misery, grief, and despair are they on fire," and that the disciple must conceive "an aversion for the eye," for all the senses, "for impressions received by the mind; and whatever sensation, pleasant, unpleasant, or indifferent, originates in dependence on impressions received by the mind," so that he may become divested of passion and hence be free and know that he is free and that "he is no more of this world."

8. "V. Spenser, *Prothalamion*" [Eliot's note]. The line is the refrain from Spenser's marriage-song, whose picture of "the silver-streaming Thames," its nymphs, and the London through which it flows are to be contrasted in detail with the same things as they are presented in Eliot's poem.

9. An echo of Psalm 137: "By the rivers of Babylon, there we sat down, yea, we wept, when we remembered Zion." Lac Léman is the Lake of Geneva, and *The Waste Land* is said to have been written at Lausanne, on its shore. *Leman* is also an archaic word for lover, mistress, or paramour.

1. Echoes Marvell's *To his Coy Mistress:* "But at my back I always hear/Time's winged chariot hurrying near."

2. "Cf. *The Tempest,* I, ii" [Eliot's note]. Ferdinand, in Shakespeare's play, just after hearing Ariel's song, "Come unto these yellow sands," and just before Ariel sings "Full fathom five thy father lies," the song inspired by the death by drowning of Ferdinand's father, describes himself as "sitting on a bank,/Weeping again the King my father's wreck./This music crept by me upon the waters."

3. "Cf. Marvell, *To His Coy Mistress*" [Eliot's note].

4. "Cf. Day, *Parliament of Bees:* "When of the sudden, listening, you shall hear,/A noise of horns and hunting, which shall bring/ Actaeon to Diana in the spring' " [Eliot's note]. The young Actaeon, discovering Diana bathing with her nymphs, was changed by the goddess to a stag, which her hounds set upon and killed.

5. "I do not know the origin of the ballad from which these lines are taken: it was reported to me from Sydney, Australia" [Eliot's note]. The ballad was popular with Australian soldiers in World War I. Sweeney (line 198) is the figure of vulgar, thoughtless sexual enterprise who figures in Eliot's *Sweeney among the Nightingales* and *Sweeney Agonistes.*

6. "V. Verlaine, *Parsifal*" [Eliot's note]. Quoted is the concluding line of Verlaine's sonnet (1886), which treats ironically Parsifal's conquering of some forms of fleshly temptation, only to be haunted—even in his purity—by others: "And, O those children's voices singing in the dome!"

So rudely forc'd.
Tereu[7]

Unreal City[8]
Under the brown fog of a winter noon
Mr. Eugenides, the Smyrna merchant
Unshaven, with a pocket full of currants
C.i.f. London: documents at sight,[9]
Asked me in demotic French[1]
To luncheon at the Cannon Street Hotel[2]
Followed by a weekend at the Metropole.

At the violet hour, when the eyes and back
Turn upward from the desk, when the human engine waits
Like a taxi throbbing waiting,
I Tiresias, though blind, throbbing between two lives,[3]
Old man with wrinkled female breasts, can see
At the violet hour, the evening hour that strives
Homeward, and brings the sailor home from sea,[4]
The typist home at teatime, clears her breakfast, lights
Her stove, and lays out food in tins.
Out of the window perilously spread
Her drying combinations touched by the sun's last rays,
On the divan are piled (at night her bed)
Stockings, slippers, camisoles, and stays.
I Tiresias, old man with wrinkled dugs
Perceived the scene, and foretold the rest—

7. These four lines reproduce the mode in which Elizabethan poets indicated the song of the nightingale, including "Tereu"—also a form of the name of Philomela's ravisher, Tereus. See Part II, lines 99–103.

8. See note to Part I, line 60.

9. "The currants were quoted at a price 'carriage and insurance free to London'; and the Bill of Lading etc. were to be handed to the buyer upon payment of the sight draft" [Eliot's note].

1. Here, simply "bad French."

2. Before the Second World War, a very large hotel in London's commercial district. The Metropole is probably the large hotel at Brighton, the beach-resort.

3. "Tiresias, although a mere spectator and not indeed a 'character,' is yet the most important personage in the poem, uniting all the rest. Just as the one-eyed merchant, seller of currants, melts into the Phoenician sailor, and the latter is not wholly distinct from Ferdinand Prince of Naples, so all the women are one woman, and the two sexes meet in Tiresias. What Tiresias *sees,* in fact, is the substance of the poem. The whole passage from Ovid is of great anthropological interest * * *" [Eliot's note]. Mythology offers three separate accounts of the reasons why Tiresias was blinded by a goddess and then granted a seer's power by Zeus. Ovid's version is contained in a passage (*Metamorphoses,* III.322 ff.) which Eliot's note cites in Latin, and which runs as follows in Golding's verse translation:

They say that Jove, disposed to mirth as he and Juno sat
A-drinking nectar after meat in sport and pleasant rate,
Did fall a-jesting with his wife, and said: "A greater pleasure
In Venus' games ye women have than men beyond all measure."
She answered, no. To try the truth, they both of them agree
The wise Tiresias in this case indifferent judge to be,
Who both the man's and woman's joys by trial understood,
For finding once two mighty snakes engend'ring in a wood,
He struck them overthwart the backs, by means whereof behold
(As strange a thing to be of truth as ever yet was told)
He being made a woman straight, seven winter livéd so.
The eighth he finding them again did say unto them tho:
"And if to strike ye have such power as for to turn their shape
That are the givers of the stripe, before you hence escape,
One stripe now shall I lend you more." He struck them as beforne
And straight returned his former shape in which he first was born.
Tiresias therefore being ta'en to judge this jesting strife,
Gave sentence on the side of Jove; the which the queen his wife
Did take a great deal more to heart than needed, and in spite
To wreak her teen upon her judge, bereft him of his sight;
But Jove (for to the gods it is unlawful to undo
The things which other of the gods by any means have do)
Did give him sight in things to come for loss of sight of eye,
And so his grievous punishment with honor did supply.

4. "This may not appear as exact as Sappho's lines, but I had in mind the 'longshore' or 'dory' fisherman, who returns at nightfall" [Eliot's note]. Sappho's poem (Number 120 in E. Diehl, *Anthologia Lyrica*), may be translated as follows: "Hesperus, all things you bring, as many as light-bringing morning has scattered abroad./You bring the sheep,/ You bring the goat, you bring the child to its mother."

I too awaited the expected guest.
He, the young man carbuncular,[5] arrives,
A small house agent's clerk, with one bold stare,
One of the low on whom assurance sits
As a silk hat on a Bradford[6] millionaire.
The time is now propitious, as he guesses,
The meal is ended, she is bored and tired,
Endeavors to engage her in caresses
Which still are unreproved, if undesired.
Flushed and decided, he assaults at once;
Exploring hands encounter no defense;
His vanity requires no response,
And makes a welcome of indifference.
(And I Tiresias have foresuffered all
Enacted on this same divan or bed;
I who have sat by Thebes below the wall[7]
And walked among the lowest of the dead.)
Bestows one final patronizing kiss,
And gropes his way, finding the stairs unlit . . .

She turns and looks a moment in the glass,
Hardly aware of her departed lover;
Her brain allows one half-formed thought to pass:
"Well now that's done: and I'm glad it's over."
When lovely woman stoops to folly and[8]
Paces about her room again, alone,
She smoothes her hair with automatic hand,
And puts a record on the gramophone.

"This music crept by me upon the waters"[9]
And along the Strand, up Queen Victoria Street.
O City city, I can sometimes hear
Beside a public bar in Lower Thames Street,
The pleasant whining of a mandolin
And a clatter and a chatter from within
Where fishmen lounge at noon: where the walls
Of Magnus Martyr[1] hold
Inexplicable splendor of Ionian white and gold.

The river sweats[2]
Oil and tar
The barges drift
With the turning tide

5. Afflicted with carbuncles, a boil-like inflammation.
6. A manufacturing town in the English Midlands.
7. The blind Theban seer (see note to line 218 above) was supposed to have lived three times as long as the average man, and his prophecies enter the lives of many legendary citizens of Thebes, including those of Oedipus and his family.
8. "V. Goldsmith, the song in *The Vicar of Wakefield*" [Eliot's note]. ("When lovely woman stoops to folly/And finds too late that men betray/What charm can soothe her melancholy,/What art can wash her guilt away?/The only art her guilt to cover,/To hide her shame from every eye,/To give repentance to her lover/And wring his bosom —is to die.")
9. "V. *The Tempest,* as above" [Eliot's note]. See note to line 191 above.
1. "The interior of St. Magnus Martyr is to my mind one of the finest among Wren's interiors. See *The Proposed Demolition of Nineteen City Churches:* (P. S. King & Son, Ltd.)" [Eliot's note]. Again in this passage (lines 257–265) it is the busy commercial East End of London that is evoked. The church of St. Magnus Martyr stands just below London Bridge, in Lower Thames Street, which skirts the north bank of the Thames between London Bridge and the Tower of London. The phrase "O City city" apostrophizes both the *City* of London, a relatively small area of the metropolis which contains its business wealth, and the generic total city.
2. "The song of the (three) Thames-daughters begins here. From line 292 to 306 inclusive they speak in turn. V. *Götterdämmerung,* III,i: the Rhine-daughters" [Eliot's note]. Lines 277–278 repeat the refrain of the Rhine-maidens in Wagner's music-drama.

Red sails
Wide
To leeward, swing on the heavy spar.
The barges wash
Drifting logs
Down Greenwich reach
Past the Isle of Dogs.[3]
Weialala leia
Wallala leialala

Elizabeth and Leicester[4]
Beating oars
The stern was formed
A gilded shell
Red and gold
The brisk swell
Rippled both shores
Southwest wind
Carried down stream
The peal of bells
White towers
Weialala leia
Wallala leialala

"Trams and dusty trees.
Highbury bore me.[5] Richmond and Kew
Undid me. By Richmond I raised my knees
Supine on the floor of a narrow canoe."

"My feet are at Moorgate,[6] and my heart
Under my feet. After the event
He wept. He promised 'a new start.'
I made no comment. What should I resent?"

"On Margate Sands.[7]
I can connect
Nothing with nothing.
The broken fingernails of dirty hands.
My people humble people who expect
Nothing."
la la

To Carthage then I came[8]

3. A tongue of land extending into the Thames opposite Greenwich.
4. "V. Froude, [*Reign of*] *Elizabeth,* Vol. I, ch. iv, letter of De Quadra to Philip of Spain: 'In the afternoon we were in a barge, watching the games on the river. (The queen) was alone with the Lord Robert and myself on the poop, when they began to talk nonsense, and went so far that Lord Robert at last said, as I was on the spot there was no reason why they should not be married if the queen pleased' " [Eliot's note]. Sir Robert Dudley (1532?–88), Earl of Leicester, was a favorite of the queen.
5. "Cf. Purgatorio, V, 133: Ricorditi di me, che son la Pia;/Siena mi fe', disfecemi Maremma" [Eliot's note]. Pia de' Tolomei, whom Dante encounters in Purgatory, after telling her story, says: "Pray, when you have returned to the world and are rested from your long journey, * * * remember me, who am la Pia; Siena made me, the Maremma unmade me"; she had been shut up by her husband in one of his castles, La Pietra in Maremma, and was there done to death by his orders. Highbury is a residential suburb in North London; Richmond is the object of a pleasant excursion up the river from London; Kew is another excursion point, chiefly because of its botanical gardens.
6. A humble district in East London.
7. A beach resort in Kent, where the Thames Estuary broadens into the Channel.
8. "V. St. Augustine's *Confessions:* 'to Carthage then I came, where a cauldron of unholy loves sang all about mine ears' " [Eliot's note].

Burning burning burning burning[9]
O Lord Thou pluckest me out[1]
O Lord Thou pluckest

burning

IV. Death by Water

Phlebas the Phoenician, a fortnight dead,
Forgot the cry of gulls, and the deep sea swell
And the profit and loss.
A current under sea
Picked his bones in whispers. As he rose and fell
He passed the stages of his age and youth
Entering the whirlpool.
Gentile or Jew
O you who turn the wheel and look to windward,
Consider Phlebas, who was once handsome and tall as you.

V. What the Thunder Said[2]

After the torchlight red on sweaty faces
After the frosty silence in the gardens
After the agony in stony places
The shouting and the crying
Prison and palace and reverberation
Of thunder of spring over distant mountains
He who was living is now dead
We who were living are now dying
With a little patience

Here is no water but only rock
Rock and no water and the sandy road
The road winding above among the mountains
Which are mountains of rock without water
If there were water we should stop and drink
Amongst the rock one cannot stop or think
Sweat is dry and feet are in the sand
If there were only water amongst the rock
Dead mountain mouth of carious teeth that cannot spit
Here one can neither stand nor lie nor sit
There is not even silence in the mountains
But dry sterile thunder without rain
There is not even solitude in the mountains
But red sullen faces sneer and snarl
From doors of mudcracked houses
If there were water
And no rock
If there were rock
And also water
And water
A spring

9. "The complete text of the Buddha's Fire Sermon (which corresponds in importance to the Sermon on the Mount) from which these words are taken, will be found translated in the late Henry Clarke Warren's *Buddhism in Translation* (Harvard Oriental Series). Mr. Warren was one of the great pioneers of Buddhist studies in the Occident" [Eliot's note].

1. "From St. Augustine's *Confessions* again. The collocation of these two representatives of eastern and western asceticism, as the culmination of this part of the poem, is not an accident" [Eliot's note].

2. "In the first part of Part V three themes are employed: the journey to Emmaus, the approach to the Chapel Perilous (see Miss Weston's book) and the present decay of eastern Europe" [Eliot's note]. For the title of Part V, see note to line 401, below.

A pool among the rock
If there were the sound of water only
Not the cicada
And dry grass singing
But sound of water over a rock
Where the hermit-thrush sings in the pine trees[3]
Drip drop drip drop drop drop drop
But there is no water

Who is the third who walks always beside you?
When I count, there are only you and I together[4]
But when I look ahead up the white road
There is always another one walking beside you
Gliding wrapt in a brown mantle, hooded
I do not know whether a man or a woman
—But who is that on the other side of you?

What is that sound high in the air[5]
Murmur of maternal lamentation
Who are those hooded hordes swarming
Over endless plains, stumbling in cracked earth
Ringed by the flat horizon only
What is the city over the mountains
Cracks and reforms and bursts in the violet air
Falling towers
Jerusalem Athens Alexandria
Vienna London
Unreal

A woman drew her long black hair out tight
And fiddled whisper music on those strings
And bats with baby faces in the violet light
Whistled, and beat their wings
And crawled head downward down a blackened wall
And upside down in air were towers
Tolling reminiscent bells, that kept the hours
And voices singing out of empty cisterns and exhausted wells.

In this decayed hole among the mountains
In the faint moonlight, the grass is singing
Over the tumbled graves, about the chapel
There is the empty chapel, only the wind's home.
It has no windows, and the door swings,
Dry bones can harm no one.
Only a cock stood on the rooftree
Co co rico co co rico
In a flash of lightning. Then a damp gust
Bringing rain

3. "This is * * * the hermit-thrush which I have heard in Quebec Province * * * Its 'water-dripping song' is justly celebrated" [Eliot's note].

4. "The following lines were stimulated by the account of one of the Antarctic expeditions (I forget which, but I think one of Shackleton's): it was related that the party of explorers, at the extremity of their strength, had the constant delusion that there was *one more member* than could actually be counted" [Eliot's note]. And compare at this point the journey of two of Christ's disciples to Emmaus, after the Crucifixion; on the way "they talked together of all these things which had happened. And * * * while they communed together and reasoned, Jesus himself drew near and went with them. But their eyes were holden that they should not know him." Luke xxiv.13–16.

5. Eliot's note to lines 366–376 quotes a passage from Hermann Hesse's *Blick ins Chaos* (*A Glimpse into Chaos*) which may be translated as follows: "Already half Europe, already at least half of Eastern Europe is on the road to Chaos, drives drunken in holy madness along the abyss and sings the while, sings drunk and hymn-like as Dmitri Karamazov sang. The bourgeois laughs, offended, at these songs, the saint and the prophet hear them with tears."

Ganga[6] was sunken, and the limp leaves
Waited for rain, while the black clouds
Gathered far distant, over Himavant.
The jungle crouched, humped in silence.
Then spoke the thunder
DA
Datta:[7] what have we given?
My friend, blood shaking my heart
The awful daring of a moment's surrender
Which an age of prudence can never retract
By this, and this only, we have existed
Which is not to be found in our obituaries
Or in memories draped by the beneficent spider[8]
Or under seals broken by the lean solicitor
In our empty rooms
DA
Dayadhvam: I have heard the key[9]
Turn in the door once and turn once only
We think of the key, each in his prison
Thinking of the key, each confirms a prison
Only at nightfall, ethereal rumors
Revive for a moment a broken Coriolanus[1]
DA
Damyata: The boat responded
Gaily, to the hand expert with sail and oar
The sea was calm, your heart would have responded
Gaily, when invited, beating obedient
To controlling hands

I sat upon the shore
Fishing, with the arid plain behind me[2]
Shall I at least set my lands in order?
London Bridge is falling down falling down falling down
Poi s'ascose nel foco che gli affina[3]
Quando fiam uti chelidon[4]—O swallow swallow

6. The River Ganges. Himavant is a peak in the Himalayas.

7. " 'Datta, dayadhvam, damyata' (Give, sympathize, control). The fable of the meaning of the Thunder is found in the *Brihadaranyaka—Upanishad,* 5, [ii] * * * [Eliot's note]. The relevant chapter of this Upanishad tells how "the three-fold offspring of Prajápati, gods, men and Asuras [demons]" in turn asked their father to tell them their duty. He replies with the one letter *Da,* which each of the three interprets differently. The gods say, " 'We do comprehend. Restrain your desires, hast thou said to us.' " The men: " 'Be liberal, hast thou said to us.' " The Asuras: " 'Be clement, hast thou said to us.' " In each case, Prajápati answers, " 'Om! you have fully comprehended.' The same is repeated by a divine voice with the force of thunder, *viz.,* the syllables *Da, Da, Da,* meaning, Be restrained (*da*myata), be liberal (*da*tta), and be clement (*da*yadhvam).

8. "Cf. Webster, *The White Devil,* V, vi: '. . . they'll remarry/Ere the worm pierce your winding-sheet, ere the spider/Make a thin curtain for your epitaphs' " [Eliot's note].

9. "Cf. *Inferno,* XXXIII, 46: 'ed io sentii chiavar l'uscio di sotto/ all' orribile torre.' Also F. H. Bradley, *Appearance and Reality,* p. 346. 'My external sensations are no less private to myself than are my thoughts or my feelings. In either case my experience falls within my own circle, a circle closed on the outside; and, with all its elements alike, every sphere is opaque to the others which surround it. . . . In brief, regarded as an existence which appears in a soul, the whole world for each is peculiar and private to that soul' " [Eliot's note]. The lines from Dante are from the section of the *Inferno* in which Count Ugolino of Pisa recounts his imprisonment with his little sons in the Hunger Tower, where they were left to starve: "and I heard them turning the key in the door of the dreadful tower, below."

1. The Roman hero of Shakespeare's tragedy, *Coriolanus,* the symbol of a truly great man whose greatness is tragically destroyed when he seeks to be utterly self-sufficient.

2. "V. Weston: *From Ritual to Romance;* chapter on the Fisher King" [Eliot's note].

3. "V. *Purgatorio,* XXVI, 148. ' "Ara vos prec per aquella valor/que vos guida al som de l'escalina,/sovegna vos a temps de ma dolor."/Poi s'ascose nel foco che gli affina' " [Eliot's note]. Arnaut Daniel, the late-12th-century poet, encountered among the lustful in Purgatory, after recounting his story, concludes with the lines quoted: " 'And so I pray you, by that Virtue which guides you to the top of the stair, be reminded in time of my pain.' Then he hid himself in the fire that purifies them."

4. "V. *Pervigilium Veneris.* Cf. Philomela in Parts I and II" [Eliot's note]. The quoted line ("When shall I become as the swallow?") is from a late Latin poem (*The Vigil of Venus*) celebrating the spring festival of Venus. It alludes to the Procne-Philomela-Tereus myth, but makes Philomela the swallow.

Le Prince d'Aquitaine à la tour abolie[5]
These fragments I have shored against my ruins
Why then Ile fit you. Hieronymo's mad againe.[6]
Datta. Dayadhvam. Damyata.
                Shantih shantih shantih[7]

1922

From FOUR QUARTETS

The Dry Salvages[8]

1

I do not know much about gods; but I think that the river[9]
Is a strong brown god—sullen, untamed and intractable,
Patient to some degree, at first recognized as a frontier;
Useful, untrustworthy, as a conveyor of commerce;
Then only a problem confronting the builder of bridges.
The problem once solved, the brown god is almost forgotten
By the dwellers in cities—ever, however, implacable,
Keeping his seasons and rages, destroyer, reminder
Of what men choose to forget. Unhonored, unpropitiated
By worshipers of the machine, but waiting, watching and waiting.
His rhythm was present in the nursery bedroom,
In the rank ailanthus[1] of the April dooryard,
In the smell of grapes on the autumn table,
And the evening circle in the winter gaslight.

The river is within us, the sea is all about us;
The sea is the land's edge also, the granite
Into which it reaches, the beaches where it tosses
Its hints of earlier and other creation:
The starfish, the hermit crab, the whale's backbone;
The pools where it offers to our curiosity
The more delicate algae and the sea anemone.
It tosses up our losses, the torn seine,° *fishing-net*
The shattered lobsterpot, the broken oar
And the gear of foreign dead men. The sea has many voices,
Many gods and many voices.
                    The salt is on the briar rose,
The fog is in the fir trees.
                    The sea howl
And the sea yelp, are different voices
Often together heard; the whine in the rigging,
The menace and caress of wave that breaks on water,
The distant rote in the granite teeth,
And the wailing warning from the approaching headland
Are all sea voices, and the heaving groaner

5. "V. Gérard de Nerval, Sonnet *El Desdichado*" [Eliot's note]. The poem (*The Disinherited*) describes "the man of shadows,—the widower,—the unconsoled,/The prince of Aquitania in the abandoned tower:/My only star is dead,—and my starred lute/Carries as its emblem the black sun of Melancholy * * *"
6. "V. Kyd's *Spanish Tragedy*" [Eliot's note]. The subtitle of Kyd's *Spanish Tragedy* (1594) is *Hieronymo's Mad Againe.* Hieronymo, driven mad by his son's death, "fits" the parts in a court masque so that in the course of it he kills his son's murderers.
7. "Shantih. Repeated as here, a formal ending to an Upanishad. 'The Peace which passeth understanding' is our nearest equivalent to this word" [Eliot's note].
8. Eliot's prefatory note to the poem is as follows: "(The Dry Salvages—presumably *les trois sauvages*—is a small group of rocks, with a beacon, off the N.E. coast of Cape Ann, Massachusetts. *Salvages* is pronounced to rhyme with *assuages. Groaner:* a whistling buoy)." The poem was published as a separate pamphlet in 1941 and took its place as the third of the *Four Quartets* in 1943.
9. The Mississippi. Eliot was born in St. Louis, Mo., and grew up there.
1. A large East Indian tree, cultivated in Europe and America for shade: "rank" because of its vigorous growth.

Rounded homewards,[2] and the seagull:
And under the oppression of the silent fog
The tolling bell
Measures time not our time, rung by the unhurried
Ground swell,[3] a time
Older than the time of chronometers, older
Than time counted by anxious worried women
Lying awake, calculating the future,
Trying to unweave, unwind, unravel
And piece together the past and the future,
Between midnight and dawn, when the past is all deception,
The future futureless, before the morning watch
When time stops and time is never ending;
And the ground swell, that is and was from the beginning,
Clangs
The bell.

2

Where is there an end of it, the soundless wailing,
The silent withering of autumn flowers
Dropping their petals and remaining motionless;
Where is there an end to the drifting wreckage,
The prayer of the bone on the beach, the unprayable
Prayer at the calamitous annunciation?[4]

There is no end, but addition: the trailing
Consequence of further days and hours,
While emotion takes to itself the emotionless
Years of living among the breakage
Of what was believed in as the most reliable—
And therefore the fittest for renunciation.

There is the final addition, the failing
Pride or resentment at failing powers,
The unattached devotion which might pass for devotionless,
In a drifting boat with a slow leakage,
The silent listening to the undeniable
Clamor of the bell of the last annunciation.

Where is the end of them, the fishermen sailing
Into the wind's tail, where the fog cowers?
We cannot think of a time that is oceanless
Or of an ocean not littered with wastage
Or of a future that is not liable
Like the past, to have no destination.

We have to think of them as forever baling,
Setting and hauling, while the North East lowers
Over shallow banks unchanging and erosionless
Or drawing their money, drying sails at dockage;
Not as making a trip that will be unpayable
For a haul that will not bear examination.

There is no end of it, the voiceless wailing,
No end to the withering of withered flowers,

2. I.e., the buoy is rounded by a ship on its way homewards.

3. Broad, deep swell of the ocean, caused by continued storm.

4. Perhaps meaning that when the annunciation is of calamity—of imminent death—it is no longer possible to pray.

To the movement of pain that is painless and motionless,
To the drift of the sea and the drifting wreckage,
The bone's prayer to Death its God. Only the hardly, barely prayable
Prayer of the one Annunciation.[5]

It seems, as one becomes older,
That the past has another pattern, and ceases to be a mere sequence—
Or even development: the latter a partial fallacy,
Encouraged by superficial notions of evolution,
Which becomes, in the popular mind, a means of disowning the past.
The moments of happiness—not the sense of well-being,
Fruition, fulfilment, security or affection,
Or even a very good dinner, but the sudden illumination—
We had the experience but missed the meaning,
And approach to the meaning restores the experience
In a different form, beyond any meaning
We can assign to happiness. I have said before
That the past experience revived in the meaning
Is not the experience of one life only
But of many generations—not forgetting
Something that is probably quite ineffable:
The backward look behind the assurance
Of recorded history, the backward half-look
Over the shoulder, towards the primitive terror.
Now, we come to discover that the moments of agony
(Whether, or not, due to misunderstanding,
Having hoped for the wrong things or dreaded the wrong things,
Is not in question) are likewise permanent
With such permanence as time has. We appreciate this better
In the agony of others, nearly experienced,
Involving ourselves, than in our own.
For our own past is covered by the currents of action,
But the torment of others remains an experience
Unqualified, unworn by subsequent attrition.
People change, and smile: but the agony abides.
Time the destroyer is time the preserver,
Like the river with its cargo of dead Negroes, cows and chicken coops,
The bitter apple and the bite in the apple.
And the ragged rock in the restless waters,
Waves wash over it, fogs conceal it;
On a halcyon day[6] it is merely a monument,
In navigable weather it is always a seamark
To lay a course by: but in the somber season
Or the sudden fury, is what it always was.

3

I sometimes wonder if that is what Krishna[7] meant—
Among other things—or one way of putting the same thing:
That the future is a faded song, a Royal Rose or a lavender spray
Of wistful regret for those who are not yet here to regret,
Pressed between yellow leaves of a book that has never been opened.
And the way up is the way down,[8] the way forward is the way back.

5. The submissive prayer made by Mary at the Annunciation by the angel that she is to become the mother of Jesus: "Behold the handmaid of the Lord; be it unto me according to thy word." See Luke i.30–38.
6. I.e., a calm day.
7. A Hindu god, called the Preserver; his teachings are preserved in the *Baghavad Gita* ("Song of the Blessed One"), which forms a part of the Hindu epic of the *Mahabharata*, and is said to be to Hindus what the Bible is to Christians, the Koran to Muslims.
8. The first of the *Four Quartets, Burnt Norton,* bears two epigraphs from the pre-Socratic philosopher Heraclitus: one of them is "The way up and the way down are one and the same."

You cannot face it steadily, but this thing is sure,
That time is no healer: the patient is no longer here.
When the train starts, and the passengers are settled
To fruit, periodicals and business letters
(And those who saw them off have left the platform)
Their faces relax from grief into relief,
To the sleepy rhythm of a hundred hours.
Fare forward, travelers! not escaping from the past
Into different lives, or into any future;
You are not the same people who left that station
Or who will arrive at any terminus,
While the narrowing rails slide together behind you;
And on the deck of the drumming liner
Watching the furrow that widens behind you,
You shall not think "the past is finished"
Or "the future is before us."
At nightfall, in the rigging and the aerial,
Is a voice descanting[9] (though not to the ear,
The murmuring shell of time, and not in any language)
"Fare forward, you who think that you are voyaging;
You are not those who saw the harbor
Receding, or those who will disembark.
Here between the hither and the farther shore
While time is withdrawn, consider the future
And the past with an equal mind.
At the moment which is not of action or inaction
You can receive this: 'on whatever sphere of being
The mind of a man may be intent
At the time of death'[1]—that is the one action
(And the time of death is every moment)
Which shall fructify in the lives of others:
And do not think of the fruit of action.
Fare forward.
O voyagers, O seamen,
You who come to port, and you whose bodies
Will suffer the trial and judgment of the sea,
Or whatever event, this is your real destination."
So Krishna, as when he admonished Arjuna
On the field of battle.
Not fare well,
But fare forward, voyagers.

4

Lady,[2] whose shrine stands on the promontory,
Pray for all those who are in ships, those
Whose business has to do with fish, and
Those concerned with every lawful traffic
And those who conduct them.

Repeat a prayer also on behalf of
Women who have seen their sons or husbands
Setting forth, and not returning:

9. Holding forth on a subject.
1. The quoted passage comes from the *Bag-havad-Gita*. Arjuna, the hero of the poem, has hesitated to fight, and Krishna says: "Whosoever at the time of death thinks only of Me, and thinking thus leaves the body and goes forth, assuredly he will know Me./ On whatever sphere of being the mind of a man may be intent at the time of death, thither will he go./ Therefore meditate always on Me, and fight; if thy mind and thy reason be fixed on Me, to Me shalt thou surely come" [tr. by Shri Purohit Swāmi].
2. The Virgin Mary.

Figlia del tuo figlio,[3]
Queen of Heaven.

Also pray for those who were in ships, and
Ended their voyage on the sand, in the sea's lips
Or in the dark throat which will not reject them
Or wherever cannot reach them the sound of the sea bell's
Perpetual angelus.[4]

5

To communicate with Mars, converse with spirits,
To report the behavior of the sea monster,
Describe the horoscope, haruspicate or scry,[5]
Observe disease in signatures, evoke
Biography from the wrinkles of the palm
And tragedy from fingers; release omens
By sortilege,[6] or tea leaves, riddle the inevitable
With playing cards, fiddle with pentagrams[7]
Or barbituric acids, or dissect
The recurrent image into pre-conscious terrors—
To explore the womb, or tomb, or dreams; all these are usual
Pastimes and drugs, and features of the press:
And always will be, some of them especially
When there is distress of nations and perplexity
Whether on the shores of Asia, or in the Edgware Road.[8]
Men's curiosity searches past and future
And clings to that dimension. But to apprehend
The point of intersection of the timeless
With time, is an occupation for the saint—
No occupation either, but something given
And taken, in a lifetime's death in love,
Ardor and selflessness and self-surrender.
For most of us, there is only the unattended
Moment, the moment in and out of time,
The distraction fit, lost in a shaft of sunlight,
The wild thyme[9] unseen, or the winter lightning
Or the waterfall, or music heard so deeply
That it is not heard at all, but you are the music
While the music lasts. These are only hints and guesses,
Hints followed by guesses; and the rest
Is prayer, observance, discipline, thought and action.
The hint half guessed, the gift half understood, is Incarnation.
Here the impossible union
Of spheres of existence is actual,
Here the past and future
Are conquered, and reconciled,
Where action were otherwise movement
Of that which is only moved
And has in it no source of movement—

3. "The daughter of Thy Son." From St. Bernard's prayer to the Virgin in Dante, *Paradiso,* XXXIII.1.
4. A devotion commemorating the Incarnation, so called from its first word (*"Angelus domini nuntiavit Mariae,"* "The angel of the lord announced to Mary"); it is repeated by Roman Catholics at morning, noon, and sunset, at the sound of a bell.
5. A horoscope foretells the future from the positions of the planets at a given time. To *haruspicate* is to interpret the will of the gods by examining the entrails of sacrificed birds or animals. To *scry* is to see visions in a crystal.
6. Divination by drawing lots.
7. Five-pointed diagrams containing figures and symbols used in divination.
8. A busy, undistinguished street in London.
9. Aromatic herb.

Driven by daemonic, chthonic[1]
Powers. And right action is freedom
From past and future also.
For most of us, this is the aim
Never here to be realized;
Who are only undefeated
Because we have gone on trying;
We, content at the last
If our temporal reversion nourish
(Not too far from the yew-tree)[2]
The life of significant soil.

1941

JOHN CROWE RANSOM (1888–1974)

Bells for John Whiteside's Daughter

There was such speed in her little body,
And such lightness in her footfall,
It is no wonder her brown study
Astonishes us all.

Her wars were bruited in our high window.
We looked among orchard trees and beyond
Where she took arms against her shadow,
Or harried unto the pond

The lazy geese, like a snow cloud
Dripping their snow on the green grass,
Tricking and stopping, sleepy and proud,
Who cried in goose, Alas,

For the tireless heart within the little
Lady with rod that made them rise
From their noon apple-dreams and scuttle
Goose-fashion under the skies!

But now go the bells, and we are ready,
In one house we are sternly stopped
To say we are vexed at her brown study,
Lying so primly propped.

1924

Piazza[1] Piece

—I am a gentleman in a dustcoat trying
To make you hear. Your ears are soft and small
And listen to an old man not at all,

1. Sprung from the earth, or from the underworld.
2. Throughout the *Four Quartets*, the yew-tree is a recurrent symbol for death, variously counterpointed or combined with the rose, a symbol of life.

1. Porch.

They want the young men's whispering and sighing.
But see the roses on your trellis dying
And hear the spectral singing of the moon;
For I must have my lovely lady soon,
I am a gentleman in a dustcoat trying.

—I am a lady young in beauty waiting
Until my truelove comes, and then we kiss.
But what gray man among the vines is this
Whose words are dry and faint as in a dream?
Back from my trellis, Sir, before I scream!
I am a lady young in beauty waiting.

1925 1927

Janet Waking

Beautifully Janet slept
Till it was deeply morning. She woke then
And thought about her dainty-feathered hen,
To see how it had kept.

One kiss she gave her mother,
Only a small one gave she to her daddy
Who would have kissed each curl of his shining baby;
No kiss at all for her brother.

"Old Chucky, old Chucky!" she cried,
Running across the world upon the grass
To Chucky's house, and listening. But alas,
Her Chucky had died.

It was a transmogrifying bee
Came droning down on Chucky's old bald head
And sat and put the poison. It scarcely bled,
But how exceedingly

And purply did the knot
Swell with the venom and communicate
Its rigor! Now the poor comb stood up straight
But Chucky did not.

So there was Janet
Kneeling on the wet grass, crying her brown hen
(Translated far beyond the daughters of men)
To rise and walk upon it.

And weeping fast as she had breath
Janet implored us, "Wake her from her sleep!"
And would not be instructed in how deep
Was the forgetful kingdom of death.

1926 1927

ISAAC ROSENBERG
(1890–1918)

Break of Day in the Trenches

The darkness crumbles away.
It is the same old druid[1] Time as ever,
Only a live thing leaps my hand,
A queer sardonic rat,
As I pull the parapet's[2] poppy
To stick behind my ear.
Droll rat, they would shoot you if they knew
Your cosmopolitan sympathies.
Now you have touched this English hand
You will do the same to a German
Soon, no doubt, if it be your pleasure
To cross the sleeping green between.
It seems you inwardly grin as you pass
Strong eyes, fine limbs, haughty athletes,
Less chanced than you for life,
Bonds to the whims of murder,
Sprawled in the bowels of the earth,
The torn fields of France.
What do you see in our eyes
At the shrieking iron and flame
Hurled through still heavens?
What quaver—what heart aghast?
Poppies whose roots are in man's veins
Drop, and are ever dropping;
But mine in my ear is safe—
Just a little white with the dust.

1922

Louse Hunting

Nudes—stark and glistening,
Yelling in lurid glee. Grinning faces
And raging limbs
Whirl over the floor one fire.
For a shirt verminously busy
Yon soldier tore from his throat, with oaths
Godhead might shrink at, but not the lice.
And soon the shirt was aflare
Over the candle he'd lit while we lay.

Then we all sprang up and stript
To hunt the verminous brood.
Soon like a demons' pantomime
The place was raging.

1. Member of an ancient Celtic order of priest-magicians.

2. Wall protecting a trench in World War I.

See the silhouettes agape,
See the gibbering shadows
Mixed with the battled arms on the wall.
See gargantuan hooked fingers
Pluck in supreme flesh
To smutch supreme littleness.
See the merry limbs in hot Highland fling
Because some wizard vermin
Charmed from the quiet this revel
When our ears were half lulled
By the dark music
Blown from Sleep's trumpet.

1922

HUGH MacDIARMID (C. M. GRIEVE) (1892–1978)

The Watergaw

Ae weet forenicht i' the yow-trummle[1]
I saw yon antrin° thing, *rare*
A watergaw[2] wi' its chitterin' licht
Ayont the on-ding;° *onset*
An' I thocht o' the last wild look ye gied
Afore ye deed!

There was nae reek i' the laverock's hoose[3]
That nicht—an' nane i' mine;
But I hae thocht o' that foolish licht
Ever sin' syne;
An' I think that mebbe at last I ken
What your look meant then.

1925

Empty Vessel[4]

I met ayont the cairney° *stone heap*
A lass wi' tousie hair
Singin' till a bairnie
That was nae langer there.

Wunds° wi' warlds to swing *winds*
Dinna sing sae sweet,
The licht° that bends owre a'thing° *light/over everything*
Is less ta'en up wi't.

1926

1. A wet early evening in the cold weather after sheepshearing." (Glosses for this poem from *Hugh MacDiarmid: Selected Poems,* selected and ed. by David Craig and John Manson, 1970.)
2. "An indistinct rainbow with its shivering light."
3. "There was no smoke in the lark's house."
4. The poem is a reworking of a folk song, the second stanza of which runs:
I met ayont the Cairnie
Jenny Nettles, Jenny Nettles
Singing til her bairnie
Robin Rattles bastart . . .

In the Children's Hospital

Does it matter? Losing your legs?—SIEGFRIED SASSOON

Now let the legless boy show the great lady
How well he can manage his crutches.
It doesn't matter though the Sister objects,
"He's not used to them yet," when such is
The will of the Princess. Come, Tommy,
Try a few desperate steps through the ward.
Then the hand of Royalty will pat your head
And life suddenly cease to be hard.
For a couple of legs are surely no miss
When the loss leads to such an honor as this!
One knows, when one sees how jealous the rest
Of the children are, it's been all for the best!—
But would the sound of your sticks on the floor
Thundered in her skull for evermore!

1935

Crystals Like Blood

I remember how, long ago, I found
Crystals like blood in a broken stone.

I picked up a broken chunk of bed-rock
And turned it this way and that,
It was heavier than one would have expected
From its size. One face was caked
With brown limestone. But the rest
Was a hard greenish-gray quartz-like stone
Faintly dappled with darker shadows,
And in this quartz ran veins and beads
Of bright magenta.

And I remember how later on I saw
How mercury is extracted from cinnebar
—The double ring of iron piledrivers
Like the multiple legs of a fantastically symmetrical spider
Rising and falling with monotonous precision,
Marching round in an endless circle
And pounding up and down with a tireless, thunderous force,
While, beyond, another conveyor drew the crumbled ore
From the bottom and raised it to an opening high
In the side of a gigantic gray-white kiln.

So I remember how mercury is got
When I contrast my living memory of you
And your dear body rotting here in the clay
—And feel once again released in me
The bright torrents of felicity, naturalness, and faith
My treadmill memory draws from you yet.

1949

ARCHIBALD MacLEISH
(1892–1982)

Ars Poetica[1]

A poem should be palpable and mute
As a globed fruit,

Dumb
As old medallions to the thumb,

Silent as the sleeve-worn stone
Of casement ledges where the moss has grown—

A poem should be wordless
As the flight of birds.

A poem should be motionless in time
As the moon climbs,

Leaving, as the moon releases
Twig by twig the night-entangled trees,

Leaving, as the moon behind the winter leaves,
Memory by memory the mind—

A poem should be motionless in time
As the moon climbs.

A poem should be equal to:
Not true.

For all the history of grief
An empty doorway and a maple leaf.

For love
The leaning grasses and two lights above the sea—

A poem should not mean
But be.

1926

You, Andrew Marvell[2]

And here face down beneath the sun
And here upon earth's noonward height
To feel the always coming on
The always rising of the night

1. "The Art of Poetry," title of a poetical treatise by the Roman poet Horace (65–8 B.C.).
2. Andrew Marvell (1621–1678) wrote *To His Coy Mistress,* the poem to which MacLeish specifically alludes.

To feel creep up the curving east
The earthy chill of dusk and slow
Upon those under lands the vast
And ever climbing shadow grow

And strange at Ecbatan[3] the trees
Take leaf by leaf the evening strange
The flooding dark about their knees
The mountains over Persia change

And now at Kermanshah the gate
Dark empty and the withered grass
And through the twilight now the late
Few travelers in the westward pass

And Baghdad darken and the bridge
Across the silent river gone
And through Arabia the edge
Of evening widen and steal on

And deepen on Palmyra's street
The wheel rut in the ruined stone
And Lebanon fade out and Crete
High through the clouds and overblown

And over Sicily the air
Still flashing with the landward gulls
And loom and slowly disappear
The sails above the shadowy hulls

And Spain go under and the shore
Of Africa the gilded sand
And evening vanish and no more
The low pale light across that land

Nor now the long light on the sea
And here face downward in the sun
To feel how swift how secretly
The shadow of the night comes on. . . .

1930

Calypso's Island[4]

I know very well, goddess, she is not beautiful
As you are: could not be. She is a woman,
Mortal, subject to the chances: duty of

Childbed, sorrow that changes cheeks, the tomb—
For unlike you she will grow gray, grow older,
Gray and older, sleep in that small room.

She is not beautiful as you, O golden!
You are immortal and will never change
And can make me immortal also, fold

3. The poet's thoughts, following the daily path of the sun, move westward, from Ecbatana, once the capital of Media Magna (part of Persia), on to Kermanshah, Baghdad, Palmyra, Sicily, and so on.

4. Where the hero of Homer's *Odyssey* tarried with the goddess Calypso for seven years before returning to his kingdom of Ithaca and his faithful wife, Penelope.

Your garment round me, make me whole and strange
As those who live forever, not the while
That we live, keep me from those dogging dangers—

Ships and the wars—in this green, far-off island,
Silent of all but sea's eternal sound
Or sea-pine's when the lull of surf is silent.

Goddess, I know how excellent this ground,
What charmed contentment of the removed heart
The bees make in the lavender where pounding

Surf sounds far off and the bird that darts
Darts through its own eternity of light,
Motionless in motion, and the startled

Hare is startled into stone, the fly
Forever golden in the flickering glance
Of leafy sunlight that still holds it. I

Know you, goddess, and your caves that answer
Ocean's confused voices with a voice:
Your poplars where the storms are turned to dances;

Arms where the heart is turned. You give the choice
To hold forever what forever passes,
To hide from what will pass, forever. Moist,

Moist are your well-stones, goddess, cool your grasses!
And she—she is a woman with that fault
Of change that will be death in her at last!

Nevertheless I long for the cold, salt,
Restless, contending sea and for the island
Where the grass dies and the seasons alter:

Where that one wears the sunlight for a while.

1962

EDNA ST. VINCENT MILLAY (1892–1950)

Euclid Alone Has Looked on Beauty Bare

Euclid[1] alone has looked on Beauty bare.
Let all who prate of Beauty hold their peace,
And lay them prone upon the earth and cease
To ponder on themselves, the while they stare
At nothing, intricately drawn nowhere
In shapes of shifting lineage; let geese
Gabble and hiss, but heroes seek release
From dusty bondage into luminous air.
O blinding hour. O holy, terrible day,
When first the shaft into his vision shone
Of light anatomized! Euclid alone

1. The Greek formulator of the science of geometry, ca. 300 B.C.

Has looked on Beauty bare. Fortunate they
Who, though once only and then but far away,
Have heard her massive sandal set on stone.

1920

I, Being Born a Woman and Distressed

I, being born a woman and distressed
By all the needs and notions of my kind,
Am urged by your propinquity to find
Your person fair, and feel a certain zest
To bear your body's weight upon my breast:
So subtly is the fume of life designed,
To clarify the pulse and cloud the mind,
And leave me once again undone, possessed.
Think not for this, however, the poor treason
Of my stout blood against my staggering brain,
I shall remember you with love, or season
My scorn with pity,—let me make it plain:
I find this frenzy insufficient reason
For conversation when we meet again.

1923

Above These Cares

Above these cares my spirit in calm abiding
Floats like a swimmer at sunrise, facing the pale sky;
Peaceful, heaved by the light infrequent lurch of the heavy wave
    serenely sliding
Under his weightless body, aware of the wide morning, aware of the gull
    on the red buoy bedaubed with guano,° aware *bird droppings*
    of his sharp cry;
Idly athirst for the sea, as who should say:
In a moment I will roll upon my mouth and drink it dry.

Painfully, under the pressure that obtains
At the sea's bottom, crushing my lungs and my brains
(For the body makes shift to breathe and after a fashion flourish
Ten fathoms deep in care,
Ten fathoms down in an element denser than air
Wherein the soul must perish)
I trap and harvest, stilling my stomach's needs;
I crawl forever, hoping never to see
Above my head the limbs of my spirit no longer free
Kicking in frenzy, a swimmer enmeshed in weeds.

1933

WILFRED OWEN
(1893–1918)

Strange Meeting

It seemed that out of battle I escaped
Down some profound dull tunnel, long since scooped
Through granites which titanic wars had groined.

Yet also there encumbered sleepers groaned,
Too fast in thought or death to be bestirred.
Then, as I probed them, one sprang up, and stared
With piteous recognition in fixed eyes,
Lifting distressful hands as if to bless.
And by his smile, I knew that sullen hall,
By his dead smile I knew we stood in Hell.
With a thousand pains that vision's face was grained;
Yet no blood reached there from the upper ground,
And no guns thumped, or down the flues made moan.
"Strange friend," I said, "here is no cause to mourn."
"None," said that other, "save the undone years,
The hopelessness. Whatever hope is yours,
Was my life also; I went hunting wild
After the wildest beauty in the world,
Which lies not calm in eyes, or braided hair,
But mocks the steady running of the hour,
And if it grieves, grieves richlier than here.
For of my glee might many men have laughed,
And of my weeping something had been left,
Which must die now. I mean the truth untold,
The pity of war, the pity war distilled.
Now men will go content with what we spoiled.
Or, discontent, boil bloody, and be spilled.
They will be swift with swiftness of the tigress,
None will break ranks, though nations trek from progress.
Courage was mine, and I had mystery,
Wisdom was mine, and I had mastery:
To miss the march of this retreating world
Into vain citadels that are not walled.
Then, when much blood had clogged their chariot wheels
I would go up and wash them from sweet wells,
Even with truths that lie too deep for taint.
I would have poured my spirit without stint
But not through wounds; not on the cess° of war. *waste*
Foreheads of men have bled where no wounds were.
I am the enemy you killed, my friend.
I knew you in this dark; for so you frowned
Yesterday through me as you jabbed and killed.
I parried; but my hands were loath and cold.
Let us sleep now. . . ."

1919 1920

Anthem for Doomed Youth

What passing-bells for these who die as cattle?
  Only the monstrous anger of the guns.
  Only the stuttering rifles' rapid rattle
Can patter out their hasty orisons.° *prayers*
No mockeries now for them; no prayers nor bells,
  Nor any voice of mourning save the choirs—
The shrill, demented choirs of wailing shells;
  And bugles calling for them from sad shires.

What candles may be held to speed them all?
  Not in the hands of boys, but in their eyes
Shall shine the holy glimmers of good-byes.

The pallor of girls' brows shall be their pall;
Their flowers the tenderness of patient minds,
And each slow dusk a drawing-down of blinds.

1917 1920

Dulce Et Decorum Est[1]

Bent double, like old beggars under sacks,
Knock-kneed, coughing like hags, we cursed through sludge,
Till on the haunting flares we turned our backs
And towards our distant rest began to trudge.
Men marched asleep. Many had lost their boots
But limped on, blood-shod. All went lame; all blind;
Drunk with fatigue; deaf even to the hoots
Of tired, outstripped Five-Nines° that dropped behind. *gas shells*

Gas! GAS! Quick, boys!—An ecstasy of fumbling,
Fitting the clumsy helmets just in time;
But someone still was yelling out and stumbling
And flound'ring like a man in fire or lime . . .
Dim, through the misty panes and thick green light,
As under a green sea, I saw him drowning.

In all my dreams, before my helpless sight,
He plunges at me, guttering, choking, drowning.

If in some smothering dreams you too could pace
Behind the wagon that we flung him in,
And watch the white eyes writhing in his face,
His hanging face, like a devil's sick of sin;
If you could hear, at every jolt, the blood
Come gargling from the froth-corrupted lungs,
Obscene as cancer, bitter as the cud
Of vile, incurable sores on innocent tongues,—
My friend, you would not tell with such high zest
To children ardent for some desperate glory,
The old Lie: Dulce et decorum est
Pro patria mori.

1920

DOROTHY PARKER
(1893–1967)

Résumé

Razors pain you;
Rivers are damp;
Acids stain you;
And drugs cause cramp.
Guns aren't lawful;
Nooses give;
Gas smells awful;
You might as well live.

1926

1. For the title and last two lines of the poem, see Horace, *Odes* III.ii.13 ("Sweet and fitting it is to die for one's country").

One Perfect Rose

A single flow'r he sent me, since we met.
  All tenderly his messenger he chose;
Deep-hearted, pure, with scented dew still wet—
  One perfect rose.

I knew the language of the floweret;
  "My fragile leaves," it said, "his heart enclose."
Love long has taken for his amulet
  One perfect rose.

Why is it no one ever sent me yet
  One perfect limousine, do you suppose?
Ah no, it's always just my luck to get
  One perfect rose.

1926

E. E. CUMMINGS
(1894–1962)

in Just-

in Just-
spring   when the world is mud-
luscious the little
lame balloonman

whistles   far   and wee

and eddieandbill come
running from marbles and
piracies and it's
spring

when the world is puddle-wonderful

the queer
old balloonman whistles
far   and   wee
and bettyandisbel come dancing

from hop-scotch and jump-rope and

it's
spring
and
        the

                goat-footed
balloonMan   whistles
far
and
wee

1923

O sweet spontaneous

O sweet spontaneous
earth how often have
the
doting

            fingers of
prurient philosophers pinched
and
poked

thee
, has the naughty thumb
of science prodded
thy

      beauty   . how
often have religions taken
thee upon their scraggy knees
squeezing and

buffeting thee that thou mightest conceive
gods
        (but
true

to the incomparable
couch of death thy
rhythmic
lover

        thou answerest

them only with

                        spring)

1923

the Cambridge ladies who live in furnished souls

the Cambridge ladies who live in furnished souls
are unbeautiful and have comfortable minds
(also, with the church's protestant blessings
daughters, unscented shapeless spirited)
they believe in Christ and Longfellow, both dead,
are invariably interested in so many things—
at the present writing one still finds
delighted fingers knitting for the is it Poles?
perhaps. While permanent faces coyly bandy
scandal of Mrs. N and Professor D
. . . . the Cambridge ladies do not care, above
Cambridge if sometimes in its box of

sky lavender and cornerless, the
moon rattles like a fragment of angry candy

1923

"next to of course god america i

"next to of course god america i
love you land of the pilgrims' and so forth oh
say can you see by the dawn's early my
country 'tis of centuries come and go
and are no more what of it we should worry
in every language even deafanddumb
thy sons acclaim your glorious name by gorry
by jingo by gee by gosh by gum
why talk of beauty what could be more beau-
tiful than these heroic happy dead
who rushed like lions to the roaring slaughter
they did not stop to think they died instead
then shall the voice of liberty be mute?"

He spoke. And drank rapidly a glass of water

1926

since feeling is first

since feeling is first
who pays any attention
to the syntax of things
will never wholly kiss you;
wholly to be a fool
while Spring is in the world

my blood approves,
and kisses are a better fate
than wisdom
lady i swear by all flowers. Don't cry
—the best gesture of my brain is less than
your eyelids' flutter which says

we are for each other: then
laugh, leaning back in my arms
for life's not a paragraph

And death i think is no parenthesis

1926

i sing of Olaf glad and big

i sing of Olaf glad and big
whose warmest heart recoiled at war:
a conscientious object-or

his wellbelovéd colonel(trig° *primly neat*
westpointer most succinctly bred)
took erring Olaf soon in hand;

but—though an host of overjoyed
noncoms(first knocking on the head
him)do through icy waters roll
that helplessness which others stroke
with brushes recently employed
anent this muddy toiletbowl,
while kindred intellects evoke
allegiance per blunt instruments—
Olaf(being to all intents
a corpse and wanting any rag
upon what God unto him gave)
responds,without getting annoyed
"I will not kiss your f.ing flag"

straightway the silver bird[1] looked grave
(departing hurriedly to shave)

but—though all kinds of officers
(a yearning nation's blueeyed pride)
their passive prey did kick and curse
until for wear their clarion
voices and boots were much the worse,
and egged the firstclassprivates on
his rectum wickedly to tease
by means of skillfully applied
bayonets roasted hot with heat—
Olaf(upon what were once knees)
does almost ceaselessly repeat
"there is some s. I will not eat"

our president,being of which
assertions duly notified
threw the yellowsonofabitch
into a dungeon,where he died

Christ(of His mercy infinite)
i pray to see;and Olaf,too

preponderatingly because
unless statistics lie he was
more brave than me:more blond than you.

1931

somewhere i have never travelled,gladly beyond

somewhere i have never travelled,gladly beyond
any experience, your eyes have their silence:
in your most frail gesture are things which enclose me,
or which i cannot touch because they are too near

your slightest look easily will unclose me
though i have closed myself as fingers,
you open always petal by petal myself as Spring opens
(touching skilfully,mysteriously)her first rose

1. The colonel; strictly speaking, his insignia of rank.

or if your wish be to close me,i and
my life will shut very beautifully,suddenly,
as when the heart of this flower imagines
the snow carefully everywhere descending;

nothing which we are to perceive in this world equals
the power of your intense fragility:whose texture
compels me with the colour of its countries,
rendering death and forever with each breathing

(i do not know what it is about you that closes
and opens;only something in me understands
the voice of your eyes is deeper than all roses)
nobody,not even the rain,has such small hands

1931

r-p-o-p-h-e-s-s-a-g-r

r-p-o-p-h-e-s-s-a-g-r
who
a)s w(e loo)k
upnowgath
PPEGORHRASS
eringint(o-
aThe):l
eA
!p:
S a
(r
rIvInG .gRrEaPsPhOs)
to
rea(be)rran(com)gi(e)ngly
,grasshopper;

1932 1935

anyone lived in a pretty how town

anyone lived in a pretty how town
(with up so floating many bells down)
spring summer autumn winter
he sang his didn't he danced his did.

Women and men(both little and small)
cared for anyone not at all
they sowed their isn't they reaped their same
sun moon stars rain

children guessed(but only a few
and down they forgot as up they grew
autumn winter spring summer)
that noone loved him more by more

when by now and tree by leaf
she laughed his joy she cried his grief
bird by snow and stir by still
anyone's any was all to her

someones married their everyones
laughed their cryings and did their dance
(sleep wake hope and then)they
said their nevers they slept their dream

stars rain sun moon
(and only the snow can begin to explain
how children are apt to forget to remember
with up so floating many bells down)

one day anyone died i guess
(and noone stooped to kiss his face)
busy folk buried them side by side
little by little and was by was

all by all and deep by deep
and more by more they dream their sleep
noone and anyone earth by april
wish by spirit and if by yes.

Women and men(both dong and ding)
summer autumn winter spring
reaped their sowing and went their came
sun moon stars rain

1940

my father moved through dooms of love

my father moved through dooms of love
through sames of am through haves of give,
singing each morning out of each night
my father moved through depths of height

this motionless forgetful where
turned at his glance to shining here;
that if(so timid air is firm)
under his eyes would stir and squirm

newly as from unburied which
floats the first who,his april touch
drove sleeping selves to swarm their fates
woke dreamers to their ghostly roots

and should some why completely weep
my father's fingers brought her sleep:
vainly no smallest voice might cry
for he could feel the mountains grow.

Lifting the valleys of the sea
my father moved through griefs of joy;
praising a forehead called the moon
singing desire into begin

joy was his song and joy so pure
a heart of star by him could steer
and pure so now and now so yes
the wrists of twilight would rejoice

keen as midsummer's keen beyond
conceiving mind of sun will stand,
so strictly(over utmost him
so hugely)stood my father's dream

his flesh was flesh his blood was blood:
no hungry man but wished him food;
no cripple wouldn't creep one mile
uphill to only see him smile.

Scorning the pomp of must and shall
my father moved through dooms of feel;
his anger was as right as rain
his pity was as green as grain

septembering arms of year extend
less humbly wealth to foe and friend
than he to foolish and to wise
offered immeasurable is

proudly and(by octobering flame
beckoned)as earth will downward climb,
so naked for immortal work
his shoulders marched against the dark

his sorrow was as true as bread:
no liar looked him in the head;
if every friend became his foe
he'd laugh and build a world with snow.

My father moved through theys of we,
singing each new leaf out of each tree
(and every child was sure that spring
danced when she heard my father sing)

then let men kill which cannot share,
let blood and flesh be mud and mire,
scheming imagine,passion willed,
freedom a drug that's bought and sold

giving to steal and cruel kind,
a heart to fear,to doubt a mind,
to differ a disease of same,
conform the pinnacle of am

though dull were all we taste as bright,
bitter all utterly things sweet,
maggoty minus and dumb death
all we inherit,all bequeath

and nothing quite so least as truth
—i say though hate were why men breathe—
because my father lived his soul
love is the whole and more than all

1940

l(a

l(a

le
af
fa

ll

s)
one
l

iness

1958

JEAN TOOMER
(1894–1967)

Face

Hair—
silver-gray,
like streams of stars,
Brows—
recurved canoes
quivered by the ripples blown by pain,
Her eyes—
mist of tears
condensing on the flesh below
And her channeled muscles
are cluster grapes of sorrow
purple in the evening sun
nearly ripe for worms.

1923

Georgia Dusk

The sky, lazily disdaining to pursue
  The setting sun, too indolent to hold
  A lengthened tournament for flashing gold,
Passively darkens for night's barbecue,

A feast of moon and men and barking hounds,
  An orgy for some genius of the South
  With blood-hot eyes and cane-lipped scented mouth,
Surprised in making folksongs from soul sounds.

The sawmill blows its whistle, buzz-saws stop,
  And silence breaks the bud of knoll and hill,
  Soft settling pollen where plowed lands fulfill
Their early promise of a bumper crop.

Smoke from the pyramidal sawdust pile
  Curls up, blue ghosts of trees, tarrying low
  Where only chips and stumps are left to show
The solid proof of former domicile.

Meanwhile, the men, with vestiges of pomp,
  Race memories of king and caravan,
  High-priests, an ostrich, and a juju-man,° *witch-doctor*
Go singing through the footpaths of the swamp.

Their voices rise . . the pine trees are guitars,
  Strumming, pine-needles fall like sheets of rain . .
  Their voices rise . . the chorus of the cane
Is caroling a vesper to the stars. .

O singers, resinous and soft your songs
  Above the sacred whisper of the pines,
  Give virgin lips to cornfield concubines,
Bring dreams of Christ to dusky cane-lipped throngs.

1923

ROBERT GRAVES
(1895–)

The Cool Web

Children are dumb to say how hot the day is,
How hot the scent is of the summer rose,
How dreadful the black wastes of evening sky,
How dreadful the tall soldiers drumming by.

But we have speech, to chill the angry day,
And speech, to dull the rose's cruel scent.
We spell away the overhanging night,
We spell away the soldiers and the fright.

There's a cool web of language winds us in,
Retreat from too much joy or too much fear:
We grow sea-green at last and coldly die
In brininess and volubility.

But if we let our tongues lose self-possession,
Throwing off language and its watery clasp
Before our death, instead of when death comes,
Facing the wide glare of the children's day,
Facing the rose, the dark sky and the drums,
We shall go mad no doubt and die that way.

1927

Warning to Children

Children, if you dare to think
Of the greatness, rareness, muchness,
Fewness of this precious only

Endless world in which you say
You live, you think of things like this:
Blocks of slate enclosing dappled
Red and green, enclosing tawny
Yellow nets, enclosing white
And black acres of dominoes,
Where a neat brown paper parcel
Tempts you to untie the string.
In the parcel a small island,
On the island a large tree,
On the tree a husky fruit.
Strip the husk and pare the rind off:
In the kernel you will see
Blocks of slate enclosed by dappled
Red and green, enclosed by tawny
Yellow nets, enclosed by white
And black acres of dominoes,
Where the same brown paper parcel—
Children, leave the string alone!
For who dares undo the parcel
Finds himself at once inside it,
On the island, in the fruit,
Blocks of slate about his head,
Finds himself enclosed by dappled
Green and red, enclosed by yellow
Tawny nets, enclosed by black
And white acres of dominoes,
With the same brown paper parcel
Still unopened on his knee.
And, if he then should dare to think
Of the fewness, muchness, rareness,
Greatness of this endless only
Precious world in which he says
He lives—he then unties the string.

1929

Down, Wanton, Down!

Down, wanton, down! Have you no shame
That at the whisper of Love's name,
Or Beauty's, presto! up you raise
Your angry head and stand at gaze?

Poor bombard-captain,[1] sworn to reach
The ravelin and effect a breach—
Indifferent what you storm or why,
So be that in the breach you die!

Love may be blind, but Love at least
Knows what is man and what mere beast;
Or Beauty wayward, but requires
More delicacy from her squires.

1. An early form of cannon that threw stones. A ravelin, in a fortification system, is "a detached work with two embankments which make a salient angle" (*Webster's*).

Tell me, my witless, whose one boast
Could be your staunchness at the post,
When were you made a man of parts
To think fine and profess the arts?

Will many-gifted Beauty come
Bowing to your bald rule of thumb,
Or Love swear loyalty to your crown?
Be gone, have done! Down, wanton, down!

1933

The Face in the Mirror

Gray haunted eyes, absent-mindedly glaring
From wide, uneven orbits; one brow drooping
Somewhat over the eye
Because of a missile fragment still inhering,
Skin deep, as a foolish record of old-world fighting.

Crookedly broken nose—low tackling caused it;
Cheeks, furrowed; coarse gray hair, flying frenetic;
Forehead, wrinkled and high;
Jowls, prominent; ears, large; jaw, pugilistic;
Teeth, few; lips, full and ruddy; mouth, ascetic.

I pause with razor poised, scowling derision
At the mirrored man whose beard needs my attention,
And once more ask him why
He still stands ready, with a boy's presumption,
To court the queen in her high silk pavilion.

1958

LOUISE BOGAN (1897–1970)

Medusa[1]

I had come to the house, in a cave of trees,
Facing a sheer sky.
Everything moved,—a bell hung ready to strike,
Sun and reflection wheeled by.

When the bare eyes were before me
And the hissing hair,
Held up at a window, seen through a door.
The stiff bald eyes, the serpents on the forehead
Formed in the air.

This is a dead scene forever now.
Nothing will ever stir.
The end will never brighten it more than this,
Nor the rain blur.

1. A Greek mythological woman of terrifying ugliness, with snakes for hair, whose glance turned people to stone.

The water will always fall, and will not fall,
And the tipped bell make no sound.
The grass will always be growing for hay
Deep on the ground.

And I shall stand here like a shadow
Under the great balanced day,
My eyes on the yellow dust, that was lifting in the wind,
And does not drift away.

1921

Song for the Last Act

Now that I have your face by heart, I look
Less at its features than its darkening frame
Where quince and melon, yellow as young flame,
Lie with quilled dahlias and the shepherd's crook.
Beyond, a garden. There, in insolent ease
The lead and marble figures watch the show
Of yet another summer loath to go
Although the scythes hang in the apple trees.

Now that I have your face by heart, I look.

Now that I have your voice by heart, I read
In the black chords upon a dulling page
Music that is not meant for music's cage,
Whose emblems mix with words that shake and bleed.
The staves are shuttled over with a stark
Unprinted silence. In a double dream
I must spell out the storm, the running stream.
The beat's too swift. The notes shift in the dark.

Now that I have your voice by heart, I read.

Now that I have your heart by heart, I see
The wharves with their great ships and architraves;
The rigging and the cargo and the slaves
On a strange beach under a broken sky.
O not departure, but a voyage done!
The bales stand on the stone; the anchor weeps
Its red rust downward, and the long vine creeps
Beside the salt herb, in the lengthening sun.

Now that I have your heart by heart, I see.

1949

HART CRANE
(1899–1932)

My Grandmother's Love Letters

There are no stars to-night
But those of memory.

Yet how much room for memory there is
In the loose girdle of soft rain.

There is even room enough
For the letters of my mother's mother,
Elizabeth,
That have been pressed so long
Into a corner of the roof
That they are brown and soft,
And liable to melt as snow.

Over the greatness of such space
Steps must be gentle.
It is all hung by an invisible white hair.
It trembles as birch limbs webbing the air.

And I ask myself:

"Are your fingers long enough to play
Old keys that are but echoes:
Is the silence strong enough
To carry back the music to its source
And back to you again
As though to her?"

Yet I would lead my grandmother by the hand
Through much of what she would not understand;
And so I stumble. And the rain continues on the roof
With such a sound of gently pitying laughter.

1926

At Melville's Tomb

Often beneath the wave, wide from this ledge
The dice[1] of drowned men's bones he saw bequeath
An embassy. Their numbers as he watched,
Beat on the dusty shore and were obscured.

And wrecks passed without sound of bells,
The calyx[2] of death's bounty giving back
A scattered chapter, livid hieroglyph,
The portent wound in corridors of shells.

Then in the circuit calm of one vast coil,
Its lashings charmed and malice reconciled,
Frosted eyes there were that lifted altars;
And silent answers crept across the stars.

Compass, quadrant and sextant[3] contrive
No farther tides . . . High in the azure steeps
Monody shall not wake the mariner.
This fabulous shadow only the sea keeps.

1926

1. Small, broken pieces.
2. Chalice, or cup-like container.
3. Instruments of measurement: the compass for describing circles or determining geographic directions; the quadrant and sextant for measuring angles and reckoning altitudes.

Voyages

1

Above the fresh ruffles of the surf
Bright striped urchins flay each other with sand.
They have contrived a conquest for shell shucks,
And their fingers crumble fragments of baked weed
Gaily digging and scattering.

And in answer to their treble interjections
The sun beats lightning on the waves,
The waves fold thunder on the sand;
And could they hear me I would tell them:

O brilliant kids, frisk with your dog,
Fondle your shells and sticks, bleached
By time and the elements; but there is a line
You must not cross nor ever trust beyond it
Spry cordage of your bodies to caresses
Too lichen-faithful from too wide a breast.
The bottom of the sea is cruel.

2

—And yet this great wink of eternity,
Of rimless floods, unfettered leewardings,
Samite[4] sheeted and processioned where
Her undinal vast belly moonward bends,
Laughing the wrapt inflections of our love;

Take this Sea, whose diapason knells
On scrolls of silver snowy sentences,
The sceptered terror of whose sessions rends
As her demeanors motion well or ill.
All but the pieties of lovers' hands.

And onward, as bells off San Salvador[5]
Salute the crocus lusters of the stars,
In these poinsettia[6] meadows of her tides—
Adagios[7] of islands, O my Prodigal,
Complete the dark confessions her veins spell.

Mark how her turning shoulders wind the hours,
And hasten while her penniless rich palms
Pass superscription of bent foam and wave—
Hasten, while they are true—sleep, death, desire,
Close round one instant in one floating flower.

Bind us in time, O Seasons clear, and awe.
O minstrel galleons of Carib[8] fire,
Bequeath us to no earthly shore until
Is answered in the vortex of our grave
The seal's wide spindrift gaze toward paradise.

4. A rich, silk fabric.
5. The Spanish name for an island of the Bahamas group, Columbus's first landfall on the first voyage.
6. Exotic flower or shrub with a small yellow blossom surrounded by bright red leaves or bracts.
7. The divisions of a composition which are musically slow and graceful.
8. Some of the West Indian islands, or the sea surrounding them.

3

Infinite consanguinity it bears—
This tendered theme of you that light
Retrieves from sea plains where the sky
Resigns a breast that every wave enthrones;
While ribboned water lanes I wind
Are laved and scattered with no stroke
Wide from your side, whereto this hour
The sea lifts, also, reliquary[9] hands.

And so, admitted through black swollen gates
That must arrest all distance otherwise,
Past whirling pillars and lithe pediments,
Light wrestling there incessantly with light,
Star kissing star through wave on wave unto
Your body rocking!
and where death, if shed,
Presumes no carnage, but this single change,
Upon the steep floor flung from dawn to dawn
The silken skilled transmemberment[1] of song;

Permit me voyage, love, into your hands . . .

4

Whose counted smile of hours and days, suppose
I know as spectrum of the sea and pledge
Vastly now parting gulf on gulf of wings
Whose circles bridge, I know, (from palms to the severe
Chilled albatross's[2] white immutability)
No stream of greater love advancing now
Than, singing, this mortality alone
Through clay aflow immortally to you.

All fragrance irrefragibly,[3] and claim
Madly meeting logically in this hour
And region that is ours to wreathe again,
Portending eyes and lips and making told
The chancel port and portion of our June—

Shall they not stem and close in our own steps
Bright staves of flowers and quills to-day as I
Must first be lost in fatal tides to tell?

In signature of the incarnate word
The harbor shoulders to resign in mingling
Mutual blood, transpiring as foreknown
And widening noon within your breast for gathering
All bright insinuations that my years have caught
For islands where must lead inviolably
Blue latitudes and levels of your eyes—

In this expectant, still exclaim receive
The secret oar and petals of all love.

5

Meticulous, past midnight in clear rime,
Infrangible and lonely, smooth as though cast

9. Characteristic of relics, or of the container for preserving them.
1. Exchange or transformation of parts.
2. A large, sometimes white sea-bird capable of long, sustained flights away from land, and in some species, nesting in the colder parts of southern lands.
3. Undeniably; unalterably.

Together in one merciless white blade—
The bay estuaries fleck the hard sky limits.

—As if too brittle or too clear to touch!
The cables of our sleep so swiftly filed,
Already hang, shred ends from remembered stars.
One frozen trackless smile . . . What words
Can strangle this deaf moonlight? For we

Are overtaken. Now no cry, no sword
Can fasten or deflect this tidal wedge,
Slow tyranny of moonlight, moonlight loved
And changed . . . "There's

Nothing like this in the world," you say,
Knowing I cannot touch your hand and look
Too, into that godless cleft of sky
Where nothing turns but dead sands flashing.

"—And never to quite understand!" No,
In all the argosy of your bright hair I dreamed
Nothing so flagless as this piracy.

But now
Draw in your head, alone and too tall here.
Your eyes already in the slant of drifting foam;
Your breath sealed by the ghosts I do not know:
Draw in your head and sleep the long way home.

6

Where icy and bright dungeons lift
Of swimmers their lost morning eyes,
And ocean rivers, churning, shift
Green borders under stranger skies,

Steadily as a shell secretes
Its beating leagues of monotone,
Or as many waters trough the sun's
Red kelson[4] past the cape's wet stone;

O rivers mingling toward the sky
And harbor of the phoenix'[5] breast—
My eyes pressed black against the prow,
—Thy derelict and blinded guest

Waiting, afire, what name, unspoke,
I cannot claim: let thy waves rear
More savage than the death of kings,
Some splintered garland for the seer.

Beyond siroccos[6] harvesting
The solstice thunders, crept away,
Like a cliff swinging or a sail
Flung into April's inmost day—

4. In a ship, the kelson (keelson) is a beam laid parallel to the keel in order to hold together the flooring and the keel.
5. In mythology, a gorgeous bird of red and gold plumage, associated with worship of the sun, and said to live a very long life, only to be consumed by fire from the ashes of which arises a new phoenix.
6. Hot, moist winds usually associated with the North African deserts.

Creation's blithe and petaled word
To the lounged goddess when she rose
Conceding dialogue with eyes
That smile unsearchable repose—

Still fervid covenant, Belle Isle,
—Unfolded floating dais before
Which rainbows twine continual hair—
Belle Isle, white echo of the oar!

The imaged Word, it is, that holds
Hushed willows anchored in its glow.
It is the unbetrayable reply
Whose accent no farewell can know.

1926

From The Bridge

Proem: To Brooklyn Bridge

How many dawns, chill from his rippling rest
The seagull's wings shall dip and pivot him,
Shedding white rings of tumult, building high
Over the chained bay waters Liberty—

Then, with inviolate curve, forsake our eyes
As apparitional as sails that cross
Some page of figures to be filed away;
—Till elevators drop us from our day . . .

I think of cinemas, panoramic sleights
With multitudes bent toward some flashing scene
Never disclosed, but hastened to again,
Foretold to other eyes on the same screen;

And Thee,[7] across the harbor, silver-paced
As though the sun took step of thee, yet left
Some motion ever unspent in thy stride—
Implicitly thy freedom staying thee!

Out of some subway scuttle, cell or loft
A bedlamite° speeds to thy parapets, *madman*
Tilting there momently, shrill shirt ballooning,
A jest falls from the speechless caravan.

Down Wall, from girder into street noon leaks,
A rip-tooth of the sky's acetylene,
All afternoon the cloud-flown derricks turn . . .
Thy cables breathe the North Atlantic still.

And obscure as that heaven of the Jews,
Thy guerdon . . . Accolade thou dost bestow
Of anonymity time cannot raise:
Vibrant reprieve and pardon thou dost show.

7. I.e., Brooklyn Bridge.

O harp and altar, of the fury fused,
(How could mere toil align thy choiring strings!)
Terrific threshold of the prophet's pledge,
Prayer of pariah, and the lover's cry—

Again the traffic lights that skim thy swift
Unfractioned idiom, immaculate sigh of stars,
Beading thy path—condense eternity:
And we have seen night lifted in thine arms.

Under thy shadow by the piers I waited;
Only in darkness is thy shadow clear.
The City's fiery parcels all undone,
Already snow submerges an iron year . . .

O Sleepless as the river under thee,
Vaulting the sea, the prairies' dreaming sod,
Unto us lowliest sometime sweep, descend
And of the curveship lend a myth to God.

1930

Royal Palm

Green rustlings, more-than-regal charities
Drift coolly from that tower of whispered light.
Amid the noontide's blazed asperities
I watched the sun's most gracious anchorite

Climb up as by communings, year on year
Uneaten of the earth or aught earth holds,
And the gray trunk, that's elephantine, rear
Its frondings sighing in ethereal folds.

Forever fruitless, and beyond that yield
Of sweat the jungle presses with hot love
And tendril till our deathward breath is sealed—
It grazes the horizons, launched above

Mortality—ascending emerald-bright,
A fountain at salute, a crown in view—
Unshackled, casual of its azured height,
As though it soared suchwise through heaven too.

1933

To Emily Dickinson[8]

You who desired so much—in vain to ask—
Yet fed your hunger like an endless task,
Dared dignify the labor, bless the quest—
Achieved that stillness ultimately best,

Being, of all, least sought for: Emily, hear!
O sweet, dead Silencer, most suddenly clear
When singing that Eternity possessed
And plundered momently in every breast;

8. American poet (1830–1886); see above.

—Truly no flower yet withers in your hand,
The harvest you descried and understand
Needs more than wit to gather, love to bind.
Some reconcilement of remotest mind—

Leaves Ormus rubyless, and Ophir chill.[9]
Else tears heap all within one clay-cold hill.

1933

ALLEN TATE (1899–1979)

Ode to the Confederate Dead

Row after row with strict impunity
The headstones yield their names to the element,
The wind whirrs without recollection;
In the riven troughs the splayed leaves
Pile up, of nature the casual sacrament
To the seasonal eternity of death;
Then driven by the fierce scrutiny
Of heaven to their election in the vast breath,
They sough the rumor of mortality.

Autumn is desolation in the plot
Of a thousand acres where these memories grow
From the inexhaustible bodies that are not
Dead, but feed the grass row after rich row.
Think of the autumns that have come and gone!
Ambitious November with the humors of the year,
With a particular zeal for every slab,
Staining the uncomfortable angels that rot
On the slabs, a wing chipped here, an arm there:
The brute curiosity of an angel's stare
Turns you, like them, to stone,
Transforms the heaving air
Till plunged to a heavier world below
You shift your sea-space blindly
Heaving, turning like the blind crab.

  Dazed by the wind, only the wind
  The leaves flying, plunge

You know who have waited by the wall
The twilight certainty of an animal,
Those midnight restitutions of the blood
You know—the immitigable° pines, the smoky frieze *unvarying*
Of the sky, the sudden call: you know the rage,
The cold pool left by the mounting flood,
Of muted Zeno and Parmenides.[1]

9. Ormus (or Ormuz), ancient city on the Persian Gulf; in the Old Testament (I Kings x.11), Solomon receives rich gifts, including gold and precious stones, from a region called Ophir.

1. Zeno and Parmenides were Greek philosophers of the Eleatic school who, among other beliefs, held that what is various and changeable, all "development," is a delusive phantom. "To be imagined and to be able to exist are the same thing, and there is no development."

You who have waited for the angry resolution
Of those desires that should be yours tomorrow,
You know the unimportant shrift of death
And praise the vision
And praise the arrogant circumstance
Of those who fall
Rank upon rank, hurried beyond decision—
Here by the sagging gate, stopped by the wall.

Seeing, seeing only the leaves
Flying, plunge and expire

Turn your eyes to the immoderate past,
Turn to the inscrutable infantry rising
Demons out of the earth—they will not last.
Stonewall, Stonewall, and the sunken fields of hemp,
Shiloh, Antietam, Malvern Hill, Bull Run.[2]
Lost in that orient of the thick and fast
You will curse the setting sun.

Cursing only the leaves crying
Like an old man in a storm

You hear the shout, the crazy hemlocks point
With troubled fingers to the silence which
Smothers you, a mummy, in time.

The hound bitch
Toothless and dying, in a musty cellar
Hears the wind only.

Now that the salt of their blood
Stiffens the saltier oblivion of the sea,
Seals the malignant purity of the flood,
What shall we who count our days and bow
Our heads with a commemorial woe
In the ribboned coats of grim felicity,
What shall we say of the bones, unclean,
Whose verdurous anonymity will grow?

The ragged arms, the ragged heads and eyes
Lost in these acres of the insane green?
The gray lean spiders come, they come and go;
In a tangle of willows without light
The singular screech-owl's tight
Invisible lyric seeds the mind
With the furious murmur of their chivalry.

We shall say only the leaves
Flying, plunge and expire

We shall say only the leaves whispering
In the improbable mist of nightfall
That flies on multiple wing:
Night is the beginning and the end
And in between the ends of distraction
Waits mute speculation, the patient curse

2. Names of important Civil War battles.

That stones the eyes, or like the jaguar leaps
For his own image in a jungle pool, his victim.

What shall we say who have knowledge
Carried to the heart? Shall we take the act
To the grave? Shall we, more hopeful, set up the grave
In the house? The ravenous grave?

Leave now
The shut gate and the decomposing wall:
The gentle serpent, green in the mulberry bush,
Riots with his tongue through the hush—
Sentinel of the grave who counts us all!

1928

LANGSTON HUGHES
(1902–1967)

The Weary Blues

Droning a drowsy syncopated tune,
Rocking back and forth to a mellow croon,
I heard a Negro play.
Down on Lenox Avenue[1] the other night
By the pale dull pallor of an old gas light
He did a lazy sway. . . .
He did a lazy sway. . . .
To the tune o' those Weary Blues.
With his ebony hands on each ivory key
He made that poor piano moan with melody.
O Blues!
Swaying to and fro on his rickety stool
He played that sad raggy tune like a musical fool.
Sweet Blues!
Coming from a black man's soul.
O Blues!
In a deep song voice with a melancholy tone
I heard that Negro sing, that old piano moan—
"Ain't got nobody in all this world,
Ain't got nobody but ma self.
I's gwine to quit ma frownin'
And put ma troubles on the shelf."
Thump, thump, thump, went his foot on the floor.
He played a few chords then he sang some more—
"I got the Weary Blues
And I can't be satisfied.
Got the Weary Blues
And can't be satisfied—
I ain't happy no mo'
And I wish that I had died."
And far into the night he crooned that tune.
The stars went out and so did the moon.
The singer stopped playing and went to bed
While the Weary Blues echoed through his head.
He slept like a rock or a man that's dead.

1926

1. A main thoroughfare in the heart of Harlem.

The Negro Speaks of Rivers

(TO W. E. B. DUBOIS)[2]

I've known rivers:
I've known rivers ancient as the world and older than the
flow of human blood in human veins.

My soul has grown deep like the rivers.

I bathed in the Euphrates when dawns were young.
I built my hut near the Congo and it lulled me to sleep.
I looked upon the Nile and raised the pyramids above it.
I heard the singing of the Mississippi when Abe Lincoln
went down to New Orleans, and I've seen its muddy
bosom turn all golden in the sunset.

I've known rivers:
Ancient, dusky rivers.

My soul has grown deep like the rivers.

1926

Harlem

What happens to a dream deferred?

Does it dry up
like a raisin in the sun?
Or fester like a sore—
And then run?
Does it stink like rotten meat?
Or crust and sugar over—
like a syrupy sweet?

Maybe it just sags
like a heavy load.

Or does it explode?

1951

Theme for English B

The instructor said,

Go home and write
a page tonight.
And let that page come out of you—
Then, it will be true.

I wonder if it's that simple?
I am twenty-two, colored, born in Winston-Salem.

2. The American historian, educator, and Negro leader (1868–1963).

I went to school there, then Durham, then here
to this college on the hill above Harlem.
I am the only colored student in my class.
The steps from the hill lead down into Harlem,
through a park, then I cross St. Nicholas,
Eighth Avenue, Seventh, and I come to the Y,
the Harlem Branch Y, where I take the elevator
up to my room, sit down, and write this page:

It's not easy to know what is true for you or me
at twenty-two, my age. But I guess I'm what
I feel and see and hear, Harlem, I hear you:
hear you, hear me—we two—you, me, talk on this page.
(I hear New York, too.) Me—who?
Well, I like to eat, sleep, drink, and be in love.
I like to work, read, learn, and understand life.
I like a pipe for a Christmas present,
or records—Bessie, bop, or Bach.
I guess being colored doesn't make me *not* like
the same things other folks like who are other races.
So will my page be colored that I write?
Being me, it will not be white.
But it will be
a part of you, instructor.
You are white—
yet a part of me, as I am a part of you.
That's American.
Sometimes perhaps you don't want to be a part of me.
Nor do I often want to be a part of you.
But we are, that's true!
I guess you learn from me—
although you're older—and white—
and somewhat more free.

This is my page for English B.

1951

OGDEN NASH
(1902–1972)

The Cow

The cow is of the bovine ilk;
One end is moo, the other, milk.

1931

Reflections on Ice-breaking

Candy
Is dandy
But liquor
Is quicker.

1931

Requiem

There was a young belle of old Natchez
Whose garments were always in patchez.
When comment arose
On the state of her clothes,
She drawled, When Ah itchez, Ah scratchez!

1935

Columbus

Once upon a time there was an Italian,
And some people thought he was a rapscallion,
But he wasn't offended,
Because other people thought he was splendid,
And he said the world was round,
And everybody made an uncomplimentary sound,
But he went and tried to borrow some money from Ferdinand
But Ferdinand said America was a bird in the bush and he'd rather have a berdinand,
But Columbus' brain was fertile, it wasn't arid,
And he remembered that Ferdinand was married,
And he thought, there is no wife like a misunderstood one,
Because if her husband thinks something is a terrible idea she is bound to think it a good one,
So he perfumed his handkerchief with bay rum and citronella,
And he went to see Isabella,
And he looked wonderful but he had never felt sillier,
And she said, I can't place the face but the aroma is familiar,
And Columbus didn't say a word,
All he said was, I am Columbus, the fifteenth-century Admiral Byrd,[1]
And, just as he thought, her disposition was very malleable,
And she said, Here are my jewels, and she wasn't penurious like Cornelia the mother of the Gracchi, she wasn't referring to her children, no, she was referring to her jewels, which were very very valuable,[2]
So Columbus said, Somebody show me the sunset and somebody did and he set sail for it,
And he discovered America and they put him in jail for it,
And the fetters gave him welts,
And they named America after somebody else,
So the sad fate of Columbus ought to be pointed out to every child and every voter,
Because it has a very important moral, which is, Don't be a discoverer, be a promoter.

1935

1. Richard Evelyn Byrd (1888–1957), American polar explorer.
2. The anecdote is told by Valerius Maximus in his *Memorable Deeds and Sayings* (1st century A.D.), 4.4. Having shown her jewels to Cornelia, mother of the illustrious tribunes Tiberius and Gaius Sempronius Gracchus, a patrician woman asked to see those of Cornelia, who sent for her sons and replied, "These are my jewels, in which alone I delight."

The Turtle

The turtle lives 'twixt plated decks
Which practically conceal its sex.
I think it clever of the turtle
In such a fix to be so fertile.

1940

Arthur

There was an old man of Calcutta,
Who coated his tonsils with butta,
Thus converting his snore
From a thunderous roar
To a soft, oleaginous mutta.

1940

STEVIE SMITH
(1902–1971)

No Categories!

I cry I cry
To God who created me
Not to you Angels who frustrated me
Let me fly, let me die,
Let me come to Him.

Not to you Angels on the wing,
With your severe faces,
And your scholarly grimaces,
And your do this and that,
And your exasperating pit-pat
Of appropriate admonishment.

That is not what the Creator meant.
In the day of his gusty creation
He made this and that
And laughed to see them grow fat.

Plod on, you Angels say, do better aspire higher
And one day you may be like us, or those next below us,
Or nearer the lowest,
Or lowest,
Doing their best.

Oh no no, you Angels, I say,
No hierarchies I pray.

Oh God, laugh not too much aside
Say not, it is a small matter.

See what your Angels do; scatter
Their pride; laugh them away.

Oh no categories I pray.

1950

The Death Sentence

Cold as No Plea,
Yet wild with all negation,
Weeping I come
To my heart's destination,
To my last bed
Between th' unhallowed boards—
The Law allows it
And the Court awards.

1950

Not Waving but Drowning

Nobody heard him, the dead man,
But still he lay moaning:
I was much further out than you thought
And not waving but drowning.

Poor chap, he always loved larking
And now he's dead
It must have been too cold for him his heart gave way,
They said.

Oh, no no no, it was too cold always
(Still the dead one lay moaning)
I was much too far out all my life
And not waving but drowning.

1957

Pretty

Why is the word pretty so underrated?
In November the leaf is pretty when it falls
The stream grows deep in the woods after rain
And in the pretty pool the pike stalks

He stalks his prey, and this is pretty too,
The prey escapes with an underwater flash
But not for long, the great fish has him now
The pike is a fish who always has his prey

And this is pretty. The water rat is pretty
His paws are not webbed, he cannot shut his nostrils
As the otter can and the beaver, he is torn between
The land and water. Not "torn," he does not mind.

The owl hunts in the evening and it is pretty
The lake water below him rustles with ice

There is frost coming from the ground, in the air mist
All this is pretty, it could not be prettier.

Yes, it could always be prettier, the eye abashes
It is becoming an eye that cannot see enough,
Out of the wood the eye climbs. This is prettier
A field in the evening, tilting up.

The field tilts to the sky. Though it is late
The sky is lighter than the hill field
All this looks easy but really it is extraordinary
Well, it is extraordinary to be so pretty.

And it is careless, and that is always pretty
This field, this owl, this pike, this pool are careless,
As Nature is always careless and indifferent
Who sees, who steps, means nothing, and this is pretty.

So a peerson can come along like a thief—pretty!—
Stealing a look, pinching the sound and feel,
Lick the icicle broken from the bank
And still say nothing at all, only cry pretty.

Cry pretty, pretty, pretty and you'll be able
Very soon not even to cry pretty
And so be delivered entirely from humanity
This is prettiest of all, it is very pretty.

1969

COUNTEE CULLEN (1903–1946)

Heritage

FOR HAROLD JACKMAN

What is Africa to me:
Copper sun or scarlet sea,
Jungle star or jungle track,
Strong bronzed men, or regal black
Women from whose loins I sprang
When the birds of Eden sang?
One three centuries removed
From the scenes his fathers loved,
Spicy grove, cinnamon tree,
What is Africa to me?

So I lie, who all day long
Want no sound except the song
Sung by wild barbaric birds
Goading massive jungle herds,
Juggernauts of flesh that pass
Trampling tall defiant grass
Where young forest lovers lie,

Plighting troth beneath the sky.
So I lie, who always hear,
Though I cram against my ear
Both my thumbs, and keep them there,
Great drums throbbing through the air.
So I lie, whose fount of pride,
Dear distress, and joy allied,
Is my somber flesh and skin,
With the dark blood dammed within
Like great pulsing tides of wine
That, I fear, must burst the fine
Channels of the chafing net
Where they surge and foam and fret.

Africa? A book one thumbs
Listlessly, till slumber comes.
Unremembered are her bats
Circling through the night, her cats
Crouching in the river reeds,
Stalking gentle flesh that feeds
By the river brink; no more
Does the bugle-throated roar
Cry that monarch claws have leapt
From the scabbards where they slept.
Silver snakes that once a year
Doff the lovely coats you wear,
Seek no covert in your fear
Lest a mortal eye should see;
What's your nakedness to me?
Here no leprous flowers rear
Fierce corollas in the air;
Here no bodies sleek and wet,
Dripping mingled rain and sweat,
Tread the savage measures of
Jungle boys and girls in love.
What is last year's snow to me,
Last year's anything? The tree
Budding yearly must forget
How its past arose or set—
Bough and blossom, flower, fruit,
Even what shy bird with mute
Wonder at her travail there,
Meekly labored in its hair.
One three centuries removed
From the scenes his fathers loved,
Spicy grove, cinnamon tree,
What is Africa to me?

So I lie, who find no peace
Night or day, no slight release
From the unremittent beat
Made by cruel padded feet
Walking through my body's street.
Up and down they go, and back,
Treading out a jungle track.
So I lie, who never quite
Safely sleep from rain at night—
I can never rest at all

When the rain begins to fall;
Like a soul gone mad with pain
I must match its weird refrain;
Ever must I twist and squirm,
Writhing like a baited worm,
While its primal measures drip
Through my body, crying, "Strip!
Doff this new exuberance.
Come and dance the Lover's Dance!"
In an old remembered way
Rain works on me night and day.

Quaint, outlandish heathen gods
Black men fashion out of rods,
Clay, and brittle bits of stone,
In a likeness like their own,
My conversion came high-priced;
I belong to Jesus Christ,
Preacher of Humility;
Heathen gods are naught to me.

Father, Son, and Holy Ghost,
So I make an idle boast;
Jesus of the twice-turned cheek,
Lamb of God, although I speak
With my mouth thus, in my heart
Do I play a double part.
Ever at Thy glowing altar
Must my heart grow sick and falter,
Wishing He I served were black,
Thinking then it would not lack
Precedent of pain to guide it,
Let who would or might deride it;
Surely then this flesh would know
Yours had borne a kindred woe.
Lord, I fashion dark gods, too,
Daring even to give You
Dark despairing features where,
Crowned with dark rebellious hair,
Patience wavers just so much as
Mortal grief compels, while touches
Quick and hot, of anger, rise
To smitten cheek and weary eyes.
Lord, forgive me if my need
Sometimes shapes a human creed.
All day long and all night through,
One thing only must I do:
Quench my pride and cool my blood,
Lest I perish in the flood,
Lest a hidden ember set
Timber that I thought was wet
Burning like the dryest flax,
Melting like the merest wax,
Lest the grave restore its dead.
Not yet has my heart or head
In the least way realized
They and I are civilized.

1925

EARLE BIRNEY
(1904–)

Bushed

He invented a rainbow but lightning struck it
shattered it into the lake-lap of a mountain
so big his mind slowed when he looked at it

Yet he built a shack on the shore
learned to roast porcupine belly and
wore the quills on his hatband

At first he was out with the dawn
whether it yellowed bright as wood-columbine
or was only a fuzzed moth in a flannel of storm
But he found the mountain was clearly alive
sent messages whizzing down every hot morning
boomed proclamations at noon and spread out
a white guard of goat
before falling asleep on its feet at sundown

When he tried his eyes on the lake   ospreys [1]
would fall like valkyries [2]
choosing the cut-throat
He took then to waiting
till the night smoke rose from the boil of the sunset

But the moon carved unknown totems
out of the lakeshore
owls in the beardusky woods derided him
moosehorned cedars circled his swamps and tossed
their antlers up to the stars
Then he knew   though the mountain slept   the winds
were shaping its peak to an arrowhead
poised

And now he could only
bar himself in and wait
for the great flint to come singing into his heart

1952

The Bear on the Delhi Road[3]

Unreal   tall as a myth
by the road the Himalayan bear
is beating the brilliant air
with his crooked arms
About him two men   bare
spindly as locusts   leap

1. Sea-hawks.
2. In Norse mythology, one of the 13 warrior-maidens of Odin; they selected the heroes who were to die in battle, and afterwards carried them to Valhalla.
3. In India.

One pulls on a ring
in the great soft nose His mate
flicks flicks with a stick
up at the rolling eyes

They have not led him here
down from the fabulous hills
to this bald alien plain
and the clamorous world to kill
but simply to teach him to dance

They are peaceful both these spare
men of Kashmir and the bear
alive is their living too
If far on the Delhi way
around him galvanic they dance
it is merely to wear wear
from his shaggy body the tranced
wish forever to stay
only an ambling bear
four-footed in berries

It is no more joyous for them
in this hot dust to prance
out of reach of the praying claws
sharpened to paw for ants
in the shadows of deodars[4]
It is not easy to free
myth from reality
or rear this fellow up
to lurch lurch with them
in the tranced dancing of men

1962 1975

C. DAY LEWIS
(1904–1972)

Song[1]

Come, live with me and be my love,
And we will all the pleasures prove
Of peace and plenty, bed and board,
That chance employment may afford.

I'll handle dainties on the docks
And thou shalt read of summer frocks:
At evening by the sour canals
We'll hope to hear some madrigals.

Care on thy maiden brow shall put
A wreath of wrinkles, and thy foot

4. East Indian cedars.
1. Compare Christopher Marlowe's "A Passionate Shepherd to His Love" and Sir Walter Ralegh's "The Nymph's Reply to the Shepherd."

Be shod with pain: not silken dress
But toil shall tire thy loveliness.

Hunger shall make thy modest zone[2]
And cheat fond death of all but bone—
If these delights thy mind may move,
Then live with me and be my love.

1935

Sheepdog Trials in Hyde Park

A shepherd stands at one end of the arena.
Five sheep are unpenned at the other. His dog runs out
In a curve to behind them, fetches them straight to the shepherd,
Then drives the flock round a triangular course
Through a couple of gates and back to his master: two
Must be sorted there from the flock, then all five penned.
Gathering, driving away, shedding and penning
Are the plain words for the miraculous game.

An abstract game. What can the sheepdog make of such
Simplified terrain?—no hills, dales, bogs, walls, tracks,
Only a quarter-mile plain of grass, dumb crowds
Like crowds on hoardings around it, and behind them
Traffic or mounds of lovers and children playing.
Well, the dog is no landscape-fancier: his whole concern
Is with his master's whistle, and of course
With the flock—sheep are sheep anywhere for him.

The sheep are the chanciest element. Why, for instance,
Go through this gate when there's on either side of it
No wall or hedge but huge and viable space?
Why not eat the grass instead of being pushed around it?
Like a blob of quicksilver on a tilting board
The flock erratically runs, dithers, breaks up,
Is reassembled: their ruling idea is the dog;
And behind the dog, though they know it not yet, is a shepherd.

The shepherd knows that time is of the essence
But haste calamitous. Between dog and sheep
There is always an ideal distance, a perfect angle;
But these are constantly varying, so the man
Should anticipate each move through the dog, his medium.
The shepherd is the brain behind the dog's brain,
But his control of dog, like dog's of sheep,
Is never absolute—that's the beauty of it.

For beautiful it is. The guided missiles,
The black-and-white angels follow each quirk and jink of
The evasive sheep, play grandmother's-steps behind them,
Freeze to the ground, or leap to head off a straggler
Almost before it knows that it wants to stray,
As if radar-controlled. But they are not machines—

2. Old word for "belt" or "girdle."

You can feel them feeling mastery, doubt, chagrin:
Machines don't frolic when their job is done.

What's needfully done in the solitude of sheep-runs—
Those rough, real tasks become this stylized game,
A demonstration of intuitive wit
Kept natural by the saving grace of error.
To lift, to fetch, to drive, to shed, to pen
Are acts I recognize, with all they mean
Of shepherding the unruly, for a kind of
Controlled woolgathering is my work too.

1958

RICHARD EBERHART
(1904–)

The Fury of Aerial Bombardment

You would think the fury of aerial bombardment
Would rouse God to relent; the infinite spaces
Are still silent. He looks on shock-pried faces.
History, even, does not know what is meant.

You would feel that after so many centuries
God would give man to repent; yet he can kill
As Cain could, but with multitudinous will,
No farther advanced than in his ancient furies.

Was man made stupid to see his own stupidity?
Is God by definition indifferent, beyond us all?
Is the eternal truth man's fighting soul
Wherein the Beast ravens in its own avidity?

Of Van Wettering I speak, and Averill,
Names on a list, whose faces I do not recall
But they are gone to early death, who late in school
Distinguished the belt feed lever from the belt holding pawl.[1]

1947

PATRICK KAVANAGH
(1905–1967)

Inniskeen Road: July Evening

The bicycles go by in twos and threes—
There's a dance in Billy Brennan's barn to-night,
And there's the half-talk code of mysteries
And the wink-and-elbow language of delight.
Half-past eight and there is not a spot

1. Parts of the .50-caliber Browning machine gun, mounted in American aircraft during World War II. Eberhart was an aerial gunnery instructor during the summer of 1944.

Upon a mile of road, no shadow thrown
That might turn out a man or woman, not
A footfall tapping secrecies of stone.

I have what every poet hates in spite
Of all the solemn talk of contemplation.
Oh, Alexander Selkirk[1] knew the plight
Of being king and government and nation.
A road, a mile of kingdom, I am king
Of banks and stones and every blooming thing.

1936

Shancoduff

My black hills have never seen the sun rising,
Eternally they look north towards Armagh.
Lot's wife would not be salt[2] if she had been
Incurious as my black hills that are happy
When dawn whitens Glassdrummond chapel.

My hills hoard the bright shillings of March
While the sun searches in every pocket.
They are my Alps and I have climbed the Matterhorn
With a sheaf of hay for three perishing calves
In the field under the Big Forth of Rocksavage.

The sleety winds fondle the rushy beards of Shancoduff
While the cattle-drovers sheltering in the Featherna Bush
Look up and say: "Who owns them hungry hills
That the water-hen and snipe must have forsaken?
A poet? Then by heavens he must be poor."
I hear and is my heart not badly shaken?

Monaghan, 1934 1942

Spraying the Potatoes

The barrels of blue potato-spray
Stood on a headland of July
Beside an orchard wall where roses
Were young girls hanging from the sky.

The flocks of green potato-stalks
Were blossoms spread for sudden flight,
The Kerr's Pinks in a frivelled° blue, *bright*
The Arran Banners[3] wearing white.

And over that potato-field
A lazy veil of woven sun.
Dandelions growing on headlands, showing
Their unloved hearts to everyone.

1. A 17th-century English seaman whose real-life experiences formed the basis for Defoe's *Robinson Crusoe*. He lived for five years on the uninhabited island of Juan Fernandez.
2. In Genesis, Lot, a nephew of Abraham, escapes the destruction of the city of Sodom. His wife, however, is turned into a pillar of salt by God when she turns, while fleeing, to look back at the burning city.
3. Kerr's Pinks and Arran Banners are varieties of potatoes.

And I was there with the knapsack sprayer
On the barrel's edge poised. A wasp was floating
Dead on a sunken briar leaf
Over a copper-poisoned ocean.

The axle-roll of a rut-locked cart
Broke the burnt stick of noon in two.
An old man came through a corn-field
Remembering his youth and some Ruth[4] he knew.

He turned my way. "God further the work."
He echoed an ancient farming prayer.
I thanked him. He eyed the potato-drills.[5]
He said: "You are bound to have good ones there."

We talked and our talk was a theme of kings,
A theme for strings. He hunkered down
In the shade of the orchard wall. O roses
The old man dies in the young girl's frown.

And poet lost to potato fields,
Remembering the lime and copper smell
Of the spraying barrels he is not lost
Or till blossomed stalks cannot weave a spell.

1947

ROBERT PENN WARREN
(1905–)

Where the Slow Fig's Purple Sloth

Where the slow fig's purple sloth
Swells, I sit and meditate the
Nature of the soul, the fig exposes,
To the blaze of afternoon, one haunch
As purple-black as Africa, a single
Leaf the rest screens, but through it, light
Burns, and for the fig's bliss
The sun dies, the sun
Has died forever—far, oh far—
For the fig's bliss, thus.

The air
Is motionless, and the fig,
Motionless in that imperial and blunt
Languor of glut, swells, and inward
The fibers relax like a sigh in that
Hot darkness, go soft, the air
Is gold.

4. The chief character in the Book of Ruth. After the death of her husband, she went with her mother-in-law, Naomi, to Bethlehem. There she worked in the fields owned by Boaz, whom she later married.
5. Long, narrow trenches in which potatoes are planted.

When you
Split the fig, you will see
Lifting from the coarse and purple seed, its
Flesh like flame, purer
Than blood.

It fills
The darkening room with light.

1968

Sila

Sila, for the Eskimo, "is the air, not the sky; movement, not wind; the very breath of life, but not physical life; he is clear-sighted energy, activating intelligence; the powerful fluid circulating 'all around' and also within each individual . . ."
—LAROUSSE WORLD MYTHOLOGY

Upgrade, past snow-tangled bramble, past
Deadfall snow-buried, there—
The ruin of old stonework, where man-heart
Long ago had once lifted
In joy, and back muscles strained. "Stay, Sila!" the boy
Commanded the tawny great husky, broad-chested,
That in harness yet stood, forward-leaning. The boy
Stamped his cross-countries. Stared
At the ruin. Thought:
Two hundred years back—and it might
Have been me.

And wondered what name the man
Might have had. Thought:
Well, summer, I'll come
And hunt for the gravestones. Then thought
How letters that crude must be weathered away—how deeper
A skull must be pulping to earth, and now grinless.
But thought: *At least, I can touch it, whatever*
It is, stone or skull.

Was young, then he thought, *young as me, maybe.*

Then felt muscles tighten and clinch
At a sudden impulse of surprise
To find here the old mark of life that for life
Once had sung, while the axe-edge glittered in sunlight.

Oh, what are the years! his heart cried, and he felt
His own muscles pulsing in joy, just as when
Hands clasp for the lift of the beauty of butt-swell.

Land benched here, great beeches,
Gray, leafless, arising parklike and artful
From snow artificial as Christmas.
"Stay, Sila!" he called, and on level ground now
Slick glided to where the blue gleam of ice-eyes
Looked up in his own, with a knowledge deeper than words.
He snapped harness loose, wrapped cords at his waist, and—
The dog exploded.

From behind a beech deadfall, the doe, it had leaped,
Cow-awkward on earth, but magically airy in flight,
And weightless as wind, forelegs airward prowing
To seem as frail as a spider's, but hooves aglitter like glass
To cleave sunlight. Then,
Suddenly knifing the ice-crust as deep
As a trap, while the husky's wide paw-spread
Had opened like snowshoes behind.
Five leaps—and first blood, at a haunch,
Flesh laid back like a hunter's thin knife-slice.

Again, two more leaps, and white slash at belly—
Red line drawn clean on the curve. The boy's order
No use now: "Stay! Damn it, stay!" Until
Hand on harness, at last and too late, for
Red blood dripped now from white fang
To whiteness of snow, and eyes blue as steel drove into
The boy's eyes brain-deep, while, that instant,
All eons of friendship fled.
Then dog-eyes went earthward. The guts
Of the doe slip forth blue on the ice-crust.

The husky, stiff as in bronze cast, waits.

Only one thing to do. Who'd leave the doe there,
Dying slow into sunset, while all the small teeth—
Fox, field mouse, and wildcat—emerge
For their nocturnal feast? So the boy's knees bend.
Break the snow-crust like prayer,
And he cuddles the doe's head, and widening brown eyes
Seem ready, almost, to forgive.

Throat fur is cream color, eyes flecked with gold glintings.
He longs for connection, to give explanation. Sudden,
The head, now helpless, drops back on his shoulder. Twin eyes
Hold his own entrapped in their depth,
But his free hand, as though unaware,
Slides slow back
To grope for the knife-sheath.

The boy could not shut his eyes to the task,
As some fool girl might, but set
Eyes deeper in eyes, as he cradled the head, and gently
Held up the soft chin
To tauten the fullness of throat, and then,
As scrupulous as a well-trained tailor, set
The knife's needle point where acuteness
Would enter without prick of pain, and
Slashed in a single, deep motion.

He was sure that the doe
Never twitched.

On snow unconsciously heaped, he let down the head,
Aware even yet of the last embracement of gaze.
He watched, bewitched by the beauty, how blood flowed,

Red petal by petal, a great rose that bloomed where he stood.
How petal on petal, curve swelling past curve,
Gleamed forth at his feet on the snow,
And each petal sparkled with flicker of ice through the crimson,
As rays of last sun found a special glory in smallness.

He lifted his head, knife yet in hand, and westward
Fixed eyes beyond beech-bench to the snow-hatched
Stone thrust of the mountain, above which sky, too,
More majestically bloomed, but petals paler as higher—
The rose of the blood of the day. Still as stone,
So he stood. Then slowly—so slowly—
He raised the blade of the knife he loved honing, and wiped
The sweet warmness and wetness across his own mouth,
And set tongue to the edge of the silk-whetted steel.

He knew he knew something at last
That he'd never before known.
No name for it—no!

He snow-cleaned the knife. Sheathed it. Called: "Come!"
The dog, now docile, obeyed. With bare hands full of snow,
The boy washed him of blood and, comblike,
With fingers ennobled the ruff.

Then suddenly clasping the creature, he,
Over raw fur, past beeches, the mountain's snow-snag,
And the sky's slow paling of petals,
Cried out into vastness
Of silence: "Oh, world!"

He felt like a fool when tears came.

Some sixty years later, propped on death's pillow,
Again will he see that same scene, and try,
Heart straining, to utter that cry?—But
Cannot, breath short.

1980

Dream, Dump-heap, and Civilization

Like the stench and smudge of the old dump-heap
Of Norwalk,[1] Connecticut, the residue

Of my dream remains, but I make no
Sense of even the fragments. They are nothing

More significant than busted iceboxes and stinking mattresses
Of Norwalk, and other such human trash from which

Smudge rose by day, or coals winked red by night,
Like a sign to the desert-walkers

1. Norwalk and Westport (line 10) are towns in Connecticut.

Blessed by God's promise. Keep your foot on the gas,
And you'll get to Westport. But

What of my dream—stench, smudge, and fragments?
And behind it all a morning shadow, like guilt, strives.

To say what? How once I had lied to my mother and hid
In a closet and said, in darkness, aloud: "I hate you"?

Or how once, in total fascination, I watched a black boy
Take a corn knife and decapitate six kittens? Did I dream

That again last night? How he said: "Too many, dem"?
Did I dream of six kitten-heads staring all night at me?

All try to say something—still now trying
By daylight? Their blood inexhaustibly drips. Did I wake

With guilt? How rarely is air here pure as in the Montana mountains!
Sometime we must probe more deeply the problem of complicity.

Is civilization possible without it?

1980

JOHN BETJEMAN
(1906–)

The Arrest of Oscar Wilde at the Cadogan Hotel[1]

He sipped at a weak hock[2] and seltzer
  As he gazed at the London skies
Through the Nottingham lace of the curtains
  Or was it his bees-winged[3] eyes?

To the right and before him Pont Street
  Did tower in her new built red,
As hard as the morning gaslight
  That shone on his unmade bed,

"I want some more hock in my seltzer,
  And Robbie,[4] please give me your hand—
Is this the end or beginning?
  How can I understand?

"So you've brought me the latest *Yellow Book*:[5]
  And Buchan[6] has got in it now:

1. On May 27, 1895, Wilde was found guilty of offenses against Section 11 of the Criminal Law Amendment Act (1885), which punished "indecencies between grown men, in public or private," and was sentenced to two years hard labor.
2. Generic term for German white wine.
3. Filmed over, from "bees-wing": "a film of tartar scales formed in port and some other wines after long keeping" (*Webster's*).
4. Robert Ross, a friend who remained loyal to Wilde after the latter's downfall.
5. *The Yellow Book* was a hard-covered, elaborately illustrated periodical which appeared quarterly from 1894 to 1897, and in which many writers associated with the aesthetic movement were represented.
6. John Buchan, later Lord Tweedsmuir (1875–1940), author of several popular novels, including *Thirty-nine Steps* (1915).

Approval of what is approved of
Is as false as a well-kept vow.

"More hock, Robbie—where is the seltzer?
Dear boy, pull again at the bell!
They are all little better than *cretins*,
Though this *is* the Cadogan Hotel.

"One astrakhan coat is at Willis's—
Another one's at the Savoy:
Do fetch my morocco portmanteau,
And bring them on later, dear boy."

A thump, and a murmur of voices—
("Oh why must they make such a din?")
As the door of the bedroom swung open
And TWO PLAIN CLOTHES POLICEMEN came in:

"Mr. Woilde, we 'ave come for tew take yew
Where felons and criminals dwell:
We must ask yew tew leave with us quoietly
For this *is* the Cadogan Hotel."

He rose, and he put down *The Yellow Book*.
He staggered—and, terrible-eyed,
He brushed past the palms on the staircase
And was helped to a hansom outside.

1937

W. H. AUDEN (1907–1973)

[For What as Easy]

For what as easy
For what though small,
For what is well
Because between,
To you simply
From me I mean.

Who goes with who
The bedclothes say,
As I and you
Go kissed away,
The data given,
The senses even.

Fate is not late,
Nor the speech rewritten,
Nor one word forgotten,
Said at the start
About heart,
By heart, for heart.

1932 1945

As I Walked Out One Evening

As I walked out one evening,
Walking down Bristol Street,
The crowds upon the pavement
Were fields of harvest wheat.

And down by the brimming river
I heard a lover sing
Under an arch of the railway:
"Love has no ending.

"I'll love you, dear, I'll love you
Till China and Africa meet,
And the river jumps over the mountain
And the salmon sing in the street,

"I'll love till the ocean
Is folded and hung up to dry
And the seven stars go squawking
Like geese about the sky.

The years shall run like rabbits,
For in my arms I hold
The Flower of the Ages,
And the first love of the world."

But all the clocks in the city
Began to whirr and chime:
"O let not Time deceive you,
You cannot conquer Time.

"In the burrows of the Nightmare
Where Justice naked is,
Time watches from the shadow
And coughs when you would kiss.

"In headaches and in worry
Vaguely life leaks away,
And Time will have his fancy
Tomorrow or today.

"Into many a green valley
Drifts the appalling snow;
Time breaks the threaded dances
And the diver's brilliant bow.

"O plunge your hands in water,
Plunge them in up to the wrist;
Stare, stare in the basin
And wonder what you've missed.

"The glacier knocks in the cupboard,
The desert sighs in the bed,

And the crack in the teacup opens
   A lane to the land of the dead.

"Where the beggars raffle the banknotes
   And the Giant is enchanting to Jack,
And the Lily-white Boy is a Roarer,
   And Jill goes down on her back.

"O look, look in the mirror,
   O look in your distress;
Life remains a blessing
   Although you cannot bless.

"O stand, stand at the window
   As the tears scald and start;
You shall love your crooked neighbor
   With your crooked heart."

It was late, late in the evening,
   The lovers they were gone;
The clocks had ceased their chiming,
   And the deep river ran on.

1940

Musée des Beaux Arts[1]

About suffering they were never wrong,
The Old Masters: how well they understood
Its human position; how it takes place
While someone else is eating or opening a window or just walking dully along;
How, when the aged are reverently, passionately waiting
For the miraculous birth, there always must be
Children who did not specially want it to happen, skating
On a pond at the edge of the wood:
They never forgot
That even the dreadful martyrdom must run its course
Anyhow in a corner, some untidy spot
Where the dogs go on with their doggy life and the torturer's horse
Scratches its innocent behind on a tree.

In Brueghel's *Icarus*,[2] for instance: how everything turns away
Quite leisurely from the disaster; the ploughman may
Have heard the splash, the forsaken cry,
But for him it was not an important failure; the sun shone
As it had to on the white legs disappearing into the green
Water; and the expensive delicate ship that must have seen
Something amazing, a boy falling out of the sky,
Had somewhere to get to and sailed calmly on.

1940

1. Museum of Fine Arts (Fr.).
2. *The Fall of Icarus*, by Pieter Brueghel (ca. 1525–69), the painting described here, is in the Musée d'Art Ancien, a section of the Musées Royaux des Beaux Arts, in Brussels. Daedalus, the greatly skilled Athenian craftsman, constructed for Minos, king of Crete, a labyrinth in which the Minotaur was kept, but was then imprisoned in it himself with his son Icarus. He made wings of feathers and wax, w th which they flew away, but Icarus flew too near the sun, the wax melted, and he fell into the sea.

Law Like Love

Law, say the gardeners, is the sun,
Law is the one
All gardeners obey
Tomorrow, yesterday, today.

Law is the wisdom of the old
The impotent grandfathers feebly scold;
The grandchildren put out a treble tongue,
Law is the senses of the young.

Law, says the priest with a priestly look,
Expounding to an unpriestly people,
Law is the words in my priestly book,
Law is my pulpit and my steeple.

Law, says the judge as he looks down his nose,
Speaking clearly and most severely,
Law is as I've told you before,
Law is as you know I suppose,
Law is but let me explain it once more,
Law is The Law.

Yet law-abiding scholars write;
Law is neither wrong nor right,
Law is only crimes
Punished by places and by times,
Law is the clothes men wear
Anytime, anywhere,
Law is Goodmorning and Goodnight.

Others say, Law is our Fate;
Others say, Law is our State;
Others say, others say
Law is no more
Law has gone away.

And always the loud angry crowd
Very angry and very loud
Law is We,
And always the soft idiot softly Me.

If we, dear, know we know no more
Than they about the Law,
If I no more than you
Know what we should and should not do
Except that all agree
Gladly or miserably
That the Law is
And that all know this,
If therefore thinking it absurd
To identify Law with some other word,
Unlike so many men
I cannot say Law is again,

No more than they can we suppress
The universal wish to guess
Or slip out of our own position
Into an unconcerned condition.
Although I can at least confine
Your vanity and mine
To stating timidly
A timid similarity,
We shall boast anyway:
Like love I say.

Like love we don't know where or why,
Like love we can't compel or fly,
Like love we often weep,
Like love we seldom keep.

1940

In Praise of Limestone

If it form the one landscape that we, the inconstant ones,
  Are consistently homesick for, this is chiefly
Because it dissolves in water. Mark these rounded slopes
  With their surface fragrance of thyme and, beneath,
A secret system of caves and conduits; hear the springs
  That spurt out everywhere with a chuckle,
Each filling a private pool for its fish and carving
  Its own little ravine whose cliffs entertain
The butterfly and the lizard; examine this region
  Of short distances and definite places:
What could be more like Mother or a fitter background
  For her son, the flirtatious male who lounges
Against a rock in the sunlight, never doubting
  That for all his faults he is loved; whose works are but
Extensions of his power to charm? From weathered outcrop
  To hilltop temple, from appearing waters to
Conspicuous fountains, from a wild to a formal vineyard,
  Are ingenious but short steps that a child's wish
To receive more attention than his brothers, whether
  By pleasing or teasing, can easily take.

Watch, then, the band of rivals as they climb up and down
  Their steep stone gennels° in twos and threes, at times *channels, passages*
Arm in arm, but never, thank God, in step; or engaged
  On the shady side of a square at midday in
Voluble discourse, knowing each other too well to think
  There are any important secrets, unable
To conceive a god whose temper tantrums are moral
  And not to be pacified by a clever line
Or a good lay: for, accustomed to a stone that responds,
  They have never had to veil their faces in awe
Of a crater whose blazing fury could not be fixed;
  Adjusted to the local needs of valleys
Where everything can be touched or reached by walking,
  Their eyes have never looked into infinite space
Through the latticework of a nomad's comb; born lucky,
  Their legs have never encountered the fungi
And insects of the jungle, the monstrous forms and lives
  With which we have nothing, we like to hope, in common.

So, when one of them goes to the bad, the way his mind works
Remains comprehensible: to become a pimp
Or deal in fake jewelry or ruin a fine tenor voice
For effects that bring down the house, could happen to all
But the best and the worst of us . . .
That is why, I suppose,
The best and worst never stayed here long but sought
Immoderate soils where the beauty was not so external,
The light less public and the meaning of life
Something more than a mad camp. "Come!" cried the granite wastes,
"How evasive is your humor, how accidental
Your kindest kiss, how permanent is death." (Saints-to-be
Slipped away sighing.) "Come!" purred the clays and gravels.
"On our plains there is room for armies to drill; rivers
Wait to be tamed and slaves to construct you a tomb
In the grand manner: soft as the earth is mankind and both
Need to be altered." (Intendant Caesars rose and
Left, slamming the door.) But the really reckless were fetched
By an older colder voice, the oceanic whisper:
"I am the solitude that asks and promises nothing;
That is how I shall set you free. There is no love;
There are only the various envies, all of them sad."
They were right, my dear, all those voices were right.
And still are; this land is not the sweet home that it looks,
Nor its peace the historical calm of a site
Where something was settled once and for all: A backward
And dilapidated province, connected
To the big busy world by a tunnel, with a certain
Seedy appeal, is that all it is now? Not quite:
It has a worldly duty which in spite of itself
It does not neglect, but calls into question
All the Great Powers assume; it disturbs our rights. The poet,
Admired for his earnest habit of calling
The sun the sun, his mind Puzzle, is made uneasy
By these marble statues which so obviously doubt
His antimythological myth; and these gamins,
Pursuing the scientist down the tiled colonnade
With such lively offers, rebuke his concern for Nature's
Remotest aspects: I, too, am reproached, for what
And how much you know. Not to lose time, not to get caught,
Not to be left behind, not, please! to resemble
The beasts who repeat themselves, or a thing like water
Or stone whose conduct can be predicted, these
Are our Common Prayer, whose greatest comfort is music
Which can be made anywhere, is invisible,
And does not smell. In so far as we have to look forward
To death as a fact, no doubt we are right: But if
Sins can be forgiven, if bodies rise from the dead,
These modifications of matter into
Innocent athletes and gesticulating fountains,
Made solely for pleasure, make a further point:
The blessed will not care what angle they are regarded from,
Having nothing to hide. Dear, I know nothing of
Either, but when I try to imagine a faultless love
Or the life to come, what I hear is the murmur
Of underground streams, what I see is a limestone landscape.

1951

A. D. HOPE
(1907–)

Australia

A Nation of trees, drab green and desolate gray
In the field uniform of modern wars,
Darkens her hills, those endless, outstretched paws
Of Sphinx[1] demolished or stone lion worn away.

They call her a young country, but they lie:
She is the last of lands, the emptiest,
A woman beyond her change of life, a breast
Still tender but within the womb is dry.

Without songs, architecture, history:
The emotions and superstitions of younger lands,
Her rivers of water drown among inland sands,
The river of her immense stupidity

Floods her monotonous tribes from Cairns to Perth.[2]
In them at last the ultimate men arrive
Whose boast is not: "we live" but "we survive,"
A type who will inhabit the dying earth.

And her five cities, like five teeming sores,
Each drains her: a vast parasite robber-state
Where second-hand Europeans pullulate
Timidly on the edge of alien shores.

Yet there are some like me turn gladly home
From the lush jungle of modern thought, to find
The Arabian desert of the human mind,
Hoping, if still from the deserts the prophets come,

Such savage and scarlet as no green hills dare
Springs in that waste, some spirit which escapes
The learned doubt, the chatter of cultured apes
Which is called civilization over there.

1939

The Elegy

VARIATIONS ON A THEME OF THE SEVENTEENTH CENTURY [3]

Madam, no more! The time has come to eat.
The spirit of man is nourished, too, with meat.
Those heroes and the warriors of old—
Feasting between their battles made them bold.

1. A reference to the monumental stone sphinx of Egypt.
2. I.e., from one end of the continent to the other. Cairns is at the far northeast of Australia, Perth at the southwest.

3. Seventeenth-century poets, such as Donne, Carew, and Marvell, revived the classical tradition of witty erotic poetry. See Donne's *Elegy XIX*, above.

When Venus in the west hung out her lamp,[4]
The rattling sons of Mars marched home to camp;
And while around the fires their wounds were dressed,
And tale was matched with tale, and jest with jest,
Flagons of wine and oxen roasted whole
Refreshed their bodies and restored the soul.

Come, leave the bed; put on your dress; efface
Awhile this dazzling armory of grace!
Flushed and rejoicing from the well-fought fight
Now day lies panting in the arms of night;
The first dews tremble on the darkening field;
Put up your naked weapons, the bright shield
Of triumph glinting to the early stars;
Call our troops home with triumpets from their wars;
And, as wise generals, let them rest and dine
And celebrate our truce with meat and wine.
See, the meek table on our service waits;
The devil in crystal winks beside our plates;
These veterans of love's war we shall repay
And crown with feasts the glories of the day.

Think no disgrace, if now they play a part
Less worthy of the soldiers of the heart.
Though these we led were granted, even as we,
Their moment's draught of immortality,
We do but snatch our instant on the height
And in the valleys still live out the night.
Yet they surrender nothing which is theirs.
Nature is frugal in her ministers;
Each to some humbler office must return,
And so must we. Then grudge it not, but learn
In this the noble irony of kind:° *sexual love*
These fierce, quick hands that rove and clasp must find
Other employment now with knife and fork;
Our mouths that groaned with joy, now eat and talk;
These chief commanders, too, without debate,
Sink to the lowliest service of the state.
Only our eyes observe no armistice;
Sparkling with love's perpetual surprise,
Their bright vedettes° keep watch from hill to hill *sentinel outposts*
And, when they meet, renew the combat still.
And yet to view you would I linger on:
This is the rarest moment, soonest gone.
While now the marching stars invest the sky
And the wide lands beneath surrendered lie,
Their streams and forests, parks and fields and farms,
Like this rich empire tranquil in my arms,
Seem lovelier in the last withdrawing light
And, as they vanish, most enchant the sight.
Still let me watch those countries as they fade
And all their lucid contours sink in shade;
The mounting thighs, the line of flank and breast,
Yet harbor a clear splendor from the west;
Though twilight draws into its shadowy reign

4. I.e., the evening star.

This breathing valley and that glimmering plain,
Still let my warrior heart with fresh delight
Rove and reflect: "Here, here began the fight;
Between those gentle hills I paused to rest,
And on this vale the kiss of triumph pressed;
There, full encircled by the frantic foe,
I rode between the lilies and the snow;
And, in this copse that parts the dark and shine,
Plundered the treasures of the hidden mine;
Down those long slopes in slow retreat I drew;
And here renewed the charge; and here, anew
Met stroke with stroke and touched, at the last breath,
The unimagined ecstasy of death."

Full darkness! Time enough the lamps were lit.
Let us to dinner, Madam; wine and wit
Must have their hour, even as love and war,
And what's to come revives what went before.
Come now, for see the Captain of my lust,
He had so stoutly fought and stiffly thrust,
Fallen, diminished on the field he lies;
Cover his face, he dreams in paradise.
We, while he sleeps, shall dine; and, when that's done,
Drink to his resurrection later on.

1955

Imperial[5] Adam

Imperial Adam, naked in the dew,
Felt his brown flanks and found the rib was gone.
Puzzled he turned and saw where, two and two,
The mighty spoor of Jahweh° marked the lawn. *Jehovah*

Then he remembered through mysterious sleep
The surgeon fingers probing at the bone,
The voice so far away, so rich and deep:
"It is not good for him to live alone."[6]

Turning once more he found Man's counterpart
In tender parody breathing at his side.
He knew her at first sight, he knew by heart
Her allegory of sense unsatisfied.

The pawpaw drooped its golden breasts above
Less generous than the honey of her flesh;
The innocent sunlight showed the place of love;
The dew on its dark hairs winked crisp and fresh.

This plump gourd severed from his virile root,
She promised on the turf of Paradise
Delicious pulp of the forbidden fruit;
Sly as the snake she loosed her sinuous thighs,

5. I.e., emperor.
6. Genesis 2.18: "And the Lord said, It is not good that the man should be alone." Eve was created from one of Adam's ribs (cf. line 6).

And waking, smiled up at him from the grass;
Her breasts rose softly and he heard her sigh—
From all the beasts whose pleasant task it was
In Eden to increase and multiply

Adam had learned the jolly deed of kind:
He took her in his arms and there and then,
Like the clean beasts, embracing from behind,
Began in joy to found the breed of men.

Then from the spurt of seed within her broke
Her terrible and triumphant female cry,
Split upward by the sexual lightning stroke.
It was the beasts now who stood watching by:

The gravid elephant, the calving hind,
The breeding bitch, the she-ape big with young
Were the first gentle midwives of mankind;
The teeming lioness rasped her with her tongue;

The proud vicuña nuzzled her as she slept
Lax on the grass; and Adam watching too
Saw how her dumb breasts at their ripening wept,
The great pod of her belly swelled and grew,

And saw its water break, and saw, in fear,
Its quaking muscles in the act of birth,
Between her legs a pigmy face appear,
And the first murderer[7] lay upon the earth.

1955

LOUIS MacNEICE
(1907–1963)

The Sunlight on the Garden

The sunlight on the garden
Hardens and grows cold,
We cannot cage the minute
Within its nets of gold,
When all is told
We cannot beg for pardon.

Our freedom as free lances
Advances towards its end;
The earth compels, upon it
Sonnets and birds descend;
And soon, my friend,
We shall have no time for dances.

The sky was good for flying
Defying the church bells

7. See Genesis 4: "And Adam knew Eve his wife; and she conceived, and bare Cain . . . and it came to pass . . . that Cain rose up against Abel his brother, and slew him."

And every evil iron
Siren and what it tells:
The earth compels,
We are dying, Egypt, dying[1]

And not expecting pardon,
Hardened in heart anew,
But glad to have sat under
Thunder and rain with you,
And grateful too
For sunlight on the garden.

1938

Bagpipe Music[2]

It's no go the merrygoround, it's no go the rickshaw,
All we want is a limousine and a ticket for the peepshow.
Their knickers[3] are made of crêpe-de-chine, their shoes are made of python,
Their halls are lined with tiger rugs and their walls with heads of bison.

John MacDonald found a corpse, put it under the sofa,
Waited till it came to life and hit it with a poker,
Sold its eyes for souvenirs, sold its blood for whiskey,
Kept its bones for dumbbells to use when he was fifty.

It's no go the Yogi-man, it's no go Blavatsky,[4]
All we want is a bank balance and a bit of skirt in a taxi.

Annie MacDougall went to milk, caught her foot in the heather,
Woke to hear a dance record playing of Old Vienna.
It's no go your maidenheads, it's no go your culture,
All we want is a Dunlop tire and the devil mend the puncture.

The Laird o' Phelps spent Hogmanay[5] declaring he was sober,
Counted his feet to prove the fact and found he had one foot over.
Mrs. Carmichael had her fifth, looked at the job with repulsion,
Said to the midwife "Take it away; I'm through with overproduction."

It's no go the gossip column, it's no go the Ceilidh,[6]
All we want is a mother's help and a sugar-stick for the baby.

Willie Murray cut his thumb, couldn't count the damage,
Took the hide of an Ayrshire cow and used it for a bandage.
His brother caught three hundred cran[7] when the seas were lavish,
Threw the bleeders back in the sea and went upon the parish.[8]

It's no go the Herring Board, it's no go the Bible,
All we want is a packet of fags° when our hands are idle. *cigarettes*

1. From *Antony and Cleopatra,* IV.xv.41, Antony's speech to Cleopatra, "I am dying, Egypt, dying."
2. The poem is set in Scotland in the 1930's, the years of the Depression, years which led up to the Munich crisis of 1938 and to the outbreak of World War II in 1939.
3. Women's undergarments.
4. Madame Helena P. Blavatsky (1831–91), Russian occultist, one of the founders of the Theosophical Society, which had flourished in London around the turn of the century and in whose writings there was renewed interest in the 1930's.
5. Scottish name given to the last day of the year.
6. (Pronounced *kaley*), Gaelic term for a round of gossiping visits.
7. A measure for the quantity of just-caught herrings.
8. I.e., went on relief.

It's no go the picture palace, it's no go the stadium,
It's no go the country cot with a pot of pink geraniums,
It's no go the Government grants, it's no go the elections,
Sit on your arse for fifty years and hang your hat on a pension.

It's no go my honey love, it's no go my poppet;
Work your hands from day to day, the winds will blow the profit.
The glass° is falling hour by hour, the glass with fall forever, *barometer*
But if you break the bloody glass you won't hold up the weather.

1938

London Rain

The rain of London pimples
The ebony street with white
And the neon-lamps of London
Stain the canals of night
And the park becomes a jungle
In the alchemy of night.

My wishes turn to violent
Horses black as coal—
The randy mares of fancy,
The stallions of the soul—
Eager to take the fences
That fence about my soul.

Across the countless chimneys
The horses ride and across
The country to the channel
Where warning beacons toss,
To a place where God and No-God
Play at pitch and toss.

Whichever wins I am happy
For God will give me bliss
But No-God will absolve me
From all I do amiss
And I need not suffer conscience
If the world was made amiss.

Under God we can reckon
On pardon when we fall
But if we are under No-God
Nothing will matter at all,
Adultery and murder
Will count for nothing at all.

So reinforced by logic
As having nothing to lose
My lust goes riding horseback
To ravish where I choose,
To burgle all the turrets
Of beauty as I choose.

But now the rain gives over
Its dance upon the town,

Logic and lust together
Come dimly tumbling down,
And neither God nor No-God
Is either up or down.

The argument was wilful,
The alternatives untrue,
We need no metaphysics
To sanction what we do
Or to muffle us in comfort
From what we did not do.

Whether the living river
Began in bog or lake,
The world is what was given,
The world is what we make.
And we only can discover
Life in the life we make.

So let the water sizzle
Upon the gleaming slates,
There will be sunshine after
When the rain abates
And rain returning duly
When the sun abates.

My wishes now come homeward,
Their gallopings in vain,
Logic and lust are quiet
And again it starts to rain;
Falling asleep I listen
To the falling London rain.

1941

Star-gazer

Forty-two years ago (to me if to no one else
The number is of some interest) it was a brilliant starry night
And the westward train was empty and had no corridors
So darting from side to side I could catch the unwonted sight
Of those almost intolerably bright
Holes, punched in the sky, which excited me partly because
Of their Latin names and partly because I had read in the textbooks
How very far off they were, it seemed their light
Had left them (some at least) long years before I was.

And this remembering now I mark that what
Light was leaving some of them at least then,
Forty-two years ago, will never arrive
In time for me to catch it, which light when
It does get here may find that there is not
Anyone left alive
To run from side to side in a late night train
Admiring it and adding noughts in vain.

1967

THEODORE ROETHKE
(1908–1963)

Root Cellar

Nothing would sleep in that cellar, dank as a ditch,
Bulbs broke out of boxes hunting for chinks in the dark,
Shoots dangled and drooped,
Lolling obscenely from mildewed crates,
Hung down long yellow evil necks, like tropical snakes.
And what a congress of stinks!
Roots ripe as old bait,
Pulpy stems, rank, silo-rich,
Leaf-mold, manure, lime, piled against slippery planks.
Nothing would give up life:
Even the dirt kept breathing a small breath.

1948

My Papa's Waltz

The whiskey on your breath
Could make a small boy dizzy;
But I hung on like death:
Such waltzing was not easy.

We romped until the pans
Slid from the kitchen shelf;
My mother's countenance
Could not unfrown itself.

The hand that held my wrist
Was battered on one knuckle;
At every step you missed
My right ear scraped a buckle.

You beat time on my head
With a palm caked hard by dirt,
Then waltzed me off to bed
Still clinging to your shirt.

1948

Elegy for Jane

MY STUDENT, THROWN BY A HORSE

I remember the neckcurls, limp and damp as tendrils;
And her quick look, a sidelong pickerel smile;
And how, once startled into talk, the light syllables leaped for her,
And she balanced in the delight of her thought,
A wren, happy, tail into the wind,
Her song trembling the twigs and small branches.
The shade sang with her;
The leaves, their whispers turned to kissing;
And the mold sang in the bleached valleys under the rose.

Oh, when she was sad, she cast herself down into such a pure depth,
Even a father could not find her:
Scraping her cheek against straw;
Stirring the clearest water.

My sparrow, you are not here,
Waiting like a fern, making a spiny shadow.
The sides of wet stones cannot console me,
Nor the moss, wound with the last light.

If only I could nudge you from this sleep,
My maimed darling, my skittery pigeon.
Over this damp grave I speak the words of my love:
I, with no rights in this matter,
Neither father nor lover.

1953

The Waking

I wake to sleep, and take my waking slow.
I feel my fate in what I cannot fear.
I learn by going where I have to go.

We think by feeling. What is there to know?
I hear my being dance from ear to ear.
I wake to sleep, and take my waking slow.

Of those so close beside me, which are you?
God bless the Ground! I shall walk softly there,
And learn by going where I have to go.

Light takes the Tree; but who can tell us how?
The lowly worm climbs up a winding stair;
I wake to sleep, and take my waking slow.

Great Nature has another thing to do
To you and me; so take the lively air,
And, lovely, learn by going where to go.

This shaking keeps me steady. I should know.
What falls away is always. And is near.
I wake to sleep, and take my waking slow.
I learn by going where I have to go.

1953

I Knew a Woman

I knew a woman, lovely in her bones,
When small birds sighed, she would sigh back at them;
Ah, when she moved, she moved more ways than one:
The shapes a bright container can contain!
Of her choice virtues only gods should speak,
Or English poets who grew up on Greek
(I'd have them sing in chorus, cheek to cheek).

How well her wishes went! She stroked my chin,
She taught me Turn, and Counter-turn, and Stand;[1]
She taught me Touch, that undulant white skin;
I nibbled meekly from her proffered hand;
She was the sickle; I, poor I, the rake,
Coming behind her for her pretty sake
(But what prodigious mowing we did make).

Love likes a gander, and adores a goose:
Her full lips pursed, the errant note to seize;
She played it quick, she played it light and loose,
My eyes, they dazzled at her flowing knees;
Her several parts could keep a pure repose,
Or one hip quiver with a mobile nose
(She moved in circles, and those circles moved).

Let seed be grass, and grass turn into hay:
I'm martyr to a motion not my own;
What's freedom for? To know eternity.
I swear she cast a shadow white as stone.
But who would count eternity in days?
These old bones live to learn her wanton ways:
(I measure time by how a body sways).

1958

The Far Field

1

I dream of journeys repeatedly:
Of flying like a bat deep into a narrowing tunnel,
Of driving alone, without luggage, out a long peninsula,
The road lined with snow-laden second growth,
A fine dry snow ticking the windshield,
Alternate snow and sleet, no on-coming traffic,
And no lights behind, in the blurred side-mirror,
The road changing from glazed tarface to a rubble of stone,
Ending at last in a hopeless sand-rut,
Where the car stalls,
Churning in a snowdrift
Until the headlights darken.

2

At the field's end, in the corner missed by the mower,
Where the turf drops off into a grass-hidden culvert,
Haunt of the cat-bird, nesting-place of the field-mouse,
Not too far away from the ever-changing flower-dump,
Among the tin cans, tires, rusted pipes, broken machinery,—
One learned of the eternal;
And in the shrunken face of a dead rat, eaten by rain and ground-beetles
(I found it lying among the rubble of an old coal bin)
And the tom-cat, caught near the pheasant-run,
Its entrails strewn over the half-grown flowers,
Blasted to death by the night watchman.

I suffered for birds, for young rabbits caught in the mower,
My grief was not excessive.

1. Literary terms, for the three parts of the Pindaric ode.

For to come upon warblers in early May
Was to forget time and death:
How they filled the oriole's elm, a twittering restless cloud, all one morning,
And I watched and watched till my eyes blurred from the bird shapes,—
Cape May, Blackburnian, Cerulean—
Moving, elusive as fish, fearless,
Hanging, bunched like young fruit, bending the end branches,
Still for a moment,
Then pitching away in half-flight,
Lighter than finches,
While the wrens bickered and sang in the half-green hedgerows,
And the flicker drummed from his dead tree in the chicken-yard.

—Or to lie naked in sand,
In the silted° shallows of a slow river, *sedimented*
Fingering a shell,
Thinking:
Once I was something like this, mindless,
Or perhaps with another mind, less peculiar;
Or to sink down to the hips in a mossy quagmire;[2]
Or, with skinny knees, to sit astride a wet log,
Believing:
I'll return again,
As a snake or a raucous bird,
Or, with luck, as a lion.

I learned not to fear infinity,
The far field, the windy cliffs of forever,
The dying of time in the white light of tomorrow,
The wheel turning away from itself,
The sprawl of the wave,
The on-coming water.

3

The river turns on itself,
The tree retreats into its own shadow.
I feel a weightless change, a moving forward
As of water quickening before a narrowing channel
When banks converge, and the wide river whitens;
Or when two rivers combine, the blue glacial torrent
And the yellowish-green from the mountainy upland,—
At first a swift rippling between rocks,
Then a long running over flat stones
Before descending to the alluvial plain,[3]
To the clay banks ,and the wild grapes hanging from the elmtrees.
The slightly trembling water
Dropping a fine yellow silt where the sun stays;
And the crabs bask near the edge,
The weedy edge, alive with small snakes and bloodsuckers—
I have come to a still, but not a deep center,
A point outside the glittering current;
My eyes stare at the bottom of a river,
At the irregular stones, iridescent sandgrains,
My mind moves in more than one place,
In a country half-land, half-water.

2. Soft, wet land.
3. Sand or soil built up from the deposits of running water.

I am renewed by death, thought of my death,
The dry scent of a dying garden in September,
The wind fanning the ash of a low fire.
What I love is near at hand,
Always, in earth and air.

4

The lost self changes,
Turning toward the sea,
A sea-shape turning around—
An old man with his feet before the fire,
In robes of green, in garments of adieu.

A man faced with his own immensity
Wakes all the waves, all their loose wandering fire.
The murmur of the absolute, the why
Of being born fails on his naked ears.
His spirit moves like monumental wind
That gentles on a sunny blue plateau.
He is the end of things, the final man.

All finite things reveal infinitude:
The mountain with its singular bright shade
Like the blue shine on freshly frozen snow,
The after-light upon ice-burdened pines;
Odor of basswood on a mountain-slope,
A scent beloved of bees;
Silence of water above a sunken tree:
The pure serene of memory in one man—
A ripple widening from a single stone
Winding around the waters of the world.

1964

Wish for a Young Wife

My lizard, my lively writher,
May your limbs never wither,
May the eyes in your face
Survive the green ice
Of envy's mean gaze;
May you live out your life
Without hate, without grief,
And your hair ever blaze,
In the sun, in the sun,
When I am undone,
When I am no one.

1964

In a Dark Time[4]

In a dark time, the eye begins to see,
I meet my shadow in the deepening shade;[5]
I hear my echo in the echoing wood—
A lord of nature[6] weeping to a tree.

4. Roethke has said that the title refers to a dark night of the soul.

5. "Deepening despair, with a hint of approaching death" (Roethke's note).

6. "A derisive epithet at this point in the poem" (Roethke's note).

I live between the heron and the wren,[7]
Beasts of the hill and serpents of the den.

What's madness but nobility of soul
At odds with circumstance? The day's on fire!
I know the purity of pure despair,
My shadow pinned against a sweating wall.
That place among the rocks—is it a cave,
Or winding path? The edge is what I have.

A steady storm of correspondences!
A night flowing with birds, a ragged moon,
And in broad day the midnight come again!
A man goes far to find out what he is—
Death of the self in a long, tearless night,
All natural shapes blazing unnatural light.

Dark, dark my light, and darker my desire.
My soul, like some heat-maddened summer fly,
Keeps buzzing at the sill. Which I is *I*?
A fallen man, I climb out of my fear.
The mind enters itself, and God the mind,
And one is One, free in the tearing[8] wind.

1964

A. M. KLEIN
(1909–1972)

Indian Reservation: Caughnawaga[1]

Where are the braves, the faces like autumn fruit,
who stared at the child from the colored frontispiece?
And the monosyllabic chief who spoke with his throat?
Where are the tribes, the feathered bestiaries?[2]—
Rank Aesop's animals erect and red,
with fur on their names to make all live things kin'—
Chief Running Deer, Black Bear, Old Buffalo Head?

Childhood, that wished me Indian, hoped that
one afterschool I'd leave the classroom chalk,
the varnish smell, the watered dust of the street,
to join the clean outdoors and the Iroquois track.
Childhood; but always,—as on a calendar,—
there stood that chief, with arms akimbo, waiting
the runaway mascot paddling to his shore.

With what strange moccasin stealth that scene is changed!
With French names, without paint, in overalls,
their bronze, like their nobility expunged,—

7. The heron is a solitary bird, the wren a sociable one—among other differences.
8. With a pun on "tearless" (line 17), according to a note of Roethke's.
1. Small Indian reservation in southern Quebec, across the St. Lawrence River from Montreal.
2. Old books describing, often with allegorical overtones, the habits of real and mythical animals; "Aesop" was the ancient Greek author of fables, many of which involved animal protagonists.

the men. Beneath their alimentary shawls
sit like black tents their squaws; while for the tourist's
brown pennies scattered at the old church door,
the ragged papooses jump, and bite the dust.

Their past is sold in a shop: the beaded shoes,
the sweetgrass basket, the curio Indian,
burnt wood and gaudy cloth and inch-canoes—
trophies and scalpings for a traveler's den.

Sometimes, it's true, they dance, but for a bribe;
after a deal don the bedraggled feather
and welcome a white mayor to the tribe.

This is a grassy ghetto, and no home.
And these are fauna in a museum kept.
The better hunters have prevailed. The game,
losing its blood, now makes these grounds its crypt.
The animals pale, the shine of the fur is lost,
bleached are their living bones. About them watch
as through a mist, the pious prosperous ghosts.

1948

STEPHEN SPENDER
(1909–)

I Think Continually of Those Who Were Truly Great

I think continually of those who were truly great.
Who, from the womb, remembered the soul's history
Through corridors of light where the hours are suns
Endless and singing. Whose lovely ambition
Was that their lips, still touched with fire,
Should tell of the Spirit clothed from head to foot in song.
And who hoarded from the Spring branches
The desires falling across their bodies like blossoms.

What is precious is never to forget
The essential delight of the blood drawn from ageless springs
Breaking through rocks in worlds before our earth.
Never to deny its pleasure in the morning simple light
Nor its grave evening demand for love.
Never to allow gradually the traffic to smother
With noise and fog the flowering of the spirit.

Near the snow, near the sun, in the highest fields
See how these names are fêted by the waving grass
And by the streamers of white cloud
And whispers of wind in the listening sky.
The names of those who in their lives fought for life
Who wore at their hearts the fire's center.
Born of the sun they traveled a short while towards the sun,
And left the vivid air signed with their honor.

1933

CHARLES OLSON
(1910–1970)

Variations Done for Gerald Van De Wiele[1]

I. Le Bonheur[2]

dogwood flakes
what is green

the petals
from the apple
blow on the road

mourning doves
mark the sway
of the afternoon, bees
dig the plum blossoms

the morning
stands up straight, the night
is blue from the full of the April moon

iris and lilac, birds
birds, yellow flowers
white flowers, the Diesel
does not let up dragging
the plow

as the whippoorwill,
the night's tractor, grinds
his song

and no other birds but us
are as busy (O saisons, o châteaux!

Délires![3]

1. Van De Wiele was a student at Black Mountain College during Olson's time as rector there.
2. The "Variations" allude repeatedly, and in complex, subtle ways, to a poem by Arthur Rimbaud (1854–91), "Le Bonheur" (Happiness), the last of the poems that occur throughout Rimbaud's poem-prose complex *Une Saison en enfer* ("A Season in Hell"), 1873. Sometimes Olson cites a word or a phrase from the poem in French, sometimes he translates a word by the English word it resembles ("*trépas*" as "trespass"), then later by the word which translates it correctly ("the hour of your flight will be the hour of your death [*trépas*]"). The poem, in couplets except for the first line, which recurs as a refrain, is as follows: "O saisons, ô châteaux! / Quelle âme est sans défauts! / J'ai fait la magique étude / Du bonheur, qu'aucun n'élude. / Salut à lui chaque fois / Que chante le coq gaulois. / Ah! je n'aurai plus d'envie: / Il s'est chargé de ma vie. / Ce charme a pris âme et corps / Et dispersé les efforts. / O saisons, ô châteaux! / L'heure de la fuite, hélas! / Sera l'heure du trépas. / O saisons, ô châteaux!" A literal translation of the poem: "O seasons, o castles! / What soul is without fault! / I have made the magic study / Of happiness, which eludes no one. / A salutation to it / Each time the Gallic cock crows. / Ah! I shall be free of desire: / It [happiness] has taken over my life. / This spell has taken body and soul / And scattered all effort. / O seasons, o castles! / Alas, the hour of flight / Will be the hour of death. / O seasons, o castles!"
3. Two sections of *Une Saison en enfer* are entitled "Délires" (Deliriums, Frenzies), "Le Bonheur" occurring in "Délires II."

What soul
is without fault?

Nobody studies
happiness

Every time the cock crows
I salute him

I have no longer any excuse
for envy. My life

has been given its orders: the seasons
seize

the soul and the body, and make mock
of any dispersed effort. The hour of death

is the only trespass

II. The Charge

dogwood flakes
the green

the petals from the apple-trees
fall for the feet to walk on

the birds are so many they are
loud, in the afternoon

they distract, as so many bees do
suddenly all over the place

With spring one knows today to see
that in the morning each thing

is separate but by noon
they have melted into each other

and by night only crazy things
like the full moon and the whippoorwill

and us, are busy. We are busy
if we can get by that whiskered bird,

that nightjar, and get across, the moon
is our conversation, she will say

what soul
isn't in default?

can you afford not to make
the magical study

which happiness is? do you hear
the cock when he crows? do you know the charge,

that you shall have no envy, that your life
has its orders, that the seasons

seize you too, that no body and soul are one
if they are not wrought

in this retort? that otherwise efforts
are efforts? And that the hour of your flight

will be the hour of your death?

III. Spring

The dogwood
lights up the day.

The April moon
flakes the night.

Birds, suddenly,
are a multitude

The flowers are ravined
by bees, the fruit blossoms

are thrown to the ground, the wind
the rain forces everything. Noise—

even the night is drummed
by whippoorwills, and we get

as busy, we plow, we move,
we break out, we love. The secret

which got lost neither hides
nor reveals itself, it shows forth

tokens. And we rush
to catch up. The body

whips the soul. In its great desire
it demands the elixir

In the roar of spring,
transmutations. Envy

drags herself off. The fault of the body and the soul
—that they are not one—

the matutinal cock clangs
and singleness: we salute you

season of no bungling

1960

The Distances

So the distances are Galatea[4]
and one does fall in love and desires
mastery
old Zeus[5]—young Augustus[6]

Love knows no distance, no place
is that far away or heat changes
into signals, and control
old Zeus—young Augustus

Death is a loving matter, then, a horror
we cannot bide, and avoid
by greedy life

we think all living things are precious
—Pygmalions

a German inventor[7] in Key West
who had a Cuban girl, and kept her, after her death
in his bed
after her family retrieved her
he stole the body again from the vault

Torso on torso in either direction,
young Augustus
out via nothing where messages
are
or in, down La Cluny's[8] steps to the old man sitting
a god throned on torsoes,

old Zeus

Sons go there hopefully as though there was a secret, the object
to undo distance?
They huddle there, at the bottom
of the shaft, against one young bum
or two loving cheeks,
Augustus?

You can teach the young nothing
all of them go away, Aphrodite

4. In Greek mythology, Pygmalion, a legendary king of Crete, fell in love with a beautiful statue of a woman (in some versions, he made the statue himself) and prayed to Aphrodite to send him a wife who would resemble the statue, upon which Aphrodite gave the statue life. In modern versions of the legend the woman is named Galatea, and its motif is a woman who is in one way or another the creation of the man who loves her.

5. In Greek mythology, Zeus, the son of the Titans Rhea and Cronos, is the chief of the Olympian gods after these have replaced the Titans.

6. Augustus was the name conferred as honorary title and surname to the first Roman emperor, Octavianus, on his elevation to the throne in 27 B.C.

7. "The allusion is to Karl Tanzler, an eighty-three-year-old X-ray technician, who fell in love with a sickly young Cuban girl. After her death he removed her body from the grave and preserved it in paraffin; he then kept her in his house for eight years, during which time he was forced to replace parts of her body with plaster casts." Paul Christensen, *Charles Olson: Call Him Ishmael* (1979), p. 115.

8. Possibly refers to a statue in the Musée de Cluny in Paris, or to one in the museum connected with the Abbaye de Cluny near Mâcon, France. (The fact that Olson calls it "La Cluny" might suggest that he has the abbey in mind.)

tricks it out,
old Zeus—young Augustus

You have love, and no object
or you have all pressed to your nose
which is too close,
old Zeus hiding in your chin your young
Galatea

the girl who makes you weep, and you keep the corpse live by all
your arts
whose cheek do you stroke when you stroke the stone face
of young Augustus, made for bed in a military camp,
o Caesar?

O love who places all where each is, as they are, for every moment,
yield
to this man
that the impossible distance
be healed,
that young Augustus
and old Zeus
be enclosed

"I wake you,
stone. Love this man."

1960

ELIZABETH BISHOP
(1911–1979)

Jerónimo's House

My house, my fairy
palace, is
of perishable
clapboards with
three rooms in all,
my gray wasps' nest
of chewed-up paper
glued with spit.

My home, my love-nest,
is endowed
with a veranda
of wooden lace,
adorned with ferns
planted in sponges,
and the front room
with red and green

left-over Christmas
decorations

looped from the corners
    to the middle
above my little
    center table
of woven wicker
    painted blue,

At night you'd think
    my house abandoned.
Come closer. You
    can see and hear
the writing-paper
    lines of light
and the voices of
    my radio

and four blue chairs
    and an affair
for the smallest baby
    with a tray
with ten big beads.
    Then on the walls
two palm-leaf fans
    and a calendar

and on the table
    one fried fish
spattered with burning
    scarlet sauce,
a little dish
    of hominy grits
and four pink tissue-
    paper roses.

Also I have
    hung on a hook,
an old French horn
    repainted with
aluminum paint.
    I play each year
in the parade
    for José Marti.[1]

singing flamencos
    in between
the lottery numbers.
    When I move
I take these things,
    not much more, from
my shelter from
    the hurricane.

1946

1. Cuban poet and revolutionary (1853–95), honored throughout Latin America for his part in the Cuban struggle for independence from Spain, was killed at the battle of Dos Rios, May 19, 1895.

The Fish

I caught a tremendous fish
and held him beside the boat
half out of water, with my hook
fast in a corner of his mouth.
He didn't fight.
He hadn't fought at all.
He hung a grunting weight,
battered and venerable
and homely. Here and there
his brown skin hung in strips
like ancient wallpaper,
and its pattern of darker brown
was like wallpaper:
shapes like full-blown roses
stained and lost through age.
He was speckled with barnacles,
fine rosettes of lime,
and infested
with tiny white sea-lice,
and underneath two or three
rags of green weed hung down.
While his gills were breathing in
the terrible oxygen
—the frightening gills,
fresh and crisp with blood,
that can cut so badly—
I thought of the coarse white flesh
packed in like feathers,
the big bones and the little bones,
the dramatic reds and blacks
of his shiny entrails,
and the pink swim-bladder
like a big peony.
I looked into his eyes
which were far larger than mine
but shallower, and yellowed,
the irises backed and packed
with tarnished tinfoil
seen through the lenses
of old scratched isinglass.[2]
They shifted a little, but not
to return my stare.
—It was more like the tipping
of an object toward the light.
I admired his sullen face,
the mechanism of his jaw,
and then I saw
that from his lower lip
—if you could call it a lip—
grim, wet, and weaponlike,

2. A more or less translucent form of mica, formerly used in thin sheets for purposes now more often served by plastics.

hung five old pieces of fish-line,
or four and a wire leader
with the swivel still attached,
with all their five big hooks
grown firmly in his mouth.
A green line, frayed at the end
where he broke it, two heavier lines,
and a fine black thread
still crimped from the strain and snap
when it broke and he got away.
Like medals with their ribbons
frayed and wavering,
a five-haired beard of wisdom
trailing from his aching jaw.
I stared and stared
and victory filled up
the little rented boat,
from the pool of bilge
where oil had spread a rainbow
around the rusted engine
to the bailer rusted orange,
the sun-cracked thwarts,
the oarlocks on their strings,
the gunnels—until everything
was rainbow, rainbow, rainbow!
And I let the fish go.

1946

At the Fishhouses

Although it is a cold evening,
down by one of the fishhouses
an old man sits netting,
his net, in the gloaming almost invisible
a dark purple-brown,
and his shuttle worn and polished.
The air smells so strong of codfish
it makes one's nose run and one's eyes water.
The five fishhouses have steeply peaked roofs
and narrow, cleated gangplanks slant up
to storerooms in the gables
for the wheelbarrows to be pushed up and down on.
All is silver: the heavy surface of the sea,
swelling slowly as if considering spilling over,
is opaque, but the silver of the benches,
the lobster pots, and masts, scattered
among the wild jagged rocks,
is of an apparent translucence
like the small old buildings with an emerald moss
growing on their shoreward walls.
The big fish tubs are completely lined
with layers of beautiful herring scales
and the wheelbarrows are similarly plastered
with creamy iridescent coats of mail,
with small iridescent flies crawling on them.

Up on the little slope behind the houses,
set in the sparse bright sprinkle of grass,
is an ancient wooden capstan,
cracked, with two long bleached handles
and some melancholy stains, like dried blood,
where the ironwork has rusted.
The old man accepts a Lucky Strike.
He was a friend of my grandfather.
We talk of the decline in the population
and of codfish and herring
while he waits for a herring boat to come in.
There are sequins on his vest and on his thumb.
He has scraped the scales, the principal beauty,
from unnumbered fish with that black old knife,
the blade of which is almost worn away.

Down at the water's edge, at the place
where they haul up the boats, up the long ramp
descending into the water, thin silver
tree trunks are laid horizontally
across the gray stones, down and down
at intervals of four or five feet.

Cold dark deep and absolutely clear,
element bearable to no mortal,
to fish and to seals . . . One seal particularly
I have seen here evening after evening.
He was curious about me. He was interested in music;
like me a believer in total immersion,
so I used to sing him Baptist hymns.
I also sang "A Mighty Fortress Is Our God."
He stood up in the water and regarded me
steadily, moving his head a little.
Then he would disappear, then suddenly emerge
almost in the same spot, with a sort of shrug
as if it were against his better judgment.
Cold dark deep and absolutely clear,
the clear gray icy water . . . Back, behind us,
the dignified tall firs begin.
Bluish, associating with their shadows,
a million Christmas trees stand
waiting for Christmas. The water seems suspended
above the rounded gray and blue-gray stones.
I have seen it over and over, the same sea, the same,
slightly, indifferently swinging above the stones,
icily free above the stones,
above the stones and then the world.
If you should dip your hand in,
your wrist would ache immediately,
your bones would begin to ache and your hand would burn
as if the water were a transmutation of fire
that feeds on stones and burns with a dark gray flame.
If you tasted it, it would first taste bitter,
then briny, then surely burn your tongue.
It is like what we imagine knowledge to be:
dark, salt, clear, moving, utterly free,

drawn from the cold hard mouth
of the world, derived from the rocky breasts
forever, flowing and drawn, and since
our knowledge is historical, flowing, and flown.

1955

Filling Station

Oh, but it is dirty!
—this little filling station,
oil-soaked, oil-permeated
to a disturbing, over-all
black translucency.
Be careful with that match!

Father wears a dirty,
oil-soaked monkey suit
that cuts him under the arms,
and several quick and saucy
and greasy sons assist him
(it's a family filling station),
all quite thoroughly dirty.

Do they live in the station?
It has a cement porch
behind the pumps, and on it
a set of crushed and grease-
impregnated wickerwork;
on the wicker sofa
a dirty dog, quite comfy.

Some comic books provide
the only note of color—
of certain color. They lie
upon a big dim doily
draping a taboret° *drum-shaped table*
(part of the set), beside
a big hirsute begonia.

Why the extraneous plant?
Why the taboret?
Why, oh why, the doily?
(Embroidered in daisy stitch
with marguerites,° I think, *small daisies*
and heavy with gray crochet.)

Somebody embroidered the doily.
Somebody waters the plant,
or oils it, maybe. Somebody
arranges the rows of cans
so that they softly say:
ESSO—SO—SO—SO
to high-strung automobiles.
Somebody loves us all.

1965

The Armadillo

FOR ROBERT LOWELL

This is the time of year
when almost every night
the frail, illegal fire balloons appear.
Climbing the mountain height,

rising toward a saint
still honored in these parts,
the paper chambers flush and fill with light
that comes and goes, like hearts.

Once up against the sky it's hard
to tell them from the stars—
planets, that is—the tinted ones:
Venus going down, or Mars,

or the pale green one. With a wind,
they flare and falter, wobble and toss;
but if it's still they steer between
the kite sticks of the Southern Cross,[3]

receding, dwindling, solemnly
and steadily forsaking us,
or, in the downdraft from a peak,
suddenly turning dangerous.

Last night another big one fell.
It splattered like an egg of fire
against the cliff behind the house.
The flame ran down. We saw the pair

of owls who nest there flying up
and up, their whirling black-and-white
stained bright pink underneath, until
they shrieked up out of sight.

The ancient owls' nest must have burned.
Hastily, all alone,
a glistening armadillo left the scene,
rose-flecked, head down, tail down,

and then a baby rabbit jumped out,
short-eared, to our surprise.
So soft!—a handful of intangible ash
with fixed, ignited eyes.

Too pretty, dreamlike mimicry!
O falling fire and piercing cry
and panic, and a weak mailed fist
clenched ignorant against the sky!

1965

3. "Four bright stars in the Southern Hemisphere, situated as if at the extremities of a Latin cross" (***Webster's***). Setting of the poem is probably Brazil, where Elizabeth Bishop lived from time to time.

Sestina

September rain falls on the house.
In the failing light, the old grandmother
sits in the kitchen with the child
beside the Little Marvel Stove,[4]
reading the jokes from the almanac,
laughing and talking to hide her tears.

She thinks that her equinoctial tears
and the rain that beats on the roof of the house
were both foretold by the almanac,
but only known to a grandmother.
The iron kettle sings on the stove.
She cuts some bread and says to the child,

It's time for tea now; but the child
is watching the teakettle's small hard tears
dance like mad on the hot black stove,
the way the rain must dance on the house.
Tidying up, the old grandmother
hangs up the clever almanac

on its string. Birdlike, the almanac
hovers half open above the child,
hovers above the old grandmother
and her teacup full of dark brown tears.
She shivers and says she thinks the house
feels chilly, and puts more wood in the stove.

It was to be, says the Marvel Stove.
I know what I know, says the almanac.
With crayons the child draws a rigid house
and a winding pathway. Then the child
puts in a man with buttons like tears
and shows it proudly to the grandmother.

But secretly, while the grandmother
busies herself about the stove,
the little moons fall down like tears
from between the pages of the almanac
into the flower bed the child
has carefully placed in the front of the house.

Time to plant tears, says the almanac.
The grandmother sings to the marvelous stove
and the child draws another inscrutable house.

1965

4. Brand name of a wood- or coal-burning stove.

JOSEPHINE MILES
(1911–)

Midweek

Plentiful people went to the Cadillac drawing,
My ticket was number nine seven two seven one,
And my friend's ticket was number nine seven two seven two,
Certainly a lucky number and easy to remember.
I thought of it all through the film, and I like Greer Garson.[1]

O heaven when the lights went up, the table trundled in,
The number called didn't even begin with a nine.
There wasn't even that much respite of hope after the happy ending.
That is the kind of change the brave buckle
Time and again to.

All those people heart-rent and rustling,
I wished the upper lights would not look down so,
The curtain not so aquamarine, the manager not in tuxedo,
Me not so pale. I wished the second feature
Dark and dreadful.

1946

Find

Diligent in the burnt fields above the sea
The boy searches for what, sticks,
Cans; he walks like a rider
The rough and stumpy ground.

And finds all morning while the sun
Travels to crest, a blooming fullness of day,
Just one ant-paste spike, rusted.
Says the boy with relish, Poison.

Often at night his fears have told him these
Dooms to find in the hills, and his heart lightens
To find them there in fact, black as intended,
But small enough.

1956

Reason

Said, Pull her up a bit will you, Mac, I want to unload there.
Said, Pull her up my rear end, first come first serve.
Said, Give her the gun, Bud, he needs a taste of his own bumper.
Then the usher came out and got into the act:

Said, Pull her up, pull her up a bit, we need this space, sir.
Said, For God's sake, is this still a free country or what?

1. A movie actress popular in the 1940s.

You go back and take care of Gary Cooper's horse
And leave me handle my own car.

Saw them unloading the lame old lady,
Ducked out under the wheel and gave her an elbow,
Said, All you needed to do was just explain;
Reason, Reason is my middle name.

1956

Student

Who is that student pale and importunate
Whom I have left with a heavy burden and forgotten all about?
Who wakes me as I fall asleep, asking
What I want done with the job now that the year's over.

And indeed I remember now he has been doing all my work,
Setting up the experiments, kidding the bystanders,
Puzzling the problems, and I have forgotten him
Till now too late, and must wait until morning.

Who is he? my thought which I deny until the dark,
Or one literal person I have now forgot
Who, early in the alphabet, recited
More than I could learn until tonight?

1956

Memorial Day

After noon, in the plaza, cries, shrill yells, running and breaking,
Students look desperately
Out of the open windows. We have to be there.
A rifle waves in the window,
Tear gas gusts in, no one to help
In the furtherance of this class in Milton's epics.
Well let's meet tomorrow at my house.
OK, we'll bring the wholegrain wheat germ raisin bread.
Up in the office floors, out in the square,
Gas of a new kind in experimentation.
I choke and cry the tears they call for.
So I say, and now we are munching
Crunchies in the front yard,
And finishing the patristic[2] part of Book VII.
Papers are due after the weekend,
Please go home and work there,
And tell your parents the story of these weeks.
Even if they believe in the war you're protesting,
They will believe you too. Tell them
The sorts of pressures, absences of aid,
Losses of understanding you are working under.
They say they've already tried: I get my dad on the phone
And he says You can't tell me.
Give me Mom, and my Mom says

2. "Of or pertaining to the study of the writings or doctrines of the early Christian Fathers" (*Webster's*), perhaps here with reference to those doctrines as they involve the story of the Creation, which figures in Book VII of *Paradise Lost*.

You can't tell me. Stay out of trouble.
The army helicopter
In its regular rounds of surveillance, drops down low—
Our twenty figures in a courtyard may mean trouble.
Couldn't we pick these flowers to throw at them?
All these camellias overgrown and wasting?

1979

WILLIAM EVERSON
(1912–)

In All These Acts

Cleave the wood and thou shalt find Me, lift the rock and I am there! —THE GOSPEL ACCORDING TO THOMAS[1]

Dawn cried out: the brutal voice of a bird
Flattened the seaglaze. Treading that surf
Hunch-headed fishers toed small agates,
Their delicate legs, iridescent, stilting the ripples.
Suddenly the cloud closed. They heard big wind
Boom back on the cliff, crunch timber over along the ridge.
They shook up their wings, crying; terror flustered their pinions.
Then hemlock, tall, torn by the roots, went crazily down,
The staggering gyrations of splintered kindling
Flung out of bracken, fleet mule deer bolted;
But the great elk, caught midway between two scissoring logs,
Arched belly-up and died, the snapped spine
Half torn out of his peeled back, his hind legs
Jerking that gasped convulsion, the kick of spasmed life,
Paunch plowed open, purple entrails
Disgorged from the basketwork ribs
Erupting out, splashed sideways, wrapping him,
Gouted in blood, flecked with the brittle sliver of bone.
Frenzied, the terrible head
Thrashed off its antlered fuzz in that rubble
And then fell still, the great tongue
That had bugled in rut, calling the cow-elk up from the glades,
Thrust agonized out, the maimed member
Bloodily stiff in the stone-smashed teeth . . .

Far down below,
The mountain torrent, that once having started
Could never be stopped, scooped up that avalanchial wrack
And strung it along, a riddle of bubble and littered duff
Spun down its thread. At the gorged river mouth
The sea plunged violently in, gasping its potholes,
Sucked and panted, answering itself in its spume.
The river, spent at last, beating driftwood up and down
In a frenzy of capitulation, pumped out its life,
Destroying itself in the mother sea,
There where the mammoth sea-grown salmon
Lurk immemorial, roe in their hulls, about to begin.

1. One of the mystic, or gnostic, Apocryphal gospels (not admitted into the New Testament).

They will beat that barbarous beauty out
On those high-stacked shallows, those headwater claims,
Back where they were born. Along that upward-racing trek
Time springs through all its loops and flanges,
The many-faced splendor and the music of the leaf,
The copulation of beasts and the watery laughter of drakes,
Too few the grave witnesses, the wakeful, vengeful beauty,
Devolving itself of its whole constraint,
Erupting as it goes.

In all these acts
Christ crouches and seethes, pitched forward
On the crucifying stroke, juvescent,[2] that will spring Him
Out of the germ, out of the belly of the dying buck,
Out of the father-phallus and the torn-up root.
These are the modes of His forth-showing,
His serene agonization. In the clicking teeth of otters
Over and over He dies and is born,
Shaping the weasel's jaw in His leap
And the staggering rush of the bass.

1962

ROBERT HAYDEN
(1913–1980)

Those Winter Sundays

Sundays too my father got up early
and put his clothes on in the blueblack cold,
then with cracked hands that ached
from labor in the weekday weather made
banked fires blaze. No one ever thanked him.

I'd wake and hear the cold splintering, breaking.
When the rooms were warm, he'd call,
and slowly I would rise and dress,
fearing the chronic angers of that house,

Speaking indifferently to him,
who had driven out the cold
and polished my good shoes as well.
What did I know, what did I know
of love's austere and lonely offices?

1962

The Night-Blooming Cereus[1]

And so for nights
we waited, hoping to see
the heavy bud
break into flower.

2. I.e., youthful. According to the poet, this is a deliberate recollection of T. S. Eliot's lines in "Gerontion," "In the juvescence of the year / Came Christ the tiger," in which the Resurrection at Easter is seen as a time of power and awesomeness; the word "juvescence" was coined by Eliot.

1. A species of cactus.

On its neck-like tube
hooking down from the edge
of the leaf-branch
nearly to the floor,

the bud packed
tight with its miracle swayed
stiffly on breaths
of air, moved

as though impelled
by stirrings within itself.
It repelled as much
as it fascinated me

sometimes—snake,
eyeless bird head,
beak that would gape
with grotesque life-squawk.

But you, my dear,
conceded less to the bizarre
than to the imminence
of bloom. Yet we agreed

we ought
to celebrate the blossom,
paint ourselves, dance
in honor of

archaic mysteries
when it appeared. Meanwhile
we waited, aware
of rigorous design.

Backster's
polygraph, I thought
would have shown
(as clearly as it had

a philodendron's
fear) tribal sentience
in the cactus, focused
energy of will.[2]

That belling of
tropic perfume—that
signaling
not meant for us;

the darkness
cloyed with summoning
fragrance. We dropped
trivial tasks

2. Cleve Backster, an American expert in the use of the polygraph (or detector), found in 1966 that he could measure and predict the responses of plants to threatening or beneficient human thoughts.

and marveling
beheld at last the achieved
flower. Its moonlight
petals were

still unfold-
ing, the spike fringe of the outer
perianth[3] recessing
as we watched.

Luna presence,
foredoomed, already dying,
it charged the room
with plangency

older than human
cries, ancient as prayers
invoking Osiris, Krishna,
Tezcátlipóca.[4]

We spoke
in whispers when
we spoke
at all . . .

1972

Paul Laurence Dunbar[5]

FOR HERBERT MARTIN

We lay red roses on his grave,
speak sorrowfully of him
as if he were but newly dead

And so it seems to us
this raw spring day, though years
before we two were born he was
a young poet dead.

Poet of our youth—
his "cri du coeur"[6] our own,
his verses "in a broken tongue"

beguiling as an elder
brother's antic lore.
Their sad blackface lilt and croon
survive him like

The happy look (subliminal
of victim, dying man)
a summer's tintypes[7] hold.

3. The covering which protects the petals in the bud.
4. Ancient deities of Egypt, India, and the Aztecs of Mexico.
5. American poet (1872–1906); see above.
6. Passionate appeal or protest (literally, "cry from the heart"). The next line is probably a reference to Dunbar's poems in dialect.
7. I.e., old photographs.

The roses flutter in the wind;
we weight their stems
with stones, then drive away.

1978

JOHN BERRYMAN
(1914–1972)

The Ball Poem

What is the boy now, who has lost his ball,
What, what is he to do? I saw it go
Merrily bouncing, down the street, and then
Merrily over—there it is in the water!
No use to say "O there are other balls":
An ultimate shaking grief fixes the boy
As he stands rigid, trembling, staring down
All his young days into the harbor where
His ball went. I would not intrude on him,
A dime, another ball, is worthless. Now
He senses first responsibility
In a world of possessions. People will take balls,
Balls will be lost always, little boy,
And no one buys a ball back. Money is external.
He is learning, well behind his desperate eyes,
The epistemology of loss, how to stand up
Knowing what every man must one day know
And most know many days, how to stand up.
And gradually light returns to the street,
A whistle blows, the ball is out of sight,
Soon part of me will explore the deep and dark
Floor of the harbor . . . I am everywhere,
I suffer and move, my mind and my heart move
With all that move me, under the water
Or whistling, I am not a little boy.

1958

Sonnet 23

They may suppose, because I would not cloy your ear—
If ever these songs by other ears are heard—
With "love" and "love," I loved you not, but blurred
Lust with strange images, warm, not quite sincere,
To switch a bedroom black. O mutineer
With me against these empty captains! gird
Your scorn again above all at *this* word
Pompous and vague on the stump of his career.

Also I fox "heart," striking a modern breast
Hollow as a drum, and "beauty" I taboo;
I want a verse fresh as a bubble breaks,
As little false . . . Blood of my sweet unrest
Runs all the same—I am in love with you—
Trapped in my rib-cage something throes and aches!

1967

From The Dream Songs[1]

1

Huffy Henry hid the day,
unappeasable Henry sulked.
I see his point,—a trying to put things over.
It was the thought that they thought
they could *do* it made Henry wicked & away.
But he should have come out and talked.

All the world like a woolen lover
once did seem on Henry's side.
Then came a departure.
Thereafter nothing fell out as it might or ought.
I don't see how Henry, pried
open for all the world to see, survived.

What he has now to say is a long
wonder the world can bear & be.
Once in a sycamore I was glad
all at the top, and I sang.
Hard on the land wears the strong sea
and empty grows every bed.

1964

29

There sat down, once, a thing on Henry's heart
so heavy, if he had a hundred years
& more, & weeping, sleepless, in all them time
Henry could not make good.
Starts again always in Henry's ears
the little cough somewhere, an odor, a chime.

And there is another thing he has in mind
like a grave Sienese[2] face a thousand years
would fail to blur the still profiled reproach of. Ghastly,
with open eyes, he attends, blind.
All the bells say: too late. This is not for tears;
thinking.

But never did Henry, as he thought he did,
end anyone and hacks her body up
and hide the pieces, where they may be found.
He knows: he went over everyone, & nobody's missing.
Often he reckons, in the dawn, them up.
Nobody is ever missing.

1964

324. An Elegy for W.C.W.,[3] The Lovely Man

Henry in Ireland to Bill underground:
Rest well, who worked so hard, who made a good sound

1. "[The Dream Songs are] essentially about an imaginary character (not the poet, not me) named Henry, a white American in early middle age sometimes in blackface, who has suffered an irreversible loss and talks about himself sometimes in the first person, sometimes in the third. sometimes even in the second; he has a friend, never named, who addresses him as Mr. Bones and variants thereof" [Berryman's note].

2. Of Siena, a center of Italian painting during the 13th century.

3. William Carlos Williams, American poet (1883–1963); see above.

constantly, for so many years:
your high-jinks delighted the continents & our ears:
you had so many girls your life was a triumph
and you loved your one wife.

At dawn you rose & wrote—the books poured forth—
you delivered infinite babies,[4] in one great birth—
and your generosity
to juniors made you deeply loved, deeply:
if envy was a Henry trademark, he would envy you,
especially the being through.

Too many journeys lie for him ahead,
too many galleys & page-proofs to be read,
he would like to lie down
in your sweet silence, to whom was not denied
the mysterious late excellence which is the crown
of our trials & our last bride.

1968

375. *His Helplessness*

I know a young lady's high-piled ashen hair
and she is miserable, threatened a thoroughfare
for pants in their desire
fondless: she drinks too dear, & feels put down,
"no one is friendly to me" she scribbles here,
of all them griefs the crown

having been her lay by her father agèd ten
from which she grew up slowly into the world of men
who headed ha for her.
She put her soul in jeopardy with pills
a week ago, she writes–Henry would offer,
only it's thousands of miles,

help to the delicate lady far in her strait,
counsel she needs, needs one to pace her fate.
I cannot spot a hole,
& I look with my heart, in her darkness over there:
dark shroud the clouds on her disordered soul
whose last letter flew like a prayer.

1968

382

At Henry's bier let some thing fall out well:
enter there none who somewhat has to sell,
the music ancient & gradual,
the voices solemn but the grief subdued,
no hairy jokes but everybody's mood
subdued, subdued,

until the Dancer comes, in a short short dress
hair black & long & loose, dark dark glasses,
uptilted face,
pallor & strangeness, the music changes
to "Give!" & "Ow!" and how! the music changes,
she kicks a backward limb

4. Williams was by profession a doctor.

on tiptoe, pirouettes, & she is free
to the knocking music, sails, dips, & suddenly
returns to the terrible gay
occasion hopeless & mad, she weaves, it's hell,
she flings to her head a leg, bobs, all is well,
she dances Henry away.

1968

RANDALL JARRELL
(1914–1965)

The Death of the Ball Turret Gunner

From my mother's sleep I fell into the State,
And I hunched in its belly till my wet fur froze.
Six miles from earth, loosed from its dream of life,
I woke to black flak and the nightmare fighters.
When I died they washed me out of the turret with a hose.

1945

A Girl in a Library[1]

An object among dreams, you sit here with your shoes off
And curl your legs up under you; your eyes
Close for a moment, your face moves toward sleep . . .
You are very human.
                                        But my mind, gone out in tenderness,
Shrinks from its object with a thoughtful sigh.
This is a waist the spirit breaks its arm on.
The gods themselves, against you, struggle in vain.[2]
This broad low strong-boned brow; these heavy eyes;
These calves, grown muscular with certainties;
This nose, three medium-sized pink strawberries
—But I exaggerate. In a little you will leave:
I'll hear, half squeal, half shriek, your laugh of greeting—
Then, *decrescendo*,[3] bars of that strange speech
In which each sound sets out to seek each other,
Murders its own father, marries its own mother,[4]
And ends as one grand transcendental vowel.

(Yet for all I know, the Egyptian Helen spoke so.)
As I look, the world contracts around you:
I see Brünnhilde had brown braids and glasses
She used for studying; Salome straight brown bangs,[5]
A calf's brown eyes, and sturdy light-brown limbs
Dusted with cinnamon, an apple-dumpling's . . .
Many a beast has gnawn a leg off and got free,

1. "*A Girl in a Library* is a poem about the New World and the Old: about a girl, a student of Home Economics and Physical Education, who has fallen asleep in the library of a Southern college; about a woman who looks out of one book, Pushkin's *Eugen Onegin*, at the girl asleep among so many; and about the *I* of the poem, a man somewhere between the two" [Jarrell's note].
2. From *The Maid of Orleans*, a play by Friedrich Schiller (1759–1805): "With stupidity the Gods themselves struggle in vain."
3. Musical term for diminishing volume.
4. Describing the chaotic effect of the girl's speech pattern; an allusion to Oedipus, who, in Greek legend, murdered his father and married his mother.
5. Helen, Brünnhilde, Salome: legendary, passionate heroines, also central figures in operas by Richard Strauss (1864–1949) (*The Egyptian Helen* and *Salome*) and Richard Wagner (1813–83) (*The Ring of the Nibelungen*).

Many a dolphin curved up from Necessity—
The trap has closed about you, and you sleep.
If someone questioned you, *What doest thou here?*
You'd knit your brows like an orangoutang
(But not so sadly; not so thoughtfully)
And answer with a pure heart, guilelessly:
I'm studying. . . .
                    If only you were not!
Assignments,
          recipes,
                    the *Official Rulebook*
Of Basketball—ah, let them go; you needn't mind.
The soul has no assignments, neither cooks
Nor referees: it wastes its time.
                              It wastes its time.
Here in this enclave there are centuries
For you to waste: the short and narrow stream
Of Life meanders into a thousand valleys
Of all that was, or might have been, or is to be.
The books, just leafed through, whisper endlessly . . .
Yet it is hard. One sees in your blurred eyes
The "uneasy half-soul" Kipling saw in dogs'.[6]
One sees it, in the glass, in one's own eyes.
In rooms alone, in galleries, in libraries,
In tears, in searchings of the heart, in staggering joys
We memorize once more our old creation,
Humanity: with what yawns the unwilling
Flesh puts on its spirit,[7] O my sister!

So many dreams! And not one troubles
Your sleep of life? no self stares shadowily
From these worn hexahedrons, beckoning
With false smiles, tears? . . .
                              Meanwhile Tatyana[8]
Larina (gray eyes nickel with the moonlight
That falls through the willows onto Lensky's tomb;
Now young and shy, now old and cold and sure)
Asks, smiling: "But what is she dreaming of, fat thing?"
I answer: She's not fat. She isn't dreaming.
She purrs or laps or runs, all in her sleep;
Believes, awake, that she is beautiful;
She never dreams.
                    Those sunrise-colored clouds
Around man's head—that inconceivable enchantment
From which, at sunset, we come back to life
To find our graves dug, families dead, selves dying:
Of all this, Tanya,[9] she is innocent.
For nineteen years she's faced reality:
They look alike already.
                              They say, man wouldn't be
The best thing in this world—and isn't he?—

6. Rudyard Kipling (1865–1936), in his poem *Supplication of the Black Aberdeen:* "This dim, distressed half-soul that hurts me so."
7. A paraphrase of Jesus' words: "The spirit is willing but the flesh is weak."
8. In the Russian novel *Eugen Onegin* (1830), by Alexander Pushkin (1799–1837), Lensky was hopelessly in love with Tatyana, who had nourished an unrequited love for Onegin when she was very young. Later, however, she marries someone else and rejects Onegin.
9. Diminutive of Tatyana.

If he were not too good for it. But she
—She's good enough for it.
                                        And yet sometimes
Her sturdy form, in its pink strapless formal,
Is as if bathed in moonlight—modulated
Into a form of joy, a Lydian mode;[1]
This Wooden Mean's[2] a kind, furred animal
That speaks, in the Wild of things, delighting riddles
To the soul that listens, trusting . . .
                                                  Poor senseless Life:
When, in the last light sleep of dawn, the messenger
Comes with his message, you will not awake.
He'll give his feathery whistle, shake you hard,
You'll look with wide eyes at the dewy yard
And dream, with calm slow factuality:
"Today's Commencement. My bachelor's degree
In Home Ec., my doctorate of philosophy
In Phys. Ed.
                [Tanya, they won't even *scan*]
Are waiting for me. . . ."
                                      Oh, Tatyana,
The Angel comes: better to squawk like a chicken
Than to say with truth, "But I'm a *good* girl,"
And Meet his Challenge with a last firm strange
Uncomprehending smile; and—then, then!—see
The blind date that has stood you up: your life.
(For all this, if it isn't, perhaps, life,
Has yet, at least, a language of its own
Different from the books'; worse than the books'.)
And yet, the ways we miss our lives are life.
Yet . . . yet . . .
                    to have one's life add up to *yet!*

You sigh a shuddering sigh. Tatyana murmurs,
"Don't cry, little peasant"; leaves us with a swift
"Good-bye, good-bye . . . Ah, don't think ill of me . . ."
Your eyes open: you sit here thoughtlessly.

I love you—and yet—and yet—I love you.

Don't cry, little peasant. Sit and dream.
One comes, a finger's width beneath your skin,
To the braided maidens singing as they spin;
There sound the shepherd's pipe, the watchman's rattle
Across the short dark distance of the years.
I am a thought of yours: and yet, you do not think . . .
The firelight of a long, blind, dreaming story
Lingers upon your lips; and I have seen
Firm, fixed forever in your closing eyes,
The Corn King beckoning to his Spring Queen.[3]

1951

1. A musical scale associated with religious tranquility.
2. As contrasted to the Golden Mean, the perfect medium.
3. "The Corn King and the Spring Queen went by many names; in the beginning they were the man and woman who, after ruling for a time, were torn to pieces and scattered over the fields in order that the grain might grow" [Jarrell's note]. The braided maidens, shepherd, and watchman mentioned earlier in this stanza are background figures in Wagner operas, through whom meaning is conveyed without their being aware of its implications.

Well Water

What a girl called 'the dailiness of life'
(Adding an errand to your errand. Saying,
'Since you're up . . .' Making you a means to
A means to a means to) is well water
Pumped from an old well at the bottom of the world.
The pump you pump the water from is rusty
And hard to move and absurd, a squirrel-wheel
A sick squirrel turns slowly, through the sunny
Inexorable hours. And yet sometimes
The wheel turns of its own weight, the rusty
Pump pumps over your sweating face the clear
Water, cold, so cold! you cup your hands
And gulp from them the dailiness of life.

1966

HENRY REED
(1914–)

From Lessons of the War

TO ALAN MITCHELL

Vixi duellis nuper idoneus
Et militavi non sine gloria[1]

1. *Naming of Parts*

Today we have naming of parts. Yesterday,
We had daily cleaning. And tomorrow morning,
We shall have what to do after firing. But today,
Today we have naming of parts. Japonica[2]
Glistens like coral in all of the neighboring gardens,
And today we have naming of parts.

This is the lower sling swivel. And this
Is the upper sling swivel, whose use you will see,
When you are given your slings. And this is the piling swivel,
Which in your case you have not got. The branches
Hold in the gardens their silent, eloquent gestures,
Which in our case we have not got.

This is the safety-catch, which is always released
With an easy flick of the thumb. And please do not let me
See anyone using his finger. You can do it quite easy
If you have any strength in your thumb. The blossoms
Are fragile and motionless, never letting anyone see
Any of them using their finger.

And this you can see is the bolt. The purpose of this
Is to open the breech, as you see. We can slide it

1. The opening lines of a poem by Horace (III.26), but with Horace's word *"puellis"* (girls) changed to *"duellis"* (war, battles): 'Lately I have lived in the midst of battles, creditably enough,/And have soldiered, not without glory."

2. The flowering quince (*Cydonia japonica*), a shrub with brilliant scarlet flowers.

Rapidly backwards and forwards: we call this
Easing the spring. And rapidly backwards and forwards
The early bees are assaulting and fumbling the flowers:
They call it easing the Spring.

They call it easing the Spring: it is perfectly easy
If you have any strength in your thumb: like the bolt,
And the breech, and the cocking-piece, and the point of balance,
Which in our case we have not got; and the almond-blossom
Silent in all of the gardens and the bees going backwards and forwards,
For today we have naming of parts.

2. *Judging Distances*

Not only how far away, but the way that you say it
Is very important. Perhaps you may never get
The knack of judging a distance, but at least you know
How to report on a landscape: the central sector,
The right of arc and that, which we had last Tuesday,
And at least you know

That maps are of time, not place, so far as the army
Happens to be concerned—the reason being,
Is one which need not delay us. Again, you know
There are three kinds of tree, three only, the fir and the poplar,
And those which have bushy tops to; and lastly
That things only seem to be things.

A barn is not called a barn, to put it more plainly,
Or a field in the distance, where sheep may be safely grazing.
You must never be over-sure. You must say, when reporting:
At five o'clock in the central sector is a dozen
Of what appear to be animals; whatever you do,
Don't call the bleeders *sheep*.

I am sure that's quite clear; and suppose, for the sake of example,
The one at the end, asleep, endeavors to tell us
What he sees over there to the west, and how far away,
After first having come to attention. There to the west,
On the fields of summer the sun and the shadows bestow
Vestments of purple and gold.

The still white dwellings are like a mirage in the heat,
And under the swaying elms a man and a woman
Lie gently together. Which is, perhaps, only to say
That there is a row of houses to the left of arc,
And that under some poplars a pair of what appear to be humans
Appear to be loving.

Well that, for an answer, is what we might rightly call
Moderately satisfactory only, the reason being,
Is that two things have been omitted, and those are important.
The human beings, now: in what direction are they,
And how far away, would you say? And do not forget
There may be dead ground[3] in between.

3. Military: "Space that cannot be reached by fire from a given weapon or a given point" [Webster's Third New International Dictionary].

There may be dead ground in between; and I may not have got
The knack of judging a distance; I will only venture
A guess that perhaps between me and the apparent lovers,
(Who, incidentally, appear by now to have finished,)
At seven o'clock from the houses, is roughly a distance
Of about one year and a half.

1946

WILLIAM STAFFORD
(1914–)

For the Grave of Daniel Boone

The farther he went the farther home grew.
Kentucky became another room;
the mansion arched over the Mississippi;
flowers were spread all over the floor.
He traced ahead a deepening home,
and better, with goldenrod:

Leaving the snakeskin of place after place,
going on—after the trees
the grass, a bird flying after a song.
Rifle so level, sighting so well
his picture freezes down to now,
a story-picture for children.

They go over the velvet falls
into the tapestry of his time,
heirs to the landscape, feeling no jar:
it is like evening; they are the quail
surrounding his fire, coming in for the kill;
their little feet move sacred sand.

Children, we live in a barbwire time
but like to follow the old hands back—
the ring in the light, the knuckle, the palm,
all the way to Daniel Boone,
hunting our own kind of deepening home.
From the land that was his I heft this rock.

Here on his grave I put it down.

1957

Traveling through the Dark

Traveling through the dark I found a deer
dead on the edge of the Wilson River road.
It is usually best to roll them into the canyon:
that road is narrow; to swerve might make more dead.

By glow of the tail-light I stumbled back of the car
and stood by the heap, a doe, a recent killing;
she had stiffened already, almost cold.
I dragged her off; she was large in the belly.

My fingers touching her side brought me the reason—
her side was warm; her fawn lay there waiting,
alive, still, never to be born.
Beside that mountain road I hesitated.

The car aimed ahead its lowered parking lights;
under the hood purred the steady engine.
I stood in the glare of the warm exhaust turning red;
around our group I could hear the wilderness listen.

I thought hard for us all—my only swerving—,
then pushed her over the edge into the river.

1960

Accountability

Cold nights outside the taverns in Wyoming
pickups and big semi's lounge idling, letting their
haunches twitch now and then in gusts of powder snow,
their owners inside for hours, forgetting as well
as they can the miles, the circling plains, the still town
that connects to nothing but cold and space and a few
stray ribbons of pavement, icy guides to nothing
but bigger towns and other taverns that glitter and wait:
Denver, Cheyenne.

Hibernating in the library of the school on the hill
a few pieces by Thomas Aquinas or Saint Teresa
and the fragmentary explorations of people like Alfred
North Whitehead[4] crouch and wait amid research folders
on energy and military recruitment posters glimpsed
by the hard stars. The school bus by the door, a yellow
mound, clangs open and shut as the wind finds a loose
door and worries it all night, letting the hollow
students count off and break up and blow away
over the frozen ground.

1977

DYLAN THOMAS
(1914–1953)

The Force That Through the Green Fuse Drives the Flower

The force that through the green fuse drives the flower
Drives my green age; that blasts the roots of trees
Is my destroyer.
And I am dumb to tell the crooked rose
My youth is bent by the same wintry fever.

4. English mathematician and philosopher (1861–1947); St. Thomas Aquinas (1225–74), Italian philosopher and theologian; St. Teresa (1515–82), Spanish Carmelite nun and mystic—all authors of major writings on the spirit and the mind.

The force that drives the water through the rocks
Drives my red blood; that dries the mouthing streams
Turns mine to wax.
And I am dumb to mouth unto my veins
How at the mountain spring the same mouth sucks.

The hand that whirls the water in the pool
Stirs the quicksand; that ropes the blowing wind
Hauls my shroud sail.
And I am dumb to tell the hanging man
How of my clay is made the hangman's lime.

The lips of time leech to the fountain head;
Love drips and gathers, but the fallen blood
Shall calm her sores.
And I am dumb to tell a weather's wind
How time has ticked a heaven round the stars.

And I am dumb to tell the lover's tomb
How at my sheet goes the same crooked worm.

1934

After the Funeral

(IN MEMORY OF ANN JONES) [1]

After the funeral, mule praises, brays,
Windshake of sailshaped ears, muffle-toed tap
Tap happily of one peg in the thick
Grave's foot, blinds down the lids, the teeth in black,
The spittled eyes, the salt ponds in the sleeves,
Morning smack of the spade that wakes up sleep,
Shakes a desolate boy who slits his throat
In the dark of the coffin and sheds dry leaves,
That breaks one bone to light with a judgment clout,
After the feast of tear-stuffed time and thistles
In a room with a stuffed fox and a stale fern,
I stand, for this memorial's sake, alone
In the sniveling hours with dead, humped Ann
Whose hooded, fountain heart once fell in puddles
Round the parched worlds of Wales and drowned each sun
(Though this for her is a monstrous image blindly
Magnified out of praise; her death was a still drop;
She would not have me sinking in the holy
Flood of her heart's fame; she would lie dumb and deep
And need no druid [2] of her broken body).
But I, Ann's bard on a raised hearth, call all
The seas to service that her wood-tongued virtue
Babble like a bellbuoy over the hymning heads,
Bow down the walls of the ferned and foxy woods
That her love sing and swing through a brown chapel,
Bless her bent spirit with four, crossing birds.
Her flesh was meek as milk, but this skyward statue

1. Ann [Williams] Jones was Dylan Thomas' aunt, his mother's sister, who had married a tenant farmer; their rented farm was Fern Hill. She died in 1933.

2. Priest, among ancient Celts of Gaul or Britain, also magician or soothsayer.

With the wild breast and blessed and giant skull
Is carved from her in a room with a wet window
In a fiercely mourning house in a crooked year.
I know her scrubbed and sour humble hands
Lie with religion in their cramp, her threadbare
Whisper in a damp word, her wits drilled hollow,
Her fist of a face died clenched on a round pain;
And sculptured Ann is seventy years of stone.
These cloud-sopped, marble hands, this monumental
Argument of the hewn voice, gesture and psalm,
Storm me forever over her grave until
The stuffed lung of the fox twitch and cry Love
And the strutting fern lay seeds on the black sill.

1939

The Hunchback in the Park

The hunchback in the park
A solitary mister
Propped between trees and water
From the opening of the garden lock
That lets the trees and water enter
Until the Sunday somber bell at dark[3]

Eating bread from a newspaper
Drinking water from the chained cup
That the children filled with gravel
In the fountain basin where I sailed my ship
Slept at night in a dog kennel
But nobody chained him up.

Like the park birds he came early
Like the water he sat down
And Mister they called Hey mister
The truant boys from the town
Running when he had heard them clearly
On out of sound

Past lake and rockery
Laughing when he shook his paper
Hunchbacked in mockery
Through the loud zoo of the willow groves
Dodging the park keeper
With his stick that picked up leaves.

And the old dog sleeper
Alone between nurses and swans
While the boys among willows
Made the tigers jump out of their eyes
To roar on the rockery stones
And the groves were blue with sailors

Made all day until bell time
A woman figure without fault
Straight as a young elm

3. The bell that warns visitors that the park gates are about to be closed for the night.

Straight and tall from his crooked bones
That she might stand in the night
After the locks and chains

All night in the unmade park
After the railings and shrubberies
The birds the grass the trees the lake
And the wild boys innocent as strawberries
Had followed the hunchback
To his kennel in the dark.

1942

A Refusal to Mourn the Death, by Fire, of a Child in London

Never until the mankind making
Bird beast and flower
Fathering and all humbling darkness
Tells with silence the last light breaking
And the still hour
Is come of the sea tumbling in harness

And I must enter again the round
Zion of the water bead
And the synagogue of the ear of corn
Shall I let pray the shadow of a sound
Or sow my salt seed
In the least valley of sackcloth to mourn

The majesty and burning of the child's death.
I shall not murder
The mankind of her going with a grave truth
Nor blaspheme down the stations of the breath
With any further
Elegy of innocence and youth.

Deep with the first dead lies London's daughter,
Robed in the long friends,
The grains beyond age, the dark veins of her mother,
Secret by the unmourning water
Of the riding Thames.
After the first death, there is no other.

1946

Fern Hill

Now as I was young and easy under the apple boughs
About the lilting house and happy as the grass was green,
      The night above the dingle starry,
            Time let me hail and climb
      Golden in the heydays of his eyes,
And honored among wagons I was prince of the apple towns
And once below a time I lordly had the trees and leaves

Trail with daisies and barley
Down the rivers of the windfall light.

And as I was green and carefree, famous among the barns
About the happy yard and singing as the farm was home,
In the sun that is young once only,
Time let me play and be
Golden in the mercy of his means,
And green and golden I was huntsman and herdsman, the calves
Sang to my horn, the foxes on the hills barked clear and cold,
And the sabbath rang slowly
In the pebbles of the holy streams.

All the sun long it was running, it was lovely, the hay
Fields high as the house, the tunes from the chimneys, it was air
And playing, lovely and watery
And fire green as grass.
And nightly under the simple stars
As I rode to sleep the owls were bearing the farm away,
All the moon long I heard, blessed among stables, the night-jars
Flying with the ricks, and the horses
Flashing into the dark.

And then to awake, and the farm, like a wanderer white
With the dew, come back, the cock on his shoulder: it was all
Shining, it was Adam and maiden,
The sky gathered again
And the sun grew round that very day.
So it must have been after the birth of the simple light
In the first, spinning place, the spellbound horses walking warm
Out of the whinnying green stable
On to the fields of praise.

And honored among foxes and pheasants by the gay house
Under the new made clouds and happy as the heart was long,
In the sun born over and over,
I ran my heedless ways,
My wishes raced through the house high hay
And nothing I cared, at my sky blue trades, that time allows
In all his tuneful turning so few and such morning songs
Before the children green and golden
Follow him out of grace,

Nothing I cared, in the lamb white days, that time would take me
Up to the swallow thronged loft by the shadow of my hand,
In the moon that is always rising,
Nor that riding to sleep
I should hear him fly with the high fields
And wake to the farm forever fled from the childless land.
Oh as I was young and easy in the mercy of his means,
Time held me green and dying
Though I sang in my chains like the sea.

1946

In My Craft or Sullen Art

In my craft or sullen art
Exercised in the still night
When only the moon rages
And the lovers lie abed
With all their griefs in their arms,
I labor by singing light
Not for ambition or bread
Or the strut and trade of charms
On the ivory stages
But for the common wages
Of their most secret heart.

Not for the proud man apart
From the raging moon I write
On these spindrift pages
Nor for the towering dead
With their nightingales and psalms
But for the lovers, their arms
Round the griefs of the ages,
Who pay no praise or wages
Nor heed my craft or art.

1946

Do Not Go Gentle into That Good Night[4]

Do not go gentle into that good night,
Old age should burn and rave at close of day;
Rage, rage against the dying of the light.

Though wise men at their end know dark is right,
Because their words had forked no lightning they
Do not go gentle into that good night.

Good men, the last wave by, crying how bright
Their frail deeds might have danced in a green bay,
Rage, rage against the dying of the light.

Wild men who caught and sang the sun in flight,
And learn, too late, they grieved it on its way,
Do not go gentle into that good night.

Grave men, near death, who see with blinding sight
Blind eyes could blaze like meteors and be gay,
Rage, rage against the dying of the light.

And you, my father, there on the sad height,
Curse, bless, me now with your fierce tears, I pray.
Do not go gentle into that good night.
Rage, rage against the dying of the light.

1952

4. The poem was written in May, 1951, during the final illness of Dylan Thomas's father.

GWENDOLYN BROOKS
(1917–)

kitchenette building

We are things of dry hours and the involuntary plan,
Grayed in, and gray. "Dream" makes a giddy sound, not strong
Like "rent," "feeding a wife," "satisfying a man."

But could a dream send up through onion fumes
Its white and violet, fight with fried potatoes
And yesterday's garbage ripening in the hall,
Flutter, or sing an aria down these rooms

Even if we were willing to let it in,
Had time to warm it, keep it very clean,
Anticipate a message, let it begin?

We wonder. But not well! not for a minute!
Since Number Five is out of the bathroom now,
We think of lukewarm water, hope to get in it.

1945

We Real Cool

The Pool Players.
Seven at the Golden Shovel.

We real cool. We
Left school. We

Lurk late. We
Strike straight. We

Sing sin. We
Thin gin. We

Jazz June. We
Die soon.

1960

Boy Breaking Glass

TO MARC CRAWFORD FROM WHOM THE COMMISSION

Whose broken window is a cry of art
(success, that winks aware
as elegance, as a treasonable faith)
is raw: is sonic: is old-eyed première.
Our beautiful flaw and terrible ornament.
Our barbarous and metal little man.

"I shall create! If not a note, a hole.
If not an overture, a desecration."

Full of pepper and light
and Salt and night and cargoes.

"Don't go down the plank
if you see there's no extension.
Each to his grief, each to
his loneliness and fidgety revenge.

Nobody knew where I was and now I am no longer there."

The only sanity is a cup of tea.
The music is in minors.

Each one other
is having different weather.

"It was you, it was you who threw away my name!
And this is everything I have for me."

Who has not Congress, lobster, love, luau,
the Regency Room, the Statue of Liberty,
runs. A sloppy amalgamation.
A mistake.
A cliff.
A hymn, a snare, and an exceeding sun.

1968

ROBERT LOWELL
(1917–1977)

The Quaker Graveyard in Nantucket

(FOR WARREN WINSLOW, DEAD AT SEA)

Let man have dominion over the fishes of the sea and the fowls of the air and the beasts and the whole earth, and every creeping creature that moveth upon the earth.[1]

1

A brackish reach of shoal off Madaket[2]
The sea was still breaking violently and night
Had steamed into our North Atlantic Fleet,
When the drowned sailor clutched the drag-net. Light
Flashed from his matted head and marble feet,
He grappled at the net
With the coiled, hurdling muscles of his thighs:
The corpse was bloodless, a botch of reds and whites,
Its open, staring eyes
Were lusterless dead-lights
Or cabin-windows on a stranded hulk
Heavy with sand.[3] We weight the body, close

1. Genesis i.26.
2. Name of a small settlement, and a bay, on Nantucket Island, Massachusetts.
3. Lines 1–12 are based on the opening chapter of Thoreau's *Cape Cod*.

Its eyes and heave it seaward whence it came,
Where the heel-headed dogfish barks its nose
On Ahab's[4] void and forehead; and the name
Is blocked in yellow chalk.
Sailors, who pitch this portent at the sea
Where dreadnaughts shall confess
Its hell-bent deity,
When you are powerless
To sand-bag this Atlantic bulwark, faced
By the earth-shaker, green, unwearied, chaste
In his steel scales: ask for no Orphean lute
To pluck life back.[5] The guns of the steeled fleet
Recoil and then repeat
The hoarse salute.

2

Whenever winds are moving and their breath
Heaves at the roped-in bulwarks of this pier,
The terns and sea-gulls tremble at your death
In these home waters. Sailor, can you hear
The Pequod's sea wings, beating landward, fall
Headlong and break on our Atlantic wall
Off 'Sconset,[6] where the yawing S-boats° splash *sailboats*
The bellbuoy, with ballooning spinnakers,
As the entangled, screeching mainsheet clears
The blocks: off Madaket, where lubbers lash
The heavy surf and throw their long lead squids
For blue-fish? Sea-gulls blink their heavy lids
Seaward. The winds' wings beat upon the stones,
Cousin, and scream for you and the claws rush
At the sea's throat and wring it in the slush
Of this old Quaker graveyard where the bones
Cry out in the long night for the hurt beast
Bobbing by Ahab's whaleboats in the East.

3

All you recovered from Poseidon died
With you, my cousin, and the harrowed brine
Is fruitless on the blue beard of the god,
Stretching beyond us to the castles in Spain,
Nantucket's westward haven. To Cape Cod
Guns, cradled on the tide,
Blast the eelgrass about a waterclock
Of bilge and backwash, roil the salt and sand
Lashing earth's scaffold, rock
Our warships in the hand
Of the great God, where time's contrition blues
Whatever it was these Quaker sailors lost
In the mad scramble of their lives. They died
When time was open-eyed,
Wooden and childish; only bones abide
There, in the nowhere, where their boats were tossed
Sky-high, where mariners had fabled news

4. Captain Ahab, who is protagonist of Herman Melville's *Moby Dick* (1851) and a recurring presence in this sequence of poems, sailed from Nantucket on the *Pequod* in pursuit of the white whale.

5. Orpheus went to the underworld to recover his wife Eurydice and so charmed its queen, Persephone, by his playing on the lyre that she allowed him to lead Eurydice up from Hades, on condition that he not look back before the end of the journey: he did look back, and Eurydice vanished forever. The "earth-shaker" is Poseidon, god of the sea.

6. Siasconset, a town on Nantucket.

Of IS, the whited monster. What it cost
Them is their secret. In the sperm-whale's slick
I see the Quakers drown and hear their cry:
"If God himself had not been on our side,
If God himself had not been on our side,
When the Atlantic rose against us, why,
Then it had swallowed us up quick."

4

This is the end of the whaleroad and the whale
Who spewed Nantucket bones on the thrashed swell
And stirred the troubled waters to whirlpools
To send the Pequod packing off to hell:
This is the end of them, three-quarters fools,
Snatching at straws to sail
Seaward and seaward on the turntail whale,
Spouting out blood and water as it rolls,
Sick as a dog to these Atlantic shoals:
Clamavimus, O depths.[7] Let the sea-gulls wail

For water, for the deep where the high tide
Mutters to its hurt self, mutters and ebbs.
Waves wallow in their wash, go out and out,
Leave only the death-rattle of the crabs,
The beach increasing, its enormous snout
Sucking the ocean's side.
This is the end of running on the waves;
We are poured out like water. Who will dance
The mast-lashed master of Leviathans
Up from this field of Quakers in their unstoned graves?

5

When the whale's viscera go and the roll
Of its corruption overruns this world
Beyond tree-swept Nantucket and Wood's Hole[8]
And Martha's Vineyard, Sailor, will your sword
Whistle and fall and sink into the fat?
In the great ash-pit of Jehoshaphat[9]
The bones cry for the blood of the white whale,
The fat flukes arch and whack about its ears,
The death-lance churns into the sanctuary, tears
The gun-blue swingle, heaving like a flail,
And hacks the coiling life out: it works and drags
And rips the sperm-whale's midriff into rags,
Gobbets of blubber spill to wind and weather,
Sailor, and gulls go round the stoven timbers
Where the morning stars sing out together
And thunder shakes the white surf and dismembers
The red flag hammered in the mast-head.[1] Hide,
Our steel, Jonas Messias,[2] in Thy side.

7. "We have cried * * * ": Psalms cxxx.1—"Out of the depths have I cried unto thee, O Lord."
8. Harbor and township in southern Massachusetts, north of the island of Martha's Vineyard, which lies to the west of Nantucket.
9. Identified by some commentators as an image for the Day of Judgment, when the world will end in fire.
1. As was the flag in the concluding chapter of *Moby Dick.*
2. For the juxtaposition of Jonah with the Messiah, see the words of Jesus in Matthew xii.39–41, and especially: "For as Jonas was three days and three nights in the whale's belly; so shall the Son of man be three days and three nights in the heart of the earth" [See Robert Lowell, *Poesie 1943–1952,* ed. Rolando Anzilotti, p. 86].

6. *Our Lady of Walsingham*[3]

There once the penitents took off their shoes
And then walked barefoot the remaining mile;
And the small trees, a stream and hedgerows file
Slowly along the munching English lane,
Like cows to the old shrine, until you lose
Track of your dragging pain.
The stream flows down under the druid tree,
Shiloah's whirlpools gurgle and make glad
The castle of God. Sailor, you were glad
And whistled Sion[4] by that stream. But see:

Our Lady, too small for her canopy,
Sits near the altar. There's no comeliness
At all or charm in that expressionless
Face with its heavy eyelids. As before,
This face, for centuries a memory,
Non est species, neque decor,
Expressionless, expresses God: it goes
Past castled Sion. She knows what God knows,
Not Calvary's Cross nor crib at Bethlehem
Now, and the world shall come to Walsingham.

7

The empty winds are creaking and the oak
Splatters and splatters on the cenotaph,[5]
The boughs are trembling and a gaff° *spar*
Bobs on the untimely stroke
Of the greased wash exploding on a shoal-bell
In the old mouth of the Atlantic. It's well;
Atlantic, you are fouled with the blue sailors,
Sea-monsters, upward angel, downward fish:[6]
Unmarried and corroding, spare of flesh
Mart once of supercilious, wing'd clippers,
Atlantic, where your bell-trap guts its spoil
You could cut the brackish winds with a knife
Here in Nantucket, and cast up the time

3. Walsingham is a small town in Norfolk, England; a shrine to the Virgin Mary, built in the 11th century, was an object of pilgrimage until it was destroyed in the Reformation. Lowell points out in a prefatory note to *Lord Weary's Castle* that " 'Our Lady of Walsingham' is an adaptation of several paragraphs from E. I. Watkin's *Catholic Art and Culture*" which describe the present Roman Catholic shrine. The passage is in part as follows: "Now once again pilgrims visit her image erected in a mediaeval chapel, where, it is said, they took off their shoes to walk barefoot the remaining mile to the shrine. * * * The road to the chapel is a quiet country lane shaded with trees, and lined on one side by a hedgerow. On the other, a stream flows down beneath the trees, the water symbol of the Holy Spirit, 'the waters of Shiloah that go softly,' the 'flow of the river making glad the city of God.' Within the chapel, an attractive example of Decorated achitecture, near an altar of mediaeval fashion, is seated Our Lady's image. It is too small for its canopy, and is not superficially beautiful. 'Non est species neque decor,' there is no comeliness or charm in that expressionless face with heavy eyelids. But let us look carefully, and allow the image, as every work of art should be allowed, to speak to us in its own language. We become aware of an inner beauty more impressive than outward grace. That expressionless countenance expresses what is beyond expression. It is the countenance of one whose spirit dwells in a region beyond emotion and thought, the centre of which mystical writers speak. Mary is beyond joy and sorrow. For her spirit is in God, and she knows as He knows, receiving His knowledge. No longer the Mother of Sorrows nor yet of the human joy of the crib, she understands the secret counsel of God to whose accomplishment Calvary and Bethlehem alike ministered. Therefore her peace, the central peace of God, is beyond the changes of earthly experience. And the inscrutability of that illegible countenance is the inscrutability of the Divine Will made known to her."

4. Sion, or Zion, was a hill in Jerusalem, the residence of King David and his successors: the heavenly city.

5. An empty tomb, or monument erected to the dead but not containing their remains; often for those lost at sea.

6. From Milton, *Paradise Lost*, I.462–63: "Dagon his name, sea monster, upward man/ And downward fish * * *"

When the Lord God formed man from the sea's slime
And breathed into his face the breath of life,
And blue-lung'd combers lumbered to the kill.
The Lord survives the rainbow of His will.[7]

1946

Mr. Edwards[8] and the Spider

I saw the spiders marching through the air,
Swimming from tree to tree that mildewed day
In latter August when the hay
Came creaking to the barn. But where
The wind is westerly,
Where gnarled November makes the spiders fly
Into the apparitions of the sky,
They purpose nothing but their ease and die
Urgently beating east to sunrise and the sea;

What are we in the hands of the great God?
It was in vain you set up thorn and briar
In battle array against the fire
And treason crackling in your blood;
For the wild thorns grow tame
And will do nothing to oppose the flame;
Your lacerations tell the losing game
You play against a sickness past your cure.
How will the hands be strong? How will the heart endure?

A very little thing, a little worm,
Or hourglass-blazoned spider,[9] it is said,
Can kill a tiger. Will the dead
Hold up his mirror and affirm

7. See Genesis ix.11–17, especially "I do set my bow in the cloud, and it shall be for a token of a covenant between me and the earth."

8. Persona of the poem is Jonathan Edwards (1703–58), Calvinist theologian, preacher, president of the College of New Jersey, and missionary to the Indians. The first stanza draws upon a paper, "On Insects," probably written ca. 1719–20, in which Edwards records his observations of the behavior of spiders. "I have several times seen, in a very calm and serene day at that time of year [i.e., August and September], multitudes of little shining webs and glistening strings of a great length, and at such a height as that one would think they were tacked to the sky by one end, were it not that they were moving and floating. * * * And once [I] saw a very large spider, to my surprise, swimming in the air in this manner, and others have assured me that they often have seen the spiders fly. * * * And without doubt they do it with a great deal of their sort of pleasure." Yet "the greater end of nature in giving spiders this way of flying * * * is at last their destruction," for by this means "almost all the spiders upon the land must necessarily be swept first and last into the sea," leaving "nothing behind them but their eggs for a new stock for the next year." Which leads us, he says, "to behold and admire at the wisdom of the Creator . . . in this wonderful contrivance of annually carrying off and burying the corrupting nauseousness of our air * * * in the bottom of the ocean where it will do no harm." (*Works of Jonathan Edwards*, ed. Wallace E. Anderson [1980], VI, pp. 154–62.)

Later stanzas draw on two of Edwards's sermons. For example, from "The Future Punishment of the Wicked Unavoidable and Intolerable": "Imagine yourself to be cast into a fiery oven . . . or into the midst of a glowing brick-kiln, or of a great furnace. * * * Imagine also that your body were to lie there for a quarter of an hour, full of fire. * * * [How] long would that quarter of an hour seem to you! * * * O then, how would your heart sink, if you thought, if you knew, that you must bear it forever and ever! * * * This is the death threatened in the law." Later, in the same sermon: "A very little thing, a little worm or spider * * * is able to kill thee. What then canst thou do in the hands of God? It is vain to set the briers and thorns in battle array against glowing flames; the points of thorns, though sharp, do nothing to withstand the fire." In a later passage: "You have often seen a spider, * * * when thrown into the midst of a fierce fire, and have observed how immediately it yields to the force of the flames. There is no long struggle, * * * no strength exerted to oppose the heat, or to fly from it; but it immediately stretches itself forth and yields." (*The Works of President Edwards*, New York [1852], IV, pp. 260–64.) From Edwards's sermon "Sinners in the Hands of an Angry God": "The God that holds you over the pit of Hell, much as one holds a spider or some loathsome insect, over the fire, abhors you, and is dreadfully provoked; his wrath towards you burns like fire." (*Works*, IV, p. 318.)

9. The black widow spider (*Latrodectus mactans*), common in North America, is marked with an hour-glass pattern on its body.

To the four winds the smell
And flash of his authority? It's well
If God who holds you to the pit of hell,
Much as one holds a spider, will destroy,
Baffle and dissipate your soul. As a small boy

On Windsor Marsh,[1] I saw the spider die
When thrown into the bowels of fierce fire:
There's no long struggle, no desire
To get up on its feet and fly—
It stretches out its feet
And dies. This is the sinner's last retreat;
Yes, and no strength exerted on the heat
Then sinews the abolished will, when sick
And full of burning, it will whistle on a brick.

But who can plumb the sinking of that soul?
Josiah Hawley,[2] picture yourself cast
Into a brick-kiln where the blast
Fans your quick vitals to a coal—
If measured by a glass,
How long would it seem burning! Let there pass
A minute, ten, ten trillion; but the blaze
Is infinite, eternal: this is death,
To die and know it. This is the Black Widow, death.

1946

My Last Afternoon with Uncle Devereux Winslow

1922: THE STONE PORCH OF MY GRANDFATHER'S SUMMER HOUSE

1

"I won't go with you. I want to stay with Grandpa!"
That's how I threw cold water
on my Mother and Father's
watery martini pipe dreams at Sunday dinner.
. . . Fontainebleau,[3] Mattapoisett, Puget Sound. . . .
Nowhere was anywhere after a summer
at my Grandfather's farm.
Diamond-pointed, athirst and Norman,[4]
its alley of poplars
paraded from Grandmother's rose garden
to a scary stand of virgin pine,
scrub, and paths forever pioneering.

One afternoon in 1922,
I sat on the stone porch, looking through
screens as black-grained as drifting coal.
Tockytock, tockytock
clumped our Alpine, Edwardian cuckoo clock,
slung with strangled, wooden game.
Our farmer was cementing a root-house[5] under the hill.

1. Near East Windsor, Connecticut, Edwards's birthplace.
2. Edwards's uncle.
3. Fontainebleau: name of an estate belonging to a member of the Lowell family.
4. The buildings were designed in the style of Norman architecture, a version of Romanesque developed in Normandy (France) ca. A.D. 950.
5. Small building, partly underground, used for storing root vegetables, bulbs, etc.

One of my hands was cool on a pile
of black earth, the other warm
on a pile of lime. All about me
were the works of my Grandfather's hands:
snapshots of his *Liberty Bell* silver mine;
his high school at *Stuttgart am Neckar;*
stogie-brown beams; fools'-gold nuggets;
octagonal red tiles,
sweaty with a secret dank, crummy with ant-stale;
a Rocky Mountain chaise longue,
its legs, shellacked saplings.
A pastel-pale Huckleberry Finn
fished with a broom straw in a basin
hollowed out of a millstone.
Like my Grandfather, the décor
was manly, comfortable,
overbearing, disproportioned.

What were those sunflowers? Pumpkins floating shoulder-high?
It was sunset, Sadie and Nellie
bearing pitchers of ice-tea,
oranges, lemons, mint, and peppermints,
and the jug of shandygaff,
which Grandpa made by blending half and half
yeasty, wheezing homemade sarsaparilla with beer.
The farm, entitled *Char-de-sa*
in the Social Register,
was named for my Grandfather's children:
Charlotte, Devereux, and Sarah.
No one had died there in my lifetime . . .
Only Cinder, our Scottie puppy
paralyzed from gobbling toads.
I sat mixing black earth and lime.

2

I was five and a half.
My formal pearl gray shorts
had been worn for three minutes.
My perfection was the Olympian
poise of my models in the imperishable autumn
display windows
of Rogers Peet's boys' store below the State House
in Boston. Distorting drops of water
pinpricked my face in the basin's mirror.
I was a stuffed toucan
with a bibulous, multicolored beak.

3

Up in the air
by the lakeview window in the billiards-room,
lurid in the doldrums of the sunset hour,
my Great Aunt Sarah
was learning *Samson and Delilah.*[6]
She thundered on the keyboard of her dummy piano,
with gauze curtains like a boudoir table,
accordionlike yet soundless.
It had been bought to spare the nerves
of my Grandmother,

6. Evidently a piano arrangement from the opera by Camille Saint-Saëns (1835–1921).

tone-deaf, quick as a cricket,
now needing a fourth for "Auction,"° *auction bridge*
and casting a thirsty eye
on Aunt Sarah,[7] risen like the phoenix
from her bed of troublesome snacks and Tauchnitz[8] classics.

Forty years earlier,
twenty, auburn headed,
grasshopper notes of genius!
Family gossip says Aunt Sarah
tilted her archaic Athenian nose
and jilted an Astor.
Each morning she practiced
on the grand piano at Symphony Hall,
deathlike in the off-season summer—
its naked Greek statues draped with purple
like the saints in Holy Week. . . .
On the recital day, she failed to appear.

4

I picked with a clean finger nail at the blue anchor
on my sailor blouse washed white as a spinnaker.
What in the world was I wishing?
. . . A sail-colored horse browsing in the bullrushes . . .
A fluff of the west wind puffing
my blouse, kiting me over our seven chimneys,
troubling the waters. . . .
As small as sapphires were the ponds: *Quittacus*, *Snippituit*,
and *Assawompset*, halved by "the Island,"
where my Uncle's duck blind
floated in a barrage of smoke-clouds.
Double-barreled shotguns
stuck out like bundles of baby crow-bars.
A single sculler in a camouflaged kayak
was quacking to the decoys. . . .

At the cabin between the waters,
the nearest windows were already boarded.
Uncle Devereux was closing camp for the winter.
As if posed for "the engagement photograph,"
he was wearing his severe
war-uniform of a volunteer Canadian officer.
Daylight from the doorway riddled his student posters,
tacked helter-skelter on walls as raw as a boardwalk.
Mr. Punch,[9] a water melon in hockey tights,
was tossing off a decanter of Scotch.
La Belle France in a red, white and blue toga
was accepting the arm of her "protector,"
the ingenu and porcine Edward VII.[1]

7. Sarah Stark Winslow, Robert Lowell's mother's aunt (see "91 Revere St.," the prose section of Lowell's *Life Studies*). "Risen like a phoenix": alludes to the legend of the phoenix, a mythological bird that lived for five hundred years, consumed itself in flames, and was then reborn from its ashes.

8. Christian Tauchnitz (1816–95), the German publisher of an extensive range of inexpensive paper-covered books, including many works by English and American authors in English.

9. A cartoon figure used as emblem for the English humor magazine *Punch, or, The London Charivari*, founded in 1841.

1. Edward VII was king of England from 1901 to 1910; his reign saw the initiation of the agreements and the era of good feeling between England and France known as "L'Entente Cordiale." The poster would have pictured Edward VII with a protective arm around the waist of a lovely young woman, Marianne, "La Belle France," the traditional emblem for France, much as Uncle Sam is an emblem for the United States.

The pre-war music hall belles
had goose necks, glorious signatures, beauty-moles,
and coils of hair like rooster tails.
The finest poster was two or three young men in khaki kilts
being bushwhacked on the veldt—[2]
They were almost life-size. . . .

My Uncle was dying at twenty-nine.
"You are behaving like children,"
said my Grandfather,
when my Uncle and Aunt left their three baby daughters,
and sailed for Europe on a last honeymoon . . .
I cowered in terror.
I wasn't a child at all—
unseen and all-seeing, I was Agrippina[3]
in the Golden House of Nero. . . .
Near me was the white measuring-door
my Grandfather had penciled with my Uncle's heights.
In 1911, he had stopped growing at just six feet.
While I sat on the tiles,
and dug at the anchor on my sailor blouse,
Uncle Devereux stood behind me.
He was as brushed as Bayard, our riding horse.
His face was putty.
His blue coat and white trousers
grew sharper and straighter.
His coat was a blue jay's tail,
his trousers were solid cream from the top of the bottle.
He was animated, hierarchical,
like a ginger snap man in a clothes-press.
He was dying of the incurable Hodgkin's disease. . . .
My hands were warm, then cool, on the piles
of earth and lime,
a black pile and a white pile. . . .
Come winter,
Uncle Devereux would blend to the one color.

1959

Skunk Hour

(FOR ELIZABETH BISHOP)[4]

Nautilus Island's hermit
heiress still lives through winter in her Spartan cottage;
her sheep still graze above the sea.
Her son's a bishop. Her farmer
is first selectman[5] in our village;
she's in her dotage.

Thirsting for
the hierarchic privacy

2. A poster from the time of the Boer War (1899–1902), fought by the British against the descendants of Dutch settlers in South Africa. "Veldt" (Afrikaans): open country in South Africa.

3. Mother of the emperor Nero, who had her murdered to remove her opposition to his divorcing Octavia in order to remarry.

4. In his essay "On 'Skunk Hour' " (see *Robert Lowell: A Collection of Critical Essays*, ed. T. Parkinson, 1968), Lowell says that his poem is modeled on Elizabeth Bishop's poem *The Armadillo*, that both poems "use short line stanzas, start with drifting description and end with a single animal."

5. Elected member of the administrative body (Board of Selectmen) of many New England towns.

of Queen Victoria's century,
she buys up all
the eyesores facing her shore,
and lets them fall.

The season's ill—
we've lost our summer millionaire,
who seemed to leap from an L. L. Bean[6]
catalogue. His nine-knot yawl
was auctioned off to lobstermen.
A red fox stain covers Blue Hill.[7]

And now our fairy
decorator brightens his shop for fall;
his fishnet's filled with orange cork,
orange, his cobbler's bench and awl;
there is no money in his work,
he'd rather marry.

One dark night,
my Tudor Ford climbed the hill's skull;
I watched for love-cars. Lights turned down,
they lay together, hull to hull,
where the graveyard shelves on the town. . . .
My mind's not right.

A car radio bleats,
"Love, O careless Love. . . ." I hear
my ill-spirit sob in each blood cell,
as if my hand were at its throat. . . .
I myself am hell;[8]
nobody's here—

only skunks, that search
in the moonlight for a bite to eat.
They march on their soles up Main Street:
white stripes, moonstruck eyes' red fire
under the chalk-dry and spar spire
of the Trinitarian Church.

I stand on top
of our back steps and breathe the rich air—
a mother skunk with her column of kittens swills the garbage pail.
She jabs her wedge-head in a cup
of sour cream, drops her ostrich tail,
and will not scare.

1957 1959

Water

It was a Maine lobster town—
each morning boatloads of hands
pushed off for granite
quarries on the islands,

6. A mail-order dealer in hunting, fishing, and camping specialties in Freeport, Me.
7. In his essay Lowell says: "The red fox stain was merely meant to describe the rusty reddish color of autumn on Blue Hill, a Maine mountain near where we were living."
8. Possibly an allusion to *Paradise Lost*, IV. 75, where Lucifer says, "Which way I fly is Hell; myself am Hell."

and left dozens of bleak
white frame houses stuck
like oyster shells
on a hill of rock,

and below us, the sea lapped
the raw little match-stick
mazes of a weir,
where the fish for bait were trapped.

Remember? We sat on a slab of rock.
From this dance in time,
it seems the color
of iris, rotting and turning purpler,

but it was only
the usual gray rock
turning the usual green
when drenched by the sea.

The sea drenched the rock
at our feet all day,
and kept tearing away
flake after flake.

One night you dreamed
you were a mermaid clinging to a wharf-pile,
and trying to pull
off the barnacles with your hands.

We wished our two souls
might return like gulls
to the rock. In the end,
the water was too cold for us.

1964

For the Union Dead[9]

"Relinquunt Omnia Servare Rem Publicam."

The old South Boston Aquarium stands
in a Sahara of snow now. Its broken windows are boarded.
The bronze weathervane cod has lost half its scales.
The airy tanks are dry.

Once my nose crawled like a snail on the glass;
my hand tingled
to burst the bubbles
drifting from the noses of the cowed, compliant fish.

9. At the edge of Boston Common, across from the Massachusetts State House, stands a monument to Colonel Robert Gould Shaw (1837–63) and the Negro troops of the 54th Massachusetts regiment whom he was leading in the assault on Fort Wagner, South Carolina, when he was killed on July 18, 1863. The memorial, by Augustus St. Gaudens, representing Shaw in equestrian high-relief, with his troops, was dedicated in 1897. In the upper right it bears the motto of the Society of the Cincinnati (slightly altered in the epigraph to Lowell's poem), *"Omnia relinquit servare rempublicam,"* "He leaves all else to serve the republic."

My hand draws back. I often sigh still
for the dark downward and vegetating kingdom
of the fish and reptile. One morning last March,
I pressed against the new barbed and galvanized

fence on the Boston Common. Behind their cage,
yellow dinosaur steamshovels were grunting
as they cropped up tons of mush and grass
to gouge their underworld garage.

Parking spaces luxuriate like civic
sandpiles in the heart of Boston.
A girdle of orange, Puritan-pumpkin colored girders
braces the tingling Statehouse,

shaking over the excavations, as it faces Colonel Shaw
and his bell-cheeked Negro infantry
on St. Gaudens' shaking Civil War relief,
propped by a plank splint against the garage's earthquake.

Two months after marching through Boston,
half the regiment was dead;
at the dedication,
William James could almost hear the bronze Negroes breathe.

Their monument sticks like a fishbone
in the city's throat.
Its Colonel is as lean
as a compass-needle.

He has an angry wrenlike vigilance,
a greyhound's gentle tautness;
he seems to wince at pleasure,
and suffocate for privacy.

He is out of bounds now. He rejoices in man's lovely,
peculiar power to choose life and die—
when he leads his black soldiers to death,
he cannot bend his back.

On a thousand small town New England greens,
the old white church holds their air
of sparse, sincere rebellion; frayed flags
quilt the graveyards of the Grand Army of the Republic

The stone statues of the abstract Union Soldier
grow slimmer and younger each year—
wasp-waisted, they doze over muskets
and muse through their sideburns . . .

Shaw's father wanted no monument
except the ditch,
where his son's body was thrown
and lost with his "niggers."

The ditch is nearer.
There are no statues for the last war here;

on Boylston Street, a commercial photograph
shows Hiroshima boiling

over a Mosler Safe, the "Rock of Ages"
that survived the blast. Space is nearer.
When I crouch to my television set,
the drained faces of Negro school-children rise like balloons.

Colonel Shaw
is riding on his bubble,
he waits
for the blessèd break.

The Aquarium is gone. Everywhere,
giant finned cars nose forward like fish;
a savage servility
slides by on grease.

1964

1930's

The vaporish closeness of this two-month fog;
forty summers back, my brightest summer:
the rounds of Dealer's Choice,[1] the housebound girls,
fog, the nightlife. Then, as now, the late curfew
boom of an unknown nightbird, local hemlock
gone black as Roman cypress, the barn-garage
below the tilted Dipper[2] lighthouse-white,
a single misanthropic frog complaining
from the water hazard on the shortest hole;
till morning! Long dreams, short nights; their faces flash
like burning shavings, scattered bait and ptomaine
caught by the gulls with groans like straining rope;
windjammer pilgrims cowled in yellow hoods,
gone like the summer in their yellow bus.

1970 1973

Harriet[3]

A repeating fly, blueback, thumbthick—so gross,
it seems apocalyptic[4] in our house—
whams back and forth across the nursery bed
manned by a madhouse of stuffed animals,
not one a fighter. It is like a plane
dusting apple orchards or Arabs on the screen—
one of the mighty . . . one of the helpless. It
bumbles and bumps its brow on this and that,
making a short, unhealthy life the shorter.
I kill it, and another instant's added

1. A version of poker in which the dealer is allowed to choose the particular mode in which the hand will be played.
2. The Big Dipper (constellation).
3. The poet's daughter, born January 4, 1945.
4. As if heralding some dire revelation.

to the horrifying mortmain[5] of
ephemera:[6] keys, drift, sea-urchin shells,
you packrat off with joy . . . a dead fly swept
under the carpet, wrinkling to fulfillment.

1970 1973

This Golden Summer

This golden summer,
this bountiful drought,
this crusting bread—
nothing in it is gold.

Its fields have the yellow-white hair
of Patriarchs who lived
on two goats and no tomorrow—
a fertility too rich to breathe.

Our cat, a new mother, put a paw
under my foot, as I held a tray;
her face went white, she streaked screaming
through an open window, an affronted woman.

Is our little season of being together
so unprecarious, I must imagine
the shadow around the corner . . .
downstairs . . . behind the door?

I see even in golden summer
the wilted blowbell spiders
ruffling up impossible angers,
as they shake threads to the light.

We have plucked the illicit corn,
seen the Scriptural
fragility of flowers—
where is our pastoral adolescence?

I will leave earth
with my shoes tied,
as if the walk
could cut bare feet.

1977

The Withdrawal

1

Only today and just for this minute,
when the sunslant finds its true angle,
you can see yellow and pinkish leaves spangle
our gentle, fluffy tree—
suddenly the green summer is momentary . . .

5. A legal term ("dead hand") meaning "possession of, or tenure by, any corporation which, by reason of the nature of corporations, may be perpetual" (*Webster's*).

6. Things or creatures of brief duration or life.

Autumn is my favorite season—
why does it change clothes and withdraw?

This week the house went on the market—
suddenly I wake among strangers;
when I go into a room, it moves
with embarrassment, and joins another room.

I don't need conversation, but you to laugh with—
you and a room and a fire,
cold starlight blowing through an open window—
whither?

2

After sunfall, heaven is melodramatic,
a temporary, puckering, burning green.
The patched-up oak
and blacker, indelible pines
have the indigestible meagerness of spines.

One wishes heaven had less solemnity:
a sensual table
with five half-filled bottles of red wine
set round the hectic carved roast—
Bohemia for ourselves
and the familiars of a lifetime
charmed to communion by resurrection—
running together in the rain to mail a single letter,
not the chafe and cling
of this despondent chaff.

3

Yet for a moment, the children
could play truant from their tuition.

4

When I look back, I see a collapsing
accordion of my receding houses,
and myself receding
to a boy of twenty-five or thirty,
too shopworn for less, too impressionable for more—
blackmaned, illmade
in a washed blue workshirt and coalblack trousers,
moving from house to house,
still seeking a boy's license
to see the countryside without arrival.

Hell?

Darling,
terror in happiness may not cure the hungry future,
the time when any illness is chronic,
and the years of discretion are spent on complaint—

until the wristwatch is taken from the wrist.

1977

Epilogue

Those blessèd structures, plot and rhyme—
why are they no help to me now
I want to make
something imagined, not recalled?
I hear the noise of my own voice:
The painter's vision is not a lens,
it trembles to caress the light.
But sometimes everything I write
with the threadbare art of my eye
seems a snapshot,
lurid, rapid, garish, grouped,
heightened from life,
yet paralyzed by fact.
All's misalliance.
Yet why not say what happened?
Pray for the grace of accuracy
Vermeer[7] gave to the sun's illumination
stealing like the tide across a map
to his girl solid with yearning.
We are poor passing facts,
warned by that to give
each figure in the photograph
his living name.

1977

P. K. PAGE
(1917–)

The Stenographers

After the brief bivouac° of Sunday, *temporary encampment*
their eyes, in the forced march of Monday to Saturday,
hoist the white flag, flutter in the snow-storm of paper,
haul it down and crack in the mid-sun of temper.

In the pause between the first draft and the carbon
they glimpse the smooth hours when they were children—
the ride in the ice-cart, the ice-man's name,
the end of the route and the long walk home;

remember the sea where floats at high tide
were sea marrows growing on the scatter-green vine
or spools of gray toffee, or wasps' nests on water;
remember the sand and the leaves of the country.

Bell rings and they go and the voice draws their pencil
like a sled across the snow; when its runners are frozen

7. Jan Vermeer of Delft, Dutch painter (1632–75).

rope snaps and the voice then is pulling no burden
but runs like a dog on the winter of paper.

Their climates are winter and summer—no wind
for the kites of their hearts—no wind for a flight;
a breeze at the most, to tumble them over
and leave them like rubbish—the boy-friends of blood.

In the inch of the noon as they move they are stagnant.
The terrible calm of the noon is their anguish;
the lip of the counter, the shapes of the straws
like icicles breaking their tongues, are invaders.

Their beds are their oceans—salt water of weeping
the waves that they know—the tide before sleep;
and fighting to drown they assemble their sheep
in columns and watch them leap desks for their fences
and stare at them with their own mirror-worn faces.

In the felt of the morning the calico-minded,
sufficiently starched, insert papers, hit keys,
efficient and sure as their adding machines;
yet they weep in the vault, they are taut as net curtains
stretched upon frames. In their eyes I have seen
the pin men of madness in marathon trim
race round the track of the stadium pupil.

1946

AL PURDY
(1918–)

Love at Roblin Lake

My ambition as I remember and
I always remember was always
to make love vulgarly and immensely
as the vulgar elephant doth
& immense reptiles did
in the open air openly
sweating and grunting together
and going
"BOING BOING BOING"
making
every lunge a hole in the great dark
for summer cottagers to fall into at a later date
and hear inside faintly (like in a football
stadium when the home team loses)
ourselves still softly
going
"boing boing boing"
as the vulgar elephant doth
& immense reptiles did
in the star-filled places of earth

that I remember we left behind long ago
and forgotten everything after
on our journey into the dark

1959

Trees at the Arctic Circle

(SALIX CORDIFOLIA—GROUND WILLOW)

They are 18 inches long
or even less
crawling under rocks
groveling among the lichens
bending and curling to escape
making themselves small
finding new ways to hide
Coward trees
I am angry to see them
like this
not proud of what they are
bowing to weather instead
careful of themselves
worried about the sky
afraid of exposing their limbs
like a Victorian married couple

I call to mind great Douglas firs
I see tall maples waving green
and oaks like gods in autumn gold
the whole horizon jungle dark
and I crouched under that continual night
But these
even the dwarf shrubs of Ontario
mock them
Coward trees

And yet—and yet—
their seed pods glow
like delicate gray earrings
their leaves are veined and intricate
like tiny parkas
They have about three months
to make sure the species does not die
and that's how they spend their time
unbothered by any human opinion
just digging in here and now
sending their roots down down down
And you know it occurs to me
about 2 feet under
those roots must touch permafrost
ice that remains ice forever
and they use it for their nourishment
they use death to remain alive

I see that I've been carried away
in my scorn of the dwarf trees

most foolish in my judgments
To take away the dignity
of any living thing
even tho it cannot understand
the scornful words
is to make life itself trivial
and yourself the Pontifex Maximus[1]
of nullity
I have been stupid in a poem
I will not alter the poem
but let the stupidity remain permanent
as the trees are
in a poem
the dwarf trees of Baffin Island

Pangnirtung[2]

1967

Wilderness Gothic

Across Roblin Lake,[3] two shores away,
they are sheathing the church spire
with new metal. Someone hangs in the sky
over there from a piece of rope,
hammering and fitting God's belly-scratcher,
working his way up along the spire
until there's nothing left to nail on—
Perhaps the workman's faith reaches beyond:
touches intangibles, wrestles with Jacob,[4]
replacing rotten timber with pine thews,
pounds hard in the blue cave of the sky,
contends heroically with difficult problems of
gravity, sky navigation and mythopeia,[5]
his volunteer time and labor donated to God,
minus sick benefits of course on a non-union job—

Fields around are yellowing into harvest,
nestling and fingerling are sky and water borne,
death is yodeling quiet in green woodlots,
and bodies of three young birds have disappeared
in the sub-surface of the new county highway—

That picture is incomplete, part left out
that might alter the whole Dürer[6] landscape:
gothic ancestors peer from medieval sky,
dour faces trapped in photograph albums escaping
to clop down iron roads with matched grays:
work-sodden wives groping inside their flesh
for what keeps moving and changing and flashing
beyond and past the long frozen Victorian day.

1. Chief priest.
2. The largest island of the Canadian Arctic. Pangnirtung is a trading post in eastern Baffin Island, just south of the Arctic Circle.
3. Small lake in southeastern Ontario.
4. The ancestor of the Hebrews, Jacob wrestled an entire night with an angel who then blessed him and gave him the name "Israel" (Genesis 32).
5. Myth-making.
6. Albrecht Dürer (1471–1528), German painter and engraver, noted for the rich and realistic detail of his work.

A sign of fire and brimstone? A two-headed calf
born in the barn last night? A sharp female agony?
An age and a faith moving into transition,
the dinner cold and new-baked bread a failure,
deep woods shiver and water drops hang pendant,
double yolked eggs and the house creaks a little—
Something is about to happen. Leaves are still.
Two shores away, a man hammering in the sky.
Perhaps he will fall.

1968

WILLIAM MEREDITH
(1919–)

Accidents of Birth

Je vois les effroyables espaces de l'Univers qui m'enferment, et je me trouve attaché à un coin de cette vaste étendue, sans savoir pourquoi je suis plutôt en ce lieu qu'en un autre, ni pourquoi ce peu de temps qui m'est donné à vivre m'est assigné à ce point plutôt qu'à un autre de toute l'éternité qui m'a précédé, et de toute qui me suit.[1]
—PENSÉES SUR LA RELIGION, *Pascal*

The approach of a man's life out of the past is history, and the approach of time out of the future is mystery. Their meeting is the present, and it is consciousness, the only time life is alive. The endless wonder of this meeting is what causes the mind, in its inward liberty of a frozen morning, to turn back and question and remember. The world is full of places. Why is it that I am here? —THE LONG-LEGGED HOUSE, *Wendell Berry*

Spared by a car- or airplane-crash or
cured of malignancy, people look
around with new eyes at a newly
praiseworthy world, blinking eyes like these.

For I've been brought back again from the
fine silt, the mud where our atoms lie
down for long naps. And I've also been
pardoned miraculously for years
by the lava of chance which runs down
the world's gullies, silting us back.
Here I am, brought back, set up, not yet
happened away.

But it's not this random
life only, throwing its sensual
astonishments upside down on
the bloody membranes behind my eyeballs,
not just me being here again, old
needer, looking for someone to need,
but you, up from the clay yourself,
as luck would have it, and inching
over the same little segment of earth-

1. "I see the terrifying spaces of the universe that enclose me, and I find myself attached to a corner of this vast expanse, without knowing why I am more in this place than in another, nor why this little time that is given me to live is assigned me at this point more than another out of all the eternity that has preceded me and out of all that will follow me" (*Thoughts on Religion*, Pascal).

ball, in the same little eon, to
meet in a room, alive in our skins,
and the whole galaxy gaping there
and the centuries whining like gnats—
you, to teach me to see it, to see
it with you, and to offer somebody
uncomprehending, impudent thanks.

1980

CHARLES BUKOWSKI
(1920–)

vegas

there was a frozen tree that I wanted to paint
but the shells came down
and in Vegas looking across at a green sunshade
at 3:30 in the morning,
I died without nails, without a copy of the *Atlantic Monthly*,
the windows screamed like doves moaning the bombing of Milan
and I went out to live with the rats
but the lights were too bright
and I thought maybe I'd better go back and sit in a
poetry class:

a marvelous description of a gazelle
is hell;
the cross sits like a fly on my window,
my mother's breath stirs small leaves
in my mind;

and I hitch-hiked back to L.A. through hangover clouds
and I pulled a letter from my pocket and read it
and the truckdriver said, what's that?
and I said, there's some gal up North who used to
sleep with Pound, she's trying to tell me that H.D.[1]
was our greatest scribe; well, Hilda gave us a few pink
Grecian gods in with the chinaware, but after reading her
I still have 140 icicles hanging from my bones.

I'm not going all the way to L.A., the truckdriver said.

it's all right, I said, the calla lilies nod to our minds
and someday we'll all go home
together.

in fact, he said, this is as far
as we go.
so I let him have it; old withered whore of time
your breasts taste the sour cream of dreaming . . .
he let me out
in the middle of the desert;

to die is to die is to die,

1. The American imagist poet Hilda Doolittle (1886–1961).

old phonographs in cellars,
joe di maggio,
magazines in with the onions . . .

an old Ford picked me up
45 minutes later
and, this time,
I kept my mouth
shut.

1963

D. J. ENRIGHT
(1920–)

The Typewriter Revolution

The typeriter is crating
A revlootion in peotry
Pishing back the frontears
And apening up fresh feels
Unherd of by Done or Bleak

Mine is a Swetish Maid
Called FACIT
Others are OLIMPYA or ARUSTOCART
RAMINTONG or LOLITEVVI

TAB e or not TAB e
i.e. the ?
Tygirl tygirl burning bride
Y, this is L
Nor-my-outfit
Anywan can od it
U 2 can b a
Tepot

C! *** stares and /// strips
Cloaca nd † -
Farty-far keys to suckcess!
A banus of +% for all futre peots!!
LSD & $$$

The trypewiter is cretin
A revultion in peotry
" "All nem r =" "
O how they £ away
@ UNDERWORDS and ALLIWETTIS
Without a.

FACIT cry I!!!

1971

HOWARD NEMEROV
(1920–)

The Goose Fish

On the long shore, lit by the moon
To show them properly alone,
Two lovers suddenly embraced
So that their shadows were as one.
The ordinary night was graced
For them by the swift tide of blood
That silently they took at flood,
And for a little time they prized
Themselves emparadised.

Then, as if shaken by stage-fright
Beneath the hard moon's bony light,
They stood together on the sand
Embarrassed in each other's sight
But still conspiring hand in hand,
Until they saw, there underfoot,
As though the world had found them out,
The goose fish turning up, though dead,
His hugely grinning head.

There in the china light he lay,
Most ancient and corrupt and gray
They hesitated at his smile,
Wondering what it seemed to say
To lovers who a little while
Before had thought to understand,
By violence upon the sand,
The only way that could be known
To make a world their own.

It was a wide and moony grin
Together peaceful and obscene;
They knew not what he would express,
So finished a comedian
He might mean failure or success,
But took it for an emblem of
Their sudden, new and guilty love
To be observed by, when they kissed,
That rigid optimist.

So he became their patriarch,
Dreadfully mild in the half-dark.
His throat that the sand seemed to choke,
His picket teeth, these left their mark
But never did explain the joke
That so amused him, lying there
While the moon went down to disappear
Along the still and tilted track
That bears the zodiac.

1960

Easter

Even this suburb has overcome Death.
Overnight, by a slow explosion, or
A rapid burning, it begins again
Bravely disturbing the brown ground
With grass and even more elaborate
Unnecessaries such as daffodils
And tulips, till the whole sordid block
Of houses turned so inward on themselves,
So keeping of a winter's secret sleep,
Looks like a lady's hat, improbably
Nodding with life, with bluejays hooting
And pigeons caracoling[1] up among
The serious chimney pots, and pairs
Of small birds speeding behind the hedges
Readying to conceal them soon. Here,
Even here, Death has been vanquished again,
What was a bramble of green barbed wire
Becomes forsythia, as the long war
Begins again, not by our doing or desiring.

1980

The Historical Judas[2]

He too has an eternal part to play,
What did he understand? that good has scope
Only from evil, flowering in filth?
Did he go smiling, kissing, to betray
Out of a fine conviction of his truth,
Or some original wreckage of our hope?

If merely mistaken, at any rate,
He had a talent for the grand mistake,
The necessary one, without which not,
And managed to incur eternal hate
For triggering what destiny had got
Arranged from the beginning, for our sake.

Let us consider, then, if not forgive
This most distinguished of our fellow sinners,
Who sponsored our redemption with his sin,
And whose name, more than ours, shall surely live
To make our meanness look like justice in
All histories commissioned by the winners.

1980

1. Half turning to either side, a term from horsemanship.

2. Judas Iscariot, the disciple who betrayed Jesus. Cf. Matthew xxvi.14–50.

RICHARD WILBUR
(1921–)

First Snow in Alsace

The snow came down last night like moths
Burned on the moon; it fell till dawn,
Covered the town with simple cloths.

Absolute snow lies rumpled on
What shellbursts scattered and deranged,
Entangled railings, crevassed lawn.

As if it did not know they'd changed,
Snow smoothly clasps the roofs of homes
Fear-gutted, trustless and estranged.

The ration stacks are milky domes;
Across the ammunition pile
The snow has climbed in sparkling combs.

You think: beyond the town a mile
Or two, this snowfall fills the eyes
Of soldiers dead a little while.

Persons and persons in disguise,
Walking the new air white and fine,
Trade glances quick with shared surprise.

At children's windows, heaped, benign,
As always, winter shines the most,
And frost makes marvelous designs.

The night guard coming from his post,
Ten first-snows back in thought, walks slow
And warms him with a boyish boast:

He was the first to see the snow.

1947

Objects

Meridians are a net
Which catches nothing; that sea-scampering bird
The gull, though shores lapse every side from sight, can yet
Sense him to land, but Hanno[1] had not heard

Hesperidean song,[2]
Had he not gone by watchful periploi:[3]

1. Carthaginian navigator who led an expedition down the west coast of Africa in the fifth century B.C.
2. The Hesperides were sweet-voiced nymphs who guarded the golden apples ("McIntoshes") given by Ge to Hera for her marriage to Zeus (see lines 12–14).
3. Plural of *periplus*, a voyage or trip around an island or a coast.

Chalk rocks, and isles like beasts, and mountain stains along
The water-hem, calmed him at last nearby

The clear high hidden chant
Blown from the spellbound coast, where under drifts
Of sunlight, under plated leaves, they guard the plant
By praising it. Among the wedding gifts

Of Herë, were a set
Of golden McIntoshes, from the Greek
Imagination. Guard and gild what's common, and forget
Uses and prices and names; have objects speak.

There's classic and there's quaint,
And then there is that devout intransitive eye
Of Pieter de Hooch:[4] see feinting from his plot of paint
The trench of light on boards, the much-mended dry

Courtyard wall of brick,
And sun submerged in beer, and streaming in glasses,
The weave of a sleeve, the careful and undulant tile. A quick
Change of the eye and all this calmly passes

Into a day, into magic.
For is there any end to true textures, to true
Integuments; do they ever desist from tacit, tragic
Fading away? Oh maculate, cracked, askew,

Gay-pocked and potsherd world
I voyage, where in every tangible tree
I see afloat among the leaves, all calm and curled,
The Cheshire smile[5] which sets me fearfully free.

1947

Museum Piece

The good gray guardians of art
Patrol the halls on spongy shoes,
Impartially protective, though
Perhaps suspicious of Toulouse.[6]

Here dozes one against the wall,
Disposed upon a funeral chair.
A Degas dancer pirouettes
Upon the parting of his hair.

See how she spins! The grace is there,
But strain as well is plain to see.
Degas loved the two together:
Beauty joined to energy.

4. Pieter de Hooch (1629–ca. 1677), Dutch genre painter.
5. In *Alice in Wonderland*, when the Cheshire cat disappeared, its smile lingered.
6. Henri de Toulouse-Lautrec (1864–1901), French painter who found his subjects in the world of music halls, theaters, and popular cafés. Other painters mentioned in the poem: Edgar Degas, the great sculptor and impressionist painter (1834–1917), and El Greco (Domenikos Theotokopoulos), Spanish painter of Greek origin (ca. 1541–1614).

Edgar Degas purchased once
A fine El Greco, which he kept
Against the wall beside his bed
To hang his pants on while he slept.

1950

The Death of a Toad

A toad the power mower caught,
Chewed and clipped of a leg, with a hobbling hop has got
To the garden verge, and sanctuaried him
Under the cineraria leaves, in the shade
Of the ashen heartshaped leaves, in a dim,
Low, and a final glade.

The rare original heartsblood goes,
Spends on the earthen hide, in the folds and wizening, flows
In the gutters of the banked and staring eyes. He lies
As still as if he would return to stone,
And soundlessly attending, dies
Toward some deep monotone,

Toward misted and ebullient seas
And cooling shores, toward lost Amphibia's emperies.[7]
Day dwindles, drowning, and at length is gone
In the wide and antique eyes, which still appear
To watch, across the castrate lawn,
The haggard daylight steer.

1950, 1957

Boy at the Window

Seeing the snowman standing all alone
In dusk and cold is more than he can bear.
The small boy weeps to hear the wind prepare
A night of gnashings and enormous moan.
His tearful sight can hardly reach to where
The pale-faced figure with bitumen eyes
Returns him such a god-forsaken stare
As outcast Adam gave to Paradise.

The man of snow is, nonetheless, content,
Having no wish to go inside and die.
Still, he is moved to see the youngster cry.
Though frozen water is his element,
He melts enough to drop from one soft eye
A trickle of the purest rain, a tear
For the child at the bright pane surrounded by
Such warmth, such light, such love, and so much fear.

1956

7. I.e., the land of amphibians.

Junk

Huru Welandes
worc ne geswiceð
monna ænigum
ðara ðe Mimming can
heardne gehealdan.
—WALDERE[8]

An axe angles
from my neighbor's ashcan;
It is hell's handiwork,
the wood not hickory,
The flow of the grain
not faithfully followed.
The shivered shaft
rises from a shellheap
Of plastic playthings,
paper plates,
And the sheer shards
of shattered tumblers
That were not annealed
for the time needful.
At the same curbside,
a cast-off cabinet
Of wavily-warped
unseasoned wood
Waits to be trundled
in the trash-man's truck.
Haul them off! Hide them!
The heart winces
For junk and gimcrack,
for jerrybuilt things
And the men who make them
for a little money,
Bartering pride
like the bought boxer
Who pulls his punches,
or the paid-off jockey
Who in the home stretch
holds in his horse.
Yet the things themselves
in thoughtless honor
Have kept composure,
like captives who would not
Talk under torture.
Tossed from a tailgate
Where the dump displays
its random dolmens,[9]
Its black barrows
and blazing valleys,

8. *Waldere* (or *Waldhere*) is the name of an Old English heroic poem. The lines quoted here translate roughly as "Weland's handiwork will fail no man who can wield sharp Mimming." Weland, or Wayland, was the mythical blacksmith and king of elves. Mimming was the name of Weland's sword.

9. Crude tombs made from rough slabs of stone.

They shall waste in the weather
toward what they were.
The sun shall glory
in the glitter of glass-chips,
Foreseeing the salvage
of the prisoned sand,
And the blistering paint
peel off in patches,
That the good grain
be discovered again.
Then burnt, bulldozed,
they shall all be buried
To the depth of diamonds,
in the making dark
Where halt Hephaestus[1]
keeps his hammer
And Wayland's work
is worn away.

1961

For K. R. on Her Sixtieth Birthday

Blow out the candles of your cake.
They will not leave you in the dark,
Who round with grace this dusky arc
Of the grand tour which souls must take.

You who have sounded William Blake,[2]
And the still pool, to Plato's[3] mark,
Blow out the candles of your cake.
They will not leave you in the dark.

Yet, for your friends' benighted sake,
Detain your upward-flying spark;
Get us that wish, though like the lark
You whet your wings till dawn shall break:
Blow out the candles of your cake.

1969

A Storm in April

FOR BEN

Some winters, taking leave,
Deal us a last, hard blow,
Salting the ground like Carthage[4]
Before they will go.

But the bright, milling snow
Which throngs the air today—
It is a way of leaving
So as to stay.

1. Greek god of the fire and forge; his Roman equivalent is Vulcan.
2. William Blake (1757–1827). English artist and mystico-philosophic-symbolist poet; see above.
3. Greek philosopher (427?-348 B.C.).
4. Ancient Phoenician city in North Africa, near the site of modern Tunis, founded in the 9th century B.C. At the end of the protracted struggles with Rome, known as the Punic Wars, the city was finally captured and destroyed by Scipio Aemilianus in 146 B.C., and the ground sown with salt to render it permanently infertile.

The light flakes do not weigh
The willows down, but sift
Through the white catkins, loose
As pedal-drift,

Or in an up-draft lift
And glitter at a height,
Dazzling as summer's leaf-stir
Chinked with light.

This storm, if I am right,
Will not be wholly over
Till green fields, here and there,
Turn white with clover,

And through chill air the puffs of milkweed hover.

1976

PHILIP LARKIN
(1922–)

Church Going

Once I am sure there's nothing going on
I step inside, letting the door thud shut.
Another church: matting, seats, and stone,
And little books; sprawlings of flowers, cut
For Sunday, brownish now; some brass and stuff
Up at the holy end; the small neat organ;
And a tense, musty, unignorable silence,
Brewed God knows how long. Hatless, I take off
My cycle-clips in awkward reverence,

Move forward, run my hand around the font.
From where I stand, the roof looks almost new—
Cleaned, or restored? Somone would know: I don't.
Mounting the lectern, I peruse a few
Hectoring large-scale verses, and pronounce
"Here endeth" much more loudly than I'd meant.
The echoes snigger briefly. Back at the door
I sign the book, donate an Irish sixpence,
Reflect the place was not worth stopping for.

Yet stop I did: in fact I often do,
And always end much at a loss like this,
Wondering what to look for; wondering, too,
When churches fall completely out of use
What we shall turn them into, if we shall keep
A few cathedrals chronically on show,
Their parchment, plate and pyx[1] in locked cases,
And let the rest rent-free to rain and sheep.
Shall we avoid them as unlucky places?

1. The vessel in which the Host is kept.

Or, after dark, will dubious women come
To make their children touch a particular stone;
Pick simples° for a cancer; or on some   herbs
Advised night see walking a dead one?
Power of some sort or other will go on
In games, in riddles, seemingly at random;
But superstition, like belief, must die,
And what remains when disbelief has gone?
Grass, weedy pavement, brambles, buttress, sky,

A shape less recognizable each week,
A purpose more obscure. I wonder who
Will be the last, the very last, to seek
This place for what it was; one of the crew
That tap and jot and know what rood-lofts were?
Some ruin-bibber, randy for antique,
Or Christmas-addict, counting on a whiff
Of gown-and-bands and organ-pipes and myrrh?
Or will he be my representative,

Bored, uninformed, knowing the ghostly silt
Dispersed, yet tending to this cross of ground
Through suburb scrub because it held unspilt
So long and equably what since is found
Only in separation—marriage, and birth,
And death, and thoughts of these—for whom was built
This special shell? For, though I've no idea
What this accoutred frowsty barn is worth,
It pleases me to stand in silence here;

A serious house on serious earth it is,
In whose blent air all our compulsions meet,
Are recognized, and robed as destinies.
And that much never can be obsolete,
Since someone will forever be surprising
A hunger in himself to be more serious,
And gravitating with it to this ground,
Which, he once heard, was proper to grow wise in,
If only that so many dead lie round.

1955

Myxomatosis [2]

Caught in the center of a soundless field
While hot inexplicable hours go by
What trap is this? Where were its teeth concealed?
You seem to ask.
                    I make a sharp reply,
Then clean my stick. I'm glad I can't explain
Just in what jaws you were to suppurate:
You may have thought things would come right again
If you could only keep quite still and wait.

1955

2. An infectious and fatal disease of rabbits, artificially introduced into Great Britain and Australia in recent years to keep down the rabbit population.

Sad Steps

Groping back to bed after a piss
I part thick curtains, and am startled by
The rapid clouds, the moon's cleanliness.

Four o'clock: wedge-shadowed gardens lie
Under a cavernous, a wind-picked sky.
There's something laughable about this,

The way the moon dashes through clouds that blow
Loosely as cannon-smoke to stand apart
(Stone-colored light sharpening the roofs below)

High and preposterous and separate—
Lozenge° of love! Medallion of art! *diamond-shaped pattern*
O wolves of memory! Immensements! No,

One shivers slightly, looking up there.
The hardness and the brightness and the plain
Far-reaching singleness of that wide stare

Is a reminder of the strength and pain
Of being young; that it can't come again,
But is for others undiminished somewhere.

1974

JAMES DICKEY
(1923–)

The Lifeguard

In a stable of boats I lie still,
From all sleeping children hidden.
The leap of a fish from its shadow
Makes the whole lake instantly tremble.
With my foot on the water, I feel
The moon outside

Take on the utmost of its power.
I rise and go out through the boats.
I set my broad sole upon silver,
On the skin of the sky, on the moonlight,
Stepping outward from earth onto water
In quest of the miracle

This village of children believed
That I could perform as I dived
For one who had sunk from my sight.
I saw his cropped haircut go under.
I leapt, and my steep body flashed
Once, in the sun.

Dark drew all the light from my eyes.
Like a man who explores his death
By the pull of his slow-moving shoulders,
I hung head down in the cold,
Wide-eyed, contained, and alone
Among the weeds,

And my fingertips turned into stone
From clutching immovable blackness.
Time after time I leapt upward
Exploding in breath, and fell back
From the change in the children's faces
At my defeat.

Beneath them I swam to the boathouse
With only my life in my arms
To wait for the lake to shine back
At the risen moon with such power
That my steps on the light of the ripples
Might be sustained.

Beneath me is nothing but brightness
Like the ghost of a snowfield in summer.
As I move toward the center of the lake,
Which is also the center of the moon,
I am thinking of how I may be
The savior of one

Who has already died in my care.
The dark trees fade from around me.
The moon's dust hovers together.
I call softly out, and the child's
Voice answers through blinding water.
Patiently, slowly,

He rises, dilating to break
The surface of stone with his forehead.
He is one I do not remember
Having ever seen in his life.
The ground I stand on is trembling
Upon his smile.

I wash the black mud from my hands.
On a light given off by the grave
I kneel in the quick of the moon
At the heart of a distant forest
And hold in my arms a child
Of water, water, water.

1962

In the Tree House at Night

And now the green household is dark.
The half-moon completely is shining
On the earth-lighted tops of the trees.
To be dead, a house must be still.
The floor and the walls wave me slowly;

I am deep in them over my head.
The needles and pine cones about me

Are full of small birds at their roundest,
Their fists without mercy gripping
Hard down through the tree to the roots
To sing back at light when they feel it.
We lie here like angels in bodies,
My brothers and I, one dead,
The other asleep from much living,

In mid-air huddled beside me.
Dark climbed to us here as we climbed
Up the nails I have hammered all day
Through the sprained, comic rungs of the ladder
Of broom handles, crate slats, and laths
Foot by foot up the trunk to the branches
Where we came out at last over lakes

Of leaves, of fields disencumbered of earth
That move with the moves of the spirit.
Each nail that sustains us I set here;
Each nail in the house is now steadied
By my dead brother's huge, freckled hand.
Through the years, he has pointed his hammer
Up into these limbs, and told us

That we must ascend, and all lie here.
Step after step he has brought me,
Embracing the trunk as his body,
Shaking its limbs with my heartbeat,
Till the pine cones danced without wind
And fell from the branches like apples.
In the arm-slender forks of our dwelling

I breathe my live brother's light hair.
The blanket around us becomes
As solid as stone, and it sways.
With all my heart, I close
The blue, timeless eye of my mind.
Wind springs, as my dead brother smiles
And touches the tree at the root;

A shudder of joy runs up
The trunk; the needles tingle;
One bird uncontrollably cries.
The wind changes round, and I stir
Within another's life. Whose life?
Who is dead? Whose presence is living?
When may I fall strangely to earth,

Who am nailed to this branch by a spirit?
Can two bodies make up a third?
To sing, must I feel the world's light?
My green, graceful bones fill the air
With sleeping birds. Alone, alone
And with them I move gently.
I move at the heart of the world.

1962

ANTHONY HECHT
(1923–)

"More Light! More Light!"

FOR HEINRICH BLÜCHER AND HANNAH ARENDT[1]

Composed in the Tower[2] before his execution
These moving verses, and being brought at that time
Painfully to the stake, submitted, declaring thus:
"I implore my God to witness that I have made no crime."

Nor was he forsaken of courage, but the death was horrible,
The sack of gunpowder failing to ignite.
His legs were blistered sticks on which the black sap
Bubbled and burst as he howled for the Kindly Light.[3]

And that was but one, and by no means one of the worst;
Permitted at least his pitiful dignity;
And such as were by made prayers in the name of Christ,
That shall judge all men, for his soul's tranquillity.

We move now to outside a German wood.[4]
Three men are there commanded to dig a hole
In which the two Jews are ordered to lie down
And be buried alive by the third, who is a Pole.

Not light from the shrine at Weimar beyond the hill
Nor light from heaven appeared. But he did refuse.
A Lüger[5] settled back deeply in its glove.
He was ordered to change places with the Jews.

Much casual death had drained away their souls.
The thick dirt mounted toward the quivering chin.
When only the head was exposed the order came
To dig him out again and to get back in.

No light, no light in the blue Polish eye.
When he finished a riding boot packed down the earth.
The Lüger hovered lightly in its glove.
He was shot in the belly and in three hours bled to death.

No prayers or incense rose up in those hours
Which grew to be years, and every day came mute
Ghosts from the ovens, sifting through crisp air,
And settled upon his eyes in a black soot.

1968

1. Husband and wife, both philosophers, notable refugees from Nazi Germany; Hannah Arendt (1906–75) wrote and lectured extensively on totalitarianism; "More light . . .": reportedly the dying words of Johann Wolfgang von Goethe (1749–1832), "the sage of Weimar," Germany's most celebrated author.
2. The Tower of London, a fortress and sometimes a prison. The author explains that no specific execution is described; but such events took place during the Catholic and Protestant persecutions in England in the 16th century.
3. An allusion to the hymn "Lead, Kindly Light," a petition for God's mercy in time of trouble.
4. Such as Buchenwald, the notorious Nazi death camp. The event is a matter of record.
5. A German military pistol.

Sestina d'Inverno[6]

Here in this bleak city of Rochester,[7]
Where there are twenty-seven words for "snow,"
Not all of them polite, the wayward mind
Basks in some Yucatan[8] of its own making,
Some coppery, sleek lagoon, or cinnamon island
Alive with lemon tints and burnished natives,

And O that we were there.[9] But here the natives
Of this gray, sunless city of Rochester
Have sown whole mines of salt about their land
(Bare ruined Carthage[1] that it is) while snow
Comes down as if The Flood[2] were in the making.
Yet on that ocean Marvell[3] called the mind

An ark sets forth which is itself the mind,
Bound for some pungent green, some shore whose natives
Blend coriander, cayenne, mint in making
Roasts that would gladden the Earl of Rochester[4]
With sinfulness, and melt a polar snow.
It might be well to remember that an island

Was a blessed haven once, more than an island,
The grand, utopian dream of a noble mind.
In that kind climate the mere thought of snow
Was but a wedding cake; the youthful natives,
Unable to conceive of Rochester,
Made love, and were acrobatic in the making.

Dream as we may, there is far more to making
Do than some wistful reverie of an island,
Especially now when hope lies with the Rochester
Gas and Electric Co., which doesn't mind
Such profitable weather, while the natives
Sink, like Pompeians,[5] under a world of snow.

The one thing indisputable here is snow,
The single verity of heaven's making,
Deeply indifferent to the dreams of the natives
And the torn hoarding-posters of some island.
Under our igloo skies the frozen mind
Holds to one truth: it is gray, and called Rochester.

No island fantasy survives Rochester,
Where to the natives destiny is snow
That is neither to our mind nor of our making.

1977

6. Sestina for winter.
7. City in upstate New York.
8. In southeast Mexico; here a symbol of an imaginary tropical paradise.
9. In heaven; a phrase from an ancient Christmas carol.
1. After defeating the kingdom of Carthage, in 146 B.C., the Romans are said to have sowed the land with salt to render it infertile; "bare ruined": a phrase from Shakespeare's sonnet 73, line 4.
2. The universal deluge (Noah's Flood); Genesis vii–viii.
3. Andrew Marvell (1621–78), in "The Garden," line 43 (see above).
4. Poet and courtier (1621–80), a notable figure in the licentious and luxurious circle around Charles II.
5. Buried under an eruption of Mount Vesuvius, near Naples, in A.D. 79.

The Feast of Stephen[6]

1

The coltish horseplay of the locker room,
Moist with the steam of the tiled shower stalls,
With shameless blends of civet, musk and sweat.
Loud with the cap-gun snapping of wet towels
Under the steel-ribbed cages of bare bulbs,
In some such setting of thick basement pipes
And janitorial realities
Boys for the first time frankly eye each other,
Inspect each others' bodies at close range,
And what they see is not so much another
As a strange, possible version of themselves,
And all the sparring dance, adrenal life,
Tense, jubilant nimbleness, is but a vague,
Busy, unfocused ballet of self-love.

2

If the heart has its reasons, perhaps the body
Has its own lumbering sort of carnal spirit,
Felt in the tingling bruises of collision,
And known to captains as *esprit de corps*.[7]
What is this brisk fraternity of timing,
Pivot and lobbing arc, or indirection,
Mens sana[8] in men's sauna, in the flush
Of health and toilets, private and corporal glee,
These fleet caroms, *pliés*[9] and genuflections
Before the salmon-leap, the leaping fountain
All sheathed in glistening light, flexed and alert?
From the vast echo-chamber of the gym,
Among the scumbled shouts and shrill of whistles
The bounced basketball sound of a leather whip.

3

Think of those barren places where men gather
To act in the terrible name of rectitude,
Of acned shame, punk's pride, muscle or turf,
The bully's thin superiority.
Think of the *Sturm-Abteilungs Kommandant*[1]
Who loves Beethoven and collects Degas,[2]
Or the blond boys in jeans whose narrowed eyes
Are focused by some hard and smothered lust,
Who lounge in a studied mimicry of ease,
Flick their live butts into the standing weeds,
And comb their hair in the mirror of cracked windows
Of an abandoned warehouse where they keep
In darkened readiness for their occasion
The rope, the chains, handcuffs and gasoline.

4

Out in the rippled heat of a neighbor's field,
In the kilowatts of noon, they've got one cornered.

6. A church festival, the day after Christmas, commemorating the death by stoning of Saint Stephen, the first Christian martyr. See Acts vii.54–60.

7. Roughly, "team spirit"; literally, "spirit of the body."

8. Latin proverb: *Mens sana in corpore sano*—"a healthy mind in a healthy body."

9. In ballet terminology, knee bends.

1. An officer of the Nazi storm troopers.

2. French painter (1834–1917).

The bugs are jumping, and the burly youths
Strip to the waist for the hot work ahead.
They go to arm themselves at the dry-stone wall,
Having flung down their wet and salty garments
At the feet of a young man whose name is Saul.[3]
He watches sharply these superbly tanned
Figures with a swimmer's chest and shoulders,
A miler's thighs, with their self-conscious grace,
And in between their sleek, converging bodies,
Brilliantly oiled and burnished by the sun,
He catches a brief glimpse of bloodied hair
And hears an unintelligible prayer.

1977

RICHARD HUGO (1923–1982)

Degrees of Gray in Philipsburg[1]

You might come here Sunday on a whim.
Say your life broke down. The last good kiss
you had was years ago. You walk these streets
laid out by the insane, past hotels
that didn't last, bars that did, the tortured try
of local drivers to accelerate their lives.
Only churches are kept up. The jail
turned 70 this year. The only prisoner
is always in, not knowing what he's done.

The principal supporting business now
is rage. Hatred of the various grays
the mountain sends, hatred of the mill,
The Silver Bill[2] repeal, the best liked girls
who leave each year for Butte. One good
restaurant and bars can't wipe the boredom out.
The 1907 boom, eight going silver mines,
a dance floor built on springs—
all memory resolves itself in gaze,
in panoramic green you know the cattle eat
or two stacks high above the town,
two dead kilns, the huge mill in collapse
for fifty years that won't fall finally down.

Isn't this your life? That ancient kiss
still burning out your eyes? Isn't this defeat
so accurate, the church bell simply seems
a pure announcement: ring and no one comes?
Don't empty houses ring? Are magnesium
and scorn sufficient to support a town,
not just Philipsburg, but towns

3. Later to become the apostle Saint Paul, he at first took part in persecuting the Christians. See Acts viii.1–3.

1. Small town in Montana which, in the early 20th century, was a thriving community supporting a silver-processing mill.

2. Law enacted in 1934 empowering the federal government to purchase silver; Butte is a city in Montana.

of towering blondes, good jazz and booze
the world will never let you have
until the town you came from dies inside?

Say no to yourself. The old man, twenty
when the jail was built, still laughs
although his lips collapse. Someday soon,
he says, I'll go to sleep and not wake up.
You tell him no. You're talking to yourself.
The car that brought you here still runs.
The money you buy lunch with,
no matter where it's mined, is silver
and the girl who serves your food
is slender and her red hair lights the wall.

1973

White Center[3]

Town or poem, I don't care how it looks. Old woman
take my hand and we'll walk one more time these streets
I believed marked me weak beneath catcalling clouds.
Long ago, the swamp behind the single row of stores
was filled and seeded. Roses today where Toughy Hassin
slapped my face to the grinning delight of his gang.
I didn't cry or run. Had I fought him
I'd have been beaten and come home bloody in tears
and you'd have told me I shouldn't be fighting.

Wasn't it all degrading, mean Mr. Kyte sweeping
the streets for no pay, believing what he'd learned
as a boy in England: "This is your community"?
I taunted him to rage, then ran. Is this the day
we call bad mothers out of the taverns and point them
sobbing for home, or issue costumes to posturing clowns
in the streets, make fun of drunk barbers, and hope
someone who left and made it returns, vowed
to buy more neon and give these people some class?

The Dugans aren't worth a dime, dirty Irish, nor days
you offered a penny for every fly I killed.
You were blind to my cheating. I saw my future certain—
that drunk who lived across the street and fell
in our garden reaching for the hoe you dropped.
All he got was our laughter. I helped him often home
when you weren't looking. I loved some terrible way
he lived in his mind and tried to be decent to others.
I loved the way we loved him behind our disdain.

Clouds. What glorious floating. They always move on
like I should have early. But your odd love and a war
taught me the world's gone evil past the first check point
and that's First Avenue South. I fell asleep each night
safe in love with my murder. The neighbor girl

3. Suburb of Seattle, Washington; when Hugo grew up there as a child, it was more like a small town.

plotted to tease every tomorrow and watch me turn
again to the woods and games too young for my age.
We never could account for the python cousin Warren
found half starved in the basement of Safeway.

It all comes back but in bites. I am the man
you beat to perversion. That was the drugstore MacCameron
flipped out in early one morning, waltzing
on his soda fountain. The siren married his shrieking.
His wife said, "We'll try again, in Des Moines."
You drove a better man into himself where he found tunes
he had no need to share. It's all beginning to blur
as it forms. Men cracking up or retreating.
Resolute women deep in hard prayer.

And it isn't the same this time. I hoped forty years
I'd write and would not write this poem. This town would die
and your grave never reopen. Or mine. Because I'm married
and happy, and across the street a foster child
from a cruel past is safe and need no longer crawl
for his meals, I walk this past with you, ghost in any field
of good crops, certain I remember everything wrong.
If not, why is this road lined thick with fern
and why do I feel no shame kicking the loose gravel home?

1980

Salt Water Story

He loved his cabin: there
nothing had happened. Then his friends were dead.
The new neighbors had different ways.
Days came heavy with regret.
He studied sea charts and charted
sea lanes out. He calculated times
to ride the tide rip, times to go ashore and rest.
He memorized the names of bays: those
with plenty of driftwood for fire,
those with oysters. He found a forest
he could draw back into
when the Coast Guard came looking, news
of him missing by now broadcast state-wide.
He made no move. He turned out lights
and lit candles and watched his face
in the window glow red.

He dreamed a raft
and dreamed this sea lane out, past
long dormant cannons and the pale hermit
who begged to go with him. A blue heron
trailed him. A second heron trailed the first,
a third the second and so on. Those who looked for him
checked the skies for a long blue line
of laboring wings.
The birds broke formation, and the world
of search and rescue lost track of his wake.
His face glowed red on the glass.

If found, he'd declare himself pro-cloud
and pro-wind and anti-flat hot days.

Then he dreamed wrong
what we owe Egypt, what we owe
sea lanes out of the slaves to ourselves
we become one morning, nothing
for us in dawn, and nothing for us in tide.
What we owe Egypt fades
into what we owe Greece and then Rome.
What we owe Rome keeps repeating
like what we owe time—namely our lives
and whatever laughter we find to pass on.
He knew grief repeats on its own.

One night late, the face in the window
glowed back at him pale. He believed that face
some bum peeking in
and waved 'hi.' The old face told him,
to navigate a lasting way out
he must learn how coins gleam
one way through water, how bones of dead fish
gleam another, and he must learn both gleams
and dive deep. He learned both gleams
and learned to dive fast and come up slow
as sky every day.

And we might think someday we'll find him
dead over his charts, the water ways out
a failed dream. Nothing like that.
His cabin stands empty and he
sails the straits. We often see him
from shore or the deck of a ferry.
We can't tell him by craft. Some days
he passes on a yacht, some days a tug.
He's young and, captain or deckhand,
he is the one who waves.

1982

DENISE LEVERTOV
(1923–   )

Triple Feature

Innocent decision: to enjoy.
And the pathos
of hopefulness, of his solicitude:

—he in mended serape,
she having plaited carefully
magenta ribbons into her hair,
the baby a round half-hidden shape
slung in her rebozo,° and the young son steadfastly *shawl*
gripping a fold of her skirt,
pale and severe under a
handed-down sombrero—

all regarding
the stills with full attention, preparing
to pay and go in—
to worlds of shadow-violence, half-
familiar, warm with popcorn, icy
with strange motives, barbarous splendors!

1959

From the Roof

This wild night, gathering the washing as if it were flowers
animal vines twisting over the line and
slapping my face lightly, soundless merriment
in the gesticulations of shirtsleeves,
I recall out of my joy a night of misery

walking in the dark and the wind over broken earth,
halfmade foundations and unfinished
drainage trenches and the spaced-out
circles of glaring light
marking streets that were to be,
walking with you but so far from you,

and now alone in October's
first decision towards winter, so close to you—
my arms full of playful rebellious linen, a freighter
going down-river two blocks away, outward bound,
the green wolf-eyes of the Harborside Terminal
glittering on the Jersey shore,
and a train somewhere under ground bringing you towards me
to our new living-place from which we can see

a river and its traffic (the Hudson and the
hidden river, who can say which it is we see, we see
something of both. Or who can say
the crippled broom-vendor yesterday, who passed
just as we needed a new broom, was not
one of the Hidden Ones?)
Crates of fruit are unloading
across the street on the cobbles,
and a brazier flaring
to warm the men and burn trash. He wished us
luck when we bought the broom. But not luck
brought us here. By design

clear air and cold wind polish
the river lights, by design
we are to live now in a new place.

1961

O Taste and See

The world is
not with us enough.[1]
O taste and see

1. Cf. Wordsworth's sonnet, *The World Is Too Much with Us,* above.

the subway Bible poster said,
meaning The Lord,[2] meaning
if anything all that lives
to the imagination's tongue,

grief, mercy, language,
tangerine, weather, to
breathe them, bite,
savor, chew, swallow, transform

into our flesh our
deaths, crossing the street, plum, quince,
living in the orchard and being

hungry, and plucking
the fruit.

1964

Tenebrae [3]

(FALL OF 1967) [4]

Heavy, heavy, heavy, hand and heart.
We are at war,
bitterly, bitterly at war.

And the buying and selling
buzzes at our heads, a swarm
of busy flies, a kind of innocence.

Gowns of gold sequins are fitted,
sharp-glinting. What harsh rustlings
of silver moiré° there are, *watered silk*
to remind me of shrapnel splinters.

And weddings are held in full solemnity
not of desire but of etiquette,
the nuptial pomp of starched lace;
a grim innocence.

And picnic parties return from the beaches
burning with stored sun in the dusk;
children promised a TV show when they get home
fall asleep in the backs of a million station wagons,
sand in their hair, the sound of waves
quietly persistent at their ears.
They are not listening.

Their parents at night
dream and forget their dreams.
They wake in the dark
and make plans. Their sequin plans

2. "O taste and see that the Lord is good (Psalms xxxiv.8).
3. *Tenebrae* (Latin, darkness), are church services for the last three days of Holy Week, to commemorate the sufferings and death of Christ; candles lighted at the beginning of the service are extinguished one by one after each psalm, in memory of the darkness at the time of the crucifixion.
4. The fall of 1967 witnessed the march on the Pentagon, in protest against the continuing presence of American troops in Vietnam.

glitter into tomorrow.
They buy, they sell.

They fill freezers with food.
Neon signs flash their intentions
into the years ahead.

And at their ears the sound
of the war. They are
not listening, not listening.

1972

KENNETH KOCH
(1925–)

You Were Wearing

You were wearing your Edgar Allan Poe printed cotton blouse.
In each divided up square of the blouse was a picture of Edgar Allan Poe.
Your hair was blonde and you were cute. You asked me, "Do most boys think that most girls are bad?"
I smelled the mould of your seaside resort hotel bedroom on your hair held in place by a John Greenleaf Whittier clip.
"No," I said, "it's girls who think that boys are bad." Then we read *Snowbound* together
And ran around in an attic, so that a little of the blue enamel was scraped off my George Washington, Father of His Country, shoes.

Mother was walking in the living room, her Strauss Waltzes comb in her hair.
We waited for a time and then joined her, only to be served tea in cups painted with pictures of Herman Melville
As well as with illustrations from his book *Moby Dick* and from his novella, *Benito Cereno.*
Father came in wearing his Dick Tracy necktie: "How about a drink, everyone?"
I said, "Let's go outside a while." Then we went onto the porch and sat on the Abraham Lincoln swing.
You sat on the eyes, mouth, and beard part, and I sat on the knees.
In the yard across the street we saw a snowman holding a garbage can lid smashed into a likeness of the mad English king, George the Third.

1962

Variations on a Theme by William Carlos Williams[5]

1

I chopped down the house that you had been saving to live in next summer.
I am sorry, but it was morning, and I had nothing to do
and its wooden beams were so inviting.

2

We laughed at the hollyhocks together
and then I sprayed them with lye.
Forgive me. I simply do not know what I am doing.

5. See "This Is Just to Say," by William Carlos Williams, above. Williams was a physician (see line 12).

3
I gave away the money that you had been saving to live on for the next ten years.
The man who asked for it was shabby
and the firm March wind on the porch was so juicy and cold.

4
Last evening we went dancing and I broke your leg.
Forgive me. I was clumsy, and
I wanted you here in the wards, where I am the doctor!

1962

A. R. AMMONS
(1926–)

Silver

I thought Silver must have snaked° logs *dragged*
when young:
she couldn't stand to have the line brush her lower hind leg:
in blinded halter she couldn't tell what had loosened behind her
and was coming
as downhill
to rush into her crippling her to the ground:

and when she almost went to sleep, me dreaming at the slow plow,
I would
at dream's end turning over the mind to a new chapter
let the line drop and touch her leg
and she would
bring the plow out of the ground with speed but wisely
fall soon again into the slow requirements of our dreams:
how we turned at the ends of rows without sense to new furrows
and went back
flicked by
cornblades and hearing the circling in
the cornblades of horseflies in pursuit:

I hitch up early, the raw spot on Silver's shoulder
sore to the collar,
get a wrench and change the plow's bull-tongue for a sweep,[1]
and go out, wrench in my hip pocket for later adjustments,
down the ditch-path
by the white-bloomed briars, wet crabgrass, cattails,
and rusting ferns,
riding the plow handles down,
keeping the sweep's point from the ground,
the smooth bar under the plow gliding,
the traces loose, the raw spot wearing its soreness out
in the gentle movement to the fields:

when snake-bitten in the spring pasture grass
Silver came up to the gate and stood head-down enchanted
in her fate

1. Cultivator blade for a plow; "bull-tongue": shovel blade for stirring soil or marking furrows.

I found her sorrowful eyes by accident and knew:
nevertheless the doctor could not keep her from all
the consequences, rolls in the sand, the blank extension
        of limbs,
        head thrown back in the dust,
useless unfocusing eyes, belly swollen
wide as I was tall
and I went out in the night and saw her in the solitude
            of her wildness:

but she lived and one day half got up
and looking round at the sober world took me back
            into her eyes
and then got up and walked and plowed again;
mornings her swollen snake-bitten leg wept bright as dew
and dried to streaks of salt leaked white from the hair.

1961

Corsons Inlet[2]

I went for a walk over the dunes again this morning
to the sea,
then turned right along
  the surf
            rounded a naked headland
            and returned

  along the inlet shore:

it was muggy sunny, the wind from the sea steady and high,
crisp in the running sand,
    some breakthroughs of sun
  but after a bit

continuous overcast:

the walk liberating, I was released from forms,
from the perpendiculars,
    straight lines, blocks, boxes, binds
of thought
into the hues, shadings, rises, flowing bends and blends
        of sight:

                I allow myself eddies of meaning:
yield to a direction of significance
running
like a stream through the geography of my work:
  you can find
in my sayings
            swerves of action
            like the inlet's cutting edge:
        there are dunes of motion,
organizations of grass, white sandy paths of remembrance
in the overall wandering of mirroring mind:

2. Located in southeast New Jersey.

but Overall is beyond me: is the sum of these events
I cannot draw, the ledger I cannot keep, the accounting
beyond the account:

in nature there are few sharp lines: there are areas of
primrose
        more or less dispersed;
disorderly orders of bayberry; between the rows
of dunes,
irregular swamps of reeds,
though not reeds alone, but grass, bayberry, yarrow, all . . .
predominantly reeds:

I have reached no conclusions, have erected no boundaries,
shutting out and shutting in, separating inside
            from outside: I have
            drawn no lines:
            as

manifold events of sand
change the dune's shape that will not be the same shape
tomorrow,

so I am willing to go along, to accept
the becoming
thought, to stake off no beginnings or ends, establish
            no walls:

by transitions the land falls from grassy dunes to creek
to undercreek: but there are no lines, though
        change in that transition is clear
        as any sharpness: but "sharpness" spread out,
allowed to occur over a wider range
than mental lines can keep:

the moon was full last night: today, low tide was low:
black shoals of mussels exposed to the risk
of air
and, earlier, of sun,
waved in and out with the waterline, waterline inexact,
caught always in the event of change:
        a young mottled gull stood free on the shoals
        and ate
to vomiting: another gull, squawking possession, cracked a crab,
picked out the entrails, swallowed the soft-shelled legs, a ruddy
turnstone running in to snatch leftover bits:

risk is full: every living thing in
siege: the demand is life, to keep life: the small
white blacklegged egret, how beautiful, quietly stalks and spears
            the shallows, darts to shore
                        to stab—what? I couldn't
        see against the black mudflats—a frightened
        fiddler crab?

            the news to my left over the dunes and
reeds and bayberry clumps was

fall: thousands of tree swallows
gathering for flight:
an order held
in constant change: a congregation
rich with entropy: nevertheless, separable, noticeable
as one event,
not chaos: preparations for
flight from winter,
cheet, cheet, cheet, cheet, wings rifling the green clumps,
beaks
at the bayberries
a perception full of wind, flight, curve,
sound:
the possibility of rule as the sum of rulelessness:
the "field" of action
with moving, incalculable center:

in the smaller view, order tight with shape:
blue tiny flowers on a leafless weed: carapace of crab:
snail shell:
pulsations of order
in the bellies of minnows: orders swallowed,
broken down, transferred through membranes
to strengthen larger orders: but in the large view, no
lines or changeless shapes: the working in and out, together
and against, of millions of events: this,
so that I make
no form
formlessness:

orders as summaries, as outcomes of actions override
or in some way result, not predictably (seeing me gain
the top of a dune,
the swallows
could take flight—some other fields of bayberry
could enter fall
berryless) and there is serenity:

no arranged terror: no forcing of image, plan,
or thought:
no propaganda, no humbling of reality to precept:

terror pervades but is not arranged, all possibilities
of escape open: no route shut, except in
the sudden loss of all routes:

I see narrow orders, limited tightness, but will
not run to that easy victory:
still around the looser, wider forces work:
I will try
to fasten into order enlarging grasps of disorder, widening
scope, but enjoying the freedom that
Scope eludes my grasp, that there is no finality of vision,
that I have perceived nothing completely,
that tomorrow a new walk is a new walk.

1965

Small Song

The reeds give
way to the

wind and give
the wind away

1970

Poetics

I look for the way
things will turn
out spiraling from a center,
the shape
things will take to come forth in

so that the birch tree white
touched black at branches
will stand out
wind-glittering
totally its apparent self:

I look for the forms
things want to come as

from what black wells of possibility,
how a thing will
unfold:

not the shape on paper—though
that, too—but the
uninterfering means on paper:

not so much looking for the shape
as being available
to any shape that may be
summoning itself
through me
from the self not mine but ours.

1971

The Put-Down Come On

You would think I'd be a specialist in contemporary
literature: novels, short stories, books of poetry,
my friends write many of them: I don't read much
and some drinks are too strong for me: my empty-headed

contemplation is still where the ideas of permanence
and transience fuse in a single body, ice, for example,
or a leaf: green pushes white up the slope: a maple
leaf gets the wobbles in a light wind and comes loose

half-ready: where what has always happened and what
has never happened before seem for an instant reconciled:
that takes up most of my time and keeps me uninformed:
but the slope, after maybe a thousand years, may spill

and the ice have a very different look withdrawing into
the lofts of cold: only a little of that kind of
thinking flashes through: but turning the permanent also
into the transient takes up all the time that's left.

1971

The City Limits

When you consider the radiance, that it does not withhold
itself but pours its abundance without selection into every
nook and cranny not overhung or hidden; when you consider

that birds' bones make no awful noise against the light but
lie low in the light as in a high testimony; when you consider
the radiance, that it will look into the guiltiest

swervings of the weaving heart and bear itself upon them,
not flinching into disguise or darkening; when you consider
the abundance of such resource as illuminates the glow-blue

bodies and gold-skeined wings of flies swarming the dumped
guts of a natural slaughter or the coil of shit and in no
way winces from its storms of generosity; when you consider

that air or vacuum, snow or shale, squid or wolf, rose or lichen,
each is accepted into as much light as it will take, then
the heart moves roomier, the man stands and looks about, the

leaf does not increase itself above the grass, and the dark
work of the deepest cells is of a tune with May bushes
and fear lit by the breadth of such calmly turns to praise.

1971

Easter Morning

I have a life that did not become,
that turned aside and stopped,
astonished:
I hold it in me like a pregnancy or
as on my lap a child
not to grow or grow old but dwell on

it is to his grave I most
frequently return and return
to ask what is wrong, what was
wrong, to see it all by
the light of a different necessity
but the grave will not heal
and the child,

stirring, must share my grave
with me, an old man having
gotten by on what was left

when I go back to my home country in these
fresh far-away days, it's convenient to visit
everybody, aunts and uncles, those who used to say,
look how he's shooting up, and the
trinket aunts who always had a little
something in their pocketbooks, cinnamon bark
or a penny or nickel, and uncles who
were the rumored fathers of cousins
who whispered of them as of great, if
troubled, presences, and school
teachers, just about everybody older
(and some younger) collected in one place
waiting, particularly, but not for
me, mother and father there, too, and others
close, close as burrowing
under skin, all in the graveyard
assembled, done for, the world they
used to wield, have trouble and joy
in, gone

the child in me that could not become
was not ready for others to go,
to go on into change, blessings and
horrors, but stands there by the road
where the mishap occurred, crying out for
help, come and fix this or we
can't get by, but the great ones who
were to return, they could not or did
not hear and went on in a flurry and
now, I say in the graveyard, here
lies the flurry, now it can't come
back with help or helpful asides, now
we all buy the bitter
incompletions, pick up the knots of
horror, silently raving, and go on
crashing into empty ends not
completions, not rondures the fullness
has come into and spent itself from
I stand on the stump
of a child, whether myself
or my little brother who died, and
yell as far as I can, I cannot leave this place, for
for me it is the dearest and the worst,
it is life nearest to life which is
life lost: it is my place where
I must stand and fail,
calling attention with tears
to the branches not lofting
boughs into space, to the barren
air that holds the world that was my world

though the incompletions
(& completions) burn out

standing in the flash high-burn
momentary structure of ash, still it
is a picture-book, letter-perfect
Easter morning: I have been for a
walk: the wind is tranquil: the brook
works without flashing in an abundant
tranquility: the birds are lively with
voice: I saw something I had
never seen before: two great birds,
maybe eagles, blackwinged, whitenecked
and -headed, came from the south oaring
the great wings steadily; they went
directly over me, high up, and kept on
due north: but then one bird,
the one behind, veered a little to the
left and the other bird kept on seeming
not to notice for a minute: the first
began to circle as if looking for
something, coasting, resting its wings
on the down side of some of the circles:
the other bird came back and they both
circled, looking perhaps for a draft;
they turned a few more times, possibly
rising—at least, clearly resting—
then flew on falling into distance till
they broke across the local bush and
trees: it was a sight of bountiful
majesty and integrity: the having
patterns and routes, breaking
from them to explore other patterns or
better ways to routes, and then the
return: a dance sacred as the sap in
the trees, permanent in its descriptions
as the ripples round the brook's
ripplestone: fresh as this particular
flood of burn breaking across us now
from the sun.

1981

Pet Panther

My attention is a wild
animal: it will if idle
make trouble where there
was no harm: it will

sniff and scratch at the
breath's sills:
it will wind itself tight
around the pulse

or, undistracted by
verbal toys, pommel the
heart frantic: it will
pounce on a stalled riddle

and wrestle the mind numb:
attention, fierce animal
I cry, as it coughs in my
face, dislodges boulders

in my belly, lie down, be
still, have mercy, here
is song, coils of song, play
it out, run with it.

1983

JAMES K. BAXTER
(1926–1972)

Lament for Barney Flanagan

LICENSEE[1] OF THE HESPERUS HOTEL

Flanagan got up on a Saturday morning,
Pulled on his pants while the coffee was warming;
He didn't remember the doctor's warning,
"Your heart's too big, Mr. Flanagan."

Barney Flanagan, sprung like a frog
From a wet root in an Irish bog—
May his soul escape from the tooth of the dog!
God have mercy on Flanagan.

Barney Flanagan R.I.P.[2]
Rode to his grave on Hennessy's
Like a bottle-cork boat in the Irish Sea.
The bell-boy rings for Flanagan.

Barney Flanagan, ripe for a coffin,
Eighteen stone[3] and brandy-rotten,
Patted the housemaid's velvet bottom—
"Oh, is it you, Mr. Flanagan?"

The sky was bright as a new milk token.[4]
Bill the Bookie and Shellshock Hogan[5]
Waited outside for the pub to open—
"Good day, Mr. Flanagan."

At noon he was drinking in the lounge bar corner
With a sergeant of police and a racehorse owner
When the Angel of Death looked over his shoulder—
"Could you spare a moment, Flanagan?"

Oh the deck was cut; the bets were laid;
But the very last card that Barney played

1. Licensed publican or tavern keeper.
2. "*Requiescat in Pace*" (Latin): "may he rest in peace."
3. I.e., weighing about 250 pounds; Hennessy's is a brand of brandy.
4. A token paid to the milkman on receipt of the daily milk delivery.
5. Hogan was a victim of "combat fatigue" as a result of shelling in World War I.

Was the Deadman's Trump, the bullet[6] of Spades—
"Would you like more air, Mr. Flanagan?"

The priest came running but the priest came late
For Barney was banging at the Pearly Gate.
St Peter said, "Quiet! You'll have to wait
For a hundred masses, Flanagan."

The regular boys and the loud accountants
Left their nips and their seven-ounces[7]
As chickens fly when the buzzard pounces—
"Have you heard about old Flanagan?"

Cold in the parlor Flanagan lay
Like a bride at the end of her marriage day.
The Waterside Workers' Band will play
A brass goodbye to Flanagan.

While publicans drink their profits still,
While lawyers flock to be in at the kill,
While Aussie barmen milk the till[8]
We will remember Flanagan.

For Barney had a send-off and no mistake.
He died like a man for his country's sake;
And the Governor-General[9] came to his wake.
Drink again to Flanagan!

Despise not, O Lord, the work of Thine own hands
And let light perpetual shine upon him.

1954

New Zealand

(FOR MONTE HOLCROFT)

These unshaped islands, on the sawyer's bench,
Wait for the chisel of the mind,
Green canyons to the south, immense and passive,
Penetrated rarely, seeded only
By the deer-culler's shot,[1] or else in the north
Tribes of the shark and the octopus,
Mangroves, black hair on a boxer's hand.

The founding fathers with their guns and bibles,
Botanist, whaler, added bones and names
To the land, to us a bridle
As if the id were a horse: the swampy towns
Like dreamers that struggle to wake,

Longing for the poet's truth
And the lover's pride. Something new and old
Explores its own pain, hearing

6. The ace.
7. I.e., their drinks at the bar.
8. I.e., steal money out of the cash register.
9. Titular head of the New Zealand government, appointed by British royalty.
1. A "deer-culler" is a kind of game warden, an agent of the government who controls the herds of deer.

The rain's choir on curtains of gray moss
Or fingers of the Tasman[2] pressing
On breasts of hardening sand, as actors
Find their own solitude in mirrors,

As one who has buried his dead,
Able at last to give with an open hand.

1969

From Jerusalem[3] Sonnets

(POEMS FOR COLIN DURNING)

1

The small gray cloudy louse that nests in my beard
Is not, as some have called it, "a pearl of God"—

No, it is a fiery tormentor
Waking me at two a.m.

Or thereabouts, when the lights are still on
In the houses in the pa,[4] to go across thick grass

Wet with rain, feet cold, to kneel
For an hour or two in front of the red flickering

Tabernacle light—what He sees inside
My meandering mind I can only guess—

A madman, a nobody, a raconteur
Whom He can joke with—"Lord," I ask Him,

"Do You or don't You expect me to put up with lice?"
His silent laugh still shakes the hills at dawn.

1970

ROBERT BLY
(1926–)

Waking from Sleep

Inside the veins there are navies setting forth,
Tiny explosions at the water lines,
And seagulls weaving in the wind of the salty blood.

It is the morning. The country has slept the whole winter.
Window seats were covered with fur skins, the yard was full
Of stiff dogs, and hands that clumsily held heavy books.

Now we wake, and rise from bed, and eat breakfast!—
Shouts rise from the harbor of the blood,
Mist, and masts rising, the knock of wooden tackle in the sunlight.

2. The Tasman Sea, to the west of New Zealand.
3. Isolated Maori settlement to which Baxter retreated during the last years of his life.
4. Village (Maori).

Now we sing, and do tiny dances on the kitchen floor.
Our whole body is like a harbor at dawn;
We know that our master has left us for the day.

1962

Driving toward the Lac Qui Parle River[1]

1

I am driving; it is dusk; Minnesota.
The stubble field catches the last growth of sun.
The soybeans are breathing on all sides.
Old men are sitting before their houses on carseats
In the small towns. I am happy,
The moon rising above the turkey sheds.

2

The small world of the car
Plunges through the deep fields of the night,
On the road from Willmar to Milan.
This solitude covered with iron
Moves through the fields of night
Penetrated by the noise of crickets.

3

Nearly to Milan, suddenly a small bridge,
And water kneeling in the moonlight.
In small towns the houses are built right on the ground;
The lamplight falls on all fours in the grass.
When I reach the river, the full moon covers it;
A few people are talking low in a boat.

1962

ROBERT CREELEY
(1926–)

A Wicker Basket

Comes the time when it's later
and onto your table the headwaiter
puts the bill, and very soon after
rings out the sound of lively laughter—

Picking up change, hands like a walrus,
and a face like a barndoor's,
and a head without an apparent size,
nothing but two eyes—

So that's you, man,
or me. I make it as I can,
I pick up, I go
faster than they know—

Out the door, the street like a night,
any night, and no one in sight,

1. "Lac Qui Parle" ("the lake that speaks"), name of a lake and a river in southwest Minnesota.

but then, well, there she is,
old friend Liz—

And she opens the door of her cadillac,
I step in back,
and we're gone.
She turns me on—

There are very huge stars, man, in the sky,
and from somewhere very far off someone hands me a slice of apple pie,
with a gob of white, white ice cream on top of it,
and I eat it—

Slowly. And while certainly
they are laughing at me, and all around me is racket
of these cats not making it, I make it

in my wicker basket.

1959

Heroes

In all those stories the hero
is beyond himself into the next
thing, be it those labors
of Hercules,[1] or Aeneas going into death.

I thought the instant of the one humanness
in Virgil's plan of it
was that it was of course human enough to die,
yet to come back, as he said, *hoc opus, hic labor est.*[2]

That was the Cumaean Sibyl speaking.
This is Robert Creeley, and Virgil
is dead now two thousand years, yet Hercules
and the *Aeneid,* yet all that industrious wis-

dom lives in the way the mountains
and the desert are waiting
for the heroes, and death also
can still propose the old labors.

1959

ALLEN GINSBERG
(1926–)

In the Baggage Room at Greyhound

1

In the depths of the Greyhound Terminal
sitting dumbly on a baggage truck looking at the sky waiting for the Los Angeles Express to depart

1. Who represents superhuman strength and courage, as revealed in his legendary 12 labors.
2. From Virgil's *Aeneid,* VI. The full quotation (in John Dryden's translation): "Smooth the descent and easy is the way:/But, to return, and view the cheerful skies—/In this the task and mighty labor lies." It is spoken by the Cumaean Sibyl, a prophetic priestess, in advising Aeneas to visit the Underworld to seek counsel in his god-appointed task of founding Rome.

worrying about eternity over the Post Office roof in the night-time red downtown heaven,
staring through my eyeglasses I realized shuddering these thoughts were not eternity, nor the poverty of our lives, irritable baggage clerks,
nor the millions of weeping relatives surrounding the buses waving goodbye,
nor other millions of the poor rushing around from city to city to see their loved ones,
nor an indian dead with fright talking to a huge cop by the Coke machine,
nor this trembling old lady with a cane taking the last trip of her life,
nor the red capped cynical porter collecting his quarters and smiling over the smashed baggage,
nor me looking around at the horrible dream,
nor mustached negro Operating Clerk named Spade, dealing out with his marvelous long hand the fate of thousands of express packages,
nor fairy Sam in the basement limping from leaden trunk to trunk,
nor Joe at the counter with his nervous breakdown smiling cowardly at the customers,
nor the grayish-green whale's stomach interior loft where we keep the baggage in hideous racks,
hundreds of suitcases full of tragedy rocking back and forth waiting to be opened,
nor the baggage that's lost, nor damaged handles, nameplates vanished, busted wires & broken ropes, whole trunks exploding on the concrete floor,
nor seabags emptied into the night in the final warehouse.

2

Yet Spade reminded me of Angel, unloading a bus,
dressed in blue overalls black face official Angel's workman cap,
pushing with his belly a huge tin horse piled high with black baggage,
looking up as he passed the yellow light bulb of the loft
and holding high on his arm an iron shepherd's crook.

3

It was the racks, I realized, sitting myself on top of them now as is my wont at lunchtime to rest my tired foot,
it was the racks, great wooden shelves and stanchions posts and beams assembled floor to roof jumbled with baggage,
—the Japanese white metal postwar trunk gaudily flowered & headed for Fort Bragg,
one Mexican green paper package in purple rope adorned with names for Nogales,
hundreds of radiators all at once for Eureka,
crates of Hawaiian underwear,
rolls of posters scattered over the Peninsula, nuts to Sacramento,
one human eye for Napa,
an aluminum box of human blood for Stockton
and a little red package of teeth for Calistoga—
it was the racks and these on the racks I saw naked in electric light the night before I quit,
the racks were created to hang our possessions, to keep us together, a temporary shift in space,
God's only way of building the rickety structure of Time,
to hold the bags to send on the roads, to carry our luggage from place to place
looking for a bus to ride us back home to Eternity where the heart was left and farewell tears began.

4

A swarm of baggage sitting by the counter as the transcontinental bus pulls in.
The clock registering 12.15 A.M., May 9, 1956, the second hand moving forward, red.
Getting ready to load my last bus.—Farewell, Walnut Creek Richmond Vallejo Portland Pacific Highway
Fleet-footed Quicksilver, God of transience.
One last package sits lone at midnight sticking up out of the Coast rack high as the dusty fluorescent light.

The wage they pay us is too low to live on. Tragedy reduced to numbers.
This for the poor shepherds. I am a communist.

Farewell ye Greyhound where I suffered so much,
hurt my knee and scraped my hand and built my pectoral muscles big as vagina.

1956 1959

To Aunt Rose

Aunt Rose—now—might I see you
with your thin face and buck tooth smile and pain
of rheumatism—and a long black heavy shoe
for your bony left leg
limping down the long hall in Newark on the running carpet
past the black grand piano
in the day room
where the parties were
and I sang Spanish loyalist songs
in a high squeaky voice
(hysterical) the committee listening
while you limped around the room
collected the money—
Aunt Honey, Uncle Sam, a stranger with a cloth arm
in his pocket
and huge young bald head
of Abraham Lincoln Brigade[1]

—your long sad face
your tears of sexual frustration
(what smothered sobs and bony hips
under the pillows of Osborne Terrace)
—the time I stood on the toilet seat naked
and you powdered my thighs with Calomine
against the poison ivy—my tender
and shamed first black curled hairs
what were you thinking in secret heart then
knowing me a man already—
and I an ignorant girl of family silence on the thin pedestal
of my legs in the bathroom—Museum of Newark.
Aunt Rose
Hitler is dead, Hitler is in Eternity; Hitler is with
Tamburlane and Emily Brontë

1. A group of American volunteers, led by Martin Wolff, in the Spanish Civil War of the 1930's.

Though I see you walking still, a ghost on Osborne Terrace
down the long dark hall to the front door
limping a little with a pinched smile
in what must have been a silken
flower dress
welcoming my father, the Poet, on his visit to Newark
—see you arriving in the living room
dancing on your crippled leg
and clapping hands his book
had been accepted by Liveright

Hitler is dead and Liveright's gone out of business
The Attic of the Past and *Everlasting Minute* are out of print
Uncle Harry sold his last silk stocking
Claire quit interpretive dancing school
Buba[2] sits a wrinkled monument in Old
Ladies Home blinking at new babies

last time I saw you was the hospital
pale skull protruding under ashen skin
blue veined unconscious girl
in an oxygen tent
the war in Spain has ended long ago
Aunt Rose

Paris 1958 1961

JAMES MERRILL
(1926–)

Upon a Second Marriage

FOR H. I. P.

Orchards, we linger here because
Women we love stand propped in your green prisons,
Obedient to such justly bending laws
Each one longs to take root,
Lives to confess whatever season's
Pride of blossom or endeavor's fruit
May to her rustling boughs have risen.

Then autumn reddens the whole mind.
No more, she vows, the dazzle of a year
Shall woo her from your bare cage of loud wind,
Promise the ring and run
To burn the altar, reappear
With apple blossoms for the credulous one.
Orchards, we wonder that we linger here!

Orchards we planted, trees we shook
To learn what you were bearing, say we stayed
Because one winter dusk we half-mistook
Frost on a bleakened bough
For blossoms, and were half-afraid

2. Yiddish for "Grandmother."

To miss the old persuasion, should we go.
And spring did come, and discourse made

Enough of weddings to us all
That, loving her for whom the whole world grows
Fragrant and white, we linger to recall
As down aisles of cut trees
How a tall trunk's cross-section shows
Concentric rings, those many marriages
That life on each live thing bestows.

1958

The Victor Dog[1]

FOR ELIZABETH BISHOP

Bix to Buxtehude to Boulez,
The little white dog on the Victor label
Listens long and hard as he is able.
It's all in a day's work, whatever plays.

From judgment, it would seem, he has refrained.
He even listens earnestly to Bloch,
Then builds a church upon our acid rock.
He's man's—no—he's the Leiermann's best friend,[2]

Or would be if hearing and listening were the same.
Does he hear? I fancy he rather smells
Those lemon-gold arpeggios in Ravel's
"Les jets d'eau du palais de ceux qui s'aiment."[3]

He ponders the Schumann Concerto's tall willow hit
By lightning, and stays put. When he surmises
Through one of Bach's eternal boxwood mazes[4]
The oboe pungent as a bitch in heat,

Or when the calypso decants its raw bay rum
Or the moon in *Wozzeck*[5] reddens ripe for murder,
He doesn't sneeze or howl; just listens harder.
Adamant° needles bear down on him from *diamond*

Whirling of outer space, too black, too near—
But he was taught as a puppy not to flinch,
Much less to imitate his bête noire Blanche
Who barked, fat foolish creature, at King Lear.[6]

Still others fought in the road's filth over Jezebel,[7]
Slavered on hearths of horned and pelted barons.

1. Until recently, the trademark on the labels of RCA Victor records was a dog listening intently to an old-fashioned gramophone, with the caption "His master's voice." In the poem, passing reference is made to jazz trumpeter Bix Beiderbecke, 18th-century composers Dietrich Buxtehude, Johann Sebastian Bach, and George Frederick Handel, to Robert Schumann (1810–1856), and to modernists Pierre Boulez, Ernest Bloch, and Maurice Ravel.

2. In Franz Schubert's song *Der Leiermann* ("The Organ-Grinder"), an old man cranks his barrel-organ in the winter cold to an audience of snarling dogs.

3. The fountains of the palace of those who are in love with each other (French).

4. A labyrinth executed in living boxwood plants, such as is to be found in the gardens of 18th-century palaces.

5. An opera by Alban Berg (1885–1935), in which the protagonist murders his unfaithful wife beneath a rising moon.

6. In the storm scene, the distraught King Lear says, "The little dogs and all./Tray, Blanche, and Sweetheart; see, they bark at me."

7. Whose body, when she died, was thrown into the street for her evil deeds. When the body was recovered for burial, dogs had eaten most of it, as had been prophesied earlier by Elijah (I Kings xxi ff.).

His forebears lacked, to say the least, forbearance.
Can nature change in him? Nothing's impossible.

The last chord fades. The night is cold and fine.
His master's voice rasps through the grooves' bare groves.
Obediently, in silence like the grave's
He sleeps there on the still-warm gramophone

Only to dream he is at the première of a Handel
Opera long thought lost—*Il Cane Minore*.[8]
Its allegorical subject is his story!
A little dog revolving round a spindle

Gives rise to harmonies beyond belief,
A cast of stars. . . . Is there in Victor's heart
No honey for the vanquished? Art is art.
The life it asks of us is a dog's life.

1972

Whitebeard on Videotape

Indigo, magenta, color of ghee,[9]
An Indian summer boiling where he sat
Put ours to shame. Six decades in the vat
Had turned his fingers emerald. Ah me.

For everyone's dirty linen here was *the*
Detergent. Zoom to combed snows on his line
—But not so fast! How fast were the colors of mine?
Was I mere printed personality

Or the real stuff, hand-woven, deep-dyed Soul?
Wasn't, as he spoke, some vital red
Already running like madras, while the whole
System churned with . . . dread? hilarity?

Bless the old fool. The rustic lecture hall
Held still. Mosquitoes dipped their needle straws
And drank our blood in perfect peace because,
Along with being holy, life was hell.

1976

FRANK O'HARA
(1926–1966)

The Day Lady[1] Died

It is 12:20 in New York a Friday
three days after Bastille day,[2] yes
it is 1959 and I go get a shoeshine

8. The Little Dog (Italian).
9. "[A] semifluid butter made chiefly in India, usually by melting buffalo butter, cooling, and pouring off the more liquid portion, which is the *ghee*" (*Webster's*).
1. Billie Holiday, called Lady Day, the black American jazz singer whom *The New Grove Dictionary of Music and Musicians* calls "the outstanding jazz singer of her day." Born in 1915, she died on July 17, 1959. Her autobiography, *Lady Sings the Blues*, was published in 1956.
2. July 14, the French national holiday that celebrates the storming of the Bastille in 1789.

because I will get off the 4:19 in Easthampton[3]
at 7:15 and then go straight to dinner
and I don't know the people who will feed me

I walk up the muggy street beginning to sun
and have a hamburger and a malted and buy
an ugly NEW WORLD WRITING to see what the poets
in Ghana are doing these days
I go on to the bank
and Miss Stillwagon (first name Linda I once heard)
doesn't even look up my balance for once in her life
and in the GOLDEN GRIFFIN[4] I get a little Verlaine
for Patsy with drawings by Bonnard although I do
think of Hesiod, trans. Richmond Lattimore or
Brendan Behan's new play or *Le Balcon* or *Les Nègres*
of Genet, but I don't, I stick with Verlaine
after practically going to sleep with quandariness

and for Mike I just stroll into the PARK LANE
Liquor Store and ask for a bottle of Strega and
then I go back where I came from to 6th Avenue
and the tobacconist in the Ziegfeld Theatre and
casually ask for a carton of Gauloises and a carton
of Picayunes, and a NEW YORK POST with her face on it

and I am sweating a lot by now and thinking of
leaning on the john door in the 5 SPOT
while she whispered a song along the keyboard
to Mal Waldron[5] and everyone and I stopped breathing

1959 1964

How to Get There

White the October air, no snow, easy to breathe
beneath the sky, lies, lies everywhere writhing and gasping
clutching and tangling, it is not easy to breathe
lies building their tendrils into dim figures
who disappear down corridors in west-side[6] apartments
into childhood's proof of being wanted, not abandoned, kidnaped
betrayal staving off loneliness, I see the fog lunge in
and hide it
where are you?
here I am on the sidewalk
under the moonlike lamplight thinking how precious moss is
so unique and greenly crushable if you can find it
on the north side of the tree where the fog binds you
and then, tearing apart into soft white lies, spreads its disease
through the primal night of an everlasting winter
which nevertheless has heat in tubes, west-side and east-side
and its intricate individual pathways of white accompanied

3. One of "the Hamptons," summer resort towns on eastern Long Island, frequented by artists and writers.
4. An avant-garde bookshop in New York, near the Museum of Modern Art where O'Hara was a curator.
5. Billie Holiday's accompanist from 1957 until her death.
6. "West-side" and "east-side" in the poem refer to neighborhoods or districts in New York City's borough of Manhattan—east or west of Fifth Avenue.

by the ringing of telephone bells beside which someone sits in
silence denying their own number, never given out! nameless
like the sound of troika[7] bells rushing past suffering
in the first storm, it is snowing now, it is already too late
the snow will go away, but nobody will be there

police cordons for lying political dignitaries ringing too
the world becomes a jangle
                                        from the index finger
to the vast empty houses filled with people, their echoes
of lies and the tendrils of fog trailing softly around their throats
now the phone can be answered, nobody calling, only an echo
all can confess to be home and waiting, all is the same
and we drift into the clear sky enthralled by our disappointment
            never to be alone again
                                                never to be loved
sailing through space: didn't I have you once for my self? West Side?
      for a couple of hours, but I am not that person

1960 1964

W. D. SNODGRASS
(1926–)

April Inventory

The green catalpa tree has turned
All white; the cherry blooms once more.
In one whole year I haven't learned
A blessed thing they pay you for.
The blossoms snow down in my hair;
The trees and I will soon be bare.

The trees have more than I to spare.
The sleek, expensive girls I teach,
Younger and pinker every year,
Bloom gradually out of reach.
The pear tree lets its petals drop
Like dandruff on a tabletop.

The girls have grown so young by now
I have to nudge myself to stare.
This year they smile and mind me how
My teeth are falling with my hair.
In thirty years I may not get
Younger, shrewder, or out of debt.

The tenth time, just a year ago,
I made myself a little list
Of all the things I'd ought to know,
Then told my parents, analyst,
And everyone who's trusted me
I'd be substantial, presently.

7. A Russian vehicle—here a sleigh—drawn by three horses abreast.

I haven't read one book about
A book or memorized one plot.
Or found a mind I did not doubt.
I learned one date. And then forgot.
And one by one the solid scholars
Get the degrees, the jobs, the dollars.

And smile above their starchy collars.
I taught my classes Whitehead's[1] notions;
One lovely girl, a song of Mahler's.[2]
Lacking a source-book or promotions,
I showed one child the colors of
A luna moth and how to love.

I taught myself to name my name,
To bark back, loosen love and crying;
To ease my woman so she came,
To ease an old man who was dying.
I have not learned how often I
Can win, can love, but choose to die.

I have not learned there is a lie
Love shall be blonder, slimmer, younger;
That my equivocating eye
Loves only by my body's hunger;
That I have forces, true to feel,
Or that the lovely world is real.

While scholars speak authority
And wear their ulcers on their sleeves,
My eyes in spectacles shall see
These trees procure and spend their leaves.
There is a value underneath
The gold and silver in my teeth.

Though trees turn bare and girls turn wives,
We shall afford our costly seasons;
There is a gentleness survives
That will outspeak and has its reasons.
There is a loveliness exists,
Preserves us, not for specialists.

1959

JOHN ASHBERY
(1927–)

The Painter

Sitting between the sea and the buildings
He enjoyed painting the sea's portrait.
But just as children imagine a prayer

1. Alfred North Whitehead (1861–1947), English philosopher.

2. Gustav Mahler (1860–1911), Austrian composer.

Is merely silence, he expected his subject
To rush up the sand, and, seizing a brush,
Plaster its own portrait on the canvas.

So there was never any paint on his canvas
Until the people who lived in the buildings
Put him to work: "Try using the brush
As a means to an end. Select, for a portrait,
Something less angry and large, and more subject
To a painter's moods, or, perhaps, to a prayer."

How could he explain to them his prayer
That nature, not art, might usurp the canvas?
He chose his wife for a new subject,
Making her vast, like ruined buildings,
As if, forgetting itself, the portrait
Had expressed itself without a brush.

Slightly encouraged, he dipped his brush
In the sea, murmuring a heartfelt prayer:
"My soul, when I paint this next portrait
Let it be you who wrecks the canvas."
The news spread like wildfire through the buildings:
He had gone back to the sea for his subject.

Imagine a painter crucified by his subject!
Too exhausted even to lift his brush,
He provoked some artists leaning from the buildings
To malicious mirth: "We haven't a prayer
Now, of putting ourselves on canvas,
Or getting the sea to sit for a portrait!"

Others declared it a self-portrait.
Finally all indications of a subject
Began to fade, leaving the canvas
Perfectly white. He put down the brush.
At once a howl, that was also a prayer,
Arose from the overcrowded buildings.

They tossed him, the portrait, from the tallest of the buildings;
And the sea devoured the canvas and the brush
As though his subject had decided to remain a prayer.

1956

Melodic Trains

A little girl with scarlet enameled fingernails
Asks me what time it is—evidently that's a toy wristwatch
She's wearing, for fun. And it is fun to wear other
Odd things, like this briar pipe and tweed coat

Like date-colored sierras with the lines of seams
Sketched in and plunging now and then into unfathomable
Valleys that can't be deduced by the shape of the person

Sitting inside it—me, and just as our way is flat across
Dales and gulches, as though our train were a pencil

Guided by a ruler held against a photomural of the Alps
We both come to see distance as something unofficial
And impersonal yet not without its curious justification
Like the time of a stopped watch—right twice a day.

Only the wait in stations is vague and
Dimensionless, like oneself. How do they decide how much
Time to spend in each? One begins to suspect there's no
Rule or that it's applied haphazardly.

Sadness of the faces of children on the platform,
Concern of the grownups for connections, for the chances
Of getting a taxi, since these have no timetable.
You get one if you can find one though in principle

You can always find one, but the segment of chance
In the circle of certainty is what gives these leaning
Tower of Pisa figures their aspect of dogged
Impatience, banking forward into the wind.

In short any stop before the final one creates
Clouds of anxiety, of sad, regretful impatience
With ourselves, our lives, the way we have been dealing
With other people up until now. Why couldn't
We have been more considerate? These figures leaving

The platform or waiting to board the train are my brothers
In a way that really wants to tell me why there is so little
Panic and disorder in the world, and so much unhappiness.
If I were to get down now to stretch, take a few steps

In the wearying and world-weary clouds of steam like great
White apples, might I just through proximity and aping
Of postures and attitudes communicate this concern of mine
To them? That their jagged attitudes correspond to mine,

That their beefing strikes answering silver bells within
My own chest, and that I know, as they do, how the last
Stop is the most anxious one of all, though it means
Getting home at last, to the pleasures and dissatisfactions of home?

It's as though a visible chorus called up the different
Stages of the journey, singing about them and being them:
Not the people in the station, not the child opposite me
With currant fingernails, but the windows, seen through,

Reflecting imperfectly, ruthlessly splitting open the bluish
Vague landscape like a zipper. Each voice has its own
Descending scale to put one in one's place at every stage;
One need never not know where one is

Unless one give up listening, sleeping, approaching a small
Western town that is nothing but a windmill. Then

The great fury of the end can drop as the solo
Voices tell about it, wreathing it somehow with an aura

Of good fortune and colossal welcomes from the mayor and
Citizens' committees tossing their hats into the air.
To hear them singing you'd think it had already happened
And we had focused back on the furniture of the air.

1977

Paradoxes and Oxymorons

This poem is concerned with language on a very plain level.
Look at it talking to you. You look out a window
Or pretend to fidget. You have it but you don't have it.
You miss it, it misses you. You miss each other.

The poem is sad because it wants to be yours, and cannot.
What's a plain level? It is that and other things,
Bringing a system of them into play. Play?
Well, actually, yes, but I consider play to be

A deeper outside thing, a dreamed role-pattern,
As in the division of grace these long August days
Without proof. Open-ended. And before you know
It gets lost in the steam and chatter of typewriters.

It has been played once more. I think you exist only
To tease me into doing it, on your level, and then you aren't there
Or have adopted a different attitude. And the poem
Has set me softly down beside you. The poem is you.

1981

GALWAY KINNELL
(1927–)

First Song

Then it was dusk in Illinois, the small boy
After an afternoon of carting dung
Hung on the rail fence, a sapped thing
Weary to crying. Dark was growing tall
And he began to hear the pond frogs all
Calling on his ear with what seemed their joy.

Soon their sound was pleasant for a boy
Listening in the smoky dusk and the nightfall
Of Illinois, and from the fields two small
Boys came bearing cornstalk violins
And they rubbed the cornstalk bows with resins
And the three sat there scraping of their joy.

It was now fine music the frogs and the boys
Did in the towering Illinois twilight make

And into dark in spite of a shoulder's ache
A boy's hunched body loved out of a stalk
The first song of his happiness, and the song woke
His heart to the darkness and into the sadness of joy.

1960

The Correspondence School Instructor Says Goodbye to His Poetry Students

Goodbye, lady in Bangor, who sent me
snapshots of yourself, after definitely hinting
you were beautiful; goodbye,
Miami Beach urologist, who enclosed plain
brown envelopes for the return of your *very*
"Clinical Sonnets"; goodbye, manufacturer
of brassieres on the Coast, whose eclogues
give the fullest treatment in literature yet
to the sagging breast motif; goodbye, you in San Quentin,
who wrote, "Being German my hero is Hitler,"
instead of "Sincerely yours," at the end of long,
neat-scripted letters demolishing
the pre-Raphaelites:[1]

I swear to you, it was just my way
of cheering myself up, as I licked
the stamped, self-addressed envelopes,
the game I had
of trying to guess which one of you, this time,
had poisoned his glue. I did care.
I did read each poem entire.
I did say what I thought was the truth
in the mildest words I knew. And now,
in this poem, or chopped prose, not any better,
I realize, than those troubled lines
I kept sending back to you,
I have to say I am relieved it is over:
at the end I could feel only pity
for that urge toward more life
your poems kept smothering in words, the smell
of which, days later, would tingle
in your nostrils as new, God-given impulses
to write.

Goodbye,
you who are, for me, the postmarks again
of shattered towns—Xenia, Burnt Cabins, Hornell—
their loneliness
given away in poems, only their solitude kept.

1968

1. A group of English poets and painters, among them Dante Gabriel Rossetti and William Morris, whose aim was to restore to art the aesthetic principles of the early Italian Renaissance—that is, before Raphael (1483–1520), the great painter.

W. S. MERWIN
(1927–)

The Drunk in the Furnace

For a good decade
The furnace stood in the naked gully, fireless
And vacant as any hat. Then when it was
No more to them than a hulking black fossil
To erode unnoticed with the rest of the junk-hill
By the poisonous creek, and rapidly to be added
To their ignorance.

They were afterwards astonished
To confirm, one morning, a twist of smoke like a pale
Resurrection, staggering out of its chewed hole,
And to remark then other tokens that someone,
Cozily bolted behind the eye-holed iron
Door of the drafty burner, had there established
His bad castle.

Where he gets his spirits
It's a mystery. But the stuff keeps him musical:
Hammer-and-anviling with poker and bottle
To his jugged bellowings, till the last groaning clang
As he collapses onto the rioting
Springs of a litter of car-seats ranged on the grates,
To sleep like an iron pig.

In their tar-paper church
On a text about stoke-holes that are sated never
Their Reverend lingers. They nod and hate trespassers.
When the furnace wakes, though, all afternoon
Their witless offspring flock like piped rats to its siren
Crescendo, and agape on the crumbling ridge
Stand in a row and learn.

1960

Odysseus[1]

FOR GEORGE KIRSTEIN

Always the setting forth was the same,
Same sea, same dangers waiting for him
As though he had got nowhere but older.
Behind him on the receding shore
The identical reproaches, and somewhere
Out before him, the unraveling patience
He was wedded to. There were the islands
Each with its woman and twining welcome

1. Hero of Homer's *Odyssey*, who spent ten years of wandering after the Trojan War before returning home. The prototype of the wanderer, he was known in Roman mythology as Ulysses.

To be navigated, and one to call "home."[2]
The knowledge of all that he betrayed
Grew till it was the same whether he stayed
Or went. Therefore he went. And what wonder
If sometimes he could not remember
Which was the one who wished on his departure
Perils that he could never sail through,
And which, improbable, remote, and true,
Was the one he kept sailing home to?

1960

Separation

Your absence has gone through me
Like thread through a needle.
Everything I do is stitched with its color.

1973

JAMES WRIGHT
(1927–1980)

A Note Left in Jimmy Leonard's Shack

Near the dry river's water-mark we found
      Your brother Minnegan,
Flopped like a fish against the muddy ground.
Beany, the kid whose yellow hair turns green,
Told me to find you, even in the rain,
      And tell you he was drowned.

I hid behind the chassis on the bank,
      The wreck of someone's Ford:
I was afraid to come and wake you drunk:
You told me once the waking up was hard,
The daylight beating at you like a board.
      Blood in my stomach sank.

Besides, you told him never to go out
      Along the river-side
Drinking and singing, clattering about.
You might have thrown a rock at me and cried
I was to blame, I let him fall in the road
      And pitch down on his side.

Well, I'll get hell enough when I get home
      For coming up this far,
Leaving the note, and running as I came.
I'll go and tell my father where you are.
You'd better go find Minnegan before
      Policemen hear and come.

Beany went home, and I got sick and ran,
      You old son of a bitch.

2. Alluding to Odysseus's adventures with the sorceress Circe and the nymph Calypso, and to his wife Penelope, waiting for him in Ithaca.

You better hurry down to Minnegan;
He's drunk or dying now, I don't know which,
Rolled in the roots and garbage like a fish,
    The poor old man.

1959

A Blessing

Just off the highway to Rochester, Minnesota,
Twilight bounds softly forth on the grass.
And the eyes of those two Indian ponies
Darken with kindness.
They have come gladly out of the willows
To welcome my friend and me.
We step over the barbed wire into the pasture
Where they have been grazing all day, alone.
They ripple tensely, they can hardly contain their happiness
That we have come.
They bow shyly as wet swans. They love each other.
There is no loneliness like theirs.
At home once more,
They begin munching the young tufts of spring in the darkness.
I would like to hold the slenderer one in my arms,
For she has walked over to me
And nuzzled my left hand.
She is black and white,
Her mane falls wild on her forehead,
And the light breeze moves me to caress her long ear
That is delicate as the skin over a girl's wrist.
Suddenly I realize
That if I stepped out of my body I would break
Into blossom.

1963

Discoveries in Arizona

All my life so far
I have been afraid
Of cactus,
Spiders,
Rattlesnakes.

The tall fourteen-year-old boy
    who led me through
The desert whispered, Come over
    this way.
Picking my steps carefully over
    an earth strangely familiar,
I found four small holes large
    enough
For a root that might have been
    torn out
Or a blacksnake hole in Ohio,
    that I hated.
What is it, I said, some cute
    prairie dog,

Or an abandoned posthole,
maybe?
No, he said, she's down there
with her children.
She doesn't hate you, she's not
afraid,
She's probably asleep, she's
probably keeping warm
With something I don't know about,
And all I know is sometimes in
sunlight
Two brown legs reach out.
It is hard to get a look at
her face.
Even in the museum she turns away.
I don't know where she is looking.

I have lived all my life in
terror
Of a tarantula,
And yet I have never even seen
A tarantula turn her face
Away from me.

That's all right, said the boy.
Maybe she's never seen you either.

1977

THOM GUNN
(1929–)

On the Move

'Man, you gotta Go.'

The blue jay scuffling in the bushes follows
Some hidden purpose, and the gust of birds
That spurts across the field, the wheeling swallows,
Have nested in the trees and undergrowth.
Seeking their instinct, or their poise, or both,
One moves with an uncertain violence
Under the dust thrown by a baffled sense
Or the dull thunder of approximate words.

On motorcycles, up the road, they come:
Small, black, as flies hanging in heat, the Boys,
Until the distance throws them forth, their hum
Bulges to thunder held by calf and thigh.
In goggles, donned impersonality,
In gleaming jackets trophied with the dust,
They strap in doubt—by hiding it, robust—
And almost hear a meaning in their noise.

Exact conclusion of their hardiness
Has no shape yet, but from known whereabouts

They ride, direction where the tires press.
They scare a flight of birds across the field:
Much that is natural, to the will must yield.
Men manufacture both machine and soul,
And use what they imperfectly control
To dare a future from the taken routes.

It is a part solution, after all.
One is not necessarily discord
On earth; or damned because, half animal,
One lacks direct instinct, because one wakes
Afloat on movement that divides and breaks.
One joins the movement in a valueless world,
Choosing it, till, both hurler and the hurled,
One moves as well, always toward, toward.

A minute holds them, who have come to go:
The self-defined, astride the created will
They burst away; the towns they travel through
Are home for neither bird nor holiness,
For birds and saints complete their purposes.
At worst, one is in motion; and at best,
Reaching no absolute, in which to rest,
One is always nearer by not keeping still.

California 1957

Back to Life

Around the little park
The lamps blink on, and make the dusk seem deeper.
I saunter toward them on the grass
That suddenly rustles from the dew,
Hearing behind, at times,
A fragmentary shout or distant bark.
I am alone, like a patrolling keeper.
And then I catch the smell of limes° *linden trees*
Coming and going faintly on the dark:
Bunched black at equal height
They stand between the lamps, yet where
They branch out toward them on each side, a few
Touching the lighted glass,
Their leaves are soft green on the night,
The closest losing even their mass,
Edged but transparent as if they too gave light.

The street is full, the quiet is broken.
I notice that the other strollers there
Extend themselves, at ease
As if just woken
To a world they have not yet recovered, though
They move across the dusk, alert,
And stare,
As I do, into shops or at the trees,
Devouring each detail, from leaf to dirt,
In the measured mildness of the air.

Here by the curb
The boys and girls walk, jostling as they grow,
Cocky with surplus strength.
And weakening with each move, the old,
Cushioned with papers or with rugs
On public seats close by,
Inch down into their loosened flesh, each fold
Being sensible of the gravity
Which tugs
And longs to bring it down
And break its hold.

I walk between the curb and bench
Conscious at length
Of sharing through each sense,
As if the light revealed us all
Sustained in delicate difference
Yet firmly growing from a single branch.

If that were all of it!
The branch that we grow on
Is not remembered easily in the dark,
Or the transparency when light is gone:
At most, a recollection
In the mind only—over a rainswept park
Held to by mere conviction
In cold and misery when the clock strikes one.
The lamp still shines.
The pale leaves shift a bit,
Now light, now shadowed, and their movement shared
A second later by the bough,
Even by the sap that runs through it:
A small full trembling through it now
As if each leaf were, so, better prepared
For falling sooner or later separate.

1967

Street Song

I am too young to grow a beard
But yes man it was me you heard
In dirty denim and dark glasses.
I look through everyone who passes
But ask him clear, I do not plead,
Keys lids acid and speed.

My grass is not oregano.
Some of it grew in Mexico.
You cannot guess the weed I hold,
Clara Green, Acapulco Gold,
Panama Red, you name it man,
Best on the street since I began.

My methedrine, my double-sun,
Will give you two lives in your one,

Five days of power before you crash.
At which time use these lumps of hash
—They burn so sweet, they smoke so smooth,
They make you sharper while they soothe.

Now here, the best I've got to show,
Made by a righteous cat I know.
Pure acid—it will scrape your brain,
And make it something else again.
Call it heaven, call it hell,
Join me and see the world I sell.

Join me, and I will take you there,
Your head will cut out from your hair
Into whichever self you choose.
With Midday Mick man you can't lose,
I'll get you anything you need.
Keys lids acid and speed.

1971

JOHN HOLLANDER
(1929–)

Adam's Task

"And Adam gave names to all cattle, and to the fowl of the air, and to every beast of the field . . ." —GEN. 2:20

Thou, paw-paw-paw; thou, glurd; thou, spotted
Glurd; thou, whitestap, lurching through
The high-grown brush; thou, pliant-footed,
Implex; thou, awagabu.

Every burrower, each flier
Came for the name he had to give:
Gay, first work, ever to be prior,
Not yet sunk to primitive.

Thou, verdle; thou, McFleery's pomma;
Thou; thou; thou—three types of grawl;
Thou, flisket; thou, kabasch; thou, comma-
Eared mashawk; thou, all; thou, all.

Were, in a fire of becoming,
Laboring to be burned away,
Then work, half-measuring, half-humming,
Would be as serious as play.

Thou, pambler; thou, rivarn; thou, greater
Wherret, and thou, lesser one;
Thou, sproal; thou, zant; thou, lily-eater.
Naming's over. Day is done.

1971

Swan and Shadow

Dusk
Above the
water hang the
loud
flies
Here
O so
gray
then
What A pale signal will appear
When Soon before its shadow fades
Where Here in this pool of opened eye
In us No Upon us As at the very edges
of where we take shape in the dark air
this object bares its image awakening
ripples of recognition that will
brush darkness up into light
even after this bird this hour both drift by atop the perfect sad instant now
already passing out of sight
toward yet-untroubled reflection
this image bears its object darkening
into memorial shades Scattered bits of
light No of water Or something across
water Breaking up No Being regathered
soon Yet by then a swan will have
gone Yes out of mind into what
vast
pale
hush
of a
place
past
sudden dark as
if a swan
sang

1969

ADRIENNE RICH
(1929–)

Aunt Jennifer's Tigers

Aunt Jennifer's tigers prance across a screen,
Bright topaz denizens of a world of green.
They do not fear the men beneath the tree;
They pace in sleek chivalric certainty.

Aunt Jennifer's fingers fluttering through her wool
Find even the ivory needle hard to pull.
The massive weight of Uncle's wedding band
Sits heavily upon Aunt Jennifer's hand.

When Aunt is dead, her terrified hands will lie
Still ringed with ordeals she was mastered by.

The tigers in the panel that she made
Will go on prancing, proud and unafraid.

1951

Living in Sin

She had thought the studio would keep itself;
no dust upon the furniture of love.
Half heresy, to wish the taps less vocal,
the panes relieved of grime. A plate of pears,
a piano with a Persian shawl, a cat
stalking the picturesque amusing mouse
had risen at his urging.
Not that at five each separate stair would writhe
under the milkman's tramp; that morning light
so coldly would delineate the scraps
of last night's cheese and three sepulchral bottles;
that on the kitchen shelf among the saucers
a pair of beetle-eyes would fix her own—
envoy from some village in the moldings . . .
Meanwhile, he, with a yawn,
sounded a dozen notes upon the keyboard,
declared it out of tune, shrugged at the mirror,
rubbed at his beard, went out for cigarettes;
while she, jeered by the minor demons,
pulled back the sheets and made the bed and found
a towel to dust the table-top,
and let the coffee-pot boil over on the stove.
By evening she was back in love again,
though not so wholly but throughout the night
she woke sometimes to feel the daylight coming
like a relentless milkman up the stairs.

1955 1975

Orion[1]

Far back when I went zig-zagging
through tamarack pastures
you were my genius, you
my cast-iron Viking, my helmed
lion-heart king in prison.[2]
Years later now you're young

my fierce half-brother, staring
down from that simplified west
your breast open, your belt dragged down
by an oldfashioned thing, a sword
the last bravado you won't give over
though it weighs you down as you stride

and the stars in it are dim
and maybe have stopped burning.
But you burn, and I know it;

1. Constellation of the winter sky (known as "the Hunter"), which appears as a giant with belt and sword.

2. Alluding to the English king Richard the Lion-Hearted (1157–99), imprisoned in Austria on his return from the Crusades.

as I throw back my head to take you in
an old transfusion happens again:
divine astronomy is nothing to it.

Indoors I bruise and blunder,
break faith, leave ill enough
alone, a dead child born in the dark.
Night cracks up over the chimney,
pieces of time, frozen geodes[3]
come showering down in the grate.

A man reaches behind my eyes
and finds them empty
a woman's head turns away
from my head in the mirror
children are dying my death
and eating crumbs of my life.

Pity is not your forte.
Calmly you ache up there
pinned aloft in your crow's nest,[4]
my speechless pirate!
You take it all for granted
and when I look you back

it's with a starlike eye
shooting its cold and egotistical[5] spear
where it can do least damage.
Breathe deep! No hurt, no pardon
out here in the cold with you
you with your back to the wall.

1965 1969

Diving into the Wreck

First having read the book of myths,
and loaded the camera,
and checked the edge of the knife-blade,
I put on
the body-armor of black rubber
the absurd flippers
the grave and awkward mask.
I am having to do this
not like Cousteau with his
assiduous team
aboard the sun-flooded schooner
but here alone.

There is a ladder.
The ladder is always there
hanging innocently

3. Small spheroid stones, with a cavity often lined with crystals.
4. Lookout post on the mast of old ships.
5. "One of two phrases suggested by Gottfried Benn's essay, *Artists and Old Age* in *Primal Vision*, edited by E. B. Ashton, New Directions" (Rich's note). Benn's advice to the modern artist is: "Don't lose sight of the cold and egotistical element in your mission. * * * With your back to the wall, care-worn and weary, in the gray light of the void, read Job and Jeremiah and keep going" (pp. 206–7).

close to the side of the schooner.
We know what it is for,
we who have used it.
otherwise
it is a piece of maritime floss
some sundry equipment.

I go down.
Rung after rung and still
the oxygen immerses me
the blue light
the clear atoms
of our human air.
I go down.
My flippers cripple me,
I crawl like an insect down the ladder
and there is no one
to tell me when the ocean
will begin.

First the air is blue and then
it is bluer and then green and then
black I am blacking out and yet
my mask is powerful
it pumps my blood with power
the sea is another story
the sea is not a question of power
I have to learn alone
to turn my body without force
in the deep element.

And now: it is easy to forget
what I came for
among so many who have always
lived here
swaying their crenellated fans
between the reefs
and besides
you breathe differently down here.

I came to explore the wreck.
The words are purposes.
The words are maps.
I came to see the damage that was done
and the treasures that prevail.
I stroke the beam of my lamp
slowly along the flank
of something more permanent
than fish or weed

the thing I came for:
the wreck and not the story of the wreck
the thing itself and not the myth
the drowned face always staring
toward the sun
the evidence of damage
worn by salt and sway into this threadbare beauty

the ribs of the disaster
curving their assertion
among the tentative haunters.

This is the place.
And I am here, the mermaid whose dark hair
streams black, the merman in his armored body.
We circle silently
about the wreck
we dive into the hold.
I am she: I am he

whose drowned face sleeps with open eyes
whose breasts still bear the stress
whose silver, copper, vermeil cargo lies
obscurely inside barrels
half-wedged and left to rot
we are the half-destroyed instruments
that once held to a course
the water-eaten log
the fouled compass

We are, I am, you are
by cowardice or courage
the one who find our way
back to this scene
carrying a knife, a camera
a book of myths
in which
our names do not appear.

1973

The Ninth Symphony of Beethoven[6] Understood at Last as a Sexual Message

A man in terror of impotence
or infertility, not knowing the difference
a man trying to tell something
howling from the climacteric[7]
music of the entirely
isolated soul
yelling at Joy from the tunnel of the ego
music without the ghost
of another person in it, music
trying to tell something the man
does not want out, would keep if he could
gagged and bound and flogged with chords of Joy
where everything is silence and the
beating of a bloody fist upon
a splintered table

1972 1973

6. Well-known work by the German composer Ludwig van Beethoven (1770–1827); the symphony reaches its climax with a choral "Hymn to Joy."

7. Period or year of life when bodily changes take place; often a synonym for menopause in men or women.

Toward the Solstice

The thirtieth of November.
Snow is starting to fall.
A peculiar silence is spreading
over the fields, the maple grove.
It is the thirtieth of May,
rain pours on ancient bushes, runs
down the youngest blade of grass.
I am trying to hold in one steady glance
all the parts of my life.
A spring torrent races
on this old slanting roof,
the slanted field below
thickens with winter's first whiteness.
Thistles dried to sticks in last year's wind
stand nakedly in the green,
stand sullenly in the slowly whitening,
field.

My brain glows
more violently, more avidly
the quieter, the thicker
the quilt of crystals settles,
the louder, more relentlessly
the torrent beats itself out
on the old boards and shingles.
It is the thirtieth of May,
the thirtieth of November,
a beginning or an end,
we are moving into the solstice
and there is so much here
I still do not understand.
If I could make sense of how
my life is still tangled
with dead weeds, thistles,
enormous burdocks, burdens
slowly shifting under
this first fall of snow,
beaten by this early, racking rain
calling all new life to declare itself strong
or die,
if I could know
in what language to address
the spirits that claim a place
beneath these low and simple ceilings,
tenants that neither speak nor stir
yet dwell in mute insistence
till I can feel utterly ghosted in this house.

If history is a spider-thread
spun over and over though brushed away
it seems I might some twilight
or dawn in the hushed country light

discern its grayness stretching
from molding or doorframe, out
into the empty dooryard
and following it climb
the path into the pinewoods,
tracing from tree to tree
in the failing light, in the slowly
lucidifying day
its constant, purposive trail,
till I reach whatever cellar hole
filling with snowflakes or lichen,
whatever fallen shack
or unremembered clearing
I am meant to have found
and there, under the first or last
star, trusting to instinct
the words would come to mind
I have failed or forgotten to say
year after year, winter
after summer, the right rune[8]
to ease the hold of the past
upon the rest of my life
and ease my hold on the past.

If some rite of separation
is still unaccomplished
between myself and the long-gone
tenants of this house,
between myself and my childhood,
and the childhood of my children,
it is I who have neglected
to perform the needed acts,
set water in corners, light and eucalyptus
in front of mirrors,
or merely pause and listen
to my own pulse vibrating
lightly as falling snow,
relentlessly as the rainstorm,
and hear what it has been saying.
It seems I am still waiting
for them to make some clear demand
some articulate sound or gesture,
for release to come from anywhere
but from inside myself.

A decade of cutting away
dead flesh, cauterizing
old scars ripped open over and over
and still it is not enough.

A decade of performing
the loving humdrum acts
of attention to this house
transplanting lilac suckers,

8. I.e., spell, incantation.

washing panes, scrubbing
wood-smoke from splitting paint,
sweeping stairs, brushing the thread
of the spider aside,
and so much yet undone,
a woman's work, the solstice nearing,
and my hand still suspended
as if above a letter
I long and dread to close.

1977 1978

Transit

When I meet the skier she is always
walking, skis and poles shouldered, toward the mountain
free-swinging in worn boots
over the path new-sifted with fresh snow
her graying dark hair almost hidden by
a cap of many colors
her fifty-year-old, strong, impatient body
dressed for cold and speed
her eyes level with mine

And when we pass each other I look into her face
wondering what we have in common
where our minds converge
for we do not pass each other, she passes me
as I halt beside the fence tangled in snow,
she passes me as I shall never pass her
in this life

Yet I remember us together
climbing Chocorua,[9] summer nineteen-forty-five
details of vegetation beyond the timberline
lichens, wildflowers, birds,
amazement when the trail broke out onto the granite ledge
sloped over blue lakes, green pines, giddy air
like dreams of flying

When sisters separate they haunt each other
as she, who I might once have been, haunts me
or is it I who do the haunting
halting and watching on the path
how she appears again through lightly-blowing
crystals, how her strong knees carry her,
how unaware she is, how simple
this is for her, how without let or hindrance
she travels in her body
until the point of passing, where the skier
and the cripple must decide
to recognize each other?

1979 1981

9. Mountain in New Hampshire.

GREGORY CORSO
(1930–)

Marriage

Should I get married? Should I be good?
Astound the girl next door with my velvet suit and faustus hood?[1]
Don't take her to movies but to cemeteries
tell all about werewolf bathtubs and forked clarinets
then desire her and kiss her and all the preliminaries
and she going just so far and I understanding why
not getting angry saying You must feel! It's beautiful to feel!
Instead take her in my arms lean against an old crooked tombstone
and woo her the entire night the constellations in the sky—

When she introduces me to her parents
back straightened, hair finally combed, strangled by a tie,
should I sit knees together on their 3rd degree sofa
and not ask Where's the bathroom?
How else to feel other than I am,
often thinking Flash Gordon soap—
O how terrible it must be for a young man
seated before a family and the family thinking
We never saw him before! He wants our Mary Lou!
After tea and homemade cookies they ask What do you do for a living?

Should I tell them? Would they like me then?
Say All right get married, we're losing a daughter
but we're gaining a son—
And should I then ask Where's the bathroom?

O God, and the wedding! All her family and her friends
and only a handful of mine all scroungy and bearded
just wait to get at the drinks and food—
And the priest! he looking at me as if I masturbated
asking me Do you take this woman for your lawful wedded wife?
And I trembling what to say say Pie Glue!
I kiss the bride all those corny men slapping me on the back
She's all yours, boy! Ha-ha-ha!
And in their eyes you could see some obscene honeymoon going on—
Then all that absurd rice and clanky cans and shoes
Niagara Falls! Hordes of us! Husbands! Wives! Flowers! Chocolates!
All streaming into cozy hotels
All going to do the same thing tonight
The indifferent clerk he knowing what was going to happen
The lobby zombies they knowing what
The whistling elevator man he knowing
The winking bellboy knowing
Everybody knowing! I'd be almost inclined not to do anything!
Stay up all night! Stare that hotel clerk in the eye!
Screaming: I deny honeymoon! I deny honeymoon!
running rampant into those almost climactic suites

1. Dr. Faustus, medieval alchemist, sold his soul to the devil. One of the rewards was renewed youth and attractiveness to young women.

yelling Radio belly! Cat shovel!
O I'd live in Niagara forever! in a dark cave beneath the Falls
I'd sit there the Mad Honeymooner
devising ways to break marriages, a sourge of bigamy
a saint of divorce—

But I should get married I should be good
How nice it'd be to come home to her
and sit by the fireplace and she in the kitchen
aproned young and lovely wanting my baby
and so happy about me she burns the roast beef
and comes crying to me and I get up from my big papa chair
saying Christmas teeth! Radiant brains! Apple deaf!
God what a husband I'd make! Yes, I should get married!
So much to do! like sneaking into Mr Jones' house late at night
and cover his golf clubs with 1920 Norwegian books
Like hanging a picture of Rimbaud [2] on the lawnmower
like pasting Tannu Tuva [3] postage stamps all over the picket fence
like when Mrs Kindhead comes to collect for the Community Chest
grab her and tell her There are unfavorable omens in the sky!
And when the mayor comes to get my vote tell him
When are you going to stop people killing whales!
And when the milkman comes leave him a note in the bottle
Penguin dust, bring me penguin dust, I want penguin dust—

Yet if I should get married and it's Connecticut and snow
and she gives birth to a child and I am sleepless, worn,
up for nights, head bowed against a quiet window, the past behind me,
finding myself in the most common of situations a trembling man
knowledged with responsibility not twig-smear nor Roman coin soup—
O what would that be like!
Surely I'd give it for a nipple a rubber Tacitus [4]
For a rattle a bag of broken Bach records
Tack Della Francesca [5] all over its crib
Sew the Greek alphabet on its bib
And build for its playpen a roofless Parthenon

No, I doubt I'd be that kind of father
Not rural not snow no quiet window
but hot smelly tight New York City
seven flights up, roaches and rats in the walls
a fat Reichian [6] wife screeching over potatoes Get a job!
And five nose running brats in love with Batman
And the neighbors all toothless and dry haired
like those hag masses of the 18th century
all wanting to come in and watch TV
The landlord wants his rent
Grocery store Blue Cross Gas & Electric Knights of Columbus
Impossible to lie back and dream Telephone snow, ghost parking—
No! I should not get married I should never get married!
But—imagine If I were married to a beautiful sophisticated woman
tall and pale wearing an elegant black dress and long black gloves
holding a cigarette holder in one hand and a highball in the other

2. Arthur Rimbaud (1854–1891), French poet.
3. A Siberian republic of the U.S.S.R.
4. (55?–117? A.D.), Roman historian.
5. Piero della Francesca (1420?–1492), Italian Renaissance painter.
6. Referring to Wilhelm Reich (1897–1957), founder of a controversial school of psychiatry.

and we lived high up in a penthouse with a huge window
from which we could see all of New York and ever farther on clearer days
No, can't imagine myself married to that pleasant prison dream—

O but what about love? I forget love
not that I am incapable of love
it's just that I see love as odd as wearing shoes—
I never wanted to marry a girl who was like my mother
And Ingrid Bergman was always impossible
And there's maybe a girl now but she's already married
And I don't like men and—
but there's got to be somebody!
Because what if I'm 60 years old and not married,
all alone in a furnished room with pee stains on my underwear
and everybody else is married! All the universe married but me!

Ah, yet well I know that were a woman possible as I am possible
then marriage would be possible—
Like SHE in her lonely alien gaud waiting her Egyptian lover[7]
so I wait—bereft of 2,000 years and the bath of life.

1960

TED HUGHES
(1930–)

The Thought-Fox

I imagine this midnight moment's forest:
Something else is alive
Beside the clock's loneliness
And this blank page where my fingers move.

Through the window I see no star:
Something more near
Though deeper within darkness
Is entering the loneliness:

Cold, delicately as the dark snow,
A fox's nose touches twig, leaf;
Two eyes serve a movement, that now
And again now, and now, and now

Sets neat prints into the snow
Between trees, and warily a lame
Shadow lags by stump and in hollow
Of a body that is bold to come

Across clearings, an eye,
A widening deepening greenness,
Brilliantly, concentratedly,
Coming about its own business

7. As in H. Rider Haggard's novel (1887), "She" gains eternal youth by bathing in a pillar of flame, and waits thousands of years for the return of her lover.

Till, with a sudden sharp hot stink of fox
It enters the dark hole of the head.
The window is starless still; the clock ticks,
The page is printed.

1957

The Bull Moses

A hoist up and I could lean over
The upper edge of the high half-door,
My left foot ledged on the hinge, and look in at the byre's[1]
Blaze of darkness: a sudden shut-eyed look
Backward into the head.
Blackness is depth
Beyond star. But the warm weight of his breathing,
The ammoniac reek of his litter, the hotly-tongued
Mash of his cud, steamed against me.
Then, slowly, as onto the mind's eye—
The brow like masonry, the deep-keeled neck:
Something come up there onto the brink of the gulf,
Hadn't heard of the world, too deep in itself to be called to,
Stood in sleep. He would swing his muzzle at a fly
But the square of sky where I hung, shouting, waving,
Was nothing to him; nothing of our light
Found any reflection in him.
Each dusk the farmer led him
Down to the pond to drink and smell the air,
And he took no pace but the farmer
Led him to take it, as if he knew nothing
Of the ages and continents of his fathers,
Shut, while he wombed, to a dark shed
And steps between his door and the duckpond;
The weight of the sun and the moon and the world hammered
To a ring of brass through his nostrils.
He would raise
His streaming muzzle and look out over the meadows,
But the grasses whispered nothing awake, the fetch
Of the distance drew nothing to momentum
In the locked black of his powers. He came strolling gently back,
Paused neither toward the pigpens on his right,
Nor toward the cow-byres on his left: something
Deliberate in his leisure, some beheld future
Founding in his quiet.
I kept the door wide,
Closed it after him and pushed the bolt.

1960

A March Calf

Right from the start he is dressed in his best—his blacks and his whites.
Little Fauntleroy—quiffed and glossy,
A Sunday suit, a wedding natty get-up,
Standing in dunged straw

1. Cattle-shed's.

Under cobwebby beams, near the mud wall,
Half of him legs,
Shining-eyed, requiring nothing more
But that mother's milk come back often.

Everything else is in order, just as it is.
Let the summer skies hold off, for the moment.
This is just as he wants it.
A little at a time, of each new thing, is best.

Too much and too sudden is too frightening—
When I block the light, a bulk from space,
To let him in to his mother for a suck,
He bolts a yard or two, then freezes,

Staring from every hair in all directions,
Ready for the worst, shut up in his hopeful religion,
A little syllogism
With a wet blue-reddish muzzle, for God's thumb.

You see all his hopes bustling
As he reaches between the worn rails towards
The topheavy oven of his mother.
He trembles to grow, stretching his curl-tip tongue—

What did cattle ever find here
To make this dear little fellow
So eager to prepare himself?
He is already in the race, and quivering to win—

His new purpled eyeball swivel-jerks
In the elbowing push of his plans.
Hungry people are getting hungrier,
Butchers developing expertise and markets.

But he just wobbles his tail—and glistens
Within his dapper profile
Unaware of how his whole lineage
Has been tied up.

He shivers for feel of the world licking his side.
He is like an ember—one glow
Of lighting himself up
With the fuel of himself, breathing and brightening.

Soon he'll plunge out, to scatter his seething joy,
To be present at the grass,
To be free on the surface of such a wideness,
To find himself himself. To stand. To moo.

1975

Deaf School

The deaf children were monkey-nimble, fish-tremulous and sudden.
Their faces were alert and simple
Like faces of little animals, small night lemurs caught in the flash-light.

They lacked a dimension,
They lacked a subtle wavering aura of sound and responses to sound.
The whole body was removed
From the vibration of air, they lived through the eyes,
The clear simple look, the instant full attention.
Their selves were not woven into a voice
Which was woven into a face
Hearing itself, its own public and audience,
An apparition in camouflage, an assertion in doubt—
Their selves were hidden, and their faces looked out of hiding.
What they spoke with was a machine,
A manipulation of fingers, a control-panel of gestures
Out there in the alien space
Separated from them—

Their unused faces were simple lenses of watchfulness
Simple pools of earnest watchfulness

Their bodies were like their hands
Nimbler than bodies, like the hammers of a piano,
A puppet agility, a simple mechanical action
A blankness of hieroglyph
A stylized lettering
Spelling out approximate signals
While the self looked through, out of the face of simple concealment
A face not merely deaf, a face in darkness, a face unaware,
A face that was simply the front skin of the self concealed and separate.

1979

GARY SNYDER
(1930–)

Mid-August at Sourdough Mountain[1] Lookout

Down valley a smoke haze
Three days heat, after five days rain
Pitch glows on the fir-cones
Across rocks and meadows
Swarms of new flies.

I cannot remember things I once read
A few friends, but they are in cities.
Drinking cold snow-water from a tin cup
Looking down for miles
Through high still air.

1959

Above Pate Valley

We finished clearing the last
Section of trail by noon,
High on the ridge-side
Two thousand feet above the creek

1. The setting of this and others of Snyder's poems is the Pacific Northwest.

Reached the pass, went on
Beyond the white pine groves,
Granite shoulders, to a small
Green meadow watered by the snow,
Edged with Aspen—sun
Straight high and blazing
But the air was cool.
Ate a cold fried trout in the
Trembling shadows. I spied
A glitter, and found a flake
Black volcanic glass—obsidian—
By a flower. Hands and knees
Pushing the Bear grass, thousands
Of arrowhead leavings over a
Hundred yards. Not one good
Head, just razor flakes
On a hill snowed all but summer,
A land of fat summer deer,
They came to camp. On their
Own trails. I followed my own
Trail here. Picked up the cold-drill,
Pick, singlejack,[2] and sack
Of dynamite.
Ten thousand years.

1959

Four Poems for Robin

Siwashing it out once in Siuslaw Forest[3]

I slept under   rhododendron
All night   blossoms fell
Shivering on   a sheet of cardboard
Feet stuck   in my pack
Hands deep   in my pockets
Barely   able   to   sleep.
I remembered   when we were in school
Sleeping together   in a big warm bed
We were   the youngest lovers
When we broke up   we were still nineteen.
Now our   friends are married
You teach   school back east
I dont mind   living this way
Green hills   the long blue beach
But sometimes   sleeping in the open
I think back   when I had you.

A spring night in Shokoku-ji[4]

Eight years ago this May
We walked under cherry blossoms
At night in an orchard in Oregon.
All that I wanted then
Is forgotten now, but you.
Here in the night
In a garden of the old capital

2. A cold-drill and singlejack (a short-handled hammer) are used to cut holes in solid rock for dynamite.
3. West of Eugene, Oregon; "siwashing": camping with light equipment, roughing it.
4. Fourteenth-century Zen monastery in Kyoto, once the capital of Japan.

I feel the trembling ghost of Yugao[5]
I remember your cool body
Naked under a summer cotton dress.

An autumn morning in Shokoku-ji

Last night watching the Pleiades,[6]
Breath smoking in the moonlight,
Bitter memory like vomit
Choked my throat.
I unrolled a sleeping bag
On mats on the porch
Under thick autumn stars.
In dream you appeared
(Three times in nine years)
Wild, cold, and accusing.
I woke shamed and angry:
The pointless wars of the heart.
Almost dawn. Venus and Jupiter.
The first time I have
Ever seen them close.

December at Yase[7]

You said, that October,
In the tall dry grass by the orchard
When you chose to be free,
"Again someday, maybe ten years."

After college I saw you
One time. You were strange.
And I was obsessed with a plan.

Now ten years and more have
Gone by: I've always known
where you were—
I might have gone to you
Hoping to win your love back.
You still are single.

I didn't.
I thought I must make it alone. I
Have done that.

Only in dream, like this dawn,
Does the grave, awed intensity
Of our young love
Return to my mind, to my flesh.

We had what the others
All crave and seek for;
We left it behind at nineteen.

5. *The Tale of Genji*, the title of Arthur Waley's translation of the medieval Japanese novel *Genji monogatori*, written between A.D. 1001 and 1006 by Murasaki-no-Shikibu, or Lady Murasaki—recounts the amorous exploits of the young Prince Genji, the setting being the imperial capital (modern Kyoto). Genji has a brief liaison with a young woman, Yugao, who dies suddenly and mysteriously, bewitched. After her death, coming upon a dress of hers, he writes a poem: "The girdle that today with tears I knot, shall we ever in some new life untie?"

6. A cluster of stars (named after the seven daughters of Atlas, in Greek mythology) in the constellation Taurus.

7. Near northeast Kyoto.

I feel ancient, as though I had
Lived many lives.

And may never now know
If I am a fool
Or have done what my
        karma[8] demands.

1968

DEREK WALCOTT
(1930–)

The Gulf

[FOR JACK AND BARBARA HARRISON]

1

The airport coffee tastes less of America.
Sour, unshaven, dreading the exertion
of tightening, racked nerves fueled with liquor,

some smoky, resinous Bourbon,
the body, buckling at its casket hole,
a roar like last night's blast racing its engines,

watches the fumes of the exhausted soul
as the trans-Texas jet, screeching, begins
its flight and friends diminish. So, to be aware

of the divine union the soul detaches
itself from created things.[1] "We're in the air,"
the Texan near me grins. All things: these matches

from LBJ's [2] campaign hotel, this rose
given me at dawn in Austin by a child,
this book of fables by Borges,[3] its prose

a stalking, moonlit tiger. What was willed
on innocent, sun-streaked Dallas,[4] the beast's claw
curled round that hairspring rifle is revealed

on every page as lunacy or feral law;
circling that wound we leave Love Field.[5]
Fondled, these objects conjure hotels,

quarrels, new friendships, brown limbs
nakedly molded as these autumn hills
memory penetrates as the jet climbs

8. "In Hinduism and Buddhism, the whole ethical consequence of one's acts considered as fixing one's lot in the future existence" (*Webster's*). Loosely, what one is fated or destined to do or be.

1. With reference to the Neo-Platonic doctrine that earthly relationships and attachments contaminate the striving for spiritual union with God; in contrast to the teaching that divine love is manifested in the created world and in human relationships.

2. Lyndon Baines Johnson (1906–1973), thirty-sixth President of the United States.

3. Jorge Luis Borges, Argentinian man of letters (1899–), best known for his short stories.

4. With an allusion to the assassination there of John F. Kennedy, November 22, 1963.

5. The Dallas airport.

the new clouds over Texas; their home means
an island suburb, forest, mountain water;
they are the simple properties for scenes

whose joy exhausts like grief, scenes where we learn,
exchanging the least gifts, this rose, this napkin,
that those we love are objects we return,

that this lens on the desert's wrinkled skin
has priced our flesh, all that we love in pawn
to that brass ball, that the gifts, multiplying

clutter and choke the heart, and that I shall
watch love reclaim its things as I lie dying.
My very flesh and blood! Each seems a petal

shriveling from its core. I watch them burn,
by the nerves' flare I catch their skeletal
candor! Best never to be born

the great dead cry.[6] Their works shine on our shelves,
by twilight tour their gilded gravestone spines,
and read until the lamplit page revolves

to a white stasis whose detachment shines
like a propeller's rainbowed radiance.
Circling like us; no comfort for their loves!

2

The cold glass darkens. Elizabeth wrote once
that we make glass the image of our pain;
I watch clouds boil past the cold, sweating pane

above the Gulf. All styles yearn to be plain
as life. The face of the loved object under glass
is plainer still. Yet, somehow, at this height,

above this cauldron boiling with its wars,
our old earth, breaking to familiar light,
that cloud-bound mummy with self-healing scars

peeled of her cerements° again looks new: *grave clothes*
some cratered valley heals itself with sage,
through that grey, fading massacre a blue

light-hearted creek flutes of some seige
to the amnesia of drumming water.
Their cause is crystalline: the divine union

of these detached, divided States, whose slaughter
darkens each summer now, as one by one,
the smoke of bursting ghettos clouds the glass

down every coast where filling-station signs
proclaim the Gulf, an air, heavy with gas,
sickens the state, from Newark to New Orleans.

6. For example, Sophocles, in *Oedipus at Colonus:* "Not to be born surpasses thought and speech./The second best is to have seen the light/And then to go back quickly whence we came."

3

Yet the South felt like home. Wrought balconies,
the sluggish river with its tidal drawl,
the tropic air charged with the extremities

of patience, a heat heavy with oil,
canebrakes, that legendary jazz. But fear
thickened my voice, that strange, familiar soil

prickled and barbed the texture of my hair,
my status as a secondary soul.
The Gulf, your gulf, is daily widening,

each blood-red rose warns of that coming night
when there's no rock cleft to go hidin' in [7]
and all the rocks catch fire, when that black might,

their stalking, moonless panthers turn from Him
whose voice they can no more believe, when the black X's [8]
mark their passover with slain seraphim.

4

The Gulf shines, dull as lead. The coast of Texas
glints like a metal rim. I have no home
as long as summer bubbling to its head

boils for that day when in the Lord God's name
the coals of fire are heaped upon the head
of all whose gospel is the whip and flame,

age after age, the uninstructing dead.

1969

Europa[9]

The full moon is so fierce that I can count the
coconuts' cross-hatched shade on bungalows,
their white walls raging with insomnia.
The stars leak drop by drop on the tin plates
of the sea almonds, and the jeering clouds
are luminously rumpled as the sheets.
The surf, insatiably promiscuous,
groans through the walls; I feel my mind
whiten to moonlight, altering that form
which daylight unambiguously designed,
from a tree to a girl's body bent in foam;
then, treading close, the black hump of a hill,
its nostrils softly snorting, nearing the
naked girl splashing her breasts with silver.
Both would have kept their proper distance still,
if the chaste moon hadn't swiftly drawn the drapes
of a dark cloud, coupling their shapes.

She teases with those flashes, yes, but once
you yield to human horniness, you see

7. A reference to the hymn which begins, "Rock of Ages, cleft for me,/Let me hide myself in thee." The "rock" signifies Christ, "cleft" in his crucifixion.
8. Such as Malcolm X, the Black Muslim leader, assassinated February 21, 1965, and the Black Panthers, a militant black organization.
9. In Greek legend the god Zeus in the form of a bull abducted the maiden Europa.

through all that moonshine what they really were,
those gods as seed-bulls, gods as rutting swans—
an overheated farmhand's literature.
Who ever saw her pale arms hook his horns,
her thighs clamped tight in their deep-plunging ride,
watched, in the hiss of the exhausted foam,
her white flesh constellate to phosphorous
as in salt darkness beast and woman come?
Nothing is there, just as it always was,
but the foam's wedge to the horizon-light,
then, wire-thin, the studded armature,
like drops still quivering on his matted hide,
the hooves and horn-points anagrammed in stars.

1981

The Season of Phantasmal[1] Peace

Then all the nations of birds lifted together
the huge net of the shadows of this earth
in multitudinous dialects, twittering tongues,
stitching and crossing it. They lifted up
the shadows of long pines down trackless slopes,
the shadows of glass-faced towers down evening streets,
the shadow of a frail plant on a city sill—
the net rising soundless as night, the birds' cries soundless, until
there was no longer dusk, or season, decline, or weather,
only this passage of phantasmal light
that not the narrowest shadow dared to sever.

And men could not see, looking up, what the wild geese drew,
what the ospreys trailed behind them in silvery ropes
that flashed in the icy sunlight; they could not hear
battalions of starlings waging peaceful cries,
bearing the net higher, covering this world
like the vines of an orchard, or a mother drawing
the trembling gauze over the trembling eyes
of a child fluttering to sleep;
                                        it was the light
that you will see at evening on the side of a hill
in yellow October, and no one hearing knew
what change had brought into the raven's cawing,
the killdeer's screech, the ember-circling chough
such an immense, soundless, and high concern
for the fields and cities where the birds belong,
except it was their seasonal passing, Love,
made seasonless, or, from the high privilege of their birth,
something brighter than pity for the wingless ones
below them who shared dark holes in windows and in houses,
and higher they lifted the net with soundless voices
above all change, betrayals of falling suns,
and this season lasted one moment, like the pause
between dusk and darkness, between fury and peace,
but, for such as our earth is now, it lasted long.

1981

1. Imaginary and perhaps unreal.

GEOFFREY HILL
(1932–)

The Guardians

The young, having risen early, had gone,
Some with excursions beyond the bay-mouth,
Some toward lakes, a fragile reflected sun.
Thunder-heads drift, awkwardly, from the south;

The old watch them. They have watched the safe
Packed harbors topple under sudden gales,
Great tides irrupt, yachts burn at the wharf
That on clean seas pitched their effective sails.

There are silences. These, too, they endure:
Soft comings-on; soft aftershocks of calm.
Quietly they wade the disturbed shore;
Gather the dead as the first dead scrape home.

1956 1959

From Mercian Hymns[1]

VI

The princes of Mercia were badger and raven. Thrall to their freedom, I dug and hoarded. Orchards fruited above clefts. I drank from honeycombs of chill sandstone.

"A boy at odds in the house, lonely among brothers." But I, who had none, fostered a strangeness; gave myself to unattainable toys.

Candles of gnarled resin, apple-branches, the tacky mistletoe. "Look" they said and again "look." But I ran slowly; the landscape flowed away, back to its source.

In the schoolyard, in the cloakrooms, the children boasted their scars of dried snot; wrists and knees garnished with impetigo.

VII

Gasholders,[2] russet among fields. Milldams, marlpools that lay unstirring. Eel-swarms. Coagulations of frogs: once, with branches and half-bricks, he battered a ditchful; then sidled away from the stillness and silence.

1. "The historical Offa reigned over Mercia (and the greater part of England south of the Humber) in the years A.D. 757–796. During early medieval times he was already becoming a creature of legend. The Offa who figures in this sequence might perhaps most usefully be regarded as the presiding genius of the West Midlands, his dominion enduring from the middle of the eighth century until the middle of the twentieth (and possibly beyond). The indication of such a timespan will, I trust, explain and to some extent justify a number of anachronisms" (Hill's note).

2. Or gasometers, large metal receptacles for gas. "Marlpools": pools in deposits of crumbling clay and chalk.

Ceolred[3] was his friend and remained so, even after the day of the lost fighter: a biplane, already obsolete and irreplaceable, two inches of heavy snub silver. Ceolred let it spin through a hole in the classroom floorboards, softly, into the rat droppings and coins.

After school he lured Ceolred, who was sniggering with fright, down to the old quarries, and flayed him. Then, leaving Ceolred, he journeyed for hours, calm and alone, in his private derelict sandlorry[4] named *Albion*.

VIII

The mad are predators. Too often lately they harbor against us. A novel heresy exculpates all maimed souls. Abjure it! I am the King of Mercia, and I know.

Threatened by phone calls at midnight, venomous letters, forewarned I have thwarted their imminent devices.

Today I name them; tomorrow I shall express the new law. I dedicate my awakening to this matter.

X

He adored the desk, its brown-oak inlaid with ebony, assorted prize pens, the seals of gold and base metal into which he had sunk his name.

It was there that he drew upon grievances from the people; attended to signatures and retributions; forgave the death-howls of his rival. And there he exchanged gifts with the Muse of History.

What should a man make of remorse, that it might profit his soul? Tell me. Tell everything to Mother, darling, and God bless.

He swayed in sunlight, in mild dreams. He tested the little pears. He smeared catmint on his palm for his cat Smut to lick. He wept, attempting to master *ancilla* and *servus*.[5]

XXX

And it seemed, while we waited, he began to walk towards us he vanished

he left behind coins, for his lodging, and traces of red mud.

1971

3. Ceolred was a 9th-century bishop of Leicester, but the name is here used as a characteristic Anglo-Saxon Mercian name.
4. Sand truck. Albion was an old Celtic name for England; it is also the name of a famous make of British truck.
5. "Maidservant" and "manservant" (or slave).

From An Apology for the Revival of Christian Architecture in England

the spiritual, Platonic old England . . .[6]
—STC, *Anima Poetae*

"Your situation," said Coningsby, looking up the green and silent valley, "is absolutely poetic."
"I try sometimes to fancy," said Mr. Millbank, with a rather fierce smile, "that I am in the New World."
—BENJAMIN DISRAELI,[7] *Coningsby*

9. *The Laurel Axe*

Autumn resumes the land, ruffles the woods
with smoky wings, entangles them. Trees shine
out from their leaves, rocks mildew to moss-green;
the avenues are spread with brittle floods.

Platonic England, house of solitudes,
rests in its laurels and its injured stone,
replete with complex fortunes that are gone,
beset by dynasties of moods and clouds.

It stands, as though at ease with its own world,
the mannerly extortions, languid praise,
all that devotion long since bought and sold,

the rooms of cedar and soft-thudding baize,[8]
tremulous boudoirs where the crystals kissed
in cabinets of amethyst and frost.

1978

SYLVIA PLATH
(1932–1963)

Black Rook in Rainy Weather

On the stiff twig up there
Hunches a wet black rook
Arranging and rearranging its feathers in the rain.
I do not expect miracle
Or an accident

To set the sight on fire
In my eye, nor seek
Any more in the desultory weather some design,
But let spotted leaves fall as they fall,
Without ceremony, or portent

6. I.e., an idealized orderly rural England. "STC": Samuel Taylor Coleridge (1772–1834). English poet and philosopher; see above.
7. British novelist and statesman (1804–81); the "New World" referred to is that of an idealized rural America.
8. I.e., billiard rooms in great old British homes; the "soft-thudding baize" refers to the soft green cloth covering billiard tables.

Although, I admit, I desire,
Occasionally, some backtalk
From the mute sky, I can't honestly complain:
A certain minor light may still
Leap incandescent

Out of kitchen table or chair
As if a celestial burning took
Possession of the most obtuse objects now and then—
Thus hallowing an interval
Otherwise inconsequent

By bestowing largesse, honor,
One might say love. At any rate, I now walk
Wary (for it could happen
Even in this dull, ruinous landscape); skeptical,
Yet politic; ignorant

Of whatever angel may choose to flare
Suddenly at my elbow. I only know that a rook
Ordering its black feathers can so shine
As to seize my senses, haul
My eyelids up, and grant

A brief respite from fear
Of total neutrality. With luck,
Trekking stubborn through this season
Of fatigue, I shall
Patch together a content

Of sorts. Miracles occur,
If you care to call those spasmodic
Tricks of radiance miracles. The wait's begun again,
The long wait for the angel,
For that rare, random descent.

1956 1971

The Colossus

I shall never get you put together entirely,
Pieced, glued, and properly jointed.
Mule-bray, pig-grunt and bawdy cackles
Proceed from your great lips.
It's worse than a barnyard.

Perhaps you consider yourself an oracle,
Mouthpiece of the dead, or of some god or other.
Thirty years now I have labored
To dredge the silt from your throat.
I am none the wiser.

Scaling little ladders with gluepots and pails of lysol
I crawl like an ant in mourning
Over the weedy acres of your brow
To mend the immense skull plates and clear
The bald, white tumuli of your eyes.

A blue sky out of the Oresteia[1]
Arches above us. O father, all by yourself
You are pithy and historical as the Roman Forum.
I open my lunch on a hill of black cypress.
Your fluted bones and acanthine[2] hair are littered

In their old anarchy to the horizon-line.
It would take more than a lightning-stroke
To create such a ruin.
Nights, I squat in the cornucopia
Of your left ear, out of the wind,

Counting the red stars and those of plum-color.
The sun rises under the pillar of your tongue.
My hours are married to shadow.
No longer do I listen for the scrape of a keel
On the blank stones of the landing.

1959 1960

Sleep in the Mojave Desert[3]

Out here there are no hearthstones,
Hot grains, simply. It is dry, dry.
And the air dangerous. Noonday acts queerly
On the mind's eye, erecting a line
Of poplars in the middle distance, the only
Object beside the mad, straight road
One can remember men and houses by.
A cool wind should inhabit those leaves
And a dew collect on them, dearer than money,
In the blue hour before sunup.
Yet they recede, untouchable as tomorrow,
Or those glittery fictions of spilt water
That glide ahead of the very thirsty.

I think of the lizards airing their tongues
In the crevice of an extremely small shadow
And the toad guarding his heart's droplet.
The desert is white as a blind man's eye,
Comfortless as salt. Snake and bird
Doze behind the old masks of fury.
We swelter like firedogs in the wind.
The sun puts its cinder out. Where we lie
The heat-cracked crickets congregate
In their black armorplate and cry.
The day-moon lights up like a sorry mother,
And the crickets come creeping into our hair
To fiddle the short night away.

1960 1971

1. A trilogy of plays by Aeschylus, performed in 458 B.C., on the story of Agamemnon, Clytemnestra, and Orestes.

2. Curled on the ends, as the leaves of the (Mediterranean) acanthus plant are curled.

3. In southern California.

Elm

FOR RUTH FAINLIGHT

I know the bottom, she says. I know it with my great tap root:
It is what you fear.
I do not fear it: I have been there.

Is it the sea you hear in me,
Its dissatisfactions?
Or the voice of nothing, that was your madness?

Love is a shadow.
How you lie and cry after it.
Listen: these are its hooves: it has gone off, like a horse.

All night I shall gallop thus, impetuously,
Till your head is a stone, your pillow a little turf,
Echoing, echoing.

Or shall I bring you the sound of poisons?
This is rain now, this big hush.
And this is the fruit of it: tin-white, like arsenic.

I have suffered the atrocity of sunsets.
Scorched to the root
My red filaments burn and stand, a hand of wires.

Now I break up in pieces that fly about like clubs.
A wind of such violence
Will tolerate no bystanding: I must shriek.

The moon, also, is merciless: she would drag me
Cruelly, being barren.
Her radiance scathes me. Or perhaps I have caught her.

I let her go. I let her go
Diminished and flat, as after radical surgery.
How your bad dreams possess and endow me.

I am inhabited by a cry.
Nightly it flaps out
Looking, with its hooks, for something to love.

I am terrified by this dark thing
That sleeps in me;
All day I feel its soft, feathery turnings, its malignity.

Clouds pass and disperse.
Are those the faces of love, those pale irretrievables?
Is it for such I agitate my heart?

I am incapable of more knowledge.
What is this, this face
So murderous in its strangle of branches?——

Its snaky acids kiss.
It petrifies the will. These are the isolate, slow faults
That kill, that kill, that kill.

1962 1965

Daddy

You do not do, you do not do
Any more, black shoe
In which I have lived like a foot
For thirty years, poor and white,
Barely daring to breathe or Achoo.

Daddy, I have had to kill you.
You died before I had time——
Marble-heavy, a bag full of God,
Ghastly statue with one gray toe
Big as a Frisco seal

And a head in the freakish Atlantic
Where it pours bean green over blue
In the waters off beautiful Nauset.
I used to pray to recover you.
Ach, du.[4]

In the German tongue, in the Polish town[5]
Scraped flat by the roller
Of wars, wars, wars.
But the name of the town is common.
My Polack friend

Says there are a dozen or two.
So I never could tell where you
Put your foot, your root,
I never could talk to you.
The tongue stuck in my jaw.

It stuck in a barb wire snare.
Ich, ich, ich, ich,[6]
I could hardly speak.
I thought every German was you.
And the language obscene

An engine, an engine
Chuffing me off like a Jew.
A Jew to Dachau, Auschwitz, Belsen.
I began to talk like a Jew.
I think I may well be a Jew.

The snows of the Tyrol, the clear beer of Vienna
Are not very pure or true.
With my gypsy ancestress and my weird luck
And my Taroc pack and my Taroc pack[7]
I may be a bit of a Jew.

4. "Oh, you" (German).
5. Grabów, in Poland, Otto Plath's birthplace.
6. "I, I, I, I" (German).
7. Taroc (or tarot), from Italian *tarocco*, a pack of cards used for fortunetelling (as, for example, in T. S. Eliot's "The Waste Land," lines 43–59, and Eliot's note: see above).

I have always been scared of *you*,
With your Luftwaffe,[8] your gobbledygoo.
And your neat moustache
And your Aryan eye, bright blue.
Panzer-man, panzer-man,[9] O You——

Bit my pretty red heart in two.
I was ten when they buried you.
At twenty I tried to die
And get back, back, back to you.
I thought even the bones would do.

But they pulled me out of the sack,
And they stuck me together with glue,
And then I knew what to do.
I made a model of you,
A man in black with a Meinkampf[1] look

And a love of the rack and the screw.
And I said I do, I do.
So daddy, I'm finally through.
The black telephone's off at the root,
The voices just can't worm through.

If I've killed one man, I've killed two——
The vampire who said he was you
And drank my blood for a year,
Seven years, if you want to know.
Daddy, you can lie back now.

There's a stake in your fat black heart
And the villagers never liked you.
They are dancing and stamping on you.
They always *knew* it was you.
Daddy, daddy, you bastard, I'm through.

1962 1965

Ariel[2]

Stasis in darkness.
Then the substanceless blue
Pour of tor and distances.

God's lioness,
How one we grow,
Pivot of heels and knees!—The furrow

Splits and passes, sister to
The brown arc
Of the neck I cannot catch,

Nigger-eye
Berries cast dark
Hooks—

8. Air Force (German).
9. Armor (German), especially, during World War II, as in armored tank and the soldiers (panzer troops) who manned them.
1. From *Mein Kampf* ("My Battle"), the title of Hitler's book about his life and political aims.
2. Sylvia Plath's horse, named for the airy spirit in Shakespeare's *The Tempest*.

Black sweet blood mouthfuls,
Shadows.
Something else

Hauls me through air—
Thighs, hair;
Flakes from my heels.

White
Godiva, I unpeel—
Dead hands, dead stringencies.

And now I
Foam to wheat, a glitter of seas.
The child's cry

Melts in the wall.
And I
Am the arrow,

The dew that flies
Suicidal, at once with the drive
Into the red

Eye, the cauldron of morning.

1962 1965

Lady Lazarus[3]

I have done it again.
One year in every ten
I manage it—

A sort of walking miracle, my skin
Bright as a Nazi lampshade,
My right foot

A paperweight,
My face a featureless, fine
Jew linen.

Peel off the napkin
O my enemy.
Do I terrify?—

The nose, the eye pits, the full set of teeth?
The sour breath
Will vanish in a day.

Soon, soon the flesh
The grave cave ate will be
At home on me

And I a smiling woman.
I am only thirty.
And like the cat I have nine times to die.

3. Lazarus was raised by Jesus from the dead (John xi.1–44).

This is Number Three.
What a trash
To annihilate each decade.

What a million filaments.
The peanut-crunching crowd
Shoves in to see

Them unwrap me hand and foot—
The big strip tease.
Gentleman, ladies,

These are my hands,
My knees.
I may be skin and bone,

Nevertheless, I am the same, identical woman.
The first time it happened I was ten.
It was an accident.

The second time I meant
To last it out and not come back at all.
I rocked shut

As a seashell.
They had to call and call
And pick the worms off me like sticky pearls.

Dying
Is an art, like everything else.
I do it exceptionally well.

I do it so it feels like hell.
I do it so it feels real.
I guess you could say I've a call.

It's easy enough to do it in a cell.
It's easy enough to do it and stay put.
It's the theatrical

Comeback in broad day
To the same place, the same face, the same brute
Amused shout:

"A miracle!"
That knocks me out.
There is a charge

For the eyeing of my scars, there is a charge
For the hearing of my heart—
It really goes.

And there is a charge, very large charge,
For a word or a touch
Or a bit of blood

Or a piece of my hair or my clothes.
So, so, Herr Doktor.
So, Herr Enemy.

I am your opus,
I am your valuable,
The pure gold baby

That melts to a shriek.
I turn and burn.
Do not think I underestimate your great concern.

Ash, ash—
You poke and stir.
Flesh, bone, there is nothing there—

A cake of soap,
A wedding ring,
A gold filling.

Herr God, Herr Lucifer,
Beware
Beware.

Out of the ash
I rise with my red hair
And I eat men like air.

1962 1965

AMIRI BARAKA (LEROI JONES) (1934–)

In Memory of Radio

Who has ever stopped to think of the divinity of Lamont Cranston?[1]
(Only Jack Kerouac, that I know of: & me.
The rest of you probably had on WCBS and Kate Smith,
Or something equally unattractive.)

What can I say?
It is better to have loved and lost
Than to put linoleum in your living rooms?

Am I a sage or something?
Mandrake's hypnotic gesture of the week?
(Remember, I do not have the healing powers of Oral Roberts . . .
I cannot, like F. J. Sheen, tell you how to get saved *& rich!*
I cannot even order you to gaschamber satori like Hitler or Goody Knight

& Love is an evil word.
Turn it backwards/see, what I mean?

1. The hero of the radio serial "The Shadow." The poem refers to prominent characters and personalities that Jones would have heard on radio as a boy. Jack Kerouac (1922–1969) was a novelist of the "Beat Generation."

An evol word. & besides
Who understands it?
I certainly wouldn't like to go out on that kind of limb.

Saturday mornings we listened to *Red Lantern* & his undersea folk.
At 11, *Let's Pretend*/& we did/& I, the poet, still do, Thank God!

What was it he used to say (after the transformation, when he was safe
& invisible & the unbelievers couldn't throw stones?) "Heh, heh, heh,
Who knows what evil lurks in the hearts of men? The Shadow knows."

O, yes he does
O, yes he does.
An evil word it is,
This Love.

1961

The New World

The sun is folding, cars stall and rise
beyond the window. The workmen leave
the street to the bums and painters' wives
pushing their babies home. Those who realize
how fitful and indecent consciousness is
stare solemnly out on the emptying street.
The mourners and soft singers. The liars,
and seekers after ridiculous righteousness. All
my doubles, and friends, whose mistakes cannot
be duplicated by machines, and this is all of our
arrogance. Being broke or broken, dribbling
at the eyes. Wasted lyricists, and men
who have seen their dreams come true, only seconds
after they knew those dreams to be horrible conceits
and plastic fantasies of gesture and extension,
shoulders, hair and tongues distributing misinformation
about the nature of the understanding. No one is that simple
or priggish, to be alone out of spite and grown strong
in its practice, mystics in two-pants suits. Our style,
and discipline, controlling the method of knowledge.
Beatniks, like Bohemians, go calmly out of style. And boys
are dying in Mexico, who did not get the word.
The lateness of their fabrication: mark their holes
with filthy needles. The lust of the world. This will not
be news. The simple damning lust,
float flat magic in low changing
evenings. Shiver your hands
in dance. Empty all of me for
knowing, and will the danger
of identification,

Let me sit and go blind in my dreaming
and be that dream in purpose and device.

A fantasy of defeat, a strong strong man
older, but no wiser than the defect of love.

1969

LEONARD COHEN
(1934–   )

As the Mist Leaves No Scar

As the mist leaves no scar
On the dark green hill,
So my body leaves no scar
On you, nor ever will.

When wind and hawk encounter,
What remains to keep?
So you and I encounter,
Then turn, then fall to sleep.

As many nights endure
Without a moon or star,
So will we endure
When one is gone and far.

1961

Suzanne Takes You Down

Suzanne takes you down
to her place near the river,
you can hear the boats go by
you can stay the night beside her.
And you know that she's half crazy
but that's why you want to be there
and she feeds you tea and oranges
that come all the way from China.
Just when you mean to tell her
that you have no gifts to give her,
she gets you on her wave-length
and she lets the river answer
that you've always been her lover.
    And you want to travel with her,
    you want to travel blind
    and you know that she can trust you
    because you've touched her perfect body
    with your mind.

Jesus was a sailor
when he walked upon the water
and he spent a long time watching
from a lonely wooden tower
and when he knew for certain
only drowning men could see him
he said All men will be sailors then
until the sea shall free them,
but he himself was broken

long before the sky would open,
forsaken, almost human,
he sank beneath your wisdom like a stone.
    And you want to travel with him,
    you want to travel blind
    and you think maybe you'll trust him
    because he touched your perfect body
    with his mind.

Suzanne takes your hand
and she leads you to the river,
she is wearing rags and feathers
from Salvation Army counters.
The sun pours down like honey
on our lady of the harbor
as she shows you where to look
among the garbage and the flowers,
there are heroes in the seaweed
there are children in the morning,
they are leaning out for love
they will learn that way forever
while Suzanne she holds the mirror.
    And you want to travel with her
    and you want to travel blind
    and you're sure that she can find you
    because she's touched her perfect body
    with her mind.

1968

AUDRE LORDE
(1934–)

From the House of Yemanjá[1]

My mother had two faces and a frying pot
where she cooked up her daughters
into girls
before she fixed our dinner.
My mother had two faces
and a broken pot
where she hid out a perfect daughter
who was not me
I am the sun and moon and forever hungry
for her eyes.

I bear two women upon my back
one dark and rich and hidden
in the ivory hungers of the other
mother
pale as a witch

1. Mother of the gods and goddesses (Orisha) of the Dahomeyan people of western Nigeria; she is also the goddess of oceans, and rivers are said to flow from her breasts.

yet steady and familiar
brings me bread and terror
in my sleep
her breasts are huge exciting anchors
in the midnight storm.

All this has been
before
in my mother's bed
time has no sense
I have no brothers
and my sisters are cruel.

Mother I need
mother I need
mother I need your blackness now
as the august earth needs rain.

I am
the sun and moon and forever hungry
the sharpened edge
where day and night shall meet
and not be
one.

1978

Recreation

Coming together
it is easier to work
after our bodies
meet
paper and pen
neither care nor profit
whether we write or not
but as your body moves
under my hands
charged and waiting
we cut the leash
you create me against your thighs
hilly with images
moving through our word countries
my body
writes into your flesh
the poem
you make of me.

Touching you I catch midnight
as moon fires set in my throat
I love you flesh into blossom
I made you
and take you made
into me.

1978

JON STALLWORTHY
(1935–)

The Source

"The dead living in their memories are, I am persuaded, the source of all that we call instinct."
—W. B. YEATS[1]

Taking me into your body
you take me out of my own,
releasing an energy,
a spirit, not mine alone

but theirs locked in my cells.
One generation after
another, the blood rose and fell
that lifts us together.

Such ancient, undiminished
longings—my longing! Such
tenderness, such famished
desires! My fathers in search

of fulfillment storm through
my body, releasing now
loved women locked in you
and hungering to be found.

1974

The Almond Tree

1

All the way to the hospital
the lights were green as peppermints.
Trees of black iron broke into leaf
ahead of me, as if
I were the lucky prince
in an enchanted wood
summoning summer with my whistle,
banishing winter with a nod.

Swung by the road from bend to bend,
I was aware that blood was running
down through the delta of my wrist
and under arches
of bright bone. Centuries,
continents it had crossed;
from an undisclosed beginning
spiraling to an unmapped end.

1. Irish poet (1865–1939); see above.

2

Crossing (at sixty) Magdalen Bridge[2]
Let it be a son, a son, said
the man in the driving mirror,
Let it be a son. The tower
held up its hand: the college
bells shook their blessing on his head.

3

I parked in an almond's
shadow blossom, for the tree
was waving, waving me
upstairs with a child's hands.

4

Up
the spinal stair
and at the top
along
a bone-white corridor
the blood tide swung
me swung me to a room
whose walls shuddered
with the shuddering womb.
Under the sheet
wave after wave, wave
after wave beat
on the bone coast, bringing
ashore—whom?
                                        New-
minted, my bright farthing![3]
Coined by our love, stamped with
our images, how you
enrich us! Both
you make one. Welcome
to your white sheet,
my best poem!

5

At seven-thirty
the visitors' bell
scissored the calm
of the corridors.
The doctor walked with me
to the slicing doors.
His hand upon my arm,
his voice—*I have to tell
you*—set another bell
beating in my head:
your son is a mongol[4]
the doctor said.

6

How easily the word went in—
clean as a bullet
leaving no mark on the skin,
stopping the heart within it.

2. Bridge over the river Cherwell in Oxford; it takes its name from one of the Oxford colleges, Magdalen College, famous for its medieval tower.

3. Small British copper coin.

4. Person suffering from congenital mental deficiency.

This was my first death.
The "*I*" ascending on a slow
last thermal breath
studied the man below

as a pilot treading air might
the buckled shell of his plane—
boot, glove, and helmet
feeling no pain

from the snapped wires' radiant ends.
Looking down from a thousand feet
I held four walls in the lens
of an eye; wall, window, the street

a torrent of windscreens, my own
car under its almond tree,
and the almond waving me down.
I wrestled against gravity,

but light was melting and the gulf
cracked open. Unfamiliar
the body of my late self
I carried to the car.

7

The hospital—its heavy freight
lashed down ship-shape ward over ward—
steamed into night with some on board
soon to be lost if the desperate

charts were known. Others would come
altered to land or find the land
altered. At their voyage's end
some would be added to, some

diminished. In a numbered cot
my son sailed from me; never to come
ashore into my kingdom
speaking my language. Better not

look that way. The almond tree
was beautiful in labor. Blood-
dark, quickening, bud after bud
split, flower after flower shook free.

On the darkening wind a pale
face floated. Out of reach. Only when
the buds, all the buds, were broken
would the tree be in full sail.

In labor the tree was becoming
itself. I, too, rooted in earth
and ringed by darkness, from the death
of myself saw myself blossoming,

wrenched from the caul[5] of my thirty
years' growing, fathered by my son,
unkindly in a kind season
by love shattered and set free.

1978

ISHMAEL REED
(1938–   )

beware : do not read this poem

tonite , thriller was
abt an ol woman , so vain she
surrounded herself w/
    many mirrors

it got so bad that finally she
locked herself indoors & her
whole life became the
    mirrors

one day the villagers broke
into her house , but she was too
swift for them . she disappeared
    into a mirror

each tenant who bought the house
after that , lost a loved one to
    the ol woman in the mirror :
    first a little girl
    then a young woman
    then the young woman/s husband

the hunger of this poem is legendary
it has taken in many victims
back off from this poem
it has drawn in yr feet
back off from this poem
it has drawn in yr legs

back off from this poem
it is a greedy mirror
you are into this poem . from
    the waist down
nobody can hear you can they ?
this poem has had you up to here
    belch
this poem aint got no manners
you cant call out frm this poem
relax now & go w/ this poem
move & roll on to this poem
do not resist this poem
this poem has yr eyes
this poem has his head
this poem has his arms

5. Membrane enclosing the skull of the fetus in the womb.

this poem has his fingers
this poem has his fingertips

this poem is the reader & the
reader this poem

statistic : the us bureau of missing persons reports
that in 1968 over 100,000 people disappeared
leaving no solid clues
nor trace only
a space in the lives of their friends

1970

CHARLES SIMIC
(1938–)

The Partial Explanation

Seems like a long time
Since the waiter took my order.
Grimy little luncheonette,
The snow falling outside.

Seems like it has grown darker
Since I last heard the kitchen door
Behind my back
Since I last noticed
Anyone pass on the street.

A glass of ice water
Keeps me company
At this table I chose myself
Upon entering.

And a longing,
Incredible longing
To eavesdrop
On the conversation
Of cooks.

1977

Charon's[1] Cosmology

With only his feeble lantern
To tell him where he is
And every time a mountain
Of fresh corpses to load up

Take them to the other side
Where there are plenty more
I'd say by now he must be confused
As to which side is which

1. In Greek mythology the shades of the dead were ferried over the river Styx to Hades by Charon, paying him an obolus (a Greek coin) as fee.

I'd say it doesn't matter
No one complains he's got
Their pockets to go through
In one a crust of bread in another a sausage

Once in a long while a mirror
Or a book which he throws
Overboard into the dark river
Swift cold and deep

1977

MARGARET ATWOOD
(1939–)

This Is a Photograph of Me

It was taken some time ago.
At first it seems to be
a smeared
print: blurred lines and gray flecks
blended with the paper;

then, as you scan
it, you see in the left-hand corner
a thing that is like a branch: part of a tree
(balsam or spruce) emerging
and, to the right, halfway up
what ought to be a gentle
slope, a small frame house.

In the background there is a lake,
and beyond that, some low hills.

(The photograph was taken
the day after I drowned.

I am in the lake, in the center
of the picture, just under the surface.

It is difficult to say where
precisely, or to say
how large or small I am:
the effect of water
on light is a distortion

but if you look long enough,
eventually
you will be able to see me.)

1966

The Animals in That Country

In that country the animals
have the faces of people:

the ceremonial
cats possessing the streets

the fox run
politely to earth, the huntsmen
standing around him, fixed
in their tapestry of manners

the bull, embroidered
with blood and given
an elegant death, trumpets, his name
stamped on him, heraldic brand
because

(when he rolled
on the sand, sword in his heart, the teeth
in his blue mouth were human)

he is really a man

even the wolves, holding resonant
conversations in their
forests thickened with legend.

In this country the animals
have the faces of
animals.

Their eyes
flash once in car headlights
and are gone.

Their deaths are not elegant.

They have the faces of
no-one.

1968

You Fit into Me

you fit into me
like a hook into an eye

a fish hook
an open eye

1971

Pig Song

This is what you changed me to:
a graypink vegetable with slug
eyes, buttock
incarnate, spreading like a slow turnip,

a skin you stuff so you may feed
in your turn, a stinking wart

of flesh, a large tuber
of blood which munches
and bloats. Very well then. Meanwhile

I have the sky, which is only half
caged, I have my weed corners,
I keep myself busy, singing
my song of roots and noses,

my song of dung. Madame,
this song offends you, these grunts
which you find oppressively sexual,
mistaking simple greed for lust.

I am yours. If you feed me garbage,
I will sing a song of garbage.
This is a hymn.

1974

You Begin

You begin this way:
this is your hand,
this is your eye,
that is a fish, blue and flat
on the paper, almost
the shape of an eye.
This is your mouth, this is an O
or a moon, whichever
you like. This is yellow.

Outside the window
is the rain, green
because it is summer, and beyond that
the trees and then the world,
which is round and has only
the colors of these nine crayons.

This is the world, which is fuller
and more difficult to learn than I have said.
You are right to smudge it that way
with the red and then
the orange: the world burns.

Once you have learned these words
you will learn that there are more
words than you can ever learn.
The word *hand* floats above your hand
like a small cloud over a lake.
The word *hand* anchors
your hand to this table,
your hand is a warm stone
I hold between two words.

This is your hand, these are my hands, this is the world,
which is round but not flat and has more colors
than we can see.

It begins, it has an end,
this is what you will
come back to, this is your hand.

1978

SEAMUS HEANEY
(1939–)

Mid-Term Break

I sat all morning in the college sick bay
Counting bells knelling classes to a close.
At two o'clock our neighbors drove me home.

In the porch I met my father crying—
He had always taken funerals in his stride—
And Big Jim Evans saying it was a hard blow.

The baby cooed and laughed and rocked the pram
When I came in, and I was embarrassed
By old men standing up to shake my hand

And tell me they were "sorry for my trouble,"
Whispers informed strangers I was the eldest,
Away at school, as my mother held my hand

In hers and coughed out angry tearless sighs.
At ten o'clock the ambulance arrived
With the corpse, stanched and bandaged by the nurses.

Next morning I went up into the room. Snowdrops
And candles soothed the bedside; I saw him
For the first time in six weeks. Paler now,

Wearing a poppy bruise on his left temple,
He lay in the four foot box as in his cot.
No gaudy scars, the bumper knocked him clear.

A four foot box, a foot for every year.

1966

Punishment[1]

I can feel the tug
of the halter at the nape
of her neck, the wind
on her naked front.

1. In 1951 the body of a young girl, who lived in the late 1st century A.D., was recovered from a bog in Windeby (Germany). As P. V. Glob describes her in *The Bog People*, she "lay naked in the hole in the peat, a bandage over the eyes and a collar round the neck. The band across the eyes was drawn tight and had cut into the neck and the base of the nose. We may feel sure that it had been used to close her eyes to this world. There was no mark of strangulation on the neck, so that it had not been used for that purpose." Her hair "had been shaved off with a razor on the left side of the head * * * When the brain was removed the convolutions and folds of the surface could be clearly seen [Glob reproduces a photograph of her brain] * * * this girl of only fourteen had had an inadequate winter diet * * * To keep the young body under, some birch branches and a big stone were laid upon her." According to the Roman historian Tacitus, the Germanic peoples punished adulterous women by shaving off their hair and then scourging them out of the village or killing them.

It blows her nipples
to amber beads,
it shakes the frail rigging
of her ribs.

I can see her drowned
body in the bog,
the weighing stone,
the floating rods and boughs.

Under which at first
she was a barked sapling
that is dug up
oak-bone, brain-firkin:[2]

her shaved head
like a stubble of black corn,
her blindfold a soiled bandage,
her noose a ring

to store
the memories of love.
Little adulteress,
before they punished you

you were flaxen-haired,
undernourished, and your
tar-black face was beautiful.
My poor scapegoat,

I almost love you
but would have cast, I know,
the stones of silence.
I am the artful voyeur

of your brain's exposed
and darkened combs,
your muscles' webbing
and all your numbered bones:

I who have stood dumb
when your betraying sisters,
cauled[3] in tar,
wept by the railings,

who would connive
in civilized outrage
yet understand the exact
and tribal, intimate revenge.

1975

Sunlight

There was a sunlit absence.
The helmeted pump in the yard

2. A small wooden cask or vessel.
3. Wrapped or enclosed. A caul is the inner fetal membrane which at birth, when it is unruptured, sometimes covers the infant's head.

heated its iron,
water honeyed

in the slung bucket
and the sun stood
like a griddle cooling
against the wall

of each long afternoon.
So, her hands scuffled
over the bakeboard,
the reddening stove

sent its plaque of heat
against her where she stood
in a floury apron
by the window.

Now she dusts the board
with a goose's wing,
now sits, broad-lapped,
with whitened nails

and measling[4] shins:
here is a space
again, the scone rising
to the tick of two clocks.

And here is love
like a tinsmith's scoop
sunk past its gleam
in the meal-bin.

1975

The Strand at Lough Beg[5]

IN MEMORY OF COLUM MCCARTNEY[6]

All round this little island, on the strand
Far down below there, where the breakers strive,
Grow the tall rushes from the oozy sand.
—DANTE, *Purgatorio*, I, 100–103

Leaving the white glow of filling stations
And a few lonely streetlamps among fields
You climbed the hills towards Newtownhamilton
Past the Fews Forest, out beneath the stars—
Along that road, a high, bare pilgrim's track
Where Sweeney[7] fled before the bloodied heads,
Goat-beards and dogs' eyes in a demon pack
Blazing out of the ground, snapping and squealing.
What blazed ahead of you? A faked road block?
The red lamp swung, the sudden brakes and stalling
Engine, voices, heads hooded and the cold-nosed gun?
Or in your driving mirror, tailing headlights

4. Mottled or spotted.
5. A lake in County Armagh, Northern Ireland.
6. A cousin of Seamus Heaney's who was killed in the sectarian violence in Northern Ireland.
7. The hero of a Middle Irish prose and poem sequence, part of which occurs in the Fews in County Armagh.

That pulled out suddenly and flagged you down
Where you weren't known and far from what you knew:
The lowland clays and waters of Lough Beg,
Church Island's[8] spire, its soft treeline of yew.

There you used hear guns fired behind the house
Long before rising time, when duck shooters
Haunted the marigolds and bulrushes,
But still were scared to find spent cartridges,
Acrid, brassy, genital, ejected,
On your way across the strand to fetch the cows.
For you and yours and yours and mine fought shy,
Spoke an old language of conspirators
And could not crack the whip or seize the day:
Big-voiced scullions,° herders, feelers round *farm hands*
Haycocks and hindquarters, talkers in byres,° *barns*
Slow arbitrators of the burial ground.

Across that strand of yours the cattle graze
Up to their bellies in an early mist
And now they turn their unbewildered gaze
To where we work our way through squeaking sedge[9]
Drowning in dew. Like a dull blade with its edge
Honed bright, Lough Beg half shines under the haze.
I turn because the sweeping of your feet
Has stopped behind me, to find you on your knees
With blood and roadside muck in your hair and eyes,
Then kneel in front of you in brimming grass
And gather up cold handfuls of the dew
To wash you, cousin. I dab you clean with moss
Fine as the drizzle out of a low cloud.
I lift you under the arms and lay you flat.
With rushes that shoot green again, I plait
Green scapulars[1] to wear over your shroud.

1979

The Guttural Muse

Late summer, and at midnight
I smelt the heat of the day:
At my window over the hotel car park
I breathed the muddied night airs off the lake
And watched a young crowd leave the discotheque.

Their voices rose up thick and comforting
As oily bubbles the feeding tench sent up
That evening at dusk—the slimy tench
Once called the "doctor fish" because his slime
Was said to heal the wounds of fish that touched it.

A girl in a white dress
Was being courted out among the cars:

8. An island in Lough Beg on which is a spire erected in 1788 by the earl of Bristol.
9. Coarse, grasslike plants.
1. Religious emblems or badges worn around the neck.

As her voice swarmed and puddled into laughs
I felt like some old pike all badged with sores
Wanting to swim in touch with soft-mouthed life.

1979

From Glanmore Sonnets[2]

10

I dreamt we slept in a moss in Donegal[3]
On turf banks under blankets, with our faces
Exposed all night in a wetting drizzle,
Pallid as the dripping sapling birches.
Lorenzo and Jessica[4] in a cold climate.
Diarmuid and Grainne[5] waiting to be found.
Darkly asperged and censed,[6] we were laid out
Like breathing effigies on a raised ground.
And in that dream I dreamt—how like you this?—
Our first night years ago in that hotel
When you came with your deliberate kiss
To raise us towards the lovely and painful
Covenants of flesh; our separateness;
The respite in our dewy dreaming faces.

1979

ROBERT HASS
(1941–)

Meditation at Lagunitas[1]

All the new thinking is about loss.
In this it resembles all the old thinking.
The idea, for example, that each particular erases
the luminous clarity of a general idea. That the clown-
faced woodpecker probing the dead sculpted trunk
of that black birch is, by his presence,
some tragic falling off from a first world
of undivided light. Or the other notion that,
because there is in this world no one thing
to which the bramble of *blackberry* corresponds,
a word is elegy to what it signifies.
We talked about it late last night and in the voice
of my friend, there was a thin wire of grief, a tone
almost querulous. After a while I understood that,
talking this way, everything dissolves: *justice,*
pine, hair, woman, you and *I*. There was a woman
I made love to and I remembered how, holding
her small shoulders in my hands sometimes,
I felt a violent wonder at her presence
like a thirst for salt, for my childhood river

2. Glanmore, in County Wicklow, was Heaney's home for four years.
3. A county in the Republic of Ireland.
4. Lovers in Shakespeare's *Merchant of Venice.*
5. Fugitive lovers of Irish legend.
6. Refers to the part of the Roman Catholic funeral rite in which the corpse is sprinkled with holy water and wafted with incense.

1. A small town in California, near San Francisco (literally, "little lake").

with its island willows, silly music from the pleasure boat,
muddy places where we caught the little orange-silver fish
called *pumpkinseed.* It hardly had to do with her.
Longing, we say, because desire is full
of endless distances. I must have been the same to her.
But I remember so much, the way her hands dismantled bread,
the thing her father said that hurt her, what
she dreamed. There are moments when the body is as numinous
as words, days that are the good flesh continuing.
Such tenderness, those afternoons and evenings,
saying *blackberry, blackberry, blackberry.*

1979

MICHAEL ONDAATJE
(1943–)

Gold and Black

At night the gold and black slashed bees come
pluck my head away. Vague thousands drift
leave brain naked stark as liver
each one carries atoms of flesh, they
walk my body in their fingers.
The mind stinks out.

In the black Kim is turning
a geiger counter to this pillow.
She cracks me open like a lightbulb.

Love, the real,
terrifies
the dreamer in his riot cell.

1973

Burning Hills

FOR KRIS AND FRED

So he came to write again
in the burnt hill region
north of Kingston.[1] A cabin
with mildew spreading down walls.
Bullfrogs on either side of him.

Hanging his lantern of Shell Vapona Strip[2]
on a hook in the center of the room
he waited a long time. Opened
the Hilroy writing pad, yellow Bic pen.
Every summer he believed would be his last.
This schizophrenic season change, June to September,
when he deviously thought out plots
across the character of his friends.
Sometimes barren as fear going nowhere

1. Town in Ontario.

2. Insect-repellant strip.

or in habit meaningless as tapwater.
One year maybe he would come and sit
for 4 months and not write a word down
would sit and investigate colors, the
insects in the room with him.
What he brought: a typewriter
tins of ginger ale, cigarettes. A copy of *StrangeLove*,
of *The Intervals*,[3] a postcard of Rousseau's *The Dream*.
His friends' words were strict as lightning
unclothing the bark of a tree, a shaved hook.
The postcard was a test pattern by the window
through which he saw growing scenery.
Also a map of a city in 1900.

Eventually the room was a time machine for him.
He closed the rotting door, sat down
thought pieces of history. The first girl
who in a park near his school
put a warm hand into his trousers
unbuttoning and finally catching the spill
across her wrist, he in the maze of her skirt.
She later played the piano
when he had tea with the parents.
He remembered that surprised—
he had forgotten for so long.
Under raincoats in the park on hot days.

The summers were layers of civilization in his memory
they were old photographs he didn't look at anymore
for girls in them were chubby not as perfect as in his mind
and his ungovernable hair was shaved to the edge of skin.
His friends leaned on bicycles
were 16 and tried to look 21
the cigarettes too big for their faces.
He could read those characters easily
undisguised as wedding pictures.
He could hardly remember their names
though they had talked all day, exchanged styles
and like dogs on a lawn hung around the houses of girls
waiting for night and the devious sex-games with their simple plots.

Sex a game of targets, of throwing firecrackers
at a couple in a field locked in hand-made orgasms,
singing dramatically in someone's ear along with the record
"How do you think I feel / you know our love's not real
The one you're mad about / Is just a gad-about
How do you think I feel"[4]
He saw all that complex tension the way his children would.

There is one picture that fuses the 5 summers.
Eight of them are leaning against a wall
arms around each other
looking into the camera and the sun

3. Books by Canadian poets; *The Dream*, by the French painter Henri Rousseau (1844–1910) depicts a naked woman on a sofa, in the middle of a dreamlike jungle.

4. From a song recorded by Elvis Presley in 1974.

trying to smile at the unseen adult photographer
trying against the glare to look 21 and confident.
The summer and friendship will last forever.
Except one who was eating an apple. That was him
oblivious to the significance of the moment.
Now he hungers to have that arm around the next shoulder.
The wretched apple is fresh and white.

Since he began burning hills
the Shell strip has taken effect.
A wasp is crawling on the floor
tumbling over, its motor fanatic.
He has smoked 5 cigarettes.
He has written slowly and carefully
with great love and great coldness.
When he finishes he will go back
hunting for the lies that are obvious.

1973

JAMES TATE
(1943–   )

The Lost Pilot

FOR MY FATHER, 1922–1944

Your face did not rot
like the others—the co-pilot,
for example, I saw him

yesterday. His face is corn-
mush: his wife and daughter,
the poor ignorant people, stare

as if he will compose soon.
He was more wronged than Job.[1]
But your face did not rot

like the others—it grew dark,
and hard like ebony;
the features progressed in their

distinction. If I could cajole
you to come back for an evening,
down from your compulsive

orbiting, I would touch you,
read your face as Dallas,
your hoodlum gunner, now,

with the blistered eyes, reads
his braille editions. I would
touch your face as a disinterested

1. Figure in the Old Testament sorely tried and afflicted by God in order to test his faith.

scholar touches an original page.
However frightening, I would
discover you, and I would not

turn you in; I would not make
you face your wife, or Dallas,
or the co-pilot, Jim. You

could return to your crazy
orbiting, and I would not try
to fully understand what

it means to you. All I know
is this: when I see you,
as I have seen you at least

once every year of my life,
spin across the wilds of the sky
like a tiny, African god,

I feel dead. I feel as if I were
the residue of a stranger's life,
that I should pursue you.

My head cocked toward the sky,
I cannot get off the ground,
and, you, passing over again,

fast, perfect, and unwilling
to tell me that you are doing
well, or that it was mistake

that placed you in that world,
and me in this; or that misfortune
placed these worlds in us.

1978 1982

ELLEN BRYANT VOIGT
(1943–)

Rescue

But if she has eaten the food of the dead,
she cannot wholly return to the upper air.[1]

All morning you squat in the weeds,
your head small and still
like the head of the snake at rest
on a green blade: no terror for you

1. Paraphrased from Robert Graves's account of the myth of Persephone in his *Greek Myths* (1955). In Greek and Roman mythology, Persephone, the daughter of Demeter, goddess of fertility, was carried off by Pluto, ruler of the underworld; she was, however, allowed to return to the earth every spring.

in his dense body, you would follow him
into the tangle of brush by the barn
to see whatever house he keeps there.

I watch you watching the snake
or gathering the fallen bird,
the dog in the road, those stiff bodies
from whom you cannot withhold your tenderness.
As if they were your children,
they call you again and again into deep water,
as I wait on the dock,
braiding the long line that knots and tangles.

1983

DOUGLAS CRASE
(1944–)

Summer

Everywhere things have been taking place
Visibly, filling vacancies as if these
Were where they accurately belonged.
Likewise with us, it is no isolated longing
We are called on to endure, encouraged
By the loose joints of each expanding afternoon,
This season we never could have made
Save for the hours that buckle and gully
Beside us with desire. Headlong as it seems,
Our momentum is still an adjunct
Of the year and the territory we cover
Is legitimately ours, as when yellow rocket
Retakes an empty field. What's to decide?
The invisible volume of richness within our grasp
Is unfathomable unless we retrieve it
In peculiar experience: a day at the beach,
A trip to the country, a morning that starts
With the loudest cardinal we ever heard.
And though these moments will ripen by themselves
We are not likely to be surprised
If they turn up heaped together one day
Like a pail of raspberries ready to be cleaned,
In total no fuller and no less than the space
That was exactly available at the time.
It's enough to occupy dimensions
As we come to them, the handsome couple
Just now appearing in the door,
And how we measure their eventual reach
We can wait for time to tell. Today though,
Today crowds the branches in busy readiness,
The abundant minutes are plentiful all around,
And immediately as the afternoon begins
The wind arrives
With the flutter of something really happening.

1981

CRAIG RAINE
(1944–)

A Martian Sends a Postcard Home

Caxtons[1] are mechanical birds with many wings
and some are treasured for their markings—

they cause the eyes to melt
or the body to shriek without pain.

I have never seen one fly, but
sometimes they perch on the hand.

Mist is when the sky is tired of flight
and rests its soft machine on ground:

then the world is dim and bookish
like engravings under tissue paper.

Rain is when the earth is television.
It has the property of making colors darker.

Model T[2] is a room with the lock inside—
a key is turned to free the world

for movement, so quick there is a film
to watch for anything missed.

But time is tied to the wrist
or kept in a box, ticking with impatience.

In homes, a haunted apparatus sleeps,
that snores when you pick it up.

If the ghost cries, they carry it
to their lips and soothe it to sleep

with sounds. And yet, they wake it up
deliberately, by tickling with a finger.

Only the young are allowed to suffer
openly. Adults go to a punishment room

with water but nothing to eat.
They lock the door and suffer the noises

alone. No one is exempt
and everyone's pain has a different smell.

1. I.e., books, which William Caxton (ca. 1422–91) was the first to print in English; in the next couplet the Martian observes the effects of books on their readers, but does not know the words for "cry" or "laugh."
2. I.e., automobiles; the "key" is the ignition key.

At night, when all the colors die,
they hide in pairs

and read about themselves—
in color, with their eyelids shut.

1979

TOM WAYMAN
(1945–)

What Good Poems Are For

To sit on a shelf in the cabin across the lake
where the young man and the young woman
have come to live—there are only a few books
in this dwelling, and one of them
is this book of poems.

To be like plants
on a sunlit windowsill
of a city apartment—all the hours of care
that go into them, the tending and watering,
and yet to the casual eye they are just present
—a brief moment of enjoyment.
Only those who work on the plant
know how slowly it grows
and changes, almost dies from its own causes
or neglect, or how other plants
can be started from this one
and used elsewhere in the house
or given to friends.
But everyone notices the absence of plants
in a residence
even those who don't have plants themselves.

There is also (though this is more rare)
Bob Smith's story about the man in the bar up north,
a man in his 50s, taking a poem from a new book Bob showed him
around from table to table, reading it aloud
to each group of drinkers because, he kept saying,
the poem was about work he did, what he knew about,
written by somebody like himself.
But where could he take it
except from table to table, past the *Fuck offs*
and the *Hey, that's pretty goods*? Over the noise
of the jukebox and the bar's TV,
past the silence of the lake,
a person is speaking
in a world full of people talking.
Out of all that is said, these particular words
put down roots in someone's mind
so that he or she likes to have them here—
these words no one was paid to write
that live with us for a while
in a small container
on the ledge where the light enters

1980

LAWRENCE RAAB
(1946–   )

Attack of the Crab Monsters

Even from the beach I could sense it—
lack of welcome, lack of abiding life,
like something in the air, a certain
lack of sound. Yesterday
there was a mountain out there.
Now it's gone. And look

at this radio, each tube neatly
sliced in half. Blow the place up!
That was my advice.
But after the storm and the earthquake,
after the tactic of the exploding plane
and the strategy of the sinking boat, it looked

like fate and I wanted to say, "Don't you see?
So what if you're a famous biochemist!
Lost with all hands is an old story."
Sure, we're on the edge
of an important breakthrough, everyone
hearing voices, everyone falling

into caves, and you're out
wandering through the jungle
in the middle of the night in your negligée.
Yes, we're way out there
on the edge of science, while the rest
of the island continues to disappear until

nothing's left except this
cliff in the middle of the ocean,
and you, in your bathing suit,
crouched behind the scuba tanks.
I'd like to tell you
not to be afraid, but I've lost

my voice. I'm not used to all these
legs, these claws, these feelers.
It's the old story, predictable
as fallout—the re-arrangement of molecules.
And everyone is surprised
and no one understands

why each man tries to kill
the thing he loves, when the change
comes over him. So now you know
what I never found the time to say.
Sweetheart, put down your flamethrower.
You know I always loved you.

1976

LESLIE MARMON SILKO
(1948–)

How to Write a Poem about the Sky

FOR THE STUDENTS OF THE BETHEL MIDDLE SCHOOL, BETHEL, ALASKA—FEB. 1975

You see the sky now
colder than the frozen river
so dense and white
little birds
walk across it.

You see the sky now
but the earth
is lost in it
and there are no horizons.
It is all
a single breath.

You see the sky
but the earth is called
by the same name
                    the moment
                    the wind shifts
sun splits it open
and bluish membranes
push through slits of skin.

You see the sky

1981

In Cold Storm Light

In cold storm light
I watch the sandrock
    canyon rim.

    The wind is wet
        with the smell of piñon.[1]
    The wind is cold
        with the sound of juniper.
                And then
                    out of the thick ice sky
                        running swiftly
                        pounding
                        swirling above the treetops
                    The snow elk come,
                    Moving, moving
                        white song
                        storm wind in the branches.

1. Small pine tree.

And when the elk have passed
behind them
a crystal train of snowflakes
strands of mist
tangled in rocks
and leaves.

1981

Prayer to the Pacific

I traveled to the ocean
distant
from my southwest land of sandrock
to the moving blue water
Big as the myth of origin.

Pale
pale water in the yellow-white light of
sun floating west
to China
where ocean herself was born.
Clouds that blow across the sand are wet.

Squat in the wet sand and speak to the Ocean:
I return to you turquoise the red coral you sent us,
sister spirit of Earth.
Four round stones in my pocket I carry back the ocean
to suck and to taste.

Thirty thousand years ago
Indians came riding across the ocean
carried by giant sea turtles.
Waves were high that day
great sea turtles waded slowly out
from the gray sundown sea.
Grandfather Turtle rolled in the sand four times
and disappeared
swimming into the sun.

And so from that time
immemorial,
as the old people say,
rain clouds drift from the west
gift from the ocean.

Green leaves in the wind
Wet earth on my feet
swallowing raindrops
clear from China.

1981

Versification

A poem is a composition written for performance by the human voice. What your eye sees on the page is the composer's verbal score, waiting for your voice to bring it alive as you read it aloud or hear it in your mind's ear. Unlike our reading of a newspaper, the best reading—that is to say, the most satisfying reading—of a poem involves a simultaneous engagement of eye and ear: the eye attentive not only to the meaning of words, but to their grouping and spacing as lines on a page; the ear attuned to the grouping and spacing of sounds. The more one understands of musical notation and the principles of musical composition, the more one will understand and appreciate a composer's score. Similarly, the more one understands of versification (the principles and practice of writing verse), the more one is likely to understand and appreciate poetry and, in particular, the intimate relationship between its form and its content. *What* a poem says or means is the result of *how* it is said, a fact that poets are often at pains to emphasize. "All my life," said W. H. Auden, "I have been more interested in technique than anything else." And T. S. Eliot claimed that "the conscious problems with which one is concerned in the actual writing are more those of a quasi-musical nature, in the arrangement of metric and pattern, than of a conscious exposition of ideas." Fortunately, the principles of versification are easier to explain than those of musical composition.

The oldest classification of poetry into three broad categories still holds:

1. **Epic:** a long narrative poem, frequently extending to several "books" (sections of several hundred lines), on a great and serious subject. See, for example, the extracts from Spenser's *The Faerie Queene* (p. 62), Milton's *Paradise Lost* (p. 165), and Wordsworth's *Prelude* (p. 276). The few poems of comparable length to have been written in the twentieth century—for example, Williams's *Paterson* and Pound's *Cantos*—have a freer, less formal structure.

2. **Dramatic:** poetry, monologue or dialogue, written in the voice of a character assumed by the poet. Space does not permit the inclusion in this anthology of speeches from the many great verse dramas of English literature, but see such dramatic monologues as Tennyson's "Ulysses" (p. 402) and Browning's "Fra Lippo Lippi" (p. 419).

3. **Lyric:** originally, a song performed in ancient Greece to the accompaniment of a small harplike instrument called a lyre. The term is now used for any fairly short poem in the voice of a single speaker, although that speaker may sometimes quote others. The reader should be wary of identifying the lyric speaker with the poet, since the "I" of a poem will frequently be that of

a fictional character invented by the poet. The majority of poems in this book are lyrics, and the principal types of lyric will be found set out under "Forms" (p. 865).

Rhythm

Poetry is the most compressed form of language, and rhythm is an essential component of language. When we speak, we hear a sequence of **syllables.** These, the basic units of pronunciation, can consist of a vowel sound alone or a vowel with attendant consonants: *oh; syl-la-ble.* Sometimes *m, n,* and *l* are counted as vowel sounds, as in *riddle, (rid-dl)* and *prism (pri-zm).* In words of two of more syllables, one is almost always given more emphasis or, as we say, is more heavily stressed than the others, so that what we hear in ordinary speech is a sequence of such units, variously stressed and unstressed as, for example:

> A **po**em is a **com**po**si**tion **writ**ten for per**for**mance by the **hu**man **voice.**

We call such an analysis of stressed and unstressed syllables **scansion** (the action or art of **scanning** a line to determine its division into metrical feet); and a simple system of signs has been evolved to denote stressed and unstressed syllables and any significant pause between them. Adding such scansion marks will produce the following:

> Ă **pó**ĕm ĭs ă **cóm**pŏ**sí**tiŏn || **wrít**tĕn fŏr pĕr**fór**mănce by̆ thĕ **hú**măn **voíce.**

The double bar known as a **caesura** (from the Latin word for *cut*), indicates a natural pause in the speaking voice, which may be short (as here) or long (as between sentences); the ◡ sign indicates an unstressed syllable, and the / sign indicates one that is stressed.

The pattern of emphasis, stress, or accent can vary from speaker to speaker and situation to situation. If someone were to contradict my definition of a poem, I might reply:

> Ă **pó**ĕm **ís** ă **cóm**pŏ**sí**tiŏn . . .

with a heavier stress on **is** than any other syllable in the sentence. The signs ◡ and / make no distinction between varying levels of stress and unstress—it being left to the reader to supply such variations—but some analysts use a third sign \ to indicate a stress falling between heavy and light.

Most people pay little or no attention to the sequence of stressed and unstressed syllables in their speaking and writing, but to a poet there is no more important element of a poem.

Meter

If a poem's rhythm is structured into a recurrence of regular—that is, approximately equal—units, we call it meter (from the Greek word for *measure*). There are four metrical systems in English poetry: the accentual; the accentual-syllabic; the syllabic; and the quantitative. Of these, the second accounts for more poems in the English language—and in this anthology—than the other three together.

Accentual meter, sometimes called "strong-stress meter," is the oldest. The earliest recorded poem in the language—that is, the oldest of Old English or Anglo-Saxon poems, Caedmon's seventh-century "Hymn"—employs a line divided in two by a heavy caesura, each half dominated by two strongly stressed syllables:

Hé **aé**rĕst scĕŏp || **aé**ldă **beá**rnŭm
[He first created for men's sons]
héofŏn tŏ **hrófĕ** || **há**lĭg **Scý**ppĕnd
[heaven as a roof holy creator]

Here, as in most Old English poetry, each line is organized by stress and by **alliteration** (the repetition of speech sounds—vowels or, more usually, consonants—in a sequence of nearby words). One and generally both of the stressed syllables in the first half-line alliterate with the first stressed syllable in the second half-line.

Accentual meter continued to be used into the late fourteenth century, as in Langland's *Piers Plowman*, which begins:

Ĭn ă **só**mĕr **sé**sŏn, || whăn **sóft** wăs thĕ **són**nĕ,
Ĭ **shópe** mĕ ĭn **shróuds**, || ăs **Í** ă **shépe** wĕre . . .

However, following the Saxons' conquest by the Normans in 1066, Saxon native meter was increasingly supplanted by the more sophisticated metrical patterns of Old French poetry brought to England in the wake of William the Conqueror. The Old English metrical system has been occasionally revived in more recent times, as for the four-stress lines of Coleridge's "Christabel" and Wilbur's "Junk" (p. 747).

Accentual-syllabic meter provided the metrical structure of the new poetry to emerge in the fourteenth century, and its basic unit was the **foot**, a combination of two or three stressed and/or unstressed syllables. The four most common metrical feet in English poetry are:

1. **Iambic** (the noun is "iamb"): an unstressed followed by a stressed syllable, as in "New **York**." Until the rise of free verse (p. 872) in this century, iambic meter was the dominant rhythm of English poetry, being closest to the natural rhythm of speech. For this reason, iambic meter is also to be found occasionally in the work of prose writers. Dickens's novel *A Tale of Two Cities*, for example, begins:

Ĭt **wàs** | thĕ **bést** | ŏf **tímes**, || ĭt **wàs** | thĕ **wórst** | ŏf **tímes** . . .

2. **Trochaic** (the noun is "trochee"): a stressed followed by an unstressed syllable, as in the word "**Lon**don" or the line from the nursery rhyme,

Lóndŏn | **brídge** ĭs | **fál**lĭng | **dówn** . . .

This is not to say that "**Lon**don" can only appear in a trochaic line. Provided its natural stress is preserved, it can take its place comfortably in an iambic line, like that from Eliot's *The Waste Land*:

Ă **crówd** | flŏwed **óv** | ĕr **Lón** | dŏn **brídge** . . .

Whereas iambic meter has a certain gravity, making it a natural choice for poems on solemn subjects, the trochaic foot has a lighter, quicker, more buoyant movement. Hence, for example, its use in Blake's "Introduction" to *Songs of Innocence* (p. 259).

3. **Anapestic** (the noun is "anapest"): two unstressed syllables followed by a stressed syllable, as in "Tennes**see**" or the opening of Byron's "The Destruction of Sennacherib".

The **Assyr** | ian came **down** | like the **wolf** | on the **fold** . . .

The last three letters of the word "Assyrian" should be heard as one syllable, a form of contraction known as **elision.**

4. **Dactylic** (the noun is "dactyl"): a stressed syllable followed by two unstressed syllables, as in "**Len**ingrad." This, like the previous "triple" (three syllable) foot, the anapest, has a naturally energetic movement, making it suitable for poems with vigorous subjects, though not these only. See Hardy's "The Voice" (p. 501), which begins:

Woman much | **missed**, how you | **call** to me, | **call** to me . . .

Iambs and anapests, which have a strong stress on the last syllable, are said to constitute a **rising meter,** whereas trochees and dactyls, ending with an unstressed syllable, constitute a **falling meter.** In addition to these four standard metrical units, there are two other (two syllable) feet that occur only as occasional variants of the others:

5. **Spondaic** (the noun is "spondee"): two successive syllables with approximately equal strong stresses, as on the words "draw back" in the second of these lines from Arnold's "Dover Beach":

Listen! | you **hear** | the **grat** | ing **roar**
Of **peb** | bles which | the **waves** | **draw back**, | and **fling** . . .

6. **Pyrrhic** (the noun is also "pyrrhic"): two successive unstressed or lightly stressed syllables, as in the second foot of the second line above, where the succession of light syllables seems to mimic the rattle of light pebbles which the heavy wave slowly draws back.

Poets, who consciously or instinctively will select a meter to suit their subject, have also a variety of line lengths from which to choose:

1. **Monometer** (one foot): see the fifth and sixth lines of each stanza of Herbert's "Easter Wings" (p. 133), which reflect, in turn, the poverty and thinness of the speaker. Herrick's "Upon His Departure Hence" is a rare example of a complete poem in iambic monometer. The fact that each line is a solitary foot (◡ ′) suggests to the eye the narrow inscription of a gravestone, and to the ear the brevity and loneliness of life.

Thus I
Pass by
And die,
As one,
Unknown,
And gone:
I'm made
A shade,
And laid
I'th grave,
There have
My cave.
Where tell
I dwell,
Farewell.

2. **Dimeter** (two feet): iambic dimeter alternates with iambic pentameter in Donne's "A Valediction: Forbidding Mourning" (p. 105); and dactylic diameter (´ ˘ ˘ | ´ ˘ ˘) gives Tennyson's "The Charge of the Light Brigade" its galloping momentum:

Cannon to right of them,
Cannon to left of them,
Cannon in front of them
  Volleyed and thundered;
Stormed at with shot and shell,
Boldly they rode and well,
Into the jaws of Death,
Into the mouth of hell
  Rode the six hundred.

Lines 4 and 9 each lack a final unstressed syllable—in technical terms such lines are **catalectic.** This shortening, which gives prominence to the stressed syllable necessary for rhyme (p. 862), is a common feature of rhyming lines in trochaic and dactylic poems.

3. **Trimeter** (three feet): Ralegh's "The Lie" (p. 60) is written in iambic trimeter; and all but the last line of each stanza of Shelley's "To a Skylark" (p. 341) in trochaic trimeter.

4. **Tetrameter** (four feet): Marvell's "To His Coy Mistress" (p. 178) is written in iambic tetrameter; and Shakespeare's "Fear No More the Heat o' the Sun" (p. 94) in trochaic tetrameter.

5. **Pentameter** (five feet): the most popular metrical line in English poetry, the iambic pentameter provides the basic rhythmical framework, or **base rhythm,** of countless poems from the fourteenth century to the twentieth, from Chaucer's "Pardoner's Tale" (p. 6) and Shakespeare's sonnets (p. 88) to Heaney's "Glanmore Sonnets" (p. 843). It even contributes to the stately prose of the Declaration of Independence:

Wĕ **hóld** | **thése trúths** | tŏ **bé** | **sélf-év** | ĭ**dént** . . .

Anapestic pentameter is to be found in Browning's "Saul":

Ăs thy̆ **lóve** | ĭs dĭs**cóv** | ĕrĕd ăl**míght** | y̆, ăl**míght** | y̆, bĕ **próved**
Thy̆ **pówer,** | thăt ĕx**ísts** | wĭth ănd **fór** | ĭt, ŏf **bé** | ĭng bĕ**lóved!**

A missing syllable in the first foot of the second line gives emphasis to the important word "power."

6. **Hexameter** (six feet): The opening sonnet of Sidney's "Astrophel and Stella" (p. 80) and Dowson's "Non sum qualis eram bonae sub regno Cynarae" (p. 532) are written in iambic hexameter a line sometimes known as an **alexandrine** (probably after a twelfth-century French poem, the *Roman d'Alexandre*). A single alexandrine is often used to provide a resonant termination to a stanza of shorter lines as, for example, the Spenserian stanza (p. 867) or Hardy's "The Convergence of the Twain" (p. 499), in which the shape of the stanza suggests the iceberg that is the poem's subject. Swinburne's "The Last Oracle" is written in trochaic hexameter:

Dáy by̆ | **dáy** thy̆ | **shád**ŏw | **shínes** ĭn | **heáven** bĕ | **hóld**ĕn . . .

7. **Heptameter** (seven feet): Kipling's "Tommy" (p. 512) is written in iambic heptameter (or **fourteeners**, as they are often called, from the number of their syllables), with an added initial syllable in three of the four lines that make up the second half of each stanza.

8. **Octameter** (eight feet): Browning's "A Toccata of Galuppi's" (p. 426) is the most famous example of the rare trochaic octameter.

Poets who write in strict conformity to a single metrical pattern will achieve the music of a metronome and soon drive their listeners away. Variation, surprise, is the very essence of every artist's trade; and one of the most important sources of metrical power and pleasure is the perpetual tension between the regular and the irregular, between the expected and the unexpected, the base rhythm and the variation.

John Hollander has spoken of the "metrical contract" which poets enter into with their readers from the first few words of the poem. When Frost begins "The Gift Outright"—

The land | was ours | before | we were | the land's

—we expect what follows to have an iambic base rhythm, but the irregularity or variation in the fourth foot tells us that we are hearing not robot speech but human speech. The stress on "we" makes it, appropriately, one of the two most important words in the line, "we" being the most important presence in the "land."

Frost's poem will serve as an example of ways in which skillful poets will vary their base rhythm:

The land | was ours | before | we were | the land's.
She was | our land || more than | a hun | dred years
Before | we were | her peo | ple. || She | was ours
In Mass | achu | setts, || in | Virgin | ia,
But we | were Eng | land's, || still | colon | ials,
Possess | ing what | we still | were un | possessed | by.
Possessed | by what | we now | no more | possessed.
Something | we were | withhold | ing made | us weak
Until | we found | it was | ourselves
We were | withhold | ing from | our land | of liv | ing,
And forth | with found | salva | tion in | surren | der.
Such as | we were | we gave | ourselves | outright
(The deed | of gift | was man | y deeds | of war)
To the land | vaguely | real | izing | westward,
But still | unstor | ied, || art | less, un | enhanced,
Such as | she was, || such as | she would | become.

The iambic pentameter gives the poem a stately movement appropriate to the unfolding history of the United States. In the trochaic "reversed feet" at the start of lines 2, 10, 12, and 16, the stress is advanced to lend emphasis to a key word or, in the case of line 8, an important syllable. Spondees in lines 2 ("our land") and 3 ("her people") bring into equal balance the two partners whose union is the theme of the poem. Such additional heavy stresses are counterbalanced by the light pyrrhic feet at the end of lines 4 and 5, in the middle of line 10, or toward the end of line 14. The multiple irregularities of that line give a wonderful impression of the land stretching westward into space, just as the variations of line 16 give a sense of the nation surging toward its destiny in time. It must be added, however, that scansion is to some extent a matter of interpretation, in which the rhetorical emphasis a particular reader prefers alters the stress pattern. Another reader might—no less correctly—prefer to begin line 9, for example:

Ŭn**tíl** | **wé** fŏund . . .

An important factor in varying the pattern of a poem is the placing of its pauses or caesurae. One falling in the middle of a line—as in line 4 above—is known as a medial caesura; one falling near the start of a line, an initial caesura; and one falling near or at the end of a line, a terminal caesura. When a caesura occurs as in lines 13 and 14 above, those lines are said to be **end-stopped.** Lines 3 and 9, however, are called **run-on lines** (or, to use a French term, they exhibit **enjambment**—"a striding over"), because the thrust of the incompleted sentence carries on over the end of the verse line. Such transitions tend to increase the pace of the poem, as the end-stopping of lines 10 through 16 slows it down.

A strikingly original and influential blending of the Old English accentual and more modern accentual-syllabic metrical systems was **sprung rhythm,** conceived and pioneeered by Gerard Manley Hopkins.

Finding the cadences of his Victorian contemporaries—what he called their "common rhythm"—too measured and mellifluous for his liking, he sought for a stronger, more muscular verse movement. Strength he equated with stress, arguing that "even one stressed syllable may make a foot, and consequently two or more stresses may come running [one after the other], which in common rhythm can, regularly speaking, never happen." In his system of sprung rhythm, each foot began with a stress and could consist of a single stressed syllable (´), a trochee (´ ˘), a dactyl (´ ˘ ˘), or what he called a **first paeon** (´ ˘ ˘ ˘). His lines will, on occasion, admit other unstressed syllables, as in the sonnet "Felix Randal" (p. 503):

> **Fé**lĭx | **Rán**dăl, || thĕ | **fár**rĭĕr, || Ŏ ĭs hĕ | **déad** thĕn? || my̆ | **dú**ty̆
>   ăll | **én**dĕd,
> **Whó** hăve | **watch**ed hĭs | **móuld** ŏf măn, || **bíg**-bonĕd ănd | **hár**dy̆-|
>   **hánd**sŏme
> **Pí**nĭng, || **pí**nĭng, || **tíll** | **tíme** whĕn | **réa**sŏn | **rám**blĕd ĭn ĭt ănd |
>   **sóme**
> **Fá**tăl | **fóur** dĭs | **ór**dĕrs, || **flesh**ed thĕre, || **áll** cŏn | **tén**dĕd?

A poetry structured on the principle that strength is stress is particularly well suited to stressful subjects, and the sprung rhythm of what Hopkins called his "terrible sonnets" (pp. 504–506), for example, gives them a dramatic urgency, a sense of anguished struggle that few poets have equalled in accentual-syllabic meter.

A number of other poets have experimented with two other metrical systems.

Syllabic meter measures only the number of syllables in a line, without regard to their stress. Being an inescapable feature of the English language, stress will of course appear in lines composed on syllabic principles, but will fall variously, and usually for rhetorical emphasis, rather than in any formal metrical pattern. When Marianne Moore wished to attack the pretentiousness of much formal "Poetry" (p. 590), she shrewdly chose to do so in **syllabics,** as lines in syllabic meter are called. The effect is carefully informal and prosaic, and few unalerted readers will notice that there are 19 syllables in the first line of each stanza; 22 in the second; 11 in the third (except for the third line of the third stanza, which has 7); 5 in the fourth; 8 in the fifth; and 13 in the sixth. That the poem succeeds in deflating Poetry (with a capital P) while at once celebrating poetry and creating it is not to be explained by Moore's talent for arithmetic so much as by her unobtrusive skill in modulating the stresses and pauses of colloquial speech. The result is a music like that of good free verse (p. 872).

Because stress plays a less important role in such Romance languages as French and Italian and in Japanese, their poetry tends to be syllabic in construction, and Pound brilliantly adapts the form of three-line, seventeen-syllable Japanese **haiku** in a poem whose title is an integral part of the whole:

In a Station of the Metro

The apparition of these faces in the crowd;
Petals on a wet, black bough.

The syllable count bears only a token relation to that of the strict Japanese pattern (5, 7, 5), but the poem succeeds largely because its internal rhymes (p. 863)—*Station*/appar*ition*; *Metro*/*pet*als/*wet*; *crowd*/*bough*—point up a series of distinct stressed syllables that suggest, in an impressionist fashion, a series of distinct white faces.

A number of other modern poets—among them Auden, Dylan Thomas, and Gunn—have written notable poems in syllabics, which cannot be said of the fourth metrical system to be considered here.

Quantitative meter measures feet according to duration of utterance rather than by their relative stress. Most Sanskrit, Greek, and later Roman poetry is quantitative, and certain English poets, familiar with one or more of these literatures, have tried to apply quantitative principles to their own language. Spenser, for example, imitates the Latin hexameter in his "Iambic Trimetrum" (bold type indicates syllables of long duration rather than heavy stress):

Un**hap** | py **verse,** | the **wit** | **ness of** | my un**hap** | py **state,**
Make thy | **self flutt** | [e] **ring** | **wings of** | thy **fast** | flying
Thought, and | fly **forth** | **un**to my | **Love, where** | soe**ver** | she **be** . . .

This metrical system is common to classical Greek and Latin poetry, being suited to the structure of those languages, but when even a poet of Spenser's skill cannot make it sound natural in English, we can understand why so few others have experimented with quantitative meter.

Rhyme

Ever since the poetry of Chaucer sprang from the fortunate marriage of Old French and Old English, rhyme (the concurrence, in two or more lines, of the last stressed vowel and of all speech sounds following that vowel) has been closely associated with rhythm in English poetry. It is to be found in the early poems and songs of many languages. Most English speakers meet it first in nursery rhymes, many of which involve numbers ("One, two,/Buckle my shoe"), a fact supporting the theory that rhyme may have had its origin in primitive religious rites and magical spells. From such beginnings poetry has been inextricably linked with music—"Caedmon's Hymn" (p. 857) and the earliest popular ballads (p. 34) were all composed to be sung—and rhyme has been a crucial element in the music of poetry. More than any other it has been responsible for making poetry memorable. Its function is a good deal more complicated than may at first appear, in that by associating one rhyme-word with another, poets may introduce a remote constellation of associations that may confirm, question, or on occasion deny the literal meaning of their words. Consider, for example, the opening 8 lines, or "octet" (p. 869), of Hopkins's sonnet "God's Grandeur" (p. 502):

1. The world is charged with the grandeur of God.
2. It will flame out, like shining from shook foil;
3. It gathers to a greatness, like the ooze of oil
4. Crushed. Why do men then now not reck his rod?
5. Generations have trod, have trod, have trod;
6. And all is seared with trade; bleared, smeared with toil;
7. And wears man's smudge and shares man's smell: the soil
8. Is bare now, nor can foot feel, being shod.

The grand statement of the first line is illustrated, not by the grand examples that the opening of lines of 2 and 3 seem to promise, but by the surprising similes of shaken tin foil and olive oil oozing from its press. The down-to-earthiness that these have in common is stressed by the *foil/oil* rhyme that will be confirmed by the *toil/soil* of lines 6 and 7. At the other end of the cosmic scale, "The grandeur of *God*" no less appropriately rhymes with "his *rod*." But what of the implicit coupling of grand God and industrial man in the ensuing *trod/shod* rhymes of lines 5 and 8? These rhymes remind Hopkins's reader that Christ, too, was a worker, a walker of hard roads, and that "the grandeur of God" is manifest in the world through which the weary generations tread.

Rhymes appearing like these at the end of a line are known as **end rhymes,** but poets frequently make use of such **internal rhyme** as the *then/men* of Hopkins's line 4; the *seared/bleared/smeared* of line 6; or the *wears/shares* of line 7. **Assonance** (the repetition of identical or similar vowel sounds) is present in the *not/rod* of line 4. This sonnet also contains two examples of a related sound effect, **onomatopoeia,** sometimes called "echoism," a combination of words whose sound seems to resemble the sound it denotes. So, in lines 3 and 4, the long, slow, alliterative vowels—"ooze of oil"—seem squeezed out by the crushing pressure of the heavily stressed verb that follows. So, too, the triple repetition of "have trod" in line 5 seems to echo the thudding boots of the laboring generations.

All the rhymes so far discussed have been what is known as **masculine rhymes** in that they consist of a single stressed syllable. Rhyme words in which a stressed syllable is followed by an unstressed syllable—*chiming/rhyming*—are known as **feminine rhymes.** Single (one syllable) and double (two syllable) rhymes are the most common, but triple and even quadruple rhymes are also to be found, usually in a comic context like that of Gilbert's "I Am the Very Model of a Modern Major-General" (p. 486) or Byron's *Don Juan*:

But—Oh! ye lords of ladies intell*ectual,*
Inform us truly, have they not hen-*pecked you all?*

If the correspondence of rhyming sounds is exact, it is called **perfect rhyme** or else "full" or "true rhyme." For many centuries almost all English writers of serious poems confined themselves to rhymes of this sort, except for an occasional **poetic license** (or violation of the rules of versification) such as **eye rhymes,** words whose endings are spelled alike, and in most instances were pronounced alike, but have in the course of time acquired a different pronunciation: *prove/love*; *daughter/laughter.* Since the nineteenth century, however, an increasing number of poets have felt the confident chimes of perfect rhymes inappropriate for poems of doubt, frustration, and grief, and have used various forms of **imperfect rhyme:**

Off-rhyme (also known as half rhyme, near rhyme, or slant rhyme) differs from perfect rhyme in changing the vowel sound and/or the concluding consonants expected of perfect rhyme. See Byron's *gone/alone* rhyme in the second stanza of "On This Day I Complete My Thirty-sixth Year" (p. 333), or Dickinson's rhyming of *Room/Storm, firm/Room,* and *be/Fly* in "I heard a Fly buzz—when I died" (p. 476).

Vowel rhyme goes beyond off-rhyme to the point at which rhyme words have only their vowel sound in common. See for example, the muted but musically effective rhymes of Dylan Thomas's "Fern Hill" (p. 716): *boughs/towns, green/leaves, starry/barley, climb/eyes/light.*

Pararhyme, in which the stressed vowel sounds differ but are flanked by identical or similar consonants, is a term coined by Edmund Blunden to describe Owen's pioneering use of such rhymes. Although they had occurred on occasion before—see *trod/trade* in lines 5 and 6 of "God's Grandeur"—Owen was the first to employ pararhyme consistently. In such a poem as "Strange Meeting" (p. 624), the second rhyme is usually lower in pitch (has a deeper vowel sound) than the first, producing effects of dissonance, failure, and unfulfillment that subtly reinforce Owen's theme. The last stanza of his "Miners" shows a further refinement:

The centuries will burn rich loads
  With which we groaned,
Whose warmth shall lull their dreaming lids,
  While songs are crooned.
But they will not dream of us poor lads,
  Left in the ground.

Here, the pitch of the pararhyme rises to reflect the dream of a happier future—*loads/lids*—before plunging to the desolate reality of *lads,* a rise and fall repeated in *groaned/crooned/ground.*

The effect of rhyming—whether the chime is loud or muted—is to a large extent dictated by one rhyme's distance from another, a factor frequently dictated by the rhyme scheme of the poet's chosen stanza form. At one extreme stands Dylan Thomas's "Author's Prologue," a poem of 102 lines, in which line 1 rhymes with line 102, line 2 with 101, and so on down to the central couplet of lines 51–52. Rhyme schemes, however, are seldom so taxing for poets (or their readers) and, as with their choice of meter, are likely to be determined consciously or subconsciously by their knowledge of earlier poems written in this or that form.

Forms

BASIC FORMS

Having looked at—and listened to—the ways in which metrical feet combine in a poetic line, one can move on to see—and hear—how such lines combine in the larger patterns of the dance, what are known as the forms of poetry.

1. **Blank verse,** at one end of the scale, consists of unrhymed (hence "blank") iambic pentameters. Introduced to England by Surrey in his translations from *The Aeneid* (1554), it soon became the standard meter for Elizabethan poetic drama. No verse form is closer to the natural rhythms of spoken English or more adaptive to different levels of speech. Following the example of Shakespeare, whose kings, clowns, and countryfolk have each their own voice when speaking blank verse, it has been used by dramatists from Marlowe to Eliot. Milton chose it for his religious epic *Paradise Lost* (p. 165), Wordsworth for his autobiographical epic *The Prelude* (p. 276), and Coleridge for his meditative lyric "Frost at Midnight" (p. 297). During the nineteenth century it became a favorite form of such **dramatic monologues** as Tennyson's "Ulysses" (p. 402) and Browning's "Fra Lippo Lippi" (p. 419), in which a single speaker (who is not the poet himself) addresses a dramatically defined listener in a specific situation and at a critical moment. All of these poems are divided into **verse paragraphs** of varying length, as distinct from the **stanzas** of equal length that make up Tennyson's "Tears, Idle Tears" (p. 404) or Stevens's "Sunday Morning" (p. 551).

2. The **couplet,** two lines of verse, usually coupled by rhyme, has been a principal unit of English poetry since rhyme entered the language. The first poem in this anthology (p. 3) is in couplets, but the first poet to use the form consistently was Chaucer, whose "Pardoner's Tale" (p. 6) exhibits great flexibility. His narrative momentum tends to overrun line endings, and his pentameter couplets are seldom the self-contained syntactic units one finds in Jonson's "On My First Son" (p. 115). The sustained use of such **closed couplets** attained its ultimate sophistication in what came to be known as **heroic couplets** ("heroic" because of their use in epic poems or plays), pioneered by Denham in the seventeenth century and perfected by Dryden and Pope in the eighteenth. The Chaucerian energies of the iambic pentameter were reigned in, and each couplet made a balanced whole within the greater balanced whole of its poem, "Mac Flecknoe" (p. 187), for example, or "The Rape of the Lock" (p. 211). As if in reaction against the elevated ("heroic or "mock heroic") diction and syntactic formality of the heroic couplet, more recent users of the couplet have tended to veer toward the other extreme of informality. Colloquialisms, frequent enjambment, and variable placing of the caesura mask the formal rhyming of Browning's "My Last Duchess" (p. 413), as the speaker of that dramatic monologue seeks to mask its diabolical organization. Owen, with the pararhymes of "Strange Meeting" (p. 624), and Yeats, with the off-rhymed tetrameters of "Under Ben Bulben" (p. 530), achieve similarly informal effects.

3. The **tercet** is a stanza of three lines usually linked with a single rhyme, although Williams's "Poem" (p. 562) is unrhymed. It may also be a three-

line section of a larger poetic structure, as, for example, the sestet of a sonnet (p. 869). Tercets can be composed of lines of equal length—iambic tetrameter in Herrick's "Upon Julia's Clothes" (p. 131), trochaic octameter in Browning's "A Toccata of Galuppi's" (p. 426)—or of different length, as in Hardy's "The Convergence of the Twain" (p. 499). An important variant of this form is the linked tercet, or **terza rima,** in which the second line of each stanza rhymes with the first and third lines of the next. A group of such stanzas is commonly concluded with a final line supplying the missing rhyme, as in Wilbur's "First Snow in Alsace" (p. 744), although Shelley expanded the conclusion to a couplet in his "Ode to the West Wind" (p. 337). No verse form in English poetry is more closely identified with its inventor than terza rima with Dante, who used it for his *Divine Comedy.* Shelley invokes the inspiration of his great predecessor in choosing the form for his "Ode" written on the outskirts of Dante's Florence, and T. S. Eliot similarly calls the *Divine Comedy* to mind with the tercets—unrhymed, but aligned on the page like Dante's—of a passage in part 2 of "Little Gidding" that ends:

"From wrong to wrong the exasperated spirit
 Proceeds, unless restored by that refining fire
 Where you must move in measure, like a dancer."
The day was breaking. In the disfigured street
 He left me, with a kind of valediction,
 And faded on the blowing of the horn.

4. The **quatrain,** a stanza of four lines, rhymed or unrhymed, is the most common of all English stanziac forms. And the most common type of quatrain is the **ballad stanza,** in which lines of iambic tetrameter alternate with iambic trimeter, rhyming *abcb* (lines 1 and 3 being unrhymed) or, less commonly, *abab.* This, the stanza of such popular ballads as "Sir Patrick Spens" (p. 38), Coleridge's literary ballad "The Rime of the Ancient Mariner" (p. 298), and Dickinson's "I taste a liquor never brewed" (p. 472), also occurs in many hymns and is there called **common meter.** The expansion of lines 2 and 4 to tetrameters produces a quatrain known (particularly in hymnbooks) as **long meter,** the form of Hardy's "Channel Firing" (p. 500). When, on the other hand, the first line is shortened to a trimeter, matching lines 2 and 4, the stanza is called **short meter.** Gascoigne uses it for "And If I Did What Then?" (p. 56) and Hardy for "I Look into my Glass" (p. 495). Stanzas of iambic pentameter rhyming *abab,* as in Gray's "Elegy Written in a Country Churchyard" (p. 248), are known as **heroic quatrains.** The pentameter stanzas of Fitzgerald's "Rubáiyát of Omar Khayyám of Naishápúr" (p. 384) are rhymed *aaba,* a rhyme scheme that Frost elaborates in "Stopping by Woods on a Snowy Evening" (p. 542), where the third line (unrhymed in the "Rubáiyát") rhymes with lines 1, 2, and 4 of the following stanza, producing an effect like that of terza rima. Quatrains can also be in **monorhyme,** like Rossetti's "The Woodspurge" (p. 467); composed of two couplets, like "Now Go'th Sun Under Wood" (p. 3), or rhymed *abba,* as in Tennyson's "In Memoriam A. H. H." (p. 405).

5. **Rhyme royal,** a seven-line iambic-pentameter stanza rhyming *ababbcc,* was introduced by Chaucer in *Troilus and Criseyde,* but it is thought to have taken its name from its later use in King James I of Scotland's "The Kingis

Quair." Another example is Wyatt's "They Flee from Me" (p. 50).

6. **Ottava rima** is an eight-line stanza, as its Italian name indicates, and it rhymes *abababcc.* Like terza rima and the sonnet (below), it was introduced to English literature by Sir Thomas Wyatt. Byron put it to brilliant use in *Don Juan* (p. 321), frequently undercutting with a comic couplet the seeming seriousness of the six preceding lines. Yeats used ottava rima more gravely in "Sailing to Byzantium" (p. 522) and "Among School Children" (p. 524).

7. The **Spenserian stanza** has nine lines, the first eight being iambic pentameter and the last an iambic hexameter (an **alexandrine**), rhyming *ababbcbcc.* Chaucer had used two such quatrains, linked by three rhymes, as the stanza form of *The Monk's Tale,* but Spenser's addition of a concluding alexandrine gave the stanza he devised for *The Faerie Queene* (p. 62) an inequality in its final couplet, a variation reducing the risk of monotony that can overtake a long series of iambic pentameters. Keats and Hopkins wrote their earliest known poems in this form, and Keats went on to achieve perhaps the fullest expression of its intricate harmonies in "The Eve of St. Agnes" (p. 360). Partly, no doubt, in tribute to that poem, Shelley used the Spenserian stanza in his great elegy on Keats, *Adonais* (p. 343); later, the form was a natural choice for the narcotic narrative of Tennyson's "The Lotos-Eaters" (p. 398).

Ottava rima and the Spenserian stanza each open with a quatrain and close with a couplet. These and other of the shorter stanzaic units similarly recur as component parts of certain lyrics with a fixed form.

8. The **sonnet,** traditionally a poem of fourteen iambic pentameters linked by an intricate rhyme scheme, is one of the oldest verse forms in English. Used by almost every notable poet in the language, there is no better example of how rhyme and meter can provide the imagination not with a prison but a theater. The sonnet originated in Italy and, since being introduced to England by Sir Thomas Wyatt (see his "Whoso List To Hunt," p. 49) in the early sixteenth century, has been the stage for the soliloquies of countless lovers and for dramatic action ranging from a dinner party (p. 469) to the rape of Leda and the fall of Troy (p. 523). There are two basic types of sonnet—the Italian or Petrarchan (named after the fourteenth-century Italian poet Petrarch) and the English or Shakespearean—and a number of variant types, of which the most important is the Spenserian. They differ in their rhyme schemes, and consequently their structure, as follows:

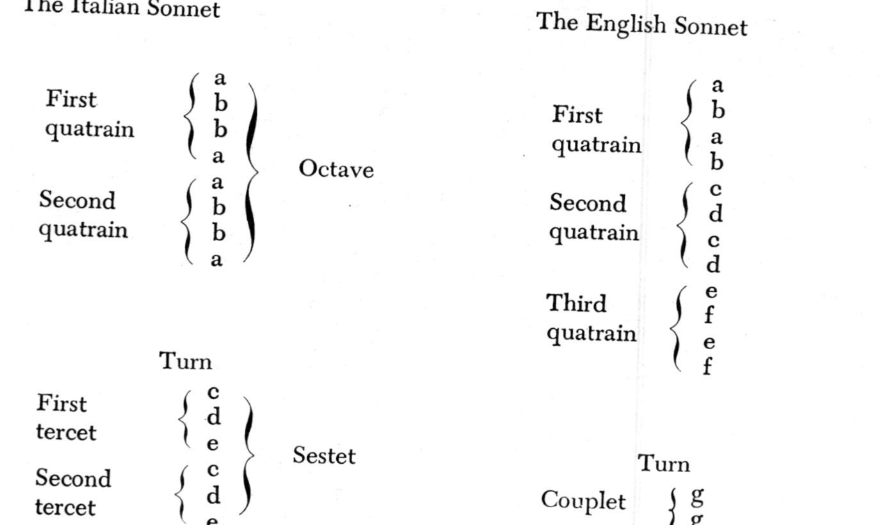

The Spenserian Sonnet

First quatrain: a b a b
couplet link: b b
Second quatrain: b c b c
couplet link: c c
Third quatrain: c d c d
Couplet: e e

The Italian sonnet, with its distinctive division into **octave** (an eight-line unit) and **sestet** (a six-line unit), is structurally suited to a statement followed by a counterstatement, as in Milton's "When I Consider How My Light Is Spent" (p. 164). The blind poet's questioning of divine justice is checked by the voice of Patience, whose haste "to prevent That murmur" is conveyed by the accelerated **turn** (change in direction of argument or narrative) on the word "but" in the last line of the octave, rather than the first of the sestet. Shelley's "Ozymandias" (p. 335) and Berryman's Sonnet 23 (p. 704) follow the same pattern of statement and counterstatement, except that their turns come in the traditional position. Another pattern common to the Italian sonnet—observation (octave) and amplifying conclusion (sestet)—underlies Keats's "On First Looking into Chapman's Homer" (p. 359) and Hill's "The Laurel Axe" (p. 818). Of these, only Milton's has a sestet conforming to the conventional rhyme scheme: others, such as Donne's "Holy Sonnets" (p. 112), end with a couplet, sometimes causing them to be mistaken for sonnets of the other type.

The English sonnet falls into three quatrains, with a turn at the end of line 12 and a concluding couplet often of a summary or epigrammatic character. M. H. Abrams has well described the unfolding of Drayton's "Since there's no help, come let us kiss and part" (p. 87): "The lover brusquely declares in the first two quatrains that he is glad the affair is cleanly broken off, pauses in the third quatrain as though at the threshold, and in the last two rhymed lines suddenly drops his swagger to make one last plea." Spenser, in the variant form that bears his name, reintroduced to the English sonnet the couplets characteristic of the Italian sonnet. This interweaving of the quatrains, as in sonnet 75 of his "Amoretti" (p. 67), makes possible a more musical and closely developed argument, and tends to reduce the sometimes excessive assertiveness of the final couplet. That last feature of the English sonnet is satirized by Brooke in his "Sonnet Reversed," which turns romantic convention upside down by *beginning* with the couplet:

> Hand trembling towards hand; the amazing lights
> Of heart and eye. They stood on supreme heights.

The three quatrains that follow record the ensuing anticlimax of suburban married life. Meredith in "Modern Love" (p. 469) stretched the sonnet to sixteen lines; Hopkins cut it short in what he termed his **curtal** (a curtailed form of "curtailed") **sonnet** "Pied Beauty" (p. 503); while Shakespeare concealed a sonnet in *Romeo and Juliet* (I.v.95 ff.). Shakespeare's 154 better-known sonnets form a carefully organized progression or **sonnet sequence,** following the precedent of such earlier sonneteers as Sidney with his "Astrophel and Stella" (p. 80) and Spenser with his "Amoretti" (p. 66). In the nineteenth century Elizabeth Barrett Browning's "Sonnets from the Portuguese" (p. 380) continued a tradition in which the author of "Berryman's Sonnets" (p. 704) has since, with that title, audaciously challenged the author of Shakespeare's sonnets.

9. The **villanelle,** a French verse form derived from an earlier Italian folk song, retains the circular pattern of a peasant dance. It consists of five tercets rhyming *aba* followed by a quatrain rhyming *abaa,* with the first line of the initial tercet recurring as the last line of the second and fourth tercets and

the third line of the initial tercet recurring as the last line of the third and fifth tercets, these two **refrains** (lines of regular recurrence) being again repeated as the last two lines of the poem. If A^1 and A^2 may be said to represent the first and third lines of the initial tercet the rhyme scheme of the villanelle will look like this:

tercet 1:	A^1 B A^2
2:	A B A^1
3:	A B A^2
4:	A B A^1
5:	A B A^2
quatrain:	A B A^1 A^2

The art of writing complicated forms like the villanelle and sestina (see below) is to give them the graceful momentum of good dancing, and the vitality of the dance informs such triumphant examples as Roethke's "The Waking" (p. 680) and Thomas's "Do Not Go Gentle into That Good Night" (p. 718).

10. The **sestina,** the most complicated of the verse forms initiated by the twelfth-century wandering singers known as troubadours, is composed of six stanzas of six lines each, followed by an **envoy,** or concluding stanza, that incorporates lines or words used before: in this case the *words* (instead of *rhymes*) end each line in the following pattern:

stanza 1:	A B C D E F
2:	F A E B D C
3:	C F D A B E
4:	E C B F A D
5:	D E A C F B
6:	B D F E C A
envoy:	E C A or A C E [these lines should contain the remaining three end words]

The earliest example in this anthology is, in fact a *double* sestina: Sidney's "Ye Goatherd Gods" (p. 77). Perhaps daunted by the intricate brilliance of this, few poets attempted the form for the next three centuries. It was reintroduced by Swinburne and Pound, who prepared the way for such notable contemporary examples as Bishop's "Sestina" (p. 697), Hecht's "Sestina D'Inverno" (p. 755, and Ashbery's "The Painter" (p. 784).

11. The **limerick** (to end this section on a lighter note) is a five-line stanza thought to take its name from an old custom at convivial parties whereby each person was required to sing an extemporized "nonsense verse," which was followed by a chorus containing the words "Will you come up to Limerick?" The acknowledged Old Master of the limerick is Edward Lear (p. 433), who required that the first and fifth lines end with the same word (usually a place name), a restriction abandoned by many Modern Masters, though triumphantly retained by the anonymous author of this:

There once was a man from Nantucket
Who kept all his cash in a bucket;
    But his daughter named Nan
    Ran away with a man,
And as for the bucket, Nantucket.

COMPOSITE FORMS

Just as good poets have always varied their base rhythm, there have always been those ready to bend, stretch, or in some way modify a fixed form to suit the demands of a particular subject. The element of the unexpected often accounts for much of the success of poems in such a composite form as Donne's "The Sun Rising" (p. 101). His stanza might be described as a combination of two quatrains (the first rhyming *abba*, the second *cdcd*), and a couplet (*ee*). That description would be accurate but inadequate in that it takes no account of the variation in line length, which is a crucial feature of the poem's structure. It opens explosively with the outrage of the interrupted lover:

> Busy old fool, unruly sun,
> Why dost thou thus
> Through windows and through curtains call on us?

Short lines, tetrameter followed by trimeter, suggest the speaker's initial shock and give place, as he begins to recover his composure, to the steadier pentameters that complete the first quatrain. Continuing irritation propels the brisk tetrameters that form the first half of the second quatrain. This, again, is completed by calmer pentameters, and the stanza rounded off like an English sonnet, with a summary pentameter couplet:

> Love, all alike, no season knows nor clime
> Nor hours, days, months, which are the rags of time.

This variation in line length achieves a different effect in the third stanza, where the brief trimeter suggests an absence contrasting with the royal presences in the preceding tetrameter:

> She's all states, and all princes, I,
> Nothing else is.

And these lines prepare, both rhetorically and visually, for the contraction and expansion so brilliantly developed in the poem's triumphant close. Similar structural considerations account for the composite stanza forms of Arnold's "The Scholar-Gypsy" (p. 458) and Lowell's "Skunk Hour" (p. 728), though variations of line length and rhyme scheme between the six-line stanzas of Lowell's poem bring it close to the line that divides composite form from the next category.

IRREGULAR FORMS

A poet writing in irregular form will use rhyme and meter but follow no fixed pattern. A classic example is Milton's "Lycidas" (p. 147), which is written in iambic pentameters interspersed with an occasional trimeter, probably modeled on the occasional half lines that intersperse the hexameters of Virgil's *Aeneid*. Milton's rhyming in this **elegy** (a formal lament for a dead person) is similarly varied, and a few lines are unrhymed. The most extensive use of irregular form is to be found in one of the three types of **ode.**

Long lyric poems of elevated style and elaborate stanzaic structure, the original odes of the Greek poet Pindar were modeled on songs sung by the chorus in Greek drama. The three-part structure of the regular **Pindaric ode** has been attempted once or twice in English, but more common and more successful has been the irregular Pindaric ode, which has no three-part structure but sections of varying length, varying line length, and varying rhyme scheme. Pindar's odes were written to celebrate someone, and celebration has been the theme of many English Pindaric odes, among them Dryden's "A Song for St. Cecilia's Day" (p. 193), Tate's "Ode to the Confederate Dead" (p. 645), and Lowell's "The Quaker Graveyard in Nantucket" (p. 720). The desire to celebrate someone or something has also prompted most English odes of the third type, those modeled on the subject matter, tone, and form of the Roman poet Horace. More meditative and restrained than the boldly irregular Pindaric ode, the **Horatian ode** is usually written in a repeated stanza form—Marvell's "An Horatian Ode upon Cronwell's Return from Ireland" in quatrains, for example, and Keats's "To Autumn" (p. 373) in a composite eleven-line stanza.

OPEN FORMS OR FREE VERSE

At the opposite end of the formal scale from the fixed forms (or, as they are sometimes called, **closed forms**) of sonnet, villanelle, and sestina, we come to what was long known as free verse, poetry that makes little or no use of traditional rhyme and meter. The term is misleading, however, suggesting to some less thoughtful champions of open forms (as free-verse structures are now increasingly called) a false analogy with political freedom as opposed to slavery, and suggesting to traditionalist opponents the disorder or anarchy implied by Frost's in/famous remark that "Writing free verse is like playing tennis with the net down." There has been much unprofitable debate in this century over the relative merits and "relevance" of closed and open forms, unprofitable because, as will be clear to any reader of this anthology, good poems continue to be written in both. It would be foolish to wish that Larkin wrote like Whitman, or Atwood like Dickinson. Poets must find voices and forms appropriate to their voices. When, around 1760, Smart chose an open form for "Jubilate Agno" (p. 253), that incantatory catalogue of the attributes of his cat Jeoffry proclaimed its descent from the King James translation of the Old Testament and, specifically, such parallel cadences as those of Psalm 150:

> Praise ye the Lord. Praise God in his sanctuary:
> praise him in the firmament of his power.
> Praise him for his mighty acts: praise him
> according to his excellent greatness.
> Praise him with the sound of the trumpet: praise
> him with the psaltery and harp.

These rhythms and rhetorical repetitions, audible also in Blake's Prophetic Books, resurfaced in the work of the nineteenth-century founder of American poetry, as we know it today. Whitman's elegy for an unknown soldier, "Vigil Strange I Kept on the Field One Night" (p. 445), may end with a traditional image of the rising sun, like Milton's "Lycidas" (p. 147), but its cadences are those of the Old Testament he read as a boy:

> And there and then and bathed by the rising sun, my son in his
> grave, in his rude-dug grave I deposited,
> Ending my vigil strange with that, vigil of night and battle-field
> dim,
> Vigil for boy of responding kisses, (never again on earth
> responding,)
> Vigil for comrade swiftly slain, vigil I never forget, how as day
> brighten'd,

I rose from the chill ground and folded my soldier well in his
blanket,
And buried him where he fell.

Whitman's breakaway from the prevailing poetic forms of his time was truly revolutionary, but certain traditional techniques he would use for special effect: the concealed *well/fell* rhyme that gives his elegy its closing chord, for example, or the bounding anapests of an earlier line:

Óne lóok | Ĭ bŭt **gáve** | whĭch yŏur **déar** | eyĕs rĕ**túrn'd** |
wĭth ă **lóok** | Ĭ shăll **név** | ĕr fŏr**gét** . . .

The poetic revolution that Whitman initiated was continued by Pound, who wrote of his predecessor:

It was you that broke the new wood,
Now is a time for carving.

Pound, the carver, unlike Whitman, the pioneer, came to open forms by way of closed forms, a progression reflected in the first four sections of Pound's partly autobiographical portrait of the artist, "Hugh Selwyn Mauberley" (p. 576). Each section is less "literary," less formal than the last, quatrains with two rhymes yielding to quatrains with one rhyme and, in section IV, to Whitmanesque free verse. A similar progression from the mastery of closed forms to the mastery of open forms can be seen in the development of such other poets as Lawrence, Eliot, Lowell, and Rich (pp. 565–571, 594–616, 720–735, 796–803, respectively).

Pound may have called himself a carver, but he, too, proved a pioneer, opening up terrain that has been more profitably mined by his successors than the highlands, the rolling cadences explored by Smart, Blake, and Whitman. Pound recovered for poets territory then inhabited only by novelists, the low ground of everyday speech, a private rather than a public language. He was aided by Williams, who, in such a poem as "The Red Wheelbarrow," used the simplest cadences of common speech to reveal the extraordinary nature of "ordinary" things:

so much depends
upon

a red wheel
barrow

glazed with rain
water

beside the white
chickens.

Each line depends upon the next to complete it, indicating the interdependence of things in the poem and, by extension, in the world. "The Red Wheelbarrow" bears out the truth of Auden's statement that in free verse "you need an infallible ear to determine where the lines should end."

Some poets have ventured even further into the no man's land between prose and poetry with **prose poems.** Hill's "Mercian Hymns" may look like prose, but the poet insists that his lines are to be printed exactly as they appear on pages 816–817; and the reader's ear will detect musical cadences no less linked and flowing than in good free verse. Eye and ear together—to return to the opening of this essay—are never more dramatically engaged than in the reading of such **shaped poems** as Herbert's "Easter Wings" (p. 133) and Hollander's "Swan and Shadow" (p. 796).

Further Reading

Poets have been making poems for as long as composers have been making music or carpenters furniture, and, just as it would be unreasonable to expect to find the lore and language of music or carpentry distilled into one short essay, so there is more to be said about the making and appreciating of poems than is said here. The fullest treatment of the subject is to be found in *A History of English Prosody from the Twelfth Century to the Present Day* by George Saintsbury (3 vols., New York, 1906–1910) and the *Princeton Encyclopedia of Poetry and Poetics*, edited by Alex Preminger, Frank J. Warnke, and O. B. Hardison, Jr. (Princeton, 1965; enl. ed., 1974). More suitable for students are *Poetic Meter and Poetic Form* by Paul Fussell (New York, 1965; rev. ed. 1979) and the appropriate entries in *A Glossary of Literary Terms* by M. H. Abrams (New York, 1957; 4th ed., 1981). Each of these has its own more detailed suggestions for further reading.

JON STALLWORTHY

Index to Versification

Index